A
Study
of
Verses Composed
of
Single Syllable Words

He that hath the Son hath life;
and he that hath not the Son of God hath not life.
1 John 5:12

A
Study
of
Verses Composed
of
Single Syllable Words

He that hath the Son hath life;
and he that hath not the Son of God hath not life.
1 John 5:12

Samuel C. Gipp, Ph. D.

DayStarPublishing
PO Box 464 • Miamitown, Ohio 45041

ISBN 978-1-890120-68-9

Printed by
Bible and Literature Missionary Foundation
713 Cannon Blvd. • Shelbyville, TN 37160
(931) 684-0304 • Email: officeblmf@bellsouth.net
www.biblelit.org

Contents

Part 1, The Reason & Rules of the Study, **page 1**

Part 2, The Study, **page 9**

Part 3, Conclusions, **page 285**

Part 4, Miscellaneous Information, **page 289**

Other Materials, **page 381**

Part 1

The Reason & Rules of the Study

Hear, ye deaf; and look, ye blind, that ye may see.
Isaiah 42:18

Why This Study?

He that hath the Son hath life;
and he that hath not the Son of God hath not life.
1 John 5:12

For many years I have heard 1 John 5:12 quoted as a testament to the simplicity of Scripture. This point is made because the verse consists of nineteen words and **all** of them have only one syllable. I never forgot that simple truth.

Then, one day the question struck me: How many verses are there in the Bible that are made up of words with only one syllable? Immediately came the next question: Since modern versions claim to be easier to read than the King James Bible, how do they render these "single syllable word" verses? Most of us remember reading the words "See Spot run" from the earliest years of our education. We were taught to read with sentences made up of single syllable words because there is no simpler way to verbally communicate.

I decided to do a study of the subject. I figured I would simply collect all the verses made up of single syllable words and then compare them in several popular modern translations. It wasn't to be quite that simple.

Isolating the Verses

The Hurdles

Following the decision to do this study, I faced the first, most daunting problem: How was I to isolate these verses? There is no computer Bible program I know of that can examine and isolate verses based strictly on the syllable count of the words used in a verse. Actually this wasn't seen as such a major problem for two reasons:

1. I **loathe** what I call "Lazy Man's Bible Study." This concept has arisen solely due to computers and Bible software. Computer Bible programs have made a bunch of lazy men think they are "Bible scholars." The process is simple: Instruct your computer Bible program to do a search for a particular word, hit "Search" and then...go mow the grass. By the time you are finished mowing your computer will have isolated all the verses with the desired word and your printer will now dutifully puke page after page of paper onto your desk. What a feeling of superiority to know "you" have just completed an "in depth" Bible study!

What's wrong with this approach? Several things, the first of which is that it isn't Bible study at all. It is simply a computer generated word search. I once had a man give me a stack of paper a half-an-inch thick. I asked him what it was. With pride he responded, "That's the word 'forever' every time it appears in the Bible." I was underwhelmed! I hadn't really been wringing my hands over how many times "forever" appeared in Scripture. I tossed the results of a word search **his computer** had worked so hard to achieve into my wastebasket.

But a bigger and more practical problem with this method is that the "searcher" will miss **every verse** that concerns the subject he is interested in that doesn't contain his key word.

There is **no substitute** for Bible reading!

2. The simple fact is that **I am** a Bible reader. The only way to isolate the single syllable word verses was to **read through the entire Bible** and record them. But it isn't that easy. No matter how carefully you read you are undoubtedly going to overlook some of the verses you are seeking. The only recourse is to read through the entire Bible **again**. But there **is still a chance** you will miss some. Yep, you know the answer...**read through the entire Bible another time!**

Reading through the entire Bible is a time-consuming process but it is one that cannot be replaced by a computer program. If you read an average of ten pages a day you will get through the Bible about three times a year. I read thirty pages per day. That puts me through the entire Bible every forty-five days, eight times per year. The study you are about to read is the result of reading through the Bible ten times. Many times I thought I had found all the verses only to find some I'd missed on the next time through the Bible. In fact, I originally tried to stop at seven times though but kept finding verses the next three times through, finally giving up after ten times through the Bible. There may still be one or two verses I've overlooked but I am confident the vast majority of single syllable word verses have been cataloged in this study.

Defining the Verses

Categories

To do this study you might think that all you have to do is record every verse made of single syllable words and begin, but it isn't that easy. It wasn't long before I found there were **several kinds** of these verses. There ended up being several categories of single syllable word verses.

1. Verses made up of words with only one syllable.

The best example of this type of verse is the one given above, 1 John 5:12. The verse is made up solely of words with only one syllable. This was the **choice of the translators**, since they could have chosen to use some multi-syllable words when translating the verse.

2. Verses made up of single syllable word but having one or more proper names in them.

There are numerous verses in the Bible that are made up of single syllable words but have names in them that are multi-syllable. These names were not rendered as multi-syllable due to a **choice made by the translators**. They are names that would have multiple syllables in **any** translation. An example of such a verse is **Genesis 6:8,** "But Noah found grace in the eyes of the LORD." As you can see, the verse is indeed made up of single syllable words with the exception of the mandatory name, "Noah." Verses such as this were also included in the study group since the name would have multiple syllables in any translation, but the other words of the verse, which were the **choice of the translators**, were all single syllable.

When a verse has a multi-syllable proper name, the reader is alerted in two ways within the text of the study. First, the verse number is followed by an asterisk (*). Secondly, the name/s in the verse are printed in boldface type so the reader can easily identify them. Single syllable names were not printed in boldface type. Thus Genesis 6:8 is rendered:

Genesis 6:8* But **Noah** found grace in the eyes of the LORD.

When printing the readout for these verses, the syllable count for the proper name/s was ignored since these names would be found to be multi-syllable no matter which version they are found in. Therefore the syllable count for Genesis 6:8 would appear as:

Genesis 6:8* But **Noah** found grace in the eyes of the LORD.
AV - **10,** 1-1,2-1,3-1,4-1,5-1,6-1,7-1,8-1,9-1,10-1,

Here is how the reader would decipher this information:

1. The asterisk following the verse number alerts the reader that the verse contains one or more multi-syllable proper names.

2. The multi-syllable proper name/s is in bold print so it can be easily identified. Single syllable proper names such as "Seth" are not printed in bold face type.

3. The "AV" tells the reader this is the "Authorized Version."

4. The bold "**10**" tells you there are ten words in the verse.

5. Then the words are counted and numbered in the order in which they appear in the verse, followed by a hyphen and the syllable count for that word. You can see that the **first** word in the verse has one syllable, 1-1. So does each word in the verse so the word/syllable count for Genesis 6:8 is: 1-1,2-1,3-1,4-1,5-1,6-1,7-1,8-1,9-1,10-1. Ten words, each with one syllable.

I have anticipated that some readers are going to scan each verse readout to alert themselves of multi-syllable words. I felt that if I printed the readout like this:
AV - **10,** 1-1,2-2,3-1,4-1,5-1,6-1,7-1,8-1,9-1,10-1 that they would halt at the "2-2" only to then find it was a proper name. Therefore, proper names are treated as single syllable words in the readout.

In the English Standard Version, Genesis 6:8 reads almost exactly like the King James Bible. The verse also has ten words. Just like the AV, the second word is the multi-syllable proper name "Noah." But the fourth word found in the Authorized Version, "grace," is rendered "favor" in the English Standard Version. Unlike the single syllable "grace" these modern translators **chose** to insert a two syllable word into the verse. For easy identification multi-syllable words appear in bold type in the readout. Thus the readout for the English Standard Version appears as:

ESV - 10, 1-1,2-1,3-1,4-**2**,5-1,6-1,7-1,8-1,9-1,10-1

The "ESV" tells you this is the English Standard Version. If a modern version's choice of words are all single syllable, the letters are not in bold face type. (ESV) If there is a multi-syllable word in the verse, the letters are in bold face (**ESV**) to alert the reader at a glance. The bold "**10**" tells you there are ten words in the verse. A number "1" follows each word in the verse indicating they have one syllable, except for word number "4" which is followed by a bold "**2**" which indicates the number of syllables in this fourth word. If it had had three or four syllables the bold number would have been "**3**" or "**4**."

By this method the reader can quickly decipher several things about each verse and version. He can tell how many words are in the Authorized Version's rendering and in the renderings of each modern version included in the study. These sometimes differ greatly. (The **number** of words in the renderings of modern versions is never counted against them as being more complex than the King

James Bible.) The reader can then tell how many multi-syllable words are in a verse and which words in the verse they are.

3. Verses made up of single syllable words but containing a number in written form.

A verse such as this would be **Genesis 41:26**, "The seven good kine are seven years; and the seven good ears are seven years: the dream is one." In this case the number "seven" appears several times. Again, these peculiarities are identified in two ways. First, the verse number is followed by a pound sign (#). As mentioned above, the words in question are printed in bold type so they can be easily identified. Numbers that were single syllable, such as "six", "seven", etc. were not printed in bold face type. Thus, the readout for Genesis 41:26 is rendered:

Genesis 41:26# The **seven** good kine are **seven** years; and the **seven** good ears are **seven** years: the dream is one.

AV - **19,** 1-1,2-1,3-1,4-1,5-1,6-1,7-1,8-1,9-1,10-1,11-1,12-1,13-1,14-1,15-1,16-1,17-1,18-1,19-1

As in the case of proper names the syllable count for the number was ignored since these numbers would be found to be multi-syllable no matter in which version they are found.

The reading for the New Living Translation for this verse appears as:

NLT - **17,** 1-1,2-1,3-**2**,4-1,5-1,6-1,7-1,8-**2**,9-1,10-1,11-1,12-1,13-**3**,14-1,15-1,16-1,17-**4**

The "NLT" tells you this is the New Living Translation, that the letters are in bold face alerts the reader that there is at least one multi-syllable word in the verse. The bold "**17**" tells you there are seventeen words in the verse as rendered by the translators of this version. The bold "**2**" following the third word tells you this word has two syllables, as does the eighth word in the verse. The thirteenth word contains three syllables and the seventeenth has four.

4. Single syllable word verses that are mostly names

If the verse is nothing but names, such as 1 Chronicles 1:1, which reads, "Adam, Sheth, Enosh," then it was excluded from the study. But, there are verses found in genealogies, such as those found in Genesis, the Chronicles and even portions of the New Testament that are top-heavy with names yet contain one or two single syllable words.

Example: Genesis 10:7 "And the sons of Cush; Seba, and Havilah, and Sabtah, and Raamah, and Sabtechah: and the sons of Raamah; Sheba, and Dedan."

Including such verses in the study greatly improved the "Percentage of Change" in favor of modern versions but I felt the study would not be honest or accurate if these verses were excluded. Besides, the goal of this study was to find out how modern versions rendered verses that had only single syllable words in the Authorized Version. Therefore I was required to include **every** single syllable word verse in the Bible

Advantages and disadvantages of the King's English:

1. Advantages - Many times the King James Bible reads "to day" where a modern version would have "today." Thus, the King James Bible would be credited with having **two** single syllable words while a modern version would be penalized for reading "today," a multi-syllable word.

This advantage was not overwhelming and mattered only on a small number of verses. In fact, I cannot think of a single verse where "today" appeared in a verse used in this study.

2. Disadvantages - Because of the "th" endings found in the King James Bible some words which are single syllable in modern versions are multi-syllable in the King James Bible, such as: "knows" vs "know-eth," "do" vs "do-est" and so on. This was a much greater factor in **disqualifying** verses that otherwise would have been included in the study.

Pronunciations

There are a couple words that are historically mispronounced as having two syllables when, in fact, they have only one. The word "saith" is **not** correctly pronounced "say-eth" but rather "seth." No one pronounces "said" as "sa-id." Neither should "saith" be pronounced "say-eth." I confess that I have a tendency to pronounce "saith" as "say-eth" when speaking but for this study it had to be viewed properly.

The other confusing word is "blessed" which is correctly pronounced with one syllable, "blessed," and not "bless-ed." I know that somehow the Sermon on the Mount sounds more holy when read as "Bless-ed are the peacemakers..." and I really have no problem with anyone doing that, but in this study it is necessary that the pronunciation be accurate rather than holy.

Interpreting the Data

Space would not allow me to reproduce each verse from each modern translation, (neither would copyright laws); therefore, I printed each verse as found in the King James Bible. I then counted the number of words as found in the King James Bible. After that I compared the word count in seven modern translations. The versions and their abbreviations used in this study are as follows:

1. AV - King James Bible
2. ESV - English Standard Version
3. HCSB - Holman Christian Standard Bible
4. NASV - New American Standard Version
5. NCV - New Century Version
6. NIV - New International Version
7. NKJV - New King James Version
8. NLT - New Living Translation
9. NRSV - New Revised Standard Version

The word count for each modern version follows its abbreviation. Thus, Genesis 1:3 appears as:

Genesis 1:3 And God said, Let there be light: and there was light.
AV - **11,** 1-1,2-1,3-1,4-1,5-1,6-1,7-1,8-1,9-1,10-1,11-1
ESV - **11,** 1-1,2-1,3-1,4-1,5-1,6-1,7-1,8-1,9-1,10-1,11-1
HCSB - **11,** 1-1,2-1,3-1,4-1,5-1,6-1,7-1,8-1,9-1,10-1,11-1
NASV - **11,** 1-1,2-1,3-1,4-1,5-1,6-1,7-1,8-1,9-1,10-1,11-1
NCV - **11,** 1-1,2-1,3-1,4-1,5-1,6-1,7-1,8-1,9-1,10-1,11-1

NIV - **11,** 1-1,2-1,3-1,4-1,5-1,6-1,7-1,8-1,9-1,10-1,11-1
NKJV - **11,** 1-1,2-1,3-1,4-1,5-1,6-1,7-1,8-1,9-1,10-1,11-1
NLT - **11,** 1-1,2-1,3-1,4-1,5-1,6-1,7-1,8-1,9-1,10-1,11-1
NRSV - **11,** 1-1,2-1,3-1,4-1,5-1,6-1,7-1,8-1,9-1,10-1,11-1
Conclusion: All versions read the same.

As you can see by the "**Conclusion**" comment all versions compared used words of only one syllable.

If a word had more than one syllable, its syllable count was printed in boldface type so as to be easily identified. The abbreviation for the version in which the word appeared is also printed in bold. Therefore, Genesis 35:13 appears like this:

Genesis 35:13 And God went up from him in the place where he talked with him.
AV - **14,** 1-1,2-1,3-1,4-1,5-1,6-1,7-1,8-1,9-1,10-1,11-1,12-1,13-1,14-1
ESV - **15,** 1-1,2-1,3-1,4-1,5-1,6-1,7-1,8-1,9-1,10-1,11-1,12-1,13-**2**,14-1,15-1
HCSB - **14,** 1-1,2-1,3-**2**,4-1,5-1,6-1,7-1,8-1,9-1,10-1,11-1,12-**2**,13-1,14-1
NASV - **15,** 1-1,2-1,3-1,4-1,5-1,6-1,7-1,8-1,9-1,10-1,11-1,12-1,13-**2**,14-1,15-1
NCV - **4,** 1-1,2-1,3-1,4-1
NIV - **15,** 1-1,2-1,3-1,4-1,5-1,6-1,7-1,8-1,9-1,10-1,11-1,12-1,13-1,14-1,15-1
NKJV - **14,** 1-1,2-1,3-1,4-1,5-1,6-1,7-1,8-1,9-1,10-1,11-1,12-1,13-1,14-1
NLT - **13,** 1-1,2-1,3-1,4-1,5-1,6-1,7-1,8-1,9-1,10-1,11-**2**,12-1,13-1
NRSV - **15,** 1-1,2-1,3-1,4-1,5-1,6-1,7-1,8-1,9-1,10-1,11-1,12-1,13-**2**,14-1,15-1
Conclusion: Five modern versions are more complex than the King James Bible. The verse is brief in the NCV because this version cuts the verse short and adds the latter portion to verse fourteen.

Here you will notice that the ESV, HCSB, NASV, NLT and the NRSV all insert multi-syllable words into the verse. Other pertinent information which concerned the NCV is also included in the comment section.

The Verse Count

The Big List

If you wish to know how many single syllable word verses there are in the Bible, simply look at the end of the list of verses and you will see the last verse, Revelation 22:21, listed as number 916. This number includes all single syllable word verses, meaning those with names, numbers or name/number combinations.

Is this the correct number? This is the correct number **as far as I could determine in ten times through the Bible**. There may well be one or two that were overlooked during those ten times.

Might I point out that if a reader of this study now runs across a verse that I overlooked, it **does not mean** they can honestly say, "I found more verses than he did." What it really means is that someone else went through the Bible ten complete times, and now the reader managed to find **one more** verse after 916 had already been identified for them. You're welcome.

The Small List

I figured there would be some who would want to know how many verses consisted of only single syllable words without names or numbers. That list can be found in the back of this study.

The Other Lists

Whenever a study such as this is performed there are always some who disapprove of the criteria by which the verses are isolated. This may be due to either prejudice or honest disagreement in the protocols used to determine the data.

I have tried to err in favor of being too inclusive in this study. My reasoning was simple. If I checked only those verses that are single syllable words, the "Small List" just mentioned, someone would say, "But there are verses that qualify as single syllable although they include names and numbers." Unfortunately they would have no way of knowing where these verses were located. I figured if I included the largest cross section of verses possible the readers could disqualify whatever verses they wished to. But if I produced only the "Small List" then the readers would be left to complete the study on their own.

I am convinced that the **three classes** of verses included in this list are the valid way to approach the subject. They are:
1. Verses made up of words with only one syllable.
2. Verses made up of single syllable words but having one or more proper names in them. (Number 4 mentioned above, "Single syllable word verses that are mostly names," would actually be within this class as described.)
3. Verses made up of single syllable words but containing a number in written form.

By including all the verses possible in the study it allows a reader who wishes to disqualify verses which contain names or numbers to do so. But if these verses were not included and a reader wanted to **include** them the reader would still have unanswered questions and a partial study with no real value.

This said there is one more "Class" of verses which I also included. This is a list of verses which included what I considered "Immutable Words," words other than names or numbers which the translator had no power to choose not to use. trying to include such verses is a "slippery slope" indeed. Since I included references to "the Father," God, then how could I reject verses that refer to a **human** "father." Of course, if "father" is included what justification would there be for excluding "mother," and then, "brother" and "sister" or "daughter." I actually began including "father" and then "mother" but soon realized it wouldn't be long before the study would prove to be irrelevant because it would be so inclusive that it would cease to actually deal with the subject at hand. So, I removed all references to brothers, sisters, daughters mothers and father. (Except in reference to God, the Father.) You can view some, not all, of these verses in the "Honorable Mention" list.

So, what words could honestly qualify as an "immutable" word? After a soul searching evaluation of many potential candidates I considered only two words as immutable, "silver" and "crucify." The word "silver" is not a translator's choice, it is mandated by the original choice of words. I found only three verses that filled the qualification of being all single syllable words except for the word "silver." These verses were **included** in the Master List and then listed separately in the

"Immutable Words" list along with their numbered location in that list so the reader can find and disqualify them if they so wish.

In the New Testament verses with the word "crucify" and its various forms were included due to the importance and impact of the word and act.

I found no other words I considered immutable. It was difficult indeed to reject verses which were single syllable but included such words as; "angel," "heaven," and a few others but being too inclusive would have led to more problems than answers.

The Conclusion

Part Three is the conclusion. This it the sum of information gleaned from the data.

Miscellaneous Information

Found in the back of this study are several lists; Immutable Words, Honorable Mention, and Single Syllable Word Verses with No Names or Numbers as well as a list of miscellaneous facts concerning verses consisting of single syllable words in our Authorized Version and some of the modern translations. Once the study was complete I tried to anticipate a few questions that might arise in the mind of the reader.

This is a legitimate study of this subject. As you read the "**Conclusion**" following each verse you will continually see the phrase "this was not counted against it" in reference to a modern version. My honest desire was not to discredit modern versions but to see how they treated these verses.

Part 2
The Study

Show me thy ways, O LORD; teach me thy paths.
Psalms 25:4

Verses Composed of Single Syllable Words

1. Genesis 1:3 And God said, Let there be light: and there was light.
AV - **11,** 1-1,2-1,3-1,4-1,5-1,6-1,7-1,8-1,9-1,10-1,11-1
ESV - **11,** 1-1,2-1,3-1,4-1,5-1,6-1,7-1,8-1,9-1,10-1,11-1
HCSB - **11,** 1-1,2-1,3-1,4-1,5-1,6-1,7-1,8-1,9-1,10-1,11-1
NASV - **11,** 1-1,2-1,3-1,4-1,5-1,6-1,7-1,8-1,9-1,10-1,11-1
NCV - **11,** 1-1,2-1,3-1,4-1,5-1,6-1,7-1,8-1,9-1,10-1,11-1
NIV - **11,** 1-1,2-1,3-1,4-1,5-1,6-1,7-1,8-1,9-1,10-1,11-1
NKJV - **11,** 1-1,2-1,3-1,4-1,5-1,6-1,7-1,8-1,9-1,10-1,11-1
NLT - **11,** 1-1,2-1,3-1,4-1,5-1,6-1,7-1,8-1,9-1,10-1,11-1
NRSV - **11,** 1-1,2-1,3-1,4-1,5-1,6-1,7-1,8-1,9-1,10-1,11-1
Conclusion: All versions read the same.

2. Genesis 5:5*# And all the days that **Adam** lived were nine **hundred** and **thirty** years: and he died.
AV - **16,** 1-1,2-1,3-1,4-1,5-1,6-1,7-1,8-1,9-1,10-1,11-1,12-1,13-1,14-1,15-1,16-1
ESV - **13,** 1-1,2-1,3-1,4-1,5-1,6-1,7-1,8-1,9-1,10-1,11-1,12-1,13-1
HCSB - 9, 1-1,2-1,3-1,4-**2**,5-1,6-1,7-1,8-1,9-1
NASV - **16,** 1-1,2-1,3-1,4-1,5-1,6-1,7-1,8-1,9-1,10-1,11-1,12-1,13-1,14-1,15-1,16-1
NCV - 12, 1-1,2-1,3-1,4-1,5-**2**,6-1,7-1,8-1,9-1,10-1,11-1,12-1
NIV - 9, 1-**4**,2-1,3-1,4-1,5-1,6-1,7-1,8-1,9-1
NKJV - **16,** 1-1,2-1,3-1,4-1,5-1,6-1,7-1,8-1,9-1,10-1,11-1,12-1,13-1,14-1,15-1,16-1
NLT - **8,** 1-1,2-1,3-1,4-1,5-1,6-1,7-1,8-1
NRSV - **15,** 1-1,2-1,3-1,4-1,5-1,6-1,7-1,8-1,9-1,10-1,11-1,12-1,13-1,14-1,15-1
Conclusion: Only three modern versions are more complex than the King James Bible.

3. Genesis 5:8# And all the days of Seth were nine **hundred** and twelve years: and he died.
AV - **15,** 1-1,2-1,3-1,4-1,5-1,6-1,7-1,8-1,9-1,10-1,11-1,12-1,13-1,14-1,15-1
ESV - **12,** 1-1,2-1,3-1,4-1,5-1,6-1,7-1,8-1,9-1,10-1,11-1,12-1
HCSB - 9, 1-1,2-1,3-1,4-**2**,5-1,6-1,7-1,8-1,9-1
NASV - **15,** 1-1,2-1,3-1,4-1,5-1,6-1,7-1,8-1,9-1,10-1,11-1,12-1,13-1,14-1,15-1
NCV - 12, 1-1,2-1,3-1,4-1,5-**2**,6-1,7-1,8-1,9-1,10-1,11-1,12-1
NIV - 9, 1-**4**,2-1,3-1,4-1,5-1,6-1,7-1,8-1,9-1
NKJV - **15,** 1-1,2-1,3-1,4-1,5-1,6-1,7-1,8-1,9-1,10-1,11-1,12-1,13-1,14-1,15-1
NLT - **8,** 1-1,2-1,3-1,4-1,5-1,6-1,7-1,8-1
NRSV - **14,** 1-1,2-1,3-1,4-1,5-1,6-1,7-1,8-1,9-1,10-1,11-1,12-1,13-1,14-1
Conclusion: Only three modern versions are more complex than the King James Bible.

4. Genesis 5:11*# And all the days of **Enos** were nine **hundred** and five years: and he died.
AV - **15,** 1-1,2-1,3-1,4-1,5-1,6-1,7-1,8-1,9-1,10-1,11-1,12-1,13-1,14-1,15-1
ESV - **12,** 1-1,2-1,3-1,4-1,5-1,6-1,7-1,8-1,9-1,10-1,11-1,12-1
HCSB - 9, 1-1,2-1,3-1,4-**2**,5-1,6-1,7-1,8-1,9-1

Samuel C. Gipp Ph.D.

NASV - **15,** 1-1,2-1,3-1,4-1,5-1,6-1,7-1,8-1,9-1,10-1,11-1,12-1,13-1,14-1,15-1
NCV - 12, 1-1,2-1,3-1,4-1,5-**2,**6-1,7-1,8-1,9-1,10-1,11-1,12-1
NIV - 9, 1-**4,**2-1,3-1,4-1,5-1,6-1,7-1,8-1,9-1
NKJV - **15,** 1-1,2-1,3-1,4-1,5-1,6-1,7-1,8-1,9-1,10-1,11-1,12-1,13-1,14-1,15-1
NLT - 8, 1-1,2-1,3-1,4-1,5-1,6-1,7-1,8-1
NRSV - **14,** 1-1,2-1,3-1,4-1,5-1,6-1,7-1,8-1,9-1,10-1,11-1,12-1,13-1,14-1
Conclusion: Only three modern versions are more complex than the King James Bible.

5. Genesis 5:14*# And all the days of **Cainan** were nine **hundred** and ten years: and he died.
AV - **15,** 1-1,2-1,3-1,4-1,5-1,6-1,7-1,8-1,9-1,10-1,11-1,12-1,13-1,14-1,15-1
ESV - **12,** 1-1,2-1,3-1,4-1,5-1,6-1,7-1,8-1,9-1,10-1,11-1,12-1
HCSB - 9, 1-1,2-1,3-1,4-**2,**5-1,6-1,7-1,8-1,9-1
NASV - **15,** 1-1,2-1,3-1,4-1,5-1,6-1,7-1,8-1,9-1,10-1,11-1,12-1,13-1,14-1,15-1
NCV - 12, 1-1,2-1,3-1,4-1,5-**2,**6-1,7-1,8-1,9-1,10-1,11-1,12-1
NIV - 9, 1-**4,**2-1,3-1,4-1,5-1,6-1,7-1,8-1,9-1
NKJV - **15,** 1-1,2-1,3-1,4-1,5-1,6-1,7-1,8-1,9-1,10-1,11-1,12-1,13-1,14-1,15-1
NLT - 8, 1-1,2-1,3-1,4-1,5-1,6-1,7-1,8-1
NRSV - **15,** 1-1,2-1,3-1,4-1,5-1,6-1,7-1,8-1,9-1,10-1,11-1,12-1,13-1,14-1,15-1
Conclusion: Only three modern versions are more complex than the King James Bible.

6. Genesis 5:17*# And all the days of **Mahalaleel** were eight **hundred ninety** and five years: and he died.
AV - **15,** 1-1,2-1,3-1,4-1,5-1,6-1,7-1,8-1,9-1,10-1,11-1,12-1,13-1,14-1,15-1
ESV - **12,** 1-1,2-1,3-1,4-1,5-1,6-1,7-1,8-1,9-1,10-1,11-1,12-1
HCSB - 9, 1-1,2-1,3-1,4-**2,**5-1,6-1,7-1,8-1,9-1
NASV - **15,** 1-1,2-1,3-1,4-1,5-1,6-1,7-1,8-1,9-1,10-1,11-1,12-1,13-1,14-1,15-1
NCV - 12, 1-1,2-1,3-1,4-1,5-**2,**6-1,7-1,8-1,9-1,10-1,11-1,12-1
NIV - 9, 1-**4,**2-1,3-1,4-1,5-1,6-1,7-1,8-1,9-1
NKJV - **15,** 1-1,2-1,3-1,4-1,5-1,6-1,7-1,8-1,9-1,10-1,11-1,12-1,13-1,14-1,15-1
NLT - 8, 1-1,2-1,3-1,4-1,5-1,6-1,7-1,8-1
NRSV - **15,** 1-1,2-1,3-1,4-1,5-1,6-1,7-1,8-1,9-1,10-1,11-1,12-1,13-1,14-1,15-1
Conclusion: Only three modern versions are more complex than the King James Bible.

7. Genesis 5:20*# And all the days of **Jared** were nine **hundred sixty** and two years: and he died.
AV - **16,** 1-1,2-1,3-1,4-1,5-1,6-1,7-1,8-1,9-1,10-1,11-1,12-1,13-1,14-1,15-1,16-1
ESV - **12,** 1-1,2-1,3-1,4-1,5-1,6-1,7-1,8-1,9-1,10-1,11-1,12-1
HCSB - 9, 1-1,2-1,3-1,4-**2,**5-1,6-1,7-1,8-1,9-1
NASV - **15,** 1-1,2-1,3-1,4-1,5-1,6-1,7-1,8-1,9-1,10-1,11-1,12-1,13-1,14-1,15-1
NCV - 12, 1-1,2-1,3-1,4-1,5-**2,**6-1,7-1,8-1,9-1,10-1,11-1,12-1
NIV - 9, 1-**4,**2-1,3-1,4-1,5-1,6-1,7-1,8-1,9-1
NKJV - **15,** 1-1,2-1,3-1,4-1,5-1,6-1,7-1,8-1,9-1,10-1,11-1,12-1,13-1,14-1,15-1
NLT - 8, 1-1,2-1,3-1,4-1,5-1,6-1,7-1,8-1
NRSV - **14,** 1-1,2-1,3-1,4-1,5-1,6-1,7-1,8-1,9-1,10-1,11-1,12-1,13-1,14-1
Conclusion: Only three modern versions are more complex than the King James Bible.

A Study of Verses Composed of Single Syllable Words

8. Genesis 5:23*# And all the days of **Enoch** were three **hundred sixty** and five years:
AV - **13,** 1-1,2-1,3-1,4-1,5-1,6-1,7-1,8-1,9-1,10-1,11-1,12-1,13-1
ESV - **9,** 1-1,2-1,3-1,4-1,5-1,6-1,7-1,8-1,9-1
HCSB - 6, 1-1,2-1,3-1,4-**2**,5-1,6-1
NASV - **12,** 1-1,2-1,3-1,4-1,5-1,6-1,7-1,8-1,9-1,10-1,11-1,12-1
NCV - 8, 1-1,2-1,3-1,4-1,5-**2**,6-1,7-1,8-1
NIV - 5, 1-**4**,2-1,3-1,4-1,5-1
NKJV - **12,** 1-1,2-1,3-1,4-1,5-1,6-1,7-1,8-1,9-1,10-1,11-1,12-1
NLT - **4,** 1-1,2-1,3-1,4-1
NRSV - **11,** 1-1,2-1,3-1,4-1,5-1,6-1,7-1,8-1,9-1,10-1,11-1
Conclusion: Only three modern versions are more complex than the King James Bible.

9. Genesis 5:24* And **Enoch** walked with God: and he was not; for God took him.
AV - **13,** 1-1,2-1,3-1,4-1,5-1,6-1,7-1,8-1,9-1,10-1,11-1,12-1,13-1
ESV - **12,** 1-1,2-1,3-1,4-1,5-1,6-1,7-1,8-1,9-1,10-1,11-1,12-1
HCSB - 13, 1-1,2-1,3-1,4-1,5-1,6-1,7-1,8-1,9-1,10-**2**,11-1,12-1,13-1
NASV - **12,** 1-1,2-1,3-1,4-1,5-1,6-1,7-1,8-1,9-1,10-1,11-1,12-1
NCV - 15, 1-1,2-1,3-1,4-1,5-1,6-1,7-1,8-1,9-1,10-1,11-1,12-**2**,13-1,14-1,15-1
NIV - 14, 1-1,2-1,3-1,4-1,5-1,6-1,7-1,8-1,9-1,10-**2**,11-1,12-1,13-1,14-1
NKJV - **13,** 1-1,2-1,3-1,4-1,5-1,6-1,7-1,8-1,9-1,10-1,11-1,12-1,13-1
NLT - 15, 1-**2**,2-1,3-1,4-**3**,5-1,6-1,7-1,8-1,9-1,10-1,11-**3**,12-**2**,13-1,14-1,15-1
NRSV - 13, 1-1,2-1,3-1,4-1,5-1,6-1,7-1,8-1,9-1,10-**2**,11-1,12-1,13-1
Conclusion: Five modern versions are more complex than the King James Bible. The NLT is the most difficult to read.

10. Genesis 5:27*# And all the days of **Methuselah** were nine **hundred sixty** and nine years: and he died.
AV - **16,** 1-1,2-1,3-1,4-1,5-1,6-1,7-1,8-1,9-1,10-1,11-1,12-1,13-1,14-1,15-1,16-1
ESV - **12,** 1-1,2-1,3-1,4-1,5-1,6-1,7-1,8-1,9-1,10-1,11-1,12-1
HCSB - 9, 1-1,2-1,3-1,4-**2**,5-1,6-1,7-1,8-1,9-1
NASV - **15,** 1-1,2-1,3-1,4-1,5-1,6-1,7-1,8-1,9-1,10-1,11-1,12-1,13-1,14-1,15-1
NCV - 12, 1-1,2-1,3-1,4-1,5-**2**,6-1,7-1,8-1,9-1,10-1,11-1,12-1
NIV - 9, 1-**4**,2-1,3-1,4-1,5-1,6-1,7-1,8-1,9-1
NKJV - **15,** 1-1,2-1,3-1,4-1,5-1,6-1,7-1,8-1,9-1,10-1,11-1,12-1,13-1,14-1,15-1
NLT - **8,** 1-1,2-1,3-1,4-1,5-1,6-1,7-1,8-1
NRSV - **14,** 1-1,2-1,3-1,4-1,5-1,6-1,7-1,8-1,9-1,10-1,11-1,12-1,13-1,14-1
Conclusion: Only three modern versions are more complex than the King James Bible.

11. Genesis 5:31*# And all the days of **Lamech** were **seven hundred seventy** and **seven** years: and he died.
AV - **16,** 1-1,2-1,3-1,4-1,5-1,6-1,7-1,8-1,9-1,10-1,11-1,12-1,13-1,14-1,15-1,16-1
ESV - **12,** 1-1,2-1,3-1,4-1,5-1,6-1,7-1,8-1,9-1,10-1,11-1,12-1
HCSB - 9, 1-1,2-1,3-1,4-**2**,5-1,6-1,7-1,8-1,9-1

Samuel C. Gipp Ph.D.

NASV - **15,** 1-1,2-1,3-1,4-1,5-1,6-1,7-1,8-1,9-1,10-1,11-1,12-1,13-1,14-1,15-1
NCV - 12, 1-1,2-1,3-1,4-1,5-**2,**6-1,7-1,8-1,9-1,10-1,11-1,12-1
NIV - 9, 1-**4,**2-1,3-1,4-1,5-1,6-1,7-1,8-1,9-1
NKJV - **15,** 1-1,2-1,3-1,4-1,5-1,6-1,7-1,8-1,9-1,10-1,11-1,12-1,13-1,14-1,15-1
NLT - **8,** 1-1,2-1,3-1,4-1,5-1,6-1,7-1,8-1
NRSV - **14,** 1-1,2-1,3-1,4-1,5-1,6-1,7-1,8-1,9-1,10-1,11-1,12-1,13-1,14-1
Conclusion: Only three modern versions are more complex than the King James Bible.

12. Genesis 6:8* But **Noah** found grace in the eyes of the LORD.
AV - **10,** 1-1,2-1,3-1,4-1,5-1,6-1,7-1,8-1,9-1,10-1
ESV - 10, 1-1,2-1,3-1,4-**2,**5-1,6-1,7-1,8-1,9-1,10-1
HCSB - 10, 1-1,2-1,3-1,4-**2,**5-1,6-1,7-1,8-1,9-1,10-1
NASV - 10, 1-1,2-1,3-1,4-**2,**5-1,6-1,7-1,8-1,9-1,10-1
NCV - **5,** 1-1,2-1,3-1,4-1,5-1
NIV - 10, 1-1,2-1,3-1,4-**2,**5-1,6-1,7-1,8-1,9-1,10-1
NKJV - **10,** 1-1,2-1,3-1,4-1,5-1,6-1,7-1,8-1,9-1,10-1
NLT - **7,** 1-1,2-1,3-1,4-1,5-1,6-1,7-1
NRSV - 10, 1-1,2-1,3-1,4-**2,**5-1,6-1,7-1,8-1,9-1,10-1
Conclusion: Five modern versions are more complex than the King James Bible.

13. Genesis 8:16 Go forth of the ark, thou, and thy wife, and thy sons, and thy sons' wives with thee.
AV - **18,** 1-1,2-1,3-1,4-1,5-1,6-1,7-1,8-1,9-1,10-1,11-1,12-1,13-1,14-1,15-1,16-1,17-1,18-1
ESV - **18,** 1-1,2-1,3-1,4-1,5-1,6-1,7-1,8-1,9-1,10-1,11-1,12-1,13-1,14-1,15-1,16-1,17-1,18-1
HCSB - **16,** 1-1,2-1,3-1,4-1,5-1,6-1,7-1,8-1,9-1,10-1,11-1,12-1,13-1,14-1,15-1,16-1
NASV - **18,** 1-1,2-1,3-1,4-1,5-1,6-1,7-1,8-1,9-1,10-1,11-1,12-1,13-1,14-1,15-1,16-1,17-1,18-1
NCV - **15,** 1-1,2-1,3-1,4-1,5-1,6-1,7-1,8-1,9-1,10-1,11-1,12-1,13-1,14-1,15-1
NIV - **15,** 1-1,2-1,3-1,4-1,5-1,6-1,7-1,8-1,9-1,10-1,11-1,12-1,13-1,14-1,15-1
NKJV - **18,** 1-1,2-1,3-1,4-1,5-1,6-1,7-1,8-1,9-1,10-1,11-1,12-1,13-1,14-1,15-1,16-1,17-1,18-1
NLT - **16,** 1-1,2-1,3-1,4-1,5-1,6-1,7-1,8-1,9-1,10-1,11-1,12-1,13-1,14-1,15-1,16-1
NRSV - **18,** 1-1,2-1,3-1,4-1,5-1,6-1,7-1,8-1,9-1,10-1,11-1,12-1,13-1,14-1,15-1,16-1,17-1,18-1
Conclusion: All versions read the same.

14. Genesis 8:18* And **Noah** went forth, and his sons, and his wife, and his sons' wives with him:
AV - **16,** 1-1,2-1,3-1,4-1,5-1,6-1,7-1,8-1,9-1,10-1,11-1,12-1,13-1,14-1,15-1,16-1
ESV - **16,** 1-1,2-1,3-1,4-1,5-1,6-1,7-1,8-1,9-1,10-1,11-1,12-1,13-1,14-1,15-1,16-1
HCSB - 14, 1-1,2-1,3-**2,**4-1,5-1,6-1,7-1,8-1,9-1,10-1,11-1,12-1,13-1,14-1
NASV - **16,** 1-1,2-1,3-1,4-1,5-1,6-1,7-1,8-1,9-1,10-1,11-1,12-1,13-1,14-1,15-1,16-1
NCV - **13,** 1-1,2-1,3-1,4-1,5-1,6-1,7-1,8-1,9-1,10-1,11-1,12-1,13-1
NIV - 15, 1-1,2-1,3-1,4-1,5-**3,**6-1,7-1,8-1,9-1,10-1,11-1,12-1,13-1,14-1,15-1
NKJV - **16,** 1-1,2-1,3-1,4-1,5-1,6-1,7-1,8-1,9-1,10-1,11-1,12-1,13-1,14-1,15-1,16-1
NLT - **13,** 1-1,2-1,3-1,4-1,5-1,6-1,7-1,8-1,9-1,10-1,11-1,12-1,13-1
NRSV - **14,** 1-1,2-1,3-1,4-1,5-1,6-1,7-1,8-1,9-1,10-1,11-1,12-1,13-1,14-1
Conclusion: Only the HCSB and NIV made the verse more complex.

15. Genesis 9:29*# And all the days of **Noah** were nine **hundred** and **fifty** years: and he died.
AV - **15,** 1-1,2-1,3-1,4-1,5-1,6-1,7-1,8-1,9-1,10-1,11-1,12-1,13-1,14-1,15-1
ESV - **11,** 1-1,2-1,3-1,4-1,5-1,6-1,7-1,8-1,9-1,10-1,11-1
HCSB - **9,** 1-1,2-1,3-1,4-**2,**5-1,6-1,7-1,8-1,9-1
NASV - **15,** 1-1,2-1,3-1,4-1,5-1,6-1,7-1,8-1,9-1,10-1,11-1,12-1,13-1,14-1,15-1
NCV - **11,** 1-1,2-1,3-1,4-1,5-**2,**6-1,7-1,8-1,9-1,10-1,11-1
NIV - **9,** 1-**4,**2-1,3-1,4-1,5-1,6-1,7-1,8-1,9-1
NKJV - **15,** 1-1,2-1,3-1,4-1,5-1,6-1,7-1,8-1,9-1,10-1,11-1,12-1,13-1,14-1,15-1
NLT - **8,** 1-1,2-1,3-1,4-1,5-1,6-1,7-1,8-1
NRSV - **13,** 1-1,2-1,3-1,4-1,5-1,6-1,7-1,8-1,9-1,10-1,11-1,12-1,13-1
Conclusion: Only three modern versions are more complex than the King James Bible.

16. Genesis 10:2* The sons of **Japheth**; **Gomer**, and **Magog**, and **Madai**, and **Javan**, and **Tubal**, and **Meshech**, and **Tiras**.
AV - **17,** 1-1,2-1,3-1,4-1,5-1,6-1,7-1,8-1,9-1,10-1,11-1,12-1,13-1,14-1,15-1,16-1,17-1
ESV - **12,** 1-1,2-1,3-1,4-1,5-1,6-1,7-1,8-1,9-1,10-1,11-1,12-1
HCSB - **10,** 1-1,2-1,3-1,4-1,5-1,6-1,7-1,8-1,9-1,10-1
NASV - **18,** 1-1,2-1,3-1,4-1,5-1,6-1,7-1,8-1,9-1,10-1,11-1,12-1,13-1,14-1,15-1,16-1,17-1,18-1
NCV - **13,** 1-1,2-1,3-1,4-1,5-1,6-1,7-1,8-1,9-1,10-1,11-1,12-1,13-1
NIV - **12,** 1-1,2-1,3-1,4-1,5-1,6-1,7-1,8-1,9-1,10-1,11-1,12-1
NKJV - **13,** 1-1,2-1,3-1,4-1,5-1,6-1,7-1,8-1,9-1,10-1,11-1,12-1,13-1
NLT - **13,** 1-1,2-**3,**3-1,4-1,5-1,6-1,7-1,8-1,9-1,10-1,11-1,12-1,13-1
NRSV - **12,** 1-1,2-**3,**3-1,4-1,5-1,6-1,7-1,8-1,9-1,10-1,11-1,12-1
Conclusion: Only the NLT and the NRSV made the verse more complex.

17. Genesis 10:3* And the sons of **Gomer**; **Ashkenaz**, and **Riphath**, and **Togarmah**.
AV - **10,** 1-1,2-1,3-1,4-1,5-1,6-1,7-1,8-1,9-1,10-1
ESV - **8,** 1-1,2-1,3-1,4-1,5-1,6-1,7-1,8-1
HCSB - **6,** 1-1,2-1,3-1,4-1,5-1,6-1
NASV - **10,** 1-1,2-1,3-1,4-1,5-1,6-1,7-1,8-1,9-1,10-1
NCV - **9,** 1-1,2-1,3-1,4-1,5-1,6-1,7-1,8-1,9-1
NIV - **8,** 1-1,2-1,3-1,4-1,5-1,6-1,7-1,8-1
NKJV - **9,** 1-1,2-1,3-1,4-1,5-1,6-1,7-1,8-1,9-1
NLT - **9,** 1-1,2-**3,**3-1,4-1,5-1,6-1,7-1,8-1,9-1
NRSV - **8,** 1-1,2-**3,**3-1,4-1,5-1,6-1,7-1,8-1
Conclusion: Only the NLT and the NRSV made the verse more complex.

18. Genesis 10:4* And the sons of **Javan**; **Elishah**, and **Tarshish**, **Kittim**, and **Dodanim**.
AV - **11,** 1-1,2-1,3-1,4-1,5-1,6-1,7-1,8-1,9-1,10-1,11-1
ESV - **9,** 1-1,2-1,3-1,4-1,5-1,6-1,7-1,8-1,9-1
HCSB - **8,** 1-1,2-1,3-1,4-1,5-1,6-1,7-1,8-1
NASV - **11,** 1-1,2-1,3-1,4-1,5-1,6-1,7-1,8-1,9-1,10-1,11-1
NCV - **10,** 1-1,2-1,3-1,4-1,5-1,6-1,7-1,8-1,9-1,10-1
NIV - **11,** 1-1,2-1,3-1,4-1,5-1,6-1,7-1,8-1,9-1,10-1,11-1

NKJV - **10,** 1-1,2-1,3-1,4-1,5-1,6-1,7-1,8-1,9-1,10-1
NLT - 10, 1-1,2-**3**,3-1,4-1,5-1,6-1,7-1,8-1,9-1,10-1
NRSV - 9, 1-1,2-**3**,3-1,4-1,5-1,6-1,7-1,8-1,9-1
Conclusion: Only the NLT and the NRSV made the verse more complex.

19. Genesis 10:6* And the sons of **Ham**; **Cush**, and **Mizraim**, and **Phut**, and **Canaan**.
AV - **12,** 1-1,2-1,3-1,4-1,5-1,6-1,7-1,8-1,9-1,10-1,11-1,12-1
ESV - **9,** 1-1,2-1,3-1,4-1,5-1,6-1,7-1,8-1,9-1
HCSB - **7,** 1-1,2-1,3-1,4-1,5-1,6-1,7-1
NASV - **12,** 1-1,2-1,3-1,4-1,5-1,6-1,7-1,8-1,9-1,10-1,11-1,12-1
NCV - **10,** 1-1,2-1,3-1,4-1,5-1,6-1,7-1,8-1,9-1,10-1
NIV - **9,** 1-1,2-1,3-1,4-1,5-1,6-1,7-1,8-1,9-1
NKJV - **10,** 1-1,2-1,3-1,4-1,5-1,6-1,7-1,8-1,9-1,10-1
NLT - 10, 1-1,2-**3**,3-1,4-1,5-1,6-1,7-1,8-1,9-1,10-1
NRSV - 9, 1-1,2-**3**,3-1,4-1,5-1,6-1,7-1,8-1,9-1
Conclusion: Only the NLT and the NRSV made the verse more complex.

20. Genesis 10:7* And the sons of **Cush**; **Seba**, and **Havilah**, and **Sabtah**, and **Raamah**, and **Sabtecha**: and the sons of **Raamah**; **Sheba**, and **Dedan**.
AV - **22,** 1-1,2-1,3-1,4-1,5-1,6-1,7-1,8-1,9-1,10-1,11-1,12-1,13-1,14-1,15-1,16-1,17-1,18-1,19-1,20-1,21-1,22-1
ESV - **17,** 1-1,2-1,3-1,4-1,5-1,6-1,7-1,8-1,9-1,10-1,11-1,12-1,13-1,14-1,15-1,16-1,17-1
HCSB - **14,** 1-1,2-1,3-1,4-1,5-1,6-1,7-1,8-1,9-1,10-1,11-1,12-1,13-1,14-1
NASV - **23,** 1-1,2-1,3-1,4-1,5-1,6-1,7-1,8-1,9-1,10-1,11-1,12-1,13-1,14-1,15-1,16-1,17-1,18-1,19-1,20-1,21-1,22-1,23-1
NCV - **19,** 1-1,2-1,3-1,4-1,5-1,6-1,7-1,8-1,9-1,10-1,11-1,12-1,13-1,14-1,15-1,16-1,17-1,18-1,19-1
NIV - **17,** 1-1,2-1,3-1,4-1,5-1,6-1,7-1,8-1,9-1,10-1,11-1,12-1,13-1,14-1,15-1,16-1,17-1
NKJV - **20,** 1-1,2-1,3-1,4-1,5-1,6-1,7-1,8-1,9-1,10-1,11-1,12-1,13-1,14-1,15-1,16-1,17-1,18-1,19-1,20-1
NLT - 19, 1-1,2-**3**,3-1,4-1,5-1,6-1,7-1,8-1,9-1,10-1,11-1,12-1,13-**3**,14-1,15-1,16-1,17-1,18-1,19-1
NRSV - 17, 1-1,2-**3**,3-1,4-1,5-1,6-1,7-1,8-1,9-1,10-1,11-1,12-**3**,13-1,14-1,15-1,16-1,17-1
Conclusion: Only the NLT and the NRSV made the verse more complex.

21. Genesis 10:14* And **Pathrusim**, and **Casluhim**, (out of whom came **Philistim**,) and **Caphtorim**.
AV - **11,** 1-1,2-1,3-1,4-1,5-1,6-1,7-1,8-1,9-1,10-1,11-1
ESV - **9,** 1-1,2-1,3-1,4-1,5-1,6-1,7-1,8-1,9-1
HCSB - **9,** 1-1,2-1,3-1,4-1,5-1,6-1,7-1,8-1,9-1
NASV - **11,** 1-1,2-1,3-1,4-1,5-1,6-1,7-1,8-1,9-1,10-1,11-1
NCV - 13, 1-1,2-1,3-1,4-1,5-**2**,6-1,7-1,8-1,9-1,10-1,11-1,12-1,13-1
NIV - **9,** 1-1,2-1,3-1,4-1,5-1,6-1,7-1,8-1,9-1
NKJV - **10,** 1-1,2-1,3-1,4-1,5-1,6-1,7-1,8-1,9-1,10-1
NLT - **10,** 1-1,2-1,3-1,4-1,5-1,6-1,7-1,8-1,9-1,10-1
NRSV - **9,** 1-1,2-1,3-1,4-1,5-1,6-1,7-1,8-1,9-1

Conclusion: Only the NCV made the verse more complex.

22. Genesis 10:16*And the **Jebusite**, and the **Amorite**, and the **Girgasite**,
AV - **9,** 1-1,2-1,3-1,4-1,5-1,6-1,7-1,8-1,9-1
ESV - **7,** 1-1,2-1,3-1,4-1,5-1,6-1,7-1
HCSB - **6,** 1-1,2-1,3-1,4-1,5-1,6-1
NASV - **9,** 1-1,2-1,3-1,4-1,5-1,6-1,7-1,8-1,9-1
NCV - 10, 1-1,2-1,3-**2**,4-1,5-**2**,6-1,7-1,8-1,9-1,10-1
NIV - **3,** 1-1,2-1,3-1
NKJV - **7,** 1-1,2-1,3-1,4-1,5-1,6-1,7-1
NLT - **3,** 1-1,2-1,3-1
NRSV - **7,** 1-1,2-1,3-1,4-1,5-1,6-1,7-1
Conclusion: Only the NCV made the verse more complex.

23. Genesis 10:17* And the **Hivite**, and the **Arkite**, and the **Sinite**,
AV - **9,** 1-1,2-1,3-1,4-1,5-1,6-1,7-1,8-1,9-1
ESV - **6,** 1-1,2-1,3-1,4-1,5-1,6-1
HCSB - **6,** 1-1,2-1,3-1,4-1,5-1,6-1
NASV - **9,** 1-1,2-1,3-1,4-1,5-1,6-1,7-1,8-1,9-1
NCV - **3,** 1-1,2-1,3-1
NIV - **3,** 1-1,2-1,3-1
NKJV - **7,** 1-1,2-1,3-1,4-1,5-1,6-1,7-1
NLT - **3,** 1-1,2-1,3-1
NRSV - **6,** 1-1,2-1,3-1,4-1,5-1,6-1
Conclusion: All versions read the same.

24. Genesis 10:27* And **Hadoram**, and **Uzal**, and **Diklah**,
AV - **6,** 1-1,2-1,3-1,4-1,5-1,6-1
ESV - **3,** 1-1,2-1,3-1
HCSB - **3,** 1-1,2-1,3-1
NASV - **6,** 1-1,2-1,3-1,4-1,5-1,6-1
NCV - **3,** 1-1,2-1,3-1
NIV - **3,** 1-1,2-1,3-1
NKJV - **3,** 1-1,2-1,3-1
NLT - **3,** 1-1,2-1,3-1
NRSV - **3,** 1-1,2-1,3-1
Conclusion: All versions read the same.

25. Genesis 10:28* And **Obal**, and **Abimael**, and **Sheba**,
AV - **6,** 1-1,2-1,3-1,4-1,5-1,6-1
ESV - **3,** 1-1,2-1,3-1
HCSB - **3,** 1-1,2-1,3-1
NASV - **6,** 1-1,2-1,3-1,4-1,5-1,6-1
NCV - **3,** 1-1,2-1,3-1

NIV - **3,** 1-1,2-1,3-1
NKJV - **3,** 1-1,2-1,3-1
NLT - **3,** 1-1,2-1,3-1
NRSV - **3,** 1-1,2-1,3-1
Conclusion: All versions read the same.

26. Genesis 10:29* And **Ophir**, and **Havilah**, and **Jobab**: all these were the sons of **Joktan**.
AV - **13,** 1-1,2-1,3-1,4-1,5-1,6-1,7-1,8-1,9-1,10-1,11-1,12-1,13-1
ESV - **11,** 1-1,2-1,3-1,4-1,5-1,6-1,7-1,8-1,9-1,10-1,11-1
HCSB - **9,** 1-1,2-1,3-1,4-1,5-1,6-1,7-1,8-1,9-1
NASV - **13,** 1-1,2-1,3-1,4-1,5-1,6-1,7-1,8-1,9-1,10-1,11-1,12-1,13-1
NCV - 12, 1-1,2-1,3-1,4-1,5-1,6-1,7-**2**,8-1,9-1,10-1,11-1,12-1
NIV - **10,** 1-1,2-1,3-1,4-1,5-1,6-1,7-1,8-1,9-1,10-1
NKJV - **11,** 1-1,2-1,3-1,4-1,5-1,6-1,7-1,8-1,9-1,10-1,11-1
NLT - 10, 1-1,2-1,3-1,4-1,5-1,6-1,7-1,8-**3**,9-1,10-1
NRSV - 11, 1-1,2-1,3-1,4-1,5-1,6-1,7-1,8-1,9-**3**,10-1,11-1
Conclusion: Only three modern versions are more complex than the King James Bible.

27. Genesis 11:32*# And the days of **Terah** were two **hundred** and five years: and **Terah** died in **Haran**.
AV - **16,** 1-1,2-1,3-1,4-1,5-1,6-1,7-1,8-1,9-1,10-1,11-1,12-1,13-1,14-1,15-1,16-1
ESV - **12,** 1-1,2-1,3-1,4-1,5-1,6-1,7-1,8-1,9-1,10-1,11-1,12-1
HCSB - **8,** 1-1,2-1,3-1,4-1,5-1,6-1,7-1,8-1
NASV - **15,** 1-1,2-1,3-1,4-1,5-1,6-1,7-1,8-1,9-1,10-1,11-1,12-1,13-1,14-1,15-1
NCV - **13,** 1-1,2-1,3-1,4-1,5-1,6-1,7-1,8-1,9-1,10-1,11-1,12-1,13-1
NIV - **9,** 1-1,2-1,3-1,4-1,5-1,6-1,7-1,8-1,9-1
NKJV - **16,** 1-1,2-1,3-1,4-1,5-1,6-1,7-1,8-1,9-1,10-1,11-1,12-1,13-1,14-1,15-1,16-1
NLT - **11,** 1-1,2-1,3-1,4-1,5-1,6-1,7-1,8-1,9-1,10-1,11-1
NRSV - **14,** 1-1,2-1,3-1,4-1,5-1,6-1,7-1,8-1,9-1,10-1,11-1,12-1,13-1,14-1
Conclusion: All versions read the same.

28. Genesis 14:2* That these made war with **Bera** king of **Sodom**, and with **Birsha** king of **Gomorrah**, **Shinab** king of **Admah**, and **Shemeber** king of **Zeboiim**, and the king of **Bela**, which is **Zoar**.
AV - **32,** 1-1,2-1,3-1,4-1,5-1,6-1,7-1,8-1,9-1,10-1,11-1,12-1,13-1,14-1,15-1,16-1,17-1,18-1,19-1,20-1,21-1,22-1,23-1,24-1,25-1,26-1,27-1,28-1,29-1,30-1,31-1,32-1
ESV - **29,** 1-1,2-1,3-1,4-1,5-1,6-1,7-1,8-1,9-1,10-1,11-1,12-1,13-1,14-1,15-1,16-1,17-1,18-1,19-1,20-1,21-1,22-1,23-1,24-1,25-1,26-1,27-1,28-1,29-1
HCSB - 30, 1-1,2-1,3-**2**,4-1,5-1,6-1,7-1,8-1,9-1,10-1,11-1,12-1,13-1,14-1,15-1,16-1,17-1,18-1,19-1,20-1,21-1,22-1,23-1,24-1,25-1,26-1,27-1,28-1,29-1,30-1
NASV - **32,** 1-1,2-1,3-1,4-1,5-1,6-1,7-1,8-1,9-1,10-1,11-1,12-1,13-1,14-1,15-1,16-1,17-1,18-1,19-1,20-1,21-1,22-1,23-1,24-1,25-1,26-1,27-1,28-1,29-1,30-1,31-1,32-1
NCV - 36, 1-1,2-1,3-1,4-1,5-1,6-1,7-**2**,8-**3**,9-**2**,10-1,11-1,12-1,13-1,14-1,15-1,16-1,17-1,18-1,19-1,20-1,21-1,22-1,23-1,24-1,25-1,26-1,27-1,28-1,29-1,30-1,31-1,32-1,33-1,34-**2**,35-1,36-1

NIV - **28,** 1-1,2-1,3-1,4-**2,**5-1,6-1,7-1,8-1,9-1,10-1,11-1,12-1,13-1,14-1,15-1,16-1,17-1,18-1,19-1,20-1,21-1,22-1,23-1,24-1,25-1,26-1,27-1,28-1

NKJV - **29,** 1-1,2-1,3-1,4-1,5-1,6-1,7-1,8-1,9-1,10-1,11-1,12-1,13-1,14-1,15-1,16-1,17-1,18-1,19-1,20-1,21-1,22-1,23-1,24-1,25-1,26-1,27-1,28-1,29-1

NLT - **26,** 1-1,2-**2,**3-1,4-1,5-1,6-1,7-1,8-1,9-1,10-1,11-1,12-1,13-1,14-1,15-1,16-1,17-1,18-1,19-1,20-1,21-1,22-1,23-1,24-**2,**25-1,26-1

NRSV - **29,** 1-1,2-1,3-1,4-1,5-1,6-1,7-1,8-1,9-1,10-1,11-1,12-1,13-1,14-1,15-1,16-1,17-1,18-1,19-1,20-1,21-1,22-1,23-1,24-1,25-1,26-1,27-1,28-1,29-1

Conclusion: Four modern versions are more complex than the King James Bible. Only the NCV made the verse more complex.

29. Genesis 14:5*# And in the **fourteenth** year came **Chedorlaomer**, and the kings that were with him, and smote the **Rephaims** in **Ashteroth Karnaim**, and the **Zuzims** in Ham, and the **Emims** in **Shaveh Kiriathaim**,

AV - **32,** 1-1,2-1,3-1,4-1,5-1,6-1,7-1,8-1,9-1,10-1,11-1,12-1,13-1,14-1,15-1,16-1,17-1,18-1,19-1,20-1,21-1,22-1,23-1,24-1,25-1,26-1,27-1,28-1,29-1,30-1,31-1,32-1

ESV - **29,** 1-1,2-1,3-1,4-1,5-1,6-1,7-1,8-1,9-1,10-1,11-1,12-1,13-1,14-1,15-**3,**16-1,17-1,18-1,19-1,20-1,21-1,22-1,23-1,24-1,25-1,26-1,27-1,28-1,29-1

HCSB - **29,** 1-1,2-1,3-1,4-1,5-1,6-1,7-1,8-1,9-1,10-1,11-1,12-1,13-1,14-1,15-**3,**16-1,17-1,18-1,19-1,20-1,21-1,22-1,23-1,24-1,25-1,26-1,27-1,28-1,29-1

NASV - **31,** 1-1,2-1,3-1,4-1,5-1,6-1,7-1,8-1,9-1,10-1,11-1,12-1,13-1,14-1,15-**3,**16-1,17-1,18-1,19-1,20-1,21-1,22-1,23-1,24-1,25-1,26-1,27-1,28-1,29-1,30-1,31-1

NCV - **29,** 1-1,2-1,3-1,4-1,5-1,6-1,7-1,8-1,9-1,10-1,11-1,12-1,13-1,14-**3,**15-1,16-1,17-1,18-1,19-1,20-1,21-1,22-1,23-1,24-1,25-1,26-1,27-1,28-1,29-1

NIV - **29,** 1-1,2-1,3-1,4-1,5-1,6-1,7-1,8-1,9-**2,**10-1,11-1,12-1,13-1,14-1,15-**3,**16-1,17-1,18-1,19-1,20-1,21-1,22-1,23-1,24-1,25-1,26-1,27-1,28-1,29-1

NKJV - **29,** 1-1,2-1,3-1,4-1,5-1,6-1,7-1,8-1,9-1,10-1,11-1,12-1,13-1,14-1,15-**2,**16-1,17-1,18-1,19-1,20-1,21-1,22-1,23-1,24-1,25-1,26-1,27-1,28-1,29-1

NLT - **24,** 1-1,2-1,3-**2,**4-1,5-1,6-1,7-**2,**8-**2,**9-1,10-**3,**11-1,12-1,13-1,14-1,15-1,16-1,17-1,18-1,19-1,20-1,21-1,22-1,23-1,24-1

NRSV - **29,** 1-1,2-1,3-1,4-1,5-1,6-1,7-1,8-1,9-1,10-1,11-1,12-1,13-1,14-1,15-**2,**16-1,17-1,18-1,19-1,20-1,21-1,22-1,23-1,24-1,25-1,26-1,27-1,28-1,29-1

Conclusion: All eight modern versions are more complex than the King James Bible. The NLT is the most difficult to read.

30. Genesis 14:18* And **Melchizedek** king of **Salem** brought forth bread and wine: and he was the priest of the most high God.

AV - **20,** 1-1,2-1,3-1,4-1,5-1,6-1,7-1,8-1,9-1,10-1,11-1,12-1,13-1,14-1,15-1,16-1,17-1,18-1,19-1,20-1

ESV - **17,** 1-1,2-1,3-1,4-1,5-1,6-1,7-1,8-1,9-1,10-1,11-1,12-1,13-1,14-1,15-1,16-1,17-1

HCSB - **18,** 1-1,2-1,3-1,4-1,5-1,6-1,7-1,8-1,9-1,10-1,11-1,12-1,13-1,14-1,15-1,16-1,17-1,18-1

NASV - **19,** 1-1,2-1,3-1,4-1,5-1,6-1,7-1,8-1,9-1,10-1,11-1,12-1,13-1,14-1,15-1,16-1,17-1,18-1,19-1

NCV - **17,** 1-1,2-1,3-1,4-1,5-1,6-1,7-1,8-1,9-1,10-1,11-1,12-1,13-1,14-1,15-1,16-1,17-1

NIV - **17,** 1-1,2-1,3-1,4-1,5-1,6-1,7-1,8-1,9-1,10-1,11-1,12-1,13-1,14-1,15-1,16-1,17-1

NKJV - **18,** 1-1,2-1,3-1,4-1,5-1,6-1,7-1,8-1,9-1,10-1,11-1,12-1,13-1,14-1,15-1,16-1,17-1,18-1
NLT - **19,** 1-1,2-1,3-1,4-1,5-1,6-1,7-1,8-1,9-1,10-1,11-1,12-1,13-1,14-1,15-1,16-1,17-1,18-1,19-1
NRSV - **17,** 1-1,2-1,3-1,4-1,5-1,6-1,7-1,8-1,9-1,10-1,11-1,12-1,13-1,14-1,15-1,16-1,17-1
Conclusion: All versions read the same.

31. Genesis 15:19* The **Kenites**, and the **Kenizzites**, and the **Kadmonites**,
AV - **8,** 1-1,2-1,3-1,4-1,5-1,6-1,7-1,8-1
ESV - **9,** 1-1,2-1,3-1,4-1,5-1,6-1,7-1,8-1,9-1
HCSB - **7,** 1-1,2-1,3-1,4-1,5-1,6-1,7-1
NASV - **8,** 1-1,2-1,3-1,4-1,5-1,6-1,7-1,8-1
NCV - **9,** 1-1,2-1,3-1,4-1,5-1,6-1,7-1,8-1,9-1
NIV - **7,** 1-1,2-1,3-1,4-1,5-1,6-1,7-1
NKJV - **6,** 1-1,2-1,3-1,4-1,5-1,6-1
NLT - **9,** 1-1,2-1,3-1,4-**3,**5-1,6-1,7-1,8-1,9-1
NRSV - **9,** 1-1,2-1,3-1,4-1,5-1,6-1,7-1,8-1,9-1
Conclusion: Only the NLT made the verse more complex.

32. Genesis 15:20* And the **Hittites**, and the **Perizzites**, and the **Rephaims**,
AV - **9,** 1-1,2-1,3-1,4-1,5-1,6-1,7-1,8-1,9-1
ESV - **6,** 1-1,2-1,3-1,4-1,5-1,6-1
HCSB - **3,** 1-1,2-1,3-1
NASV - **9,** 1-1,2-1,3-1,4-1,5-1,6-1,7-1,8-1,9-1
NCV - **3,** 1-1,2-1,3-1
NIV - **3,** 1-1,2-1,3-1
NKJV - **6,** 1-1,2-1,3-1,4-1,5-1,6-1
NLT - **3,** 1-1,2-1,3-1
NRSV - **6,** 1-1,2-1,3-1,4-1,5-1,6-1
Conclusion: All versions read the same.

33. Genesis 15:21* And the **Amorites**, and the **Canaanites**, and the **Girgashites**, and the **Jebusites**.
AV - **12,** 1-1,2-1,3-1,4-1,5-1,6-1,7-1,8-1,9-1,10-1,11-1,12-1
ESV - **9,** 1-1,2-1,3-1,4-1,5-1,6-1,7-1,8-1,9-1
HCSB - **5,** 1-1,2-1,3-1,4-1,5-1
NASV - **12,** 1-1,2-1,3-1,4-1,5-1,6-1,7-1,8-1,9-1,10-1,11-1,12-1
NCV - **5,** 1-1,2-1,3-1,4-1,5-1
NIV - **5,** 1-1,2-1,3-1,4-1,5-1
NKJV - **9,** 1-1,2-1,3-1,4-1,5-1,6-1,7-1,8-1,9-1
NLT - **5,** 1-1,2-1,3-1,4-1,5-1
NRSV - **9,** 1-1,2-1,3-1,4-1,5-1,6-1,7-1,8-1,9-1
Conclusion: All versions read the same.

34. Genesis 16:15* And **Hagar** bare **Abram** a son: and **Abram** called his son's name, which **Hagar** bare, **Ishmael**.
AV - **16,** 1-1,2-1,3-1,4-1,5-1,6-1,7-1,8-1,9-1,10-1,11-1,12-1,13-1,14-1,15-1,16-1

20

ESV - **18,** 1-1,2-1,3-1,4-1,5-1,6-1,7-1,8-1,9-1,10-1,11-1,12-1,13-1,14-1,15-1,16-1,17-1,18-1
HCSB - **18,** 1-1,2-1,3-1,4-1,5-1,6-1,7-1,8-1,9-1,10-1,11-1,12-1,13-1,14-1,15-1,16-1,17-1,18-1
NASV - **18,** 1-1,2-1,3-1,4-1,5-1,6-1,7-1,8-1,9-1,10-1,11-1,12-1,13-1,14-1,15-1,16-1,17-1,18-1
NCV - **13,** 1-1,2-1,3-1,4-1,5-1,6-1,7-1,8-1,9-1,10-1,11-1,12-1,13-1
NIV - **18,** 1-1,2-1,3-1,4-1,5-1,6-1,7-1,8-1,9-1,10-1,11-1,12-1,13-1,14-1,15-1,16-1,17-1,18-1
NKJV - **15,** 1-1,2-1,3-1,4-1,5-1,6-1,7-1,8-1,9-1,10-1,11-1,12-1,13-1,14-1,15-1
NLT - **11,** 1-1,2-1,3-1,4-1,5-1,6-1,7-1,8-1,9-1,10-1,11-1
NRSV - **14,** 1-1,2-1,3-1,4-1,5-1,6-1,7-1,8-1,9-1,10-1,11-1,12-1,13-1,14-1
Conclusion: All versions read the same.

35. Genesis 16:16*# And **Abram** was **fourscore** and six years old, when **Hagar** bare **Ishmael** to **Abram**.
AV - **14,** 1-1,2-1,3-1,4-1,5-1,6-1,7-1,8-1,9-1,10-1,11-1,12-1,13-1,14-1
ESV - **11,** 1-1,2-1,3-1,4-1,5-1,6-1,7-1,8-1,9-1,10-1,11-1
HCSB - **11,** 1-1,2-1,3-1,4-1,5-1,6-1,7-1,8-1,9-1,10-1,11-1
NASV - **11,** 1-1,2-1,3-1,4-1,5-1,6-1,7-1,8-1,9-1,10-1,11-1
NCV - **11,** 1-1,2-1,3-1,4-1,5-1,6-1,7-1,8-1,9-1,10-1,11-1
NIV - **10,** 1-1,2-1,3-1,4-1,5-1,6-1,7-1,8-1,9-1,10-1
NKJV - **11,** 1-1,2-1,3-1,4-1,5-1,6-1,7-1,8-1,9-1,10-1,11-1
NLT - **9,** 1-1,2-1,3-1,4-1,5-1,6-1,7-1,8-1,9-1
NRSV - **10,** 1-1,2-1,3-1,4-1,5-1,6-1,7-1,8-1,9-1,10-1
Conclusion: All versions read the same.

36. Genesis 18:16* And the men rose up from thence, and looked toward **Sodom**: and **Abraham** went with them to bring them on the way.
AV - **22,** 1-1,2-1,3-1,4-1,5-1,6-1,7-1,8-1,9-1,10-1,11-1,12-1,13-1,14-1,15-1,16-1,17-1,18-1,19-1,20-1,21-1,22-1
ESV - **24,** 1-1,2-1,3-1,4-1,5-1,6-1,7-1,8-1,9-1,10-1,11-1,12-1,13-1,14-1,15-1,16-1,17-1,18-1,19-1,20-1,21-1,22-1,23-1,24-1
HCSB - **21,** 1-1,2-1,3-1,4-1,5-1,6-1,7-1,8-1,9-1,10-**2,**11-1,12-1,13-1,14-1,15-**2,**16-1,17-1,18-1,19-1,20-1,21-1
NASV - **22,** 1-1,2-1,3-1,4-1,5-1,6-1,7-1,8-1,9-1,10-1,11-1,12-1,13-1,14-1,15-1,16-**2,**17-1,18-1,19-1,20-1,21-1,22-1
NCV - **26,** 1-1,2-1,3-1,4-1,5-1,6-1,7-1,8-1,9-**2,**10-1,11-1,12-1,13-1,14-1,15-**2,**16-1,17-1,18-1,19-1,20-1,21-1,22-1,23-1,24-1,25-1,26-1
NIV - **24,** 1-1,2-1,3-1,4-1,5-1,6-1,7-1,8-1,9-1,10-1,11-1,12-1,13-1,14-1,15-1,16-**2,**17-1,18-1,19-1,20-1,21-1,22-1,23-1,24-1
NKJV - **21,** 1-1,2-1,3-1,4-1,5-1,6-1,7-1,8-1,9-1,10-1,11-1,12-1,13-1,14-1,15-1,16-1,17-1,18-1,19-1,20-1,21-1
NLT - **26,** 1-1,2-1,3-1,4-1,5-1,6-1,7-1,8-1,9-1,10-1,11-1,12-1,13-1,14-1,15-1,16-1,17-1,18-1,19-1,20-1,21-1,22-1,23-1,24-1,25-1,26-1
NRSV - **23,** 1-1,2-1,3-1,4-1,5-1,6-1,7-1,8-1,9-1,10-1,11-1,12-1,13-1,14-1,15-1,16-1,17-1,18-1,19-1,20-1,21-1,22-1,23-1
Conclusion: Four modern versions are more complex than the King James Bible.

Samuel C. Gipp Ph.D.

37. Genesis 18:17* And the LORD said, Shall I hide from **Abraham** that thing which I do;
AV - **14,** 1-1,2-1,3-1,4-1,5-1,6-1,7-1,8-1,9-1,10-1,11-1,12-1,13-1,14-1
ESV - 14, 1-1,2-1,3-1,4-1,5-1,6-1,7-1,8-1,9-1,10-1,11-1,12-**2**,13-1,14-1
HCSB - 15, 1-1,2-1,3-1,4-1,5-1,6-1,7-1,8-1,9-1,10-1,11-1,12-1,13-**2**,14-1,15-1
NASV - 14, 1-1,2-1,3-1,4-1,5-1,6-1,7-1,8-1,9-1,10-1,11-1,12-**2**,13-1,14-1
NCV - 14, 1-1,2-1,3-1,4-1,5-1,6-1,7-1,8-1,9-1,10-1,11-**2**,12-1,13-1,14-1
NIV - 15, 1-1,2-1,3-1,4-1,5-1,6-1,7-1,8-1,9-1,10-1,11-1,12-1,13-**2**,14-1,15-1
NKJV - 13, 1-1,2-1,3-1,4-1,5-1,6-1,7-1,8-1,9-1,10-1,11-1,12-1,13-**2**
NLT - **10,** 1-1,2-1,3-1,4-1,5-1,6-1,7-1,8-1,9-1,10-1
NRSV - 14, 1-1,2-1,3-1,4-1,5-1,6-1,7-1,8-1,9-1,10-1,11-1,12-**2**,13-1,14-1
Conclusion: Seven modern versions are more complex than the King James Bible.

38. Genesis 21:6* And **Sarah** said, God hath made me to laugh, so that all that hear will laugh with me.
AV - **18,** 1-1,2-1,3-1,4-1,5-1,6-1,7-1,8-1,9-1,10-1,11-1,12-1,13-1,14-1,15-1,16-1,17-1,18-1
ESV - 16, 1-1,2-1,3-1,4-1,5-1,6-1,7-**2**,8-1,9-1,10-**4**,11-1,12-1,13-1,14-1,15-**2**,16-1
HCSB - 15, 1-1,2-1,3-1,4-1,5-1,6-1,7-1,8-1,9-**4**,10-1,11-1,12-1,13-1,14-1,15-1
NASV - 14, 1-1,2-1,3-1,4-1,5-**2**,6-1,7-1,8-**4**,9-1,10-1,11-1,12-1,13-1,14-1
NCV - 17, 1-1,2-1,3-1,4-1,5-1,6-1,7-1,8-1,9-**4**,10-1,11-1,12-1,13-1,14-1,15-1,16-1,17-1
NIV - 17, 1-1,2-1,3-1,4-1,5-1,6-1,7-**2**,8-1,9-**4**,10-1,11-1,12-1,13-1,14-1,15-1,16-1,17-1
NKJV - **16,** 1-1,2-1,3-1,4-1,5-1,6-1,7-1,8-1,9-1,10-1,11-1,12-1,13-1,14-1,15-1,16-1
NLT - 17, 1-1,2-1,3-**2**,4-1,5-1,6-1,7-1,8-**2**,9-1,10-1,11-1,12-**2**,13-1,14-1,15-1,16-1,17-1
NRSV - 16, 1-1,2-1,3-1,4-1,5-1,6-1,7-**2**,8-1,9-1,10-**4**,11-1,12-1,13-1,14-1,15-1,16-1
Conclusion: Seven modern versions are more complex than the King James Bible.

39. Genesis 21:8* And the child grew, and was weaned: and **Abraham** made a great feast the same day that **Isaac** was weaned.
AV - **20,** 1-1,2-1,3-1,4-1,5-1,6-1,7-1,8-1,9-1,10-1,11-1,12-1,13-1,14-1,15-1,16-1,17-1,18-1,19-1,20-1
ESV - **20,** 1-1,2-1,3-1,4-1,5-1,6-1,7-1,8-1,9-1,10-1,11-1,12-1,13-1,14-1,15-1,16-1,17-1,18-1,19-1,20-1
HCSB - **18,** 1-1,2-1,3-1,4-1,5-1,6-1,7-1,8-1,9-1,10-1,11-1,12-1,13-1,14-1,15-1,16-1,17-1,18-1
NASV - **19,** 1-1,2-1,3-1,4-1,5-1,6-1,7-1,8-1,9-1,10-1,11-1,12-1,13-1,14-1,15-1,16-1,17-1,18-1,19-1
NCV - 16, 1-1,2-1,3-1,4-1,5-1,6-**2**,7-1,8-**2**,9-1,10-1,11-1,12-1,13-1,14-1,15-1,16-1
NIV - **18,** 1-1,2-1,3-1,4-1,5-1,6-1,7-1,8-1,9-1,10-1,11-1,12-1,13-1,14-1,15-1,16-1,17-1,18-1
NKJV - **21,** 1-1,2-1,3-1,4-1,5-1,6-1,7-1,8-1,9-1,10-1,11-1,12-1,13-1,14-1,15-1,16-1,17-1,18-1,19-1,20-1,21-1
NLT - 19, 1-1,2-1,3-1,4-1,5-1,6-1,7-**2**,8-1,9-1,10-1,11-1,12-**2**,13-1,14-1,15-1,16-1,17-**3**,18-1,19-**3**
NRSV - **19,** 1-1,2-1,3-1,4-1,5-1,6-1,7-1,8-1,9-1,10-1,11-1,12-1,13-1,14-1,15-1,16-1,17-1,18-1,19-1
Conclusion: Only the NCV and NLT are more complex than the King James Bible. The NLT is the most difficult to read.

40. Genesis 21:24* And **Abraham** said, I will swear.
AV - **6,** 1-1,2-1,3-1,4-1,5-1,6-1

ESV - **6,** 1-1,2-1,3-1,4-1,5-1,6-1
HCSB - **6,** 1-1,2-1,3-1,4-1,5-1,6-1
NASV - **5,** 1-1,2-1,3-1,4-1,5-1
NCV - **5,** 1-1,2-1,3-1,4-1,5-**2**
NIV - **5,** 1-1,2-1,3-1,4-1,5-1
NKJV - **6,** 1-1,2-1,3-1,4-1,5-1,6-1
NLT - **7,** 1-1,2-**2,**3-1,4-1,5-1,6-1,7-1
NRSV - **6,** 1-1,2-1,3-1,4-1,5-1,6-1
Conclusion: Only the NCV and NLT are more complex than the King James Bible.

41. Genesis 22:10* And **Abraham** stretched forth his hand, and took the knife to slay his son.
AV - **14,** 1-1,2-1,3-1,4-1,5-1,6-1,7-1,8-1,9-1,10-1,11-1,12-1,13-1,14-1
ESV - **14,** 1-1,2-1,3-1,4-1,5-1,6-1,7-1,8-1,9-1,10-1,11-1,12-**2,**13-1,14-1
HCSB - **12,** 1-1,2-1,3-1,4-1,5-1,6-1,7-1,8-1,9-1,10-**2,**11-1,12-1
NASV - **13,** 1-1,2-1,3-1,4-1,5-1,6-1,7-1,8-1,9-1,10-1,11-1,12-1,13-1
NCV - **12,** 1-1,2-1,3-1,4-1,5-1,6-1,7-1,8-1,9-1,10-1,11-1,12-1
NIV - **14,** 1-1,2-1,3-1,4-1,5-1,6-1,7-1,8-1,9-1,10-1,11-1,12-1,13-1,14-1
NKJV - **14,** 1-1,2-1,3-1,4-1,5-1,6-1,7-1,8-1,9-1,10-1,11-1,12-1,13-1,14-1
NLT - **13,** 1-1,2-1,3-1,4-1,5-1,6-1,7-1,8-1,9-1,10-1,11-1,12-1,13-**3**
NRSV - **14,** 1-1,2-1,3-1,4-1,5-1,6-1,7-1,8-1,9-1,10-1,11-1,12-1,13-1,14-1
Conclusion: Three modern versions are more complex than the King James Bible.

42. Genesis 22:14* And **Abraham** called the name of that place **Jehovahjireh**: as it is said to this day, In the mount of the LORD it shall be seen.
AV - **26,**1-1,2-1,3-1,4-1,5-1,6-1,7-1,8-1,9-1,10-1,11-1,12-1,13-1,14-1,15-1,16-1,17-1,18-1,19-1,20-1,21-1,22-1,23-1,24-1,25-1,26-1
ESV - **29,** 1-1,2-1,3-1,4-1,5-1,6-1,7-1,8-1,9-1,10-1,11-1,12-1,13-1,14-1,15-1,16-1,17-1,18-1,19-1,20-1,21-1,22-1,23-1,24-1,25-1,26-1,27-1,28-1,29-**3**
HCSB - **22,**1-1,2-1,3-1,4-1,5-1,6-1,7-1,8-1,9-1,10-1,11-1,12-1,13-1,14-1,15-1,16-1,17-1,18-**3,**19-1,20-1,21-1,22-**2**
NASV - **28,**1-1,2-1,3-1,4-1,5-1,6-1,7-1,8-1,9-1,10-1,11-1,12-1,13-1,14-1,15-1,16-1,17-1,18-1,19-1,20-1,21-1,22-1,23-1,24-1,25-1,26-1,27-1,28-**3**
NCV - **22,** 1-1,2-1,3-1,4-1,5-1,6-1,7-1,8-1,9-1,10-1,11-1,12-1,13-1,14-1,15-**2,**16-1,17-1,18-1,19-1,20-1,21-1,22-**3**
NIV - **26,** 1-1,2-1,3-1,4-1,5-1,6-1,7-1,8-1,9-1,10-1,11-1,12-1,13-1,14-1,15-1,16-1,17-1,18-1,19-**2,**20-1,21-1,22-1,23-1,24-1,25-1,26-**3**
NKJV - **29,**1-1,2-1,3-1,4-1,5-1,6-1,7-1,8-1,9-1,10-1,11-1,12-1,13-1,14-1,15-1,16-1,17-1,18-1,19-1,20-1,21-1,22-1,23-1,24-1,25-1,26-1,27-1,28-1,29-**3**
NLT - **33,** 1-1,2-1,3-1,4-1,5-1,6-1,7-1,8-1,9-1,10-1,11-1,12-1,13-1,14-1,15-1,16-**2,**17-1,18-1,19-1,20-1,21-1,22-1,23-**2,**24-1,25-1,26-**2,**27-1,28-1,29-1,30-1, 31-1,32-1,33-**3**
NRSV - **26,**1-1,2-1,3-1,4-1,5-1,6-1,7-1,8-1,9-1,10-1,11-1,12-1,13-1,14-1,15-1,16-1,17-1,18-1,19-**2,**20-1,21-1,22-1,23-1,24-1,25-1,26-**3**
Conclusion: All eight modern versions are more complex than the King James Bible. Rather than transliterate the Hebrew name "Jehovahjireh" several modern versions translated it as "The LORD

will provide." Since this is used within the name it is counted as one syllable, just like "Jehovahjireh." But where the word "provided" appears elsewhere in a verse it is counted for its multi-syllables. The New Living Translation is the most difficult to read.

43. Genesis 22:22* And **Chesed**, and **Hazo**, and **Pildash**, and **Jidlaph**, and **Bethuel**.
AV - **10,** 1-1,2-1,3-1,4-1,5-1,6-1,7-1,8-1,9-1,10-1
ESV - **6,** 1-1,2-1,3-1,4-1,5-1,6-1
HCSB - **6,** 1-1,2-1,3-1,4-1,5-1,6-1
NASV - **10,** 1-1,2-1,3-1,4-1,5-1,6-1,7-1,8-1,9-1,10-1
NCV - **9,** 1-1,2-1,3-1,4-1,5-1,6-1,7-1,8-1,9-1
NIV - **6,** 1-1,2-1,3-1,4-1,5-1,6-1
NKJV - **6,** 1-1,2-1,3-1,4-1,5-1,6-1
NLT - **6,** 1-1,2-1,3-1,4-1,5-1,6-1
NRSV - **6,** 1-1,2-1,3-1,4-1,5-1,6-1
Conclusion: All versions read the same.

44. Genesis 23:1*# And **Sarah** was an **hundred** and **seven** and **twenty** years old: these were the years of the life of **Sarah**.
AV - **20,** 1-1,2-1,3-1,4-1,5-1,6-1,7-1,8-1,9-1,10-1,11-1,12-1,13-1,14-1,15-1,16-1,17-1,18-1,19-1,20-1
ESV - **13,** 1-1,2-1,3-1,4-1,5-1,6-1,7-1,8-1,9-1,10-1,11-1,12-1,13-1
HCSB - **13,** 1-1,2-1,3-1,4-1,5-1,6-1,7-1,8-1,9-1,10-1,11-1,12-1,13-1
NASV - **18,** 1-1,2-1,3-1,4-1,5-1,6-1,7-1,8-1,9-1,10-1,11-1,12-1,13-1,14-1,15-1,16-1,17-1,18-1
NCV - **10,** 1-1,2-1,3-1,4-1,5-1,6-1,7-1,8-1,9-1,10-1
NIV - **11,** 1-1,2-1,3-1,4-1,5-1,6-1,7-1,8-1,9-1,10-1,11-1
NKJV - **17,** 1-1,2-1,3-1,4-1,5-1,6-1,7-1,8-1,9-1,10-1,11-1,12-1,13-1,14-1,15-1,16-1,17-1
NLT - **6,** 1-1,2-1,3-1,4-1,5-1,6-1
NRSV - **14,** 1-1,2-1,3-1,4-1,5-1,6-1,7-1,8-1,9-1,10-1,11-1,12-1,13-1,14-1
Conclusion: All versions read the same.

45. Genesis 23:2* And **Sarah** died in **Kirjatharba**; the same is **Hebron** in the land of **Canaan**: and **Abraham** came to mourn for **Sarah**, and to weep for her.
AV - **26,** 1-1,2-1,3-1,4-1,5-1,6-1,7-1,8-1,9-1,10-1,11-1,12-1,13-1,14-1,15-1,16-1,17-1,18-1,19-1,20-1,21-1,22-1,23-1,24-1,25-1,26-1
ESV - **26,** 1-1,2-1,3-1,4-1,5-1,6-1,7-1,8-1,9-1,10-1,11-1,12-1,13-1,14-1,15-1,16-1,17-1,18-1,19-1,20-1,21-1,22-1,23-1,24-1,25-1,26-1
HCSB - **25,** 1-1,2-1,3-1,4-1,5-1,6-1,7-1,8-1,9-1,10-1,11-1,12-1,13-1,14-1,15-1,16-1,17-1,18-1,19-1,20-1,21-1,22-1,23-1,24-1,25-1
NASV - **25,** 1-1,2-1,3-1,4-1,5-1,6-1,7-1,8-1,9-1,10-1,11-1,12-1,13-1,14-1,15-1,16-1,17-1,18-1,19-1,20-1,21-1,22-1,23-1,24-1,25-1
NCV - **22,** 1-1,2-1,3-1,4-1,5-1,6-1,7-1,8-1,9-1,10-1,11-1,12-1,13-1,14-1,15-1,16-**2**,17-1,18-1,19-1,20-**2**,21-1,22-1
NIV - **25,** 1-1,2-1,3-1,4-1,5-1,6-1,7-1,8-1,9-1,10-1,11-1,12-1,13-1,14-1,15-1,16-1,17-1,18-1,19-1,20-1,21-1,22-1,23-1,24-**2**,25-1

NKJV - **26,** 1-1,2-1,3-1,4-1,5-1,6-1,7-1,8-1,9-1,10-1,11-1,12-1,13-1,14-1,15-1,16-1,17-1,18-1,19-1,20-1,21-1,22-1,23-1,24-1,25-1,26-1

NLT - **19,** 1-1,2-1,3-1,4-1,5-1,6-1,7-1,8-1,9-1,10-1,11-1,12-1,13-1,14-1,15-1,16-1,17-1,18-1,19-1

NRSV - **26,** 1-1,2-1,3-1,4-1,5-1,6-1,7-1,8-1,9-1,10-1,11-1,12-1,13-1,14-1,15-1,16-1,17-1,18-1,19-1,20-1,21-1,22-1,23-1,24-1,25-1,26-1

Conclusion: Only the NCV and the NIV made the verse more complex.

46. Genesis 25:2* And she bare him **Zimran**, and **Jokshan**, and **Medan**, and **Midian**, and **Ishbak**, and **Shuah**.

AV - **15,** 1-1,2-1,3-1,4-1,5-1,6-1,7-1,8-1,9-1,10-1,11-1,12-1,13-1,14-1,15-1

ESV - **10,** 1-1,2-1,3-1,4-1,5-1,6-1,7-1,8-1,9-1,10-1

HCSB - **11,** 1-1,2-1,3-1,4-1,5-1,6-1,7-1,8-1,9-1,10-1,11-1

NASV - **15,** 1-1,2-1,3-1,4-1,5-1,6-1,7-1,8-1,9-1,10-1,11-1,12-1,13-1,14-1,15-1

NCV - **11,** 1-1,2-1,3-1,4-1,5-1,6-1,7-1,8-1,9-1,10-1,11-1

NIV - **10,** 1-1,2-1,3-1,4-1,5-1,6-1,7-1,8-1,9-1,10-1

NKJV - **11,** 1-1,2-1,3-1,4-1,5-1,6-1,7-1,8-1,9-1,10-1,11-1

NLT - **11,** 1-1,2-1,3-1,4-1,5-1,6-1,7-1,8-1,9-1,10-1,11-1

NRSV - **10,** 1-1,2-1,3-1,4-1,5-1,6-1,7-1,8-1,9-1,10-1

Conclusion: All versions read the same.

47. Genesis 25:7*# And these are the days of the years of **Abraham's** life which he lived, an **hundred threescore** and **fifteen** years.

AV - **20,** 1-1,2-1,3-1,4-1,5-1,6-1,7-1,8-1,9-1,10-1,11-1,12-1,13-1,14-1,15-1,16-1,17-1,18-1,19-1,20-1

ESV - **12,** 1-1,2-1,3-1,4-1,5-1,6-1,7-1,8-1,9-1,10-1,11-1,12-1

HCSB - **9,** 1-1,2-1,3-1,4-1,5-1,6-1,7-1,8-1,9-1

NASV - **17,** 1-1,2-1,3-1,4-1,5-1,6-1,7-1,8-1,9-1,10-1,11-1,12-1,13-1,14-1,15-1,16-1,17-1

NCV - **10,** 1-1,2-1,3-1,4-1,5-1,6-1,7-1,8-1,9-1,10-1

NIV - 9, 1-4,2-1,3-1,4-1,5-1,6-1,7-1,8-1,9-1

NKJV - **19,** 1-1,2-1,3-1,4-1,5-1,6-1,7-1,8-1,9-1,10-1,11-1,12-1,13-1,14-1,15-1,16-1,17-1,18-1,19-1

NLT - **5,** 1-1,2-1,3-1,4-1,5-1

NRSV - **12,** 1-1,2-1,3-1,4-1,5-1,6-1,7-1,8-1,9-1,10-1,11-1,12-1

Conclusion: Only the NIV made the verse more complex.

48. Genesis 25:14* And **Mishma**, and **Dumah**, and **Massa**,

AV - **6,** 1-1,2-1,3-1,4-1,5-1,6-1

ESV - **3,** 1-1,2-1,3-1

HCSB - **3,** 1-1,2-1,3-1

NASV - **6,** 1-1,2-1,3-1,4-1,5-1,6-1

NCV - **3,** 1-1,2-1,3-1

NIV - **3,** 1-1,2-1,3-1

NKJV - **3,** 1-1,2-1,3-1

NLT - **3,** 1-1,2-1,3-1

NRSV - **3,** 1-1,2-1,3-1

Conclusion: All versions read the same.

49. Genesis 25:15* Hadar, and **Tema**, **Jetur**, **Naphish**, and **Kedemah**:
AV - **7,** 1-1,2-1,3-1,4-1,5-1,6-1,7-1
ESV - **6,** 1-1,2-1,3-1,4-1,5-1,6-1
HCSB - **6,** 1-1,2-1,3-1,4-1,5-1,6-1
NASV - **7,** 1-1,2-1,3-1,4-1,5-1,6-1,7-1
NCV - **6,** 1-1,2-1,3-1,4-1,5-1,6-1
NIV - **6,** 1-1,2-1,3-1,4-1,5-1,6-1
NKJV - **6,** 1-1,2-1,3-1,4-1,5-1,6-1
NLT - **6,** 1-1,2-1,3-1,4-1,5-1,6-1
NRSV - **6,** 1-1,2-1,3-1,4-1,5-1,6-1
Conclusion: All versions read the same.

50. Genesis 26:6* And **Isaac** dwelt in **Gerar**:
AV - **5,** 1-1,2-1,3-1,4-1,5-1
ESV - **5,** 1-1,2-1,3-**2**,4-1,5-1
HCSB - **5,** 1-1,2-1,3-**2**,4-1,5-1
NASV - **5,** 1-1,2-1,3-1,4-1,5-1
NCV - **5,** 1-1,2-1,3-1,4-1,5-1
NIV - **5,** 1-1,2-1,3-1,4-1,5-1
NKJV - **5,** 1-1,2-1,3-1,4-1,5-1
NLT - **5,** 1-1,2-1,3-1,4-1,5-1
NRSV - **5,** 1-1,2-1,3-**2**,4-1,5-1
Conclusion: Three modern versions are more complex than the King James Bible.

51. Genesis 26:23* And he went up from thence to **Beersheba**.
AV - **8,** 1-1,2-1,3-1,4-1,5-1,6-1,7-1,8-1
ESV - **7,** 1-1,2-1,3-1,4-1,5-1,6-1,7-1
HCSB - **7,** 1-1,2-1,3-1,4-1,5-1,6-1,7-1
NASV - **8,** 1-1,2-1,3-1,4-1,5-1,6-1,7-1,8-1
NCV - **6,** 1-1,2-1,3-1,4-1,5-1,6-1
NIV - **7,** 1-1,2-1,3-1,4-1,5-1,6-1,7-1
NKJV - **8,** 1-1,2-1,3-1,4-1,5-1,6-1,7-1,8-1
NLT - **6,** 1-1,2-1,3-1,4-1,5-1,6-1
NRSV - **7,** 1-1,2-1,3-1,4-1,5-1,6-1,7-1
Conclusion: All versions read the same.

52. Genesis 26:30 And he made them a feast, and they did eat and drink.
AV - **12,** 1-1,2-1,3-1,4-1,5-1,6-1,7-1,8-1,9-1,10-1,11-1,12-1
ESV - **11,** 1-1,2-1,3-1,4-1,5-1,6-1,7-1,8-1,9-1,10-1,11-1
HCSB - **12,** 1-1,2-1,3-**2**,4-1,5-**2**,6-1,7-1,8-1,9-1,10-1,11-1,12-1
NASV - **11,** 1-1,2-1,3-1,4-1,5-1,6-1,7-1,8-1,9-1,10-1,11-1
NCV - **12,** 1-1,2-1,3-**2**,4-1,5-1,6-1,7-1,8-1,9-1,10-1,11-1,12-1

NIV - **12,** 1-1,2-1,3-1,4-1,5-1,6-1,7-1,8-1,9-1,10-1,11-1,12-1
NKJV - **11,** 1-1,2-1,3-1,4-1,5-1,6-1,7-1,8-1,9-1,10-1,11-1
NLT - 16, 1-1,2-1,3-**2,**4-1,5-**3,**6-1,7-1,8-**3,**9-1,10-**2,**11-1,12-1,13-1,14-1,15-1,16-**3**
NRSV - **11,** 1-1,2-1,3-1,4-1,5-1,6-1,7-1,8-1,9-1,10-1,11-1
Conclusion: Three modern versions are more complex than the King James Bible. The NLT is the most difficult to read.

53. Genesis 30:10* And **Zilpah Leah's** maid bare **Jacob** a son.
AV - **8,** 1-1,2-1,3-1,4-1,5-1,6-1,7-1,8-1
ESV - 8, 1-1,2-1,3-**2,**4-1,5-1,6-1,7-1,8-1
HCSB - **7,** 1-1,2-1,3-1,4-1,5-1,6-1,7-1
NASV - **7,** 1-1,2-1,3-1,4-1,5-1,6-1,7-1
NCV - **5,** 1-1,2-1,3-1,4-1,5-1
NIV - **7,** 1-1,2-1,3-1,4-1,5-1,6-1,7-1
NKJV - **8,** 1-1,2-1,3-1,4-1,5-1,6-1,7-1,8-1
NLT - 7, 1-1,2-1,3-**3,**4-1,5-1,6-1,7-1
NRSV - **8,** 1-1,2-1,3-1,4-1,5-1,6-1,7-1,8-1
Conclusion: Only the ESV and NLT are more complex than the King James Bible.

54. Genesis 30:12*# And **Zilpah Leah's** maid bare **Jacob** a **second** son.
AV - **9,** 1-1,2-1,3-1,4-1,5-1,6-1,7-1,8-1,9-1
ESV - 8, 1-1,2-**2,**3-1,4-1,5-1,6-1,7-1,8-1
HCSB - **9,** 1-1,2-1,3-1,4-1,5-1,6-1,7-1,8-1,9-1
NASV - **8,** 1-1,2-1,3-1,4-1,5-1,6-1,7-1,8-1
NCV - 6, 1-1,2-1,3-1,4-1,5-**3,**6-1
NIV - 8, 1-1,2-**2,**3-1,4-1,5-1,6-1,7-1,8-1
NKJV - **9,** 1-1,2-1,3-1,4-1,5-1,6-1,7-1,8-1,9-1
NLT - **7,** 1-1,2-1,3-1,4-1,5-1,6-1,7-1
NRSV - **8,** 1-1,2-1,3-1,4-1,5-1,6-1,7-1,8-1
Conclusion: Only three modern versions are more complex than the King James Bible.

55. Genesis 31:22* And it was told **Laban** on the third day that **Jacob** was fled.
AV - **13,** 1-1,2-1,3-1,4-1,5-1,6-1,7-1,8-1,9-1,10-1,11-1,12-1,13-1
ESV - **13,** 1-1,2-1,3-1,4-1,5-1,6-1,7-1,8-1,9-1,10-1,11-1,12-1,13-1
HCSB - **11,** 1-1,2-1,3-1,4-1,5-1,6-1,7-1,8-1,9-1,10-1,11-1
NASV - **13,** 1-1,2-1,3-1,4-1,5-1,6-1,7-1,8-1,9-1,10-1,11-1,12-1,13-1
NCV - 10, 1-1,2-1,3-**2,**4-1,5-1,6-1,7-1,8-1,9-1,10-**2**
NIV - **11,** 1-1,2-1,3-1,4-1,5-1,6-1,7-1,8-1,9-1,10-1,11-1
NKJV - **12,** 1-1,2-1,3-1,4-1,5-1,6-1,7-1,8-1,9-1,10-1,11-1,12-1
NLT - 10, 1-1,2-1,3-**2,**4-1,5-1,6-1,7-1,8-1,9-1,10-1
NRSV - **11,** 1-1,2-1,3-1,4-1,5-1,6-1,7-1,8-1,9-1,10-1,11-1
Conclusion: Only the NCV and NLT are more complex than the King James Bible.

56. Genesis 32:2* And when **Jacob** saw them, he said, This is God's host: and he called the name of that place **Mahanaim**.

AV - **20,** 1-1,2-1,3-1,4-1,5-1,6-1,7-1,8-1,9-1,10-1,11-1,12-1,13-1,14-1,15-1,16-1,17-1,18-1,19-1,20-1

ESV - **20,** 1-1,2-1,3-1,4-1,5-1,6-1,7-1,8-1,9-1,10-1,11-1,12-1,13-1,14-1,15-1,16-1,17-1,18-1,19-1,20-1

HCSB - **16,** 1-1,2-1,3-1,4-1,5-1,6-1,7-1,8-1,9-1,10-1,11-1,12-1,13-1,14-1,15-1,16-1

NASV - **16,** 1-1,2-1,3-1,4-1,5-1,6-1,7-1,8-1,9-1,10-1,11-1,12-1,13-1,14-1,15-1,16-1

NCV - **18,** 1-1,2-1,3-1,4-1,5-1,6-1,7-1,8-1,9-1,10-1,11-1,12-1,13-1,14-1,15-1,16-1,17-1,18-1

NIV - **18,** 1-1,2-1,3-1,4-1,5-1,6-1,7-1,8-1,9-1,10-1,11-1,12-1,13-1,14-1,15-1,16-1,17-1,18-1

NKJV - **19,** 1-1,2-1,3-1,4-1,5-1,6-1,7-1,8-1,9-1,10-1,11-1,12-1,13-1,14-1,15-1,16-1,17-1,18-1,19-1

NLT - 16, 1-1,2-1,3-1,4-1,5-1,6-**2**,7-1,8-1,9-1,10-1,11-1,12-1,13-1,14-1,15-1,16-1

NRSV - **17,** 1-1,2-1,3-1,4-1,5-1,6-1,7-1,8-1,9-1,10-1,11-1,12-1,13-1,14-1,15-1,16-1,17-1

Conclusion: Only the NLT made the verse more complex.

57. Genesis 32:14# Two **hundred** she goats, and **twenty** he goats, two **hundred** ewes, and **twenty** rams,

AV - **14,** 1-1,2-1,3-1,4-1,5-1,6-1,7-1,8-1,9-1,10-1,11-1,12-1,13-1,14-1

ESV - 14, 1-1,2-1,3-**2**,4-1,5-1,6-1,7-1,8-1,9-1,10-1,11-1,12-1,13-1,14-1

HCSB - 10, 1-1,2-**2**,3-1,4-1,5-1,6-1,7-1,8-1,9-1,10-1

NASV - 14, 1-1,2-1,3-**2**,4-1,5-1,6-1,7-1,8-1,9-1,10-1,11-1,12-1,13-1,14-1

NCV - 16, 1-1,2-1,3-**2**,4-1,5-1,6-1,7-1,8-1,9-1,10-1,11-**2**,12-1,13-1,14-1,15-1,16-1

NIV - 14, 1-1,2-1,3-**2**,4-1,5-1,6-1,7-1,8-1,9-1,10-1,11-1,12-1,13-1,14-1

NKJV - 14, 1-1,2-1,3-**2**,4-1,5-1,6-1,7-1,8-1,9-1,10-1,11-1,12-1,13-1,14-1

NLT - 14, 1-1,2-1,3-**2**,4-1,5-1,6-1,7-1,8-1,9-1,10-1,11-1,12-1,13-1,14-1

NRSV - 14, 1-1,2-1,3-**2**,4-1,5-1,6-1,7-1,8-1,9-1,10-1,11-1,12-1,13-1,14-1

Conclusion: All eight modern versions are more complex than the King James Bible.

58. Genesis 34:18* And their words pleased **Hamor**, and **Shechem Hamor's** son.

AV - **9,** 1-1,2-1,3-1,4-1,5-1,6-1,7-1,8-1,9-1

ESV - **8,** 1-1,2-1,3-1,4-1,5-1,6-1,7-1,8-1

HCSB - **13,** 1-1,2-1,3-1,4-1,5-1,6-1,7-1,8-1,9-1,10-1,11-1,12-1,13-1

NASV - 11, 1-1,2-1,3-1,4-1,5-**4**,6-1,7-1,8-1,9-1,10-1,11-1

NCV - **9,** 1-1,2-1,3-1,4-1,5-1,6-1,7-1,8-1,9-1

NIV - 10, 1-1,2-**3**,3-1,4-1,5-1,6-1,7-1,8-1,9-1,10-1

NKJV - **9,** 1-1,2-1,3-1,4-1,5-1,6-1,7-1,8-1,9-1

NLT - 9, 1-1,2-1,3-1,4-1,5-1,6-**2**,7-1,8-1,9-**4**

NRSV - **8,** 1-1,2-1,3-1,4-1,5-1,6-1,7-1,8-1

Conclusion: Three modern versions are more complex than the King James Bible.

59. Genesis 35:13 And God went up from him in the place where he talked with him.

AV - **14,** 1-1,2-1,3-1,4-1,5-1,6-1,7-1,8-1,9-1,10-1,11-1,12-1,13-1,14-1

ESV - 15, 1-1,2-1,3-1,4-1,5-1,6-1,7-1,8-1,9-1,10-1,11-1,12-1,13-**2**,14-1,15-1

HCSB - 14, 1-1,2-1,3-**2**,4-1,5-1,6-1,7-1,8-1,9-1,10-1,11-1,12-**2**,13-1,14-1

NASV - 15, 1-1,2-1,3-1,4-1,5-1,6-1,7-1,8-1,9-1,10-1,11-1,12-1,13-**2**,14-1,15-1
NCV - **4,** 1-1,2-1,3-1,4-1
NIV - **15,** 1-1,2-1,3-1,4-1,5-1,6-1,7-1,8-1,9-1,10-1,11-1,12-1,13-1,14-1,15-1
NKJV - **14,** 1-1,2-1,3-1,4-1,5-1,6-1,7-1,8-1,9-1,10-1,11-1,12-1,13-1,14-1
NLT - 13, 1-1,2-1,3-1,4-1,5-1,6-1,7-1,8-1,9-1,10-1,11-**2**,12-1,13-1
NRSV - 15, 1-1,2-1,3-1,4-1,5-1,6-1,7-1,8-1,9-1,10-1,11-1,12-1,13-**2**,14-1,15-1
Conclusion: Five modern versions are more complex than the King James Bible. The verse is brief in the NCV because this version cuts the verse short and adds the latter portion to verse fourteen.

60. Genesis 35:15* And **Jacob** called the name of the place where God spake with him, **Bethel**.
AV - **14,** 1-1,2-1,3-1,4-1,5-1,6-1,7-1,8-1,9-1,10-1,11-1,12-1,13-1,14-1
ESV - 15, 1-1,2-1,3-1,4-1,5-1,6-1,7-1,8-1,9-1,10-1,11-1,12-**2**,13-1,14-1,15-1
HCSB - 11, 1-1,2-1,3-1,4-1,5-1,6-1,7-1,8-**2**,9-1,10-1,11-1
NASV - 12, 1-1,2-1,3-1,4-1,5-1,6-1,7-1,8-1,9-**2**,10-1,11-1,12-1
NCV - **6,** 1-1,2-1,3-1,4-1,5-1,6-1
NIV - **11,** 1-1,2-1,3-1,4-1,5-1,6-1,7-1,8-1,9-1,10-1,11-1
NKJV - **14,** 1-1,2-1,3-1,4-1,5-1,6-1,7-1,8-1,9-1,10-1,11-1,12-1,13-1,14-1
NLT - 15, 1-1,2-1,3-1,4-1,5-1,6-1,7-1,8-1,9-1,10-1,11-1,12-**2**,13-1,14-1,15-**2**
NRSV - 12, 1-1,2-1,3-1,4-1,5-1,6-1,7-1,8-1,9-**2**,10-1,11-1,12-1
Conclusion: Five modern versions are more complex than the King James Bible.

61. Genesis 35:24* The sons of **Rachel**; **Joseph**, and **Benjamin**:
AV - **7,** 1-1,2-1,3-1,4-1,5-1,6-1,7-1
ESV - **7,** 1-1,2-1,3-1,4-1,5-1,6-1,7-1
HCSB - **6,** 1-1,2-1,3-1,4-1,5-1,6-1
NASV - **7,** 1-1,2-1,3-1,4-1,5-1,6-1,7-1
NCV - **11,** 1-1,2-1,3-1,4-1,5-1,6-1,7-1,8-1,9-1,10-1,11-1
NIV - **7,** 1-1,2-1,3-1,4-1,5-1,6-1,7-1
NKJV - **7,** 1-1,2-1,3-1,4-1,5-1,6-1,7-1
NLT - **7,** 1-1,2-1,3-1,4-1,5-1,6-1,7-1
NRSV - **7,** 1-1,2-1,3-1,4-1,5-1,6-1,7-1
Conclusion: All versions read the same.

62. Genesis 35:28*# And the days of **Isaac** were an **hundred** and **fourscore** years.
AV - **11,** 1-1,2-1,3-1,4-1,5-1,6-1,7-1,8-1,9-1,10-1,11-1
ESV - **8,** 1-1,2-1,3-1,4-1,5-1,6-1,7-1,8-1
HCSB - **4,** 1-1,2-1,3-1,4-1
NASV - **11,** 1-1,2-1,3-1,4-1,5-1,6-1,7-1,8-1,9-1,10-1,11-1
NCV - **6,** 1-1,2-1,3-1,4-1,5-1,6-1
NIV - **7,** 1-1,2-1,3-1,4-1,5-1,6-1,7-1
NKJV - **11,** 1-1,2-1,3-1,4-1,5-1,6-1,7-1,8-1,9-1,10-1,11-1
NLT - **5,** 1-1,2-1,3-1,4-1,5-1
NRSV - **10,** 1-1,2-1,3-1,4-1,5-1,6-1,7-1,8-1,9-1,10-1
Conclusion: All versions read the same.

63. Genesis 36:4* And **Adah** bare to **Esau Eliphaz**; and **Bashemath** bare **Reuel**;
AV - **10,** 1-1,2-1,3-1,4-1,5-1,6-1,7-1,8-1,9-1,10-1
ESV - **9,** 1-1,2-1,3-1,4-1,5-1,6-1,7-1,8-1,9-1
HCSB - **8,** 1-1,2-1,3-1,4-1,5-1,6-1,7-1,8-1
NASV - **9,** 1-1,2-1,3-1,4-1,5-1,6-1,7-1,8-1,9-1
NCV - **11,** 1-1,2-1,3-1,4-1,5-1,6-1,7-1,8-1,9-1,10-1,11-1
NIV - **8,** 1-1,2-1,3-1,4-1,5-1,6-1,7-1,8-1
NKJV - **10,** 1-1,2-1,3-1,4-1,5-1,6-1,7-1,8-1,9-1,10-1
NLT - **18,** 1-1,2-1,3-1,4-1,5-1,6-1,7-1,8-1,9-1,10-1,11-1,12-1,13-1,14-1,15-1,16-1,17-1,18-1
NRSV - **8,** 1-1,2-1,3-1,4-1,5-1,6-1,7-1,8-1
Conclusion: All versions read the same.

64. Genesis 36:8* Thus dwelt **Esau** in mount **Seir**: **Esau** is **Edom**.
AV - **9,** 1-1,2-1,3-1,4-1,5-1,6-1,7-1,8-1,9-1
ESV - 12, 1-1,2-1,3-**2**,4-1,5-1,6-1,7-**2**,8-1,9-1,10-1,11-1,12-1
HCSB - 11, 1-1,2-1,3-1,4-1,5-1,6-1,7-1,8-1,9-**2**,10-1,11-1
NASV - 12, 1-1,2-1,3-1,4-1,5-1,6-1,7-**2**,8-1,9-1,10-1,11-1,12-1
NCV - 13, 1-1,2-1,3-1,4-1,5-1,6-**2**,7-1,8-1,9-1,10-1,11-**2**,12-1,13-1
NIV - 12, 1-1,2-1,3-1,4-1,5-1,6-**2**,7-1,8-1,9-1,10-**2**,11-1,12-1
NKJV - **9,** 1-1,2-1,3-1,4-1,5-1,6-1,7-1,8-1,9-1
NLT - 13, 1-1,2-1,3-**2**,4-1,5-1,6-1,7-**2**,8-1,9-1,10-1,11-**2**,12-1,13-1
NRSV - 12, 1-1,2-1,3-**2**,4-1,5-1,6-1,7-**2**,8-1,9-1,10-1,11-1,12-1
Conclusion: Seven modern versions are more complex than the King James Bible.

65. Genesis 36:10* These are the names of **Esau's** sons; **Eliphaz** the son of **Adah** the wife of **Esau**, **Reuel** the son of **Bashemath** the wife of **Esau**.
AV - **25,** 1-1,2-1,3-1,4-1,5-1,6-1,7-1,8-1,9-1,10-1,11-1,12-1,13-1,14-1,15-1,16-1,17-1,18-1,19-1,20-1,21-1,22-1,23-1,24-1,25-1
ESV - **25,** 1-1,2-1,3-1,4-1,5-1,6-1,7-1,8-1,9-1,10-1,11-1,12-1,13-1,14-1,15-1,16-1,17-1,18-1,19-1,20-1,21-1,22-1,23-1,24-1,25-1
HCSB - **20,** 1-1,2-1,3-1,4-1,5-1,6-1,7-1,8-1,9-1,10-1,11-1,12-1,13-1,14-1,15-1,16-1,17-1,18-1,19-1,20-1
NASV - **21,** 1-1,2-1,3-1,4-1,5-1,6-1,7-1,8-1,9-1,10-1,11-1,12-1,13-1,14-1,15-1,16-1,17-1,18-1,19-1,20-1,21-1
NCV - **16,** 1-1,2-1,3-1,4-1,5-1,6-1,7-1,8-1,9-1,10-1,11-1,12-1,13-1,14-1,15-1,16-1
NIV - **22,** 1-1,2-1,3-1,4-1,5-1,6-1,7-1,8-1,9-1,10-1,11-1,12-1,13-1,14-1,15-1,16-1,17-1,18-1,19-1,20-1,21-1,22-1
NKJV - **26,** 1-1,2-1,3-1,4-1,5-1,6-1,7-1,8-1,9-1,10-1,11-1,12-1,13-1,14-1,15-1,16-1,17-1,18-1,19-1,20-1,21-1,22-1,23-1,24-1,25-1,26-1
NLT - **22,** 1-1,2-1,3-1,4-1,5-1,6-1,7-1,8-1,9-1,10-1,11-1,12-1,13-1,14-1,15-1,16-1,17-1,18-1,19-1,20-1,21-1,22-1
NRSV - **22,** 1-1,2-1,3-1,4-1,5-1,6-1,7-1,8-1,9-1,10-1,11-1,12-1,13-1,14-1,15-1,16-1,17-1,18-1,19-1,20-1,21-1,22-1
Conclusion: All versions read the same.

66. Genesis 36:11* And the sons of **Eliphaz** were **Teman**, **Omar**, **Zepho**, and **Gatam**, and **Kenaz**.
AV - **13,** 1-1,2-1,3-1,4-1,5-1,6-1,7-1,8-1,9-1,10-1,11-1,12-1,13-1
ESV - **11,** 1-1,2-1,3-1,4-1,5-1,6-1,7-1,8-1,9-1,10-1,11-1
HCSB - **11,** 1-1,2-1,3-1,4-1,5-1,6-1,7-1,8-1,9-1,10-1,11-1
NASV - **13,** 1-1,2-1,3-1,4-1,5-1,6-1,7-1,8-1,9-1,10-1,11-1,12-1,13-1
NCV - **10,** 1-1,2-1,3-1,4-1,5-1,6-1,7-1,8-1,9-1,10-1
NIV - **10,** 1-1,2-1,3-1,4-1,5-1,6-1,7-1,8-1,9-1,10-1
NKJV - **13,** 1-1,2-1,3-1,4-1,5-1,6-1,7-1,8-1,9-1,10-1,11-1,12-1,13-1
NLT - **11,** 1-1,2-**3**,3-1,4-1,5-1,6-1,7-1,8-1,9-1,10-1,11-1
NRSV - **11,** 1-1,2-1,3-1,4-1,5-1,6-1,7-1,8-1,9-1,10-1,11-1
Conclusion: Only the NLT made the verse more complex.

67. Genesis 36:13* And these are the sons of **Reuel**; **Nahath**, and **Zerah**, **Shammah**, and **Mizzah**: these were the sons of **Bashemath Esau's** wife.
AV - **21,** 1-1,2-1,3-1,4-1,5-1,6-1,7-1,8-1,9-1,10-1,11-1,12-1,13-1,14-1,15-1,16-1,17-1,18-1,19-1,20-1,21-1
ESV -**19,** 1-1,2-1,3-1,4-1,5-1,6-1,7-1,8-1,9-1,10-1,11-1,12-1,13-1,14-1,15-1,16-1,17-1,18-1,19-1
HCSB - **17,** 1-1,2-1,3-1,4-1,5-1,6-1,7-1,8-1,9-1,10-1,11-1,12-1,13-1,14-1,15-1,16-1,17-1
NASV - **20,** 1-1,2-1,3-1,4-1,5-1,6-1,7-1,8-1,9-1,10-1,11-1,12-1,13-1,14-1,15-1,16-1,17-1,18-1,19-1,20-1
NCV - **17,** 1-1,2-1,3-1,4-1,5-1,6-1,7-1,8-1,9-1,10-1,11-1,12-1,13-**2**,14-1,15-1,16-1,17-1
NIV - **16,** 1-1,2-1,3-1,4-1,5-1,6-1,7-1,8-1,9-1,10-1,11-1,12-**2**,13-1,14-1,15-1,16-1
NKJV - **19,** 1-1,2-1,3-1,4-1,5-1,6-1,7-1,8-1,9-1,10-1,11-1,12-1,13-1,14-1,15-1,16-1,17-1,18-1,19-1
NLT - **18,** 1-1,2-**3**,3-1,4-1,5-1,6-1,7-1,8-1,9-1,10-1,11-1,12-1,13-1,14-**3**,15-1,16-1,17-1,18-1
NRSV - **19,** 1-1,2-1,3-1,4-1,5-1,6-1,7-1,8-1,9-1,10-1,11-1,12-1,13-1,14-1,15-1,16-1,17-1,18-1,19-1
Conclusion: Three modern versions are more complex than the King James Bible.

68. Genesis 36:16* Duke **Korah**, duke **Gatam**, and duke **Amalek**: these are the dukes that came of **Eliphaz** in the land of **Edom**; these were the sons of **Adah**.
AV - **26,** 1-1,2-1,3-1,4-1,5-1,6-1,7-1,8-1,9-1,10-1,11-1,12-1,13-1,14-1,15-1,16-1,17-1,18-1,19-1,20-1,21-1,22-1,23-1,24-1,25-1,26-1
ESV - **21,** 1-1,2-1,3-1,4-1,5-1,6-1,7-1,8-1,9-1,10-1,11-1,12-1,13-1,14-1,15-1,16-1,17-1,18-1,19-1,20-1,21-1
HCSB - **21,** 1-1,2-1,3-1,4-1,5-1,6-1,7-1,8-1,9-1,10-1,11-1,12-1,13-1,14-1,15-1,16-1,17-1,18-1,19-1,20-1,21-1
NASV - **24,** 1-1,2-1,3-1,4-1,5-1,6-1,7-1,8-1,9-1,10-1,11-**3**,12-1,13-1,14-1,15-1,16-1,17-1,18-1,19-1,20-1,21-1,22-1,23-1,24-1
NCV - **23,** 1-1,2-1,3-1,4-1,5-1,6-1,7-1,8-**2**,9-1,10-1,11-1,12-1,13-1,14-1,15-1,16-1,17-1,18-1,19-1,20-1,21-**2**,22-1,23-1
NIV - **18,** 1-1,2-1,3-1,4-1,5-1,6-1,7-1,8-1,9-**3**,10-1,11-1,12-1,13-1,14-1,15-1,16-**2**,17-1,18-1
NKJV - **24,** 1-1,2-1,3-1,4-1,5-1,6-1,7-1,8-1,9-1,10-1,11-1,12-1,13-1,14-1,15-1,16-1,17-1,18-1,19-1,20-1,21-1,22-1,23-1,24-1
NLT - **26,** 1-1,2-1,3-1,4-1,5-1,6-1,7-1,8-1,9-**2**,10-1,11-1,12-1,13-1,14-1,15-1,16-**3**,17-1,18-1,19-1,20-1,21-1,22-**3**,23-1,24-1,25-1,26-1

NRSV - **21,** 1-1,2-1,3-1,4-1,5-1,6-1,7-1,8-1,9-1,10-1,11-1,12-1,13-1,14-1,15-1,16-1,17-1,18-1,19-1,20-1,21-1

Conclusion: Four modern versions are more complex than the King James Bible.

69. Genesis 36:17* And these are the sons of **Reuel Esau's** son; duke **Nahath**, duke **Zerah**, duke **Shammah**, duke **Mizzah**: these are the dukes that came of **Reuel** in the land of **Edom**; these are the sons of **Bashemath Esau's** wife.

AV - **38,** 1-1,2-1,3-1,4-1,5-1,6-1,7-1,8-1,9-1,10-1,11-1,12-1,13-1,14-1,15-1,16-1,17-1,18-1,19-1,20-1,21-1,22-1,23-1,24-1,25-1,26-1,27-1,28-1,29-1,30-1,31-1,32-1,33-1,34-1,35-1,36-1,37-1,38-1

ESV - **34,** 1-1,2-1,3-1,4-1,5-1,6-1,7-1,8-1,9-1,10-1,11-1,12-1,13-1,14-1,15-1,16-1,17-1,18-1,19-1,20-1,21-1,22-1,23-1,24-1,25-1,26-1,27-1,28-1,29-1,30-1,31-1,32-1,33-1,34-1

HCSB - **33,** 1-1,2-1,3-1,4-1,5-1,6-1,7-1,8-1,9-1,10-1,11-1,12-1,13-1,14-1,15-1,16-1,17-1,18-1,19-1,20-1,21-1,22-1,23-1,24-1,25-1,26-1,27-1,28-1,29-1,30-1,31-1,32-1,33-1

NASV - **36,** 1-1,2-1,3-1,4-1,5-1,6-1,7-1,8-1,9-1,10-1,11-1,12-1,13-1,14-1,15-1,16-1,17-1,18-1,19-1,20-1,21-**3,**22-1,23-1,24-1,25-1,26-1,27-1,28-1,29-1,30-1,31-1,32-1,33-1,34-1,35-1,36-1

NCV - **35,** 1-1,2-1,3-1,4-1,5-1,6-**2,**7-1,8-1,9-**2,**10-1,11-1,12-1,13-1,14-1,15-1,16-1,17-1,18-**2,**19-1,20-1,21-1,22-1,23-1,24-1,25-1,26-1,27-1,28-1,29-1,30-1,31-**2,**32-1,33-1,34-1,35-1

NIV - **28,** 1-1,2-1,3-1,4-1,5-1,6-1,7-1,8-1,9-1,10-1,11-1,12-1,13-1,14-1,15-1,16-1,17-**3,**18-1,19-1,20-1,21-1,22-1,23-1,24-**2,**25-1,26-1,27-1,28-1

NKJV - **36,** 1-1,2-1,3-1,4-1,5-1,6-1,7-1,8-1,9-1,10-1,11-1,12-1,13-1,14-1,15-1,16-1,17-1,18-1,19-1,20-1,21-1,22-1,23-1,24-1,25-1,26-1,27-1,28-1,29-1,30-1,31-1,32-1,33-1,34-1,35-1,36-1

NLT - **40,** 1-1,2-**3,**3-1,4-1,5-1,6-1,7-**2,**8-1,9-**2,**10-1,11-1,12-1,13-1,14-1,15-1,16-1,17-1,18-1,19-1,20-1,21-1,22-1,23-**2,**24-1,25-1,26-1,27-1,28-1,29-1,30-**3,**31-1,32-1,33-1,34-1,35-1,36-**3,**37-1,38-1,39-1,40-1

NRSV - **34,** 1-1,2-1,3-1,4-1,5-1,6-1,7-1,8-1,9-1,10-1,11-1,12-1,13-1,14-1,15-1,16-1,17-1,18-1,19-1,20-1,21-1,22-1,23-1,24-1,25-1,26-1,27-1,28-1,29-1,30-1,31-1,32-1,33-1,34-1

Conclusion: Four modern versions are more complex than the King James Bible. The NLT is the most difficult to read.

70. Genesis 36:19* These are the sons of **Esau**, who is **Edom**, and these are their dukes.

AV - **14,** 1-1,2-1,3-1,4-1,5-1,6-1,7-1,8-1,9-1,10-1,11-1,12-1,13-1,14-1

ESV - **14,** 1-1,2-1,3-1,4-1,5-1,6-1,7-1,8-1,9-1,10-1,11-1,12-1,13-1,14-1

HCSB - **14,** 1-1,2-1,3-1,4-1,5-1,6-1,7-1,8-1,9-1,10-1,11-1,12-1,13-1,14-1

NASV - **14,** 1-1,2-1,3-1,4-1,5-1,6-1,7-1,8-1,9-1,10-1,11-1,12-1,13-1,14-1

NCV - **14,** 1-1,2-1,3-1,4-1,5-1,6-1,7-**2,**8-1,9-1,10-1,11-1,12-1,13-1,14-**2**

NIV - **14,** 1-1,2-1,3-1,4-1,5-1,6-1,7-1,8-1,9-1,10-1,11-1,12-1,13-1,14-1

NKJV - **14,** 1-1,2-1,3-1,4-1,5-1,6-1,7-1,8-1,9-1,10-1,11-1,12-1,13-1,14-1

NLT - **16,** 1-1,2-1,3-1,4-1,5-**3,**6-1,7-1,8-**2,**9-1,10-1,11-1,12-**4,**13-1,14-1,15-1,16-**2**

NRSV - **14,** 1-1,2-1,3-1,4-1,5-1,6-1,7-1,8-1,9-1,10-1,11-1,12-1,13-1,14-1

Conclusion: Only the NCV and NLT made the verse more complex.

71. Genesis 36:29* These are the dukes that came of the **Horites**; duke **Lotan**, duke **Shobal**, duke **Zibeon**, duke **Anah**,

AV - **17,** 1-1,2-1,3-1,4-1,5-1,6-1,7-1,8-1,9-1,10-1,11-1,12-1,13-1,14-1,15-1,16-1,17-1

ESV - **13,** 1-1,2-1,3-1,4-1,5-1,6-1,7-1,8-1,9-1,10-1,11-1,12-1,13-1
HCSB - **12,** 1-1,2-1,3-1,4-1,5-1,6-1,7-1,8-1,9-1,10-1,11-1,12-1
NASV - 16, 1-1,2-1,3-1,4-1,5-**3**,6-1,7-1,8-1,9-1,10-1,11-1,12-1,13-1,14-1,15-1,16-1
NCV - 12, 1-1,2-1,3-1,4-1,5-1,6-1,7-1,8-**2**,9-1,10-1,11-1,12-1
NIV - **9,** 1-1,2-1,3-1,4-1,5-1,6-1,7-1,8-1,9-1
NKJV - **15,** 1-1,2-1,3-1,4-1,5-1,6-1,7-1,8-1,9-1,10-1,11-1,12-1,13-1,14-1,15-1
NLT - 13, 1-1,2-1,3-1,4-1,5-**2**,6-1,7-1,8-1,9-1,10-1,11-1,12-1,13-1
NRSV - **13,** 1-1,2-1,3-1,4-1,5-1,6-1,7-1,8-1,9-1,10-1,11-1,12-1,13-1
Conclusion: Three modern versions are more complex than the King James Bible.

72. Genesis 36:33* And **Bela** died, and **Jobab** the son of **Zerah** of **Bozrah** reigned in his stead.
AV - **15,** 1-1,2-1,3-1,4-1,5-1,6-1,7-1,8-1,9-1,10-1,11-1,12-1,13-1,14-1,15-1
ESV - **14,** 1-1,2-1,3-1,4-1,5-1,6-1,7-1,8-1,9-1,10-1,11-1,12-1,13-1,14-1
HCSB - **13,** 1-1,2-1,3-1,4-1,5-1,6-1,7-1,8-1,9-1,10-1,11-1,12-1,13-1
NASV - 16, 1-1,2-1,3-1,4-1,5-1,6-1,7-1,8-1,9-1,10-1,11-1,12-**2**,13-1,14-1,15-1,16-1
NCV - 13, 1-1,2-1,3-1,4-1,5-1,6-1,7-1,8-**2**,9-1,10-1,11-1,12-1,13-1
NIV - 13, 1-1,2-1,3-1,4-1,5-1,6-1,7-1,8-1,9-1,10-**3**,11-1,12-1,13-1
NKJV - **15,** 1-1,2-1,3-1,4-1,5-1,6-1,7-1,8-1,9-1,10-1,11-1,12-1,13-1,14-1,15-1
NLT - 14, 1-**2**,2-1,3-1,4-1,5-1,6-1,7-1,8-1,9-1,10-**2**,11-1,12-1,13-1,14-1
NRSV - 13, 1-1,2-1,3-1,4-1,5-1,6-1,7-1,8-1,9-1,10-**3**,11-1,12-1,13-1
Conclusion: Five modern versions are more complex than the King James Bible.

73. Genesis 36:34* And **Jobab** died, and **Husham** of the land of **Temani** reigned in his stead.
AV - **14,** 1-1,2-1,3-1,4-1,5-1,6-1,7-1,8-1,9-1,10-1,11-1,12-1,13-1,14-1
ESV - **14,** 1-1,2-1,3-1,4-1,5-1,6-1,7-1,8-1,9-1,10-1,11-1,12-1,13-1,14-1
HCSB - **14,** 1-1,2-1,3-1,4-1,5-1,6-1,7-1,8-1,9-1,10-1,11-1,12-1,13-1,14-1
NASV - 16, 1-1,2-1,3-1,4-1,5-1,6-1,7-1,8-1,9-1,10-1,11-1,12-**2**,13-1,14-1,15-1,16-1
NCV - 14, 1-1,2-1,3-1,4-1,5-**2**,6-1,7-1,8-1,9-1,10-1,11-1,12-1,13-1,14-1
NIV - 14, 1-1,2-1,3-1,4-1,5-1,6-1,7-1,8-1,9-1,10-1,11-**3**,12-1,13-1,14-1
NKJV - **14,** 1-1,2-1,3-1,4-1,5-1,6-1,7-1,8-1,9-1,10-1,11-1,12-1,13-1,14-1
NLT - 15, 1-**2**,2-1,3-1,4-1,5-1,6-1,7-1,8-1,9-1,10-1,11-**2**,12-1,13-1,14-1,15-1
NRSV - **14,** 1-1,2-1,3-1,4-1,5-1,6-1,7-1,8-1,9-1,10-1,11-1,12-1,13-1,14-1
Conclusion: Four modern versions are more complex than the King James Bible.

74. Genesis 36:36* And **Hadad** died, and **Samlah** of **Masrekah** reigned in his stead.
AV - **11,** 1-1,2-1,3-1,4-1,5-1,6-1,7-1,8-1,9-1,10-1,11-1
ESV - **10,** 1-1,2-1,3-1,4-1,5-1,6-1,7-1,8-1,9-1,10-1
HCSB - **10,** 1-1,2-1,3-1,4-1,5-1,6-1,7-1,8-1,9-1,10-1
NASV - 12, 1-1,2-1,3-1,4-1,5-1,6-1,7-1,8-**2**,9-1,10-1,11-1,12-1
NCV - 10, 1-1,2-1,3-1,4-1,5-**2**,6-1,7-1,8-1,9-1,10-1
NIV - 10, 1-1,2-1,3-1,4-1,5-1,6-1,7-**3**,8-1,9-1,10-1
NKJV - **10,** 1-1,2-1,3-1,4-1,5-1,6-1,7-1,8-1,9-1,10-1
NLT - 14, 1-**2**,2-1,3-1,4-1,5-1,6-1,7-**2**,8-1,9-1,10-**2**,11-1,12-1,13-1,14-1
NRSV - 10, 1-1,2-1,3-1,4-1,5-1,6-1,7-**3**,8-1,9-1,10-1

Conclusion: Five modern versions are more complex than the King James Bible. The NLT is the most difficult to read.

75. Genesis 36:38* And Saul died, and **Baalhanan** the son of **Achbor** reigned in his stead.
AV - **13,** 1-1,2-1,3-1,4-1,5-1,6-1,7-1,8-1,9-1,10-1,11-1,12-1,13-1
ESV - **12,** 1-1,2-1,3-1,4-1,5-1,6-1,7-1,8-1,9-1,10-1,11-1,12-1
HCSB - **11,** 1-1,2-1,3-1,4-1,5-1,6-1,7-1,8-1,9-1,10-1,11-1
NASV - 14, 1-1,2-1,3-1,4-1,5-1,6-1,7-1,8-1,9-1,10-**2**,11-1,12-1,13-1,14-1
NCV - 9, 1-1,2-1,3-1,4-1,5-1,6-1,7-1,8-**2**,9-1
NIV - 11, 1-1,2-1,3-1,4-1,5-1,6-1,7-1,8-**3**,9-1,10-1,11-1
NKJV - **12,** 1-1,2-1,3-1,4-1,5-1,6-1,7-1,8-1,9-1,10-1,11-1,12-1
NLT - 12, 1-**2**,2-1,3-1,4-1,5-1,6-1,7-1,8-**2**,9-1,10-1,11-1,12-1
NRSV - 11, 1-1,2-1,3-1,4-1,5-1,6-1,7-1,8-**3**,9-1,10-1,11-1
Conclusion: Five modern versions are more complex than the King James Bible. The NLT is the most difficult to read.

76. Genesis 36:41* Duke **Aholibamah**, duke **Elah**, duke **Pinon**,
AV - **6,** 1-1,2-1,3-1,4-1,5-1,6-1
ESV - **3,** 1-1,2-1,3-1
HCSB - **3,** 1-1,2-1,3-1
NASV - **6,** 1-1,2-1,3-1,4-1,5-1,6-1
NCV - **3,** 1-1,2-1,3-1
NIV - **3,** 1-1,2-1,3-1
NKJV - **6,** 1-1,2-1,3-1,4-1,5-1,6-1
NLT - **3,** 1-1,2-1,3-1
NRSV - **3,** 1-1,2-1,3-1
Conclusion: All versions read the same.

77. Genesis 36:42* Duke **Kenaz**, duke **Teman**, duke **Mibzar**,
AV - **6,** 1-1,2-1,3-1,4-1,5-1,6-1
ESV - **3,** 1-1,2-1,3-1
HCSB - **3,** 1-1,2-1,3-1
NASV - **6,** 1-1,2-1,3-1,4-1,5-1,6-1
NCV - **3,** 1-1,2-1,3-1
NIV - **3,** 1-1,2-1,3-1
NKJV - **6,** 1-1,2-1,3-1,4-1,5-1,6-1
NLT - **3,** 1-1,2-1,3-1
NRSV - **3,** 1-1,2-1,3-1
Conclusion: All versions read the same.

78. Genesis 37:31* And they took **Joseph's** coat, and killed a kid of the goats, and dipped the coat in the blood;
AV - **19,** 1-1,2-1,3-1,4-1,5-1,6-1,7-1,8-1,9-1,10-1,11-1,12-1,13-1,14-1,15-1,16-1,17-1,18-1,19-1
ESV - 16, 1-1,2-1,3-1,4-1,5-1,6-1,7-**2**,8-1,9-1,10-1,11-1,12-1,13-1,14-1,15-1,16-1

HCSB - 16, 1-1,2-1,3-1,4-1,5-1,6-**2**,7-1,8-1,9-1,10-1,11-1,12-1,13-1,14-1,15-1,16-1
NASV - 17, 1-1,2-1,3-1,4-1,5-**2**,6-1,7-**2**,8-1,9-1,10-1,11-1,12-1,13-1,14-**2**,15-1,16-1,17-1
NCV - 12, 1-1,2-**2**,3-1,4-1,5-1,6-1,7-1,8-1,9-1,10-1,11-1,12-1
NIV - 15, 1-1,2-1,3-1,4-1,5-1,6-**2**,7-1,8-1,9-1,10-1,11-1,12-1,13-1,14-1,15-1
NKJV - 18, 1-1,2-1,3-1,4-1,5-**2**,6-1,7-1,8-1,9-1,10-1,11-1,12-1,13-1,14-1,15-**2**,16-1,17-1,18-1
NLT - 14, 1-1,2-1,3-**2**,4-1,5-1,6-1,7-1,8-1,9-1,10-1,11-1,12-1,13-1,14-1
NRSV - 15, 1-1,2-1,3-1,4-1,5-1,6-**2**,7-1,8-1,9-1,10-1,11-1,12-1,13-1,14-1,15-1
Conclusion: All eight modern versions are more complex than the King James Bible.

79. Genesis 38:17 And he said, I will send thee a kid from the flock. And she said, Wilt thou give me a pledge, till thou send it?
AV - **25,** 1-1,2-1,3-1,4-1,5-1,6-1,7-1,8-1,9-1,10-1,11-1,12-1,13-1,14-1,15-1,16-1,17-1,18-1,19-1,20-1,21-1,22-1,23-1,24-1,25-1
ESV - 25, 1-1,2-**2**,3-1,4-1,5-1,6-1,7-1,8-1,9-1,10-1,11-1,12-1,13-1,14-1,15-1,16-1,17-1,18-1,19-1,20-1,21-1,22-**2**,23-1,24-1,25-1
HCSB - 26, 1-1,2-1,3-1,4-1,5-1,6-1,7-1,8-1,9-1,10-1,11-1,12-**2**,13-1,14-1,15-1,16-**2**,17-1,18-1,19-1,20-1,21-1,22-1,23-1,24-1,25-1,26-1
NASV - 25, 1-1,2-1,3-**2**,4-1,5-1,6-1,7-1,8-1,9-1,10-1,11-1,12-1,13-1,14-1,15-1,16-**2**,17-1,18-1,19-1,20-1,21-1,22-**2**,23-1,24-1,25-1
NCV - 28, 1-1,2-**2**,3-1,4-1,5-1,6-1,7-1,8-1,9-1,10-1,11-1,12-1,13-1,14-**2**,15-1,16-1,17-1,18-**2**,19-1,20-1,21-1,22-1,23-**3**,24-**2**,25-1,26-1,27-1,28-1
NIV - 24, 1-1,2-1,3-1,4-1,5-1,6-1,7-1,8-1,9-1,10-1,11-1,12-1,13-1,14-1,15-**2**,16-1,17-1,18-1,19-**2**,20-1,21-1,22-1,23-1,24-1
NKJV - **25,** 1-1,2-1,3-1,4-1,5-1,6-1,7-1,8-1,9-1,10-1,11-1,12-1,13-1,14-1,15-1,16-1,17-1,18-1,19-1,20-1,21-1,22-1,23-1,24-1,25-1
NLT - 27, 1-1,2-1,3-1,4-1,5-1,6-1,7-1,8-1,9-1,10-1,11-**2**,12-1,13-1,14-1,15-1,16-1,17-1,18-1,19-**3**,20-1,21-1,22-1,23-1,24-1,25-1,26-1,27-1
NRSV - 25, 1-1,2-**2**,3-1,4-1,5-1,6-1,7-1,8-1,9-1,10-1,11-1,12-1,13-1,14-1,15-**2**,16-1,17-1,18-1,19-1,20-1,21-1,22-**2**,23-1,24-1,25-1
Conclusion: Seven modern versions are more complex than the King James Bible. The NCV and the NLT are the most difficult to read.

80. Genesis 41:26# The **seven** good kine are **seven** years; and the **seven** good ears are **seven** years: the dream is one.
AV - **19,** 1-1,2-1,3-1,4-1,5-1,6-1,7-1,8-1,9-1,10-1,11-1,12-1,13-1,14-1,15-1,16-1,17-1,18-1,19-1
ESV - **19,** 1-1,2-1,3-1,4-1,5-1,6-1,7-1,8-1,9-1,10-1,11-1,12-1,13-1,14-1,15-1,16-1,17-1,18-1,19-1
HCSB - **21,** 1-1,2-1,3-1,4-1,5-1,6-1,7-1,8-1,9-1,10-1,11-1,12-1,13-1,14-1,15-1,16-1,17-1,18-1,19-1,20-1,21-1
NASV - **22,** 1-1,2-1,3-1,4-1,5-1,6-1,7-1,8-1,9-1,10-1,11-1,12-1,13-1,14-1,15-1,16-1,17-1,18-1,19-1,20-1,21-1,22-1
NCV - **25,** 1-1,2-1,3-1,4-1,5-1,6-1,7-1,8-1,9-1,10-1,11-1,12-1,13-1,14-1,15-1,16-1,17-1,18-1,19-1,20-1,21-1,22-1,23-1,24-1,25-1
NIV - **24,** 1-1,2-1,3-1,4-1,5-1,6-1,7-1,8-1,9-1,10-1,11-1,12-1,13-1,14-1,15-1,16-1,17-1,18-1,19-1,20-1,21-1,22-1,23-1,24-1

NKJV - **19,** 1-1,2-1,3-1,4-1,5-1,6-1,7-1,8-1,9-1,10-1,11-1,12-1,13-1,14-1,15-1,16-1,17-1,18-1,19-1
NLT - 17, 1-1,2-1,3-**2,**4-1,5-1,6-1,7-1,8-**2,**9-1,10-1,11-1,12-1,13-**3,**14-1,15-1,16-1,17-**4**
NRSV - **19,** 1-1,2-1,3-1,4-1,5-1,6-1,7-1,8-1,9-1,10-1,11-1,12-1,13-1,14-1,15-1,16-1,17-1,18-1,19-1
Conclusion: Only the NLT made the verse more complex.

81. Genesis 46:9* And the sons of **Reuben**; **Hanoch**, and **Phallu**, and **Hezron**, and **Carmi**.
AV - **12,** 1-1,2-1,3-1,4-1,5-1,6-1,7-1,8-1,9-1,10-1,11-1,12-1
ESV - **10,** 1-1,2-1,3-1,4-1,5-1,6-1,7-1,8-1,9-1,10-1
HCSB - **7,** 1-1,2-1,3-1,4-1,5-1,6-1,7-1
NASV - **11,** 1-1,2-1,3-1,4-1,5-1,6-1,7-1,8-1,9-1,10-1,11-1
NCV - **8,** 1-1,2-1,3-1,4-1,5-1,6-1,7-1,8-1
NIV - **9,** 1-1,2-1,3-1,4-1,5-1,6-1,7-1,8-1,9-1
NKJV - **10,** 1-1,2-1,3-1,4-1,5-1,6-1,7-1,8-1,9-1,10-1
NLT - **10,** 1-1,2-1,3-1,4-1,5-1,6-1,7-1,8-1,9-1,10-1
NRSV - 10, 1-1,2-1,3-**2,**4-1,5-1,6-1,7-1,8-1,9-1,10-1
Conclusion: Only the NRSV made the verse more complex.

82. Genesis 46:11* And the sons of **Levi**; **Gershon**, **Kohath**, and **Merari**.
AV - **9,** 1-1,2-1,3-1,4-1,5-1,6-1,7-1,8-1,9-1
ESV - **8,** 1-1,2-1,3-1,4-1,5-1,6-1,7-1,8-1
HCSB - **6,** 1-1,2-1,3-1,4-1,5-1,6-1
NASV - **8,** 1-1,2-1,3-1,4-1,5-1,6-1,7-1,8-1
NCV - **8,** 1-1,2-1,3-1,4-1,5-1,6-1,7-1,8-1
NIV - **8,** 1-1,2-1,3-1,4-1,5-1,6-1,7-1,8-1
NKJV - **9,** 1-1,2-1,3-1,4-1,5-1,6-1,7-1,8-1,9-1
NLT - **9,** 1-1,2-1,3-1,4-1,5-1,6-1,7-1,8-1,9-1
NRSV - 8, 1-1,2-**2,**3-1,4-1,5-1,6-1,7-1,8-1
Conclusion: Only the NRSV made the verse more complex.

83. Genesis 46:12* And the sons of **Judah**; Er, and **Onan**, and **Shelah**, and **Pharez**, and **Zerah**: but Er and **Onan** died in the land of **Canaan**. And the sons of **Pharez** were **Hezron** and **Hamul**.
AV - **33,** 1-1,2-1,3-1,4-1,5-1,6-1,7-1,8-1,9-1,10-1,11-1,12-1,13-1,14-1,15-1,16-1,17-1,18-1,19-1,20-1,21-1,22-1,23-1,24-1,25-1,26-1,27-1,28-1,29-1,30-1,31-1,32-1,33-1
ESV - **29,** 1-1,2-1,3-1,4-1,5-1,6-1,7-1,8-1,9-1,10-1,11-1,12-1,13-1,14-1,15-1,16-1,17-1,18-1,19-1,20-1,21-1,22-1,23-1,24-1,25-1,26-1,27-1,28-1,29-1
HCSB - **23,** 1-1,2-1,3-1,4-1,5-1,6-1,7-1,8-1,9-1,10-1,11-1,12-1,13-1,14-1,15-1,16-1,17-1,18-1,19-1,20-1,21-1,22-1,23-1
NASV - **32,** 1-1,2-1,3-1,4-1,5-1,6-1,7-1,8-1,9-1,10-1,11-1,12-1,13-1,14-1,15-1,16-1,17-1,18-1,19-1,20-1,21-1,22-1,23-1,24-1,25-1,26-1,27-1,28-1,29-1,30-1,31-1,32-1
NCV - **26,** 1-1,2-1,3-1,4-1,5-1,6-1,7-1,8-1,9-1,10-1,11-1,12-1,13-1,14-1,15-1,16-1,17-1,18-1,19-1,20-1,21-1,22-1,23-1,24-1,25-1,26-1
NIV - **28,** 1-1,2-1,3-1,4-1,5-1,6-1,7-1,8-1,9-1,10-1,11-1,12-1,13-1,14-1,15-1,16-1,17-1,18-1,19-1,20-1,21-1,22-1,23-1,24-1,25-1,26-1,27-1,28-1

NKJV - **29,** 1-1,2-1,3-1,4-1,5-1,6-1,7-1,8-1,9-1,10-1,11-1,12-1,13-1,14-1,15-1,16-1,17-1,18-1,19-1,20-1,21-1,22-1,23-1,24-1,25-1,26-1,27-1,28-1,29-1

NLT - **30,** 1-1,2-1,3-1,4-1,5-1,6-1,7-1,8-1,9-1,10-1,11-1,12-1,13-1,14-1,15-1,16-1,17-1,18-1,19-1,20-1,21-1,22-1,23-1,24-1,25-1,26-1,27-1,28-1,29-1,30-1

NRSV - **29,** 1-1,2-**2**,3-1,4-1,5-1,6-1,7-1,8-1,9-1,10-1,11-1,12-1,13-1,14-1,15-1,16-1,17-1,18-1,19-1,20-1,21-1,22-1,23-**2**,24-1,25-1,26-1,27-1,28-1,29-1

Conclusion: Only the NRSV made the verse more complex.

84. Genesis 46:13* And the sons of **Issachar**; **Tola**, and **Phuvah**, and Job, and **Shimron**.
AV - **12,** 1-1,2-1,3-1,4-1,5-1,6-1,7-1,8-1,9-1,10-1,11-1,12-1
ESV - **9,** 1-1,2-1,3-1,4-1,5-1,6-1,7-1,8-1,9-1
HCSB - **7,** 1-1,2-1,3-1,4-1,5-1,6-1,7-1
NASV - **11,** 1-1,2-1,3-1,4-1,5-1,6-1,7-1,8-1,9-1,10-1,11-1
NCV - **8,** 1-1,2-1,3-1,4-1,5-1,6-1,7-1,8-1
NIV - **9,** 1-1,2-1,3-1,4-1,5-1,6-1,7-1,8-1,9-1
NKJV - **10,** 1-1,2-1,3-1,4-1,5-1,6-1,7-1,8-1,9-1,10-1
NLT - **10,** 1-1,2-1,3-1,4-1,5-1,6-1,7-1,8-1,9-1,10-1
NRSV - **9,** 1-1,2-**2**,3-1,4-1,5-1,6-1,7-1,8-1,9-1
Conclusion: Only the NRSV made the verse more complex.

85. Genesis 46:14* And the sons of **Zebulun**; **Sered**, and **Elon**, and **Jahleel**.
AV - **10,** 1-1,2-1,3-1,4-1,5-1,6-1,7-1,8-1,9-1,10-1
ESV - **8,** 1-1,2-1,3-1,4-1,5-1,6-1,7-1,8-1
HCSB - **6,** 1-1,2-1,3-1,4-1,5-1,6-1
NASV - **9,** 1-1,2-1,3-1,4-1,5-1,6-1,7-1,8-1,9-1
NCV - **7,** 1-1,2-1,3-1,4-1,5-1,6-1,7-1
NIV - **8,** 1-1,2-1,3-1,4-1,5-1,6-1,7-1,8-1
NKJV - **9,** 1-1,2-1,3-1,4-1,5-1,6-1,7-1,8-1,9-1
NLT - **9,** 1-1,2-1,3-1,4-1,5-1,6-1,7-1,8-1,9-1
NRSV - **8,** 1-1,2-**2**,3-1,4-1,5-1,6-1,7-1,8-1
Conclusion: Only the NRSV made the verse more complex.

86. Genesis 46:16* And the sons of Gad; **Ziphion**, and **Haggi**, **Shuni**, and **Ezbon**, **Eri**, and **Arodi**, and **Areli**.
AV - **16,** 1-1,2-1,3-1,4-1,5-1,6-1,7-1,8-1,9-1,10-1,11-1,12-1,13-1,14-1,15-1,16-1
ESV - **12,** 1-1,2-1,3-1,4-1,5-1,6-1,7-1,8-1,9-1,10-1,11-1,12-1
HCSB - **10,** 1-1,2-1,3-1,4-1,5-1,6-1,7-1,8-1,9-1,10-1
NASV - **15,** 1-1,2-1,3-1,4-1,5-1,6-1,7-1,8-1,9-1,10-1,11-1,12-1,13-1,14-1,15-1
NCV - **11,** 1-1,2-1,3-1,4-1,5-1,6-1,7-1,8-1,9-1,10-1,11-1
NIV - **12,** 1-1,2-1,3-1,4-1,5-1,6-1,7-1,8-1,9-1,10-1,11-1,12-1
NKJV - **13,** 1-1,2-1,3-1,4-1,5-1,6-1,7-1,8-1,9-1,10-1,11-1,12-1,13-1
NLT - **13,** 1-1,2-1,3-1,4-1,5-1,6-1,7-1,8-1,9-1,10-1,11-1,12-1,13-1
NRSV - **12,** 1-1,2-**2**,3-1,4-1,5-1,6-1,7-1,8-1,9-1,10-1,11-1,12-1
Conclusion: Only the NRSV made the verse more complex.

87. Genesis 46:19* The sons of **Rachel Jacob's** wife; **Joseph**, and **Benjamin**.
AV - **9,** 1-1,2-1,3-1,4-1,5-1,6-1,7-1,8-1,9-1
ESV - **9,** 1-1,2-1,3-1,4-1,5-1,6-1,7-1,8-1,9-1
HCSB - **9,** 1-1,2-1,3-1,4-1,5-1,6-1,7-1,8-1,9-1
NASV - **9,** 1-1,2-1,3-1,4-1,5-1,6-1,7-1,8-1,9-1
NCV - **10,** 1-1,2-1,3-1,4-1,5-1,6-1,7-1,8-1,9-1,10-1
NIV - **9,** 1-1,2-1,3-1,4-1,5-1,6-1,7-1,8-1,9-1
NKJV - **10,** 1-1,2-1,3-1,4-1,5-1,6-1,7-1,8-1,9-1,10-1
NLT - **10,** 1-1,2-1,3-1,4-1,5-1,6-1,7-1,8-1,9-1,10-1
NRSV - **9,** 1-1,2-**2**,3-1,4-1,5-1,6-1,7-1,8-1,9-1
Conclusion: Only the NRSV made the verse more complex.

88. Genesis 46:22*# These are the sons of **Rachel**, which were born to **Jacob**: all the souls were **fourteen**.
AV - **16,** 1-1,2-1,3-1,4-1,5-1,6-1,7-1,8-1,9-1,10-1,11-1,12-1,13-1,14-1,15-1,16-1
ESV - **15,** 1-1,2-1,3-1,4-1,5-1,6-1,7-1,8-1,9-1,10-1,11-1,12-1,13-**2**,14-1,15-1
HCSB - **11,** 1-1,2-1,3-1,4-1,5-1,6-1,7-1,8-1,9-1,10-1,11-**2**
NASV - **17,** 1-1,2-1,3-1,4-1,5-1,6-1,7-1,8-1,9-1,10-1,11-1,12-1,13-1,14-1,15-**2**,16-1,17-1
NCV - **20,** 1-1,2-1,3-1,4-1,5-1,6-1,7-1,8-1,9-1,10-1,11-1,12-1,13-1,14-**2**,15-1,16-1,17-1,18-1,19-1,20-**3**
NIV - **14,** 1-1,2-1,3-1,4-1,5-1,6-1,7-1,8-1,9-1,10-1,11-1,12-1,13-1,14-1
NKJV - **15,** 1-1,2-1,3-1,4-1,5-1,6-1,7-1,8-1,9-1,10-1,11-1,12-1,13-**2**,14-1,15-1
NLT - **17,** 1-1,2-1,3-1,4-1,5-1,6-1,7-1,8-1,9-1,10-**2**,11-1,12-1,13-**3**,14-1,15-1,16-1,17-1
NRSV - **15,** 1-1,2-1,3-1,4-**2**,5-1,6-1,7-1,8-1,9-1,10-1,11-1,12-1,13-**2**,14-1,15-1
Conclusion: Seven modern versions are more complex than the King James Bible.

89. Genesis 46:23* And the sons of Dan; **Hushim**.
AV - **6,** 1-1,2-1,3-1,4-1,5-1,6-1
ESV -**5,** 1-1,2-1,3-1,4-1,5-1
HCSB - **3,** 1-1,2-1,3-1
NASV -**5,** 1-1,2-1,3-1,4-1,5-1
NCV - **4,** 1-1,2-1,3-1,4-1
NIV - **5,** 1-1,2-1,3-1,4-1,5-1
NKJV - **6,** 1-1,2-1,3-1,4-1,5-1,6-1
NLT - **6,** 1-1,2-1,3-1,4-1,5-1,6-1
NRSV - **5,** 1-1,2-**2**,3-1,4-1,5-1
Conclusion: Only the NRSV made the verse more complex.

90. Genesis 47:28*# And **Jacob** lived in the land of **Egypt seventeen** years: so the whole age of **Jacob** was an **hundred forty** and **seven** years.
AV - **23,** 1-1,2-1,3-1,4-1,5-1,6-1,7-1,8-1,9-1,10-1,11-1,12-1,13-1,14-1,15-1,16-1,17-1,18-1,19-1,20-1,21-1,22-1,23-1

ESV - **23,** 1-1,2-1,3-1,4-1,5-1,6-1,7-1,8-1,9-1,10-1,11-1,12-1,13-1,14-1,15-1,16-1,17-1,18-1,19-1,20-1,21-1,22-1,23-1

HCSB - **17,** 1-1,2-1,3-1,4-1,5-1,6-1,7-1,8-1,9-1,10-1,11-1,12-1,13-1,14-1,15-1,16-1,17-1

NASV - **21,** 1-1,2-1,3-1,4-1,5-1,6-1,7-1,8-1,9-1,10-1,11-1,12-1,13-1,14-1,15-1,16-1,17-1,18-1,19-1,20-1,21-1

NCV - **16,** 1-1,2-1,3-1,4-1,5-1,6-1,7-1,8-1,9-1,10-1,11-1,12-1,13-1,14-1,15-1,16-1

NIV - **17,** 1-1,2-1,3-1,4-1,5-1,6-1,7-1,8-1,9-1,10-1,11-1,12-1,13-1,14-1,15-1,16-1,17-1

NKJV - **22,** 1-1,2-1,3-1,4-1,5-1,6-1,7-1,8-1,9-1,10-1,11-1,12-1,13-1,14-1,15-1,16-1,17-1,18-1,19-1,20-1,21-1,22-1

NLT - **17,** 1-1,2-1,3-1,4-1,5-1,6-**2,**7-1,8-**3,**9-1,10-1,11-1,12-1,13-1,14-1,15-1,16-1,17-1

NRSV - **24,** 1-1,2-1,3-1,4-1,5-1,6-1,7-1,8-1,9-1,10-1,11-1,12-1,13-1,14-1,15-1,16-1,17-1,18-1,19-1,20-1,21-1,22-1,23-1,24-1

Conclusion: Only the NLT made the verse more complex.

91. Genesis 49:12 His eyes shall be red with wine, and his teeth white with milk.

AV - **13,** 1-1,2-1,3-1,4-1,5-1,6-1,7-1,8-1,9-1,10-1,11-1,12-1,13-1

ESV - **12,** 1-1,2-1,3-1,4-**2,**5-1,6-1,7-1,8-1,9-1,10-**2,**11-1,12-1

HCSB - **13,** 1-1,2-1,3-1,4-**2,**5-1,6-1,7-1,8-1,9-1,10-1,11-**2,**12-1,13-1

NASV - **12,** 1-1,2-1,3-1,4-1,5-1,6-1,7-1,8-1,9-1,10-1,11-1,12-1

NCV - **20,** 1-1,2-1,3-1,4-1,5-1,6-1,7-**2,**8-1,9-1,10-1,11-1,12-1,13-1,14-1,15-1,16-1,17-1,18-**2,**19-1,20-1

NIV - **12,** 1-1,2-1,3-1,4-1,5-**2,**6-1,7-1,8-1,9-1,10-**2,**11-1,12-1

NKJV - **12,** 1-1,2-1,3-1,4-**2,**5-1,6-1,7-1,8-1,9-1,10-**2,**11-1,12-1

NLT - **13,** 1-1,2-1,3-1,4-**2,**5-1,6-1,7-1,8-1,9-1,10-1,11-**2,**12-1,13-1

NRSV - **12,** 1-1,2-1,3-1,4-**2,**5-1,6-1,7-1,8-1,9-1,10-**2,**11-1,12-1

Conclusion: Seven modern versions are more complex than the King James Bible.

92. Exodus 1:2* Reuben, **Simeon**, **Levi**, and **Judah,**

AV - **5,** 1-1,2-1,3-1,4-1,5-1

ESV - **5,** 1-1,2-1,3-1,4-1,5-1

HCSB - **5,** 1-1,2-1,3-1,4-1,5-1

NASV - **5,** 1-1,2-1,3-1,4-1,5-1

NCV - **4,** 1-1,2-1,3-1,4-1

NIV - **5,** 1-1,2-1,3-1,4-1,5-1

NKJV - **5,** 1-1,2-1,3-1,4-1,5-1

NLT - **4,** 1-1,2-1,3-1,4-1

NRSV - **5,** 1-1,2-1,3-1,4-1,5-1

Conclusion: All versions read the same.

93. Exodus 1:3* Issachar, **Zebulun**, and **Benjamin,**

AV - **4,** 1-1,2-1,3-1,4-1

ESV - **4,** 1-1,2-1,3-1,4-1

HCSB - **4,** 1-1,2-1,3-1,4-1

NASV - **4,** 1-1,2-1,3-1,4-1

NCV - **3,** 1-1,2-1,3-1
NIV - **4,** 1-1,2-1,3-1,4-1
NKJV - **4,** 1-1,2-1,3-1,4-1
NLT - **3,** 1-1,2-1,3-1
NRSV - **4,** 1-1,2-1,3-1,4-1
Conclusion: All versions read the same.

94. Exodus 1:4* Dan, and **Naphtali**, Gad, and **Asher**.
AV - **6,** 1-1,2-1,3-1,4-1,5-1,6-1
ESV - **6,** 1-1,2-1,3-1,4-1,5-1,6-1
HCSB - **6,** 1-1,2-1,3-1,4-1,5-1,6-1
NASV - **6,** 1-1,2-1,3-1,4-1,5-1,6-1
NCV - **5,** 1-1,2-1,3-1,4-1,5-1
NIV - **6,** 1-1,2-1,3-1,4-1,5-1,6-1
NKJV - **5,** 1-1,2-1,3-1,4-1,5-1
NLT - **5,** 1-1,2-1,3-1,4-1,5-1
NRSV - **6,** 1-1,2-1,3-1,4-1,5-1,6-1
Conclusion: All versions read the same.

95. Exodus 2:12* And he looked this way and that way, and when he saw that there was no man, he slew the **Egyptian**, and hid him in the sand.
AV - **27,** 1-1,2-1,3-1,4-1,5-1,6-1,7-1,8-1,9-1,10-1,11-1,12-1,13-1,14-1,15-1,16-1,17-1,18-1,19-1,20-1,21-1,22-1,23-1,24-1,25-1,26-1,27-1
ESV - **21,** 1-1,2-1,3-1,4-1,5-1,6-1,7-1,8-**2**,9-1,10-1,11-1,12-1,13-1,14-1,15-1,16-1,17-1,18-1,19-1,20-1,21-1
HCSB - **18,** 1-**2**,2-1,3-**2**,4-1,5-**2**,6-1,7-1,8-1,9-1,10-1,11-1,12-1,13-1,14-1,15-1,16-1,17-1,18-1
NASV - **27,** 1-1,2-1,3-1,4-1,5-1,6-1,7-1,8-1,9-1,10-1,11-1,12-1,13-1,14-1,15-1,16-**2**,17-1,18-1,19-1,20-1,21-1,22-1,23-1,24-1,25-1,26-1,27-1
NCV - **23,** 1-1,2-1,3-1,4-**2**,5-1,6-1,7-1,8-1,9-1,10-1,11-**2**,12-1,13-1,14-1,15-1,16-1,17-1,18-1,19-1,20-**2**,21-1,22-1,23-1
NIV - **19,** 1-**2**,2-1,3-1,4-1,5-1,6-1,7-**2**,8-1,9-1,10-1,11-1,12-1,13-1,14-1,15-1,16-1,17-1,18-1,19-1
NKJV - **24,** 1-1,2-1,3-1,4-1,5-1,6-1,7-1,8-1,9-1,10-1,11-1,12-1,13-1,14-1,15-1,16-1,17-1,18-1,19-1,20-1,21-1,22-1,23-1,24-1
NLT - **23,** 1-**2**,2-**2**,3-1,4-1,5-**3**,6-1,7-1,8-1,9-1,10-1,11-1,12-**2**,13-1,14-1,15-1,16-1,17-1,18-1,19-1,20-1,21-1,22-1,23-1
NRSV - **20,** 1-1,2-1,3-1,4-1,5-1,6-1,7-1,8-**2**,9-1,10-1,11-1,12-1,13-1,14-1,15-1,16-1,17-1,18-1,19-1,20-1
Conclusion: Seven modern versions are more complex than the King James Bible. The NCV and the NLT are the most difficult to read.

96. Exodus 4:13 And he said, O my Lord, send, I pray thee, by the hand of him whom thou wilt send.
AV - **19,** 1-1,2-1,3-1,4-1,5-1,6-1,7-1,8-1,9-1,10-1,11-1,12-1,13-1,14-1,15-1,16-1,17-1,18-1,19-1
ESV - **10,** 1-1,2-1,3-1,4-1,5-1,6-1,7-1,8-1,9-**2**,10-1

HCSB - 7, 1-1,2-1,3-1,4-1,5-1,6-**2**,7-1
NASV - 13, 1-1,2-1,3-1,4-1,5-1,6-1,7-1,8-1,9-**2**,10-1,11-**2**,12-1,13-1
NCV - 8, 1-1,2-1,3-1,4-1,5-1,6-1,7-**2**,8-1
NIV - 12, 1-1,2-1,3-1,4-1,5-1,6-1,7-1,8-**2**,9-1,10-1,11-1,12-1
NKJV - 17, 1-1,2-1,3-1,4-1,5-1,6-1,7-1,8-1,9-1,10-1,11-1,12-1,13-**2**,14-1,15-1,16-1,17-1
NLT - 9, 1-1,2-1,3-**2**,4-**2**,5-1,6-1,7-1,8-**2**,9-1
NRSV - 10, 1-1,2-1,3-1,4-1,5-1,6-1,7-1,8-1,9-**2**,10-1
Conclusion: All eight modern versions are more complex than the King James Bible. The NLT is the most difficult to read.

97. Exodus 4:24 And it came to pass by the way in the inn, that the LORD met him, and sought to kill him.
AV - **21,** 1-1,2-1,3-1,4-1,5-1,6-1,7-1,8-1,9-1,10-1,11-1,12-1,13-1,14-1,15-1,16-1,17-1,18-1,19-1,20-1,21-1
ESV - 18, 1-1,2-1,3-**2**,4-1,5-1,6-1,7-1,8-1,9-1,10-1,11-1,12-1,13-1,14-1,15-1,16-1,17-1,18-1
HCSB - 21, 1-1,2-1,3-1,4-1,5-1,6-**3**,7-**2**,8-1,9-**2**,10-1,11-1,12-1,13-**3**,14-1,15-1,16-1,17-1,18-1,19-1,20-1,21-1
NASV - 23, 1-1,2-1,3-1,4-1,5-1,6-1,7-**2**,8-1,9-1,10-1,11-1,12-1,13-1,14-1,15-1,16-1,17-1,18-1,19-1,20-1,21-1,22-1,23-1
NCV - 27, 1-1,2-1,3-1,4-1,5-1,6-1,7-1,8-1,9-1,10-1,11-1,12-1,13-**2**,14-1,15-1,16-1,17-1,18-1,19-1,20-1,21-1,22-1,23-1,24-1,25-1,26-1,27-1
NIV - 17, 1-1,2-1,3-**2**,4-1,5-1,6-1,7-1,8-1,9-1,10-1,11-1,12-1,13-1,14-1,15-1,16-1,17-1
NKJV - 21, 1-1,2-1,3-1,4-1,5-1,6-1,7-1,8-1,9-1,10-1,11-**3**,12-1,13-1,14-1,15-1,16-1,17-1,18-1,19-1,20-1,21-1
NLT - 28, 1-1,2-1,3-1,4-1,5-1,6-1,7-1,8-1,9-1,10-1,11-1,12-1,13-1,14-1,15-1,16-1,17-1,18-1,19-1,20-1,21-**3**,22-1,23-1,24-1,25-1,26-1,27-1,28-1
NRSV - **20,** 1-1,2-1,3-1,4-1,5-1,6-1,7-1,8-1,9-1,10-1,11-1,12-1,13-1,14-1,15-1,16-1,17-1,18-1,19-1,20-1
Conclusion: Seven modern versions are more complex than the King James Bible. The HCSB is the most difficult to read.

98. Exodus 5:20* And they met **Moses** and **Aaron**, who stood in the way, as they came forth from **Pharaoh**:
AV - **17,** 1-1,2-1,3-1,4-1,5-1,6-1,7-1,8-1,9-1,10-1,11-1,12-1,13-1,14-1,15-1,16-1,17-1
ESV - 16, 1-1,2-1,3-1,4-1,5-1,6-1,7-1,8-**2**,9-1,10-1,11-1,12-1,13-1,14-1,15-1,16-1
HCSB - 15, 1-1,2-1,3-1,4-1,5-1,6-**3**,7-1,8-1,9-1,10-1,11-1,12-**2**,13-1,14-1,15-1
NASV - 16, 1-1,2-1,3-1,4-1,5-**2**,6-1,7-1,8-1,9-1,10-1,11-1,12-1,13-1,14-**2**,15-1,16-1
NCV - 19, 1-1,2-1,3-1,4-**2**,5-1,6-**2**,7-1,8-1,9-1,10-1,11-1,12-1,13-1,14-1,15-1,16-1,17-**2**,18-1,19-1
NIV - 13, 1-1,2-1,3-1,4-1,5-1,6-1,7-1,8-1,9-1,10-**2**,11-1,12-1,13-1
NKJV - **18,** 1-1,2-1,3-1,4-1,5-1,6-1,7-1,8-1,9-1,10-1,11-1,12-1,13-1,14-1,15-1,16-1,17-1,18-1
NLT - 16, 1-1,2-1,3-1,4-1,5-1,6-1,7-**3**,8-1,9-1,10-1,11-1,12-1,13-**2**,14-**2**,15-1,16-1
NRSV - 16, 1-1,2-1,3-1,4-1,5-1,6-1,7-**2**,8-1,9-1,10-1,11-1,12-1,13-**2**,14-1,15-1,16-1
Conclusion: Seven modern versions are more complex than the King James Bible.

99. Exodus 6:18*# And the sons of **Kohath**; **Amram**, and **Izhar**, and **Hebron**, and **Uzziel**: and the years of the life of **Kohath** were an **hundred thirty** and three years.
AV - **27,** 1-1,2-1,3-1,4-1,5-1,6-1,7-1,8-1,9-1,10-1,11-1,12-1,13-1,14-1,15-1,16-1,17-1,18-1,19-1,20-1,21-1,22-1,23-1,24-1,25-1,26-1,27-1
ESV - **19,** 1-1,2-1,3-1,4-1,5-1,6-1,7-1,8-1,9-1,10-1,11-1,12-1,13-1,14-1,15-1,16-1,17-**2**,18-1,19-1
HCSB - **13,** 1-1,2-1,3-1,4-1,5-1,6-1,7-1,8-1,9-1,10-1,11-1,12-1,13-1
NASV - **23,** 1-1,2-1,3-1,4-1,5-1,6-1,7-1,8-1,9-1,10-1,11-1,12-1,13-1,14-1,15-1,16-1,17-1,18-1,19-1,20-1,21-1,22-1,23-1
NCV - **16,** 1-1,2-1,3-1,4-1,5-1,6-1,7-1,8-1,9-1,10-1,11-1,12-1,13-1,14-1,15-1,16-1
NIV - **14,** 1-1,2-1,3-1,4-1,5-1,6-1,7-1,8-1,9-1,10-1,11-1,12-1,13-1,14-1
NKJV - **24,** 1-1,2-1,3-1,4-1,5-1,6-1,7-1,8-1,9-1,10-1,11-1,12-1,13-1,14-1,15-1,16-1,17-1,18-1,19-1,20-1,21-1,22-1,23-1,24-1
NLT - **17,** 1-1,2-**3**,3-1,4-1,5-1,6-**3**,7-1,8-1,9-1,10-1,11-1,12-1,13-1,14-1,15-1,16-1,17-1
NRSV - **20,** 1-1,2-1,3-1,4-1,5-1,6-1,7-1,8-1,9-1,10-1,11-1,12-1,13-1,14-1,15-1,16-1,17-1,18-1,19-1,20-1
Conclusion: Only the ESV and the NLT made the verse more complex.

100. Exodus 6:21* And the sons of **Izhar**; **Korah**, and **Nepheg**, and **Zichri**.
AV - **10,** 1-1,2-1,3-1,4-1,5-1,6-1,7-1,8-1,9-1,10-1
ESV - **8,** 1-1,2-1,3-1,4-1,5-1,6-1,7-1,8-1
HCSB - **8,** 1-1,2-1,3-1,4-1,5-1,6-1,7-1,8-1
NASV - **9,** 1-1,2-1,3-1,4-1,5-1,6-1,7-1,8-1,9-1
NCV - **7,** 1-1,2-1,3-1,4-1,5-1,6-1,7-1
NIV - **9,** 1-1,2-1,3-1,4-1,5-1,6-1,7-1,8-1,9-1
NKJV - **9,** 1-1,2-1,3-1,4-1,5-1,6-1,7-1,8-1,9-1
NLT - **9,** 1-1,2-1,3-1,4-1,5-1,6-1,7-1,8-1,9-1
NRSV - **8,** 1-1,2-1,3-1,4-1,5-1,6-1,7-1,8-1
Conclusion: All versions read the same.

101. Exodus 6:22* And the sons of **Uzziel**; **Mishael**, and **Elzaphan**, and **Zithri**.
AV - **10,** 1-1,2-1,3-1,4-1,5-1,6-1,7-1,8-1,9-1,10-1
ESV - **8,** 1-1,2-1,3-1,4-1,5-1,6-1,7-1,8-1
HCSB - **8,** 1-1,2-1,3-1,4-1,5-1,6-1,7-1,8-1
NASV - **9,** 1-1,2-1,3-1,4-1,5-1,6-1,7-1,8-1,9-1
NCV - **7,** 1-1,2-1,3-1,4-1,5-1,6-1,7-1
NIV - **9,** 1-1,2-1,3-1,4-1,5-1,6-1,7-1,8-1,9-1
NKJV - **10,** 1-1,2-1,3-1,4-1,5-1,6-1,7-1,8-1,9-1,10-1
NLT - **9,** 1-1,2-1,3-1,4-1,5-1,6-1,7-1,8-1,9-1
NRSV - **8,** 1-1,2-1,3-1,4-1,5-1,6-1,7-1,8-1
Conclusion: All versions read the same.

102. Exodus 13:4* This day came ye out in the month **Abib**.
AV - **8,** 1-1,2-1,3-1,4-1,5-1,6-1,7-1,8-1
ESV - **10,** 1-**2**,2-1,3-1,4-1,5-1,6-1,7-1,8-1,9-**2**,10-1

HCSB - 9, 1-1,2-1,3-1,4-1,5-1,6-1,7-1,8-1,9-**3**
NASV - 14, 1-1,2-1,3-1,4-1,5-1,6-1,7-1,8-1,9-1,10-1,11-**2**,12-1,13-1,14-1
NCV - 10, 1-**2**,2-1,3-1,4-1,5-1,6-1,7-1,8-1,9-**2**,10-1
NIV - 9, 1-**2**,2-1,3-1,4-1,5-1,6-1,7-1,8-1,9-**2**
NKJV - 11, 1-1,2-1,3-1,4-1,5-1,6-**2**,7-1,8-1,9-1,10-1,11-1
NLT - 11, 1-1,2-1,3-1,4-1,5-**2**,6-1,7-1,8-1,9-1,10-1,11-1
NRSV - 10, 1-**2**,2-1,3-1,4-1,5-1,6-1,7-1,8-1,9-**2**,10-1
Conclusion: All eight modern versions are more complex than the King James Bible.

103. Exodus 14:14 The LORD shall fight for you, and ye shall hold your peace.
AV - **12,** 1-1,2-1,3-1,4-1,5-1,6-1,7-1,8-1,9-1,10-1,11-1,12-1
ESV - 13, 1-1,2-1,3-1,4-1,5-1,6-1,7-1,8-1,9-1,10-1,11-1,12-1,13-**2**
HCSB - 10, 1-1,2-1,3-1,4-1,5-1,6-1,7-1,8-1,9-1,10-**2**
NASV - 10, 1-1,2-1,3-1,4-1,5-1,6-1,7-1,8-1,9-1,10-**2**
NCV - 12, 1-1,2-**2**,3-1,4-1,5-**2**,6-1,7-1,8-1,9-1,10-1,11-1,12-1
NIV - 12, 1-1,2-1,3-1,4-1,5-1,6-1,7-1,8-1,9-**2**,10-1,11-1,12-1
NKJV - **12,** 1-1,2-1,3-1,4-1,5-1,6-1,7-1,8-1,9-1,10-1,11-1,12-1
NLT - 10, 1-1,2-1,3-**2**,4-1,5-1,6-1,7-1,8-1,9-1,10-1
NRSV - 13, 1-1,2-1,3-1,4-1,5-1,6-1,7-1,8-1,9-1,10-**2**,11-1,12-1,13-1
Conclusion: Seven modern versions are more complex than the King James Bible.

104. Exodus 15:3 The LORD is a man of war: the LORD is his name.
AV - **12,** 1-1,2-1,3-1,4-1,5-1,6-1,7-1,8-1,9-1,10-1,11-1,12-1
ESV - **12,** 1-1,2-1,3-1,4-1,5-1,6-1,7-1,8-1,9-1,10-1,11-1,12-1
HCSB - 9, 1-1,2-1,3-1,4-1,5-**2**,6-1,7-1,8-1,9-1
NASV - 10, 1-1,2-1,3-1,4-1,5-**2**,6-1,7-1,8-1,9-1,10-1
NCV - 10, 1-1,2-1,3-1,4-1,5-**2**,6-1,7-1,8-1,9-1,10-1
NIV - 10, 1-1,2-1,3-1,4-1,5-**2**,6-1,7-1,8-1,9-1,10-1
NKJV - **12,** 1-1,2-1,3-1,4-1,5-1,6-1,7-1,8-1,9-1,10-1,11-1,12-1
NLT - 9, 1-1,2-1,3-1,4-1,5-**2**,6-1,7-1,8-1,9-1
NRSV - 10, 1-1,2-1,3-1,4-1,5-**2**,6-1,7-1,8-1,9-1,10-1
Conclusion: Six modern versions are more complex than the King James Bible. In the HCSB and the NLT the sixth word in the verse is transliterated, "Yahweh" but it was counted as one syllable because it is a name.

105. Exodus 17:8* Then came **Amalek**, and fought with **Israel** in **Rephidim**.
AV - **9,** 1-1,2-1,3-1,4-1,5-1,6-1,7-1,8-1,9-1
ESV - **9,** 1-1,2-1,3-1,4-1,5-1,6-1,7-1,8-1,9-1
HCSB - 8, 1-1,2-1,3-1,4-1,5-1,6-1,7-**2**,8-1
NASV - 9, 1-1,2-1,3-1,4-1,5-1,6-**2**,7-1,8-1,9-1
NCV - **9,** 1-1,2-1,3-1,4-1,5-1,6-1,7-1,8-1,9-1
NIV - 9, 1-1,2-1,3-1,4-1,5-**2**,6-1,7-1,8-1,9-1
NKJV - **9,** 1-1,2-1,3-1,4-1,5-1,6-1,7-1,8-1,9-1
NLT - 15, 1-1,2-1,3-**2**,4-1,5-1,6-1,7-1,8-1,9-1,10-1,11-**2**,12-1,13-1,14-**2**,15-1

NRSV - **9,** 1-1,2-1,3-1,4-1,5-1,6-1,7-1,8-1,9-1
Conclusion: Four modern versions are more complex than the King James Bible. The NLT is the most difficult to read.

106. Exodus 17:10* So **Joshua** did as **Moses** had said to him, and fought with **Amalek**: and **Moses**, **Aaron**, and Hur went up to the top of the hill.
AV - **26,** 1-1,2-1,3-1,4-1,5-1,6-1,7-1,8-1,9-1,10-1,11-1,12-1,13-1,14-1,15-1,16-1,17-1,18-1,19-1,20-1,21-1,22-1,23-1,24-1,25-1,26-1
ESV - **24,** 1-1,2-1,3-1,4-1,5-1,6-1,7-1,8-1,9-1,10-1,11-1,12-1,13-1,14-1,15-1,16-1,17-1,18-1,19-1,20-1,21-1,22-1,23-1,24-1
HCSB - **24,** 1-1,2-1,3-1,4-1,5-1,6-1,7-1,8-1,9-1,10-**2**,11-1,12-1,13-1,14-1,15-1,16-1,17-1,18-1,19-1,20-1,21-1,22-1,23-1,24-1
NASV - **23,** 1-1,2-1,3-1,4-1,5-1,6-1,7-1,8-1,9-**2**,10-1,11-1,12-1,13-1,14-1,15-1,16-1,17-1,18-1,19-1,20-1,21-1,22-1,23-1
NCV - **21,** 1-1,2-**2**,3-1,4-1,5-1,6-1,7-1,8-1,9-1,10-1,11-1,12-1,13-1,14-1,15-1,16-1,17-1,18-1,19-1,20-1,21-1
NIV - **21,** 1-1,2-1,3-1,4-1,5-1,6-1,7-1,8-1,9-**2**,10-1,11-1,12-1,13-1,14-1,15-1,16-1,17-1,18-1,19-1,20-1,21-1
NKJV - **25,** 1-1,2-1,3-1,4-1,5-1,6-1,7-1,8-1,9-1,10-1,11-1,12-1,13-1,14-1,15-1,16-1,17-1,18-1,19-1,20-1,21-1,22-1,23-1,24-1,25-1
NLT - **26,** 1-1,2-1,3-1,4-1,5-1,6-1,7-**3**,8-1,9-1,10-1,11-**2**,12-1,13-1,14-**2**,15-1,16-1,17-1,18-1,19-1,20-1,21-1,22-1,23-1,24-1,25-**2**,26-1
NRSV - **24,** 1-1,2-1,3-1,4-1,5-1,6-1,7-1,8-1,9-1,10-1,11-1,12-1,13-1,14-1,15-1,16-1,17-1,18-1,19-1,20-1,21-1,22-1,23-1,24-1
Conclusion: Five modern versions are more complex than the King James Bible. The NLT is the most difficult to read.

107. Exodus 20:13 Thou shalt not kill.
AV - **4,** 1-1,2-1,3-1,4-1
ESV - **4,** 1-1,2-1,3-1,4-**2**
HCSB - **3,** 1-1,2-1,3-**2**
NASV - **4,** 1-1,2-1,3-1,4-**2**
NCV - **5,** 1-1,2-1,3-1,4-**2**,5-**2**
NIV - **4,** 1-1,2-1,3-1,4-**2**
NKJV - **4,** 1-1,2-1,3-1,4-**2**
NLT - **4,** 1-1,2-1,3-1,4-**2**
NRSV - **4,** 1-1,2-1,3-1,4-**2**
Conclusion: All eight modern versions are more complex than the King James Bible. The NCV is the most difficult to read.

108. Exodus 20:15 Thou shalt not steal.
AV - **4,** 1-1,2-1,3-1,4-1
ESV - **4,** 1-1,2-1,3-1,4-1
HCSB - **3,** 1-1,2-1,3-1

NASV - **4,** 1-1,2-1,3-1,4-1
NCV - **4,** 1-1,2-1,3-1,4-1
NIV - **4,** 1-1,2-1,3-1,4-1
NKJV - **4,** 1-1,2-1,3-1,4-1
NLT - **4,** 1-1,2-1,3-1,4-1
NRSV - **4,** 1-1,2-1,3-1,4-1
Conclusion: All versions read the same.

109. Exodus 21:24 Eye for eye, tooth for tooth, hand for hand, foot for foot,
AV - **12,** 1-1,2-1,3-1,4-1,5-1,6-1,7-1,8-1,9-1,10-1,11-1,12-1
ESV - **12,** 1-1,2-1,3-1,4-1,5-1,6-1,7-1,8-1,9-1,10-1,11-1,12-1
HCSB -**12,** 1-1,2-1,3-1,4-1,5-1,6-1,7-1,8-1,9-1,10-1,11-1,12-1
NASV - **12,** 1-1,2-1,3-1,4-1,5-1,6-1,7-1,8-1,9-1,10-1,11-1,12-1
NCV - **12,** 1-1,2-1,3-1,4-1,5-1,6-1,7-1,8-1,9-1,10-1,11-1,12-1
NIV - **12,** 1-1,2-1,3-1,4-1,5-1,6-1,7-1,8-1,9-1,10-1,11-1,12-1
NKJV - **12,** 1-1,2-1,3-1,4-1,5-1,6-1,7-1,8-1,9-1,10-1,11-1,12-1
NLT - **20,** 1-1,2-1,3-1,4-1,5-1,6-1,7-1,8-1,9-1,10-1,11-1,12-1,13-1,14-1,15-1,16-1,17-1,18-1,19-1,20-1
NRSV - **12,** 1-1,2-1,3-1,4-1,5-1,6-1,7-1,8-1,9-1,10-1,11-1,12-1
Conclusion: All versions read the same. The NLT found a longer way to say the same thing.

110. Exodus 31:2* See, I have called by name **Bezaleel** the son of **Uri**, the son of Hur, of the tribe of **Judah**:
AV - **20,** 1-1,2-1,3-1,4-1,5-1,6-1,7-1,8-1,9-1,10-1,11-1,12-1,13-1,14-1,15-1,16-1,17-1,18-1,19-1,20-1
ESV - **19,** 1-1,2-1,3-1,4-1,5-1,6-1,7-1,8-1,9-1,10-1,11-1,12-1,13-1,14-1,15-1,16-1,17-1,18-1,19-1
HCSB - **18,** 1-1,2-1,3-1,4-**3**,5-1,6-1,7-1,8-1,9-1,10-1,11-1,12-1,13-1,14-1,15-1,16-1,17-1,18-1
NASV - **20,** 1-1,2-1,3-1,4-1,5-1,6-1,7-1,8-1,9-1,10-1,11-1,12-1,13-1,14-1,15-1,16-1,17-1,18-1,19-1,20-1
NCV - **19,** 1-1,2-1,3-1,4-**2**,5-1,6-1,7-1,8-1,9-1,10-1,11-1,12-1,13-1,14-1,15-1,16-1,17-1,18-1,19-1
NIV - **17,** 1-1,2-1,3-1,4-**2**,5-1,6-1,7-1,8-1,9-1,10-1,11-1,12-1,13-1,14-1,15-1,16-1,17-1
NKJV - **20,** 1-1,2-1,3-1,4-1,5-1,6-1,7-1,8-1,9-1,10-1,11-1,12-1,13-1,14-1,15-1,16-1,17-1,18-1,19-1,20-1
NLT - **17,** 1-1,2-1,3-1,4-**5**,5-**2**,6-1,7-1,8-1,9-1,10-**2**,11-1,12-1,13-1,14-1,15-1,16-1,17-1
NRSV - **18,** 1-1,2-1,3-1,4-1,5-1,6-1,7-1,8-1,9-1,10-1,11-1,12-1,13-1,14-1,15-1,16-1,17-1,18-1
Conclusion: Four modern versions are more complex than the King James Bible.

111. Exodus 33:20 And he said, Thou canst not see my face: for there shall no man see me, and live.
AV - **18,** 1-1,2-1,3-1,4-1,5-1,6-1,7-1,8-1,9-1,10-1,11-1,12-1,13-1,14-1,15-1,16-1,17-1,18-1
ESV - **16,** 1-1,2-1,3-1,4-1,5-**2**,6-1,7-1,8-1,9-1,10-1,11-1,12-1,13-1,14-1,15-1,16-1
HCSB - **16,** 1-1,2-1,3-**2**,4-1,5-**2**,6-1,7-1,8-1,9-1,10-1,11-1,12-1,13-1,14-1,15-1,16-1
NASV - **16,** 1-1,2-1,3-1,4-1,5-**2**,6-1,7-1,8-1,9-1,10-1,11-1,12-1,13-1,14-1,15-1,16-1
NCV - **14,** 1-1,2-1,3-**2**,4-1,5-1,6-1,7-**2**,8-1,9-1,10-1,11-1,12-1,13-1,14-1
NIV - **16,** 1-1,2-1,3-1,4-1,5-**2**,6-1,7-1,8-1,9-1,10-1,11-1,12-1,13-1,14-1,15-1,16-1

NKJV - 16, 1-1,2-1,3-1,4-1,5-**2**,6-1,7-1,8-1,9-1,10-1,11-1,12-1,13-1,14-1,15-1,16-1
NLT - 17, 1-1,2-1,3-1,4-1,5-1,6-**3**,7-1,8-1,9-1,10-1,11-1,12-1,13-1,14-1,15-1,16-1,17-1
NRSV - 16, 1-1,2-1,3-1,4-1,5-**2**,6-1,7-1,8-1,9-1,10-1,11-1,12-1,13-1,14-1,15-1,16-1
Conclusion: All eight modern versions are more complex than the King James Bible.

112. Exodus 40:14 And thou shalt bring his sons, and clothe them with coats:
AV - 11, 1-1,2-1,3-1,4-1,5-1,6-1,7-1,8-1,9-1,10-1,11-1
ESV - 11, 1-1,2-1,3-1,4-1,5-1,6-**2**,7-1,8-1,9-1,10-1,11-1
HCSB - 10, 1-1,2-1,3-1,4-1,5-**2**,6-1,7-1,8-1,9-1,10-**2**
NASV - 10, 1-1,2-1,3-1,4-1,5-1,6-1,7-1,8-**2**,9-1,10-1
NCV - 10, 1-1,2-1,3-1,4-1,5-1,6-1,7-**2**,8-1,9-1,10-1
NIV - 8, 1-1,2-1,3-1,4-1,5-1,6-1,7-1,8-**2**
NKJV - 11, 1-1,2-1,3-1,4-1,5-1,6-1,7-1,8-1,9-1,10-1,11-**2**
NLT - 10, 1-1,2-**2**,3-1,4-1,5-1,6-1,7-1,8-1,9-1,10-**2**
NRSV - 11, 1-1,2-1,3-1,4-1,5-1,6-1,7-1,8-1,9-**2**,10-1,11-1
Conclusion: All eight modern versions are more complex than the King James Bible. The NCT says "Aaron's" where most say "his" but this was not counted as multi-syllable.

113. Leviticus 14:38# Then the priest shall go out of the house to the door of the house, and shut up the house **seven** days:
AV - 22, 1-1,2-1,3-1,4-1,5-1,6-1,7-1,8-1,9-1,10-1,11-1,12-1,13-1,14-1,15-1,16-1,17-1,18-1,19-1,20-1,21-1,22-1
ESV - 22, 1-1,2-1,3-1,4-1,5-1,6-1,7-1,8-1,9-1,10-1,11-1,12-1,13-1,14-1,15-1,16-1,17-1,18-1,19-1,20-1,21-1,22-1
HCSB - 18, 1-1,2-1,3-1,4-1,5-1,6-**2**,7-1,8-1,9-1,10-1,11-**2**,12-1,13-**3**,14-1,15-1,16-1,17-1,18-1
NASV - 19, 1-1,2-1,3-1,4-1,5-1,6-1,7-1,8-1,9-1,10-1,11-1,12-**2**,13-1,14-**3**,15-1,16-1,17-1,18-1,19-1
NCV - **12,** 1-1,2-1,3-1,4-1,5-1,6-1,7-1,8-1,9-1,10-1,11-1,12-1
NIV - 17, 1-1,2-1,3-1,4-1,5-1,6-1,7-**2**,8-1,9-1,10-1,11-1,12-1,13-1,14-1,15-1,16-1,17-1
NKJV - **22,** 1-1,2-1,3-1,4-1,5-1,6-1,7-1,8-1,9-1,10-1,11-1,12-1,13-1,14-1,15-1,16-1,17-1,18-1,19-1,20-1,21-1,22-1
NLT - 16, 1-1,2-1,3-1,4-1,5-**2**,6-1,7-1,8-1,9-1,10-1,11-1,12-1,13-**3**,14-1,15-1,16-1
NRSV - 18, 1-1,2-1,3-1,4-1,5-**2**,6-1,7-1,8-1,9-1,10-1,11-1,12-1,13-1,14-1,15-1,16-1,17-1,18-1
Conclusion: Five modern versions are more complex than the King James Bible.

114. Leviticus 22:33* That brought you out of the land of **Egypt**, to be your God: I am the LORD.
AV - **17,** 1-1,2-1,3-1,4-1,5-1,6-1,7-1,8-1,9-1,10-1,11-1,12-1,13-1,14-1,15-1,16-1,17-1
ESV - 17, 1-1,2-1,3-1,4-1,5-1,6-1,7-1,8-1,9-1,10-1,11-1,12-1,13-1,14-1,15-1,16-1,17-1
HCSB - **19,** 1-1,2-1,3-1,4-1,5-1,6-1,7-1,8-1,9-1,10-1,11-1,12-1,13-1,14-1,15-1,16-1,17-1,18-1,19-1
NASV - **17,** 1-1,2-1,3-1,4-1,5-1,6-1,7-1,8-1,9-1,10-1,11-1,12-1,13-1,14-1,15-1,16-1,17-1
NCV - **14,** 1-1,2-1,3-1,4-1,5-1,6-1,7-1,8-1,9-1,10-1,11-1,12-1,13-1,14-1
NIV - **15,** 1-1,2-1,3-1,4-1,5-1,6-1,7-1,8-1,9-1,10-1,11-1,12-1,13-1,14-1,15-1
NKJV - **17,** 1-1,2-1,3-1,4-1,5-1,6-1,7-1,8-1,9-1,10-1,11-1,12-1,13-1,14-1,15-1,16-1,17-1
NLT - 21, 1-1,2-1,3-1,4-1,5-**2**,6-1,7-1,8-1,9-1,10-1,11-1,12-1,13-1,14-1,15-1,16-1,17-1,18-1,19-1,20-1,21-1

NRSV - **18,** 1-1,2-1,3-1,4-1,5-1,6-1,7-1,8-1,9-1,10-1,11-1,12-1,13-1,14-1,15-1,16-1,17-1,18-1
Conclusion: Only the NLT makes the verse more complex.

115. Leviticus 23:42*# Ye shall dwell in booths **seven** days; all that are **Israelites** born shall dwell in booths:
AV - **16,** 1-1,2-1,3-1,4-1,5-1,6-1,7-1,8-1,9-1,10-1,11-1,12-1,13-1,14-1,15-1,16-1
ESV - 15, 1-1,2-1,3-1,4-1,5-1,6-1,7-1,8-1,9-1,10-**2,**11-1,12-1,13-1,14-1,15-1
HCSB - 19, 1-1,2-1,3-1,4-1,5-1,6-1,7-1,8-1,9-1,10-1,11-1,12-**2,**13-1,14-1,15-1,16-1,17-1,18-1,19-1
NASV - 18, 1-1,2-1,3-1,4-1,5-1,6-1,7-1,8-1,9-1,10-1,11-**2,**12-1,13-1,14-1,15-1,16-1,17-1,18-1
NCV - 16, 1-1,2-1,3-**2,**4-1,5-1,6-1,7-1,8-1,9-**2,**10-1,11-1,12-1,13-1,14-1,15-1,16-**2**
NIV - 15, 1-1,2-1,3-1,4-1,5-1,6-1,7-1,8-**2,**9-1,10-1,11-1,12-1,13-1,14-1,15-1
NKJV - 17, 1-1,2-1,3-1,4-1,5-1,6-1,7-1,8-1,9-1,10-1,11-1,12-**2,**13-1,14-1,15-1,16-1,17-1
NLT - 18, 1-1,2-1,3-1,4-1,5-1,6-1,7-**2,**8-1,9-**2,**10-**2,**11-1,12-**2,**13-1,14-1,15-1,16-1,17-1,18-**2**
NRSV - 18, 1-1,2-1,3-1,4-1,5-1,6-1,7-1,8-1,9-1,10-1,11-1,12-**3,**13-1,14-1,15-1,16-1,17-1,18-1
Conclusion: All eight modern versions are more complex than the King James Bible. Once again the NCV and the NLT competed for "most complex" and once again the NLT won.

116. Leviticus 24:12 And they put him in ward, that the mind of the LORD might be showed them.
AV - **16,** 1-1,2-1,3-1,4-1,5-1,6-1,7-1,8-1,9-1,10-1,11-1,12-1,13-1,14-1,15-1,16-1
ESV - 17, 1-1,2-1,3-1,4-1,5-1,6-**3,**7-1,8-1,9-1,10-1,11-1,12-1,13-1,14-1,15-1,16-1,17-1
HCSB - 15, 1-1,2-1,3-1,4-1,5-**3,**6-**2,**7-1,8-1,9-**3,**10-1,11-1,12-1,13-1,14-1,15-1
NASV - 18, 1-1,2-1,3-1,4-1,5-**3,**6-1,7-1,8-1,9-**2,**10-1,11-1,12-1,13-1,14-1,15-1,16-1,17-1,18-1
NCV - 20, 1-1,2-**2,**3-1,4-1,5-1,6-1,7-**3,**8-1,9-1,10-**2,**11-1,12-1,13-1,14-**2,**15-1,16-1,17-1,18-1,19-1,20-1
NIV - 17, 1-1,2-1,3-1,4-1,5-**3,**6-**2,**7-1,8-1,9-1,10-1,11-1,12-1,13-1,14-1,15-1,16-1,17-1
NKJV - 17, 1-1,2-1,3-1,4-1,5-1,6-**3,**7-1,8-1,9-1,10-1,11-1,12-1,13-1,14-1,15-1,16-1,17-1
NLT - 18, 1-1,2-1,3-1,4-1,5-1,6-**3,**7-**2,**8-1,9-1,10-1,11-1,12-1,13-**2,**14-1,15-**2,**16-1,17-1,18-1
NRSV - 18, 1-1,2-1,3-1,4-1,5-1,6-**3,**7-**2,**8-1,9-**3,**10-1,11-1,12-1,13-1,14-1,15-1,16-1,17-1,18-1
Conclusion: All eight modern versions are more complex than the King James Bible.

117. Leviticus 25:38* I am the LORD your God, which brought you forth out of the land of **Egypt,** to give you the land of **Canaan,** and to be your God.
AV - **28,** 1-1,2-1,3-1,4-1,5-1,6-1,7-1,8-1,9-1,10-1,11-1,12-1,13-1,14-1,15-1,16-1,17-1,18-1,19-1,20-1,21-1,22-1,23-1,24-1,25-1,26-1,27-1,28-1
ESV - **27,** 1-1,2-1,3-1,4-1,5-1,6-1,7-1,8-1,9-1,10-1,11-1,12-1,13-1,14-1,15-1,16-1,17-1,18-1,19-1,20-1,21-1,22-1,23-1,24-1,25-1,26-1,27-1
HCSB - **27,** 1-1,2-1,3-1,4-1,5-1,6-1,7-1,8-1,9-1,10-1,11-1,12-1,13-1,14-1,15-1,16-1,17-1,18-1,19-1,20-1,21-1,22-1,23-1,24-1,25-1,26-1,27-1
NASV - **27,** 1-1,2-1,3-1,4-1,5-1,6-1,7-1,8-1,9-1,10-1,11-1,12-1,13-1,14-1,15-1,16-1,17-1,18-1,19-1,20-1,21-1,22-1,23-1,24-1,25-1,26-1,27-1
NCV - 28, 1-1,2-1,3-1,4-1,5-1,6-1,7-1,8-1,9-1,10-1,11-1,12-1,13-1,14-1,15-1,16-1,17-1,18-1,19-1,20-1,21-1,22-1,23-1,24-1,25-1,26-**2,**27-1,28-1
NIV - **24,** 1-1,2-1,3-1,4-1,5-1,6-1,7-1,8-1,9-1,10-1,11-1,12-1,13-1,14-1,15-1,16-1,17-1,18-1,19-1,20-1,21-1,22-1,23-1,24-1

NKJV - **27,** 1-1,2-1,3-1,4-1,5-1,6-1,7-1,8-1,9-1,10-1,11-1,12-1,13-1,14-1,15-1,16-1,17-1,18-1,19-1,20-1,21-1,22-1,23-1,24-1,25-1,26-1,27-1

NLT - **27,** 1-1,2-1,3-1,4-1,5-1,6-1,7-1,8-1,9-1,10-1,11-1,12-1,13-1,14-1,15-1,16-1,17-1,18-1,19-1,20-1,21-1,22-1,23-1,24-1,25-1,26-1,27-1

NRSV - **26,** 1-1,2-1,3-1,4-1,5-1,6-1,7-1,8-1,9-1,10-1,11-1,12-1,13-1,14-1,15-1,16-1,17-1,18-1,19-1,20-1,21-1,22-1,23-1,24-1,25-1,26-1

Conclusion: Only the NCV made the verse more complex.

118. Numbers 1:5* And these are the names of the men that shall stand with you: of the tribe of **Reuben**; **Elizur** the son of **Shedeur**.

AV - **23,** 1-1,2-1,3-1,4-1,5-1,6-1,7-1,8-1,9-1,10-1,11-1,12-1,13-1,14-1,15-1,16-1,17-1,18-1,19-1,20-1,21-1,22-1,23-1

ESV - **19,** 1-1,2-1,3-1,4-1,5-1,6-1,7-1,8-1,9-1,10-1,11-**2**,12-1,13-1,14-1,15-1,16-1,17-1,18-1,19-1

HCSB - **18,** 1-1,2-1,3-1,4-1,5-1,6-1,7-1,8-1,9-1,10-1,11-**2**,12-1,13-1,14-1,15-1,16-1,17-1,18-1

NASV - **20,** 1-1,2-1,3-1,4-1,5-1,6-1,7-1,8-1,9-1,10-1,11-1,12-1,13-1,14-1,15-1,16-1,17-1,18-1,19-1,20-1

NCV - **20,** 1-1,2-1,3-1,4-1,5-1,6-1,7-1,8-1,9-1,10-1,11-1,12-1,13-1,14-1,15-1,16-1,17-1,18-1,19-1,20-1

NIV - **18,** 1-1,2-1,3-1,4-1,5-1,6-1,7-1,8-1,9-1,10-1,11-**2**,12-1,13-1,14-1,15-1,16-1,17-1,18-1

NKJV - **19,** 1-1,2-1,3-1,4-1,5-1,6-1,7-1,8-1,9-1,10-1,11-1,12-1,13-1,14-1,15-1,16-1,17-1,18-1,19-1

NLT - **21,** 1-1,2-1,3-1,4-1,5-1,6-1,7-1,8-1,9-1,10-**2**,11-1,12-1,13-**2**,14-1,15-1,16-1,17-**2**,18-1,19-1,20-1,21-1

NRSV - **17,** 1-1,2-1,3-1,4-1,5-1,6-1,7-1,8-1,9-1,10-**2**,11-1,12-1,13-1,14-1,15-1,16-1,17-1

Conclusion: Five modern versions are more complex than the King James Bible. The NLT is the most difficult to read.

119. Numbers 1:6* Of **Simeon**; **Shelumiel** the son of **Zurishaddai**.

AV - **7,** 1-1,2-1,3-1,4-1,5-1,6-1,7-1

ESV - **7,** 1-1,2-1,3-1,4-1,5-1,6-1,7-1

HCSB - **6,** 1-1,2-1,3-1,4-1,5-1,6-1

NASV - **7,** 1-1,2-1,3-1,4-1,5-1,6-1,7-1

NCV - **9,** 1-1,2-1,3-1,4-1,5-1,6-1,7-1,8-1,9-1

NIV - **6,** 1-1,2-1,3-1,4-1,5-1,6-1

NKJV - **7,** 1-1,2-1,3-1,4-1,5-1,6-1,7-1

NLT - **5,** 1-1,2-1,3-1,4-1,5-1

NRSV - **6,** 1-1,2-1,3-1,4-1,5-1,6-1

Conclusion: All versions read the same.

120. Numbers 1:7* Of **Judah**; **Nahshon** the son of **Amminadab**.

AV - **7,** 1-1,2-1,3-1,4-1,5-1,6-1,7-1

ESV - **7,** 1-1,2-1,3-1,4-1,5-1,6-1,7-1

HCSB - **6,** 1-1,2-1,3-1,4-1,5-1,6-1

NASV - **7,** 1-1,2-1,3-1,4-1,5-1,6-1,7-1

NCV - **9,** 1-1,2-1,3-1,4-1,5-1,6-1,7-1,8-1,9-1

NIV - **6,** 1-1,2-1,3-1,4-1,5-1,6-1
NKJV - **7,** 1-1,2-1,3-1,4-1,5-1,6-1,7-1
NLT - **5,** 1-1,2-1,3-1,4-1,5-1
NRSV - **6,** 1-1,2-1,3-1,4-1,5-1,6-1
Conclusion: All versions read the same.

121. Numbers 1:8* Of **Issachar**; **Nethaneel** the son of **Zuar**.
AV - **7,** 1-1,2-1,3-1,4-1,5-1,6-1,7-1
ESV - **7,** 1-1,2-1,3-1,4-1,5-1,6-1,7-1
HCSB - **6,** 1-1,2-1,3-1,4-1,5-1,6-1
NASV - **7,** 1-1,2-1,3-1,4-1,5-1,6-1,7-1
NCV - **9,** 1-1,2-1,3-1,4-1,5-1,6-1,7-1,8-1,9-1
NIV - **6,** 1-1,2-1,3-1,4-1,5-1,6-1
NKJV - **7,** 1-1,2-1,3-1,4-1,5-1,6-1,7-1
NLT - **5,** 1-1,2-1,3-1,4-1,5-1
NRSV - **6,** 1-1,2-1,3-1,4-1,5-1,6-1
Conclusion: All versions read the same.

122. Numbers 1:9* Of **Zebulun**; **Eliab** the son of **Helon**.
AV - **7,** 1-1,2-1,3-1,4-1,5-1,6-1,7-1
ESV - **7,** 1-1,2-1,3-1,4-1,5-1,6-1,7-1
HCSB - **6,** 1-1,2-1,3-1,4-1,5-1,6-1
NASV - **7,** 1-1,2-1,3-1,4-1,5-1,6-1,7-1
NCV - **9,** 1-1,2-1,3-1,4-1,5-1,6-1,7-1,8-1,9-1
NIV - **6,** 1-1,2-1,3-1,4-1,5-1,6-1
NKJV - **7,** 1-1,2-1,3-1,4-1,5-1,6-1,7-1
NLT - **5,** 1-1,2-1,3-1,4-1,5-1
NRSV - **6,** 1-1,2-1,3-1,4-1,5-1,6-1
Conclusion: All versions read the same.

123. Numbers 1:11* Of **Benjamin**; **Abidan** the son of **Gideoni**.
AV - **7,** 1-1,2-1,3-1,4-1,5-1,6-1,7-1
ESV - **7,** 1-1,2-1,3-1,4-1,5-1,6-1,7-1
HCSB - **6,** 1-1,2-1,3-1,4-1,5-1,6-1
NASV - **7,** 1-1,2-1,3-1,4-1,5-1,6-1,7-1
NCV - **9,** 1-1,2-1,3-1,4-1,5-1,6-1,7-1,8-1,9-1
NIV - **6,** 1-1,2-1,3-1,4-1,5-1,6-1
NKJV - **7,** 1-1,2-1,3-1,4-1,5-1,6-1,7-1
NLT - **5,** 1-1,2-1,3-1,4-1,5-1
NRSV - **6,** 1-1,2-1,3-1,4-1,5-1,6-1
Conclusion: All versions read the same.

124. Numbers 1:12* Of Dan; **Ahiezer** the son of **Ammishaddai**.
AV - **7,** 1-1,2-1,3-1,4-1,5-1,6-1,7-1

ESV - **7,** 1-1,2-1,3-1,4-1,5-1,6-1,7-1
HCSB - **6,** 1-1,2-1,3-1,4-1,5-1,6-1
NASV - **7,** 1-1,2-1,3-1,4-1,5-1,6-1,7-1
NCV - **9,** 1-1,2-1,3-1,4-1,5-1,6-1,7-1,8-1,9-1
NIV - **6,** 1-1,2-1,3-1,4-1,5-1,6-1
NKJV - **7,** 1-1,2-1,3-1,4-1,5-1,6-1,7-1
NLT - **5,** 1-1,2-1,3-1,4-1,5-1
NRSV - **6,** 1-1,2-1,3-1,4-1,5-1,6-1
Conclusion: All versions read the same.

125. Numbers 1:13* Of **Asher**; **Pagiel** the son of **Ocran**.
AV - **7,** 1-1,2-1,3-1,4-1,5-1,6-1,7-1
ESV - **7,** 1-1,2-1,3-1,4-1,5-1,6-1,7-1
HCSB - **6,** 1-1,2-1,3-1,4-1,5-1,6-1
NASV - **7,** 1-1,2-1,3-1,4-1,5-1,6-1,7-1
NCV - **9,** 1-1,2-1,3-1,4-1,5-1,6-1,7-1,8-1,9-1
NIV - **6,** 1-1,2-1,3-1,4-1,5-1,6-1
NKJV - **7,** 1-1,2-1,3-1,4-1,5-1,6-1,7-1
NLT - **5,** 1-1,2-1,3-1,4-1,5-1
NRSV - **6,** 1-1,2-1,3-1,4-1,5-1,6-1
Conclusion: All versions read the same.

126. Numbers 1:14* Of Gad; **Eliasaph** the son of **Deuel**.
AV - **7,** 1-1,2-1,3-1,4-1,5-1,6-1,7-1
ESV - **7,** 1-1,2-1,3-1,4-1,5-1,6-1,7-1
HCSB - **6,** 1-1,2-1,3-1,4-1,5-1,6-1
NASV - **7,** 1-1,2-1,3-1,4-1,5-1,6-1,7-1
NCV - **9,** 1-1,2-1,3-1,4-1,5-1,6-1,7-1,8-1,9-1
NIV - **6,** 1-1,2-1,3-1,4-1,5-1,6-1
NKJV - **7,** 1-1,2-1,3-1,4-1,5-1,6-1,7-1
NLT - **5,** 1-1,2-1,3-1,4-1,5-1
NRSV - **6,** 1-1,2-1,3-1,4-1,5-1,6-1
Conclusion: All versions read the same.

127. Numbers 1:15* Of **Naphtali**; **Ahira** the son of **Enan**.
AV - **7,** 1-1,2-1,3-1,4-1,5-1,6-1,7-1
ESV - **7,** 1-1,2-1,3-1,4-1,5-1,6-1,7-1
HCSB - **6,** 1-1,2-1,3-1,4-1,5-1,6-1
NASV - **7,** 1-1,2-1,3-1,4-1,5-1,6-1,7-1
NCV - **9,** 1-1,2-1,3-1,4-1,5-1,6-1,7-1,8-1,9-1
NIV - **6,** 1-1,2-1,3-1,4-1,5-1,6-1
NKJV - **7,** 1-1,2-1,3-1,4-1,5-1,6-1,7-1
NLT - **5,** 1-1,2-1,3-1,4-1,5-1
NRSV - **6,** 1-1,2-1,3-1,4-1,5-1,6-1

50

Conclusion: All versions read the same.

128. Numbers 3:17* And these were the sons of **Levi** by their names; **Gershon**, and **Kohath**, and **Merari**.
AV - **15,** 1-1,2-1,3-1,4-1,5-1,6-1,7-1,8-1,9-1,10-1,11-1,12-1,13-1,14-1,15-1
ESV - **15,** 1-1,2-1,3-1,4-1,5-1,6-1,7-1,8-1,9-1,10-1,11-1,12-1,13-1,14-1,15-1
HCSB - **10,** 1-1,2-1,3-1,4-1,5-1,6-1,7-1,8-1,9-1,10-1
NASV - **15,** 1-1,2-1,3-1,4-1,5-1,6-1,7-1,8-1,9-1,10-1,11-1,12-1,13-1,14-1,15-1
NCV - **11,** 1-1,2-1,3-1,4-1,5-1,6-1,7-1,8-1,9-1,10-1,11-1
NIV - **13,** 1-1,2-1,3-1,4-1,5-1,6-1,7-1,8-1,9-1,10-1,11-1,12-1,13-1
NKJV - **13,** 1-1,2-1,3-1,4-1,5-1,6-1,7-1,8-1,9-1,10-1,11-1,12-1,13-1
NLT - **11,** 1-1,2-1,3-1,4-1,5-1,6-1,7-1,8-1,9-1,10-1,11-1
NRSV - **14,** 1-1,2-**3,**3-1,4-1,5-1,6-1,7-1,8-1,9-1,10-1,11-1,12-1,13-1,14-1
Conclusion: Only the NRSV made the verse more complex.

129. Numbers 6:24 The LORD bless thee, and keep thee:
AV - **7,** 1-1,2-1,3-1,4-1,5-1,6-1,7-1
ESV - **7,** 1-1,2-1,3-1,4-1,5-1,6-1,7-1
HCSB - **7,** 1-1,2-1,3-1,4-1,5-1,6-**2,**7-1
NASV - **7,** 1-1,2-1,3-1,4-1,5-1,6-1,7-1
NCV - **8,** 1-1,2-1,3-1,4-1,5-1,6-1,7-1,8-1
NIV - **7,** 1-1,2-1,3-1,4-1,5-1,6-1,7-1
NKJV - **7,** 1-1,2-1,3-1,4-1,5-1,6-1,7-1
NLT - **8,** 1-1,2-1,3-1,4-1,5-1,6-1,7-**2,**8-1
NRSV - **7,** 1-1,2-1,3-1,4-1,5-1,6-1,7-1
Conclusion: Only the HCSB and the NLT made the verse more complex.

130. Numbers 13:4* And these were their names: of the tribe of **Reuben**, **Shammua** the son of **Zaccur**.
AV - **15,** 1-1,2-1,3-1,4-1,5-1,6-1,7-1,8-1,9-1,10-1,11-1,12-1,13-1,14-1,15-1
ESV - **15,** 1-1,2-1,3-1,4-1,5-1,6-1,7-1,8-1,9-1,10-1,11-1,12-1,13-1,14-1,15-1
HCSB - **13,** 1-1,2-1,3-1,4-1,5-1,6-1,7-1,8-1,9-1,10-1,11-1,12-1,13-1
NASV - **15,** 1-1,2-1,3-1,4-1,5-1,6-1,7-1,8-1,9-1,10-1,11-1,12-1,13-1,14-1,15-1
NCV - **13,** 1-1,2-1,3-1,4-1,5-1,6-1,7-1,8-1,9-1,10-1,11-1,12-1,13-1
NIV - **13,** 1-1,2-1,3-1,4-1,5-1,6-1,7-1,8-1,9-1,10-1,11-1,12-1,13-1
NKJV - **13,** 1-1,2-1,3-1,4-1,5-1,6-1,7-1,8-1,9-1,10-1,11-1,12-1,13-1
NLT - **17,** 1-1,2-1,3-1,4-1,5-1,6-1,7-1,8-1,9-1,10-**2,**11-1,12-1,13-**2,**14-1,15-1,16-1,17-1
NRSV - **13,** 1-1,2-1,3-1,4-1,5-1,6-1,7-1,8-1,9-1,10-1,11-1,12-1,13-1
Conclusion: Only the NLT found a way to make this simple verse more complex.

131. Numbers 13:5* Of the tribe of **Simeon**, **Shaphat** the son of **Hori**.
AV - **10,** 1-1,2-1,3-1,4-1,5-1,6-1,7-1,8-1,9-1,10-1
ESV - **10,** 1-1,2-1,3-1,4-1,5-1,6-1,7-1,8-1,9-1,10-1
HCSB - **9,** 1-1,2-1,3-1,4-1,5-1,6-1,7-1,8-1,9-1

Samuel C. Gipp Ph.D.

NASV - **10,** 1-1,2-1,3-1,4-1,5-1,6-1,7-1,8-1,9-1,10-1
NCV - **9,** 1-1,2-1,3-1,4-1,5-1,6-1,7-1,8-1,9-1
NIV - **9,** 1-1,2-1,3-1,4-1,5-1,6-1,7-1,8-1,9-1
NKJV - **10,** 1-1,2-1,3-1,4-1,5-1,6-1,7-1,8-1,9-1,10-1
NLT - **5,** 1-1,2-1,3-1,4-1,5-1
NRSV - **9,** 1-1,2-1,3-1,4-1,5-1,6-1,7-1,8-1,9-1
Conclusion: All versions read the same.

132. Numbers 13:6* Of the tribe of **Judah, Caleb** the son of **Jephunneh.**
AV - **10,** 1-1,2-1,3-1,4-1,5-1,6-1,7-1,8-1,9-1,10-1
ESV - **10,** 1-1,2-1,3-1,4-1,5-1,6-1,7-1,8-1,9-1,10-1
HCSB - **9,** 1-1,2-1,3-1,4-1,5-1,6-1,7-1,8-1,9-1
NASV - **10,** 1-1,2-1,3-1,4-1,5-1,6-1,7-1,8-1,9-1,10-1
NCV - **9,** 1-1,2-1,3-1,4-1,5-1,6-1,7-1,8-1,9-1
NIV - **9,** 1-1,2-1,3-1,4-1,5-1,6-1,7-1,8-1,9-1
NKJV - **10,** 1-1,2-1,3-1,4-1,5-1,6-1,7-1,8-1,9-1,10-1
NLT - **5,** 1-1,2-1,3-1,4-1,5-1
NRSV - **9,** 1-1,2-1,3-1,4-1,5-1,6-1,7-1,8-1,9-1
Conclusion: All versions read the same.

133. Numbers 13:7* Of the tribe of **Issachar, Igal** the son of **Joseph.**
AV - **10,** 1-1,2-1,3-1,4-1,5-1,6-1,7-1,8-1,9-1,10-1
ESV - **10,** 1-1,2-1,3-1,4-1,5-1,6-1,7-1,8-1,9-1,10-1
HCSB - **9,** 1-1,2-1,3-1,4-1,5-1,6-1,7-1,8-1,9-1
NASV - **10,** 1-1,2-1,3-1,4-1,5-1,6-1,7-1,8-1,9-1,10-1
NCV - **9,** 1-1,2-1,3-1,4-1,5-1,6-1,7-1,8-1,9-1
NIV - **9,** 1-1,2-1,3-1,4-1,5-1,6-1,7-1,8-1,9-1
NKJV - **10,** 1-1,2-1,3-1,4-1,5-1,6-1,7-1,8-1,9-1,10-1
NLT - **5,** 1-1,2-1,3-1,4-1,5-1
NRSV - **9,** 1-1,2-1,3-1,4-1,5-1,6-1,7-1,8-1,9-1
Conclusion: All versions read the same.

134. Numbers 13:8* Of the tribe of **Ephraim, Oshea** the son of Nun.
AV - **10,** 1-1,2-1,3-1,4-1,5-1,6-1,7-1,8-1,9-1,10-1
ESV - **10,** 1-1,2-1,3-1,4-1,5-1,6-1,7-1,8-1,9-1,10-1
HCSB - **9,** 1-1,2-1,3-1,4-1,5-1,6-1,7-1,8-1,9-1
NASV - **10,** 1-1,2-1,3-1,4-1,5-1,6-1,7-1,8-1,9-1,10-1
NCV - **9,** 1-1,2-1,3-1,4-1,5-1,6-1,7-1,8-1,9-1
NIV - **9,** 1-1,2-1,3-1,4-1,5-1,6-1,7-1,8-1,9-1
NKJV - **10,** 1-1,2-1,3-1,4-1,5-1,6-1,7-1,8-1,9-1,10-1
NLT - **5,** 1-1,2-1,3-1,4-1,5-1
NRSV - **9,** 1-1,2-1,3-1,4-1,5-1,6-1,7-1,8-1,9-1
Conclusion: All versions read the same.

135. Numbers 13:9* Of the tribe of **Benjamin**, **Palti** the son of **Raphu**.
AV - **10,** 1-1,2-1,3-1,4-1,5-1,6-1,7-1,8-1,9-1,10-1
ESV - **10,** 1-1,2-1,3-1,4-1,5-1,6-1,7-1,8-1,9-1,10-1
HCSB - **9,** 1-1,2-1,3-1,4-1,5-1,6-1,7-1,8-1,9-1
NASV - **10,** 1-1,2-1,3-1,4-1,5-1,6-1,7-1,8-1,9-1,10-1
NCV - **9,** 1-1,2-1,3-1,4-1,5-1,6-1,7-1,8-1,9-1
NIV - **9,** 1-1,2-1,3-1,4-1,5-1,6-1,7-1,8-1,9-1
NKJV - **10,** 1-1,2-1,3-1,4-1,5-1,6-1,7-1,8-1,9-1,10-1
NLT - **5,** 1-1,2-1,3-1,4-1,5-1
NRSV - **9,** 1-1,2-1,3-1,4-1,5-1,6-1,7-1,8-1,9-1
Conclusion: All versions read the same.

136. Numbers 13:10* Of the tribe of **Zebulun**, **Gaddiel** the son of **Sodi**.
AV - **10,** 1-1,2-1,3-1,4-1,5-1,6-1,7-1,8-1,9-1,10-1
ESV - **10,** 1-1,2-1,3-1,4-1,5-1,6-1,7-1,8-1,9-1,10-1
HCSB - **9,** 1-1,2-1,3-1,4-1,5-1,6-1,7-1,8-1,9-1
NASV - **10,** 1-1,2-1,3-1,4-1,5-1,6-1,7-1,8-1,9-1,10-1
NCV - **9,** 1-1,2-1,3-1,4-1,5-1,6-1,7-1,8-1,9-1
NIV - **9,** 1-1,2-1,3-1,4-1,5-1,6-1,7-1,8-1,9-1
NKJV - **10,** 1-1,2-1,3-1,4-1,5-1,6-1,7-1,8-1,9-1,10-1
NLT - **5,** 1-1,2-1,3-1,4-1,5-1
NRSV - **9,** 1-1,2-1,3-1,4-1,5-1,6-1,7-1,8-1,9-1
Conclusion: All versions read the same.

137. Numbers 13:12* Of the tribe of Dan, **Ammiel** the son of **Gemalli**.
AV - **10,** 1-1,2-1,3-1,4-1,5-1,6-1,7-1,8-1,9-1,10-1
ESV - **10,** 1-1,2-1,3-1,4-1,5-1,6-1,7-1,8-1,9-1,10-1
HCSB - **9,** 1-1,2-1,3-1,4-1,5-1,6-1,7-1,8-1,9-1
NASV - **10,** 1-1,2-1,3-1,4-1,5-1,6-1,7-1,8-1,9-1,10-1
NCV - **9,** 1-1,2-1,3-1,4-1,5-1,6-1,7-1,8-1,9-1
NIV - **9,** 1-1,2-1,3-1,4-1,5-1,6-1,7-1,8-1,9-1
NKJV - **10,** 1-1,2-1,3-1,4-1,5-1,6-1,7-1,8-1,9-1,10-1
NLT - **5,** 1-1,2-1,3-1,4-1,5-1
NRSV - **9,** 1-1,2-1,3-1,4-1,5-1,6-1,7-1,8-1,9-1
Conclusion: All versions read the same.

138. Numbers 13:13* Of the tribe of **Asher**, **Sethur** the son of **Michael**.
AV - **10,** 1-1,2-1,3-1,4-1,5-1,6-1,7-1,8-1,9-1,10-1
ESV - **10,** 1-1,2-1,3-1,4-1,5-1,6-1,7-1,8-1,9-1,10-1
HCSB - **9,** 1-1,2-1,3-1,4-1,5-1,6-1,7-1,8-1,9-1
NASV - **10,** 1-1,2-1,3-1,4-1,5-1,6-1,7-1,8-1,9-1,10-1
NCV - **9,** 1-1,2-1,3-1,4-1,5-1,6-1,7-1,8-1,9-1
NIV - **9,** 1-1,2-1,3-1,4-1,5-1,6-1,7-1,8-1,9-1
NKJV - **10,** 1-1,2-1,3-1,4-1,5-1,6-1,7-1,8-1,9-1,10-1

NLT - **5,** 1-1,2-1,3-1,4-1,5-1
NRSV - **9,** 1-1,2-1,3-1,4-1,5-1,6-1,7-1,8-1,9-1
Conclusion: All versions read the same.

139. Numbers 13:14* Of the tribe of **Naphtali, Nahbi** the son of **Vophsi**.
AV - **10,** 1-1,2-1,3-1,4-1,5-1,6-1,7-1,8-1,9-1,10-1
ESV - **10,** 1-1,2-1,3-1,4-1,5-1,6-1,7-1,8-1,9-1,10-1
HCSB - **9,** 1-1,2-1,3-1,4-1,5-1,6-1,7-1,8-1,9-1
NASV - **10,** 1-1,2-1,3-1,4-1,5-1,6-1,7-1,8-1,9-1,10-1
NCV - **9,** 1-1,2-1,3-1,4-1,5-1,6-1,7-1,8-1,9-1
NIV - **9,** 1-1,2-1,3-1,4-1,5-1,6-1,7-1,8-1,9-1
NKJV - **10,** 1-1,2-1,3-1,4-1,5-1,6-1,7-1,8-1,9-1,10-1
NLT - **5,** 1-1,2-1,3-1,4-1,5-1
NRSV - **9,** 1-1,2-1,3-1,4-1,5-1,6-1,7-1,8-1,9-1
Conclusion: All versions read the same.

140. Numbers 13:15* Of the tribe of Gad, **Geuel** the son of **Machi**.
AV - **10,** 1-1,2-1,3-1,4-1,5-1,6-1,7-1,8-1,9-1,10-1
ESV - **10,** 1-1,2-1,3-1,4-1,5-1,6-1,7-1,8-1,9-1,10-1
HCSB - **9,** 1-1,2-1,3-1,4-1,5-1,6-1,7-1,8-1,9-1
NASV - **10,** 1-1,2-1,3-1,4-1,5-1,6-1,7-1,8-1,9-1,10-1
NCV - **9,** 1-1,2-1,3-1,4-1,5-1,6-1,7-1,8-1,9-1
NIV - **9,** 1-1,2-1,3-1,4-1,5-1,6-1,7-1,8-1,9-1
NKJV - **10,** 1-1,2-1,3-1,4-1,5-1,6-1,7-1,8-1,9-1,10-1
NLT - **5,** 1-1,2-1,3-1,4-1,5-1
NRSV - **9,** 1-1,2-1,3-1,4-1,5-1,6-1,7-1,8-1,9-1
Conclusion: All versions read the same.

141. Numbers 13:16* These are the names of the men which **Moses** sent to spy out the land. And **Moses** called **Oshea** the son of Nun **Jehoshua**.
AV - **24,** 1-1,2-1,3-1,4-1,5-1,6-1,7-1,8-1,9-1,10-1,11-1,12-1,13-1,14-1,15-1,16-1,17-1,18-1,19-1,20-1,21-1,22-1,23-1,24-1
ESV - **24,** 1-1,2-1,3-1,4-1,5-1,6-1,7-1,8-1,9-1,10-1,11-1,12-1,13-1,14-1,15-1,16-1,17-1,18-1,19-1,20-1,21-1,22-1,23-1,24-1
HCSB - **22,** 1-1,2-1,3-1,4-1,5-1,6-1,7-1,8-1,9-1,10-1,11-1,12-1,13-1,14-1,15-1,16-1,17-**2,**18-1,19-1,20-1,21-1,22-1
NASV - **24,** 1-1,2-1,3-1,4-1,5-1,6-1,7-1,8-1,9-1,10-1,11-1,12-1,13-1,14-1,15-1,16-1,17-1,18-1,19-1,20-1,21-1,22-1,23-1,24-1
NCV - **23,** 1-1,2-1,3-1,4-1,5-1,6-1,7-1,8-1,9-1,10-1,11-**2,**12-1,13-1,14-1,15-1,16-1,17-1,18-1,19-1,20-1,21-1,22-1,23-1
NIV - **23,** 1-1,2-1,3-1,4-1,5-1,6-1,7-1,8-1,9-1,10-1,11-**2,**12-1,13-1,14-1,15-1,16-1,17-1,18-1,19-1,20-1,21-1,22-1,23-1
NKJV - **24,** 1-1,2-1,3-1,4-1,5-1,6-1,7-1,8-1,9-1,10-1,11-1,12-1,13-1,14-1,15-1,16-1,17-1,18-1,19-1,20-1,21-1,22-1,23-1,24-1

NLT - 24, 1-1,2-1,3-1,4-1,5-1,6-1,7-1,8-1,9-1,10-1,11-1,12-**2**,13-1,14-1,15-1,16-1,17-1,18-1,19-1,20-1,21-1,22-1,23-1,24-1

NRSV - 27, 1-1,2-1,3-1,4-1,5-1,6-1,7-1,8-1,9-1,10-1,11-1,12-1,13-1,14-1,15-1,16-1,17-1,18-1,19-1,20-1,21-1,22-1,23-1,24-1,25-1,26-1,27-1

Conclusion: Four modern versions are more complex than the King James Bible.

142. Numbers 14:6* And **Joshua** the son of Nun, and **Caleb** the son of **Jephunneh**, which were of them that searched the land, rent their clothes:

AV - 23, 1-1,2-1,3-1,4-1,5-1,6-1,7-1,8-1,9-1,10-1,11-1,12-1,13-1,14-1,15-1,16-1,17-1,18-1,19-1,20-1,21-1,22-1,23-1

ESV - 25, 1-1,2-1,3-1,4-1,5-1,6-1,7-1,8-1,9-1,10-1,11-1,12-1,13-1,14-1,15-**2**,16-1,17-1,18-1,19-1,20-1,21-1,22-1,23-1,24-1,25-1

HCSB - 21, 1-1,2-1,3-1,4-1,5-1,6-1,7-1,8-1,9-1,10-1,11-1,12-**2**,13-1,14-1,15-**2**,16-1,17-1,18-1,19-1,20-1,21-1

NASV - 22, 1-1,2-1,3-1,4-1,5-1,6-1,7-1,8-1,9-1,10-1,11-1,12-1,13-1,14-1,15-1,16-1,17-1,18-1,19-1,20-1,21-1,22-1

NCV - 17, 1-1,2-1,3-1,4-1,5-1,6-1,7-1,8-1,9-1,10-1,11-1,12-**2**,13-1,14-1,15-1,16-1,17-1

NIV - 21, 1-1,2-1,3-1,4-1,5-1,6-1,7-1,8-1,9-1,10-1,11-1,12-**2**,13-1,14-1,15-1,16-**2**,17-1,18-1,19-1,20-1,21-1

NKJV - 25, 1-1,2-1,3-1,4-1,5-1,6-1,7-1,8-1,9-1,10-1,11-1,12-1,13-1,14-1,15-**2**,16-1,17-1,18-1,19-1,20-1,21-1,22-1,23-1,24-1,25-1

NLT - 21, 1-1,2-1,3-1,4-1,5-1,6-1,7-**2**,8-1,9-1,10-1,11-1,12-1,13-1,14-1,15-1,16-1,17-1,18-1,19-1,20-1,21-**2**

NRSV - 23, 1-1,2-1,3-1,4-1,5-1,6-1,7-1,8-1,9-1,10-1,11-1,12-1,13-**2**,14-1,15-1,16-1,17-1,18-1,19-1,20-1,21-1,22-1,23-1

Conclusion: Seven modern versions are more complex than the King James Bible.

143. Numbers 14:38* But **Joshua** the son of Nun, and **Caleb** the son of **Jephunneh**, which were of the men that went to search the land, lived still.

AV - 25, 1-1,2-1,3-1,4-1,5-1,6-1,7-1,8-1,9-1,10-1,11-1,12-1,13-1,14-1,15-1,16-1,17-1,18-1,19-1,20-1,21-1,22-1,23-1,24-1,25-1

ESV - 24, 1-1,2-1,3-1,4-1,5-1,6-1,7-1,8-1,9-1,10-1,11-**2**,12-1,13-1,14-1,15-1,16-1,17-1,18-1,19-1,20-1,21-1,22-1,23-**2**,24-**2**

HCSB - 22, 1-**2**,2-1,3-1,4-1,5-1,6-1,7-1,8-1,9-1,10-1,11-**2**,12-**2**,13-1,14-1,15-1,16-1,17-1,18-1,19-1,20-1,21-1,22-1

NASV - 25, 1-1,2-1,3-1,4-1,5-1,6-1,7-1,8-1,9-1,10-1,11-1,12-1,13-**2**,14-**2**,15-1,16-1,17-1,18-1,19-1,20-1,21-1,22-1,23-1,24-1,25-1

NCV - 21, 1-**2**,2-1,3-1,4-1,5-1,6-1,7-**2**,8-1,9-1,10-1,11-1,12-1,13-1,14-1,15-1,16-1,17-1,18-1,19-1,20-1,21-1

NIV - 20, 1-1,2-1,3-1,4-1,5-1,6-1,7-**2**,8-1,9-1,10-**2**,11-1,12-1,13-1,14-1,15-1,16-1,17-1,18-1,19-1,20-**2**

NKJV - 24, 1-1,2-1,3-1,4-1,5-1,6-1,7-1,8-1,9-1,10-1,11-1,12-1,13-**2**,14-**2**,15-1,16-1,17-1,18-1,19-1,20-1,21-1,22-1,23-1,24-1

NLT - 14, 1-1,2-1,3-1,4-1,5-1,6-**2**,7-1,8-1,9-**2**,10-1,11-1,12-1,13-**2**,14-**2**

NRSV - 23, 1-1,2-1,3-1,4-1,5-1,6-1,7-1,8-1,9-1,10-1,11-**2**,12-**2**,13-**2**,14-1,15-1,16-1,17-1,18-1,19-1,20-1,21-1,22-1,23-1

Conclusion: All eight modern versions are more complex than the King James Bible.

144. Numbers 15:41* I am the LORD your God, which brought you out of the land of **Egypt**, to be your God: I am the LORD your God.

AV - **25,** 1-1,2-1,3-1,4-1,5-1,6-1,7-1,8-1,9-1,10-1,11-1,12-1,13-1,14-1,15-1,16-1,17-1,18-1,19-1,20-1,21-1,22-1,23-1,24-1,25-1

ESV - **25,** 1-1,2-1,3-1,4-1,5-1,6-1,7-1,8-1,9-1,10-1,11-1,12-1,13-1,14-1,15-1,16-1,17-1,18-1,19-1,20-1,21-1,22-1,23-1,24-1,25-1

HCSB - **25,** 1-1,2-1,3-1,4-1,5-1,6-1,7-1,8-1,9-1,10-1,11-1,12-1,13-1,14-1,15-1,16-1,17-1,18-1,19-1,20-1,21-1,22-1,23-1,24-1,25-1

NASV - **25,** 1-1,2-1,3-1,4-1,5-1,6-1,7-1,8-1,9-1,10-1,11-1,12-1,13-1,14-1,15-1,16-1,17-1,18-1,19-1,20-1,21-1,22-1,23-1,24-1,25-1

NCV - **22,** 1-1,2-1,3-1,4-1,5-1,6-1,7-1,8-1,9-1,10-1,11-1,12-1,13-1,14-1,15-1,16-1,17-1,18-1,19-1,20-1,21-1,22-1

NIV - **22,** 1-1,2-1,3-1,4-1,5-1,6-1,7-1,8-1,9-1,10-1,11-1,12-1,13-1,14-1,15-1,16-1,17-1,18-1,19-1,20-1,21-1,22-1

NKJV - **25,** 1-1,2-1,3-1,4-1,5-1,6-1,7-1,8-1,9-1,10-1,11-1,12-1,13-1,14-1,15-1,16-1,17-1,18-1,19-1,20-1,21-1,22-1,23-1,24-1,25-1

NLT - **27,** 1-1,2-1,3-1,4-1,5-1,6-1,7-1,8-1,9-1,10-1,11-1,12-1,13-1,14-1,15-1,16-1,17-1,18-1,19-1,20-1,21-1,22-1,23-1,24-1,25-1,26-1,27-1

NRSV - **25,** 1-1,2-1,3-1,4-1,5-1,6-1,7-1,8-1,9-1,10-1,11-1,12-1,13-1,14-1,15-1,16-1,17-1,18-1,19-1,20-1,21-1,22-1,23-1,24-1,25-1

Conclusion: All versions read the same.

145. Numbers 16:1* Now **Korah**, the son of **Izhar**, the son of **Kohath**, the son of **Levi**, and **Dathan** and **Abiram**, the sons of **Eliab**, and On, the son of **Peleth**, sons of **Reuben**, took men:

AV - **33,** 1-1,2-1,3-1,4-1,5-1,6-1,7-1,8-1,9-1,10-1,11-1,12-1,13-1,14-1,15-1,16-1,17-1,18-1,19-1,20-1,21-1,22-1,23-1,24-1,25-1,26-1,27-1,28-1,29-1,30-1,31-1,32-1,33-1

ESV - **31,** 1-1,2-1,3-1,4-1,5-1,6-1,7-1,8-1,9-1,10-1,11-1,12-1,13-1,14-1,15-1,16-1,17-1,18-1,19-1,20-1,21-1,22-1,23-1,24-1,25-1,26-1,27-1,28-1,29-1,30-1,31-1

HCSB - **27,** 1-1,2-1,3-1,4-1,5-1,6-1,7-1,8-1,9-1,10-1,11-1,12-1,13-1,14-1,15-1,16-1,17-1,18-1,19-1,20-1,21-1,22-1,23-1,24-1,25-1,26-1,27-1

NASV - **33,** 1-1,2-1,3-1,4-1,5-1,6-1,7-1,8-1,9-1,10-1,11-1,12-1,13-1,14-1,15-1,16-1,17-1,18-1,19-1,20-1,21-1,22-1,23-1,24-1,25-1,26-1,27-1,28-1,29-1,30-1,31-1,32-1,33-**2**

NCV - **48,** 1-1,2-1,3-1,4-1,5-1,6-1,7-**2**,8-1,9-1,10-1,11-1,12-1,13-1,14-1,15-1,16-1,17-1,18-1,19-1,20-1,21-1,22-1,23-1,24-1,25-1,26-1,27-**2**,28-1,29-1,30-1,31-1,32-1,33-1,34-1,35-1,36-1,37-1,38-1,39-1,40-1,41-1,42-1,43-1,44-1,45-1,46-1,47-1,48-1

NIV - **28,** 1-1,2-1,3-1,4-1,5-1,6-1,7-1,8-1,9-1,10-1,11-1,12-1,13-1,14-**2**,15-1,16-1,17-1,18-1,19-1,20-1,21-1,22-1,23-1,24-1,25-1,26-1,27-**2**,28-**3**

NKJV - **33,** 1-1,2-1,3-1,4-1,5-1,6-1,7-1,8-1,9-1,10-1,11-1,12-1,13-1,14-1,15-1,16-1,17-1,18-1,19-1,20-1,21-1,22-1,23-1,24-1,25-1,26-1,27-1,28-1,29-1,30-1,31-1,32-1,33-1

NLT - **32,** 1-1,2-1,3-1,4-1,5-1,6-1,7-1,8-**3,**9-1,10-1,11-1,12-1,13-1,14-**3,**15-1,16-1,17-1,18-1,19-1,20-1,21-1,22-1,23-1,24-1,25-1,26-1,27-1,28-1,29-1,30-1,31-1,32-1

NRSV - **28,** 1-1,2-1,3-1,4-1,5-1,6-1,7-1,8-1,9-1,10-1,11-1,12-**2,**13-1,14-1,15-1,16-1,17-1,18-1,19-1,20-1,21-1,22-1,23-1,24-1,25-**3,**26-1,27-1,28-1

Conclusion: Five modern versions are more complex than the King James Bible.

146. Numbers 16:12* And **Moses** sent to call **Dathan** and **Abiram**, the sons of **Eliab**: which said, We will not come up:

AV - **19,** 1-1,2-1,3-1,4-1,5-1,6-1,7-1,8-1,9-1,10-1,11-1,12-1,13-1,14-1,15-1,16-1,17-1,18-1,19-1

ESV - **20,** 1-1,2-1,3-1,4-1,5-1,6-1,7-1,8-1,9-1,10-1,11-1,12-1,13-1,14-1,15-1,16-1,17-1,18-1,19-1,20-1

HCSB - **17,** 1-1,2-1,3-1,4-1,5-1,6-1,7-1,8-1,9-1,10-1,11-1,12-1,13-1,14-1,15-1,16-1,17-1

NASV - **21,** 1-1,2-1,3-1,4-1,5-**2,**6-1,7-1,8-1,9-1,10-1,11-1,12-1,13-1,14-1,15-1,16-1,17-1,18-1,19-1,20-1,21-1

NCV - **17,** 1-1,2-1,3-**2,**4-1,5-1,6-1,7-1,8-1,9-1,10-1,11-1,12-1,13-1,14-1,15-1,16-1,17-1

NIV - **17,** 1-1,2-1,3-1,4-1,5-1,6-1,7-1,8-1,9-1,10-1,11-1,12-1,13-1,14-1,15-1,16-1,17-1

NKJV - **20,** 1-1,2-1,3-1,4-1,5-1,6-1,7-1,8-1,9-1,10-1,11-1,12-1,13-1,14-1,15-1,16-1,17-1,18-1,19-1,20-1

NLT - **19,** 1-1,2-1,3-**2,**4-1,5-1,6-1,7-1,8-1,9-1,10-1,11-1,12-1,13-**2,**14-1,15-**2,**16-1,17-1,18-**2,**19-1

NRSV - **16,** 1-1,2-1,3-1,4-1,5-1,6-1,7-1,8-1,9-1,10-1,11-1,12-1,13-1,14-1,15-1,16-1

Conclusion: While only three modern versions are more complex than the King James Bible the NLT managed to make the verse wildly more complex.

147. Numbers 21:31* Thus **Israel** dwelt in the land of the **Amorites**.

AV - **9,** 1-1,2-1,3-1,4-1,5-1,6-1,7-1,8-1,9-1

ESV - **9,** 1-1,2-1,3-1,4-1,5-1,6-1,7-1,8-1,9-1

HCSB - **7,** 1-1,2-1,3-1,4-1,5-1,6-1,7-1

NASV - **9,** 1-1,2-1,3-1,4-1,5-1,6-1,7-1,8-1,9-1

NCV - **9,** 1-1,2-1,3-1,4-1,5-1,6-1,7-1,8-1,9-1

NIV - **9,** 1-1,2-1,3-**2,**4-1,5-1,6-1,7-1,8-1,9-1

NKJV - **9,** 1-1,2-1,3-1,4-1,5-1,6-1,7-1,8-1,9-1

NLT - **11,** 1-1,2-1,3-**2,**4-1,5-1,6-**3,**7-1,8-**4,**9-1,10-1,11-1

NRSV - **9,** 1-1,2-1,3-**2,**4-1,5-1,6-1,7-1,8-1,9-1

Conclusion: Only three modern versions are more complex than the King James Bible. The NLT is the most difficult to read.

148. Numbers 22:2* And **Balak** the son of **Zippor** saw all that **Israel** had done to the **Amorites**.

AV - **15,** 1-1,2-1,3-1,4-1,5-1,6-1,7-1,8-1,9-1,10-1,11-1,12-1,13-1,14-1,15-1

ESV - **15,** 1-1,2-1,3-1,4-1,5-1,6-1,7-1,8-1,9-1,10-1,11-1,12-1,13-1,14-1,15-1

HCSB - **14,** 1-1,2-1,3-1,4-1,5-1,6-1,7-1,8-1,9-1,10-1,11-1,12-1,13-1,14-1

NASV - **15,** 1-1,2-1,3-1,4-1,5-1,6-1,7-1,8-1,9-1,10-1,11-1,12-1,13-1,14-1,15-1

NCV - **13,** 1-1,2-1,3-1,4-1,5-1,6-**4,**7-1,8-1,9-1,10-1,11-1,12-1,13-1

NIV - **14,** 1-1,2-1,3-1,4-1,5-1,6-1,7-1,8-1,9-1,10-1,11-1,12-1,13-1,14-1

NKJV - **15,** 1-1,2-1,3-1,4-1,5-1,6-1,7-1,8-1,9-1,10-1,11-1,12-1,13-1,14-1,15-1

NLT - 16, 1-1,2-1,3-1,4-1,5-1,6-1,7-1,8-1,9-1,10-**4**,11-1,12-1,13-1,14-1,15-1,16-1
NRSV - 14, 1-1,2-1,3-1,4-1,5-1,6-1,7-1,8-1,9-1,10-1,11-1,12-1,13-1,14-1
Conclusion: Only the NCV and NLT made the verse more complex. Both of these versions used "Israelites" in reference to Israel and the NLT added "the Moabite king" to the verse. The syllable count for these added words was not counted against either of these versions.

149. Numbers 25:9# And those that died in the plague were **twenty** and four **thousand.**
AV - **12,** 1-1,2-1,3-1,4-1,5-1,6-1,7-1,8-1,9-1,10-1,11-1,12-1
ESV - 11, 1-**3**,2-1,3-1,4-1,5-1,6-1,7-1,8-1,9-1,10-1,11-1
HCSB - 9, 1-1,2-1,3-1,4-1,5-1,6-1,7-1,8-**2**,9-1
NASV - **8,** 1-1,2-1,3-1,4-1,5-1,6-1,7-1,8-1
NCV - 8, 1-1,2-**2**,3-1,4-1,5-1,6-1,7-1,8-**2**
NIV - 9, 1-1,2-1,3-1,4-1,5-1,6-1,7-1,8-**2**,9-1
NKJV - **11,** 1-1,2-1,3-1,4-1,5-1,6-1,7-1,8-1,9-1,10-1,11-1
NLT - 7, 1-1,2-1,3-**2**,4-1,5-**2**,6-1,7-1
NRSV - 11, 1-**3**,2-1,3-1,4-1,5-1,6-1,7-1,8-1,9-1,10-1,11-1
Conclusion: Six modern versions are more complex than the King James Bible.

150. Numbers 25:17* Vex the **Midianites,** and smite them:
AV - **6,** 1-1,2-1,3-1,4-1,5-1,6-1
ESV - 7, 1-**2**,2-1,3-1,4-1,5-1,6-1,7-1
HCSB - 7, 1-**2**,2-1,3-1,4-1,5-1,6-1,7-1
NASV - 8, 1-1,2-**2**,3-1,4-1,5-1,6-1,7-1,8-1
NCV - 10, 1-1,2-1,3-1,4-1,5-**3**,6-1,7-1,8-1,9-1,10-1
NIV - 8, 1-1,2-1,3-1,4-1,5-**3**,6-1,7-1,8-1
NKJV - 6, 1-**2**,2-1,3-1,4-1,5-**2**,6-1
NLT - 6, 1-**2**,2-1,3-1,4-1,5-**2**,6-1
NRSV - 6, 1-**2**,2-1,3-1,4-1,5-**2**,6-1
Conclusion: All eight modern versions are more complex than the King James Bible.

151. Numbers 26:8* And the sons of **Pallu**; **Eliab.**
AV - **6,** 1-1,2-1,3-1,4-1,5-1,6-1
ESV - **6,** 1-1,2-1,3-1,4-1,5-1,6-1
HCSB - **6,** 1-1,2-1,3-1,4-1,5-1,6-1
NASV - **5,** 1-1,2-1,3-1,4-1,5-1
NCV - **6,** 1-1,2-1,3-1,4-1,5-1,6-1
NIV - **6,** 1-1,2-1,3-1,4-1,5-1,6-1
NKJV - **7,** 1-1,2-1,3-1,4-1,5-1,6-1,7-1
NLT - 6, 1-1,2-1,3-1,4-**3**,5-1,6-1
NRSV - 6, 1-1,2-1,3-**3**,4-1,5-1,6-1
Conclusion: Only the NLT and the NRSV made the verse more complex.

152. Numbers 26:19* The sons of **Judah** were Er and **Onan**: and Er and **Onan** died in the land of **Canaan**.
AV - **18,** 1-1,2-1,3-1,4-1,5-1,6-1,7-1,8-1,9-1,10-1,11-1,12-1,13-1,14-1,15-1,16-1,17-1,18-1
ESV - **18,** 1-1,2-1,3-1,4-1,5-1,6-1,7-1,8-1,9-1,10-1,11-1,12-1,13-1,14-1,15-1,16-1,17-1,18-1
HCSB - 14, 1-1,2-1,3-**3,**4-1,5-1,6-1,7-1,8-1,9-1,10-1,11-1,12-1,13-1,14-1
NASV - **18,** 1-1,2-1,3-1,4-1,5-1,6-1,7-1,8-1,9-1,10-1,11-1,12-1,13-1,14-1,15-1,16-1,17-1,18-1
NCV - **10,** 1-1,2-1,3-1,4-1,5-1,6-1,7-1,8-1,9-1,10-1
NIV - **12,** 1-1,2-1,3-1,4-1,5-1,6-1,7-1,8-1,9-1,10-1,11-1,12-1
NKJV - **18,** 1-1,2-1,3-1,4-1,5-1,6-1,7-1,8-1,9-1,10-1,11-1,12-1,13-1,14-1,15-1,16-1,17-1,18-1
NLT - **15,** 1-1,2-1,3-1,4-1,5-1,6-1,7-1,8-1,9-1,10-1,11-1,12-1,13-1,14-1,15-1
NRSV - **16,** 1-1,2-1,3-1,4-1,5-1,6-1,7-1,8-1,9-1,10-1,11-1,12-1,13-1,14-1,15-1,16-1
Conclusion: Only the HCSB made the verse more complex.

153. Numbers 31:11 And they took all the spoil, and all the prey, both of men and of beasts.
AV - **16,** 1-1,2-1,3-1,4-1,5-1,6-1,7-1,8-1,9-1,10-1,11-1,12-1,13-1,14-1,15-1,16-1
ESV - **15,** 1-1,2-1,3-1,4-1,5-1,6-1,7-1,8-1,9-**2,**10-1,11-1,12-1,13-1,14-1,15-1
HCSB - 15, 1-1,2-1,3-**2,**4-1,5-1,6-1,7-1,8-1,9-1,10-1,11-**2,**12-1,13-**2,**14-1,15-**3**
NASV - **15,** 1-1,2-1,3-1,4-1,5-1,6-1,7-1,8-1,9-1,10-1,11-1,12-1,13-1,14-1,15-1
NCV - 10, 1-1,2-1,3-1,4-1,5-1,6-**2,**7-1,8-**3,**9-1,10-1
NIV - 12, 1-1,2-1,3-1,4-1,5-**2,**6-1,7-1,8-**3,**9-1,10-**2,**11-1,12-**3**
NKJV - **14,** 1-1,2-1,3-1,4-1,5-1,6-1,7-1,8-1,9-1,10-**2,**11-1,12-1,13-1,14-1
NLT - 12, 1-**2,**2-1,3-1,4-**2,**5-1,6-**2,**7-1,8-**2,**9-1,10-1,11-**2,**12-**3**
NRSV - 14, 1-1,2-1,3-1,4-1,5-1,6-1,7-1,8-1,9-1,10-**2,**11-1,12-**2,**13-1,14-**3**
Conclusion: Seven modern versions are more complex than the King James Bible. The NLT is the most difficult to read.

154. Numbers 31:22* Only the gold, and the **silver**, the brass, the iron, the tin, and the lead,
AV - **15,** 1-1,2-1,3-1,4-1,5-1,6-1,7-1,8-1,9-1,10-1,11-1,12-1,13-1,14-1,15-1
ESV - **14,** 1-**2,**2-1,3-1,4-1,5-1,6-1,7-1,8-1,9-1,10-1,11-1,12-1,13-1,14-1
HCSB - 9, 1-**2,**2-1,3-1,4-1,5-1,6-1,7-1,8-1,9-1
NASV - 15, 1-**2,**2-1,3-1,4-1,5-1,6-1,7-1,8-1,9-1,10-1,11-1,12-1,13-1,14-1,15-1
NCV - 9, 1-1,2-**2,**3-1,4-1,5-1,6-1,7-1,8-1,9-1
NIV - **6,** 1-1,2-1,3-1,4-1,5-1,6-1
NKJV - 14, 1-**2,**2-1,3-1,4-1,5-1,6-1,7-1,8-1,9-1,10-1,11-1,12-1,13-1,14-1
NLT - 10, 1-**3,**2-1,3-1,4-1,5-1,6-1,7-1,8-1,9-1,10-1
NRSV - **7,** 1-1,2-1,3-1,4-1,5-1,6-1,7-1
Conclusion: Six modern versions are more complex than the King James Bible.

155. Numbers 32:3* Ataroth, and **Dibon**, and **Jazer**, and **Nimrah**, and **Heshbon**, and **Elealeh**, and **Shebam**, and **Nebo**, and **Beon**,
AV - **17,** 1-1,2-1,3-1,4-1,5-1,6-1,7-1,8-1,9-1,10-1,11-1,12-1,13-1,14-1,15-1,16-1,17-1
ESV - **10,** 1-1,2-1,3-1,4-1,5-1,6-1,7-1,8-1,9-1,10-1
HCSB - 13, 1-1,2-**4,**3-1,4-1,5-1,6-1,7-1,8-1,9-1,10-1,11-1,12-1,13-1
NASV - **10,** 1-1,2-1,3-1,4-1,5-1,6-1,7-1,8-1,9-1,10-1

NCV - **13,** 1-1,2-1,3-**2,**4-1,5-1,6-1,7-1,8-1,9-1,10-1,11-1,12-1,13-1
NIV - **10,** 1-1,2-1,3-1,4-1,5-1,6-1,7-1,8-1,9-1,10-1
NKJV - **10,** 1-1,2-1,3-1,4-1,5-1,6-1,7-1,8-1,9-1,10-1
NLT - **13,** 1-**2,**2-1,3-1,4-1,5-1,6-1,7-1,8-1,9-1,10-1,11-1,12-1,13-1
NRSV - **10,** 1-1,2-1,3-1,4-1,5-1,6-1,7-1,8-1,9-1,10-1
Conclusion: Only three modern versions are more complex than the King James Bible. The NCV combined and reversed verses 3 and 4 resulting in a total of 36 words which is reproduced below. For this study the portion prior to the dash, verse 4, was ignored and only the thirteen words following the dash were counted, which still contained in one multi-syllable word.
NCV Numbers 32:3* They said, We, your servants, have flocks and herds. The Lord has captured for the Israelites a land that is good for animals—the land around Ataroth, Dibon, Jazer, Nimrah, Heshbon, Elealeh, Sebam, Nebo, and Beon.

156. Numbers 32:35* And **Atroth**, **Shophan**, and **Jaazer**, and **Jogbehah**,
AV - **7,** 1-1,2-1,3-1,4-1,5-1,6-1,7-1
ESV - **3,** 1-1,2-1,3-1
HCSB - **3,** 1-1,2-1,3-1
NASV - **6,** 1-1,2-1,3-1,4-1,5-1,6-1
NCV - **4,** 1-1,2-1,3-1,4-1
NIV - **4,** 1-1,2-1,3-1,4-1
NKJV - **7,** 1-1,2-1,3-1,4-1,5-1,6-1,7-1
NLT - **3,** 1-1,2-1,3-1
NRSV - **3,** 1-1,2-1,3-1
Conclusion: All versions read the same.

157. Numbers 33:29* And they went from **Mithcah**, and pitched in **Hashmonah**.
AV - **9,** 1-1,2-1,3-1,4-1,5-1,6-1,7-1,8-1,9-1
ESV - **10,** 1-1,2-1,3-1,4-1,5-1,6-1,7-1,8-1,9-1,10-1
HCSB - 8, 1-1,2-**3,**3-1,4-1,5-1,6-1,7-1,8-1
NASV - 8, 1-1,2-**2,**3-1,4-1,5-1,6-1,7-1,8-1
NCV - **7,** 1-1,2-1,3-1,4-1,5-1,6-1,7-1
NIV - **7,** 1-1,2-1,3-1,4-1,5-1,6-1,7-1
NKJV - **8,** 1-1,2-1,3-1,4-1,5-1,6-1,7-1,8-1
NLT - **7,** 1-1,2-1,3-1,4-1,5-1,6-1,7-1
NRSV - **9,** 1-1,2-1,3-1,4-1,5-1,6-1,7-1,8-1,9-1
Conclusion: Only the HCSB and the NASV made the verse more complex.

158. Numbers 33:33* And they went from **Horhagidgad**, and pitched in **Jotbathah**.
AV - **9,** 1-1,2-1,3-1,4-1,5-1,6-1,7-1,8-1,9-1
ESV - **10,** 1-1,2-1,3-1,4-1,5-1,6-1,7-1,8-1,9-1,10-1
HCSB - 8, 1-1,2-**3,**3-1,4-1,5-1,6-1,7-1,8-1
NASV - 8, 1-1,2-**2,**3-1,4-1,5-1,6-1,7-1,8-1
NCV - **8,** 1-1,2-1,3-1,4-1,5-1,6-1,7-1,8-1
NIV - **8,** 1-1,2-1,3-1,4-1,5-1,6-1,7-1,8-1

NKJV - **9,** 1-1,2-1,3-1,4-1,5-1,6-1,7-1,8-1,9-1
NLT - **7,** 1-1,2-1,3-1,4-1,5-1,6-1,7-1
NRSV - **10,** 1-1,2-1,3-1,4-1,5-1,6-1,7-1,8-1,9-1,10-1
Conclusion: Only the HCSB and the NASV made the verse more complex.

159. Numbers 33:39*# And **Aaron** was an **hundred** and **twenty** and three years old when he died in mount Hor.
AV - **17,** 1-1,2-1,3-1,4-1,5-1,6-1,7-1,8-1,9-1,10-1,11-1,12-1,13-1,14-1,15-1,16-1,17-1
ESV - **12,** 1-1,2-1,3-1,4-1,5-1,6-1,7-1,8-1,9-1,10-1,11-1,12-1
HCSB - **11,** 1-1,2-1,3-1,4-1,5-1,6-1,7-1,8-1,9-1,10-1,11-1
NASV - **14,** 1-1,2-1,3-1,4-1,5-1,6-1,7-1,8-1,9-1,10-1,11-1,12-1,13-1,14-1
NCV - **11,** 1-1,2-1,3-1,4-1,5-1,6-1,7-1,8-1,9-1,10-1,11-1
NIV - **15,** 1-1,2-1,3-1,4-1,5-1,6-1,7-1,8-1,9-1,10-1,11-1,12-1,13-1,14-1,15-1
NKJV - **15,** 1-1,2-1,3-1,4-1,5-1,6-1,7-1,8-1,9-1,10-1,11-1,12-1,13-1,14-1,15-1
NLT - **12,** 1-1,2-1,3-1,4-1,5-1,6-1,7-1,8-1,9-1,10-1,11-1,12-1
NRSV - **14,** 1-1,2-1,3-1,4-1,5-1,6-1,7-1,8-1,9-1,10-1,11-1,12-1,13-1,14-1
Conclusion: All versions read the same.

160. Numbers 34:19* And the names of the men are these: Of the tribe of **Judah**, **Caleb** the son of **Jephunneh**.
AV - **18,** 1-1,2-1,3-1,4-1,5-1,6-1,7-1,8-1,9-1,10-1,11-1,12-1,13-1,14-1,15-1,16-1,17-1,18-1
ESV - **17,** 1-1,2-1,3-1,4-1,5-1,6-1,7-1,8-1,9-1,10-1,11-1,12-1,13-1,14-1,15-1,16-1,17-1
HCSB - **16,** 1-1,2-1,3-1,4-1,5-1,6-1,7-1,8-1,9-1,10-1,11-1,12-1,13-1,14-1,15-1,16-1
NASV - **16,** 1-1,2-1,3-1,4-1,5-1,6-1,7-1,8-1,9-1,10-1,11-1,12-1,13-1,14-1,15-1,16-1
NCV - **17,** 1-1,2-1,3-1,4-1,5-1,6-1,7-1,8-1,9-1,10-1,11-1,12-1,13-1,14-1,15-1,16-1,17-1
NIV - **16,** 1-1,2-1,3-1,4-1,5-1,6-1,7-**2**,8-1,9-1,10-1,11-1,12-1,13-1,14-1,15-1,16-1
NKJV - **13,** 1-1,2-1,3-1,4-1,5-1,6-1,7-1,8-1,9-1,10-1,11-1,12-1,13-1
NLT - **17,** 1-1,2-1,3-1,4-1,5-1,6-1,7-1,8-1,9-1,10-**2**,11-1,12-1,13-**2**,14-1,15-1,16-1,17-1
NRSV - **16,** 1-1,2-1,3-1,4-1,5-1,6-1,7-1,8-1,9-1,10-1,11-1,12-1,13-1,14-1,15-1,16-1
Conclusion: Only the NIV and the NLT made the verse more complex.

161. Numbers 34:21* Of the tribe of **Benjamin**, **Elidad** the son of **Chislon**.
AV - **10,** 1-1,2-1,3-1,4-1,5-1,6-1,7-1,8-1,9-1,10-1
ESV - **10,** 1-1,2-1,3-1,4-1,5-1,6-1,7-1,8-1,9-1,10-1
HCSB - **9,** 1-1,2-1,3-1,4-1,5-1,6-1,7-1,8-1,9-1
NASV - **10,** 1-1,2-1,3-1,4-1,5-1,6-1,7-1,8-1,9-1,10-1
NCV - **9,** 1-1,2-1,3-1,4-1,5-1,6-1,7-1,8-1,9-1
NIV - **9,** 1-1,2-1,3-1,4-1,5-1,6-1,7-1,8-1,9-1
NKJV - **10,** 1-1,2-1,3-1,4-1,5-1,6-1,7-1,8-1,9-1,10-1
NLT - **5,** 1-1,2-1,3-1,4-1,5-1
NRSV - **9,** 1-1,2-1,3-1,4-1,5-1,6-1,7-1,8-1,9-1
Conclusion: All versions read the same.

162. Deuteronomy 3:9* (Which **Hermon** the **Sidonians** call **Sirion**; and the **Amorites** call it
Shenir;)
AV - **12,** 1-1,2-1,3-1,4-1,5-1,6-1,7-1,8-1,9-1,10-1,11-1,12-1
ESV - **11,** 1-1,2-1,3-1,4-1,5-1,6-1,7-1,8-1,9-1,10-1,11-1
HCSB - **10,** 1-1,2-1,3-1,4-1,5-1,6-1,7-1,8-1,9-1,10-1
NASV - **10,** 1-1,2-1,3-1,4-1,5-1,6-1,7-1,8-1,9-1,10-1
NCV - 14, 1-1,2-1,3-1,4-1,5-1,6-1,7-1,8-**2,**9-1,10-1,11-1,12-1,13-1,14-1
NIV - **12,** 1-1,2-1,3-1,4-1,5-1,6-1,7-1,8-1,9-1,10-1,11-1,12-1
NKJV - **11,** 1-1,2-1,3-1,4-1,5-1,6-1,7-1,8-1,9-1,10-1,11-1
NLT - **14,** 1-1,2-1,3-1,4-1,5-1,6-1,7-1,8-1,9-1,10-1,11-1,12-1,13-1,14-1
NRSV - **11,** 1-1,2-1,3-1,4-1,5-1,6-1,7-1,8-1,9-1,10-1,11-1
Conclusion: Only the NCV made the verse more complex.

163. Deuteronomy 3:22 Ye shall not fear them: for the LORD your God he shall fight for you.
AV - **15,** 1-1,2-1,3-1,4-1,5-1,6-1,7-1,8-1,9-1,10-1,11-1,12-1,13-1,14-1,15-1
ESV - **16,** 1-1,2-1,3-1,4-1,5-1,6-1,7-1,8-1,9-1,10-1,11-1,12-1,13-1,14-1,15-1,16-1
HCSB - 13, 1-1,2-1,3-**2,**4-1,5-1,6-1,7-1,8-1,9-1,10-1,11-1,12-1,13-1
NASV - 15, 1-1,2-1,3-1,4-1,5-1,6-1,7-1,8-1,9-1,10-1,11-1,12-1,13-**2,**14-1,15-1
NCV - 14, 1-1,2-1,3-**2,**4-1,5-1,6-**2,**7-1,8-1,9-1,10-1,11-1,12-1,13-1,14-1
NIV - 15, 1-1,2-1,3-1,4-**2,**5-1,6-1,7-1,8-1,9-1,10-1,11-**2,**12-1,13-1,14-1,15-1
NKJV - 14, 1-1,2-1,3-1,4-1,5-1,6-1,7-1,8-1,9-1,10-1,11-**2,**12-1,13-1,14-1
NLT - 17, 1-1,2-1,3-1,4-**2,**5-1,6-1,7-**2,**8-1,9-1,10-1,11-1,12-1,13-1,14-1,15-1,16-1,17-1
NRSV - **15,** 1-1,2-1,3-1,4-1,5-1,6-1,7-1,8-1,9-1,10-1,11-1,12-1,13-1,14-1,15-1
Conclusion: Six modern versions are more complex than the King James Bible.

164. Deuteronomy 4:29 But if from thence thou shalt seek the LORD thy God, thou shalt find him,
if thou seek him with all thy heart and with all thy soul.
AV - **28,** 1-1,2-1,3-1,4-1,5-1,6-1,7-1,8-1,9-1,10-1,11-1,12-1,13-1,14-1,15-1,16-1,17-1,18-1,19-1,20-
1,21-1,22-1,23-1,24-1,25-1,26-1,27-1,28-1
ESV - 29, 1-1,2-1,3-1,4-1,5-1,6-1,7-1,8-1,9-1,10-1,11-1,12-1,13-1,14-1,15-1,16-1,17-1,18-1,19-
2,20-1,21-1,22-1,23-1,24-1,25-1,26-1,27-1,28-1,29-1
HCSB - **28,** 1-1,2-1,3-1,4-1,5-1,6-1,7-1,8-1,9-1,10-1,11-1,12-1,13-1,14-1,15-1,16-1,17-1,18-1,19-
1,20-1,21-1,22-1,23-1,24-1,25-1,26-1,27-1,28-1
NASV - **28,** 1-1,2-1,3-1,4-1,5-1,6-1,7-1,8-1,9-1,10-1,11-1,12-1,13-1,14-1,15-1,16-1,17-1,18-1,19-
1,20-1,21-1,22-1,23-1,24-1,25-1,26-1,27-1,28-1
NCV - 25, 1-1,2-**2,**3-1,4-1,5-1,6-1,7-1,8-1,9-1,10-1,11-1,12-1,13-1,14-1,15-1,16-1,17-1,18-1,19-
1,20-1,21-1,22-1,23-1,24-1,25-**2**
NIV - **28,** 1-1,2-1,3-1,4-1,5-1,6-1,7-1,8-1,9-1,10-1,11-1,12-1,13-1,14-1,15-1,16-1,17-1,18-1,19-1,20-
1,21-1,22-1,23-1,24-1,25-1,26-1,27-1,28-1
NKJV - **28,** 1-1,2-1,3-1,4-1,5-1,6-1,7-1,8-1,9-1,10-1,11-1,12-1,13-1,14-1,15-1,16-1,17-1,18-1,19-
1,20-1,21-1,22-1,23-1,24-1,25-1,26-1,27-1,28-1
NLT - 28, 1-1,2-1,3-1,4-1,5-1,6-1,7-**2,**8-1,9-1,10-1,11-1,12-1,13-1,14-1,15-1,16-1,17-1,18-1,19-
1,20-1,21-1,22-1,23-1,24-1,25-1,26-1,27-1,28-1

NRSV - 25, 1-1,2-1,3-1,4-1,5-1,6-1,7-1,8-1,9-1,10-1,11-1,12-1,13-1,14-1,15-1,16-1,17-1,18-**2**,19-1,20-1,21-1,22-1,23-1,24-1,25-1
Conclusion: Four modern versions are more complex than the King James Bible.

165. Deuteronomy 5:4 The LORD talked with you face to face in the mount out of the midst of the fire,
AV - **18,** 1-1,2-1,3-1,4-1,5-1,6-1,7-1,8-1,9-1,10-1,11-1,12-1,13-1,14-1,15-1,16-1,17-1,18-1
ESV - 18, 1-1,2-1,3-1,4-1,5-1,6-1,7-1,8-1,9-1,10-1,11-**2**,12-1,13-1,14-1,15-1,16-1,17-1,18-1
HCSB - 14, 1-1,2-1,3-1,4-1,5-1,6-1,7-1,8-1,9-1,10-1,11-1,12-1,13-1,14-**2**
NASV - 17, 1-1,2-1,3-1,4-1,5-1,6-1,7-1,8-1,9-1,10-1,11-**2**,12-1,13-1,14-1,15-1,16-1,17-1
NCV - 14, 1-1,2-1,3-1,4-1,5-1,6-1,7-1,8-1,9-1,10-1,11-1,12-1,13-1,14-**2**
NIV - 15, 1-1,2-1,3-1,4-1,5-1,6-1,7-1,8-1,9-1,10-1,11-1,12-1,13-1,14-1,15-**2**
NKJV - 17, 1-1,2-1,3-1,4-1,5-1,6-1,7-1,8-1,9-1,10-1,11-**2**,12-1,13-1,14-1,15-1,16-1,17-1
NLT - **17,** 1-1,2-1,3-1,4-1,5-1,6-1,7-1,8-1,9-1,10-1,11-1,12-1,13-1,14-1,15-1,16-1,17-1
NRSV - 15, 1-1,2-1,3-1,4-1,5-1,6-1,7-1,8-1,9-1,10-1,11-**2**,12-1,13-1,14-1,15-1
Conclusion: Seven modern versions are more complex than the King James Bible.

166. Deuteronomy 5:17 Thou shalt not kill.
AV - **4,** 1-1,2-1,3-1,4-1
ESV - 4, 1-1,2-1,3-1,4-**2**
HCSB - 3, 1-1,2-1,3-**2**
NASV - 4, 1-1,2-1,3-1,4-**2**
NCV - 5, 1-1,2-1,3-1,4-**2**,5-**2**
NIV - 4, 1-1,2-1,3-1,4-**2**
NKJV - 4, 1-1,2-1,3-1,4-**2**
NLT - 4, 1-1,2-1,3-1,4-**2**
NRSV - 4, 1-1,2-1,3-1,4-**2**
Conclusion: All eight modern versions are more complex than the King James Bible. The NCV is the most difficult to read.

167. Deuteronomy 6:4* Hear, O **Israel**: The LORD our God is one LORD:
AV - **10,** 1-1,2-1,3-1,4-1,5-1,6-1,7-1,8-1,9-1,10-1
ESV - **11,** 1-1,2-1,3-1,4-1,5-1,6-1,7-1,8-1,9-1,10-1,11-1
HCSB - 10, 1-**2**,2-1,3-1,4-1,5-1,6-1,7-1,8-1,9-1,10-1
NASV - **12,** 1-1,2-1,3-1,4-1,5-1,6-1,7-1,8-1,9-1,10-1,11-1,12-1
NCV - 12, 1-**2**,2-**2**,3-1,4-1,5-1,6-1,7-1,8-1,9-1,10-1,11-1,12-1
NIV - **11,** 1-1,2-1,3-1,4-1,5-1,6-1,7-1,8-1,9-1,10-1,11-1
NKJV - **11,** 1-1,2-1,3-1,4-1,5-1,6-1,7-1,8-1,9-1,10-1,11-1
NLT - 11, 1-**2**,2-1,3-1,4-1,5-1,6-1,7-1,8-1,9-1,10-1,11-**2**
NRSV - 11, 1-1,2-1,3-1,4-1,5-1,6-1,7-1,8-1,9-1,10-1,11-**2**
Conclusion: Four modern versions are more complex than the King James Bible.

168. Deuteronomy 6:5 And thou shalt love the LORD thy God with all thine heart, and with all thy soul, and with all thy might.

AV - **22,** 1-1,2-1,3-1,4-1,5-1,6-1,7-1,8-1,9-1,10-1,11-1,12-1,13-1,14-1,15-1,16-1,17-1,18-1,19-1,20-1,21-1,22-1

ESV - **21,** 1-1,2-1,3-1,4-1,5-1,6-1,7-1,8-1,9-1,10-1,11-1,12-1,13-1,14-1,15-1,16-1,17-1,18-1,19-1,20-1,21-1

HCSB - **18,** 1-1,2-1,3-1,4-1,5-1,6-1,7-1,8-1,9-1,10-1,11-1,12-1,13-1,14-1,15-1,16-1,17-1,18-1

NASV - **21,** 1-1,2-1,3-1,4-1,5-1,6-1,7-1,8-1,9-1,10-1,11-1,12-1,13-1,14-1,15-1,16-1,17-1,18-1,19-1,20-1,21-1

NCV - **16,** 1-1,2-1,3-1,4-1,5-1,6-1,7-1,8-1,9-1,10-1,11-1,12-1,13-1,14-1,15-1,16-1

NIV - **19,** 1-1,2-1,3-1,4-1,5-1,6-1,7-1,8-1,9-1,10-1,11-1,12-1,13-1,14-1,15-1,16-1,17-1,18-1,19-1

NKJV - **20,** 1-1,2-1,3-1,4-1,5-1,6-1,7-1,8-1,9-1,10-1,11-1,12-1,13-1,14-1,15-1,16-1,17-1,18-1,19-1,20-1

NLT - **19,** 1-1,2-1,3-1,4-1,5-1,6-1,7-1,8-1,9-1,10-1,11-1,12-1,13-1,14-1,15-1,16-1,17-1,18-1,19-1

NRSV - **21,** 1-1,2-1,3-1,4-1,5-1,6-1,7-1,8-1,9-1,10-1,11-1,12-1,13-1,14-1,15-1,16-1,17-1,18-1,19-1,20-1,21-1

Conclusion: All versions read the same.

169. Deuteronomy 6:13 Thou shalt fear the LORD thy God, and serve him, and shalt swear by his name.

AV - **16,** 1-1,2-1,3-1,4-1,5-1,6-1,7-1,8-1,9-1,10-1,11-1,12-1,13-1,14-1,15-1,16-1

ESV - **20,** 1-1,2-1,3-1,4-1,5-1,6-1,7-1,8-1,9-1,10-1,11-1,12-1,13-1,14-1,15-1,16-1,17-1,18-1,19-1,20-1

HCSB - 14, 1-1,2-1,3-1,4-1,5-1,6-**2,**7-1,8-1,9-1,10-1,11-1,12-1,13-1,14-1

NASV - 18, 1-1,2-1,3-1,4-**2,**5-1,6-1,7-1,8-1,9-1,10-1,11-1,12-**2,**13-1,14-1,15-1,16-1,17-1,18-1

NCV - 17, 1-**2,**2-1,3-1,4-1,5-1,6-1,7-1,8-**2,**9-1,10-1,11-1,12-1,13-**3,**14-1,15-1,16-1,17-1

NIV - 15, 1-1,2-1,3-1,4-1,5-1,6-1,7-1,8-**2,**9-1,10-1,11-1,12-1,13-1,14-1,15-1

NKJV - **17,** 1-1,2-1,3-1,4-1,5-1,6-1,7-1,8-1,9-1,10-1,11-1,12-1,13-1,14-1,15-1,16-1,17-1

NLT - 21, 1-1,2-1,3-1,4-1,5-1,6-1,7-1,8-1,9-1,10-1,11-1,12-1,13-1,14-1,15-1,16-1,17-1,18-1,19-**2,**20-1,21-1

NRSV - 19, 1-1,2-1,3-1,4-1,5-1,6-1,7-1,8-1,9-1,10-1,11-1,12-1,13-1,14-1,15-1,16-**2,**17-1,18-1,19-1

Conclusion: Six modern versions are more complex than the King James Bible. The NCV is the most difficult to read.

170. Deuteronomy 10:20 Thou shalt fear the LORD thy God; him shalt thou serve, and to him shalt thou cleave, and swear by his name.

AV - **22,** 1-1,2-1,3-1,4-1,5-1,6-1,7-1,8-1,9-1,10-1,11-1,12-1,13-1,14-1,15-1,16-1,17-1,18-1,19-1,20-1,21-1,22-1

ESV - **23,** 1-1,2-1,3-1,4-1,5-1,6-1,7-1,8-1,9-1,10-1,11-1,12-1,13-1,14-1,15-1,16-1,17-1,18-1,19-1,20-1,21-1,22-1,23-1

HCSB - 21, 1-1,2-1,3-1,4-1,5-1,6-1,7-1,8-1,9-1,10-**2,**11-1,12-**2,**13-**2,**14-1,15-1,16-1,17-1,18-1,19-1,20-1,21-1

NASV - **22,** 1-1,2-1,3-1,4-1,5-1,6-1,7-1,8-1,9-1,10-1,11-1,12-1,13-1,14-1,15-1,16-1,17-1,18-1,19-1,20-1,21-1,22-1

NCV - **19,** 1-**2**,2-1,3-1,4-1,5-1,6-1,7-1,8-1,9-1,10-**2**,11-1,12-1,13-1,14-1,15-1,16-**3**,17-1,18-1,19-1
NIV - **19,** 1-1,2-1,3-1,4-1,5-1,6-1,7-1,8-1,9-1,10-1,11-1,12-1,13-1,14-1,15-1,16-1,17-1,18-1,19-1
NKJV - **24,** 1-1,2-1,3-1,4-1,5-1,6-1,7-1,8-1,9-1,10-1,11-1,12-1,13-1,14-1,15-1,16-1,17-1,18-1,19-1,20-1,21-1,22-1,23-1,24-1
NLT - **22,** 1-1,2-1,3-1,4-1,5-1,6-1,7-1,8-1,9-**2**,10-1,11-1,12-1,13-1,14-1,15-1,16-1,17-1,18-1,19-1,20-1,21-1,22-**2**
NRSV - **25,** 1-1,2-1,3-1,4-1,5-1,6-1,7-1,8-1,9-**2**,10-1,11-1,12-**2**,13-1,14-1,15-1,16-1,17-1,18-1,19-1,20-1,21-1,22-1,23-1,24-1,25-1
Conclusion: Four modern versions are more complex than the King James Bible.

171. Deuteronomy 11:7 But your eyes have seen all the great acts of the LORD which he did.
AV - **15,** 1-1,2-1,3-1,4-1,5-1,6-1,7-1,8-1,9-1,10-1,11-1,12-1,13-1,14-1,15-1
ESV - **16,** 1-1,2-1,3-1,4-1,5-1,6-1,7-1,8-1,9-1,10-1,11-1,12-1,13-1,14-1,15-1,16-1
HCSB - **12,** 1-1,2-1,3-1,4-1,5-1,6-**2**,7-1,8-1,9-1,10-1,11-1,12-1
NASV - **16,** 1-1,2-1,3-1,4-1,5-1,6-1,7-1,8-1,9-1,10-1,11-1,12-1,13-1,14-1,15-1,16-1
NCV - **13,** 1-1,2-1,3-1,4-1,5-1,6-1,7-1,8-1,9-1,10-1,11-1,12-1,13-1
NIV - **16,** 1-1,2-1,3-1,4-1,5-1,6-1,7-1,8-1,9-1,10-1,11-1,12-1,13-1,14-1,15-1,16-1
NKJV - **14,** 1-1,2-1,3-1,4-1,5-1,6-**2**,7-1,8-1,9-1,10-1,11-1,12-1,13-1,14-1
NLT - **15,** 1-1,2-1,3-1,4-1,5-1,6-1,7-**2**,8-1,9-1,10-**2**,11-1,12-1,13-1,14-1,15-1
NRSV - **16,** 1-1,2-1,3-1,4-1,5-1,6-1,7-1,8-1,9-1,10-**2**,11-1,12-1,13-1,14-1,15-1,16-1
Conclusion: Four modern versions are more complex than the King James Bible.

172. Deuteronomy 14:4 These are the beasts which ye shall eat: the ox, the sheep, and the goat,
AV - **15,** 1-1,2-1,3-1,4-1,5-1,6-1,7-1,8-1,9-1,10-1,11-1,12-1,13-1,14-1,15-1
ESV - **13,** 1-1,2-1,3-1,4-**3**,5-1,6-1,7-1,8-1,9-1,10-1,11-1,12-1,13-1
HCSB - **13,** 1-1,2-1,3-1,4-**3**,5-1,6-1,7-1,8-1,9-1,10-1,11-1,12-1,13-1
NASV - **14,** 1-1,2-1,3-1,4-**3**,5-1,6-1,7-1,8-1,9-1,10-1,11-1,12-1,13-1,14-1
NCV - **10,** 1-1,2-1,3-1,4-**3**,5-1,6-1,7-1,8-**2**,9-1,10-1
NIV - **13,** 1-1,2-1,3-1,4-**3**,5-1,6-1,7-1,8-1,9-1,10-1,11-1,12-1,13-1
NKJV - **14,** 1-1,2-1,3-1,4-**3**,5-1,6-1,7-1,8-1,9-1,10-1,11-1,12-1,13-1,14-1
NLT - **13,** 1-1,2-1,3-1,4-**3**,5-1,6-1,7-1,8-1,9-1,10-1,11-1,12-1,13-1
NRSV - **13,** 1-1,2-1,3-1,4-**3**,5-1,6-1,7-1,8-1,9-1,10-1,11-1,12-1,13-1
Conclusion: All eight modern versions are more complex than the King James Bible. Ironically the NCV has the smallest word count but the highest syllable count.

173. Deuteronomy 14:11 Of all clean birds ye shall eat.
AV - **7,** 1-1,2-1,3-1,4-1,5-1,6-1,7-1
ESV - **6,** 1-1,2-1,3-1,4-1,5-1,6-1
HCSB - **6,** 1-1,2-1,3-1,4-1,5-1,6-1
NASV - **6,** 1-1,2-1,3-1,4-1,5-1,6-1
NCV - **6,** 1-1,2-1,3-1,4-1,5-1,6-1
NIV - **6,** 1-1,2-1,3-1,4-1,5-1,6-1
NKJV - **6,** 1-1,2-1,3-1,4-1,5-1,6-1
NLT - **9,** 1-1,2-1,3-1,4-1,5-1,6-1,7-1,8-**6**,9-1

NRSV - **6,** 1-1,2-1,3-1,4-1,5-1,6-1
Conclusion: It is remarkable that, when all other modern versions kept such a short verse to single syllable words the one that would be expected to be the simplest, the NLT, is once again the most difficult to read.

174. Deuteronomy 14:20 But of all clean fowls ye may eat.
AV - **8,** 1-1,2-1,3-1,4-1,5-1,6-1,7-1,8-1
ESV - **7,** 1-1,2-1,3-1,4-1,5-1,6-1,7-1
HCSB - 9, 1-1,2-1,3-1,4-1,5-**3**,6-1,7-1,8-**2**,9-**2**
NASV - 6, 1-1,2-1,3-1,4-**2**,5-1,6-1
NCV - 11, 1-**2**,2-1,3-1,4-1,5-1,6-1,7-1,8-1,9-1,10-1,11-1
NIV - 10, 1-1,2-**2**,3-1,4-**2**,5-1,6-1,7-1,8-1,9-1,10-1
NKJV - **6,** 1-1,2-1,3-1,4-1,5-1,6-1
NLT - 13, 1-1,2-1,3-1,4-1,5-**2**,6-1,7-1,8-1,9-**2**,10-1,11-1,12-**6**,13-1
NRSV - 7, 1-1,2-1,3-1,4-**2**,5-1,6-1,7-**2**
Conclusion: Six modern versions are more complex than the King James Bible. Once again the NLT is the most difficult to read.

175. Deuteronomy 21:12 Then thou shalt bring her home to thine house; and she shall shave her head, and pare her nails;
AV - **19,** 1-1,2-1,3-1,4-1,5-1,6-1,7-1,8-1,9-1,10-1,11-1,12-1,13-1,14-1,15-1,16-1,17-1,18-1,19-1
ESV - **17,** 1-1,2-1,3-1,4-1,5-1,6-1,7-1,8-1,9-1,10-1,11-1,12-1,13-1,14-1,15-1,16-1,17-1
HCSB - 16, 1-1,2-1,3-1,4-1,5-1,6-**2**,7-1,8-1,9-1,10-1,11-1,12-1,13-1,14-1,15-1,16-1
NASV - **19,** 1-1,2-1,3-1,4-1,5-1,6-1,7-1,8-1,9-1,10-1,11-1,12-1,13-1,14-1,15-1,16-1,17-1,18-1,19-1
NCV - 15, 1-1,2-1,3-**2**,4-1,5-1,6-1,7-1,8-1,9-1,10-1,11-1,12-1,13-1,14-1,15-1
NIV - 14, 1-1,2-1,3-**2**,4-1,5-1,6-1,7-1,8-1,9-1,10-1,11-1,12-1,13-1,14-1
NKJV - **19,** 1-1,2-1,3-1,4-1,5-1,6-1,7-1,8-1,9-1,10-1,11-1,12-1,13-1,14-1,15-1,16-1,17-1,18-1,19-1
NLT - 19, 1-1,2-1,3-**2**,4-1,5-1,6-1,7-1,8-1,9-1,10-1,11-1,12-1,13-1,14-1,15-1,16-1,17-1,18-1,19-1
NRSV - **17,** 1-1,2-1,3-1,4-1,5-1,6-1,7-1,8-1,9-1,10-1,11-1,12-1,13-1,14-1,15-1,16-1,17-1
Conclusion: Four modern versions are more complex than the King James Bible.

176. Deuteronomy 24:12 And if the man be poor, thou shalt not sleep with his pledge:
AV - **13,** 1-1,2-1,3-1,4-1,5-1,6-1,7-1,8-1,9-1,10-1,11-1,12-1,13-1
ESV - **14,** 1-1,2-1,3-1,4-1,5-1,6-1,7-1,8-1,9-1,10-1,11-1,12-1,13-1,14-1
HCSB - 18, 1-1,2-1,3-1,4-1,5-1,6-1,7-1,8-1,9-1,10-1,11-1,12-1,13-**2**,14-1,15-1,16-**2**,17-1,18-**4**
NASV - **13,** 1-1,2-1,3-1,4-1,5-1,6-1,7-1,8-1,9-1,10-1,11-1,12-1,13-1
NCV - 18, 1-1,2-1,3-1,4-**2**,5-1,6-1,7-1,8-1,9-1,10-1,11-1,12-1,13-1,14-1,15-1,16-1,17-1,18-**2**
NIV - 16, 1-1,2-1,3-1,4-1,5-1,6-1,7-1,8-1,9-1,10-1,11-1,12-1,13-1,14-1,15-1,16-**3**
NKJV - 13, 1-1,2-1,3-1,4-1,5-1,6-1,7-1,8-1,9-1,10-1,11-1,12-1,13-**3**
NLT - 21, 1-1,2-1,3-**2**,4-1,5-1,6-1,7-1,8-1,9-1,10-1,11-1,12-**4**,13-1,14-1,15-1,16-1,17-1,18-1,19-1,20-1,21-**3**
NRSV - 17, 1-1,2-1,3-**2**,4-1,5-1,6-1,7-1,8-1,9-1,10-1,11-1,12-**2**,13-**2**,14-1,15-1,16-1,17-1
Conclusion: Six modern versions are more complex than the King James Bible. Once again the NLT is the most difficult to read.

177. Deuteronomy 25:10* And his name shall be called in **Israel**, The house of him that hath his shoe loosed.
AV - **17,** 1-1,2-1,3-1,4-1,5-1,6-1,7-1,8-1,9-1,10-1,11-1,12-1,13-1,14-1,15-1,16-1,17-1
ESV - **21,** 1-1,2-1,3-1,4-1,5-1,6-1,7-1,8-1,9-1,10-1,11-1,12-1,13-1,14-1,15-1,16-1,17-1,18-1,19-2,20-1,21-1
HCSB - 18, 1-1,2-1,3-**3**,4-1,5-1,6-1,7-1,8-1,9-1,10-1,11-1,12-1,13-1,14-1,15-1,16-**2**,17-1,18-**2**
NASV - 15, 1-1,2-1,3-1,4-1,5-1,6-1,7-1,8-1,9-1,10-1,11-1,12-1,13-**2**,14-1,15-**2**
NCV - 15, 1-1,2-1,3-1,4-**3**,5-1,6-1,7-1,8-1,9-1,10-1,11-1,12-**3**,13-1,14-1,15-**2**
NIV - 14, 1-1,2-1,3-1,4-1,5-1,6-1,7-1,8-1,9-1,10-1,11-**3**,12-1,13-1,14-**2**
NKJV - 17, 1-1,2-1,3-1,4-1,5-1,6-1,7-1,8-1,9-1,10-1,11-1,12-1,13-1,14-1,15-1,16-**2**,17-**2**
NLT - 21, 1-**2**,2-**3**,3-1,4-1,5-1,6-**3**,7-1,8-1,9-**2**,10-1,11-1,12-1,13-**3**,14-1,15-1,16-1,17-1,18-**2**,19-1,20-1,21-1
NRSV - 17, 1-**2**,2-1,3-1,4-**3**,5-1,6-1,7-1,8-1,9-1,10-1,11-1,12-1,13-1,14-**2**,15-1,16-1,17-1
Conclusion: All eight modern versions are more complex than the King James Bible. Why is it not surprising that the NLT is the most difficult to read?

178. Deuteronomy 28:34 So that thou shalt be mad for the sight of thine eyes which thou shalt see.
AV - **16,** 1-1,2-1,3-1,4-1,5-1,6-1,7-1,8-1,9-1,10-1,11-1,12-1,13-1,14-1,15-1,16-1
ESV - **13,** 1-1,2-1,3-1,4-1,5-**2**,6-1,7-1,8-1,9-1,10-1,11-1,12-1,13-1
HCSB - 9, 1-1,2-1,3-1,4-**2**,5-1,6-1,7-1,8-1,9-1
NASV - 12, 1-1,2-1,3-1,4-**2**,5-1,6-1,7-1,8-1,9-1,10-1,11-1,12-1
NCV - **10,** 1-1,2-1,3-1,4-1,5-1,6-1,7-1,8-1,9-1,10-1
NIV - **8,** 1-1,2-1,3-1,4-1,5-1,6-1,7-1,8-1
NKJV - 14, 1-1,2-1,3-1,4-1,5-**2**,6-1,7-**2**,8-1,9-1,10-1,11-1,12-1,13-1,14-1
NLT - 13, 1-1,2-1,3-1,4-1,5-**2**,6-1,7-1,8-1,9-**3**,10-1,11-1,12-**2**,13-1
NRSV - 11, 1-1,2-**2**,3-1,4-1,5-1,6-1,7-1,8-1,9-1,10-1,11-1
Conclusion: Six modern versions are more complex than the King James Bible. It is surprising to see the NKJV, which usually tends to be more conservative, be one of the most complex. But, never fear, the NLT is the most difficult to read.

179. Deuteronomy 28:44 He shall lend to thee, and thou shalt not lend to him: he shall be the head, and thou shalt be the tail.
AV - **23,** 1-1,2-1,3-1,4-1,5-1,6-1,7-1,8-1,9-1,10-1,11-1,12-1,13-1,14-1,15-1,16-1,17-1,18-1,19-1,20-1,21-1,22-1,23-1
ESV - **23,** 1-1,2-1,3-1,4-1,5-1,6-1,7-1,8-1,9-1,10-1,11-1,12-1,13-1,14-1,15-1,16-1,17-1,18-1,19-1,20-1,21-1,22-1,23-1
HCSB - **22,** 1-1,2-1,3-1,4-1,5-1,6-1,7-1,8-1,9-1,10-1,11-1,12-1,13-1,14-1,15-1,16-1,17-1,18-1,19-1,20-1,21-1,22-1
NASV - **23,** 1-1,2-1,3-1,4-1,5-1,6-1,7-1,8-1,9-1,10-1,11-1,12-1,13-1,14-1,15-1,16-1,17-1,18-1,19-1,20-1,21-1,22-1,23-1
NCV - **29,** 1-**3**,2-1,3-1,4-**2**,5-1,6-1,7-1,8-1,9-1,10-1,11-1,12-**2**,13-1,14-1,15-1,16-1,17-1,18-1,19-1,20-1,21-1,22-1,23-1,24-1,25-1,26-1,27-1,28-1,29-1
NIV - **23,** 1-1,2-1,3-1,4-1,5-1,6-1,7-1,8-1,9-1,10-1,11-1,12-1,13-1,14-1,15-1,16-1,17-1,18-1,19-1,20-1,21-1,22-1,23-1

NKJV - **23,** 1-1,2-1,3-1,4-1,5-1,6-1,7-1,8-1,9-1,10-1,11-1,12-1,13-1,14-1,15-1,16-1,17-1,18-1,19-1,20-1,21-1,22-1,23-1

NLT - 24, 1-1,2-1,3-1,4-**2**,5-1,6-1,7-1,8-1,9-1,10-1,11-1,12-1,13-1,14-1,15-1,16-1,17-1,18-1,19-1,20-1,21-1,22-1,23-1,24-1

NRSV - **23,** 1-1,2-1,3-1,4-1,5-1,6-1,7-1,8-1,9-1,10-1,11-1,12-1,13-1,14-1,15-1,16-1,17-1,18-1,19-1,20-1,21-1,22-1,23-1

Conclusion: Only the NCV and the NLT made the verse more complex. The NCV is the most difficult to read.

180. Deuteronomy 33:6* Let **Reuben** live, and not die; and let not his men be few.
AV - **13,** 1-1,2-1,3-1,4-1,5-1,6-1,7-1,8-1,9-1,10-1,11-1,12-1,13-1
ESV - **12,** 1-1,2-1,3-1,4-1,5-1,6-1,7-1,8-1,9-1,10-1,11-1,12-1
HCSB - 11, 1-1,2-1,3-1,4-1,5-1,6-1,7-1,8-1,9-**2**,10-**2**,11-1
NASV - **11,** 1-1,2-1,3-1,4-1,5-1,6-1,7-1,8-1,9-1,10-1,11-1
NCV - 15, 1-1,2-1,3-**2**,4-1,5-1,6-1,7-1,8-1,9-1,10-1,11-1,12-1,13-**2**,14-1,15-1
NIV - **11,** 1-1,2-1,3-1,4-1,5-1,6-1,7-1,8-1,9-1,10-1,11-1
NKJV - **12,** 1-1,2-1,3-1,4-1,5-1,6-1,7-1,8-1,9-1,10-1,11-1,12-1
NLT - 24, 1-1,2-1,3-1,4-**2**,5-1,6-1,7-1,8-1,9-1,10-1,11-1,12-1,13-1,14-1,15-1,16-1,17-1,18-1,19-1,20-1,21-1,22-1,23-1,24-**2**
NRSV - 13, 1-1,2-1,3-1,4-1,5-1,6-1,7-1,8-**2**,9-1,10-1,11-**2**,12-1,13-1
Conclusion: Four modern versions are more complex than the King James Bible. The NLT stands out by how complicated it made a simple verse.

181. Deuteronomy 33:25 Thy shoes shall be iron and brass; and as thy days, so shall thy strength be.
AV - **16,** 1-1,2-1,3-1,4-1,5-1,6-1,7-1,8-1,9-1,10-1,11-1,12-1,13-1,14-1,15-1,16-1
ESV - **16,** 1-1,2-1,3-1,4-1,5-1,6-1,7-1,8-1,9-1,10-1,11-1,12-1,13-1,14-1,15-1,16-1
HCSB - **19,** 1-1,2-1,3-1,4-1,5-1,6-1,7-1,8-1,9-1,10-1,11-1,12-1,13-1,14-1,15-1,16-1,17-1,18-1,19-1
NASV - 18, 1-1,2-1,3-1,4-1,5-1,6-1,7-1,8-1,9-**3**,10-1,11-1,12-1,13-1,14-1,15-1,16-**3**,17-1,18-1
NCV - **19,** 1-1,2-1,3-1,4-1,5-1,6-1,7-1,8-1,9-1,10-1,11-1,12-1,13-1,14-1,15-1,16-1,17-1,18-1,19-1
NIV - 17, 1-1,2-1,3-1,4-1,5-1,6-1,7-1,8-1,9-1,10-1,11-1,12-1,13-1,14-1,15-**2**,16-1,17-1
NKJV - 15, 1-1,2-**2**,3-1,4-1,5-1,6-1,7-1,8-1,9-1,10-1,11-1,12-1,13-1,14-1,15-1
NLT - 18, 1-1,2-1,3-1,4-1,5-1,6-1,7-1,8-1,9-1,10-1,11-1,12-1,13-1,14-1,15-**3**,16-1,17-1,18-1
NRSV - **14,** 1-1,2-1,3-1,4-1,5-1,6-1,7-1,8-1,9-1,10-1,11-1,12-1,13-1,14-1
Conclusion: Four modern versions are more complex than the King James Bible.

182. Joshua 4:20* And those twelve stones, which they took out of **Jordan**, did **Joshua** pitch in **Gilgal**.
AV - **15,** 1-1,2-1,3-1,4-1,5-1,6-1,7-1,8-1,9-1,10-1,11-1,12-1,13-1,14-1,15-1
ESV - **16,** 1-1,2-1,3-1,4-1,5-1,6-1,7-1,8-1,9-1,10-1,11-1,12-1,13-1,14-1,15-1,16-1
HCSB - 15, 1-1,2-1,3-1,4-1,5-1,6-1,7-1,8-1,9-1,10-1,11-1,12-**2**,13-1,14-1,15-1
NASV - 15, 1-1,2-1,3-1,4-1,5-1,6-1,7-**2**,8-1,9-1,10-1,11-1,12-1,13-1,14-1,15-1
NCV - 18, 1-1,2-**2**,3-1,4-1,5-1,6-1,7-1,8-**2**,9-1,10-1,11-1,12-1,13-1,14-1,15-1,16-1,17-1,18-1
NIV - 16, 1-1,2-1,3-1,4-1,5-1,6-1,7-1,8-1,9-1,10-1,11-1,12-**2**,13-1,14-1,15-1,16-1

68

NKJV - **16,** 1-1,2-1,3-1,4-1,5-1,6-1,7-1,8-1,9-1,10-1,11-1,12-1,13-1,14-1,15-1,16-1
NLT - 17, 1-1,2-1,3-1,4-1,5-1,6-1,7-1,8-1,9-1,10-1,11-1,12-1,13-**2**,14-1,15-1,16-1,17-1
NRSV - 16, 1-1,2-1,3-1,4-1,5-1,6-1,7-**2**,8-1,9-1,10-1,11-1,12-1,13-1,14-1,15-1,16-1
Conclusion: Six modern versions are more complex than the King James Bible. The NCV made the verse most complex.

183. Joshua 11:18* Joshua made war a long time with all those kings.
AV - **10,** 1-1,2-1,3-1,4-1,5-1,6-1,7-1,8-1,9-1,10-1
ESV - **10,** 1-1,2-1,3-1,4-1,5-1,6-1,7-1,8-1,9-1,10-1
HCSB - **11,** 1-1,2-1,3-1,4-1,5-1,6-1,7-1,8-1,9-1,10-1,11-1
NASV - **10,** 1-1,2-1,3-1,4-1,5-1,6-1,7-1,8-1,9-1,10-1
NCV - 7, 1-1,2-1,3-**2**,4-1,5-1,6-**2**,7-1
NIV - 11, 1-1,2-1,3-1,4-**2**,5-1,6-1,7-1,8-1,9-1,10-1,11-1
NKJV - **10,** 1-1,2-1,3-1,4-1,5-1,6-1,7-1,8-1,9-1,10-1
NLT - 9, 1-**2**,2-1,3-1,4-1,5-1,6-1,7-1,8-**3**,9-1
NRSV - **10,** 1-1,2-1,3-1,4-1,5-1,6-1,7-1,8-1,9-1,10-1
Conclusion: Only three modern versions are more complex than the King James Bible. Ironically the NCV and NLT have the smallest word count but the highest syllable count.

184. Joshua 12:10* The king of **Jerusalem**, one; the king of **Hebron**, one;
AV - **10,** 1-1,2-1,3-1,4-1,5-1,6-1,7-1,8-1,9-1,10-1
ESV - **10,** 1-1,2-1,3-1,4-1,5-1,6-1,7-1,8-1,9-1,10-1
HCSB - **10,** 1-1,2-1,3-1,4-1,5-1,6-1,7-1,8-1,9-1,10-1
NASV - **10,** 1-1,2-1,3-1,4-1,5-1,6-1,7-1,8-1,9-1,10-1
NCV - **2,** 1-1,2-1
NIV - **10,** 1-1,2-1,3-1,4-1,5-1,6-1,7-1,8-1,9-1,10-1
NKJV - **10,** 1-1,2-1,3-1,4-1,5-1,6-1,7-1,8-1,9-1,10-1
NLT - **8,** 1-1,2-1,3-1,4-1,5-1,6-1,7-1,8-1
NRSV - **10,** 1-1,2-1,3-1,4-1,5-1,6-1,7-1,8-1,9-1,10-1
Conclusion: All versions read the same.

185. Joshua 12:11* The king of **Jarmuth**, one; the king of **Lachish**, one;
AV - **10,** 1-1,2-1,3-1,4-1,5-1,6-1,7-1,8-1,9-1,10-1
ESV - **10,** 1-1,2-1,3-1,4-1,5-1,6-1,7-1,8-1,9-1,10-1
HCSB - **10,** 1-1,2-1,3-1,4-1,5-1,6-1,7-1,8-1,9-1,10-1
NASV - **10,** 1-1,2-1,3-1,4-1,5-1,6-1,7-1,8-1,9-1,10-1
NCV - **2,** 1-1,2-1
NIV - **10,** 1-1,2-1,3-1,4-1,5-1,6-1,7-1,8-1,9-1,10-1
NKJV - **10,** 1-1,2-1,3-1,4-1,5-1,6-1,7-1,8-1,9-1,10-1
NLT - **8,** 1-1,2-1,3-1,4-1,5-1,6-1,7-1,8-1
NRSV - **10,** 1-1,2-1,3-1,4-1,5-1,6-1,7-1,8-1,9-1,10-1
Conclusion: All versions read the same.

186. Joshua 12:12* The king of **Eglon**, one; the king of **Gezer**, one;
AV - **10,** 1-1,2-1,3-1,4-1,5-1,6-1,7-1,8-1,9-1,10-1
ESV - **10,** 1-1,2-1,3-1,4-1,5-1,6-1,7-1,8-1,9-1,10-1
HCSB - **10,** 1-1,2-1,3-1,4-1,5-1,6-1,7-1,8-1,9-1,10-1
NASV - **10,** 1-1,2-1,3-1,4-1,5-1,6-1,7-1,8-1,9-1,10-1
NCV - **2,** 1-1,2-1
NIV - **10,** 1-1,2-1,3-1,4-1,5-1,6-1,7-1,8-1,9-1,10-1
NKJV - **10,** 1-1,2-1,3-1,4-1,5-1,6-1,7-1,8-1,9-1,10-1
NLT - **8,** 1-1,2-1,3-1,4-1,5-1,6-1,7-1,8-1
NRSV - **10,** 1-1,2-1,3-1,4-1,5-1,6-1,7-1,8-1,9-1,10-1
Conclusion: All versions read the same.

187. Joshua 12:13* The king of **Debir**, one; the king of **Geder**, one;
AV - **10,** 1-1,2-1,3-1,4-1,5-1,6-1,7-1,8-1,9-1,10-1
ESV - **10,** 1-1,2-1,3-1,4-1,5-1,6-1,7-1,8-1,9-1,10-1
HCSB - **10,** 1-1,2-1,3-1,4-1,5-1,6-1,7-1,8-1,9-1,10-1
NASV - **10,** 1-1,2-1,3-1,4-1,5-1,6-1,7-1,8-1,9-1,10-1
NCV - **2,** 1-1,2-1
NIV - **10,** 1-1,2-1,3-1,4-1,5-1,6-1,7-1,8-1,9-1,10-1
NKJV - **10,** 1-1,2-1,3-1,4-1,5-1,6-1,7-1,8-1,9-1,10-1
NLT - **8,** 1-1,2-1,3-1,4-1,5-1,6-1,7-1,8-1
NRSV - **10,** 1-1,2-1,3-1,4-1,5-1,6-1,7-1,8-1,9-1,10-1
Conclusion: All versions read the same.

188. Joshua 12:14* The king of **Hormah**, one; the king of **Arad**, one;
AV - **10,** 1-1,2-1,3-1,4-1,5-1,6-1,7-1,8-1,9-1,10-1
ESV - **10,** 1-1,2-1,3-1,4-1,5-1,6-1,7-1,8-1,9-1,10-1
HCSB - **10,** 1-1,2-1,3-1,4-1,5-1,6-1,7-1,8-1,9-1,10-1
NASV - **10,** 1-1,2-1,3-1,4-1,5-1,6-1,7-1,8-1,9-1,10-1
NCV - **2,** 1-1,2-1
NIV - **10,** 1-1,2-1,3-1,4-1,5-1,6-1,7-1,8-1,9-1,10-1
NKJV - **10,** 1-1,2-1,3-1,4-1,5-1,6-1,7-1,8-1,9-1,10-1
NLT - **8,** 1-1,2-1,3-1,4-1,5-1,6-1,7-1,8-1
NRSV - **10,** 1-1,2-1,3-1,4-1,5-1,6-1,7-1,8-1,9-1,10-1
Conclusion: All versions read the same.

189. Joshua 12:15* The king of **Libnah**, one; the king of **Adullam**, one;
AV - **10,** 1-1,2-1,3-1,4-1,5-1,6-1,7-1,8-1,9-1,10-1
ESV - **10,** 1-1,2-1,3-1,4-1,5-1,6-1,7-1,8-1,9-1,10-1
HCSB - **10,** 1-1,2-1,3-1,4-1,5-1,6-1,7-1,8-1,9-1,10-1
NASV - **10,** 1-1,2-1,3-1,4-1,5-1,6-1,7-1,8-1,9-1,10-1
NCV - **2,** 1-1,2-1
NIV - **10,** 1-1,2-1,3-1,4-1,5-1,6-1,7-1,8-1,9-1,10-1
NKJV - **10,** 1-1,2-1,3-1,4-1,5-1,6-1,7-1,8-1,9-1,10-1

NLT - **8,** 1-1,2-1,3-1,4-1,5-1,6-1,7-1,8-1
NRSV - **10,** 1-1,2-1,3-1,4-1,5-1,6-1,7-1,8-1,9-1,10-1
Conclusion: All versions read the same.

190. Joshua 12:16* The king of **Makkedah**, one; the king of **Bethel**, one;
AV - **10,** 1-1,2-1,3-1,4-1,5-1,6-1,7-1,8-1,9-1,10-1
ESV - **10,** 1-1,2-1,3-1,4-1,5-1,6-1,7-1,8-1,9-1,10-1
HCSB - **10,** 1-1,2-1,3-1,4-1,5-1,6-1,7-1,8-1,9-1,10-1
NASV - **10,** 1-1,2-1,3-1,4-1,5-1,6-1,7-1,8-1,9-1,10-1
NCV - **2,** 1-1,2-1
NIV - **10,** 1-1,2-1,3-1,4-1,5-1,6-1,7-1,8-1,9-1,10-1
NKJV - **10,** 1-1,2-1,3-1,4-1,5-1,6-1,7-1,8-1,9-1,10-1
NLT - **8,** 1-1,2-1,3-1,4-1,5-1,6-1,7-1,8-1
NRSV - **10,** 1-1,2-1,3-1,4-1,5-1,6-1,7-1,8-1,9-1,10-1
Conclusion: All versions read the same.

191. Joshua 12:17* The king of **Tappuah**, one; the king of **Hepher**, one;
AV - **10,** 1-1,2-1,3-1,4-1,5-1,6-1,7-1,8-1,9-1,10-1
ESV - **10,** 1-1,2-1,3-1,4-1,5-1,6-1,7-1,8-1,9-1,10-1
HCSB - **10,** 1-1,2-1,3-1,4-1,5-1,6-1,7-1,8-1,9-1,10-1
NASV - **10,** 1-1,2-1,3-1,4-1,5-1,6-1,7-1,8-1,9-1,10-1
NCV - **2,** 1-1,2-1
NIV - **10,** 1-1,2-1,3-1,4-1,5-1,6-1,7-1,8-1,9-1,10-1
NKJV - **10,** 1-1,2-1,3-1,4-1,5-1,6-1,7-1,8-1,9-1,10-1
NLT - **8,** 1-1,2-1,3-1,4-1,5-1,6-1,7-1,8-1
NRSV - **10,** 1-1,2-1,3-1,4-1,5-1,6-1,7-1,8-1,9-1,10-1
Conclusion: All versions read the same.

192. Joshua 12:18* The king of **Aphek**, one; the king of **Lasharon**, one;
AV - **10,** 1-1,2-1,3-1,4-1,5-1,6-1,7-1,8-1,9-1,10-1
ESV - **10,** 1-1,2-1,3-1,4-1,5-1,6-1,7-1,8-1,9-1,10-1
HCSB - **10,** 1-1,2-1,3-1,4-1,5-1,6-1,7-1,8-1,9-1,10-1
NASV - **10,** 1-1,2-1,3-1,4-1,5-1,6-1,7-1,8-1,9-1,10-1
NCV - **2,** 1-1,2-1
NIV - **10,** 1-1,2-1,3-1,4-1,5-1,6-1,7-1,8-1,9-1,10-1
NKJV - **10,** 1-1,2-1,3-1,4-1,5-1,6-1,7-1,8-1,9-1,10-1
NLT - **8,** 1-1,2-1,3-1,4-1,5-1,6-1,7-1,8-1
NRSV - **10,** 1-1,2-1,3-1,4-1,5-1,6-1,7-1,8-1,9-1,10-1
Conclusion: All versions read the same.

193. Joshua 12:19* The king of **Madon**, one; the king of **Hazor**, one;
AV - **10,** 1-1,2-1,3-1,4-1,5-1,6-1,7-1,8-1,9-1,10-1
ESV - **10,** 1-1,2-1,3-1,4-1,5-1,6-1,7-1,8-1,9-1,10-1
HCSB - **10,** 1-1,2-1,3-1,4-1,5-1,6-1,7-1,8-1,9-1,10-1

NASV - **10,** 1-1,2-1,3-1,4-1,5-1,6-1,7-1,8-1,9-1,10-1
NCV - **2,** 1-1,2-1
NIV - **10,** 1-1,2-1,3-1,4-1,5-1,6-1,7-1,8-1,9-1,10-1
NKJV - **10,** 1-1,2-1,3-1,4-1,5-1,6-1,7-1,8-1,9-1,10-1
NLT - **8,** 1-1,2-1,3-1,4-1,5-1,6-1,7-1,8-1
NRSV - **10,** 1-1,2-1,3-1,4-1,5-1,6-1,7-1,8-1,9-1,10-1
Conclusion: All versions read the same.

194. Joshua 12:20* The king of **Shimronmeron**, one; the king of **Achshaph**, one;
AV - **10,** 1-1,2-1,3-1,4-1,5-1,6-1,7-1,8-1,9-1,10-1
ESV - **10,** 1-1,2-1,3-1,4-1,5-1,6-1,7-1,8-1,9-1,10-1
HCSB - **10,** 1-1,2-1,3-1,4-1,5-1,6-1,7-1,8-1,9-1,10-1
NASV - **10,** 1-1,2-1,3-1,4-1,5-1,6-1,7-1,8-1,9-1,10-1
NCV - **3,** 1-1,2-1,3-1
NIV - **11,** 1-1,2-1,3-1,4-1,5-1,6-1,7-1,8-1,9-1,10-1,11-1
NKJV - **11,** 1-1,2-1,3-1,4-1,5-1,6-1,7-1,8-1,9-1,10-1,11-1
NLT - **8,** 1-1,2-1,3-1,4-1,5-1,6-1,7-1,8-1
NRSV - **10,** 1-1,2-1,3-1,4-1,5-1,6-1,7-1,8-1,9-1,10-1
Conclusion: All versions read the same.

195. Joshua 12:21* The king of **Taanach**, one; the king of **Megiddo**, one;
AV - **10,** 1-1,2-1,3-1,4-1,5-1,6-1,7-1,8-1,9-1,10-1
ESV - **10,** 1-1,2-1,3-1,4-1,5-1,6-1,7-1,8-1,9-1,10-1
HCSB - **10,** 1-1,2-1,3-1,4-1,5-1,6-1,7-1,8-1,9-1,10-1
NASV - **10,** 1-1,2-1,3-1,4-1,5-1,6-1,7-1,8-1,9-1,10-1
NCV - **2,** 1-1,2-1
NIV - **10,** 1-1,2-1,3-1,4-1,5-1,6-1,7-1,8-1,9-1,10-1
NKJV - **10,** 1-1,2-1,3-1,4-1,5-1,6-1,7-1,8-1,9-1,10-1
NLT - **8,** 1-1,2-1,3-1,4-1,5-1,6-1,7-1,8-1
NRSV - **10,** 1-1,2-1,3-1,4-1,5-1,6-1,7-1,8-1,9-1,10-1
Conclusion: All versions read the same.

196. Joshua 12:22* The king of **Kedesh**, one; the king of **Jokneam** of **Carmel**, one;
AV - **12,** 1-1,2-1,3-1,4-1,5-1,6-1,7-1,8-1,9-1,10-1,11-1,12-1
ESV - **12,** 1-1,2-1,3-1,4-1,5-1,6-1,7-1,8-1,9-1,10-1,11-1,12-1
HCSB - **12,** 1-1,2-1,3-1,4-1,5-1,6-1,7-1,8-1,9-1,10-1,11-1,12-1
NASV - **12,** 1-1,2-1,3-1,4-1,5-1,6-1,7-1,8-1,9-1,10-1,11-1,12-1
NCV - **4,** 1-1,2-1,3-1,4-1
NIV - **12,** 1-1,2-1,3-1,4-1,5-1,6-1,7-1,8-1,9-1,10-1,11-1,12-1
NKJV - **12,** 1-1,2-1,3-1,4-1,5-1,6-1,7-1,8-1,9-1,10-1,11-1,12-1
NLT - **10,** 1-1,2-1,3-1,4-1,5-1,6-1,7-1,8-1,9-1,10-1
NRSV - **12,** 1-1,2-1,3-1,4-1,5-1,6-1,7-1,8-1,9-1,10-1,11-1,12-1
Conclusion: All versions read the same.

197. Joshua 12:24*# The king of **Tirzah**, one: all the kings **thirty** and one.
AV - **11,** 1-1,2-1,3-1,4-1,5-1,6-1,7-1,8-1,9-1,10-1,11-1
ESV - **10,** 1-1,2-1,3-1,4-1,5-1,6-1,7-1,8-1,9-1,10-1
HCSB - 12, 1-1,2-1,3-1,4-1,5-1,6-1,7-**2**,8-**2**,9-1,10-1,11-1,12-1
NASV - **10,** 1-1,2-1,3-1,4-1,5-1,6-1,7-1,8-1,9-1,10-1
NCV - 9, 1-1,2-1,3-**2**,4-**2**,5-1,6-1,7-1,8-1,9-1
NIV - **10,** 1-1,2-1,3-1,4-1,5-1,6-1,7-1,8-1,9-1,10-1
NKJV - **10,** 1-1,2-1,3-1,4-1,5-1,6-1,7-1,8-1,9-1,10-1
NLT - 11, 1-1,2-1,3-1,4-1,5-1,6-1,7-1,8-1,9-1,10-1,11-**3**
NRSV - **10,** 1-1,2-1,3-1,4-1,5-1,6-1,7-1,8-1,9-1,10-1
Conclusion: Three modern versions are more complex than the King James Bible.

198. Joshua 13:18* And **Jahazah**, and **Kedemoth**, and **Mephaath**,
AV - **6,** 1-1,2-1,3-1,4-1,5-1,6-1
ESV - **6,** 1-1,2-1,3-1,4-1,5-1,6-1
HCSB - **3,** 1-1,2-1,3-1
NASV - **6,** 1-1,2-1,3-1,4-1,5-1,6-1
NCV - **3,** 1-1,2-1,3-1
NIV - **3,** 1-1,2-1,3-1
NKJV - **3,** 1-1,2-1,3-1
NLT - **3,** 1-1,2-1,3-1
NRSV - **6,** 1-1,2-1,3-1,4-1,5-1,6-1
Conclusion: All versions read the same.

199. Joshua 13:20* And **Bethpeor**, and **Ashdothpisgah**, and **Bethjeshimoth**,
AV - **6,** 1-1,2-1,3-1,4-1,5-1,6-1
ESV - **11,** 1-1,2-1,3-1,4-1,5-1,6-1,7-1,8-1,9-1,10-1,11-1
HCSB - **9,** 1-1,2-1,3-1,4-1,5-1,6-1,7-1,8-1,9-1
NASV - **11,** 1-1,2-1,3-1,4-1,5-1,6-1,7-1,8-1,9-1,10-1,11-1
NCV - **9,** 1-1,2-1,3-1,4-1,5-1,6-1,7-1,8-1,9-1
NIV - **9,** 1-1,2-1,3-1,4-1,5-1,6-1,7-1,8-1,9-1
NKJV - **9,** 1-1,2-1,3-1,4-1,5-1,6-1,7-1,8-1,9-1
NLT - **9,** 1-1,2-1,3-1,4-1,5-1,6-1,7-1,8-1,9-1
NRSV - **11,** 1-1,2-1,3-1,4-1,5-1,6-1,7-1,8-1,9-1,10-1,11-1
Conclusion: All versions read the same.

200. Joshua 15:22* And **Kinah**, and **Dimonah**, and **Adadah**,
AV - **6,** 1-1,2-1,3-1,4-1,5-1,6-1
ESV - **3,** 1-1,2-1,3-1
HCSB - **3,** 1-1,2-1,3-1
NASV - **6,** 1-1,2-1,3-1,4-1,5-1,6-1
NCV - **3,** 1-1,2-1,3-1
NIV - **3,** 1-1,2-1,3-1
NKJV - **3,** 1-1,2-1,3-1

NLT - **3,** 1-1,2-1,3-1
NRSV - **3,** 1-1,2-1,3-1
Conclusion: All versions read the same.

201. Joshua 15:23* And **Kedesh**, and **Hazor**, and **Ithnan**,
AV - **6,** 1-1,2-1,3-1,4-1,5-1,6-1
ESV - **3,** 1-1,2-1,3-1
HCSB - **3,** 1-1,2-1,3-1
NASV - **6,** 1-1,2-1,3-1,4-1,5-1,6-1
NCV - **3,** 1-1,2-1,3-1
NIV - **3,** 1-1,2-1,3-1
NKJV - **3,** 1-1,2-1,3-1
NLT - **3,** 1-1,2-1,3-1
NRSV - **3,** 1-1,2-1,3-1
Conclusion: All versions read the same.

202. Joshua 15:24* Ziph, and **Telem**, and **Bealoth**,
AV - **5,** 1-1,2-1,3-1,4-1,5-1
ESV - **3,** 1-1,2-1,3-1
HCSB - **3,** 1-1,2-1,3-1
NASV - **5,** 1-1,2-1,3-1,4-1,5-1
NCV - **3,** 1-1,2-1,3-1
NIV - **3,** 1-1,2-1,3-1
NKJV - **3,** 1-1,2-1,3-1
NLT - **3,** 1-1,2-1,3-1
NRSV - **3,** 1-1,2-1,3-1
Conclusion: All versions read the same.

203. Joshua 15:25* And **Hazor**, **Hadattah**, and **Kerioth**, and **Hezron**, which is **Hazor**,
AV - **10,** 1-1,2-1,3-1,4-1,5-1,6-1,7-1,8-1,9-1,10-1
ESV - **7,** 1-1,2-1,3-1,4-1,5-1,6-1,7-1
HCSB - **7,** 1-1,2-1,3-1,4-1,5-1,6-1,7-1
NASV - **9,** 1-1,2-1,3-1,4-1,5-1,6-1,7-1,8-1,9-1
NCV - 7, 1-1,2-1,3-1,4-1,5-**2**,6-1,7-1
NIV - **7,** 1-1,2-1,3-1,4-1,5-1,6-1,7-1
NKJV - **7,** 1-1,2-1,3-1,4-1,5-1,6-1,7-1
NLT - **7,** 1-1,2-1,3-1,4-1,5-1,6-1,7-1
NRSV - **7,** 1-1,2-1,3-1,4-1,5-1,6-1,7-1
Conclusion: Only the NCV made the verse more complex.

204. Joshua 15:26* **Amam**, and **Shema**, and **Moladah**,
AV - **5,** 1-1,2-1,3-1,4-1,5-1
ESV - **3,** 1-1,2-1,3-1
HCSB - **3,** 1-1,2-1,3-1

NASV - **5,** 1-1,2-1,3-1,4-1,5-1
NCV - **3,** 1-1,2-1,3-1
NIV - **3,** 1-1,2-1,3-1
NKJV - **3,** 1-1,2-1,3-1
NLT - **3,** 1-1,2-1,3-1
NRSV - **3,** 1-1,2-1,3-1
Conclusion: All versions read the same.

205. Joshua 15:27* And **Hazargaddah**, and **Heshmon**, and **Bethpalet**,
AV - **6,** 1-1,2-1,3-1,4-1,5-1,6-1
ESV - **5,** 1-1,2-1,3-1,4-1,5-1
HCSB - **5,** 1-1,2-1,3-1,4-1,5-1
NASV - **6,** 1-1,2-1,3-1,4-1,5-1,6-1
NCV - **5,** 1-1,2-1,3-1,4-1,5-1
NIV - **5,** 1-1,2-1,3-1,4-1,5-1
NKJV - **5,** 1-1,2-1,3-1,4-1,5-1
NLT - **5,** 1-1,2-1,3-1,4-1,5-1
NRSV - **5,** 1-1,2-1,3-1,4-1,5-1
Conclusion: All versions read the same.

206. Joshua 15:28* And **Hazarshual**, and **Beersheba**, and **Bizjothjah**,
AV - **6,** 1-1,2-1,3-1,4-1,5-1,6-1
ESV - **3,** 1-1,2-1,3-1
HCSB - **3,** 1-1,2-1,3-1
NASV - **6,** 1-1,2-1,3-1,4-1,5-1,6-1
NCV - **3,** 1-1,2-1,3-1
NIV - **3,** 1-1,2-1,3-1
NKJV - **3,** 1-1,2-1,3-1
NLT - **3,** 1-1,2-1,3-1
NRSV - **3,** 1-1,2-1,3-1
Conclusion: All versions read the same.

207. Joshua 15:29* **Baalah**, and Iim, and **Azem**,
AV - **5,** 1-1,2-1,3-1,4-1,5-1
ESV - **3,** 1-1,2-1,3-1
HCSB - **3,** 1-1,2-1,3-1
NASV - **5,** 1-1,2-1,3-1,4-1,5-1
NCV - **3,** 1-1,2-1,3-1
NIV - **3,** 1-1,2-1,3-1
NKJV - **3,** 1-1,2-1,3-1
NLT - **3,** 1-1,2-1,3-1
NRSV - **3,** 1-1,2-1,3-1
Conclusion: All versions read the same.

208. Joshua 15:30* And **Eltolad**, and **Chesil**, and **Hormah**,
AV - **6,** 1-1,2-1,3-1,4-1,5-1,6-1
ESV - **3,** 1-1,2-1,3-1
HCSB - **3,** 1-1,2-1,3-1
NASV - **6,** 1-1,2-1,3-1,4-1,5-1,6-1
NCV - **3,** 1-1,2-1,3-1
NIV - **3,** 1-1,2-1,3-1
NKJV - **3,** 1-1,2-1,3-1
NLT - **3,** 1-1,2-1,3-1
NRSV - **3,** 1-1,2-1,3-1
Conclusion: All versions read the same.

209. Joshua 15:31* And **Ziklag**, and **Madmannah**, and **Sansannah**,
AV - **6,** 1-1,2-1,3-1,4-1,5-1,6-1
ESV - **3,** 1-1,2-1,3-1
HCSB - **3,** 1-1,2-1,3-1
NASV - **6,** 1-1,2-1,3-1,4-1,5-1,6-1
NCV - **3,** 1-1,2-1,3-1
NIV - **3,** 1-1,2-1,3-1
NKJV - **3,** 1-1,2-1,3-1
NLT - **3,** 1-1,2-1,3-1
NRSV - **3,** 1-1,2-1,3-1
Conclusion: All versions read the same.

210. Joshua 15:34* And **Zanoah**, and **Engannim**, **Tappuah**, and **Enam**,
AV - **7,** 1-1,2-1,3-1,4-1,5-1,6-1,7-1
ESV - **4,** 1-1,2-1,3-1,4-1
HCSB - **4,** 1-1,2-1,3-1,4-1
NASV - **7,** 1-1,2-1,3-1,4-1,5-1,6-1,7-1
NCV - **4,** 1-1,2-1,3-1,4-1
NIV - **4,** 1-1,2-1,3-1,4-1
NKJV - **4,** 1-1,2-1,3-1,4-1
NLT - **4,** 1-1,2-1,3-1,4-1
NRSV - **4,** 1-1,2-1,3-1,4-1
Conclusion: All versions read the same.

211. Joshua 15:35* **Jarmuth**, and **Adullam**, **Socoh**, and **Azekah**,
AV - **6,** 1-1,2-1,3-1,4-1,5-1,6-1
ESV - **4,** 1-1,2-1,3-1,4-1
HCSB - **4,** 1-1,2-1,3-1,4-1
NASV - **6,** 1-1,2-1,3-1,4-1,5-1,6-1
NCV - **4,** 1-1,2-1,3-1,4-1
NIV - **4,** 1-1,2-1,3-1,4-1
NKJV - **4,** 1-1,2-1,3-1,4-1

NLT - **4,** 1-1,2-1,3-1,4-1
NRSV - **4,** 1-1,2-1,3-1,4-1
Conclusion: All versions read the same.

212. Joshua 15:37* Zenan, and **Hadashah,** and **Migdalgad,**
AV - **5,** 1-1,2-1,3-1,4-1,5-1
ESV - **3,** 1-1,2-1,3-1
HCSB - **3,** 1-1,2-1,3-1
NASV - **5,** 1-1,2-1,3-1,4-1,5-1
NCV - 14, 1-1,2-1,3-**2,**4-**2,**5-1,6-1,7-1,8-1,9-**2,**10-1,11-1,12-1,13-1,14-1
NIV - **4,** 1-1,2-1,3-1,4-1
NKJV - **4,** 1-1,2-1,3-1,4-1
NLT - 6, 1-**2,**2-**3,**3-1,4-1,5-1,6-1
NRSV - **3,** 1-1,2-1,3-1
Conclusion: Only the NCV and the NLT made the verse more complex.

213. Joshua 15:38* And **Dilean,** and **Mizpeh,** and **Joktheel,**
AV - **6,** 1-1,2-1,3-1,4-1,5-1,6-1
ESV - **3,** 1-1,2-1,3-1
HCSB - **3,** 1-1,2-1,3-1
NASV - **6,** 1-1,2-1,3-1,4-1,5-1,6-1
NCV - **3,** 1-1,2-1,3-1
NIV - **3,** 1-1,2-1,3-1
NKJV - **3,** 1-1,2-1,3-1
NLT - **3,** 1-1,2-1,3-1
NRSV - **3,** 1-1,2-1,3-1
Conclusion: All versions read the same.

214. Joshua 15:39* Lachish, and **Bozkath,** and **Eglon,**
AV - **5,** 1-1,2-1,3-1,4-1,5-1
ESV - **3,** 1-1,2-1,3-1
HCSB - **3,** 1-1,2-1,3-1
NASV - **5,** 1-1,2-1,3-1,4-1,5-1
NCV - **3,** 1-1,2-1,3-1
NIV - **3,** 1-1,2-1,3-1
NKJV - **3,** 1-1,2-1,3-1
NLT - **3,** 1-1,2-1,3-1
NRSV - **3,** 1-1,2-1,3-1
Conclusion: All versions read the same.

215. Joshua 15:40* And **Cabbon,** and **Lahmam,** and **Kithlish,**
AV - **6,** 1-1,2-1,3-1,4-1,5-1,6-1
ESV - **3,** 1-1,2-1,3-1
HCSB - **3,** 1-1,2-1,3-1

NASV - **6,** 1-1,2-1,3-1,4-1,5-1,6-1
NCV - **3,** 1-1,2-1,3-1
NIV - **3,** 1-1,2-1,3-1
NKJV - **3,** 1-1,2-1,3-1
NLT - **3,** 1-1,2-1,3-1
NRSV - **3,** 1-1,2-1,3-1
Conclusion: All versions read the same.

216. Joshua 15:42* Libnah, and **Ether**, and **Ashan**,
AV - **5,** 1-1,2-1,3-1,4-1,5-1
ESV - **3,** 1-1,2-1,3-1
HCSB - **3,** 1-1,2-1,3-1
NASV - **5,** 1-1,2-1,3-1,4-1,5-1
NCV - 13, 1-1,2-1,3-**2**,4-**2**,5-1,6-1,7-1,8-1,9-**2**,10-1,11-1,12-1,13-1
NIV - **3,** 1-1,2-1,3-1
NKJV - **3,** 1-1,2-1,3-1
NLT - 7, 1-**2**,2-1,3-1,4-1,5-1,6-1,7-1
NRSV - **3,** 1-1,2-1,3-1
Conclusion: Only the NCV and the NLT made the verse more complex.

217. Joshua 15:43* And Jiphtah, and **Ashnah**, and **Nezib**,
AV - **6,** 1-1,2-1,3-1,4-1,5-1,6-1
ESV - **3,** 1-1,2-1,3-1
HCSB - **3,** 1-1,2-1,3-1
NASV - **6,** 1-1,2-1,3-1,4-1,5-1,6-1
NCV - **3,** 1-1,2-1,3-1
NIV - **3,** 1-1,2-1,3-1
NKJV - **3,** 1-1,2-1,3-1
NLT - **3,** 1-1,2-1,3-1
NRSV - **3,** 1-1,2-1,3-1
Conclusion: All versions read the same.

218. Joshua 15:49* And Dannah, and **Kirjathsannah**, which is **Debir**,
AV - **7,** 1-1,2-1,3-1,4-1,5-1,6-1,7-1
ESV - **6,** 1-1,2-1,3-1,4-1,5-1,6-1
HCSB - **6,** 1-1,2-1,3-1,4-1,5-1,6-1
NASV - **8,** 1-1,2-1,3-1,4-1,5-1,6-1,7-1,8-1
NCV - 6, 1-1,2-1,3-1,4-**2**,5-1,6-1
NIV - **6,** 1-1,2-1,3-1,4-1,5-1,6-1
NKJV - **6,** 1-1,2-1,3-1,4-1,5-1,6-1
NLT - **6,** 1-1,2-1,3-1,4-1,5-1,6-1
NRSV - **6,** 1-1,2-1,3-1,4-1,5-1,6-1
Conclusion: Only the NCV made the verse more complex.

219. Joshua 15:50* And **Anab**, and **Eshtemoh**, and **Anim**,
AV - **6,** 1-1,2-1,3-1,4-1,5-1,6-1
ESV - **3,** 1-1,2-1,3-1
HCSB - **3,** 1-1,2-1,3-1
NASV - **6,** 1-1,2-1,3-1,4-1,5-1,6-1
NCV - **3,** 1-1,2-1,3-1
NIV - **3,** 1-1,2-1,3-1
NKJV - **3,** 1-1,2-1,3-1
NLT - **3,** 1-1,2-1,3-1
NRSV - **3,** 1-1,2-1,3-1
Conclusion: All versions read the same.

220. Joshua 15:52* **Arab**, and **Dumah**, and **Eshean**,
AV - **5,** 1-1,2-1,3-1,4-1,5-1
ESV - **3,** 1-1,2-1,3-1
HCSB - **3,** 1-1,2-1,3-1
NASV - **5,** 1-1,2-1,3-1,4-1,5-1
NCV - 12, 1-1,2-1,3-**2,**4-**2,**5-1,6-1,7-1,8-1,9-**2,**10-1,11-1,12-1
NIV - **3,** 1-1,2-1,3-1
NKJV - **3,** 1-1,2-1,3-1
NLT - 9, 1-**2,**2-**3,**3-1,4-1,5-1,6-1,7-1,8-1,9-1
NRSV - **3,** 1-1,2-1,3-1
Conclusion: Only the NCV and the NLT made the verse more complex.

221. Joshua 15:53* And **Janum**, and **Bethtappuah**, and **Aphekah**,
AV - **6,** 1-1,2-1,3-1,4-1,5-1,6-1
ESV - **3,** 1-1,2-1,3-1
HCSB - **3,** 1-1,2-1,3-1
NASV - **6,** 1-1,2-1,3-1,4-1,5-1,6-1
NCV - **3,** 1-1,2-1,3-1
NIV - **4,** 1-1,2-1,3-1,4-1
NKJV - **4,** 1-1,2-1,3-1,4-1
NLT - **3,** 1-1,2-1,3-1
NRSV - **3,** 1-1,2-1,3-1
Conclusion: All versions read the same.

222. Joshua 15:55* **Maon**, **Carmel**, and **Ziph**, and **Juttah**,
AV - **6,** 1-1,2-1,3-1,4-1,5-1,6-1
ESV - **4,** 1-1,2-1,3-1,4-1
HCSB - **4,** 1-1,2-1,3-1,4-1
NASV - **6,** 1-1,2-1,3-1,4-1,5-1,6-1
NCV - 13, 1-1,2-1,3-**2,**4-**2,**5-1,6-1,7-1,8-1,9-**2,**10-1,11-1,12-1,13-1
NIV - **4,** 1-1,2-1,3-1,4-1
NKJV - **4,** 1-1,2-1,3-1,4-1

NLT - 8, 1-**2**,2-1,3-1,4-1,5-1,6-1,7-1,8-1
NRSV - **4,** 1-1,2-1,3-1,4-1
Conclusion: Only the NCV and the NLT made the verse more complex.

223. Joshua 15:56* And **Jezreel**, and **Jokdeam**, and **Zanoah**,
AV - **6,** 1-1,2-1,3-1,4-1,5-1,6-1
ESV - **3,** 1-1,2-1,3-1
HCSB - **3,** 1-1,2-1,3-1
NASV - **6,** 1-1,2-1,3-1,4-1,5-1,6-1
NCV - **3,** 1-1,2-1,3-1
NIV - **3,** 1-1,2-1,3-1
NKJV - **3,** 1-1,2-1,3-1
NLT - **3,** 1-1,2-1,3-1
NRSV - **3,** 1-1,2-1,3-1
Conclusion: All versions read the same.

224. Joshua 15:58* **Halhul**, **Bethzur**, and **Gedor**,
AV - **4,** 1-1,2-1,3-1,4-1
ESV - **3,** 1-1,2-1,3-1
HCSB - **3,** 1-1,2-1,3-1
NASV - **4,** 1-1,2-1,3-1,4-1
NCV - 13, 1-1,2-1,3-**2**,4-**2**,5-1,6-1,7-1,8-1,9-**2**,10-1,11-1,12-1,13-1
NIV - **4,** 1-1,2-1,3-1,4-1
NKJV - **4,** 1-1,2-1,3-1,4-1
NLT - 7, 1-1,2-**3**,3-1,4-1,5-1,6-1,7-1
NRSV - **3,** 1-1,2-1,3-1
Conclusion: Only the NCV and the NLT made the verse more complex.

225. Joshua 16:7* And it went down from **Janohah** to **Ataroth**, and to **Naarath**, and came to **Jericho**, and went out at **Jordan**.
AV - **20,** 1-1,2-1,3-1,4-1,5-1,6-1,7-1,8-1,9-1,10-1,11-1,12-1,13-1,14-1,15-1,16-1,17-1,18-1,19-1,20-1
ESV - 18, 1-1,2-1,3-1,4-1,5-1,6-1,7-1,8-1,9-1,10-1,11-1,12-1,13-**2**,14-1,15-**2**,16-1,17-1,18-1
HCSB - 17, 1-1,2-1,3-1,4-**3**,5-1,6-1,7-1,8-1,9-1,10-1,11-1,12-1,13-1,14-1,15-1,16-1,17-1
NASV - **19,** 1-1,2-1,3-1,4-1,5-1,6-1,7-1,8-1,9-1,10-1,11-1,12-1,13-1,14-1,15-1,16-1,17-1,18-1,19-1
NCV - 23, 1-1,2-1,3-1,4-1,5-1,6-1,7-1,8-1,9-1,10-1,11-1,12-1,13-**3**,14-**2**,15-1,16-1,17-1,18-1,19-1,20-1,21-1,22-1,23-**2**
NIV - **18,** 1-1,2-1,3-1,4-1,5-1,6-1,7-1,8-1,9-1,10-1,11-1,12-1,13-1,14-1,15-1,16-1,17-1,18-1
NKJV - **19,** 1-1,2-1,3-1,4-1,5-1,6-1,7-1,8-1,9-1,10-1,11-1,12-1,13-1,14-1,15-1,16-1,17-1,18-1,19-1
NLT - 17, 1-1,2-1,3-1,4-1,5-**2**,6-1,7-1,8-1,9-1,10-1,11-1,12-1,13-**2**,14-1,15-1,16-1,17-**2**
NRSV - 18, 1-1,2-1,3-1,4-1,5-1,6-1,7-1,8-1,9-1,10-1,11-1,12-1,13-**2**,14-1,15-**2**,16-1,17-1,18-1
Conclusion: Five modern versions are more complex than the King James Bible.

226. Joshua 18:22* And **Betharabah**, and **Zemaraim**, and **Bethel**,
AV - **6,** 1-1,2-1,3-1,4-1,5-1,6-1
ESV - **3,** 1-1,2-1,3-1
HCSB - **3,** 1-1,2-1,3-1
NASV - **6,** 1-1,2-1,3-1,4-1,5-1,6-1
NCV - **3,** 1-1,2-1,3-1
NIV - **4,** 1-1,2-1,3-1,4-1
NKJV - **4,** 1-1,2-1,3-1,4-1
NLT - **3,** 1-1,2-1,3-1
NRSV - **3,** 1-1,2-1,3-1
Conclusion: All versions read the same.

227. Joshua 18:23* And **Avim**, and **Pharah**, and **Ophrah**,
AV - **6,** 1-1,2-1,3-1,4-1,5-1,6-1
ESV - **3,** 1-1,2-1,3-1
HCSB - **3,** 1-1,2-1,3-1
NASV - **6,** 1-1,2-1,3-1,4-1,5-1,6-1
NCV - **3,** 1-1,2-1,3-1
NIV - **3,** 1-1,2-1,3-1
NKJV - **3,** 1-1,2-1,3-1
NLT - **3,** 1-1,2-1,3-1
NRSV - **3,** 1-1,2-1,3-1
Conclusion: All versions read the same.

228. Joshua 18:25* **Gibeon**, and **Ramah**, and **Beeroth**,
AV - **5,** 1-1,2-1,3-1,4-1,5-1
ESV - **3,** 1-1,2-1,3-1
HCSB - **3,** 1-1,2-1,3-1
NASV - **5,** 1-1,2-1,3-1,4-1,5-1
NCV - 9, 1-1,2-1,3-1,4-1,5-**2,**6-**2,**7-1,8-1,9-1
NIV - **3,** 1-1,2-1,3-1
NKJV - **3,** 1-1,2-1,3-1
NLT - 4, 1-**2,**2-1,3-1,4-1
NRSV - **3,** 1-1,2-1,3-1
Conclusion: Only the NCV and the NLT made the verse more complex.

229. Joshua 18:26* And **Mizpeh**, and **Chephirah**, and **Mozah**,
AV - **6,** 1-1,2-1,3-1,4-1,5-1,6-1
ESV - **3,** 1-1,2-1,3-1
HCSB - **3,** 1-1,2-1,3-1
NASV - **6,** 1-1,2-1,3-1,4-1,5-1,6-1
NCV - **3,** 1-1,2-1,3-1
NIV - **3,** 1-1,2-1,3-1
NKJV - **3,** 1-1,2-1,3-1

NLT - **3,** 1-1,2-1,3-1
NRSV - **3,** 1-1,2-1,3-1
Conclusion: All versions read the same.

230. Joshua 18:27* And **Rekem**, and **Irpeel**, and **Taralah**,
AV - **6,** 1-1,2-1,3-1,4-1,5-1,6-1
ESV - **3,** 1-1,2-1,3-1
HCSB - **3,** 1-1,2-1,3-1
NASV - **6,** 1-1,2-1,3-1,4-1,5-1,6-1
NCV - **3,** 1-1,2-1,3-1
NIV - **3,** 1-1,2-1,3-1
NKJV - **3,** 1-1,2-1,3-1
NLT - **3,** 1-1,2-1,3-1
NRSV - **3,** 1-1,2-1,3-1
Conclusion: All versions read the same.

231. Joshua 19:3* And **Hazarshual**, and **Balah**, and **Azem**,
AV - **6,** 1-1,2-1,3-1,4-1,5-1,6-1
ESV - **3,** 1-1,2-1,3-1
HCSB - **3,** 1-1,2-1,3-1
NASV - **6,** 1-1,2-1,3-1,4-1,5-1,6-1
NCV - **4,** 1-1,2-1,3-1,4-1
NIV - **4,** 1-1,2-1,3-1,4-1
NKJV - **4,** 1-1,2-1,3-1,4-1
NLT - **3,** 1-1,2-1,3-1
NRSV - **3,** 1-1,2-1,3-1
Conclusion: All versions read the same.

232. Joshua 19:4* And **Eltolad**, and **Bethul**, and **Hormah**,
AV - **6,** 1-1,2-1,3-1,4-1,5-1,6-1
ESV - **3,** 1-1,2-1,3-1
HCSB - **3,** 1-1,2-1,3-1
NASV - **6,** 1-1,2-1,3-1,4-1,5-1,6-1
NCV - **3,** 1-1,2-1,3-1
NIV - **3,** 1-1,2-1,3-1
NKJV - **3,** 1-1,2-1,3-1
NLT - **3,** 1-1,2-1,3-1
NRSV - **3,** 1-1,2-1,3-1
Conclusion: All versions read the same.

233. Joshua 19:5* And **Ziklag**, and **Bethmarcaboth**, and **Hazarsusah**,
AV - **6,** 1-1,2-1,3-1,4-1,5-1,6-1
ESV - **3,** 1-1,2-1,3-1
HCSB - **3,** 1-1,2-1,3-1

NASV - **6,** 1-1,2-1,3-1,4-1,5-1,6-1
NCV - **5,** 1-1,2-1,3-1,4-1,5-1
NIV - **5,** 1-1,2-1,3-1,4-1,5-1
NKJV - **5,** 1-1,2-1,3-1,4-1,5-1
NLT - **3,** 1-1,2-1,3-1
NRSV - **3,** 1-1,2-1,3-1
Conclusion: All versions read the same.

234. Joshua 19:19* And **Haphraim**, and **Shihon**, and **Anaharath**,
AV - **6,** 1-1,2-1,3-1,4-1,5-1,6-1
ESV - **3,** 1-1,2-1,3-1
HCSB - **3,** 1-1,2-1,3-1
NASV - **6,** 1-1,2-1,3-1,4-1,5-1,6-1
NCV - **3,** 1-1,2-1,3-1
NIV - **3,** 1-1,2-1,3-1
NKJV - **3,** 1-1,2-1,3-1
NLT - **3,** 1-1,2-1,3-1
NRSV - **3,** 1-1,2-1,3-1
Conclusion: All versions read the same.

235. Joshua 19:20* And **Rabbith**, and **Kishion**, and **Abez**,
AV - **6,** 1-1,2-1,3-1,4-1,5-1,6-1
ESV - **3,** 1-1,2-1,3-1
HCSB - **3,** 1-1,2-1,3-1
NASV - **6,** 1-1,2-1,3-1,4-1,5-1,6-1
NCV - **3,** 1-1,2-1,3-1
NIV - **3,** 1-1,2-1,3-1
NKJV - **3,** 1-1,2-1,3-1
NLT - **3,** 1-1,2-1,3-1
NRSV - **3,** 1-1,2-1,3-1
Conclusion: All versions read the same.

236. Joshua 19:21* And **Remeth**, and **Engannim**, and **Enhaddah**, and **Bethpazzez**;
AV - **8,** 1-1,2-1,3-1,4-1,5-1,6-1,7-1,8-1
ESV - **4,** 1-1,2-1,3-1,4-1
HCSB - **4,** 1-1,2-1,3-1,4-1
NASV - **8,** 1-1,2-1,3-1,4-1,5-1,6-1,7-1,8-1
NCV - **8,** 1-1,2-1,3-1,4-1,5-1,6-1,7-1,8-1
NIV - **8,** 1-1,2-1,3-1,4-1,5-1,6-1,7-1,8-1
NKJV - **8,** 1-1,2-1,3-1,4-1,5-1,6-1,7-1,8-1
NLT - **5,** 1-1,2-1,3-1,4-1,5-1
NRSV - **4,** 1-1,2-1,3-1,4-1
Conclusion: All versions read the same.

237. Joshua 19:36* And **Adamah**, and **Ramah**, and **Hazor**,
AV - **6,** 1-1,2-1,3-1,4-1,5-1,6-1
ESV - **3,** 1-1,2-1,3-1
HCSB - **3,** 1-1,2-1,3-1
NASV - **6,** 1-1,2-1,3-1,4-1,5-1,6-1
NCV - **3,** 1-1,2-1,3-1
NIV - **3,** 1-1,2-1,3-1
NKJV - **3,** 1-1,2-1,3-1
NLT - **3,** 1-1,2-1,3-1
NRSV - **3,** 1-1,2-1,3-1
Conclusion: All versions read the same.

238. Joshua 19:37* And **Kedesh**, and **Edrei**, and **Enhazor**,
AV - **6,** 1-1,2-1,3-1,4-1,5-1,6-1
ESV - **3,** 1-1,2-1,3-1
HCSB - **3,** 1-1,2-1,3-1
NASV - **6,** 1-1,2-1,3-1,4-1,5-1,6-1
NCV - **4,** 1-1,2-1,3-1,4-1
NIV - **4,** 1-1,2-1,3-1,4-1
NKJV - **4,** 1-1,2-1,3-1,4-1
NLT - **3,** 1-1,2-1,3-1
NRSV - **3,** 1-1,2-1,3-1
Conclusion: All versions read the same.

239. Joshua 19:42* And **Shaalabbin**, and **Ajalon**, and **Jethlah**,
AV - **6,** 1-1,2-1,3-1,4-1,5-1,6-1
ESV - **3,** 1-1,2-1,3-1
HCSB - **3,** 1-1,2-1,3-1
NASV - **6,** 1-1,2-1,3-1,4-1,5-1,6-1
NCV - **3,** 1-1,2-1,3-1
NIV - **3,** 1-1,2-1,3-1
NKJV - **3,** 1-1,2-1,3-1
NLT - **3,** 1-1,2-1,3-1
NRSV - **3,** 1-1,2-1,3-1
Conclusion: All versions read the same.

240. Joshua 19:43* And **Elon**, and **Thimnathah**, and **Ekron**,
AV - **6,** 1-1,2-1,3-1,4-1,5-1,6-1
ESV - **3,** 1-1,2-1,3-1
HCSB - **3,** 1-1,2-1,3-1
NASV - **6,** 1-1,2-1,3-1,4-1,5-1,6-1
NCV - **3,** 1-1,2-1,3-1
NIV - **3,** 1-1,2-1,3-1
NKJV - **3,** 1-1,2-1,3-1

NLT - **3,** 1-1,2-1,3-1
NRSV - **3,** 1-1,2-1,3-1
Conclusion: All versions read the same.

241. Joshua 19:44* And **Eltekeh**, and **Gibbethon**, and **Baalath**,
AV - **6,** 1-1,2-1,3-1,4-1,5-1,6-1
ESV - **3,** 1-1,2-1,3-1
HCSB - **3,** 1-1,2-1,3-1
NASV - **6,** 1-1,2-1,3-1,4-1,5-1,6-1
NCV - **3,** 1-1,2-1,3-1
NIV - **3,** 1-1,2-1,3-1
NKJV - **3,** 1-1,2-1,3-1
NLT - **3,** 1-1,2-1,3-1
NRSV - **3,** 1-1,2-1,3-1
Conclusion: All versions read the same.

242. Joshua 19:45* And **Jehud**, and **Beneberak**, and **Gathrimmon**,
AV - **6,** 1-1,2-1,3-1,4-1,5-1,6-1
ESV - **3,** 1-1,2-1,3-1
HCSB - **3,** 1-1,2-1,3-1
NASV - **6,** 1-1,2-1,3-1,4-1,5-1,6-1
NCV - **5,** 1-1,2-1,3-1,4-1,5-1
NIV - **5,** 1-1,2-1,3-1,4-1,5-1
NKJV - **5,** 1-1,2-1,3-1,4-1,5-1
NLT - **3,** 1-1,2-1,3-1
NRSV - **3,** 1-1,2-1,3-1
Conclusion: All versions read the same.

243. Joshua 22:1* Then **Joshua** called the **Reubenites**, and the **Gadites**, and the half tribe of **Manasseh**,
AV - **14,** 1-1,2-1,3-1,4-1,5-1,6-1,7-1,8-1,9-1,10-1,11-1,12-1,13-1,14-1
ESV - **16,** 1-1,2-1,3-1,4-1,5-**2**,6-1,7-1,8-1,9-1,10-1,11-1,12-1,13-1,14-1,15-1,16-1
HCSB - **11,** 1-1,2-**2**,3-1,4-1,5-1,6-1,7-1,8-1,9-1,10-1,11-1
NASV - **14,** 1-1,2-1,3-**2**,4-1,5-1,6-1,7-1,8-1,9-1,10-1,11-1,12-1,13-1,14-1
NCV - **18,** 1-1,2-1,3-1,4-1,5-**2**,6-1,7-1,8-1,9-**2**,10-1,11-1,12-1,13-1,14-1,15-1,16-1,17-1,18-1
NIV - **13,** 1-1,2-1,3-**2**,4-1,5-1,6-1,7-1,8-1,9-1,10-1,11-1,12-1,13-1
NKJV - **13,** 1-1,2-1,3-1,4-1,5-1,6-1,7-1,8-1,9-1,10-1,11-1,12-1,13-1
NLT - **15,** 1-1,2-1,3-1,4-**3**,5-1,6-1,7-1,8-1,9-1,10-1,11-1,12-1,13-1,14-1,15-1
NRSV - **13,** 1-1,2-1,3-**2**,4-1,5-1,6-1,7-1,8-1,9-1,10-1,11-1,12-1,13-1
Conclusion: Seven modern versions are more complex than the King James Bible.

244. Judges 3:11*# And the land had rest **forty** years. And **Othniel** the son of **Kenaz** died.
AV - **14,** 1-1,2-1,3-1,4-1,5-1,6-1,7-1,8-1,9-1,10-1,11-1,12-1,13-1,14-1
ESV - **14,** 1-1,2-1,3-1,4-1,5-1,6-1,7-1,8-1,9-1,10-1,11-1,12-1,13-1,14-1

HCSB - **13,** 1-1,2-1,3-1,4-1,5-**2**,6-1,7-1,8-1,9-1,10-1,11-1,12-1,13-1
NASV - **14,** 1-1,2-1,3-1,4-1,5-1,6-1,7-1,8-1,9-1,10-1,11-1,12-1,13-1,14-1
NCV - **15,** 1-1,2-1,3-1,4-1,5-1,6-1,7-1,8-1,9-1,10-1,11-1,12-1,13-1,14-1,15-1
NIV - **14,** 1-1,2-1,3-1,4-1,5-1,6-1,7-1,8-1,9-**2**,10-1,11-1,12-1,13-1,14-1
NKJV - **15,** 1-1,2-1,3-1,4-1,5-1,6-1,7-1,8-1,9-1,10-1,11-1,12-1,13-1,14-1,15-1
NLT - **16,** 1-1,2-1,3-1,4-1,5-1,6-1,7-1,8-1,9-1,10-1,11-1,12-1,13-1,14-1,15-1,16-1
NRSV - **13,** 1-1,2-1,3-1,4-1,5-1,6-1,7-1,8-1,9-1,10-1,11-1,12-1,13-1
Conclusion: Only the HCSB and the NIV made the verse more complex.

245. Judges 4:10*# And **Barak** called **Zebulun** and **Naphtali** to **Kedesh**; and he went up with ten **thousand** men at his feet: and **Deborah** went up with him.
AV - **25,** 1-1,2-1,3-1,4-1,5-1,6-1,7-1,8-1,9-1,10-1,11-1,12-1,13-1,14-1,15-1,16-1,17-1,18-1,19-1,20-1,21-1,22-1,23-1,24-1,25-1
ESV - **23,** 1-1,2-1,3-1,4-1,5-1,6-1,7-1,8-1,9-1,10-1,11-1,12-1,13-1,14-1,15-1,16-1,17-1,18-1,19-1,20-1,21-1,22-1,23-1
HCSB - **17,** 1-1,2-**2**,3-1,4-1,5-1,6-1,7-1,8-1,9-1,10-**2**,11-1,12-1,13-1,14-**2**,15-1,16-1,17-1
NASV - **22,** 1-1,2-1,3-1,4-1,5-1,6-**3**,7-1,8-1,9-1,10-1,11-1,12-1,13-1,14-1,15-1,16-1,17-1,18-**2**,19-1,20-1,21-1,22-1
NCV - **27,** 1-1,2-1,3-1,4-1,5-1,6-**2**,7-1,8-1,9-1,10-1,11-**3**,12-1,13-1,14-1,15-**2**,16-1,17-1,18-1,19-1,20-**2**,21-1,22-1,23-1,24-1,25-1,26-1,27-1
NIV - **17,** 1-1,2-1,3-**2**,4-1,5-1,6-1,7-1,8-1,9-1,10-**2**,11-1,12-1,13-1,14-**2**,15-1,16-1,17-1
NKJV - **24,** 1-1,2-1,3-1,4-1,5-1,6-1,7-1,8-1,9-1,10-1,11-1,12-1,13-1,14-1,15-1,16-**2**,17-1,18-**2**,19-1,20-1,21-1,22-1,23-1,24-1
NLT - **23,** 1-1,2-1,3-1,4-1,5-**3**,6-1,7-1,8-1,9-1,10-1,11-1,12-1,13-1,14-**3**,15-1,16-1,17-1,18-1,19-1,20-**2**,21-1,22-1,23-1
NRSV - **21,** 1-1,2-**2**,3-1,4-1,5-1,6-1,7-1,8-1,9-1,10-1,11-**3**,12-1,13-1,14-**2**,15-1,16-1,17-1,18-1,19-1,20-1,21-1
Conclusion: Seven modern versions are more complex than the King James Bible.

246. Judges 4:12* And they shewed **Sisera** that **Barak** the son of **Abinoam** was gone up to mount **Tabor**.
AV - **16,** 1-1,2-1,3-1,4-1,5-1,6-1,7-1,8-1,9-1,10-1,11-1,12-1,13-1,14-1,15-1,16-1
ESV - **16,** 1-1,2-1,3-1,4-1,5-1,6-1,7-1,8-1,9-1,10-1,11-1,12-1,13-1,14-1,15-1,16-1
HCSB - **15,** 1-1,2-1,3-**3**,4-1,5-1,6-1,7-1,8-1,9-1,10-1,11-1,12-1,13-1,14-1,15-1
NASV - **16,** 1-1,2-1,3-1,4-1,5-1,6-1,7-1,8-1,9-1,10-1,11-1,12-1,13-1,14-1,15-1,16-1
NCV - **14,** 1-1,2-1,3-1,4-1,5-1,6-1,7-1,8-1,9-1,10-1,11-1,12-1,13-1,14-1
NIV - **15,** 1-1,2-1,3-1,4-1,5-1,6-1,7-1,8-1,9-1,10-1,11-1,12-1,13-1,14-1,15-1
NKJV - **17,** 1-1,2-1,3-**3**,4-1,5-1,6-1,7-1,8-1,9-1,10-1,11-1,12-1,13-1,14-1,15-1,16-1,17-1
NLT - **15,** 1-1,2-1,3-1,4-1,5-1,6-1,7-1,8-1,9-1,10-1,11-1,12-1,13-1,14-1,15-1
NRSV - **15,** 1-1,2-1,3-1,4-1,5-1,6-1,7-1,8-1,9-1,10-1,11-1,12-1,13-1,14-1,15-1
Conclusion: Only the HCSB and the NKJV made the verse more complex. Odd it is that the NKJV would be more complex than most modern versions.

247. Judges 5:27 At her feet he bowed, he fell, he lay down: at her feet he bowed, he fell: where he bowed, there he fell down dead.

AV - **25,** 1-1,2-1,3-1,4-1,5-1,6-1,7-1,8-1,9-1,10-1,11-1,12-1,13-1,14-1,15-1,16-1,17-1,18-1,19-1,20-1,21-1,22-1,23-1,24-1,25-1

ESV - **24,** 1-**2**,2-1,3-1,4-1,5-1,6-1,7-1,8-1,9-1,10-1,11-**2**,12-1,13-1,14-1,15-1,16-1,17-1,18-1,19-1,20-1,21-1,22-1,23-1,24-1

HCSB - **24,** 1-1,2-**2**,3-1,4-1,5-1,6-1,7-1,8-1,9-1,10-1,11-1,12-**2**,13-1,14-1,15-1,16-1,17-1,18-1,19-1,20-**2**,21-1,22-1,23-1,24-1

NASV - **23,** 1-**2**,2-1,3-1,4-1,5-1,6-1,7-1,8-1,9-1,10-**2**,11-1,12-1,13-1,14-1,15-1,16-1,17-1,18-1,19-1,20-1,21-1,22-1,23-1

NCV - **25,** 1-1,2-1,3-1,4-1,5-1,6-1,7-1,8-1,9-1,10-1,11-1,12-1,13-1,14-1,15-1,16-1,17-1,18-1,19-1,20-1,21-1,22-1,23-1,24-1,25-1

NIV - **24,** 1-1,2-1,3-1,4-1,5-1,6-1,7-1,8-1,9-1,10-1,11-1,12-1,13-1,14-1,15-1,16-1,17-1,18-1,19-1,20-1,21-1,22-1,23-1,24-1

NKJV - **24,** 1-1,2-1,3-1,4-1,5-1,6-1,7-1,8-1,9-1,10-1,11-1,12-1,13-1,14-1,15-1,16-1,17-1,18-1,19-1,20-1,21-1,22-1,23-1,24-1

NLT - **17,** 1-1,2-1,3-1,4-1,5-1,6-1,7-1,8-1,9-1,10-1,11-1,12-1,13-1,14-1,15-1,16-1,17-1

NRSV - **24,** 1-1,2-1,3-1,4-1,5-1,6-1,7-1,8-1,9-1,10-1,11-1,12-1,13-1,14-1,15-1,16-1,17-1,18-1,19-1,20-1,21-1,22-1,23-1,24-1

Conclusion: Only three modern versions are more complex than the King James Bible.

248. Judges 8:29* And **Jerubbaal** the son of **Joash** went and dwelt in his own house.
AV - **13,** 1-1,2-1,3-1,4-1,5-1,6-1,7-1,8-1,9-1,10-1,11-1,12-1,13-1
ESV - **12,** 1-1,2-1,3-1,4-1,5-1,6-1,7-1,8-1,9-1,10-1,11-1,12-1
HCSB - **14,** 1-1,2-1,3-1,4-1,5-1,6-1,7-1,8-1,9-1,10-1,11-1,12-1,13-1,14-1
NASV - **13,** 1-1,2-1,3-1,4-1,5-1,6-1,7-1,8-1,9-1,10-1,11-1,12-1,13-1
NCV - **10,** 1-1,2-1,3-1,4-1,5-1,6-1,7-1,8-1,9-1,10-1
NIV - **9,** 1-1,2-1,3-1,4-1,5-1,6-1,7-1,8-1,9-1
NKJV - **13,** 1-1,2-1,3-1,4-1,5-1,6-1,7-1,8-1,9-1,10-1,11-1,12-1,13-1
NLT - **7,** 1-1,2-1,3-1,4-1,5-1,6-**2**,7-1
NRSV - **11,** 1-1,2-1,3-1,4-1,5-1,6-1,7-1,8-1,9-1,10-1,11-1
Conclusion: Only the NLT made the verse more complex.

249. Judges 15:20*# And he judged **Israel** in the days of the **Philistines twenty** years.
AV - **12,** 1-1,2-1,3-1,4-1,5-1,6-1,7-1,8-1,9-1,10-1,11-1,12-1
ESV - **12,** 1-1,2-1,3-1,4-1,5-1,6-1,7-1,8-1,9-1,10-1,11-1,12-1
HCSB - **12,** 1-1,2-1,3-1,4-1,5-1,6-1,7-1,8-1,9-1,10-1,11-1,12-1
NASV - **12,** 1-1,2-1,3-1,4-1,5-1,6-1,7-1,8-1,9-1,10-1,11-1,12-1
NCV - **12,** 1-1,2-1,3-1,4-1,5-1,6-1,7-1,8-1,9-1,10-1,11-1,12-1
NIV - **12,** 1-1,2-1,3-1,4-1,5-1,6-1,7-1,8-1,9-1,10-1,11-1,12-1
NKJV - **12,** 1-1,2-1,3-1,4-1,5-1,6-1,7-1,8-1,9-1,10-1,11-1,12-1
NLT - **15,** 1-1,2-1,3-1,4-1,5-1,6-1,7-**2**,8-1,9-**3**,10-1,11-1,12-1,13-**4**,14-1,15-1
NRSV - **12,** 1-1,2-1,3-1,4-1,5-1,6-1,7-1,8-1,9-1,10-1,11-1,12-1
Conclusion: Only the NLT made the verse more complex.

250. Judges 17:1* And there was a man of mount **Ephraim**, whose name was **Micah**.
AV - **12,** 1-1,2-1,3-1,4-1,5-1,6-1,7-1,8-1,9-1,10-1,11-1,12-1
ESV - **14,** 1-1,2-1,3-1,4-1,5-1,6-1,7-1,8-**2**,9-1,10-1,11-1,12-1,13-1,14-1
HCSB - 12, 1-1,2-1,3-1,4-1,5-1,6-1,7-1,8-**2**,9-1,10-1,11-1,12-1
NASV - **15,** 1-1,2-1,3-1,4-1,5-1,6-1,7-1,8-1,9-**2**,10-1,11-1,12-1,13-1,14-1,15-1
NCV - **13,** 1-1,2-1,3-1,4-1,5-1,6-1,7-1,8-1,9-1,10-1,11-**2**,12-1,13-1
NIV - **11,** 1-1,2-1,3-1,4-1,5-1,6-1,7-1,8-1,9-**2**,10-1,11-1
NKJV - **14,** 1-1,2-1,3-1,4-1,5-1,6-1,7-1,8-**2**,9-1,10-1,11-1,12-1,13-1,14-1
NLT - **14,** 1-1,2-1,3-1,4-1,5-1,6-1,7-1,8-1,9-1,10-1,11-1,12-**2**,13-1,14-1
NRSV - **14,** 1-1,2-1,3-1,4-1,5-1,6-1,7-1,8-**2**,9-1,10-1,11-1,12-1,13-1,14-1
Conclusion: All eight modern versions are more complex than the King James Bible.

251. 1 Samuel 2:12* Now the sons of **Eli** were sons of **Belial**; they knew not the LORD.
AV - **14,** 1-1,2-1,3-1,4-1,5-1,6-1,7-1,8-1,9-1,10-1,11-1,12-1,13-1,14-1
ESV - **14,** 1-1,2-1,3-1,4-1,5-1,6-1,7-**2**,8-1,9-1,10-1,11-1,12-1,13-1,14-1
HCSB - 12, 1-1,2-1,3-1,4-**2**,5-1,6-1,7-1,8-1,9-**2**,10-1,11-1,12-1
NASV - **14,** 1-1,2-1,3-1,4-1,5-1,6-1,7-**2**,8-1,9-1,10-1,11-1,12-1,13-1,14-1
NCV - **13,** 1-1,2-1,3-1,4-1,5-**2**,6-1,7-1,8-1,9-1,10-1,11-**2**,12-1,13-1
NIV - **12,** 1-1,2-1,3-1,4-**2**,5-1,6-1,7-1,8-1,9-**2**,10-1,11-1,12-1
NKJV - **13,** 1-1,2-1,3-1,4-1,5-1,6-1,7-**2**,8-1,9-1,10-1,11-1,12-1,13-1
NLT - **14,** 1-1,2-1,3-1,4-1,5-1,6-1,7-**2**,8-1,9-1,10-1,11-**2**,12-1,13-1,14-1
NRSV - **14,** 1-1,2-1,3-1,4-1,5-1,6-1,7-**2**,8-1,9-1,10-1,11-**2**,12-1,13-1,14-1
Conclusion: All eight modern versions are more complex than the King James Bible.

252. 1 Samuel 3:19* And **Samuel** grew, and the LORD was with him, and did let none of his words fall to the ground.
AV - **20,** 1-1,2-1,3-1,4-1,5-1,6-1,7-1,8-1,9-1,10-1,11-1,12-1,13-1,14-1,15-1,16-1,17-1,18-1,19-1,20-1
ESV - **19,** 1-1,2-1,3-1,4-1,5-1,6-1,7-1,8-1,9-1,10-1,11-1,12-1,13-1,14-1,15-1,16-1,17-1,18-1,19-1
HCSB - 15, 1-1,2-1,3-1,4-1,5-1,6-1,7-1,8-1,9-1,10-1,11-**2**,12-1,13-1,14-1,15-1
NASV - **16,** 1-1,2-1,3-1,4-1,5-1,6-1,7-1,8-1,9-1,10-1,11-1,12-1,13-1,14-1,15-1,16-1
NCV - **21,** 1-1,2-1,3-1,4-1,5-1,6-1,7-1,8-1,9-1,10-1,11-1,12-1,13-1,14-**2**,15-1,16-1,17-**3**,18-1,19-1,20-1,21-1
NIV - **20,** 1-1,2-1,3-1,4-1,5-1,6-1,7-1,8-1,9-1,10-1,11-1,12-1,13-1,14-1,15-1,16-1,17-1,18-1,19-1,20-1
NKJV - **19,** 1-1,2-1,3-1,4-1,5-1,6-1,7-1,8-1,9-1,10-1,11-1,12-1,13-1,14-1,15-1,16-1,17-1,18-1,19-1
NLT - 17, 1-1,2-1,3-1,4-1,5-1,6-1,7-1,8-1,9-1,10-1,11-**4**,12-1,13-1,14-1,15-1,16-1,17-**4**
NRSV - **19,** 1-1,2-1,3-1,4-1,5-1,6-1,7-1,8-1,9-1,10-1,11-1,12-1,13-1,14-1,15-1,16-1,17-1,18-1,19-1
Conclusion: Only three modern versions are more complex than the King James Bible.

253. 1 Samuel 4:15*# Now **Eli** was **ninety** and eight years old; and his eyes were dim, that he could not see.
AV - **18,** 1-1,2-1,3-1,4-1,5-1,6-1,7-1,8-1,9-1,10-1,11-1,12-1,13-1,14-1,15-1,16-1,17-1,18-1
ESV - **17,** 1-1,2-1,3-1,4-1,5-1,6-1,7-1,8-1,9-1,10-1,11-1,12-1,13-1,14-1,15-1,16-1,17-1

HCSB - 17, 1-1,2-1,3-1,4-1,5-1,6-1,7-1,8-1,9-1,10-1,11-1,12-1,13-1,14-**2**,15-1,16-**2**,17-1
NASV - **17,** 1-1,2-1,3-1,4-1,5-1,6-1,7-1,8-1,9-1,10-1,11-1,12-1,13-1,14-1,15-1,16-1,17-1
NCV - **10,** 1-1,2-1,3-1,4-1,5-1,6-1,7-1,8-1,9-1,10-1
NIV - **16,** 1-1,2-1,3-1,4-1,5-1,6-1,7-1,8-1,9-1,10-1,11-1,12-1,13-1,14-1,15-1,16-1
NKJV - **16,** 1-1,2-1,3-1,4-1,5-1,6-1,7-1,8-1,9-1,10-1,11-1,12-1,13-1,14-1,15-1,16-1
NLT - **7,** 1-1,2-1,3-1,4-1,5-1,6-1,7-1
NRSV - **17,** 1-1,2-1,3-1,4-1,5-1,6-1,7-1,8-1,9-1,10-1,11-1,12-1,13-1,14-1,15-1,16-1,17-1
Conclusion: Only the HCSB made the verse more complex.

254. 1 Samuel 6:10 And the men did so; and took two milch kine, and tied them to the cart, and shut up their calves at home:
AV - **23,** 1-1,2-1,3-1,4-1,5-1,6-1,7-1,8-1,9-1,10-1,11-1,12-1,13-1,14-1,15-1,16-1,17-1,18-1,19-1,20-1,21-1,22-1,23-1
ESV - **22,** 1-1,2-1,3-1,4-1,5-1,6-1,7-1,8-1,9-1,10-1,11-1,12-1,13-1,14-1,15-1,16-1,17-1,18-1,19-1,20-1,21-1,22-1
HCSB - **21,** 1-1,2-1,3-1,4-1,5-1,6-1,7-1,8-1,9-1,10-1,11-1,12-1,13-1,14-1,15-1,16-**2**,17-1,18-1,19-1,20-1,21-1
NASV - **23,** 1-1,2-1,3-1,4-1,5-1,6-1,7-1,8-1,9-1,10-1,11-1,12-1,13-1,14-1,15-1,16-1,17-1,18-1,19-1,20-1,21-1,22-1,23-1
NCV - **31,** 1-1,2-**2**,3-1,4-1,5-1,6-1,7-1,8-**3**,9-1,10-1,11-1,12-1,13-1,14-1,15-1,16-1,17-1,18-1,19-1,20-1,21-1,22-1,23-1,24-1,25-1,26-1,27-1,28-1,29-1,30-1,31-1
NIV - **20,** 1-1,2-1,3-1,4-1,5-1,6-1,7-1,8-1,9-1,10-1,11-1,12-1,13-1,14-1,15-1,16-1,17-1,18-1,19-1,20-1
NKJV - **22,** 1-1,2-1,3-1,4-1,5-1,6-1,7-1,8-1,9-1,10-1,11-1,12-1,13-1,14-1,15-1,16-1,17-1,18-1,19-1,20-1,21-1,22-1
NLT - **23,** 1-1,2-1,3-**3**,4-1,5-**2**,6-1,7-1,8-1,9-1,10-1,11-1,12-1,13-1,14-1,15-1,16-**2**,17-1,18-1,19-1,20-1,21-1,22-1,23-1
NRSV - **22,** 1-1,2-1,3-1,4-1,5-1,6-1,7-1,8-1,9-1,10-1,11-1,12-1,13-1,14-1,15-1,16-1,17-1,18-1,19-1,20-1,21-1,22-1
Conclusion: Only three modern versions are more complex than the King James Bible.

255. 1 Samuel 7:15* And **Samuel** judged **Israel** all the days of his life.
AV - **10,** 1-1,2-1,3-1,4-1,5-1,6-1,7-1,8-1,9-1,10-1
ESV - **9,** 1-1,2-1,3-1,4-1,5-1,6-1,7-1,8-1,9-1
HCSB - **6,** 1-1,2-1,3-1,4-**2**,5-1,6-1
NASV - **10,** 1-1,2-1,3-1,4-1,5-1,6-1,7-1,8-1,9-1,10-1
NCV - **9,** 1-1,2-**3**,3-1,4-1,5-1,6-1,7-1,8-1,9-1
NIV - **12,** 1-1,2-**3**,3-1,4-1,5-**2**,6-1,7-1,8-1,9-1,10-1,11-1,12-1
NKJV - **10,** 1-1,2-1,3-1,4-1,5-1,6-1,7-1,8-1,9-1,10-1
NLT - **11,** 1-1,2-**3**,3-1,4-1,5-1,6-1,7-1,8-1,9-1,10-1,11-1
NRSV - **9,** 1-1,2-1,3-1,4-1,5-1,6-1,7-1,8-1,9-1
Conclusion: Four modern versions are more complex than the King James Bible.

256. 1 Samuel 15:34* Then **Samuel** went to **Ramah**; and Saul went up to his house to **Gibeah** of Saul.
AV - **16,** 1-1,2-1,3-1,4-1,5-1,6-1,7-1,8-1,9-1,10-1,11-1,12-1,13-1,14-1,15-1,16-1
ESV - **16,** 1-1,2-1,3-1,4-1,5-1,6-1,7-1,8-1,9-1,10-1,11-1,12-1,13-1,14-1,15-1,16-1
HCSB - **15,** 1-1,2-1,3-1,4-1,5-1,6-1,7-1,8-1,9-1,10-1,11-1,12-1,13-1,14-1,15-1
NASV - **16,** 1-1,2-1,3-1,4-1,5-1,6-1,7-1,8-1,9-1,10-1,11-1,12-1,13-1,14-1,15-1,16-1
NCV - **16,** 1-1,2-1,3-1,4-1,5-1,6-1,7-1,8-1,9-1,10-1,11-1,12-1,13-1,14-1,15-1,16-1
NIV - **16,** 1-1,2-1,3-1,4-1,5-1,6-1,7-1,8-1,9-1,10-1,11-1,12-1,13-1,14-1,15-1,16-1
NKJV - **16,** 1-1,2-1,3-1,4-1,5-1,6-1,7-1,8-1,9-1,10-1,11-1,12-1,13-1,14-1,15-1,16-1
NLT - **16,** 1-1,2-1,3-1,4-1,5-1,6-1,7-1,8-1,9-**2**,10-1,11-1,12-1,13-1,14-1,15-1,16-1
NRSV - **16,** 1-1,2-1,3-1,4-1,5-1,6-1,7-1,8-1,9-1,10-1,11-1,12-1,13-1,14-1,15-1,16-1
Conclusion: Only the New Living Translation made the verse more complex.

257. 1 Samuel 17:29* And **David** said, What have I now done? Is there not a cause?
AV - **13,** 1-1,2-1,3-1,4-1,5-1,6-1,7-1,8-1,9-1,10-1,11-1,12-1,13-1
ESV - **14,** 1-1,2-1,3-1,4-1,5-1,6-1,7-1,8-1,9-1,10-1,11-1,12-1,13-1,14-1
HCSB - **12,** 1-1,2-1,3-1,4-1,5-1,6-**2**,7-1,8-1,9-1,10-1,11-1,12-**2**
NASV - **14,** 1-1,2-1,3-1,4-1,5-1,6-1,7-1,8-1,9-1,10-1,11-1,12-1,13-1,14-**2**
NCV - **12,** 1-1,2-1,3-1,4-1,5-1,6-1,7-1,8-1,9-1,10-1,11-**2**,12-1
NIV - **11,** 1-1,2-1,3-1,4-1,5-1,6-1,7-1,8-1,9-1,10-**2**,11-1
NKJV - **13,** 1-1,2-1,3-1,4-1,5-1,6-1,7-1,8-1,9-1,10-1,11-1,12-1,13-1
NLT - **13,** 1-1,2-1,3-1,4-1,5-1,6-1,7-**2**,8-1,9-1,10-1,11-**2**,12-1,13-**2**
NRSV - **12,** 1-1,2-1,3-1,4-1,5-1,6-1,7-1,8-1,9-1,10-**2**,11-1,12-**2**
Conclusion: Six modern versions are more complex than the King James Bible. Once again the New Living Translation is the most difficult to read.

258. 1 Samuel 22:21* And **Abiathar** shewed **David** that Saul had slain the LORD's priests.
AV - **11,** 1-1,2-1,3-1,4-1,5-1,6-1,7-1,8-1,9-1,10-1,11-1
ESV - **13,** 1-1,2-1,3-1,4-1,5-1,6-1,7-1,8-1,9-1,10-1,11-1,12-1,13-1
HCSB - **12,** 1-1,2-1,3-1,4-1,5-1,6-1,7-1,8-1,9-1,10-1,11-1,12-1
NASV - **12,** 1-1,2-1,3-1,4-1,5-1,6-1,7-1,8-1,9-1,10-1,11-1,12-1
NCV - **10,** 1-1,2-1,3-1,4-1,5-1,6-1,7-1,8-1,9-1,10-1
NIV - **12,** 1-1,2-1,3-1,4-1,5-1,6-1,7-1,8-1,9-1,10-1,11-1,12-1
NKJV - **11,** 1-1,2-1,3-1,4-1,5-1,6-1,7-1,8-1,9-1,10-1,11-1
NLT - **13,** 1-1,2-1,3-1,4-1,5-1,6-1,7-1,8-1,9-1,10-1,11-1,12-1,13-1
NRSV - **12,** 1-1,2-1,3-1,4-1,5-1,6-1,7-1,8-1,9-1,10-1,11-1,12-1
Conclusion: All versions read the same.

259. 1 Samuel 23:29* And **David** went up from thence, and dwelt in strong holds at **Engedi**.
AV - **13,** 1-1,2-1,3-1,4-1,5-1,6-1,7-1,8-1,9-1,10-1,11-1,12-1,13-1
ESV - **13,** 1-1,2-1,3-1,4-1,5-1,6-1,7-1,8-1,9-1,10-1,11-1,12-1,13-1
HCSB - **12,** 1-1,2-1,3-1,4-1,5-1,6-1,7-1,8-1,9-1,10-1,11-1,12-1
NASV - **12,** 1-1,2-1,3-1,4-1,5-1,6-1,7-1,8-1,9-1,10-1,11-1,12-1
NCV - **15,** 1-1,2-**2**,3-1,4-1,5-**2**,6-1,7-1,8-1,9-1,10-1,11-1,12-**2**,13-1,14-1,15-1

NIV - **14,** 1-1,2-1,3-1,4-1,5-1,6-1,7-1,8-1,9-1,10-1,11-1,12-1,13-1,14-1

NKJV - **13,** 1-1,2-1,3-1,4-1,5-1,6-1,7-1,8-1,9-1,10-1,11-1,12-1,13-1

NLT - **10,** 1-1,2-1,3-1,4-1,5-1,6-1,7-1,8-1,9-1,10-1

NRSV - **14,** 1-1,2-1,3-1,4-1,5-1,6-1,7-1,8-1,9-1,10-1,11-1,12-1,13-1,14-1

Conclusion: Only the NCV made the verse more complex.

260. 1 Samuel 25:32* And **David** said to **Abigail**, Blessed be the LORD God of **Israel**, which sent thee this day to meet me:

AV - **20,** 1-1,2-1,3-1,4-1,5-1,6-1,7-1,8-1,9-1,10-1,11-1,12-1,13-1,14-1,15-1,16-1,17-1,18-1,19-1,20-1

ESV - **21,** 1-1,2-1,3-1,4-1,5-1,6-1,7-1,8-1,9-1,10-1,11-1,12-1,13-1,14-1,15-1,16-1,17-1,18-1,19-1,20-1,21-1

HCSB - **19,** 1-1,2-1,3-1,4-1,5-1,6-1,7-1,8-1,9-1,10-1,11-1,12-1,13-1,14-1,15-1,16-1,17-1,18-1,19-**2**

NASV - **20,** 1-1,2-1,3-1,4-1,5-1,6-1,7-1,8-1,9-1,10-1,11-1,12-1,13-1,14-1,15-1,16-1,17-1,18-1,19-1,20-1

NCV - **16,** 1-1,2-**2**,3-1,4-1,5-1,6-1,7-1,8-1,9-1,10-1,11-1,12-1,13-1,14-1,15-1,16-1

NIV - **21,** 1-1,2-1,3-1,4-1,5-1,6-1,7-1,8-1,9-1,10-1,11-1,12-1,13-1,14-1,15-1,16-1,17-1,18-**2**,19-1,20-1,21-1

NKJV - **20,** 1-1,2-1,3-1,4-1,5-1,6-1,7-1,8-1,9-1,10-1,11-1,12-1,13-1,14-1,15-1,16-1,17-1,18-1,19-1,20-1

NLT - **19,** 1-1,2-**2**,3-1,4-1,5-1,6-1,7-1,8-1,9-1,10-1,11-1,12-1,13-1,14-1,15-1,16-1,17-1,18-1,19-**2**

NRSV - **19,** 1-1,2-1,3-1,4-1,5-1,6-1,7-1,8-1,9-1,10-1,11-1,12-1,13-1,14-1,15-1,16-1,17-1,18-1,19-**2**

Conclusion: Five modern versions are more complex than the King James Bible.

261. 1 Samuel 26:17* And Saul knew **David's** voice, and said, Is this thy voice, my son **David**? And **David** said, It is my voice, my lord, O king.

AV - **25,** 1-1,2-1,3-1,4-1,5-1,6-1,7-1,8-1,9-1,10-1,11-1,12-1,13-1,14-1,15-1,16-1,17-1,18-1,19-1,20-1,21-1,22-1,23-1,24-1,25-1

ESV - **24,** 1-1,2-**3**,3-1,4-1,5-1,6-1,7-1,8-1,9-1,10-1,11-1,12-1,13-1,14-1,15-1,16-1,17-1,18-1,19-1,20-1,21-1,22-1,23-1,24-1

HCSB - **23,** 1-1,2-**3**,3-1,4-1,5-1,6-1,7-1,8-1,9-1,10-1,11-1,12-1,13-1,14-1,15-1,16-1,17-1,18-1,19-1,20-1,21-1,22-1,23-1

NASV - **25,** 1-1,2-1,3-**3**,4-1,5-1,6-1,7-1,8-1,9-1,10-1,11-1,12-1,13-1,14-1,15-1,16-1,17-1,18-1,19-1,20-1,21-1,22-1,23-1,24-1,25-1

NCV - **22,** 1-1,2-1,3-1,4-1,5-1,6-1,7-1,8-1,9-1,10-1,11-1,12-1,13-1,14-1,15-**2**,16-1,17-1,18-1,19-1,20-**2**,21-1,22-1

NIV - **22,** 1-1,2-**2**,3-1,4-1,5-1,6-1,7-1,8-1,9-1,10-1,11-1,12-1,13-1,14-1,15-**2**,16-1,17-1,18-1,19-1,20-1,21-1,22-1

NKJV - **24,** 1-1,2-1,3-1,4-1,5-1,6-1,7-1,8-1,9-1,10-1,11-1,12-1,13-1,14-1,15-1,16-1,17-1,18-1,19-1,20-1,21-1,22-1,23-1,24-1

NLT - **21,** 1-1,2-**3**,3-1,4-1,5-1,6-1,7-1,8-1,9-1,10-1,11-1,12-1,13-1,14-1,15-1,16-**2**,17-1,18-1,19-1,20-1,21-1

NRSV - **23,** 1-1,2-**2**,3-1,4-1,5-1,6-1,7-1,8-1,9-1,10-1,11-1,12-1,13-1,14-1,15-1,16-1,17-1,18-1,19-1,20-1,21-1,22-1,23-1

Conclusion: Seven modern versions are more complex than the King James Bible.

262. 1 Samuel 30:27* To them which were in **Bethel**, and to them which were in south **Ramoth**, and to them which were in **Jattir**,
AV - **21,** 1-1,2-1,3-1,4-1,5-1,6-1,7-1,8-1,9-1,10-1,11-1,12-1,13-1,14-1,15-1,16-1,17-1,18-1,19-1,20-1,21-1
ESV - **13,** 1-1,2-1,3-1,4-1,5-1,6-1,7-1,8-1,9-1,10-1,11-1,12-1,13-1
HCSB - **15,** 1-1,2-1,3-1,4-1,5-1,6-1,7-1,8-1,9-1,10-1,11-1,12-1,13-1,14-1,15-1
NASV - **23,** 1-1,2-1,3-1,4-1,5-1,6-1,7-1,8-1,9-1,10-1,11-1,12-1,13-1,14-1,15-1,16-1,17-1,18-1,19-1,20-1,21-1,22-1,23-1
NCV - **18,** 1-1,2-**2,**3-1,4-1,5-1,6-1,7-1,8-**2,**9-1,10-1,11-1,12-1,13-1,14-**2,**15-1,16-1,17-1,18-1
NIV - **13,** 1-1,2-1,3-1,4-1,5-1,6-1,7-1,8-1,9-1,10-1,11-1,12-1,13-1
NKJV - **19,** 1-1,2-1,3-1,4-1,5-1,6-1,7-1,8-1,9-1,10-1,11-1,12-1,13-1,14-1,15-1,16-1,17-1,18-1,19-1
NLT - **18,** 1-1,2-1,3-1,4-1,5-1,6-1,7-**2,**8-1,9-1,10-**3,**11-1,12-1,13-1,14-**3,**15-1,16-1,17-1,18-1
NRSV - **13,** 1-1,2-1,3-1,4-1,5-1,6-1,7-1,8-1,9-1,10-1,11-1,12-1,13-1
Conclusion: Only the NCV and the NLT made the verse more complex.

263. 1 Samuel 30:28* And to them which were in **Aroer**, and to them which were in **Siphmoth**, and to them which were in **Eshtemoa**,
AV - **21,** 1-1,2-1,3-1,4-1,5-1,6-1,7-1,8-1,9-1,10-1,11-1,12-1,13-1,14-1,15-1,16-1,17-1,18-1,19-1,20-1,21-1
ESV - **5,** 1-1,2-1,3-1,4-1,5-1
HCSB - **9,** 1-1,2-1,3-1,4-1,5-1,6-1,7-1,8-1,9-1
NASV - **21,** 1-1,2-1,3-1,4-1,5-1,6-1,7-1,8-1,9-1,10-1,11-1,12-1,13-1,14-1,15-1,16-1,17-1,18-1,19-1,20-1,21-1
NCV - **3,** 1-1,2-1,3-1
NIV - **6,** 1-1,2-1,3-1,4-1,5-1,6-1
NKJV - **15,** 1-1,2-1,3-1,4-1,5-1,6-1,7-1,8-1,9-1,10-1,11-1,12-1,13-1,14-1,15-1
NLT - **3,** 1-1,2-1,3-1
NRSV - **6,** 1-1,2-1,3-1,4-1,5-1,6-1
Conclusion: All versions read the same.

264. 1 Samuel 30:30* And to them which were in **Hormah**, and to them which were in **Chorashan**, and to them which were in **Athach**,
AV - **21,** 1-1,2-1,3-1,4-1,5-1,6-1,7-1,8-1,9-1,10-1,11-1,12-1,13-1,14-1,15-1,16-1,17-1,18-1,19-1,20-1,21-1
ESV - **6,** 1-1,2-1,3-1,4-1,5-1,6-1
HCSB - **9,** 1-1,2-1,3-1,4-1,5-1,6-1,7-1,8-1,9-1
NASV - **21,** 1-1,2-1,3-1,4-1,5-1,6-1,7-1,8-1,9-1,10-1,11-1,12-1,13-1,14-1,15-1,16-1,17-1,18-1,19-1,20-1,21-1
NCV - **4,** 1-1,2-1,3-1,4-1
NIV - **7,** 1-1,2-1,3-1,4-1,5-1,6-1,7-1
NKJV - **15,** 1-1,2-1,3-1,4-1,5-1,6-1,7-1,8-1,9-1,10-1,11-1,12-1,13-1,14-1,15-1
NLT - **3,** 1-1,2-1,3-1

NRSV - **6,** 1-1,2-1,3-1,4-1,5-1,6-1
Conclusion: All versions read the same.

265. 2 Samuel 2:18* And there were three sons of **Zeruiah** there, **Joab**, and **Abishai**, and **Asahel**: and **Asahel** was as light of foot as a wild roe.
AV - **24,** 1-1,2-1,3-1,4-1,5-1,6-1,7-1,8-1,9-1,10-1,11-1,12-1,13-1,14-1,15-1,16-1,17-1,18-1,19-1,20-1,21-1,22-1,23-1,24-1
ESV - **25,** 1-1,2-1,3-1,4-1,5-1,6-1,7-1,8-1,9-1,10-1,11-1,12-1,13-1,14-1,15-1,16-1,17-1,18-1,19-1,20-1,21-1,22-1,23-**2**,24-1,25-1
HCSB - **22,** 1-1,2-1,3-1,4-1,5-1,6-1,7-1,8-1,9-1,10-1,11-1,12-1,13-1,14-1,15-1,16-**2**,17-1,18-1,19-1,20-1,21-1,22-**2**
NASV - **29,** 1-1,2-1,3-1,4-1,5-1,6-1,7-1,8-1,9-1,10-1,11-1,12-1,13-1,14-1,15-1,16-1,17-1,18-1,19-**2**,20-1,21-1,22-1,23-1,24-**2**,25-1,26-1,27-1,28-1,29-1
NCV - **23,** 1-1,2-1,3-1,4-1,5-1,6-1,7-1,8-1,9-1,10-1,11-1,12-1,13-1,14-1,15-**2**,16-1,17-1,18-1,19-1,20-1,21-1,22-1,23-1
NIV - **21,** 1-1,2-1,3-1,4-1,5-1,6-1,7-1,8-1,9-1,10-1,11-1,12-1,13-1,14-1,15-1,16-1,17-**2**,18-1,19-1,20-1,21-**2**
NKJV - **24,** 1-1,2-1,3-1,4-1,5-1,6-1,7-1,8-1,9-1,10-1,11-1,12-1,13-1,14-1,15-1,16-1,17-1,18-1,19-1,20-1,21-1,22-1,23-1,24-**2**
NLT - **21,** 1-1,2-1,3-1,4-1,5-1,6-1,7-1,8-1,9-1,10-1,11-**2**,12-1,13-**2**,14-1,15-1,16-1,17-1,18-1,19-1,20-1,21-**2**
NRSV - **22,** 1-1,2-1,3-1,4-1,5-1,6-1,7-1,8-1,9-1,10-1,11-1,12-1,13-1,14-1,15-1,16-1,17-1,18-1,19-1,20-1,21-1,22-**2**
Conclusion: All eight modern versions are more complex than the King James Bible.

266. 2 Samuel 3:4* And the fourth, **Adonijah** the son of **Haggith**; and the fifth, **Shephatiah** the son of **Abital**;
AV - **16,** 1-1,2-1,3-1,4-1,5-1,6-1,7-1,8-1,9-1,10-1,11-1,12-1,13-1,14-1,15-1,16-1
ESV - **16,** 1-1,2-1,3-1,4-1,5-1,6-1,7-1,8-1,9-1,10-1,11-1,12-1,13-1,14-1,15-1,16-1
HCSB - **14,** 1-1,2-1,3-1,4-1,5-1,6-1,7-1,8-1,9-1,10-1,11-1,12-1,13-1,14-1
NASV - **16,** 1-1,2-1,3-1,4-1,5-1,6-1,7-1,8-1,9-1,10-1,11-1,12-1,13-1,14-1,15-1,16-1
NCV - **18,** 1-1,2-1,3-1,4-1,5-1,6-1,7-**2**,8-1,9-1,10-1,11-1,12-1,13-1,14-1,15-1,16-**2**,17-1,18-1
NIV - **14,** 1-1,2-1,3-1,4-1,5-1,6-1,7-1,8-1,9-1,10-1,11-1,12-1,13-1,14-1
NKJV - **14,** 1-1,2-1,3-1,4-1,5-1,6-1,7-1,8-1,9-1,10-1,11-1,12-1,13-1,14-1
NLT - **16,** 1-1,2-1,3-1,4-1,5-1,6-**2**,7-1,8-1,9-1,10-1,11-1,12-1,13-1,14-**2**,15-1,16-1
NRSV - **12,** 1-1,2-1,3-1,4-1,5-1,6-1,7-1,8-1,9-1,10-1,11-1,12-1
Conclusion: Only the NCV and the NLT made the verse more complex.

267. 2 Samuel 3:5* And the sixth, **Ithream**, by **Eglah David's** wife. These were born to **David** in **Hebron**.
AV - **15,** 1-1,2-1,3-1,4-1,5-1,6-1,7-1,8-1,9-1,10-1,11-1,12-1,13-1,14-1,15-1
ESV - **15,** 1-1,2-1,3-1,4-1,5-1,6-1,7-1,8-1,9-1,10-1,11-1,12-1,13-1,14-1,15-1
HCSB - **15,** 1-1,2-1,3-1,4-1,5-1,6-1,7-1,8-1,9-1,10-1,11-1,12-1,13-1,14-1,15-1
NASV - **15,** 1-1,2-1,3-1,4-1,5-1,6-1,7-1,8-1,9-1,10-1,11-1,12-1,13-1,14-1,15-1

NCV - **19,** 1-1,2-1,3-1,4-1,5-1,6-1,7-**2,**8-1,9-1,10-1,11-1,12-1,13-1,14-1,15-1,16-1,17-1,18-1,19-1

NIV - **17,** 1-1,2-1,3-1,4-1,5-1,6-1,7-1,8-1,9-1,10-1,11-1,12-1,13-1,14-1,15-1,16-1,17-1

NKJV - **15,** 1-1,2-1,3-1,4-1,5-1,6-1,7-1,8-1,9-1,10-1,11-1,12-1,13-1,14-1,15-1

NLT - **19,** 1-1,2-1,3-1,4-1,5-1,6-**2,**7-1,8-1,9-1,10-1,11-1,12-1,13-1,14-1,15-1,16-1,17-1,18-1,19-1

NRSV - **15,** 1-1,2-1,3-1,4-1,5-1,6-1,7-1,8-1,9-1,10-1,11-1,12-1,13-1,14-1,15-1

Conclusion: Only the NCV and the NLT made the verse more complex.

268. 2 Samuel 3:20*# So **Abner** came to **David** to **Hebron**, and **twenty** men with him. And **David** made **Abner** and the men that were with him a feast.

AV - **25,** 1-1,2-1,3-1,4-1,5-1,6-1,7-1,8-1,9-1,10-1,11-1,12-1,13-1,14-1,15-1,16-1,17-1,18-1,19-1,20-1,21-1,22-1,23-1,24-1,25-1

ESV - **23,** 1-1,2-1,3-1,4-1,5-1,6-1,7-1,8-1,9-1,10-1,11-1,12-1,13-1,14-1,15-1,16-1,17-1,18-1,19-1,20-1,21-1,22-1,23-1

HCSB - **19,** 1-1,2-1,3-1,4-1,5-1,6-1,7-1,8-1,9-1,10-1,11-1,12-1,13-1,14-**2,**15-1,16-1,17-1,18-1,19-1

NASV - **26,** 1-1,2-1,3-1,4-1,5-1,6-1,7-1,8-1,9-1,10-1,11-1,12-1,13-1,14-1,15-1,16-1,17-1,18-1,19-1,20-1,21-1,22-1,23-1,24-1,25-1,26-1

NCV - **19,** 1-1,2-1,3-1,4-1,5-1,6-1,7-1,8-1,9-1,10-1,11-1,12-**2,**13-1,14-1,15-1,16-1,17-1,18-1,19-1

NIV - **22,** 1-1,2-1,3-1,4-1,5-1,6-1,7-1,8-1,9-1,10-1,11-1,12-1,13-1,14-1,15-**2,**16-1,17-1,18-1,19-1,20-1,21-1,22-1

NKJV - **26,** 1-1,2-1,3-1,4-1,5-1,6-1,7-1,8-1,9-1,10-1,11-1,12-1,13-1,14-1,15-1,16-1,17-1,18-1,19-1,20-1,21-1,22-1,23-1,24-1,25-1,26-1

NLT - **17,** 1-1,2-1,3-1,4-1,5-1,6-1,7-1,8-1,9-1,10-1,11-1,12-**3,**13-1,14-1,15-1,16-1,17-1

NRSV - **23,** 1-1,2-1,3-1,4-1,5-1,6-1,7-1,8-1,9-1,10-1,11-1,12-1,13-1,14-1,15-1,16-1,17-1,18-1,19-1,20-1,21-1,22-1,23-1

Conclusion: Four modern versions are more complex than the King James Bible.

269. 2 Samuel 5:10* And **David** went on, and grew great, and the LORD God of hosts was with him.

AV - **16,** 1-1,2-1,3-1,4-1,5-1,6-1,7-1,8-1,9-1,10-1,11-1,12-1,13-1,14-1,15-1,16-1

ESV - **16,** 1-1,2-1,3-**2,**4-**2,**5-1,6-**2,**7-1,8-1,9-1,10-1,11-1,12-1,13-1,14-1,15-1,16-1

HCSB - **15,** 1-1,2-**2,**3-1,4-1,5-1,6-**3,**7-1,8-1,9-1,10-1,11-1,12-1,13-1,14-1,15-1

NASV - **14,** 1-1,2-**2,**3-**2,**4-1,5-**2,**6-1,7-1,8-1,9-1,10-1,11-1,12-1,13-1,14-1

NCV - **14,** 1-1,2-**2,**3-**2,**4-1,5-**2,**6-**2,**7-1,8-1,9-1,10-1,11-**3,**12-1,13-1,14-1

NIV - **15,** 1-1,2-1,3-**2,**4-1,5-1,6-1,7-**3,**8-**2,**9-1,10-1,11-1,12-**3,**13-1,14-1,15-1

NKJV - **15,** 1-1,2-1,3-1,4-1,5-1,6-**2,**7-1,8-1,9-1,10-1,11-1,12-1,13-1,14-1,15-1

NLT - **17,** 1-1,2-1,3-**2,**4-1,5-1,6-1,7-**3,**8-**2,**9-1,10-1,11-1,12-1,13-2,14-2,15-1,16-1,17-1

NRSV - **16,** 1-1,2-1,3-**2,**4-**2,**5-1,6-**2,**7-1,8-1,9-1,10-1,11-1,12-1,13-1,14-1,15-1,16-1

Conclusion: All eight modern versions are more complex than the King James Bible. The NIV inserted the title "Almighty" and the NLT inserted "Heaven's Armies" for "God of hosts." Since either of these titles would have been allowed in the AV they were not counted against them, but they were indicated by the number "2" above, though not in bold print.

270. 2 Samuel 5:16* And **Elishama**, and **Eliada**, and **Eliphalet**.

AV - **6,** 1-1,2-1,3-1,4-1,5-1,6-1

ESV - **4,** 1-1,2-1,3-1,4-1
HCSB - **4,** 1-1,2-1,3-1,4-1
NASV - **4,** 1-1,2-1,3-1,4-1
NCV - **4,** 1-1,2-1,3-1,4-1
NIV - **4,** 1-1,2-1,3-1,4-1
NKJV - **4,** 1-1,2-1,3-1,4-1
NLT - **4,** 1-1,2-1,3-1,4-1
NRSV - **4,** 1-1,2-1,3-1,4-1
Conclusion: All versions read the same.

271. 2 Samuel 7:3* And **Nathan** said to the king, Go, do all that is in thine heart; for the LORD is with thee.
AV - **20,** 1-1,2-1,3-1,4-1,5-1,6-1,7-1,8-1,9-1,10-1,11-1,12-1,13-1,14-1,15-1,16-1,17-1,18-1,19-1,20-1
ESV - **20,** 1-1,2-1,3-1,4-1,5-1,6-1,7-1,8-1,9-1,10-1,11-1,12-1,13-1,14-1,15-1,16-1,17-1,18-1,19-1,20-1
HCSB - **20,** 1-1,2-1,3-1,4-1,5-1,6-1,7-1,8-1,9-1,10-1,11-1,12-1,13-1,14-1,15-1,16-1,17-1,18-1,19-1,20-1
NASV - **19,** 1-1,2-1,3-1,4-1,5-1,6-1,7-1,8-1,9-1,10-1,11-1,12-1,13-1,14-1,15-1,16-1,17-1,18-1,19-1
NCV - **20,** 1-1,2-1,3-1,4-1,5-1,6-1,7-1,8-1,9-1,10-1,11-**2**,12-1,13-1,14-1,15-**2**,16-1,17-1,18-1,19-1,20-1
NIV - **21,** 1-1,2-**2**,3-1,4-1,5-1,6-**3**,7-1,8-1,9-1,10-1,11-1,12-**2**,13-1,14-1,15-1,16-1,17-1,18-1,19-1,20-1,21-1
NKJV - **20,** 1-1,2-1,3-1,4-1,5-1,6-1,7-1,8-1,9-1,10-1,11-1,12-1,13-1,14-1,15-1,16-1,17-1,18-1,19-1,20-1
NLT - **20,** 1-1,2-**2**,3-1,4-1,5-1,6-1,7-**2**,8-1,9-1,10-**3**,11-1,12-1,13-1,14-1,15-1,16-1,17-1,18-1,19-1,20-1
NRSV - **19,** 1-1,2-1,3-1,4-1,5-1,6-1,7-1,8-1,9-1,10-1,11-1,12-1,13-1,14-1,15-1,16-1,17-1,18-1,19-1
Conclusion: Only three modern versions are more complex than the King James Bible.

272. 2 Samuel 8:17* And **Zadok** the son of **Ahitub**, and **Ahimelech** the son of **Abiathar**, were the priests; and **Seraiah** was the scribe;
AV - **20,** 1-1,2-1,3-1,4-1,5-1,6-1,7-1,8-1,9-1,10-1,11-1,12-1,13-1,14-1,15-1,16-1,17-1,18-1,19-1,20-1
ESV - 18, 1-1,2-1,3-1,4-1,5-1,6-1,7-1,8-1,9-1,10-1,11-1,12-1,13-1,14-1,15-1,16-1,17-1,18-**4**
HCSB - 15, 1-1,2-1,3-1,4-1,5-1,6-1,7-1,8-1,9-1,10-1,11-1,12-1,13-1,14-1,15-**4**
NASV - 17, 1-1,2-1,3-1,4-1,5-1,6-1,7-1,8-1,9-1,10-1,11-1,12-1,13-1,14-1,15-1,16-1,17-**4**
NCV - 16, 1-1,2-1,3-1,4-1,5-1,6-1,7-1,8-1,9-1,10-1,11-1,12-1,13-1,14-1,15-**2**,16-**4**
NIV - 14, 1-1,2-1,3-1,4-1,5-1,6-1,7-1,8-1,9-1,10-1,11-1,12-1,13-1,14-**4**
NKJV - **18,** 1-1,2-1,3-1,4-1,5-1,6-1,7-1,8-1,9-1,10-1,11-1,12-1,13-1,14-1,15-1,16-1,17-1,18-1
NLT - 17, 1-1,2-1,3-1,4-1,5-1,6-1,7-1,8-1,9-1,10-1,11-1,12-1,13-1,14-1,15-1,16-1,17-**4**
NRSV - 14, 1-1,2-1,3-1,4-1,5-1,6-1,7-1,8-1,9-1,10-1,11-1,12-1,13-1,14-**4**
Conclusion: Seven modern versions are more complex than the King James Bible.

273. 2 Samuel 9:5* Then king **David** sent, and fetched him out of the house of **Machir**, the son of **Ammiel**, from **Lodebar**.
AV - **19,** 1-1,2-1,3-1,4-1,5-1,6-1,7-1,8-1,9-1,10-1,11-1,12-1,13-1,14-1,15-1,16-1,17-1,18-1,19-1
ESV - **18,** 1-1,2-1,3-1,4-1,5-1,6-1,7-1,8-1,9-1,10-1,11-1,12-1,13-1,14-1,15-1,16-1,17-1,18-1
HCSB - **16,** 1-1,2-1,3-1,4-1,5-1,6-1,7-1,8-1,9-1,10-1,11-1,12-1,13-1,14-1,15-1,16-1
NASV - **18,** 1-1,2-1,3-1,4-1,5-1,6-1,7-1,8-1,9-1,10-1,11-1,12-1,13-1,14-1,15-1,16-1,17-1,18-1
NCV - **19,** 1-1,2-1,3-1,4-1,5-**2**,6-1,7-1,8-1,9-1,10-1,11-1,12-1,13-1,14-1,15-1,16-1,17-1,18-1,19-1
NIV - **17,** 1-1,2-1,3-1,4-1,5-1,6-1,7-1,8-1,9-1,10-1,11-1,12-1,13-1,14-1,15-1,16-1,17-1
NKJV - **20,** 1-1,2-1,3-1,4-1,5-1,6-1,7-1,8-1,9-1,10-1,11-1,12-1,13-1,14-1,15-1,16-1,17-1,18-1,19-1,20-1
NLT - **11,** 1-1,2-1,3-1,4-1,5-1,6-1,7-1,8-1,9-1,10-1,11-1
NRSV - **17,** 1-1,2-1,3-1,4-1,5-1,6-1,7-1,8-1,9-1,10-1,11-1,12-1,13-1,14-1,15-1,16-1,17-1
Conclusion: Only the NCV made the verse more complex.

274. 2 Samuel 13:27* But **Absalom** pressed him, that he let **Amnon** and all the king's sons go with him.
AV - **16,** 1-1,2-1,3-1,4-1,5-1,6-1,7-1,8-1,9-1,10-1,11-1,12-1,13-1,14-1,15-1,16-1
ESV - **16,** 1-1,2-1,3-1,4-1,5-**2**,6-1,7-1,8-1,9-1,10-1,11-1,12-1,13-1,14-1,15-1,16-1
HCSB - **13,** 1-1,2-1,3-1,4-1,5-1,6-1,7-1,8-1,9-1,10-1,11-1,12-1,13-1
NASV - **16,** 1-1,2-1,3-1,4-1,5-1,6-1,7-1,8-1,9-1,10-1,11-1,12-1,13-1,14-1,15-1,16-1
NCV - **16,** 1-1,2-1,3-**2**,4-1,5-**2**,6-1,7-1,8-1,9-1,10-1,11-1,12-1,13-1,14-1,15-1,16-1
NIV - **17,** 1-1,2-1,3-1,4-1,5-1,6-1,7-1,8-1,9-1,10-1,11-1,12-1,13-1,14-1,15-1,16-1,17-1
NKJV - **16,** 1-1,2-1,3-1,4-1,5-1,6-1,7-1,8-1,9-1,10-1,11-1,12-1,13-1,14-1,15-1,16-1
NLT - **19,** 1-1,2-1,3-1,4-1,5-**2**,6-1,7-1,8-**2**,9-1,10-**3**,11-**2**,12-1,13-1,14-1,15-1,16-1,17-**2**,18-**3**,19-1
NRSV - **24,** 1-1,2-1,3-1,4-1,5-**2**,6-1,7-1,8-1,9-1,10-1,11-1,12-1,13-1,14-1,15-1,16-1,17-1,18-1,19-1,20-1,21-1,22-1,23-1,24-1
Conclusion: Four modern versions are more complex than the King James Bible. The New Living Translation is amazing in its ability to be the most difficult to read.

275. 2 Samuel 13:38* So **Absalom** fled, and went to **Geshur**, and was there three years.
AV - **12,** 1-1,2-1,3-1,4-1,5-1,6-1,7-1,8-1,9-1,10-1,11-1,12-1
ESV - **12,** 1-1,2-1,3-1,4-1,5-1,6-1,7-1,8-1,9-1,10-1,11-1,12-1
HCSB - **12,** 1-1,2-1,3-1,4-1,5-1,6-1,7-1,8-1,9-1,10-1,11-1,12-1
NASV - **13,** 1-1,2-1,3-1,4-1,5-1,6-1,7-1,8-1,9-1,10-1,11-1,12-1,13-1
NCV - **12,** 1-**2**,2-1,3-1,4-**2**,5-1,6-1,7-1,8-1,9-1,10-1,11-1,12-1
NIV - **12,** 1-**2**,2-1,3-1,4-1,5-1,6-1,7-1,8-1,9-1,10-1,11-1,12-1
NKJV - **12,** 1-1,2-1,3-1,4-1,5-1,6-1,7-1,8-1,9-1,10-1,11-1,12-1
NLT - **8,** 1-1,2-1,3-1,4-1,5-1,6-1,7-1,8-1
NRSV - **9,** 1-1,2-**2**,3-1,4-1,5-1,6-1,7-1,8-1,9-1
Conclusion: Only three modern versions are more complex than the King James Bible.

276. 2 Samuel 14:28* So **Absalom** dwelt two full years in **Jerusalem**, and saw not the king's face.
AV - **14,** 1-1,2-1,3-1,4-1,5-1,6-1,7-1,8-1,9-1,10-1,11-1,12-1,13-1,14-1
ESV - **14,** 1-1,2-1,3-1,4-1,5-1,6-1,7-1,8-1,9-**2**,10-**2**,11-**2**,12-1,13-1,14-**2**

HCSB - 11, 1-1,2-**3**,3-1,4-1,5-1,6-1,7-1,8-**2**,9-1,10-1,11-1
NASV - 15, 1-1,2-1,3-1,4-1,5-1,6-1,7-1,8-1,9-1,10-1,11-1,12-1,13-1,14-1,15-1
NCV - 12, 1-1,2-1,3-1,4-1,5-1,6-1,7-1,8-1,9-**2**,10-**2**,11-1,12-1
NIV - 11, 1-1,2-1,3-1,4-1,5-1,6-1,7-**2**,8-**2**,9-1,10-1,11-1
NKJV - 15, 1-1,2-1,3-1,4-1,5-1,6-1,7-1,8-1,9-1,10-1,11-1,12-1,13-1,14-1,15-1
NLT - 15, 1-1,2-1,3-1,4-1,5-1,6-1,7-1,8-1,9-1,10-**2**,11-1,12-1,13-1,14-1,15-1
NRSV - 14, 1-1,2-1,3-1,4-1,5-1,6-1,7-1,8-1,9-**2**,10-**2**,11-1,12-1,13-1,14-**2**
Conclusion: Six modern versions are more complex than the King James Bible. The ESV is the most difficult to read. There seems to be a pattern of agreement between the NASV and the NKJV, almost as though the translators of the NKJV consulted the NASV for guidance and followed it frequently.

277. 2 Samuel 17:26* So **Israel** and **Absalom** pitched in the land of **Gilead**.
AV - **10,** 1-1,2-1,3-1,4-1,5-1,6-1,7-1,8-1,9-1,10-1
ESV - 10, 1-1,2-1,3-1,4-1,5-**2**,6-1,7-1,8-1,9-1,10-1
HCSB - **10,** 1-1,2-1,3-1,4-1,5-1,6-1,7-1,8-1,9-1,10-1
NASV - **10,** 1-1,2-1,3-1,4-1,5-1,6-1,7-1,8-1,9-1,10-1
NCV - **10,** 1-1,2-1,3-1,4-1,5-1,6-1,7-1,8-1,9-1,10-1
NIV - **10,** 1-1,2-1,3-1,4-1,5-1,6-1,7-1,8-1,9-1,10-1
NKJV - 10, 1-1,2-1,3-1,4-1,5-**2**,6-1,7-1,8-1,9-1,10-1
NLT - 13, 1-1,2-1,3-1,4-1,5-**2**,6-1,7-1,8-1,9-1,10-1,11-1,12-1,13-1
NRSV - 10, 1-1,2-1,3-1,4-1,5-**2**,6-1,7-1,8-1,9-1,10-1
Conclusion: Four modern versions are more complex than the King James Bible. Several modern versions used "Israelites" instead of "Israel" but this was not counted against them.

278. 2 Samuel 20:25* And **Sheva** was scribe: and **Zadok** and **Abiathar** were the priests:
AV - **11,** 1-1,2-1,3-1,4-1,5-1,6-1,7-1,8-1,9-1,10-1,11-1
ESV - 10, 1-1,2-1,3-1,4-**4**,5-1,6-1,7-1,8-1,9-1,10-1
HCSB - 9, 1-1,2-1,3-1,4-**4**,5-1,6-1,7-1,8-1,9-1
NASV - **10,** 1-1,2-1,3-1,4-1,5-1,6-1,7-1,8-1,9-1,10-1
NCV - 11, 1-1,2-1,3-1,4-**2**,5-**4**,6-1,7-1,8-1,9-1,10-1,11-1
NIV - 8, 1-1,2-1,3-**4**,4-1,5-1,6-1,7-1,8-1
NKJV - **9,** 1-1,2-1,3-1,4-1,5-1,6-1,7-1,8-1,9-1
NLT - 10, 1-1,2-1,3-1,4-**4**,5-1,6-1,7-1,8-1,9-1,10-1
NRSV - 8, 1-1,2-1,3-**4**,4-1,5-1,6-1,7-1,8-1
Conclusion: Six modern versions are more complex than the King James Bible.

279. 2 Samuel 22:32 For who is God, save the LORD? and who is a rock, save our God?
AV - **15,** 1-1,2-1,3-1,4-1,5-1,6-1,7-1,8-1,9-1,10-1,11-1,12-1,13-1,14-1,15-1
ESV - 15, 1-1,2-1,3-1,4-1,5-1,6-1,7-1,8-1,9-1,10-1,11-1,12-1,13-**2**,14-1,15-1
HCSB - 15, 1-1,2-1,3-1,4-1,5-**2**,6-1,7-1,8-1,9-1,10-1,11-1,12-1,13-**2**,14-1,15-1
NASV - 15, 1-1,2-1,3-1,4-1,5-**2**,6-1,7-1,8-1,9-1,10-1,11-1,12-1,13-**2**,14-1,15-1
NCV - 13, 1-1,2-1,3-1,4-**2**,5-1,6-1,7-1,8-1,9-1,10-1,11-**2**,12-1,13-1
NIV - 15, 1-1,2-1,3-1,4-1,5-**2**,6-1,7-1,8-1,9-1,10-1,11-1,12-1,13-**2**,14-1,15-1

NKJV - 15, 1-1,2-1,3-1,4-1,5-**2**,6-1,7-1,8-1,9-1,10-1,11-1,12-1,13-**2**,14-1,15-1
NLT - 15, 1-1,2-1,3-1,4-1,5-**2**,6-1,7-1,8-1,9-1,10-1,11-1,12-1,13-1,14-**2**,15-1
NRSV - 15, 1-1,2-1,3-1,4-1,5-1,6-1,7-1,8-1,9-1,10-1,11-1,12-1,13-**2**,14-1,15-1
Conclusion: All eight modern versions are more complex than the King James Bible.

280. 2 Samuel 23:2* The **Spirit** of the LORD spake by me, and his word was in my tongue.
AV - **15,** 1-1,2-1,3-1,4-1,5-1,6-1,7-1,8-1,9-1,10-1,11-1,12-1,13-1,14-1,15-1
ESV - **14,** 1-1,2-1,3-1,4-1,5-1,6-1,7-1,8-1,9-1,10-1,11-1,12-1,13-1,14-1
HCSB - **13,** 1-1,2-1,3-1,4-1,5-1,6-1,7-1,8-1,9-1,10-1,11-1,12-1,13-1
NASV - **15,** 1-1,2-1,3-1,4-1,5-1,6-1,7-1,8-1,9-1,10-1,11-1,12-1,13-1,14-1,15-1
NCV - **13,** 1-1,2-1,3-1,4-1,5-1,6-1,7-1,8-1,9-1,10-1,11-1,12-1,13-1
NIV - **14,** 1-1,2-1,3-1,4-1,5-1,6-1,7-1,8-1,9-1,10-1,11-1,12-1,13-1,14-1
NKJV - **15,** 1-1,2-1,3-1,4-1,5-1,6-1,7-1,8-1,9-1,10-1,11-1,12-1,13-1,14-1,15-1
NLT - 14, 1-1,2-1,3-1,4-1,5-1,6-1,7-1,8-1,9-1,10-1,11-1,12-**2**,13-1,14-1
NRSV - 14, 1-1,2-1,3-1,4-1,5-1,6-1,7-1,8-1,9-1,10-1,11-1,12-**2**,13-1,14-1
Conclusion: Only the NLT and the NRSV made the verse more complex. The NRSV is the only version examined that did not capitalize "spirit" in the verse.

281. 2 Samuel 23:25* Shammah the **Harodite, Elika** the **Harodite,**
AV - **6,** 1-1,2-1,3-1,4-1,5-1,6-1
ESV - **6,** 1-1,2-1,3-1,4-1,5-1,6-1
HCSB - **6,** 1-1,2-1,3-1,4-1,5-1,6-1
NASV - **6,** 1-1,2-1,3-1,4-1,5-1,6-1
NCV - **6,** 1-1,2-1,3-1,4-1,5-1,6-1
NIV - **6,** 1-1,2-1,3-1,4-1,5-1,6-1
NKJV - **6,** 1-1,2-1,3-1,4-1,5-1,6-1
NLT - **6,** 1-1,2-1,3-1,4-1,5-1,6-1
NRSV - **6,** 1-1,2-1,3-1,4-1,5-1,6-1
Conclusion: All versions read the same.

282. 2 Samuel 23:26* Helez the **Paltite, Ira** the son of **Ikkesh** the **Tekoite,**
AV - **10,** 1-1,2-1,3-1,4-1,5-1,6-1,7-1,8-1,9-1,10-1
ESV - **10,** 1-1,2-1,3-1,4-1,5-1,6-1,7-1,8-1,9-1,10-1
HCSB - **9,** 1-1,2-1,3-1,4-1,5-1,6-1,7-1,8-1,9-1
NASV - **10,** 1-1,2-1,3-1,4-1,5-1,6-1,7-1,8-1,9-1,10-1
NCV - **9,** 1-1,2-1,3-1,4-1,5-1,6-1,7-1,8-1,9-1
NIV - **9,** 1-1,2-1,3-1,4-1,5-1,6-1,7-1,8-1,9-1
NKJV - **10,** 1-1,2-1,3-1,4-1,5-1,6-1,7-1,8-1,9-1,10-1
NLT - **9,** 1-1,2-1,3-1,4-1,5-1,6-1,7-1,8-1,9-1
NRSV - **8,** 1-1,2-1,3-1,4-1,5-1,6-1,7-1,8-1
Conclusion: All versions read the same.

283. 2 Samuel 23:27* Abiezer the **Anethothite, Mebunnai** the **Hushathite,**
AV - **6,** 1-1,2-1,3-1,4-1,5-1,6-1

ESV - **6,** 1-1,2-1,3-1,4-1,5-1,6-1
HCSB - **6,** 1-1,2-1,3-1,4-1,5-1,6-1
NASV - **6,** 1-1,2-1,3-1,4-1,5-1,6-1
NCV - **6,** 1-1,2-1,3-1,4-1,5-1,6-1
NIV - **6,** 1-1,2-1,3-1,4-1,5-1,6-1
NKJV - **6,** 1-1,2-1,3-1,4-1,5-1,6-1
NLT - **6,** 1-1,2-1,3-1,4-1,5-1,6-1
NRSV - **6,** 1-1,2-1,3-1,4-1,5-1,6-1
Conclusion: All versions read the same.

284. 2 Samuel 23:28* Zalmon the **Ahohite, Maharai** the **Netophathite,**
AV - **6,** 1-1,2-1,3-1,4-1,5-1,6-1
ESV - **6,** 1-1,2-1,3-1,4-1,5-1,6-1
HCSB - **6,** 1-1,2-1,3-1,4-1,5-1,6-1
NASV - **6,** 1-1,2-1,3-1,4-1,5-1,6-1
NCV - **6,** 1-1,2-1,3-1,4-1,5-1,6-1
NIV - **6,** 1-1,2-1,3-1,4-1,5-1,6-1
NKJV - **6,** 1-1,2-1,3-1,4-1,5-1,6-1
NLT - **6,** 1-1,2-1,3-1,4-1,5-1,6-1
NRSV - **6,** 1-1,2-1,3-1,4-1,5-1,6-1
Conclusion: All versions read the same.

285. 2 Samuel 23:30* Benaiah the **Pirathonite, Hiddai** of the brooks of **Gaash,**
AV - **9,** 1-1,2-1,3-1,4-1,5-1,6-1,7-1,8-1,9-1
ESV - **9,** 1-1,2-1,3-1,4-1,5-1,6-1,7-1,8-1,9-1
HCSB - **9,** 1-1,2-1,3-1,4-1,5-1,6-1,7-1,8-1,9-1
NASV - **9,** 1-1,2-1,3-1,4-1,5-1,6-1,7-1,8-1,9-1
NCV - **9,** 1-1,2-1,3-1,4-1,5-1,6-1,7-**2,**8-1,9-1
NIV - **9,** 1-1,2-1,3-1,4-1,5-1,6-1,7-**2,**8-1,9-1
NKJV - **9,** 1-1,2-1,3-1,4-1,5-1,6-1,7-1,8-1,9-1
NLT - **6,** 1-1,2-1,3-1,4-1,5-1,6-1
NRSV - **9,** 1-1,2-1,3-1,4-1,5-1,6-1,7-**2,**8-1,9-1
Conclusion: Only three modern versions are more complex than the King James Bible.

286. 2 Samuel 23:31* Abialbon the **Arbathite, Azmaveth** the **Barhumite,**
AV - **6,** 1-1,2-1,3-1,4-1,5-1,6-1
ESV - **6,** 1-1,2-1,3-1,4-1,5-1,6-1
HCSB - **6,** 1-1,2-1,3-1,4-1,5-1,6-1
NASV - **6,** 1-1,2-1,3-1,4-1,5-1,6-1
NCV - **6,** 1-1,2-1,3-1,4-1,5-1,6-1
NIV - **6,** 1-1,2-1,3-1,4-1,5-1,6-1
NKJV - **6,** 1-1,2-1,3-1,4-1,5-1,6-1
NLT - **6,** 1-1,2-1,3-1,4-1,5-1,6-1
NRSV - **6,** 1-1,2-1,3-1,4-1,5-1,6-1

Conclusion: All versions read the same.

287. 2 Samuel 23:32* Eliahba the **Shaalbonite**, of the sons of **Jashen, Jonathan,**
AV - **9,** 1-1,2-1,3-1,4-1,5-1,6-1,7-1,8-1,9-1
ESV - **8,** 1-1,2-1,3-1,4-1,5-1,6-1,7-1,8-1
HCSB - **10,** 1-1,2-1,3-1,4-1,5-1,6-1,7-1,8-1,9-1,10-1
NASV - **8,** 1-1,2-1,3-1,4-1,5-1,6-1,7-1,8-1
NCV - **8,** 1-1,2-1,3-1,4-1,5-1,6-1,7-1,8-1
NIV - **8,** 1-1,2-1,3-1,4-1,5-1,6-1,7-1,8-1
NKJV - **9,** 1-1,2-1,3-1,4-1,5-1,6-1,7-1,8-1,9-1
NLT - **7,** 1-1,2-1,3-1,4-1,5-1,6-1,7-1
NRSV - **8,** 1-1,2-1,3-1,4-1,5-1,6-1,7-1,8-1
Conclusion: All versions read the same.

288. 2 Samuel 23:33* Shammah the **Hararite, Ahiam** the son of **Sharar** the **Hararite,**
AV - **10,** 1-1,2-1,3-1,4-1,5-1,6-1,7-1,8-1,9-1,10-1
ESV - **10,** 1-1,2-1,3-1,4-1,5-1,6-1,7-1,8-1,9-1,10-1
HCSB - **9,** 1-1,2-1,3-1,4-1,5-1,6-1,7-1,8-1,9-1
NASV - **10,** 1-1,2-1,3-1,4-1,5-1,6-1,7-1,8-1,9-1,10-1
NCV - **11,** 1-1,2-1,3-1,4-1,5-1,6-1,7-1,8-1,9-1,10-1,11-1
NIV - **11,** 1-1,2-1,3-1,4-1,5-1,6-1,7-1,8-1,9-1,10-1,11-1
NKJV - **10,** 1-1,2-1,3-1,4-1,5-1,6-1,7-1,8-1,9-1,10-1
NLT - **12,** 1-1,2-1,3-1,4-1,5-1,6-1,7-1,8-1,9-1,10-1,11-1,12-1
NRSV - **11,** 1-1,2-1,3-1,4-1,5-1,6-1,7-1,8-1,9-1,10-1,11-1
Conclusion: All versions read the same.

289. 2 Samuel 23:34* Eliphelet the son of **Ahasbai,** the son of the **Maachathite, Eliam** the son of **Ahithophel** the **Gilonite,**
AV - **17,** 1-1,2-1,3-1,4-1,5-1,6-1,7-1,8-1,9-1,10-1,11-1,12-1,13-1,14-1,15-1,16-1,17-1
ESV - **14,** 1-1,2-1,3-1,4-1,5-1,6-1,7-1,8-1,9-1,10-1,11-1,12-1,13-1,14-1
HCSB - **14,** 1-1,2-1,3-1,4-1,5-1,6-1,7-1,8-1,9-1,10-1,11-1,12-1,13-1,14-1
NASV - **17,** 1-1,2-1,3-1,4-1,5-1,6-1,7-1,8-1,9-1,10-1,11-1,12-1,13-1,14-1,15-1,16-1,17-1
NCV - **12,** 1-1,2-1,3-1,4-1,5-1,6-1,7-1,8-1,9-1,10-1,11-1,12-1
NIV - **12,** 1-1,2-1,3-1,4-1,5-1,6-1,7-1,8-1,9-1,10-1,11-1,12-1
NKJV - **17,** 1-1,2-1,3-1,4-1,5-1,6-1,7-1,8-1,9-1,10-1,11-1,12-1,13-1,14-1,15-1,16-1,17-1
NLT - **12,** 1-1,2-1,3-1,4-1,5-1,6-1,7-1,8-1,9-1,10-1,11-1,12-1
NRSV - **12,** 1-1,2-1,3-1,4-1,5-1,6-1,7-1,8-1,9-1,10-1,11-1,12-1
Conclusion: All versions read the same.

290. 2 Samuel 23:35* Hezrai the **Carmelite, Paarai** the **Arbite,**
AV - **6,** 1-1,2-1,3-1,4-1,5-1,6-1
ESV - **6,** 1-1,2-1,3-1,4-1,5-1,6-1
HCSB - **6,** 1-1,2-1,3-1,4-1,5-1,6-1
NASV - **6,** 1-1,2-1,3-1,4-1,5-1,6-1

NCV - **6,** 1-1,2-1,3-1,4-1,5-1,6-1
NIV - **6,** 1-1,2-1,3-1,4-1,5-1,6-1
NKJV - **6,** 1-1,2-1,3-1,4-1,5-1,6-1
NLT - **6,** 1-1,2-1,3-1,4-1,5-1,6-1
NRSV - **6,** 1-1,2-1,3-1,4-1,5-1,6-1
Conclusion: All versions read the same.

291. 2 Samuel 23:36* Igal the son of **Nathan** of **Zobah**, **Bani** the **Gadite**,
AV - **10,** 1-1,2-1,3-1,4-1,5-1,6-1,7-1,8-1,9-1,10-1
ESV - **10,** 1-1,2-1,3-1,4-1,5-1,6-1,7-1,8-1,9-1,10-1
HCSB - **9,** 1-1,2-1,3-1,4-1,5-1,6-1,7-1,8-1,9-1
NASV - **10,** 1-1,2-1,3-1,4-1,5-1,6-1,7-1,8-1,9-1,10-1
NCV - **10,** 1-1,2-1,3-1,4-1,5-1,6-1,7-1,8-1,9-1,10-1
NIV - **10,** 1-1,2-1,3-1,4-1,5-1,6-1,7-1,8-1,9-1,10-1
NKJV - **10,** 1-1,2-1,3-1,4-1,5-1,6-1,7-1,8-1,9-1,10-1
NLT - **9,** 1-1,2-1,3-1,4-1,5-1,6-1,7-1,8-1,9-1
NRSV - **9,** 1-1,2-1,3-1,4-1,5-1,6-1,7-1,8-1,9-1
Conclusion: All versions read the same.

292. 2 Samuel 23:38* Ira an **Ithrite**, **Gareb** an **Ithrite**,
AV - **6,** 1-1,2-1,3-1,4-1,5-1,6-1
ESV - **6,** 1-1,2-1,3-1,4-1,5-1,6-1
HCSB - **6,** 1-1,2-1,3-1,4-1,5-1,6-1
NASV - **6,** 1-1,2-1,3-1,4-1,5-1,6-1
NCV - **6,** 1-1,2-1,3-1,4-1,5-1,6-1
NIV - **6,** 1-1,2-1,3-1,4-1,5-1,6-1
NKJV - **6,** 1-1,2-1,3-1,4-1,5-1,6-1
NLT - **6,** 1-1,2-1,3-1,4-1,5-1,6-1
NRSV - **6,** 1-1,2-1,3-1,4-1,5-1,6-1
Conclusion: All versions read the same.

293. 2 Samuel 23:39*# Uriah the **Hittite**: **thirty** and **seven** in all.
AV - **8,** 1-1,2-1,3-1,4-1,5-1,6-1,7-1,8-1
ESV - **7,** 1-1,2-1,3-1,4-1,5-1,6-1,7-1
HCSB - **9,** 1-1,2-1,3-1,4-1,5-1,6-1,7-1,8-1,9-1
NASV - **7,** 1-1,2-1,3-1,4-1,5-1,6-1,7-1
NCV - **10,** 1-1,2-1,3-1,4-1,5-1,6-1,7-1,8-1,9-1,10-1
NIV - **10,** 1-1,2-1,3-1,4-1,5-1,6-1,7-1,8-1,9-1,10-1
NKJV - **8,** 1-1,2-1,3-1,4-1,5-1,6-1,7-1,8-1
NLT - **9,** 1-1,2-1,3-1,4-1,5-1,6-1,7-1,8-1,9-1
NRSV - **7,** 1-1,2-1,3-1,4-1,5-1,6-1,7-1
Conclusion: All versions read the same.

294. 2 Samuel 24:8*# So when they had gone through all the land, they came to **Jerusalem** at the end of nine months and **twenty** days.
AV - **22,** 1-1,2-1,3-1,4-1,5-1,6-1,7-1,8-1,9-1,10-1,11-1,12-1,13-1,14-1,15-1,16-1,17-1,18-1,19-1,20-1,21-1,22-1
ESV - **22,** 1-1,2-1,3-1,4-1,5-1,6-1,7-1,8-1,9-1,10-1,11-1,12-1,13-1,14-1,15-1,16-1,17-1,18-1,19-1,20-1,21-1,22-1
HCSB - **21,** 1-1,2-1,3-1,4-1,5-1,6-1,7-1,8-1,9-1,10-**2,**11-1,12-1,13-1,14-1,15-1,16-1,17-1,18-1,19-1,20-1,21-1
NASV - **23,** 1-1,2-1,3-1,4-1,5-1,6-**2,**7-1,8-1,9-1,10-1,11-1,12-1,13-1,14-1,15-1,16-1,17-1,18-1,19-1,20-1,21-1,22-1,23-1
NCV - **19,** 1-**2,**2-1,3-1,4-1,5-1,6-1,7-1,8-1,9-1,10-1,11-1,12-1,13-1,14-1,15-1,16-1,17-1,18-1,19-1
NIV - **22,** 1-**2,**2-1,3-1,4-1,5-1,6-1,7-**2,**8-1,9-1,10-1,11-1,12-1,13-1,14-1,15-1,16-1,17-1,18-1,19-1,20-1,21-1,22-1
NKJV - **22,** 1-1,2-1,3-1,4-1,5-1,6-1,7-1,8-1,9-1,10-1,11-1,12-1,13-1,14-1,15-1,16-1,17-1,18-1,19-1,20-1,21-1,22-1
NLT - **16,** 1-**2,**2-1,3-1,4-1,5-**2,**6-1,7-1,8-1,9-1,10-1,11-1,12-1,13-1,14-**2,**15-1,16-1
NRSV - **23,** 1-1,2-1,3-1,4-1,5-1,6-1,7-1,8-1,9-1,10-1,11-1,12-1,13-1,14-1,15-1,16-1,17-1,18-1,19-1,20-1,21-1,22-1,23-1
Conclusion: Five modern versions are more complex than the King James Bible.

295. 1 Kings 3:10* And the speech pleased the Lord, that **Solomon** had asked this thing.
AV - **12,** 1-1,2-1,3-1,4-1,5-1,6-1,7-1,8-1,9-1,10-1,11-1,12-1
ESV - **9,** 1-1,2-1,3-1,4-1,5-1,6-1,7-1,8-1,9-1
HCSB - **10,** 1-1,2-1,3-1,4-1,5-1,6-1,7-1,8-1,9-**3,**10-1
NASV - **15,** 1-1,2-1,3-**2,**4-1,5-1,6-1,7-1,8-1,9-1,10-1,11-1,12-1,13-1,14-1,15-1
NCV - **9,** 1-1,2-1,3-1,4-1,5-1,6-1,7-1,8-1,9-1
NIV - **10,** 1-1,2-1,3-1,4-1,5-1,6-1,7-1,8-1,9-1,10-1
NKJV - **11,** 1-1,2-1,3-1,4-1,5-1,6-1,7-1,8-1,9-1,10-1,11-1
NLT - **10,** 1-1,2-1,3-1,4-1,5-1,6-1,7-1,8-1,9-1,10-**2**
NRSV - **9,** 1-1,2-1,3-1,4-1,5-1,6-1,7-1,8-1,9-1
Conclusion: Only three modern versions are more complex than the King James Bible.

296. 1 Kings 4:8* And these are their names: The son of Hur, in mount **Ephraim**:
AV - **12,** 1-1,2-1,3-1,4-1,5-1,6-1,7-1,8-1,9-1,10-1,11-1,12-1
ESV - **11,** 1-1,2-1,3-1,4-1,5-1,6-1,7-1,8-1,9-**2,**10-1,11-1
HCSB - **11,** 1-1,2-1,3-1,4-1,5-1,6-1,7-1,8-1,9-**2,**10-1,11-1
NASV - **11,** 1-1,2-1,3-1,4-1,5-1,6-1,7-1,8-1,9-**2,**10-1,11-1
NCV - **17,** 1-1,2-1,3-1,4-1,5-1,6-1,7-1,8-**3,**9-1,10-1,11-**3,**12-1,13-1,14-**2,**15-**2,**16-1,17-1
NIV - **11,** 1-1,2-1,3-1,4-1,5-1,6-1,7-1,8-1,9-**2,**10-1,11-1
NKJV - **10,** 1-1,2-1,3-1,4-1,5-1,6-1,7-1,8-**2,**9-1,10-1
NLT - **15,** 1-1,2-1,3-1,4-1,5-1,6-1,7-1,8-**3,**9-1,10-1,11-1,12-1,13-**2,**14-1,15-1
NRSV - **11,** 1-1,2-1,3-1,4-1,5-1,6-1,7-1,8-1,9-**2,**10-1,11-1
Conclusion: All eight modern versions are more complex than the King James Bible. The NCV is the most difficult to read.

297. 1 Kings 4:9* The son of **Dekar**, in **Makaz**, and in **Shaalbim**, and **Bethshemesh**, and **Elonbethhanan**:
AV - **13,** 1-1,2-1,3-1,4-1,5-1,6-1,7-1,8-1,9-1,10-1,11-1,12-1,13-1
ESV - **7,** 1-1,2-1,3-1,4-1,5-1,6-1,7-1
HCSB - **7,** 1-1,2-1,3-1,4-1,5-1,6-1,7-1
NASV - **9,** 1-1,2-1,3-1,4-1,5-1,6-1,7-1,8-1,9-1
NCV - **11,** 1-1,2-1,3-**3,**4-1,5-1,6-1,7-1,8-1,9-1,10-1,11-1
NIV - **9,** 1-1,2-1,3-1,4-1,5-1,6-1,7-1,8-1,9-1
NKJV - **10,** 1-1,2-1,3-1,4-1,5-1,6-1,7-1,8-1,9-1,10-1
NLT - **7,** 1-1,2-1,3-1,4-1,5-1,6-1,7-1
NRSV - **7,** 1-1,2-1,3-1,4-1,5-1,6-1,7-1
Conclusion: Only the NCV made the verse more complex.

298. 1 Kings 4:14* **Ahinadab** the son of **Iddo** had **Mahanaim**:
AV - **7,** 1-1,2-1,3-1,4-1,5-1,6-1,7-1
ESV - **7,** 1-1,2-1,3-1,4-1,5-1,6-1,7-1
HCSB - **6,** 1-1,2-1,3-1,4-1,5-1,6-1
NASV - **7,** 1-1,2-1,3-1,4-1,5-1,6-1,7-1
NCV - **8,** 1-1,2-1,3-1,4-1,5-1,6-**3,**7-1,8-1
NIV - **6,** 1-1,2-1,3-1,4-1,5-1,6-1
NKJV - **7,** 1-1,2-1,3-1,4-1,5-1,6-1,7-1
NLT - **6,** 1-1,2-1,3-1,4-1,5-1,6-1
NRSV - **6,** 1-1,2-1,3-1,4-1,5-1,6-1
Conclusion: Only the NCV made the verse more complex.

299. 1 Kings 4:16* **Baanah** the son of **Husha** was in **Asher** and in **Aloth**:
AV - **11,** 1-1,2-1,3-1,4-1,5-1,6-1,7-1,8-1,9-1,10-1,11-1
ESV - **9,** 1-1,2-1,3-1,4-1,5-1,6-1,7-1,8-1,9-1
HCSB - **8,** 1-1,2-1,3-1,4-1,5-1,6-1,7-1,8-1
NASV - **9,** 1-1,2-1,3-1,4-1,5-1,6-1,7-1,8-1,9-1
NCV - **10,** 1-1,2-1,3-1,4-1,5-1,6-**3,**7-1,8-1,9-1,10-1
NIV - **9,** 1-1,2-1,3-1,4-1,5-1,6-1,7-1,8-1,9-1
NKJV - **9,** 1-1,2-1,3-1,4-1,5-1,6-1,7-1,8-1,9-1
NLT - **9,** 1-1,2-1,3-1,4-1,5-1,6-1,7-1,8-1,9-1
NRSV - **8,** 1-1,2-1,3-1,4-1,5-1,6-1,7-1,8-1
Conclusion: Only the NCV made the verse more complex.

300. 1 Kings 4:17* **Jehoshaphat** the son of **Paruah**, in **Issachar**:
AV - **7,** 1-1,2-1,3-1,4-1,5-1,6-1,7-1
ESV - **7,** 1-1,2-1,3-1,4-1,5-1,6-1,7-1
HCSB - **6,** 1-1,2-1,3-1,4-1,5-1,6-1
NASV - **7,** 1-1,2-1,3-1,4-1,5-1,6-1,7-1
NCV - **8,** 1-1,2-1,3-1,4-1,5-1,6-**3,**7-1,8-1
NIV - **6,** 1-1,2-1,3-1,4-1,5-1,6-1

NKJV - **7,** 1-1,2-1,3-1,4-1,5-1,6-1,7-1
NLT - **6,** 1-1,2-1,3-1,4-1,5-1,6-1
NRSV - **6,** 1-1,2-1,3-1,4-1,5-1,6-1
Conclusion: Only the NCV made the verse more complex.

301. 1 Kings 4:18* Shimei the son of **Elah**, in **Benjamin**:
AV - **7,** 1-1,2-1,3-1,4-1,5-1,6-1,7-1
ESV - **7,** 1-1,2-1,3-1,4-1,5-1,6-1,7-1
HCSB - **6,** 1-1,2-1,3-1,4-1,5-1,6-1
NASV - **7,** 1-1,2-1,3-1,4-1,5-1,6-1,7-1
NCV - 8, 1-1,2-1,3-1,4-1,5-1,6-**3,**7-1,8-1
NIV - **6,** 1-1,2-1,3-1,4-1,5-1,6-1
NKJV - **7,** 1-1,2-1,3-1,4-1,5-1,6-1,7-1
NLT - **6,** 1-1,2-1,3-1,4-1,5-1,6-1
NRSV - **6,** 1-1,2-1,3-1,4-1,5-1,6-1
Conclusion: Only the NCV made the verse more complex.

302. 1 Kings 7:13* And king **Solomon** sent and fetched **Hiram** out of Tyre.
AV - **10,** 1-1,2-1,3-1,4-1,5-1,6-1,7-1,8-1,9-1,10-1
ESV - **9,** 1-1,2-1,3-1,4-1,5-1,6-1,7-1,8-1,9-1
HCSB - **7,** 1-1,2-1,3-1,4-1,5-1,6-1,7-1
NASV - **9,** 1-1,2-1,3-1,4-1,5-1,6-1,7-1,8-1,9-1
NCV - **11,** 1-1,2-1,3-1,4-1,5-1,6-1,7-1,8-1,9-1,10-1,11-1
NIV - **8,** 1-1,2-1,3-1,4-1,5-1,6-1,7-1,8-1
NKJV - **9,** 1-1,2-1,3-1,4-1,5-1,6-1,7-1,8-1,9-1
NLT - **13,** 1-1,2-1,3-1,4-1,5-1,6-1,7-1,8-1,9-1,10-1,11-1,12-1,13-1
NRSV - 9, 1-1,2-1,3-1,4-**3,**5-1,6-**2,**7-1,8-1,9-1
Conclusion: Only the NRSV made the verse more complex.

303. 1 Kings 14:1* At that time **Abijah** the son of **Jeroboam** fell sick.
AV - **10,** 1-1,2-1,3-1,4-1,5-1,6-1,7-1,8-1,9-1,10-1
ESV - **10,** 1-1,2-1,3-1,4-1,5-1,6-1,7-1,8-1,9-1,10-1
HCSB - 9, 1-1,2-1,3-1,4-1,5-1,6-1,7-1,8-**2,**9-1
NASV - 10, 1-1,2-1,3-1,4-1,5-1,6-1,7-1,8-1,9-**2,**10-1
NCV - 9, 1-1,2-1,3-1,4-1,5-1,6-1,7-**2,**8-**2,**9-1
NIV - 9, 1-1,2-1,3-1,4-1,5-1,6-1,7-1,8-**2,**9-1
NKJV - 10, 1-1,2-1,3-1,4-1,5-1,6-1,7-1,8-1,9-**2,**10-1
NLT - 9, 1-1,2-1,3-1,4-1,5-1,6-1,7-**2,**8-**2,**9-1
NRSV - **9,** 1-1,2-1,3-1,4-1,5-1,6-1,7-1,8-1,9-1
Conclusion: Six modern versions are more complex than the King James Bible.

304. 1 Kings 18:16* So **Obadiah** went to meet **Ahab**, and told him: and **Ahab** went to meet **Elijah**.
AV - **15,** 1-1,2-1,3-1,4-1,5-1,6-1,7-1,8-1,9-1,10-1,11-1,12-1,13-1,14-1,15-1
ESV - **15,** 1-1,2-1,3-1,4-1,5-1,6-1,7-1,8-1,9-1,10-1,11-1,12-1,13-1,14-1,15-1

HCSB - 15, 1-1,2-1,3-1,4-1,5-1,6-1,7-**2**,8-1,9-1,10-1,11-1,12-1,13-1,14-1,15-1
NASV - 15, 1-1,2-1,3-1,4-1,5-1,6-1,7-1,8-1,9-1,10-1,11-1,12-1,13-1,14-1,15-1
NCV - 17, 1-1,2-1,3-1,4-1,5-1,6-1,7-1,8-1,9-1,10-1,11-1,12-1,13-1,14-1,15-1,16-1,17-1
NIV - 15, 1-1,2-1,3-1,4-1,5-1,6-1,7-1,8-1,9-1,10-1,11-1,12-1,13-1,14-1,15-1
NKJV - 15, 1-1,2-1,3-1,4-1,5-1,6-1,7-1,8-1,9-1,10-1,11-1,12-1,13-1,14-1,15-1
NLT - 17, 1-1,2-1,3-1,4-1,5-1,6-1,7-1,8-1,9-1,10-1,11-1,12-1,13-1,14-1,15-1,16-1,17-1
NRSV - 15, 1-1,2-1,3-1,4-1,5-1,6-1,7-1,8-1,9-1,10-1,11-1,12-1,13-1,14-1,15-1
Conclusion: Only the HCSB made the verse more complex.

305. 1 Kings 18:34# And he said, Do it the **second** time. And they did it the **second** time. And he said, Do it the third time. And they did it the third time.
AV - **30,** 1-1,2-1,3-1,4-1,5-1,6-1,7-1,8-1,9-1,10-1,11-1,12-1,13-1,14-1,15-1,16-1,17-1,18-1,19-1,20-1,21-1,22-1,23-1,24-1,25-1,26-1,27-1,28-1,29-1,30-1
ESV - **30,** 1-1,2-1,3-1,4-1,5-1,6-1,7-1,8-1,9-1,10-1,11-1,12-1,13-1,14-1,15-1,16-1,17-1,18-1,19-1,20-1,21-1,22-1,23-1,24-1,25-1,26-1,27-1,28-1,29-1,30-1
HCSB - **27,** 1-1,2-1,3-1,4-1,5-1,6-1,7-1,8-1,9-1,10-1,11-1,12-1,13-1,14-1,15-1,16-1,17-1,18-1,19-1,20-1,21-1,22-1,23-1,24-1,25-1,26-1,27-1
NASV - **49/30,** 1-1,2-1,3-1,4-1,5-1,6-**2**,7-1,8-**2**,9-1,10-1,11-1,12-1,13-1,14-1,15-**3**,16-1,17-1,18-1,19-1,-----20-1,21-1,22-1,23-1,24-1,25-1,26-1,27-1,28-1,29-1,30-1,31-1,32-1,33-1,34-1,35-1,36-1,37-1,38-1,39-1,40-1,41-1,42-1,43-1,44-1,45-1,46-1,47-1,48-1, 49-1
NCV - **44/26,** 1-1,2-1,3-1,4-1,5-1,6-1,7-1,8-**2**,9-1,10-1,11-1,12-1,13-1,14-1,15-1,16-1,17-1,18-1,-----19-1,20-1,21-1,22-1,23-1,24-**2**,25-1,26-1,27-1,28-1,29-**2**,30-1,31-1,32-1,33-1,34-1,35-1,36-1,37-1,38-1,39-1,40-1,41-1,42-1,43-1,44-1
NIV - **24,** 1-1,2-1,3-**2**,4-1,5-1,6-1,7-1,8-1,9-1,10-**2**,11-1,12-1,13-1,14-1,15-1,16-1,17-**2**,18-1,19-1,20-1,21-1,22-1,23-1,24-1
NKJV - **30,** 1-1,2-1,3-1,4-1,5-1,6-1,7-1,8-1,9-1,10-1,11-1,12-1,13-1,14-1,15-1,16-1,17-1,18-1,19-1,20-1,21-1,22-1,23-1,24-1,25-1,26-1,27-1,28-1,29-1,30-1
NLT - **31,** 1-**2**,2-1,3-1,4-1,5-1,6-1,7-1,8-1,9-1,10-1,11-1,12-**2**,13-1,14-1,15-1,16-1,17-**2**,18-1,19-1,20-1,21-1,22-1,23-1,24-1,25-1,26-1,27-1,28-1,29-1,30-1,31-1
NRSV - **30,** 1-1,2-1,3-1,4-1,5-1,6-1,7-1,8-1,9-1,10-1,11-1,12-1,13-1,14-1,15-1,16-1,17-1,18-1,19-1,20-1,21-1,22-1,23-1,24-1,25-1,26-1,27-1,28-1,29-1,30-1
Conclusion: Five modern versions are more complex than the King James Bible. This verse is unique. The NIV and NCV split verse 33 and add the last half of it to verse 34 elongating the verse to 49 and 44 words respectively. In the NIV the first 19 words are added from the preceding verse and the three words which have more than one syllable are all in these nineteen added words. The remaining 30 words, which parallel the 30 words of the AV are all single syllable. If it were not for the added 19 words the verse would not be penalized in which case you could say that "four," rather than "five," modern versions are more complex than the King James Bible.

In the case of the NCV the first 18 words are added from the preceding verse. One of the three words which have more than one syllable are found within these eighteen added words. The remaining 26 words, which parallel the 30 words of the AV also added two multi-syllable words. Even if 18 words had not been added from the preceding verse the two multi-syllable words found in the last 26 words would have made the verse more complex than the AV.

306. 1 Kings 22:2* And it came to pass in the third year, that **Jehoshaphat** the king of **Judah** came down to the king of **Israel**.

AV - **22,** 1-1,2-1,3-1,4-1,5-1,6-1,7-1,8-1,9-1,10-1,11-1,12-1,13-1,14-1,15-1,16-1,17-1,18-1,19-1,20-1,21-1,22-1

ESV - **17,** 1-1,2-1,3-1,4-1,5-1,6-1,7-1,8-1,9-1,10-1,11-1,12-1,13-1,14-1,15-1,16-1,17-1

HCSB - **16,** 1-**3**,2-1,3-1,4-1,5-1,6-1,7-1,8-1,9-1,10-1,11-1,12-**2**,13-1,14-1,15-1,16-1

NASV - **16,** 1-1,2-1,3-1,4-1,5-1,6-1,7-1,8-1,9-1,10-1,11-1,12-1,13-1,14-1,15-1,16-1

NCV - **15,** 1-**2**,2-1,3-1,4-1,5-1,6-1,7-1,8-1,9-1,10-1,11-**2**,12-1,13-1,14-1,15-1

NIV - **17,** 1-1,2-1,3-1,4-1,5-1,6-1,7-1,8-1,9-1,10-1,11-1,12-1,13-1,14-1,15-1,16-1,17-1

NKJV - **23,** 1-1,2-1,3-1,4-1,5-1,6-1,7-1,8-1,9-1,10-1,11-1,12-1,13-1,14-1,15-1,16-1,17-1,18-1,19-1,20-1,21-1,22-1,23-1

NLT - **16,** 1-1,2-**2**,3-1,4-1,5-1,6-1,7-1,8-1,9-1,10-1,11-1,12-**2**,13-1,14-1,15-1,16-1

NRSV - **16,** 1-1,2-1,3-1,4-1,5-1,6-1,7-1,8-1,9-1,10-1,11-1,12-1,13-1,14-1,15-1,16-1

Conclusion: Only three modern versions are more complex than the King James Bible. Both the NCV and NLT inserted the name Ahab as the king of Israel ut this was not counted against them since proper names are accepted in this study.

307. 1 Kings 22:44* And **Jehoshaphat** made peace with the king of **Israel**.

AV - **9,** 1-1,2-1,3-1,4-1,5-1,6-1,7-1,8-1,9-1

ESV - **9,** 1-1,2-**2**,3-1,4-1,5-1,6-1,7-1,8-1,9-1

HCSB - **9,** 1-1,2-**2**,3-1,4-1,5-1,6-1,7-1,8-1,9-1

NASV - **9,** 1-1,2-**2**,3-1,4-1,5-1,6-1,7-1,8-1,9-1

NCV - **9,** 1-1,2-1,3-1,4-1,5-1,6-1,7-1,8-1,9-1

NIV - **10,** 1-1,2-1,3-**2**,4-1,5-1,6-1,7-1,8-1,9-1,10-1

NKJV - **9,** 1-**2**,2-1,3-1,4-1,5-1,6-1,7-1,8-1,9-1

NLT - **9,** 1-1,2-**2**,3-1,4-1,5-1,6-1,7-1,8-1,9-1

NRSV - **9,** 1-1,2-**2**,3-1,4-1,5-1,6-1,7-1,8-1,9-1

Conclusion: Seven modern versions are more complex than the King James Bible.

308. 2 Kings 3:12* And **Jehoshaphat** said, The word of the LORD is with him. So the king of **Israel** and **Jehoshaphat** and the king of **Edom** went down to him.

AV - **27,** 1-1,2-1,3-1,4-1,5-1,6-1,7-1,8-1,9-1,10-1,11-1,12-1,13-1,14-1,15-1,16-1,17-1,18-1,19-1,20-1,21-1,22-1,23-1,24-1,25-1,26-1,27-1

ESV - **27,** 1-1,2-1,3-1,4-1,5-1,6-1,7-1,8-1,9-1,10-1,11-1,12-1,13-1,14-1,15-1,16-1,17-1,18-1,19-1,20-1,21-1,22-1,23-1,24-1,25-1,26-1,27-1

HCSB - **23,** 1-1,2-**2**,3-1,4-1,5-1,6-1,7-1,8-1,9-1,10-1,11-1,12-1,13-1,14-1,15-1,16-1,17-1,18-1,19-1,20-1,21-1,22-1,23-1

NASV - **26,** 1-1,2-1,3-1,4-1,5-1,6-1,7-1,8-1,9-1,10-1,11-1,12-1,13-1,14-1,15-1,16-1,17-1,18-1,19-1,20-1,21-1,22-1,23-1,24-1,25-1,26-1

NCV - **24,** 1-1,2-1,3-1,4-1,5-1,6-1,7-1,8-1,9-1,10-1,11-1,12-1,13-1,14-1,15-1,16-1,17-1,18-1,19-1,20-1,21-1,22-1,23-1,24-1

NIV - **26,** 1-1,2-1,3-1,4-1,5-1,6-1,7-1,8-1,9-1,10-1,11-1,12-1,13-1,14-1,15-1,16-1,17-1,18-1,19-1,20-1,21-1,22-1,23-1,24-1,25-1,26-1

NKJV - **27,** 1-1,2-1,3-1,4-1,5-1,6-1,7-1,8-1,9-1,10-1,11-1,12-1,13-1,14-1,15-1,16-1,17-1,18-1,19-1,20-1,21-1,22-1,23-1,24-1,25-1,26-1,27-1

NLT - **21,** 1-1,2-1,3-1,4-1,5-1,6-1,7-1,8-1,9-1,10-1,11-1,12-1,13-1,14-1,15-1,16-1,17-1,18-1,19-**2**,20-1,21-1

NRSV - **26,** 1-1,2-1,3-1,4-1,5-1,6-1,7-1,8-1,9-1,10-1,11-1,12-1,13-1,14-1,15-1,16-1,17-1,18-1,19-1,20-1,21-1,22-1,23-1,24-1,25-1,26-1

Conclusion: Only the HCSB and the NLT made the verse more complex.

309. 2 Kings 4:15 And he said, Call her. And when he had called her, she stood in the door.

AV - **16,** 1-1,2-1,3-1,4-1,5-1,6-1,7-1,8-1,9-1,10-1,11-1,12-1,13-1,14-1,15-1,16-1

ESV - **15,** 1-1,2-1,3-1,4-1,5-1,6-1,7-1,8-1,9-1,10-1,11-1,12-1,13-1,14-1,15-**2**

HCSB - **14,** 1-1,2-1,3-1,4-1,5-1,6-1,7-1,8-1,9-1,10-1,11-1,12-1,13-1,14-**2**

NASV - **14,** 1-1,2-1,3-1,4-1,5-1,6-1,7-1,8-1,9-1,10-1,11-1,12-1,13-1,14-**2**

NCV - **21,** 1-1,2-1,3-1,4-**2**,5-1,6-1,7-1,8-1,9-1,10-**2**,11-**2**,12-1,13-1,14-1,15-1,16-1,17-1,18-1,19-1,20-1,21-**2**

NIV - **15,** 1-1,2-1,3-1,4-1,5-1,6-1,7-1,8-1,9-1,10-1,11-1,12-1,13-1,14-1,15-**2**

NKJV - **15,** 1-1,2-1,3-1,4-1,5-1,6-1,7-1,8-1,9-1,10-1,11-1,12-1,13-1,14-1,15-**2**

NLT - **16,** 1-1,2-1,3-1,4-1,5-1,6-1,7-1,8-1,9-1,10-1,11-1,12-1,13-1,14-1,15-1,16-**2**

NRSV - **14,** 1-1,2-1,3-1,4-1,5-1,6-1,7-1,8-1,9-1,10-1,11-1,12-1,13-1,14-1

Conclusion: Seven modern versions are more complex than the King James Bible. The NCV seemed to go out of its way to make this verse difficult to read.

310. 2 Kings 6:4* So he went with them. And when they came to **Jordan**, they cut down wood.

AV - **15,** 1-1,2-1,3-1,4-1,5-1,6-1,7-1,8-1,9-1,10-1,11-1,12-1,13-1,14-1,15-1

ESV - **16,** 1-1,2-1,3-1,4-1,5-1,6-1,7-1,8-1,9-1,10-1,11-1,12-1,13-1,14-1,15-1,16-1

HCSB - **16,** 1-1,2-1,3-1,4-1,5-1,6-1,7-1,8-1,9-1,10-1,11-1,12-1,13-1,14-1,15-1,16-1

NASV - **16,** 1-1,2-1,3-1,4-1,5-1,6-1,7-1,8-1,9-1,10-1,11-1,12-1,13-1,14-1,15-1,16-1

NCV - **16,** 1-1,2-1,3-1,4-1,5-1,6-1,7-1,8-**2**,9-1,10-1,11-1,12-1,13-1,14-1,15-1,16-1

NIV - **16,** 1-1,2-1,3-1,4-1,5-1,6-1,7-1,8-1,9-1,10-1,11-1,12-**2**,13-1,14-1,15-1,16-1

NKJV - **16,** 1-1,2-1,3-1,4-1,5-1,6-1,7-1,8-1,9-1,10-1,11-1,12-1,13-1,14-1,15-1,16-1

NLT - **16,** 1-1,2-1,3-1,4-1,5-1,6-1,7-1,8-**2**,9-1,10-1,11-1,12-1,13-**2**,14-**2**,15-1,16-1

NRSV - **15,** 1-1,2-1,3-1,4-1,5-1,6-1,7-1,8-1,9-1,10-1,11-1,12-1,13-1,14-1,15-1

Conclusion: Only three modern versions are more complex than the King James Bible. The NLT is the most difficult to read.

311. 2 Kings 14:1*# In the **second** year of **Joash** son of **Jehoahaz** king of **Israel** reigned **Amaziah** the son of **Joash** king of **Judah**.

AV - **21,** 1-1,2-1,3-1,4-1,5-1,6-1,7-1,8-1,9-1,10-1,11-1,12-1,13-1,14-1,15-1,16-1,17-1,18-1,19-1,20-1,21-1

ESV - **24,** 1-1,2-1,3-1,4-1,5-1,6-1,7-1,8-1,9-1,10-1,11-1,12-1,13-1,14-1,15-1,16-1,17-1,18-1,19-1,20-1,21-1,22-**2**,23-1,24-1

HCSB - **19,** 1-1,2-1,3-1,4-1,5-1,6-1,7-1,8-1,9-1,10-1,11-1,12-1,13-1,14-1,15-1,16-**2**,17-1,18-1,19-1

NASV - **21,** 1-1,2-1,3-1,4-1,5-1,6-1,7-1,8-1,9-1,10-1,11-1,12-1,13-1,14-1,15-1,16-1,17-1,18-1,19-1,20-**2**,21-1

NCV - 20, 1-1,2-1,3-1,4-1,5-**2**,6-1,7-1,8-1,9-**2**,10-1,11-1,12-1,13-1,14-1,15-1,16-1,17-1,18-1,19-1,20-1

NIV - 22, 1-1,2-1,3-1,4-1,5-1,6-1,7-1,8-1,9-1,10-1,11-1,12-1,13-1,14-1,15-1,16-1,17-1,18-1,19-1,20-**2**,21-1,22-1

NKJV - 23, 1-1,2-1,3-1,4-1,5-1,6-1,7-1,8-1,9-1,10-1,11-1,12-1,13-1,14-1,15-1,16-1,17-1,18-1,19-1,20-1,21-1,22-**2**,23-1

NLT - 21, 1-1,2-1,3-1,4-1,5-**2**,6-1,7-1,8-**2**,9-1,10-1,11-1,12-1,13-1,14-1,15-1,16-1,17-1,18-1,19-1,20-1,21-1

NRSV - 22, 1-1,2-1,3-1,4-1,5-1,6-1,7-1,8-1,9-1,10-1,11-1,12-1,13-1,14-1,15-1,16-1,17-1,18-1,19-1,20-**2**,21-1,22-1

Conclusion: All eight modern versions are more complex than the King James Bible.

312. 2 Kings 17:30* And the men of **Babylon** made **Succothbenoth**, and the men of Cuth made **Nergal**, and the men of **Hamath** made **Ashima**,

AV - 21, 1-1,2-1,3-1,4-1,5-1,6-1,7-1,8-1,9-1,10-1,11-1,12-1,13-1,14-1,15-1,16-1,17-1,18-1,19-1,20-1,21-1

ESV - 18, 1-1,2-1,3-1,4-1,5-1,6-1,7-1,8-1,9-1,10-1,11-1,12-1,13-1,14-1,15-1,16-1,17-1,18-1

HCSB - 18, 1-1,2-1,3-1,4-1,5-1,6-1,7-1,8-1,9-1,10-1,11-1,12-1,13-1,14-1,15-1,16-1,17-1,18-1

NASV - 18, 1-1,2-1,3-1,4-1,5-1,6-1,7-1,8-1,9-1,10-1,11-1,12-1,13-1,14-1,15-1,16-1,17-1,18-1

NCV - 20, 1-1,2-**2**,3-1,4-1,5-1,6-1,7-1,8-1,9-1,10-1,11-**2**,12-1,13-1,14-**2**,15-1,16-**2**,17-1,18-1,19-**2**,20-1

NIV - 20, 1-1,2-1,3-1,4-1,5-1,6-1,7-1,8-1,9-1,10-1,11-1,12-1,13-1,14-1,15-1,16-1,17-1,18-1,19-1,20-1

NKJV - 19, 1-1,2-1,3-1,4-1,5-1,6-1,7-1,8-1,9-1,10-1,11-1,12-1,13-1,14-1,15-1,16-1,17-1,18-1,19-1

NLT - 22, 1-1,2-1,3-1,4-**2**,5-**2**,6-1,7-1,8-1,9-1,10-1,11-1,12-1,13-**2**,14-1,15-1,16-1,17-1,18-1,19-1,20-1,21-**2**,22-1

NRSV - 18, 1-1,2-**2**,3-1,4-1,5-1,6-1,7-1,8-**2**,9-1,10-1,11-1,12-1,13-1,14-**2**,15-1,16-1,17-1,18-1

Conclusion: Only three modern versions are more complex than the King James Bible.

313. 2 Kings 22:11 And it came to pass, when the king had heard the words of the book of the law, that he rent his clothes.

AV - 23, 1-1,2-1,3-1,4-1,5-1,6-1,7-1,8-1,9-1,10-1,11-1,12-1,13-1,14-1,15-1,16-1,17-1,18-1,19-1,20-1,21-1,22-1,23-1

ESV - 16, 1-1,2-1,3-1,4-1,5-1,6-1,7-1,8-1,9-1,10-1,11-1,12-1,13-1,14-1,15-1,16-1

HCSB - 16, 1-1,2-1,3-1,4-1,5-1,6-1,7-1,8-1,9-1,10-1,11-1,12-1,13-1,14-1,15-1,16-1

NASV - 16, 1-1,2-1,3-1,4-1,5-1,6-1,7-1,8-1,9-1,10-1,11-1,12-1,13-1,14-1,15-1,16-1

NCV - 22, 1-1,2-1,3-1,4-1,5-1,6-1,7-1,8-1,9-1,10-1,11-1,12-**2**,13-1,14-1,15-1,16-1,17-1,18-1,19-1,20-**2**,21-1,22-1

NIV - 16, 1-1,2-1,3-1,4-1,5-1,6-1,7-1,8-1,9-1,10-1,11-1,12-1,13-1,14-1,15-1,16-1

NKJV - 20, 1-1,2-1,3-**2**,4-1,5-1,6-1,7-1,8-1,9-1,10-1,11-1,12-1,13-1,14-1,15-1,16-1,17-1,18-1,19-1,20-1

NLT - 19, 1-1,2-1,3-1,4-1,5-1,6-1,7-**2**,8-1,9-1,10-1,11-1,12-1,13-1,14-1,15-1,16-1,17-1,18-1,19-**2**

NRSV - 16, 1-1,2-1,3-1,4-1,5-1,6-1,7-1,8-1,9-1,10-1,11-1,12-1,13-1,14-1,15-1,16-1

Conclusion: Only three modern versions are more complex than the King James Bible. This is one of the rare times that the NKJV was more complex than either the NCV, HCSB, NASV, NIV or NRSV.

314. 1 Chronicles 1:4* **Noah**, Shem, Ham, and **Japheth**.
AV - **5,** 1-1,2-1,3-1,4-1,5-1
ESV - **5,** 1-1,2-1,3-1,4-1,5-1
HCSB - **7,** 1-1,2-1,3-1,4-1,5-1,6-1,7-1
NASV - **5,** 1-1,2-1,3-1,4-1,5-1
NCV - **9,** 1-1,2-1,3-1,4-1,5-1,6-1,7-1,8-1,9-1
NIV - **8,** 1-1,2-1,3-1,4-1,5-1,6-1,7-1,8-1
NKJV - **5,** 1-1,2-1,3-1,4-1,5-1
NLT - **11,** 1-1,2-1,3-1,4-1,5-1,6-1,7-1,8-1,9-1,10-1,11-1
NRSV - **5,** 1-1,2-1,3-1,4-1,5-1
Conclusion: All versions read the same.

315. 1 Chronicles 1:5* The sons of **Japheth**; **Gomer**, and **Magog**, and **Madai**, and **Javan**, and **Tubal**, and **Meshech**, and **Tiras**.
AV - **17,** 1-1,2-1,3-1,4-1,5-1,6-1,7-1,8-1,9-1,10-1,11-1,12-1,13-1,14-1,15-1,16-1,17-1
ESV - **12,** 1-1,2-1,3-1,4-1,5-1,6-1,7-1,8-1,9-1,10-1,11-1,12-1
HCSB - **10,** 1-1,2-1,3-1,4-1,5-1,6-1,7-1,8-1,9-1,10-1
NASV - **13,** 1-1,2-1,3-1,4-1,5-1,6-1,7-1,8-1,9-1,10-1,11-1,12-1,13-1
NCV - **11,** 1-1,2-1,3-1,4-1,5-1,6-1,7-1,8-1,9-1,10-1,11-1
NIV - **12,** 1-1,2-1,3-1,4-1,5-1,6-1,7-1,8-1,9-1,10-1,11-1,12-1
NKJV - **13,** 1-1,2-1,3-1,4-1,5-1,6-1,7-1,8-1,9-1,10-1,11-1,12-1,13-1
NLT - **13,** 1-1,2-3,3-1,4-1,5-1,6-1,7-1,8-1,9-1,10-1,11-1,12-1,13-1
NRSV - **12,** 1-1,2-3,3-1,4-1,5-1,6-1,7-1,8-1,9-1,10-1,11-1,12-1
Conclusion: Only the NLT and the NRSV made the verse more complex.

316. 1 Chronicles 1:6* And the sons of **Gomer**; **Ashchenaz**, and **Riphath**, and **Togarmah**.
AV - **10,** 1-1,2-1,3-1,4-1,5-1,6-1,7-1,8-1,9-1,10-1
ESV - **8,** 1-1,2-1,3-1,4-1,5-1,6-1,7-1,8-1
HCSB - **6,** 1-1,2-1,3-1,4-1,5-1,6-1
NASV - **9,** 1-1,2-1,3-1,4-1,5-1,6-1,7-1,8-1,9-1
NCV - **7,** 1-1,2-1,3-1,4-1,5-1,6-1,7-1
NIV - **8,** 1-1,2-1,3-1,4-1,5-1,6-1,7-1,8-1
NKJV - **9,** 1-1,2-1,3-1,4-1,5-1,6-1,7-1,8-1,9-1
NLT - **9,** 1-1,2-3,3-1,4-1,5-1,6-1,7-1,8-1,9-1
NRSV - **8,** 1-1,2-3,3-1,4-1,5-1,6-1,7-1,8-1
Conclusion: Only the NLT and the NRSV made the verse more complex.

317. 1 Chronicles 1:7* And the sons of **Javan**; **Elishah**, and **Tarshish**, **Kittim**, and **Dodanim**.
AV - **11,** 1-1,2-1,3-1,4-1,5-1,6-1,7-1,8-1,9-1,10-1,11-1
ESV - **9,** 1-1,2-1,3-1,4-1,5-1,6-1,7-1,8-1,9-1

HCSB - **7,** 1-1,2-1,3-1,4-1,5-1,6-1,7-1
NASV - **10,** 1-1,2-1,3-1,4-1,5-1,6-1,7-1,8-1,9-1,10-1
NCV - **8,** 1-1,2-1,3-1,4-1,5-1,6-1,7-1,8-1
NIV - **11,** 1-1,2-1,3-1,4-1,5-1,6-1,7-1,8-1,9-1,10-1,11-1
NKJV - **10,** 1-1,2-1,3-1,4-1,5-1,6-1,7-1,8-1,9-1,10-1
NLT - **10,** 1-1,2-**3**,3-1,4-1,5-1,6-1,7-1,8-1,9-1,10-1
NRSV - **9,** 1-1,2-**3**,3-1,4-1,5-1,6-1,7-1,8-1,9-1
Conclusion: Only the NLT and the NRSV made the verse more complex.

318. 1 Chronicles 1:8* The sons of Ham; Cush, and **Mizraim**, Put, and **Canaan**.
AV - **10,** 1-1,2-1,3-1,4-1,5-1,6-1,7-1,8-1,9-1,10-1
ESV - **9,** 1-1,2-1,3-1,4-1,5-1,6-1,7-1,8-1,9-1
HCSB - **7,** 1-1,2-1,3-1,4-1,5-1,6-1,7-1
NASV - **10,** 1-1,2-1,3-1,4-1,5-1,6-1,7-1,8-1,9-1,10-1
NCV - **8,** 1-1,2-1,3-1,4-1,5-1,6-1,7-1,8-1
NIV - **9,** 1-1,2-1,3-1,4-1,5-1,6-1,7-1,8-1,9-1
NKJV - **10,** 1-1,2-1,3-1,4-1,5-1,6-1,7-1,8-1,9-1,10-1
NLT - **10,** 1-1,2-**3**,3-1,4-1,5-1,6-1,7-1,8-1,9-1,10-1
NRSV - **9,** 1-1,2-**3**,3-1,4-1,5-1,6-1,7-1,8-1,9-1
Conclusion: Only the NLT and the NRSV made the verse more complex.

319. 1 Chronicles 1:9* And the sons of Cush; **Seba**, and **Havilah**, and **Sabta**, and **Raamah**, and **Sabtecha**. And the sons of **Raamah**; **Sheba**, and **Dedan**.
AV - **22,** 1-1,2-1,3-1,4-1,5-1,6-1,7-1,8-1,9-1,10-1,11-1,12-1,13-1,14-1,15-1,16-1,17-1,18-1,19-1,20-1,21-1,22-1
ESV - **17,** 1-1,2-1,3-1,4-1,5-1,6-1,7-1,8-1,9-1,10-1,11-1,12-1,13-1,14-1,15-1,16-1,17-1
HCSB - **13,** 1-1,2-1,3-1,4-1,5-1,6-1,7-1,8-1,9-1,10-1,11-1,12-1,13-1
NASV - **20,** 1-1,2-1,3-1,4-1,5-1,6-1,7-1,8-1,9-1,10-1,11-1,12-1,13-1,14-1,15-1,16-1,17-1,18-1,19-1,20-1
NCV - **15,** 1-1,2-1,3-1,4-1,5-1,6-1,7-1,8-1,9-1,10-1,11-1,12-1,13-1,14-1,15-1
NIV - **17,** 1-1,2-1,3-1,4-1,5-1,6-1,7-1,8-1,9-1,10-1,11-1,12-1,13-1,14-1,15-1,16-1,17-1
NKJV - **19,** 1-1,2-1,3-1,4-1,5-1,6-1,7-1,8-1,9-1,10-1,11-1,12-1,13-1,14-1,15-1,16-1,17-1,18-1,19-1
NLT - **19,** 1-1,2-**3**,3-1,4-1,5-1,6-1,7-1,8-1,9-1,10-1,11-1,12-1,13-**3**,14-1,15-1,16-1,17-1,18-1,19-1
NRSV - **17,** 1-1,2-**3**,3-1,4-1,5-1,6-1,7-1,8-1,9-1,10-1,11-1,12-**3**,13-1,14-1,15-1,16-1,17-1
Conclusion: Only the NLT and the NRSV made the verse more complex.

320. 1 Chronicles 1:12* And **Pathrusim**, and **Casluhim**, (of whom came the **Philistines**,) and **Caphthorim**.
AV - **11,** 1-1,2-1,3-1,4-1,5-1,6-1,7-1,8-1,9-1,10-1,11-1
ESV - **9,** 1-1,2-1,3-1,4-1,5-1,6-1,7-1,8-1,9-1
HCSB - **9,** 1-1,2-1,3-1,4-1,5-1,6-1,7-1,8-1,9-1
NASV - **9,** 1-1,2-1,3-1,4-1,5-1,6-1,7-1,8-1,9-1
NCV - **10,** 1-1,2-1,3-1,4-1,5-1,6-1,7-1,8-1,9-1,10-1
NIV - **9,** 1-1,2-1,3-1,4-1,5-1,6-1,7-1,8-1,9-1

NKJV - **10,** 1-1,2-1,3-1,4-1,5-1,6-1,7-1,8-1,9-1,10-1
NLT - **10,** 1-1,2-1,3-1,4-1,5-1,6-1,7-1,8-1,9-1,10-1
NRSV - **9,** 1-1,2-1,3-1,4-1,5-1,6-1,7-1,8-1,9-1
Conclusion: All versions read the same.

321. 1 Chronicles 1:15* And the **Hivite**, and the **Arkite**, and the **Sinite**,
AV - **9,** 1-1,2-1,3-1,4-1,5-1,6-1,7-1,8-1,9-1
ESV - **6,** 1-1,2-1,3-1,4-1,5-1,6-1
HCSB - **3,** 1-1,2-1,3-1
NASV - **6,** 1-1,2-1,3-1,4-1,5-1,6-1
NCV - **3,** 1-1,2-1,3-1
NIV - **3,** 1-1,2-1,3-1
NKJV - **6,** 1-1,2-1,3-1,4-1,5-1,6-1
NLT - **3,** 1-1,2-1,3-1
NRSV - **6,** 1-1,2-1,3-1,4-1,5-1,6-1
Conclusion: All versions read the same.

322. 1 Chronicles 1:16* And the **Arvadite**, and the **Zemarite**, and the **Hamathite**.
AV - **9,** 1-1,2-1,3-1,4-1,5-1,6-1,7-1,8-1,9-1
ESV - **6,** 1-1,2-1,3-1,4-1,5-1,6-1
HCSB - **4,** 1-1,2-1,3-1,4-1
NASV - **6,** 1-1,2-1,3-1,4-1,5-1,6-1
NCV - **4,** 1-1,2-1,3-1,4-1
NIV - **4,** 1-1,2-1,3-1,4-1
NKJV - **6,** 1-1,2-1,3-1,4-1,5-1,6-1
NLT - **4,** 1-1,2-1,3-1,4-1
NRSV - **6,** 1-1,2-1,3-1,4-1,5-1,6-1
Conclusion: All versions read the same.

323. 1 Chronicles 1:17* The sons of Shem; **Elam**, and **Asshur**, and **Arphaxad**, and Lud, and **Aram**, and Uz, and Hul, and **Gether**, and **Meshech**.
AV - **21,** 1-1,2-1,3-1,4-1,5-1,6-1,7-1,8-1,9-1,10-1,11-1,12-1,13-1,14-1,15-1,16-1,17-1,18-1,19-1,20-1,21-1
ESV - **20,** 1-1,2-1,3-1,4-1,5-1,6-1,7-1,8-1,9-1,10-1,11-1,12-1,13-1,14-1,15-1,16-1,17-1,18-1,19-1,20-1
HCSB - **12,** 1-1,2-1,3-1,4-1,5-1,6-1,7-1,8-1,9-1,10-1,11-1,12-1
NASV - **15,** 1-1,2-1,3-1,4-1,5-1,6-1,7-1,8-1,9-1,10-1,11-1,12-1,13-1,14-1,15-1
NCV - **17,** 1-1,2-1,3-1,4-1,5-1,6-1,7-1,8-1,9-1,10-1,11-1,12-1,13-1,14-1,15-1,16-1,17-1
NIV - **19,** 1-1,2-1,3-1,4-1,5-1,6-1,7-1,8-1,9-1,10-1,11-1,12-1,13-1,14-1,15-1,16-1,17-1,18-1,19-1
NKJV - **15,** 1-1,2-1,3-1,4-1,5-1,6-1,7-1,8-1,9-1,10-1,11-1,12-1,13-1,14-1,15-1
NLT - **21,** 1-1,2-**3,**3-1,4-1,5-1,6-1,7-1,8-1,9-1,10-1,11-1,12-1,13-**3,**14-1,15-1,16-1,17-1,18-1,19-1,20-1,21-1
NRSV - **14,** 1-1,2-**3,**3-1,4-1,5-1,6-1,7-1,8-1,9-1,10-1,11-1,12-1,13-1,14-1
Conclusion: Only the NLT and the NRSV made the verse more complex.

324. 1 Chronicles 1:22* And **Ebal**, and **Abimael**, and **Sheba**,
AV - **6,** 1-1,2-1,3-1,4-1,5-1,6-1
ESV - **3,** 1-1,2-1,3-1
HCSB - **3,** 1-1,2-1,3-1
NASV - **3,** 1-1,2-1,3-1
NCV - **3,** 1-1,2-1,3-1
NIV - **3,** 1-1,2-1,3-1
NKJV - **3,** 1-1,2-1,3-1
NLT - **3,** 1-1,2-1,3-1
NRSV - **3,** 1-1,2-1,3-1
Conclusion: All versions read the same.

325. 1 Chronicles 1:23* And **Ophir**, and **Havilah**, and **Jobab**. All these were the sons of **Joktan**.
AV - **13,** 1-1,2-1,3-1,4-1,5-1,6-1,7-1,8-1,9-1,10-1,11-1,12-1,13-1
ESV - **11,** 1-1,2-1,3-1,4-1,5-1,6-1,7-1,8-1,9-1,10-1,11-1
HCSB - **10,** 1-1,2-1,3-1,4-1,5-1,6-1,7-1,8-1,9-1,10-1
NASV - **11,** 1-1,2-1,3-1,4-1,5-1,6-1,7-1,8-1,9-1,10-1,11-1
NCV - **9,** 1-1,2-1,3-1,4-1,5-1,6-1,7-1,8-1,9-1
NIV - **10,** 1-1,2-1,3-1,4-1,5-1,6-1,7-1,8-1,9-1,10-1
NKJV - **11,** 1-1,2-1,3-1,4-1,5-1,6-1,7-1,8-1,9-1,10-1,11-1
NLT - **10,** 1-1,2-1,3-1,4-1,5-1,6-1,7-1,8-**3**,9-1,10-1
NRSV - **11,** 1-1,2-1,3-1,4-1,5-1,6-1,7-1,8-1,9-**3**,10-1,11-1
Conclusion: Only the NLT and the NRSV made the verse more complex.

326. 1 Chronicles 1:27* **Abram**; the same is **Abraham**.
AV - **5,** 1-1,2-1,3-1,4-1,5-1
ESV - **4,** 1-1,2-1,3-1,4-1
HCSB - **5,** 1-1,2-1,3-1,4-1,5-1
NASV - **4,** 1-1,2-1,3-1,4-1
NCV - **6,** 1-1,2-1,3-1,4-1,5-1,6-1
NIV - **5,** 1-1,2-1,3-1,4-1,5-1
NKJV - **5,** 1-1,2-1,3-1,4-1,5-1
NLT - **6,** 1-1,2-1,3-**2**,4-1,5-1,6-1
NRSV - **4,** 1-1,2-1,3-1,4-1
Conclusion: Only the NLT made the verse more complex.

327. 1 Chronicles 1:28* The sons of **Abraham**; **Isaac**, and **Ishmael**.
AV - **7,** 1-1,2-1,3-1,4-1,5-1,6-1,7-1
ESV - **7,** 1-1,2-1,3-1,4-1,5-1,6-1,7-1
HCSB - **5,** 1-1,2-1,3-1,4-1,5-1
NASV - **8,** 1-1,2-1,3-1,4-1,5-1,6-1,7-1,8-1
NCV - **6,** 1-1,2-1,3-1,4-1,5-1,6-1
NIV - **7,** 1-1,2-1,3-1,4-1,5-1,6-1,7-1
NKJV - **8,** 1-1,2-1,3-1,4-1,5-1,6-1,7-1,8-1

NLT - **8,** 1-1,2-1,3-1,4-1,5-1,6-1,7-1,8-1
NRSV - **7,** 1-1,2-1,3-1,4-1,5-1,6-1,7-1
Conclusion: All versions read the same.

328. 1 Chronicles 1:31* **Jetur**, **Naphish**, and **Kedemah**. These are the sons of **Ishmael**.
AV - **10,** 1-1,2-1,3-1,4-1,5-1,6-1,7-1,8-1,9-1,10-1
ESV - **10,** 1-1,2-1,3-1,4-1,5-1,6-1,7-1,8-1,9-1,10-1
HCSB - **8,** 1-1,2-1,3-1,4-1,5-1,6-1,7-1,8-1
NASV - **10,** 1-1,2-1,3-1,4-1,5-1,6-1,7-1,8-1,9-1,10-1
NCV - **8,** 1-1,2-1,3-1,4-1,5-1,6-1,7-1,8-1
NIV - **10,** 1-1,2-1,3-1,4-1,5-1,6-1,7-1,8-1,9-1,10-1
NKJV - **10,** 1-1,2-1,3-1,4-1,5-1,6-1,7-1,8-1,9-1,10-1
NLT - **10,** 1-1,2-1,3-1,4-1,5-1,6-1,7-1,8-1,9-1,10-1
NRSV - **10,** 1-1,2-1,3-1,4-1,5-1,6-1,7-1,8-1,9-1,10-1
Conclusion: All versions read the same.

329. 1 Chronicles 1:33* And the sons of **Midian**; **Ephah**, and **Epher**, and **Henoch**, and **Abida**, and **Eldaah**. All these are the sons of **Keturah**.
AV - **21,** 1-1,2-1,3-1,4-1,5-1,6-1,7-1,8-1,9-1,10-1,11-1,12-1,13-1,14-1,15-1,16-1,17-1,18-1,19-1,20-1,21-1
ESV - **17,** 1-1,2-1,3-1,4-1,5-1,6-1,7-1,8-1,9-1,10-1,11-1,12-1,13-1,14-1,15-**3**,16-1,17-1
HCSB - **14,** 1-1,2-1,3-1,4-1,5-1,6-1,7-1,8-1,9-1,10-1,11-1,12-1,13-1,14-1
NASV - **18,** 1-1,2-1,3-1,4-1,5-1,6-1,7-1,8-1,9-1,10-1,11-1,12-1,13-1,14-1,15-1,16-1,17-1,18-1
NCV - **15,** 1-1,2-1,3-1,4-1,5-1,6-1,7-1,8-1,9-1,10-1,11-1,12-1,13-**3**,14-1,15-1
NIV - **16,** 1-1,2-1,3-1,4-1,5-1,6-1,7-1,8-1,9-1,10-1,11-1,12-1,13-1,14-**3**,15-1,16-1
NKJV - **18,** 1-1,2-1,3-1,4-1,5-1,6-1,7-1,8-1,9-1,10-1,11-1,12-1,13-1,14-1,15-1,16-**2**,17-1,18-1
NLT - **21,** 1-1,2-1,3-1,4-1,5-1,6-1,7-1,8-1,9-1,10-1,11-1,12-1,13-1,14-1,15-**3**,16-1,17-1,18-1,19-1,20-**3**,21-1
NRSV - **17,** 1-1,2-1,3-1,4-1,5-1,6-1,7-1,8-1,9-1,10-1,11-1,12-1,13-1,14-1,15-**3**,16-1,17-1
Conclusion: Six modern versions are more complex than the King James Bible.

330. 1 Chronicles 1:35* The sons of **Esau**; **Eliphaz**, **Reuel**, and **Jeush**, and **Jaalam**, and **Korah**.
AV - **12,** 1-1,2-1,3-1,4-1,5-1,6-1,7-1,8-1,9-1,10-1,11-1,12-1
ESV - **10,** 1-1,2-1,3-1,4-1,5-1,6-1,7-1,8-1,9-1,10-1
HCSB - **8,** 1-1,2-1,3-1,4-1,5-1,6-1,7-1,8-1
NASV - **11,** 1-1,2-1,3-1,4-1,5-1,6-1,7-1,8-1,9-1,10-1,11-1
NCV - **9,** 1-1,2-1,3-1,4-1,5-1,6-1,7-1,8-1,9-1
NIV - **10,** 1-1,2-1,3-1,4-1,5-1,6-1,7-1,8-1,9-1,10-1
NKJV - **11,** 1-1,2-1,3-1,4-1,5-1,6-1,7-1,8-1,9-1,10-1,11-1
NLT - **11,** 1-1,2-1,3-1,4-1,5-1,6-1,7-1,8-1,9-1,10-1,11-1
NRSV - **10,** 1-1,2-1,3-1,4-1,5-1,6-1,7-1,8-1,9-1,10-1
Conclusion: All versions read the same.

331. 1 Chronicles 1:36* The sons of **Eliphaz**; **Teman**, and **Omar**, **Zephi**, and **Gatam**, **Kenaz**, and **Timna**, and **Amalek**.
AV - **15,** 1-1,2-1,3-1,4-1,5-1,6-1,7-1,8-1,9-1,10-1,11-1,12-1,13-1,14-1,15-1
ESV - **13,** 1-1,2-1,3-1,4-1,5-1,6-1,7-1,8-1,9-1,10-1,11-1,12-1,13-1
HCSB - **12,** 1-1,2-1,3-1,4-1,5-1,6-1,7-1,8-1,9-1,10-1,11-1,12-1
NASV - **13,** 1-1,2-1,3-1,4-1,5-1,6-1,7-1,8-1,9-1,10-1,11-1,12-1,13-1
NCV - **11,** 1-1,2-1,3-1,4-1,5-1,6-1,7-1,8-1,9-1,10-1,11-1
NIV - **13,** 1-1,2-1,3-1,4-1,5-1,6-1,7-1,8-1,9-1,10-1,11-1,12-1,13-1
NKJV - **16,** 1-1,2-1,3-1,4-1,5-1,6-1,7-1,8-1,9-1,10-1,11-1,12-1,13-1,14-1,15-1,16-1
NLT - **17,** 1-1,2-1,3-1,4-1,5-1,6-1,7-1,8-1,9-1,10-1,11-1,12-1,13-1,14-1,15-1,16-1,17-1
NRSV - **12,** 1-1,2-1,3-1,4-1,5-1,6-1,7-1,8-1,9-1,10-1,11-1,12-1
Conclusion: All versions read the same.

332. 1 Chronicles 1:37* The sons of **Reuel**; **Nahath**, **Zerah**, **Shammah**, and **Mizzah**.
AV - **9,** 1-1,2-1,3-1,4-1,5-1,6-1,7-1,8-1,9-1
ESV - **9,** 1-1,2-1,3-1,4-1,5-1,6-1,7-1,8-1,9-1
HCSB - **7,** 1-1,2-1,3-1,4-1,5-1,6-1,7-1
NASV - **10,** 1-1,2-1,3-1,4-1,5-1,6-1,7-1,8-1,9-1,10-1
NCV - **8,** 1-1,2-1,3-1,4-1,5-1,6-1,7-1,8-1
NIV - **9,** 1-1,2-1,3-1,4-1,5-1,6-1,7-1,8-1,9-1
NKJV - **10,** 1-1,2-1,3-1,4-1,5-1,6-1,7-1,8-1,9-1,10-1
NLT - **10,** 1-1,2-1,3-1,4-1,5-1,6-1,7-1,8-1,9-1,10-1
NRSV - **9,** 1-1,2-1,3-1,4-1,5-1,6-1,7-1,8-1,9-1
Conclusion: All versions read the same.

333. 1 Chronicles 1:38* And the sons of Seir; **Lotan**, and **Shobal**, and **Zibeon**, and **Anah**, and **Dishon**, and **Ezer**, and **Dishan**.
AV - **18,** 1-1,2-1,3-1,4-1,5-1,6-1,7-1,8-1,9-1,10-1,11-1,12-1,13-1,14-1,15-1,16-1,17-1,18-1
ESV - **12,** 1-1,2-1,3-1,4-1,5-1,6-1,7-1,8-1,9-1,10-1,11-1,12-1
HCSB - **10,** 1-1,2-1,3-1,4-1,5-1,6-1,7-1,8-1,9-1,10-1
NASV - **13,** 1-1,2-1,3-1,4-1,5-1,6-1,7-1,8-1,9-1,10-1,11-1,12-1,13-1
NCV - **11,** 1-1,2-1,3-1,4-1,5-1,6-1,7-1,8-1,9-1,10-1,11-1
NIV - **12,** 1-1,2-1,3-1,4-1,5-1,6-1,7-1,8-1,9-1,10-1,11-1,12-1
NKJV - **13,** 1-1,2-1,3-1,4-1,5-1,6-1,7-1,8-1,9-1,10-1,11-1,12-1,13-1
NLT - **13,** 1-1,2-1,3-1,4-1,5-1,6-1,7-1,8-1,9-1,10-1,11-1,12-1,13-1
NRSV - **12,** 1-1,2-1,3-1,4-1,5-1,6-1,7-1,8-1,9-1,10-1,11-1,12-1
Conclusion: All versions read the same.

334. 1 Chronicles 1:40* The sons of **Shobal**; **Alian**, and **Manahath**, and **Ebal**, **Shephi**, and **Onam**. And the sons of **Zibeon**; **Aiah**, and **Anah**.
AV - **20,** 1-1,2-1,3-1,4-1,5-1,6-1,7-1,8-1,9-1,10-1,11-1,12-1,13-1,14-1,15-1,16-1,17-1,18-1,19-1,20-1
ESV - **17,** 1-1,2-1,3-1,4-1,5-1,6-1,7-1,8-1,9-1,10-1,11-1,12-1,13-1,14-1,15-1,16-1,17-1
HCSB - **13,** 1-1,2-1,3-1,4-1,5-1,6-1,7-1,8-1,9-1,10-1,11-1,12-1,13-1

NASV - **20,** 1-1,2-1,3-1,4-1,5-1,6-1,7-1,8-1,9-1,10-1,11-1,12-1,13-1,14-1,15-1,16-1,17-1,18-1,19-1,20-1
NCV - **15,** 1-1,2-1,3-1,4-1,5-1,6-1,7-1,8-1,9-1,10-1,11-1,12-1,13-1,14-1,15-1
NIV - **17,** 1-1,2-1,3-1,4-1,5-1,6-1,7-1,8-1,9-1,10-1,11-1,12-1,13-1,14-1,15-1,16-1,17-1
NKJV - **19,** 1-1,2-1,3-1,4-1,5-1,6-1,7-1,8-1,9-1,10-1,11-1,12-1,13-1,14-1,15-1,16-1,17-1,18-1,19-1
NLT - **19,** 1-1,2-1,3-1,4-1,5-1,6-1,7-1,8-1,9-1,10-1,11-1,12-1,13-1,14-1,15-1,16-1,17-1,18-1,19-1
NRSV - **17,** 1-1,2-1,3-1,4-1,5-1,6-1,7-1,8-1,9-1,10-1,11-1,12-1,13-1,14-1,15-1,16-1,17-1
Conclusion: All versions read the same.

335. 1 Chronicles 1:41* The sons of **Anah**; **Dishon**. And the sons of **Dishon**; **Amram**, and **Eshban**, and **Ithran**, and **Cheran**.
AV - **17,** 1-1,2-1,3-1,4-1,5-1,6-1,7-1,8-1,9-1,10-1,11-1,12-1,13-1,14-1,15-1,16-1,17-1
ESV - **14,** 1-1,2-1,3-1,4-1,5-1,6-1,7-1,8-1,9-1,10-1,11-1,12-1,13-1,14-1
HCSB - **10,** 1-1,2-1,3-1,4-1,5-1,6-1,7-1,8-1,9-1,10-1
NASV - **17,** 1-1,2-1,3-1,4-1,5-1,6-1,7-1,8-1,9-1,10-1,11-1,12-1,13-1,14-1,15-1,16-1,17-1
NCV - **12,** 1-1,2-1,3-1,4-1,5-1,6-1,7-1,8-1,9-1,10-1,11-1,12-1
NIV - **14,** 1-1,2-1,3-1,4-1,5-1,6-1,7-1,8-1,9-1,10-1,11-1,12-1,13-1,14-1
NKJV - **16,** 1-1,2-1,3-1,4-1,5-1,6-1,7-1,8-1,9-1,10-1,11-1,12-1,13-1,14-1,15-1,16-1
NLT - **16,** 1-1,2-1,3-1,4-1,5-1,6-1,7-1,8-1,9-1,10-1,11-1,12-1,13-1,14-1,15-1,16-1
NRSV - **14,** 1-1,2-1,3-1,4-1,5-1,6-1,7-1,8-1,9-1,10-1,11-1,12-1,13-1,14-1
Conclusion: All versions read the same.

336. 1 Chronicles 1:42* The sons of **Ezer**; **Bilhan**, and **Zavan**, and **Jakan**. The sons of **Dishan**; Uz, and **Aran**.
AV - **16,** 1-1,2-1,3-1,4-1,5-1,6-1,7-1,8-1,9-1,10-1,11-1,12-1,13-1,14-1,15-1,16-1
ESV - **15,** 1-1,2-1,3-1,4-1,5-1,6-1,7-1,8-1,9-1,10-1,11-1,12-1,13-1,14-1,15-1
HCSB - **11,** 1-1,2-1,3-1,4-1,5-1,6-1,7-1,8-1,9-1,10-1,11-1
NASV - **17,** 1-1,2-1,3-1,4-1,5-1,6-1,7-1,8-1,9-1,10-1,11-1,12-1,13-1,14-1,15-1,16-1,17-1
NCV - **13,** 1-1,2-1,3-1,4-1,5-1,6-1,7-1,8-1,9-1,10-1,11-1,12-1,13-1
NIV - **15,** 1-1,2-1,3-1,4-1,5-1,6-1,7-1,8-1,9-1,10-1,11-1,12-1,13-1,14-1,15-1
NKJV - **17,** 1-1,2-1,3-1,4-1,5-1,6-1,7-1,8-1,9-1,10-1,11-1,12-1,13-1,14-1,15-1,16-1,17-1
NLT - **17,** 1-1,2-1,3-1,4-1,5-1,6-1,7-1,8-1,9-1,10-1,11-1,12-1,13-1,14-1,15-1,16-1,17-1
NRSV - **17,** 1-1,2-1,3-1,4-1,5-1,6-1,7-1,8-1,9-1,10-1,11-1,12-1,13-1,14-1,15-1,16-1,17-1
Conclusion: All versions read the same.

337. 1 Chronicles 1:44* And when **Bela** was dead, **Jobab** the son of **Zerah** of **Bozrah** reigned in his stead.
AV - **16,** 1-1,2-1,3-1,4-1,5-1,6-1,7-1,8-1,9-1,10-1,11-1,12-1,13-1,14-1,15-1,16-1
ESV - **14,** 1-1,2-1,3-1,4-1,5-1,6-1,7-1,8-1,9-1,10-1,11-1,12-1,13-1,14-1
HCSB - **13,** 1-1,2-1,3-1,4-1,5-1,6-1,7-1,8-1,9-1,10-1,11-1,12-1,13-1
NASV - 15, 1-1,2-1,3-1,4-1,5-1,6-1,7-1,8-1,9-1,10-1,11-**2**,12-1,13-1,14-1,15-1
NCV - 13, 1-1,2-1,3-1,4-1,5-1,6-1,7-1,8-**2**,9-1,10-1,11-1,12-1,13-1
NIV - 13, 1-1,2-1,3-1,4-1,5-1,6-1,7-1,8-1,9-1,10-**3**,11-1,12-1,13-1
NKJV - **15,** 1-1,2-1,3-1,4-1,5-1,6-1,7-1,8-1,9-1,10-1,11-1,12-1,13-1,14-1,15-1

NLT - **11,** 1-1,2-1,3-1,4-1,5-1,6-1,7-1,8-1,9-1,10-**2**,11-1
NRSV - **11,** 1-1,2-1,3-1,4-1,5-1,6-1,7-1,8-1,9-1,10-**3**,11-1
Conclusion: Five modern versions are more complex than the King James Bible.

338. 1 Chronicles 1:45* And when **Jobab** was dead, **Husham** of the land of the **Temanites** reigned in his stead.
AV - **16,** 1-1,2-1,3-1,4-1,5-1,6-1,7-1,8-1,9-1,10-1,11-1,12-1,13-1,14-1,15-1,16-1
ESV - **14,** 1-1,2-1,3-1,4-1,5-1,6-1,7-1,8-1,9-1,10-1,11-1,12-1,13-1,14-1
HCSB - **14,** 1-1,2-1,3-1,4-1,5-1,6-1,7-1,8-1,9-1,10-1,11-1,12-1,13-1,14-1
NASV - 15, 1-1,2-1,3-1,4-1,5-1,6-1,7-1,8-1,9-1,10-1,11-**2**,12-1,13-1,14-1,15-1
NCV - 14, 1-1,2-1,3-1,4-1,5-**2**,6-1,7-1,8-1,9-1,10-1,11-1,12-1,13-1,14-1
NIV - 14, 1-1,2-1,3-1,4-1,5-1,6-1,7-1,8-1,9-1,10-1,11-**3**,12-1,13-1,14-1
NKJV - **14,** 1-1,2-1,3-1,4-1,5-1,6-1,7-1,8-1,9-1,10-1,11-1,12-1,13-1,14-1
NLT - 12, 1-1,2-1,3-1,4-1,5-1,6-1,7-1,8-1,9-1,10-1,11-**2**,12-1
NRSV - 12, 1-1,2-1,3-1,4-1,5-1,6-1,7-1,8-1,9-1,10-1,11-**3**,12-1
Conclusion: Five modern versions are more complex than the King James Bible.

339. 1 Chronicles 1:47* And when **Hadad** was dead, **Samlah** of **Masrekah** reigned in his stead.
AV - **12,** 1-1,2-1,3-1,4-1,5-1,6-1,7-1,8-1,9-1,10-1,11-1,12-1
ESV - **10,** 1-1,2-1,3-1,4-1,5-1,6-1,7-1,8-1,9-1,10-1
HCSB - **10,** 1-1,2-1,3-1,4-1,5-1,6-1,7-1,8-1,9-1,10-1
NASV - 11, 1-1,2-1,3-1,4-1,5-1,6-1,7-**2**,8-1,9-1,10-1,11-1
NCV - 10, 1-1,2-1,3-1,4-1,5-**2**,6-1,7-1,8-1,9-1,10-1
NIV - 10, 1-1,2-1,3-1,4-1,5-1,6-1,7-**3**,8-1,9-1,10-1
NKJV - **10,** 1-1,2-1,3-1,4-1,5-1,6-1,7-1,8-1,9-1,10-1
NLT - 11, 1-1,2-1,3-1,4-1,5-1,6-1,7-**2**,8-1,9-1,10-**2**,11-1
NRSV - 8, 1-1,2-1,3-1,4-1,5-1,6-1,7-**3**,8-1
Conclusion: Five modern versions are more complex than the King James Bible.

340. 1 Chronicles 1:49* And when Shaul was dead, **Baalhanan** the son of **Achbor** reigned in his stead.
AV - **14,** 1-1,2-1,3-1,4-1,5-1,6-1,7-1,8-1,9-1,10-1,11-1,12-1,13-1,14-1
ESV - **12,** 1-1,2-1,3-1,4-1,5-1,6-1,7-1,8-1,9-1,10-1,11-1,12-1
HCSB - **11,** 1-1,2-1,3-1,4-1,5-1,6-1,7-1,8-1,9-1,10-1,11-1
NASV - 13, 1-1,2-1,3-1,4-1,5-1,6-1,7-1,8-1,9-**2**,10-1,11-1,12-1,13-1
NCV - 9, 1-1,2-1,3-1,4-1,5-1,6-1,7-1,8-**2**,9-1
NIV - 11, 1-1,2-1,3-1,4-1,5-1,6-1,7-1,8-**3**,9-1,10-1,11-1
NKJV - **12,** 1-1,2-1,3-1,4-1,5-1,6-1,7-1,8-1,9-1,10-1,11-1,12-1
NLT - 9, 1-1,2-1,3-1,4-1,5-1,6-1,7-1,8-**2**,9-1
NRSV - 9, 1-1,2-1,3-1,4-1,5-1,6-1,7-1,8-**3**,9-1
Conclusion: Five modern versions are more complex than the King James Bible.

341. 1 Chronicles 1:52* Duke **Aholibamah**, duke **Elah**, duke **Pinon**,
AV - **6,** 1-1,2-1,3-1,4-1,5-1,6-1

ESV - **3,** 1-1,2-1,3-1
HCSB - **3,** 1-1,2-1,3-1
NASV - **6,** 1-1,2-1,3-1,4-1,5-1,6-1
NCV - **3,** 1-1,2-1,3-1
NIV - **3,** 1-1,2-1,3-1
NKJV - **6,** 1-1,2-1,3-1,4-1,5-1,6-1
NLT - **3,** 1-1,2-1,3-1
NRSV - **3,** 1-1,2-1,3-1
Conclusion: All versions read the same.

342. 1 Chronicles 1:53* Duke **Kenaz**, duke **Teman**, duke **Mibzar**,
AV - **6,** 1-1,2-1,3-1,4-1,5-1,6-1
ESV - **3,** 1-1,2-1,3-1
HCSB - **3,** 1-1,2-1,3-1
NASV - **6,** 1-1,2-1,3-1,4-1,5-1,6-1
NCV - **3,** 1-1,2-1,3-1
NIV - **3,** 1-1,2-1,3-1
NKJV - **6,** 1-1,2-1,3-1,4-1,5-1,6-1
NLT - **3,** 1-1,2-1,3-1
NRSV - **3,** 1-1,2-1,3-1
Conclusion: All versions read the same.

343. 1 Chronicles 1:54* Duke **Magdiel**, duke **Iram**. These are the dukes of **Edom**.
AV - **10,** 1-1,2-1,3-1,4-1,5-1,6-1,7-1,8-1,9-1,10-1
ESV - **9,** 1-1,2-1,3-1,4-1,5-1,6-1,7-1,8-1,9-1
HCSB - **7,** 1-1,2-1,3-1,4-1,5-1,6-1,7-1
NASV - **10,** 1-1,2-1,3-1,4-1,5-1,6-1,7-1,8-1,9-1,10-1
NCV - 9, 1-1,2-1,3-1,4-1,5-1,6-1,7-**2,**8-1,9-1
NIV - **9,** 1-1,2-1,3-1,4-1,5-1,6-1,7-1,8-1,9-1
NKJV - **11,** 1-1,2-1,3-1,4-1,5-1,6-1,7-1,8-1,9-1,10-1,11-1
NLT - 10, 1-1,2-1,3-1,4-1,5-1,6-1,7-1,8-**2,**9-1,10-1
NRSV - **9,** 1-1,2-1,3-1,4-1,5-1,6-1,7-1,8-1,9-1
Conclusion: Only the NCV and the NLT made the verse more complex.

344. 1 Chronicles 2:1* These are the sons of **Israel**; **Reuben**, **Simeon**, **Levi**, and **Judah**, **Issachar**, and **Zebulun**,
AV - **14,** 1-1,2-1,3-1,4-1,5-1,6-1,7-1,8-1,9-1,10-1,11-1,12-1,13-1,14-1
ESV - **12,** 1-1,2-1,3-1,4-1,5-1,6-1,7-1,8-1,9-1,10-1,11-1,12-1
HCSB - **10,** 1-1,2-1,3-1,4-1,5-1,6-1,7-1,8-1,9-1,10-1
NASV - **12,** 1-1,2-1,3-1,4-1,5-1,6-1,7-1,8-1,9-1,10-1,11-1,12-1
NCV - **11,** 1-1,2-1,3-1,4-1,5-1,6-1,7-1,8-1,9-1,10-1,11-1
NIV - **12,** 1-1,2-1,3-1,4-1,5-1,6-1,7-1,8-1,9-1,10-1,11-1,12-1
NKJV - **12,** 1-1,2-1,3-1,4-1,5-1,6-1,7-1,8-1,9-1,10-1,11-1,12-1
NLT - **11,** 1-1,2-1,3-1,4-1,5-1,6-1,7-1,8-1,9-1,10-1,11-1

NRSV - **12,** 1-1,2-1,3-1,4-1,5-1,6-1,7-1,8-1,9-1,10-1,11-1,12-1
Conclusion: All versions read the same.

345. 1 Chronicles 2:2* Dan, **Joseph**, and **Benjamin**, **Naphtali**, Gad, and **Asher**.
AV - **8,** 1-1,2-1,3-1,4-1,5-1,6-1,7-1,8-1
ESV - **7,** 1-1,2-1,3-1,4-1,5-1,6-1,7-1
HCSB - **7,** 1-1,2-1,3-1,4-1,5-1,6-1,7-1
NASV - **7,** 1-1,2-1,3-1,4-1,5-1,6-1,7-1
NCV - **7,** 1-1,2-1,3-1,4-1,5-1,6-1,7-1
NIV - **7,** 1-1,2-1,3-1,4-1,5-1,6-1,7-1
NKJV - **7,** 1-1,2-1,3-1,4-1,5-1,6-1,7-1
NLT - **7,** 1-1,2-1,3-1,4-1,5-1,6-1,7-1
NRSV - **7,** 1-1,2-1,3-1,4-1,5-1,6-1,7-1
Conclusion: All versions read the same.

346. 1 Chronicles 2:5* The sons of **Pharez**; **Hezron**, and **Hamul**.
AV - **7,** 1-1,2-1,3-1,4-1,5-1,6-1,7-1
ESV - **7,** 1-1,2-1,3-1,4-1,5-1,6-1,7-1
HCSB - **5,** 1-1,2-1,3-1,4-1,5-1
NASV - **8,** 1-1,2-1,3-1,4-1,5-1,6-1,7-1,8-1
NCV - **6,** 1-1,2-1,3-1,4-1,5-1,6-1
NIV - **7,** 1-1,2-1,3-1,4-1,5-1,6-1,7-1
NKJV - **8,** 1-1,2-1,3-1,4-1,5-1,6-1,7-1,8-1
NLT - **8,** 1-1,2-1,3-1,4-1,5-1,6-1,7-1,8-1
NRSV - **7,** 1-1,2-1,3-1,4-1,5-1,6-1,7-1
Conclusion: All versions read the same.

347. 1 Chronicles 2:6* And the sons of **Zerah**; **Zimri**, and **Ethan**, and **Heman**, and **Calcol**, and **Dara**: five of them in all.
AV - **19,** 1-1,2-1,3-1,4-1,5-1,6-1,7-1,8-1,9-1,10-1,11-1,12-1,13-1,14-1,15-1,16-1,17-1,18-1,19-1
ESV - **13,** 1-1,2-1,3-1,4-1,5-1,6-1,7-1,8-1,9-1,10-1,11-1,12-1,13-1
HCSB - **11,** 1-1,2-1,3-1,4-1,5-1,6-1,7-1,8-1,9-1,10-1,11-1
NASV - **16,** 1-1,2-1,3-1,4-1,5-1,6-1,7-1,8-1,9-1,10-1,11-1,12-1,13-1,14-1,15-1,16-1
NCV - **10,** 1-1,2-1,3-1,4-1,5-1,6-1,7-1,8-1,9-1,10-1
NIV - **13,** 1-1,2-1,3-1,4-1,5-1,6-1,7-1,8-1,9-1,10-1,11-1,12-1,13-1
NKJV - **16,** 1-1,2-1,3-1,4-1,5-1,6-1,7-1,8-1,9-1,10-1,11-1,12-1,13-1,14-1,15-1,16-1
NLT - **14,** 1-1,2-1,3-1,4-1,5-1,6-1,7-1,8-1,9-1,10-1,11-1,12-1,13-1,14-1
NRSV - **13,** 1-1,2-1,3-1,4-1,5-1,6-1,7-1,8-1,9-1,10-1,11-1,12-1,13-1
Conclusion: All versions read the same.

348. 1 Chronicles 2:8* And the sons of **Ethan**; **Azariah**.
AV - **6,** 1-1,2-1,3-1,4-1,5-1,6-1
ESV - **5,** 1-1,2-1,3-1,4-1,5-1
HCSB - **3,** 1-1,2-1,3-1

NASV - **6,** 1-1,2-1,3-1,4-1,5-1,6-1
NCV - **4,** 1-1,2-1,3-1,4-1
NIV - **5,** 1-1,2-1,3-1,4-1,5-1
NKJV - **6,** 1-1,2-1,3-1,4-1,5-1,6-1
NLT - **6,** 1-1,2-1,3-1,4-1,5-1,6-1
NRSV - **5,** 1-1,2-1,3-1,4-1,5-1
Conclusion: All versions read the same.

349. 1 Chronicles 2:14* **Nethaneel** the fourth, **Raddai** the fifth,
AV - **6,** 1-1,2-1,3-1,4-1,5-1,6-1
ESV - **6,** 1-1,2-1,3-1,4-1,5-1,6-1
HCSB - **4,** 1-1,2-1,3-1,4-1
NASV - **6,** 1-1,2-1,3-1,4-1,5-1,6-1
NCV - **8,** 1-1,2-1,3-1,4-1,5-1,6-1,7-1,8-1
NIV - **6,** 1-1,2-1,3-1,4-1,5-1,6-1
NKJV - **6,** 1-1,2-1,3-1,4-1,5-1,6-1
NLT - **8,** 1-1,2-1,3-1,4-1,5-1,6-1,7-1,8-1
NRSV - **6,** 1-1,2-1,3-1,4-1,5-1,6-1
Conclusion: All versions read the same.

350. 1 Chronicles 2:15*# **Ozem** the sixth, **David** the **seventh**:
AV - **6,** 1-1,2-1,3-1,4-1,5-1,6-1
ESV - **6,** 1-1,2-1,3-1,4-1,5-1,6-1
HCSB - **5,** 1-1,2-1,3-1,4-1,5-1
NASV - **6,** 1-1,2-1,3-1,4-1,5-1,6-1
NCV - **10,** 1-1,2-1,3-1,4-1,5-1,6-1,7-1,8-1,9-1,10-1
NIV - **7,** 1-1,2-1,3-1,4-1,5-1,6-1,7-1
NKJV - **7,** 1-1,2-1,3-1,4-1,5-1,6-1,7-1
NLT - **9,** 1-1,2-1,3-1,4-1,5-1,6-1,7-1,8-1,9-1
NRSV - **6,** 1-1,2-1,3-1,4-1,5-1,6-1
Conclusion: All versions read the same.

351. 1 Chronicles 2:28* And the sons of **Onam** were, **Shammai**, and **Jada**. And the sons of **Shammai**; **Nadab**, and **Abishur**.
AV - **17,** 1-1,2-1,3-1,4-1,5-1,6-1,7-1,8-1,9-1,10-1,11-1,12-1,13-1,14-1,15-1,16-1,17-1
ESV - **14,** 1-1,2-1,3-1,4-1,5-1,6-1,7-1,8-1,9-1,10-1,11-1,12-1,13-1,14-1
HCSB - **10,** 1-1,2-1,3-1,4-1,5-1,6-1,7-1,8-1,9-1,10-1
NASV - **17,** 1-1,2-1,3-1,4-1,5-1,6-1,7-1,8-1,9-1,10-1,11-1,12-1,13-1,14-1,15-1,16-1,17-1
NCV - **12,** 1-1,2-1,3-1,4-1,5-1,6-1,7-1,8-1,9-1,10-1,11-1,12-1
NIV - **14,** 1-1,2-1,3-1,4-1,5-1,6-1,7-1,8-1,9-1,10-1,11-1,12-1,13-1,14-1
NKJV - **16,** 1-1,2-1,3-1,4-1,5-1,6-1,7-1,8-1,9-1,10-1,11-1,12-1,13-1,14-1,15-1,16-1
NLT - **16,** 1-1,2-1,3-1,4-1,5-1,6-1,7-1,8-1,9-1,10-1,11-1,12-1,13-1,14-1,15-1,16-1
NRSV - **14,** 1-1,2-1,3-1,4-1,5-1,6-1,7-1,8-1,9-1,10-1,11-1,12-1,13-1,14-1
Conclusion: All versions read the same.

352. 1 Chronicles 2:29* And the name of the wife of **Abishur** was **Abihail**, and she bare him **Ahban**, and **Molid**.
AV - **17,** 1-1,2-1,3-1,4-1,5-1,6-1,7-1,8-1,9-1,10-1,11-1,12-1,13-1,14-1,15-1,16-1,17-1
ESV - **14,** 1-1,2-1,3-1,4-1,5-1,6-1,7-1,8-1,9-1,10-1,11-1,12-1,13-1,14-1
HCSB - **11,** 1-1,2-1,3-1,4-1,5-1,6-1,7-1,8-1,9-1,10-1,11-1
NASV - **14,** 1-1,2-1,3-1,4-1,5-1,6-1,7-1,8-1,9-1,10-1,11-1,12-1,13-1,14-1
NCV - **12,** 1-1,2-1,3-1,4-1,5-1,6-1,7-1,8-1,9-1,10-1,11-1,12-1
NIV - **11,** 1-1,2-1,3-1,4-1,5-1,6-1,7-1,8-1,9-1,10-1,11-1
NKJV - **17,** 1-1,2-1,3-1,4-1,5-1,6-1,7-1,8-1,9-1,10-1,11-1,12-1,13-1,14-1,15-1,16-1,17-1
NLT - **12,** 1-1,2-1,3-1,4-1,5-1,6-1,7-1,8-1,9-1,10-1,11-1,12-1
NRSV - **14,** 1-1,2-1,3-1,4-1,5-1,6-1,7-1,8-1,9-1,10-1,11-1,12-1,13-1,14-1
Conclusion: All versions read the same.

353. 1 Chronicles 2:33* And the sons of **Jonathan**; **Peleth**, and **Zaza**. These were the sons of **Jerahmeel**.
AV - **14,** 1-1,2-1,3-1,4-1,5-1,6-1,7-1,8-1,9-1,10-1,11-1,12-1,13-1,14-1
ESV - 13, 1-1,2-1,3-1,4-1,5-1,6-1,7-1,8-1,9-1,10-1,11-**3**,12-1,13-1
HCSB - 11, 1-1,2-1,3-1,4-1,5-1,6-1,7-1,8-1,9-**3**,10-1,11-1
NASV - **14,** 1-1,2-1,3-1,4-1,5-1,6-1,7-1,8-1,9-1,10-1,11-1,12-1,13-1,14-1
NCV - 10, 1-1,2-1,3-1,4-1,5-1,6-1,7-1,8-1,9-1,10-**3**
NIV - 13, 1-1,2-1,3-1,4-1,5-1,6-1,7-1,8-1,9-1,10-1,11-**3**,12-1,13-1
NKJV - **14,** 1-1,2-1,3-1,4-1,5-1,6-1,7-1,8-1,9-1,10-1,11-1,12-1,13-1,14-1
NLT - 15, 1-1,2-1,3-1,4-1,5-1,6-1,7-1,8-1,9-1,10-1,11-1,12-1,13-**3**,14-1,15-1
NRSV - 13, 1-1,2-1,3-1,4-1,5-1,6-1,7-1,8-1,9-1,10-1,11-**3**,12-1,13-1
Conclusion: Six modern versions are more complex than the King James Bible.

354. 1 Chronicles 2:43* And the sons of **Hebron**; **Korah**, and **Tappuah**, and **Rekem**, and **Shema**.
AV - **12,** 1-1,2-1,3-1,4-1,5-1,6-1,7-1,8-1,9-1,10-1,11-1,12-1
ESV - **9,** 1-1,2-1,3-1,4-1,5-1,6-1,7-1,8-1,9-1
HCSB - **7,** 1-1,2-1,3-1,4-1,5-1,6-1,7-1
NASV - **12,** 1-1,2-1,3-1,4-1,5-1,6-1,7-1,8-1,9-1,10-1,11-1,12-1
NCV - **8,** 1-1,2-1,3-1,4-1,5-1,6-1,7-1,8-1
NIV - **9,** 1-1,2-1,3-1,4-1,5-1,6-1,7-1,8-1,9-1
NKJV - **10,** 1-1,2-1,3-1,4-1,5-1,6-1,7-1,8-1,9-1,10-1
NLT - **10,** 1-1,2-1,3-1,4-1,5-1,6-1,7-1,8-1,9-1,10-1
NRSV - **9,** 1-1,2-1,3-1,4-1,5-1,6-1,7-1,8-1,9-1
Conclusion: All versions read the same.

355. 1 Chronicles 2:47* And the sons of **Jahdai**; **Regem**, and **Jotham**, and **Geshan**, and **Pelet**, and **Ephah**, and **Shaaph**.
AV - **16,** 1-1,2-1,3-1,4-1,5-1,6-1,7-1,8-1,9-1,10-1,11-1,12-1,13-1,14-1,15-1,16-1
ESV - **11,** 1-1,2-1,3-1,4-1,5-1,6-1,7-1,8-1,9-1,10-1,11-1
HCSB - **9,** 1-1,2-1,3-1,4-1,5-1,6-1,7-1,8-1,9-1

NASV - **12,** 1-1,2-1,3-1,4-1,5-1,6-1,7-1,8-1,9-1,10-1,11-1,12-1
NCV - **10,** 1-1,2-1,3-1,4-1,5-1,6-1,7-1,8-1,9-1,10-1
NIV - **11,** 1-1,2-1,3-1,4-1,5-1,6-1,7-1,8-1,9-1,10-1,11-1
NKJV - **13,** 1-1,2-1,3-1,4-1,5-1,6-1,7-1,8-1,9-1,10-1,11-1,12-1,13-1
NLT - **12,** 1-1,2-1,3-1,4-1,5-1,6-1,7-1,8-1,9-1,10-1,11-1,12-1
NRSV - **11,** 1-1,2-1,3-1,4-1,5-1,6-1,7-1,8-1,9-1,10-1,11-1
Conclusion: All versions read the same.

356. 1 Chronicles 2:54* The sons of **Salma**; **Bethlehem**, and the **Netophathites**, **Ataroth**, the house of **Joab**, and half of the **Manahethites**, the **Zorites**.
AV - **20,** 1-1,2-1,3-1,4-1,5-1,6-1,7-1,8-1,9-1,10-1,11-1,12-1,13-1,14-1,15-1,16-1,17-1,18-1,19-1,20-1
ESV - **15,** 1-1,2-1,3-1,4-1,5-1,6-1,7-1,8-1,9-1,10-1,11-1,12-1,13-1,14-1,15-1
HCSB - **13,** 1-1,2-1,3-1,4-1,5-1,6-1,7-1,8-1,9-1,10-1,11-1,12-1,13-1
NASV - **17,** 1-1,2-1,3-1,4-1,5-1,6-1,7-1,8-1,9-1,10-1,11-1,12-1,13-1,14-1,15-1,16-1,17-1
NCV - **15,** 1-1,2-**3**,3-1,4-1,5-1,6-1,7-1,8-1,9-1,10-1,11-1,12-1,13-1,14-1,15-1
NIV - **15,** 1-1,2-**3**,3-1,4-1,5-1,6-1,7-1,8-1,9-1,10-1,11-1,12-1,13-1,14-1,15-1
NKJV - **18,** 1-1,2-1,3-1,4-1,5-1,6-1,7-1,8-1,9-1,10-1,11-1,12-1,13-1,14-1,15-1,16-1,17-1,18-1
NLT - **20,** 1-1,2-**3**,3-1,4-1,5-1,6-1,7-**2**,8-1,9-1,10-1,11-1,12-1,13-1,14-**2**,15-1,16-1,17-1,18-1,19-1,20-1
NRSV - **15,** 1-1,2-1,3-1,4-1,5-1,6-1,7-1,8-1,9-1,10-1,11-1,12-1,13-1,14-1,15-1
Conclusion: Only three modern versions are more complex than the King James Bible. The NLT is the most difficult to read.

357. 1 Chronicles 3:3* The fifth, **Shephatiah** of **Abital**: the sixth, **Ithream** by **Eglah** his wife.
AV - **12,** 1-1,2-1,3-1,4-1,5-1,6-1,7-1,8-1,9-1,10-1,11-1,12-1
ESV - **12,** 1-1,2-1,3-1,4-1,5-1,6-1,7-1,8-1,9-1,10-1,11-1,12-1
HCSB - **13,** 1-1,2-1,3-1,4-1,5-1,6-1,7-1,8-1,9-1,10-1,11-1,12-1,13-1
NASV - **14,** 1-1,2-1,3-1,4-1,5-1,6-1,7-1,8-1,9-1,10-1,11-1,12-1,13-1,14-1
NCV - **18,** 1-1,2-1,3-1,4-1,5-1,6-1,7-**2**,8-1,9-1,10-1,11-1,12-1,13-1,14-1,15-1,16-**2**,17-1,18-1
NIV - **15,** 1-1,2-1,3-1,4-1,5-1,6-1,7-1,8-1,9-1,10-1,11-1,12-1,13-1,14-1,15-1
NKJV - **12,** 1-1,2-1,3-1,4-1,5-1,6-1,7-1,8-1,9-1,10-1,11-1,12-1
NLT - **18,** 1-1,2-1,3-1,4-1,5-1,6-**2**,7-1,8-1,9-1,10-1,11-1,12-1,13-1,14-**2**,15-1,16-1,17-1,18-1
NRSV - **12,** 1-1,2-1,3-1,4-1,5-1,6-1,7-1,8-1,9-1,10-1,11-1,12-1
Conclusion: Only the NCV and the NLT made the verse more complex.

358. 1 Chronicles 3:7* And **Nogah**, and **Nepheg**, and **Japhia**,
AV - **6,** 1-1,2-1,3-1,4-1,5-1,6-1
ESV - **3,** 1-1,2-1,3-1
HCSB - **3,** 1-1,2-1,3-1
NASV - **3,** 1-1,2-1,3-1
NCV - **15,** 1-1,2-**2**,3-1,4-**2**,5-1,6-1,7-1,8-1,9-1,10-1,11-1,12-1,13-1,14-1,15-1
NIV - **3,** 1-1,2-1,3-1
NKJV - **3,** 1-1,2-1,3-1

NLT - **3,** 1-1,2-1,3-1
NRSV - **3,** 1-1,2-1,3-1
Conclusion: Only the NCV made the verse more complex. That version eliminates verses 7 and 8 and combines them in verse six. It reads as follows:

  1 Chronicles 3:6 (NCV) "David's other nine children were Ibhar, Elishua, Eliphelet, Nogah, Nepheg, Japhia, Elishama, Eliada, and Eliphelet."

359. 1 Chronicles 3:8* And **Elishama**, and **Eliada**, and **Eliphelet**, nine.
AV - **7,** 1-1,2-1,3-1,4-1,5-1,6-1,7-1
ESV - **5,** 1-1,2-1,3-1,4-1,5-1
HCSB - **6,** 1-1,2-1,3-1,4-1,5-1,6-1
NASV - **5,** 1-1,2-1,3-1,4-1,5-1
NCV - (See information for 1 Chron. 3:7.)
NIV - **7,** 1-1,2-1,3-1,4-1,5-1,6-1,7-1
NKJV - **7,** 1-1,2-1,3-1,4-1,5-1,6-1,7-1
NLT - **4,** 1-1,2-1,3-1,4-1
NRSV - **5,** 1-1,2-1,3-1,4-1,5-1
Conclusion: Only the NCV made the verse more complex. See comments on the previous verse.

360. 1 Chronicles 3:10* And **Solomon's** son was **Rehoboam**, **Abia** his son, **Asa** his son, **Jehoshaphat** his son,
AV - **14,** 1-1,2-1,3-1,4-1,5-1,6-1,7-1,8-1,9-1,10-1,11-1,12-1,13-1,14-1
ESV - **15,** 1-1,2-1,3-1,4-1,5-1,6-1,7-1,8-1,9-1,10-1,11-1,12-1,13-1,14-1,15-1
HCSB - **14,** 1-1,2-1,3-1,4-1,5-1,6-1,7-1,8-1,9-1,10-1,11-1,12-1,13-1,14-1
NASV - **15,** 1-1,2-1,3-1,4-1,5-1,6-1,7-1,8-1,9-1,10-1,11-1,12-1,13-1,14-1,15-1
NCV - **16,** 1-1,2-1,3-1,4-1,5-1,6-1,7-1,8-1,9-1,10-1,11-1,12-1,13-1,14-1,15-1,16-1
NIV - **13,** 1-1,2-1,3-1,4-1,5-1,6-1,7-1,8-1,9-1,10-1,11-1,12-1,13-1
NKJV - **14,** 1-1,2-1,3-1,4-1,5-1,6-1,7-1,8-1,9-1,10-1,11-1,12-1,13-1,14-1
NLT - **9,** 1-1,2-**3,**3-1,4-1,5-1,6-1,7-1,8-1,9-1
NRSV - **14,** 1-1,2-**3,**3-1,4-1,5-1,6-1,7-1,8-1,9-1,10-1,11-1,12-1,13-1,14-1
Conclusion: Only the NLT and the NRSV made the verse more complex.

361. 1 Chronicles 3:11* **Joram** his son, **Ahaziah** his son, **Joash** his son,
AV - **9,** 1-1,2-1,3-1,4-1,5-1,6-1,7-1,8-1,9-1
ESV - **9,** 1-1,2-1,3-1,4-1,5-1,6-1,7-1,8-1,9-1
HCSB - **9,** 1-1,2-1,3-1,4-1,5-1,6-1,7-1,8-1,9-1
NASV - **9,** 1-1,2-1,3-1,4-1,5-1,6-1,7-1,8-1,9-1
NCV - **12,** 1-1,2-1,3-1,4-1,5-1,6-1,7-1,8-1,9-1,10-1,11-1,12-1
NIV - **9,** 1-1,2-1,3-1,4-1,5-1,6-1,7-1,8-1,9-1
NKJV - **9,** 1-1,2-1,3-1,4-1,5-1,6-1,7-1,8-1,9-1
NLT - **3,** 1-1,2-1,3-1
NRSV - **9,** 1-1,2-1,3-1,4-1,5-1,6-1,7-1,8-1,9-1
Conclusion: All versions read the same.

362. 1 Chronicles 3:12* **Amaziah** his son, **Azariah** his son, **Jotham** his son,
AV - **9,** 1-1,2-1,3-1,4-1,5-1,6-1,7-1,8-1,9-1
ESV - **9,** 1-1,2-1,3-1,4-1,5-1,6-1,7-1,8-1,9-1
HCSB - **9,** 1-1,2-1,3-1,4-1,5-1,6-1,7-1,8-1,9-1
NASV - **9,** 1-1,2-1,3-1,4-1,5-1,6-1,7-1,8-1,9-1
NCV - **12,** 1-1,2-1,3-1,4-1,5-1,6-1,7-1,8-1,9-1,10-1,11-1,12-1
NIV - **9,** 1-1,2-1,3-1,4-1,5-1,6-1,7-1,8-1,9-1
NKJV - **9,** 1-1,2-1,3-1,4-1,5-1,6-1,7-1,8-1,9-1
NLT - **3,** 1-1,2-1,3-1
NRSV - **9,** 1-1,2-1,3-1,4-1,5-1,6-1,7-1,8-1,9-1
Conclusion: All versions read the same.

363. 1 Chronicles 3:13* **Ahaz** his son, **Hezekiah** his son, **Manasseh** his son,
AV - **9,** 1-1,2-1,3-1,4-1,5-1,6-1,7-1,8-1,9-1
ESV - **9,** 1-1,2-1,3-1,4-1,5-1,6-1,7-1,8-1,9-1
HCSB - **9,** 1-1,2-1,3-1,4-1,5-1,6-1,7-1,8-1,9-1
NASV - **9,** 1-1,2-1,3-1,4-1,5-1,6-1,7-1,8-1,9-1
NCV - **12,** 1-1,2-1,3-1,4-1,5-1,6-1,7-1,8-1,9-1,10-1,11-1,12-1
NIV - **9,** 1-1,2-1,3-1,4-1,5-1,6-1,7-1,8-1,9-1
NKJV - **9,** 1-1,2-1,3-1,4-1,5-1,6-1,7-1,8-1,9-1
NLT - **3,** 1-1,2-1,3-1
NRSV - **9,** 1-1,2-1,3-1,4-1,5-1,6-1,7-1,8-1,9-1
Conclusion: All versions read the same.

364. 1 Chronicles 3:14* **Amon** his son, **Josiah** his son.
AV - **6,** 1-1,2-1,3-1,4-1,5-1,6-1
ESV - **6,** 1-1,2-1,3-1,4-1,5-1,6-1
HCSB - **7,** 1-1,2-1,3-1,4-1,5-1,6-1,7-1
NASV - **6,** 1-1,2-1,3-1,4-1,5-1,6-1
NCV - **9,** 1-1,2-1,3-1,4-1,5-1,6-1,7-1,8-1,9-1
NIV - **6,** 1-1,2-1,3-1,4-1,5-1,6-1
NKJV - **6,** 1-1,2-1,3-1,4-1,5-1,6-1
NLT - **3,** 1-1,2-1,3-1
NRSV - **6,** 1-1,2-1,3-1,4-1,5-1,6-1
Conclusion: All versions read the same.

365. 1 Chronicles 3:16* And the sons of **Jehoiakim**: **Jeconiah** his son, **Zedekiah** his son.
AV - **11,** 1-1,2-1,3-1,4-1,5-1,6-1,7-1,8-1,9-1,10-1,11-1
ESV - 10, 1-1,2-**3,**3-1,4-1,5-1,6-1,7-1,8-1,9-1,10-1
HCSB - **7,** 1-1,2-1,3-1,4-1,5-1,6-1,7-1
NASV - **11,** 1-1,2-1,3-1,4-1,5-1,6-1,7-1,8-1,9-1,10-1,11-1
NCV - 11, 1-1,2-1,3-**2,**4-1,5-1,6-1,7-1,8-1,9-**2,**10-1,11-1
NIV - 9, 1-1,2-**3,**3-1,4-1,5-1,6-1,7-1,8-1,9-1
NKJV - **12,** 1-1,2-1,3-1,4-1,5-1,6-1,7-1,8-1,9-1,10-1,11-1,12-1

NLT - **12,** 1-1,2-**3**,3-1,4-1,5-1,6-1,7-1,8-1,9-1,10-1,11-**2**,12-1
NRSV - **10,** 1-1,2-**3**,3-1,4-1,5-1,6-1,7-1,8-1,9-1,10-1
Conclusion: Five modern versions are more complex than the King James Bible.

366. 1 Chronicles 3:17* And the sons of **Jeconiah**; **Assir, Salathiel** his son,
AV - **9,** 1-1,2-1,3-1,4-1,5-1,6-1,7-1,8-1,9-1
ESV - 10, 1-1,2-1,3-1,4-1,5-1,6-1,7-**2**,8-1,9-1,10-1
HCSB - 9, 1-1,2-1,3-1,4-1,5-1,6-**2**,7-1,8-1,9-1
NASV - 10, 1-1,2-1,3-1,4-1,5-1,6-**3**,7-1,8-1,9-1,10-1
NCV - 10, 1-1,2-1,3-**2**,4-1,5-1,6-**3**,7-1,8-1,9-1,10-1
NIV - **9,** 1-1,2-**3**,3-1,4-1,5-1,6-**2**,7-1,8-1,9-1
NKJV - **10,** 1-1,2-1,3-1,4-1,5-1,6-1,7-1,8-1,9-1,10-1
NLT - 13, 1-1,2-1,3-1,4-1,5-1,6-1,7-**2**,8-**3**,9-1,10-1,11-1,12-1,13-1
NRSV - 10, 1-1,2-1,3-1,4-1,5-1,6-1,7-**2**,8-1,9-1,10-1
Conclusion: Seven modern versions are more complex than the King James Bible.

367. 1 Chronicles 3:20* And **Hashubah**, and **Ohel**, and **Berechiah**, and **Hasadiah**, **Jushabhesed**, five.
AV - **10,** 1-1,2-1,3-1,4-1,5-1,6-1,7-1,8-1,9-1,10-1
ESV - **8,** 1-1,2-1,3-1,4-1,5-1,6-1,7-1,8-1
HCSB - 9, 1-1,2-1,3-**2**,4-1,5-1,6-1,7-1,8-1,9-1
NASV - **8,** 1-1,2-1,3-1,4-1,5-1,6-1,7-1,8-1
NCV - 12, 1-1,2-**2**,3-1,4-1,5-**2**,6-1,7-1,8-1,9-1,10-1,11-1,12-1
NIV - 11, 1-1,2-1,3-**2**,4-1,5-**2**,6-1,7-1,8-1,9-1,10-1,11-1
NKJV - **10,** 1-1,2-1,3-1,4-1,5-1,6-1,7-1,8-1,9-1,10-1
NLT - 11, 1-1,2-1,3-**2**,4-1,5-1,6-1,7-1,8-1,9-1,10-1,11-1
NRSV - **8,** 1-1,2-1,3-1,4-1,5-1,6-1,7-1,8-1
Conclusion: Four modern versions are more complex than the King James Bible.

368. 1 Chronicles 3:21* And the sons of **Hananiah**; **Pelatiah**, and **Jesaiah**: the sons of **Rephaiah**, the sons of **Arnan**, the sons of **Obadiah**, the sons of **Shechaniah**.
AV - **24,** 1-1,2-1,3-1,4-1,5-1,6-1,7-1,8-1,9-1,10-1,11-1,12-1,13-1,14-1,15-1,16-1,17-1,18-1,19-1,20-1,21-1,22-1,23-1,24-1
ESV - **19,** 1-1,2-1,3-1,4-1,5-1,6-1,7-1,8-1,9-1,10-1,11-1,12-1,13-1,14-1,15-1,16-1,17-1,18-1,19-1
HCSB - 13, 1-1,2-**3**,3-1,4-1,5-1,6-1,7-1,8-1,9-1,10-1,11-1,12-1,13-1
NASV - **24,** 1-1,2-1,3-1,4-1,5-1,6-1,7-1,8-1,9-1,10-1,11-1,12-1,13-1,14-1,15-1,16-1,17-1,18-1,19-1,20-1,21-1,22-1,23-1,24-1
NCV - 15, 1-1,2-**3**,3-1,4-1,5-1,6-1,7-1,8-1,9-1,10-1,11-1,12-1,13-1,14-1,15-1
NIV - 19, 1-1,2-**3**,3-1,4-1,5-1,6-1,7-1,8-1,9-1,10-1,11-1,12-1,13-1,14-1,15-1,16-1,17-1,18-1,19-1
NKJV - **25,** 1-1,2-1,3-1,4-1,5-1,6-1,7-1,8-1,9-1,10-1,11-1,12-1,13-1,14-1,15-1,16-1,17-1,18-1,19-1,20-1,21-1,22-1,23-1,24-1,25-1
NLT - **24,** 1-1,2-1,3-1,4-1,5-1,6-1,7-1,8-1,9-1,10-1,11-1,12-1,13-1,14-1,15-1,16-1,17-1,18-1,19-1,20-1,21-1,22-1,23-1,24-1
NRSV - **19,** 1-1,2-1,3-1,4-1,5-1,6-1,7-1,8-1,9-1,10-1,11-1,12-1,13-1,14-1,15-1,16-1,17-1,18-1,19-1

Conclusion: Only three modern versions are more complex than the King James Bible.

369. 1 Chronicles 3:22* And the sons of **Shechaniah**; **Shemaiah**: and the sons of **Shemaiah**; **Hattush**, and **Igeal**, and **Bariah**, and **Neariah**, and **Shaphat**, six.
AV - **21,** 1-1,2-1,3-1,4-1,5-1,6-1,7-1,8-1,9-1,10-1,11-1,12-1,13-1,14-1,15-1,16-1,17-1,18-1,19-1,20-1,21-1
ESV - **17,** 1-1,2-1,3-1,4-1,5-1,6-1,7-1,8-1,9-1,10-1,11-1,12-1,13-1,14-1,15-1,16-1,17-1
HCSB - **14,** 1-1,2-1,3-1,4-1,5-1,6-1,7-1,8-1,9-1,10-1,11-1,12-1,13-1,14-1
NASV - 18, 1-1,2-**3**,3-1,4-1,5-1,6-1,7-1,8-1,9-1,10-1,11-1,12-1,13-1,14-1,15-1,16-1,17-1,18-1
NCV - **18,** 1-1,2-1,3-1,4-1,5-1,6-1,7-1,8-1,9-1,10-1,11-1,12-1,13-1,14-1,15-1,16-1,17-1,18-1
NIV - 17, 1-1,2-**3**,3-1,4-1,5-1,6-1,7-1,8-1,9-1,10-1,11-1,12-1,13-1,14-1,15-1,16-1,17-1
NKJV - **20,** 1-1,2-1,3-1,4-1,5-1,6-1,7-1,8-1,9-1,10-1,11-1,12-1,13-1,14-1,15-1,16-1,17-1,18-1,19-1,20-1
NLT - 18, 1-1,2-**3**,3-1,4-1,5-1,6-1,7-1,8-1,9-1,10-1,11-1,12-1,13-1,14-1,15-1,16-1,17-1,18-1
NRSV - **17,** 1-1,2-1,3-1,4-1,5-1,6-1,7-1,8-1,9-1,10-1,11-1,12-1,13-1,14-1,15-1,16-1,17-1
Conclusion: Only three modern versions are more complex than the King James Bible.

370. 1 Chronicles 3:23* And the sons of **Neariah**; **Elioenai**, and **Hezekiah**, and **Azrikam**, three.
AV - **11,** 1-1,2-1,3-1,4-1,5-1,6-1,7-1,8-1,9-1,10-1,11-1
ESV - **9,** 1-1,2-1,3-1,4-1,5-1,6-1,7-1,8-1,9-1
HCSB - **7,** 1-1,2-1,3-1,4-1,5-1,6-1,7-1
NASV - **10,** 1-1,2-1,3-1,4-1,5-1,6-1,7-1,8-1,9-1,10-1
NCV - **8,** 1-1,2-1,3-1,4-1,5-1,6-1,7-1,8-1
NIV - **11,** 1-1,2-1,3-1,4-1,5-1,6-1,7-1,8-1,9-1,10-1,11-1
NKJV - **12,** 1-1,2-1,3-1,4-1,5-1,6-1,7-1,8-1,9-1,10-1,11-1,12-1
NLT - **12,** 1-1,2-1,3-1,4-1,5-1,6-1,7-1,8-1,9-1,10-1,11-1,12-1
NRSV - **9,** 1-1,2-1,3-1,4-1,5-1,6-1,7-1,8-1,9-1
Conclusion: All versions read the same.

371. 1 Chronicles 3:24*# And the sons of **Elioenai** were, **Hodaiah**, and **Eliashib**, and **Pelaiah**, and **Akkub**, and **Johanan**, and **Dalaiah**, and **Anani**, **seven**.
AV - **20,** 1-1,2-1,3-1,4-1,5-1,6-1,7-1,8-1,9-1,10-1,11-1,12-1,13-1,14-1,15-1,16-1,17-1,18-1,19-1,20-1
ESV - **13,** 1-1,2-1,3-1,4-1,5-1,6-1,7-1,8-1,9-1,10-1,11-1,12-1,13-1
HCSB - **11,** 1-1,2-1,3-1,4-1,5-1,6-1,7-1,8-1,9-1,10-1,11-1
NASV - **14,** 1-1,2-1,3-1,4-1,5-1,6-1,7-1,8-1,9-1,10-1,11-1,12-1,13-1,14-1
NCV - **12,** 1-1,2-1,3-1,4-1,5-1,6-1,7-1,8-1,9-1,10-1,11-1,12-1
NIV - **15,** 1-1,2-1,3-1,4-1,5-1,6-1,7-1,8-1,9-1,10-1,11-1,12-1,13-1,14-1,15-1
NKJV - **16,** 1-1,2-1,3-1,4-1,5-1,6-1,7-1,8-1,9-1,10-1,11-1,12-1,13-1,14-1,15-1,16-1
NLT - **16,** 1-1,2-1,3-1,4-1,5-1,6-1,7-1,8-1,9-1,10-1,11-1,12-1,13-1,14-1,15-1,16-1
NRSV - **13,** 1-1,2-1,3-1,4-1,5-1,6-1,7-1,8-1,9-1,10-1,11-1,12-1,13-1
Conclusion: All versions read the same.

372. 1 Chronicles 4:1* The sons of **Judah**; **Pharez**, **Hezron**, and **Carmi**, and Hur, and **Shobal**.
AV - **12,** 1-1,2-1,3-1,4-1,5-1,6-1,7-1,8-1,9-1,10-1,11-1,12-1
ESV - **10,** 1-1,2-1,3-1,4-1,5-1,6-1,7-1,8-1,9-1,10-1
HCSB - **8,** 1-1,2-1,3-1,4-1,5-1,6-1,7-1,8-1
NASV - **11,** 1-1,2-1,3-1,4-1,5-1,6-1,7-1,8-1,9-1,10-1,11-1
NCV - **9,** 1-1,2-**3**,3-1,4-1,5-1,6-1,7-1,8-1,9-1
NIV - **10,** 1-1,2-**3**,3-1,4-1,5-1,6-1,7-1,8-1,9-1,10-1
NKJV - **11,** 1-1,2-1,3-1,4-1,5-1,6-1,7-1,8-1,9-1,10-1,11-1
NLT - **11,** 1-1,2-**3**,3-1,4-1,5-1,6-1,7-1,8-1,9-1,10-1,11-1
NRSV - **10,** 1-1,2-1,3-1,4-1,5-1,6-1,7-1,8-1,9-1,10-1
Conclusion: Only three modern versions are more complex than the King James Bible.

373. 1 Chronicles 4:6* And **Naarah** bare him **Ahuzam**, and **Hepher**, and **Temeni**, and **Haahashtari**. These were the sons of **Naarah**.
AV - **17,** 1-1,2-1,3-1,4-1,5-1,6-1,7-1,8-1,9-1,10-1,11-1,12-1,13-1,14-1,15-1,16-1,17-1
ESV - **14,** 1-1,2-1,3-1,4-1,5-1,6-1,7-1,8-1,9-1,10-1,11-1,12-1,13-1,14-1
HCSB - **12,** 1-1,2-1,3-1,4-1,5-1,6-1,7-1,8-1,9-1,10-1,11-1,12-1
NASV - **14,** 1-1,2-1,3-1,4-1,5-1,6-1,7-1,8-1,9-1,10-1,11-1,12-1,13-1,14-1
NCV - **18,** 1-1,2-1,3-1,4-1,5-1,6-1,7-1,8-1,9-1,10-1,11-1,12-1,13-1,14-1,15-1,16-**3**,17-1,18-1
NIV - **14,** 1-1,2-1,3-1,4-1,5-1,6-1,7-1,8-1,9-1,10-1,11-1,12-**3**,13-1,14-1
NKJV - **14,** 1-1,2-1,3-1,4-1,5-1,6-1,7-1,8-1,9-1,10-1,11-1,12-1,13-1,14-1
NLT - **9,** 1-1,2-1,3-1,4-1,5-1,6-1,7-1,8-1,9-1
NRSV - **14,** 1-1,2-1,3-1,4-1,5-1,6-1,7-1,8-1,9-1,10-1,11-1,12-1,13-1,14-1
Conclusion: Only the NCV and the NIV made the verse more complex.

374. 1 Chronicles 4:7* And the sons of **Helah** were, **Zereth**, and **Jezoar**, and **Ethnan**.
AV - **11,** 1-1,2-1,3-1,4-1,5-1,6-1,7-1,8-1,9-1,10-1,11-1
ESV - **8,** 1-1,2-1,3-1,4-1,5-1,6-1,7-1,8-1
HCSB - **6,** 1-1,2-1,3-1,4-1,5-1,6-1
NASV - **9,** 1-1,2-1,3-1,4-1,5-1,6-1,7-1,8-1,9-1
NCV - **6,** 1-1,2-1,3-1,4-1,5-1,6-1
NIV - **7,** 1-1,2-1,3-1,4-1,5-1,6-1,7-1
NKJV - **9,** 1-1,2-1,3-1,4-1,5-1,6-1,7-1,8-1,9-1
NLT - **7,** 1-1,2-1,3-1,4-1,5-1,6-1,7-1
NRSV - **8,** 1-1,2-1,3-1,4-1,5-1,6-1,7-1,8-1
Conclusion: All versions read the same.

375. 1 Chronicles 4:13* And the sons of **Kenaz**; **Othniel**, and **Seraiah**: and the sons of **Othniel**; **Hathath**.
AV - **14,** 1-1,2-1,3-1,4-1,5-1,6-1,7-1,8-1,9-1,10-1,11-1,12-1,13-1,14-1
ESV - **15,** 1-1,2-1,3-1,4-1,5-1,6-1,7-1,8-1,9-1,10-1,11-1,12-1,13-1,14-1,15-1
HCSB - **10,** 1-1,2-1,3-1,4-1,5-1,6-1,7-1,8-1,9-1,10-1
NASV - **18,** 1-1,2-1,3-1,4-1,5-1,6-1,7-1,8-1,9-1,10-1,11-1,12-1,13-1,14-1,15-1,16-1,17-1,18-1
NCV - **14,** 1-1,2-1,3-1,4-1,5-1,6-1,7-1,8-1,9-1,10-1,11-1,12-1,13-1,14-1

NIV - **14,** 1-1,2-1,3-1,4-1,5-1,6-1,7-1,8-1,9-1,10-1,11-1,12-1,13-1,14-1
NKJV - **14,** 1-1,2-1,3-1,4-1,5-1,6-1,7-1,8-1,9-1,10-1,11-1,12-1,13-1,14-1
NLT - **14,** 1-1,2-1,3-1,4-1,5-1,6-1,7-1,8-1,9-1,10-1,11-1,12-1,13-1,14-1
NRSV - **15,** 1-1,2-1,3-1,4-1,5-1,6-1,7-1,8-1,9-1,10-1,11-1,12-1,13-1,14-1,15-1
Conclusion: All versions read the same.

376. 1 Chronicles 4:15* And the sons of **Caleb** the son of **Jephunneh**; **Iru, Elah,** and Naam: and the sons of **Elah,** even **Kenaz.**
AV - **20,** 1-1,2-1,3-1,4-1,5-1,6-1,7-1,8-1,9-1,10-1,11-1,12-1,13-1,14-1,15-1,16-1,17-1,18-1,19-1,20-1
ESV - **18,** 1-1,2-1,3-1,4-1,5-1,6-1,7-1,8-1,9-1,10-1,11-1,12-1,13-1,14-1,15-1,16-1,17-1,18-1
HCSB - **14,** 1-1,2-1,3-1,4-1,5-1,6-1,7-1,8-1,9-1,10-1,11-1,12-1,13-1,14-1
NASV - **20,** 1-1,2-1,3-1,4-1,5-1,6-1,7-1,8-1,9-1,10-1,11-1,12-1,13-1,14-1,15-1,16-1,17-1,18-1,19-1,20-1
NCV - **15,** 1-1,2-1,3-1,4-1,5-1,6-1,7-1,8-1,9-1,10-1,11-1,12-1,13-1,14-1,15-1
NIV - **16,** 1-1,2-1,3-1,4-1,5-1,6-1,7-1,8-1,9-1,10-1,11-1,12-1,13-1,14-1,15-1,16-1
NKJV - **19,** 1-1,2-1,3-1,4-1,5-1,6-1,7-1,8-1,9-1,10-1,11-1,12-1,13-1,14-1,15-1,16-1,17-1,18-1,19-1
NLT - **18,** 1-1,2-1,3-1,4-1,5-1,6-1,7-1,8-1,9-1,10-1,11-1,12-1,13-1,14-1,15-1,16-1,17-1,18-1
NRSV - **17,** 1-1,2-1,3-1,4-1,5-1,6-1,7-1,8-1,9-1,10-1,11-1,12-1,13-1,14-1,15-1,16-1,17-1
Conclusion: All versions read the same.

377. 1 Chronicles 4:16* And the sons of **Jehaleleel**; Ziph, and **Ziphah, Tiria,** and **Asareel.**
AV - **11,** 1-1,2-1,3-1,4-1,5-1,6-1,7-1,8-1,9-1,10-1,11-1
ESV - **9,** 1-1,2-1,3-1,4-1,5-1,6-1,7-1,8-1,9-1
HCSB - **7,** 1-1,2-1,3-1,4-1,5-1,6-1,7-1
NASV - **11,** 1-1,2-1,3-1,4-1,5-1,6-1,7-1,8-1,9-1,10-1,11-1
NCV - **8,** 1-1,2-1,3-1,4-1,5-1,6-1,7-1,8-1
NIV - **9,** 1-1,2-1,3-1,4-1,5-1,6-1,7-1,8-1,9-1
NKJV - **10,** 1-1,2-1,3-1,4-1,5-1,6-1,7-1,8-1,9-1,10-1
NLT - **10,** 1-1,2-1,3-1,4-1,5-1,6-1,7-1,8-1,9-1,10-1
NRSV - **9,** 1-1,2-1,3-1,4-1,5-1,6-1,7-1,8-1,9-1
Conclusion: All versions read the same.

378. 1 Chronicles 4:20* And the sons of **Shimon** were, **Amnon,** and **Rinnah, Benhanan,** and **Tilon**. And the sons of **Ishi** were, **Zoheth,** and **Benzoheth.**
AV - **21,** 1-1,2-1,3-1,4-1,5-1,6-1,7-1,8-1,9-1,10-1,11-1,12-1,13-1,14-1,15-1,16-1,17-1,18-1,19-1,20-1,21-1
ESV - **16,** 1-1,2-1,3-1,4-1,5-1,6-1,7-1,8-1,9-1,10-1,11-1,12-1,13-1,14-1,15-1,16-1
HCSB - **12,** 1-1,2-1,3-1,4-1,5-1,6-1,7-1,8-1,9-1,10-1,11-1,12-1
NASV - **20,** 1-1,2-1,3-1,4-1,5-1,6-1,7-1,8-1,9-1,10-1,11-1,12-1,13-1,14-1,15-1,16-1,17-1,18-1,19-1,20-1
NCV - **14,** 1-1,2-1,3-1,4-1,5-1,6-1,7-1,8-1,9-1,10-1,11-1,12-1,13-1,14-1
NIV - **16,** 1-1,2-1,3-1,4-1,5-1,6-1,7-1,8-1,9-1,10-1,11-**3**,12-1,13-1,14-1,15-1,16-1

NKJV - **20,** 1-1,2-1,3-1,4-1,5-1,6-1,7-1,8-1,9-1,10-1,11-1,12-1,13-1,14-1,15-1,16-1,17-1,18-1,19-1,20-1
NLT - 18, 1-1,2-1,3-1,4-1,5-1,6-1,7-1,8-1,9-1,10-1,11-1,12-**3,**13-1,14-1,15-1,16-1,17-1,18-1
NRSV - **16,** 1-1,2-1,3-1,4-1,5-1,6-1,7-1,8-1,9-1,10-1,11-1,12-1,13-1,14-1,15-1,16-1
Conclusion: Only the NIV and the NLT made the verse more complex.

379. 1 Chronicles 4:24* The sons of **Simeon** were, **Nemuel**, and **Jamin**, **Jarib**, **Zerah**, and **Shaul**:
AV - **12,** 1-1,2-1,3-1,4-1,5-1,6-1,7-1,8-1,9-1,10-1,11-1,12-1
ESV - **9,** 1-1,2-1,3-1,4-1,5-1,6-1,7-1,8-1,9-1
HCSB - **8,** 1-1,2-1,3-1,4-1,5-1,6-1,7-1,8-1
NASV - **11,** 1-1,2-1,3-1,4-1,5-1,6-1,7-1,8-1,9-1,10-1,11-1
NCV - **9,** 1-1,2-1,3-1,4-1,5-1,6-1,7-1,8-1,9-1
NIV - 10, 1-1,2-**3,**3-1,4-1,5-1,6-1,7-1,8-1,9-1,10-1
NKJV - **11,** 1-1,2-1,3-1,4-1,5-1,6-1,7-1,8-1,9-1,10-1,11-1
NLT - **11,** 1-1,2-1,3-1,4-1,5-1,6-1,7-1,8-1,9-1,10-1,11-1
NRSV - **9,** 1-1,2-1,3-1,4-1,5-1,6-1,7-1,8-1,9-1
Conclusion: Only the NIV made the verse more complex.

380. 1 Chronicles 4:25* Shallum his son, **Mibsam** his son, **Mishma** his son.
AV - **9,** 1-1,2-1,3-1,4-1,5-1,6-1,7-1,8-1,9-1
ESV - **10,** 1-1,2-1,3-1,4-1,5-1,6-1,7-1,8-1,9-1,10-1
HCSB - **12,** 1-1,2-1,3-1,4-1,5-1,6-1,7-1,8-1,9-1,10-1,11-1,12-1
NASV - **9,** 1-1,2-1,3-1,4-1,5-1,6-1,7-1,8-1,9-1
NCV - **12,** 1-1,2-1,3-1,4-1,5-1,6-1,7-1,8-1,9-1,10-1,11-1,12-1
NIV - **11,** 1-1,2-1,3-1,4-1,5-1,6-1,7-1,8-1,9-1,10-1,11-1
NKJV - **10,** 1-1,2-1,3-1,4-1,5-1,6-1,7-1,8-1,9-1,10-1
NLT - 9, 1-1,2-**3,**3-1,4-1,5-1,6-1,7-1,8-1,9-1
NRSV - **10,** 1-1,2-1,3-1,4-1,5-1,6-1,7-1,8-1,9-1,10-1
Conclusion: Only the NLT made the verse more complex.

381. 1 Chronicles 4:26* And the sons of **Mishma**; **Hamuel** his son, **Zacchur** his son, **Shimei** his son.
AV - **14,** 1-1,2-1,3-1,4-1,5-1,6-1,7-1,8-1,9-1,10-1,11-1,12-1,13-1,14-1
ESV - **13,** 1-1,2-1,3-1,4-1,5-1,6-1,7-1,8-1,9-1,10-1,11-1,12-1,13-1
HCSB - **12,** 1-1,2-1,3-1,4-1,5-1,6-1,7-1,8-1,9-1,10-1,11-1,12-1
NASV - **14,** 1-1,2-1,3-1,4-1,5-1,6-1,7-1,8-1,9-1,10-1,11-1,12-1,13-1,14-1
NCV - **12,** 1-1,2-1,3-1,4-1,5-1,6-1,7-1,8-1,9-1,10-1,11-1,12-1
NIV - 14, 1-1,2-**3,**3-1,4-1,5-1,6-1,7-1,8-1,9-1,10-1,11-1,12-1,13-1,14-1
NKJV - **16,** 1-1,2-1,3-1,4-1,5-1,6-1,7-1,8-1,9-1,10-1,11-1,12-1,13-1,14-1,15-1,16-1
NLT - 9, 1-1,2-**3,**3-1,4-1,5-1,6-1,7-1,8-1,9-1
NRSV - **13,** 1-1,2-1,3-1,4-1,5-1,6-1,7-1,8-1,9-1,10-1,11-1,12-1,13-1
Conclusion: Only the NIV and the NLT made the verse more complex.

382. 1 Chronicles 4:28* And they dwelt at **Beersheba**, and **Moladah**, and **Hazarshual**,
AV - **9,** 1-1,2-1,3-1,4-1,5-1,6-1,7-1,8-1,9-1
ESV - **6,** 1-1,2-1,3-1,4-1,5-1,6-1
HCSB - **6,** 1-1,2-1,3-1,4-1,5-1,6-1
NASV - **7,** 1-1,2-1,3-1,4-1,5-1,6-1,7-1
NCV - **8,** 1-1,2-**2**,3-1,4-1,5-1,6-1,7-1,8-1
NIV - **7,** 1-1,2-1,3-1,4-1,5-1,6-1,7-1
NKJV - **7,** 1-1,2-1,3-1,4-1,5-1,6-1,7-1
NLT - **6,** 1-1,2-1,3-1,4-1,5-1,6-1
NRSV - **6,** 1-1,2-1,3-1,4-1,5-1,6-1
Conclusion: Only the NCV made the verse more complex.

383. 1 Chronicles 4:29* And at **Bilhah**, and at **Ezem**, and at **Tolad**,
AV - **9,** 1-1,2-1,3-1,4-1,5-1,6-1,7-1,8-1,9-1
ESV - **3,** 1-1,2-1,3-1
HCSB - **3,** 1-1,2-1,3-1
NASV - **3,** 1-1,2-1,3-1
NCV - **3,** 1-1,2-1,3-1
NIV - **3,** 1-1,2-1,3-1
NKJV - **3,** 1-1,2-1,3-1
NLT - **3,** 1-1,2-1,3-1
NRSV - **3,** 1-1,2-1,3-1
Conclusion: All versions read the same.

384. 1 Chronicles 4:30* And at **Bethuel**, and at **Hormah**, and at **Ziklag**,
AV - **9,** 1-1,2-1,3-1,4-1,5-1,6-1,7-1,8-1,9-1
ESV - **3,** 1-1,2-1,3-1
HCSB - **3,** 1-1,2-1,3-1
NASV - **3,** 1-1,2-1,3-1
NCV - **3,** 1-1,2-1,3-1
NIV - **3,** 1-1,2-1,3-1
NKJV - **3,** 1-1,2-1,3-1
NLT - **3,** 1-1,2-1,3-1
NRSV - **3,** 1-1,2-1,3-1
Conclusion: All versions read the same.

385. 1 Chronicles 4:34* And **Meshobab**, and **Jamlech**, and **Joshah** the son of **Amaziah**,
AV - **10,** 1-1,2-1,3-1,4-1,5-1,6-1,7-1,8-1,9-1,10-1
ESV - **7,** 1-1,2-1,3-1,4-1,5-1,6-1,7-1
HCSB - **6,** 1-1,2-1,3-1,4-1,5-1,6-1
NASV - **9,** 1-1,2-1,3-1,4-1,5-1,6-1,7-1,8-1,9-1
NCV - **79,** 1-1,2-1,3-1,4-1,5-1,6-1,7-**2**,8-1,9-1,10-**3**,11-1,12-1,13-1,14-1,15-1,16-1,17-1,18-1,19-1,20-1,21-1,22-1,23-1,24-1,25-1,26-1,27-1,28-1,29-1,30-1,31-1,32-1,33-1,34-1,35-1,36-1,37-1,38-1,39-1,40-1,41-1,42-1,43-1,44-1,45-1,46-1,47-1,48-1,49-1,50-1,51-1,52-1,53-1,54-1,55-1,56-1,57-

1,58-1,59-1,60-1,61-1,62-1,63-1,64-1,65-1,66-1,67-1,68-1,69-1,70-1,71-1,72-1,73-1,74-1,75-1,76-**3**,77-1,78-**2**,79-1

NIV - **6,** 1-1,2-1,3-1,4-1,5-1,6-1

NKJV - **8,** 1-1,2-1,3-1,4-1,5-1,6-1,7-1,8-1

NLT - 11, 1-1,2-**3**,3-1,4-1,5-**3**,6-1,7-1,8-1,9-1,10-1,11-1

NRSV - **6,** 1-1,2-1,3-1,4-1,5-1,6-1

Conclusion: Only the NCV and the NLT made the verse more complex. The NCV combined verses 1 Chron. 4:34 -38 to produce a massive, seventy-nine word verse which reads as follows:

> **1 Chronicles 4:34** (NCV) "The men in this list were leaders of their family groups: Meshobab, Jamlech, Joshah son of Amaziah, Joel, Jehu son of Joshibiah (Joshibiah was the son of Seraiah, who was the son of Asiel), Elioenai, Jaakobah, Jeshohaiah, Asaiah, Adiel, Jesimiel, Benaiah, and Ziza. (Ziza was the son of Shiphi, who was the son of Allon. Allon was the son of Jedaiah, who was the son of Shimri. And Shimri was the son of Shemaiah.) These families grew very large."

386. 1 Chronicles 4:35* And **Joel**, and **Jehu** the son of **Josibiah**, the son of **Seraiah**, the son of **Asiel**,

AV - **16,** 1-1,2-1,3-1,4-1,5-1,6-1,7-1,8-1,9-1,10-1,11-1,12-1,13-1,14-1,15-1,16-1

ESV - **12,** 1-1,2-1,3-1,4-1,5-1,6-1,7-1,8-1,9-1,10-1,11-1,12-1

HCSB - **11,** 1-1,2-1,3-1,4-1,5-1,6-1,7-1,8-1,9-1,10-1,11-1

NASV - **16,** 1-1,2-1,3-1,4-1,5-1,6-1,7-1,8-1,9-1,10-1,11-1,12-1,13-1,14-1,15-1,16-1

NCV - (See information for 1 Chron. 4:34.)

NIV - **13,** 1-1,2-1,3-1,4-1,5-1,6-1,7-1,8-1,9-1,10-1,11-1,12-1,13-1

NKJV - **15,** 1-1,2-1,3-1,4-1,5-1,6-1,7-1,8-1,9-1,10-1,11-1,12-1,13-1,14-1,15-1

NLT - **11,** 1-1,2-1,3-1,4-1,5-1,6-1,7-1,8-1,9-1,10-1,11-1

NRSV - **11,** 1-1,2-1,3-1,4-1,5-1,6-1,7-1,8-1,9-1,10-1,11-1

Conclusion: Only the NCV made the verse more complex. See comments on the previous verse.

387. 1 Chronicles 4:36* And **Elioenai**, and **Jaakobah**, and **Jeshohaiah**, and **Asaiah**, and **Adiel**, and **Jesimiel**, and **Benaiah**,

AV - **14,** 1-1,2-1,3-1,4-1,5-1,6-1,7-1,8-1,9-1,10-1,11-1,12-1,13-1,14-1

ESV - **7,** 1-1,2-1,3-1,4-1,5-1,6-1,7-1

HCSB - **7,** 1-1,2-1,3-1,4-1,5-1,6-1,7-1

NASV - **8,** 1-1,2-1,3-1,4-1,5-1,6-1,7-1,8-1

NCV - (See information for 1 Chron. 4:34.)

NIV - **8,** 1-**2**,2-1,3-1,4-1,5-1,6-1,7-1,8-1

NKJV - **8,** 1-1,2-1,3-1,4-1,5-1,6-1,7-1,8-1

NLT - **7,** 1-1,2-1,3-1,4-1,5-1,6-1,7-1

NRSV - **7,** 1-1,2-1,3-1,4-1,5-1,6-1,7-1

Conclusion: Only the NCV and the NIV made the verse more complex. See comments on 1 Chron. 4:34.

388. 1 Chronicles 4:37* And **Ziza** the son of **Shiphi**, the son of **Allon**, the son of **Jedaiah**, the son of **Shimri**, the son of **Shemaiah**;
AV - **22,** 1-1,2-1,3-1,4-1,5-1,6-1,7-1,8-1,9-1,10-1,11-1,12-1,13-1,14-1,15-1,16-1,17-1,18-1,19-1,20-1,21-1,22-1
ESV - **17,** 1-1,2-1,3-1,4-1,5-1,6-1,7-1,8-1,9-1,10-1,11-1,12-1,13-1,14-1,15-1,16-1,17-1
HCSB - **17,** 1-1,2-1,3-1,4-1,5-1,6-1,7-1,8-1,9-1,10-1,11-1,12-1,13-1,14-1,15-1,16-1,17-1
NASV - **21,** 1-1,2-1,3-1,4-1,5-1,6-1,7-1,8-1,9-1,10-1,11-1,12-1,13-1,14-1,15-1,16-1,17-1,18-1,19-1,20-1,21-1
NCV - (See information for 1 Chron. 4:34.)
NIV - **21,** 1-1,2-1,3-1,4-1,5-1,6-1,7-1,8-1,9-1,10-1,11-1,12-1,13-1,14-1,15-1,16-1,17-1,18-1,19-1,20-1,21-1
NKJV - **21,** 1-1,2-1,3-1,4-1,5-1,6-1,7-1,8-1,9-1,10-1,11-1,12-1,13-1,14-1,15-1,16-1,17-1,18-1,19-1,20-1,21-1
NLT - **17,** 1-1,2-1,3-1,4-1,5-1,6-1,7-1,8-1,9-1,10-1,11-1,12-1,13-1,14-1,15-1,16-1,17-1
NRSV - **16,** 1-1,2-1,3-1,4-1,5-1,6-1,7-1,8-1,9-1,10-1,11-1,12-1,13-1,14-1,15-1,16-1
Conclusion: Only the NCV made the verse more complex. See comments on 1 Chron. 4:34.

389. 1 Chronicles 5:4* The sons of **Joel**; **Shemaiah** his son, **Gog** his son, **Shimei** his son,
AV - **13,** 1-1,2-1,3-1,4-1,5-1,6-1,7-1,8-1,9-1,10-1,11-1,12-1,13-1
ESV - **13,** 1-1,2-1,3-1,4-1,5-1,6-1,7-1,8-1,9-1,10-1,11-1,12-1,13-1
HCSB - **11,** 1-1,2-1,3-1,4-1,5-1,6-1,7-1,8-1,9-1,10-1,11-1
NASV - **14,** 1-1,2-1,3-1,4-1,5-1,6-1,7-1,8-1,9-1,10-1,11-1,12-1,13-1,14-1
NCV - **18,** 1-1,2-1,3-1,4-**3,**5-1,6-1,7-1,8-1,9-1,10-1,11-1,12-1,13-1,14-1,15-1,16-1,17-1,18-1
NIV - **13,** 1-1,2-**3,**3-1,4-1,5-1,6-1,7-1,8-1,9-1,10-1,11-1,12-1,13-1
NKJV - **14,** 1-1,2-1,3-1,4-1,5-1,6-1,7-1,8-1,9-1,10-1,11-1,12-1,13-1,14-1
NLT - **8,** 1-1,2-**3,**3-1,4-1,5-1,6-1,7-1,8-1
NRSV - **13,** 1-1,2-1,3-1,4-1,5-1,6-1,7-1,8-1,9-1,10-1,11-1,12-1,13-1
Conclusion: Only three modern versions are more complex than the King James Bible.

390. 1 Chronicles 5:5* **Micah** his son, **Reaia** his son, **Baal** his son,
AV - **9,** 1-1,2-1,3-1,4-1,5-1,6-1,7-1,8-1,9-1
ESV - **9,** 1-1,2-1,3-1,4-1,5-1,6-1,7-1,8-1,9-1
HCSB - **9,** 1-1,2-1,3-1,4-1,5-1,6-1,7-1,8-1,9-1
NASV - **9,** 1-1,2-1,3-1,4-1,5-1,6-1,7-1,8-1,9-1
NCV - **12,** 1-1,2-1,3-1,4-1,5-1,6-1,7-1,8-1,9-1,10-1,11-1,12-1
NIV - **9,** 1-1,2-1,3-1,4-1,5-1,6-1,7-1,8-1,9-1
NKJV - **9,** 1-1,2-1,3-1,4-1,5-1,6-1,7-1,8-1,9-1
NLT - **3,** 1-1,2-1,3-1
NRSV - **9,** 1-1,2-1,3-1,4-1,5-1,6-1,7-1,8-1,9-1
Conclusion: All versions read the same.

391. 1 Chronicles 5:12* **Joel** the chief, and **Shapham** the next, and **Jaanai**, and **Shaphat** in **Bashan**.
AV - **13,** 1-1,2-1,3-1,4-1,5-1,6-1,7-1,8-1,9-1,10-1,11-1,12-1,13-1

Samuel C. Gipp Ph.D.

ESV - **11,** 1-1,2-1,3-1,4-1,5-1,6-**2**,7-1,8-1,9-1,10-1,11-1
HCSB - **13,** 1-1,2-1,3-1,4-1,5-1,6-**2**,7-1,8-**2**,9-1,10-1,11-1,12-1,13-1
NASV - **14,** 1-1,2-1,3-1,4-1,5-1,6-1,7-1,8-**2**,9-1,10-1,11-1,12-1,13-1,14-1
NCV - **17,** 1-1,2-1,3-1,4-1,5-**2**,6-1,7-1,8-**2**,9-1,10-1,11-1,12-1,13-1,14-1,15-**2**,16-1,17-1
NIV - **13,** 1-1,2-1,3-1,4-1,5-1,6-1,7-**2**,8-1,9-1,10-1,11-1,12-1,13-1
NKJV - **13,** 1-1,2-1,3-1,4-1,5-1,6-1,7-1,8-1,9-1,10-1,11-1,12-1,13-1
NLT - **20,** 1-1,2-1,3-1,4-**2**,5-1,6-1,7-1,8-1,9-1,10-1,11-1,12-1,13-**2**,14-1,15-**2**,16-**2**,17-1,18-1,19-1,20-1
NRSV - **11,** 1-1,2-1,3-1,4-1,5-1,6-**2**,7-1,8-1,9-1,10-1,11-1
Conclusion: Seven modern versions are more complex than the King James Bible.

392. 1 Chronicles 5:19* And they made war with the **Hagarites**, with **Jetur**, and **Nephish**, and **Nodab**.
AV - **13,** 1-1,2-1,3-1,4-1,5-1,6-1,7-1,8-1,9-1,10-1,11-1,12-1,13-1
ESV - **10,** 1-1,2-1,3-1,4-**2**,5-1,6-1,7-1,8-1,9-1,10-1
HCSB - **10,** 1-1,2-1,3-1,4-**2**,5-1,6-1,7-1,8-1,9-1,10-1
NASV - **10,** 1-1,2-1,3-1,4-**2**,5-1,6-1,7-1,8-1,9-1,10-1
NCV - **15,** 1-1,2-**2**,3-1,4-1,5-**2**,6-1,7-1,8-1,9-1,10-**2**,11-1,12-1,13-1,14-1,15-1
NIV - **10,** 1-1,2-1,3-1,4-**2**,5-1,6-1,7-1,8-1,9-1,10-1
NKJV - **10,** 1-1,2-1,3-1,4-1,5-1,6-1,7-1,8-1,9-1,10-1
NLT - **13,** 1-1,2-1,3-1,4-**2**,5-1,6-1,7-1,8-1,9-1,10-1,11-1,12-1,13-1
NRSV - **10,** 1-1,2-1,3-1,4-1,5-1,6-1,7-1,8-1,9-1,10-1
Conclusion: Six modern versions are more complex than the King James Bible. The NCV is the most difficult to read.

393. 1 Chronicles 6:1* The sons of **Levi**; **Gershon**, **Kohath**, and **Merari**.
AV - **8,** 1-1,2-1,3-1,4-1,5-1,6-1,7-1,8-1
ESV - **8,** 1-1,2-1,3-1,4-1,5-1,6-1,7-1,8-1
HCSB - **6,** 1-1,2-1,3-1,4-1,5-1,6-1
NASV - **9,** 1-1,2-1,3-1,4-1,5-1,6-1,7-1,8-1,9-1
NCV - **7,** 1-1,2-1,3-1,4-1,5-1,6-1,7-1
NIV - **8,** 1-1,2-1,3-1,4-1,5-1,6-1,7-1,8-1
NKJV - **9,** 1-1,2-1,3-1,4-1,5-1,6-1,7-1,8-1,9-1
NLT - **9,** 1-1,2-1,3-1,4-1,5-1,6-1,7-1,8-1,9-1
NRSV - **8,** 1-1,2-1,3-1,4-1,5-1,6-1,7-1,8-1
Conclusion: All versions read the same.

394. 1 Chronicles 6:2* And the sons of **Kohath**; **Amram**, **Izhar**, and **Hebron**, and **Uzziel**.
AV - **11,** 1-1,2-1,3-1,4-1,5-1,6-1,7-1,8-1,9-1,10-1,11-1
ESV - **9,** 1-1,2-1,3-1,4-1,5-1,6-1,7-1,8-1,9-1
HCSB - **7,** 1-1,2-1,3-1,4-1,5-1,6-1,7-1
NASV - **10,** 1-1,2-1,3-1,4-1,5-1,6-1,7-1,8-1,9-1,10-1
NCV - **8,** 1-1,2-1,3-1,4-1,5-1,6-1,7-1,8-1
NIV - **9,** 1-1,2-1,3-1,4-1,5-1,6-1,7-1,8-1,9-1

NKJV - **10,** 1-1,2-1,3-1,4-1,5-1,6-1,7-1,8-1,9-1,10-1
NLT - **10,** 1-1,2-**3**,3-1,4-1,5-**3**,6-1,7-1,8-1,9-1,10-1
NRSV - **9,** 1-1,2-1,3-1,4-1,5-1,6-1,7-1,8-1,9-1
Conclusion: Only the NLT made the verse more complex.

395. 1 Chronicles 6:16* The sons of **Levi**; **Gershom**, **Kohath**, and **Merari**.
AV - **8,** 1-1,2-1,3-1,4-1,5-1,6-1,7-1,8-1
ESV - **8,** 1-1,2-1,3-1,4-1,5-1,6-1,7-1,8-1
HCSB - **6,** 1-1,2-1,3-1,4-1,5-1,6-1
NASV - **9,** 1-1,2-1,3-1,4-1,5-1,6-1,7-1,8-1,9-1
NCV - **7,** 1-1,2-1,3-1,4-1,5-1,6-1,7-1
NIV - **8,** 1-1,2-1,3-1,4-1,5-1,6-1,7-1,8-1
NKJV - **9,** 1-1,2-1,3-1,4-1,5-1,6-1,7-1,8-1,9-1
NLT - **9,** 1-1,2-1,3-1,4-1,5-1,6-1,7-1,8-1,9-1
NRSV - **8,** 1-1,2-1,3-1,4-1,5-1,6-1,7-1,8-1
Conclusion: All versions read the same.

396. 1 Chronicles 6:17* And these be the names of the sons of **Gershom**; **Libni**, and **Shimei**.
AV - **13,** 1-1,2-1,3-1,4-1,5-1,6-1,7-1,8-1,9-1,10-1,11-1,12-1,13-1
ESV - **13,** 1-1,2-1,3-1,4-1,5-1,6-1,7-1,8-1,9-1,10-1,11-1,12-1,13-1
HCSB - **10,** 1-1,2-1,3-1,4-1,5-1,6-1,7-1,8-1,9-1,10-1
NASV - **12,** 1-1,2-1,3-1,4-1,5-1,6-1,7-1,8-1,9-1,10-1,11-1,12-1
NCV - **9,** 1-1,2-1,3-1,4-1,5-1,6-1,7-1,8-1,9-1
NIV - **12,** 1-1,2-1,3-1,4-1,5-1,6-1,7-1,8-1,9-1,10-1,11-1,12-1
NKJV - **12,** 1-1,2-1,3-1,4-1,5-1,6-1,7-1,8-1,9-1,10-1,11-1,12-1
NLT - **8,** 1-1,2-**3**,3-1,4-1,5-**3**,6-1,7-1,8-1
NRSV - **12,** 1-1,2-1,3-1,4-1,5-1,6-1,7-1,8-1,9-1,10-1,11-1,12-1
Conclusion: The NLT managed to translate the verse with the fewest words while at the same time making it more complex.

397. 1 Chronicles 6:20* Of **Gershom**; **Libni** his son, **Jahath** his son, **Zimmah** his son,
AV - **11,** 1-1,2-1,3-1,4-1,5-1,6-1,7-1,8-1,9-1,10-1,11-1
ESV - **11,** 1-1,2-1,3-1,4-1,5-1,6-1,7-1,8-1,9-1,10-1,11-1
HCSB - **11,** 1-1,2-1,3-1,4-1,5-1,6-1,7-1,8-1,9-1,10-1,11-1
NASV - **11,** 1-1,2-1,3-1,4-1,5-1,6-1,7-1,8-1,9-1,10-1,11-1
NCV - **12,** 1-1,2-1,3-1,4-1,5-1,6-1,7-1,8-1,9-1,10-1,11-1,12-1
NIV - **11,** 1-1,2-1,3-1,4-1,5-1,6-1,7-1,8-1,9-1,10-1,11-1
NKJV - **12,** 1-1,2-1,3-1,4-1,5-1,6-1,7-1,8-1,9-1,10-1,11-1,12-1
NLT - **8,** 1-1,2-**3**,3-1,4-1,5-**3**,6-1,7-1,8-1
NRSV - **11,** 1-1,2-1,3-1,4-1,5-1,6-1,7-1,8-1,9-1,10-1,11-1
Conclusion: Only the NLT made the verse more complex.

398. 1 Chronicles 6:21* **Joah** his son, **Iddo** his son, **Zerah** his son, **Jeaterai** his son.
AV - **12,** 1-1,2-1,3-1,4-1,5-1,6-1,7-1,8-1,9-1,10-1,11-1,12-1

ESV - **12,** 1-1,2-1,3-1,4-1,5-1,6-1,7-1,8-1,9-1,10-1,11-1,12-1
HCSB - **13,** 1-1,2-1,3-1,4-1,5-1,6-1,7-1,8-1,9-1,10-1,11-1,12-1,13-1
NASV - **12,** 1-1,2-1,3-1,4-1,5-1,6-1,7-1,8-1,9-1,10-1,11-1,12-1
NCV - **17,** 1-1,2-1,3-1,4-1,5-1,6-1,7-1,8-1,9-1,10-1,11-1,12-1,13-1,14-1,15-1,16-1,17-1
NIV - **13,** 1-1,2-1,3-1,4-1,5-1,6-1,7-1,8-1,9-1,10-1,11-1,12-1,13-1
NKJV - **13,** 1-1,2-1,3-1,4-1,5-1,6-1,7-1,8-1,9-1,10-1,11-1,12-1,13-1
NLT - **5,** 1-1,2-1,3-1,4-1,5-1
NRSV - **12,** 1-1,2-1,3-1,4-1,5-1,6-1,7-1,8-1,9-1,10-1,11-1,12-1
Conclusion: All versions read the same.

399. 1 Chronicles 6:22* The sons of **Kohath**; **Amminadab** his son, **Korah** his son, **Assir** his son,
AV - **13,** 1-1,2-1,3-1,4-1,5-1,6-1,7-1,8-1,9-1,10-1,11-1,12-1,13-1
ESV - **13,** 1-1,2-1,3-1,4-1,5-1,6-1,7-1,8-1,9-1,10-1,11-1,12-1,13-1
HCSB - **11,** 1-1,2-1,3-1,4-1,5-1,6-1,7-1,8-1,9-1,10-1,11-1
NASV - **14,** 1-1,2-1,3-1,4-1,5-1,6-1,7-1,8-1,9-1,10-1,11-1,12-1,13-1,14-1
NCV - **12,** 1-1,2-1,3-1,4-1,5-1,6-1,7-1,8-1,9-1,10-1,11-1,12-1
NIV - **13,** 1-1,2-**3**,3-1,4-1,5-1,6-1,7-1,8-1,9-1,10-1,11-1,12-1,13-1
NKJV - **14,** 1-1,2-1,3-1,4-1,5-1,6-1,7-1,8-1,9-1,10-1,11-1,12-1,13-1,14-1
NLT - **8,** 1-1,2-**3**,3-1,4-1,5-**3**,6-1,7-1,8-1
NRSV - **13,** 1-1,2-1,3-1,4-1,5-1,6-1,7-1,8-1,9-1,10-1,11-1,12-1,13-1
Conclusion: Only the NIV and the NLT made the verse more complex.

400. 1 Chronicles 6:23* **Elkanah** his son, and **Ebiasaph** his son, and **Assir** his son,
AV - **11,** 1-1,2-1,3-1,4-1,5-1,6-1,7-1,8-1,9-1,10-1,11-1
ESV - **9,** 1-1,2-1,3-1,4-1,5-1,6-1,7-1,8-1,9-1
HCSB - **9,** 1-1,2-1,3-1,4-1,5-1,6-1,7-1,8-1,9-1
NASV - **10,** 1-1,2-1,3-1,4-1,5-1,6-1,7-1,8-1,9-1,10-1
NCV - **12,** 1-1,2-1,3-1,4-1,5-1,6-1,7-1,8-1,9-1,10-1,11-1,12-1
NIV - **9,** 1-1,2-1,3-1,4-1,5-1,6-1,7-1,8-1,9-1
NKJV - **9,** 1-1,2-1,3-1,4-1,5-1,6-1,7-1,8-1,9-1
NLT - **3,** 1-1,2-1,3-1
NRSV - **9,** 1-1,2-1,3-1,4-1,5-1,6-1,7-1,8-1,9-1
Conclusion: All versions read the same.

401. 1 Chronicles 6:24* **Tahath** his son, **Uriel** his son, **Uzziah** his son, and **Shaul** his son.
AV - **13,** 1-1,2-1,3-1,4-1,5-1,6-1,7-1,8-1,9-1,10-1,11-1,12-1,13-1
ESV - **13,** 1-1,2-1,3-1,4-1,5-1,6-1,7-1,8-1,9-1,10-1,11-1,12-1,13-1
HCSB - **13,** 1-1,2-1,3-1,4-1,5-1,6-1,7-1,8-1,9-1,10-1,11-1,12-1,13-1
NASV - **13,** 1-1,2-1,3-1,4-1,5-1,6-1,7-1,8-1,9-1,10-1,11-1,12-1,13-1
NCV - **17,** 1-1,2-1,3-1,4-1,5-1,6-1,7-1,8-1,9-1,10-1,11-1,12-1,13-1,14-1,15-1,16-1,17-1
NIV - **13,** 1-1,2-1,3-1,4-1,5-1,6-1,7-1,8-1,9-1,10-1,11-1,12-1,13-1
NKJV - **13,** 1-1,2-1,3-1,4-1,5-1,6-1,7-1,8-1,9-1,10-1,11-1,12-1,13-1
NLT - **5,** 1-1,2-1,3-1,4-1,5-1
NRSV - **13,** 1-1,2-1,3-1,4-1,5-1,6-1,7-1,8-1,9-1,10-1,11-1,12-1,13-1

Conclusion: All versions read the same.

402. 1 Chronicles 6:25* And the sons of **Elkanah**; **Amasai**, and **Ahimoth**.
AV - **8,** 1-1,2-1,3-1,4-1,5-1,6-1,7-1,8-1
ESV - **7,** 1-1,2-1,3-1,4-1,5-1,6-1,7-1
HCSB - **5,** 1-1,2-1,3-1,4-1,5-1
NASV - **8,** 1-1,2-1,3-1,4-1,5-1,6-1,7-1,8-1
NCV - **6,** 1-1,2-1,3-1,4-1,5-1,6-1
NIV - 6, 1-1,2-**3**,3-1,4-1,5-1,6-1
NKJV - **8,** 1-1,2-1,3-1,4-1,5-1,6-1,7-1,8-1
NLT - 7, 1-1,2-**3**,3-1,4-1,5-**3**,6-1,7-1
NRSV - **7,** 1-1,2-1,3-1,4-1,5-1,6-1,7-1
Conclusion: Only the NIV and the NLT made the verse more complex.

403. 1 Chronicles 6:26* As for **Elkanah**: the sons of **Elkanah**; **Zophai** his son, and **Nahath** his son,
AV - **14,** 1-1,2-1,3-1,4-1,5-1,6-1,7-1,8-1,9-1,10-1,11-1,12-1,13-1,14-1
ESV - **9,** 1-1,2-1,3-1,4-1,5-1,6-1,7-1,8-1,9-1
HCSB - **9,** 1-1,2-1,3-1,4-1,5-1,6-1,7-1,8-1,9-1
NASV - **15,** 1-1,2-1,3-1,4-1,5-1,6-1,7-1,8-1,9-1,10-1,11-1,12-1,13-1,14-1,15-1
NCV - **12,** 1-1,2-1,3-1,4-1,5-1,6-1,7-1,8-1,9-1,10-1,11-1,12-1
NIV - **9,** 1-1,2-1,3-1,4-1,5-1,6-1,7-1,8-1,9-1
NKJV - **14,** 1-1,2-1,3-1,4-1,5-1,6-1,7-1,8-1,9-1,10-1,11-1,12-1,13-1,14-1
NLT - **3,** 1-1,2-1,3-1
NRSV - **9,** 1-1,2-1,3-1,4-1,5-1,6-1,7-1,8-1,9-1
Conclusion: All versions read the same.

404. 1 Chronicles 6:27* **Eliab** his son, **Jeroham** his son, **Elkanah** his son.
AV - **9,** 1-1,2-1,3-1,4-1,5-1,6-1,7-1,8-1,9-1
ESV - **9,** 1-1,2-1,3-1,4-1,5-1,6-1,7-1,8-1,9-1
HCSB - **10,** 1-1,2-1,3-1,4-1,5-1,6-1,7-1,8-1,9-1,10-1
NASV - **9,** 1-1,2-1,3-1,4-1,5-1,6-1,7-1,8-1,9-1
NCV - **17,** 1-1,2-1,3-1,4-1,5-1,6-1,7-1,8-1,9-1,10-1,11-1,12-1,13-1,14-1,15-1,16-1,17-1
NIV - **13,** 1-1,2-1,3-1,4-1,5-1,6-1,7-1,8-1,9-1,10-1,11-1,12-1,13-1
NKJV - **10,** 1-1,2-1,3-1,4-1,5-1,6-1,7-1,8-1,9-1,10-1
NLT - **5,** 1-1,2-1,3-1,4-1,5-1
NRSV - **9,** 1-1,2-1,3-1,4-1,5-1,6-1,7-1,8-1,9-1
Conclusion: All versions read the same.

405. 1 Chronicles 6:29* The sons of **Merari**; **Mahli**, **Libni** his son, **Shimei** his son, **Uzza** his son,
AV - **14,** 1-1,2-1,3-1,4-1,5-1,6-1,7-1,8-1,9-1,10-1,11-1,12-1,13-1,14-1
ESV - **14,** 1-1,2-1,3-1,4-1,5-1,6-1,7-1,8-1,9-1,10-1,11-1,12-1,13-1,14-1
HCSB - **12,** 1-1,2-1,3-1,4-1,5-1,6-1,7-1,8-1,9-1,10-1,11-1,12-1
NASV - **15,** 1-1,2-1,3-1,4-1,5-1,6-1,7-1,8-1,9-1,10-1,11-1,12-1,13-1,14-1,15-1

NCV - **16,** 1-1,2-1,3-1,4-1,5-1,6-1,7-1,8-1,9-1,10-1,11-1,12-1,13-1,14-1,15-1,16-1
NIV - 14, 1-1,2-**3,**3-1,4-1,5-1,6-1,7-1,8-1,9-1,10-1,11-1,12-1,13-1,14-1
NKJV - **15,** 1-1,2-1,3-1,4-1,5-1,6-1,7-1,8-1,9-1,10-1,11-1,12-1,13-1,14-1,15-1
NLT - 9, 1-1,2-**3,**3-1,4-1,5-**3,**6-1,7-1,8-1,9-1
NRSV - **14,** 1-1,2-1,3-1,4-1,5-1,6-1,7-1,8-1,9-1,10-1,11-1,12-1,13-1,14-1
Conclusion: Only the NIV and the NLT made the verse more complex.

406. 1 Chronicles 6:30* Shimea his son, **Haggiah** his son, **Asaiah** his son.
AV - **9,** 1-1,2-1,3-1,4-1,5-1,6-1,7-1,8-1,9-1
ESV - **10,** 1-1,2-1,3-1,4-1,5-1,6-1,7-1,8-1,9-1,10-1
HCSB - **10,** 1-1,2-1,3-1,4-1,5-1,6-1,7-1,8-1,9-1,10-1
NASV - **9,** 1-1,2-1,3-1,4-1,5-1,6-1,7-1,8-1,9-1
NCV - **13,** 1-1,2-1,3-1,4-1,5-1,6-1,7-1,8-1,9-1,10-1,11-1,12-1,13-1
NIV - **10,** 1-1,2-1,3-1,4-1,5-1,6-1,7-1,8-1,9-1,10-1
NKJV - **10,** 1-1,2-1,3-1,4-1,5-1,6-1,7-1,8-1,9-1,10-1
NLT - **4,** 1-1,2-1,3-1,4-1
NRSV - **10,** 1-1,2-1,3-1,4-1,5-1,6-1,7-1,8-1,9-1,10-1
Conclusion: All versions read the same.

407. 1 Chronicles 6:34* The son of **Elkanah**, the son of **Jeroham**, the son of **Eliel**, the son of
Toah,
AV - **16,** 1-1,2-1,3-1,4-1,5-1,6-1,7-1,8-1,9-1,10-1,11-1,12-1,13-1,14-1,15-1,16-1
ESV - **12,** 1-1,2-1,3-1,4-1,5-1,6-1,7-1,8-1,9-1,10-1,11-1,12-1
HCSB - **12,** 1-1,2-1,3-1,4-1,5-1,6-1,7-1,8-1,9-1,10-1,11-1,12-1
NASV - **16,** 1-1,2-1,3-1,4-1,5-1,6-1,7-1,8-1,9-1,10-1,11-1,12-1,13-1,14-1,15-1,16-1
NCV - **16,** 1-1,2-1,3-1,4-1,5-1,6-1,7-1,8-1,9-1,10-1,11-1,12-1,13-1,14-1,15-1,16-1
NIV - **16,** 1-1,2-1,3-1,4-1,5-1,6-1,7-1,8-1,9-1,10-1,11-1,12-1,13-1,14-1,15-1,16-1
NKJV - **16,** 1-1,2-1,3-1,4-1,5-1,6-1,7-1,8-1,9-1,10-1,11-1,12-1,13-1,14-1,15-1,16-1
NLT - **4,** 1-1,2-1,3-1,4-1
NRSV - **12,** 1-1,2-1,3-1,4-1,5-1,6-1,7-1,8-1,9-1,10-1,11-1,12-1
Conclusion: All versions read the same.

408. 1 Chronicles 6:35* The son of Zuph, the son of **Elkanah**, the son of **Mahath**, the son of
Amasai,
AV - **16,** 1-1,2-1,3-1,4-1,5-1,6-1,7-1,8-1,9-1,10-1,11-1,12-1,13-1,14-1,15-1,16-1
ESV - **12,** 1-1,2-1,3-1,4-1,5-1,6-1,7-1,8-1,9-1,10-1,11-1,12-1
HCSB - **12,** 1-1,2-1,3-1,4-1,5-1,6-1,7-1,8-1,9-1,10-1,11-1,12-1
NASV - **16,** 1-1,2-1,3-1,4-1,5-1,6-1,7-1,8-1,9-1,10-1,11-1,12-1,13-1,14-1,15-1,16-1
NCV - **16,** 1-1,2-1,3-1,4-1,5-1,6-1,7-1,8-1,9-1,10-1,11-1,12-1,13-1,14-1,15-1,16-1
NIV - **16,** 1-1,2-1,3-1,4-1,5-1,6-1,7-1,8-1,9-1,10-1,11-1,12-1,13-1,14-1,15-1,16-1
NKJV - **16,** 1-1,2-1,3-1,4-1,5-1,6-1,7-1,8-1,9-1,10-1,11-1,12-1,13-1,14-1,15-1,16-1
NLT - **4,** 1-1,2-1,3-1,4-1
NRSV - **12,** 1-1,2-1,3-1,4-1,5-1,6-1,7-1,8-1,9-1,10-1,11-1,12-1
Conclusion: All versions read the same.

409. 1 Chronicles 6:36* The son of **Elkanah**, the son of **Joel**, the son of **Azariah**, the son of **Zephaniah**,
AV - **16,** 1-1,2-1,3-1,4-1,5-1,6-1,7-1,8-1,9-1,10-1,11-1,12-1,13-1,14-1,15-1,16-1
ESV - **12,** 1-1,2-1,3-1,4-1,5-1,6-1,7-1,8-1,9-1,10-1,11-1,12-1
HCSB - **12,** 1-1,2-1,3-1,4-1,5-1,6-1,7-1,8-1,9-1,10-1,11-1,12-1
NASV - **16,** 1-1,2-1,3-1,4-1,5-1,6-1,7-1,8-1,9-1,10-1,11-1,12-1,13-1,14-1,15-1,16-1
NCV - **16,** 1-1,2-1,3-1,4-1,5-1,6-1,7-1,8-1,9-1,10-1,11-1,12-1,13-1,14-1,15-1,16-1
NIV - **16,** 1-1,2-1,3-1,4-1,5-1,6-1,7-1,8-1,9-1,10-1,11-1,12-1,13-1,14-1,15-1,16-1
NKJV - **16,** 1-1,2-1,3-1,4-1,5-1,6-1,7-1,8-1,9-1,10-1,11-1,12-1,13-1,14-1,15-1,16-1
NLT - **4,** 1-1,2-1,3-1,4-1
NRSV - **12,** 1-1,2-1,3-1,4-1,5-1,6-1,7-1,8-1,9-1,10-1,11-1,12-1
Conclusion: All versions read the same.

410. 1 Chronicles 6:37* The son of **Tahath**, the son of **Assir**, the son of **Ebiasaph**, the son of **Korah**,
AV - **16,** 1-1,2-1,3-1,4-1,5-1,6-1,7-1,8-1,9-1,10-1,11-1,12-1,13-1,14-1,15-1,16-1
ESV - **12,** 1-1,2-1,3-1,4-1,5-1,6-1,7-1,8-1,9-1,10-1,11-1,12-1
HCSB - **12,** 1-1,2-1,3-1,4-1,5-1,6-1,7-1,8-1,9-1,10-1,11-1,12-1
NASV - **16,** 1-1,2-1,3-1,4-1,5-1,6-1,7-1,8-1,9-1,10-1,11-1,12-1,13-1,14-1,15-1,16-1
NCV - **16,** 1-1,2-1,3-1,4-1,5-1,6-1,7-1,8-1,9-1,10-1,11-1,12-1,13-1,14-1,15-1,16-1
NIV - **16,** 1-1,2-1,3-1,4-1,5-1,6-1,7-1,8-1,9-1,10-1,11-1,12-1,13-1,14-1,15-1,16-1
NKJV - **16,** 1-1,2-1,3-1,4-1,5-1,6-1,7-1,8-1,9-1,10-1,11-1,12-1,13-1,14-1,15-1,16-1
NLT - **4,** 1-1,2-1,3-1,4-1
NRSV - **12,** 1-1,2-1,3-1,4-1,5-1,6-1,7-1,8-1,9-1,10-1,11-1,12-1
Conclusion: All versions read the same.

411. 1 Chronicles 6:38* The son of **Izhar**, the son of **Kohath**, the son of **Levi**, the son of **Israel**.
AV - **16,** 1-1,2-1,3-1,4-1,5-1,6-1,7-1,8-1,9-1,10-1,11-1,12-1,13-1,14-1,15-1,16-1
ESV - **12,** 1-1,2-1,3-1,4-1,5-1,6-1,7-1,8-1,9-1,10-1,11-1,12-1
HCSB - **12,** 1-1,2-1,3-1,4-1,5-1,6-1,7-1,8-1,9-1,10-1,11-1,12-1
NASV - **16,** 1-1,2-1,3-1,4-1,5-1,6-1,7-1,8-1,9-1,10-1,11-1,12-1,13-1,14-1,15-1,16-1
NCV - **16,** 1-1,2-1,3-1,4-1,5-1,6-1,7-1,8-1,9-1,10-1,11-1,12-1,13-1,14-1,15-1,16-1
NIV - **16,** 1-1,2-1,3-1,4-1,5-1,6-1,7-1,8-1,9-1,10-1,11-1,12-1,13-1,14-1,15-1,16-1
NKJV - **16,** 1-1,2-1,3-1,4-1,5-1,6-1,7-1,8-1,9-1,10-1,11-1,12-1,13-1,14-1,15-1,16-1
NLT - **5,** 1-1,2-1,3-1,4-1,5-1
NRSV - **12,** 1-1,2-1,3-1,4-1,5-1,6-1,7-1,8-1,9-1,10-1,11-1,12-1
Conclusion: All versions read the same.

412. 1 Chronicles 6:40* The son of **Michael**, the son of **Baaseiah**, the son of **Malchiah**,
AV - **12,** 1-1,2-1,3-1,4-1,5-1,6-1,7-1,8-1,9-1,10-1,11-1,12-1
ESV - **9,** 1-1,2-1,3-1,4-1,5-1,6-1,7-1,8-1,9-1
HCSB - **9,** 1-1,2-1,3-1,4-1,5-1,6-1,7-1,8-1,9-1
NASV - **12,** 1-1,2-1,3-1,4-1,5-1,6-1,7-1,8-1,9-1,10-1,11-1,12-1

NCV - **12,** 1-1,2-1,3-1,4-1,5-1,6-1,7-1,8-1,9-1,10-1,11-1,12-1
NIV - **12,** 1-1,2-1,3-1,4-1,5-1,6-1,7-1,8-1,9-1,10-1,11-1,12-1
NKJV - **12,** 1-1,2-1,3-1,4-1,5-1,6-1,7-1,8-1,9-1,10-1,11-1,12-1
NLT - **3,** 1-1,2-1,3-1
NRSV - **9,** 1-1,2-1,3-1,4-1,5-1,6-1,7-1,8-1,9-1
Conclusion: All versions read the same.

413. 1 Chronicles 6:41* The son of **Ethni**, the son of **Zerah**, the son of **Adaiah**,
AV - **12,** 1-1,2-1,3-1,4-1,5-1,6-1,7-1,8-1,9-1,10-1,11-1,12-1
ESV - **9,** 1-1,2-1,3-1,4-1,5-1,6-1,7-1,8-1,9-1
HCSB - **9,** 1-1,2-1,3-1,4-1,5-1,6-1,7-1,8-1,9-1
NASV - **12,** 1-1,2-1,3-1,4-1,5-1,6-1,7-1,8-1,9-1,10-1,11-1,12-1
NCV - **12,** 1-1,2-1,3-1,4-1,5-1,6-1,7-1,8-1,9-1,10-1,11-1,12-1
NIV - **12,** 1-1,2-1,3-1,4-1,5-1,6-1,7-1,8-1,9-1,10-1,11-1,12-1
NKJV - **12,** 1-1,2-1,3-1,4-1,5-1,6-1,7-1,8-1,9-1,10-1,11-1,12-1
NLT - **3,** 1-1,2-1,3-1
NRSV - **9,** 1-1,2-1,3-1,4-1,5-1,6-1,7-1,8-1,9-1
Conclusion: All versions read the same.

414. 1 Chronicles 6:42* The son of **Ethan**, the son of **Zimmah**, the son of **Shimei**,
AV - **12,** 1-1,2-1,3-1,4-1,5-1,6-1,7-1,8-1,9-1,10-1,11-1,12-1
ESV - **9,** 1-1,2-1,3-1,4-1,5-1,6-1,7-1,8-1,9-1
HCSB - **9,** 1-1,2-1,3-1,4-1,5-1,6-1,7-1,8-1,9-1
NASV - **12,** 1-1,2-1,3-1,4-1,5-1,6-1,7-1,8-1,9-1,10-1,11-1,12-1
NCV - **12,** 1-1,2-1,3-1,4-1,5-1,6-1,7-1,8-1,9-1,10-1,11-1,12-1
NIV - **12,** 1-1,2-1,3-1,4-1,5-1,6-1,7-1,8-1,9-1,10-1,11-1,12-1
NKJV - **12,** 1-1,2-1,3-1,4-1,5-1,6-1,7-1,8-1,9-1,10-1,11-1,12-1
NLT - **3,** 1-1,2-1,3-1
NRSV - **9,** 1-1,2-1,3-1,4-1,5-1,6-1,7-1,8-1,9-1
Conclusion: All versions read the same.

415. 1 Chronicles 6:43* The son of **Jahath**, the son of **Gershom**, the son of **Levi**.
AV - **12,** 1-1,2-1,3-1,4-1,5-1,6-1,7-1,8-1,9-1,10-1,11-1,12-1
ESV - **9,** 1-1,2-1,3-1,4-1,5-1,6-1,7-1,8-1,9-1
HCSB - **9,** 1-1,2-1,3-1,4-1,5-1,6-1,7-1,8-1,9-1
NASV - **12,** 1-1,2-1,3-1,4-1,5-1,6-1,7-1,8-1,9-1,10-1,11-1,12-1
NCV - **13,** 1-1,2-1,3-1,4-1,5-1,6-1,7-1,8-1,9-1,10-1,11-1,12-1,13-1
NIV - **12,** 1-1,2-1,3-1,4-1,5-1,6-1,7-1,8-1,9-1,10-1,11-1,12-1
NKJV - **12,** 1-1,2-1,3-1,4-1,5-1,6-1,7-1,8-1,9-1,10-1,11-1,12-1
NLT - **4,** 1-1,2-1,3-1,4-1
NRSV - **9,** 1-1,2-1,3-1,4-1,5-1,6-1,7-1,8-1,9-1
Conclusion: All versions read the same.

416. 1 Chronicles 6:45* The son of **Hashabiah**, the son of **Amaziah**, the son of **Hilkiah**,
AV - **12,** 1-1,2-1,3-1,4-1,5-1,6-1,7-1,8-1,9-1,10-1,11-1,12-1
ESV - **9,** 1-1,2-1,3-1,4-1,5-1,6-1,7-1,8-1,9-1
HCSB - **9,** 1-1,2-1,3-1,4-1,5-1,6-1,7-1,8-1,9-1
NASV - **12,** 1-1,2-1,3-1,4-1,5-1,6-1,7-1,8-1,9-1,10-1,11-1,12-1
NCV - **12,** 1-1,2-1,3-1,4-1,5-1,6-1,7-1,8-1,9-1,10-1,11-1,12-1
NIV - **12,** 1-1,2-1,3-1,4-1,5-1,6-1,7-1,8-1,9-1,10-1,11-1,12-1
NKJV - **12,** 1-1,2-1,3-1,4-1,5-1,6-1,7-1,8-1,9-1,10-1,11-1,12-1
NLT - **3,** 1-1,2-1,3-1
NRSV - **9,** 1-1,2-1,3-1,4-1,5-1,6-1,7-1,8-1,9-1
Conclusion: All versions read the same.

417. 1 Chronicles 6:46* The son of **Amzi**, the son of **Bani**, the son of **Shamer**,
AV - **12,** 1-1,2-1,3-1,4-1,5-1,6-1,7-1,8-1,9-1,10-1,11-1,12-1
ESV - **9,** 1-1,2-1,3-1,4-1,5-1,6-1,7-1,8-1,9-1
HCSB - **9,** 1-1,2-1,3-1,4-1,5-1,6-1,7-1,8-1,9-1
NASV - **12,** 1-1,2-1,3-1,4-1,5-1,6-1,7-1,8-1,9-1,10-1,11-1,12-1
NCV - **12,** 1-1,2-1,3-1,4-1,5-1,6-1,7-1,8-1,9-1,10-1,11-1,12-1
NIV - **12,** 1-1,2-1,3-1,4-1,5-1,6-1,7-1,8-1,9-1,10-1,11-1,12-1
NKJV - **12,** 1-1,2-1,3-1,4-1,5-1,6-1,7-1,8-1,9-1,10-1,11-1,12-1
NLT - **3,** 1-1,2-1,3-1
NRSV - **9,** 1-1,2-1,3-1,4-1,5-1,6-1,7-1,8-1,9-1
Conclusion: All versions read the same.

418. 1 Chronicles 6:47* The son of **Mahli**, the son of **Mushi**, the son of **Merari**, the son of **Levi**.
AV - **16,** 1-1,2-1,3-1,4-1,5-1,6-1,7-1,8-1,9-1,10-1,11-1,12-1,13-1,14-1,15-1,16-1
ESV - **12,** 1-1,2-1,3-1,4-1,5-1,6-1,7-1,8-1,9-1,10-1,11-1,12-1
HCSB - **12,** 1-1,2-1,3-1,4-1,5-1,6-1,7-1,8-1,9-1,10-1,11-1,12-1
NASV - **16,** 1-1,2-1,3-1,4-1,5-1,6-1,7-1,8-1,9-1,10-1,11-1,12-1,13-1,14-1,15-1,16-1
NCV - **17,** 1-1,2-1,3-1,4-1,5-1,6-1,7-1,8-1,9-1,10-1,11-1,12-1,13-1,14-1,15-1,16-1,17-1
NIV - **16,** 1-1,2-1,3-1,4-1,5-1,6-1,7-1,8-1,9-1,10-1,11-1,12-1,13-1,14-1,15-1,16-1
NKJV - **16,** 1-1,2-1,3-1,4-1,5-1,6-1,7-1,8-1,9-1,10-1,11-1,12-1,13-1,14-1,15-1,16-1
NLT - **5,** 1-1,2-1,3-1,4-1,5-1
NRSV - **12,** 1-1,2-1,3-1,4-1,5-1,6-1,7-1,8-1,9-1,10-1,11-1,12-1
Conclusion: All versions read the same.

419. 1 Chronicles 6:50* And these are the sons of **Aaron**; **Eleazar** his son, **Phinehas** his son, **Abishua** his son,
AV - **16,** 1-1,2-1,3-1,4-1,5-1,6-1,7-1,8-1,9-1,10-1,11-1,12-1,13-1,14-1,15-1,16-1
ESV - **15,** 1-1,2-1,3-1,4-1,5-1,6-1,7-1,8-1,9-1,10-1,11-1,12-1,13-1,14-1,15-1
HCSB - **13,** 1-1,2-1,3-1,4-1,5-1,6-1,7-1,8-1,9-1,10-1,11-1,12-1,13-1
NASV - **15,** 1-1,2-1,3-1,4-1,5-1,6-1,7-1,8-1,9-1,10-1,11-1,12-1,13-1,14-1,15-1
NCV - **16,** 1-1,2-1,3-1,4-1,5-1,6-1,7-1,8-1,9-1,10-1,11-1,12-1,13-1,14-1,15-1,16-1
NIV - **15,** 1-1,2-1,3-1,4-**3**,5-1,6-1,7-1,8-1,9-1,10-1,11-1,12-1,13-1,14-1,15-1

NKJV - **16,** 1-1,2-1,3-1,4-1,5-1,6-1,7-1,8-1,9-1,10-1,11-1,12-1,13-1,14-1,15-1,16-1
NLT - 8, 1-1,2-**3,**3-1,4-1,5-1,6-1,7-1,8-1
NRSV - **15,** 1-1,2-1,3-1,4-1,5-1,6-1,7-1,8-1,9-1,10-1,11-1,12-1,13-1,14-1,15-1
Conclusion: Only the NIV and the NLT made the verse more complex.

420. 1 Chronicles 6:51* Bukki his son, **Uzzi** his son, **Zerahiah** his son,
AV - **9,** 1-1,2-1,3-1,4-1,5-1,6-1,7-1,8-1,9-1
ESV - **9,** 1-1,2-1,3-1,4-1,5-1,6-1,7-1,8-1,9-1
HCSB - **9,** 1-1,2-1,3-1,4-1,5-1,6-1,7-1,8-1,9-1
NASV - **9,** 1-1,2-1,3-1,4-1,5-1,6-1,7-1,8-1,9-1
NCV - **12,** 1-1,2-1,3-1,4-1,5-1,6-1,7-1,8-1,9-1,10-1,11-1,12-1
NIV - **9,** 1-1,2-1,3-1,4-1,5-1,6-1,7-1,8-1,9-1
NKJV - **9,** 1-1,2-1,3-1,4-1,5-1,6-1,7-1,8-1,9-1
NLT - **3,** 1-1,2-1,3-1
NRSV - **9,** 1-1,2-1,3-1,4-1,5-1,6-1,7-1,8-1,9-1
Conclusion: All versions read the same.

421. 1 Chronicles 6:52* Meraioth his son, **Amariah** his son, **Ahitub** his son,
AV - **9,** 1-1,2-1,3-1,4-1,5-1,6-1,7-1,8-1,9-1
ESV - **9,** 1-1,2-1,3-1,4-1,5-1,6-1,7-1,8-1,9-1
HCSB - **9,** 1-1,2-1,3-1,4-1,5-1,6-1,7-1,8-1,9-1
NASV - **9,** 1-1,2-1,3-1,4-1,5-1,6-1,7-1,8-1,9-1
NCV - **12,** 1-1,2-1,3-1,4-1,5-1,6-1,7-1,8-1,9-1,10-1,11-1,12-1
NIV - **9,** 1-1,2-1,3-1,4-1,5-1,6-1,7-1,8-1,9-1
NKJV - **9,** 1-1,2-1,3-1,4-1,5-1,6-1,7-1,8-1,9-1
NLT - **3,** 1-1,2-1,3-1
NRSV - **9,** 1-1,2-1,3-1,4-1,5-1,6-1,7-1,8-1,9-1
Conclusion: All versions read the same.

422. 1 Chronicles 6:53* Zadok his son, **Ahimaaz** his son.
AV - **6,** 1-1,2-1,3-1,4-1,5-1,6-1
ESV - **6,** 1-1,2-1,3-1,4-1,5-1,6-1
HCSB - **7,** 1-1,2-1,3-1,4-1,5-1,6-1,7-1
NASV - **6,** 1-1,2-1,3-1,4-1,5-1,6-1
NCV - **9,** 1-1,2-1,3-1,4-1,5-1,6-1,7-1,8-1,9-1
NIV - **7,** 1-1,2-1,3-1,4-1,5-1,6-1,7-1
NKJV - **7,** 1-1,2-1,3-1,4-1,5-1,6-1,7-1
NLT - **3,** 1-1,2-1,3-1
NRSV - **6,** 1-1,2-1,3-1,4-1,5-1,6-1
Conclusion: All versions read the same.

423. 1 Chronicles 7:1* Now the sons of **Issachar** were, **Tola**, and **Puah**, **Jashub**, and **Shimron**, four.
AV - **13,** 1-1,2-1,3-1,4-1,5-1,6-1,7-1,8-1,9-1,10-1,11-1,12-1,13-1

ESV - **10,** 1-1,2-1,3-1,4-1,5-1,6-1,7-1,8-1,9-1,10-1
HCSB - **8,** 1-1,2-1,3-1,4-1,5-1,6-1,7-1,8-1
NASV - **12,** 1-1,2-1,3-1,4-1,5-1,6-1,7-1,8-1,9-1,10-1,11-1,12-1
NCV - **9,** 1-1,2-1,3-1,4-1,5-1,6-1,7-1,8-1,9-1
NIV - **12,** 1-1,2-1,3-1,4-1,5-1,6-1,7-1,8-1,9-1,10-1,11-1,12-1
NKJV - **13,** 1-1,2-1,3-1,4-1,5-1,6-1,7-1,8-1,9-1,10-1,11-1,12-1,13-1
NLT - **11,** 1-1,2-1,3-1,4-1,5-1,6-1,7-1,8-1,9-1,10-1,11-1
NRSV - **10,** 1-1,2-1,3-1,4-1,5-1,6-1,7-1,8-1,9-1,10-1
Conclusion: All versions read the same.

424. 1 Chronicles 7:3* And the sons of **Uzzi**; **Izrahiah**: and the sons of **Izrahiah**; **Michael**, and **Obadiah**, and Joel, **Ishiah**, five: all of them chief men.
AV - **23,** 1-1,2-1,3-1,4-1,5-1,6-1,7-1,8-1,9-1,10-1,11-1,12-1,13-1,14-1,15-1,16-1,17-1,18-1,19-1,20-1,21-1,22-1,23-1
ESV - **22,** 1-1,2-1,3-1,4-1,5-1,6-1,7-1,8-1,9-1,10-1,11-1,12-1,13-1,14-1,15-1,16-1,17-1,18-1,19-1,20-1,21-1,22-1
HCSB - **15,** 1-1,2-1,3-1,4-1,5-1,6-1,7-1,8-1,9-1,10-1,11-1,12-1,13-1,14-1,15-1
NASV - **23,** 1-1,2-1,3-1,4-1,5-1,6-1,7-1,8-1,9-1,10-1,11-1,12-1,13-1,14-1,15-1,16-1,17-1,18-1,19-1,20-1,21-1,22-1,23-1
NCV - **18,** 1-1,2-1,3-1,4-1,5-1,6-1,7-1,8-1,9-1,10-1,11-1,12-1,13-1,14-1,15-1,16-1,17-1,18-**2**
NIV - **20,** 1-1,2-1,3-1,4-1,5-1,6-1,7-1,8-1,9-1,10-1,11-1,12-1,13-1,14-1,15-1,16-1,17-1,18-1,19-1,20-1
NKJV - **24,** 1-1,2-1,3-1,4-1,5-1,6-1,7-1,8-1,9-1,10-1,11-1,12-1,13-1,14-1,15-1,16-1,17-1,18-1,19-1,20-1,21-1,22-1,23-1,24-1
NLT - **23,** 1-1,2-1,3-1,4-1,5-1,6-1,7-1,8-1,9-1,10-1,11-1,12-1,13-1,14-1,15-1,16-1,17-1,18-1,19-**2**,20-1,21-**2**,22-1,23-1
NRSV - **20,** 1-1,2-1,3-1,4-1,5-1,6-1,7-1,8-1,9-1,10-1,11-1,12-1,13-1,14-1,15-1,16-1,17-1,18-1,19-1,20-1
Conclusion: Only the NCV and the NLT made the verse more complex.

425. 1 Chronicles 7:6* The sons of **Benjamin**; **Bela**, and **Becher**, and **Jediael**, three.
AV - **10,** 1-1,2-1,3-1,4-1,5-1,6-1,7-1,8-1,9-1,10-1
ESV - **9,** 1-1,2-1,3-1,4-1,5-1,6-1,7-1,8-1,9-1
HCSB - **8,** 1-1,2-1,3-1,4-1,5-1,6-1,7-1,8-1
NASV - **11,** 1-1,2-1,3-1,4-1,5-1,6-1,7-1,8-1,9-1,10-1,11-1
NCV - **8,** 1-1,2-1,3-1,4-1,5-1,6-1,7-1,8-1
NIV - **8,** 1-1,2-1,3-1,4-1,5-1,6-1,7-1,8-1
NKJV - **12,** 1-1,2-1,3-1,4-1,5-1,6-1,7-1,8-1,9-1,10-1,11-1,12-1
NLT - **9,** 1-1,2-1,3-1,4-1,5-1,6-1,7-1,8-1,9-1
NRSV - **9,** 1-1,2-1,3-1,4-1,5-1,6-1,7-1,8-1,9-1
Conclusion: All versions read the same.

426. 1 Chronicles 7:8* And the sons of **Becher**; **Zemira**, and **Joash**, and **Eliezer**, and **Elioenai**, and **Omri**, and **Jerimoth**, and **Abiah**, and **Anathoth**, and **Alameth**. All these are the sons of **Becher**.

AV - **29,** 1-1,2-1,3-1,4-1,5-1,6-1,7-1,8-1,9-1,10-1,11-1,12-1,13-1,14-1,15-1,16-1,17-1,18-1,19-1,20-1,21-1,22-1,23-1,24-1,25-1,26-1,27-1,28-1,29-1

ESV - **21,** 1-1,2-1,3-1,4-1,5-1,6-1,7-1,8-1,9-1,10-1,11-1,12-1,13-1,14-1,15-1,16-1,17-1,18-1,19-1,20-1,21-1

HCSB - **17,** 1-1,2-1,3-1,4-1,5-1,6-1,7-1,8-1,9-1,10-1,11-1,12-1,13-1,14-1,15-1,16-1,17-1

NASV - **22,** 1-1,2-1,3-1,4-1,5-1,6-1,7-1,8-1,9-1,10-1,11-1,12-1,13-1,14-1,15-1,16-1,17-1,18-1,19-1,20-1,21-1,22-1

NCV - **18,** 1-1,2-1,3-1,4-1,5-1,6-1,7-1,8-1,9-1,10-1,11-1,12-1,13-1,14-1,15-1,16-1,17-1,18-1

NIV - **21,** 1-1,2-1,3-1,4-1,5-1,6-1,7-1,8-1,9-1,10-1,11-1,12-1,13-1,14-1,15-1,16-1,17-1,18-1,19-1,20-1,21-1

NKJV - **22,** 1-1,2-1,3-1,4-1,5-1,6-1,7-1,8-1,9-1,10-1,11-1,12-1,13-1,14-1,15-1,16-1,17-1,18-1,19-1,20-1,21-1,22-1

NLT - **15,** 1-1,2-1,3-1,4-1,5-1,6-1,7-1,8-1,9-1,10-1,11-1,12-1,13-1,14-1,15-1

NRSV - **21,** 1-1,2-1,3-1,4-1,5-1,6-1,7-1,8-1,9-1,10-1,11-1,12-1,13-1,14-1,15-1,16-1,17-1,18-1,19-1,20-1,21-1

Conclusion: All versions read the same.

427. 1 Chronicles 7:13* The sons of **Naphtali**; **Jahziel**, and **Guni**, and **Jezer**, and **Shallum**, the sons of **Bilhah**.

AV - **15,** 1-1,2-1,3-1,4-1,5-1,6-1,7-1,8-1,9-1,10-1,11-1,12-1,13-1,14-1,15-1

ESV - 13, 1-1,2-1,3-1,4-1,5-1,6-1,7-1,8-1,9-1,10-1,11-**3**,12-1,13-1

HCSB - **18,** 1-1,2-1,3-1,4-1,5-1,6-1,7-1,8-1,9-1,10-1,11-1,12-1,13-1,14-1,15-1,16-1,17-1,18-1

NASV - **14,** 1-1,2-1,3-1,4-1,5-1,6-1,7-1,8-1,9-1,10-1,11-1,12-1,13-1,14-1

NCV - 12, 1-1,2-1,3-1,4-1,5-1,6-1,7-1,8-1,9-1,10-1,11-1,12-**2**

NIV - 13, 1-1,2-1,3-1,4-1,5-1,6-1,7-1,8-1,9-1,10-1,11-**3**,12-1,13-1

NKJV - **14,** 1-1,2-1,3-1,4-1,5-1,6-1,7-1,8-1,9-1,10-1,11-1,12-1,13-1,14-1

NLT - 18, 1-1,2-1,3-1,4-1,5-1,6-1,7-1,8-1,9-1,10-1,11-1,12-1,13-1,14-**3**,15-1,16-1,17-**3**,18-1

NRSV - 13, 1-1,2-**3**,3-1,4-1,5-1,6-1,7-1,8-1,9-1,10-1,11-**3**,12-1,13-1

Conclusion: Five modern versions are more complex than the King James Bible.

428. 1 Chronicles 7:17* And the sons of **Ulam**; **Bedan**. These were the sons of **Gilead**, the son of **Machir**, the son of **Manasseh**.

AV - **20,** 1-1,2-1,3-1,4-1,5-1,6-1,7-1,8-1,9-1,10-1,11-1,12-1,13-1,14-1,15-1,16-1,17-1,18-1,19-1,20-1

ESV - **18,** 1-1,2-1,3-1,4-1,5-1,6-1,7-1,8-1,9-1,10-1,11-1,12-1,13-1,14-1,15-1,16-1,17-1,18-1

HCSB - **15,** 1-1,2-1,3-1,4-1,5-1,6-1,7-1,8-1,9-1,10-1,11-1,12-1,13-1,14-1,15-1

NASV - **20,** 1-1,2-1,3-1,4-1,5-1,6-1,7-1,8-1,9-1,10-1,11-1,12-1,13-1,14-1,15-1,16-1,17-1,18-1,19-1,20-1

NCV - **20,** 1-1,2-1,3-1,4-1,5-1,6-1,7-1,8-1,9-1,10-1,11-1,12-1,13-1,14-1,15-1,16-1,17-1,18-1,19-1,20-1

NIV - **18,** 1-1,2-1,3-1,4-1,5-1,6-1,7-1,8-1,9-1,10-1,11-1,12-1,13-1,14-1,15-1,16-1,17-1,18-1

NKJV - 20, 1-1,2-1,3-1,4-1,5-1,6-1,7-1,8-1,9-1,10-**3**,11-1,12-1,13-1,14-1,15-1,16-1,17-1,18-1,19-1,20-1

NLT - 17, 1-1,2-1,3-1,4-1,5-1,6-1,7-1,8-1,9-1,10-**3**,11-1,12-**3**,13-1,14-1,15-1,16-1,17-1

NRSV - **17,** 1-1,2-1,3-1,4-1,5-1,6-1,7-1,8-1,9-1,10-1,11-1,12-1,13-1,14-1,15-1,16-1,17-1
Conclusion: Only the NKJV and the NLT made the verse more complex.

429. 1 Chronicles 7:19* And the sons of **Shemida** were, **Ahian**, and **Shechem**, and **Likhi**, and **Aniam**.
AV - **13,** 1-1,2-1,3-1,4-1,5-1,6-1,7-1,8-1,9-1,10-1,11-1,12-1,13-1
ESV - **10,** 1-1,2-1,3-1,4-1,5-1,6-1,7-1,8-1,9-1,10-1
HCSB - **7,** 1-1,2-1,3-1,4-1,5-1,6-1,7-1
NASV - **12,** 1-1,2-1,3-1,4-1,5-1,6-1,7-1,8-1,9-1,10-1,11-1,12-1
NCV - **10,** 1-1,2-1,3-1,4-1,5-1,6-1,7-1,8-1,9-1,10-1
NIV - **10,** 1-1,2-1,3-1,4-1,5-1,6-1,7-1,8-1,9-1,10-1
NKJV - **11,** 1-1,2-1,3-1,4-1,5-1,6-1,7-1,8-1,9-1,10-1,11-1
NLT - **10,** 1-1,2-1,3-1,4-1,5-1,6-1,7-1,8-1,9-1,10-1
NRSV - **10,** 1-1,2-1,3-1,4-1,5-1,6-1,7-1,8-1,9-1,10-1
Conclusion: All versions read the same.

430. 1 Chronicles 7:20* And the sons of **Ephraim**; **Shuthelah**, and **Bered** his son, and **Tahath** his son, and **Eladah** his son, and **Tahath** his son,
AV - **22,** 1-1,2-1,3-1,4-1,5-1,6-1,7-1,8-1,9-1,10-1,11-1,12-1,13-1,14-1,15-1,16-1,17-1,18-1,19-1,20-1,21-1,22-1
ESV - **18,** 1-1,2-1,3-1,4-1,5-1,6-1,7-1,8-1,9-1,10-1,11-1,12-1,13-1,14-1,15-1,16-1,17-1,18-1
HCSB - **16,** 1-1,2-1,3-1,4-1,5-1,6-1,7-1,8-1,9-1,10-1,11-1,12-1,13-1,14-1,15-1,16-1
NASV - **19,** 1-1,2-1,3-1,4-1,5-1,6-1,7-1,8-1,9-1,10-1,11-1,12-1,13-1,14-1,15-1,16-1,17-1,18-1,19-1
NCV - 27, 1-1,2-1,3-1,4-1,5-1,6-1,7-**3**,8-1,9-1,10-1,11-1,12-1,13-1,14-1,15-1,16-1,17-1,18-1,19-1,20-1,21-1,22-1,23-1,24-1,25-1,26-1,27-1
NIV - 17, 1-1,2-**3**,3-1,4-1,5-1,6-1,7-1,8-1,9-1,10-1,11-1,12-1,13-1,14-1,15-1,16-1,17-1
NKJV - **18,** 1-1,2-1,3-1,4-1,5-1,6-1,7-1,8-1,9-1,10-1,11-1,12-1,13-1,14-1,15-1,16-1,17-1,18-1
NLT - 10, 1-1,2-**3**,3-1,4-1,5-1,6-1,7-1,8-1,9-1,10-1
NRSV - **18,** 1-1,2-1,3-1,4-1,5-1,6-1,7-1,8-1,9-1,10-1,11-1,12-1,13-1,14-1,15-1,16-1,17-1,18-1
Conclusion: Only three modern versions are more complex than the King James Bible.

431. 1 Chronicles 7:26* **Laadan** his son, **Ammihud** his son, **Elishama** his son,
AV - **9,** 1-1,2-1,3-1,4-1,5-1,6-1,7-1,8-1,9-1
ESV - **9,** 1-1,2-1,3-1,4-1,5-1,6-1,7-1,8-1,9-1
HCSB - **9,** 1-1,2-1,3-1,4-1,5-1,6-1,7-1,8-1,9-1
NASV - **9,** 1-1,2-1,3-1,4-1,5-1,6-1,7-1,8-1,9-1
NCV - **12,** 1-1,2-1,3-1,4-1,5-1,6-1,7-1,8-1,9-1,10-1,11-1,12-1
NIV - **9,** 1-1,2-1,3-1,4-1,5-1,6-1,7-1,8-1,9-1
NKJV - **9,** 1-1,2-1,3-1,4-1,5-1,6-1,7-1,8-1,9-1
NLT - **3,** 1-1,2-1,3-1
NRSV - **9,** 1-1,2-1,3-1,4-1,5-1,6-1,7-1,8-1,9-1
Conclusion: All versions read the same.

432. 1 Chronicles 7:27* Non his son, **Jehoshua** his son.
AV - **6,** 1-1,2-1,3-1,4-1,5-1,6-1
ESV - **6,** 1-1,2-1,3-1,4-1,5-1,6-1
HCSB - **7,** 1-1,2-1,3-1,4-1,5-1,6-1,7-1
NASV - **7,** 1-1,2-1,3-1,4-1,5-1,6-1,7-1
NCV - **11,** 1-1,2-1,3-1,4-1,5-1,6-1,7-1,8-1,9-1,10-1,11-1
NIV - **7,** 1-1,2-1,3-1,4-1,5-1,6-1,7-1
NKJV - **7,** 1-1,2-1,3-1,4-1,5-1,6-1,7-1
NLT - **3,** 1-1,2-1,3-1
NRSV - **6,** 1-1,2-1,3-1,4-1,5-1,6-1
Conclusion: All versions read the same.

433. 1 Chronicles 7:34* And the sons of **Shamer**; **Ahi**, and **Rohgah, Jehubbah,** and **Aram**.
AV - **11,** 1-1,2-1,3-1,4-1,5-1,6-1,7-1,8-1,9-1,10-1,11-1
ESV - 10, 1-1,2-1,3-1,4-1,5-1,6-**2**,7-1,8-1,9-1,10-1
HCSB - **7,** 1-1,2-1,3-1,4-1,5-1,6-1,7-1
NASV - **11,** 1-1,2-1,3-1,4-1,5-1,6-1,7-1,8-1,9-1,10-1,11-1
NCV - 11, 1-1,2-**2**,3-1,4-1,5-1,6-1,7-1,8-1,9-1,10-1,11-1
NIV - **9,** 1-1,2-1,3-1,4-1,5-1,6-1,7-1,8-1,9-1
NKJV - **10,** 1-1,2-1,3-1,4-1,5-1,6-1,7-1,8-1,9-1,10-1
NLT - **10,** 1-1,2-1,3-1,4-1,5-1,6-1,7-1,8-1,9-1,10-1
NRSV - **9,** 1-1,2-1,3-1,4-1,5-1,6-1,7-1,8-1,9-1
Conclusion: Only the ESV and the NCV made the verse more complex.

434. 1 Chronicles 7:36* The sons of **Zophah**; **Suah**, and **Harnepher**, and Shual, and **Beri**, and **Imrah**,
AV - **13,** 1-1,2-1,3-1,4-1,5-1,6-1,7-1,8-1,9-1,10-1,11-1,12-1,13-1
ESV - **9,** 1-1,2-1,3-1,4-1,5-1,6-1,7-1,8-1,9-1
HCSB - **7,** 1-1,2-1,3-1,4-1,5-1,6-1,7-1
NASV - **11,** 1-1,2-1,3-1,4-1,5-1,6-1,7-1,8-1,9-1,10-1,11-1
NCV - **8,** 1-1,2-1,3-1,4-1,5-1,6-1,7-1,8-1
NIV - **9,** 1-1,2-1,3-1,4-1,5-1,6-1,7-1,8-1,9-1
NKJV - **10,** 1-1,2-1,3-1,4-1,5-1,6-1,7-1,8-1,9-1,10-1
NLT - **10,** 1-1,2-1,3-1,4-1,5-1,6-1,7-1,8-1,9-1,10-1
NRSV - **9,** 1-1,2-1,3-1,4-1,5-1,6-1,7-1,8-1,9-1
Conclusion: All versions read the same.

435. 1 Chronicles 7:37* **Bezer**, and Hod, and **Shamma**, and **Shilshah**, and **Ithran**, and **Beera**.
AV - **11,** 1-1,2-1,3-1,4-1,5-1,6-1,7-1,8-1,9-1,10-1,11-1
ESV - **7,** 1-1,2-1,3-1,4-1,5-1,6-1,7-1
HCSB - **7,** 1-1,2-1,3-1,4-1,5-1,6-1,7-1
NASV - **7,** 1-1,2-1,3-1,4-1,5-1,6-1,7-1
NCV - **7,** 1-1,2-1,3-1,4-1,5-1,6-1,7-1
NIV - **7,** 1-1,2-1,3-1,4-1,5-1,6-1,7-1

NKJV - **7,** 1-1,2-1,3-1,4-1,5-1,6-1,7-1
NLT - **7,** 1-1,2-1,3-1,4-1,5-1,6-1,7-1
NRSV - **7,** 1-1,2-1,3-1,4-1,5-1,6-1,7-1
Conclusion: All versions read the same.

436. 1 Chronicles 7:38* And the sons of **Jether**; **Jephunneh**, and **Pispah**, and **Ara**.
AV - **10,** 1-1,2-1,3-1,4-1,5-1,6-1,7-1,8-1,9-1,10-1
ESV - **8,** 1-1,2-1,3-1,4-1,5-1,6-1,7-1,8-1
HCSB - **6,** 1-1,2-1,3-1,4-1,5-1,6-1
NASV - **9,** 1-1,2-1,3-1,4-1,5-1,6-1,7-1,8-1,9-1
NCV - **7,** 1-1,2-1,3-1,4-1,5-1,6-1,7-1
NIV - **8,** 1-1,2-1,3-1,4-1,5-1,6-1,7-1,8-1
NKJV - **9,** 1-1,2-1,3-1,4-1,5-1,6-1,7-1,8-1,9-1
NLT - **9,** 1-1,2-1,3-1,4-1,5-1,6-1,7-1,8-1,9-1
NRSV - **8,** 1-1,2-1,3-1,4-1,5-1,6-1,7-1,8-1
Conclusion: All versions read the same.

437. 1 Chronicles 7:39* And the sons of **Ulla**; **Arah**, and **Haniel**, and **Rezia**.
AV - **10,** 1-1,2-1,3-1,4-1,5-1,6-1,7-1,8-1,9-1,10-1
ESV - **8,** 1-1,2-1,3-1,4-1,5-1,6-1,7-1,8-1
HCSB - **6,** 1-1,2-1,3-1,4-1,5-1,6-1
NASV - **9,** 1-1,2-1,3-1,4-1,5-1,6-1,7-1,8-1,9-1
NCV - **7,** 1-1,2-1,3-1,4-1,5-1,6-1,7-1
NIV - **8,** 1-1,2-1,3-1,4-1,5-1,6-1,7-1,8-1
NKJV - **9,** 1-1,2-1,3-1,4-1,5-1,6-1,7-1,8-1,9-1
NLT - **9,** 1-1,2-1,3-1,4-1,5-1,6-1,7-1,8-1,9-1
NRSV - **8,** 1-1,2-1,3-1,4-1,5-1,6-1,7-1,8-1
Conclusion: All versions read the same.

438. 1 Chronicles 8:2* **Nohah** the fourth, and **Rapha** the fifth.
AV - **7,** 1-1,2-1,3-1,4-1,5-1,6-1,7-1
ESV - **7,** 1-1,2-1,3-1,4-1,5-1,6-1,7-1
HCSB - **5,** 1-1,2-1,3-1,4-1,5-1
NASV - **7,** 1-1,2-1,3-1,4-1,5-1,6-1,7-1
NCV - **10,** 1-1,2-1,3-1,4-1,5-1,6-1,7-1,8-1,9-1,10-1
NIV - **7,** 1-1,2-1,3-1,4-1,5-1,6-1,7-1
NKJV - **7,** 1-1,2-1,3-1,4-1,5-1,6-1,7-1
NLT - **9,** 1-1,2-1,3-1,4-1,5-1,6-1,7-1,8-1,9-1
NRSV - **7,** 1-1,2-1,3-1,4-1,5-1,6-1,7-1
Conclusion: All versions read the same.

439. 1 Chronicles 8:3* And the sons of **Bela** were, **Addar**, and **Gera**, and **Abihud**,
AV - **11,** 1-1,2-1,3-1,4-1,5-1,6-1,7-1,8-1,9-1,10-1,11-1
ESV - **7,** 1-1,2-1,3-1,4-1,5-1,6-1,7-1

HCSB - **5,** 1-1,2-1,3-1,4-1,5-1
NASV - **6,** 1-1,2-1,3-1,4-1,5-1,6-1
NCV - **6,** 1-1,2-1,3-1,4-1,5-1,6-1
NIV - **8,** 1-1,2-1,3-1,4-1,5-1,6-1,7-1,8-1
NKJV - **8,** 1-1,2-1,3-1,4-1,5-1,6-1,7-1,8-1
NLT - **8,** 1-1,2-1,3-1,4-1,5-1,6-1,7-1,8-1
NRSV - **7,** 1-1,2-1,3-1,4-1,5-1,6-1,7-1
Conclusion: All versions read the same.

440. 1 Chronicles 8:4* And **Abishua**, and **Naaman**, and **Ahoah**,
AV - **6,** 1-1,2-1,3-1,4-1,5-1,6-1
ESV - **3,** 1-1,2-1,3-1
HCSB - **3,** 1-1,2-1,3-1
NASV - **3,** 1-1,2-1,3-1
NCV - **3,** 1-1,2-1,3-1
NIV - **3,** 1-1,2-1,3-1
NKJV - **3,** 1-1,2-1,3-1
NLT - **3,** 1-1,2-1,3-1
NRSV - **3,** 1-1,2-1,3-1
Conclusion: All versions read the same.

441. 1 Chronicles 8:5* And **Gera**, and **Shephuphan**, and **Huram**.
AV - **6,** 1-1,2-1,3-1,4-1,5-1,6-1
ESV - **4,** 1-1,2-1,3-1,4-1
HCSB - **4,** 1-1,2-1,3-1,4-1
NASV - **4,** 1-1,2-1,3-1,4-1
NCV - **4,** 1-1,2-1,3-1,4-1
NIV - **4,** 1-1,2-1,3-1,4-1
NKJV - **4,** 1-1,2-1,3-1,4-1
NLT - **4,** 1-1,2-1,3-1,4-1
NRSV - **4,** 1-1,2-1,3-1,4-1
Conclusion: All versions read the same.

442. 1 Chronicles 8:14* And **Ahio, Shashak,** and **Jeremoth,**
AV - **5,** 1-1,2-1,3-1,4-1,5-1
ESV - **5,** 1-1,2-1,3-1,4-1,5-1
HCSB - **4,** 1-1,2-1,3-1,4-1
NASV - **5,** 1-1,2-1,3-1,4-1,5-1
NCV - **6,** 1-1,2-1,3-1,4-1,5-1,6-1
NIV - **3,** 1-1,2-1,3-1
NKJV - **3,** 1-1,2-1,3-1
NLT - **3,** 1-1,2-1,3-1
NRSV - **5,** 1-1,2-1,3-1,4-1,5-1
Conclusion: All versions read the same.

443. 1 Chronicles 8:15* And **Zebadiah**, and **Arad**, and **Ader**,
AV - **6,** 1-1,2-1,3-1,4-1,5-1,6-1
ESV - **3,** 1-1,2-1,3-1
HCSB - **3,** 1-1,2-1,3-1
NASV - **3,** 1-1,2-1,3-1
NCV - **3,** 1-1,2-1,3-1
NIV - **3,** 1-1,2-1,3-1
NKJV - **3,** 1-1,2-1,3-1
NLT - **3,** 1-1,2-1,3-1
NRSV - **3,** 1-1,2-1,3-1
Conclusion: All versions read the same.

444. 1 Chronicles 8:16* And **Michael**, and **Ispah**, and **Joha**, the sons of **Beriah**;
AV - **10,** 1-1,2-1,3-1,4-1,5-1,6-1,7-1,8-1,9-1,10-1
ESV - **8,** 1-1,2-1,3-1,4-1,5-1,6-1,7-1,8-1
HCSB - **7,** 1-1,2-1,3-1,4-1,5-1,6-1,7-1
NASV - **9,** 1-1,2-1,3-1,4-1,5-1,6-1,7-1,8-1,9-1
NCV - **4,** 1-1,2-1,3-1,4-1
NIV - **9,** 1-1,2-1,3-1,4-1,5-1,6-1,7-1,8-1,9-1
NKJV - **9,** 1-1,2-1,3-1,4-1,5-1,6-1,7-1,8-1,9-1
NLT - **9,** 1-1,2-1,3-1,4-1,5-1,6-1,7-1,8-1,9-1
NRSV - **8,** 1-1,2-1,3-1,4-1,5-1,6-1,7-1,8-1
Conclusion: All versions read the same.

445. 1 Chronicles 8:17* And **Zebadiah**, and **Meshullam**, and **Hezeki**, and **Heber**,
AV - **8,** 1-1,2-1,3-1,4-1,5-1,6-1,7-1,8-1
ESV - **4,** 1-1,2-1,3-1,4-1
HCSB - **4,** 1-1,2-1,3-1,4-1
NASV - **4,** 1-1,2-1,3-1,4-1
NCV - **7,** 1-1,2-1,3-1,4-1,5-1,6-1,7-1
NIV - **4,** 1-1,2-1,3-1,4-1
NKJV - **4,** 1-1,2-1,3-1,4-1
NLT - **4,** 1-1,2-1,3-1,4-1
NRSV - **4,** 1-1,2-1,3-1,4-1
Conclusion: All versions read the same.

446. 1 Chronicles 8:19* And **Jakim**, and **Zichri**, and **Zabdi**,
AV - **6,** 1-1,2-1,3-1,4-1,5-1,6-1
ESV - **3,** 1-1,2-1,3-1
HCSB - **3,** 1-1,2-1,3-1
NASV - **3,** 1-1,2-1,3-1
NCV - **6,** 1-1,2-1,3-1,4-1,5-1,6-1
NIV - **3,** 1-1,2-1,3-1

NKJV - **3,** 1-1,2-1,3-1
NLT - **3,** 1-1,2-1,3-1
NRSV - **3,** 1-1,2-1,3-1
Conclusion: All versions read the same.

447. 1 Chronicles 8:20* And **Elienai**, and **Zilthai**, and **Eliel**,
AV - **6,** 1-1,2-1,3-1,4-1,5-1,6-1
ESV - **3,** 1-1,2-1,3-1
HCSB - **3,** 1-1,2-1,3-1
NASV - **3,** 1-1,2-1,3-1
NCV - **3,** 1-1,2-1,3-1
NIV - **3,** 1-1,2-1,3-1
NKJV - **3,** 1-1,2-1,3-1
NLT - **3,** 1-1,2-1,3-1
NRSV - **3,** 1-1,2-1,3-1
Conclusion: All versions read the same.

448. 1 Chronicles 8:21* And **Adaiah**, and **Beraiah**, and **Shimrath**, the sons of **Shimhi**;
AV - **10,** 1-1,2-1,3-1,4-1,5-1,6-1,7-1,8-1,9-1,10-1
ESV - **9,** 1-1,2-1,3-1,4-1,5-1,6-1,7-1,8-1,9-1
HCSB - **7,** 1-1,2-1,3-1,4-1,5-1,6-1,7-1
NASV - **9,** 1-1,2-1,3-1,4-1,5-1,6-1,7-1,8-1,9-1
NCV - **4,** 1-1,2-1,3-1,4-1
NIV - **9,** 1-1,2-1,3-1,4-1,5-1,6-1,7-1,8-1,9-1
NKJV - **9,** 1-1,2-1,3-1,4-1,5-1,6-1,7-1,8-1,9-1
NLT - **9,** 1-1,2-1,3-1,4-1,5-1,6-1,7-1,8-1,9-1
NRSV - **9,** 1-1,2-1,3-1,4-1,5-1,6-1,7-1,8-1,9-1
Conclusion: All versions read the same.

449. 1 Chronicles 8:22* And **Ishpan**, and **Heber**, and **Eliel**,
AV - **6,** 1-1,2-1,3-1,4-1,5-1,6-1
ESV - **3,** 1-1,2-1,3-1
HCSB - **3,** 1-1,2-1,3-1
NASV - **3,** 1-1,2-1,3-1
NCV - **6,** 1-1,2-1,3-1,4-1,5-1,6-1
NIV - **3,** 1-1,2-1,3-1
NKJV - **3,** 1-1,2-1,3-1
NLT - **3,** 1-1,2-1,3-1
NRSV - **3,** 1-1,2-1,3-1
Conclusion: All versions read the same.

450. 1 Chronicles 8:23* And **Abdon**, and **Zichri**, and **Hanan**,
AV - **6,** 1-1,2-1,3-1,4-1,5-1,6-1
ESV - **3,** 1-1,2-1,3-1

HCSB - **3,** 1-1,2-1,3-1
NASV - **3,** 1-1,2-1,3-1
NCV - **3,** 1-1,2-1,3-1
NIV - **3,** 1-1,2-1,3-1
NKJV - **3,** 1-1,2-1,3-1
NLT - **3,** 1-1,2-1,3-1
NRSV - **3,** 1-1,2-1,3-1
Conclusion: All versions read the same.

451. 1 Chronicles 8:24* And **Hananiah**, and **Elam**, and **Antothijah**,
AV - **6,** 1-1,2-1,3-1,4-1,5-1,6-1
ESV - **3,** 1-1,2-1,3-1
HCSB - **3,** 1-1,2-1,3-1
NASV - **3,** 1-1,2-1,3-1
NCV - **3,** 1-1,2-1,3-1
NIV - **3,** 1-1,2-1,3-1
NKJV - **3,** 1-1,2-1,3-1
NLT - **3,** 1-1,2-1,3-1
NRSV - **3,** 1-1,2-1,3-1
Conclusion: All versions read the same.

452. 1 Chronicles 8:25* And **Iphedeiah**, and **Penuel**, the sons of **Shashak**;
AV - **8,** 1-1,2-1,3-1,4-1,5-1,6-1,7-1,8-1
ESV - **8,** 1-1,2-1,3-1,4-1,5-1,6-1,7-1,8-1
HCSB - **6,** 1-1,2-1,3-1,4-1,5-1,6-1
NASV - **8,** 1-1,2-1,3-1,4-1,5-1,6-1,7-1,8-1
NCV - **3,** 1-1,2-1,3-1
NIV - **8,** 1-1,2-1,3-1,4-1,5-1,6-1,7-1,8-1
NKJV - **8,** 1-1,2-1,3-1,4-1,5-1,6-1,7-1,8-1
NLT - **8,** 1-1,2-1,3-1,4-1,5-1,6-1,7-1,8-1
NRSV - **8,** 1-1,2-1,3-1,4-1,5-1,6-1,7-1,8-1
Conclusion: All versions read the same.

453. 1 Chronicles 8:26* And **Shamsherai**, and **Shehariah**, and **Athaliah**,
AV - **6,** 1-1,2-1,3-1,4-1,5-1,6-1
ESV - **3,** 1-1,2-1,3-1
HCSB - **3,** 1-1,2-1,3-1
NASV - **3,** 1-1,2-1,3-1
NCV - **6,** 1-1,2-1,3-1,4-1,5-1,6-1
NIV - **3,** 1-1,2-1,3-1
NKJV - **3,** 1-1,2-1,3-1
NLT - **3,** 1-1,2-1,3-1
NRSV - **3,** 1-1,2-1,3-1
Conclusion: All versions read the same.

454. 1 Chronicles 8:27* And **Jaresiah**, and **Eliah**, and **Zichri**, the sons of **Jeroham**.
AV - **10,** 1-1,2-1,3-1,4-1,5-1,6-1,7-1,8-1,9-1,10-1
ESV - **9,** 1-1,2-1,3-1,4-1,5-1,6-1,7-1,8-1,9-1
HCSB - **7,** 1-1,2-1,3-1,4-1,5-1,6-1,7-1
NASV - **9,** 1-1,2-1,3-1,4-1,5-1,6-1,7-1,8-1,9-1
NCV - **4,** 1-1,2-1,3-1,4-1
NIV - **9,** 1-1,2-1,3-1,4-1,5-1,6-1,7-1,8-1,9-1
NKJV - **9,** 1-1,2-1,3-1,4-1,5-1,6-1,7-1,8-1,9-1
NLT - **9,** 1-1,2-1,3-1,4-1,5-1,6-1,7-1,8-1,9-1
NRSV - **9,** 1-1,2-1,3-1,4-1,5-1,6-1,7-1,8-1,9-1
Conclusion: All versions read the same.

455. 1 Chronicles 8:31* And **Gedor**, and **Ahio**, and **Zacher**.
AV - **6,** 1-1,2-1,3-1,4-1,5-1,6-1
ESV - **3,** 1-1,2-1,3-1
HCSB - **3,** 1-1,2-1,3-1
NASV - **4,** 1-1,2-1,3-1,4-1
NCV - **3,** 1-1,2-1,3-1
NIV - **3,** 1-1,2-1,3-1
NKJV - **3,** 1-1,2-1,3-1
NLT - **3,** 1-1,2-1,3-1
NRSV - **3,** 1-1,2-1,3-1
Conclusion: All versions read the same.

456. 1 Chronicles 8:35* And the sons of **Micah** were, **Pithon**, and **Melech**, and **Tarea**, and **Ahaz**.
AV - **13,** 1-1,2-1,3-1,4-1,5-1,6-1,7-1,8-1,9-1,10-1,11-1,12-1,13-1
ESV - **9,** 1-1,2-1,3-1,4-1,5-1,6-1,7-1,8-1,9-1
HCSB - **8,** 1-1,2-1,3-1,4-1,5-1,6-1,7-1,8-1
NASV - **10,** 1-1,2-1,3-1,4-1,5-1,6-1,7-1,8-1,9-1,10-1
NCV - **8,** 1-1,2-1,3-1,4-1,5-1,6-1,7-1,8-1
NIV - **9,** 1-1,2-1,3-1,4-1,5-1,6-1,7-1,8-1,9-1
NKJV - **10,** 1-1,2-1,3-1,4-1,5-1,6-1,7-1,8-1,9-1,10-1
NLT - **10,** 1-1,2-1,3-1,4-**2**,5-1,6-1,7-1,8-1,9-1,10-1
NRSV - **9,** 1-1,2-1,3-1,4-1,5-1,6-1,7-1,8-1,9-1
Conclusion: Only the NLT made the verse more complex.

457. 1 Chronicles 8:38* And **Azel** had six sons, whose names are these, **Azrikam**, **Bocheru**, and **Ishmael**, and **Sheariah**, and **Obadiah**, and **Hanan**. All these were the sons of **Azel**.
AV - **26,** 1-1,2-1,3-1,4-1,5-1,6-1,7-1,8-1,9-1,10-1,11-1,12-1,13-1,14-1,15-1,16-1,17-1,18-1,19-1,20-1,21-1,22-1,23-1,24-1,25-1,26-1
ESV - **23,** 1-1,2-1,3-1,4-1,5-1,6-1,7-1,8-1,9-1,10-1,11-1,12-1,13-1,14-1,15-1,16-1,17-1,18-1,19-1,20-1,21-1,22-1,23-1

HCSB - **21,** 1-1,2-1,3-1,4-1,5-1,6-1,7-1,8-1,9-1,10-1,11-1,12-1,13-1,14-1,15-1,16-1,17-1,18-1,19-1,20-1,21-1

NASV - **23,** 1-1,2-1,3-1,4-1,5-1,6-1,7-1,8-1,9-1,10-1,11-1,12-1,13-1,14-1,15-1,16-1,17-1,18-1,19-1,20-1,21-1,22-1,23-1

NCV - **16,** 1-1,2-1,3-1,4-1,5-1,6-1,7-1,8-1,9-1,10-1,11-1,12-1,13-1,14-1,15-1,16-1

NIV - **23,** 1-1,2-1,3-1,4-1,5-1,6-1,7-1,8-1,9-1,10-1,11-1,12-1,13-1,14-1,15-1,16-1,17-1,18-1,19-1,20-1,21-1,22-1,23-1

NKJV - **22,** 1-1,2-1,3-1,4-1,5-1,6-1,7-1,8-1,9-1,10-1,11-1,12-1,13-1,14-1,15-1,16-1,17-1,18-1,19-1,20-1,21-1,22-1

NLT - **17,** 1-1,2-1,3-1,4-1,5-1,6-1,7-1,8-1,9-1,10-1,11-1,12-1,13-1,14-1,15-1,16-1,17-1

NRSV - **23,** 1-1,2-1,3-1,4-1,5-1,6-1,7-1,8-1,9-1,10-1,11-1,12-1,13-1,14-1,15-1,16-1,17-1,18-1,19-1,20-1,21-1,22-1,23-1

Conclusion: All versions read the same.

458. 1 Chronicles 9:7* And of the sons of **Benjamin**; **Sallu** the son of **Meshullam**, the son of **Hodaviah**, the son of **Hasenuah**,
AV - **19,** 1-1,2-1,3-1,4-1,5-1,6-1,7-1,8-1,9-1,10-1,11-1,12-1,13-1,14-1,15-1,16-1,17-1,18-1,19-1
ESV - **14,** 1-1,2-1,3-1,4-1,5-1,6-1,7-1,8-1,9-1,10-1,11-1,12-1,13-1,14-1
HCSB - **12,** 1-1,2-1,3-1,4-1,5-1,6-1,7-1,8-1,9-1,10-1,11-1,12-1
NASV - **19,** 1-1,2-1,3-1,4-1,5-1,6-1,7-1,8-1,9-1,10-1,11-1,12-1,13-1,14-1,15-1,16-1,17-1,18-1,19-1
NCV - **20,** 1-1,2-1,3-1,4-1,5-1,6-1,7-1,8-1,9-1,10-1,11-1,12-1,13-1,14-1,15-1,16-1,17-1,18-1,19-1,20-1
NIV - **15,** 1-1,2-1,3-1,4-1,5-1,6-1,7-1,8-1,9-1,10-1,11-1,12-1,13-1,14-1,15-1
NKJV - **18,** 1-1,2-1,3-1,4-1,5-1,6-1,7-1,8-1,9-1,10-1,11-1,12-1,13-1,14-1,15-1,16-1,17-1,18-1
NLT - **16,** 1-1,2-1,3-1,4-1,5-1,6-1,7-1,8-1,9-1,10-1,11-1,12-1,13-1,14-1,15-1,16-1
NRSV - **13,** 1-1,2-1,3-1,4-1,5-1,6-1,7-1,8-1,9-1,10-1,11-1,12-1,13-1
Conclusion: All versions read the same.

459. 1 Chronicles 9:8* And **Ibneiah** the son of **Jeroham**, and **Elah** the son of **Uzzi**, the son of **Michri**, and **Meshullam** the son of **Shephathiah**, the son of **Reuel**, the son of **Ibnijah**;
AV - **30,** 1-1,2-1,3-1,4-1,5-1,6-1,7-1,8-1,9-1,10-1,11-1,12-1,13-1,14-1,15-1,16-1,17-1,18-1,19-1,20-1,21-1,22-1,23-1,24-1,25-1,26-1,27-1,28-1,29-1,30-1
ESV - **25,** 1-1,2-1,3-1,4-1,5-1,6-1,7-1,8-1,9-1,10-1,11-1,12-1,13-1,14-1,15-1,16-1,17-1,18-1,19-1,20-1,21-1,22-1,23-1,24-1,25-1
HCSB - **21,** 1-1,2-1,3-1,4-1,5-1,6-1,7-1,8-1,9-1,10-1,11-1,12-1,13-1,14-1,15-1,16-1,17-1,18-1,19-1,20-1,21-1
NASV - **30,** 1-1,2-1,3-1,4-1,5-1,6-1,7-1,8-1,9-1,10-1,11-1,12-1,13-1,14-1,15-1,16-1,17-1,18-1,19-1,20-1,21-1,22-1,23-1,24-1,25-1,26-1,27-1,28-1,29-1,30-1
NCV - **32,** 1-1,2-1,3-**2,**4-1,5-1,6-1,7-1,8-1,9-1,10-1,11-1,12-1,13-1,14-1,15-1,16-1,17-1,18-1,19-1,20-1,21-1,22-1,23-1,24-1,25-1,26-1,27-1,28-1,29-1,30-1,31-1,32-1
NIV - **25,** 1-1,2-1,3-1,4-1,5-1,6-1,7-1,8-1,9-1,10-1,11-1,12-1,13-1,14-1,15-1,16-1,17-1,18-1,19-1,20-1,21-1,22-1,23-1,24-1,25-1
NKJV - **27,** 1-1,2-1,3-1,4-1,5-1,6-1,7-1,8-1,9-1,10-1,11-1,12-1,13-1,14-1,15-1,16-1,17-1,18-1,19-1,20-1,21-1,22-1,23-1,24-1,25-1,26-1,27-1

NLT - **22,** 1-1,2-1,3-1,4-1,5-1,6-1,7-1,8-1,9-1,10-1,11-1,12-1,13-1,14-1,15-1,16-1,17-1,18-1,19-1,20-1,21-1,22-1

NRSV - **22,** 1-1,2-1,3-1,4-1,5-1,6-1,7-1,8-1,9-1,10-1,11-1,12-1,13-1,14-1,15-1,16-1,17-1,18-1,19-1,20-1,21-1,22-1

Conclusion: Only the NCV made the verse more complex.

460. 1 Chronicles 9:10* And of the priests; **Jedaiah**, and **Jehoiarib**, and **Jachin**,
AV - **9,** 1-1,2-1,3-1,4-1,5-1,6-1,7-1,8-1,9-1
ESV - **6,** 1-1,2-1,3-1,4-1,5-1,6-1
HCSB - **5,** 1-1,2-1,3-1,4-1,5-1
NASV - **7,** 1-1,2-1,3-1,4-1,5-1,6-1,7-1
NCV - **9,** 1-1,2-1,3-1,4-1,5-1,6-1,7-1,8-1,9-1
NIV - **6,** 1-1,2-1,3-1,4-1,5-1,6-1
NKJV - **7,** 1-1,2-1,3-1,4-1,5-1,6-1,7-1
NLT - **9,** 1-**2**,2-1,3-1,4-1,5-**2**,6-1,7-1,8-1,9-1
NRSV - **6,** 1-1,2-1,3-1,4-1,5-1,6-1
Conclusion: Only the NLT made the verse more complex.

461. 1 Chronicles 9:12* And **Adaiah** the son of **Jeroham**, the son of **Pashur**, the son of **Malchijah**, and **Maasiai** the son of **Adiel**, the son of **Jahzerah**, the son of **Meshullam**, the son of **Meshillemith**, the son of **Immer**;
AV - **36,** 1-1,2-1,3-1,4-1,5-1,6-1,7-1,8-1,9-1,10-1,11-1,12-1,13-1,14-1,15-1,16-1,17-1,18-1,19-1,20-1,21-1,22-1,23-1,24-1,25-1,26-1,27-1,28-1,29-1,30-1,31-1,32-1,33-1,34-1,35-1,36-1
ESV - **30,** 1-1,2-1,3-1,4-1,5-1,6-1,7-1,8-1,9-1,10-1,11-1,12-1,13-1,14-1,15-1,16-1,17-1,18-1,19-1,20-1,21-1,22-1,23-1,24-1,25-1,26-1,27-1,28-1,29-1,30-1
HCSB - **26,** 1-1,2-1,3-1,4-1,5-1,6-1,7-1,8-1,9-1,10-1,11-1,12-1,13-1,14-1,15-1,16-1,17-1,18-1,19-1,20-1,21-1,22-1,23-1,24-1,25-1,26-1
NASV - **36,** 1-1,2-1,3-1,4-1,5-1,6-1,7-1,8-1,9-1,10-1,11-1,12-1,13-1,14-1,15-1,16-1,17-1,18-1,19-1,20-1,21-1,22-1,23-1,24-1,25-1,26-1,27-1,28-1,29-1,30-1,31-1,32-1,33-1,34-1,35-1,36-1
NCV - **40,** 1-**2**,2-1,3-1,4-1,5-1,6-1,7-1,8-1,9-1,10-1,11-1,12-1,13-1,14-1,15-1,16-1,17-1,18-1,19-1,20-1,21-1,22-1,23-1,24-1,25-1,26-1,27-1,28-1,29-1,30-1,31-1,32-1,33-1,34-1,35-1,36-1,37-1,38-1,39-1,40-1
NIV - **33,** 1-1,2-1,3-1,4-1,5-1,6-1,7-1,8-1,9-1,10-1,11-1,12-1,13-1,14-1,15-1,16-1,17-1,18-1,19-1,20-1,21-1,22-1,23-1,24-1,25-1,26-1,27-1,28-1,29-1,30-1,31-1,32-1,33-1
NKJV - **34,** 1-1,2-1,3-1,4-1,5-1,6-1,7-1,8-1,9-1,10-1,11-1,12-1,13-1,14-1,15-1,16-1,17-1,18-1,19-1,20-1,21-1,22-1,23-1,24-1,25-1,26-1,27-1,28-1,29-1,30-1,31-1,32-1,33-1,34-1
NLT - **31,** 1-**2**,2-**3**,3-1,4-1,5-1,6-1,7-1,8-1,9-1,10-1,11-1,12-1,13-1,14-1,15-1,16-1,17-1,18-1,19-1,20-1,21-1,22-1,23-1,24-1,25-1,26-1,27-1,28-1,29-1,30-1,31-1
NRSV - **28,** 1-1,2-1,3-1,4-1,5-1,6-1,7-1,8-1,9-1,10-1,11-1,12-1,13-1,14-1,15-1,16-1,17-1,18-1,19-1,20-1,21-1,22-1,23-1,24-1,25-1,26-1,27-1,28-1
Conclusion: Only the NCV and the NLT made the verse more complex.

462. 1 Chronicles 9:14* And of the **Levites**; **Shemaiah** the son of **Hasshub**, the son of **Azrikam**, the son of **Hashabiah**, of the sons of **Merari**;
AV - **22,** 1-1,2-1,3-1,4-1,5-1,6-1,7-1,8-1,9-1,10-1,11-1,12-1,13-1,14-1,15-1,16-1,17-1,18-1,19-1,20-1,21-1,22-1
ESV - **19,** 1-1,2-1,3-1,4-1,5-1,6-1,7-1,8-1,9-1,10-1,11-1,12-1,13-1,14-1,15-1,16-1,17-1,18-1,19-1
HCSB - **15,** 1-1,2-1,3-1,4-1,5-1,6-1,7-1,8-1,9-1,10-1,11-1,12-1,13-1,14-1,15-1
NASV - **22,** 1-1,2-1,3-1,4-1,5-1,6-1,7-1,8-1,9-1,10-1,11-1,12-1,13-1,14-1,15-1,16-1,17-1,18-1,19-1,20-1,21-1,22-1
NCV - **24,** 1-1,2-1,3-1,4-1,5-1,6-1,7-1,8-1,9-1,10-1,11-1,12-1,13-1,14-1,15-1,16-1,17-1,18-1,19-1,20-1,21-1,22-**3**,23-1,24-1
NIV - **17,** 1-1,2-1,3-1,4-1,5-1,6-1,7-1,8-1,9-1,10-1,11-1,12-1,13-1,14-1,15-1,16-1,17-1
NKJV - **21,** 1-1,2-1,3-1,4-1,5-1,6-1,7-1,8-1,9-1,10-1,11-1,12-1,13-1,14-1,15-1,16-1,17-1,18-1,19-1,20-1,21-1
NLT - **19,** 1-1,2-1,3-1,4-**2**,5-1,6-1,7-1,8-1,9-1,10-1,11-1,12-1,13-1,14-1,15-1,16-1,17-**3**,18-1,19-1
NRSV - **18,** 1-1,2-1,3-1,4-1,5-1,6-1,7-1,8-1,9-1,10-1,11-1,12-1,13-1,14-1,15-1,16-1,17-1,18-1
Conclusion: Only the NCV and the NLT made the verse more complex.

463. 1 Chronicles 9:15* And **Bakbakkar**, **Heresh**, and **Galal**, and **Mattaniah** the son of **Micah**, the son of **Zichri**, the son of **Asaph**;
AV - **19,** 1-1,2-1,3-1,4-1,5-1,6-1,7-1,8-1,9-1,10-1,11-1,12-1,13-1,14-1,15-1,16-1,17-1,18-1,19-1
ESV - **16,** 1-1,2-1,3-1,4-1,5-1,6-1,7-1,8-1,9-1,10-1,11-1,12-1,13-1,14-1,15-1,16-1
HCSB - **14,** 1-1,2-1,3-1,4-1,5-1,6-1,7-1,8-1,9-1,10-1,11-1,12-1,13-1,14-1
NASV - **19,** 1-1,2-1,3-1,4-1,5-1,6-1,7-1,8-1,9-1,10-1,11-1,12-1,13-1,14-1,15-1,16-1,17-1,18-1,19-1
NCV - **20,** 1-1,2-1,3-**2**,4-1,5-1,6-1,7-1,8-1,9-1,10-1,11-1,12-1,13-1,14-1,15-1,16-1,17-1,18-1,19-1,20-1
NIV - **16,** 1-1,2-1,3-1,4-1,5-1,6-1,7-1,8-1,9-1,10-1,11-1,12-1,13-1,14-1,15-1,16-1
NKJV - **17,** 1-1,2-1,3-1,4-1,5-1,6-1,7-1,8-1,9-1,10-1,11-1,12-1,13-1,14-1,15-1,16-1,17-1
NLT - **13,** 1-1,2-1,3-1,4-1,5-1,6-1,7-1,8-1,9-1,10-1,11-1,12-1,13-1
NRSV - **15,** 1-1,2-1,3-1,4-1,5-1,6-1,7-1,8-1,9-1,10-1,11-1,12-1,13-1,14-1,15-1
Conclusion: Only the NCV made the verse more complex.

464. 1 Chronicles 9:37* And **Gedor**, and **Ahio**, and **Zechariah**, and **Mikloth**.
AV - **8,** 1-1,2-1,3-1,4-1,5-1,6-1,7-1,8-1
ESV - **5,** 1-1,2-1,3-1,4-1,5-1
HCSB - **5,** 1-1,2-1,3-1,4-1,5-1
NASV - **5,** 1-1,2-1,3-1,4-1,5-1
NCV - **5,** 1-1,2-1,3-1,4-1,5-1
NIV - **5,** 1-1,2-1,3-1,4-1,5-1
NKJV - **5,** 1-1,2-1,3-1,4-1,5-1
NLT - **5,** 1-1,2-1,3-1,4-1,5-1
NRSV - **5,** 1-1,2-1,3-1,4-1,5-1
Conclusion: All versions read the same.

465. 1 Chronicles 9:41* And the sons of **Micah** were, **Pithon**, and **Melech**, and **Tahrea**, and **Ahaz**.
AV - **13,** 1-1,2-1,3-1,4-1,5-1,6-1,7-1,8-1,9-1,10-1,11-1,12-1,13-1
ESV - **9,** 1-1,2-1,3-1,4-1,5-1,6-1,7-1,8-1,9-1
HCSB - **7,** 1-1,2-1,3-1,4-1,5-1,6-1,7-1
NASV - **10,** 1-1,2-1,3-1,4-1,5-1,6-1,7-1,8-1,9-1,10-1
NCV - **8,** 1-1,2-1,3-1,4-1,5-1,6-1,7-1,8-1
NIV - **9,** 1-1,2-1,3-1,4-1,5-1,6-1,7-1,8-1,9-1
NKJV - **10,** 1-1,2-1,3-1,4-1,5-1,6-1,7-1,8-1,9-1,10-1
NLT - **10,** 1-1,2-1,3-1,4-1,5-1,6-1,7-1,8-1,9-1,10-1
NRSV - **9,** 1-1,2-1,3-1,4-1,5-1,6-1,7-1,8-1,9-1
Conclusion: All versions read the same.

466. 1 Chronicles 9:44* And **Azel** had six sons, whose names are these, **Azrikam**, **Bocheru**, and **Ishmael**, and **Sheariah**, and **Obadiah**, and **Hanan**: these were the sons of **Azel**.
AV - **25,** 1-1,2-1,3-1,4-1,5-1,6-1,7-1,8-1,9-1,10-1,11-1,12-1,13-1,14-1,15-1,16-1,17-1,18-1,19-1,20-1,21-1,22-1,23-1,24-1,25-1
ESV - **22,** 1-1,2-1,3-1,4-1,5-1,6-1,7-1,8-1,9-1,10-1,11-1,12-1,13-1,14-1,15-1,16-1,17-1,18-1,19-1,20-1,21-1,22-1
HCSB - **20,** 1-1,2-1,3-1,4-1,5-1,6-1,7-1,8-1,9-1,10-1,11-1,12-1,13-1,14-1,15-1,16-1,17-1,18-1,19-1,20-1
NASV - **24,** 1-1,2-1,3-1,4-1,5-1,6-1,7-1,8-1,9-1,10-1,11-1,12-1,13-1,14-1,15-1,16-1,17-1,18-1,19-1,20-1,21-1,22-1,23-1,24-1
NCV - **15,** 1-1,2-1,3-1,4-1,5-1,6-1,7-1,8-1,9-1,10-1,11-1,12-1,13-1,14-1,15-1
NIV - **22,** 1-1,2-1,3-1,4-1,5-1,6-1,7-1,8-1,9-1,10-1,11-1,12-1,13-1,14-1,15-1,16-1,17-1,18-1,19-1,20-1,21-1,22-1
NKJV - **22,** 1-1,2-1,3-1,4-1,5-1,6-1,7-1,8-1,9-1,10-1,11-1,12-1,13-1,14-1,15-1,16-1,17-1,18-1,19-1,20-1,21-1,22-1
NLT - **20,** 1-1,2-1,3-1,4-1,5-1,6-1,7-1,8-1,9-1,10-1,11-1,12-1,13-1,14-1,15-1,16-1,17-1,18-1,19-1,20-1
NRSV - **22,** 1-1,2-1,3-1,4-1,5-1,6-1,7-1,8-1,9-1,10-1,11-1,12-1,13-1,14-1,15-1,16-1,17-1,18-1,19-1,20-1,21-1,22-1
Conclusion: All versions read the same.

467. 1 Chronicles 10:11* And when all **Jabeshgilead** heard all that the **Philistines** had done to Saul,
AV - **13,** 1-1,2-1,3-1,4-1,5-1,6-1,7-1,8-1,9-1,10-1,11-1,12-1,13-1
ESV - **14,** 1-1,2-1,3-1,4-1,5-1,6-1,7-1,8-1,9-1,10-1,11-1,12-1,13-1,14-1
HCSB - 13, 1-1,2-1,3-1,4-1,5-1,6-1,7-**4**,8-1,9-1,10-1,11-1,12-1,13-1
NASV - **13,** 1-1,2-1,3-1,4-1,5-1,6-1,7-1,8-1,9-1,10-1,11-1,12-1,13-1
NCV - 14, 1-1,2-1,3-**2**,4-1,5-1,6-1,7-1,8-1,9-1,10-1,11-1,12-1,13-1,14-1
NIV - 16, 1-1,2-1,3-1,4-**4**,5-1,6-1,7-1,8-1,9-1,10-**4**,11-1,12-1,13-1,14-1,15-1,16-1
NKJV - **14,** 1-1,2-1,3-1,4-1,5-1,6-1,7-1,8-1,9-1,10-1,11-1,12-1,13-1,14-1
NLT - 15, 1-1,2-1,3-**4**,4-1,5-1,6-1,7-1,8-1,9-**4**,10-1,11-1,12-1,13-1,14-1,15-1
NRSV - 14, 1-1,2-1,3-1,4-1,5-1,6-1,7-**4**,8-1,9-1,10-1,11-1,12-1,13-1,14-1

Conclusion: Five modern versions are more complex than the King James Bible.

468. 1 Chronicles 11:27* Shammoth the **Harorite, Helez** the **Pelonite,**
AV - **6,** 1-1,2-1,3-1,4-1,5-1,6-1
ESV - **6,** 1-1,2-1,3-1,4-1,5-1,6-1
HCSB - **6,** 1-1,2-1,3-1,4-1,5-1,6-1
NASV - **6,** 1-1,2-1,3-1,4-1,5-1,6-1
NCV - **6,** 1-1,2-1,3-1,4-1,5-1,6-1
NIV - **6,** 1-1,2-1,3-1,4-1,5-1,6-1
NKJV - **6,** 1-1,2-1,3-1,4-1,5-1,6-1
NLT - **6,** 1-1,2-1,3-1,4-1,5-1,6-1
NRSV - **6,** 1-1,2-1,3-1,4-1,5-1,6-1
Conclusion: All versions read the same.

469. 1 Chronicles 11:28* Ira the son of **Ikkesh** the **Tekoite, Abiezer** the **Antothite,**
AV - **10,** 1-1,2-1,3-1,4-1,5-1,6-1,7-1,8-1,9-1,10-1
ESV - **10,** 1-1,2-1,3-1,4-1,5-1,6-1,7-1,8-1,9-1,10-1
HCSB - **9,** 1-1,2-1,3-1,4-1,5-1,6-1,7-1,8-1,9-1
NASV - **10,** 1-1,2-1,3-1,4-1,5-1,6-1,7-1,8-1,9-1,10-1
NCV - **9,** 1-1,2-1,3-1,4-1,5-1,6-1,7-1,8-1,9-1
NIV - **9,** 1-1,2-1,3-1,4-1,5-1,6-1,7-1,8-1,9-1
NKJV - **10,** 1-1,2-1,3-1,4-1,5-1,6-1,7-1,8-1,9-1,10-1
NLT - **9,** 1-1,2-1,3-1,4-1,5-1,6-1,7-1,8-1,9-1
NRSV - **9,** 1-1,2-1,3-1,4-1,5-1,6-1,7-1,8-1,9-1
Conclusion: All versions read the same.

470. 1 Chronicles 11:29* Sibbecai the **Hushathite, Ilai** the **Ahohite,**
AV - **6,** 1-1,2-1,3-1,4-1,5-1,6-1
ESV - **6,** 1-1,2-1,3-1,4-1,5-1,6-1
HCSB - **6,** 1-1,2-1,3-1,4-1,5-1,6-1
NASV - **6,** 1-1,2-1,3-1,4-1,5-1,6-1
NCV - **6,** 1-1,2-1,3-1,4-1,5-1,6-1
NIV - **6,** 1-1,2-1,3-1,4-1,5-1,6-1
NKJV - **6,** 1-1,2-1,3-1,4-1,5-1,6-1
NLT - **6,** 1-1,2-1,3-1,4-1,5-1,6-1
NRSV - **6,** 1-1,2-1,3-1,4-1,5-1,6-1
Conclusion: All versions read the same.

471. 1 Chronicles 11:30* Maharai the **Netophathite, Heled** the son of **Baanah** the **Netophathite,**
AV - **10,** 1-1,2-1,3-1,4-1,5-1,6-1,7-1,8-1,9-1,10-1
ESV - **10,** 1-1,2-1,3-1,4-1,5-1,6-1,7-1,8-1,9-1,10-1
HCSB - **9,** 1-1,2-1,3-1,4-1,5-1,6-1,7-1,8-1,9-1
NASV - **10,** 1-1,2-1,3-1,4-1,5-1,6-1,7-1,8-1,9-1,10-1
NCV - **9,** 1-1,2-1,3-1,4-1,5-1,6-1,7-1,8-1,9-1

NIV - **9,** 1-1,2-1,3-1,4-1,5-1,6-1,7-1,8-1,9-1
NKJV - **10,** 1-1,2-1,3-1,4-1,5-1,6-1,7-1,8-1,9-1,10-1
NLT - **9,** 1-1,2-1,3-1,4-1,5-1,6-1,7-1,8-1,9-1
NRSV - **9,** 1-1,2-1,3-1,4-1,5-1,6-1,7-1,8-1,9-1
Conclusion: All versions read the same.

472. 1 Chronicles 11:32* Hurai of the brooks of **Gaash, Abiel** the **Arbathite,**
AV - **9,** 1-1,2-1,3-1,4-1,5-1,6-1,7-1,8-1,9-1
ESV - **9,** 1-1,2-1,3-1,4-1,5-1,6-1,7-1,8-1,9-1
HCSB - 9, 1-1,2-1,3-1,4-**2**,5-1,6-1,7-1,8-1,9-1
NASV - **9,** 1-1,2-1,3-1,4-1,5-1,6-1,7-1,8-1,9-1
NCV - 9, 1-1,2-1,3-1,4-**2**,5-1,6-1,7-1,8-1,9-1
NIV - 9, 1-1,2-1,3-1,4-**2**,5-1,6-1,7-1,8-1,9-1
NKJV - **9,** 1-1,2-1,3-1,4-1,5-1,6-1,7-1,8-1,9-1
NLT - **7,** 1-1,2-1,3-1,4-1,5-1,6-1,7-1
NRSV - 9, 1-1,2-1,3-1,4-**2**,5-1,6-1,7-1,8-1,9-1
Conclusion: Four modern versions are more complex than the King James Bible.

473. 1 Chronicles 11:33* Azmaveth the **Baharumite, Eliahba** the **Shaalbonite,**
AV - **6,** 1-1,2-1,3-1,4-1,5-1,6-1
ESV - **6,** 1-1,2-1,3-1,4-1,5-1,6-1
HCSB - **6,** 1-1,2-1,3-1,4-1,5-1,6-1
NASV - **6,** 1-1,2-1,3-1,4-1,5-1,6-1
NCV - **6,** 1-1,2-1,3-1,4-1,5-1,6-1
NIV - **6,** 1-1,2-1,3-1,4-1,5-1,6-1
NKJV - **6,** 1-1,2-1,3-1,4-1,5-1,6-1
NLT - **6,** 1-1,2-1,3-1,4-1,5-1,6-1
NRSV - **6,** 1-1,2-1,3-1,4-1,5-1,6-1
Conclusion: All versions read the same.

474. 1 Chronicles 11:34* The sons of **Hashem** the **Gizonite, Jonathan** the son of Shage the **Hararite,**
AV - **13,** 1-1,2-1,3-1,4-1,5-1,6-1,7-1,8-1,9-1,10-1,11-1,12-1,13-1
ESV - **10,** 1-1,2-1,3-1,4-1,5-1,6-1,7-1,8-1,9-1,10-1
HCSB - **12,** 1-1,2-1,3-1,4-1,5-1,6-1,7-1,8-1,9-1,10-1,11-1,12-1
NASV - **13,** 1-1,2-1,3-1,4-1,5-1,6-1,7-1,8-1,9-1,10-1,11-1,12-1,13-1
NCV - **12,** 1-1,2-1,3-1,4-1,5-1,6-1,7-1,8-1,9-1,10-1,11-1,12-1
NIV - **12,** 1-1,2-1,3-1,4-1,5-1,6-1,7-1,8-1,9-1,10-1,11-1,12-1
NKJV - **13,** 1-1,2-1,3-1,4-1,5-1,6-1,7-1,8-1,9-1,10-1,11-1,12-1,13-1
NLT - **12,** 1-1,2-1,3-1,4-1,5-1,6-1,7-1,8-1,9-1,10-1,11-1,12-1
NRSV - **9,** 1-1,2-1,3-1,4-1,5-1,6-1,7-1,8-1,9-1
Conclusion: All versions read the same.

475. 1 Chronicles 11:35* Ahiam the son of **Sacar** the **Hararite, Eliphal** the son of Ur,
AV - **12,** 1-1,2-1,3-1,4-1,5-1,6-1,7-1,8-1,9-1,10-1,11-1,12-1
ESV - **12,** 1-1,2-1,3-1,4-1,5-1,6-1,7-1,8-1,9-1,10-1,11-1,12-1
HCSB - **10,** 1-1,2-1,3-1,4-1,5-1,6-1,7-1,8-1,9-1,10-1
NASV - **12,** 1-1,2-1,3-1,4-1,5-1,6-1,7-1,8-1,9-1,10-1,11-1,12-1
NCV - **10,** 1-1,2-1,3-1,4-1,5-1,6-1,7-1,8-1,9-1,10-1
NIV - **10,** 1-1,2-1,3-1,4-1,5-1,6-1,7-1,8-1,9-1,10-1
NKJV - **12,** 1-1,2-1,3-1,4-1,5-1,6-1,7-1,8-1,9-1,10-1,11-1,12-1
NLT - **10,** 1-1,2-1,3-1,4-1,5-1,6-1,7-1,8-1,9-1,10-1
NRSV - **10,** 1-1,2-1,3-1,4-1,5-1,6-1,7-1,8-1,9-1,10-1
Conclusion: All versions read the same.

476. 1 Chronicles 11:36* Hepher the **Mecherathite, Ahijah** the **Pelonite,**
AV - **6,** 1-1,2-1,3-1,4-1,5-1,6-1
ESV - **6,** 1-1,2-1,3-1,4-1,5-1,6-1
HCSB - **6,** 1-1,2-1,3-1,4-1,5-1,6-1
NASV - **6,** 1-1,2-1,3-1,4-1,5-1,6-1
NCV - **6,** 1-1,2-1,3-1,4-1,5-1,6-1
NIV - **6,** 1-1,2-1,3-1,4-1,5-1,6-1
NKJV - **6,** 1-1,2-1,3-1,4-1,5-1,6-1
NLT - **6,** 1-1,2-1,3-1,4-1,5-1,6-1
NRSV - **6,** 1-1,2-1,3-1,4-1,5-1,6-1
Conclusion: All versions read the same.

477. 1 Chronicles 11:37* Hezro the **Carmelite, Naarai** the son of **Ezbai,**
AV - **8,** 1-1,2-1,3-1,4-1,5-1,6-1,7-1,8-1
ESV - **8,** 1-1,2-1,3-1,4-1,5-1,6-1,7-1,8-1
HCSB - **7,** 1-1,2-1,3-1,4-1,5-1,6-1,7-1
NASV - **8,** 1-1,2-1,3-1,4-1,5-1,6-1,7-1,8-1
NCV - **6,** 1-1,2-1,3-1,4-1,5-1,6-1
NIV - **7,** 1-1,2-1,3-1,4-1,5-1,6-1,7-1
NKJV - **8,** 1-1,2-1,3-1,4-1,5-1,6-1,7-1,8-1
NLT - **7,** 1-1,2-1,3-1,4-1,5-1,6-1,7-1
NRSV - **7,** 1-1,2-1,3-1,4-1,5-1,6-1,7-1
Conclusion: All versions read the same.

478. 1 Chronicles 11:40* Ira the **Ithrite, Gareb** the **Ithrite,**
AV - **6,** 1-1,2-1,3-1,4-1,5-1,6-1
ESV - **6,** 1-1,2-1,3-1,4-1,5-1,6-1
HCSB - **6,** 1-1,2-1,3-1,4-1,5-1,6-1
NASV - **6,** 1-1,2-1,3-1,4-1,5-1,6-1
NCV - **6,** 1-1,2-1,3-1,4-1,5-1,6-1
NIV - **6,** 1-1,2-1,3-1,4-1,5-1,6-1
NKJV - **6,** 1-1,2-1,3-1,4-1,5-1,6-1

NLT - **6,** 1-1,2-1,3-1,4-1,5-1,6-1
NRSV - **6,** 1-1,2-1,3-1,4-1,5-1,6-1
Conclusion: All versions read the same.

479. 1 Chronicles 11:41* Uriah the **Hittite, Zabad** the son of **Ahlai,**
AV - **8,** 1-1,2-1,3-1,4-1,5-1,6-1,7-1,8-1
ESV - **8,** 1-1,2-1,3-1,4-1,5-1,6-1,7-1,8-1
HCSB - **7,** 1-1,2-1,3-1,4-1,5-1,6-1,7-1
NASV - **8,** 1-1,2-1,3-1,4-1,5-1,6-1,7-1,8-1
NCV - **7,** 1-1,2-1,3-1,4-1,5-1,6-1,7-1
NIV - **7,** 1-1,2-1,3-1,4-1,5-1,6-1,7-1
NKJV - **8,** 1-1,2-1,3-1,4-1,5-1,6-1,7-1,8-1
NLT - **7,** 1-1,2-1,3-1,4-1,5-1,6-1,7-1
NRSV - **7,** 1-1,2-1,3-1,4-1,5-1,6-1,7-1
Conclusion: All versions read the same.

480. 1 Chronicles 11:43* Hanan the son of **Maachah,** and **Joshaphat** the **Mithnite,**
AV - **9,** 1-1,2-1,3-1,4-1,5-1,6-1,7-1,8-1,9-1
ESV - **9,** 1-1,2-1,3-1,4-1,5-1,6-1,7-1,8-1,9-1
HCSB - **7,** 1-1,2-1,3-1,4-1,5-1,6-1,7-1
NASV - **9,** 1-1,2-1,3-1,4-1,5-1,6-1,7-1,8-1,9-1
NCV - **7,** 1-1,2-1,3-1,4-1,5-1,6-1,7-1
NIV - **7,** 1-1,2-1,3-1,4-1,5-1,6-1,7-1
NKJV - **8,** 1-1,2-1,3-1,4-1,5-1,6-1,7-1,8-1
NLT - **7,** 1-1,2-1,3-1,4-1,5-1,6-1,7-1
NRSV - **8,** 1-1,2-1,3-1,4-1,5-1,6-1,7-1,8-1
Conclusion: All versions read the same.

481. 1 Chronicles 11:44* Uzzia the **Ashterathite, Shama** and **Jehiel** the sons of **Hothan** the **Aroerite,**
AV - **12,** 1-1,2-1,3-1,4-1,5-1,6-1,7-1,8-1,9-1,10-1,11-1,12-1
ESV - **12,** 1-1,2-1,3-1,4-1,5-1,6-1,7-1,8-1,9-1,10-1,11-1,12-1
HCSB - **12,** 1-1,2-1,3-1,4-1,5-1,6-1,7-1,8-1,9-1,10-1,11-1,12-1
NASV - **12,** 1-1,2-1,3-1,4-1,5-1,6-1,7-1,8-1,9-1,10-1,11-1,12-1
NCV - **11,** 1-1,2-1,3-1,4-1,5-1,6-1,7-1,8-1,9-1,10-1,11-1
NIV - **12,** 1-1,2-1,3-1,4-1,5-1,6-1,7-1,8-1,9-1,10-1,11-1,12-1
NKJV - **12,** 1-1,2-1,3-1,4-1,5-1,6-1,7-1,8-1,9-1,10-1,11-1,12-1
NLT - **12,** 1-1,2-1,3-1,4-1,5-1,6-1,7-1,8-1,9-1,10-1,11-1,12-1
NRSV - **11,** 1-1,2-1,3-1,4-1,5-1,6-1,7-1,8-1,9-1,10-1,11-1
Conclusion: All versions read the same.

482. 1 Chronicles 11:46* Eliel the **Mahavite,** and **Jeribai,** and **Joshaviah,** the sons of **Elnaam,** and **Ithmah** the **Moabite,**
AV - **15,** 1-1,2-1,3-1,4-1,5-1,6-1,7-1,8-1,9-1,10-1,11-1,12-1,13-1,14-1,15-1

ESV - **15,** 1-1,2-1,3-1,4-1,5-1,6-1,7-1,8-1,9-1,10-1,11-1,12-1,13-1,14-1,15-1
HCSB - **13,** 1-1,2-1,3-1,4-1,5-1,6-1,7-1,8-1,9-1,10-1,11-1,12-1,13-1
NASV - **15,** 1-1,2-1,3-1,4-1,5-1,6-1,7-1,8-1,9-1,10-1,11-1,12-1,13-1,14-1,15-1
NCV - **11,** 1-1,2-1,3-1,4-1,5-1,6-1,7-1,8-1,9-1,10-1,11-1
NIV - **13,** 1-1,2-1,3-1,4-1,5-1,6-1,7-1,8-1,9-1,10-1,11-1,12-1,13-1
NKJV - **13,** 1-1,2-1,3-1,4-1,5-1,6-1,7-1,8-1,9-1,10-1,11-1,12-1,13-1
NLT - **13,** 1-1,2-1,3-1,4-1,5-1,6-1,7-1,8-1,9-1,10-1,11-1,12-1,13-1
NRSV - **14,** 1-1,2-1,3-1,4-1,5-1,6-1,7-1,8-1,9-1,10-1,11-1,12-1,13-1,14-1
Conclusion: All versions read the same.

483. 1 Chronicles 11:47* Eliel, and **Obed**, and **Jasiel** the **Mesobaite**.
AV - **7,** 1-1,2-1,3-1,4-1,5-1,6-1,7-1
ESV - **7,** 1-1,2-1,3-1,4-1,5-1,6-1,7-1
HCSB - **6,** 1-1,2-1,3-1,4-1,5-1,6-1
NASV - **7,** 1-1,2-1,3-1,4-1,5-1,6-1,7-1
NCV - **6,** 1-1,2-1,3-1,4-1,5-1,6-1
NIV - **6,** 1-1,2-1,3-1,4-1,5-1,6-1
NKJV - **6,** 1-1,2-1,3-1,4-1,5-1,6-1
NLT - **6,** 1-1,2-1,3-1,4-1,5-1,6-1
NRSV - **7,** 1-1,2-1,3-1,4-1,5-1,6-1,7-1
Conclusion: All versions read the same.

484. 1 Chronicles 12:3* The chief was **Ahiezer**, then **Joash**, the sons of **Shemaah** the **Gibeathite**; and **Jeziel**, and **Pelet**, the sons of **Azmaveth**; and **Berachah**, and **Jehu** the **Antothite**,
AV - **26,** 1-1,2-1,3-1,4-1,5-1,6-1,7-1,8-1,9-1,10-1,11-1,12-1,13-1,14-1,15-1,16-1,17-1,18-1,19-1,20-1,21-1,22-1,23-1,24-1,25-1,26-1
ESV - 24, 1-1,2-1,3-1,4-1,5-1,6-1,7-1,8-1,9-1,10-1,11-1,12-1,13-**2**,14-1,15-1,16-1,17-1,18-1,19-1,20-1,21-1,22-1,23-1,24-1
HCSB - 25, 1-1,2-1,3-1,4-1,5-1,6-1,7-1,8-1,9-1,10-1,11-1,12-1,13-1,14-**2**,15-1,16-1,17-1,18-1,19-1,20-1,21-1,22-1,23-1,24-1,25-1
NASV - **26,** 1-1,2-1,3-1,4-1,5-1,6-1,7-1,8-1,9-1,10-1,11-1,12-1,13-1,14-1,15-1,16-1,17-1,18-1,19-1,20-1,21-1,22-1,23-1,24-1,25-1,26-1
NCV - 42, 1-1,2-1,3-1,4-**2**,5-1,6-1,7-1,8-1,9-1,10-1,11-1,12-1,13-1,14-1,15-1,16-1,17-1,18-1,19-1,20-1,21-1,22-1,23-1,24-1,25-**2**,26-1,27-1,28-1,29-1,30-1,31-1,32-1,33-1,34-1,35-1,36-1,37-1,38-1,39-1,40-1,41-1,42-1
NIV - **22,** 1-1,2-1,3-1,4-1,5-1,6-1,7-1,8-1,9-1,10-1,11-1,12-1,13-1,14-1,15-1,16-1,17-1,18-1,19-1,20-1,21-1,22-1
NKJV - **24,** 1-1,2-1,3-1,4-1,5-1,6-1,7-1,8-1,9-1,10-1,11-1,12-1,13-1,14-1,15-1,16-1,17-1,18-1,19-1,20-1,21-1,22-1,23-1,24-1
NLT - 31, 1-1,2-**2**,3-1,4-1,5-1,6-1,7-1,8-1,9-1,10-1,11-1,12-1,13-1,14-**2**,15-1,16-**2**,17-1,18-1,19-1,20-**2**,21-**3**,22-1,23-1,24-1,25-1,26-1,27-1,28-1,29-1,30-1,31-1
NRSV - 23, 1-1,2-1,3-1,4-1,5-1,6-1,7-1,8-1,9-1,10-1,11-1,12-1,13-**2**,14-1,15-1,16-1,17-1,18-1,19-1,20-1,21-1,22-1,23-1

Conclusion: While five modern versions are more complex than the King James Bible the NCV and NLT worked quite hard to make their renderings both wordy and complex.

485. 1 Chronicles 12:5* Eluzai, and **Jerimoth**, and **Bealiah**, and **Shemariah**, and **Shephatiah** the **Haruphite**,
AV - **11,** 1-1,2-1,3-1,4-1,5-1,6-1,7-1,8-1,9-1,10-1,11-1
ESV - **7,** 1-1,2-1,3-1,4-1,5-1,6-1,7-1
HCSB - **7,** 1-1,2-1,3-1,4-1,5-1,6-1,7-1
NASV - **7,** 1-1,2-1,3-1,4-1,5-1,6-1,7-1
NCV - **12,** 1-1,2-1,3-1,4-1,5-1,6-1,7-1,8-1,9-1,10-1,11-1,12-1
NIV - **8,** 1-1,2-1,3-1,4-1,5-1,6-1,7-1,8-1
NKJV - **8,** 1-1,2-1,3-1,4-1,5-1,6-1,7-1,8-1
NLT - **8,** 1-1,2-1,3-1,4-1,5-1,6-1,7-1,8-1
NRSV - **7,** 1-1,2-1,3-1,4-1,5-1,6-1,7-1
Conclusion: All versions read the same.

486. 1 Chronicles 12:7* And **Joelah**, and **Zebadiah**, the sons of **Jeroham** of **Gedor**.
AV - **10,** 1-1,2-1,3-1,4-1,5-1,6-1,7-1,8-1,9-1,10-1
ESV - **10,** 1-1,2-1,3-1,4-1,5-1,6-1,7-1,8-1,9-1,10-1
HCSB - **10,** 1-1,2-1,3-1,4-1,5-1,6-1,7-1,8-1,9-1,10-1
NASV - **10,** 1-1,2-1,3-1,4-1,5-1,6-1,7-1,8-1,9-1,10-1
NCV - **15,** 1-1,2-1,3-1,4-1,5-1,6-1,7-1,8-1,9-1,10-1,11-1,12-1,13-1,14-1,15-1
NIV - **10,** 1-1,2-1,3-1,4-1,5-1,6-1,7-1,8-1,9-1,10-1
NKJV - **10,** 1-1,2-1,3-1,4-1,5-1,6-1,7-1,8-1,9-1,10-1
NLT - **8,** 1-1,2-1,3-1,4-1,5-1,6-1,7-1,8-1
NRSV - **9,** 1-1,2-1,3-1,4-1,5-1,6-1,7-1,8-1,9-1
Conclusion: All versions read the same.

487. 1 Chronicles 12:9*# Ezer the first, **Obadiah** the **second**, **Eliab** the third,
AV - **9,** 1-1,2-1,3-1,4-1,5-1,6-1,7-1,8-1,9-1
ESV - **7,** 1-1,2-1,3-1,4-1,5-1,6-1,7-1
HCSB - **8,** 1-1,2-1,3-1,4-1,5-1,6-1,7-1,8-1
NASV - **10,** 1-1,2-1,3-1,4-1,5-1,6-1,7-1,8-1,9-1,10-1
NCV - 16, 1-1,2-1,3-1,4-**2**,5-1,6-1,7-**2**,8-1,9-1,10-1,11-**2**,12-1,13-**2**,14-1,15-1,16-1
NIV - 12, 1-1,2-1,3-1,4-1,5-1,6-1,7-**2**,8-1,9-**2**,10-1,11-1,12-1
NKJV - **9,** 1-1,2-1,3-1,4-1,5-1,6-1,7-1,8-1,9-1
NLT - 10, 1-1,2-1,3-1,4-**2**,5-1,6-1,7-**2**,8-1,9-1,10-1
NRSV - 8, 1-1,2-1,3-1,4-1,5-**2**,6-1,7-1,8-1
Conclusion: Four modern versions are more complex than the King James Bible. The NCV is the most difficult to read.

488. 1 Chronicles 12:10* Mishmannah the fourth, **Jeremiah** the fifth,
AV - **6,** 1-1,2-1,3-1,4-1,5-1,6-1
ESV - **4,** 1-1,2-1,3-1,4-1

HCSB - **4,** 1-1,2-1,3-1,4-1
NASV - **6,** 1-1,2-1,3-1,4-1,5-1,6-1
NCV - **6,** 1-1,2-1,3-1,4-1,5-1,6-1
NIV - **6,** 1-1,2-1,3-1,4-1,5-1,6-1
NKJV - **6,** 1-1,2-1,3-1,4-1,5-1,6-1
NLT - **6,** 1-1,2-1,3-1,4-1,5-1,6-1
NRSV - **4,** 1-1,2-1,3-1,4-1
Conclusion: All versions read the same.

489. 1 Chronicles 12:11*# Attai the sixth, **Eliel** the **seventh,**
AV - **6,** 1-1,2-1,3-1,4-1,5-1,6-1
ESV - **4,** 1-1,2-1,3-1,4-1
HCSB - **4,** 1-1,2-1,3-1,4-1
NASV - **6,** 1-1,2-1,3-1,4-1,5-1,6-1
NCV - **6,** 1-1,2-1,3-1,4-1,5-1,6-1
NIV - **6,** 1-1,2-1,3-1,4-1,5-1,6-1
NKJV - **6,** 1-1,2-1,3-1,4-1,5-1,6-1
NLT - **6,** 1-1,2-1,3-1,4-1,5-1,6-1
NRSV - **4,** 1-1,2-1,3-1,4-1
Conclusion: All versions read the same.

490. 1 Chronicles 12:12* Johanan the eighth, **Elzabad** the ninth,
AV - **6,** 1-1,2-1,3-1,4-1,5-1,6-1
ESV - **4,** 1-1,2-1,3-1,4-1
HCSB - **4,** 1-1,2-1,3-1,4-1
NASV - **6,** 1-1,2-1,3-1,4-1,5-1,6-1
NCV - **6,** 1-1,2-1,3-1,4-1,5-1,6-1
NIV - **6,** 1-1,2-1,3-1,4-1,5-1,6-1
NKJV - **6,** 1-1,2-1,3-1,4-1,5-1,6-1
NLT - **6,** 1-1,2-1,3-1,4-1,5-1,6-1
NRSV - **4,** 1-1,2-1,3-1,4-1
Conclusion: All versions read the same.

491. 1 Chronicles 12:13*# Jeremiah the tenth, **Machbanai** the **eleventh.**
AV - **6,** 1-1,2-1,3-1,4-1,5-1,6-1
ESV - **4,** 1-1,2-1,3-1,4-1
HCSB - **5,** 1-1,2-1,3-1,4-1,5-1
NASV - **6,** 1-1,2-1,3-1,4-1,5-1,6-1
NCV - 9, 1-1,2-1,3-1,4-1,5-1,6-1,7-1,8-1,9-**2**
NIV - **7,** 1-1,2-1,3-1,4-1,5-1,6-1,7-1
NKJV - **7,** 1-1,2-1,3-1,4-1,5-1,6-1,7-1
NLT - **6,** 1-1,2-1,3-1,4-1,5-1,6-1
NRSV - **4,** 1-1,2-1,3-1,4-1
Conclusion: Only the NCV made the verse more complex.

492. 1 Chronicles 14:5* And **Ibhar**, and **Elishua**, and **Elpalet**,
AV - **6,** 1-1,2-1,3-1,4-1,5-1,6-1
ESV - **3,** 1-1,2-1,3-1
HCSB - **3,** 1-1,2-1,3-1
NASV - **3,** 1-1,2-1,3-1
NCV - **3,** 1-1,2-1,3-1
NIV - **3,** 1-1,2-1,3-1
NKJV - **3,** 1-1,2-1,3-1
NLT - **3,** 1-1,2-1,3-1
NRSV - **4,** 1-1,2-1,3-1,4-1
Conclusion: All versions read the same.

493. 1 Chronicles 14:6* And **Nogah**, and **Nepheg**, and **Japhia**,
AV - **6,** 1-1,2-1,3-1,4-1,5-1,6-1
ESV - **3,** 1-1,2-1,3-1
HCSB - **3,** 1-1,2-1,3-1
NASV - **3,** 1-1,2-1,3-1
NCV - **3,** 1-1,2-1,3-1
NIV - **3,** 1-1,2-1,3-1
NKJV - **3,** 1-1,2-1,3-1
NLT - **3,** 1-1,2-1,3-1
NRSV - **4,** 1-1,2-1,3-1,4-1
Conclusion: All versions read the same.

494. 1 Chronicles 14:7* And **Elishama**, and **Beeliada**, and **Eliphalet**.
AV - **6,** 1-1,2-1,3-1,4-1,5-1,6-1
ESV - **4,** 1-1,2-1,3-1,4-1
HCSB - **4,** 1-1,2-1,3-1,4-1
NASV - **4,** 1-1,2-1,3-1,4-1
NCV - **4,** 1-1,2-1,3-1,4-1
NIV - **4,** 1-1,2-1,3-1,4-1
NKJV - **4,** 1-1,2-1,3-1,4-1
NLT - **4,** 1-1,2-1,3-1,4-1
NRSV - **4,** 1-1,2-1,3-1,4-1
Conclusion: All versions read the same.

495. 1 Chronicles 15:11* And **David** called for **Zadok** and **Abiathar** the priests, and for the **Levites**, for **Uriel**, **Asaiah**, and Joel, **Shemaiah**, and **Eliel**, and **Amminadab**,
AV - **23,** 1-1,2-1,3-1,4-1,5-1,6-1,7-1,8-1,9-1,10-1,11-1,12-1,13-1,14-1,15-1,16-1,17-1,18-1,19-1,20-1,21-1,22-1,23-1
ESV - 18, 1-1,2-1,3-**2**,4-1,5-1,6-1,7-1,8-1,9-1,10-1,11-1,12-1,13-1,14-1,15-1,16-1,17-1,18-1
HCSB - **23,** 1-1,2-1,3-1,4-1,5-1,6-1,7-1,8-1,9-1,10-1,11-1,12-1,13-1,14-1,15-1,16-1,17-1,18-1,19-1,20-1,21-1,22-1,23-1

NASV - **21,** 1-1,2-1,3-1,4-1,5-1,6-1,7-1,8-1,9-1,10-1,11-1,12-1,13-1,14-1,15-1,16-1,17-1,18-1,19-1,20-1,21-1

NCV - **22,** 1-1,2-1,3-1,4-1,5-1,6-1,7-1,8-1,9-1,10-1,11-1,12-1,13-1,14-1,15-1,16-1,17-1,18-1,19-1,20-1,21-1,22-1

NIV - 18, 1-1,2-1,3-**2,**4-1,5-1,6-1,7-1,8-1,9-1,10-1,11-1,12-1,13-1,14-1,15-1,16-1,17-1,18-1

NKJV - **21,** 1-1,2-1,3-1,4-1,5-1,6-1,7-1,8-1,9-1,10-1,11-1,12-1,13-1,14-1,15-1,16-1,17-1,18-1,19-1,20-1,21-1

NLT - 19, 1-1,2-1,3-**2,**4-1,5-1,6-1,7-1,8-1,9-1,10-1,11-1,12-1,13-1,14-1,15-1,16-1,17-1,18-1,19-1

NRSV - 17, 1-1,2-**2,**3-1,4-1,5-1,6-1,7-1,8-1,9-1,10-1,11-1,12-1,13-1,14-1,15-1,16-1,17-1

Conclusion: Four modern versions are more complex than the King James Bible.

496. 1 Chronicles 18:5*# And when the **Syrians** of **Damascus** came to help **Hadarezer** king of **Zobah**, **David** slew of the **Syrians** two and **twenty thousand** men.

AV - **23,** 1-1,2-1,3-1,4-1,5-1,6-1,7-1,8-1,9-1,10-1,11-1,12-1,13-1,14-1,15-1,16-1,17-1,18-1,19-1,20-1,21-1,22-1,23-1

ESV - **21,** 1-1,2-1,3-1,4-1,5-1,6-1,7-1,8-1,9-1,10-1,11-1,12-1,13-1,14-1,15-1,16-1,17-1,18-1,19-1,20-1,21-1

HCSB - 18, 1-1,2-1,3-1,4-1,5-1,6-1,7-1,8-**2,**9-1,10-1,11-1,12-1,13-1,14-1,15-1,16-1,17-1,18-1

NASV - **19,** 1-1,2-1,3-1,4-1,5-1,6-1,7-1,8-1,9-1,10-1,11-1,12-1,13-1,14-1,15-1,16-1,17-1,18-1,19-1

NCV - **18,** 1-1,2-1,3-1,4-1,5-1,6-1,7-1,8-1,9-1,10-1,11-1,12-1,13-1,14-1,15-1,16-1,17-1,18-1

NIV - **20,** 1-1,2-1,3-1,4-1,5-1,6-1,7-1,8-1,9-1,10-1,11-1,12-1,13-1,14-1,15-1,16-1,17-1,18-1,19-1,20-1

NKJV - **20,** 1-1,2-1,3-1,4-1,5-1,6-1,7-1,8-1,9-1,10-1,11-1,12-1,13-1,14-1,15-1,16-1,17-1,18-1,19-1,20-1

NLT - 14, 1-1,2-1,3-1,4-1,5-**2,**6-1,7-1,8-1,9-1,10-1,11-1,12-1,13-1,14-1

NRSV - **18,** 1-1,2-1,3-1,4-1,5-1,6-1,7-1,8-1,9-1,10-1,11-1,12-1,13-1,14-1,15-1,16-1,17-1,18-1

Conclusion: Only the HCSB and the NLT made the verse more complex.

497. 1 Chronicles 18:16* And **Zadok** the son of **Ahitub**, and **Abimelech** the son of **Abiathar**, were the priests; and **Shavsha** was scribe;

AV - **19,** 1-1,2-1,3-1,4-1,5-1,6-1,7-1,8-1,9-1,10-1,11-1,12-1,13-1,14-1,15-1,16-1,17-1,18-1,19-1

ESV - 18, 1-1,2-1,3-1,4-1,5-1,6-1,7-1,8-1,9-1,10-1,11-1,12-1,13-1,14-1,15-1,16-1,17-1,18-**4**

HCSB - 15, 1-1,2-1,3-1,4-1,5-1,6-1,7-1,8-1,9-1,10-1,11-1,12-1,13-1,14-1,15-**4**

NASV - 18, 1-1,2-1,3-1,4-1,5-1,6-1,7-1,8-1,9-1,10-1,11-1,12-1,13-1,14-1,15-1,16-1,17-1,18-**4**

NCV - 16, 1-1,2-1,3-1,4-1,5-1,6-1,7-1,8-1,9-1,10-1,11-1,12-1,13-1,14-1,15-**2,**16-**4**

NIV - 14, 1-1,2-1,3-1,4-1,5-1,6-1,7-1,8-1,9-1,10-1,11-1,12-1,13-1,14-**4**

NKJV - **18,** 1-1,2-1,3-1,4-1,5-1,6-1,7-1,8-1,9-1,10-1,11-1,12-1,13-1,14-1,15-1,16-1,17-1,18-1

NLT - 17, 1-1,2-1,3-1,4-1,5-1,6-1,7-1,8-1,9-1,10-1,11-1,12-1,13-1,14-1,15-1,16-1,17-**4**

NRSV - 14, 1-1,2-1,3-1,4-1,5-1,6-1,7-1,8-1,9-1,10-1,11-1,12-1,13-1,14-**4**

Conclusion: Seven modern versions are more complex than the King James Bible.

498. 1 Chronicles 18:29* So the king of **Israel** and **Jehoshaphat** the king of **Judah** went up to **Ramothgilead.**

AV - **15,** 1-1,2-1,3-1,4-1,5-1,6-1,7-1,8-1,9-1,10-1,11-1,12-1,13-1,14-1,15-1

ESV - **15,** 1-1,2-1,3-1,4-1,5-1,6-1,7-1,8-1,9-1,10-1,11-1,12-1,13-1,14-1,15-1
HCSB - **15,** 1-1,2-1,3-1,4-1,5-1,6-1,7-1,8-1,9-1,10-1,11-1,12-1,13-1,14-1,15-1
NASV - **14,** 1-1,2-1,3-1,4-1,5-1,6-1,7-1,8-1,9-1,10-1,11-1,12-1,13-**2,**14-1
NCV - **15,** 1-1,2-1,3-1,4-1,5-1,6-1,7-1,8-1,9-1,10-1,11-1,12-1,13-1,14-1,15-1
NIV - **15,** 1-1,2-1,3-1,4-1,5-1,6-1,7-1,8-1,9-1,10-1,11-1,12-1,13-1,14-1,15-1
NKJV - **16,** 1-1,2-1,3-1,4-1,5-1,6-1,7-1,8-1,9-1,10-1,11-1,12-1,13-1,14-1,15-1,16-1
NLT - **15,** 1-1,2-1,3-1,4-1,5-1,6-1,7-1,8-1,9-1,10-1,11-1,12-1,13-**2,**14-**2,**15-1
NRSV - **14,** 1-1,2-1,3-1,4-1,5-1,6-1,7-1,8-1,9-1,10-1,11-1,12-1,13-1,14-1
Conclusion: Only the NASV and the NLT made the verse more complex. Both the NCV and NLT added the proper name "Ahab" for the King of Israel. This was not counted against them.

499. 1 Chronicles 22:6* Then he called for **Solomon** his son, and charged him to build an house for the LORD God of **Israel**.
AV - **20,** 1-1,2-1,3-1,4-1,5-1,6-1,7-1,8-1,9-1,10-1,11-1,12-1,13-1,14-1,15-1,16-1,17-1,18-1,19-1,20-1
ESV - **21,** 1-1,2-1,3-1,4-1,5-1,6-1,7-1,8-1,9-1,10-1,11-1,12-1,13-1,14-1,15-1,16-1,17-1,18-1,19-1,20-1,21-1
HCSB - **19,** 1-1,2-1,3-**2,**4-1,5-1,6-1,7-1,8-**3,**9-1,10-1,11-1,12-1,13-1,14-1,15-1,16-1,17-1,18-1,19-1
NASV - **20,** 1-1,2-1,3-1,4-1,5-1,6-1,7-1,8-1,9-1,10-1,11-1,12-1,13-1,14-1,15-1,16-1,17-1,18-1,19-1,20-1
NCV - **21,** 1-1,2-1,3-1,4-1,5-1,6-1,7-1,8-1,9-1,10-1,11-1,12-1,13-1,14-1,15-1,16-1,17-1,18-1,19-1,20-1,21-1
NIV - **21,** 1-1,2-1,3-1,4-1,5-1,6-1,7-1,8-1,9-1,10-1,11-1,12-1,13-1,14-1,15-1,16-1,17-1,18-1,19-1,20-1,21-1
NKJV - **20,** 1-1,2-1,3-1,4-1,5-1,6-1,7-1,8-1,9-1,10-1,11-1,12-1,13-1,14-1,15-1,16-1,17-1,18-1,19-1,20-1
NLT - **21,** 1-1,2-1,3-1,4-1,5-1,6-1,7-1,8-1,9-**3,**10-1,11-1,12-1,13-1,14-1,15-1,16-1,17-1,18-1,19-1,20-1,21-1
NRSV - **21,** 1-1,2-1,3-1,4-1,5-1,6-1,7-1,8-1,9-1,10-1,11-1,12-1,13-1,14-1,15-1,16-1,17-1,18-1,19-1,20-1,21-1
Conclusion: Only the HCSB and the NLT made the verse more complex. The NCV, which did not complicate the verse, and the NLT, which did, both inserted the word "temple" for "house." This word, which would have been accepted under other conditions was not counted against them.

500. 1 Chronicles 23:7* Of the **Gershonites** were, **Laadan**, and **Shimei**.
AV - **7,** 1-1,2-1,3-1,4-1,5-1,6-1,7-1
ESV - **8,** 1-1,2-1,3-1,4-1,5-1,6-1,7-1,8-1
HCSB - **5,** 1-1,2-1,3-1,4-1,5-1
NASV - **7,** 1-1,2-1,3-1,4-1,5-1,6-1,7-1
NCV - **10,** 1-1,2-1,3-**2,**4-1,5-1,6-1,7-1,8-1,9-1,10-1
NIV - **7,** 1-**3,**2-1,3-1,4-1,5-1,6-1,7-1
NKJV - **6,** 1-1,2-1,3-1,4-1,5-1,6-1
NLT - **18,** 1-1,2-1,3-**3,**4-**2,**5-**2,**6-1,7-1,8-1,9-1,10-**2,**11-1,12-1,13-1,14-1,15-1,16-1,17-1,18-1
NRSV - **8,** 1-1,2-1,3-1,4-1,5-1,6-1,7-1,8-1

Conclusion: Only three modern versions are more complex than the King James Bible. The NLT was breathtakingly complex!

501. 1 Chronicles 23:8* The sons of **Laadan**; the chief was **Jehiel**, and **Zetham**, and **Joel**, three.
AV - **13,** 1-1,2-1,3-1,4-1,5-1,6-1,7-1,8-1,9-1,10-1,11-1,12-1,13-1
ESV - **12,** 1-1,2-1,3-1,4-1,5-1,6-1,7-1,8-1,9-1,10-1,11-1,12-1
HCSB - **11,** 1-1,2-1,3-1,4-1,5-1,6-1,7-1,8-1,9-1,10-1,11-1
NASV - **13,** 1-1,2-1,3-1,4-1,5-1,6-1,7-1,8-1,9-1,10-1,11-1,12-1,13-1
NCV - **17,** 1-1,2-1,3-1,4-1,5-1,6-1,7-1,8-1,9-1,10-1,11-1,12-**2**,13-1,14-1,15-1,16-1,17-1
NIV - **13,** 1-1,2-1,3-1,4-1,5-1,6-1,7-1,8-1,9-1,10-1,11-1,12-1,13-1
NKJV - **14,** 1-1,2-1,3-1,4-1,5-1,6-1,7-1,8-1,9-1,10-1,11-1,12-1,13-1,14-1
NLT - **14,** 1-1,2-1,3-1,4-**3**,5-1,6-1,7-1,8-1,9-1,10-**3**,11-**2**,12-1,13-1,14-1
NRSV - **11,** 1-1,2-1,3-1,4-1,5-1,6-1,7-1,8-1,9-1,10-1,11-1
Conclusion: Only the NCV and the NLT made the verse more complex.

502. 1 Chronicles 23:10* And the sons of **Shimei** were, **Jahath**, **Zina**, and **Jeush**, and **Beriah**. These four were the sons of **Shimei**.
AV - **19,** 1-1,2-1,3-1,4-1,5-1,6-1,7-1,8-1,9-1,10-1,11-1,12-1,13-1,14-1,15-1,16-1,17-1,18-1,19-1
ESV - **18,** 1-1,2-1,3-1,4-1,5-1,6-1,7-1,8-1,9-1,10-1,11-1,12-1,13-1,14-1,15-1,16-1,17-1,18-1
HCSB - **12,** 1-1,2-1,3-1,4-1,5-1,6-1,7-1,8-1,9-1,10-1,11-1,12-1
NASV - **17,** 1-1,2-1,3-1,4-1,5-1,6-1,7-1,8-1,9-1,10-1,11-1,12-1,13-1,14-1,15-1,16-1,17-1
NCV - **9,** 1-1,2-1,3-1,4-1,5-1,6-1,7-1,8-1,9-1
NIV - **19,** 1-1,2-1,3-1,4-1,5-1,6-1,7-1,8-1,9-1,10-1,11-1,12-1,13-1,14-1,15-1,16-1,17-1,18-1,19-1
NKJV - **17,** 1-1,2-1,3-1,4-1,5-1,6-1,7-1,8-1,9-1,10-1,11-1,12-1,13-1,14-1,15-1,16-1,17-1
NLT - **11,** 1-1,2-**2**,3-**3**,4-1,5-1,6-1,7-1,8-1,9-1,10-1,11-1
NRSV - **17,** 1-1,2-1,3-1,4-1,5-1,6-1,7-1,8-1,9-1,10-1,11-1,12-1,13-1,14-1,15-1,16-1,17-1
Conclusion: Only the NLT made the verse more complex.

503. 1 Chronicles 23:12* The sons of **Kohath**; **Amram**, **Izhar**, **Hebron**, and **Uzziel**, four.
AV - **10,** 1-1,2-1,3-1,4-1,5-1,6-1,7-1,8-1,9-1,10-1
ESV - **10,** 1-1,2-1,3-1,4-1,5-1,6-1,7-1,8-1,9-1,10-1
HCSB - **8,** 1-1,2-1,3-1,4-1,5-1,6-1,7-1,8-1
NASV - **11,** 1-1,2-1,3-1,4-1,5-1,6-1,7-1,8-1,9-1,10-1,11-1
NCV - **9,** 1-1,2-1,3-1,4-1,5-1,6-1,7-1,8-1,9-1
NIV - **12,** 1-1,2-1,3-1,4-1,5-1,6-1,7-1,8-1,9-1,10-1,11-1,12-1
NKJV - **12,** 1-1,2-1,3-1,4-1,5-1,6-1,7-1,8-1,9-1,10-1,11-1,12-1
NLT - **12,** 1-1,2-1,3-1,4-**3**,5-1,6-1,7-1,8-1,9-1,10-1,11-1,12-1
NRSV - **10,** 1-1,2-1,3-1,4-1,5-1,6-1,7-1,8-1,9-1,10-1
Conclusion: Only the NLT made the verse more complex.

504. 1 Chronicles 23:15* The sons of **Moses** were, **Gershom**, and **Eliezer**.
AV - **8,** 1-1,2-1,3-1,4-1,5-1,6-1,7-1,8-1
ESV - **7,** 1-1,2-1,3-1,4-1,5-1,6-1,7-1
HCSB - **5,** 1-1,2-1,3-1,4-1,5-1

NASV - **8,** 1-1,2-1,3-1,4-1,5-1,6-1,7-1,8-1
NCV - **6,** 1-1,2-1,3-1,4-1,5-1,6-1
NIV - **7,** 1-1,2-1,3-1,4-1,5-1,6-1,7-1
NKJV - **8,** 1-1,2-1,3-1,4-1,5-1,6-1,7-1,8-1
NLT - **8,** 1-1,2-1,3-1,4-1,5-1,6-1,7-1,8-1
NRSV - **7,** 1-1,2-1,3-1,4-1,5-1,6-1,7-1
Conclusion: All versions read the same.

505. 1 Chronicles 23:16* Of the sons of **Gershom**, **Shebuel** was the chief.
AV - **9,** 1-1,2-1,3-1,4-1,5-1,6-1,7-1,8-1,9-1
ESV - **7,** 1-1,2-1,3-1,4-1,5-1,6-1,7-1
HCSB - **4,** 1-1,2-1,3-1,4-1
NASV - **8,** 1-1,2-1,3-1,4-1,5-1,6-1,7-1,8-1
NCV - **5,** 1-1,2-1,3-1,4-1,5-1
NIV - **9,** 1-1,2-**3**,3-1,4-1,5-1,6-1,7-1,8-1,9-1
NKJV - **9,** 1-1,2-1,3-1,4-1,5-1,6-1,7-1,8-1,9-1
NLT - **9,** 1-1,2-**3**,3-1,4-1,5-**3**,6-1,7-1,8-**3**,9-**2**
NRSV - **7,** 1-1,2-1,3-1,4-1,5-1,6-1,7-1
Conclusion: Only the NIV and the NLT made the verse more complex.

506. 1 Chronicles 23:18* Of the sons of **Izhar**; **Shelomith** the chief.
AV - **8,** 1-1,2-1,3-1,4-1,5-1,6-1,7-1,8-1
ESV - **7,** 1-1,2-1,3-1,4-1,5-1,6-1,7-1
HCSB - **5,** 1-1,2-1,3-1,4-1,5-1
NASV - **8,** 1-1,2-1,3-1,4-1,5-1,6-1,7-1,8-1
NCV - **5,** 1-1,2-1,3-1,4-1,5-1
NIV - **8,** 1-1,2-1,3-1,4-1,5-1,6-1,7-1,8-1
NKJV - **9,** 1-1,2-1,3-1,4-1,5-1,6-1,7-1,8-1,9-1
NLT - **9,** 1-1,2-**3**,3-1,4-1,5-**3**,6-1,7-1,8-**3**,9-**2**
NRSV - **7,** 1-1,2-1,3-1,4-1,5-1,6-1,7-1
Conclusion: While the seven other modern versions kept to single syllable words the NLT did a masterful job of making the verse extremely complex.

507. 1 Chronicles 23:19*# Of the sons of **Hebron**; **Jeriah** the first, **Amariah** the **second**, **Jahaziel** the third, and **Jekameam** the fourth.
AV - **18,** 1-1,2-1,3-1,4-1,5-1,6-1,7-1,8-1,9-1,10-1,11-1,12-1,13-1,14-1,15-1,16-1,17-1,18-1
ESV - **17,** 1-1,2-1,3-1,4-1,5-1,6-1,7-1,8-1,9-1,10-1,11-1,12-1,13-1,14-1,15-1,16-1,17-1
HCSB - **12,** 1-1,2-1,3-1,4-1,5-1,6-1,7-1,8-1,9-1,10-1,11-1,12-1
NASV - **18,** 1-1,2-1,3-1,4-1,5-1,6-1,7-1,8-1,9-1,10-1,11-1,12-1,13-1,14-1,15-1,16-1,17-1,18-1
NCV - **18,** 1-1,2-1,3-1,4-1,5-1,6-1,7-1,8-1,9-1,10-1,11-1,12-1,13-1,14-1,15-1,16-1,17-1,18-1
NIV - **17,** 1-1,2-1,3-1,4-1,5-1,6-1,7-1,8-1,9-1,10-1,11-1,12-1,13-1,14-1,15-1,16-1,17-1
NKJV - **19,** 1-1,2-1,3-1,4-1,5-1,6-1,7-1,8-1,9-1,10-1,11-1,12-1,13-1,14-1,15-1,16-1,17-1,18-1,19-1
NLT - **19,** 1-1,2-**3**,3-1,4-1,5-**3**,6-1,7-1,8-**3**,9-**2**,10-1,11-1,12-1,13-1,14-1,15-1,16-1,17-1,18-1,19-1
NRSV - **17,** 1-1,2-1,3-1,4-1,5-1,6-1,7-1,8-1,9-1,10-1,11-1,12-1,13-1,14-1,15-1,16-1,17-1

Conclusion: Once again the seven other modern versions kept to single syllable words while the NLT made the verse extremely complex.

508. 1 Chronicles 23:20*# Of the sons of **Uzziel**; **Michah** the first, and **Jesiah** the **second**.
AV - **12,** 1-1,2-1,3-1,4-1,5-1,6-1,7-1,8-1,9-1,10-1,11-1,12-1
ESV - **11,** 1-1,2-1,3-1,4-1,5-1,6-1,7-1,8-1,9-1,10-1,11-1
HCSB - **8,** 1-1,2-1,3-1,4-1,5-1,6-1,7-1,8-1
NASV - **12,** 1-1,2-1,3-1,4-1,5-1,6-1,7-1,8-1,9-1,10-1,11-1,12-1
NCV - **10,** 1-1,2-1,3-1,4-1,5-1,6-1,7-1,8-1,9-1,10-1
NIV - **11,** 1-1,2-1,3-1,4-1,5-1,6-1,7-1,8-1,9-1,10-1,11-1
NKJV - **13,** 1-1,2-1,3-1,4-1,5-1,6-1,7-1,8-1,9-1,10-1,11-1,12-1,13-1
NLT - **13,** 1-1,2-**3,**3-1,4-1,5-**3,**6-1,7-1,8-**3,**9-**2,**10-1,11-1,12-1,13-1
NRSV - **11,** 1-1,2-1,3-1,4-1,5-1,6-1,7-1,8-1,9-1,10-1,11-1
Conclusion: As in the two previous cases the seven other modern versions kept to single syllable words while the NLT made the verse extremely complex.

509. 1 Chronicles 23:21* The sons of **Merari**; **Mahli**, and **Mushi**. The sons of **Mahli**; **Eleazar**, and Kish.
AV - **14,** 1-1,2-1,3-1,4-1,5-1,6-1,7-1,8-1,9-1,10-1,11-1,12-1,13-1,14-1
ESV - **14,** 1-1,2-1,3-1,4-1,5-1,6-1,7-1,8-1,9-1,10-1,11-1,12-1,13-1,14-1
HCSB - **10,** 1-1,2-1,3-1,4-1,5-1,6-1,7-1,8-1,9-1,10-1
NASV - **16,** 1-1,2-1,3-1,4-1,5-1,6-1,7-1,8-1,9-1,10-1,11-1,12-1,13-1,14-1,15-1,16-1
NCV - **12,** 1-1,2-1,3-1,4-1,5-1,6-1,7-1,8-1,9-1,10-1,11-1,12-1
NIV - **14,** 1-1,2-1,3-1,4-1,5-1,6-1,7-1,8-1,9-1,10-1,11-1,12-1,13-1,14-1
NKJV - **16,** 1-1,2-1,3-1,4-1,5-1,6-1,7-1,8-1,9-1,10-1,11-1,12-1,13-1,14-1,15-1,16-1
NLT - **16,** 1-1,2-**3,**3-1,4-1,5-1,6-**3,**7-1,8-1,9-1,10-1,11-1,12-1,13-1,14-1,15-1,16-1
NRSV - **14,** 1-1,2-1,3-1,4-1,5-1,6-1,7-1,8-1,9-1,10-1,11-1,12-1,13-1,14-1
Conclusion: Only the NLT made the verse more complex.

510. 1 Chronicles 23:23* The sons of **Mushi**; **Mahli**, and **Eder**, and **Jeremoth**, three.
AV - **10,** 1-1,2-1,3-1,4-1,5-1,6-1,7-1,8-1,9-1,10-1
ESV - **9,** 1-1,2-1,3-1,4-1,5-1,6-1,7-1,8-1,9-1
HCSB - **7,** 1-1,2-1,3-1,4-1,5-1,6-1,7-1
NASV - **10,** 1-1,2-1,3-1,4-1,5-1,6-1,7-1,8-1,9-1,10-1
NCV - **8,** 1-1,2-1,3-1,4-1,5-1,6-1,7-1,8-1
NIV - **11,** 1-1,2-1,3-1,4-1,5-1,6-1,7-1,8-1,9-1,10-1,11-1
NKJV - **12,** 1-1,2-1,3-1,4-1,5-1,6-1,7-1,8-1,9-1,10-1,11-1,12-1
NLT - **11,** 1-1,2-1,3-1,4-**3,**5-1,6-1,7-1,8-1,9-1,10-1,11-1
NRSV - **9,** 1-1,2-1,3-1,4-1,5-1,6-1,7-1,8-1,9-1
Conclusion: Only the NLT made the verse more complex.

511. 1 Chronicles 24:7*# Now the first lot came forth to **Jehoiarib**, the **second** to **Jedaiah**,
AV - **12,** 1-1,2-1,3-1,4-1,5-1,6-1,7-1,8-1,9-1,10-1,11-1,12-1
ESV - **10,** 1-1,2-1,3-1,4-1,5-1,6-1,7-1,8-1,9-1,10-1

HCSB - **10,** 1-1,2-1,3-1,4-1,5-1,6-1,7-1,8-1,9-1,10-1
NASV - **12,** 1-1,2-1,3-1,4-1,5-1,6-1,7-1,8-1,9-1,10-1,11-1,12-1
NCV - **10,** 1-1,2-1,3-1,4-**2,**5-1,6-1,7-1,8-1,9-1,10-1
NIV - **10,** 1-1,2-1,3-1,4-1,5-1,6-1,7-1,8-1,9-1,10-1
NKJV - **11,** 1-1,2-1,3-1,4-1,5-1,6-1,7-1,8-1,9-1,10-1,11-1
NLT - **12,** 1-1,2-1,3-1,4-1,5-1,6-1,7-1,8-1,9-1,10-1,11-1,12-1
NRSV - **10,** 1-1,2-1,3-1,4-1,5-1,6-1,7-1,8-1,9-1,10-1
Conclusion: Only the NCV made the verse more complex.

512. 1 Chronicles 24:8* The third to **Harim**, the fourth to **Seorim**,
AV - **8,** 1-1,2-1,3-1,4-1,5-1,6-1,7-1,8-1
ESV - **8,** 1-1,2-1,3-1,4-1,5-1,6-1,7-1,8-1
HCSB - **8,** 1-1,2-1,3-1,4-1,5-1,6-1,7-1,8-1
NASV - **8,** 1-1,2-1,3-1,4-1,5-1,6-1,7-1,8-1
NCV - **8,** 1-1,2-1,3-1,4-1,5-1,6-1,7-1,8-1
NIV - **8,** 1-1,2-1,3-1,4-1,5-1,6-1,7-1,8-1
NKJV - **8,** 1-1,2-1,3-1,4-1,5-1,6-1,7-1,8-1
NLT - **12,** 1-1,2-1,3-1,4-1,5-1,6-1,7-1,8-1,9-1,10-1,11-1,12-1
NRSV - **8,** 1-1,2-1,3-1,4-1,5-1,6-1,7-1,8-1
Conclusion: All versions read the same.

513. 1 Chronicles 24:9* The fifth to **Malchijah**, the sixth to **Mijamin**,
AV - **8,** 1-1,2-1,3-1,4-1,5-1,6-1,7-1,8-1
ESV - **8,** 1-1,2-1,3-1,4-1,5-1,6-1,7-1,8-1
HCSB - **8,** 1-1,2-1,3-1,4-1,5-1,6-1,7-1,8-1
NASV - **8,** 1-1,2-1,3-1,4-1,5-1,6-1,7-1,8-1
NCV - **8,** 1-1,2-1,3-1,4-1,5-1,6-1,7-1,8-1
NIV - **8,** 1-1,2-1,3-1,4-1,5-1,6-1,7-1,8-1
NKJV - **8,** 1-1,2-1,3-1,4-1,5-1,6-1,7-1,8-1
NLT - **12,** 1-1,2-1,3-1,4-1,5-1,6-1,7-1,8-1,9-1,10-1,11-1,12-1
NRSV - **8,** 1-1,2-1,3-1,4-1,5-1,6-1,7-1,8-1
Conclusion: All versions read the same.

514. 1 Chronicles 24:10*# The **seventh** to **Hakkoz**, the eighth to **Abijah**,
AV - **8,** 1-1,2-1,3-1,4-1,5-1,6-1,7-1,8-1
ESV - **8,** 1-1,2-1,3-1,4-1,5-1,6-1,7-1,8-1
HCSB - **8,** 1-1,2-1,3-1,4-1,5-1,6-1,7-1,8-1
NASV - **8,** 1-1,2-1,3-1,4-1,5-1,6-1,7-1,8-1
NCV - **8,** 1-1,2-1,3-1,4-1,5-1,6-1,7-1,8-1
NIV - **8,** 1-1,2-1,3-1,4-1,5-1,6-1,7-1,8-1
NKJV - **8,** 1-1,2-1,3-1,4-1,5-1,6-1,7-1,8-1
NLT - **12,** 1-1,2-1,3-1,4-1,5-1,6-1,7-1,8-1,9-1,10-1,11-1,12-1
NRSV - **8,** 1-1,2-1,3-1,4-1,5-1,6-1,7-1,8-1
Conclusion: All versions read the same.

515. 1 Chronicles 24:11* The ninth to **Jeshua**, the tenth to **Shecaniah**,
AV - **8,** 1-1,2-1,3-1,4-1,5-1,6-1,7-1,8-1
ESV - **8,** 1-1,2-1,3-1,4-1,5-1,6-1,7-1,8-1
HCSB - **8,** 1-1,2-1,3-1,4-1,5-1,6-1,7-1,8-1
NASV - **8,** 1-1,2-1,3-1,4-1,5-1,6-1,7-1,8-1
NCV - **8,** 1-1,2-1,3-1,4-1,5-1,6-1,7-1,8-1
NIV - **8,** 1-1,2-1,3-1,4-1,5-1,6-1,7-1,8-1
NKJV - **8,** 1-1,2-1,3-1,4-1,5-1,6-1,7-1,8-1
NLT - **12,** 1-1,2-1,3-1,4-1,5-1,6-1,7-1,8-1,9-1,10-1,11-1,12-1
NRSV - **8,** 1-1,2-1,3-1,4-1,5-1,6-1,7-1,8-1
Conclusion: All versions read the same.

516. 1 Chronicles 24:12*# The **eleventh** to **Eliashib**, the twelfth to **Jakim**,
AV - **8,** 1-1,2-1,3-1,4-1,5-1,6-1,7-1,8-1
ESV - **8,** 1-1,2-1,3-1,4-1,5-1,6-1,7-1,8-1
HCSB - **8,** 1-1,2-1,3-1,4-1,5-1,6-1,7-1,8-1
NASV - **8,** 1-1,2-1,3-1,4-1,5-1,6-1,7-1,8-1
NCV - **8,** 1-1,2-1,3-1,4-1,5-1,6-1,7-1,8-1
NIV - **8,** 1-1,2-1,3-1,4-1,5-1,6-1,7-1,8-1
NKJV - **8,** 1-1,2-1,3-1,4-1,5-1,6-1,7-1,8-1
NLT - **12,** 1-1,2-1,3-1,4-1,5-1,6-1,7-1,8-1,9-1,10-1,11-1,12-1
NRSV - **8,** 1-1,2-1,3-1,4-1,5-1,6-1,7-1,8-1
Conclusion: All versions read the same.

517. 1 Chronicles 24:13*# The **thirteenth** to **Huppah**, the **fourteenth** to **Jeshebeab**,
AV - **8,** 1-1,2-1,3-1,4-1,5-1,6-1,7-1,8-1
ESV - **8,** 1-1,2-1,3-1,4-1,5-1,6-1,7-1,8-1
HCSB - **8,** 1-1,2-1,3-1,4-1,5-1,6-1,7-1,8-1
NASV - **8,** 1-1,2-1,3-1,4-1,5-1,6-1,7-1,8-1
NCV - **8,** 1-1,2-1,3-1,4-1,5-1,6-1,7-1,8-1
NIV - **8,** 1-1,2-1,3-1,4-1,5-1,6-1,7-1,8-1
NKJV - **8,** 1-1,2-1,3-1,4-1,5-1,6-1,7-1,8-1
NLT - **12,** 1-1,2-1,3-1,4-1,5-1,6-1,7-1,8-1,9-1,10-1,11-1,12-1
NRSV - **8,** 1-1,2-1,3-1,4-1,5-1,6-1,7-1,8-1
Conclusion: All versions read the same.

518. 1 Chronicles 24:14*# The **fifteenth** to **Bilgah**, the **sixteenth** to **Immer**,
AV - **8,** 1-1,2-1,3-1,4-1,5-1,6-1,7-1,8-1
ESV - **8,** 1-1,2-1,3-1,4-1,5-1,6-1,7-1,8-1
HCSB - **8,** 1-1,2-1,3-1,4-1,5-1,6-1,7-1,8-1
NASV - **8,** 1-1,2-1,3-1,4-1,5-1,6-1,7-1,8-1
NCV - **8,** 1-1,2-1,3-1,4-1,5-1,6-1,7-1,8-1
NIV - **8,** 1-1,2-1,3-1,4-1,5-1,6-1,7-1,8-1
NKJV - **8,** 1-1,2-1,3-1,4-1,5-1,6-1,7-1,8-1

NLT - **12,** 1-1,2-1,3-1,4-1,5-1,6-1,7-1,8-1,9-1,10-1,11-1,12-1
NRSV - **8,** 1-1,2-1,3-1,4-1,5-1,6-1,7-1,8-1
Conclusion: All versions read the same.

519. 1 Chronicles 24:15*# The **seventeenth** to **Hezir**, the **eighteenth** to **Aphses**,
AV - **8,** 1-1,2-1,3-1,4-1,5-1,6-1,7-1,8-1
ESV - **8,** 1-1,2-1,3-1,4-1,5-1,6-1,7-1,8-1
HCSB - **8,** 1-1,2-1,3-1,4-1,5-1,6-1,7-1,8-1
NASV - **8,** 1-1,2-1,3-1,4-1,5-1,6-1,7-1,8-1
NCV - **8,** 1-1,2-1,3-1,4-1,5-1,6-1,7-1,8-1
NIV - **8,** 1-1,2-1,3-1,4-1,5-1,6-1,7-1,8-1
NKJV - **8,** 1-1,2-1,3-1,4-1,5-1,6-1,7-1,8-1
NLT - **12,** 1-1,2-1,3-1,4-1,5-1,6-1,7-1,8-1,9-1,10-1,11-1,12-1
NRSV - **8,** 1-1,2-1,3-1,4-1,5-1,6-1,7-1,8-1
Conclusion: All versions read the same.

520. 1 Chronicles 24:16*# The **nineteenth** to **Pethahiah**, the **twentieth** to **Jehezekel**,
AV - **8,** 1-1,2-1,3-1,4-1,5-1,6-1,7-1,8-1
ESV - **8,** 1-1,2-1,3-1,4-1,5-1,6-1,7-1,8-1
HCSB - **8,** 1-1,2-1,3-1,4-1,5-1,6-1,7-1,8-1
NASV - **8,** 1-1,2-1,3-1,4-1,5-1,6-1,7-1,8-1
NCV - **8,** 1-1,2-1,3-1,4-1,5-1,6-1,7-1,8-1
NIV - **8,** 1-1,2-1,3-1,4-1,5-1,6-1,7-1,8-1
NKJV - **8,** 1-1,2-1,3-1,4-1,5-1,6-1,7-1,8-1
NLT - **12,** 1-1,2-1,3-1,4-1,5-1,6-1,7-1,8-1,9-1,10-1,11-1,12-1
NRSV - **8,** 1-1,2-1,3-1,4-1,5-1,6-1,7-1,8-1
Conclusion: All versions read the same.

521. 1 Chronicles 24:17*# The one and **twentieth** to **Jachin**, the two and **twentieth** to **Gamul**,
AV - **12,** 1-1,2-1,3-1,4-1,5-1,6-1,7-1,8-1,9-1,10-1,11-1,12-1
ESV - **10,** 1-1,2-1,3-1,4-1,5-1,6-1,7-1,8-1,9-1,10-1
HCSB - **10,** 1-1,2-1,3-1,4-1,5-1,6-1,7-1,8-1,9-1,10-1
NASV - **10,** 1-1,2-1,3-1,4-1,5-1,6-1,7-1,8-1,9-1,10-1
NCV - **10,** 1-1,2-1,3-1,4-1,5-1,6-1,7-1,8-1,9-1,10-1
NIV - **10,** 1-1,2-1,3-1,4-1,5-1,6-1,7-1,8-1,9-1,10-1
NKJV - **10,** 1-1,2-1,3-1,4-1,5-1,6-1,7-1,8-1,9-1,10-1
NLT - **14,** 1-1,2-1,3-1,4-1,5-1,6-1,7-1,8-1,9-1,10-1,11-1,12-1,13-1,14-1
NRSV - **10,** 1-1,2-1,3-1,4-1,5-1,6-1,7-1,8-1,9-1,10-1
Conclusion: All versions read the same.

522. 1 Chronicles 24:18*# The three and **twentieth** to **Delaiah**, the four and **twentieth** to **Maaziah**.
AV - **12,** 1-1,2-1,3-1,4-1,5-1,6-1,7-1,8-1,9-1,10-1,11-1,12-1
ESV - **10,** 1-1,2-1,3-1,4-1,5-1,6-1,7-1,8-1,9-1,10-1
HCSB -**11,** 1-1,2-1,3-1,4-1,5-1,6-1,7-1,8-1,9-1,10-1,11-1

NASV - **10,** 1-1,2-1,3-1,4-1,5-1,6-1,7-1,8-1,9-1,10-1
NCV - **10,** 1-1,2-1,3-1,4-1,5-1,6-1,7-1,8-1,9-1,10-1
NIV - **11,** 1-1,2-1,3-1,4-1,5-1,6-1,7-1,8-1,9-1,10-1,11-1
NKJV - **10,** 1-1,2-1,3-1,4-1,5-1,6-1,7-1,8-1,9-1,10-1
NLT - **14,** 1-1,2-1,3-1,4-1,5-1,6-1,7-1,8-1,9-1,10-1,11-1,12-1,13-1,14-1
NRSV - **10,** 1-1,2-1,3-1,4-1,5-1,6-1,7-1,8-1,9-1,10-1
Conclusion: All versions read the same.

523. 1 Chronicles 24:20* And the rest of the sons of **Levi** were these: Of the sons of **Amram**; **Shubael**: of the sons of **Shubael**; **Jehdeiah**.
AV - **22,** 1-1,2-1,3-1,4-1,5-1,6-1,7-1,8-1,9-1,10-1,11-1,12-1,13-1,14-1,15-1,16-1,17-1,18-1,19-1,20-1,21-1,22-1
ESV - **21,** 1-1,2-1,3-1,4-1,5-1,6-1,7-1,8-1,9-1,10-1,11-1,12-1,13-1,14-1,15-1,16-1,17-1,18-1,19-1,20-1,21-1
HCSB - **15,** 1-1,2-1,3-1,4-1,5-1,6-1,7-1,8-1,9-1,10-1,11-1,12-1,13-1,14-1,15-1
NASV - **21,** 1-1,2-1,3-1,4-1,5-1,6-1,7-1,8-1,9-1,10-1,11-1,12-1,13-1,14-1,15-1,16-1,17-1,18-1,19-1,20-1,21-1
NCV - **23,** 1-1,2-1,3-1,4-1,5-1,6-1,7-1,8-1,9-1,10-**3**,11-1,12-1,13-1,14-**3**,15-1,16-1,17-1,18-1,19-1,20-1,21-**3**,22-1,23-1
NIV - **21,** 1-1,2-1,3-1,4-1,5-1,6-1,7-**3**,8-1,9-1,10-1,11-1,12-1,13-1,14-1,15-1,16-1,17-1,18-1,19-1,20-1,21-1
NKJV - **20,** 1-1,2-1,3-1,4-1,5-1,6-1,7-1,8-1,9-1,10-1,11-1,12-1,13-1,14-1,15-1,16-1,17-1,18-1,19-1,20-1
NLT - **27,** 1-1,2-1,3-1,4-**2**,5-**3**,6-**2**,7-**3**,8-1,9-1,10-1,11-1,12-**3**,13-1,14-1,15-1,16-**2**,17-1,18-1,19-1,20-1,21-**3**,22-1,23-1,24-1,25-**2**,26-1,27-1
NRSV - **21,** 1-1,2-1,3-1,4-1,5-1,6-1,7-1,8-1,9-1,10-1,11-1,12-1,13-1,14-1,15-1,16-1,17-1,18-1,19-1,20-1,21-1
Conclusion: Only three modern versions made the verse more complex. The NLT is the most difficult to read.

524. 1 Chronicles 24:22* Of the **Izharites**; **Shelomoth**: of the sons of **Shelomoth**; **Jahath**.
AV - **10,** 1-1,2-1,3-1,4-1,5-1,6-1,7-1,8-1,9-1,10-1
ESV - **10,** 1-1,2-1,3-1,4-1,5-1,6-1,7-1,8-1,9-1,10-1
HCSB - **8,** 1-1,2-1,3-1,4-1,5-1,6-1,7-1,8-1
NASV - **10,** 1-1,2-1,3-1,4-1,5-1,6-1,7-1,8-1,9-1,10-1
NCV - **15,** 1-1,2-1,3-1,4-**3**,5-1,6-1,7-1,8-1,9-1,10-1,11-1,12-1,13-**3**,14-1,15-1
NIV - **10,** 1-1,2-1,3-1,4-1,5-1,6-1,7-1,8-1,9-1,10-1
NKJV - **10,** 1-1,2-1,3-1,4-1,5-1,6-1,7-1,8-1,9-1,10-1
NLT - **18,** 1-1,2-1,3-**3**,4-1,5-1,6-1,7-**2**,8-1,9-1,10-1,11-1,12-**3**,13-1,14-1,15-1,16-**2**,17-1,18-1
NRSV - **10,** 1-1,2-1,3-1,4-1,5-1,6-1,7-1,8-1,9-1,10-1
Conclusion: Only the NCV and the NLT made the verse more complex.

525. 1 Chronicles 24:23*# And the sons of **Hebron**; **Jeriah** the first, **Amariah** the **second**, **Jahaziel** the third, **Jekameam** the fourth.

AV - **17,** 1-1,2-1,3-1,4-1,5-1,6-1,7-1,8-1,9-1,10-1,11-1,12-1,13-1,14-1,15-1,16-1,17-1
ESV - **16,** 1-1,2-1,3-1,4-1,5-1,6-1,7-1,8-1,9-1,10-1,11-1,12-1,13-1,14-1,15-1,16-1
HCSB - **15,** 1-1,2-1,3-1,4-1,5-1,6-1,7-1,8-1,9-1,10-1,11-1,12-1,13-1,14-1,15-1
NASV - **16,** 1-1,2-1,3-1,4-1,5-1,6-1,7-1,8-1,9-1,10-1,11-1,12-1,13-1,14-1,15-1,16-1
NCV - **18,** 1-1,2-1,3-1,4-1,5-1,6-1,7-1,8-1,9-1,10-1,11-1,12-1,13-1,14-1,15-1,16-1,17-1,18-1
NIV - **17,** 1-1,2-1,3-1,4-1,5-1,6-1,7-1,8-1,9-1,10-1,11-1,12-1,13-1,14-1,15-1,16-1,17-1
NKJV - **19,** 1-1,2-1,3-1,4-1,5-1,6-1,7-1,8-1,9-1,10-1,11-1,12-1,13-1,14-1,15-1,16-1,17-1,18-1,19-1
NLT - **19,** 1-1,2-1,3-**3**,4-1,5-1,6-1,7-1,8-1,9-**2**,10-1,11-1,12-1,13-1,14-1,15-1,16-1,17-1,18-1,19-1
NRSV - **16,** 1-1,2-1,3-1,4-1,5-1,6-1,7-1,8-1,9-1,10-1,11-1,12-1,13-1,14-1,15-1,16-1
Conclusion: Only the NLT made the verse more complex.

526. 1 Chronicles 24:24* Of the sons of **Uzziel**; **Michah**: of the sons of **Michah**; **Shamir**.
AV - **12,** 1-1,2-1,3-1,4-1,5-1,6-1,7-1,8-1,9-1,10-1,11-1,12-1
ESV - **11,** 1-1,2-1,3-1,4-1,5-1,6-1,7-1,8-1,9-1,10-1,11-1
HCSB - **8,** 1-1,2-1,3-1,4-1,5-1,6-1,7-1,8-1
NASV - **12,** 1-1,2-1,3-1,4-1,5-1,6-1,7-1,8-1,9-1,10-1,11-1,12-1
NCV - **8,** 1-1,2-1,3-1,4-1,5-1,6-1,7-1,8-1
NIV - **11,** 1-1,2-1,3-1,4-1,5-1,6-1,7-1,8-1,9-1,10-1,11-1
NKJV - **12,** 1-1,2-1,3-1,4-1,5-1,6-1,7-1,8-1,9-1,10-1,11-1,12-1
NLT - **18,** 1-1,2-1,3-**3**,4-1,5-1,6-1,7-**2**,8-1,9-1,10-1,11-1,12-**3**,13-1,14-1,15-1,16-**2**,17-1,18-1
NRSV - **11,** 1-1,2-1,3-1,4-1,5-1,6-1,7-1,8-1,9-1,10-1,11-1
Conclusion: Only the NLT made the verse more complex.

527. 1 Chronicles 24:26* The sons of **Merari** were **Mahli** and **Mushi**: the sons of **Jaaziah**; **Beno**.
AV - **13,** 1-1,2-1,3-1,4-1,5-1,6-1,7-1,8-1,9-1,10-1,11-1,12-1,13-1
ESV - **12,** 1-1,2-1,3-1,4-1,5-1,6-1,7-1,8-1,9-1,10-1,11-1,12-1
HCSB - **12,** 1-1,2-1,3-1,4-1,5-1,6-1,7-1,8-1,9-1,10-1,11-1,12-1
NASV - **12,** 1-1,2-1,3-1,4-1,5-1,6-1,7-1,8-1,9-1,10-1,11-1,12-1
NCV - **11,** 1-1,2-**3**,3-1,4-1,5-1,6-1,7-1,8-1,9-1,10-1,11-1
NIV - **12,** 1-1,2-1,3-1,4-1,5-1,6-1,7-1,8-1,9-1,10-1,11-1,12-1
NKJV - **13,** 1-1,2-1,3-1,4-1,5-1,6-1,7-1,8-1,9-1,10-1,11-1,12-1,13-1
NLT - **20,** 1-1,2-1,3-**3**,4-1,5-1,6-1,7-**2**,8-1,9-1,10-1,11-1,12-1,13-1,14-**3**,15-1,16-1,17-1,18-**2**,19-1,20-1
NRSV - **12,** 1-1,2-1,3-1,4-1,5-1,6-1,7-1,8-1,9-1,10-1,11-1,12-1
Conclusion: Only the NCV and the NLT made the verse more complex.

528. 1 Chronicles 24:27* The sons of **Merari** by **Jaaziah**; **Beno**, and **Shoham**, and **Zaccur**, and **Ibri**.
AV - **13,** 1-1,2-1,3-1,4-1,5-1,6-1,7-1,8-1,9-1,10-1,11-1,12-1,13-1
ESV - **11,** 1-1,2-1,3-1,4-1,5-1,6-1,7-1,8-1,9-1,10-1,11-1
HCSB - **10,** 1-1,2-1,3-1,4-1,5-1,6-1,7-1,8-1,9-1,10-1
NASV - **12,** 1-1,2-1,3-1,4-1,5-1,6-1,7-1,8-1,9-1,10-1,11-1,12-1
NCV - **11,** 1-1,2-1,3-1,4-1,5-1,6-1,7-1,8-1,9-1,10-1,11-1
NIV - **11,** 1-1,2-1,3-1,4-1,5-1,6-1,7-1,8-1,9-1,10-1,11-1

NKJV - **12,** 1-1,2-1,3-1,4-1,5-1,6-1,7-1,8-1,9-1,10-1,11-1,12-1
NLT - 15, 1-1,2-1,3-**3,**4-1,5-1,6-1,7-1,8-1,9-**2,**10-1,11-1,12-1,13-1,14-1,15-1
NRSV - **11,** 1-1,2-1,3-1,4-1,5-1,6-1,7-1,8-1,9-1,10-1,11-1
Conclusion: Only the NLT made the verse more complex.

529. 1 Chronicles 24:28* Of **Mahli** came **Eleazar**, who had no sons.
AV - **8,** 1-1,2-1,3-1,4-1,5-1,6-1,7-1,8-1
ESV - **7,** 1-1,2-1,3-1,4-1,5-1,6-1,7-1
HCSB - **7,** 1-1,2-1,3-1,4-1,5-1,6-1,7-1
NASV - **7,** 1-1,2-1,3-1,4-1,5-1,6-1,7-1
NCV - 11, 1-1,2-1,3-1,4-1,5-1,6-1,7-1,8-1,9-1,10-**2,**11-1
NIV - **7,** 1-1,2-1,3-1,4-1,5-1,6-1,7-1
NKJV - **7,** 1-1,2-1,3-1,4-1,5-1,6-1,7-1
NLT - 14, 1-1,2-1,3-**3,**4-1,5-1,6-1,7-**2,**8-1,9-1,10-1,11-1,12-1,13-1,14-1
NRSV - **7,** 1-1,2-1,3-1,4-1,5-1,6-1,7-1
Conclusion: Only the NCV and the NLT made the verse more complex.

530. 1 Chronicles 25:4* Of **Heman**: the sons of **Heman**; **Bukkiah**, **Mattaniah**, **Uzziel**, **Shebuel**, and **Jerimoth**, **Hananiah**, **Hanani**, **Eliathah**, **Giddalti**, and **Romamtiezer**, **Joshbekashah**, **Mallothi**, **Hothir**, and **Mahazioth**:
AV - **23,** 1-1,2-1,3-1,4-1,5-1,6-1,7-1,8-1,9-1,10-1,11-1,12-1,13-1,14-1,15-1,16-1,17-1,18-1,19-1,20-1,21-1,22-1,23-1
ESV - **22,** 1-1,2-1,3-1,4-1,5-1,6-1,7-1,8-1,9-1,10-1,11-1,12-1,13-1,14-1,15-1,16-1,17-1,18-1,19-1,20-1,21-1,22-1
HCSB - **19,** 1-1,2-1,3-1,4-1,5-1,6-1,7-1,8-1,9-1,10-1,11-1,12-1,13-1,14-1,15-1,16-1,17-1,18-1,19-1
NASV - **23,** 1-1,2-1,3-1,4-1,5-1,6-1,7-1,8-1,9-1,10-1,11-1,12-1,13-1,14-1,15-1,16-1,17-1,18-1,19-1,20-1,21-1,22-1,23-1
NCV - **20,** 1-1,2-1,3-1,4-1,5-1,6-1,7-1,8-1,9-1,10-1,11-1,12-1,13-1,14-1,15-1,16-1,17-1,18-1,19-1,20-1
NIV - **23,** 1-1,2-1,3-1,4-1,5-1,6-1,7-1,8-1,9-1,10-1,11-1,12-1,13-1,14-1,15-1,16-1,17-1,18-1,19-1,20-1,21-1,22-1,23-1
NKJV - **21,** 1-1,2-1,3-1,4-1,5-1,6-1,7-1,8-1,9-1,10-1,11-1,12-1,13-1,14-1,15-1,16-1,17-1,18-1,19-1,20-1,21-1
NLT - **22,** 1-1,2-1,3-1,4-1,5-1,6-1,7-1,8-1,9-1,10-1,11-1,12-1,13-1,14-1,15-1,16-1,17-1,18-1,19-1,20-1,21-1,22-1
NRSV - **22,** 1-1,2-1,3-1,4-1,5-1,6-1,7-1,8-1,9-1,10-1,11-1,12-1,13-1,14-1,15-1,16-1,17-1,18-1,19-1,20-1,21-1,22-1
Conclusion: All versions read the same.

531. 1 Chronicles 26:3*# **Elam** the fifth, **Jehohanan** the sixth, **Elioenai** the **seventh**.
AV - **9,** 1-1,2-1,3-1,4-1,5-1,6-1,7-1,8-1,9-1
ESV - **9,** 1-1,2-1,3-1,4-1,5-1,6-1,7-1,8-1,9-1
HCSB - **10,** 1-1,2-1,3-1,4-1,5-1,6-1,7-1,8-1,9-1,10-1
NASV - **9,** 1-1,2-1,3-1,4-1,5-1,6-1,7-1,8-1,9-1

NCV - **10,** 1-1,2-1,3-1,4-1,5-1,6-1,7-1,8-1,9-1,10-1
NIV - **10,** 1-1,2-1,3-1,4-1,5-1,6-1,7-1,8-1,9-1,10-1
NKJV - **9,** 1-1,2-1,3-1,4-1,5-1,6-1,7-1,8-1,9-1
NLT - **10,** 1-1,2-1,3-1,4-1,5-1,6-1,7-1,8-1,9-1,10-1
NRSV - **9,** 1-1,2-1,3-1,4-1,5-1,6-1,7-1,8-1,9-1
Conclusion: All versions read the same.

532. 1 Chronicles 26:5*# **Ammiel** the sixth, **Issachar** the **seventh**, **Peulthai** the eighth: for God blessed him.
AV - **13,** 1-1,2-1,3-1,4-1,5-1,6-1,7-1,8-1,9-1,10-1,11-1,12-1,13-1
ESV - **13,** 1-1,2-1,3-1,4-1,5-1,6-1,7-1,8-1,9-1,10-1,11-1,12-1,13-1
HCSB - **14,** 1-1,2-1,3-1,4-1,5-1,6-1,7-1,8-1,9-1,10-1,11-1,12-1,13-1,14-1
NASV - 15, 1-1,2-1,3-1,4-1,5-1,6-1,7-1,8-1,9-1,10-1,11-1,12-1,13-**2**,14-1,15-1
NCV - 16, 1-1,2-1,3-1,4-1,5-1,6-1,7-1,8-1,9-1,10-1,11-1,12-1,13-1,14-1,15-1,16-**2**
NIV - **16,** 1-1,2-1,3-1,4-1,5-1,6-1,7-1,8-1,9-1,10-1,11-1,12-1,13-1,14-1,15-1,16-1
NKJV - **13,** 1-1,2-1,3-1,4-1,5-1,6-1,7-1,8-1,9-1,10-1,11-1,12-1,13-1
NLT - 16, 1-1,2-1,3-1,4-1,5-1,6-1,7-1,8-1,9-1,10-1,11-1,12-1,13-**2**,14-1,15-1,16-1
NRSV - **13,** 1-1,2-1,3-1,4-1,5-1,6-1,7-1,8-1,9-1,10-1,11-1,12-1,13-1
Conclusion: Only three modern versions made the verse more complex.

533. 1 Chronicles 26:23* Of the **Amramites**, and the **Izharites**, the **Hebronites**, and the **Uzzielites**:
AV - **11,** 1-1,2-1,3-1,4-1,5-1,6-1,7-1,8-1,9-1,10-1,11-1
ESV - **10,** 1-1,2-1,3-1,4-1,5-1,6-1,7-1,8-1,9-1,10-1
HCSB - **10,** 1-1,2-1,3-1,4-1,5-1,6-1,7-1,8-1,9-1,10-1
NASV - **11,** 1-1,2-1,3-1,4-1,5-1,6-1,7-1,8-1,9-1,10-1,11-1
NCV - 14, 1-**2**,2-**2**,3-1,4-**2**,5-1,6-1,7-**3**,8-1,9-1,10-1,11-1,12-1,13-1,14-1
NIV - **10,** 1-1,2-1,3-1,4-1,5-1,6-1,7-1,8-1,9-1,10-1
NKJV - **10,** 1-1,2-1,3-1,4-1,5-1,6-1,7-1,8-1,9-1,10-1
NLT - 12, 1-1,2-1,3-1,4-**2**,5-1,6-**3**,7-1,8-1,9-1,10-1,11-1,12-1
NRSV - **10,** 1-1,2-1,3-1,4-1,5-1,6-1,7-1,8-1,9-1,10-1
Conclusion: Only the NCV and the NLT made the verse more complex.

534. 1 Chronicles 27:17* Of the **Levites, Hashabiah** the son of **Kemuel**: of the **Aaronites, Zadok**:
AV - **12,** 1-1,2-1,3-1,4-1,5-1,6-1,7-1,8-1,9-1,10-1,11-1,12-1
ESV - **10,** 1-1,2-1,3-1,4-1,5-1,6-1,7-1,8-1,9-1,10-1
HCSB - **10,** 1-1,2-1,3-1,4-1,5-1,6-1,7-1,8-1,9-1,10-1
NASV - **10,** 1-1,2-1,3-1,4-1,5-1,6-1,7-1,8-1,9-1,10-1
NCV - 17, 1-1,2-1,3-1,4-1,5-1,6-**2**,7-1,8-1,9-1,10-1,11-1,12-1,13-**2**,14-1,15-**2**,16-1,17-1
NIV - 9, 1-**2**,2-1,3-1,4-1,5-1,6-1,7-**2**,8-1,9-1
NKJV - 12, 1-**2**,2-1,3-1,4-1,5-1,6-1,7-1,8-1,9-**2**,10-1,11-1,12-1
NLT - **9,** 1-1,2-1,3-1,4-1,5-1,6-1,7-1,8-1,9-1
NRSV - **9,** 1-1,2-1,3-1,4-1,5-1,6-1,7-1,8-1,9-1
Conclusion: Only three modern versions are more complex than the King James Bible.

535. 1 Chronicles 27:19* Of **Zebulun**, **Ishmaiah** the son of **Obadiah**: of **Naphtali**, **Jerimoth** the son of **Azriel**:
AV - **14,** 1-1,2-1,3-1,4-1,5-1,6-1,7-1,8-1,9-1,10-1,11-1,12-1,13-1,14-1
ESV - **14,** 1-1,2-1,3-1,4-1,5-1,6-1,7-1,8-1,9-1,10-1,11-1,12-1,13-1,14-1
HCSB - **12,** 1-1,2-1,3-1,4-1,5-1,6-1,7-1,8-1,9-1,10-1,11-1,12-1
NASV - **14,** 1-1,2-1,3-1,4-1,5-1,6-1,7-1,8-1,9-1,10-1,11-1,12-1,13-1,14-1
NCV - **20,** 1-1,2-1,3-1,4-1,5-1,6-**2,**7-1,8-1,9-1,10-1,11-1,12-1,13-1,14-1,15-1,16-**2,**17-1,18-1,19-1,20-1
NIV - **12,** 1-**2,**2-1,3-1,4-1,5-1,6-1,7-**2,**8-1,9-1,10-1,11-1,12-1
NKJV - **14,** 1-**2,**2-1,3-1,4-1,5-1,6-1,7-1,8-**2,**9-1,10-1,11-1,12-1,13-1,14-1
NLT - **10,** 1-1,2-1,3-1,4-1,5-1,6-1,7-1,8-1,9-1,10-1
NRSV - **12,** 1-1,2-1,3-1,4-1,5-1,6-1,7-1,8-1,9-1,10-1,11-1,12-1
Conclusion: Only three modern versions are more complex than the King James Bible.

536. 1 Chronicles 27:21* Of the half tribe of **Manasseh** in **Gilead**, **Iddo** the son of **Zechariah**: of **Benjamin**, **Jaasiel** the son of **Abner**:
AV - **20,** 1-1,2-1,3-1,4-1,5-1,6-1,7-1,8-1,9-1,10-1,11-1,12-1,13-1,14-1,15-1,16-1,17-1,18-1,19-1,20-1
ESV - **19,** 1-1,2-1,3-1,4-1,5-1,6-1,7-1,8-1,9-1,10-1,11-1,12-1,13-1,14-1,15-1,16-1,17-1,18-1,19-1
HCSB - **18,** 1-1,2-1,3-1,4-1,5-1,6-1,7-1,8-1,9-1,10-1,11-1,12-1,13-1,14-1,15-1,16-1,17-1,18-1
NASV - **19,** 1-1,2-1,3-1,4-1,5-1,6-1,7-1,8-1,9-1,10-1,11-1,12-1,13-1,14-1,15-1,16-1,17-1,18-1,19-1
NCV - **18,** 1-1,2-1,3-1,4-1,5-1,6-**2,**7-1,8-1,9-1,10-1,11-1,12-1,13-1,14-**2,**15-1,16-1,17-1,18-1
NIV - **17,** 1-**2,**2-1,3-1,4-1,5-1,6-1,7-1,8-1,9-1,10-1,11-1,12-**2,**13-1,14-1,15-1,16-1,17-1
NKJV - **19,** 1-**2**-1,3-1,4-1,5-1,6-1,7-1,8-1,9-1,10-1,11-1,12-1,13-**2,**14-1,15-1,16-1,17-1,18-1,19-1
NLT - **13,** 1-1,2-1,3-1,4-1,5-1,6-1,7-1,8-1,9-1,10-1,11-1,12-1,13-1
NRSV - **17,** 1-1,2-1,3-1,4-1,5-1,6-1,7-1,8-1,9-1,10-1,11-1,12-1,13-1,14-1,15-1,16-1,17-1
Conclusion: Only three modern versions are more complex than the King James Bible.

537. 2 Chronicles 8:17* Then went **Solomon** to **Eziongeber**, and to **Eloth**, at the sea side in the land of **Edom**.
AV - **17,** 1-1,2-1,3-1,4-1,5-1,6-1,7-1,8-1,9-1,10-1,11-1,12-1,13-1,14-1,15-1,16-1,17-1
ESV - **19,** 1-1,2-1,3-1,4-1,5-1,6-1,7-1,8-1,9-1,10-1,11-1,12-1,13-1,14-1,15-1,16-1,17-1,18-1,19-1
HCSB - 19, 1-1,2-1,3-1,4-1,5-1,6-1,7-1,8-1,9-1,10-1,11-1,12-1,13-1,14-**2,**15-1,16-1,17-1,18-1,19-1
NASV - 17, 1-1,2-1,3-1,4-1,5-1,6-1,7-1,8-1,9-1,10-1,11-1,12-**2,**13-1,14-1,15-1,16-1,17-1
NCV - **20,** 1-1,2-1,3-1,4-1,5-1,6-1,7-1,8-1,9-1,10-1,11-1,12-1,13-1,14-1,15-1,16-1,17-1,18-1,19-1,20-1
NIV - **13,** 1-1,2-1,3-1,4-1,5-1,6-1,7-1,8-1,9-1,10-1,11-1,12-1,13-1
NKJV - 16, 1-1,2-1,3-1,4-1,5-1,6-1,7-1,8-1,9-1,10-1,11-**2,**12-1,13-1,14-1,15-1,16-1
NLT - 21, 1-**2,**2-1,3-1,4-1,5-1,6-1,7-1,8-1,9-1,10-**2,**11-1,12-1,13-1,14-1,15-1,16-1,17-1,18-1,19-1,20-1,21-1
NRSV - **19,** 1-1,2-1,3-1,4-1,5-1,6-1,7-1,8-1,9-1,10-1,11-1,12-1,13-1,14-1,15-1,16-1,17-1,18-1,19-1
Conclusion: Four modern versions are more complex than the King James Bible.

538. 2 Chronicles 11:7* And **Bethzur**, and **Shoco**, and **Adullam**,
AV - **6,** 1-1,2-1,3-1,4-1,5-1,6-1
ESV - **3,** 1-1,2-1,3-1
HCSB - **3,** 1-1,2-1,3-1
NASV - **3,** 1-1,2-1,3-1
NCV - **3,** 1-1,2-1,3-1
NIV - **3,** 1-1,2-1,3-1
NKJV - **3,** 1-1,2-1,3-1
NLT - **3,** 1-1,2-1,3-1
NRSV - **3,** 1-1,2-1,3-1
Conclusion: All versions read the same.

539. 2 Chronicles 11:8* And Gath, and **Mareshah**, and **Ziph**,
AV - **6,** 1-1,2-1,3-1,4-1,5-1,6-1
ESV - **3,** 1-1,2-1,3-1
HCSB - **3,** 1-1,2-1,3-1
NASV - **3,** 1-1,2-1,3-1
NCV - **3,** 1-1,2-1,3-1
NIV - **3,** 1-1,2-1,3-1
NKJV - **3,** 1-1,2-1,3-1
NLT - **3,** 1-1,2-1,3-1
NRSV - **3,** 1-1,2-1,3-1
Conclusion: All versions read the same.

540. 2 Chronicles 11:9* And **Adoraim**, and **Lachish**, and **Azekah**,
AV - **6,** 1-1,2-1,3-1,4-1,5-1,6-1
ESV - **3,** 1-1,2-1,3-1
HCSB - **3,** 1-1,2-1,3-1
NASV - **3,** 1-1,2-1,3-1
NCV - **3,** 1-1,2-1,3-1
NIV - **3,** 1-1,2-1,3-1
NKJV - **3,** 1-1,2-1,3-1
NLT - **3,** 1-1,2-1,3-1
NRSV - **3,** 1-1,2-1,3-1
Conclusion: All versions read the same.

541. 2 Chronicles 14:2* And **Asa** did that which was good and right in the eyes of the LORD his God:
AV - **17,** 1-1,2-1,3-1,4-1,5-1,6-1,7-1,8-1,9-1,10-1,11-1,12-1,13-1,14-1,15-1,16-1,17-1
ESV - **16,** 1-1,2-1,3-1,4-1,5-1,6-1,7-1,8-1,9-1,10-1,11-1,12-1,13-1,14-1,15-1,16-1
HCSB - **15,** 1-1,2-1,3-1,4-1,5-1,6-1,7-1,8-1,9-1,10-1,11-1,12-1,13-1,14-1,15-1
NASV - **13,** 1-1,2-1,3-1,4-1,5-1,6-1,7-1,8-1,9-1,10-1,11-1,12-1,13-1
NCV - **12,** 1-1,2-1,3-1,4-1,5-1,6-1,7-1,8-1,9-1,10-1,11-1,12-1
NIV - **15,** 1-1,2-1,3-1,4-1,5-1,6-1,7-1,8-1,9-1,10-1,11-1,12-1,13-1,14-1,15-1

NKJV - **15,** 1-1,2-1,3-1,4-1,5-1,6-1,7-1,8-1,9-1,10-1,11-1,12-1,13-1,14-1,15-1
NLT - **15,** 1-1,2-1,3-1,4-1,5-**2**,6-1,7-1,8-1,9-1,10-1,11-1,12-1,13-1,14-1,15-1
NRSV - **15,** 1-1,2-1,3-1,4-1,5-1,6-1,7-1,8-1,9-1,10-1,11-1,12-1,13-1,14-1,15-1
Conclusion: The NLT is the most difficult to read.

542. 2 Chronicles 24:2* And **Joash** did that which was right in the sight of the LORD all the days of **Jehoiada** the priest.
AV - **20,** 1-1,2-1,3-1,4-1,5-1,6-1,7-1,8-1,9-1,10-1,11-1,12-1,13-1,14-1,15-1,16-1,17-1,18-1,19-1,20-1
ESV - **19,** 1-1,2-1,3-1,4-1,5-1,6-1,7-1,8-1,9-1,10-1,11-1,12-1,13-1,14-1,15-1,16-1,17-1,18-1,19-1
HCSB - **16,** 1-**2**,2-1,3-1,4-1,5-1,6-1,7-1,8-1,9-1,10-1,11-1,12-1,13-1,14-1,15-1,16-1
NASV - **18,** 1-1,2-1,3-1,4-1,5-1,6-1,7-1,8-1,9-1,10-1,11-1,12-1,13-1,14-1,15-1,16-1,17-1,18-1
NCV - **16,** 1-1,2-1,3-1,4-1,5-1,6-1,7-1,8-1,9-1,10-1,11-1,12-1,13-1,14-1,15-1,16-**2**
NIV - **18,** 1-1,2-1,3-1,4-1,5-1,6-1,7-1,8-1,9-1,10-1,11-1,12-1,13-1,14-1,15-1,16-1,17-1,18-1
NKJV - **18,** 1-1,2-1,3-1,4-1,5-1,6-1,7-1,8-1,9-1,10-1,11-1,12-1,13-1,14-1,15-1,16-1,17-1,18-1
NLT - **16,** 1-1,2-1,3-1,4-1,5-**2**,6-1,7-1,8-1,9-1,10-**2**,11-**2**,12-1,13-1,14-1,15-1,16-1
NRSV - **18,** 1-1,2-1,3-1,4-1,5-1,6-1,7-1,8-1,9-1,10-1,11-1,12-1,13-1,14-1,15-1,16-1,17-1,18-1
Conclusion: Only three modern versions are more complex than the King James Bible. The NLT is the most difficult to read.

543. 2 Chronicles 24:15*# But **Jehoiada** waxed old, and was full of days when he died; an **hundred** and **thirty** years old was he when he died.
AV - **23,** 1-1,2-1,3-1,4-1,5-1,6-1,7-1,8-1,9-1,10-1,11-1,12-1,13-1,14-1,15-1,16-1,17-1,18-1,19-1,20-1,21-1,22-1,23-1
ESV - **18,** 1-1,2-1,3-1,4-1,5-1,6-1,7-1,8-1,9-1,10-1,11-1,12-1,13-1,14-1,15-1,16-1,17-1,18-1
HCSB - **18,** 1-1,2-1,3-1,4-1,5-1,6-1,7-1,8-1,9-1,10-1,11-1,12-1,13-1,14-1,15-1,16-1,17-1,18-1
NASV - **21,** 1-1,2-1,3-1,4-1,5-1,6-1,7-1,8-1,9-1,10-1,11-1,12-1,13-1,14-1,15-1,16-1,17-1,18-1,19-1,20-1,21-1
NCV - **18,** 1-1,2-1,3-1,4-1,5-1,6-**2**,7-1,8-1,9-1,10-1,11-1,12-1,13-1,14-1,15-1,16-1,17-1,18-1
NIV - **19,** 1-1,2-1,3-1,4-1,5-1,6-1,7-1,8-1,9-1,10-1,11-1,12-1,13-1,14-1,15-1,16-1,17-1,18-1,19-1
NKJV - **23,** 1-1,2-1,3-1,4-1,5-1,6-1,7-1,8-1,9-1,10-1,11-1,12-1,13-1,14-1,15-1,16-1,17-1,18-1,19-1,20-1,21-1,22-1,23-1
NLT - **11,** 1-1,2-1,3-1,4-1,5-**2**,6-1,7-1,8-**3**,9-**2**,10-1,11-1
NRSV - **20,** 1-1,2-1,3-1,4-1,5-1,6-1,7-1,8-1,9-1,10-1,11-1,12-1,13-1,14-1,15-1,16-1,17-1,18-1,19-1,20-1
Conclusion: Only the NCV and NLT made the verse more complex. Amazingly the NLT reduced the number of words in the verse by more than half of those in the AV and still managed to be the most difficult to read, incorporating three multi-syllable words in the verse.

544. 2 Chronicles 27:3* He built the high gate of the house of the LORD, and on the wall of **Ophel** he built much.
AV - **20,** 1-1,2-1,3-1,4-1,5-1,6-1,7-1,8-1,9-1,10-1,11-1,12-1,13-1,14-1,15-1,16-1,17-1,18-1,19-1,20-1

ESV - **20,** 1-1,2-1,3-1,4-**2**,5-1,6-1,7-1,8-1,9-1,10-1,11-1,12-1,13-1,14-1,15-**2**,16-1,17-1,18-1,19-1,20-1

HCSB - **18,** 1-1,2-1,3-1,4-**2**,5-1,6-1,7-1,8-1,9-1,10-1,11-1,12-1,13-**4**,14-1,15-1,16-1,17-1,18-1

NASV - **19,** 1-1,2-1,3-1,4-**2**,5-1,6-1,7-1,8-1,9-1,10-1,11-1,12-1,13-1,14-1,15-**4**,16-1,17-1,18-1,19-1

NCV - **20,** 1-1,2-**2**,3-1,4-**2**,5-1,6-1,7-1,8-1,9-1,10-1,11-1,12-1,13-1,14-**2**,15-**2**,16-1,17-1,18-1,19-1,20-1

NIV - **23,** 1-1,2-**2**,3-1,4-**2**,5-1,6-1,7-1,8-1,9-1,10-1,11-1,12-1,13-1,14-**3**,15-1,16-1,17-1,18-1,19-1,20-1,21-1,22-1,23-1

NKJV - **20,** 1-1,2-1,3-1,4-**2**,5-1,6-1,7-1,8-1,9-1,10-1,11-1,12-1,13-1,14-1,15-**4**,16-1,17-1,18-1,19-1,20-1

NLT - **23,** 1-1,2-**2**,3-1,4-**2**,5-1,6-1,7-1,8-1,9-1,10-1,11-1,12-1,13-**2**,14-**3**,15-**3**,16-1,17-1,18-1,19-1,20-1,21-1,22-1,23-1

NRSV - **20,** 1-1,2-1,3-1,4-**2**,5-1,6-1,7-1,8-1,9-1,10-1,11-1,12-1,13-1,14-**3**,15-**2**,16-1,17-1,18-1,19-1,20-1

Conclusion: All eight modern versions are more complex than the King James Bible. The HCSB, NCV, NIV and NLT inserted "temple" for "house" but this was not counted against them since it would be accepted under other circumstances.

545. 2 Chronicles 29:13* And of the sons of **Elizaphan**; **Shimri**, and **Jeiel**: and of the sons of **Asaph**; **Zechariah**, and **Mattaniah**:

AV - **18,** 1-1,2-1,3-1,4-1,5-1,6-1,7-1,8-1,9-1,10-1,11-1,12-1,13-1,14-1,15-1,16-1,17-1,18-1

ESV - **18,** 1-1,2-1,3-1,4-1,5-1,6-1,7-1,8-1,9-1,10-1,11-1,12-1,13-1,14-1,15-1,16-1,17-1,18-1

HCSB - **12,** 1-1,2-1,3-1,4-1,5-1,6-1,7-1,8-1,9-1,10-1,11-1,12-1

NASV - **18,** 1-1,2-1,3-1,4-1,5-1,6-1,7-1,8-1,9-1,10-1,11-1,12-1,13-1,14-1,15-1,16-1,17-1,18-1

NCV - **16,** 1-1,2-1,3-**3**,4-1,5-1,6-1,7-1,8-1,9-1,10-1,11-**3**,12-1,13-1,14-1,15-1,16-1

NIV - **16,** 1-1,2-1,3-**3**,4-1,5-1,6-1,7-1,8-1,9-1,10-1,11-**3**,12-1,13-1,14-1,15-1,16-1

NKJV - **16,** 1-1,2-1,3-1,4-1,5-1,6-1,7-1,8-1,9-1,10-1,11-1,12-1,13-1,14-1,15-1,16-1

NLT - **16,** 1-1,2-1,3-**3**,4-1,5-1,6-1,7-1,8-1,9-1,10-1,11-**3**,12-1,13-1,14-1,15-1,16-1

NRSV - **18,** 1-1,2-1,3-1,4-1,5-1,6-1,7-1,8-1,9-1,10-1,11-1,12-1,13-1,14-1,15-1,16-1,17-1,18-1

Conclusion: Only three modern versions are more complex than the King James Bible.

546. 2 Chronicles 29:14* And of the sons of **Heman**; **Jehiel**, and **Shimei**: and of the sons of **Jeduthun**; **Shemaiah**, and **Uzziel**.

AV - **18,** 1-1,2-1,3-1,4-1,5-1,6-1,7-1,8-1,9-1,10-1,11-1,12-1,13-1,14-1,15-1,16-1,17-1,18-1

ESV - **18,** 1-1,2-1,3-1,4-1,5-1,6-1,7-1,8-1,9-1,10-1,11-1,12-1,13-1,14-1,15-1,16-1,17-1,18-1

HCSB - **12,** 1-1,2-1,3-1,4-1,5-1,6-1,7-1,8-1,9-1,10-1,11-1,12-1

NASV - **18,** 1-1,2-1,3-1,4-1,5-1,6-1,7-1,8-1,9-1,10-1,11-1,12-1,13-1,14-1,15-1,16-1,17-1,18-1

NCV - **16,** 1-1,2-1,3-**3**,4-1,5-1,6-1,7-1,8-1,9-1,10-1,11-**3**,12-1,13-1,14-1,15-1,16-1

NIV - **16,** 1-1,2-1,3-**3**,4-1,5-1,6-1,7-1,8-1,9-1,10-1,11-**3**,12-1,13-1,14-1,15-1,16-1

NKJV - **17,** 1-1,2-1,3-1,4-1,5-1,6-1,7-1,8-1,9-1,10-1,11-1,12-1,13-1,14-1,15-1,16-1,17-1

NLT - **16,** 1-1,2-1,3-**3**,4-1,5-1,6-1,7-1,8-1,9-1,10-1,11-**3**,12-1,13-1,14-1,15-1,16-1

NRSV - **18,** 1-1,2-1,3-1,4-1,5-1,6-1,7-1,8-1,9-1,10-1,11-1,12-1,13-1,14-1,15-1,16-1,17-1,18-1

Conclusion: Only three modern versions are more complex than the King James Bible.

547. 2 Chronicles 34:19 And it came to pass, when the king had heard the words of the law, that he rent his clothes.

AV - **20,** 1-1,2-1,3-1,4-1,5-1,6-1,7-1,8-1,9-1,10-1,11-1,12-1,13-1,14-1,15-1,16-1,17-1,18-1,19-1,20-1

ESV - **14,** 1-1,2-1,3-1,4-1,5-1,6-1,7-1,8-1,9-1,10-1,11-1,12-1,13-1,14-1

HCSB - **13,** 1-1,2-1,3-1,4-1,5-1,6-1,7-1,8-1,9-1,10-1,11-1,12-1,13-1

NASV - **13,** 1-1,2-1,3-1,4-1,5-1,6-1,7-1,8-1,9-1,10-1,11-1,12-1,13-1

NCV - **19,** 1-1,2-1,3-1,4-1,5-1,6-1,7-1,8-1,9-**2**,10-1,11-1,12-1,13-1,14-1,15-1,16-1,17-**2**,18-1,19-1

NIV - **13,** 1-1,2-1,3-1,4-1,5-1,6-1,7-1,8-1,9-1,10-1,11-1,12-1,13-1

NKJV - **17,** 1-1,2-1,3-**2**,4-1,5-1,6-1,7-1,8-1,9-1,10-1,11-1,12-1,13-1,14-1,15-1,16-1,17-1

NLT - **16,** 1-1,2-1,3-1,4-1,5-1,6-1,7-**2**,8-1,9-1,10-1,11-1,12-1,13-1,14-1,15-1,16-**2**

NRSV - **13,** 1-1,2-1,3-1,4-1,5-1,6-1,7-1,8-1,9-1,10-1,11-1,12-1,13-1

Conclusion: Only three modern versions are more complex than the King James Bible.

548. Ezra 2:22*# The men of **Netophah, fifty** and six.

AV - **7,** 1-1,2-1,3-1,4-1,5-1,6-1,7-1

ESV - **5,** 1-1,2-1,3-1,4-1,5-1

HCSB - **3,** 1-1,2-1,3-1

NASV - **5,** 1-1,2-1,3-1,4-1,5-1

NCV - **3,** 1-1,2-1,3-1

NIV - **3,** 1-1,2-1,3-1

NKJV - **6,** 1-1,2-1,3-1,4-1,5-1,6-1

NLT - **5,** 1-1,2-**2**,3-1,4-1,5-1

NRSV - **6,** 1-1,2-**2**,3-1,4-1,5-1,6-1

Conclusion: Only the NLT and the NRSV made the verse more complex.

549. Ezra 2:23*# The men of **Anathoth, an hundred twenty** and eight.

AV - **9,** 1-1,2-1,3-1,4-1,5-1,6-1,7-1,8-1,9-1

ESV - **5,** 1-1,2-1,3-1,4-1,5-1

HCSB - **3,** 1-1,2-1,3-1

NASV - **5,** 1-1,2-1,3-1,4-1,5-1

NCV - **3,** 1-1,2-1,3-1

NIV - **3,** 1-1,2-1,3-1

NKJV - **9,** 1-1,2-1,3-1,4-1,5-1,6-1,7-1,8-1,9-1

NLT - **5,** 1-1,2-**2**,3-1,4-1,5-1

NRSV - **6,** 1-1,2-1,3-1,4-1,5-1,6-1

Conclusion: Only the NLT made the verse more complex.

550. Ezra 2:27*# The men of **Michmas, an hundred twenty** and two.

AV - **9,** 1-1,2-1,3-1,4-1,5-1,6-1,7-1,8-1,9-1

ESV - **5,** 1-1,2-1,3-1,4-1,5-1

HCSB - **3,** 1-1,2-1,3-1

NASV - **5,** 1-1,2-1,3-1,4-1,5-1

NCV - **3,** 1-1,2-1,3-1

NIV - **3,** 1-1,2-1,3-1
NKJV - **9,** 1-1,2-1,3-1,4-1,5-1,6-1,7-1,8-1,9-1
NLT - **5,** 1-1,2-1,3-1,4-1,5-1
NRSV - **8,** 1-1,2-**2**,3-1,4-1,5-1,6-1,7-1,8-1
Conclusion: Only the NRSV made the verse more complex.

551. Ezra 2:28*# The men of **Bethel** and **Ai**, two **hundred twenty** and three.
AV - **11,** 1-1,2-1,3-1,4-1,5-1,6-1,7-1,8-1,9-1,10-1,11-1
ESV - **7,** 1-1,2-1,3-1,4-1,5-1,6-1,7-1
HCSB - **5,** 1-1,2-1,3-1,4-1,5-1
NASV - **7,** 1-1,2-1,3-1,4-1,5-1,6-1,7-1
NCV - **5,** 1-1,2-1,3-1,4-1,5-1
NIV - **5,** 1-1,2-1,3-1,4-1,5-1
NKJV - **11,** 1-1,2-1,3-1,4-1,5-1,6-1,7-1,8-1,9-1,10-1,11-1
NLT - **7,** 1-1,2-**2**,3-1,4-1,5-1,6-1,7-1
NRSV - **8,** 1-1,2-1,3-1,4-1,5-1,6-1,7-1,8-1
Conclusion: Only the NLT made the verse more complex.

552. Ezra 7:2* The son of **Shallum**, the son of **Zadok**, the son of **Ahitub**,
AV - **12,** 1-1,2-1,3-1,4-1,5-1,6-1,7-1,8-1,9-1,10-1,11-1,12-1
ESV - **9,** 1-1,2-1,3-1,4-1,5-1,6-1,7-1,8-1,9-1
HCSB - **6,** 1-1,2-1,3-1,4-1,5-1,6-1
NASV - **9,** 1-1,2-1,3-1,4-1,5-1,6-1,7-1,8-1,9-1
NCV - **12,** 1-1,2-1,3-1,4-1,5-1,6-1,7-1,8-1,9-1,10-1,11-1,12-1
NIV - **12,** 1-1,2-1,3-1,4-1,5-1,6-1,7-1,8-1,9-1,10-1,11-1,12-1
NKJV - **12,** 1-1,2-1,3-1,4-1,5-1,6-1,7-1,8-1,9-1,10-1,11-1,12-1
NLT - **9,** 1-1,2-1,3-1,4-1,5-1,6-1,7-1,8-1,9-1
NRSV - **9,** 1-1,2-1,3-1,4-1,5-1,6-1,7-1,8-1,9-1
Conclusion: All versions read the same.

553. Ezra 7:3* The son of **Amariah**, the son of **Azariah**, the son of **Meraioth**,
AV - **12,** 1-1,2-1,3-1,4-1,5-1,6-1,7-1,8-1,9-1,10-1,11-1,12-1
ESV - **9,** 1-1,2-1,3-1,4-1,5-1,6-1,7-1,8-1,9-1
HCSB - **6,** 1-1,2-1,3-1,4-1,5-1,6-1
NASV - **9,** 1-1,2-1,3-1,4-1,5-1,6-1,7-1,8-1,9-1
NCV - **12,** 1-1,2-1,3-1,4-1,5-1,6-1,7-1,8-1,9-1,10-1,11-1,12-1
NIV - **12,** 1-1,2-1,3-1,4-1,5-1,6-1,7-1,8-1,9-1,10-1,11-1,12-1
NKJV - **12,** 1-1,2-1,3-1,4-1,5-1,6-1,7-1,8-1,9-1,10-1,11-1,12-1
NLT - **9,** 1-1,2-1,3-1,4-1,5-1,6-1,7-1,8-1,9-1
NRSV - **9,** 1-1,2-1,3-1,4-1,5-1,6-1,7-1,8-1,9-1
Conclusion: All versions read the same.

554. Ezra 7:4* The son of **Zerahiah**, the son of **Uzzi**, the son of **Bukki**,
AV - **12,** 1-1,2-1,3-1,4-1,5-1,6-1,7-1,8-1,9-1,10-1,11-1,12-1

ESV - **9,** 1-1,2-1,3-1,4-1,5-1,6-1,7-1,8-1,9-1
HCSB - **6,** 1-1,2-1,3-1,4-1,5-1,6-1
NASV - **9,** 1-1,2-1,3-1,4-1,5-1,6-1,7-1,8-1,9-1
NCV - **12,** 1-1,2-1,3-1,4-1,5-1,6-1,7-1,8-1,9-1,10-1,11-1,12-1
NIV - **12,** 1-1,2-1,3-1,4-1,5-1,6-1,7-1,8-1,9-1,10-1,11-1,12-1
NKJV - **12,** 1-1,2-1,3-1,4-1,5-1,6-1,7-1,8-1,9-1,10-1,11-1,12-1
NLT - **9,** 1-1,2-1,3-1,4-1,5-1,6-1,7-1,8-1,9-1
NRSV - **9,** 1-1,2-1,3-1,4-1,5-1,6-1,7-1,8-1,9-1
Conclusion: All versions read the same.

555. Ezra 7:5* The son of **Abishua**, the son of **Phinehas**, the son of **Eleazar**, the son of **Aaron** the chief priest:
AV - **19,** 1-1,2-1,3-1,4-1,5-1,6-1,7-1,8-1,9-1,10-1,11-1,12-1,13-1,14-1,15-1,16-1,17-1,18-1,19-1
ESV - **15,** 1-1,2-1,3-1,4-1,5-1,6-1,7-1,8-1,9-1,10-1,11-1,12-1,13-1,14-1,15-1
HCSB - **11,** 1-1,2-1,3-1,4-1,5-1,6-1,7-1,8-1,9-1,10-1,11-1
NASV - **15,** 1-1,2-1,3-1,4-1,5-1,6-1,7-1,8-1,9-1,10-1,11-1,12-1,13-1,14-1,15-1
NCV - **15,** 1-1,2-1,3-1,4-1,5-1,6-1,7-1,8-1,9-1,10-1,11-1,12-1,13-1,14-1,15-1
NIV - **19,** 1-1,2-1,3-1,4-1,5-1,6-1,7-1,8-1,9-1,10-1,11-1,12-1,13-1,14-1,15-1,16-1,17-1,18-1,19-1
NKJV - **19,** 1-1,2-1,3-1,4-1,5-1,6-1,7-1,8-1,9-1,10-1,11-1,12-1,13-1,14-1,15-1,16-1,17-1,18-1,19-1
NLT - **15,** 1-1,2-1,3-1,4-1,5-1,6-1,7-1,8-1,9-1,10-1,11-1,12-1,13-1,14-1,15-1
NRSV - **15,** 1-1,2-1,3-1,4-1,5-1,6-1,7-1,8-1,9-1,10-1,11-1,12-1,13-1,14-1,15-1
Conclusion: All versions read the same.

556. Ezra 7:8*# And he came to **Jerusalem** in the fifth month, which was in the **seventh** year of the king.
AV - **18,** 1-1,2-1,3-1,4-1,5-1,6-1,7-1,8-1,9-1,10-1,11-1,12-1,13-1,14-1,15-1,16-1,17-1,18-1
ESV - **18,** 1-1,2-1,3-1,4-1,5-1,6-1,7-1,8-1,9-1,10-1,11-1,12-1,13-1,14-1,15-1,16-1,17-1,18-1
HCSB - **15,** 1-1,2-1,3-1,4-1,5-1,6-1,7-1,8-1,9-**2**,10-1,11-1,12-1,13-1,14-1,15-1
NASV - **17,** 1-1,2-1,3-1,4-1,5-1,6-1,7-1,8-1,9-1,10-1,11-1,12-1,13-1,14-1,15-1,16-1,17-1
NCV - **14,** 1-1,2-**2**,3-1,4-1,5-1,6-1,7-1,8-1,9-1,10-1,11-1,12-1,13-1,14-1
NIV - **15,** 1-1,2-**2**,3-1,4-1,5-1,6-1,7-1,8-1,9-1,10-1,11-1,12-1,13-1,14-1,15-1
NKJV - **18,** 1-1,2-1,3-1,4-1,5-1,6-1,7-1,8-1,9-1,10-1,11-1,12-1,13-1,14-1,15-1,16-1,17-1,18-1
NLT - **9,** 1-1,2-**2**,3-1,4-1,5-1,6-1,7-1,8-1,9-1
NRSV - **17,** 1-1,2-1,3-1,4-1,5-1,6-1,7-1,8-1,9-1,10-1,11-1,12-1,13-1,14-1,15-1,16-1,17-1
Conclusion: Four modern versions are more complex than the King James Bible.

557. Ezra 8:2* Of the sons of **Phinehas**; **Gershom**: of the sons of **Ithamar**; **Daniel**: of the sons of **David**; **Hattush**:
AV - **18,** 1-1,2-1,3-1,4-1,5-1,6-1,7-1,8-1,9-1,10-1,11-1,12-1,13-1,14-1,15-1,16-1,17-1,18-1
ESV - **18,** 1-1,2-1,3-1,4-1,5-1,6-1,7-1,8-1,9-1,10-1,11-1,12-1,13-1,14-1,15-1,16-1,17-1,18-1
HCSB - **12,** 1-1,2-1,3-1,4-**3**,5-1,6-1,7-1,8-**3**,9-1,10-1,11-1,12-**3**
NASV - **18,** 1-1,2-1,3-1,4-1,5-1,6-1,7-1,8-1,9-1,10-1,11-1,12-1,13-1,14-1,15-1,16-1,17-1,18-1
NCV - **18,** 1-1,2-1,3-**3**,4-1,5-1,6-1,7-1,8-1,9-**3**,10-1,11-1,12-1,13-1,14-1,15-**3**,16-1,17-1,18-1
NIV - **18,** 1-1,2-1,3-**3**,4-1,5-1,6-1,7-1,8-1,9-**3**,10-1,11-1,12-1,13-1,14-1,15-**3**,16-1,17-1,18-1

NKJV - **18,** 1-1,2-1,3-1,4-1,5-1,6-1,7-1,8-1,9-1,10-1,11-1,12-1,13-1,14-1,15-1,16-1,17-1,18-1
NLT - **18,** 1-1,2-1,3-1,4-1,5-1,6-1,7-1,8-1,9-1,10-1,11-1,12-1,13-1,14-1,15-1,16-1,17-1,18-1
NRSV - 12, 1-1,2-1,3-**3,**4-1,5-1,6-1,7-1,8-1,9-1,10-1,11-1,12-1
Conclusion: Four modern versions are more complex than the King James Bible.

558. Ezra 8:4*# Of the sons of **Pahathmoab**; **Elihoenai** the son of **Zerahiah**, and with him two **hundred** males.
AV - **16,** 1-1,2-1,3-1,4-1,5-1,6-1,7-1,8-1,9-1,10-1,11-1,12-1,13-1,14-1,15-1,16-1
ESV - **16,** 1-1,2-1,3-1,4-1,5-1,6-1,7-1,8-1,9-1,10-1,11-1,12-1,13-1,14-1,15-1,16-1
HCSB - 13, 1-1,2-1,3-1,4-1,5-1,6-1,7-1,8-**3,**9-1,10-1,11-1,12-1,13-1
NASV - **16,** 1-1,2-1,3-1,4-1,5-1,6-1,7-1,8-1,9-1,10-1,11-1,12-1,13-1,14-1,15-1,16-1
NCV - 14, 1-1,2-1,3-**3,**4-1,5-1,6-1,7-1,8-1,9-1,10-1,11-1,12-1,13-1,14-1
NIV - 15, 1-1,2-1,3-**3,**4-1,5-1,6-1,7-1,8-1,9-1,10-1,11-1,12-1,13-1,14-1,15-1
NKJV - **17,** 1-1,2-1,3-1,4-1,5-1,6-1,7-1,8-1,9-1,10-1,11-1,12-1,13-1,14-1,15-1,16-1,17-1
NLT - 14, 1-1,2-1,3-**3,**4-1,5-1,6-1,7-1,8-1,9-1,10-1,11-1,12-1,13-**2,**14-1
NRSV - 16, 1-1,2-1,3-**3,**4-1,5-1,6-1,7-1,8-1,9-1,10-1,11-1,12-1,13-1,14-1,15-1,16-1
Conclusion: Five modern versions are more complex than the King James Bible.

559. Ezra 8:5*# Of the sons of **Shechaniah**; the son of **Jahaziel**, and with him three **hundred** males.
AV - **15,** 1-1,2-1,3-1,4-1,5-1,6-1,7-1,8-1,9-1,10-1,11-1,12-1,13-1,14-1,15-1
ESV - **15,** 1-1,2-1,3-1,4-1,5-1,6-1,7-1,8-1,9-1,10-1,11-1,12-1,13-1,14-1,15-1
HCSB - 12, 1-1,2-1,3-1,4-1,5-1,6-1,7-**3,**8-1,9-1,10-1,11-1,12-1
NASV - **15,** 1-1,2-1,3-1,4-1,5-1,6-1,7-1,8-1,9-1,10-1,11-1,12-1,13-1,14-1,15-1
NCV - 13, 1-1,2-1,3-**3,**4-1,5-1,6-1,7-1,8-1,9-1,10-1,11-1,12-1,13-1
NIV - 14, 1-1,2-1,3-**3,**4-1,5-1,6-1,7-1,8-1,9-1,10-1,11-1,12-1,13-1,14-1
NKJV - **13,** 1-1,2-1,3-1,4-1,5-1,6-1,7-1,8-1,9-1,10-1,11-1,12-1,13-1
NLT - 13, 1-1,2-1,3-**3,**4-1,5-1,6-1,7-1,8-1,9-1,10-1,11-1,12-**2,**13-1
NRSV - 15, 1-1,2-1,3-**3,**4-1,5-1,6-1,7-1,8-1,9-1,10-1,11-1,12-1,13-1,14-1,15-1
Conclusion: Five modern versions are more complex than the King James Bible.

560. Ezra 8:7*# And of the sons of **Elam**; **Jeshaiah** the son of **Athaliah**, and with him **seventy** males.
AV - **16,** 1-1,2-1,3-1,4-1,5-1,6-1,7-1,8-1,9-1,10-1,11-1,12-1,13-1,14-1,15-1,16-1
ESV - **15,** 1-1,2-1,3-1,4-1,5-1,6-1,7-1,8-1,9-1,10-1,11-1,12-1,13-1,14-1,15-1
HCSB - 12, 1-1,2-1,3-1,4-1,5-1,6-1,7-**3,**8-1,9-1,10-1,11-1,12-1
NASV - **16,** 1-1,2-1,3-1,4-1,5-1,6-1,7-1,8-1,9-1,10-1,11-1,12-1,13-1,14-1,15-1,16-1
NCV - 12, 1-1,2-1,3-**3,**4-1,5-1,6-1,7-1,8-1,9-1,10-1,11-1,12-1
NIV - 14, 1-1,2-1,3-**3,**4-1,5-1,6-1,7-1,8-1,9-1,10-1,11-1,12-1,13-1,14-1
NKJV - **15,** 1-1,2-1,3-1,4-1,5-1,6-1,7-1,8-1,9-1,10-1,11-1,12-1,13-1,14-1,15-1
NLT - 13, 1-1,2-1,3-**3,**4-1,5-1,6-1,7-1,8-1,9-1,10-1,11-1,12-**2,**13-1
NRSV - 14, 1-1,2-1,3-**3,**4-1,5-1,6-1,7-1,8-1,9-1,10-1,11-1,12-1,13-1,14-1
Conclusion: Five modern versions are more complex than the King James Bible.

561. Ezra 8:8*# And of the sons of **Shephatiah**; **Zebadiah** the son of **Michael**, and with him **fourscore** males.

AV - **16,** 1-1,2-1,3-1,4-1,5-1,6-1,7-1,8-1,9-1,10-1,11-1,12-1,13-1,14-1,15-1,16-1
ESV - **15,** 1-1,2-1,3-1,4-1,5-1,6-1,7-1,8-1,9-1,10-1,11-1,12-1,13-1,14-1,15-1
HCSB - 12, 1-1,2-1,3-1,4-1,5-1,6-1,7-**3**,8-1,9-1,10-1,11-1,12-1
NASV - **16,** 1-1,2-1,3-1,4-1,5-1,6-1,7-1,8-1,9-1,10-1,11-1,12-1,13-1,14-1,15-1,16-1
NCV - 12, 1-1,2-1,3-**3**,4-1,5-1,6-1,7-1,8-1,9-1,10-1,11-1,12-1
NIV - 14, 1-1,2-1,3-**3**,4-1,5-1,6-1,7-1,8-1,9-1,10-1,11-1,12-1,13-1,14-1
NKJV - **15,** 1-1,2-1,3-1,4-1,5-1,6-1,7-1,8-1,9-1,10-1,11-1,12-1,13-1,14-1,15-1
NLT - 13, 1-1,2-1,3-**3**,4-1,5-1,6-1,7-1,8-1,9-1,10-1,11-1,12-**2**,13-1
NRSV - 14, 1-1,2-1,3-**3**,4-1,5-1,6-1,7-1,8-1,9-1,10-1,11-1,12-1,13-1,14-1
Conclusion: Five modern versions are more complex than the King James Bible.

562. Ezra 8:9*# Of the sons of **Joab**; **Obadiah** the son of **Jehiel**, and with him two **hundred** and **eighteen** males.

AV - **18,** 1-1,2-1,3-1,4-1,5-1,6-1,7-1,8-1,9-1,10-1,11-1,12-1,13-1,14-1,15-1,16-1,17-1,18-1
ESV - **15,** 1-1,2-1,3-1,4-1,5-1,6-1,7-1,8-1,9-1,10-1,11-1,12-1,13-1,14-1,15-1
HCSB - 12, 1-1,2-1,3-1,4-1,5-1,6-1,7-**3**,8-1,9-1,10-1,11-1,12-1
NASV - **15,** 1-1,2-1,3-1,4-1,5-1,6-1,7-1,8-1,9-1,10-1,11-1,12-1,13-1,14-1,15-1
NCV - 14, 1-1,2-1,3-**3**,4-1,5-1,6-1,7-1,8-1,9-1,10-1,11-1,12-1,13-1,14-1
NIV - 14, 1-1,2-1,3-**3**,4-1,5-1,6-1,7-1,8-1,9-1,10-1,11-1,12-1,13-1,14-1
NKJV - **18,** 1-1,2-1,3-1,4-1,5-1,6-1,7-1,8-1,9-1,10-1,11-1,12-1,13-1,14-1,15-1,16-1,17-1,18-1
NLT - 13, 1-1,2-1,3-**3**,4-1,5-1,6-1,7-1,8-1,9-1,10-1,11-1,12-**2**,13-1
NRSV - 16, 1-1,2-1,3-**3**,4-1,5-1,6-1,7-1,8-1,9-1,10-1,11-1,12-1,13-1,14-1,15-1,16-1
Conclusion: Five modern versions are more complex than the King James Bible.

563. Ezra 8:10*# And of the sons of **Shelomith**; the son of **Josiphiah**, and with him an **hundred** and **threescore** males.

AV - **18,** 1-1,2-1,3-1,4-1,5-1,6-1,7-1,8-1,9-1,10-1,11-1,12-1,13-1,14-1,15-1,16-1,17-1,18-1
ESV - **15,** 1-1,2-1,3-1,4-1,5-1,6-1,7-1,8-1,9-1,10-1,11-1,12-1,13-1,14-1,15-1
HCSB - 12, 1-1,2-1,3-1,4-1,5-1,6-1,7-**3**,8-1,9-1,10-1,11-1,12-1
NASV - **16,** 1-1,2-1,3-1,4-1,5-1,6-1,7-1,8-1,9-1,10-1,11-1,12-1,13-1,14-1,15-1,16-1
NCV - 14, 1-1,2-1,3-**3**,4-1,5-1,6-1,7-1,8-1,9-1,10-1,11-1,12-1,13-1,14-1
NIV - 14, 1-1,2-1,3-**3**,4-1,5-1,6-1,7-1,8-1,9-1,10-1,11-1,12-1,13-1,14-1
NKJV - **15,** 1-1,2-1,3-1,4-1,5-1,6-1,7-1,8-1,9-1,10-1,11-1,12-1,13-1,14-1,15-1
NLT - 13, 1-1,2-1,3-**3**,4-1,5-1,6-1,7-1,8-1,9-1,10-1,11-1,12-**2**,13-1
NRSV - 16, 1-1,2-1,3-**3**,4-1,5-1,6-1,7-1,8-1,9-1,10-1,11-1,12-1,13-1,14-1,15-1,16-1
Conclusion: Five modern versions are more complex than the King James Bible.

564. Ezra 8:11*# And of the sons of **Bebai**; **Zechariah** the son of **Bebai**, and with him **twenty** and eight males.

AV - **18,** 1-1,2-1,3-1,4-1,5-1,6-1,7-1,8-1,9-1,10-1,11-1,12-1,13-1,14-1,15-1,16-1,17-1,18-1
ESV - **15,** 1-1,2-1,3-1,4-1,5-1,6-1,7-1,8-1,9-1,10-1,11-1,12-1,13-1,14-1,15-1
HCSB - 12, 1-1,2-1,3-1,4-1,5-1,6-1,7-**3**,8-1,9-1,10-1,11-1,12-1

NASV - **16,** 1-1,2-1,3-1,4-1,5-1,6-1,7-1,8-1,9-1,10-1,11-1,12-1,13-1,14-1,15-1,16-1
NCV - 13, 1-1,2-1,3-**3**,4-1,5-1,6-1,7-1,8-1,9-1,10-1,11-1,12-1,13-1
NIV - 14, 1-1,2-1,3-**3**,4-1,5-1,6-1,7-1,8-1,9-1,10-1,11-1,12-1,13-1,14-1
NKJV - **16,** 1-1,2-1,3-1,4-1,5-1,6-1,7-1,8-1,9-1,10-1,11-1,12-1,13-1,14-1,15-1,16-1
NLT - 13, 1-1,2-1,3-**3**,4-1,5-1,6-1,7-1,8-1,9-1,10-1,11-1,12-**2**,13-1
NRSV - 15, 1-1,2-1,3-**3**,4-1,5-1,6-1,7-1,8-1,9-1,10-1,11-1,12-1,13-1,14-1,15-1
Conclusion: Five modern versions are more complex than the King James Bible.

565. Ezra 8:12*# And of the sons of **Azgad**; **Johanan** the son of **Hakkatan**, and with him an **hundred** and ten males.
AV - **19,** 1-1,2-1,3-1,4-1,5-1,6-1,7-1,8-1,9-1,10-1,11-1,12-1,13-1,14-1,15-1,16-1,17-1,18-1,19-1
ESV - **15,** 1-1,2-1,3-1,4-1,5-1,6-1,7-1,8-1,9-1,10-1,11-1,12-1,13-1,14-1,15-1
HCSB - 12, 1-1,2-1,3-1,4-1,5-1,6-1,7-**3**,8-1,9-1,10-1,11-1,12-1
NASV - **16,** 1-1,2-1,3-1,4-1,5-1,6-1,7-1,8-1,9-1,10-1,11-1,12-1,13-1,14-1,15-1,16-1
NCV - 14, 1-1,2-1,3-**3**,4-1,5-1,6-1,7-1,8-1,9-1,10-1,11-1,12-1,13-1,14-1
NIV - 14, 1-1,2-1,3-**3**,4-1,5-1,6-1,7-1,8-1,9-1,10-1,11-1,12-1,13-1,14-1
NKJV - **18,** 1-1,2-1,3-1,4-1,5-1,6-1,7-1,8-1,9-1,10-1,11-1,12-1,13-1,14-1,15-1,16-1,17-1,18-1
NLT - 13, 1-1,2-1,3-**3**,4-1,5-1,6-1,7-1,8-1,9-1,10-1,11-1,12-**2**,13-1
NRSV - 16, 1-1,2-1,3-**3**,4-1,5-1,6-1,7-1,8-1,9-1,10-1,11-1,12-1,13-1,14-1,15-1,16-1
Conclusion: Five modern versions are more complex than the King James Bible.

566. Ezra 8:13*# And of the last sons of **Adonikam**, whose names are these, **Eliphelet**, **Jeiel**, and **Shemaiah**, and with them **threescore** males.
AV - **20,** 1-1,2-1,3-1,4-1,5-1,6-1,7-1,8-1,9-1,10-1,11-1,12-1,13-1,14-1,15-1,16-1,17-1,18-1,19-1,20-1
ESV - 21, 1-1,2-1,3-1,4-1,5-1,6-1,7-1,8-1,9-**2**,10-1,11-1,12-**2**,13-1,14-1,15-1,16-1,17-1,18-1,19-1,20-1,21-1
HCSB - 21, 1-1,2-1,3-1,4-1,5-1,6-1,7-1,8-**3**,9-1,10-1,11-1,12-1,13-1,14-1,15-1,16-1,17-1,18-1,19-1,20-1,21-1
NASV - 22, 1-1,2-1,3-1,4-1,5-1,6-1,7-1,8-1,9-1,10-1,11-**2**,12-1,13-1,14-1,15-1,16-1,17-1,18-1,19-1,20-1,21-1,22-1
NCV - 17, 1-1,2-1,3-**3**,4-1,5-1,6-1,7-1,8-1,9-1,10-1,11-1,12-1,13-1,14-1,15-1,16-1,17-1
NIV - 20, 1-1,2-1,3-**3**,4-1,5-1,6-1,7-1,8-1,9-1,10-1,11-1,12-1,13-1,14-1,15-1,16-1,17-1,18-1,19-1,20-1
NKJV - **19,** 1-1,2-1,3-1,4-1,5-1,6-1,7-1,8-1,9-1,10-1,11-1,12-1,13-1,14-1,15-1,16-1,17-1,18-1,19-1
NLT - 15, 1-1,2-1,3-**3**,4-1,5-1,6-1,7-1,8-**2**,9-1,10-1,11-1,12-1,13-1,14-**2**,15-1
NRSV - 21, 1-1,2-1,3-**3**,4-1,5-1,6-1,7-1,8-1,9-**2**,10-1,11-1,12-**2**,13-1,14-1,15-1,16-1,17-1,18-1,19-1,20-1,21-1
Conclusion: Seven modern versions are more complex than the King James Bible.

567. Ezra 10:20 * And of the sons of **Immer**; **Hanani**, and **Zebadiah**.
AV - **9,** 1-1,2-1,3-1,4-1,5-1,6-1,7-1,8-1,9-1
ESV - **8,** 1-1,2-1,3-1,4-1,5-1,6-1,7-1,8-1
HCSB - 6, 1-1,2-1,3-1,4-1,5-1,6-**3**

NASV - **10,** 1-1,2-1,3-1,4-1,5-1,6-1,7-1,8-1,9-1,10-1
NCV - **8,** 1-1,2-1,3-**3**,4-1,5-1,6-1,7-1,8-1
NIV - **8,** 1-1,2-1,3-**3**,4-1,5-1,6-1,7-1,8-1
NKJV - **9,** 1-**2**,2-1,3-1,4-1,5-1,6-1,7-1,8-1,9-1
NLT - **8,** 1-1,2-1,3-**3**,4-1,5-1,6-1,7-1,8-1
NRSV - **8,** 1-1,2-1,3-**3**,4-1,5-1,6-1,7-1,8-1
Conclusion: Six modern versions are more complex than the King James Bible.

568. Ezra 10:21* And of the sons of **Harim**; **Maaseiah**, and **Elijah**, and **Shemaiah**, and **Jehiel**, and **Uzziah**.
AV - **15,** 1-1,2-1,3-1,4-1,5-1,6-1,7-1,8-1,9-1,10-1,11-1,12-1,13-1,14-1,15-1
ESV - **11,** 1-1,2-1,3-1,4-1,5-1,6-1,7-1,8-1,9-1,10-1,11-1
HCSB - **9,** 1-1,2-1,3-1,4-1,5-1,6-1,7-1,8-1,9-**3**
NASV - **12,** 1-1,2-1,3-1,4-1,5-1,6-1,7-1,8-1,9-1,10-1,11-1,12-1
NCV - **11,** 1-1,2-1,3-**3**,4-1,5-1,6-1,7-1,8-1,9-1,10-1,11-1
NIV - **11,** 1-1,2-1,3-**3**,4-1,5-1,6-1,7-1,8-1,9-1,10-1,11-1
NKJV - **11,** 1-1,2-1,3-1,4-1,5-1,6-1,7-1,8-1,9-1,10-1,11-1
NLT - **11,** 1-1,2-1,3-**3**,4-1,5-1,6-1,7-1,8-1,9-1,10-1,11-1
NRSV - **11,** 1-1,2-1,3-**3**,4-1,5-1,6-1,7-1,8-1,9-1,10-1,11-1
Conclusion: Five modern versions are more complex than the King James Bible.

569. Ezra 10:22* And of the sons of **Pashur**; **Elioenai, Maaseiah, Ishmael, Nethaneel, Jozabad,** and **Elasah**.
AV - **13,** 1-1,2-1,3-1,4-1,5-1,6-1,7-1,8-1,9-1,10-1,11-1,12-1,13-1
ESV - **12,** 1-1,2-1,3-1,4-1,5-1,6-1,7-1,8-1,9-1,10-1,11-1,12-1
HCSB - **10,** 1-1,2-1,3-1,4-1,5-1,6-1,7-1,8-1,9-1,10-**3**
NASV - **13,** 1-1,2-1,3-1,4-1,5-1,6-1,7-1,8-1,9-1,10-1,11-1,12-1,13-1
NCV - **12,** 1-1,2-1,3-**3**,4-1,5-1,6-1,7-1,8-1,9-1,10-1,11-1,12-1
NIV - **12,** 1-1,2-1,3-**3**,4-1,5-1,6-1,7-1,8-1,9-1,10-1,11-1,12-1
NKJV - **12,** 1-1,2-1,3-1,4-1,5-1,6-1,7-1,8-1,9-1,10-1,11-1,12-1
NLT - **12,** 1-1,2-1,3-**3**,4-1,5-1,6-1,7-1,8-1,9-1,10-1,11-1,12-1
NRSV - **12,** 1-1,2-1,3-**3**,4-1,5-1,6-1,7-1,8-1,9-1,10-1,11-1,12-1
Conclusion: Five modern versions are more complex than the King James Bible.

570. Ezra 10:26* And of the sons of **Elam**; **Mattaniah, Zechariah,** and **Jehiel,** and **Abdi,** and **Jeremoth,** and **Eliah**.
AV - **16,** 1-1,2-1,3-1,4-1,5-1,6-1,7-1,8-1,9-1,10-1,11-1,12-1,13-1,14-1,15-1,16-1
ESV - **12,** 1-1,2-1,3-1,4-1,5-1,6-1,7-1,8-1,9-1,10-1,11-1,12-1
HCSB - **9,** 1-1,2-**3**,3-1,4-1,5-1,6-1,7-1,8-1,9-1
NASV - **13,** 1-1,2-1,3-1,4-1,5-1,6-1,7-1,8-1,9-1,10-1,11-1,12-1,13-1
NCV - **12,** 1-1,2-1,3-**3**,4-1,5-1,6-1,7-1,8-1,9-1,10-1,11-1,12-1
NIV - **12,** 1-1,2-1,3-**3**,4-1,5-1,6-1,7-1,8-1,9-1,10-1,11-1,12-1
NKJV - **12,** 1-1,2-1,3-1,4-1,5-1,6-1,7-1,8-1,9-1,10-1,11-1,12-1
NLT - **12,** 1-1,2-1,3-**3**,4-1,5-1,6-1,7-1,8-1,9-1,10-1,11-1,12-1

NRSV - 12, 1-1,2-1,3-**3**,4-1,5-1,6-1,7-1,8-1,9-1,10-1,11-1,12-1
Conclusion: Five modern versions are more complex than the King James Bible.

571. Ezra 10:27* And of the sons of **Zattu**; **Elioenai**, **Eliashib**, **Mattaniah**, and **Jeremoth**, and **Zabad**, and **Aziza**.
AV - **15,** 1-1,2-1,3-1,4-1,5-1,6-1,7-1,8-1,9-1,10-1,11-1,12-1,13-1,14-1,15-1
ESV - **12,** 1-1,2-1,3-1,4-1,5-1,6-1,7-1,8-1,9-1,10-1,11-1,12-1
HCSB - 9, 1-1,2-**3**,3-1,4-1,5-1,6-1,7-1,8-1,9-1
NASV - **13,** 1-1,2-1,3-1,4-1,5-1,6-1,7-1,8-1,9-1,10-1,11-1,12-1,13-1
NCV - 12, 1-1,2-1,3-**3**,4-1,5-1,6-1,7-1,8-1,9-1,10-1,11-1,12-1
NIV - 12, 1-1,2-1,3-**3**,4-1,5-1,6-1,7-1,8-1,9-1,10-1,11-1,12-1
NKJV - **12,** 1-1,2-1,3-1,4-1,5-1,6-1,7-1,8-1,9-1,10-1,11-1,12-1
NLT - 12, 1-1,2-1,3-**3**,4-1,5-1,6-1,7-1,8-1,9-1,10-1,11-1,12-1
NRSV - 12, 1-1,2-1,3-**3**,4-1,5-1,6-1,7-1,8-1,9-1,10-1,11-1,12-1
Conclusion: Five modern versions are more complex than the King James Bible.

572. Ezra 10:29* And of the sons of **Bani**; **Meshullam**, **Malluch**, and **Adaiah**, **Jashub**, and Sheal, and **Ramoth**.
AV - **15,** 1-1,2-1,3-1,4-1,5-1,6-1,7-1,8-1,9-1,10-1,11-1,12-1,13-1,14-1,15-1
ESV - **13,** 1-1,2-1,3-1,4-1,5-1,6-1,7-1,8-1,9-1,10-1,11-1,12-1,13-1
HCSB - 9, 1-1,2-**3**,3-1,4-1,5-1,6-1,7-1,8-1,9-1
NASV - **14,** 1-1,2-1,3-1,4-1,5-1,6-1,7-1,8-1,9-1,10-1,11-1,12-1,13-1,14-1
NCV - 12, 1-1,2-1,3-**3**,4-1,5-1,6-1,7-1,8-1,9-1,10-1,11-1,12-1
NIV - 12, 1-1,2-1,3-**3**,4-1,5-1,6-1,7-1,8-1,9-1,10-1,11-1,12-1
NKJV - **12,** 1-1,2-1,3-1,4-1,5-1,6-1,7-1,8-1,9-1,10-1,11-1,12-1
NLT - 12, 1-1,2-1,3-**3**,4-1,5-1,6-1,7-1,8-1,9-1,10-1,11-1,12-1
NRSV - 12, 1-1,2-1,3-**3**,4-1,5-1,6-1,7-1,8-1,9-1,10-1,11-1,12-1
Conclusion: Five modern versions are more complex than the King James Bible.

573. Ezra 10:30* And of the sons of **Pahathmoab**; **Adna**, and **Chelal**, **Benaiah**, **Maaseiah**, **Mattaniah**, **Bezaleel**, and **Binnui**, and **Manasseh**.
AV - **17,** 1-1,2-1,3-1,4-1,5-1,6-1,7-1,8-1,9-1,10-1,11-1,12-1,13-1,14-1,15-1,16-1,17-1
ESV - **14,** 1-1,2-1,3-1,4-1,5-1,6-1,7-1,8-1,9-1,10-1,11-1,12-1,13-1,14-1
HCSB - 11, 1-1,2-**3**,3-1,4-1,5-1,6-1,7-1,8-1,9-1,10-1,11-1
NASV - **15,** 1-1,2-1,3-1,4-1,5-1,6-1,7-1,8-1,9-1,10-1,11-1,12-1,13-1,14-1,15-1
NCV - 14, 1-1,2-1,3-**3**,4-1,5-1,6-1,7-1,8-1,9-1,10-1,11-1,12-1,13-1,14-1
NIV - 14, 1-1,2-1,3-**3**,4-1,5-1,6-1,7-1,8-1,9-1,10-1,11-1,12-1,13-1,14-1
NKJV - **14,** 1-1,2-1,3-1,4-1,5-1,6-1,7-1,8-1,9-1,10-1,11-1,12-1,13-1,14-1
NLT - 14, 1-1,2-1,3-**3**,4-1,5-1,6-1,7-1,8-1,9-1,10-1,11-1,12-1,13-1,14-1
NRSV - 14, 1-1,2-1,3-**3**,4-1,5-1,6-1,7-1,8-1,9-1,10-1,11-1,12-1,13-1,14-1
Conclusion: Five modern versions are more complex than the King James Bible.

574. Ezra 10:31* And of the sons of **Harim**; **Eliezer**, **Ishijah**, **Malchiah**, **Shemaiah**, **Shimeon**,
AV - **11,** 1-1,2-1,3-1,4-1,5-1,6-1,7-1,8-1,9-1,10-1,11-1

ESV - **10,** 1-1,2-1,3-1,4-1,5-1,6-1,7-1,8-1,9-1,10-1
HCSB - **7,** 1-1,2-**3,**3-1,4-1,5-1,6-1,7-1
NASV - **11,** 1-1,2-1,3-1,4-1,5-1,6-1,7-1,8-1,9-1,10-1,11-1
NCV - **10,** 1-1,2-1,3-**3,**4-1,5-1,6-1,7-1,8-1,9-1,10-1
NIV - **10,** 1-1,2-1,3-**3,**4-1,5-1,6-1,7-1,8-1,9-1,10-1
NKJV - **10,** 1-1,2-1,3-1,4-1,5-1,6-1,7-1,8-1,9-1,10-1
NLT - **10,** 1-1,2-1,3-**3,**4-1,5-1,6-1,7-1,8-1,9-1,10-1
NRSV - **10,** 1-1,2-1,3-**3,**4-1,5-1,6-1,7-1,8-1,9-1,10-1
Conclusion: Five modern versions are more complex than the King James Bible.

575. Ezra 10:32 * Benjamin, Malluch, and Shemariah.
AV - **4,** 1-1,2-1,3-1,4-1
ESV - **4,** 1-1,2-1,3-1,4-1
HCSB - **4,** 1-1,2-1,3-1,4-1
NASV - **4,** 1-1,2-1,3-1,4-1
NCV - **4,** 1-1,2-1,3-1,4-1
NIV - **4,** 1-1,2-1,3-1,4-1
NKJV - **4,** 1-1,2-1,3-1,4-1
NLT - **4,** 1-1,2-1,3-1,4-1
NRSV - **4,** 1-1,2-1,3-1,4-1
Conclusion: All versions read the same.

576. Ezra 10:33* Of the sons of Hashum; Mattenai, Mattathah, Zabad, Eliphelet, Jeremai, Manasseh, and Shimei.
AV - **13,** 1-1,2-1,3-1,4-1,5-1,6-1,7-1,8-1,9-1,10-1,11-1,12-1,13-1
ESV - **13,** 1-1,2-1,3-1,4-1,5-1,6-1,7-1,8-1,9-1,10-1,11-1,12-1,13-1
HCSB - **10,** 1-1,2-**3,**3-1,4-1,5-1,6-1,7-1,8-1,9-1,10-1
NASV - **13,** 1-1,2-1,3-1,4-1,5-1,6-1,7-1,8-1,9-1,10-1,11-1,12-1,13-1
NCV - **13,** 1-1,2-1,3-**3,**4-1,5-1,6-1,7-1,8-1,9-1,10-1,11-1,12-1,13-1
NIV - **13,** 1-1,2-1,3-**3,**4-1,5-1,6-1,7-1,8-1,9-1,10-1,11-1,12-1,13-1
NKJV - **13,** 1-1,2-1,3-1,4-1,5-1,6-1,7-1,8-1,9-1,10-1,11-1,12-1,13-1
NLT - **13,** 1-1,2-1,3-**3,**4-1,5-1,6-1,7-1,8-1,9-1,10-1,11-1,12-1,13-1
NRSV - **13,** 1-1,2-1,3-**3,**4-1,5-1,6-1,7-1,8-1,9-1,10-1,11-1,12-1,13-1
Conclusion: Five modern versions are more complex than the King James Bible.

577. Ezra 10:34* Of the sons of Bani; Maadai, Amram, and Uel,
AV - **9,** 1-1,2-1,3-1,4-1,5-1,6-1,7-1,8-1,9-1
ESV - **8,** 1-1,2-1,3-1,4-1,5-1,6-1,7-1,8-1
HCSB - **5,** 1-1,2-**3,**3-1,4-1,5-1
NASV - **8,** 1-1,2-1,3-1,4-1,5-1,6-1,7-1,8-1
NCV - **8,** 1-1,2-1,3-**3,**4-1,5-1,6-1,7-1,8-1
NIV - **8,** 1-1,2-1,3-**3,**4-1,5-1,6-1,7-1,8-1
NKJV - **8,** 1-1,2-1,3-1,4-1,5-1,6-1,7-1,8-1
NLT - **8,** 1-1,2-1,3-**3,**4-1,5-1,6-1,7-1,8-1

NRSV - 8, 1-1,2-1,3-**3**,4-1,5-1,6-1,7-1,8-1
Conclusion: Five modern versions are more complex than the King James Bible.

578. Ezra 10:37* Mattaniah, **Mattenai**, and **Jaasau**,
AV - **4,** 1-1,2-1,3-1,4-1
ESV - **3,** 1-1,2-1,3-1
HCSB - **3,** 1-1,2-1,3-1
NASV - **3,** 1-1,2-1,3-1
NCV - **4,** 1-1,2-1,3-1,4-1
NIV - **4,** 1-1,2-1,3-1,4-1
NKJV - **3,** 1-1,2-1,3-1
NLT - **4,** 1-1,2-1,3-1,4-1
NRSV - **4,** 1-1,2-1,3-1,4-1
Conclusion: All versions read the same.

579. Ezra 10:38* And Bani, and **Binnui**, **Shimei**,
AV - **5,** 1-1,2-1,3-1,4-1,5-1
ESV - **6,** 1-1,2-1,3-1,4-1,5-1,6-1
HCSB - **3,** 1-1,2-1,3-1
NASV - **3,** 1-1,2-1,3-1
NCV - 6, 1-1,2-1,3-**3**,4-1,5-1,6-1
NIV - 6, 1-1,2-1,3-**3**,4-1,5-1,6-1
NKJV - **3,** 1-1,2-1,3-1
NLT - 6, 1-1,2-1,3-**3**,4-1,5-1,6-1
NRSV - 6, 1-1,2-1,3-**3**,4-1,5-1,6-1
Conclusion: Four modern versions are more complex than the King James Bible.

580. Ezra 10:39* And Shelemiah, and **Nathan**, and **Adaiah**,
AV - **6,** 1-1,2-1,3-1,4-1,5-1,6-1
ESV - **3,** 1-1,2-1,3-1
HCSB - **3,** 1-1,2-1,3-1
NASV - **3,** 1-1,2-1,3-1
NCV - **3,** 1-1,2-1,3-1
NIV - **3,** 1-1,2-1,3-1
NKJV - **3,** 1-1,2-1,3-1
NLT - **3,** 1-1,2-1,3-1
NRSV - **3,** 1-1,2-1,3-1
Conclusion: All versions read the same.

581. Ezra 10:41* Azareel, and **Shelemiah**, **Shemariah**,
AV - **4,** 1-1,2-1,3-1,4-1
ESV - **3,** 1-1,2-1,3-1
HCSB - **3,** 1-1,2-1,3-1
NASV - **3,** 1-1,2-1,3-1

NCV - **3,** 1-1,2-1,3-1
NIV - **3,** 1-1,2-1,3-1
NKJV - **3,** 1-1,2-1,3-1
NLT - **3,** 1-1,2-1,3-1
NRSV - **3,** 1-1,2-1,3-1
Conclusion: All versions read the same.

582. Ezra 10:42* Shallum, Amariah, and **Joseph.**
AV - **4,** 1-1,2-1,3-1,4-1
ESV - **4,** 1-1,2-1,3-1,4-1
HCSB - **4,** 1-1,2-1,3-1,4-1
NASV - **4,** 1-1,2-1,3-1,4-1
NCV - **4,** 1-1,2-1,3-1,4-1
NIV - **4,** 1-1,2-1,3-1,4-1
NKJV - **4,** 1-1,2-1,3-1,4-1
NLT - **4,** 1-1,2-1,3-1,4-1
NRSV - **4,** 1-1,2-1,3-1,4-1
Conclusion: All versions read the same.

583. Ezra 10:43* Of the sons of **Nebo; Jeiel, Mattithiah, Zabad, Zebina, Jadau,** and Joel, **Benaiah.**
AV - **13,** 1-1,2-1,3-1,4-1,5-1,6-1,7-1,8-1,9-1,10-1,11-1,12-1,13-1
ESV - **13,** 1-1,2-1,3-1,4-1,5-1,6-1,7-1,8-1,9-1,10-1,11-1,12-1,13-1
HCSB - 10, 1-1,2-**3**,3-1,4-1,5-1,6-1,7-1,8-1,9-1,10-1
NASV - **15,** 1-1,2-1,3-1,4-1,5-1,6-1,7-1,8-1,9-1,10-1,11-1,12-1,13-1,14-1,15-1
NCV - 13, 1-1,2-1,3-**3**,4-1,5-1,6-1,7-1,8-1,9-1,10-1,11-1,12-1,13-1
NIV - 13, 1-1,2-1,3-**3**,4-1,5-1,6-1,7-1,8-1,9-1,10-1,11-1,12-1,13-1
NKJV - **13,** 1-1,2-1,3-1,4-1,5-1,6-1,7-1,8-1,9-1,10-1,11-1,12-1,13-1
NLT - 13, 1-1,2-1,3-**3**,4-1,5-1,6-1,7-1,8-1,9-1,10-1,11-1,12-1,13-1
NRSV - 13, 1-1,2-1,3-**3**,4-1,5-1,6-1,7-1,8-1,9-1,10-1,11-1,12-1,13-1
Conclusion: Five modern versions are more complex than the King James Bible.

584. Nehemiah 2:11* So I came to **Jerusalem,** and was there three days.
AV - **10,** 1-1,2-1,3-1,4-1,5-1,6-1,7-1,8-1,9-1,10-1
ESV - **10,** 1-1,2-1,3-1,4-1,5-1,6-1,7-1,8-1,9-1,10-1
HCSB - 11, 1-**2**,2-1,3-**2**,4-1,5-1,6-1,7-1,8-1,9-1,10-1,11-1
NASV - **10,** 1-1,2-1,3-1,4-1,5-1,6-1,7-1,8-1,9-1,10-1
NCV - **9,** 1-1,2-1,3-1,4-1,5-1,6-1,7-1,8-1,9-1
NIV - 10, 1-1,2-1,3-1,4-1,5-1,6-**2**,7-**2**,8-1,9-1,10-1
NKJV - **10,** 1-1,2-1,3-1,4-1,5-1,6-1,7-1,8-1,9-1,10-1
NLT - 10, 1-1,2-1,3-**2**,4-1,5-1,6-1,7-1,8-**2**,9-1,10-1
NRSV - **11,** 1-1,2-1,3-1,4-1,5-1,6-1,7-1,8-1,9-1,10-1,11-1
Conclusion: Three modern versions are more complex than the King James Bible.

585. Nehemiah 7:26*# The men of **Bethlehem** and **Netophah**, an **hundred fourscore** and eight.
AV - **11,** 1-1,2-1,3-1,4-1,5-1,6-1,7-1,8-1,9-1,10-1,11-1
ESV - **7,** 1-1,2-1,3-1,4-1,5-1,6-1,7-1
HCSB - **5,** 1-1,2-1,3-1,4-1,5-1
NASV - **7,** 1-1,2-1,3-1,4-1,5-1,6-1,7-1
NCV - 12, 1-1,2-1,3-1,4-**2**,5-1,6-1,7-1,8-1,9-1,10-1,11-1,12-1
NIV - **7,** 1-1,2-1,3-1,4-1,5-1,6-1,7-1
NKJV - **11,** 1-1,2-1,3-1,4-1,5-1,6-1,7-1,8-1,9-1,10-1,11-1
NLT - 7, 1-1,2-**2**,3-1,4-1,5-1,6-1,7-1
NRSV - 10, 1-1,2-**2**,3-1,4-1,5-1,6-1,7-1,8-1,9-1,10-1
Conclusion: Three modern versions are more complex than the King James Bible.

586. Nehemiah 7:27*# The men of **Anathoth**, an **hundred twenty** and eight.
AV - **9,** 1-1,2-1,3-1,4-1,5-1,6-1,7-1,8-1,9-1
ESV - **5,** 1-1,2-1,3-1,4-1,5-1
HCSB - **3,** 1-1,2-1,3-1
NASV - **5,** 1-1,2-1,3-1,4-1,5-1
NCV - **3,** 1-1,2-1,3-1
NIV - **3,** 1-1,2-1,3-1
NKJV - **9,** 1-1,2-1,3-1,4-1,5-1,6-1,7-1,8-1,9-1
NLT - 5, 1-1,2-**2**,3-1,4-1,5-1
NRSV - **6,** 1-1,2-1,3-1,4-1,5-1,6-1
Conclusion: Only the NLT made the verse more complex.

587. Nehemiah 7:28*# The men of **Bethazmaveth**, **forty** and two.
AV - **7,** 1-1,2-1,3-1,4-1,5-1,6-1,7-1
ESV - **5,** 1-1,2-1,3-1,4-1,5-1
HCSB - **3,** 1-1,2-1,3-1
NASV - **5,** 1-1,2-1,3-1,4-1,5-1
NCV - **4,** 1-1,2-1,3-1,4-1
NIV - **4,** 1-1,2-1,3-1,4-1
NKJV - **7,** 1-1,2-1,3-1,4-1,5-1,6-1,7-1
NLT - 5, 1-1,2-**2**,3-1,4-1,5-1
NRSV - **4,** 1-1,2-1,3-1,4-1
Conclusion: Only the NLT made the verse more complex.

588. Nehemiah 7:29*# The men of **Kirjathjearim, Chephirah,** and **Beeroth, seven hundred forty** and three.
AV - **12,** 1-1,2-1,3-1,4-1,5-1,6-1,7-1,8-1,9-1,10-1,11-1,12-1
ESV - **8,** 1-1,2-1,3-1,4-1,5-1,6-1,7-1,8-1
HCSB - **6,** 1-1,2-1,3-1,4-1,5-1,6-1
NASV - **8,** 1-1,2-1,3-1,4-1,5-1,6-1,7-1,8-1
NCV - **7,** 1-1,2-1,3-1,4-1,5-1,6-1,7-1
NIV - **7,** 1-1,2-1,3-1,4-1,5-1,6-1,7-1

NKJV - **12,** 1-1,2-1,3-1,4-1,5-1,6-1,7-1,8-1,9-1,10-1,11-1,12-1
NLT - **8,** 1-1,2-1,3-1,4-1,5-1,6-1,7-1,8-1
NRSV - **8,** 1-1,2-1,3-1,4-1,5-1,6-1,7-1,8-1
Conclusion: All versions read the same.

589. Nehemiah 7:30*# The men of **Ramah** and **Geba**, six **hundred twenty** and one.
AV - **11,** 1-1,2-1,3-1,4-1,5-1,6-1,7-1,8-1,9-1,10-1,11-1
ESV - **7,** 1-1,2-1,3-1,4-1,5-1,6-1,7-1
HCSB - **5,** 1-1,2-1,3-1,4-1,5-1
NASV - **7,** 1-1,2-1,3-1,4-1,5-1,6-1,7-1
NCV - **5,** 1-1,2-1,3-1,4-1,5-1
NIV - **5,** 1-1,2-1,3-1,4-1,5-1
NKJV - **11,** 1-1,2-1,3-1,4-1,5-1,6-1,7-1,8-1,9-1,10-1,11-1
NLT - 7, 1-1,2-**2**,3-1,4-1,5-1,6-1,7-1
NRSV - **8,** 1-1,2-1,3-1,4-1,5-1,6-1,7-1,8-1
Conclusion: Only the NLT made the verse more complex.

590. Nehemiah 7:31*# The men of **Michmas**, an **hundred** and **twenty** and two.
AV - **10,** 1-1,2-1,3-1,4-1,5-1,6-1,7-1,8-1,9-1,10-1
ESV - **5,** 1-1,2-1,3-1,4-1,5-1
HCSB - **3,** 1-1,2-1,3-1
NASV - **5,** 1-1,2-1,3-1,4-1,5-1
NCV - **3,** 1-1,2-1,3-1
NIV - **3,** 1-1,2-1,3-1
NKJV - **9,** 1-1,2-1,3-1,4-1,5-1,6-1,7-1,8-1,9-1
NLT - 5, 1-1,2-**2**,3-1,4-1,5-1
NRSV - **6,** 1-1,2-1,3-1,4-1,5-1,6-1
Conclusion: Only the NLT made the verse more complex.

591. Nehemiah 7:32*# The men of **Bethel** and **Ai**, an **hundred twenty** and three.
AV - **11,** 1-1,2-1,3-1,4-1,5-1,6-1,7-1,8-1,9-1,10-1,11-1
ESV - **7,** 1-1,2-1,3-1,4-1,5-1,6-1,7-1
HCSB - **5,** 1-1,2-1,3-1,4-1,5-1
NASV - **7,** 1-1,2-1,3-1,4-1,5-1,6-1,7-1
NCV - **5,** 1-1,2-1,3-1,4-1,5-1
NIV - **5,** 1-1,2-1,3-1,4-1,5-1
NKJV - **11,** 1-1,2-1,3-1,4-1,5-1,6-1,7-1,8-1,9-1,10-1,11-1
NLT - 7, 1-1,2-**2**,3-1,4-1,5-1,6-1,7-1
NRSV - **8,** 1-1,2-1,3-1,4-1,5-1,6-1,7-1,8-1
Conclusion: Only the NLT made the verse more complex.

592. Nehemiah 10:1* Now those that sealed were, **Nehemiah**, the **Tirshatha**, the son of **Hachaliah**, and **Zidkijah**,
AV - **14,** 1-1,2-1,3-1,4-1,5-1,6-1,7-1,8-1,9-1,10-1,11-1,12-1,13-1,14-1

ESV - **15,** 1-1,2-1,3-1,4-1,5-1,6-1,7-1,8-1,9-1,10-1,11-1,12-1,13-1,14-1,15-1
HCSB - **16,** 1-1,2-1,3-1,4-1,5-1,6-1,7-**3,**8-1,9-1,10-1,11-1,12-1,13-1,14-1,15-1,16-1
NASV - **18,** 1-1,2-1,3-1,4-1,5-**3,**6-1,7-1,8-1,9-1,10-1,11-1,12-1,13-1,14-1,15-1,16-1,17-1,18-1
NCV - **15,** 1-1,2-1,3-1,4-1,5-1,6-1,7-1,8-**3,**9-1,10-1,11-1,12-1,13-1,14-1,15-1
NIV - **13,** 1-1,2-1,3-1,4-1,5-1,6-1,7-1,8-1,9-1,10-1,11-1,12-1,13-1
NKJV - **19,**1-1,2-1,3-1,4-1,5-1,6-1,7-1,8-1,9-**3,**10-1,11-1,12-1,13-1,14-1,15-1,16-1,17-1,18-1,19-1
NLT - **19,** 1-1,2-**3,**3-1,4-**3,**5-1,6-1,7-1,8-1,9-**3,**10-1,11-1,12-1,13-1,14-1,15-1,16-1,17-1,18-**2,**19-1
NRSV - **16,** 1-**2,**2-1,3-1,4-**3,**5-1,6-1,7-1,8-1,9-1,10-1,11-1,12-1,13-1,14-1,15-1,16-1
Conclusion: Six modern versions are more complex than the King James Bible. Each modern version examined replaced "Tirshatha" with "governor" but this was not counted against them. The NLT is the most difficult to read.

593. Nehemiah 10:8* **Maaziah**, **Bilgai**, **Shemaiah**: these were the priests.
AV - **7,** 1-1,2-1,3-1,4-1,5-1,6-1,7-1
ESV - **7,** 1-1,2-1,3-1,4-1,5-1,6-1,7-1
HCSB - **8,** 1-1,2-1,3-1,4-1,5-1,6-1,7-1,8-1
NASV - **7,** 1-1,2-1,3-1,4-1,5-1,6-1,7-1
NCV - **8,** 1-1,2-1,3-1,4-1,5-1,6-1,7-1,8-1
NIV - **8,** 1-1,2-1,3-1,4-1,5-1,6-1,7-1,8-1
NKJV - **8,** 1-1,2-1,3-1,4-1,5-1,6-1,7-1,8-1
NLT - **8,** 1-1,2-1,3-1,4-1,5-1,6-1,7-1,8-1
NRSV - **7,** 1-1,2-1,3-1,4-1,5-1,6-1,7-1
Conclusion: All versions read the same.

594. Nehemiah 10:9* And the **Levites**: both **Jeshua** the son of **Azaniah**, **Binnui** of the sons of **Henadad**, **Kadmiel**;
AV - **16,** 1-1,2-1,3-1,4-1,5-1,6-1,7-1,8-1,9-1,10-1,11-1,12-1,13-1,14-1,15-1,16-1
ESV - **15,** 1-1,2-1,3-1,4-1,5-1,6-1,7-1,8-1,9-1,10-1,11-1,12-1,13-1,14-1,15-1
HCSB - **14,** 1-1,2-1,3-1,4-1,5-1,6-1,7-1,8-1,9-1,10-1,11-1,12-1,13-1,14-1
NASV - **15,** 1-1,2-1,3-1,4-1,5-1,6-1,7-1,8-1,9-1,10-1,11-1,12-1,13-1,14-1,15-1
NCV - **18,** 1-1,2-1,3-1,4-1,5-1,6-1,7-1,8-1,9-1,10-1,11-1,12-1,13-1,14-1,15-1,16-1,17-1,18-1
NIV - **13,** 1-1,2-1,3-1,4-1,5-1,6-1,7-1,8-1,9-1,10-1,11-1,12-1,13-1
NKJV - **15,** 1-1,2-1,3-1,4-1,5-1,6-1,7-1,8-1,9-1,10-1,11-1,12-1,13-1,14-1,15-1
NLT - **14,** 1-1,2-**3,**3-1,4-1,5-1,6-1,7-1,8-1,9-1,10-1,11-**3,**12-1,13-1,14-1
NRSV - **14,** 1-1,2-1,3-1,4-1,5-1,6-1,7-1,8-1,9-1,10-1,11-1,12-1,13-1,14-1
Conclusion: Only the NLT made the verse more complex.

595. Nehemiah 10:26* And **Ahijah**, **Hanan**, **Anan**,
AV - **4,** 1-1,2-1,3-1,4-1
ESV - **3,** 1-1,2-1,3-1
HCSB - **3,** 1-1,2-1,3-1
NASV - **3,** 1-1,2-1,3-1
NCV - **3,** 1-1,2-1,3-1
NIV - **3,** 1-1,2-1,3-1

NKJV - **3,** 1-1,2-1,3-1
NLT - **3,** 1-1,2-1,3-1
NRSV - **3,** 1-1,2-1,3-1
Conclusion: All versions read the same.

596. Nehemiah 11:5* And **Maaseiah** the son of **Baruch**, the son of **Colhozeh**, the son of **Hazaiah**, the son of **Adaiah**, the son of **Joiarib**, the son of **Zechariah**, the son of **Shiloni**.
AV - **30,** 1-1,2-1,3-1,4-1,5-1,6-1,7-1,8-1,9-1,10-1,11-1,12-1,13-1,14-1,15-1,16-1,17-1,18-1,19-1,20-1,21-1,22-1,23-1,24-1,25-1,26-1,27-1,28-1,29-1,30-1
ESV - **25,** 1-1,2-1,3-1,4-1,5-1,6-1,7-1,8-1,9-1,10-1,11-1,12-1,13-1,14-1,15-1,16-1,17-1,18-1,19-1,20-1,21-1,22-1,23-1,24-1,25-1
HCSB - **25,** 1-1,2-1,3-1,4-1,5-1,6-1,7-1,8-1,9-1,10-1,11-1,12-1,13-1,14-1,15-1,16-1,17-1,18-1,19-1,20-1,21-1,22-**3**,23-1,24-1,25-1
NASV - **31,** 1-1,2-1,3-1,4-1,5-1,6-1,7-1,8-1,9-1,10-1,11-1,12-1,13-1,14-1,15-1,16-1,17-1,18-1,19-1,20-1,21-1,22-1,23-1,24-1,25-1,26-1,27-1,28-1,29-1,30-1,31-1
NCV - **37,** 1-1,2-1,3-**2**,4-1,5-1,6-1,7-1,8-1,9-1,10-1,11-1,12-1,13-1,14-1,15-1,16-1,17-1,18-1,19-1,20-1,21-1,22-1,23-1,24-1,25-1,26-1,27-1,28-1,29-1,30-1,31-1,32-1,33-1,34-1,35-**3**,36-1,37-1
NIV - **29,** 1-1,2-1,3-1,4-1,5-1,6-1,7-1,8-1,9-1,10-1,11-1,12-1,13-1,14-1,15-1,16-1,17-1,18-1,19-1,20-1,21-1,22-1,23-1,24-1,25-1,26-1,27-**3**,28-1,29-1
NKJV - **30,** 1-1,2-1,3-1,4-1,5-1,6-1,7-1,8-1,9-1,10-1,11-1,12-1,13-1,14-1,15-1,16-1,17-1,18-1,19-1,20-1,21-1,22-1,23-1,24-1,25-1,26-1,27-1,28-1,29-1,30-1
NLT - **25,** 1-**2**,2-1,3-1,4-1,5-1,6-1,7-1,8-1,9-1,10-1,11-1,12-1,13-1,14-1,15-1,16-1,17-1,18-1,19-1,20-1,21-1,22-1,23-**3**,24-1,25-1
NRSV - **24,** 1-1,2-1,3-1,4-1,5-1,6-1,7-1,8-1,9-1,10-1,11-1,12-1,13-1,14-1,15-1,16-1,17-1,18-1,19-1,20-1,21-1,22-1,23-1,24-1
Conclusion: Four modern versions are more complex than the King James Bible.

597. Nehemiah 11:7* And these are the sons of **Benjamin**; **Sallu** the son of **Meshullam**, the son of Joed, the son of **Pedaiah**, the son of **Kolaiah**, the son of **Maaseiah**, the son of **Ithiel**, the son of **Jesaiah**.
AV - **36,** 1-1,2-1,3-1,4-1,5-1,6-1,7-1,8-1,9-1,10-1,11-1,12-1,13-1,14-1,15-1,16-1,17-1,18-1,19-1,20-1,21-1,22-1,23-1,24-1,25-1,26-1,27-1,28-1,29-1,30-1,31-1,32-1,33-1,34-1,35-1,36-1
ESV - **30,** 1-1,2-1,3-1,4-1,5-1,6-1,7-1,8-1,9-1,10-1,11-1,12-1,13-1,14-1,15-1,16-1,17-1,18-1,19-1,20-1,21-1,22-1,23-1,24-1,25-1,26-1,27-1,28-1,29-1,30-1
HCSB - **26,** 1-1,2-1,3-1,4-**3**,5-1,6-1,7-1,8-1,9-1,10-1,11-1,12-1,13-1,14-1,15-1,16-1,17-1,18-1,19-1,20-1,21-1,22-1,23-1,24-1,25-1,26-1
NASV - **36,** 1-1,2-1,3-1,4-1,5-1,6-1,7-1,8-1,9-1,10-1,11-1,12-1,13-1,14-1,15-1,16-1,17-1,18-1,19-1,20-1,21-1,22-1,23-1,24-1,25-1,26-1,27-1,28-1,29-1,30-1,31-1,32-1,33-1,34-1,35-1,36-1
NCV - **45,** 1-1,2-1,3-**3**,4-1,5-1,6-1,7-1,8-**2**,9-1,10-1,11-1,12-1,13-1,14-1,15-1,16-1,17-1,18-1,19-1,20-1,21-1,22-1,23-1,24-1,25-1,26-1,27-1,28-1,29-1,30-1,31-1,32-1,33-1,34-1,35-1,36-1,37-1,38-1,39-1,40-1,41-1,42-1,43-1,44-1,45-1
NIV - **33,** 1-1,2-1,3-**3**,4-1,5-1,6-1,7-1,8-1,9-1,10-1,11-1,12-1,13-1,14-1,15-1,16-1,17-1,18-1,19-1,20-1,21-1,22-1,23-1,24-1,25-1,26-1,27-1,28-1,29-1,30-1,31-1,32-1,33-1

NKJV - **36,** 1-1,2-1,3-1,4-1,5-1,6-1,7-1,8-1,9-1,10-1,11-1,12-1,13-1,14-1,15-1,16-1,17-1,18-1,19-1,20-1,21-1,22-1,23-1,24-1,25-1,26-1,27-1,28-1,29-1,30-1,31-1,32-1,33-1,34-1,35-1,36-1
NLT - **27,** 1-1,2-1,3-1,4-1,5-1,6-1,7-1,8-1,9-1,10-1,11-1,12-1,13-1,14-1,15-1,16-1,17-1,18-1,19-1,20-1,21-1,22-1,23-1,24-1,25-1,26-1,27-1
NRSV - **27,** 1-1,2-1,3-1,4-1,5-1,6-1,7-1,8-1,9-1,10-1,11-1,12-1,13-1,14-1,15-1,16-1,17-1,18-1,19-1,20-1,21-1,22-1,23-1,24-1,25-1,26-1,27-1
Conclusion: Only three modern versions are more complex than the King James Bible.

598. Nehemiah 11:10* Of the priests: **Jedaiah** the son of **Joiarib, Jachin.**
AV - **9,** 1-1,2-1,3-1,4-1,5-1,6-1,7-1,8-1,9-1
ESV - **9,** 1-1,2-1,3-1,4-1,5-1,6-1,7-1,8-1,9-1
HCSB - **8,** 1-1,2-1,3-1,4-1,5-1,6-1,7-1,8-1
NASV - **9,** 1-1,2-1,3-1,4-1,5-1,6-1,7-1,8-1,9-1
NCV - 15, 1-1,2-1,3-1,4-1,5-1,6-1,7-**2**,8-**4**,9-1,10-1,11-1,12-1,13-1,14-1,15-1
NIV - **9,** 1-1,2-1,3-1,4-1,5-1,6-1,7-1,8-1,9-1
NKJV - **10,** 1-1,2-1,3-1,4-1,5-1,6-1,7-1,8-1,9-1,10-1
NLT - **8,** 1-1,2-1,3-1,4-1,5-1,6-1,7-1,8-1
NRSV - **8,** 1-1,2-1,3-1,4-1,5-1,6-1,7-1,8-1
Conclusion: Only the NCV made the verse more complex. This version adds, "These are the priests who moved into Jerusalem..." to the beginning of the verse. This phrase is fabricated out of thin air and is not carried over from verse nine, therefore the four syllable "Jerusalem" was counted against it.

599. Nehemiah 11:26* And at **Jeshua**, and at **Moladah**, and at **Bethphelet**,
AV - **9,** 1-1,2-1,3-1,4-1,5-1,6-1,7-1,8-1,9-1
ESV - **8,** 1-1,2-1,3-1,4-1,5-1,6-1,7-1,8-1
HCSB - **4,** 1-1,2-1,3-1,4-1
NASV - **7,** 1-1,2-1,3-1,4-1,5-1,6-1,7-1
NCV - **5,** 1-1,2-1,3-1,4-1,5-1
NIV - **7,** 1-1,2-1,3-1,4-1,5-1,6-1,7-1
NKJV - **5,** 1-1,2-1,3-1,4-1,5-1
NLT - 7, 1-1,2-**2**,3-1,4-1,5-1,6-1,7-1
NRSV - **8,** 1-1,2-1,3-1,4-1,5-1,6-1,7-1,8-1
Conclusion: Only the NLT made the verse more complex.

600. Nehemiah 11:29* And at **Enrimmon**, and at **Zareah**, and at **Jarmuth**,
AV - **9,** 1-1,2-1,3-1,4-1,5-1,6-1,7-1,8-1,9-1
ESV - **6,** 1-1,2-1,3-1,4-1,5-1,6-1
HCSB - **5,** 1-1,2-1,3-1,4-1,5-1
NASV - **8,** 1-1,2-1,3-1,4-1,5-1,6-1,7-1,8-1
NCV - **5,** 1-1,2-1,3-1,4-1,5-1
NIV - **7,** 1-1,2-1,3-1,4-1,5-1,6-1,7-1
NKJV - **5,** 1-1,2-1,3-1,4-1,5-1
NLT - 7, 1-1,2-**2**,3-1,4-1,5-1,6-1,7-1

NRSV - **6,** 1-1,2-1,3-1,4-1,5-1,6-1
Conclusion: Only the NLT made the verse more complex.

601. Nehemiah 11:32* And at **Anathoth**, Nob, **Ananiah,**
AV - **5,** 1-1,2-1,3-1,4-1,5-1
ESV - **3,** 1-1,2-1,3-1
HCSB - **3,** 1-1,2-1,3-1
NASV - **3,** 1-1,2-1,3-1
NCV - **3,** 1-1,2-1,3-1
NIV - **4,** 1-1,2-1,3-1,4-1
NKJV - **3,** 1-1,2-1,3-1
NLT - **7,** 1-1,2-**2,**3-1,4-1,5-1,6-1,7-1
NRSV - **3,** 1-1,2-1,3-1
Conclusion: Only the NLT made the verse more complex.

602. Nehemiah 12:1* Now these are the priests and the **Levites** that went up with **Zerubbabel** the son of **Shealtiel**, and **Jeshua**: **Seraiah, Jeremiah, Ezra,**
AV - **22,** 1-1,2-1,3-1,4-1,5-1,6-1,7-1,8-1,9-1,10-1,11-1,12-1,13-1,14-1,15-1,16-1,17-1,18-1,19-1,20-1,21-1,22-1
ESV - **21,** 1-1,2-1,3-1,4-1,5-1,6-1,7-1,8-1,9-1,10-1,11-1,12-1,13-1,14-1,15-1,16-1,17-1,18-1,19-1,20-1,21-1
HCSB - **20,** 1-1,2-1,3-1,4-1,5-1,6-1,7-1,8-1,9-1,10-1,11-1,12-1,13-1,14-1,15-1,16-1,17-1,18-1,19-1,20-1
NASV - **22,** 1-1,2-1,3-1,4-1,5-1,6-1,7-1,8-1,9-1,10-1,11-1,12-1,13-1,14-1,15-1,16-1,17-1,18-1,19-1,20-1,21-1,22-1
NCV - **21,** 1-1,2-1,3-1,4-1,5-1,6-1,7-1,8-**2,**9-1,10-1,11-1,12-1,13-1,14-1,15-1,16-1,17-1,18-1,19-1,20-1,21-1
NIV - **19,** 1-1,2-1,3-1,4-1,5-1,6-1,7-1,8-**2,**9-1,10-1,11-1,12-1,13-1,14-1,15-1,16-1,17-1,18-1,19-1
NKJV - **22,** 1-1,2-1,3-1,4-1,5-1,6-1,7-1,8-1,9-1,10-1,11-1,12-1,13-1,14-1,15-1,16-1,17-1,18-1,19-1,20-1,21-1,22-1
NLT - **24,** 1-1,2-1,3-1,4-1,5-1,6-1,7-1,8-1,9-1,10-1,11-**2,**12-1,13-1,14-1,15-1,16-1,17-1,18-1,19-1,20-1,21-1,22-1,23-1,24-1
NRSV - **20,** 1-1,2-1,3-1,4-1,5-1,6-1,7-1,8-1,9-1,10-1,11-1,12-1,13-1,14-1,15-1,16-1,17-1,18-1,19-1,20-1
Conclusion: Only three modern versions are more complex than the King James Bible.

603. Nehemiah 12:6* **Shemaiah**, and **Joiarib, Jedaiah,**
AV - **4,** 1-1,2-1,3-1,4-1
ESV - **3,** 1-1,2-1,3-1
HCSB - **3,** 1-1,2-1,3-1
NASV - **4,** 1-1,2-1,3-1,4-1
NCV - **3,** 1-1,2-1,3-1
NIV - **3,** 1-1,2-1,3-1
NKJV - **3,** 1-1,2-1,3-1

NLT - **3,** 1-1,2-1,3-1
NRSV - **3,** 1-1,2-1,3-1
Conclusion: All versions read the same.

604. Nehemiah 12:13* Of **Ezra, Meshullam;** of **Amariah, Jehohanan;**
AV - **6,** 1-1,2-1,3-1,4-1,5-1,6-1
ESV - **6,** 1-1,2-1,3-1,4-1,5-1,6-1
HCSB - **6,** 1-1,2-1,3-1,4-1,5-1,6-1
NASV - **6,** 1-1,2-1,3-1,4-1,5-1,6-1
NCV - 8, 1-1,2-1,3-1,4-**3,**5-1,6-1,7-1,8-**3**
NIV - **6,** 1-1,2-1,3-1,4-1,5-1,6-1
NKJV - **6,** 1-1,2-1,3-1,4-1,5-1,6-1
NLT - 16, 1-1,2-1,3-**2,**4-1,5-1,6-**3,**7-1,8-1,9-1,10-1,11-**2,**12-1,13-1,14-**3,**15-1,16-1
NRSV - **6,** 1-1,2-1,3-1,4-1,5-1,6-1
Conclusion: Only the NCV and the NLT made the verse more complex.

605. Nehemiah 12:14* Of **Melicu, Jonathan;** of **Shebaniah, Joseph;**
AV - **6,** 1-1,2-1,3-1,4-1,5-1,6-1
ESV - **6,** 1-1,2-1,3-1,4-1,5-1,6-1
HCSB - **6,** 1-1,2-1,3-1,4-1,5-1,6-1
NASV - **6,** 1-1,2-1,3-1,4-1,5-1,6-1
NCV - 8, 1-1,2-1,3-1,4-**3,**5-1,6-1,7-1,8-**3**
NIV - **6,** 1-1,2-1,3-1,4-1,5-1,6-1
NKJV - **6,** 1-1,2-1,3-1,4-1,5-1,6-1
NLT - 16, 1-1,2-1,3-**2,**4-1,5-1,6-**3,**7-1,8-1,9-1,10-1,11-**2,**12-1,13-1,14-**3,**15-1,16-1
NRSV - **6,** 1-1,2-1,3-1,4-1,5-1,6-1
Conclusion: Only the NCV and the NLT made the verse more complex.

606. Nehemiah 12:15* Of **Harim, Adna;** of **Meraioth, Helkai;**
AV - **6,** 1-1,2-1,3-1,4-1,5-1,6-1
ESV - **6,** 1-1,2-1,3-1,4-1,5-1,6-1
HCSB - **6,** 1-1,2-1,3-1,4-1,5-1,6-1
NASV - **6,** 1-1,2-1,3-1,4-1,5-1,6-1
NCV - 8, 1-1,2-1,3-1,4-**3,**5-1,6-1,7-1,8-**3**
NIV - **6,** 1-1,2-1,3-1,4-1,5-1,6-1
NKJV - **6,** 1-1,2-1,3-1,4-1,5-1,6-1
NLT - 16, 1-1,2-1,3-**2,**4-1,5-1,6-**3,**7-1,8-1,9-1,10-1,11-**2,**12-1,13-1,14-**3,**15-1,16-1
NRSV - **6,** 1-1,2-1,3-1,4-1,5-1,6-1
Conclusion: Only the NCV and the NLT made the verse more complex.

607. Nehemiah 12:16* Of **Iddo, Zechariah;** of **Ginnethon, Meshullam;**
AV - **6,** 1-1,2-1,3-1,4-1,5-1,6-1
ESV - **6,** 1-1,2-1,3-1,4-1,5-1,6-1
HCSB - **6,** 1-1,2-1,3-1,4-1,5-1,6-1

NASV - **6,** 1-1,2-1,3-1,4-1,5-1,6-1
NCV - **8,** 1-1,2-1,3-1,4-**3**,5-1,6-1,7-1,8-**3**
NIV - **6,** 1-1,2-1,3-1,4-1,5-1,6-1
NKJV - **6,** 1-1,2-1,3-1,4-1,5-1,6-1
NLT - **16,** 1-1,2-1,3-**2**,4-1,5-1,6-**3**,7-1,8-1,9-1,10-1,11-**2**,12-1,13-1,14-**3**,15-1,16-1
NRSV - **6,** 1-1,2-1,3-1,4-1,5-1,6-1
Conclusion: Only the NCV and the NLT made the verse more complex.

608. Nehemiah 12:17* Of **Abijah**, **Zichri**; of **Miniamin**, of **Moadiah**, **Piltai**;
AV - **8,** 1-1,2-1,3-1,4-1,5-1,6-1,7-1,8-1
ESV - **8,** 1-1,2-1,3-1,4-1,5-1,6-1,7-1,8-1
HCSB - **6,** 1-1,2-1,3-1,4-1,5-1,6-1
NASV - **8,** 1-1,2-1,3-1,4-1,5-1,6-1,7-1,8-1
NCV - **10,** 1-1,2-1,3-1,4-**3**,5-1,6-1,7-1,8-1,9-1,10-**3**
NIV - **9,** 1-1,2-1,3-1,4-1,5-1,6-1,7-1,8-1,9-1
NKJV - **10,** 1-1,2-1,3-1,4-1,5-1,6-1,7-1,8-1,9-1,10-1
NLT - **26,** 1-1,2-1,3-**2**,4-1,5-1,6-**3**,7-1,8-1,9-1,10-1,11-**2**,12-1,13-**2**,14-1,15-1,16-**3**,17-1,18-1,19-1,20-1,21-**2**,22-1,23-1,24-**3**,25-1,26-1
NRSV - **8,** 1-1,2-1,3-1,4-1,5-1,6-1,7-1,8-1
Conclusion: Once again, only the NCV and the NLT made the verse more complex, but the translators of the NLT have done their usual masterful job of swelling their rendering of the verse to more than three times the size of the smallest rendering of the other translations.

609. Nehemiah 12:18* Of **Bilgah**, **Shammua**; of **Shemaiah**, **Jehonathan**;
AV - **6,** 1-1,2-1,3-1,4-1,5-1,6-1
ESV - **6,** 1-1,2-1,3-1,4-1,5-1,6-1
HCSB - **6,** 1-1,2-1,3-1,4-1,5-1,6-1
NASV - **6,** 1-1,2-1,3-1,4-1,5-1,6-1
NCV - **8,** 1-1,2-1,3-1,4-**3**,5-1,6-1,7-1,8-**3**
NIV - **6,** 1-1,2-1,3-1,4-1,5-1,6-1
NKJV - **6,** 1-1,2-1,3-1,4-1,5-1,6-1
NLT - **16,** 1-1,2-1,3-**2**,4-1,5-1,6-**3**,7-1,8-1,9-1,10-1,11-**2**,12-1,13-1,14-**3**,15-1,16-1
NRSV - **6,** 1-1,2-1,3-1,4-1,5-1,6-1
Conclusion: Only the NCV and the NLT made the verse more complex. Another wordy rendering by the producers of the NLT.

610. Nehemiah 12:19* And of **Joiarib**, **Mattenai**; of **Jedaiah**, **Uzzi**;
AV - **6,** 1-1,2-1,3-1,4-1,5-1,6-1
ESV - **6,** 1-1,2-1,3-1,4-1,5-1,6-1
HCSB - **6,** 1-1,2-1,3-1,4-1,5-1,6-1
NASV - **6,** 1-1,2-1,3-1,4-1,5-1,6-1
NCV - **8,** 1-1,2-1,3-1,4-**3**,5-1,6-1,7-1,8-**3**
NIV - **6,** 1-1,2-1,3-1,4-1,5-1,6-1
NKJV - **6,** 1-1,2-1,3-1,4-1,5-1,6-1

NLT - **16,** 1-1,2-1,3-**2,**4-1,5-1,6-**3,**7-1,8-1,9-1,10-1,11-**2,**12-1,13-1,14-**3,**15-1,16-1
NRSV - **6,** 1-1,2-1,3-1,4-1,5-1,6-1
Conclusion: Only the NCV and the NLT made the verse more complex.

611. Nehemiah 12:20* Of **Sallai, Kallai**; of **Amok, Eber;**
AV - **6,** 1-1,2-1,3-1,4-1,5-1,6-1
ESV - **6,** 1-1,2-1,3-1,4-1,5-1,6-1
HCSB - **6,** 1-1,2-1,3-1,4-1,5-1,6-1
NASV - **6,** 1-1,2-1,3-1,4-1,5-1,6-1
NCV - 8, 1-1,2-1,3-1,4-**3,**5-1,6-1,7-1,8-**3**
NIV - **6,** 1-1,2-1,3-1,4-1,5-1,6-1
NKJV - **6,** 1-1,2-1,3-1,4-1,5-1,6-1
NLT - **16,** 1-1,2-1,3-**2,**4-1,5-1,6-**3,**7-1,8-1,9-1,10-1,11-**2,**12-1,13-1,14-**3,**15-1,16-1
NRSV - **6,** 1-1,2-1,3-1,4-1,5-1,6-1
Conclusion: Only the NCV and the NLT made the verse more complex.

612. Nehemiah 12:21* Of **Hilkiah, Hashabiah**; of **Jedaiah, Nethaneel.**
AV - **6,** 1-1,2-1,3-1,4-1,5-1,6-1
ESV - **6,** 1-1,2-1,3-1,4-1,5-1,6-1
HCSB - **6,** 1-1,2-1,3-1,4-1,5-1,6-1
NASV - **6,** 1-1,2-1,3-1,4-1,5-1,6-1
NCV - 8, 1-1,2-1,3-1,4-**3,**5-1,6-1,7-1,8-**3**
NIV - **6,** 1-1,2-1,3-1,4-1,5-1,6-1
NKJV - **6,** 1-1,2-1,3-1,4-1,5-1,6-1
NLT - **16,** 1-1,2-1,3-**2,**4-1,5-1,6-**3,**7-1,8-1,9-1,10-1,11-**2,**12-1,13-1,14-**3,**15-1,16-1
NRSV - **6,** 1-1,2-1,3-1,4-1,5-1,6-1
Conclusion: Only the NCV and the NLT made the verse more complex.

613. Nehemiah 12:33* And **Azariah, Ezra,** and **Meshullam,**
AV - **5,** 1-1,2-1,3-1,4-1,5-1
ESV - **4,** 1-1,2-1,3-1,4-1
HCSB - **3,** 1-1,2-1,3-1
NASV - **4,** 1-1,2-1,3-1,4-1
NCV - **3,** 1-1,2-1,3-1
NIV - 5, 1-**2,**2-1,3-1,4-1,5-1
NKJV - **4,** 1-1,2-1,3-1,4-1
NLT - 5, 1-**2,**2-1,3-1,4-1,5-1
NRSV - **4,** 1-1,2-1,3-1,4-1
Conclusion: Only the NIV and the NLT made the verse more complex.

614. Nehemiah 12:34* **Judah,** and **Benjamin,** and **Shemaiah,** and **Jeremiah,**
AV - **7,** 1-1,2-1,3-1,4-1,5-1,6-1,7-1
ESV - **5,** 1-1,2-1,3-1,4-1,5-1
HCSB - **5,** 1-1,2-1,3-1,4-1,5-1

NASV - **4,** 1-1,2-1,3-1,4-1
NCV - 7, 1-1,2-1,3-1,4-1,5-1,6-**2,**7-1
NIV - **4,** 1-1,2-1,3-1,4-1
NKJV - **4,** 1-1,2-1,3-1,4-1
NLT - **5,** 1-1,2-1,3-1,4-1,5-1
NRSV - **5,** 1-1,2-1,3-1,4-1,5-1
Conclusion: Only the NCV made the verse more complex.

615. Nehemiah 12:41* And the priests; **Eliakim, Maaseiah, Miniamin, Michaiah, Elioenai, Zechariah,** and **Hananiah,** with **trumpets;**
AV - **13,** 1-1,2-1,3-1,4-1,5-1,6-1,7-1,8-1,9-1,10-1,11-1,12-1,13-1
ESV - **13,** 1-1,2-1,3-1,4-1,5-1,6-1,7-1,8-1,9-1,10-1,11-1,12-1,13-1
HCSB - **12,** 1-1,2-1,3-1,4-1,5-1,6-1,7-1,8-1,9-1,10-1,11-1,12-1
NASV - **14,** 1-1,2-1,3-1,4-1,5-1,6-1,7-1,8-1,9-1,10-1,11-1,12-1,13-1,14-1
NCV - **15,** 1-1,2-1,3-1,4-1,5-1,6-1,7-1,8-1,9-1,10-1,11-1,12-1,13-1,14-1,15-1
NIV - **16,** 1-1,2-1,3-1,4-1,5-1,6-1,7-1,8-1,9-1,10-1,11-1,12-1,13-1,14-1,15-1,16-1
NKJV - **13,** 1-1,2-1,3-1,4-1,5-1,6-1,7-1,8-1,9-1,10-1,11-1,12-1,13-1
NLT - 16, 1-1,2-1,3-**3,**4-1,5-1,6-1,7-**2,**8-1,9-1,10-1,11-1,12-1,13-1,14-1,15-1,16-1
NRSV - **13,** 1-1,2-1,3-1,4-1,5-1,6-1,7-1,8-1,9-1,10-1,11-1,12-1,13-1
Conclusion: Only the NLT made the verse more complex.

616. Esther 4:9* And **Hatach** came and told **Esther** the words of **Mordecai.**
AV - **10,** 1-1,2-1,3-1,4-1,5-1,6-1,7-1,8-1,9-1,10-1
ESV - **10,** 1-1,2-1,3-1,4-1,5-1,6-1,7-1,8-1,9-1,10-1
HCSB - 8, 1-1,2-1,3-1,4-**3,**5-1,6-**2,**7-1,8-1
NASV - 9, 1-1,2-1,3-1,4-1,5-**3,**6-1,7-1,8-1,9-1
NCV - 11, 1-1,2-1,3-1,4-1,5-**3,**6-1,7-1,8-**4,**9-1,10-1,11-1
NIV - 11, 1-1,2-1,3-1,4-1,5-**3,**6-1,7-1,8-1,9-1,10-1,11-1
NKJV - 10, 1-1,2-1,3-**2,**4-1,5-1,6-1,7-1,8-1,9-1,10-1
NLT - 8, 1-1,2-1,3-**2,**4-1,5-1,6-1,7-1,8-**2**
NRSV - **9,** 1-1,2-1,3-1,4-1,5-1,6-1,7-1,8-1,9-1
Conclusion: Six modern versions are more complex than the King James Bible.

617. Esther 4:12* And they told to **Mordecai Esther's** words.
AV - **7,** 1-1,2-1,3-1,4-1,5-1,6-1,7-1
ESV - **8,** 1-1,2-1,3-1,4-1,5-1,6-1,7-1,8-1
HCSB - 6, 1-1,2-**2,**3-1,4-**3,**5-1,6-1
NASV - 6, 1-1,2-**3,**3-1,4-1,5-1,6-1
NCV - 6, 1-1,2-**2,**3-1,4-**2,**5-1,6-1
NIV - 7, 1-1,2-1,3-1,4-1,5-**3,**6-1,7-1
NKJV - **6,** 1-1,2-1,3-1,4-1,5-1,6-1
NLT - 7, 1-1,2-1,3-1,4-1,5-**2,**6-1,7-1
NRSV - **8,** 1-1,2-1,3-1,4-1,5-1,6-1,7-1,8-1
Conclusion: Five modern versions are more complex than the King James Bible.

618. Esther 9:7* And **Parshandatha**, and **Dalphon**, and **Aspatha**,
AV - **6,** 1-1,2-1,3-1,4-1,5-1,6-1
ESV - **8,** 1-1,2-**2**,3-1,4-1,5-1,6-1,7-1,8-1
HCSB - **4,** 1-**3**,2-1,3-1,4-1
NASV - **4,** 1-1,2-1,3-1,4-1
NCV - **6,** 1-1,2-**2**,3-1,4-1,5-1,6-1
NIV - **6,** 1-1,2-**2**,3-1,4-1,5-1,6-1
NKJV - **4,** 1-**2**,2-1,3-1,4-1
NLT - **6,** 1-1,2-**2**,3-1,4-1,5-1,6-1
NRSV - **5,** 1-1,2-1,3-1,4-1,5-1
Conclusion: Six modern versions are more complex than the King James Bible.

619. Esther 9:8* And **Poratha**, and **Adalia**, and **Aridatha**,
AV - **6,** 1-1,2-1,3-1,4-1,5-1,6-1
ESV - **3,** 1-1,2-1,3-1
HCSB - **3,** 1-1,2-1,3-1
NASV - **3,** 1-1,2-1,3-1
NCV - **3,** 1-1,2-1,3-1
NIV - **3,** 1-1,2-1,3-1
NKJV - **3,** 1-1,2-1,3-1
NLT - **3,** 1-1,2-1,3-1
NRSV - **3,** 1-1,2-1,3-1
Conclusion: All versions read the same.

620. Esther 9:9* And **Parmashta**, and **Arisai**, and **Aridai**, and **Vajezatha**,
AV - **8,** 1-1,2-1,3-1,4-1,5-1,6-1,7-1,8-1
ESV - **8,** 1-1,2-1,3-1,4-1,5-1,6-1,7-1,8-1
HCSB - **5,** 1-1,2-1,3-1,4-1,5-1
NASV - **5,** 1-1,2-1,3-1,4-1,5-1
NCV - **5,** 1-1,2-1,3-1,4-1,5-1
NIV - **5,** 1-1,2-1,3-1,4-1,5-1
NKJV - **5,** 1-1,2-1,3-1,4-1,5-1
NLT - **5,** 1-1,2-1,3-1,4-1,5-1
NRSV - **4,** 1-1,2-1,3-1,4-1
Conclusion: All versions read the same.

621. Job 1:11 But put forth thine hand now, and touch all that he hath, and he will curse thee to thy face.
AV - **20,** 1-1,2-1,3-1,4-1,5-1,6-1,7-1,8-1,9-1,10-1,11-1,12-1,13-1,14-1,15-1,16-1,17-1,18-1,19-1,20-1
ESV - **19,** 1-1,2-1,3-1,4-1,5-1,6-1,7-1,8-1,9-1,10-1,11-1,12-1,13-1,14-1,15-1,16-1,17-1,18-1,19-1
HCSB - **19,** 1-1,2-1,3-1,4-1,5-1,6-1,7-1,8-**4**,9-1,10-1,11-1,12-1,13-1,14-**2**,15-1,16-1,17-1,18-1,19-1
NASV - **20,** 1-1,2-1,3-1,4-1,5-1,6-1,7-1,8-1,9-1,10-1,11-1,12-1,13-1,14-1,15-**2**,16-1,17-1,18-1,19-1,20-1

NCV - 18, 1-1,2-1,3-1,4-1,5-1,6-1,7-**2**,8-**4**,9-1,10-1,11-1,12-1,13-1,14-1,15-1,16-1,17-1,18-1

NIV - 19, 1-1,2-1,3-1,4-1,5-1,6-1,7-1,8-**4**,9-1,10-1,11-1,12-1,13-1,14-**2**,15-1,16-1,17-1,18-1,19-1

NKJV - 21, 1-1,2-1,3-1,4-1,5-1,6-1,7-1,8-1,9-1,10-1,11-1,12-1,13-1,14-1,15-1,16-**2**,17-1,18-1,19-1,20-1,21-1

NLT - 18, 1-1,2-1,3-1,4-1,5-1,6-**2**,7-**4**,8-1,9-1,10-1,11-1,12-1,13-**2**,14-1,15-1,16-1,17-1,18-1

NRSV - **20,** 1-1,2-1,3-1,4-1,5-1,6-1,7-1,8-1,9-1,10-1,11-1,12-1,13-1,14-1,15-1,16-1,17-1,18-1,19-1,20-1

Conclusion: Six modern versions are more complex than the King James Bible.

622. Job 2:5 But put forth thine hand now, and touch his bone and his flesh, and he will curse thee to thy face.

AV - **20,** 1-1,2-1,3-1,4-1,5-1,6-1,7-1,8-1,9-1,10-1,11-1,12-1,13-1,14-1,15-1,16-1,17-1,18-1,19-1,20-1

ESV - **20,** 1-1,2-1,3-1,4-1,5-1,6-1,7-1,8-1,9-1,10-1,11-1,12-1,13-1,14-1,15-1,16-1,17-1,18-1,19-1,20-1

HCSB - **20,** 1-1,2-1,3-1,4-1,5-1,6-1,7-1,8-1,9-1,10-1,11-1,12-1,13-1,14-1,15-**2**,16-1,17-1,18-1,19-1,20-1

NASV - **20,** 1-**3**,2-1,3-1,4-1,5-1,6-1,7-1,8-1,9-1,10-1,11-1,12-1,13-1,14-1,15-1,16-1,17-1,18-1,19-1,20-1

NCV - 19, 1-1,2-1,3-1,4-1,5-1,6-1,7-**2**,8-1,9-1,10-1,11-1,12-1,13-1,14-1,15-1,16-1,17-1,18-1,19-1

NIV - **20,** 1-1,2-1,3-1,4-1,5-1,6-1,7-1,8-1,9-1,10-1,11-1,12-1,13-1,14-1,15-**2**,16-1,17-1,18-1,19-1,20-1

NKJV - 22, 1-1,2-1,3-1,4-1,5-1,6-1,7-1,8-1,9-1,10-1,11-1,12-1,13-1,14-1,15-1,16-1,17-**2**,18-1,19-1,20-1,21-1,22-1

NLT - 17, 1-1,2-1,3-1,4-1,5-1,6-**2**,7-1,8-1,9-1,10-1,11-1,12-**2**,13-1,14-1,15-1,16-1,17-1

NRSV - **21,** 1-1,2-1,3-1,4-1,5-1,6-1,7-1,8-1,9-1,10-1,11-1,12-1,13-1,14-1,15-1,16-1,17-1,18-1,19-1,20-1,21-1

Conclusion: Six modern versions are more complex than the King James Bible.

623. Job 3:2 And Job spake, and said.

AV - **5,** 1-1,2-1,3-1,4-1,5-1

ESV - **3,** 1-1,2-1,3-1

HCSB - **2,** 1-1,2-1

NASV - **3,** 1-1,2-1,3-1

NCV - **1,** 1-1

NIV - **2,** 1-1,2-1

NKJV - **5,** 1-1,2-1,3-1,4-1,5-1

NLT - **2,** 1-1,2-1

NRSV - **2,** 1-1,2-1

Conclusion: All versions read the same. For this verse the NCV simply has the lone word, "saying:" with no capital letter or any other word. I imagine this qualifies this verse as "the shortest verse in the bible" concerning the NCV.

624. Job 5:27 Lo this, we have searched it, so it is; hear it, and know thou it for thy good.
AV - **18,** 1-1,2-1,3-1,4-1,5-1,6-1,7-1,8-1,9-1,10-1,11-1,12-1,13-1,14-1,15-1,16-1,17-1,18-1
ESV - 16, 1-**2**,2-1,3-1,4-1,5-1,6-1,7-1,8-1,9-1,10-1,11-1,12-1,13-1,14-1,15-1,16-1
HCSB - 15, 1-1,2-1,3-**5**,4-1,5-1,6-1,7-1,8-1,9-1,10-1,11-1,12-**3**,13-1,14-1,15-**2**
NASV - 16, 1-**2**,2-1,3-1,4-1,5-**5**,6-1,7-1,8-1,9-1,10-1,11-1,12-1,13-1,14-1,15-1,16-**2**
NCV - 18, 1-1,2-1,3-1,4-1,5-1,6-1,7-1,8-1,9-1,10-1,11-1,12-1,13-**2**,14-1,15-1,16-1,17-1,18-1
NIV - 16, 1-1,2-1,3-**3**,4-1,5-1,6-1,7-1,8-1,9-1,10-1,11-1,12-1,13-**2**,14-1,15-1,16-**2**
NKJV - 15, 1-**2**,2-1,3-1,4-1,5-1,6-1,7-1,8-1,9-1,10-1,11-1,12-1,13-1,14-1,15-**2**
NLT - 20, 1-1,2-1,3-**2**,4-1,5-1,6-1,7-1,8-1,9-1,10-1,11-1,12-**2**,13-1,14-1,15-**2**,16-1,17-**2**,18-1,19-1,20-**2**
NRSV - 15, 1-1,2-1,3-1,4-1,5-1,6-1,7-1,8-1,9-1,10-1,11-1,12-1,13-1,14-1,15-**2**
Conclusion: All eight modern versions are more complex than the King James Bible. The NLT is the most difficult to read.

625. Job 6:12 Is my strength the strength of stones? or is my flesh of brass?
AV - **13,** 1-1,2-1,3-1,4-1,5-1,6-1,7-1,8-1,9-1,10-1,11-1,12-1,13-1
ESV - **12,** 1-1,2-1,3-1,4-1,5-1,6-1,7-1,8-1,9-1,10-1,11-1,12-1
HCSB - **12,** 1-1,2-1,3-1,4-1,5-1,6-1,7-1,8-1,9-1,10-1,11-1,12-1
NASV - **12,** 1-1,2-1,3-1,4-1,5-1,6-1,7-1,8-1,9-1,10-1,11-1,12-1
NCV - **13,** 1-1,2-1,3-1,4-1,5-1,6-1,7-1,8-1,9-1,10-1,11-1,12-1,13-1
NIV - **11,** 1-1,2-1,3-1,4-1,5-1,6-1,7-1,8-1,9-1,10-1,11-1
NKJV - **12,** 1-1,2-1,3-1,4-1,5-1,6-1,7-1,8-1,9-1,10-1,11-1,12-1
NLT - **12,** 1-1,2-1,3-1,4-1,5-1,6-1,7-1,8-1,9-1,10-1,11-1,12-1
NRSV - **12,** 1-1,2-1,3-1,4-1,5-1,6-1,7-1,8-1,9-1,10-1,11-1,12-1
Conclusion: All versions read the same.

626. Job 8:2 How long wilt thou speak these things? and how long shall the words of thy mouth be like a strong wind?
AV - **21,** 1-1,2-1,3-1,4-1,5-1,6-1,7-1,8-1,9-1,10-1,11-1,12-1,13-1,14-1,15-1,16-1,17-1,18-1,19-1,20-1,21-1
ESV - **17,** 1-1,2-1,3-1,4-1,5-1,6-1,7-1,8-1,9-1,10-1,11-1,12-1,13-1,14-1,15-1,16-1,17-1
HCSB - 16, 1-1,2-1,3-1,4-1,5-1,6-1,7-**2**,8-1,9-1,10-1,11-1,12-1,13-1,14-1,15-1,16-1
NASV - 17, 1-1,2-1,3-1,4-1,5-1,6-1,7-1,8-1,9-1,10-1,11-1,12-1,13-1,14-1,15-1,16-**2**,17-1
NCV - **14,** 1-1,2-1,3-1,4-1,5-1,6-1,7-1,8-1,9-1,10-1,11-1,12-1,13-1,14-1
NIV - 13, 1-1,2-1,3-1,4-1,5-1,6-1,7-1,8-1,9-1,10-1,11-1,12-**3**,13-1
NKJV - **18,** 1-1,2-1,3-1,4-1,5-1,6-1,7-1,8-1,9-1,10-1,11-1,12-1,13-1,14-1,15-1,16-1,17-1,18-1
NLT - 14, 1-1,2-1,3-1,4-1,5-1,6-1,7-1,8-1,9-1,10-1,11-1,12-1,13-**3**,14-1
NRSV - **17,** 1-1,2-1,3-1,4-1,5-1,6-1,7-1,8-1,9-1,10-1,11-1,12-1,13-1,14-1,15-1,16-1,17-1
Conclusion: Four modern versions are more complex than the King James Bible.

627. Job 9:2 I know it is so of a truth: but how should man be just with God?
AV - **16,** 1-1,2-1,3-1,4-1,5-1,6-1,7-1,8-1,9-1,10-1,11-1,12-1,13-1,14-1,15-1,16-1
ESV - 18, 1-**2**,2-1,3-1,4-1,5-1,6-1,7-1,8-1,9-1,10-1,11-1,12-1,13-1,14-1,15-1,16-1,17-**2**,18-1
HCSB - 17, 1-1,2-1,3-1,4-1,5-1,6-1,7-1,8-1,9-1,10-1,11-1,12-1,13-**2**,14-1,15-**3**,16-**2**,17-1

NASV - 19, 1-1,2-1,3-1,4-1,5-1,6-1,7-1,8-1,9-1,10-1,11-1,12-1,13-1,14-1,15-1,16-1,17-1,18-**2**,19-1
NCV - 18, 1-1,2-1,3-1,4-1,5-1,6-1,7-1,8-1,9-1,10-1,11-**3**,12-1,13-1,14-1,15-1,16-**2**,17-1,18-1
NIV - 16, 1-**2**,2-1,3-1,4-1,5-1,6-1,7-1,8-1,9-1,10-1,11-1,12-**2**,13-1,14-**3**,15-**2**,16-1
NKJV - 15, 1-**2**,2-1,3-1,4-1,5-1,6-1,7-1,8-1,9-1,10-1,11-1,12-1,13-**3**,14-**2**,15-1
NLT - 20, 1-1,2-1,3-1,4-1,5-1,6-1,7-1,8-1,9-**3**,10-1,11-1,12-1,13-1,14-**2**,15-1,16-**2**,17-**3**,18-1,19-1,20-1
NRSV - 16, 1-**2**,2-1,3-1,4-1,5-1,6-1,7-1,8-1,9-1,10-1,11-1,12-**2**,13-1,14-1,15-**2**,16-1
Conclusion: All eight modern versions are more complex than the King James Bible. The New Living Translation is the most difficult to read.

628. Job 9:35 Then would I speak, and not fear him; but it is not so with me.
AV - 15, 1-1,2-1,3-1,4-1,5-1,6-1,7-1,8-1,9-1,10-1,11-1,12-1,13-1,14-1,15-1
ESV - 15, 1-1,2-1,3-1,4-1,5-**2**,6-1,7-1,8-1,9-1,10-1,11-1,12-1,13-1,14-1,15-**2**
HCSB - 19, 1-1,2-1,3-1,4-1,5-1,6-1,7-1,8-1,9-1,10-1,11-1,12-1,13-1,14-1,15-1,16-1,17-1,18-1,19-1
NASV - 16, 1-1,2-1,3-1,4-1,5-1,6-1,7-1,8-1,9-1,10-1,11-1,12-1,13-1,14-1,15-1,16-**2**
NCV - 15, 1-1,2-1,3-1,4-1,5-**2**,6-**2**,7-**2**,8-1,9-1,10-1,11-1,12-**2**,13-1,14-1,15-1
NIV - 18, 1-1,2-1,3-1,4-1,5-1,6-**2**,7-1,8-1,9-1,10-1,11-1,12-1,13-1,14-1,15-1,16-1,17-1,18-**2**
NKJV - **15,** 1-1,2-1,3-1,4-1,5-1,6-1,7-1,8-1,9-1,10-1,11-1,12-1,13-1,14-1,15-1
NLT - 17, 1-1,2-1,3-1,4-1,5-1,6-1,7-**2**,8-1,9-1,10-1,11-**2**,12-1,13-1,14-1,15-1,16-1,17-1
NRSV - 20, 1-1,2-1,3-1,4-1,5-**2**,6-1,7-1,8-1,9-1,10-1,11-1,12-1,13-1,14-1,15-1,16-1,17-1,18-1,19-1,20-1
Conclusion: Six modern versions are more complex than the King James Bible. The NCV is the most difficult to read.

629. Job 10:5 Are thy days as the days of man? are thy years as man's days,
AV - 14, 1-1,2-1,3-1,4-1,5-1,6-1,7-1,8-1,9-1,10-1,11-1,12-1,13-1,14-1
ESV - 15, 1-1,2-1,3-1,4-1,5-1,6-1,7-1,8-1,9-1,10-1,11-1,12-1,13-1,14-1,15-1
HCSB - 16, 1-1,2-1,3-1,4-1,5-1,6-1,7-1,8-**2**,9-1,10-1,11-1,12-1,13-1,14-1,15-1,16-1
NASV - 15, 1-1,2-1,3-1,4-1,5-1,6-1,7-1,8-1,9-**2**,10-1,11-1,12-1,13-1,14-1,15-1
NCV - 14, 1-1,2-1,3-1,4-1,5-1,6-1,7-1,8-**2**,9-1,10-1,11-1,12-1,13-1,14-1
NIV - 16, 1-1,2-1,3-1,4-1,5-1,6-1,7-1,8-**2**,9-1,10-1,11-1,12-1,13-1,14-1,15-1,16-1
NKJV - 20, 1-1,2-1,3-1,4-1,5-1,6-1,7-1,8-1,9-**2**,10-1,11-1,12-1,13-1,14-1,15-1,16-1,17-1,18-1,19-**2**,20-1
NLT - 13, 1-1,2-1,3-**2**,4-1,5-1,6-1,7-1,8-1,9-1,10-1,11-1,12-1,13-1
NRSV - 14, 1-1,2-1,3-1,4-1,5-1,6-1,7-1,8-**2**,9-1,10-1,11-1,12-1,13-**2**,14-1
Conclusion: Seven modern versions are more complex than the King James Bible.

630. Job 10:13 And these things hast thou hid in thine heart: I know that this is with thee.
AV - 16, 1-1,2-1,3-1,4-1,5-1,6-1,7-1,8-1,9-1,10-1,11-1,12-1,13-1,14-1,15-1,16-1
ESV - 15, 1-1,2-1,3-1,4-1,5-1,6-1,7-1,8-1,9-1,10-1,11-1,12-1,13-1,14-1,15-**2**
HCSB - 16, 1-1,2-1,3-**2**,4-1,5-1,6-1,7-1,8-1,9-1,10-1,11-1,12-1,13-1,14-1,15-**2**,16-1
NASV - 16, 1-1,2-1,3-1,4-1,5-1,6-**2**,7-1,8-1,9-1,10-1,11-1,12-1,13-1,14-1,15-**2**,16-1
NCV - 15, 1-1,2-1,3-1,4-1,5-1,6-1,7-**2**,8-1,9-1,10-1,11-1,12-1,13-1,14-1,15-1
NIV - 7, 1-1,2-1,3-1,4-**2**,5-1,6-1,7-**2**

NKJV - **16,** 1-1,2-1,3-1,4-1,5-1,6-**2**,7-1,8-1,9-1,10-1,11-1,12-1,13-1,14-1,15-1,16-1
NLT - **18,** 1-1,2-1,3-1,4-1,5-1,6-**2**,7-1,8-1,9-1,10-1,11-1,12-1,13-1,14-1,15-1,16-1,17-1,18-1
NRSV - **15,** 1-1,2-1,3-1,4-1,5-1,6-1,7-1,8-1,9-1,10-1,11-1,12-1,13-1,14-1,15-**2**
Conclusion: All eight modern versions are more complex than the King James Bible.

631. Job 12:7 But ask now the beasts, and they shall teach thee; and the fowls of the air, and they shall tell thee:
AV - **21,** 1-1,2-1,3-1,4-1,5-1,6-1,7-1,8-1,9-1,10-1,11-1,12-1,13-1,14-1,15-1,16-1,17-1,18-1,19-1,20-1,21-1
ESV - **19,** 1-1,2-1,3-1,4-1,5-1,6-1,7-1,8-1,9-1,10-1,11-1,12-1,13-1,14-**2**,15-1,16-1,17-1,18-1,19-1
HCSB - **20,** 1-1,2-1,3-1,4-**3**,5-1,6-1,7-1,8-**2**,9-1,10-1,11-1,12-1,13-1,14-1,15-1,16-1,17-1,18-1,19-1,20-1
NASV - **21,** 1-1,2-1,3-1,4-1,5-1,6-1,7-1,8-1,9-1,10-1,11-1,12-1,13-1,14-1,15-1,16-**2**,17-1,18-1,19-1,20-1,21-1
NCV - **21,** 1-1,2-1,3-1,4-**3**,5-1,6-1,7-1,8-1,9-1,10-1,11-1,12-1,13-1,14-1,15-1,16-1,17-1,18-1,19-1,20-1,21-1
NIV - **20,** 1-1,2-1,3-1,4-**3**,5-1,6-1,7-1,8-1,9-1,10-1,11-1,12-1,13-1,14-1,15-1,16-1,17-1,18-1,19-1,20-1
NKJV - **21,** 1-1,2-1,3-1,4-1,5-1,6-1,7-1,8-1,9-1,10-1,11-1,12-1,13-1,14-1,15-1,16-1,17-1,18-1,19-1,20-1,21-1
NLT - **20,** 1-1,2-1,3-1,4-**3**,5-1,6-1,7-1,8-1,9-1,10-1,11-1,12-1,13-1,14-1,15-1,16-1,17-1,18-1,19-1,20-1
NRSV - **19,** 1-1,2-1,3-1,4-**3**,5-1,6-1,7-1,8-1,9-1,10-1,11-1,12-1,13-1,14-1,15-1,16-1,17-1,18-1,19-1
Conclusion: Seven modern versions are more complex than the King James Bible. The HCSB is the most difficult to read.

632. Job 12:11 Doth not the ear try words? and the mouth taste his meat?
AV - **12,** 1-1,2-1,3-1,4-1,5-1,6-1,7-1,8-1,9-1,10-1,11-1,12-1
ESV - **11,** 1-1,2-1,3-1,4-1,5-1,6-1,7-1,8-1,9-**2**,10-1,11-1
HCSB - **10,** 1-**2**,2-1,3-1,4-1,5-1,6-1,7-1,8-**2**,9-1,10-1
NASV - **12,** 1-1,2-1,3-1,4-1,5-1,6-1,7-1,8-1,9-**2**,10-1,11-1,12-1
NCV - **9,** 1-1,2-1,3-1,4-1,5-1,6-1,7-1,8-1,9-1
NIV - **11,** 1-1,2-1,3-1,4-1,5-1,6-1,7-1,8-1,9-1,10-1,11-1
NKJV - **12,** 1-1,2-1,3-1,4-1,5-1,6-1,7-1,8-1,9-1,10-1,11-1,12-1
NLT - **14,** 1-1,2-1,3-1,4-1,5-1,6-1,7-1,8-1,9-1,10-1,11-1,12-**4**,13-**2**,14-1
NRSV - **11,** 1-1,2-1,3-1,4-1,5-1,6-1,7-1,8-1,9-**2**,10-1,11-1
Conclusion: Five modern versions are more complex than the King James Bible. The NLT is the most difficult to read.

633. Job 13:19 Who is he that will plead with me? for now, if I hold my tongue, I shall give up the ghost.
AV - **21,** 1-1,2-1,3-1,4-1,5-1,6-1,7-1,8-1,9-1,10-1,11-1,12-1,13-1,14-1,15-1,16-1,17-1,18-1,19-1,20-1,21-1
ESV - **16,** 1-1,2-1,3-1,4-1,5-1,6-**2**,7-1,8-1,9-1,10-1,11-1,12-1,13-1,14-**2**,15-1,16-1

HCSB - 12, 1-1,2-**2**,3-**2**,4-1,5-1,6-1,7-1,8-1,9-1,10-**2**,11-1,12-1
NASV - 13, 1-1,2-1,3-**2**,4-1,5-1,6-1,7-1,8-1,9-1,10-1,11-**2**,12-1,13-1
NCV - 17, 1-1,2-1,3-1,4-**2**,5-1,6-1,7-**2**,8-1,9-1,10-**2**,11-1,12-1,13-1,14-1,15-1,16-1,17-1
NIV - 14, 1-1,2-**2**,3-1,4-**2**,5-**2**,6-1,7-1,8-1,9-1,10-1,11-1,12-**2**,13-1,14-1
NKJV - 16, 1-1,2-1,3-1,4-1,5-1,6-**2**,7-1,8-1,9-1,10-1,11-1,12-1,13-1,14-1,15-1,16-**2**
NLT - 20, 1-1,2-1,3-**2**,4-1,5-1,6-**2**,7-1,8-1,9-1,10-1,11-1,12-1,13-1,14-1,15-1,16-**2**,17-**2**,18-1,19-1,20-1
NRSV - 16, 1-1,2-1,3-1,4-1,5-1,6-**2**,7-1,8-1,9-1,10-1,11-1,12-1,13-1,14-**2**,15-1,16-1
Conclusion: All eight modern versions are more complex than the King James Bible.

634. Job 17:15 And where is now my hope? as for my hope, who shall see it?
AV - **14,** 1-1,2-1,3-1,4-1,5-1,6-1,7-1,8-1,9-1,10-1,11-1,12-1,13-1,14-1
ESV - **10,** 1-1,2-1,3-1,4-1,5-1,6-1,7-1,8-1,9-1,10-1
HCSB - 12, 1-1,2-1,3-1,4-1,5-1,6-1,7-1,8-1,9-**2**,10-1,11-1,12-1
NASV - 10, 1-1,2-1,3-1,4-1,5-1,6-1,7-1,8-**2**,9-1,10-1
NCV - 12, 1-1,2-1,3-1,4-1,5-1,6-1,7-1,8-1,9-**2**,10-1,11-1,12-1
NIV - 12, 1-1,2-1,3-1,4-1,5-1,6-1,7-1,8-1,9-**2**,10-1,11-1,12-1
NKJV - 13, 1-1,2-1,3-1,4-1,5-1,6-1,7-1,8-1,9-**2**,10-1,11-1,12-1,13-1
NLT - 9, 1-1,2-1,3-1,4-1,5-1,6-1,7-**3**,8-1,9-1
NRSV - **10,** 1-1,2-1,3-1,4-1,5-1,6-1,7-1,8-1,9-1,10-1
Conclusion: Six modern versions are more complex than the King James Bible.

635. Job 18:10 The snare is laid for him in the ground, and a trap for him in the way.
AV - **17,** 1-1,2-1,3-1,4-1,5-1,6-1,7-1,8-1,9-1,10-1,11-1,12-1,13-1,14-1,15-1,16-1,17-1
ESV - 16, 1-1,2-1,3-1,4-**2**,5-1,6-1,7-1,8-1,9-1,10-1,11-1,12-1,13-1,14-1,15-1,16-1
HCSB - 18, 1-1,2-1,3-1,4-**2**,5-1,6-1,7-1,8-1,9-1,10-1,11-1,12-1,13-1,14-1,15-1,16-**2**,17-1,18-1
NASV - 17, 1-1,2-1,3-1,4-1,5-1,6-**2**,7-1,8-1,9-1,10-1,11-1,12-1,13-1,14-1,15-1,16-1,17-1
NCV - 13, 1-1,2-1,3-1,4-1,5-1,6-**2**,7-1,8-1,9-1,10-1,11-1,12-1,13-1
NIV - 15, 1-1,2-1,3-1,4-**2**,5-1,6-1,7-1,8-1,9-1,10-1,11-1,12-1,13-1,14-1,15-1
NKJV - 17, 1-1,2-1,3-1,4-**2**,5-1,6-1,7-1,8-1,9-1,10-1,11-1,12-1,13-1,14-1,15-1,16-1,17-1
NLT - 14, 1-1,2-1,3-1,4-**2**,5-1,6-1,7-1,8-1,9-1,10-1,11-1,12-**2**,13-1,14-1
NRSV - **16,** 1-1,2-1,3-1,4-1,5-1,6-1,7-1,8-1,9-1,10-1,11-1,12-1,13-1,14-1,15-1,16-1
Conclusion: Seven modern versions are more complex than the King James Bible.

636. Job 20:11 His bones are full of the sin of his youth, which shall lie down with him in the dust.
AV - **19,** 1-1,2-1,3-1,4-1,5-1,6-1,7-1,8-1,9-1,10-1,11-1,12-1,13-1,14-1,15-1,16-1,17-1,18-1,19-1
ESV - 18, 1-1,2-1,3-1,4-1,5-1,6-1,7-**2**,8-**2**,9-1,10-1,11-1,12-1,13-1,14-1,15-1,16-1,17-1,18-1
HCSB - 18, 1-1,2-1,3-1,4-1,5-1,6-1,7-**2**,8-**2**,9-1,10-1,11-1,12-1,13-1,14-1,15-1,16-1,17-1,18-1
NASV - 17, 1-1,2-1,3-1,4-1,5-1,6-1,7-**2**,8-**2**,9-1,10-1,11-1,12-1,13-1,14-1,15-1,16-1,17-1
NCV - **21,** 1-1,2-1,3-1,4-1,5-1,6-1,7-1,8-1,9-1,10-1,11-1,12-1,13-1,14-1,15-1,16-1,17-1,18-1,19-1,20-1,21-1
NIV - 14, 1-1,2-**2**,3-**2**,4-1,5-1,6-1,7-1,8-1,9-1,10-1,11-1,12-1,13-1,14-1
NKJV - 18, 1-1,2-1,3-1,4-1,5-1,6-1,7-**2**,8-**2**,9-1,10-1,11-1,12-1,13-1,14-1,15-1,16-1,17-1,18-1
NLT - **11,** 1-1,2-1,3-1,4-1,5-1,6-1,7-1,8-1,9-1,10-1,11-1

NRSV - 14, 1-1,2-**2**,3-1,4-1,5-1,6-1,7-1,8-1,9-1,10-1,11-1,12-1,13-1,14-1

Conclusion: Six modern versions are more complex than the King James Bible. In an extremely rare turnabout the NCV and NLT are the only modern version that **do not** make the verse more complex.

637. Job 22:24* Then shalt thou lay up gold as dust, and the gold of **Ophir** as the stones of the brooks.

AV - 19, 1-1,2-1,3-1,4-1,5-1,6-1,7-1,8-1,9-1,10-1,11-1,12-1,13-1,14-1,15-1,16-1,17-1,18-1,19-1

ESV - 18, 1-1,2-1,3-1,4-1,5-1,6-1,7-1,8-1,9-1,10-1,11-1,12-**2**,13-1,14-1,15-1,16-1,17-**2**,18-1

HCSB - 17, 1-1,2-**2**,3-1,4-1,5-1,6-1,7-1,8-1,9-1,10-1,11-1,12-1,13-1,14-1,15-1,16-1,17-**2**

NASV - 18, 1-1,2-1,3-1,4-1,5-1,6-1,7-1,8-1,9-1,10-1,11-1,12-1,13-**2**,14-1,15-1,16-1,17-1,18-1

NCV - 17, 1-1,2-1,3-1,4-**2**,5-**2**,6-1,7-1,8-1,9-1,10-1,11-1,12-**2**,13-1,14-1,15-1,16-1,17-**2**

NIV - 17, 1-1,2-**2**,3-1,4-**2**,5-1,6-1,7-1,8-1,9-1,10-1,11-1,12-1,13-1,14-1,15-1,16-1,17-**2**

NKJV - 20, 1-1,2-1,3-1,4-1,5-1,6-1,7-1,8-1,9-1,10-1,11-1,12-1,13-1,14-1,15-**2**,16-1,17-1,18-1,19-1,20-1

NLT - 16, 1-1,2-1,3-1,4-1,5-1,6-1,7-1,8-**2**,9-1,10-1,11-1,12-**2**,13-1,14-**2**,15-1,16-**2**

NRSV - 17, 1-1,2-1,3-1,4-1,5-1,6-1,7-1,8-1,9-1,10-1,11-1,12-1,13-1,14-1,15-1,16-**2**,17-1

Conclusion: All eight modern versions are more complex than the King James Bible. Both the ESV and NRSV inserted "torrent beds" for "brooks."

638. Job 25:6 How much less man, that is a worm? and the son of man, which is a worm?

AV - 17, 1-1,2-1,3-1,4-1,5-1,6-1,7-1,8-1,9-1,10-1,11-1,12-1,13-1,14-1,15-1,16-1,17-1

ESV - 17, 1-1,2-1,3-1,4-1,5-1,6-1,7-1,8-**2**,9-1,10-1,11-1,12-1,13-1,14-1,15-1,16-1,17-1

HCSB - 17, 1-1,2-1,3-1,4-1,5-1,6-1,7-1,8-**2**,9-1,10-1,11-1,12-1,13-1,14-1,15-1,16-1,17-1

NASV - 13, 1-1,2-1,3-1,4-1,5-1,6-**2**,7-1,8-1,9-1,10-1,11-1,12-1,13-1

NCV - 12, 1-**2**,2-1,3-1,4-1,5-1,6-1,7-1,8-**2**,9-1,10-1,11-**2**,12-1

NIV - 18, 1-1,2-1,3-1,4-1,5-1,6-1,7-1,8-1,9-**2**,10-1,11-1,12-1,13-1,14-1,15-1,16-**2**,17-1,18-1

NKJV - 17, 1-1,2-1,3-1,4-1,5-1,6-1,7-1,8-**2**,9-1,10-1,11-1,12-1,13-1,14-1,15-1,16-1,17-1

NLT - 10, 1-1,2-**4**,3-**2**,4-1,5-**2**,6-1,7-**2**,8-1,9-1,10-1

NRSV - 17, 1-1,2-1,3-1,4-1,5-**2**,6-1,7-1,8-1,9-**2**,10-1,11-1,12-**2**,13-**2**,14-1,15-1,16-1,17-1

Conclusion: All eight modern versions are more complex than the King James Bible. Both the NLT and the NRSV have four words that are multi-syllable, but the NLT manages to achieve that with only ten words, and one of those even has four syllables.

639. Job 27:23 Men shall clap their hands at him, and shall hiss him out of his place.

AV - 15, 1-1,2-1,3-1,4-1,5-1,6-1,7-1,8-1,9-1,10-1,11-1,12-1,13-1,14-1,15-1

ESV - 13, 1-1,2-1,3-1,4-1,5-1,6-1,7-1,8-**2**,9-1,10-1,11-1,12-1,13-1

HCSB - 12, 1-1,2-1,3-1,4-1,5-1,6-1,7-1,8-1,9-1,10-1,11-1,12-1

NASV - 14, 1-1,2-1,3-1,4-1,5-1,6-1,7-1,8-1,9-1,10-1,11-1,12-1,13-1,14-1

NCV - 22, 1-1,2-1,3-1,4-1,5-1,6-1,7-1,8-1,9-**2**,10-1,11-1,12-1,13-1,14-**2**,15-1,16-1,17-1,18-1,19-1,20-1,21-1,22-1

NIV - 13, 1-1,2-1,3-1,4-1,5-1,6-**3**,7-1,8-**2**,9-1,10-1,11-1,12-1,13-1

NKJV - 15, 1-1,2-1,3-1,4-1,5-1,6-1,7-1,8-1,9-1,10-1,11-1,12-1,13-1,14-1,15-1

NLT - 8, 1-1,2-**3**,3-1,4-1,5-1,6-1,7-1,8-1

NRSV - 13, 1-1,2-1,3-1,4-1,5-1,6-1,7-1,8-**2**,9-1,10-1,11-1,12-1,13-1

Conclusion: Five modern versions are more complex than the King James Bible.

640. Job 28:14 The depth saith, It is not in me: and the sea saith, It is not with me.
AV - **17,** 1-1,2-1,3-1,4-1,5-1,6-1,7-1,8-1,9-1,10-1,11-1,12-1,13-1,14-1,15-1,16-1,17-1
ESV - **17,** 1-1,2-1,3-1,4-1,5-1,6-1,7-1,8-1,9-1,10-1,11-1,12-1,13-1,14-1,15-1,16-1,17-1
HCSB - 16, 1-1,2-**2**,3-1,4-1,5-1,6-1,7-1,8-1,9-1,10-1,11-1,12-**2**,13-1,14-1,15-1,16-1
NASV - **17,** 1-1,2-1,3-1,4-1,5-1,6-1,7-1,8-1,9-1,10-1,11-1,12-1,13-1,14-1,15-1,16-1,17-1
NCV - 15, 1-1,2-1,3-**2**,4-1,5-1,6-1,7-1,8-1,9-1,10-1,11-1,12-1,13-1,14-1,15-1
NIV - **16,** 1-1,2-1,3-1,4-1,5-1,6-1,7-1,8-1,9-1,10-1,11-1,12-1,13-1,14-1,15-1,16-1
NKJV - **17,** 1-1,2-1,3-1,4-1,5-1,6-1,7-1,8-1,9-1,10-1,11-1,12-1,13-1,14-1,15-1,16-1,17-1
NLT - 14, 1-1,2-1,3-1,4-1,5-1,6-1,7-**2**,8-1,9-1,10-1,11-1,12-1,13-1,14-1
NRSV - **17,** 1-1,2-1,3-1,4-1,5-1,6-1,7-1,8-1,9-1,10-1,11-1,12-1,13-1,14-1,15-1,16-1,17-1
Conclusion: Only three modern versions are more complex than the King James Bible.

641. Job 29:15 I was eyes to the blind, and feet was I to the lame.
AV - **13,** 1-1,2-1,3-1,4-1,5-1,6-1,7-1,8-1,9-1,10-1,11-1,12-1,13-1
ESV - **11,** 1-1,2-1,3-1,4-1,5-1,6-1,7-1,8-1,9-1,10-1,11-1
HCSB - **11,** 1-1,2-1,3-1,4-1,5-1,6-1,7-1,8-1,9-1,10-1,11-1
NASV - **11,** 1-1,2-1,3-1,4-1,5-1,6-1,7-1,8-1,9-1,10-1,11-1
NCV - **11,** 1-1,2-1,3-1,4-1,5-1,6-1,7-1,8-1,9-1,10-1,11-1
NIV - **11,** 1-1,2-1,3-1,4-1,5-1,6-1,7-1,8-1,9-1,10-1,11-1
NKJV - **13,** 1-1,2-1,3-1,4-1,5-1,6-1,7-1,8-1,9-1,10-1,11-1,12-1,13-1
NLT - **12,** 1-1,2-1,3-1,4-1,5-1,6-1,7-1,8-1,9-1,10-1,11-1,12-1
NRSV - **11,** 1-1,2-1,3-1,4-1,5-1,6-1,7-1,8-1,9-1,10-1,11-1
Conclusion: All versions read the same.

642. Job 31:4 Doth not he see my ways, and count all my steps?
AV - **11,** 1-1,2-1,3-1,4-1,5-1,6-1,7-1,8-1,9-1,10-1,11-1
ESV - 11, 1-1,2-1,3-1,4-1,5-1,6-1,7-1,8-**2**,9-1,10-1,11-1
HCSB - 11, 1-1,2-1,3-1,4-1,5-1,6-1,7-1,8-**2**,9-1,10-1,11-1
NASV - 11, 1-1,2-1,3-1,4-1,5-1,6-1,7-1,8-**2**,9-1,10-1,11-1
NCV - 10, 1-1,2-1,3-1,4-1,5-1,6-1,7-**2**,8-1,9-1,10-1
NIV - **11,** 1-1,2-1,3-1,4-1,5-1,6-1,7-1,8-1,9-1,10-1,11-1
NKJV - **11,** 1-1,2-1,3-1,4-1,5-1,6-1,7-1,8-1,9-1,10-1,11-1
NLT - 11, 1-**2**,2-1,3-1,4-**3**,5-1,6-1,7-1,8-**2**,9-1,10-1,11-1
NRSV - 11, 1-1,2-1,3-1,4-1,5-1,6-1,7-1,8-**2**,9-1,10-1,11-1
Conclusion: Six modern versions are more complex than the King James Bible. Once again, the NLT is the most difficult to read.

643. Job 31:20 If his loins have not blessed me, and if he were not warmed with the fleece of my sheep;
AV - **19,** 1-1,2-1,3-1,4-1,5-1,6-1,7-1,8-1,9-1,10-1,11-1,12-1,13-1,14-1,15-1,16-1,17-1,18-1,19-1
ESV - 19, 1-1,2-1,3-**2**,4-1,5-1,6-1,7-1,8-1,9-1,10-1,11-1,12-1,13-1,14-1,15-1,16-1,17-1,18-1,19-1
HCSB - 15, 1-1,2-1,3-1,4-1,5-1,6-1,7-1,8-**2**,9-**2**,10-1,11-1,12-1,13-1,14-1,15-1

NASV - **20,** 1-1,2-1,3-1,4-1,5-1,6-1,7-1,8-1,9-1,10-1,11-1,12-1,13-1,14-1,15-1,16-1,17-1,18-1,19-1,20-1

NCV - **15,** 1-1,2-**2,**3-1,4-1,5-1,6-**2,**7-1,8-1,9-1,10-1,11-1,12-1,13-1,14-1,15-1

NIV - **16,** 1-1,2-1,3-1,4-1,5-1,6-1,7-1,8-1,9-**2,**10-1,11-1,12-1,13-1,14-1,15-1,16-1

NKJV - **19,** 1-1,2-1,3-1,4-1,5-1,6-1,7-1,8-1,9-1,10-1,11-1,12-1,13-1,14-1,15-1,16-1,17-1,18-1,19-1

NLT - **13,** 1-1,2-1,3-1,4-1,5-1,6-1,7-**3,**8-1,9-**2,**10-1,11-1,12-1,13-1

NRSV - **17,** 1-1,2-1,3-1,4-1,5-1,6-1,7-1,8-1,9-1,10-1,11-1,12-1,13-1,14-1,15-1,16-1,17-1

Conclusion: Five modern versions are more complex than the King James Bible.

644. Job 39:5 Who hath sent out the wild ass free? or who hath loosed the bands of the wild ass?

AV - **18,** 1-1,2-1,3-1,4-1,5-1,6-1,7-1,8-1,9-1,10-1,11-1,12-1,13-1,14-1,15-1,16-1,17-1,18-1

ESV - **17,** 1-1,2-1,3-1,4-1,5-1,6-**2,**7-1,8-1,9-1,10-1,11-1,12-1,13-1,14-1,15-1,16-1,17-**2**

HCSB - **14,** 1-1,2-1,3-1,4-1,5-**2,**6-1,7-1,8-**2,**9-1,10-1,11-**2,**12-1,13-1,14-**2**

NASV - **16,** 1-1,2-1,3-1,4-1,5-1,6-**2,**7-1,8-1,9-1,10-1,11-1,12-1,13-1,14-1,15-1,16-**2**

NCV - **11,** 1-1,2-1,3-1,4-1,5-**2,**6-1,7-1,8-1,9-**2,**10-1,11-1

NIV - **11,** 1-1,2-1,3-1,4-1,5-**2,**6-1,7-1,8-1,9-**2,**10-1,11-1

NKJV - **13,** 1-1,2-1,3-1,4-1,5-**2,**6-1,7-1,8-1,9-1,10-1,11-1,12-1,13-**3**

NLT - **11,** 1-1,2-1,3-1,4-1,5-**2,**6-1,7-**2,**8-1,9-**2,**10-1,11-1

NRSV - **17,** 1-1,2-1,3-1,4-1,5-1,6-1,7-1,8-1,9-1,10-1,11-1,12-1,13-1,14-1,15-1,16-1,17-1

Conclusion: Seven modern versions are more complex than the King James Bible. Only the NRSV retained the Authorized Version's "ass" where six of the remaining seven changed it to "donkey" both times. But, for some reason the NKJV used "donkey" for the first reference and "onager" in the second. The HCSB is the most difficult to read.

645. Job 41:7 Canst thou fill his skin with barbed irons? or his head with fish spears?

AV - **14,** 1-1,2-1,3-1,4-1,5-1,6-1,7-1,8-1,9-1,10-1,11-1,12-1,13-1,14-1

ESV - **13,** 1-1,2-1,3-1,4-1,5-1,6-1,7-**2,**8-1,9-1,10-1,11-1,12-**2,**13-1

HCSB - **13,** 1-1,2-1,3-1,4-1,5-1,6-1,7-**2,**8-1,9-1,10-1,11-1,12-**2,**13-1

NASV - **13,** 1-1,2-1,3-1,4-1,5-1,6-1,7-**2,**8-1,9-1,10-1,11-1,12-**2,**13-1

NCV - **15,** 1-1,2-1,3-1,4-1,5-1,6-**2,**7-1,8-1,9-1,10-1,11-1,12-1,13-1,14-**2,**15-1

NIV - **13,** 1-1,2-1,3-1,4-1,5-1,6-1,7-**2,**8-1,9-1,10-1,11-1,12-**2,**13-1

NKJV - **13,** 1-1,2-1,3-1,4-1,5-1,6-1,7-**2,**8-1,9-1,10-1,11-1,12-**2,**13-1

NLT - **13,** 1-1,2-1,3-1,4-1,5-1,6-1,7-1,8-1,9-1,10-1,11-1,12-1,13-**2**

NRSV - **13,** 1-1,2-1,3-1,4-1,5-1,6-1,7-**2,**8-1,9-1,10-1,11-1,12-**2,**13-1

Conclusion: All eight modern versions are more complex than the King James Bible.

646. Job 42:14*# And he called the name of the first, **Jemima**; and the name of the **second, Kezia**; and the name of the third, **Kerenhappuch**.

AV - **23,** 1-1,2-1,3-1,4-1,5-1,6-1,7-1,8-1,9-1,10-1,11-1,12-1,13-1,14-1,15-1,16-1,17-1,18-1,19-1,20-1,21-1,22-1,23-1

ESV - **24,** 1-1,2-1,3-1,4-1,5-1,6-1,7-1,8-1,9-**2,**10-1,11-1,12-1,13-1,14-1,15-1,16-1,17-1,18-1,19-1,20-1,21-1,22-1,23-1,24-1

HCSB - **13,** 1-1,2-1,3-1,4-1,5-**2,**6-1,7-1,8-1,9-1,10-1,11-1,12-1,13-1

NASV - **13,** 1-1,2-1,3-1,4-1,5-1,6-1,7-1,8-1,9-1,10-1,11-1,12-1,13-1

NCV - 15, 1-1,2-1,3-1,4-1,5-**2**,6-1,7-1,8-1,9-**2**,10-1,11-1,12-1,13-1,14-**2**,15-1
NIV - 13, 1-1,2-1,3-**2**,4-1,5-1,6-1,7-1,8-1,9-1,10-1,11-1,12-1,13-1
NKJV - **22,** 1-1,2-1,3-1,4-1,5-1,6-1,7-1,8-1,9-1,10-1,11-1,12-1,13-1,14-1,15-1,16-1,17-1,18-1,19-1,20-1,21-1,22-1
NLT - 13, 1-1,2-1,3-1,4-1,5-**2**,6-1,7-1,8-1,9-1,10-1,11-1,12-1,13-1
NRSV - **12,** 1-1,2-1,3-1,4-1,5-1,6-1,7-1,8-1,9-1,10-1,11-1,12-1
Conclusion: Five modern versions are more complex than the King James Bible. The NCV is the most difficult to read.

647. Psalms 18:1 I will love thee, O LORD, my strength.
AV - **8,** 1-1,2-1,3-1,4-1,5-1,6-1,7-1,8-1
ESV - **7,** 1-1,2-1,3-1,4-1,5-1,6-1,7-1
HCSB - **6,** 1-1,2-1,3-1,4-1,5-1,6-1
NASV - **7,** 1-1,2-1,3-1,4-1,5-1,6-1,7-1
NCV - **8,** 1-1,2-1,3-1,4-1,5-1,6-1,7-1,8-1
NIV - **7,** 1-1,2-1,3-1,4-1,5-1,6-1,7-1
NKJV - **8,** 1-1,2-1,3-1,4-1,5-1,6-1,7-1,8-1
NLT - **8,** 1-1,2-1,3-1,4-1,5-1,6-1,7-1,8-1
NRSV - **7,** 1-1,2-1,3-1,4-1,5-1,6-1,7-1
Conclusion: All versions read the same.

648. Psalms 18:31 For who is God save the LORD? or who is a rock save our God?
AV - **15,** 1-1,2-1,3-1,4-1,5-1,6-1,7-1,8-1,9-1,10-1,11-1,12-1,13-1,14-1,15-1
ESV - 15, 1-1,2-1,3-1,4-1,5-1,6-1,7-1,8-1,9-1,10-1,11-1,12-1,13-**2**,14-1,15-1
HCSB - 15, 1-1,2-1,3-1,4-1,5-**2**,6-1,7-1,8-1,9-1,10-1,11-1,12-1,13-**2**,14-1,15-1
NASV - 15, 1-1,2-1,3-1,4-1,5-**2**,6-1,7-1,8-1,9-1,10-1,11-1,12-1,13-**2**,14-1,15-1
NCV - 13, 1-1,2-1,3-1,4-**2**,5-1,6-1,7-1,8-1,9-1,10-1,11-**2**,12-1,13-1
NIV - 15, 1-1,2-1,3-1,4-1,5-**2**,6-1,7-1,8-1,9-1,10-1,11-1,12-1,13-**2**,14-1,15-1
NKJV - 15, 1-1,2-1,3-1,4-1,5-**2**,6-1,7-1,8-1,9-1,10-1,11-1,12-1,13-**2**,14-1,15-1
NLT - 15, 1-1,2-1,3-1,4-1,5-**2**,6-1,7-1,8-1,9-1,10-1,11-1,12-1,13-1,14-**2**,15-1
NRSV - 15, 1-1,2-1,3-1,4-1,5-**2**,6-1,7-1,8-1,9-1,10-1,11-1,12-1,13-**2**,14-1,15-1
Conclusion: All eight modern versions are more complex than the King James Bible. With the exception of the NRSV these results mirror those of 2 Samuel 22:32. In 2 Samuel 22:32 the NRSV uses a one syllable word for its fifth word in the verse. In Psalm 18:1 it uses a two syllable word as its fifth word.

649. Psalms 20:9 Save, LORD: let the king hear us when we call.
AV - **10,** 1-1,2-1,3-1,4-1,5-1,6-1,7-1,8-1,9-1,10-1
ESV - 12, 1-1,2-1,3-1,4-1,5-1,6-1,7-1,8-**2**,9-1,10-1,11-1,12-1
HCSB - 16, 1-1,2-1,3-**3**,4-1,5-1,6-1,7-1,8-1,9-**2**,10-1,11-1,12-1,13-1,14-1,15-1,16-1
NASV - 13, 1-1,2-1,3-1,4-1,5-1,6-1,7-**2**,8-1,9-1,10-1,11-1,12-1,13-1
NCV - 11, 1-1,2-1,3-1,4-1,5-**2**,6-1,7-1,8-1,9-1,10-1,11-1
NIV - 10, 1-1,2-1,3-1,4-1,5-1,6-**2**,7-1,8-1,9-1,10-1
NKJV - 10, 1-1,2-1,3-1,4-1,5-1,6-**2**,7-1,8-1,9-1,10-1

NLT - 12, 1-1,2-**3**,3-1,4-1,5-1,6-1,7-1,8-**2**,9-1,10-1,11-1,12-1
NRSV - 12, 1-1,2-**3**,3-1,4-1,5-1,6-1,7-1,8-**2**,9-1,10-1,11-1,12-1
Conclusion: All eight modern versions are more complex than the King James Bible.

650. Psalms 22:19 But be not thou far from me, O LORD: O my strength, haste thee to help me.
AV - **17,** 1-1,2-1,3-1,4-1,5-1,6-1,7-1,8-1,9-1,10-1,11-1,12-1,13-1,14-1,15-1,16-1,17-1
ESV - 18, 1-1,2-1,3-1,4-1,5-1,6-1,7-1,8-1,9-1,10-1,11-1,12-1,13-1,14-1,15-**2**,16-1,17-1,18-1
HCSB - 14, 1-1,2-1,3-1,4-1,5-1,6-1,7-**2**,8-1,9-1,10-1,11-**2**,12-1,13-1,14-1
NASV - 16, 1-1,2-1,3-1,4-1,5-1,6-1,7-1,8-1,9-1,10-1,11-1,12-1,13-**2**,14-1,15-1,16-**2**
NCV - 14, 1-1,2-1,3-1,4-1,5-1,6-**2**,7-1,8-1,9-1,10-1,11-**2**,12-1,13-1,14-1
NIV - 16, 1-1,2-1,3-1,4-1,5-1,6-1,7-1,8-1,9-1,10-1,11-1,12-1,13-**2**,14-1,15-1,16-1
NKJV - 17, 1-1,2-1,3-1,4-1,5-1,6-1,7-1,8-1,9-1,10-1,11-1,12-1,13-1,14-**2**,15-1,16-1,17-1
NLT - 16, 1-1,2-1,3-1,4-1,5-1,6-1,7-**2**,8-1,9-1,10-1,11-1,12-1,13-**2**,14-1,15-1,16-1
NRSV - 17, 1-1,2-1,3-1,4-1,5-1,6-1,7-1,8-1,9-**2**,10-1,11-1,12-1,13-1,14-**2**,15-1,16-1,17-1
Conclusion: All eight modern versions are more complex than the King James Bible.

651. Psalms 25:4 Show me thy ways, O LORD; teach me thy paths.
AV - **10,** 1-1,2-1,3-1,4-1,5-1,6-1,7-1,8-1,9-1,10-1
ESV - **12,** 1-1,2-1,3-1,4-1,5-1,6-1,7-1,8-1,9-1,10-1,11-1,12-1
HCSB - **11,** 1-1,2-1,3-1,4-1,5-1,6-1,7-1,8-1,9-1,10-1,11-1
NASV - **11,** 1-1,2-1,3-1,4-1,5-1,6-1,7-1,8-1,9-1,10-1,11-1
NCV - **10,** 1-1,2-1,3-1,4-1,5-1,6-1,7-1,8-1,9-1,10-1
NIV - **10,** 1-1,2-1,3-1,4-1,5-1,6-1,7-1,8-1,9-1,10-1
NKJV - **10,** 1-1,2-1,3-1,4-1,5-1,6-1,7-1,8-1,9-1,10-1
NLT - 15, 1-1,2-**2**,3-1,4-1,5-1,6-1,7-1,8-1,9-1,10-1,11-1,12-1,13-1,14-1,15-1
NRSV - **12,** 1-1,2-1,3-1,4-1,5-1,6-1,7-1,8-1,9-1,10-1,11-1,12-1
Conclusion: Only the NLT made the verse more complex.

652. Psalms 33:4 For the word of the LORD is right; and all his works are done in truth.
AV - **16,** 1-1,2-1,3-1,4-1,5-1,6-1,7-1,8-1,9-1,10-1,11-1,12-1,13-1,14-1,15-1,16-1
ESV - 16, 1-1,2-1,3-1,4-1,5-1,6-1,7-1,8-**2**,9-1,10-1,11-1,12-1,13-1,14-1,15-1,16-**3**
HCSB - 14, 1-1,2-1,3-1,4-1,5-1,6-1,7-1,8-1,9-1,10-1,11-1,12-1,13-1,14-**3**
NASV - 16, 1-1,2-1,3-1,4-1,5-1,6-1,7-1,8-**2**,9-1,10-1,11-1,12-1,13-1,14-1,15-1,16-**3**
NCV - 10, 1-1,2-1,3-1,4-1,5-1,6-**4**,7-1,8-1,9-1,10-1
NIV - 17, 1-1,2-1,3-1,4-1,5-1,6-1,7-1,8-1,9-1,10-1,11-1,12-1,13-**2**,14-1,15-1,16-1,17-1
NKJV - **16,** 1-1,2-1,3-1,4-1,5-1,6-1,7-1,8-1,9-1,10-1,11-1,12-1,13-1,14-1,15-1,16-1
NLT - 15, 1-1,2-1,3-1,4-1,5-1,6-1,7-1,8-1,9-1,10-1,11-1,12-1,13-**4**,14-1,15-1
NRSV - 16, 1-1,2-1,3-1,4-1,5-1,6-1,7-1,8-**2**,9-1,10-1,11-1,12-1,13-1,14-1,15-1,16-**3**
Conclusion: Seven modern versions are more complex than the King James Bible.

653. Psalms 34:9 O fear the LORD, ye his saints: for there is no want to them that fear him.
AV - **17,** 1-1,2-1,3-1,4-1,5-1,6-1,7-1,8-1,9-1,10-1,11-1,12-1,13-1,14-1,15-1,16-1,17-1
ESV - **15,** 1-1,2-1,3-1,4-1,5-1,6-1,7-1,8-1,9-1,10-1,11-1,12-1,13-1,14-1,15-1
HCSB - 13, 1-1,2-1,3-1,4-1,5-1,6-1,7-1,8-1,9-1,10-1,11-1,12-1,13-**2**

NASV - **17,** 1-1,2-1,3-1,4-1,5-1,6-1,7-1,8-1,9-1,10-1,11-1,12-1,13-1,14-1,15-1,16-1,17-1
NCV - **17,** 1-1,2-1,3-**2,**4-1,5-1,6-1,7-1,8-1,9-1,10-1,11-1,12-1,13-1,14-1,15-**4,**16-1,17-1
NIV - 13, 1-1,2-1,3-1,4-1,5-1,6-1,7-1,8-1,9-1,10-1,11-1,12-1,13-**2**
NKJV - **16,** 1-1,2-1,3-1,4-1,5-1,6-1,7-1,8-1,9-1,10-1,11-1,12-1,13-1,14-1,15-1,16-1
NLT - 17, 1-1,2-1,3-1,4-1,5-1,6-**2,**7-**2,**8-1,9-1,10-1,11-1,12-1,13-1,14-1,15-1,16-1,17-1
NRSV - 16, 1-1,2-1,3-1,4-1,5-1,6-1,7-**2,**8-1,9-1,10-1,11-1,12-1,13-1,14-1,15-1,16-1
Conclusion: Five modern versions are more complex than the King James Bible.

654. Psalm 37:31 The law of his God is in his heart; none of his steps shall slide.
AV - **15,** 1-1,2-1,3-1,4-1,5-1,6-1,7-1,8-1,9-1,10-1,11-1,12-1,13-1,14-1,15-1
ESV - **14,** 1-1,2-1,3-1,4-1,5-1,6-1,7-1,8-1,9-1,10-1,11-1,12-1,13-1,14-1
HCSB - 15, 1-1,2-**3,**3-1,4-1,5-1,6-1,7-1,8-1,9-1,10-1,11-1,12-1,13-1,14-1,15-**2**
NASV - **14,** 1-1,2-1,3-1,4-1,5-1,6-1,7-1,8-1,9-1,10-1,11-1,12-1,13-1,14-1
NCV - 17, 1-1,2-**2,**3-1,4-1,5-1,6-1,7-1,8-1,9-1,10-1,11-1,12-1,13-1,14-1,15-1,16-1,17-1
NIV - **14,** 1-1,2-1,3-1,4-1,5-1,6-1,7-1,8-1,9-1,10-1,11-1,12-1,13-1,14-1
NKJV - **15,** 1-1,2-1,3-1,4-1,5-1,6-1,7-1,8-1,9-1,10-1,11-1,12-1,13-1,14-1,15-1
NLT - 15, 1-1,2-1,3-1,4-1,5-1,6-1,7-1,8-1,9-1,10-1,11-**2,**12-1,13-1,14-1,15-1
NRSV - **14,** 1-1,2-1,3-1,4-1,5-1,6-1,7-1,8-1,9-1,10-1,11-1,12-1,13-1,14-1
Conclusion: Only three modern versions are more complex than the King James Bible.

655. Psalms 38:15 For in thee, O LORD, do I hope: thou wilt hear, O Lord my God.
AV - **15,** 1-1,2-1,3-1,4-1,5-1,6-1,7-1,8-1,9-1,10-1,11-1,12-1,13-1,14-1,15-1
ESV - 18, 1-1,2-1,3-1,4-1,5-1,6-1,7-1,8-1,9-1,10-1,11-1,12-1,13-1,14-1,15-1,16-1,17-1,18-**2**
HCSB - 13, 1-1,2-1,3-1,4-1,5-1,6-1,7-1,8-1,9-1,10-**2,**11-1,12-1,13-1
NASV - 14, 1-1,2-1,3-1,4-1,5-1,6-1,7-1,8-1,9-1,10-**2,**11-1,12-1,13-1,14-1
NCV - 11, 1-1,2-1,3-1,4-1,5-1,6-1,7-**2,**8-1,9-1,10-1,11-1
NIV - 13, 1-1,2-1,3-1,4-1,5-1,6-1,7-1,8-1,9-**2,**10-1,11-1,12-1,13-1
NKJV - **14,** 1-1,2-1,3-1,4-1,5-1,6-1,7-1,8-1,9-1,10-1,11-1,12-1,13-1,14-1
NLT - 17, 1-1,2-1,3-1,4-**2,**5-1,6-1,7-1,8-1,9-1,10-1,11-**2,**12-1,13-1,14-1,15-1,16-1,17-1
NRSV - 20, 1-1,2-1,3-1,4-1,5-1,6-1,7-1,8-1,9-1,10-1,11-1,12-1,13-1,14-1,15-1,16-1,17-1,18-1,19-1,20-**2**
Conclusion: Seven modern versions are more complex than the King James Bible.

656. Psalms 39:7 And now, Lord, what wait I for? my hope is in thee.
AV - **12,** 1-1,2-1,3-1,4-1,5-1,6-1,7-1,8-1,9-1,10-1,11-1,12-1
ESV - **14,** 1-1,2-1,3-1,4-1,5-1,6-1,7-1,8-1,9-1,10-1,11-1,12-1,13-1,14-1
HCSB - **12,** 1-1,2-1,3-1,4-1,5-1,6-1,7-1,8-1,9-1,10-1,11-1,12-1
NASV - **13,** 1-1,2-1,3-1,4-1,5-1,6-1,7-1,8-1,9-1,10-1,11-1,12-1,13-1
NCV - **11,** 1-1,2-1,3-1,4-1,5-1,6-1,7-1,8-1,9-1,10-1,11-1
NIV - **13,** 1-1,2-1,3-1,4-1,5-1,6-1,7-1,8-1,9-1,10-1,11-1,12-1,13-1
NKJV - **13,** 1-1,2-1,3-1,4-1,5-1,6-1,7-1,8-1,9-1,10-1,11-1,12-1,13-1
NLT - **15,** 1-1,2-1,3-1,4-1,5-1,6-1,7-1,8-1,9-1,10-1,11-1,12-1,13-1,14-1,15-1
NRSV - **14,** 1-1,2-1,3-1,4-1,5-1,6-1,7-1,8-1,9-1,10-1,11-1,12-1,13-1,14-1
Conclusion: All versions read the same.

Samuel C. Gipp Ph.D.

657. Psalms 50:13 Will I eat the flesh of bulls, or drink the blood of goats?
AV - **13,** 1-1,2-1,3-1,4-1,5-1,6-1,7-1,8-1,9-1,10-1,11-1,12-1,13-1
ESV - **13,** 1-1,2-1,3-1,4-1,5-1,6-1,7-1,8-1,9-1,10-1,11-1,12-1,13-1
HCSB - **13,** 1-1,2-1,3-1,4-1,5-1,6-1,7-1,8-1,9-1,10-1,11-1,12-1,13-1
NASV - **14,** 1-1,2-1,3-1,4-1,5-1,6-1,7-1,8-1,9-1,10-1,11-1,12-1,13-1,14-1
NCV - **13,** 1-1,2-1,3-1,4-1,5-1,6-1,7-1,8-1,9-1,10-1,11-1,12-1,13-1
NIV - **13,** 1-1,2-1,3-1,4-1,5-1,6-1,7-1,8-1,9-1,10-1,11-1,12-1,13-1
NKJV - **13,** 1-1,2-1,3-1,4-1,5-1,6-1,7-1,8-1,9-1,10-1,11-1,12-1,13-1
NLT - **14,** 1-1,2-1,3-1,4-1,5-1,6-1,7-1,8-1,9-1,10-1,11-1,12-1,13-1,14-1
NRSV - **13,** 1-1,2-1,3-1,4-1,5-1,6-1,7-1,8-1,9-1,10-1,11-1,12-1,13-1
Conclusion: All versions read the same.

658. Psalms 54:1 Save me, O God, by thy name, and judge me by thy strength.
AV - **13,** 1-1,2-1,3-1,4-1,5-1,6-1,7-1,8-1,9-1,10-1,11-1,12-1,13-1
ESV - 13, 1-1,2-1,3-1,4-1,5-1,6-1,7-1,8-1,9-**3**,10-1,11-1,12-1,13-1
HCSB - 12, 1-1,2-1,3-1,4-1,5-1,6-1,7-1,8-**3**,9-1,10-1,11-1,12-1
NASV - 13, 1-1,2-1,3-1,4-1,5-1,6-1,7-1,8-1,9-**3**,10-1,11-1,12-1,13-1
NCV - 16, 1-1,2-1,3-1,4-**2**,5-1,6-1,7-1,8-1,9-1,10-1,11-1,12-1,13-1,14-1,15-1,16-**3**
NIV - 12, 1-1,2-1,3-1,4-1,5-1,6-1,7-1,8-**3**,9-1,10-1,11-1,12-1
NKJV - 13, 1-1,2-1,3-1,4-1,5-1,6-1,7-1,8-1,9-**3**,10-1,11-1,12-1,13-1
NLT - 14, 1-1,2-1,3-1,4-**2**,5-1,6-1,7-1,8-**2**,9-1,10-**2**,11-1,12-1,13-1,14-1
NRSV - 13, 1-1,2-1,3-1,4-1,5-1,6-1,7-1,8-1,9-**3**,10-1,11-1,12-1,13-1
Conclusion: All eight modern versions are more complex than the King James Bible.

659. Psalms 54:2 Hear my prayer, O God; give ear to the words of my mouth.
AV - **13,** 1-1,2-1,3-1,4-1,5-1,6-1,7-1,8-1,9-1,10-1,11-1,12-1,13-1
ESV - **13,** 1-1,2-1,3-1,4-1,5-1,6-1,7-1,8-1,9-1,10-1,11-1,12-1,13-1
HCSB - 11, 1-1,2-1,3-1,4-1,5-**2**,6-1,7-1,8-1,9-1,10-1,11-1
NASV - **13,** 1-1,2-1,3-1,4-1,5-1,6-1,7-1,8-1,9-1,10-1,11-1,12-1,13-1
NCV - 9, 1-1,2-1,3-1,4-1,5-**2**,6-1,7-1,8-1,9-1
NIV - 12, 1-1,2-1,3-1,4-1,5-1,6-**2**,7-1,8-1,9-1,10-1,11-1,12-1
NKJV - **13,** 1-1,2-1,3-1,4-1,5-1,6-1,7-1,8-1,9-1,10-1,11-1,12-1,13-1
NLT - 11, 1-**2**,2-1,3-1,4-1,5-1,6-1,7-1,8-**3**,9-1,10-1,11-1
NRSV - 13, 1-1,2-1,3-1,4-1,5-1,6-1,7-1,8-1,9-1,10-1,11-1,12-1,13-1
Conclusion: Four modern versions are more complex than the King James Bible.

660. Psalm 56:10 In God will I praise his word: in the LORD will I praise his word.
AV - **15,** 1-1,2-1,3-1,4-1,5-1,6-1,7-1,8-1,9-1,10-1,11-1,12-1,13-1,14-1,15-1
ESV - **13,** 1-1,2-1,3-1,4-1,5-1,6-1,7-1,8-1,9-1,10-1,11-1,12-1,13-1
HCSB - **13,** 1-1,2-1,3-1,4-1,5-1,6-1,7-1,8-1,9-1,10-1,11-1,12-1,13-1
NASV - **13,** 1-1,2-1,3-1,4-1,5-1,6-1,7-1,8-1,9-1,10-1,11-1,12-1,13-1
NCV - **15,** 1-1,2-1,3-1,4-1,5-1,6-1,7-1,8-1,9-1,10-1,11-1,12-1,13-1,14-1,15-1
NIV - **13,** 1-1,2-1,3-1,4-1,5-1,6-1,7-1,8-1,9-1,10-1,11-1,12-1,13-1
NKJV - **15,** 1-1,2-1,3-1,4-1,5-1,6-1,7-1,8-1,9-1,10-1,11-1,12-1,13-1,14-1,15-1

NLT - 18, 1-1,2-1,3-1,4-1,5-1,6-1,7-1,8-**2**,9-1,10-1,11-1,12-1,13-1,14-1,15-1,16-1,17-1,18-**2**
NRSV - **13,** 1-1,2-1,3-1,4-1,5-1,6-1,7-1,8-1,9-1,10-1,11-1,12-1,13-1
Conclusion: Only the NLT made the verse more complex.

661. Psalm 57:7 My heart is fixed, O God, my heart is fixed: I will sing and give praise.
AV - **16,** 1-1,2-1,3-1,4-1,5-1,6-1,7-1,8-1,9-1,10-1,11-1,12-1,13-1,14-1,15-1,16-1
ESV - 16, 1-1,2-1,3-1,4-**2**,5-1,6-1,7-1,8-1,9-1,10-**2**,11-1,12-1,13-1,14-1,15-1,16-**3**
HCSB - 16, 1-1,2-1,3-1,4-**2**,5-1,6-1,7-1,8-1,9-1,10-**2**,11-1,12-1,13-1,14-1,15-1,16-**2**
NASV - 18, 1-1,2-1,3-1,4-**2**,5-1,6-1,7-1,8-1,9-1,10-**2**,11-1,12-1,13-1,14-1,15-1,16-1,17-1,18-**2**
NCV - 15, 1-1,2-1,3-1,4-**2**,5-1,6-1,7-1,8-1,9-**2**,10-1,11-1,12-1,13-1,14-1,15-1
NIV - 16, 1-1,2-1,3-1,4-**2**,5-1,6-1,7-1,8-1,9-1,10-**2**,11-1,12-1,13-1,14-1,15-1,16-**2**
NKJV - 16, 1-1,2-1,3-1,4-**2**,5-1,6-1,7-1,8-1,9-1,10-**2**,11-1,12-1,13-1,14-1,15-1,16-1
NLT - 19, 1-1,2-1,3-1,4-**3**,5-1,6-1,7-1,8-1,9-1,10-1,11-1,12-**3**,13-1,14-**2**,15-1,16-1,17-1,18-1,19-**2**
NRSV - 16, 1-1,2-1,3-1,4-**2**,5-1,6-1,7-1,8-1,9-1,10-**2**,11-1,12-1,13-1,14-1,15-1,16-**3**
Conclusion: All eight modern versions are more complex than the King James Bible. The NLT is the most difficult to read.

662. Psalms 63:4 Thus will I bless thee while I live: I will lift up my hands in thy name.
AV - **17,** 1-1,2-1,3-1,4-1,5-1,6-1,7-1,8-1,9-1,10-1,11-1,12-1,13-1,14-1,15-1,16-1,17-1
ESV - **19,** 1-1,2-1,3-1,4-1,5-1,6-1,7-1,8-1,9-1,10-1,11-1,12-1,13-1,14-1,15-1,16-1,17-1,18-1,19-1
HCSB - **19,** 1-1,2-1,3-1,4-1,5-1,6-1,7-1,8-1,9-1,10-1,11-1,12-1,13-1,14-1,15-1,16-1,17-1,18-1,19-1
NASV - **19,** 1-1,2-1,3-1,4-1,5-1,6-1,7-1,8-1,9-1,10-1,11-1,12-1,13-1,14-1,15-1,16-1,17-1,18-1,19-1
NCV - **20,** 1-1,2-1,3-1,4-1,5-1,6-1,7-1,8-1,9-1,10-1,11-1,12-1,13-1,14-1,15-1,16-1,17-1,18-1,19-1,20-1
NIV - **19,** 1-1,2-1,3-1,4-1,5-1,6-1,7-1,8-1,9-1,10-1,11-1,12-1,13-1,14-1,15-1,16-1,17-1,18-1,19-1
NKJV - **17,** 1-1,2-1,3-1,4-1,5-1,6-1,7-1,8-1,9-1,10-1,11-1,12-1,13-1,14-1,15-1,16-1,17-1
NLT - 17, 1-1,2-1,3-1,4-1,5-1,6-1,7-1,8-1,9-1,10-**2**,11-1,12-1,13-1,14-1,15-1,16-1,17-1
NRSV - **21,** 1-1,2-1,3-1,4-1,5-1,6-1,7-1,8-1,9-1,10-1,11-1,12-1,13-1,14-1,15-1,16-1,17-1,18-1,19-1,20-1,21-1
Conclusion: Only the NLT made the verse more complex.

663. Psalms 67:7 God shall bless us; and all the ends of the earth shall fear him.
AV - **14,** 1-1,2-1,3-1,4-1,5-1,6-1,7-1,8-1,9-1,10-1,11-1,12-1,13-1,14-1
ESV - **13,** 1-1,2-1,3-1,4-1,5-1,6-1,7-1,8-1,9-1,10-1,11-1,12-1,13-1
HCSB - **14,** 1-1,2-1,3-1,4-1,5-1,6-1,7-1,8-1,9-1,10-1,11-1,12-1,13-1,14-1
NASV - **13,** 1-1,2-1,3-1,4-1,5-1,6-1,7-1,8-1,9-1,10-1,11-1,12-1,13-1
NCV - 12, 1-1,2-**2**,3-1,4-1,5-**2**,6-1,7-**2**,8-1,9-1,10-1,11-1,12-1
NIV - **14,** 1-1,2-1,3-1,4-1,5-1,6-1,7-1,8-1,9-1,10-1,11-1,12-1,13-1,14-1
NKJV - **14,** 1-1,2-1,3-1,4-1,5-1,6-1,7-1,8-1,9-1,10-1,11-1,12-1,13-1,14-1
NLT - 14, 1-1,2-1,3-1,4-1,5-1,6-1,7-**2**,8-1,9-**2**,10-1,11-**2**,12-1,13-1,14-1
NRSV - 15, 1-1,2-1,3-**3**,4-1,5-1,6-1,7-1,8-1,9-1,10-1,11-1,12-1,13-1,14-**2**,15-1
Conclusion: Only three modern versions are more complex than the King James Bible.

664. Psalms 68:15* The hill of God is as the hill of **Bashan**; an high hill as the hill of **Bashan**.
AV - **18,** 1-1,2-1,3-1,4-1,5-1,6-1,7-1,8-1,9-1,10-1,11-1,12-1,13-1,14-1,15-1,16-1,17-1,18-1
ESV - 14, 1-1,2-**2**,3-1,4-1,5-**2**,6-1,7-1,8-1,9-**2**,10-1,11-**2**,12-**2**,13-1,14-1
HCSB - 14, 1-1,2-1,3-1,4-1,5-**3**,6-**2**,7-1,8-1,9-1,10-1,11-**2**,12-1,13-**2**,14-1
NASV - 19, 1-1,2-**2**,3-1,4-1,5-1,6-1,7-**2**,8-1,9-1,10-1,11-**2**,12-1,13-**2**,14-1,15-1,16-1,17-**2**,18-1,19-1
NCV - 13, 1-1,2-**2**,3-1,4-1,5-1,6-1,7-1,8-**2**,9-1,10-1,11-1,12-**2**,13-1
NIV - 13, 1-1,2-**2**,3-1,4-1,5-1,6-**3**,7-**2**,8-**2**,9-1,10-1,11-**2**,12-1,13-1
NKJV - 19, 1-1,2-**2**,3-1,4-1,5-1,6-1,7-**2**,8-1,9-1,10-1,11-**2**,12-1,13-**2**,14-1,15-1,16-1,17-**2**,18-1,19-1
NLT - 15, 1-1,2-**2**,3-1,4-1,5-1,6-**3**,7-1,8-**2**,9-1,10-1,11-**2**,12-1,13-**2**,14-1,15-1
NRSV - 13, 1-1,2-**2**,3-**2**,4-**2**,5-1,6-1,7-1,8-**2**,9-1,10-**2**,11-**2**,12-1,13-1
Conclusion: All eight modern versions are radically more complex than the King James Bible. In a series where each modern version has its own unique approach the NASV & NKJV read identical.

665. Psalms 71:5 For thou art my hope, O Lord GOD: thou art my trust from my youth.
AV - **15,** 1-1,2-1,3-1,4-1,5-1,6-1,7-1,8-1,9-1,10-1,11-1,12-1,13-1,14-1,15-1
ESV - 14, 1-1,2-1,3-1,4-1,5-1,6-1,7-1,8-1,9-1,10-1,11-1,12-1,13-1,14-1
HCSB - 12, 1-1,2-1,3-1,4-1,5-1,6-1,7-1,8-1,9-**3**,10-1,11-1,12-1
NASV - 15, 1-1,2-1,3-1,4-1,5-1,6-1,7-1,8-1,9-1,10-1,11-1,12-**3**,13-1,14-1,15-1
NCV - 13, 1-1,2-1,3-1,4-1,5-1,6-1,7-1,8-**2**,9-1,10-1,11-1,12-1,13-1
NIV - 14, 1-1,2-1,3-1,4-1,5-1,6-1,7-1,8-**3**,9-1,10-1,11-**3**,12-1,13-1,14-1
NKJV - 15, 1-1,2-1,3-1,4-1,5-1,6-1,7-1,8-1,9-1,10-1,11-1,12-1,13-1,14-1,15-1
NLT - 14, 1-1,2-1,3-1,4-**2**,5-1,6-1,7-1,8-1,9-**2**,10-1,11-1,12-1,13-1,14-**2**
NRSV - **14,** 1-1,2-1,3-1,4-1,5-1,6-1,7-1,8-1,9-1,10-1,11-1,12-1,13-1,14-1
Conclusion: Five modern versions made the verse more complex. As Psalm 68:15 illustrated how the NKJV often slavishly follows the NASV this verse indicates its other favorite version to duplicate, the King James Bible.

666. Psalms 71:12 O God, be not far from me: O my God, make haste for my help.
AV - **15,** 1-1,2-1,3-1,4-1,5-1,6-1,7-1,8-1,9-1,10-1,11-1,12-1,13-1,14-1,15-1
ESV - 15, 1-1,2-1,3-1,4-1,5-1,6-1,7-1,8-1,9-1,10-1,11-1,12-1,13-1,14-1,15-1
HCSB - 13, 1-1,2-1,3-1,4-1,5-1,6-1,7-1,8-1,9-1,10-**2**,11-1,12-1,13-1
NASV - 15, 1-1,2-1,3-1,4-1,5-1,6-1,7-1,8-1,9-1,10-1,11-1,12-**2**,13-1,14-1,15-1
NCV - 11, 1-1,2-1,3-1,4-1,5-1,6-1,7-1,8-**2**,9-1,10-1,11-1
NIV - 15, 1-1,2-1,3-1,4-1,5-1,6-1,7-1,8-1,9-**2**,10-1,11-1,12-1,13-1,14-1,15-1
NKJV - 16, 1-1,2-1,3-1,4-1,5-1,6-1,7-1,8-1,9-1,10-1,11-1,12-1,13-1,14-1,15-1,16-1
NLT - 12, 1-1,2-1,3-1,4-1,5-**2**,6-1,7-1,8-1,9-**2**,10-1,11-1,12-1
NRSV - **16,** 1-1,2-1,3-1,4-1,5-1,6-1,7-1,8-1,9-1,10-1,11-1,12-1,13-1,14-1,15-1,16-1
Conclusion: Five modern versions are more complex than the King James Bible. The NLT is the most difficult to read.

667. Psalms 73:4 For there are no bands in their death: but their strength is firm.
AV - **13,** 1-1,2-1,3-1,4-1,5-1,6-1,7-1,8-1,9-1,10-1,11-1,12-1,13-1
ESV - 13, 1-1,2-1,3-1,4-1,5-1,6-**2**,7-1,8-1,9-**2**,10-1,11-1,12-1,13-1
HCSB - 14, 1-1,2-1,3-1,4-**2**,5-1,6-**2**,7-1,8-1,9-1,10-1,11-**2**,12-1,13-1,14-1

NASV - 13, 1-1,2-1,3-1,4-1,5-1,6-1,7-1,8-1,9-1,10-1,11-**2**,12-1,13-1
NCV - 9 , 1-1,2-1,3-1,4-**3**,5-1,6-1,7-**2**,8-1,9-1
NIV - 10, 1-1,2-1,3-1,4-**2**,5-1,6-**2**,7-1,8-**2**,9-1,10-1
NKJV - **13,** 1-1,2-1,3-1,4-1,5-1,6-1,7-1,8-1,9-1,10-1,11-1,12-1,13-1
NLT - 14, 1-1,2-1,3-1,4-1,5-1,6-**2**,7-1,8-1,9-**2**,10-1,11-1,12-**2**,13-1,14-1
NRSV - 11, 1-1,2-1,3-1,4-1,5-1,6-1,7-**2**,8-1,9-1,10-1,11-1
Conclusion: Seven modern versions are more complex than the King James Bible.

668. Psalms 73:21 Thus my heart was grieved, and I was pricked in my reins.
AV - **12,** 1-1,2-1,3-1,4-1,5-1,6-1,7-1,8-1,9-1,10-1,11-1,12-1
ESV - 11, 1-1,2-1,3-1,4-1,5-**3**,6-1,7-1,8-1,9-1,10-1,11-1
HCSB - 10, 1-1,2-1,3-**2**,4-**3**,5-1,6-1,7-**3**,8-**2**,9-1,10-**2**
NASV - 10, 1-1,2-1,3-1,4-1,5-**3**,6-1,7-1,8-1,9-1,10-**2**
NCV - 9, 1-1,2-1,3-1,4-1,5-1,6-1,7-1,8-1,9-**2**
NIV - 9, 1-1,2-1,3-1,4-1,5-1,6-1,7-1,8-**2**,9-**3**
NKJV - **12,** 1-1,2-1,3-1,4-1,5-1,6-1,7-1,8-1,9-1,10-1,11-1,12-1
NLT - 15, 1-1,2-1,3-**3**,4-1,5-1,6-1,7-1,8-**2**,9-1,10-1,11-1,12-1,13-1,14-1,15-**2**
NRSV - 11, 1-1,2-1,3-1,4-1,5-**3**,6-1,7-1,8-1,9-1,10-1,11-1
Conclusion: Seven modern versions are more complex than the King James Bible. The HCSB is the most difficult to read.

669. Psalms 75:5 Lift not up your horn on high: speak not with a stiff neck.
AV - **13,** 1-1,2-1,3-1,4-1,5-1,6-1,7-1,8-1,9-1,10-1,11-1,12-1,13-1
ESV - 13, 1-1,2-1,3-1,4-1,5-1,6-1,7-1,8-1,9-1,10-1,11-1,12-**2**,13-1
HCSB - 11, 1-1,2-1,3-1,4-1,5-1,6-1,7-**2**,8-**2**,9-1,10-1,11-**4**
NASV - 14, 1-1,2-1,3-1,4-1,5-1,6-1,7-1,8-1,9-1,10-1,11-1,12-1,13-**4**,14-1
NCV - 11, 1-1,2-1,3-1,4-1,5-1,6-**2**,7-**2**,8-**2**,9-1,10-1,11-**2**
NIV - 13, 1-1,2-1,3-1,4-1,5-1,6-**2**,7-**2**,8-1,9-1,10-1,11-1,12-**2**,13-1
NKJV - **15,** 1-1,2-1,3-1,4-1,5-1,6-1,7-1,8-1,9-1,10-1,11-1,12-1,13-1,14-1,15-1
NLT - 14, 1-1,2-1,3-1,4-1,5-1,6-**3**,7-1,8-1,9-**2**,10-1,11-1,12-1,13-1,14-**3**
NRSV - 13, 1-1,2-1,3-1,4-1,5-1,6-1,7-1,8-1,9-1,10-1,11-1,12-**3**,13-1
Conclusion: Seven modern versions are more complex than the King James Bible.

670. Psalm 76:1* In **Judah** is God known: his name is great in **Israel.**
AV - **11,** 1-1,2-1,3-1,4-1,5-1,6-1,7-1,8-1,9-1,10-1,11-1
ESV - **11,** 1-1,2-1,3-1,4-1,5-1,6-1,7-1,8-1,9-1,10-1,11-1
HCSB - **11,** 1-1,2-1,3-1,4-1,5-1,6-1,7-1,8-1,9-1,10-1,11-1
NASV - **11,** 1-1,2-1,3-1,4-1,5-1,6-1,7-1,8-1,9-1,10-1,11-1
NCV - 11, 1-**2**,2-1,3-1,4-1,5-1,6-1,7-1,8-1,9-1,10-1,11-1
NIV - **11,** 1-1,2-1,3-1,4-1,5-1,6-1,7-1,8-1,9-1,10-1,11-1
NKJV - **11,** 1-1,2-1,3-1,4-1,5-1,6-1,7-1,8-1,9-1,10-1,11-1
NLT - 11, 1-1,2-1,3-**2**,4-1,5-1,6-1,7-1,8-1,9-1,10-1,11-1
NRSV - **11,** 1-1,2-1,3-1,4-1,5-1,6-1,7-1,8-1,9-1,10-1,11-1
Conclusion: Only the NCV and NLT made the verse more complex.

671. Psalm 78:68* But chose the tribe of **Judah**, the mount **Zion** which he loved.
AV - **12,** 1-1,2-1,3-1,4-1,5-1,6-1,7-1,8-1,9-1,10-1,11-1,12-1
ESV - **12,** 1-1,2-1,3-1,4-1,5-1,6-1,7-1,8-1,9-1,10-1,11-1,12-1
HCSB - **12,** 1-1,2-1,3-**2**,4-1,5-1,6-1,7-1,8-1,9-1,10-1,11-1,12-1
NASV - **11,** 1-1,2-1,3-1,4-1,5-1,6-1,7-1,8-1,9-1,10-1,11-1
NCV - **13,** 1-**2**,2-1,3-1,4-1,5-1,6-1,7-1,8-1,9-1,10-1,11-1,12-1,13-1
NIV - **12,** 1-1,2-1,3-1,4-1,5-1,6-1,7-1,8-1,9-1,10-1,11-1,12-1
NKJV - **11,** 1-1,2-1,3-1,4-1,5-1,6-1,7-1,8-1,9-1,10-1,11-1
NLT - **13,** 1-1,2-1,3-**2**,4-1,5-1,6-1,7-1,8-1,9-1,10-1,11-1,12-1,13-1
NRSV - **12,** 1-1,2-1,3-1,4-1,5-1,6-1,7-1,8-1,9-1,10-1,11-1,12-1
Conclusion: Only three modern versions are more complex than the King James Bible.

672. Psalms 84:5 Blessed is the man whose strength is in thee; in whose heart are the ways of them.
AV - **17,** 1-1,2-1,3-1,4-1,5-1,6-1,7-1,8-1,9-1,10-1,11-1,12-1,13-1,14-1,15-1,16-1,17-1
ESV - **16,** 1-1,2-1,3-1,4-1,5-1,6-1,7-1,8-1,9-1,10-1,11-1,12-1,13-1,14-**2**,15-1,16-**2**
HCSB - **15,** 1-**2**,2-1,3-1,4-**2**,5-1,6-1,7-1,8-1,9-1,10-1,11-1,12-1,13-1,14-1,15-**3**
NASV - **18,** 1-1,2-1,3-1,4-1,5-1,6-1,7-1,8-1,9-1,10-1,11-1,12-1,13-1,14-1,15-1,16-**2**,17-1,18-**2**
NCV - **14,** 1-**2**,2-1,3-1,4-1,5-1,6-1,7-1,8-1,9-1,10-1,11-1,12-**2**,13-1,14-**4**
NIV - **15,** 1-1,2-1,3-1,4-1,5-1,6-1,7-1,8-1,9-1,10-1,11-1,12-1,13-1,14-1,15-**3**
NKJV - **15,** 1-1,2-1,3-1,4-1,5-1,6-1,7-1,8-1,9-1,10-1,11-1,12-1,13-1,14-1,15-**3**
NLT - **20,** 1-1,2-1,3-1,4-1,5-1,6-1,7-1,8-1,9-1,10-1,11-1,12-1,13-1,14-1,15-1,16-1,17-1,18-**3**,19-1,20-**4**
NRSV - **16,** 1-**2**,2-1,3-1,4-1,5-1,6-1,7-1,8-1,9-1,10-1,11-1,12-1,13-1,14-**2**,15-1,16-**2**
Conclusion: All eight modern versions are more complex than the King James Bible.

673. Psalm 84:8* O LORD God of hosts, hear my prayer: give ear, O God of **Jacob**. **Selah**.
AV - **15,** 1-1,2-1,3-1,4-1,5-1,6-1,7-1,8-1,9-1,10-1,11-1,12-1,13-1,14-1,15-1
ESV - **15,** 1-1,2-1,3-1,4-1,5-1,6-1,7-1,8-1,9-1,10-1,11-1,12-1,13-1,14-1,15-1
HCSB - **12,** 1-1,2-1,3-1,4-1,5-1,6-1,7-1,8-**2**,9-1,10-1,11-1,12-1
NASV - **15,** 1-1,2-1,3-1,4-1,5-1,6-1,7-1,8-1,9-1,10-1,11-1,12-1,13-1,14-1,15-1
NCV - **14,** 1-1,2-1,3-1,4-**3**,5-1,6-1,7-1,8-1,9-1,10-1,11-**2**,12-1,13-1,14-1
NIV - **15,** 1-1,2-1,3-1,4-1,5-1,6-1,7-1,8-**2**,9-1,10-1,11-1,12-1,13-1,14-1,15-1
NKJV - **15,** 1-1,2-1,3-1,4-1,5-1,6-1,7-1,8-1,9-1,10-1,11-1,12-1,13-1,14-1,15-1
NLT - **15,** 1-1,2-1,3-1,4-1,5-1,6-1,7-1,8-1,9-1,10-**2**,11-1,12-1,13-1,14-1,15-1
NRSV - **15,** 1-1,2-1,3-1,4-1,5-1,6-1,7-1,8-1,9-1,10-1,11-1,12-1,13-1,14-1,15-1
Conclusion: Four modern versions are more complex than the King James Bible. The NIV inserted "Almighty" for "hosts." The NLT inserted "Heaven's Armies" for "hosts" and "Interlude" for "Selah." None of these changes were counted against them.

674. Psalms 95:5 The sea is his, and he made it: and his hands formed the dry land.
AV - **15,** 1-1,2-1,3-1,4-1,5-1,6-1,7-1,8-1,9-1,10-1,11-1,12-1,13-1,14-1,15-1
ESV - **15,** 1-1,2-1,3-1,4-1,5-1,6-1,7-1,8-1,9-1,10-1,11-1,12-1,13-1,14-1,15-1
HCSB - **13,** 1-1,2-1,3-1,4-1,5-1,6-1,7-1,8-1,9-1,10-1,11-1,12-1,13-1

NASV - **18,** 1-1,2-1,3-1,4-1,5-1,6-1,7-1,8-1,9-1,10-1,11-1,12-1,13-1,14-1,15-1,16-1,17-1,18-1
NCV - 16, 1-1,2-1,3-1,4-**2**,5-1,6-1,7-1,8-1,9-1,10-**3**,11-1,12-1,13-1,14-1,15-1,16-1
NIV - **15,** 1-1,2-1,3-1,4-1,5-1,6-1,7-1,8-1,9-1,10-1,11-1,12-1,13-1,14-1,15-1
NKJV - **15,** 1-1,2-1,3-1,4-1,5-1,6-1,7-1,8-1,9-1,10-1,11-1,12-1,13-1,14-1,15-1
NLT - 16, 1-1,2-1,3-**2**,4-1,5-1,6-1,7-1,8-1,9-1,10-1,11-1,12-1,13-1,14-1,15-1,16-1
NRSV - **17,** 1-1,2-1,3-1,4-1,5-1,6-1,7-1,8-1,9-1,10-1,11-1,12-1,13-1,14-1,15-1,16-1,17-1
Conclusion: Only the NCV and the NLT made the verse more complex.

675. Psalms 102:27 But thou art the same, and thy years shall have no end.
AV - **12,** 1-1,2-1,3-1,4-1,5-1,6-1,7-1,8-1,9-1,10-1,11-1,12-1
ESV - **11,** 1-1,2-1,3-1,4-1,5-1,6-1,7-1,8-1,9-1,10-1,11-1
HCSB - 11, 1-1,2-1,3-1,4-1,5-1,6-1,7-1,8-1,9-1,10-**2**,11-1
NASV - **14,** 1-1,2-1,3-1,4-1,5-1,6-1,7-1,8-1,9-1,10-1,11-1,12-1,13-1,14-1
NCV - 10, 1-1,2-1,3-**2**,4-1,5-1,6-1,7-1,8-1,9-**2**,10-1
NIV - 11, 1-1,2-1,3-**2**,4-1,5-1,6-1,7-1,8-1,9-1,10-**2**,11-1
NKJV - **12,** 1-1,2-1,3-1,4-1,5-1,6-1,7-1,8-1,9-1,10-1,11-1,12-1
NLT - 9, 1-1,2-1,3-1,4-**2**,5-1,6-1,7-1,8-1,9-**3**
NRSV - **11,** 1-1,2-1,3-1,4-1,5-1,6-1,7-1,8-1,9-1,10-1,11-1
Conclusion: Four modern versions are more complex than the King James Bible.

676. Psalms 104:17 Where the birds make their nests: as for the stork, the fir trees are her house.
AV - **16,** 1-1,2-1,3-1,4-1,5-1,6-1,7-1,8-1,9-1,10-1,11-1,12-1,13-1,14-1,15-1,16-1
ESV - **16,** 1-1,2-1,3-1,4-1,5-1,6-1,7-1,8-1,9-1,10-1,11-1,12-1,13-1,14-1,15-1,16-1
HCSB - **15,** 1-1,2-1,3-1,4-1,5-1,6-1,7-1,8-1,9-1,10-1,11-1,12-1,13-1,14-1,15-1
NASV - **15,** 1-1,2-1,3-1,4-1,5-1,6-1,7-1,8-1,9-1,10-1,11-1,12-1,13-1,14-1,15-1
NCV - **14,** 1-1,2-1,3-1,4-1,5-1,6-1,7-1,8-1,9-1,10-1,11-1,12-1,13-1,14-1
NIV - **15,** 1-1,2-1,3-1,4-1,5-1,6-1,7-1,8-1,9-1,10-1,11-1,12-1,13-1,14-1,15-1
NKJV - **15,** 1-1,2-1,3-1,4-1,5-1,6-1,7-1,8-1,9-1,10-1,11-1,12-1,13-1,14-1,15-1
NLT - 15, 1-1,2-1,3-1,4-1,5-1,6-1,7-1,8-1,9-1,10-1,11-1,12-1,13-1,14-1,15-**3**
NRSV - **16,** 1-1,2-1,3-1,4-1,5-1,6-1,7-1,8-1,9-1,10-1,11-1,12-1,13-1,14-1,15-1,16-1
Conclusion: Only the NLT made the verse more complex.

677. Psalms 108:11 Wilt not thou, O God, who hast cast us off? and wilt not thou, O God, go forth with our hosts?
AV - **21,** 1-1,2-1,3-1,4-1,5-1,6-1,7-1,8-1,9-1,10-1,11-1,12-1,13-1,14-1,15-1,16-1,17-1,18-1,19-1,20-1,21-1
ESV - 17, 1-1,2-1,3-1,4-**3**,5-1,6-1,7-1,8-1,9-1,10-1,11-1,12-1,13-1,14-1,15-1,16-1,17-**2**
HCSB - 15, 1-1,2-1,3-1,4-**3**,5-1,6-1,7-1,8-1,9-1,10-1,11-1,12-1,13-1,14-1,15-**2**
NASV - 19, 1-1,2-1,3-1,4-**2**,5-1,6-1,7-**3**,8-1,9-1,10-1,11-1,12-1,13-1,14-1,15-1,16-1,17-**2**,18-1,19-1
NCV - 14, 1-1,2-**2**,3-1,4-1,5-**3**,6-1,7-1,8-1,9-1,10-1,11-1,12-1,13-1,14-**2**
NIV - 19, 1-1,2-1,3-1,4-1,5-1,6-1,7-1,8-1,9-1,10-**3**,11-1,12-1,13-1,14-**2**,15-1,16-1,17-1,18-1,19-**2**
NKJV - 22, 1-1,2-1,3-1,4-1,5-1,6-1,7-1,8-1,9-1,10-1,11-1,12-1,13-1,14-1,15-1,16-1,17-1,18-1,19-1,20-1,21-1,22-**2**
NLT - 14, 1-1,2-1,3-**3**,4-1,5-1,6-1,7-1,8-1,9-1,10-**2**,11-1,12-1,13-1,14-**2**

NRSV - 17, 1-1,2-1,3-1,4-**3**,5-1,6-1,7-1,8-1,9-1,10-1,11-1,12-1,13-1,14-1,15-1,16-1,17-**2**
Conclusion: All eight modern versions are more complex than the King James Bible.

678. Psalms 109:1 Hold not thy peace, O God of my praise;
AV - **9,** 1-1,2-1,3-1,4-1,5-1,6-1,7-1,8-1,9-1
ESV - 8, 1-1,2-1,3-**2**,4-1,5-1,6-1,7-1,8-1
HCSB - 8, 1-1,2-1,3-1,4-1,5-1,6-1,7-1,8-**2**
NASV - 9, 1-1,2-1,3-1,4-1,5-1,6-1,7-1,8-1,9-**2**
NCV - 8, 1-1,2-1,3-1,4-1,5-1,6-1,7-1,8-**2**
NIV - 9, 1-1,2-1,3-1,4-1,5-1,6-1,7-1,8-**2**,9-**2**
NKJV - 9, 1-1,2-1,3-1,4-**2**,5-1,6-1,7-1,8-1,9-1
NLT - 10, 1-1,2-1,3-1,4-1,5-1,6-1,7-1,8-**2**,9-1,10-**2**
NRSV - 9, 1-1,2-1,3-1,4-**2**,5-1,6-1,7-1,8-1,9-1
Conclusion: All eight modern versions are more complex than the King James Bible.

679. Psalms 109:27 That they may know that this is thy hand; that thou, LORD, hast done it.
AV - **15,** 1-1,2-1,3-1,4-1,5-1,6-1,7-1,8-1,9-1,10-1,11-1,12-1,13-1,14-1,15-1
ESV - **14,** 1-1,2-1,3-1,4-1,5-1,6-1,7-1,8-1,9-1,10-1,11-1,12-1,13-1,14-1
HCSB - **16,** 1-1,2-1,3-1,4-1,5-1,6-1,7-1,8-1,9-1,10-1,11-1,12-1,13-1,14-1,15-1,16-1
NASV - **14,** 1-1,2-1,3-1,4-1,5-1,6-1,7-1,8-1,9-1,10-1,11-1,12-1,13-1,14-1
NCV - 19, 1-1,2-1,3-1,4-1,5-1,6-1,7-**2**,8-1,9-1,10-1,11-1,12-1,13-1,14-1,15-1,16-1,17-1,18-1,19-1
NIV - **15,** 1-1,2-1,3-1,4-1,5-1,6-1,7-1,8-1,9-1,10-1,11-1,12-1,13-1,14-1,15-1
NKJV - **15,** 1-1,2-1,3-1,4-1,5-1,6-1,7-1,8-1,9-1,10-1,11-1,12-1,13-1,14-1,15-1
NLT - 15, 1-1,2-1,3-1,4-1,5-1,6-1,7-1,8-**2**,9-1,10-1,11-1,12-1,13-1,14-1,15-**2**
NRSV - **14,** 1-1,2-1,3-1,4-1,5-1,6-1,7-1,8-1,9-1,10-1,11-1,12-1,13-1,14-1
Conclusion: Only the NCV and the NLT made the verse more complex.

680. Psalms 110:5 The Lord at thy right hand shall strike through kings in the day of his wrath.
AV - **16,** 1-1,2-1,3-1,4-1,5-1,6-1,7-1,8-1,9-1,10-1,11-1,12-1,13-1,14-1,15-1,16-1
ESV - 17, 1-1,2-1,3-1,4-1,5-1,6-1,7-1,8-1,9-1,10-**2**,11-1,12-1,13-1,14-1,15-1,16-1,17-1
HCSB - 16, 1-1,2-1,3-1,4-1,5-1,6-1,7-1,8-1,9-1,10-1,11-1,12-1,13-1,14-1,15-1,16-**2**
NASV - 17, 1-1,2-1,3-1,4-1,5-1,6-1,7-1,8-1,9-1,10-**2**,11-1,12-1,13-1,14-1,15-1,16-1,17-1
NCV - 16, 1-1,2-1,3-1,4-**2**,5-1,6-1,7-1,8-1,9-1,10-1,11-**2**,12-**2**,13-1,14-1,15-1,16-1
NIV - **17,** 1-1,2-1,3-1,4-1,5-1,6-1,7-1,8-1,9-1,10-1,11-1,12-1,13-1,14-1,15-1,16-1,17-1
NKJV - 17, 1-1,2-1,3-1,4-1,5-1,6-1,7-1,8-1,9-1,10-**3**,11-1,12-1,13-1,14-1,15-1,16-1,17-1
NLT - 20, 1-1,2-1,3-1,4-1,5-1,6-1,7-1,8-1,9-**2**,10-1,11-1,12-1,13-1,14-1,15-**2**,16-1,17-1,18-1,19-**2**,20-**2**
NRSV - 17, 1-1,2-1,3-1,4-1,5-1,6-1,7-1,8-1,9-1,10-**2**,11-1,12-1,13-1,14-1,15-1,16-1,17-1
Conclusion: Seven modern versions are more complex than the King James Bible. The NLT is the most difficult to read.

681. Psalms 115:5 They have mouths, but they speak not: eyes have they, but they see not:
AV - **14,** 1-1,2-1,3-1,4-1,5-1,6-1,7-1,8-1,9-1,10-1,11-1,12-1,13-1,14-1
ESV - **12,** 1-1,2-1,3-1,4-1,5-1,6-1,7-1,8-1,9-1,10-1,11-1,12-1

HCSB - 10, 1-1,2-1,3-1,4-1,5-**2**,6-1,7-1,8-1,9-**2**,10-1
NASV - 14, 1-1,2-1,3-1,4-1,5-1,6-**2**,7-1,8-1,9-1,10-1,11-1,12-1,13-**2**,14-1
NCV - 14, 1-1,2-1,3-1,4-1,5-1,6-**2**,7-1,8-1,9-1,10-1,11-1,12-1,13-**2**,14-1
NIV - 10, 1-1,2-1,3-1,4-1,5-**2**,6-1,7-1,8-1,9-**2**,10-1
NKJV - **16,** 1-1,2-1,3-1,4-1,5-1,6-1,7-1,8-1,9-1,10-1,11-1,12-1,13-1,14-1,15-1,16-1
NLT - 11, 1-1,2-1,3-1,4-1,5-**2**,6-1,7-1,8-1,9-1,10-**2**,11-1
NRSV - **12,** 1-1,2-1,3-1,4-1,5-1,6-1,7-1,8-1,9-1,10-1,11-1,12-1
Conclusion: Five modern versions are more complex than the King James Bible.

682. Psalms 115:9* O **Israel**, trust thou in the LORD: he is their help and their shield.
AV - **14,** 1-1,2-1,3-1,4-1,5-1,6-1,7-1,8-1,9-1,10-1,11-1,12-1,13-1,14-1
ESV - **13,** 1-1,2-1,3-1,4-1,5-1,6-1,7-1,8-1,9-1,10-1,11-1,12-1,13-1
HCSB - **11,** 1-1,2-1,3-1,4-1,5-1,6-1,7-1,8-1,9-1,10-1,11-1
NASV - **13,** 1-1,2-1,3-1,4-1,5-1,6-1,7-1,8-1,9-1,10-1,11-1,12-1,13-1
NCV - 13, 1-**3**,2-1,3-1,4-1,5-1,6-1,7-1,8-1,9-1,10-**2**,11-1,12-1,13-**3**
NIV - **14,** 1-1,2-1,3-1,4-1,5-1,6-1,7-1,8-1,9-1,10-1,11-1,12-1,13-1,14-1
NKJV - **13,** 1-1,2-1,3-1,4-1,5-1,6-1,7-1,8-1,9-1,10-1,11-1,12-1,13-1
NLT - 12, 1-1,2-1,3-1,4-1,5-1,6-1,7-1,8-1,9-**2**,10-1,11-1,12-1
NRSV - **13,** 1-1,2-1,3-1,4-1,5-1,6-1,7-1,8-1,9-1,10-1,11-1,12-1,13-1
Conclusion: Only the NCV and the NLT made the verse more complex.

683. Psalms 115:10* O house of **Aaron**, trust in the LORD: he is their help and their shield.
AV - **15,** 1-1,2-1,3-1,4-1,5-1,6-1,7-1,8-1,9-1,10-1,11-1,12-1,13-1,14-1,15-1
ESV - **15,** 1-1,2-1,3-1,4-1,5-1,6-1,7-1,8-1,9-1,10-1,11-1,12-1,13-1,14-1,15-1
HCSB - **13,** 1-1,2-1,3-1,4-1,5-1,6-1,7-1,8-1,9-1,10-1,11-1,12-1,13-1
NCV - **13,** 1-**3**,2-1,3-1,4-1,5-1,6-1,7-1,8-1,9-1,10-**2**,11-1,12-1,13-**3**
NIV - **14,** 1-1,2-1,3-1,4-1,5-1,6-1,7-1,8-1,9-1,10-1,11-1,12-1,13-1,14-1
NKJV - **15,** 1-1,2-1,3-1,4-1,5-1,6-1,7-1,8-1,9-1,10-1,11-1,12-1,13-1,14-1,15-1
NLT - 15, 1-1,2-1,3-**3**,4-1,5-1,6-1,7-1,8-1,9-1,10-1,11-1,12-**2**,13-1,14-1,15-1
NRSV - **15,** 1-1,2-1,3-1,4-1,5-1,6-1,7-1,8-1,9-1,10-1,11-1,12-1,13-1,14-1,15-1
Conclusion: Only two modern versions are more complex than the King James Bible. The NLT is the most difficult to read.

684. Psalms 115:11 Ye that fear the LORD, trust in the LORD: he is their help and their shield.
AV - **16,** 1-1,2-1,3-1,4-1,5-1,6-1,7-1,8-1,9-1,10-1,11-1,12-1,13-1,14-1,15-1,16-1
ESV - **16,** 1-1,2-1,3-1,4-1,5-1,6-1,7-1,8-1,9-1,10-1,11-1,12-1,13-1,14-1,15-1,16-1
HCSB - **15,** 1-1,2-1,3-1,4-1,5-1,6-1,7-1,8-1,9-1,10-1,11-1,12-1,13-1,14-1,15-1
NASV - **16,** 1-1,2-1,3-1,4-1,5-1,6-1,7-1,8-1,9-1,10-1,11-1,12-1,13-1,14-1,15-1,16-1
NCV - 15, 1-1,2-1,3-**2**,4-1,5-1,6-1,7-1,8-1,9-1,10-1,11-1,12-**2**,13-1,14-1,15-**3**
NIV - **14,** 1-1,2-1,3-1,4-1,5-1,6-1,7-1,8-1,9-1,10-1,11-1,12-1,13-1,14-1
NKJV - **16,** 1-1,2-1,3-1,4-1,5-1,6-1,7-1,8-1,9-1,10-1,11-1,12-1,13-1,14-1,15-1,16-1
NLT - 16, 1-1,2-1,3-1,4-1,5-1,6-1,7-1,8-1,9-1,10-1,11-1,12-1,13-**2**,14-1,15-1,16-1
NRSV - **16,** 1-1,2-1,3-1,4-1,5-1,6-1,7-1,8-1,9-1,10-1,11-1,12-1,13-1,14-1,15-1,16-1

Conclusion: Only two modern versions are more complex than the King James Bible. The NCV is the most difficult to read.

685. Psalms 115:13 He will bless them that fear the LORD, both small and great.
AV - **12,** 1-1,2-1,3-1,4-1,5-1,6-1,7-1,8-1,9-1,10-1,11-1,12-1
ESV - **14,** 1-1,2-1,3-1,4-1,5-1,6-1,7-1,8-1,9-1,10-1,11-1,12-1,13-1,14-1
HCSB - **12,** 1-1,2-1,3-1,4-1,5-1,6-1,7-1,8-1,9-1,10-1,11-1,12-1
NASV - **14,** 1-1,2-1,3-1,4-1,5-1,6-1,7-1,8-1,9-1,10-1,11-**3**,12-1,13-1,14-1
NCV - **14,** 1-1,2-1,3-1,4-1,5-1,6-1,7-**2**,8-1,9-1,10-1,11-**2**,12-1,13-1,14-**2**
NIV - **12,** 1-1,2-1,3-1,4-1,5-1,6-1,7-1,8-1,9-1,10-1,11-1,12-**2**
NKJV - **12,** 1-1,2-1,3-1,4-1,5-1,6-1,7-1,8-1,9-1,10-1,11-1,12-1
NLT - **12,** 1-1,2-1,3-1,4-1,5-1,6-1,7-1,8-1,9-1,10-1,11-1,12-**2**
NRSV - **12,** 1-1,2-1,3-1,4-1,5-1,6-1,7-1,8-1,9-1,10-1,11-1,12-1
Conclusion: Four modern versions are more complex than the King James Bible. The NCV is the most difficult to read.

686. Psalms 116:19* In the courts of the Lord's house, in the midst of thee, O **Jerusalem**. Praise ye the LORD.
AV - **18,** 1-1,2-1,3-1,4-1,5-1,6-1,7-1,8-1,9-1,10-1,11-1,12-1,13-1,14-1,15-1,16-1,17-1,18-1
ESV - **17,** 1-1,2-1,3-1,4-1,5-1,6-1,7-1,8-1,9-1,10-1,11-1,12-1,13-1,14-1,15-1,16-1,17-1
HCSB - **11,** 1-1,2-1,3-1,4-1,5-1,6-1,7-1,8-**2**,9-1,10-1,11-1
NASV - **17,** 1-1,2-1,3-1,4-1,5-1,6-1,7-1,8-1,9-1,10-1,11-1,12-1,13-1,14-1,15-1,16-1,17-1
NCV - **17,** 1-1,2-1,3-1,4-1,5-1,6-1,7-1,8-1,9-1,10-1,11-1,12-1,13-1,14-1,15-1,16-1,17-1
NIV - **9,** 1-1,2-1,3-**2**,4-**2**,5-1,6-1,7-1,8-1,9-1
NKJV - **17,** 1-1,2-1,3-1,4-1,5-1,6-1,7-1,8-1,9-1,10-1,11-1,12-1,13-1,14-1,15-1,16-1,17-1
NLT - **14,** 1-1,2-1,3-1,4-1,5-1,6-1,7-1,8-1,9-1,10-1,11-1,12-1,13-1,14-1
NRSV - **17,** 1-1,2-1,3-1,4-1,5-1,6-1,7-1,8-1,9-1,10-1,11-1,12-1,13-1,14-1,15-1,16-1,17-1
Conclusion: Only the HCSB and the NIV made the verse more complex. The phrase "Praise the Lord" found in the other versions is rendered "Hallelujah" in the HCSB. This was not counted against it as a multi-syllable word.

687. Psalms 118:13 Thou hast thrust sore at me that I might fall: but the LORD helped me.
AV - **15,** 1-1,2-1,3-1,4-1,5-1,6-1,7-1,8-1,9-1,10-1,11-1,12-1,13-1,14-1,15-1
ESV, **14,** 1-1,2-1,3-1,4-1,5-1,6-1,7-1,8-1,9-**2**,10-1,11-1,12-1,13-1,14-1
HCSB - **13,** 1-1,2-1,3-1,4-1,5-1,6-1,7-1,8-1,9-1,10-1,11-1,12-1,13-1
NASV - **14,** 1-1,2-1,3-1,4-**4**,5-1,6-1,7-1,8-1,9-**2**,10-1,11-1,12-1,13-1,14-1
NCV - **13,** 1-1,2-1,3-1,4-**2**,5-1,6-1,7-**2**,8-**3**,9-1,10-1,11-1,12-1,13-1
NIV - **13,** 1-1,2-1,3-1,4-1,5-1,6-1,7-1,8-1,9-1,10-1,11-1,12-1,13-1
NKJV - **13,** 1-1,2-1,3-1,4-**4**,5-1,6-1,7-1,8-1,9-1,10-1,11-1,12-1,13-1
NLT - **13,** 1-1,2-**3**,3-1,4-1,5-1,6-1,7-1,8-1,9-1,10-1,11-1,12-**2**,13-1
NRSV - **14,** 1-1,2-1,3-1,4-1,5-1,6-1,7-1,8-1,9-**2**,10-1,11-1,12-1,13-1,14-1
Conclusion: Six modern versions are more complex than the King James Bible. The NCV is the most difficult to read.

688. Psalms 119:113 I hate vain thoughts: but thy law do I love.
AV - **10,** 1-1,2-1,3-1,4-1,5-1,6-1,7-1,8-1,9-1,10-1
ESV - **10,** 1-1,2-1,3-1,4-**2**,5-**2**,6-1,7-1,8-1,9-1,10-1
HCSB - **10,** 1-1,2-1,3-1,4-**2**,5-**2**,6-1,7-1,8-1,9-1,10-**3**
NASV - **12,** 1-1,2-1,3-1,4-1,5-1,6-**2**,7-**2**,8-1,9-1,10-1,11-1,12-1
NCV - **9,** 1-1,2-1,3-**2**,4-**2**,5-1,6-1,7-1,8-1,9-**2**
NIV - **10,** 1-1,2-1,3-**2**,4-**2**,5-1,6-1,7-1,8-1,9-1,10-1
NKJV - **10,** 1-1,2-1,3-1,4-**2**,5-**2**,6-1,7-1,8-1,9-1,10-1
NLT - **11,** 1-1,2-1,3-1,4-1,5-**3**,6-**3**,7-1,8-1,9-1,10-1,11-**3**
NRSV - **10,** 1-1,2-1,3-1,4-**2**,5-**2**,6-1,7-1,8-1,9-1,10-1
Conclusion: All eight modern versions are more complex than the King James Bible. Just as the NKJV often mimics the NASV it appears the ESV often does the same thing using the NRSV as its template.

689. Psalms 119:126 It is time for thee, LORD, to work: for they have made void thy law.
AV - **15,** 1-1,2-1,3-1,4-1,5-1,6-1,7-1,8-1,9-1,10-1,11-1,12-1,13-1,14-1,15-1
ESV - **14,** 1-1,2-1,3-1,4-1,5-1,6-1,7-1,8-1,9-1,10-1,11-1,12-1,13-1,14-**2**
HCSB - **14,** 1-1,2-1,3-1,4-1,5-1,6-1,7-1,8-1,9-1,10-1,11-1,12-**2**,13-1,14-1
NASV - **14,** 1-1,2-1,3-1,4-1,5-1,6-1,7-1,8-1,9-1,10-1,11-1,12-**2**,13-1,14-1
NCV - **15,** 1-1,2-1,3-1,4-1,5-1,6-1,7-1,8-1,9-**2**,10-**2**,11-**2**,12-1,13-**3**,14-1,15-**2**
NIV - **14,** 1-1,2-1,3-1,4-1,5-1,6-1,7-1,8-1,9-1,10-1,11-1,12-1,13-**2**,14-**2**
NKJV - **17,** 1-1,2-1,3-**3**,4-1,5-1,6-1,7-1,8-1,9-1,10-1,11-1,12-1,13-1,14-1,15-1,16-1,17-1
NLT - **16,** 1-1,2-1,3-1,4-1,5-1,6-1,7-1,8-1,9-1,10-1,11-**2**,12-**2**,13-1,14-**4**,15-1,16-**3**
NRSV - **14,** 1-1,2-1,3-1,4-1,5-1,6-1,7-1,8-1,9-1,10-1,11-1,12-1,13-1,14-**2**
Conclusion: All eight modern versions are more complex than the King James Bible. The translators of the NCV and NLT should be credited for their fertile imaginations in managing to make such a simple verse so overwhelmingly complicated.

690. Psalms 120:7 I am for peace: but when I speak, they are for war.
AV - **12,** 1-1,2-1,3-1,4-1,5-1,6-1,7-1,8-1,9-1,10-1,11-1,12-1
ESV - **12,** 1-1,2-1,3-1,4-1,5-1,6-1,7-1,8-1,9-1,10-1,11-1,12-1
HCSB - **12,** 1-1,2-1,3-1,4-1,5-1,6-1,7-1,8-1,9-1,10-1,11-1,12-1
NASV - **12,** 1-1,2-1,3-1,4-1,5-1,6-1,7-1,8-1,9-1,10-1,11-1,12-1
NCV - **7,** 1-1,2-1,3-1,4-1,5-1,6-1,7-1
NIV - **14,** 1-1,2-1,3-1,4-1,5-1,6-1,7-1,8-1,9-1,10-1,11-1,12-1,13-1,14-1
NKJV - **12,** 1-1,2-1,3-1,4-1,5-1,6-1,7-1,8-1,9-1,10-1,11-1,12-1
NLT - **13,** 1-1,2-1,3-1,4-1,5-1,6-1,7-1,8-1,9-1,10-1,11-1,12-1,13-1
NRSV - **12,** 1-1,2-1,3-1,4-1,5-1,6-1,7-1,8-1,9-1,10-1,11-1,12-1
Conclusion: All versions read the same.

691. Psalm 121:6 The sun shall not smite thee by day, nor the moon by night.
AV - **13,** 1-1,2-1,3-1,4-1,5-1,6-1,7-1,8-1,9-1,10-1,11-1,12-1,13-1
ESV - **13,** 1-1,2-1,3-1,4-1,5-1,6-1,7-1,8-1,9-1,10-1,11-1,12-1,13-1
HCSB - **13,** 1-1,2-1,3-1,4-1,5-1,6-1,7-1,8-1,9-1,10-1,11-1,12-1,13-1

NASV - **13,** 1-1,2-1,3-1,4-1,5-1,6-1,7-1,8-1,9-1,10-1,11-1,12-1,13-1
NCV - 16, 1-1,2-1,3-**2,**4-1,5-1,6-**2,**7-1,8-1,9-1,10-1,11-1,12-**2,**13-1,14-1,15-1,16-1
NIV - **13,** 1-1,2-1,3-1,4-1,5-1,6-1,7-1,8-1,9-1,10-1,11-1,12-1,13-1
NKJV - **13,** 1-1,2-1,3-1,4-1,5-1,6-1,7-1,8-1,9-1,10-1,11-1,12-1,13-1
NLT - **13,** 1-1,2-1,3-1,4-1,5-1,6-1,7-1,8-1,9-1,10-1,11-1,12-1,13-1
NRSV - **13,** 1-1,2-1,3-1,4-1,5-1,6-1,7-1,8-1,9-1,10-1,11-1,12-1,13-1
Conclusion: Only the NCV made the verse more complex, and that royally.

692. Psalms 124:1* If it had not been the LORD who was on our side, now may **Israel** say;
AV - **16,** 1-1,2-1,3-1,4-1,5-1,6-1,7-1,8-1,9-1,10-1,11-1,12-1,13-1,14-1,15-1,16-1
ESV - **16,** 1-1,2-1,3-1,4-1,5-1,6-1,7-1,8-1,9-1,10-1,11-1,12-1,13-1,14-1,15-1,16-1
HCSB - **12,** 1-1,2-1,3-1,4-1,5-1,6-1,7-1,8-1,9-1,10-1,11-1,12-1
NASV - **15,** 1-1,2-1,3-1,4-1,5-1,6-1,7-1,8-1,9-1,10-1,11-1,12-1,13-1,14-1,15-1
NCV - 14, 1-1,2-1,3-1,4-1,5-1,6-1,7-1,8-1,9-1,10-1,11-1,12-1,13-**2,**14-1
NIV - **12,** 1-1,2-1,3-1,4-1,5-1,6-1,7-1,8-1,9-1,10-1,11-1,12-1
NLT - 14, 1-1,2-1,3-1,4-1,5-1,6-1,7-1,8-1,9-1,10-1,11-1,12-1,13-1,14-**2**
NRSV - **16,** 1-1,2-1,3-1,4-1,5-1,6-1,7-1,8-1,9-1,10-1,11-1,12-1,13-1,14-1,15-1,16-1
Conclusion: Only the NCV and the NLT made the verse more complex. These two versions have set up a pattern of making the simple difficult. Possibly their translators once held jobs for the government...or do now.

693. Psalms 126:5 They that sow in tears shall reap in joy.
AV - **9,** 1-1,2-1,3-1,4-1,5-1,6-1,7-1,8-1,9-1
ESV - **11,** 1-1,2-1,3-1,4-1,5-1,6-1,7-1,8-1,9-1,10-1,11-1
HCSB - **11,** 1-1,2-1,3-1,4-1,5-1,6-1,7-1,8-1,9-1,10-1,11-1
NASV - 10, 1-1,2-1,3-1,4-1,5-1,6-1,7-1,8-1,9-**2,**10-**2**
NCV - 12, 1-1,2-1,3-1,4-1,5-1,6-1,7-1,8-1,9-1,10-1,11-**2,**12-1
NIV - **11,** 1-1,2-1,3-1,4-1,5-1,6-1,7-1,8-1,9-1,10-1,11-1
NKJV - **9,** 1-1,2-1,3-1,4-1,5-1,6-1,7-1,8-1,9-1
NLT - 11, 1-1,2-1,3-1,4-1,5-1,6-1,7-**2,**8-1,9-1,10-1,11-1
NRSV - **11,** 1-1,2-1,3-1,4-1,5-1,6-1,7-1,8-1,9-1,10-1,11-1
Conclusion: Only three modern versions are more complex than the King James Bible. The NASV is the most difficult to read.

694. Psalm 128:5* The LORD shall bless thee out of **Zion**: and thou shalt see the good of **Jerusalem** all the days of thy life.
AV - **22,** 1-1,2-1,3-1,4-1,5-1,6-1,7-1,8-1,9-1,10-1,11-1,12-1,13-1,14-1,15-1,16-1,17-1,18-1,19-1,20-1,21-1,22-1
ESV - 19, 1-1,2-1,3-1,4-1,5-1,6-1,7-1,8-1,9-1,10-1,11-**4,**12-1,13-1,14-1,15-1,16-1,17-1,18-1,19-1
HCSB - 22, 1-1,2-1,3-1,4-1,5-1,6-1,7-1,8-1,9-1,10-1,11-1,12-1,13-1,14-**4,**15-1,16-1,17-1,18-1,19-1,20-1,21-1,22-1
NASV - 20, 1-1,2-1,3-1,4-1,5-1,6-1,7-1,8-1,9-1,10-1,11-1,12-**4,**13-1,14-1,15-1,16-1,17-1,18-1,19-1,20-1

NCV - 19, 1-1,2-1,3-1,4-1,5-1,6-1,7-1,8-1,9-1,10-1,11-**2**,12-1,13-1,14-1,15-1,16-1,17-1,18-1,19-1
NIV - 20, 1-1,2-1,3-1,4-1,5-1,6-1,7-1,8-1,9-1,10-1,11-1,12-1,13-1,14-1,15-1,16-1,17-1,18-**4**,19-1,20-1
NKJV - 21, 1-1,2-1,3-1,4-1,5-1,6-1,7-1,8-1,9-1,10-1,11-1,12-1,13-1,14-1,15-1,16-1,17-1,18-1,19-1,20-1,21-1
NLT - 19, 1-1,2-1,3-1,4-**5**,5-1,6-1,7-1,8-1,9-1,10-1,11-1,12-1,13-1,14-**2**,15-1,16-1,17-1,18-1,19-1
NRSV - 19, 1-1,2-1,3-1,4-1,5-1,6-1,7-1,8-1,9-1,10-1,11-**4**,12-1,13-1,14-1,15-1,16-1,17-1,18-1,19-1
Conclusion: Seven modern versions are more complex than the King James Bible.

695. Psalms 130:5 I wait for the LORD, my soul doth wait, and in his word do I hope.
AV - **16,** 1-1,2-1,3-1,4-1,5-1,6-1,7-1,8-1,9-1,10-1,11-1,12-1,13-1,14-1,15-1,16-1
ESV - **14,** 1-1,2-1,3-1,4-1,5-1,6-1,7-1,8-1,9-1,10-1,11-1,12-1,13-1,14-1
HCSB - **14,** 1-1,2-1,3-1,4-1,5-1,6-1,7-1,8-1,9-1,10-1,11-1,12-1,13-1,14-1
NASV - **16,** 1-1,2-1,3-1,4-1,5-1,6-1,7-1,8-1,9-1,10-1,11-1,12-1,13-1,14-1,15-1,16-1
NCV - **13,** 1-1,2-1,3-1,4-1,5-1,6-1,7-1,8-1,9-1,10-1,11-1,12-1,13-1
NIV - **16,** 1-1,2-1,3-1,4-1,5-1,6-1,7-1,8-1,9-1,10-1,11-1,12-1,13-1,14-1,15-1,16-1
NKJV - **15,** 1-1,2-1,3-1,4-1,5-1,6-1,7-1,8-1,9-1,10-1,11-1,12-1,13-1,14-1,15-1
NLT - 20, 1-1,2-1,3-**2**,4-1,5-1,6-1,7-1,8-1,9-1,10-**2**,11-1,12-1,13-1,14-1,15-1,16-1,17-1,18-1,19-1,20-1
NRSV - **14,** 1-1,2-1,3-1,4-1,5-1,6-1,7-1,8-1,9-1,10-1,11-1,12-1,13-1,14-1
Conclusion: Only the NLT made the verse more complex.

696. Psalm 132:6* Lo, we heard of it at **Ephratah**: we found it in the fields of the wood.
AV - **16,** 1-1,2-1,3-1,4-1,5-1,6-1,7-1,8-1,9-1,10-1,11-1,12-1,13-1,14-1,15-1,16-1
ESV - 15, 1-**2**,2-1,3-1,4-1,5-1,6-1,7-1,8-1,9-1,10-1,11-1,12-1,13-1,14-1,15-1
HCSB - **15,** 1-1,2-1,3-1,4-1,5-1,6-1,7-1,8-1,9-1,10-1,11-1,12-1,13-1,14-1,15-1
NASV - 15, 1-**2**,2-1,3-1,4-1,5-1,6-1,7-1,8-1,9-1,10-1,11-1,12-1,13-1,14-1,15-1
NCV - 13, 1-1,2-1,3-**2**,4-1,5-1,6-1,7-1,8-1,9-1,10-1,11-1,12-1,13-1
NIV - 14, 1-1,2-1,3-1,4-1,5-1,6-1,7-1,8-**2**,9-1,10-1,11-1,12-1,13-1,14-1
NKJV - 16, 1-**2**,2-1,3-1,4-1,5-1,6-1,7-1,8-1,9-1,10-1,11-1,12-1,13-1,14-1,15-1,16-1
NLT - 18, 1-1,2-1,3-1,4-1,5-1,6-1,7-1,8-1,9-1,10-1,11-1,12-1,13-1,14-1,15-**2**,16-**3**,17-1,18-1
NRSV - **14,** 1-1,2-1,3-1,4-1,5-1,6-1,7-1,8-1,9-1,10-1,11-1,12-1,13-1,14-1
Conclusion: Six modern versions are more complex than the King James Bible.

697. Psalms 135:2 Ye that stand in the house of the LORD, in the courts of the house of our God,
AV - **18,** 1-1,2-1,3-1,4-1,5-1,6-1,7-1,8-1,9-1,10-1,11-1,12-1,13-1,14-1,15-1,16-1,17-1,18-1
ESV - **17,** 1-1,2-1,3-1,4-1,5-1,6-1,7-1,8-1,9-1,10-1,11-1,12-1,13-1,14-1,15-1,16-1,17-1
HCSB - **17,** 1-1,2-1,3-1,4-1,5-1,6-1,7-1,8-1,9-1,10-1,11-1,12-1,13-1,14-1,15-1,16-1,17-1
NASV - **18,** 1-1,2-1,3-1,4-1,5-1,6-1,7-1,8-1,9-1,10-1,11-1,12-1,13-1,14-1,15-1,16-1,17-1,18-1
NCV - 13, 1-1,2-1,3-1,4-1,5-1,6-1,7-**2**,8-1,9-1,10-1,11-**2**,12-1,13-**2**
NIV - 18, 1-1,2-1,3-**3**,4-1,5-1,6-1,7-1,8-1,9-1,10-1,11-1,12-1,13-1,14-1,15-1,16-1,17-1,18-1
NKJV - **18,** 1-1,2-1,3-1,4-1,5-1,6-1,7-1,8-1,9-1,10-1,11-1,12-1,13-1,14-1,15-1,16-1,17-1,18-1
NLT - **18,** 1-1,2-1,3-1,4-1,5-1,6-1,7-1,8-1,9-1,10-1,11-1,12-1,13-1,14-1,15-1,16-1,17-1,18-1
NRSV - **18,** 1-1,2-1,3-1,4-1,5-1,6-1,7-1,8-1,9-1,10-1,11-1,12-1,13-1,14-1,15-1,16-1,17-1,18-1

Conclusion: Only the NCV and the NIV made the verse more complex. The NCV is the most difficult to read.

698. Psalms 135:16 They have mouths, but they speak not; eyes have they, but they see not;
AV - **14,** 1-1,2-1,3-1,4-1,5-1,6-1,7-1,8-1,9-1,10-1,11-1,12-1,13-1,14-1
ESV - **14,** 1-1,2-1,3-1,4-1,5-1,6-1,7-1,8-1,9-1,10-1,11-1,12-1,13-1,14-1
HCSB - **10,** 1-1,2-1,3-1,4-1,5-**2,**6-1,7-1,8-1,9-**2,**10-1
NASV - **16,** 1-1,2-1,3-1,4-1,5-1,6-1,7-1,8-1,9-1,10-1,11-1,12-1,13-1,14-1,15-1,16-1
NCV - **14,** 1-1,2-1,3-1,4-1,5-1,6-**2,**7-1,8-1,9-1,10-1,11-1,12-1,13-**2,**14-1
NIV - **11,** 1-1,2-1,3-1,4-1,5-**2,**6-1,7-1,8-1,9-1,10-**2,**11-1
NKJV - **16,** 1-1,2-1,3-1,4-1,5-1,6-1,7-1,8-1,9-1,10-1,11-1,12-1,13-1,14-1,15-1,16-1
NLT - **11,** 1-1,2-1,3-1,4-1,5-**2,**6-1,7-1,8-1,9-1,10-**2,**11-1
NRSV - **16,** 1-1,2-1,3-1,4-1,5-1,6-1,7-1,8-1,9-1,10-1,11-1,12-1,13-1,14-1,15-1,16-1
Conclusion: Four modern versions are more complex than the King James Bible.

699. Psalm 135:19* Bless the LORD, O house of **Israel**: bless the LORD, O house of **Aaron**:
AV - **14,** 1-1,2-1,3-1,4-1,5-1,6-1,7-1,8-1,9-1,10-1,11-1,12-1,13-1,14-1
ESV - **14,** 1-1,2-1,3-1,4-1,5-1,6-1,7-1,8-1,9-1,10-1,11-1,12-1,13-1,14-1
HCSB - **12,** 1-1,2-1,3-1,4-1,5-1,6-1,7-1,8-1,9-1,10-1,11-1,12-1
NASV - **14,** 1-1,2-1,3-1,4-1,5-1,6-1,7-1,8-1,9-1,10-1,11-1,12-1,13-1,14-1
NCV - **12,** 1-**3,**2-1,3-1,4-1,5-1,6-1,7-**3,**8-1,9-1,10-1,11-1,12-1
NIV - **14,** 1-1,2-1,3-1,4-1,5-1,6-1,7-1,8-1,9-1,10-1,11-1,12-1,13-1,14-1
NKJV - **14,** 1-1,2-1,3-1,4-1,5-1,6-1,7-1,8-1,9-1,10-1,11-1,12-1,13-1,14-1
NLT - **13,** 1-1,2-1,3-1,4-1,5-1,6-1,7-1,8-**3,**9-1,10-1,11-1,12-1,13-1
NRSV - **14,** 1-1,2-1,3-1,4-1,5-1,6-1,7-1,8-1,9-1,10-1,11-1,12-1,13-1,14-1
Conclusion: Only the NCV and the NLT made the verse more complex.

700. Psalm 135:20* Bless the LORD, O house of **Levi**: ye that fear the LORD, bless the LORD.
AV - **15,** 1-1,2-1,3-1,4-1,5-1,6-1,7-1,8-1,9-1,10-1,11-1,12-1,13-1,14-1,15-1
ESV - **15,** 1-1,2-1,3-1,4-1,5-1,6-1,7-1,8-1,9-1,10-1,11-1,12-1,13-1,14-1,15-1
HCSB - **14,** 1-1,2-1,3-1,4-1,5-1,6-1,7-1,8-1,9-**2,**10-1,11-1,12-1,13-1,14-1
NASV - **15,** 1-1,2-1,3-1,4-1,5-1,6-1,7-1,8-1,9-1,10-**2,**11-1,12-1,13-1,14-1,15-1
NCV - **14,** 1-**3,**2-1,3-1,4-1,5-1,6-1,7-1,8-1,9-**2,**10-1,11-1,12-1,13-1,14-1
NIV - **14,** 1-1,2-1,3-1,4-1,5-1,6-1,7-1,8-1,9-1,10-1,11-1,12-1,13-1,14-1
NKJV - **15,** 1-1,2-1,3-1,4-1,5-1,6-1,7-1,8-1,9-1,10-1,11-1,12-1,13-1,14-1,15-1
NLT - **14,** 1-1,2-1,3-1,4-1,5-1,6-1,7-1,8-1,9-1,10-1,11-1,12-1,13-1,14-1
NRSV - **15,** 1-1,2-1,3-1,4-1,5-1,6-1,7-1,8-1,9-1,10-1,11-1,12-1,13-1,14-1,15-1
Conclusion: Only three modern versions are more complex than the King James Bible. The NLT inserted "Levites" for "house of Levi." This was not counted against it.

701. Psalms 137:4 How shall we sing the Lord's song in a strange land?
AV - **11,** 1-1,2-1,3-1,4-1,5-1,6-1,7-1,8-1,9-1,10-1,11-1
ESV - **11,** 1-1,2-1,3-1,4-1,5-1,6-1,7-1,8-1,9-1,10-**2,**11-1
HCSB - **10,** 1-1,2-1,3-1,4-1,5-1,6-1,7-1,8-1,9-**2,**10-1

NASV - 11, 1-1,2-1,3-1,4-1,5-1,6-1,7-1,8-1,9-1,10-**2**,11-1
NCV - 15, 1-1,2-1,3-**2**,4-1,5-1,6-**2**,7-1,8-1,9-1,10-1,11-1,12-1,13-1,14-**2**,15-**2**
NIV - 14, 1-1,2-1,3-1,4-1,5-1,6-1,7-1,8-1,9-1,10-1,11-1,12-1,13-**2**,14-1
NKJV - 11, 1-1,2-1,3-1,4-1,5-1,6-1,7-1,8-1,9-1,10-**2**,11-1
NLT - 15, 1-1,2-1,3-1,4-1,5-1,6-1,7-1,8-1,9-1,10-1,11-1,12-1,13-1,14-**2**,15-1
NRSV - 11, 1-1,2-1,3-1,4-1,5-1,6-1,7-1,8-1,9-1,10-**2**,11-1
Conclusion: All eight modern versions are more complex than the King James Bible. Once again, the NCV is the most difficult to read.

702. Psalms 138:4 All the kings of the earth shall praise thee, O LORD, when they hear the words of thy mouth.
AV - **19,** 1-1,2-1,3-1,4-1,5-1,6-1,7-1,8-1,9-1,10-1,11-1,12-1,13-1,14-1,15-1,16-1,17-1,18-1,19-1
ESV - **21,** 1-1,2-1,3-1,4-1,5-1,6-1,7-1,8-1,9-1,10-1,11-1,12-1,13-1,14-1,15-1,16-1,17-1,18-1,19-1,20-1,21-1
HCSB - 17, 1-1,2-1,3-1,4-1,5-1,6-1,7-1,8-1,9-1,10-1,11-1,12-1,13-1,14-1,15-1,16-1,17-**2**
NASV - **22,** 1-1,2-1,3-1,4-1,5-1,6-1,7-1,8-1,9-1,10-1,11-1,12-1,13-1,14-1,15-1,16-1,17-1,18-1,19-1,20-1,21-1,22-1
NCV - **17,** 1-1,2-1,3-1,4-1,5-1,6-1,7-1,8-1,9-1,10-1,11-1,12-1,13-1,14-1,15-1,16-1,17-1
NIV - **19,** 1-1,2-1,3-1,4-1,5-1,6-1,7-1,8-1,9-1,10-1,11-1,12-1,13-1,14-1,15-1,16-1,17-1,18-1,19-1
NKJV - **19,** 1-1,2-1,3-1,4-1,5-1,6-1,7-1,8-1,9-1,10-1,11-1,12-1,13-1,14-1,15-1,16-1,17-1,18-1,19-1
NLT - 18, 1-**3**,2-1,3-1,4-1,5-1,6-1,7-1,8-1,9-1,10-1,11-1,12-1,13-1,14-1,15-1,16-1,17-1,18-1
NRSV - **20,** 1-1,2-1,3-1,4-1,5-1,6-1,7-1,8-1,9-1,10-1,11-1,12-1,13-1,14-1,15-1,16-1,17-1,18-1,19-1,20-1
Conclusion: Only the HCSB and the NLT made the verse more complex.

703. Psalms 139:1 O LORD, thou hast searched me, and known me.
AV - **9,** 1-1,2-1,3-1,4-1,5-1,6-1,7-1,8-1,9-1
ESV - **9,** 1-1,2-1,3-1,4-1,5-1,6-1,7-1,8-1,9-1
HCSB - **8,** 1-1,2-1,3-1,4-1,5-1,6-1,7-1,8-1
NASV - **9,** 1-1,2-1,3-1,4-1,5-1,6-1,7-1,8-1,9-1
NCV - 10, 1-1,2-1,3-1,4-**3**,5-1,6-1,7-1,8-1,9-**2**,10-1
NIV - **10,** 1-1,2-1,3-1,4-1,5-1,6-1,7-1,8-1,9-1,10-1
NKJV - **9,** 1-1,2-1,3-1,4-1,5-1,6-1,7-1,8-1,9-1
NLT - 12, 1-1,2-1,3-1,4-1,5-**3**,6-1,7-1,8-1,9-1,10-**4**,11-1,12-1
NRSV - **9,** 1-1,2-1,3-1,4-1,5-1,6-1,7-1,8-1,9-1
Conclusion: Once again the NCV and the NLT are the most difficult to read.

704. Psalms 139:23 Search me, O God, and know my heart: try me, and know my thoughts:
AV - **14,** 1-1,2-1,3-1,4-1,5-1,6-1,7-1,8-1,9-1,10-1,11-1,12-1,13-1,14-1
ESV - **14,** 1-1,2-1,3-1,4-1,5-1,6-1,7-1,8-1,9-1,10-1,11-1,12-1,13-1,14-1
HCSB - 13, 1-1,2-1,3-1,4-1,5-1,6-1,7-1,8-1,9-1,10-1,11-1,12-1,13-**2**
NASV - 15, 1-1,2-1,3-1,4-1,5-1,6-1,7-1,8-1,9-1,10-1,11-1,12-1,13-1,14-**2**,15-1
NCV - 14, 1-1,2-**3**,3-1,4-1,5-1,6-1,7-1,8-1,9-1,10-1,11-1,12-1,13-**2**,14-1
NIV - 15, 1-1,2-1,3-1,4-1,5-1,6-1,7-1,8-1,9-1,10-1,11-1,12-1,13-1,14-**2**,15-1

NKJV - 14, 1-1,2-1,3-1,4-1,5-1,6-1,7-1,8-1,9-1,10-1,11-1,12-1,13-1,14-**4**
NLT - 15, 1-1,2-1,3-1,4-1,5-1,6-1,7-1,8-1,9-1,10-1,11-1,12-1,13-1,14-**2**,15-1
NRSV - **14,** 1-1,2-1,3-1,4-1,5-1,6-1,7-1,8-1,9-1,10-1,11-1,12-1,13-1,14-1
Conclusion: Six modern versions are more complex than the King James Bible. The NCV is the most difficult to read.

705. Psalms 145:10 All thy works shall praise thee, O LORD; and thy saints shall bless thee.
AV - **14,** 1-1,2-1,3-1,4-1,5-1,6-1,7-1,8-1,9-1,10-1,11-1,12-1,13-1,14-1
ESV - **17,** 1-1,2-1,3-1,4-1,5-1,6-1,7-1,8-1,9-1,10-1,11-1,12-1,13-1,14-1,15-1,16-1,17-1
HCSB - 13, 1-1,2-1,3-1,4-1,5-1,6-1,7-1,8-1,9-1,10-**2**,11-1,12-1,13-1
NASV - 17, 1-1,2-1,3-1,4-1,5-1,6-1,7-1,8-1,9-1,10-1,11-1,12-1,13-**2**,14-1,15-1,16-1,17-1
NCV - 16, 1-1,2-**4**,3-1,4-1,5-1,6-1,7-1,8-1,9-1,10-1,11-**2**,12-1,13-1,14-1,15-1,16-1
NIV - 14, 1-1,2-1,3-1,4-1,5-1,6-1,7-1,8-1,9-1,10-1,11-1,12-1,13-**2**,14-1
NKJV - **14,** 1-1,2-1,3-1,4-1,5-1,6-1,7-1,8-1,9-1,10-1,11-1,12-1,13-1,14-1
NLT - 15, 1-1,2-1,3-1,4-1,5-1,6-1,7-1,8-1,9-1,10-1,11-**2**,12-**3**,13-1,14-1,15-1
NRSV - 17, 1-1,2-1,3-1,4-1,5-1,6-1,7-1,8-1,9-1,10-1,11-1,12-1,13-1,14-**2**,15-1,16-1,17-1
Conclusion: Six modern versions are more complex than the King James Bible.

706. Psalm 146:1 Praise ye the LORD. Praise the LORD, O my soul.
AV - **10,** 1-1,2-1,3-1,4-1,5-1,6-1,7-1,8-1,9-1,10-1
ESV - **9,** 1-1,2-1,3-1,4-1,5-1,6-1,7-1,8-1,9-1
HCSB - **6,** 1-1,2-1,3-1,4-1,5-1,6-1
NASV - **9,** 1-1,2-1,3-1,4-1,5-1,6-1,7-1,8-1,9-1
NCV - 9, 1-1,2-1,3-1,4-1,5-1,6-**2**,7-1,8-1,9-1
NIV - **9,** 1-1,2-1,3-1,4-1,5-1,6-1,7-1,8-1,9-1
NKJV - **9,** 1-1,2-1,3-1,4-1,5-1,6-1,7-1,8-1,9-1
NLT - **11,** 1-1,2-1,3-1,4-1,5-1,6-1,7-1,8-1,9-1,10-1,11-1
NRSV - **9,** 1-1,2-1,3-1,4-1,5-1,6-1,7-1,8-1,9-1
Conclusion: Only the NCV made the verse more complex. The HCSB inserted "Hallelujah" for "Praise the LORD" but this was not counted against it.

707. Psalm 147:12* Praise the LORD, O **Jerusalem**; praise thy God, O **Zion**.
AV - **10,** 1-1,2-1,3-1,4-1,5-1,6-1,7-1,8-1,9-1,10-1
ESV - **10,** 1-1,2-1,3-1,4-1,5-1,6-1,7-1,8-1,9-1,10-1
HCSB - 8, 1-**2**,2-1,3-1,4-1,5-1,6-1,7-1,8-1
NASV - **10,** 1-1,2-1,3-1,4-1,5-1,6-1,7-1,8-1,9-1,10-1
NCV - **8,** 1-1,2-1,3-1,4-1,5-1,6-1,7-1,8-1
NIV - 10, 1-**2**,2-1,3-1,4-1,5-1,6-1,7-1,8-1,9-1,10-1
NKJV - **10,** 1-1,2-1,3-1,4-1,5-1,6-1,7-1,8-1,9-1,10-1
NLT - 10, 1-**3**,2-1,3-1,4-1,5-1,6-1,7-1,8-1,9-1,10-1
NRSV - **10,** 1-1,2-1,3-1,4-1,5-1,6-1,7-1,8-1,9-1,10-1
Conclusion: Only three made the verse more complex.

708. Psalm 148:3 Praise ye him, sun and moon: praise him, all ye stars of light.
AV - **13,** 1-1,2-1,3-1,4-1,5-1,6-1,7-1,8-1,9-1,10-1,11-1,12-1,13-1
ESV - 11, 1-1,2-1,3-1,4-1,5-1,6-1,7-1,8-1,9-1,10-**2**,11-1
HCSB - 11, 1-1,2-1,3-1,4-1,5-1,6-1,7-1,8-1,9-1,10-**2**,11-1
NASV - 11, 1-1,2-1,3-1,4-1,5-1,6-1,7-1,8-1,9-1,10-1,11-1
NCV - 11, 1-1,2-1,3-1,4-1,5-1,6-1,7-1,8-1,9-1,10-**2**,11-1
NIV - 11, 1-1,2-1,3-1,4-1,5-1,6-1,7-1,8-1,9-1,10-**2**,11-1
NKJV - **12,** 1-1,2-1,3-1,4-1,5-1,6-1,7-1,8-1,9-1,10-1,11-1,12-1
NLT - 11, 1-1,2-1,3-1,4-1,5-1,6-1,7-1,8-1,9-1,10-**2**,11-1
NRSV - 11, 1-1,2-1,3-1,4-1,5-1,6-1,7-1,8-1,9-1,10-**2**,11-1
Conclusion: Six modern versions are more complex than the King James Bible.

709. Proverbs 3:2 For length of days, and long life, and peace, shall they add to thee.
AV - **14,** 1-1,2-1,3-1,4-1,5-1,6-1,7-1,8-1,9-1,10-1,11-1,12-1,13-1,14-1
ESV - **15,** 1-1,2-1,3-1,4-1,5-1,6-1,7-1,8-1,9-1,10-1,11-1,12-1,13-1,14-1,15-1
HCSB - 13, 1-1,2-1,3-1,4-1,5-1,6-**2**,7-1,8-1,9-1,10-1,11-1,12-1,13-**2**
NASV - 15, 1-1,2-1,3-1,4-1,5-1,6-1,7-1,8-1,9-1,10-1,11-1,12-1,13-1,14-1,15-1
NCV - 13, 1-1,2-1,3-1,4-1,5-1,6-1,7-1,8-1,9-1,10-1,11-1,12-1,13-**3**
NIV - 13, 1-1,2-1,3-1,4-**2**,5-1,6-1,7-**2**,8-1,9-1,10-1,11-1,12-**4**
NKJV - **14,** 1-1,2-1,3-1,4-1,5-1,6-1,7-1,8-1,9-1,10-1,11-1,12-1,13-1,14-1
NLT - 15, 1-1,2-1,3-1,4-1,5-1,6-1,7-1,8-**2**,9-1,10-1,11-1,12-1,13-1,14-1,15-**4**
NRSV - 15, 1-1,2-1,3-1,4-1,5-1,6-1,7-1,8-1,9-1,10-**3**,11-**2**,12-1,13-1,14-1,15-1
Conclusion: Five modern versions are more complex than the King James Bible.

710. Proverbs 5:5 Her feet go down to death; her steps take hold on hell.
AV - **12,** 1-1,2-1,3-1,4-1,5-1,6-1,7-1,8-1,9-1,10-1,11-1,12-1
ESV - 13, 1-1,2-1,3-1,4-1,5-1,6-1,7-1,8-1,9-**2**,10-1,11-1,12-1,13-1
HCSB - **12,** 1-1,2-1,3-1,4-1,5-1,6-1,7-1,8-1,9-1,10-1,11-1,12-1
NASV - **12,** 1-1,2-1,3-1,4-1,5-1,6-1,7-1,8-1,9-1,10-1,11-1,12-1
NCV - 15, 1-1,2-1,3-1,4-1,5-1,6-1,7-1,8-1,9-1,10-1,11-**2**,12-1,13-1,14-1,15-1
NIV - **13,** 1-1,2-1,3-1,4-1,5-1,6-1,7-1,8-1,9-1,10-1,11-1,12-1,13-1
NKJV - **12,** 1-1,2-1,3-1,4-1,5-1,6-1,7-1,8-1,9-1,10-1,11-1,12-1
NLT - **13,** 1-1,2-1,3-1,4-1,5-1,6-1,7-1,8-1,9-1,10-1,11-1,12-1,13-1
NRSV - 13, 1-1,2-1,3-1,4-1,5-1,6-1,7-1,8-1,9-**2**,10-1,11-1,12-1,13-1
Conclusion: Only three modern versions, the ESV, NCV and the NRSV, made the verse more complex.

The NCV, NIV and NLT say "grave" in place of "hell." The ESV, HCSB, NASV and NRSV say "Sheol" which was counted as one syllable. Only the NKJV says "hell" like the Authorized Version.

711. Proverbs 20:9 Who can say, I have made my heart clean, I am pure from my sin?
AV - **15,** 1-1,2-1,3-1,4-1,5-1,6-1,7-1,8-1,9-1,10-1,11-1,12-1,13-1,14-1,15-1
ESV - 15, 1-1,2-1,3-1,4-1,5-1,6-1,7-1,8-1,9-1,10-1,11-1,12-1,13-1,14-1,15-1
HCSB - 15, 1-1,2-1,3-1,4-1,5-1,6-1,7-1,8-1,9-1,10-1,11-1,12-1,13-1,14-1,15-1

NASV - **14,** 1-1,2-1,3-1,4-1,5-1,6-1,7-1,8-1,9-1,10-1,11-1,12-1,13-1,14-1
NCV - 13, 1-1,2-1,3-1,4-1,5-1,6-1,7-**3,**8-1,9-1,10-**2,**11-1,12-**3,**13-1
NIV - 15, 1-1,2-1,3-1,4-1,5-1,6-1,7-1,8-1,9-1,10-1,11-1,12-1,13-1,14-**2,**15-1
NKJV - 15, 1-1,2-1,3-1,4-1,5-1,6-1,7-1,8-1,9-1,10-1,11-1,12-1,13-1,14-1,15-1
NLT - 15, 1-1,2-1,3-1,4-1,5-1,6-1,7-1,8-1,9-1,10-1,11-1,12-1,13-1,14-1,15-1
NRSV - 15, 1-1,2-1,3-1,4-1,5-1,6-1,7-1,8-1,9-1,10-1,11-1,12-1,13-1,14-1,15-1
Conclusion: Only the NCV and the NIV made the verse more complex. The NCV is the most difficult to read.

712. Proverbs 22:23 For the LORD will plead their cause, and spoil the soul of those that spoiled them.
AV - **16,** 1-1,2-1,3-1,4-1,5-1,6-1,7-1,8-1,9-1,10-1,11-1,12-1,13-1,14-1,15-1,16-1
ESV - 15, 1-1,2-1,3-1,4-1,5-1,6-1,7-1,8-1,9-1,10-1,11-1,12-1,13-1,14-1,15-1
HCSB - 15, 1-1,2-1,3-1,4-1,5-1,6-1,7-1,8-1,9-1,10-1,11-**2,**12-1,13-1,14-**2,**15-1
NASV - **16,** 1-1,2-1,3-1,4-1,5-1,6-1,7-1,8-1,9-1,10-1,11-1,12-1,13-1,14-1,15-1,16-1
NCV - 19, 1-1,2-1,3-1,4-**2,**5-1,6-1,7-1,8-1,9-1,10-1,11-1,12-1,13-1,14-1,15-1,16-1,17-**2,**18-1,19-1
NIV - 15, 1-1,2-1,3-1,4-1,5-1,6-1,7-1,8-1,9-1,10-1,11-**2,**12-1,13-1,14-**2,**15-1
NKJV - 16, 1-1,2-1,3-1,4-1,5-1,6-1,7-1,8-1,9-**2,**10-1,11-1,12-1,13-1,14-1,15-**2,**16-1
NLT - 13, 1-1,2-1,3-1,4-1,5-1,6-**3,**7-1,8-1,9-**2,**10-**3,**11-1,12-**2,**13-1
NRSV - 14, 1-1,2-1,3-1,4-1,5-1,6-1,7-1,8-**2,**9-1,10-1,11-1,12-1,13-**2,**14-1
Conclusion: Six modern versions are more complex than the King James Bible. The NLT did its usual masterful job of complicating the simple.

713. Proverbs 22:25 Lest thou learn his ways, and get a snare to thy soul.
AV - **12,** 1-1,2-1,3-1,4-1,5-1,6-1,7-1,8-1,9-1,10-1,11-1,12-1
ESV - 11, 1-1,2-1,3-1,4-1,5-1,6-1,7-**3,**8-**2,**9-1,10-1,11-1
HCSB - 12, 1-1,2-1,3-1,4-1,5-1,6-1,7-1,8-**3,**9-**2,**10-1,11-1,12-1
NASV - 12, 1-1,2-1,3-1,4-1,5-1,6-1,7-1,8-1,9-1,10-1,11-1,12-**2**
NCV - 15, 1-1,2-1,3-1,4-1,5-1,6-1,7-1,8-1,9-1,10-1,11-1,12-1,13-1,14-1,15-**2**
NIV - 10, 1-1,2-1,3-1,4-1,5-1,6-1,7-1,8-1,9-**2,**10-**2**
NKJV - **12,** 1-1,2-1,3-1,4-1,5-1,6-1,7-1,8-1,9-1,10-1,11-1,12-1
NLT - 12, 1-1,2-1,3-1,4-1,5-1,6-1,7-1,8-1,9-1,10-**3,**11-1,12-1
NRSV - 12, 1-1,2-1,3-1,4-1,5-1,6-1,7-1,8-**3,**9-**2,**10-1,11-1,12-1
Conclusion: Seven modern versions are more complex than the King James Bible.

714. Proverbs 23:19 Hear thou, my son, and be wise, and guide thine heart in the way.
AV - **14,** 1-1,2-1,3-1,4-1,5-1,6-1,7-1,8-1,9-1,10-1,11-1,12-1,13-1,14-1
ESV - 13, 1-1,2-1,3-1,4-1,5-1,6-1,7-1,8-**2,**9-1,10-1,11-1,12-1,13-1
HCSB - 13, 1-**2,**2-1,3-1,4-1,5-1,6-1,7-1,8-1,9-1,10-1,11-1,12-1,13-1
NASV - 13, 1-**2,**2-1,3-1,4-1,5-1,6-1,7-1,8-**2,**9-1,10-1,11-1,12-1,13-1
NCV - 13, 1-**2,**2-1,3-1,4-1,5-1,6-1,7-1,8-1,9-1,10-1,11-1,12-1,13-1
NIV - 14, 1-**2,**2-1,3-1,4-1,5-1,6-1,7-1,8-1,9-1,10-1,11-1,12-1,13-1,14-1
NKJV - **13,** 1-1,2-1,3-1,4-1,5-1,6-1,7-1,8-1,9-1,10-1,11-1,12-1,13-1
NLT - 13, 1-1,2-1,3-**2,**4-1,5-1,6-1,7-1,8-1,9-1,10-1,11-1,12-1,13-1

NRSV - 13, 1-1,2-1,3-1,4-1,5-1,6-1,7-1,8-**2**,9-1,10-1,11-1,12-1,13-1
Conclusion: Seven modern versions are more complex than the King James Bible.

715. Proverbs 31:2 What, my son? and what, the son of my womb? and what, the son of my vows?
AV - **17,** 1-1,2-1,3-1,4-1,5-1,6-1,7-1,8-1,9-1,10-1,11-1,12-1,13-1,14-1,15-1,16-1,17-1
ESV - **22,** 1-1,2-1,3-1,4-**2**,5-1,6-1,7-1,8-1,9-1,10-**2**,11-1,12-1,13-1,14-1,15-1,16-1,17-1,18-**2**,19-1,20-1,21-1,22-1
HCSB - **16,** 1-1,2-1,3-1,4-1,5-1,6-1,7-1,8-1,9-1,10-1,11-1,12-1,13-1,14-1,15-1,16-1
NASV - **18,** 1-1,2-1,3-1,4-1,5-1,6-1,7-1,8-1,9-1,10-1,11-1,12-1,13-1,14-1,15-1,16-1,17-1,18-1
NCV - **14,** 1-1,2-1,3-1,4-1,5-1,6-1,7-1,8-1,9-1,10-1,11-1,12-1,13-1,14-1
NIV - **13,** 1-1,2-1,3-1,4-1,5-1,6-1,7-1,8-1,9-1,10-1,11-1,12-1,13-1
NKJV - **15,** 1-1,2-1,3-1,4-1,5-1,6-1,7-1,8-1,9-1,10-1,11-1,12-1,13-1,14-1,15-1
NLT - **13,** 1-1,2-1,3-1,4-1,5-1,6-1,7-1,8-1,9-1,10-1,11-1,12-1,13-1
NRSV - **13,** 1-1,2-1,3-1,4-1,5-1,6-1,7-1,8-1,9-1,10-1,11-1,12-1,13-1
Conclusion: Only the ESV made the verse more complex. The NCV renders the verse in all single syllable words as do the remaining modern versions, but where the other versions all share the same basic format, the rendering of the NCV is both stunning and humorous. It merits reproduction here. Where it came from one can only guess.
  Pro. 31:2 (NCV) "My son, I gave birth to you. You are the son I prayed for."

716. Proverbs 31:31 Give her of the fruit of her hands; and let her own works praise her in the gates.
AV - **18,** 1-1,2-1,3-1,4-1,5-1,6-1,7-1,8-1,9-1,10-1,11-1,12-1,13-1,14-1,15-1,16-1,17-1,18-1
ESV - **17,** 1-1,2-1,3-1,4-1,5-1,6-1,7-1,8-1,9-1,10-1,11-1,12-1,13-1,14-1,15-1,16-1,17-1
HCSB - **17,** 1-1,2-1,3-1,4-**2**,5-1,6-1,7-**2**,8-1,9-1,10-1,11-1,12-1,13-1,14-1,15-1,16-**2**,17-1
NASV - **16,** 1-1,2-1,3-1,4-**2**,5-1,6-1,7-1,8-1,9-1,10-1,11-1,12-1,13-1,14-1,15-1,16-1
NCV - **18,** 1-1,2-1,3-1,4-**2**,5-1,6-1,7-1,8-1,9-1,10-1,11-1,12-1,13-**2**,14-1,15-1,16-1,17-1,18-1
NIV - **18,** 1-1,2-1,3-1,4-**2**,5-1,6-1,7-1,8-1,9-1,10-1,11-1,12-1,13-1,14-1,15-1,16-1,17-1,18-1
NKJV - **18,** 1-1,2-1,3-1,4-1,5-1,6-1,7-1,8-1,9-1,10-1,11-1,12-1,13-1,14-1,15-1,16-1,17-1,18-1
NLT - **14,** 1-**2**,2-1,3-1,4-1,5-1,6-1,7-1,8-1,9-1,10-1,11-**3**,12-**2**,13-1,14-1
NRSV - **20,** 1-1,2-1,3-1,4-1,5-1,6-1,7-1,8-1,9-1,10-1,11-1,12-1,13-1,14-1,15-1,16-1,17-1,18-1,19-**2**,20-1
Conclusion: Six modern versions are more complex than the King James Bible. The HCSB and the NLT made the verse more complex.

717. Ecclesiastes 1:1* The words of the **Preacher**, the son of **David**, king in **Jerusalem**.
AV - **12,** 1-1,2-1,3-1,4-1,5-1,6-1,7-1,8-1,9-1,10-1,11-1,12-1
ESV - **12,** 1-1,2-1,3-1,4-1,5-1,6-1,7-1,8-1,9-1,10-1,11-1,12-1
HCSB - **11,** 1-1,2-1,3-1,4-1,5-1,6-1,7-1,8-1,9-1,10-1,11-1
NASV - **12,** 1-1,2-1,3-1,4-1,5-1,6-1,7-1,8-1,9-1,10-1,11-1,12-1
NCV - **14,** 1-1,2-1,3-1,4-1,5-1,6-1,7-1,8-1,9-1,10-1,11-1,12-1,13-1,14-1
NIV - **11,** 1-1,2-1,3-1,4-1,5-1,6-1,7-1,8-1,9-1,10-1,11-1
NKJV - **12,** 1-1,2-1,3-1,4-1,5-1,6-1,7-1,8-1,9-1,10-1,11-1,12-1
NLT - **14,** 1-1,2-1,3-1,4-1,5-1,6-1,7-1,8-1,9-1,10-1,11-1,12-1,13-1,14-1
NRSV - **12,** 1-1,2-1,3-1,4-1,5-1,6-1,7-1,8-1,9-1,10-1,11-1,12-1

Conclusion: All versions read the same.

718. Ecclesiastes 3:3 A time to kill, and a time to heal; a time to break down, and a time to build up;
AV - **20,** 1-1,2-1,3-1,4-1,5-1,6-1,7-1,8-1,9-1,10-1,11-1,12-1,13-1,14-1,15-1,16-1,17-1,18-1,19-1,20-1
ESV - **20,** 1-1,2-1,3-1,4-1,5-1,6-1,7-1,8-1,9-1,10-1,11-1,12-1,13-1,14-1,15-1,16-1,17-1,18-1,19-1,20-1
HCSB - **19,** 1-1,2-1,3-1,4-1,5-1,6-1,7-1,8-1,9-1,10-1,11-1,12-1,13-1,14-1,15-1,16-1,17-1,18-1,19-1
NASV - **20,** 1-1,2-1,3-1,4-1,5-1,6-1,7-1,8-1,9-1,10-1,11-1,12-1,13-1,14-1,15-1,16-1,17-1,18-1,19-1,20-1
NCV - **22,** 1-1,2-1,3-1,4-1,5-1,6-1,7-1,8-1,9-1,10-1,11-1,12-1,13-1,14-1,15-1,16-1,17-**2,**18-1,19-1,20-1,21-1,22-1
NIV - **19,** 1-1,2-1,3-1,4-1,5-1,6-1,7-1,8-1,9-1,10-1,11-1,12-1,13-1,14-1,15-1,16-1,17-1,18-1,19-1
NKJV - **20,** 1-1,2-1,3-1,4-1,5-1,6-1,7-1,8-1,9-1,10-1,11-1,12-1,13-1,14-1,15-1,16-1,17-1,18-1,19-1,20-1
NLT - **20,** 1-1,2-1,3-1,4-1,5-1,6-1,7-1,8-1,9-1,10-1,11-1,12-1,13-1,14-1,15-1,16-1,17-1,18-1,19-1,20-1
NRSV - **20,** 1-1,2-1,3-1,4-1,5-1,6-1,7-1,8-1,9-1,10-1,11-1,12-1,13-1,14-1,15-1,16-1,17-1,18-1,19-1,20-1
Conclusion: Only the NCV made the verse more complex.

719. Ecclesiastes 3:4 A time to weep, and a time to laugh; a time to mourn, and a time to dance;
AV - **18,** 1-1,2-1,3-1,4-1,5-1,6-1,7-1,8-1,9-1,10-1,11-1,12-1,13-1,14-1,15-1,16-1,17-1,18-1
ESV - **18,** 1-1,2-1,3-1,4-1,5-1,6-1,7-1,8-1,9-1,10-1,11-1,12-1,13-1,14-1,15-1,16-1,17-1,18-1
HCSB - **18,** 1-1,2-1,3-1,4-1,5-1,6-1,7-1,8-1,9-1,10-1,11-1,12-1,13-1,14-1,15-1,16-1,17-1,18-1
NASV - **18,** 1-1,2-1,3-1,4-1,5-1,6-1,7-1,8-1,9-1,10-1,11-1,12-1,13-1,14-1,15-1,16-1,17-1,18-1
NCV - **23,** 1-1,2-1,3-1,4-1,5-1,6-1,7-1,8-1,9-1,10-1,11-1,12-1,13-1,14-1,15-1,16-1,17-1,18-1,19-1,20-1,21-1,22-1,23-1
NIV - **18,** 1-1,2-1,3-1,4-1,5-1,6-1,7-1,8-1,9-1,10-1,11-1,12-1,13-1,14-1,15-1,16-1,17-1,18-1
NKJV - **18,** 1-1,2-1,3-1,4-1,5-1,6-1,7-1,8-1,9-1,10-1,11-1,12-1,13-1,14-1,15-1,16-1,17-1,18-1
NLT - **18,** 1-1,2-1,3-1,4-1,5-1,6-1,7-1,8-1,9-1,10-1,11-1,12-1,13-1,14-1,15-1,16-1,17-1,18-1
NRSV - **18,** 1-1,2-1,3-1,4-1,5-1,6-1,7-1,8-1,9-1,10-1,11-1,12-1,13-1,14-1,15-1,16-1,17-1,18-1
Conclusion: All versions read the same.

720. Ecclesiastes 3:8 A time to love, and a time to hate; a time of war, and a time of peace.
AV - **18,** 1-1,2-1,3-1,4-1,5-1,6-1,7-1,8-1,9-1,10-1,11-1,12-1,13-1,14-1,15-1,16-1,17-1,18-1
ESV - **18,** 1-1,2-1,3-1,4-1,5-1,6-1,7-1,8-1,9-1,10-1,11-1,12-1,13-1,14-1,15-1,16-1,17-1,18-1
HCSB - **18,** 1-1,2-1,3-1,4-1,5-1,6-1,7-1,8-1,9-1,10-1,11-1,12-1,13-1,14-1,15-1,16-1,17-1,18-1
NASV - **18,** 1-1,2-1,3-1,4-1,5-1,6-1,7-1,8-1,9-1,10-1,11-1,12-1,13-1,14-1,15-1,16-1,17-1,18-1
NCV - **22,** 1-1,2-1,3-1,4-1,5-1,6-1,7-1,8-1,9-1,10-1,11-1,12-1,13-1,14-1,15-1,16-1,17-1,18-1,19-1,20-1,21-1,22-1
NIV - **18,** 1-1,2-1,3-1,4-1,5-1,6-1,7-1,8-1,9-1,10-1,11-1,12-1,13-1,14-1,15-1,16-1,17-1,18-1
NKJV - **18,** 1-1,2-1,3-1,4-1,5-1,6-1,7-1,8-1,9-1,10-1,11-1,12-1,13-1,14-1,15-1,16-1,17-1,18-1
NLT - **18,** 1-1,2-1,3-1,4-1,5-1,6-1,7-1,8-1,9-1,10-1,11-1,12-1,13-1,14-1,15-1,16-1,17-1,18-1

NRSV - **18,** 1-1,2-1,3-1,4-1,5-1,6-1,7-1,8-1,9-1,10-1,11-1,12-1,13-1,14-1,15-1,16-1,17-1,18-1
Conclusion: All versions read the same.

721. Ecclesiastes 6:6# Yea, though he live a **thousand** years twice told, yet hath he seen no good: do not all go to one place?
AV - **22,** 1-1,2-1,3-1,4-1,5-1,6-1,7-1,8-1,9-1,10-1,11-1,12-1,13-1,14-1,15-1,16-1,17-1,18-1,19-1,20-1,21-1,22-1
ESV - **22,** 1-**2**,2-1,3-1,4-1,5-1,6-1,7-1,8-1,9-1,10-**2**,11-1,12-**2**,13-1,14-1,15-1,16-1,17-1,18-1,19-1,20-1,21-1,22-1
HCSB - **21,** 1-1,2-1,3-1,4-1,5-1,6-1,7-1,8-1,9-1,10-1,11-1,12-**4**,13-**3**,14-1,15-1,16-1,17-1,18-1,19-1,20-1,21-1
NASV - **23,** 1-**2**,2-1,3-1,4-**2**,5-1,6-1,7-1,8-1,9-1,10-1,11-1,12-1,13-1,14-**2**,15-1,16-1,17-1,18-1,19-1,20-1,21-1,22-1,23-1
NCV - **22,** 1-**2**,2-1,3-1,4-1,5-1,6-1,7-1,8-1,9-**2**,10-**2**,11-1,12-1,13-1,14-1,15-1,16-**4**,17-1,18-**2**,19-1,20-1,21-1,22-1
NIV - **23,** 1-**2**,2-1,3-1,4-1,5-1,6-1,7-1,8-1,9-**2**,10-1,11-1,12-1,13-**2**,14-1,15-**4**,16-1,17-1,18-1,19-1,20-1,21-1,22-1,23-1
NKJV - **20,** 1-**2**,2-1,3-1,4-1,5-1,6-1,7-1,8-1,9-1,10-1,11-1,12-1,13-**2**,14-1,15-1,16-1,17-1,18-1,19-1,20-1
NLT - **25,** 1-1,2-1,3-1,4-1,5-1,6-1,7-1,8-**2**,9-1,10-1,11-1,12-1,13-**3**,14-1,15-1,16-1,17-1,18-1,19-1,20-**4**,21-1,22-1,23-1,24-1,25-1
NRSV - **22,** 1-**2**,2-1,3-1,4-1,5-1,6-1,7-1,8-1,9-1,10-**2**,11-1,12-**2**,13-1,14-1,15-1,16-1,17-1,18-1,19-1,20-1,21-1,22-1
Conclusion: All eight modern versions are more complex than the King James Bible.

722. Ecclesiastes 10:2 A wise man's heart is at his right hand; but a fool's heart at his left.
AV - **16,** 1-1,2-1,3-1,4-1,5-1,6-1,7-1,8-1,9-1,10-1,11-1,12-1,13-1,14-1,15-1,16-1
ESV - **16,** 1-1,2-1,3-1,4-1,5-**2**,6-1,7-1,8-1,9-1,10-1,11-1,12-1,13-1,14-1,15-1,16-1
HCSB - **15,** 1-1,2-1,3-1,4-1,5-1,6-1,7-1,8-1,9-1,10-1,11-1,12-1,13-1,14-1,15-1
NASV - **19,** 1-1,2-1,3-1,4-1,5-**2**,6-1,7-1,8-1,9-1,10-1,11-1,12-1,13-1,14-1,15-**2**,16-1,17-1,18-1,19-1
NCV - **17,** 1-1,2-1,3-1,4-1,5-1,6-1,7-1,8-1,9-1,10-1,11-1,12-1,13-1,14-1,15-1,16-1,17-1
NIV - **18,** 1-1,2-1,3-1,4-1,5-1,6-**2**,7-1,8-1,9-1,10-1,11-1,12-1,13-1,14-1,15-1,16-1,17-1,18-1
NKJV - **16,** 1-1,2-1,3-1,4-1,5-1,6-1,7-1,8-1,9-1,10-1,11-1,12-1,13-1,14-1,15-1,16-1
NLT - **13,** 1-1,2-1,3-**2**,4-**2**,5-1,6-1,7-1,8-1,9-1,10-1,11-1,12-1,13-1
NRSV - **18,** 1-1,2-1,3-1,4-1,5-1,6-**2**,7-1,8-1,9-1,10-1,11-1,12-1,13-1,14-1,15-1,16-1,17-1,18-1
Conclusion: Five modern versions are more complex than the King James Bible.

723. Song of Solomon 1:1* The song of songs, which is **Solomon's**.
AV - **7,** 1-1,2-1,3-1,4-1,5-1,6-1,7-1
ESV - **7,** 1-1,2-1,3-1,4-1,5-1,6-1,7-1
HCSB - **3,** 1-1,2-**2**,3-1
NASV - **7,** 1-1,2-1,3-1,4-1,5-1,6-1,7-1
NCV - **4,** 1-1,2-1,3-1,4-1
NIV - **4,** 1-1,2-1,3-1,4-1

NKJV - **7,** 1-1,2-1,3-1,4-1,5-1,6-1,7-1
NLT - 11, 1-1,2-1,3-1,4-1,5-1,6-1,7-1,8-**3,**9-1,10-1,11-**2**
NRSV - **7,** 1-1,2-1,3-1,4-1,5-1,6-1,7-1
Conclusion: Only the HCSB and the NLT made the verse more complex. Those "Masters of Complexity" over at the NLT have struck again!

724. Song of Solomon 4:7 Thou art all fair, my love; there is no spot in thee.
AV - **12,** 1-1,2-1,3-1,4-1,5-1,6-1,7-1,8-1,9-1,10-1,11-1,12-1
ESV - 12, 1-1,2-1,3-**4,**4-**3,**5-1,6-1,7-1,8-1,9-1,10-1,11-1,12-1
HCSB - 11, 1-1,2-1,3-**4,**4-**3,**5-1,6-**2,**7-1,8-1,9-**4,**10-1,11-1
NASV - 13, 1-1,2-1,3-1,4-**3,**5-**4,**6-**2,**7-1,8-1,9-1,10-1,11-**2,**12-1,13-1
NCV - 16, 1-1,2-**2,**3-**4,**4-**2,**5-1,6-1,7-**3,**8-1,9-1,10-1,11-**2,**12-1,13-1,14-1,15-1,16-1
NIV - 12, 1-1,2-**3,**3-1,4-1,5-1,6-**2,**7-1,8-1,9-1,10-1,11-1,12-1
NKJV - **13,** 1-1,2-1,3-1,4-1,5-1,6-1,7-1,8-1,9-1,10-1,11-1,12-1,13-1
NLT - 10, 1-1,2-1,3-**4,**4-**3,**5-1,6-**2,**7-**3,**8-1,9-**3,**10-1
NRSV - 12, 1-1,2-1,3-**4,**4-**3,**5-1,6-1,7-1,8-1,9-1,10-1,11-1,12-1
Conclusion: Seven modern versions are more complex than the King James Bible. The modern versions produce an amazing array of complexity.

725. Song of Solomon 7:3 Thy two breasts are like two young roes that are twins.
AV - **11,** 1-1,2-1,3-1,4-1,5-1,6-1,7-1,8-1,9-1,10-1,11-1
ESV - 11, 1-1,2-1,3-1,4-1,5-1,6-1,7-1,8-1,9-1,10-1,11-**2**
HCSB - 10, 1-1,2-1,3-1,4-1,5-1,6-1,7-1,8-1,9-1,10-**2**
NASV - 11, 1-1,2-1,3-1,4-1,5-1,6-1,7-1,8-1,9-1,10-1,11-**2**
NCV - 11, 1-1,2-1,3-1,4-1,5-1,6-1,7-1,8-1,9-1,10-1,11-**2**
NIV - 10, 1-1,2-1,3-1,4-1,5-1,6-1,7-1,8-1,9-1,10-**2**
NKJV - 11, 1-1,2-1,3-1,4-1,5-1,6-1,7-1,8-1,9-1,10-1,11-**2**
NLT - 11, 1-1,2-1,3-1,4-1,5-1,6-1,7-1,8-1,9-1,10-1,11-**2**
NRSV - 11, 1-1,2-1,3-1,4-1,5-1,6-1,7-1,8-1,9-1,10-1,11-**2**
Conclusion: All eight modern versions are more complex than the King James Bible. In case you are wondering, the two syllable word added to every modern version is "gazelle" and in all eight it appears at the end of the verse.

726. Isaiah 2:5* O house of **Jacob**, come ye, and let us walk in the light of the LORD.
AV - **16,** 1-1,2-1,3-1,4-1,5-1,6-1,7-1,8-1,9-1,10-1,11-1,12-1,13-1,14-1,15-1,16-1
ESV - **14,** 1-1,2-1,3-1,4-1,5-1,6-1,7-1,8-1,9-1,10-1,11-1,12-1,13-1,14-1
HCSB - **12,** 1-1,2-1,3-1,4-1,5-1,6-1,7-1,8-1,9-1,10-1,11-1,12-1
NASV - **14,** 1-1,2-1,3-1,4-1,5-1,6-1,7-1,8-1,9-1,10-1,11-1,12-1,13-1,14-1
NCV - 14, 1-1,2-**3,**3-1,4-1,5-1,6-1,7-1,8-1,9-**2,**10-1,11-1,12-1,13-1,14-1
NIV - **14,** 1-1,2-1,3-1,4-1,5-1,6-1,7-1,8-1,9-1,10-1,11-1,12-1,13-1,14-1
NKJV - **15,** 1-1,2-1,3-1,4-1,5-1,6-1,7-1,8-1,9-1,10-1,11-1,12-1,13-1,14-1,15-1
NLT - 13, 1-1,2-**3,**3-1,4-1,5-1,6-1,7-1,8-1,9-1,10-1,11-1,12-1,13-1
NRSV - **14,** 1-1,2-1,3-1,4-1,5-1,6-1,7-1,8-1,9-1,10-1,11-1,12-1,13-1,14-1

Conclusion: Those "Masters of Complexity" who translated the NCV and NLT have again managed to find complexity where it didn't exist.

727. Isaiah 3:21 The rings, and nose jewels,
AV - **5,** 1-1,2-1,3-1,4-1,5-1
ESV - 6, 1-1,2-**2**,3-1,4-1,5-1,6-1
HCSB - 4, 1-**2**,2-1,3-1,4-1
NASV - 4, 1-**2**,2-1,3-1,4-1
NCV - 5, 1-1,2-**2**,3-1,4-1,5-1
NIV - 6, 1-1,2-**2**,3-1,4-1,5-1,6-1
NKJV - **6,** 1-1,2-1,3-1,4-1,5-1,6-1
NLT - **2,** 1-1,2-1
NRSV - 6, 1-1,2-**2**,3-1,4-1,5-1,6-1
Conclusion: Six modern versions are more complex than the King James Bible.

728. Isaiah 6:4 And the posts of the door moved at the voice of him that cried, and the house was filled with smoke.
AV - **21,** 1-1,2-1,3-1,4-1,5-1,6-1,7-1,8-1,9-1,10-1,11-1,12-1,13-1,14-1,15-1,16-1,17-1,18-1,19-1,20-1,21-1
ESV - 21, 1-1,2-1,3-**3**,4-1,5-1,6-**2**,7-1,8-1,9-1,10-1,11-1,12-1,13-1,14-1,15-1,16-1,17-1,18-1,19-1,20-1,21-1
HCSB - 19, 1-1,2-**3**,3-1,4-1,5-**2**,6-1,7-1,8-1,9-1,10-1,11-1,12-1,13-1,14-1,15-**2**,16-1,17-1,18-1,19-1
NASV - 22, 1-1,2-1,3-**3**,4-1,5-1,6-**2**,7-**2**,8-1,9-1,10-1,11-1,12-1,13-1,14-1,15-1,16-1,17-1,18-**2**,19-1,20-**2**,21-1,22-1
NCV - 16, 1-1,2-**2**,3-1,4-1,5-1,6-**2**,7-1,8-1,9-1,10-1,11-1,12-1,13-**2**,14-1,15-1,16-1
NIV - 18, 1-1,2-1,3-1,4-1,5-1,6-1,7-1,8-**2**,9-1,10-**2**,11-1,12-1,13-1,14-**2**,15-1,16-1,17-1,18-1
NKJV - 23, 1-1,2-1,3-1,4-1,5-1,6-1,7-1,8-**2**,9-1,10-1,11-1,12-1,13-1,14-1,15-1,16-1,17-1,18-1,19-1,20-1,21-1,22-1,23-1
NLT - 16, 1-1,2-**2**,3-1,4-1,5-**2**,6-1,7-1,8-**3**,9-1,10-1,11-**2**,12-**2**,13-1,14-1,15-1,16-1
NRSV - 19, 1-1,2-**2**,3-1,4-1,5-**2**,6-1,7-1,8-1,9-**2**,10-1,11-1,12-1,13-1,14-1,15-1,16-1,17-1,18-1,19-1
Conclusion: All eight modern versions are more complex than the King James Bible.

729. Isaiah 10:9* Is not **Calno** as **Carchemish**? is not **Hamath** as **Arpad**? is not **Samaria** as **Damascus**?
AV - **15,** 1-1,2-1,3-1,4-1,5-1,6-1,7-1,8-1,9-1,10-1,11-1,12-1,13-1,14-1,15-1
ESV - **15,** 1-1,2-1,3-1,4-1,5-1,6-1,7-1,8-1,9-1,10-1,11-1,12-1,13-1,14-1,15-1
HCSB - 13, 1-**2**,2-1,3-1,4-1,5-**2**,6-1,7-1,8-1,9-**2**,10-1,11-1,12-1,13-1
NASV - 13, 1-1,2-1,3-1,4-1,5-1,6-1,7-1,8-1,9-1,10-1,11-1,12-1,13-1
NCV - 24, 1-1,2-**2**,3-1,4-1,5-1,6-1,7-**2**,8-1,9-1,10-**2**,11-1,12-1,13-1,14-1,15-**2**,16-1,17-1,18-**2**,19-1,20-1,21-1,22-1,23-**2**,24-1
NIV - **15,** 1-1,2-1,3-1,4-1,5-1,6-1,7-1,8-1,9-1,10-1,11-1,12-1,13-1,14-1,15-1
NKJV - **15,** 1-1,2-1,3-1,4-1,5-1,6-1,7-1,8-1,9-1,10-1,11-1,12-1,13-1,14-1,15-1
NLT - 24, 1-1,2-**2**,3-1,4-1,5-1,6-1,7-1,8-1,9-1,10-1,11-**2**,12-1,13-1,14-1,15-1,16-1,17-1,18-**2**,19-1,20-1,21-1,22-1,23-1,24-1

NRSV - **15,** 1-1,2-1,3-1,4-1,5-1,6-1,7-1,8-1,9-1,10-1,11-1,12-1,13-1,14-1,15-1
Conclusion: Only three modern versions are more complex than the King James Bible. After a tough competition, the NCV beat out the NLT as the most difficult to read.

730. Isaiah 11:1* And there shall come forth a rod out of the stem of **Jesse**, and a **Branch** shall grow out of his roots:
AV - **22,** 1-1,2-1,3-1,4-1,5-1,6-1,7-1,8-1,9-1,10-1,11-1,12-1,13-1,14-1,15-1,16-1,17-1,18-1,19-1,20-1,21-1,22-1
ESV - **20,** 1-1,2-1,3-1,4-1,5-1,6-1,7-1,8-1,9-1,10-1,11-1,12-1,13-1,14-1,15-1,16-1,17-1,18-1,19-1,20-1
HCSB - **19,** 1-1,2-1,3-1,4-1,5-1,6-1,7-1,8-1,9-1,10-1,11-1,12-1,13-1,14-1,15-1,16-1,17-1,18-1,19-1
NASV - **19,** 1-1,2-1,3-1,4-1,5-1,6-1,7-1,8-1,9-1,10-1,11-1,12-1,13-1,14-1,15-1,16-1,17-1,18-1,19-1
NCV - **22,** 1-1,2-1,3-1,4-1,5-1,6-1,7-1,8-1,9-1,10-1,11-1,12-1,13-1,14-1,15-1,16-1,17-1,18-1,19-1,20-**3**,21-1,22-1
NIV - **18,** 1-1,2-1,3-1,4-1,5-1,6-1,7-1,8-1,9-1,10-1,11-1,12-1,13-1,14-1,15-1,16-1,17-1,18-1
NKJV - **20,** 1-1,2-1,3-1,4-1,5-1,6-1,7-1,8-1,9-1,10-1,11-1,12-1,13-1,14-1,15-1,16-1,17-1,18-1,19-1,20-1
NLT - **21,** 1-1,2-1,3-1,4-1,5-1,6-1,7-**3**,8-1,9-1,10-1,11-1,12-1,13-1,14-1,15-1,16-**2**,17-1,18-1,19-1,20-1,21-1
NRSV - **19,** 1-1,2-1,3-1,4-1,5-1,6-1,7-1,8-1,9-1,10-1,11-1,12-1,13-1,14-1,15-1,16-1,17-1,18-1,19-1
Conclusion: Only the NCV and the NLT made the verse more complex.

731. Isaiah 14:15 Yet thou shalt be brought down to hell, to the sides of the pit.
AV - **14,** 1-1,2-1,3-1,4-1,5-1,6-1,7-1,8-1,9-1,10-1,11-1,12-1,13-1,14-1
ESV - **14,** 1-1,2-1,3-1,4-1,5-1,6-1,7-1,8-1,9-1,10-1,11-**2**,12-1,13-1,14-1
HCSB - **15,** 1-1,2-1,3-1,4-1,5-1,6-1,7-1,8-1,9-**2**,10-1,11-**2**,12-**2**,13-1,14-1,15-1
NASV - **14,** 1-**4**,2-1,3-1,4-1,5-1,6-1,7-1,8-1,9-1,10-1,11-**3**,12-1,13-1,14-1
NCV - **16,** 1-1,2-1,3-1,4-1,5-1,6-1,7-1,8-1,9-1,10-1,11-1,12-**2**,13-1,14-1,15-1,16-1
NIV - **14,** 1-1,2-1,3-1,4-1,5-1,6-1,7-1,8-1,9-1,10-1,11-1,12-1,13-1,14-1
NKJV - **15,** 1-1,2-1,3-1,4-1,5-1,6-1,7-1,8-1,9-1,10-1,11-**2**,12-1,13-1,14-1,15-1
NLT - **17,** 1-**2**,2-1,3-1,4-1,5-1,6-1,7-1,8-1,9-1,10-1,11-1,12-1,13-1,14-1,15-1,16-**2**,17-1
NRSV - **13,** 1-1,2-1,3-1,4-1,5-1,6-1,7-1,8-1,9-1,10-1,11-1,12-1,13-1
Conclusion: Six modern versions are more complex than the King James Bible. The ESV, HCSB, NASV and NRSV all replace "hell" with "Sheol" but it was not counted as a multi-syllable word. None of the eight versions examined contain the word "hell."

732. Isaiah 23:14* Howl, ye ships of **Tarshish**: for your strength is laid waste.
AV - **11,** 1-1,2-1,3-1,4-1,5-1,6-1,7-1,8-1,9-1,10-1,11-1
ESV - **11,** 1-1,2-1,3-1,4-1,5-1,6-1,7-1,8-**2**,9-1,10-1,11-1
HCSB - **9,** 1-1,2-1,3-1,4-1,5-**2**,6-1,7-**2**,8-1,9-**2**
NASV - **10,** 1-1,2-1,3-1,4-1,5-1,6-1,7-1,8-**2**,9-1,10-**2**
NCV - **12,** 1-1,2-1,3-1,4-1,5-**2**,6-1,7-**2**,8-1,9-1,10-**2**,11-1,12-**2**
NIV - **9,** 1-1,2-1,3-1,4-1,5-1,6-1,7-**2**,8-1,9-**2**
NKJV - **11,** 1-1,2-1,3-1,4-1,5-1,6-1,7-1,8-1,9-1,10-1,11-1

234

NLT - 10, 1-1,2-1,3-1,4-1,5-1,6-1,7-1,8-**2**,9-1,10-**2**
NRSV - 10, 1-1,2-1,3-1,4-1,5-1,6-1,7-1,8-**2**,9-1,10-**2**
Conclusion: Seven modern versions are more complex than the King James Bible. The NCV is the most difficult to read.

733. Isaiah 27:5 Or let him take hold of my strength, that he may make peace with me; and he shall make peace with me.
AV - **22,** 1-1,2-1,3-1,4-1,5-1,6-1,7-1,8-1,9-1,10-1,11-1,12-1,13-1,14-1,15-1,16-1,17-1,18-1,19-1,20-1,21-1,22-1
ESV - **20,** 1-1,2-1,3-1,4-1,5-1,6-1,7-1,8-**3**,9-1,10-1,11-1,12-1,13-1,14-1,15-1,16-1,17-1,18-1,19-1,20-1
HCSB - **18,** 1-1,2-1,3-1,4-1,5-1,6-1,7-1,8-1,9-1,10-1,11-1,12-1,13-1,14-1,15-1,16-1,17-1,18-1
NASV - **19,** 1-1,2-1,3-1,4-**2**,5-1,6-1,7-**3**,8-1,9-1,10-1,11-1,12-1,13-1,14-1,15-1,16-1,17-1,18-1,19-1
NCV - **23,** 1-1,2-1,3-**3**,4-1,5-1,6-1,7-1,8-**2**,9-1,10-1,11-1,12-1,13-1,14-1,15-1,16-1,17-1,18-1,19-1,20-1,21-1,22-1,23-1
NIV - **22,** 1-1,2-1,3-1,4-1,5-1,6-1,7-1,8-1,9-**2**,10-1,11-1,12-1,13-1,14-1,15-1,16-1,17-1,18-1,19-1,20-1,21-1,22-1
NKJV - **22,** 1-1,2-1,3-1,4-1,5-1,6-1,7-1,8-1,9-1,10-1,11-1,12-1,13-1,14-1,15-1,16-1,17-1,18-1,19-1,20-1,21-1,22-1
NLT - **20,** 1-**2**,2-1,3-1,4-1,5-1,6-1,7-1,8-1,9-1,10-1,11-1,12-1,13-1,14-1,15-1,16-1,17-1,18-1,19-1,20-1
NRSV - **21,** 1-1,2-1,3-1,4-1,5-1,6-1,7-1,8-1,9-**3**,10-1,11-1,12-1,13-1,14-1,15-1,16-1,17-1,18-1,19-1,20-1,21-1
Conclusion: Six modern versions are more complex than the King James Bible.

734. Isaiah 39:5* Then said **Isaiah** to **Hezekiah**, Hear the word of the LORD of hosts:
AV - **13,** 1-1,2-1,3-1,4-1,5-1,6-1,7-1,8-1,9-1,10-1,11-1,12-1,13-1
ESV - **13,** 1-1,2-1,3-1,4-1,5-1,6-1,7-1,8-1,9-1,10-1,11-1,12-1,13-1
HCSB - **13,** 1-1,2-1,3-1,4-1,5-1,6-1,7-1,8-1,9-1,10-1,11-1,12-1,13-1
NASV - **13,** 1-1,2-1,3-1,4-1,5-1,6-1,7-1,8-1,9-1,10-1,11-1,12-1,13-1
NCV - **13,** 1-1,2-1,3-1,4-1,5-1,6-**2**,7-1,8-1,9-1,10-1,11-1,12-1,13-**3**
NIV - **12,** 1-1,2-1,3-1,4-1,5-1,6-1,7-1,8-1,9-1,10-1,11-1,12-1
NKJV - **13,** 1-1,2-1,3-1,4-1,5-1,6-1,7-1,8-1,9-1,10-1,11-1,12-1,13-1
NLT - **15,** 1-1,2-1,3-1,4-1,5-1,6-**2**,7-1,8-1,9-**2**,10-1,11-1,12-1,13-1,14-1,15-**2**
NRSV - **13,** 1-1,2-1,3-1,4-1,5-1,6-1,7-1,8-1,9-1,10-1,11-1,12-1,13-1
Conclusion: Only the NCV and the NLT made the verse more complex. The NIV inserted "Lord Almighty" for "Lord of Hosts" but this wasn't counted against it.

735. Isaiah 42:2 He shall not cry, nor lift up, nor cause his voice to be heard in the street.
AV - **17,** 1-1,2-1,3-1,4-1,5-1,6-1,7-1,8-1,9-1,10-1,11-1,12-1,13-1,14-1,15-1,16-1,17-1
ESV - **17,** 1-1,2-1,3-1,4-1,5-**2**,6-1,7-1,8-1,9-1,10-1,11-1,12-1,13-1,14-1,15-1,16-1,17-1
HCSB - **15,** 1-1,2-1,3-1,4-1,5-1,6-1,7-1,8-1,9-1,10-1,11-1,12-1,13-1,14-1,15-1
NASV - **17,** 1-1,2-1,3-1,4-1,5-1,6-1,7-1,8-1,9-1,10-1,11-1,12-1,13-1,14-1,15-1,16-1,17-1
NCV - **13,** 1-1,2-1,3-1,4-1,5-1,6-1,7-1,8-1,9-1,10-**2**,11-1,12-1,13-1

Samuel C. Gipp Ph.D.

NIV - **14,** 1-1,2-1,3-1,4-1,5-1,6-1,7-1,8-1,9-1,10-1,11-1,12-1,13-1,14-1
NKJV - **19,** 1-1,2-1,3-1,4-1,5-1,6-1,7-1,8-1,9-1,10-1,11-1,12-1,13-1,14-1,15-1,16-1,17-1,18-1,19-1
NLT - 10, 1-1,2-1,3-1,4-1,5-1,6-1,7-1,8-1,9-1,10-**2**
NRSV - **16,** 1-1,2-1,3-1,4-1,5-1,6-1,7-1,8-1,9-1,10-1,11-1,12-1,13-1,14-1,15-1,16-1
Conclusion: Only three modern versions are more complex than the King James Bible.

736. Isaiah 42:18 Hear, ye deaf; and look, ye blind, that ye may see.
AV - **11,** 1-1,2-1,3-1,4-1,5-1,6-1,7-1,8-1,9-1,10-1,11-1
ESV - **11,** 1-1,2-1,3-1,4-1,5-1,6-1,7-1,8-1,9-1,10-1,11-1
HCSB - 11, 1-**2**,2-1,3-1,4-1,5-1,6-1,7-1,8-1,9-1,10-1,11-1
NASV - **11,** 1-1,2-1,3-1,4-1,5-1,6-1,7-1,8-1,9-1,10-1,11-1
NCV - **13,** 1-1,2-1,3-1,4-1,5-1,6-1,7-1,8-1,9-1,10-1,11-1,12-1,13-1
NIV - **8,** 1-1,2-1,3-1,4-1,5-1,6-1,7-1,8-1
NKJV - **11,** 1-1,2-1,3-1,4-1,5-1,6-1,7-1,8-1,9-1,10-1,11-1
NLT - 10, 1-**2**,2-1,3-1,4-1,5-1,6-1,7-1,8-1,9-1,10-1
NRSV - 14, 1-**2**,2-1,3-1,4-1,5-1,6-1,7-1,8-1,9-1,10-1,11-1,12-1,13-1,14-1
Conclusion: Only three modern versions are more complex than the King James Bible.

737. Isaiah 66:9 Shall I bring to the birth, and not cause to bring forth? saith the LORD: shall I cause to bring forth, and shut the womb? saith thy God.
AV - **28,** 1-1,2-1,3-1,4-1,5-1,6-1,7-1,8-1,9-1,10-1,11-1,12-1,13-1,14-1,15-1,16-1,17-1,18-1,19-1,20-1,21-1,22-1,23-1,24-1,25-1,26-1,27-1,28-1
ESV - **30,** 1-1,2-1,3-1,4-1,5-1,6-1,7-1,8-1,9-1,10-1,11-1,12-1,13-1,14-1,15-1,16-1,17-1,18-1,19-1,20-1,21-1,22-1,23-1,24-1,25-1,26-1,27-1,28-1,29-1,30-1
HCSB - 27, 1-1,2-1,3-1,4-**2**,5-1,6-1,7-1,8-1,9-1,10-1,11-1,12-**3**,13-1,14-1,15-1,16-1,17-1,18-1,19-1,20-1,21-**3**,22-1,23-1,24-1,25-1,26-1,27-1
NASV - 27, 1-1,2-1,3-1,4-1,5-1,6-1,7-1,8-1,9-1,10-1,11-1,12-**4**,13-1,14-1,15-1,16-1,17-1,18-1,19-1,20-1,21-**4**,22-1,23-1,24-1,25-1,26-1,27-1
NCV - **40,** 1-1,2-1,3-1,4-1,5-1,6-1,7-1,8-1,9-1,10-**2**,11-**3**,12-**2**,13-1,14-1,15-1,16-1,17-1,18-1,19-1,20-1,21-1,22-1,23-1,24-1,25-1,26-1,27-1,28-1,29-1,30-1,31-1,32-**2**,33-1,34-1,35-1,36-1,37-1,38-1,39-1,40-1
NIV - **29,** 1-1,2-1,3-1,4-1,5-1,6-**2**,7-1,8-1,9-1,10-1,11-1,12-**4**,13-1,14-1,15-1,16-1,17-1,18-1,19-1,20-1,21-1,22-1,23-1,24-1,25-1,26-**4**,27-1,28-1,29-1
NKJV - 27, 1-1,2-1,3-1,4-1,5-1,6-1,7-1,8-1,9-1,10-1,11-1,12-**4**,13-1,14-1,15-1,16-1,17-1,18-1,19-1,20-**4**,21-1,22-1,23-1,24-1,25-1,26-1,27-1
NLT - 32, 1-1,2-1,3-**2**,4-1,5-1,6-**2**,7-1,8-1,9-1,10-1,11-1,12-1,13-1,14-1,15-**3**,16-1,17-1,18-1,19-1,20-1,21-1,22-1,23-**2**,24-1,25-1,26-**2**,27-1,28-**2**,29-1,30-1,31-1,32-1
NRSV - 23, 1-1,2-1,3-**2**,4-1,5-1,6-1,7-1,8-**3**,9-1,10-1,11-1,12-1,13-1,14-1,15-1,16-1,17-**3**,18-1,19-1,20-1,21-1,22-1,23-1
Conclusion: Seven modern versions are more complex than the King James Bible. In a strange twist, the ESV has 30 words in the verse and they are all single syllable.

738. Jeremiah 1:1* The words of **Jeremiah** the son of **Hilkiah**, of the priests that were in **Anathoth** in the land of **Benjamin**:

AV - **20,** 1-1,2-1,3-1,4-1,5-1,6-1,7-1,8-1,9-1,10-1,11-1,12-1,13-1,14-1,15-1,16-1,17-1,18-1,19-1,20-1

ESV - **21,** 1-1,2-1,3-1,4-1,5-1,6-1,7-1,8-1,9-1,10-1,11-1,12-1,13-1,14-1,15-1,16-1,17-1,18-1,19-1,20-1,21-1

HCSB - **20,** 1-1,2-1,3-1,4-1,5-1,6-1,7-1,8-1,9-1,10-1,11-1,12-1,13-**2**,14-1,15-1,16-1,17-1,18-**4**,19-1,20-1

NASV - **20,** 1-1,2-1,3-1,4-1,5-1,6-1,7-1,8-1,9-1,10-1,11-1,12-1,13-1,14-1,15-1,16-1,17-1,18-1,19-1,20-1

NCV - **28,** 1-1,2-1,3-1,4-1,5-1,6-1,7-1,8-1,9-1,10-1,11-**2**,12-1,13-1,14-**3**,15-1,16-1,17-1,18-1,19-1,20-1,21-1,22-1,23-1,24-1,25-1,26-1,27-1,28-1

NIV - **18,** 1-1,2-1,3-1,4-1,5-1,6-1,7-1,8-1,9-1,10-1,11-1,12-1,13-1,14-1,15-1,16-**4**,17-1,18-1

NKJV - **20,** 1-1,2-1,3-1,4-1,5-1,6-1,7-1,8-1,9-1,10-1,11-1,12-1,13-1,14-1,15-1,16-1,17-1,18-1,19-1,20-1

NLT - **23,** 1-1,2-1,3-1,4-1,5-1,6-1,7-1,8-1,9-1,10-1,11-1,12-1,13-1,14-1,15-1,16-1,17-1,18-1,19-1,20-1,21-1,22-1,23-1

NRSV - **19,** 1-1,2-1,3-1,4-1,5-1,6-1,7-1,8-1,9-1,10-1,11-1,12-1,13-1,14-1,15-1,16-1,17-1,18-1,19-1

Conclusion: Only three modern versions are more complex than the King James Bible.

739. Jeremiah 1:2*# To whom the word of the LORD came in the days of **Josiah** the son of **Amon** king of **Judah**, in the **thirteenth** year of his reign.

AV - **27,** 1-1,2-1,3-1,4-1,5-1,6-1,7-1,8-1,9-1,10-1,11-1,12-1,13-1,14-1,15-1,16-1,17-1,18-1,19-1,20-1,21-1,22-1,23-1,24-1,25-1,26-1,27-1

ESV - **27,** 1-1,2-1,3-1,4-1,5-1,6-1,7-1,8-1,9-1,10-1,11-1,12-1,13-1,14-1,15-1,16-1,17-1,18-1,19-1,20-1,21-1,22-1,23-1,24-1,25-1,26-1,27-1

HCSB - **23,** 1-1,2-1,3-1,4-1,5-1,6-1,7-1,8-1,9-1,10-1,11-1,12-1,13-1,14-1,15-1,16-1,17-1,18-1,19-1,20-1,21-1,22-1,23-1

NASV - **27,** 1-1,2-1,3-1,4-1,5-1,6-1,7-1,8-1,9-1,10-1,11-1,12-1,13-1,14-1,15-1,16-1,17-1,18-1,19-1,20-1,21-1,22-1,23-1,24-1,25-1,26-1,27-1

NCV - **20,** 1-1,2-1,3-1,4-1,5-1,6-1,7-1,8-**2**,9-1,10-1,11-1,12-1,13-1,14-1,15-1,16-1,17-1,18-1,19-1,20-1

NIV - **23,** 1-1,2-1,3-1,4-1,5-1,6-1,7-1,8-1,9-1,10-1,11-1,12-1,13-1,14-1,15-1,16-1,17-1,18-1,19-1,20-1,21-1,22-1,23-1

NKJV - **27,** 1-1,2-1,3-1,4-1,5-1,6-1,7-1,8-1,9-1,10-1,11-1,12-1,13-1,14-1,15-1,16-1,17-1,18-1,19-1,20-1,21-1,22-1,23-1,24-1,25-1,26-1,27-1

NLT - **22,** 1-1,2-1,3-1,4-1,5-**3**,6-1,7-1,8-**2**,9-1,10-1,11-1,12-1,13-1,14-1,15-1,16-1,17-1,18-1,19-1,20-1,21-1,22-1

NRSV - **26,** 1-1,2-1,3-1,4-1,5-1,6-1,7-1,8-1,9-1,10-1,11-1,12-1,13-1,14-1,15-1,16-1,17-1,18-1,19-1,20-1,21-1,22-1,23-1,24-1,25-1,26-1

Conclusion: Only the NCV and the NLT made the verse more complex.

740. Jeremiah 17:14 Heal me, O LORD, and I shall be healed; save me, and I shall be saved: for thou art my praise.

AV - **21,** 1-1,2-1,3-1,4-1,5-1,6-1,7-1,8-1,9-1,10-1,11-1,12-1,13-1,14-1,15-1,16-1,17-1,18-1,19-1,20-1,21-1

ESV - **21,** 1-1,2-1,3-1,4-1,5-1,6-1,7-1,8-1,9-1,10-1,11-1,12-1,13-1,14-1,15-1,16-1,17-1,18-1,19-1,20-1,21-1

HCSB - **20,** 1-1,2-1,3-1,4-1,5-1,6-1,7-1,8-1,9-1,10-1,11-1,12-1,13-1,14-1,15-1,16-1,17-1,18-1,19-1,20-1

NASV - **21,** 1-1,2-1,3-1,4-1,5-1,6-1,7-1,8-1,9-1,10-1,11-1,12-1,13-1,14-1,15-1,16-1,17-1,18-1,19-1,20-1,21-1

NCV - **23,** 1-1,2-1,3-1,4-1,5-1,6-1,7-**2**,8-1,9-1,10-1,11-1,12-1,13-1,14-1,15-**2**,16-1,17-1,18-1,19-1,20-1,21-1,22-1,23-1

NIV - **23,** 1-1,2-1,3-1,4-1,5-1,6-1,7-1,8-1,9-1,10-1,11-1,12-1,13-1,14-1,15-1,16-1,17-1,18-1,19-1,20-1,21-1,22-1,23-1

NKJV - **21,** 1-1,2-1,3-1,4-1,5-1,6-1,7-1,8-1,9-1,10-1,11-1,12-1,13-1,14-1,15-1,16-1,17-1,18-1,19-1,20-1,21-1

NLT - **26,** 1-1,2-1,3-1,4-1,5-1,6-1,7-1,8-1,9-1,10-**2**,11-1,12-1,13-1,14-1,15-1,16-1,17-1,18-1,19-**2**,20-1,21-1,22-1,23-1,24-1,25-1,26-**2**

NRSV - **21,** 1-1,2-1,3-1,4-1,5-1,6-1,7-1,8-1,9-1,10-1,11-1,12-1,13-1,14-1,15-1,16-1,17-1,18-1,19-1,20-1,21-1

Conclusion: Only the NCV and the NLT made the verse more complex.

741. Jeremiah 22:1* Thus saith the LORD; Go down to the house of the king of **Judah**, and speak there this word,

AV - **19,** 1-1,2-1,3-1,4-1,5-1,6-1,7-1,8-1,9-1,10-1,11-1,12-1,13-1,14-1,15-1,16-1,17-1,18-1,19-1

ESV - **19,** 1-1,2-1,3-1,4-1,5-1,6-1,7-1,8-1,9-1,10-1,11-1,12-1,13-1,14-1,15-1,16-1,17-1,18-1,19-1

HCSB - **21,** 1-1,2-1,3-1,4-1,5-1,6-1,7-1,8-1,9-1,10-1,11-**2**,12-1,13-1,14-1,15-1,16-1,17-1,18-**2**,19-1,20-1,21-1

NASV - **19,** 1-1,2-1,3-1,4-1,5-1,6-1,7-1,8-1,9-1,10-1,11-1,12-1,13-1,14-1,15-1,16-1,17-1,18-1,19-1

NCV - **21,** 1-1,2-1,3-1,4-1,5-1,6-1,7-1,8-1,9-1,10-1,11-**2**,12-1,13-1,14-1,15-1,16-1,17-1,18-**3**,19-1,20-**2**,21-1

NIV - **21,** 1-1,2-1,3-1,4-1,5-1,6-1,7-1,8-1,9-1,10-1,11-**2**,12-1,13-1,14-1,15-1,16-1,17-1,18-**2**,19-1,20-**2**,21-1

NKJV - **19,** 1-1,2-1,3-1,4-1,5-1,6-1,7-1,8-1,9-1,10-1,11-1,12-1,13-1,14-1,15-1,16-1,17-1,18-1,19-1

NLT - **21,** 1-1,2-1,3-1,4-1,5-1,6-1,7-1,8-1,9-1,10-**2**,11-1,12-1,13-**3**,14-1,15-1,16-1,17-1,18-1,19-1,20-1,21-1

NRSV - **19,** 1-1,2-1,3-1,4-1,5-1,6-1,7-1,8-1,9-1,10-1,11-1,12-1,13-1,14-1,15-1,16-1,17-1,18-1,19-1

Conclusion: Four modern versions are more complex than the King James Bible.

742. Jeremiah 22:29 O earth, earth, earth, hear the word of the LORD.

AV - **10,** 1-1,2-1,3-1,4-1,5-1,6-1,7-1,8-1,9-1,10-1

ESV - **10,** 1-1,2-1,3-1,4-1,5-1,6-1,7-1,8-1,9-1,10-1

HCSB - **9,** 1-1,2-1,3-1,4-1,5-1,6-1,7-1,8-1,9-1

NASV - **10,** 1-1,2-1,3-1,4-1,5-1,6-1,7-1,8-1,9-1,10-1

NCV - **11,** 1-1,2-1,3-1,4-1,5-**2**,6-1,7-1,8-1,9-1,10-1,11-1

NIV - **10,** 1-1,2-1,3-1,4-1,5-1,6-1,7-1,8-1,9-1,10-1

238

NKJV - **10,** 1-1,2-1,3-1,4-1,5-1,6-1,7-1,8-1,9-1,10-1
NLT - 11, 1-1,2-1,3-1,4-1,5-**2**,6-1,7-1,8-**2**,9-1,10-1,11-1
NRSV - **10,** 1-1,2-1,3-1,4-1,5-1,6-1,7-1,8-1,9-1,10-1

Conclusion: Only the NCV and the NLT made the verse more complex. The ESV, NASV, NCV, NIV and the NRSV replaced "earth" with "land" which greatly curtails the scope of the prophecy. The NCV rendered "earth" as, "land of Judah." This was counted against it because, although "Judah" would be accepted as a proper name elsewhere, there is no authority for the insertion in this case. The NLT is the most difficult to read.

743. Jeremiah 25:25* And all the kings of **Zimri**, and all the kings of **Elam**, and all the kings of the Medes,
AV - **19,** 1-1,2-1,3-1,4-1,5-1,6-1,7-1,8-1,9-1,10-1,11-1,12-1,13-1,14-1,15-1,16-1,17-1,18-1,19-1
ESV - **16,** 1-1,2-1,3-1,4-1,5-1,6-1,7-1,8-1,9-1,10-1,11-1,12-1,13-1,14-1,15-1,16-1
HCSB - **16,** 1-1,2-1,3-1,4-1,5-1,6-1,7-1,8-1,9-1,10-1,11-1,12-1,13-1,14-1,15-1,16-1
NASV - **17,** 1-1,2-1,3-1,4-1,5-1,6-1,7-1,8-1,9-1,10-1,11-1,12-1,13-1,14-1,15-1,16-1,17-1
NCV - **8,** 1-1,2-1,3-1,4-1,5-1,6-1,7-1,8-1
NIV - **8,** 1-1,2-1,3-1,4-1,5-1,6-1,7-1,8-1
NKJV - **17,** 1-1,2-1,3-1,4-1,5-1,6-1,7-1,8-1,9-1,10-1,11-1,12-1,13-1,14-1,15-1,16-1,17-1
NLT - **9,** 1-1,2-1,3-1,4-1,5-1,6-1,7-1,8-1,9-1
NRSV - **16,** 1-1,2-1,3-1,4-1,5-1,6-1,7-1,8-1,9-1,10-1,11-1,12-1,13-1,14-1,15-1,16-1
Conclusion: All versions read the same.

744. Jeremiah 29:13 And ye shall seek me, and find me, when ye shall search for me with all your heart.
AV - **18,** 1-1,2-1,3-1,4-1,5-1,6-1,7-1,8-1,9-1,10-1,11-1,12-1,13-1,14-1,15-1,16-1,17-1,18-1
ESV - **15,** 1-1,2-1,3-1,4-1,5-1,6-1,7-1,8-1,9-1,10-1,11-1,12-1,13-1,14-1,15-1
HCSB - **16,** 1-1,2-1,3-1,4-1,5-1,6-1,7-1,8-1,9-1,10-1,11-1,12-1,13-1,14-1,15-1,16-1
NASV - **16,** 1-1,2-1,3-1,4-1,5-1,6-1,7-1,8-1,9-1,10-1,11-1,12-1,13-1,14-1,15-1,16-1
NCV - **19,** 1-1,2-1,3-1,4-1,5-1,6-1,7-1,8-1,9-1,10-1,11-1,12-1,13-1,14-1,15-1,16-1,17-1,18-1,19-1
NIV - **15,** 1-1,2-1,3-1,4-1,5-1,6-1,7-1,8-1,9-1,10-1,11-1,12-1,13-1,14-1,15-1
NKJV - **17,** 1-1,2-1,3-1,4-1,5-1,6-1,7-1,8-1,9-1,10-1,11-1,12-1,13-1,14-1,15-1,16-1,17-1
NLT - 10, 1-1,2-1,3-1,4-1,5-1,6-**4**,7-1,8-1,9-1,10-1
NRSV - **17,** 1-1,2-1,3-1,4-1,5-1,6-1,7-1,8-1,9-1,10-1,11-1,12-1,13-1,14-1,15-1,16-1,17-1
Conclusion: Only the NLT made the verse more complex, which although it had the smallest word count inserted a four syllable word.

745. Jeremiah 34:4* Yet hear the word of the LORD, O **Zedekiah** king of **Judah**; Thus saith the LORD of thee, Thou shalt not die by the sword:
AV - **25,** 1-1,2-1,3-1,4-1,5-1,6-1,7-1,8-1,9-1,10-1,11-1,12-1,13-1,14-1,15-1,16-1,17-1,18-1,19-1,20-1,21-1,22-1,23-1,24-1,25-1
ESV - 25, 1-1,2-1,3-1,4-1,5-1,6-1,7-1,8-1,9-1,10-1,11-1,12-1,13-1,14-1,15-1,16-1,17-**3**,18-1,19-1,20-1,21-1,22-1,23-1,24-1,25-1
HCSB - 24, 1-1,2-1,3-1,4-1,5-1,6-1,7-1,8-1,9-1,10-1,11-1,12-1,13-1,14-1,15-1,16-**3**,17-1,18-1,19-1,20-1,21-1,22-1,23-1,24-1

NASV - 25, 1-1,2-1,3-1,4-1,5-1,6-1,7-1,8-1,9-1,10-1,11-1,12-1,13-1,14-1,15-1,16-1,17-**3**,18-1,19-1,20-1,21-1,22-1,23-1,24-1,25-1

NCV - 28, 1-1,2-1,3-1,4-1,5-1,6-**2**,7-1,8-1,9-**2**,10-1,11-1,12-1,13-1,14-1,15-1,16-1,17-1,18-1,19-**2**,20-1,21-1,22-1,23-1,24-1,25-1,26-1,27-1,28-1

NIV - 27, 1-1,2-1,3-1,4-**2**,5-1,6-1,7-1,8-1,9-1,10-1,11-1,12-1,13-1,14-1,15-1,16-1,17-1,18-1,19-**3**,20-1,21-1,22-1,23-1,24-1,25-1,26-1,27-1

NKJV - 25, 1-1,2-1,3-1,4-1,5-1,6-1,7-1,8-1,9-1,10-1,11-1,12-1,13-1,14-1,15-1,16-1,17-**3**,18-1,19-1,20-1,21-1,22-1,23-1,24-1,25-1

NLT - 26, 1-1,2-**2**,3-1,4-1,5-**2**,6-1,7-1,8-1,9-1,10-1,11-1,12-1,13-1,14-1,15-1,16-1,17-1,18-1,19-1,20-1,21-1,22-1,23-1,24-1,25-1,26-1

NRSV - 25, 1-1,2-1,3-1,4-1,5-1,6-1,7-1,8-1,9-1,10-1,11-1,12-1,13-1,14-1,15-1,16-1,17-**3**,18-1,19-1,20-1,21-1,22-1,23-1,24-1,25-1

Conclusion: All eight modern versions are more complex than the King James Bible.

746. Jeremiah 51:4* Thus the slain shall fall in the land of the **Chaldeans**, and they that are thrust through in her street.

AV - **20,** 1-1,2-1,3-1,4-1,5-1,6-1,7-1,8-1,9-1,10-1,11-1,12-1,13-1,14-1,15-1,16-1,17-1,18-1,19-1,20-1

ESV - 16, 1-1,2-1,3-1,4-1,5-1,6-1,7-1,8-1,9-1,10-1,11-1,12-1,13-**2**,14-1,15-1,16-1

HCSB - **20,** 1-1,2-1,3-1,4-1,5-1,6-1,7-1,8-1,9-1,10-1,11-1,12-1,13-1,14-1,15-1,16-1,17-1,18-1,19-1,20-1

NASV - **17,** 1-1,2-1,3-1,4-1,5-1,6-1,7-1,8-1,9-1,10-1,11-1,12-1,13-1,14-1,15-1,16-1,17-1

NCV - **16,** 1-1,2-1,3-1,4-1,5-1,6-1,7-1,8-1,9-1,10-1,11-1,12-1,13-1,14-1,15-1,16-1

NIV - 12, 1-1,2-1,3-1,4-1,5-1,6-1,7-1,8-**3**,9-**2**,10-1,11-1,12-1

NKJV - **18,** 1-1,2-1,3-1,4-1,5-1,6-1,7-1,8-1,9-1,10-1,11-1,12-1,13-1,14-1,15-1,16-1,17-1,18-1

NLT - **16,** 1-1,2-1,3-1,4-1,5-1,6-1,7-1,8-1,9-1,10-1,11-1,12-1,13-1,14-1,15-1,16-1

NRSV - 16, 1-1,2-1,3-1,4-1,5-1,6-1,7-1,8-1,9-1,10-1,11-1,12-1,13-**2**,14-1,15-1,16-1

Conclusion: Only three modern versions are more complex than the King James Bible. Only the NIV made the verse more complex.

747. Jeremiah 51:49* As **Babylon** hath caused the slain of **Israel** to fall, so at **Babylon** shall fall the slain of all the earth.

AV - **21,** 1-1,2-1,3-1,4-1,5-1,6-1,7-1,8-1,9-1,10-1,11-1,12-1,13-1,14-1,15-1,16-1,17-1,18-1,19-1,20-1,21-1

ESV - 20, 1-1,2-1,3-1,4-1,5-1,6-1,7-1,8-1,9-1,10-1,11-1,12-1,13-1,14-**2**,15-1,16-1,17-1,18-1,19-1,20-1

HCSB - 21, 1-1,2-1,3-1,4-**2**,5-1,6-1,7-1,8-1,9-1,10-**2**,11-1,12-1,13-1,14-1,15-1,16-1,17-1,18-1,19-**2**,20-1,21-1

NASV - 22, 1-**2**,2-1,3-1,4-1,5-1,6-1,7-1,8-1,9-1,10-1,11-1,12-**2**,13-1,14-1,15-1,16-1,17-1,18-1,19-1,20-1,21-1,22-**2**

NCV - 16, 1-1,2-1,3-1,4-**2**,5-1,6-1,7-**2**,8-1,9-1,10-1,11-1,12-**2**,13-1,14-**2**,15-1,16-1

NIV - 20, 1-1,2-1,3-1,4-**2**,5-1,6-1,7-1,8-1,9-1,10-1,11-1,12-1,13-1,14-1,15-1,16-1,17-**2**,18-**2**,19-1,20-1

NKJV - **21,** 1-1,2-1,3-1,4-1,5-1,6-1,7-1,8-1,9-1,10-1,11-1,12-1,13-1,14-1,15-1,16-1,17-1,18-1,19-1,20-1,21-1

NLT - **19,** 1-1,2-1,3-1,4-1,5-1,6-**2,**7-1,8-1,9-1,10-**2,**11-**2,**12-1,13-1,14-1,15-1,16-1,17-**2,**18-1,19-1

NRSV - **20,** 1-1,2-1,3-1,4-1,5-1,6-1,7-1,8-1,9-1,10-1,11-1,12-1,13-1,14-1,15-1,16-1,17-**2,**18-**2,**19-1,20-1

Conclusion: Seven modern versions are more complex than the King James Bible.

748. Lamentations 3:27 It is good for a man that he bear the yoke in his youth.
AV - **14,** 1-1,2-1,3-1,4-1,5-1,6-1,7-1,8-1,9-1,10-1,11-1,12-1,13-1,14-1
ESV - **14,** 1-1,2-1,3-1,4-1,5-1,6-1,7-1,8-1,9-1,10-1,11-1,12-1,13-1,14-1
HCSB - **15,** 1-1,2-1,3-1,4-1,5-1,6-1,7-1,8-1,9-1,10-1,11-1,12-1,13-1,14-1,15-1
NASV - **15,** 1-1,2-1,3-1,4-1,5-1,6-1,7-1,8-1,9-1,10-1,11-1,12-1,13-1,14-1,15-1
NCV - **12,** 1-1,2-1,3-1,4-1,5-**2,**6-1,7-1,8-1,9-1,10-1,11-1,12-1
NIV - **14,** 1-1,2-1,3-1,4-1,5-1,6-1,7-1,8-1,9-1,10-1,11-1,12-1,13-1,14-1
NKJV - **13,** 1-1,2-1,3-1,4-1,5-1,6-1,7-1,8-1,9-1,10-1,11-1,12-1,13-1
NLT - **18,** 1-1,2-1,3-1,4-1,5-1,6-**2,**7-1,8-**2,**9-1,10-1,11-**2,**12-1,13-1,14-1,15-1,16-1,17-1,18-**3**
NRSV - **11,** 1-1,2-1,3-1,4-1,5-1,6-1,7-1,8-1,9-1,10-1,11-1

Conclusion: Only the NCV and the NLT made the verse more complex. The NLT mustered an olympic effort to complicate the simple.

749. Lamentations 3:59 O LORD, thou hast seen my wrong: judge thou my cause.
AV - **11,** 1-1,2-1,3-1,4-1,5-1,6-1,7-1,8-1,9-1,10-1,11-1
ESV - **13,** 1-1,2-1,3-1,4-1,5-1,6-1,7-1,8-1,9-1,10-1,11-1,12-1,13-1
HCSB - **11,** 1-1,2-1,3-1,4-1,5-1,6-1,7-1,8-1,9-1,10-1,11-1
NASV - **10,** 1-1,2-1,3-1,4-1,5-1,6-1,7-**3,**8-1,9-1,10-1
NCV - **15,** 1-1,2-1,3-1,4-1,5-1,6-1,7-1,8-1,9-1,10-1,11-1,12-1,13-1,14-1,15-1
NIV - **13,** 1-1,2-1,3-1,4-1,5-1,6-1,7-1,8-1,9-1,10-1,11-**2,**12-1,13-1
NKJV - **12,** 1-1,2-1,3-1,4-1,5-1,6-1,7-1,8-1,9-1,10-1,11-1,12-1
NLT - **18,** 1-1,2-1,3-1,4-1,5-1,6-1,7-1,8-1,9-1,10-1,11-1,12-1,13-1,14-1,15-1,16-1,17-1,18-1
NRSV - **13,** 1-1,2-1,3-1,4-1,5-1,6-1,7-1,8-1,9-1,10-1,11-1,12-1,13-1

Conclusion: Only the NASV and the NIV made the verse more complex.

750. Lamentations 5:17 For this our heart is faint; for these things our eyes are dim.
AV - **13,** 1-1,2-1,3-1,4-1,5-1,6-1,7-1,8-1,9-1,10-1,11-1,12-1,13-1
ESV - **15,** 1-1,2-1,3-1,4-1,5-1,6-**2,**7-1,8-1,9-1,10-1,11-1,12-1,13-1,14-1,15-1
HCSB - **14,** 1-**2,**2-1,3-1,4-1,5-1,6-1,7-1,8-**2,**9-1,10-1,11-1,12-1,13-1,14-1
NASV - **15,** 1-**2,**2-1,3-1,4-1,5-1,6-1,7-1,8-**2,**9-1,10-1,11-1,12-1,13-1,14-1,15-1
NCV - **12,** 1-**2,**2-1,3-1,4-1,5-1,6-1,7-1,8-1,9-1,10-1,11-1,12-1
NIV - **15,** 1-**2,**2-1,3-1,4-1,5-1,6-1,7-1,8-**2,**9-1,10-1,11-1,12-1,13-1,14-1,15-1
NKJV - **15,** 1-**2,**2-1,3-1,4-1,5-1,6-1,7-1,8-**2,**9-1,10-1,11-1,12-1,13-1,14-1,15-1
NLT - **13,** 1-1,2-1,3-1,4-1,5-1,6-**2,**7-1,8-1,9-1,10-1,11-1,12-1,13-1
NRSV - **16,** 1-**2,**2-1,3-1,4-1,5-1,6-1,7-1,8-**2,**9-1,10-1,11-1,12-1,13-1,14-1,15-1,16-1

Conclusion: All eight modern versions are more complex than the King James Bible.

751. Ezekiel 6:7 And the slain shall fall in the midst of you, and ye shall know that I am the LORD.
AV - **19,** 1-1,2-1,3-1,4-1,5-1,6-1,7-1,8-1,9-1,10-1,11-1,12-1,13-1,14-1,15-1,16-1,17-1,18-1,19-1
ESV - **17,** 1-1,2-1,3-1,4-1,5-1,6-1,7-1,8-1,9-1,10-1,11-1,12-1,13-1,14-1,15-1,16-1,17-1
HCSB - 15, 1-1,2-1,3-1,4-1,5-**2**,6-1,7-1,8-1,9-1,10-1,11-1,12-1,13-1,14-1,15-1
NASV - 15, 1-1,2-1,3-1,4-1,5-**2**,6-1,7-1,8-1,9-1,10-1,11-1,12-1,13-1,14-1,15-1
NCV - **18,** 1-1,2-**2**,3-1,4-1,5-1,6-1,7-1,8-**2**,9-1,10-1,11-1,12-1,13-1,14-1,15-1,16-1,17-1,18-1
NIV - 16, 1-1,2-**2**,3-1,4-1,5-1,6-**2**,7-1,8-1,9-1,10-1,11-1,12-1,13-1,14-1,15-1,16-1
NKJV - **16,** 1-1,2-1,3-1,4-1,5-1,6-1,7-1,8-1,9-1,10-1,11-1,12-1,13-1,14-1,15-1,16-1
NLT - **17,** 1-1,2-1,3-1,4-1,5-**2**,6-1,7-**2**,8-1,9-1,10-1,11-1,12-1,13-1,14-**2**,15-1,16-1,17-1
NRSV - **16,** 1-1,2-1,3-1,4-1,5-1,6-1,7-1,8-1,9-1,10-1,11-1,12-1,13-1,14-1,15-1,16-1
Conclusion: Five modern versions are more complex than the King James Bible. Again, the NLT won the prize for complexity.

752. Ezekiel 26:13 And I will cause the noise of thy songs to cease; and the sound of thy harps shall be no more heard.
AV - **22,** 1-1,2-1,3-1,4-1,5-1,6-1,7-1,8-1,9-1,10-1,11-1,12-1,13-1,14-1,15-1,16-1,17-1,18-1,19-1,20-1,21-1,22-1
ESV - 20, 1-1,2-1,3-1,4-1,5-1,6-**2**,7-1,8-1,9-1,10-1,11-1,12-1,13-1,14-1,15-1,16-1,17-1,18-1,19-1,20-1
HCSB - 22, 1-1,2-1,3-1,4-1,5-1,6-1,7-1,8-1,9-1,10-1,11-1,12-1,13-1,14-1,15-1,16-1,17-1,18-1,19-1,20-**2**,21-1,22-1
NASV - 20, 1-1,2-1,3-1,4-**2**,5-1,6-1,7-1,8-1,9-1,10-1,11-1,12-1,13-1,14-1,15-1,16-1,17-1,18-1,19-1,20-1
NCV - 16, 1-1,2-1,3-1,4-1,5-1,6-1,7-1,8-**2**,9-1,10-1,11-1,12-1,13-1,14-1,15-1,16-**3**
NIV - 20, 1-1,2-1,3-1,4-1,5-1,6-1,7-1,8-**2**,9-1,10-1,11-1,12-**2**,13-1,14-1,15-1,16-1,17-1,18-1,19-1,20-1
NKJV - **22,** 1-1,2-1,3-1,4-1,5-1,6-1,7-1,8-1,9-1,10-1,11-1,12-1,13-1,14-1,15-1,16-1,17-1,18-1,19-1,20-1,21-1,22-1
NLT - 20, 1-1,2-1,3-1,4-1,5-**2**,6-1,7-1,8-1,9-1,10-1,11-1,12-1,13-1,14-1,15-1,16-1,17-1,18-**2**,19-1,20-**2**
NRSV - 18, 1-1,2-1,3-**2**,4-1,5-**2**,6-1,7-1,8-1,9-1,10-1,11-1,12-1,13-1,14-1,15-1,16-1,17-1,18-1
Conclusion: Seven modern versions are more complex than the King James Bible. The NLT is the most difficult to read.

753. Ezekiel 28:8 They shall bring thee down to the pit, and thou shalt die the deaths of them that are slain in the midst of the seas.
AV - **25,** 1-1,2-1,3-1,4-1,5-1,6-1,7-1,8-1,9-1,10-1,11-1,12-1,13-1,14-1,15-1,16-1,17-1,18-1,19-1,20-1,21-1,22-1,23-1,24-1,25-1
ESV - 23, 1-1,2-1,3-1,4-1,5-1,6-**2**,7-1,8-1,9-1,10-1,11-1,12-1,13-1,14-1,15-1,16-1,17-1,18-1,19-1,20-1,21-1,22-1,23-1
HCSB - 21, 1-1,2-1,3-1,4-1,5-1,6-1,7-1,8-1,9-1,10-1,11-1,12-1,13-1,14-**3**,15-1,16-1,17-1,18-1,19-1,20-1,21-1
NASV - **25,** 1-1,2-1,3-1,4-1,5-1,6-1,7-1,8-1,9-1,10-1,11-1,12-1,13-1,14-1,15-1,16-1,17-1,18-1,19-1,20-1,21-1,22-1,23-1,24-1,25-1

NCV - 17, 1-1,2-1,3-1,4-1,5-1,6-1,7-1,8-1,9-**3**,10-1,11-1,12-1,13-1,14-1,15-1,16-1,17-1
NIV - 21, 1-1,2-1,3-1,4-1,5-1,6-1,7-1,8-1,9-1,10-1,11-1,12-1,13-1,14-**3**,15-1,16-1,17-1,18-1,19-1,20-1,21-1
NKJV - 23, 1-1,2-1,3-1,4-1,5-1,6-**2**,7-1,8-1,9-1,10-1,11-1,12-1,13-1,14-1,15-1,16-1,17-1,18-1,19-1,20-1,21-1,22-1,23-1
NLT - 22, 1-1,2-1,3-1,4-1,5-1,6-1,7-1,8-1,9-1,10-1,11-1,12-1,13-1,14-1,15-1,16-1,17-1,18-1,19-1,20-1,21-**2**,22-1
NRSV - 21, 1-1,2-1,3-1,4-1,5-1,6-1,7-1,8-1,9-1,10-1,11-1,12-1,13-1,14-**3**,15-1,16-1,17-1,18-1,19-1,20-1,21-1
Conclusion: Seven modern versions are more complex than the King James Bible.

754. Ezekiel 34:3 Ye eat the fat, and ye clothe you with the wool, ye kill them that are fed: but ye feed not the flock.
AV - 23, 1-1,2-1,3-1,4-1,5-1,6-1,7-1,8-1,9-1,10-1,11-1,12-1,13-1,14-1,15-1,16-1,17-1,18-1,19-1,20-1,21-1,22-1,23-1
ESV - 22, 1-1,2-1,3-1,4-1,5-1,6-1,7-1,8-**2**,8-1,9-1,10-1,11-1,12-**2**,13-1,14-1,15-1,16-1,17-1,18-1,19-1,20-1,21-1,22-1
HCSB - 18, 1-1,2-1,3-1,4-1,5-1,6-1,7-1,8-1,9-**2**,10-1,11-**2**,12-1,13-1,14-1,15-1,16-1,17-1,18-1
NASV - 19, 1-1,2-1,3-1,4-1,5-1,6-1,7-**2**,8-1,9-1,10-1,11-1,12-**2**,13-1,14-1,15-1,16-**2**,17-**2**,18-1,19-1
NCV - 24, 1-1,2-1,3-1,4-1,5-1,6-1,7-1,8-1,9-**2**,10-1,11-1,12-1,13-1,14-1,15-1,16-1,17-1,18-1,19-1,20-1,21-1,22-1,23-1,24-1
NIV - 23, 1-1,2-1,3-1,4-1,5-1,6-**2**,7-1,8-1,9-1,10-1,11-**2**,12-1,13-1,14-**3**,15-1,16-1,17-1,18-1,19-1,20-1,21-1,22-1,23-1
NKJV - 21, 1-1,2-1,3-1,4-1,5-1,6-1,7-**2**,8-1,9-1,10-1,11-1,12-**2**,13-1,14-**2**,15-1,16-1,17-1,18-1,19-1,20-1,21-1
NLT - 18, 1-1,2-1,3-1,4-1,5-1,6-1,7-1,8-1,9-**2**,10-1,11-1,12-**3**,13-1,14-1,15-1,16-1,17-1,18-1
NRSV - 21, 1-1,2-1,3-1,4-1,5-1,6-1,7-**2**,8-1,9-1,10-1,11-1,12-**2**,13-1,14-**2**,15-1,16-1,17-1,18-1,19-1,20-1,21-1
Conclusion: All eight modern versions are more complex than the King James Bible.

755. Ezekiel 34:15 I will feed my flock, and I will cause them to lie down, saith the Lord GOD.
AV - 17, 1-1,2-1,3-1,4-1,5-1,6-1,7-1,8-1,9-1,10-1,11-1,12-1,13-1,14-1,15-1,16-1,17-1
ESV - 21, 1-1,2-**2**,3-1,4-1,5-1,6-**2**,7-1,8-1,9-1,10-1,11-1,12-**2**,13-1,14-1,15-1,16-1,17-1,18-**2**,19-1,20-1,21-1
HCSB - 18, 1-1,2-1,3-1,4-1,5-1,6-1,7-1,8-1,9-1,10-1,11-1,12-1,13-1,14-**4**,15-1,16-1,17-1,18-1
NASV - 16, 1-1,2-1,3-1,4-1,5-1,6-1,7-1,8-1,9-1,10-1,11-1,12-1,13-**2**,14-1,15-1,16-1
NCV - **14,** 1-1,2-1,3-1,4-1,5-1,6-1,7-1,8-1,9-1,10-1,11-1,12-1,13-1,14-1
NIV - **15,** 1-1,2-**2**,3-1,4-1,5-1,6-1,7-1,8-1,9-1,10-1,11-1,12-**2**,13-1,14-**3**,15-1
NKJV - **16,** 1-1,2-1,3-1,4-1,5-1,6-1,7-1,8-1,9-1,10-1,11-1,12-1,13-1,14-1,15-1,16-1
NLT - 20, 1-1,2-**2**,3-1,4-1,5-1,6-1,7-1,8-1,9-1,10-1,11-1,12-1,13-1,14-1,15-1,16-1,17-1,18-1,19-**3**,20-1
NRSV - 20, 1-1,2-**2**,3-1,4-1,5-1,6-**2**,7-1,8-1,9-1,10-1,11-1,12-1,13-1,14-1,15-1,16-1,17-1,18-1,19-1,20-1
Conclusion: Six modern versions are more complex than the King James Bible.

Samuel C. Gipp Ph.D.

756. Daniel 2:33: His legs of iron, his feet part of iron and part of clay.
AV - **13,** 1-1,2-1,3-1,4-1,5-1,6-1,7-1,8-1,9-1,10-1,11-1,12-1,13-1
ESV - 13, 1-1,2-1,3-1,4-1,5-1,6-1,7-**2**,8-1,9-1,10-1,11-**2**,12-1,13-1
HCSB - 14, 1-1,2-1,3-1,4-1,5-1,6-1,7-1,8-1,9-**2**,10-1,11-1,12-**2**,13-1,14-1
NASV - 13, 1-1,2-1,3-1,4-1,5-1,6-1,7-**2**,8-1,9-1,10-1,11-**2**,12-1,13-1
NCV - 23, 1-1,2-**2**,3-1,4-1,5-1,6-1,7-1,8-1,9-1,10-1,11-1,12-1,13-1,14-1,15-1,16-**2**,17-1,18-1,19-1,20-**2**,21-1,22-1,23-1
NIV - 14, 1-1,2-1,3-1,4-1,5-1,6-1,7-**2**,8-1,9-1,10-1,11-**2**,12-1,13-1,14-1
NKJV - 13, 1-1,2-1,3-1,4-1,5-1,6-1,7-**2**,8-1,9-1,10-1,11-**2**,12-1,13-1
NLT - 15, 1-1,2-1,3-1,4-1,5-1,6-1,7-1,8-1,9-1,10-**4**,11-1,12-1,13-1,14-1,15-1
NRSV - 13, 1-1,2-1,3-1,4-1,5-1,6-1,7-**2**,8-1,9-1,10-1,11-**2**,12-1,13-1
Conclusion: All eight modern versions are more complex than the King James Bible. The NCV made the verse more complex.

757. Daniel 5:4* They drank wine, and praised the gods of gold, and of **silver**, of brass, of iron, of wood, and of stone.
AV - **21,** 1-1,2-1,3-1,4-1,5-1,6-1,7-1,8-1,9-1,10-1,11-1,12-1,13-1,14-1,15-1,16-1,17-1,18-1,19-1,20-1,21-1
ESV - **16,** 1-1,2-1,3-1,4-1,5-1,6-1,7-1,8-1,9-1,10-1,11-1,12-1,13-1,14-1,15-1,16-1
HCSB - **18,** 1-1,2-1,3-1,4-1,5-1,6-1,7-1,8-1,9-1,10-1,11-1,12-1,13-1,14-1,15-1,16-1,17-1,18-1
NASV - **18,** 1-1,2-1,3-1,4-1,5-1,6-1,7-1,8-1,9-1,10-1,11-1,12-1,13-1,14-1,15-1,16-1,17-1,18-1
NCV - 19, 1-1,2-1,3-1,4-**2**,5-1,6-1,7-1,8-1,9-1,10-1,11-1,12-1,13-1,14-1,15-1,16-1,17-1,18-1,19-1
NIV - **19,** 1-1,2-1,3-1,4-1,5-1,6-1,7-1,8-1,9-1,10-1,11-1,12-1,13-1,14-1,15-1,16-1,17-1,18-1,19-1
NKJV - **17,** 1-1,2-1,3-1,4-1,5-1,6-1,7-1,8-1,9-1,10-1,11-1,12-1,13-1,14-1,15-1,16-1,17-1
NLT - 18, 1-1,2-1,3-1,4-1,5-1,6-1,7-1,8-1,9-**2**,10-1,11-1,12-1,13-1,14-1,15-1,16-1,17-1,18-1
NRSV - **17,** 1-1,2-1,3-1,4-1,5-1,6-1,7-1,8-1,9-1,10-1,11-1,12-1,13-1,14-1,15-1,16-1,17-1
Conclusion: Only the NCV and the NLT made the verse more complex.

758. Daniel 5:30* In that night was **Belshazzar** the king of the **Chaldeans** slain.
AV - **11,** 1-1,2-1,3-1,4-1,5-1,6-1,7-1,8-1,9-1,10-1,11-1
ESV - **9,** 1-1,2-**2**,3-1,4-1,5-1,6-1,7-1,8-1,9-1
HCSB - **11,** 1-1,2-**2**,3-1,4-1,5-1,6-1,7-1,8-1,9-1,10-1,11-1
NASV - **9,** 1-1,2-1,3-1,4-1,5-1,6-1,7-1,8-1,9-1
NCV - **12,** 1-1,2-**2**,3-1,4-1,5-1,6-1,7-1,8-1,9-1,10-**2**,11-1,12-1
NIV - 10, 1-1,2-**2**,3-1,4-1,5-1,6-1,7-1,8-1,9-1,10-1
NKJV - 10, 1-1,2-**2**,3-1,4-1,5-1,6-1,7-1,8-1,9-1,10-1
NLT - 9, 1-1,2-**2**,3-1,4-1,5-1,6-1,7-1,8-1,9-1
NRSV - 9, 1-1,2-**2**,3-1,4-1,5-1,6-1,7-1,8-1,9-1
Conclusion: Seven modern versions are more complex than the King James Bible.

759. Daniel 12:13 But go thou thy way till the end be: for thou shalt rest, and stand in thy lot at the end of the days.
AV - **24,** 1-1,2-1,3-1,4-1,5-1,6-1,7-1,8-1,9-1,10-1,11-1,12-1,13-1,14-1,15-1,16-1,17-1,18-1,19-1,20-1,21-1,22-1,23-1,24-1

ESV - 24, 1-1,2-1,3-1,4-1,5-1,6-1,7-1,8-1,9-1,10-1,11-1,12-1,13-1,14-1,15-1,16-1,17-**3**,18-1,19-1,20-1,21-1,22-1,23-1,24-1

HCSB - 25, 1-1,2-1,3-1,4-1,5-1,6-1,7-1,8-1,9-1,10-1,11-1,12-1,13-1,14-1,15-1,16-1,17-1,18-1,19-**3**,20-1,21-1,22-1,23-1,24-1,25-1

NASV - 29, 1-1,2-1,3-1,4-1,5-1,6-1,7-1,8-1,9-1,10-1,11-1,12-1,13-1,14-**2**,15-**2**,16-1,17-1,18-1,19-**2**,20-1,21-1,22-**3**,23-**2**,24-1,25-1,26-1,27-1,28-1,29-1

NCV - 26, 1-1,2-1,3-1,4-1,5-1,6-1,7-1,8-**2**,9-1,10-1,11-1,12-1,13-1,14-1,15-1,16-1,17-1,18-1,19-1,20-1,21-1,22-1,23-1,24-**2**,25-1,26-**2**

NIV - 28, 1-1,2-1,3-1,4-1,5-1,6-1,7-1,8-1,9-1,10-1,11-1,12-1,13-1,14-1,15-1,16-1,17-1,18-1,19-1,20-1,21-1,22-1,23-1,24-1,25-**2**,26-1,27-**3**,28-**4**

NKJV - 24, 1-1,2-1,3-1,4-1,5-1,6-1,7-1,8-1,9-1,10-1,11-1,12-1,13-1,14-1,15-**2**,16-1,17-1,18-**4**,19-1,20-1,21-1,22-1,23-1,24-1

NLT - 32, 1-1,2-1,3-1,4-1,5-1,6-1,7-**2**,8-1,9-1,10-1,11-1,12-1,13-1,14-1,15-1,16-1,17-1,18-1,19-1,20-1,21-1,22-1,23-1,24-**2**,25-1,26-**2**,27-1,28-**4**,29-1,30-**2**,31-1,32-1

NRSV - 19, 1-1,2-1,3-1,4-1,5-1,6-1,7-1,8-1,9-1,10-1,11-1,12-1,13-**2**,14-1,15-1,16-1,17-1,18-1,19-1

Conclusion: All eight modern versions are more complex than the King James Bible.

760. Hosea 2:16* And it shall be at that day, saith the LORD, that thou shalt call me **Ishi**; and shalt call me no more **Baali**.

AV - 23, 1-1,2-1,3-1,4-1,5-1,6-1,7-1,8-1,9-1,10-1,11-1,12-1,13-1,14-1,15-1,16-1,17-1,18-1,19-1,20-1,21-1,22-1,23-1

ESV - 22, 1-1,2-1,3-1,4-1,5-**2**,6-1,7-1,8-1,9-1,10-1,11-1,12-1,13-1,14-1,15-1,16-**2**,17-1,18-1,19-1,20-1,21-1,22-1

HCSB - 19, 1-1,2-1,3-1,4-1,5-1,6-**4**,7-1,8-1,9-1,10-1,11-1,12-1,13-1,14-1,15-**2**,16-1,17-1,18-1,19-1

NASV - 23, 1-1,2-1,3-1,4-**2**,5-1,6-1,7-1,8-**2**,9-1,10-1,11-1,12-1,13-1,14-1,15-1,16-1,17-1,18-1,19-1,20-**2**,21-1,22-1,23-1

NCV - 20, 1-1,2-1,3-1,4-1,5-1,6-**2**,7-1,8-1,9-1,10-1,11-1,12-1,13-1,14-**2**,15-1,16-1,17-1,18-1,19-1,20-1

NIV - 20, 1-1,2-1,3-1,4-**2**,5-1,6-1,7-1,8-1,9-1,10-1,11-1,12-1,13-1,14-1,15-1,16-**2**,17-1,18-1,19-1,20-1

NKJV - 24, 1-1,2-1,3-1,4-1,5-1,6-1,7-1,8-1,9-1,10-1,11-1,12-1,13-1,14-1,15-1,16-1,17-1,18-1,19-1,20-**2**,21-1,22-1,23-1,24-1

NLT - 17, 1-1,2-1,3-1,4-1,5-1,6-1,7-1,8-1,9-1,10-1,11-1,12-1,13-1,14-**2**,15-1,16-1,17-1

NRSV - 21, 1-1,2-1,3-1,4-1,5-1,6-1,7-1,8-1,9-1,10-1,11-1,12-1,13-1,14-1,15-**2**,16-1,17-1,18-1,19-1,20-1,21-1

Conclusion: All eight modern versions are more complex than the King James Bible. The ESV, HCSB, NCV, NIV, NKJV, NLT and the NRSV translated "Ishi" as "husband" but this was not counted against them. The NIV, NKJV, and NLT translated "Baali" as "master" but this was not counted against them.

761. Hosea 2:22* And the earth shall hear the corn, and the wine, and the oil; and they shall hear **Jezreel**.

AV - 18, 1-1,2-1,3-1,4-1,5-1,6-1,7-1,8-1,9-1,10-1,11-1,12-1,13-1,14-1,15-1,16-1,17-1,18-1

ESV - 17, 1-1,2-1,3-1,4-1,5-**2**,6-1,7-1,8-1,9-1,10-1,11-1,12-1,13-1,14-1,15-1,16-**2**,17-1

HCSB - **19,** 1-1,2-1,3-1,4-**2**,5-1,6-1,7-1,8-1,9-1,10-1,11-1,12-1,13-1,14-1,15-1,16-1,17-**2**,18-1,19-1
NASV - **22,** 1-1,2-1,3-1,4-1,5-**2**,6-1,7-1,8-1,9-1,10-1,11-1,12-1,13-1,14-1,15-1,16-1,17-1,18-1,19-1,20-**2**,21-1,22-1
NCV - **18,** 1-1,2-1,3-1,4-**2**,5-1,6-1,7-1,8-1,9-1,10-1,11-1,12-1,13-**2**,14-1,15-**2**,16-1,17-1,18-1
NIV - **19,** 1-1,2-1,3-1,4-1,5-**2**,6-1,7-1,8-1,9-1,10-1,11-1,12-1,13-1,14-1,15-1,16-1,17-**2**,18-1,19-1
NKJV - **16,** 1-1,2-1,3-1,4-**2**,5-1,6-1,7-1,8-1,9-1,10-1,11-1,12-1,13-1,14-1,15-**2**,16-1
NLT - **26,** 1-1,2-1,3-1,4-1,5-**2**,6-1,7-**2**,8-1,9-1,10-1,11-1,12-1,13-**2**,14-1,15-1,16-**2**,17-1,18-1,19-1,20-1,21-1,22-1,23-**2**,24-1,25-1,26-1
NRSV - **17,** 1-1,2-1,3-1,4-1,5-**2**,6-1,7-1,8-1,9-1,10-1,11-1,12-1,13-1,14-1,15-1,16-**2**,17-1
Conclusion: All eight modern versions are more complex than the King James Bible. The NLT is the most difficult to read.

762. Hosea 11:1* When **Israel** was a child, then I loved him, and called my son out of **Egypt**.
AV - **16,** 1-1,2-1,3-1,4-1,5-1,6-1,7-1,8-1,9-1,10-1,11-1,12-1,13-1,14-1,15-1,16-1
ESV - **16,** 1-1,2-1,3-1,4-1,5-1,6-1,7-1,8-1,9-1,10-1,11-1,12-1,13-1,14-1,15-1,16-1
HCSB - **16,** 1-1,2-1,3-1,4-1,5-1,6-1,7-1,8-1,9-1,10-1,11-1,12-1,13-1,14-1,15-1,16-1
NASV - **16,** 1-1,2-1,3-1,4-1,5-1,6-1,7-1,8-1,9-1,10-1,11-1,12-1,13-1,14-1,15-1,16-1
NCV - **16,** 1-1,2-1,3-1,4-1,5-1,6-1,7-1,8-1,9-1,10-1,11-1,12-1,13-1,14-1,15-1,16-1
NIV - **16,** 1-1,2-1,3-1,4-1,5-1,6-1,7-1,8-1,9-1,10-1,11-1,12-1,13-1,14-1,15-1,16-1
NKJV - **16,** 1-1,2-1,3-1,4-1,5-1,6-1,7-1,8-1,9-1,10-1,11-1,12-1,13-1,14-1,15-1,16-1
NLT - **16,** 1-1,2-1,3-1,4-1,5-1,6-1,7-1,8-1,9-1,10-1,11-1,12-1,13-1,14-1,15-1,16-1
NRSV - **16,** 1-1,2-1,3-1,4-1,5-1,6-1,7-1,8-1,9-1,10-1,11-1,12-1,13-1,14-1,15-1,16-1
Conclusion: All versions read the same, even in word count.

763. Joel 1:1* The word of the LORD that came to **Joel** the son of **Pethuel**.
AV - **13,** 1-1,2-1,3-1,4-1,5-1,6-1,7-1,8-1,9-1,10-1,11-1,12-1,13-1
ESV - **13,** 1-1,2-1,3-1,4-1,5-1,6-1,7-1,8-1,9-1,10-1,11-1,12-1,13-1
HCSB - **12,** 1-1,2-1,3-1,4-1,5-1,6-1,7-1,8-1,9-1,10-1,11-1,12-1
NASV - **13,** 1-1,2-1,3-1,4-1,5-1,6-1,7-1,8-1,9-1,10-1,11-1,12-1,13-1
NCV - **10,** 1-1,2-1,3-1,4-1,5-1,6-1,7-1,8-1,9-1,10-1
NIV - **12,** 1-1,2-1,3-1,4-1,5-1,6-1,7-1,8-1,9-1,10-1,11-1,12-1
NKJV - **13,** 1-1,2-1,3-1,4-1,5-1,6-1,7-1,8-1,9-1,10-1,11-1,12-1,13-1
NLT - **10,** 1-1,2-1,3-1,4-1,5-**2**,6-1,7-1,8-1,9-1,10-1
NRSV - **12,** 1-1,2-1,3-1,4-1,5-1,6-1,7-1,8-1,9-1,10-1,11-1,12-1
Conclusion: Only the NLT made the verse more complex.

764. Zephaniah 3:16* In that day it shall be said to **Jerusalem**, Fear thou not: and to **Zion**, Let not thine hands be slack.
AV - **21,** 1-1,2-1,3-1,4-1,5-1,6-1,7-1,8-1,9-1,10-1,11-1,12-1,13-1,14-1,15-1,16-1,17-1,18-1,19-1,20-1,21-1
ESV - **19,** 1-1,2-1,3-1,4-1,5-1,6-1,7-1,8-1,9-1,10-1,11-1,12-1,13-1,14-1,15-1,16-1,17-1,18-1,19-1
HCSB - **20,** 1-1,2-1,3-1,4-1,5-1,6-1,7-1,8-1,9-1,10-1,11-1,12-1,13-1,14-1,15-1,16-1,17-1,18-1,19-1,20-1

NASV - **22,** 1-1,2-1,3-1,4-1,5-1,6-1,7-1,8-1,9-1,10-1,11-1,12-1,13-1,14-1,15-1,16-1,17-1,18-1,19-1,20-1,21-1,22-1

NCV - 16, 1-1,2-1,3-1,4-1,5-1,6-1,7-1,8-1,9-1,10-**2,**11-**2,**12-1,13-1,14-1,15-1,16-1

NIV - **20,** 1-1,2-1,3-1,4-1,5-1,6-1,7-1,8-1,9-1,10-1,11-1,12-1,13-1,14-1,15-1,16-1,17-1,18-1,19-1,20-1

NKJV - **19,** 1-1,2-1,3-1,4-1,5-1,6-1,7-1,8-1,9-1,10-1,11-1,12-1,13-1,14-1,15-1,16-1,17-1,18-1,19-1

NLT - 15, 1-1,2-1,3-1,4-1,5-**3,**6-1,7-1,8-1,9-1,10-1,11-1,12-1,13-1,14-1,15-1

NRSV - **21,** 1-1,2-1,3-1,4-1,5-1,6-1,7-1,8-1,9-1,10-1,11-1,12-1,13-1,14-1,15-1,16-1,17-1,18-1,19-1,20-1,21-1

Conclusion: Amazingly the NCV and NLT have the shortest word count but are the only two modern versions that made the verse more complex.

765. Haggai 1:15*# In the four and **twentieth** day of the sixth month, in the **second** year of **Darius** the king.
AV - **18,** 1-1,2-1,3-1,4-1,5-1,6-1,7-1,8-1,9-1,10-1,11-1,12-1,13-1,14-1,15-1,16-1,17-1,18-1
ESV - **20,** 1-1,2-1,3-1,4-1,5-1,6-1,7-1,8-1,9-1,10-1,11-1,12-1,13-1,14-1,15-1,16-1,17-1,18-1,19-1,20-1
HCSB - **16,** 1-1,2-1,3-1,4-1,5-1,6-1,7-1,8-1,9-1,10-1,11-1,12-1,13-1,14-1,15-1,16-1
NASV - **17,** 1-1,2-1,3-1,4-1,5-1,6-1,7-1,8-1,9-1,10-1,11-1,12-1,13-1,14-1,15-1,16-1,17-1
NCV - 18, 1-1,2-**2,**3-1,4-1,5-1,6-1,7-1,8-1,9-1,10-1,11-1,12-1,13-1,14-1,15-1,16-1,17-1,18-1
NIV - **16,** 1-1,2-1,3-1,4-1,5-1,6-1,7-1,8-1,9-1,10-1,11-1,12-1,13-1,14-1,15-1,16-1
NKJV - **16,** 1-1,2-1,3-1,4-1,5-1,6-1,7-1,8-1,9-1,10-1,11-1,12-1,13-1,14-1,15-1,16-1
NLT - **11,** 1-1,2-1,3-1,4-1,5-1,6-1,7-1,8-1,9-1,10-1,11-1
NRSV - **19,** 1-1,2-1,3-1,4-1,5-1,6-1,7-1,8-1,9-1,10-1,11-1,12-1,13-1,14-1,15-1,16-1,17-1,18-1,19-1
Conclusion: All versions read the same. Rather than "sixth month" the NCV says "September" which was not held against it.

766. Haggai 2:8* The **silver** is mine, and the gold is mine, saith the LORD of hosts.
AV - **14,** 1-1,2-1,3-1,4-1,5-1,6-1,7-1,8-1,9-1,10-1,11-1,12-1,13-1,14-1
ESV - 14, 1-1,2-1,3-1,4-1,5-1,6-1,7-1,8-1,9-1,10-**2,**11-1,12-1,13-1,14-1
HCSB - 14, 1-1,2-1,3-1,4-1,5-**2,**6-1,7-1,8-1,9-**4,**10-1,11-1,12-1,13-1,14-1
NASV - 14, 1-1,2-1,3-1,4-1,5-1,6-1,7-1,8-1,9-1,10-**2,**11-1,12-1,13-1,14-1
NCV - **14,** 1-1,2-1,3-1,4-1,5-1,6-1,7-1,8-1,9-1,10-1,11-1,12-1,13-1,14-1
NIV - 13, 1-1,2-1,3-1,4-1,5-**2,**6-1,7-1,8-1,9-**4,**10-1,11-1,12-1,13-1
NKJV - **14,** 1-1,2-1,3-1,4-1,5-1,6-1,7-1,8-1,9-1,10-1,11-1,12-1,13-1,14-1
NLT - **15,** 1-1,2-1,3-1,4-1,5-1,6-1,7-1,8-1,9-1,10-1,11-1,12-1,13-1,14-1,15-1
NRSV - **14,** 1-1,2-1,3-1,4-1,5-1,6-1,7-1,8-1,9-1,10-1,11-1,12-1,13-1,14-1
Conclusion: Four modern versions are more complex than the King James Bible. Rather than "Lord of Hosts" the NCV says "Lord All-Powerful" the NIV says, "Lord Almighty" and the NLT says "Lord of Heaven's Armies" none of these were held against these modern versions.

767. Zechariah 14:6 And it shall come to pass in that day, that the light shall not be clear, nor dark:
AV - **18,** 1-1,2-1,3-1,4-1,5-1,6-1,7-1,8-1,9-1,10-1,11-1,12-1,13-1,14-1,15-1,16-1,17-1,18-1
ESV - **11,** 1-1,2-1,3-1,4-1,5-1,6-1,7-1,8-1,9-1,10-1,11-1

HCSB -14, 1-1,2-1,3-1,4-1,5-1,6-1,7-1,8-1,9-1,10-**2**,11-1,12-**2**,13-1,14-**3**
NASV - 12, 1-1,2-1,3-1,4-1,5-1,6-1,7-1,8-1,9-1,10-**4**,11-1,12-**2**
NCV - **11,** 1-1,2-1,3-1,4-1,5-1,6-1,7-1,8-1,9-1,10-1,11-1
NIV - **12,** 1-1,2-1,3-1,4-1,5-1,6-1,7-1,8-1,9-1,10-1,11-1,12-1
NKJV - 18, 1-1,2-1,3-1,4-1,5-1,6-1,7-1,8-1,9-1,10-1,11-1,12-1,13-1,14-1,15-1,16-1,17-1,18-**3**
NLT - 11, 1-1,2-1,3-1,4-1,5-**2**,6-1,7-1,8-1,9-1,10-**2**,11-1
NRSV - 11, 1-1,2-1,3-1,4-1,5-1,6-1,7-1,8-**2**,9-1,10-1,11-1
Conclusion: Five modern versions are more complex than the King James Bible. The HCSB made the verse more complex.

768. Matthew 5:8 Blessed are the pure in heart: for they shall see God.
AV - **11,** 1-1,2-1,3-1,4-1,5-1,6-1,7-1,8-1,9-1,10-1,11-1
ESV - **11,** 1-1,2-1,3-1,4-1,5-1,6-1,7-1,8-1,9-1,10-1,11-1
HCSB - 11, 1-1,2-1,3-1,4-1,5-1,6-1,7-**2**,8-1,9-1,10-1,11-1
NASV - **11,** 1-1,2-1,3-1,4-1,5-1,6-1,7-1,8-1,9-1,10-1,11-1
NCV - **12,** 1-1,2-1,3-1,4-1,5-1,6-1,7-1,8-1,9-1,10-1,11-1,12-1
NIV - **11,** 1-1,2-1,3-1,4-1,5-1,6-1,7-1,8-1,9-1,10-1,11-1
NKJV - **11,** 1-1,2-1,3-1,4-1,5-1,6-1,7-1,8-1,9-1,10-1,11-1
NLT - 12, 1-1,2-**2**,3-1,4-1,5-1,6-1,7-1,8-1,9-1,10-1,11-1,12-1
NRSV - **11,** 1-1,2-1,3-1,4-1,5-1,6-1,7-1,8-1,9-1,10-1,11-1
Conclusion: Only the HCSB and the NLT made the verse more complex.

769. Matthew 5:38 Ye have heard that it hath been said, An eye for an eye, and a tooth for a tooth:
AV - **19,** 1-1,2-1,3-1,4-1,5-1,6-1,7-1,8-1,9-1,10-1,11-1,12-1,13-1,14-1,15-1,16-1,17-1,18-1,19-1
ESV - **18,** 1-1,2-1,3-1,4-1,5-1,6-1,7-1,8-1,9-1,10-1,11-1,12-1,13-1,14-1,15-1,16-1,17-1,18-1
HCSB - **18,** 1-1,2-1,3-1,4-1,5-1,6-1,7-1,8-1,9-1,10-1,11-1,12-1,13-1,14-1,15-1,16-1,17-1,18-1
NASV - **18,** 1-1,2-1,3-1,4-1,5-1,6-1,7-1,8-1,9-1,10-1,11-1,12-1,13-1,14-1,15-1,16-1,17-1,18-1
NCV - **18,** 1-1,2-1,3-1,4-1,5-1,6-1,7-1,8-1,9-1,10-1,11-1,12-1,13-1,14-1,15-1,16-1,17-1,18-1
NIV - **14,** 1-1,2-1,3-1,4-1,5-1,6-1,7-1,8-1,9-1,10-1,11-1,12-1,13-1,14-1
NKJV - **18,** 1-1,2-1,3-1,4-1,5-1,6-1,7-1,8-1,9-1,10-1,11-1,12-1,13-1,14-1,15-1,16-1,17-1,18-1
NLT - 24, 1-1,2-1,3-1,4-1,5-1,6-1,7-1,8-1,9-**3**,10-1,11-1,12-1,13-**3**,14-1,15-1,16-1,17-1,18-1,19-1,20-1,21-1,22-1,23-1,24-1
NRSV - **18,** 1-1,2-1,3-1,4-1,5-1,6-1,7-1,8-1,9-1,10-1,11-1,12-1,13-1,14-1,15-1,16-1,17-1,18-1
Conclusion: Only the NLT made the verse more complex.

770. Matthew 7:1 Judge not, that ye be not judged.
AV - **7,** 1-1,2-1,3-1,4-1,5-1,6-1,7-1
ESV - **7,** 1-1,2-1,3-1,4-1,5-1,6-1,7-1
HCSB - **9,** 1-1,2-1,3-1,4-1,5-1,6-1,7-1,8-1,9-1
NASV - **10,** 1-1,2-1,3-1,4-1,5-1,6-1,7-1,8-1,9-1,10-1
NCV - **8,** 1-1,2-1,3-1,4-1,5-1,6-1,7-1,8-1
NIV - **9,** 1-1,2-1,3-1,4-1,5-1,6-1,7-1,8-1,9-1
NKJV - **7,** 1-1,2-1,3-1,4-1,5-1,6-1,7-1
NLT - 10, 1-1,2-1,3-1,4-**2**,5-1,6-1,7-1,8-1,9-1,10-1

NRSV - **10,** 1-1,2-1,3-1,4-1,5-1,6-1,7-1,8-1,9-1,10-1
Conclusion: Only the NLT found a way to make such a simple statement complex.

771. Matthew 7:9 Or what man is there of you, whom if his son ask bread, will he give him a stone?
AV - **19,** 1-1,2-1,3-1,4-1,5-1,6-1,7-1,8-1,9-1,10-1,11-1,12-1,13-1,14-1,15-1,16-1,17-1,18-1,19-1
ESV - **17,** 1-1,2-1,3-1,4-1,5-1,6-1,7-1,8-1,9-1,10-1,11-1,12-1,13-1,14-1,15-1,16-1,17-1
HCSB - **16,** 1-1,2-1,3-**2,**4-1,5-1,6-1,7-1,8-1,9-1,10-1,11-1,12-1,13-1,14-1,15-1,16-1
NASV - **20,** 1-1,2-1,3-1,4-1,5-1,6-**2,**7-1,8-1,9-1,10-1,11-1,12-1,13-1,14-1,15-1,16-1,17-1,18-1,19-1,20-1
NCV - **14,** 1-1,2-1,3-**2,**4-1,5-1,6-1,7-1,8-1,9-1,10-1,11-1,12-1,13-1,14-1
NIV - **14,** 1-1,2-1,3-1,4-1,5-1,6-1,7-1,8-1,9-1,10-1,11-1,12-1,13-1,14-1
NKJV - **19,** 1-1,2-1,3-1,4-1,5-1,6-**2,**7-1,8-1,9-1,10-1,11-1,12-1,13-1,14-1,15-1,16-1,17-1,18-1,19-1
NLT - **18,** 1-1,2-**2,**3-1,4-1,5-**2,**6-1,7-1,8-1,9-1,10-1,11-1,12-1,13-1,14-1,15-1,16-1,17-1,18-**2**
NRSV - **16,** 1-1,2-1,3-**3,**4-**2,**5-1,6-1,7-1,8-1,9-1,10-1,11-1,12-1,13-1,14-1,15-1,16-1
Conclusion: Six modern versions are more complex than the King James Bible. The NLT is the most difficult to read.

772. Matthew 10:34 Think not that I am come to send peace on earth: I came not to send peace, but a sword.
AV - **20,** 1-1,2-1,3-1,4-1,5-1,6-1,7-1,8-1,9-1,10-1,11-1,12-1,13-1,14-1,15-1,16-1,17-1,18-1,19-1,20-1
ESV - **23,** 1-1,2-1,3-1,4-1,5-1,6-1,7-1,8-1,9-1,10-1,11-1,12-1,13-1,14-1,15-1,16-1,17-1,18-1,19-1,20-1,21-1,22-1,23-1
HCSB - **21,** 1-1,2-**2,**3-1,4-1,5-1,6-1,7-1,8-1,9-1,10-1,11-1,12-1,13-1,14-1,15-1,16-1,17-1,18-1,19-1,20-1,21-1
NASV - **22,** 1-1,2-1,3-1,4-1,5-1,6-1,7-1,8-1,9-1,10-1,11-1,12-1,13-1,14-1,15-1,16-1,17-1,18-1,19-1,20-1,21-1,22-1
NCV - **21,** 1-1,2-1,3-1,4-1,5-1,6-1,7-1,8-1,9-1,10-1,11-1,12-1,13-1,14-1,15-1,16-1,17-1,18-1,19-1,20-1,21-1
NIV - **23,** 1-1,2-1,3-**2,**4-1,5-1,6-1,7-1,8-1,9-1,10-1,11-1,12-1,13-1,14-1,15-1,16-1,17-1,18-1,19-1,20-1,21-1,22-1,23-1
NKJV - **21,** 1-1,2-1,3-1,4-1,5-1,6-1,7-1,8-1,9-1,10-1,11-1,12-1,13-1,14-1,15-1,16-1,17-1,18-1,19-1,20-1,21-1
NLT - **21,** 1-1,2-**3,**3-1,4-1,5-1,6-1,7-1,8-1,9-1,10-1,11-1,12-1,13-1,14-1,15-1,16-1,17-1,18-1,19-1,20-1,21-1
NRSV - **23,** 1-1,2-1,3-1,4-1,5-1,6-1,7-1,8-1,9-1,10-1,11-1,12-1,13-1,14-1,15-1,16-1,17-1,18-1,19-1,20-1,21-1,22-1,23-1
Conclusion: Only the HCSB, the NIV and the NLT made the verse more complex.

773. Matthew 11:15 He that hath ears to hear, let him hear.
AV - **9,** 1-1,2-1,3-1,4-1,5-1,6-1,7-1,8-1,9-1
ESV - **9,** 1-1,2-1,3-1,4-1,5-1,6-1,7-1,8-1,9-1
HCSB - **6,** 1-**3,**2-1,3-1,4-1,5-1,6-**2**
NASV - **9,** 1-1,2-1,3-1,4-1,5-1,6-1,7-1,8-1,9-1

NCV - **7,** 1-1,2-1,3-1,4-1,5-1,6-1,7-1
NIV - **9,** 1-1,2-1,3-1,4-1,5-1,6-1,7-1,8-1,9-1
NKJV - **9,** 1-1,2-1,3-1,4-1,5-1,6-1,7-1,8-1,9-1
NLT - 9, 1-**3,**2-1,3-1,4-1,5-1,6-1,7-**2,**8-1,9-**3**
NRSV - 5, 1-1,2-**3,**3-1,4-1,5-**2**
Conclusion: Only three modern versions are more complex than the King James Bible. The NLT is the most difficult to read.

774. Matthew 12:16 And charged them that they should not make him known:
AV - **10,** 1-1,2-1,3-1,4-1,5-1,6-1,7-1,8-1,9-1,10-1
ESV - 8, 1-1,2-**2,**3-1,4-1,5-1,6-1,7-1,8-1
HCSB - **8,** 1-1,2-1,3-1,4-1,5-1,6-1,7-1,8-1
NASV - **9,** 1-1,2-1,3-1,4-1,5-1,6-1,7-1,8-1,9-1
NCV - 11, 1-1,2-1,3-1,4-1,5-**2,**6-1,7-1,8-1,9-1,10-1,11-1
NIV - 8, 1-**2,**2-1,3-1,4-1,5-1,6-1,7-1,8-1
NKJV - **9,** 1-1,2-1,3-1,4-1,5-1,6-1,7-1,8-1,9-1
NLT - 10, 1-1,2-1,3-1,4-1,5-1,6-1,7-**2,**8-1,9-1,10-1
NRSV - 9, 1-1,2-1,3-**2,**4-1,5-1,6-1,7-1,8-1,9-1
Conclusion: Five modern versions are more complex than the King James Bible. The NCV inserted "Jesus" for "him" but it was not counted as a multi-syllable word.

775. Matthew 12:21* And in his name shall the **Gentiles** trust.
AV - **8,** 1-1,2-1,3-1,4-1,5-1,6-1,7-1,8-1
ESV - **8,** 1-1,2-1,3-1,4-1,5-1,6-1,7-1,8-1
HCSB - **9,** 1-1,2-1,3-1,4-1,5-1,6-1,7-1,8-1,9-1
NASV - **8,** 1-1,2-1,3-1,4-1,5-1,6-1,7-1,8-1
NCV - **9,** 1-1,2-1,3-1,4-1,5-1,6-1,7-1,8-1,9-1
NIV - **9,** 1-1,2-1,3-1,4-1,5-1,6-1,7-1,8-1,9-1
NKJV - **7,** 1-1,2-1,3-1,4-1,5-1,6-1,7-1
NLT - **11,** 1-1,2-1,3-1,4-1,5-1,6-1,7-1,8-1,9-1,10-1,11-1
NRSV - **8,** 1-1,2-1,3-1,4-1,5-1,6-1,7-1,8-1
Conclusion: All versions read **basically** the same: the HCSB and NIV inserted "nations" for "Gentiles" while the NCV rendered the word as "non-Jewish people" and the NLT said "the hope of all the world." Since "Gentile" is multi-syllable none of these renderings were counted against any of these versions.

776. Matthew 13:1* The same day went **Jesus** out of the house, and sat by the sea side.
AV - **15,** 1-1,2-1,3-1,4-1,5-1,6-1,7-1,8-1,9-1,10-1,11-1,12-1,13-1,14-1,15-1
ESV - **14,** 1-1,2-1,3-1,4-1,5-1,6-1,7-1,8-1,9-1,10-1,11-1,12-1,13-1,14-1
HCSB - 15, 1-1,2-1,3-1,4-1,5-1,6-1,7-1,8-1,9-1,10-1,11-1,12-**2,**13-1,14-1,15-1
NASV - 14, 1-1,2-1,3-1,4-1,5-1,6-1,7-1,8-1,9-1,10-1,11-**2,**12-1,13-1,14-1
NCV - **14,** 1-1,2-1,3-1,4-1,5-1,6-1,7-1,8-1,9-1,10-1,11-1,12-1,13-1,14-1
NIV - **14,** 1-1,2-1,3-1,4-1,5-1,6-1,7-1,8-1,9-1,10-1,11-1,12-1,13-1,14-1
NKJV - **15,** 1-1,2-1,3-1,4-1,5-1,6-1,7-1,8-1,9-1,10-1,11-1,12-1,13-1,14-1,15-1

NLT - 13, 1-**2**,2-1,3-1,4-1,5-1,6-1,7-1,8-1,9-1,10-1,11-**2**,12-1,13-1
NRSV - 14, 1-1,2-1,3-1,4-1,5-1,6-1,7-1,8-1,9-1,10-1,11-1,12-**2**,13-1,14-1
Conclusion: Four modern versions are more complex than the King James Bible.

777. Matthew 13:9 Who hath ears to hear, let him hear.
AV - **8,** 1-1,2-1,3-1,4-1,5-1,6-1,7-1,8-1
ESV - **7,** 1-1,2-1,3-1,4-1,5-1,6-1,7-1
HCSB - 6, 1-**3**,2-1,3-1,4-1,5-1,6-**2**
NASV - **7,** 1-1,2-1,3-1,4-1,5-1,6-1,7-1
NCV - 8, 1-1,2-1,3-1,4-1,5-1,6-1,7-1,8-**2**
NIV - **7,** 1-1,2-1,3-1,4-1,5-1,6-1,7-1
NKJV - **9,** 1-1,2-1,3-1,4-1,5-1,6-1,7-1,8-1,9-1
NLT - 9, 1-**3**,2-1,3-1,4-1,5-1,6-1,7-**2**,8-1,9-**3**
NRSV - 5, 1-1,2-**3**,3-1,4-1,5-**2**
Conclusion: Four modern versions are more complex than the King James Bible. The NLT is the most difficult to read.

778. Matthew 13:16 But blessed are your eyes, for they see: and your ears, for they hear.
AV - **14,** 1-1,2-1,3-1,4-1,5-1,6-1,7-1,8-1,9-1,10-1,11-1,12-1,13-1,14-1
ESV - **14,** 1-1,2-1,3-1,4-1,5-1,6-1,7-1,8-1,9-1,10-1,11-1,12-1,13-1,14-1
HCSB - 16, 1-1,2-1,3-1,4-1,5-1,6-**2**,7-1,8-1,9-1,10-1,11-1,12-1,13-**2**,14-1,15-1,16-1
NASV - 14, 1-1,2-1,3-1,4-1,5-1,6-**2**,7-1,8-1,9-1,10-1,11-1,12-**2**,13-1,14-1
NCV - 15, 1-1,2-1,3-1,4-1,5-**2**,6-1,7-1,8-1,9-1,10-1,11-1,12-1,13-1,14-1,15-1
NIV - 14, 1-1,2-1,3-1,4-1,5-1,6-**2**,7-1,8-1,9-1,10-1,11-1,12-**2**,13-1,14-1
NKJV - **14,** 1-1,2-1,3-1,4-1,5-1,6-1,7-1,8-1,9-1,10-1,11-1,12-1,13-1,14-1
NLT - 14, 1-1,2-1,3-1,4-1,5-1,6-**2**,7-1,8-1,9-1,10-1,11-1,12-**2**,13-1,14-1
NRSV - **14,** 1-1,2-1,3-1,4-1,5-1,6-1,7-1,8-1,9-1,10-1,11-1,12-1,13-1,14-1
Conclusion: Five modern versions are more complex than the King James Bible.

779. Matthew 13:46 Who, when he had found one pearl of great price, went and sold all that he had, and bought it.
AV - **20,** 1-1,2-1,3-1,4-1,5-1,6-1,7-1,8-1,9-1,10-1,11-1,12-1,13-1,14-1,15-1,16-1,17-1,18-1,19-1,20-1
ESV - 18, 1-1,2-1,3-**2**,4-1,5-1,6-1,7-1,8-**2**,9-1,10-1,11-1,12-1,13-1,14-1,15-1,16-1,17-1,18-1
HCSB - 16, 1-1,2-1,3-1,4-1,5-**2**,6-1,7-1,8-1,9-1,10-1,11-**4**,12-1,13-1,14-1,15-1,16-1
NASV - 19, 1-1,2-**2**,3-**2**,4-1,5-1,6-1,7-1,8-**2**,9-1,10-1,11-1,12-1,13-1,14-1,15-1,16-1,17-1,18-1,19-1
NCV - 17, 1-1,2-1,3-1,4-1,5-**2**,6-**4**,7-1,8-1,9-1,10-1,11-1,12-**4**,13-1,14-1,15-1,16-1,17-1
NIV - 18, 1-1,2-1,3-1,4-1,5-1,6-1,7-**2**,8-1,9-1,10-**2**,11-1,12-1,13-**4**,14-1,15-1,16-1,17-1,18-1
NKJV - **20,** 1-1,2-1,3-1,4-1,5-1,6-1,7-1,8-1,9-1,10-1,11-1,12-1,13-1,14-1,15-1,16-1,17-1,18-1,19-1,20-1
NLT - 16, 1-1,2-1,3-**3**,4-1,5-1,6-1,7-1,8-**2**,9-1,10-1,11-**4**,12-1,13-1,14-1,15-1,16-1
NRSV - 18, 1-1,2-**2**,3-1,4-1,5-1,6-1,7-1,8-1,9-1,10-1,11-1,12-1,13-1,14-1,15-1,16-1,17-1,18-1
Conclusion: Seven modern versions are more complex than the King James Bible.

780. Matthew 18:11 For the Son of man is come to save that which was lost.
AV - **13,** 1-1,2-1,3-1,4-1,5-1,6-1,7-1,8-1,9-1,10-1,11-1,12-1,13-1
ESV - The verse is omitted.
HCSB - **[11,** 1-1,2-1,3-1,4-1,5-1,6-1,7-1,8-1,9-1,10-1,11-1**]**
NASV - **[13,** 1-1,2-1,3-1,4-1,5-1,6-1,7-1,8-1,9-1,10-1,11-1,12-1,13-1**]**
NCV - **[9,** 1-1,2-1,3-1,4-1,5-1,6-1,7-1,8-1,9-2**]**
NIV - The verse is omitted.
NKJV - **13,** 1-1,2-1,3-1,4-1,5-1,6-1,7-1,8-1,9-1,10-1,11-1,12-1,13-1
NLT - The verse is omitted.
NRSV - The verse is omitted.
Conclusion: Four modern versions omit the verse entirely. The HCSB, the NASV and the NCV have the verse in brackets. Only the NKJV does not put the verse in brackets.

781. Matthew 22:45* If **David** then call him Lord, how is he his son?
AV - **11,** 1-1,2-1,3-1,4-1,5-1,6-1,7-1,8-1,9-1,10-1,11-1
ESV - **11,** 1-1,2-1,3-1,4-1,5-1,6-1,7-1,8-1,9-1,10-1,11-1
HCSB - **13,** 1-1,2-1,3-1,4-1,5-1,6-1,7-1,8-1,9-1,10-1,11-1,12-1,13-1
NASV - **11,** 1-1,2-1,3-1,4-1,5-1,6-1,7-1,8-1,9-1,10-1,11-1
NCV - **13,** 1-1,2-1,3-1,4-1,5-1,6-1,7-1,8-1,9-1,10-1,11-1,12-1,13-1
NIV - **12,** 1-1,2-1,3-1,4-1,5-1,6-1,7-1,8-1,9-1,10-1,11-1,12-1
NKJV - **11,** 1-1,2-1,3-1,4-1,5-1,6-1,7-1,8-1,9-1,10-1,11-1
NLT - **14,** 1-1,2-1,3-1,4-1,5-1,6-1,7-1,8-1,9-1,10-1,11-1,12-1,13-1,14-1
NRSV - **12,** 1-1,2-1,3-1,4-1,5-1,6-1,7-1,8-1,9-1,10-1,11-1,12-1
Conclusion: All versions basically read the same. Both the HCSB and the NLT insert the name "Messiah" (the NLT twice) but this was not counted against them since "Messiah" would be accepted as a proper name under other circumstances.

782. Matthew 25:33 And he shall set the sheep on his right hand, but the goats on the left
AV - **16,** 1-1,2-1,3-1,4-1,5-1,6-1,7-1,8-1,9-1,10-1,11-1,12-1,13-1,14-1,15-1,16-1
ESV - **15,** 1-1,2-1,3-1,4-1,5-1,6-1,7-1,8-1,9-1,10-1,11-1,12-1,13-1,14-1,15-1
HCSB - **14,** 1-1,2-1,3-1,4-1,5-1,6-1,7-1,8-1,9-1,10-1,11-1,12-1,13-1,14-1
NASV - **15,** 1-1,2-1,3-1,4-1,5-1,6-1,7-1,8-1,9-1,10-1,11-1,12-1,13-1,14-1,15-1
NCV - **17,** 1-1,2-1,3-1,4-1,5-1,6-1,7-1,8-1,9-1,10-1,11-1,12-1,13-1,14-1,15-1,16-1,17-1
NIV - **14,** 1-1,2-1,3-1,4-1,5-1,6-1,7-1,8-1,9-1,10-1,11-1,12-1,13-1,14-1
NKJV - **16,** 1-1,2-1,3-1,4-1,5-1,6-1,7-1,8-1,9-1,10-1,11-1,12-1,13-1,14-1,15-1,16-1
NLT - **15,** 1-1,2-1,3-1,4-1,5-1,6-1,7-1,8-1,9-1,10-1,11-1,12-1,13-1,14-1,15-1
NRSV - **16,** 1-1,2-1,3-1,4-1,5-1,6-1,7-1,8-1,9-1,10-1,11-1,12-1,13-1,14-1,15-1,16-1
Conclusion: All versions read the same.

783. Mark 3:18* And **Andrew,** and **Philip,** and **Bartholomew,** and **Matthew,** and **Thomas,** and James the son of **Alphaeus,** and **Thaddaeus,** and **Simon** the **Canaanite,**
AV - **22,** 1-1,2-1,3-1,4-1,5-1,6-1,7-1,8-1,9-1,10-1,11-1,12-1,13-1,14-1,15-1,16-1,17-1,18-1,19-1,20-1,21-1,22-1

ESV - **21,** 1-1,2-1,3-1,4-1,5-1,6-1,7-1,8-1,9-1,10-1,11-1,12-1,13-1,14-1,15-1,16-1,17-1,18-1,19-1,20-1,21-1

HCSB - **17,** 1-1,2-1,3-1,4-1,5-1,6-1,7-1,8-1,9-1,10-1,11-1,12-1,13-1,14-1,15-1,16-1,17-1

NASV - **21,** 1-1,2-1,3-1,4-1,5-1,6-1,7-1,8-1,9-1,10-1,11-1,12-1,13-1,14-1,15-1,16-1,17-1,18-1,19-1,20-1,21-1

NCV - **14,** 1-1,2-1,3-1,4-1,5-1,6-1,7-1,8-1,9-1,10-1,11-1,12-1,13-1,14-1

NIV - **13,** 1-1,2-1,3-1,4-1,5-1,6-1,7-1,8-1,9-1,10-1,11-1,12-1,13-1

NKJV - **14,** 1-1,2-1,3-1,4-1,5-1,6-1,7-1,8-1,9-1,10-1,11-1,12-1,13-1,14-1

NLT - **13,** 1-1,2-1,3-1,4-1,5-1,6-1,7-1,8-1,9-1,10-1,11-1,12-1,13-1

NRSV - **21,** 1-1,2-1,3-1,4-1,5-1,6-1,7-1,8-1,9-1,10-1,11-1,12-1,13-1,14-1,15-1,16-1,17-1,18-1,19-1,20-1,21-1

Conclusion: While all versions read the same the HCSB, NCV and the NLT all replaced "Canaanite" with "Zealot." Since this was the change of a multi-syllable word with a different multi-syllable word this was not counted against these versions.

784. Mark 6:40# And they sat down in ranks, by **hundreds**, and by **fifties**.

AV - **11,** 1-1,2-1,3-1,4-1,5-1,6-1,7-1,8-1,9-1,10-1,11-1

ESV - **11,** 1-1,2-1,3-1,4-1,5-1,6-1,7-1,8-1,9-1,10-1,11-1

HCSB - **10,** 1-1,2-1,3-1,4-1,5-1,6-1,7-1,8-1,9-1,10-1

NASV - **10,** 1-1,2-1,3-1,4-1,5-1,6-1,7-1,8-1,9-1,10-1

NCV - **10,** 1-1,2-1,3-1,4-1,5-1,6-1,7-1,8-1,9-1,10-1

NIV - **10,** 1-1,2-1,3-1,4-1,5-1,6-1,7-1,8-1,9-1,10-1

NKJV - **11,** 1-1,2-1,3-1,4-1,5-1,6-1,7-1,8-1,9-1,10-1,11-1

NLT - **11,** 1-1,2-1,3-1,4-1,5-1,6-1,7-1,8-1,9-1,10-1,11-1

NRSV - **11,** 1-1,2-1,3-1,4-1,5-1,6-1,7-1,8-1,9-1,10-1,11-1

Conclusion: All versions read the same.

785. Mark 6:42 And they did all eat, and were filled.

AV - **8,** 1-1,2-1,3-1,4-1,5-1,6-1,7-1,8-1

ESV - 7, 1-1,2-1,3-1,4-1,5-1,6-1,7-**3**

HCSB - 5, 1-**4**,2-1,3-1,4-1,5-1

NASV - 6, 1-1,2-1,3-1,4-1,5-1,6-**3**

NCV - 7, 1-1,2-1,3-**2**,4-1,5-1,6-1,7-**3**

NIV - 6, 1-1,2-1,3-1,4-1,5-1,6-**3**

NKJV - **7,** 1-1,2-1,3-1,4-1,5-1,6-1,7-1

NLT - 8, 1-1,2-1,3-1,4-1,5-1,6-1,7-1,8-**2**

NRSV - **6,** 1-1,2-1,3-1,4-1,5-1,6-1

Conclusion: Six modern versions are more complex than the King James Bible. The NCV is the most difficult to read.

786. Mark 8:30 And he charged them that they should tell no man of him.

AV - **12,** 1-1,2-1,3-1,4-1,5-1,6-1,7-1,8-1,9-1,10-1,11-1,12-1

ESV - 11, 1-1,2-1,3-**2**,4-1,5-1,6-1,7-1,8-1,9-1,10-**2**,11-1

HCSB - 11, 1-1,2-1,3-**2**,4-1,5-1,6-1,7-1,8-1,9-1,10-**2**,11-1

NASV - **10,** 1-1,2-1,3-1,4-1,5-1,6-1,7-1,8-1,9-**2**,10-1
NCV - **11,** 1-1,2-1,3-1,4-**3**,5-1,6-1,7-1,8-**3**,9-1,10-1,11-1
NIV - **9,** 1-1,2-1,3-1,4-1,5-1,6-1,7-**3**,8-**2**,9-1
NKJV - **13,** 1-1,2-1,3-**2**,4-1,5-1,6-1,7-1,8-1,9-1,10-1,11-1,12-**2**,13-1
NLT - **10,** 1-1,2-1,3-1,4-1,5-1,6-1,7-1,8-**3**,9-**2**,10-1
NRSV - **11,** 1-1,2-1,3-**2**,4-**2**,5-1,6-1,7-1,8-1,9-**3**,10-**2**,11-1
Conclusion: All eight modern versions are more complex than the King James Bible. The NRSV is the most difficult to read.

787. Mark 10:8 And they twain shall be one flesh: so then they are no more twain, but one flesh.
AV - **17,** 1-1,2-1,3-1,4-1,5-1,6-1,7-1,8-1,9-1,10-1,11-1,12-1,13-1,14-1,15-1,16-1,17-1
ESV - **15,** 1-1,2-1,3-1,4-**2**,5-1,6-1,7-1,8-1,9-1,10-1,11-**2**,12-1,13-1,14-1,15-1
HCSB - **16,** 1-1,2-1,3-1,4-1,5-**2**,6-1,7-1,8-1,9-1,10-1,11-1,12-**2**,13-1,14-1,15-1,16-1
NASV - **16,** 1-1,2-1,3-1,4-1,5-**2**,6-1,7-1,8-1,9-1,10-1,11-1,12-**2**,13-1,14-1,15-1,16-1
NCV - **14,** 1-1,2-1,3-1,4-1,5-**2**,6-1,7-1,8-1,9-1,10-1,11-1,12-1,13-1,14-1
NIV - **15,** 1-1,2-1,3-1,4-1,5-**2**,6-1,7-1,8-1,9-1,10-1,11-1,12-**2**,13-1,14-1,15-1
NKJV - **16,** 1-1,2-1,3-1,4-1,5-**2**,6-1,7-1,8-1,9-1,10-1,11-1,12-**2**,13-1,14-1,15-1,16-1
NLT - **15,** 1-1,2-1,3-1,4-1,5-**3**,6-**2**,7-1,8-1,9-1,10-1,11-1,12-**2**,13-1,14-1,15-1
NRSV - **16,** 1-1,2-1,3-1,4-1,5-**2**,6-1,7-1,8-1,9-1,10-1,11-1,12-**2**,13-1,14-1,15-1,16-1
Conclusion: All eight modern versions are more complex than the King James Bible. The NLT is the most difficult to read.

788. Mark 13:17 But woe to them that are with child, and to them that give suck in those days!
AV - **17,** 1-1,2-1,3-1,4-1,5-1,6-1,7-1,8-1,9-1,10-1,11-1,12-1,13-1,14-1,15-1,16-1,17-1
ESV - **17,** 1-1,2-**2**,3-1,4-**2**,5-1,6-1,7-**2**,8-1,9-1,10-1,11-1,12-1,13-**2**,14-**2**,15-1,16-1,17-1
HCSB - **10,** 1-1,2-1,3-**2**,4-**2**,5-1,6-**2**,7-**2**,8-1,9-1,10-1
NASV - **17,** 1-1,2-1,3-1,4-1,5-1,6-1,7-**2**,8-1,9-1,10-1,11-1,12-1,13-**2**,14-**2**,15-1,16-1,17-1
NCV - **17,** 1-1,2-1,3-1,4-1,5-**3**,6-1,7-1,8-1,9-1,10-**2**,11-1,12-1,13-**2**,14-1,15-1,16-**2**,17-**2**
NIV - **14,** 1-1,2-**2**,3-1,4-1,5-1,6-1,7-1,8-1,9-1,10-**2**,11-**2**,12-1,13-**2**,14-**2**
NKJV - **17,** 1-1,2-1,3-1,4-1,5-1,6-1,7-**2**,8-1,9-1,10-1,11-1,12-1,13-**2**,14-**2**,15-1,16-1,17-1
NLT - **15,** 1-1,2-**3**,3-1,4-1,5-1,6-1,7-**2**,8-**2**,9-1,10-1,11-**2**,12-**2**,13-1,14-1,15-1
NRSV - **16,** 1-1,2-1,3-1,4-1,5-1,6-**2**,7-1,8-1,9-1,10-1,11-1,12-**2**,13-**2**,14-1,15-1,16-1
Conclusion: All eight modern versions are more complex than the King James Bible.

789. Mark 13:33 Take ye heed, watch and pray: for ye know not when the time is.
AV - **14,** 1-1,2-1,3-1,4-1,5-1,6-1,7-1,8-1,9-1,10-1,11-1,12-1,13-1,14-1
ESV - **15,** 1-1,2-1,3-1,4-1,5-**2**,6-1,7-1,8-1,9-1,10-1,11-1,12-1,13-1,14-1,15-1
HCSB - **12,** 1-1,2-1,3-**2**,4-1,5-1,6-1,7-1,8-1,9-1,10-1,11-1,12-**2**
NASV - **17,** 1-1,2-1,3-1,4-1,5-1,6-**2**,7-1,8-1,9-1,10-1,11-1,12-1,13-1,14-**3**,15-1,16-1,17-1
NCV - **14,** 1-1,2-**2**,3-**2**,4-1,5-**2**,6-**2**,7-1,8-1,9-1,10-1,11-1,12-1,13-1,14-1
NIV - **14,** 1-1,2-1,3-1,4-1,5-**2**,6-1,7-1,8-1,9-1,10-1,11-1,12-1,13-1,14-1
NKJV - **14,** 1-1,2-1,3-1,4-1,5-1,6-1,7-1,8-1,9-1,10-1,11-1,12-1,13-1,14-1
NLT - **15,** 1-1,2-1,3-1,4-1,5-1,6-1,7-1,8-1,9-1,10-1,11-1,12-1,13-1,14-1,15-**2**
NRSV - **13,** 1-**2**,2-1,3-**2**,4-1,5-1,6-1,7-1,8-1,9-1,10-1,11-1,12-1,13-1

254

Conclusion: Seven modern versions are more complex than the King James Bible.

790. Mark 14:46 And they laid their hands on him, and took him.
AV - **10,** 1-1,2-1,3-1,4-1,5-1,6-1,7-1,8-1,9-1,10-1
ESV - **9,** 1-1,2-1,3-1,4-1,5-1,6-1,7-1,8-1,9-1
HCSB - 9, 1-1,2-1,3-1,4-1,5-1,6-1,7-1,8-**3**,9-1
NASV - **8,** 1-1,2-1,3-1,4-1,5-1,6-1,7-1,8-1
NCV - 8, 1-1,2-1,3-**2**,4-1,5-1,6-1,7-**3**,8-1
NIV - 7, 1-1,2-1,3-1,4-1,5-1,6-**3**,7-1
NKJV - **10,** 1-1,2-1,3-1,4-1,5-1,6-1,7-1,8-1,9-1,10-1
NLT - 8, 1-1,2-1,3-**2**,4-1,5-1,6-1,7-**3**,8-1
NRSV - 9, 1-1,2-1,3-1,4-1,5-1,6-1,7-1,8-**3**,9-1
Conclusion: Five modern versions are more complex than the King James Bible. Both the NCV and the NIV inserted the name "Jesus" but this was not counted against them since "Jesus" would be accepted as a proper name under other circumstances.

791. Mark 15:25* And it was the third hour, and they **crucified** him.
AV - **10,** 1-1,2-1,3-1,4-1,5-1,6-1,7-1,8-1,9-1,10-1
ESV - **10,** 1-1,2-1,3-1,4-1,5-1,6-1,7-1,8-1,9-1,10-1
HCSB - 11, 1-1,2-1,3-1,4-1,5-1,6-1,7-**2**,8-1,9-1,10-1,11-1
NASV - **9,** 1-1,2-1,3-1,4-1,5-1,6-1,7-1,8-1,9-1
NCV - 11, 1-1,2-1,3-1,4-**2**,5-1,6-1,7-**2**,8-1,9-1,10-1,11-1
NIV - **9,** 1-1,2-1,3-1,4-1,5-1,6-1,7-1,8-1,9-1
NKJV - **10,** 1-1,2-1,3-1,4-1,5-1,6-1,7-1,8-1,9-1,10-1
NLT - 11, 1-1,2-1,3-1,4-**2**,5-1,6-1,7-**2**,8-1,9-1,10-1,11-1
NRSV - 11, 1-1,2-1,3-1,4-**2**,5-1,6-1,7-**2**,8-1,9-1,10-1,11-1
Conclusion: Four modern versions are more complex than the King James Bible.

792. Mark 15:27* And with him they **crucify** two thieves; the one on his right hand, and the other on his left.
AV - **19,** 1-1,2-1,3-1,4-1,5-1,6-1,7-1,8-1,9-1,10-1,11-1,12-1,13-1,14-1,15-1,16-1,17-1,18-1,19-1
ESV - **16,** 1-1,2-1,3-1,4-1,5-1,6-1,7-**2**,8-1,9-1,10-1,11-1,12-1,13-1,14-1,15-1,16-1
HCSB - 15, 1-1,2-1,3-1,4-**3**,5-1,6-1,7-1,8-1,9-1,10-1,11-1,12-1,13-1,14-1,15-1
NASV - 15, 1-1,2-1,3-1,4-**2**,5-1,6-1,7-1,8-1,9-1,10-1,11-1,12-1,13-1,14-1,15-1
NCV - **19,** 1-1,2-**2**,3-1,4-1,5-**2**,6-1,7-**2**,8-**2**,9-1,10-1,11-1,12-1,13-1,14-1,15-1,16-**2**,17-1,18-1,19-1
NIV - **15,** 1-1,2-1,3-1,4-**2**,5-1,6-1,7-1,8-1,9-1,10-1,11-1,12-1,13-1,14-1,15-1
NKJV - **17,** 1-1,2-1,3-1,4-**2**,5-1,6-1,7-**2**,8-1,9-1,10-1,11-1,12-1,13-1,14-**2**,15-1,16-1,17-1
NLT - 15, 1-1,2-**6**,3-1,4-1,5-1,6-1,7-1,8-1,9-1,10-1,11-1,12-1,13-1,14-1,15-1
NRSV - 16, 1-1,2-1,3-1,4-1,5-1,6-1,7-**2**,8-1,9-1,10-1,11-1,12-1,13-1,14-1,15-1,16-1
Conclusion: While all eight modern versions are more complex than the King James Bible this is one of those rare occasions when the NKJV was more complex than ever other modern version except the NCV, which made the verse the most complex.

793. Mark 15:37* And **Jesus** cried with a loud voice, and gave up the ghost.
AV - **12,** 1-1,2-1,3-1,4-1,5-1,6-1,7-1,8-1,9-1,10-1,11-1,12-1
ESV - 10, 1-1,2-1,3-**2,**4-1,5-1,6-1,7-1,8-1,9-1,10-1
HCSB - **11,** 1-1,2-1,3-1,4-1,5-1,6-1,7-1,8-1,9-1,10-1,11-1
NASV - 10, 1-1,2-1,3-**2,**4-1,5-1,6-1,7-1,8-1,9-1,10-1
NCV - **9,** 1-1,2-1,3-1,4-1,5-1,6-1,7-1,8-1,9-1
NIV - **8,** 1-1,2-1,3-1,4-1,5-1,6-1,7-1,8-1
NKJV - **12,** 1-1,2-1,3-1,4-1,5-1,6-1,7-1,8-1,9-1,10-1,11-1,12-1
NLT - 10, 1-1,2-1,3-**2,**4-**3,**5-1,6-1,7-1,8-1,9-1,10-1
NRSV - **10,** 1-1,2-1,3-1,4-1,5-1,6-1,7-1,8-1,9-1,10-1
Conclusion: Three modern versions are more complex than the King James Bible.

794. Mark 16:10 And she went and told them that had been with him, as they mourned and wept.
AV - **16,** 1-1,2-1,3-1,4-1,5-1,6-1,7-1,8-1,9-1,10-1,11-1,12-1,13-1,14-1,15-1,16-1
ESV - **15,** 1-1,2-1,3-1,4-1,5-1,6-1,7-1,8-1,9-1,10-1,11-1,12-1,13-1,14-1,15-1
HCSB - 17, 1-1,2-1,3-1,4-**3,**5-1,6-1,7-1,8-1,9-1,10-1,11-1,12-1,13-1,14-1,15-**2,**16-1,17-**2**
NASV - 17, 1-1,2-1,3-1,4-**3,**5-1,6-1,7-1,8-1,9-1,10-1,11-1,12-1,13-1,14-1,15-**2,**16-1,17-**2**
NCV - 17, 1-**2,**2-1,3-1,4-1,5-1,6-1,7-1,8-1,9-1,10-**3,**11-1,12-1,13-1,14-1,15-1,16-1,17-**2**
NIV - 16, 1-1,2-1,3-1,4-1,5-1,6-1,7-1,8-1,9-1,10-1,11-1,12-1,13-1,14-**2,**15-1,16-**2**
NKJV - **15,** 1-1,2-1,3-1,4-1,5-1,6-1,7-1,8-1,9-1,10-1,11-1,12-1,13-1,14-1,15-1
NLT - 16, 1-1,2-1,3-1,4-1,5-**3,**6-1,7-1,8-**2,**9-1,10-**2,**11-1,12-1,13-1,14-1,15-1,16-**2**
NRSV - 17, 1-1,2-1,3-1,4-1,5-1,6-1,7-1,8-1,9-1,10-1,11-1,12-1,13-1,14-1,15-**2,**16-1,17-**2**
Conclusion: Six modern versions are more complex than the King James Bible. The NCV inserts the names "Mary" and "Jesus" but this was not counted against it since these names would be accepted as a proper names under other circumstances.

795. Luke 2:28 Then took he him up in his arms, and blessed God, and said,
AV - **13,** 1-1,2-1,3-1,4-1,5-1,6-1,7-1,8-1,9-1,10-1,11-1,12-1,13-1
ESV - **12,** 1-1,2-1,3-1,4-1,5-1,6-1,7-1,8-1,9-1,10-1,11-1,12-1
HCSB - **11,** 1-1,2-1,3-1,4-1,5-1,6-1,7-1,8-1,9-1,10-1,11-1
NASV - 12, 1-1,2-1,3-1,4-1,5-**2,**6-1,7-1,8-1,9-1,10-1,11-1,12-1
NCV - 10, 1-1,2-1,3-1,4-**2,**5-1,6-1,7-1,8-1,9-1,10-1
NIV - 14, 1-1,2-1,3-1,4-1,5-1,6-1,7-1,8-1,9-1,10-1,11-1,12-1,13-1,14-**2**
NKJV - **12,** 1-1,2-1,3-1,4-1,5-1,6-1,7-1,8-1,9-1,10-1,11-1,12-1
NLT - 10, 1-1,2-1,3-1,4-1,5-1,6-1,7-1,8-1,9-1,10-**2**
NRSV - 10, 1-1,2-1,3-1,4-1,5-1,6-1,7-1,8-1,9-1,10-**2**
Conclusion: Five modern versions are more complex than the King James Bible. The HCSB, NCV, NIV, NLT and the NRSV insert the name "Simeon" but this was not counted against them since "Simeon" would be accepted as a proper name under other circumstances.

796. Luke 3:24* Which was the son of **Matthat**, which was the son of **Levi**, which was the son of **Melchi**, which was the son of **Janna**, which was the son of **Joseph**,
AV - **30,** 1-1,2-1,3-1,4-1,5-1,6-1,7-1,8-1,9-1,10-1,11-1,12-1,13-1,14-1,15-1,16-1,17-1,18-1,19-1,20-1,21-1,22-1,23-1,24-1,25-1,26-1,27-1,28-1,29-1,30-1

ESV - **20,** 1-1,2-1,3-1,4-1,5-1,6-1,7-1,8-1,9-1,10-1,11-1,12-1,13-1,14-1,15-1,16-1,17-1,18-1,19-1,20-1

HCSB - **15,** 1-1,2-1,3-1,4-1,5-1,6-1,7-1,8-1,9-1,10-1,11-1,12-1,13-1,14-1,15-1

NASV - **20,** 1-1,2-1,3-1,4-1,5-1,6-1,7-1,8-1,9-1,10-1,11-1,12-1,13-1,14-1,15-1,16-1,17-1,18-1,19-1,20-1

NCV - **30,** 1-1,2-1,3-1,4-1,5-1,6-1,7-1,8-1,9-1,10-1,11-1,12-1,13-1,14-1,15-1,16-1,17-1,18-1,19-1,20-1,21-1,22-1,23-1,24-1,25-1,26-1,27-1,28-1,29-1,30-1

NIV - **20,** 1-1,2-1,3-1,4-1,5-1,6-1,7-1,8-1,9-1,10-1,11-1,12-1,13-1,14-1,15-1,16-1,17-1,18-1,19-1,20-1

NKJV - **20,** 1-1,2-1,3-1,4-1,5-1,6-1,7-1,8-1,9-1,10-1,11-1,12-1,13-1,14-1,15-1,16-1,17-1,18-1,19-1,20-1

NLT - **30,** 1-1,2-1,3-1,4-1,5-1,6-1,7-1,8-1,9-1,10-1,11-1,12-1,13-1,14-1,15-1,16-1,17-1,18-1,19-1,20-1,21-1,22-1,23-1,24-1,25-1,26-1,27-1,28-1,29-1,30-1

NRSV - **15,** 1-1,2-1,3-1,4-1,5-1,6-1,7-1,8-1,9-1,10-1,11-1,12-1,13-1,14-1,15-1

Conclusion: All versions read the same.

797. Luke 3:25* Which was the son of **Mattathias**, which was the son of **Amos**, which was the son of Naum, which was the son of **Esli**, which was the son of **Nagge**,

AV - **30,** 1-1,2-1,3-1,4-1,5-1,6-1,7-1,8-1,9-1,10-1,11-1,12-1,13-1,14-1,15-1,16-1,17-1,18-1,19-1,20-1,21-1,22-1,23-1,24-1,25-1,26-1,27-1,28-1,29-1,30-1

ESV - **20,** 1-1,2-1,3-1,4-1,5-1,6-1,7-1,8-1,9-1,10-1,11-1,12-1,13-1,14-1,15-1,16-1,17-1,18-1,19-1,20-1

HCSB - **15,** 1-1,2-1,3-1,4-1,5-1,6-1,7-1,8-1,9-1,10-1,11-1,12-1,13-1,14-1,15-1

NASV - **20,** 1-1,2-1,3-1,4-1,5-1,6-1,7-1,8-1,9-1,10-1,11-1,12-1,13-1,14-1,15-1,16-1,17-1,18-1,19-1,20-1

NCV - **30,** 1-1,2-1,3-1,4-1,5-1,6-1,7-1,8-1,9-1,10-1,11-1,12-1,13-1,14-1,15-1,16-1,17-1,18-1,19-1,20-1,21-1,22-1,23-1,24-1,25-1,26-1,27-1,28-1,29-1,30-1

NIV - **20,** 1-1,2-1,3-1,4-1,5-1,6-1,7-1,8-1,9-1,10-1,11-1,12-1,13-1,14-1,15-1,16-1,17-1,18-1,19-1,20-1

NKJV - **20,** 1-1,2-1,3-1,4-1,5-1,6-1,7-1,8-1,9-1,10-1,11-1,12-1,13-1,14-1,15-1,16-1,17-1,18-1,19-1,20-1

NLT - **30,** 1-1,2-1,3-1,4-1,5-1,6-1,7-1,8-1,9-1,10-1,11-1,12-1,13-1,14-1,15-1,16-1,17-1,18-1,19-1,20-1,21-1,22-1,23-1,24-1,25-1,26-1,27-1,28-1,29-1,30-1

NRSV - **15,** 1-1,2-1,3-1,4-1,5-1,6-1,7-1,8-1,9-1,10-1,11-1,12-1,13-1,14-1,15-1

Conclusion: All versions read the same.

798. Luke 3:26* Which was the son of Maath, which was the son of **Mattathias**, which was the son of **Semei,** which was the son of **Joseph**, which was the son of **Juda,**

AV - **30,** 1-1,2-1,3-1,4-1,5-1,6-1,7-1,8-1,9-1,10-1,11-1,12-1,13-1,14-1,15-1,16-1,17-1,18-1,19-1,20-1,21-1,22-1,23-1,24-1,25-1,26-1,27-1,28-1,29-1,30-1

ESV - **20,** 1-1,2-1,3-1,4-1,5-1,6-1,7-1,8-1,9-1,10-1,11-1,12-1,13-1,14-1,15-1,16-1,17-1,18-1,19-1,20-1

HCSB - **15,** 1-1,2-1,3-1,4-1,5-1,6-1,7-1,8-1,9-1,10-1,11-1,12-1,13-1,14-1,15-1

NASV - **20,** 1-1,2-1,3-1,4-1,5-1,6-1,7-1,8-1,9-1,10-1,11-1,12-1,13-1,14-1,15-1,16-1,17-1,18-1,19-1,20-1

NCV - **30,** 1-1,2-1,3-1,4-1,5-1,6-1,7-1,8-1,9-1,10-1,11-1,12-1,13-1,14-1,15-1,16-1,17-1,18-1,19-1,20-1,21-1,22-1,23-1,24-1,25-1,26-1,27-1,28-1,29-1,30-1

NIV - **20,** 1-1,2-1,3-1,4-1,5-1,6-1,7-1,8-1,9-1,10-1,11-1,12-1,13-1,14-1,15-1,16-1,17-1,18-1,19-1,20-1

NKJV - **20,** 1-1,2-1,3-1,4-1,5-1,6-1,7-1,8-1,9-1,10-1,11-1,12-1,13-1,14-1,15-1,16-1,17-1,18-1,19-1,20-1

NLT - **30,** 1-1,2-1,3-1,4-1,5-1,6-1,7-1,8-1,9-1,10-1,11-1,12-1,13-1,14-1,15-1,16-1,17-1,18-1,19-1,20-1,21-1,22-1,23-1,24-1,25-1,26-1,27-1,28-1,29-1,30-1

NRSV - **15,** 1-1,2-1,3-1,4-1,5-1,6-1,7-1,8-1,9-1,10-1,11-1,12-1,13-1,14-1,15-1

Conclusion: All versions read the same.

799. Luke 3:27* Which was the son of **Joanna**, which was the son of **Rhesa**, which was the son of **Zorobabel**, which was the son of **Salathiel**, which was the son of **Neri**,

AV - **30,** 1-1,2-1,3-1,4-1,5-1,6-1,7-1,8-1,9-1,10-1,11-1,12-1,13-1,14-1,15-1,16-1,17-1,18-1,19-1,20-1,21-1,22-1,23-1,24-1,25-1,26-1,27-1,28-1,29-1,30-1

ESV - **20,** 1-1,2-1,3-1,4-1,5-1,6-1,7-1,8-1,9-1,10-1,11-1,12-1,13-1,14-1,15-1,16-1,17-1,18-1,19-1,20-1

HCSB - **15,** 1-1,2-1,3-1,4-1,5-1,6-1,7-1,8-1,9-1,10-1,11-1,12-1,13-1,14-1,15-1

NASV - **20,** 1-1,2-1,3-1,4-1,5-1,6-1,7-1,8-1,9-1,10-1,11-1,12-1,13-1,14-1,15-1,16-1,17-1,18-1,19-1,20-1

NCV - **30,** 1-1,2-1,3-1,4-1,5-1,6-1,7-1,8-1,9-1,10-1,11-1,12-1,13-1,14-1,15-1,16-1,17-1,18-1,19-1,20-1,21-1,22-**2,**23-1,24-1,25-1,26-1,27-1,28-1,29-1,30-1

NIV - **20,** 1-1,2-1,3-1,4-1,5-1,6-1,7-1,8-1,9-1,10-1,11-1,12-1,13-1,14-1,15-1,16-1,17-1,18-1,19-1,20-1

NKJV - **20,** 1-1,2-1,3-1,4-1,5-1,6-1,7-1,8-1,9-1,10-1,11-1,12-1,13-1,14-1,15-1,16-1,17-1,18-1,19-1,20-1

NLT - **30,** 1-1,2-1,3-1,4-1,5-1,6-1,7-1,8-1,9-1,10-1,11-1,12-1,13-1,14-1,15-1,16-1,17-1,18-1,19-1,20-1,21-1,22-1,23-1,24-1,25-1,26-1,27-1,28-1,29-1,30-1

NRSV - **15,** 1-1,2-1,3-1,4-1,5-1,6-1,7-1,8-1,9-1,10-1,11-1,12-1,13-1,14-1,15-1

Conclusion: Only the NCV made the verse more complex.

800. Luke 3:28* Which was the son of **Melchi**, which was the son of **Addi**, which was the son of **Cosam**, which was the son of **Elmodam**, which was the son of Er,

AV - **30,** 1-1,2-1,3-1,4-1,5-1,6-1,7-1,8-1,9-1,10-1,11-1,12-1,13-1,14-1,15-1,16-1,17-1,18-1,19-1,20-1,21-1,22-1,23-1,24-1,25-1,26-1,27-1,28-1,29-1,30-1

ESV - **20,** 1-1,2-1,3-1,4-1,5-1,6-1,7-1,8-1,9-1,10-1,11-1,12-1,13-1,14-1,15-1,16-1,17-1,18-1,19-1,20-1

HCSB - **15,** 1-1,2-1,3-1,4-1,5-1,6-1,7-1,8-1,9-1,10-1,11-1,12-1,13-1,14-1,15-1

NASV - **20,** 1-1,2-1,3-1,4-1,5-1,6-1,7-1,8-1,9-1,10-1,11-1,12-1,13-1,14-1,15-1,16-1,17-1,18-1,19-1,20-1

NCV - **30,** 1-1,2-1,3-1,4-1,5-1,6-1,7-1,8-1,9-1,10-1,11-1,12-1,13-1,14-1,15-1,16-1,17-1,18-1,19-1,20-1,21-1,22-1,23-1,24-1,25-1,26-1,27-1,28-1,29-1,30-1

NIV - **20,** 1-1,2-1,3-1,4-1,5-1,6-1,7-1,8-1,9-1,10-1,11-1,12-1,13-1,14-1,15-1,16-1,17-1,18-1,19-1,20-1

NKJV - **20,** 1-1,2-1,3-1,4-1,5-1,6-1,7-1,8-1,9-1,10-1,11-1,12-1,13-1,14-1,15-1,16-1,17-1,18-1,19-1,20-1

NLT - **30,** 1-1,2-1,3-1,4-1,5-1,6-1,7-1,8-1,9-1,10-1,11-1,12-1,13-1,14-1,15-1,16-1,17-1,18-1,19-1,20-1,21-1,22-1,23-1,24-1,25-1,26-1,27-1,28-1,29-1,30-1

NRSV - **15,** 1-1,2-1,3-1,4-1,5-1,6-1,7-1,8-1,9-1,10-1,11-1,12-1,13-1,14-1,15-1

Conclusion: All versions read the same.

801. Luke 3:29* Which was the son of Jose, which was the son of **Eliezer**, which was the son of **Jorim**, which was the son of **Matthat**, which was the son of **Levi**,

AV - **30,** 1-1,2-1,3-1,4-1,5-1,6-1,7-1,8-1,9-1,10-1,11-1,12-1,13-1,14-1,15-1,16-1,17-1,18-1,19-1,20-1,21-1,22-1,23-1,24-1,25-1,26-1,27-1,28-1,29-1,30-1

ESV - **20,** 1-1,2-1,3-1,4-1,5-1,6-1,7-1,8-1,9-1,10-1,11-1,12-1,13-1,14-1,15-1,16-1,17-1,18-1,19-1,20-1

HCSB - **15,** 1-1,2-1,3-1,4-1,5-1,6-1,7-1,8-1,9-1,10-1,11-1,12-1,13-1,14-1,15-1

NASV - **20,** 1-1,2-1,3-1,4-1,5-1,6-1,7-1,8-1,9-1,10-1,11-1,12-1,13-1,14-1,15-1,16-1,17-1,18-1,19-1,20-1

NCV - **30,** 1-1,2-1,3-1,4-1,5-1,6-1,7-1,8-1,9-1,10-1,11-1,12-1,13-1,14-1,15-1,16-1,17-1,18-1,19-1,20-1,21-1,22-1,23-1,24-1,25-1,26-1,27-1,28-1,29-1,30-1

NIV - **20,** 1-1,2-1,3-1,4-1,5-1,6-1,7-1,8-1,9-1,10-1,11-1,12-1,13-1,14-1,15-1,16-1,17-1,18-1,19-1,20-1

NKJV - **20,** 1-1,2-1,3-1,4-1,5-1,6-1,7-1,8-1,9-1,10-1,11-1,12-1,13-1,14-1,15-1,16-1,17-1,18-1,19-1,20-1

NLT - **30,** 1-1,2-1,3-1,4-1,5-1,6-1,7-1,8-1,9-1,10-1,11-1,12-1,13-1,14-1,15-1,16-1,17-1,18-1,19-1,20-1,21-1,22-1,23-1,24-1,25-1,26-1,27-1,28-1,29-1,30-1

NRSV - **15,** 1-1,2-1,3-1,4-1,5-1,6-1,7-1,8-1,9-1,10-1,11-1,12-1,13-1,14-1,15-1

Conclusion: All versions read the same.

802. Luke 3:30* Which was the son of **Simeon**, which was the so of **Juda**, which was the son of **Joseph**, which was the son of **Jonan**, which was the son of **Eliakim**,

AV - **30,** 1-1,2-1,3-1,4-1,5-1,6-1,7-1,8-1,9-1,10-1,11-1,12-1,13-1,14-1,15-1,16-1,17-1,18-1,19-1,20-1,21-1,22-1,23-1,24-1,25-1,26-1,27-1,28-1,29-1,30-1

ESV - **20,** 1-1,2-1,3-1,4-1,5-1,6-1,7-1,8-1,9-1,10-1,11-1,12-1,13-1,14-1,15-1,16-1,17-1,18-1,19-1,20-1

HCSB - **15,** 1-1,2-1,3-1,4-1,5-1,6-1,7-1,8-1,9-1,10-1,11-1,12-1,13-1,14-1,15-1

NASV - **20,** 1-1,2-1,3-1,4-1,5-1,6-1,7-1,8-1,9-1,10-1,11-1,12-1,13-1,14-1,15-1,16-1,17-1,18-1,19-1,20-1

NCV - **30,** 1-1,2-1,3-1,4-1,5-1,6-1,7-1,8-1,9-1,10-1,11-1,12-1,13-1,14-1,15-1,16-1,17-1,18-1,19-1,20-1,21-1,22-1,23-1,24-1,25-1,26-1,27-1,28-1,29-1,30-1

NIV - **20,** 1-1,2-1,3-1,4-1,5-1,6-1,7-1,8-1,9-1,10-1,11-1,12-1,13-1,14-1,15-1,16-1,17-1,18-1,19-1,20-1

NKJV - **20,** 1-1,2-1,3-1,4-1,5-1,6-1,7-1,8-1,9-1,10-1,11-1,12-1,13-1,14-1,15-1,16-1,17-1,18-1,19-1,20-1

NLT - **30,** 1-1,2-1,3-1,4-1,5-1,6-1,7-1,8-1,9-1,10-1,11-1,12-1,13-1,14-1,15-1,16-1,17-1,18-1,19-1,20-1,21-1,22-1,23-1,24-1,25-1,26-1,27-1,28-1,29-1,30-1

NRSV - **15,** 1-1,2-1,3-1,4-1,5-1,6-1,7-1,8-1,9-1,10-1,11-1,12-1,13-1,14-1,15-1

Conclusion: All versions read the same.

803. Luke 3:31* Which was the son of **Melea**, which was the son of **Menan**, which was the son of **Mattatha**, which was the son of **Nathan**, which was the son of **David**,

AV - **30,** 1-1,2-1,3-1,4-1,5-1,6-1,7-1,8-1,9-1,10-1,11-1,12-1,13-1,14-1,15-1,16-1,17-1,18-1,19-1,20-1,21-1,22-1,23-1,24-1,25-1,26-1,27-1,28-1,29-1,30-1

ESV - **20,** 1-1,2-1,3-1,4-1,5-1,6-1,7-1,8-1,9-1,10-1,11-1,12-1,13-1,14-1,15-1,16-1,17-1,18-1,19-1,20-1

HCSB - **15,** 1-1,2-1,3-1,4-1,5-1,6-1,7-1,8-1,9-1,10-1,11-1,12-1,13-1,14-1,15-1

NASV - **20,** 1-1,2-1,3-1,4-1,5-1,6-1,7-1,8-1,9-1,10-1,11-1,12-1,13-1,14-1,15-1,16-1,17-1,18-1,19-1,20-1

NCV - **30,** 1-1,2-1,3-1,4-1,5-1,6-1,7-1,8-1,9-1,10-1,11-1,12-1,13-1,14-1,15-1,16-1,17-1,18-1,19-1,20-1,21-1,22-1,23-1,24-1,25-1,26-1,27-1,28-1,29-1,30-1

NIV - **20,** 1-1,2-1,3-1,4-1,5-1,6-1,7-1,8-1,9-1,10-1,11-1,12-1,13-1,14-1,15-1,16-1,17-1,18-1,19-1,20-1

NKJV - **20,** 1-1,2-1,3-1,4-1,5-1,6-1,7-1,8-1,9-1,10-1,11-1,12-1,13-1,14-1,15-1,16-1,17-1,18-1,19-1,20-1

NLT - **30,** 1-1,2-1,3-1,4-1,5-1,6-1,7-1,8-1,9-1,10-1,11-1,12-1,13-1,14-1,15-1,16-1,17-1,18-1,19-1,20-1,21-1,22-1,23-1,24-1,25-1,26-1,27-1,28-1,29-1,30-1

NRSV - **15,** 1-1,2-1,3-1,4-1,5-1,6-1,7-1,8-1,9-1,10-1,11-1,12-1,13-1,14-1,15-1

Conclusion: All versions read the same.

804. Luke 3:32* Which was the son of **Jesse**, which was the son of **Obed**, which was the son of Booz, which was the son of Salmon, which was the son of **Naasson**,

AV - **30,** 1-1,2-1,3-1,4-1,5-1,6-1,7-1,8-1,9-1,10-1,11-1,12-1,13-1,14-1,15-1,16-1,17-1,18-1,19-1,20-1,21-1,22-1,23-1,24-1,25-1,26-1,27-1,28-1,29-1,30-1

ESV - **20,** 1-1,2-1,3-1,4-1,5-1,6-1,7-1,8-1,9-1,10-1,11-1,12-1,13-1,14-1,15-1,16-1,17-1,18-1,19-1,20-1

HCSB - **15,** 1-1,2-1,3-1,4-1,5-1,6-1,7-1,8-1,9-1,10-1,11-1,12-1,13-1,14-1,15-1

NASV - **20,** 1-1,2-1,3-1,4-1,5-1,6-1,7-1,8-1,9-1,10-1,11-1,12-1,13-1,14-1,15-1,16-1,17-1,18-1,19-1,20-1

NCV - **30,** 1-1,2-1,3-1,4-1,5-1,6-1,7-1,8-1,9-1,10-1,11-1,12-1,13-1,14-1,15-1,16-1,17-1,18-1,19-1,20-1,21-1,22-1,23-1,24-1,25-1,26-1,27-1,28-1,29-1,30-1

NIV - **20,** 1-1,2-1,3-1,4-1,5-1,6-1,7-1,8-1,9-1,10-1,11-1,12-1,13-1,14-1,15-1,16-1,17-1,18-1,19-1,20-1

NKJV - **20,** 1-1,2-1,3-1,4-1,5-1,6-1,7-1,8-1,9-1,10-1,11-1,12-1,13-1,14-1,15-1,16-1,17-1,18-1,19-1,20-1

NLT - **30,** 1-1,2-1,3-1,4-1,5-1,6-1,7-1,8-1,9-1,10-1,11-1,12-1,13-1,14-1,15-1,16-1,17-1,18·1,19-1,20-1,21-1,22-1,23-1,24-1,25-1,26-1,27-1,28-1,29-1,30-1

NRSV - **15,** 1-1,2-1,3-1,4-1,5-1,6-1,7-1,8-1,9-1,10-1,11-1,12-1,13-1,14-1,15-1

Conclusion: All versions read the same.

805. Luke 3:33* Which was the son of **Aminadab**, which was the son of **Aram**, which was the son of **Esrom**, which was the son of **Phares**, which was the son of **Juda**,

AV - **30,** 1-1,2-1,3-1,4-1,5-1,6-1,7-1,8-1,9-1,10-1,11-1,12-1,13-1,14-1,15-1,16-1,17-1,18-1,19-1,20-1,21-1,22-1,23-1,24-1,25-1,26-1,27-1,28-1,29-1,30-1

ESV - **20,** 1-1,2-1,3-1,4-1,5-1,6-1,7-1,8-1,9-1,10-1,11-1,12-1,13-1,14-1,15-1,16-1,17-1,18-1,19-1,20-1

HCSB - **15,** 1-1,2-1,3-1,4-1,5-1,6-1,7-1,8-1,9-1,10-1,11-1,12-1,13-1,14-1,15-1

NASV - **20,** 1-1,2-1,3-1,4-1,5-1,6-1,7-1,8-1,9-1,10-1,11-1,12-1,13-1,14-1,15-1,16-1,17-1,18-1,19-1,20-1

NCV - **30,** 1-1,2-1,3-1,4-1,5-1,6-1,7-1,8-1,9-1,10-1,11-1,12-1,13-1,14-1,15-1,16-1,17-1,18-1,19-1,20-1,21-1,22-1,23-1,24-1,25-1,26-1,27-1,28-1,29-1,30-1

NIV - **20,** 1-1,2-1,3-1,4-1,5-1,6-1,7-1,8-1,9-1,10-1,11-1,12-1,13-1,14-1,15-1,16-1,17-1,18-1,19-1,20-1

NKJV - **20,** 1-1,2-1,3-1,4-1,5-1,6-1,7-1,8-1,9-1,10-1,11-1,12-1,13-1,14-1,15-1,16-1,17-1,18-1,19-1,20-1

NLT - **30,** 1-1,2-1,3-1,4-1,5-1,6-1,7-1,8-1,9-1,10-1,11-1,12-1,13-1,14-1,15-1,16-1,17-1,18-1,19-1,20-1,21-1,22-1,23-1,24-1,25-1,26-1,27-1,28-1,29-1,30-1

NRSV - **15,** 1-1,2-1,3-1,4-1,5-1,6-1,7-1,8-1,9-1,10-1,11-1,12-1,13-1,14-1,15-1

Conclusion: All versions read the same.

806. Luke 3:34* Which was the son of **Jacob**, which was the son of **Isaac**, which was the son of **Abraham**, which was the son of **Thara**, which was the son of **Nachor**,

AV - **30,** 1-1,2-1,3-1,4-1,5-1,6-1,7-1,8-1,9-1,10-1,11-1,12-1,13-1,14-1,15-1,16-1,17-1,18-1,19-1,20-1,21-1,22-1,23-1,24-1,25-1,26-1,27-1,28-1,29-1,30-1

ESV - **20,** 1-1,2-1,3-1,4-1,5-1,6-1,7-1,8-1,9-1,10-1,11-1,12-1,13-1,14-1,15-1,16-1,17-1,18-1,19-1,20-1

HCSB - **15,** 1-1,2-1,3-1,4-1,5-1,6-1,7-1,8-1,9-1,10-1,11-1,12-1,13-1,14-1,15-1

NASV - **20,** 1-1,2-1,3-1,4-1,5-1,6-1,7-1,8-1,9-1,10-1,11-1,12-1,13-1,14-1,15-1,16-1,17-1,18-1,19-1,20-1

NCV - **30,** 1-1,2-1,3-1,4-1,5-1,6-1,7-1,8-1,9-1,10-1,11-1,12-1,13-1,14-1,15-1,16-1,17-1,18-1,19-1,20-1,21-1,22-1,23-1,24-1,25-1,26-1,27-1,28-1,29-1,30-1

NIV - **20,** 1-1,2-1,3-1,4-1,5-1,6-1,7-1,8-1,9-1,10-1,11-1,12-1,13-1,14-1,15-1,16-1,17-1,18-1,19-1,20-1

NKJV - **20,** 1-1,2-1,3-1,4-1,5-1,6-1,7-1,8-1,9-1,10-1,11-1,12-1,13-1,14-1,15-1,16-1,17-1,18-1,19-1,20-1

NLT - **30,** 1-1,2-1,3-1,4-1,5-1,6-1,7-1,8-1,9-1,10-1,11-1,12-1,13-1,14-1,15-1,16-1,17-1,18-1,19-1,20-1,21-1,22-1,23-1,24-1,25-1,26-1,27-1,28-1,29-1,30-1

NRSV - **15,** 1-1,2-1,3-1,4-1,5-1,6-1,7-1,8-1,9-1,10-1,11-1,12-1,13-1,14-1,15-1

Conclusion: All versions read the same.

807. Luke 3:35* Which was the son of **Saruch**, which was the son of **Ragau**, which was the son of **Phalec**, which was the son of **Heber**, which was the son of **Sala**,

AV - **30,** 1-1,2-1,3-1,4-1,5-1,6-1,7-1,8-1,9-1,10-1,11-1,12-1,13-1,14-1,15-1,16-1,17-1,18-1,19-1,20-1,21-1,22-1,23-1,24-1,25-1,26-1,27-1,28-1,29-1,30-1

ESV - **20,** 1-1,2-1,3-1,4-1,5-1,6-1,7-1,8-1,9-1,10-1,11-1,12-1,13-1,14-1,15-1,16-1,17-1,18-1,19-1,20-1

HCSB - **15,** 1-1,2-1,3-1,4-1,5-1,6-1,7-1,8-1,9-1,10-1,11-1,12-1,13-1,14-1,15-1

NASV - **20,** 1-1,2-1,3-1,4-1,5-1,6-1,7-1,8-1,9-1,10-1,11-1,12-1,13-1,14-1,15-1,16-1,17-1,18-1,19-1,20-1

NCV - **30,** 1-1,2-1,3-1,4-1,5-1,6-1,7-1,8-1,9-1,10-1,11-1,12-1,13-1,14-1,15-1,16-1,17-1,18-1,19-1,20-1,21-1,22-1,23-1,24-1,25-1,26-1,27-1,28-1,29-1,30-1

NIV - **20,** 1-1,2-1,3-1,4-1,5-1,6-1,7-1,8-1,9-1,10-1,11-1,12-1,13-1,14-1,15-1,16-1,17-1,18-1,19-1,20-1

NKJV - **20,** 1-1,2-1,3-1,4-1,5-1,6-1,7-1,8-1,9-1,10-1,11-1,12-1,13-1,14-1,15-1,16-1,17-1,18-1,19-1,20-1

NLT - **30,** 1-1,2-1,3-1,4-1,5-1,6-1,7-1,8-1,9-1,10-1,11-1,12-1,13-1,14-1,15-1,16-1,17-1,18-1,19-1,20-1,21-1,22-1,23-1,24-1,25-1,26-1,27-1,28-1,29-1,30-1

NRSV - **15,** 1-1,2-1,3-1,4-1,5-1,6-1,7-1,8-1,9-1,10-1,11-1,12-1,13-1,14-1,15-1

Conclusion: All versions read the same.

808. Luke 3:36* Which was the son of **Cainan**, which was the son of **Arphaxad**, which was the son of Sem, which was the son of Noe, which was the son of **Lamech**,

AV - **30,** 1-1,2-1,3-1,4-1,5-1,6-1,7-1,8-1,9-1,10-1,11-1,12-1,13-1,14-1,15-1,16-1,17-1,18-1,19-1,20-1,21-1,22-1,23-1,24-1,25-1,26-1,27-1,28-1,29-1,30-1

ESV - **20,** 1-1,2-1,3-1,4-1,5-1,6-1,7-1,8-1,9-1,10-1,11-1,12-1,13-1,14-1,15-1,16-1,17-1,18-1,19-1,20-1

HCSB - **15,** 1-1,2-1,3-1,4-1,5-1,6-1,7-1,8-1,9-1,10-1,11-1,12-1,13-1,14-1,15-1

NASV - **20,** 1-1,2-1,3-1,4-1,5-1,6-1,7-1,8-1,9-1,10-1,11-1,12-1,13-1,14-1,15-1,16-1,17-1,18-1,19-1,20-1

NCV - **30,** 1-1,2-1,3-1,4-1,5-1,6-1,7-1,8-1,9-1,10-1,11-1,12-1,13-1,14-1,15-1,16-1,17-1,18-1,19-1,20-1,21-1,22-1,23-1,24-1,25-1,26-1,27-1,28-1,29-1,30-1

NIV - **20,** 1-1,2-1,3-1,4-1,5-1,6-1,7-1,8-1,9-1,10-1,11-1,12-1,13-1,14-1,15-1,16-1,17-1,18-1,19-1,20-1

NKJV - **20,** 1-1,2-1,3-1,4-1,5-1,6-1,7-1,8-1,9-1,10-1,11-1,12-1,13-1,14-1,15-1,16-1,17-1,18-1,19-1,20-1

NLT - **30,** 1-1,2-1,3-1,4-1,5-1,6-1,7-1,8-1,9-1,10-1,11-1,12-1,13-1,14-1,15-1,16-1,17-1,18-1,19-1,20-1,21-1,22-1,23-1,24-1,25-1,26-1,27-1,28-1,29-1,30-1

NRSV - **15,** 1-1,2-1,3-1,4-1,5-1,6-1,7-1,8-1,9-1,10-1,11-1,12-1,13-1,14-1,15-1

Conclusion: All versions read the same.

809. Luke 3:37* Which was the son of **Mathusala**, which was the son of **Enoch**, which was the son of **Jared**, which was the son of **Maleleel**, which was the son of **Cainan**,

AV - **30,** 1-1,2-1,3-1,4-1,5-1,6-1,7-1,8-1,9-1,10-1,11-1,12-1,13-1,14-1,15-1,16-1,17-1,18-1,19-1,20-1,21-1,22-1,23-1,24-1,25-1,26-1,27-1,28-1,29-1,30-1

ESV - **20,** 1-1,2-1,3-1,4-1,5-1,6-1,7-1,8-1,9-1,10-1,11-1,12-1,13-1,14-1,15-1,16-1,17-1,18-1,19-1,20-1

HCSB - **15,** 1-1,2-1,3-1,4-1,5-1,6-1,7-1,8-1,9-1,10-1,11-1,12-1,13-1,14-1,15-1
NASV - **20,** 1-1,2-1,3-1,4-1,5-1,6-1,7-1,8-1,9-1,10-1,11-1,12-1,13-1,14-1,15-1,16-1,17-1,18-1,19-1,20-1
NCV - **30,** 1-1,2-1,3-1,4-1,5-1,6-1,7-1,8-1,9-1,10-1,11-1,12-1,13-1,14-1,15-1,16-1,17-1,18-1,19-1,20-1,21-1,22-1,23-1,24-1,25-1,26-1,27-1,28-1,29-1,30-1
NIV - **20,** 1-1,2-1,3-1,4-1,5-1,6-1,7-1,8-1,9-1,10-1,11-1,12-1,13-1,14-1,15-1,16-1,17-1,18-1,19-1,20-1
NKJV - **20,** 1-1,2-1,3-1,4-1,5-1,6-1,7-1,8-1,9-1,10-1,11-1,12-1,13-1,14-1,15-1,16-1,17-1,18-1,19-1,20-1
NLT - **30,** 1-1,2-1,3-1,4-1,5-1,6-1,7-1,8-1,9-1,10-1,11-1,12-1,13-1,14-1,15-1,16-1,17-1,18-1,19-1,20-1,21-1,22-1,23-1,24-1,25-1,26-1,27-1,28-1,29-1,30-1
NRSV - **15,** 1-1,2-1,3-1,4-1,5-1,6-1,7-1,8-1,9-1,10-1,11-1,12-1,13-1,14-1,15-1
Conclusion: All versions read the same.

810. Luke 3:38* Which was the son of **Enos**, which was the son of Seth, which was the son of **Adam**, which was the son of God.
AV - **24,** 1-1,2-1,3-1,4-1,5-1,6-1,7-1,8-1,9-1,10-1,11-1,12-1,13-1,14-1,15-1,16-1,17-1,18-1,19-1,20-1,21-1,22-1,23-1,24-1
ESV - **16,** 1-1,2-1,3-1,4-1,5-1,6-1,7-1,8-1,9-1,10-1,11-1,12-1,13-1,14-1,15-1,16-1
HCSB - **12,** 1-1,2-1,3-1,4-1,5-1,6-1,7-1,8-1,9-1,10-1,11-1,12-1
NASV - **16,** 1-1,2-1,3-1,4-1,5-1,6-1,7-1,8-1,9-1,10-1,11-1,12-1,13-1,14-1,15-1,16-1
NCV - **24,** 1-1,2-1,3-1,4-1,5-1,6-1,7-1,8-1,9-1,10-1,11-1,12-1,13-1,14-1,15-1,16-1,17-1,18-1,19-1,20-1,21-1,22-1,23-1,24-1
NIV - **16,** 1-1,2-1,3-1,4-1,5-1,6-1,7-1,8-1,9-1,10-1,11-1,12-1,13-1,14-1,15-1,16-1
NKJV - **16,** 1-1,2-1,3-1,4-1,5-1,6-1,7-1,8-1,9-1,10-1,11-1,12-1,13-1,14-1,15-1,16-1
NLT - **24,** 1-1,2-1,3-1,4-1,5-1,6-1,7-1,8-1,9-1,10-1,11-1,12-1,13-1,14-1,15-1,16-1,17-1,18-1,19-1,20-1,21-1,22-1,23-1,24-1
NRSV - **12,** 1-1,2-1,3-1,4-1,5-1,6-1,7-1,8-1,9-1,10-1,11-1,12-1
Conclusion: All versions read the same.

811. Luke 6:15* Matthew and **Thomas**, James the son of **Alphaeus**, and **Simon** called **Zelotes,**
AV - **12,** 1-1,2-1,3-1,4-1,5-1,6-1,7-1,8-1,9-1,10-1,11-1,12-1
ESV - **17,** 1-1,2-1,3-1,4-1,5-1,6-1,7-1,8-1,9-1,10-1,11-1,12-1,13-1,14-1,15-1,16-1,17-1
HCSB - **13,** 1-1,2-1,3-1,4-1,5-1,6-1,7-1,8-1,9-1,10-1,11-1,12-1,13-1
NASV - **16,** 1-1,2-1,3-1,4-1,5-1,6-1,7-1,8-1,9-1,10-1,11-1,12-1,13-1,14-1,15-1,16-1
NCV - **10,** 1-1,2-1,3-1,4-1,5-1,6-1,7-1,8-1,9-1,10-1
NIV - **12,** 1-1,2-1,3-1,4-1,5-1,6-1,7-1,8-1,9-1,10-1,11-1,12-1
NKJV - **13,** 1-1,2-1,3-1,4-1,5-1,6-1,7-1,8-1,9-1,10-1,11-1,12-1,13-1
NLT - **12,** 1-1,2-1,3-1,4-1,5-1,6-1,7-1,8-1,9-1,10-1,11-1,12-1
NRSV - **16,** 1-1,2-1,3-1,4-1,5-1,6-1,7-1,8-1,9-1,10-1,11-1,12-1,13-1,14-1,15-1,16-1
Conclusion: All versions read the same.

812. Luke 6:46 And why call ye me, Lord, Lord, and do not the things which I say?
AV - **15,** 1-1,2-1,3-1,4-1,5-1,6-1,7-1,8-1,9-1,10-1,11-1,12-1,13-1,14-1,15-1

ESV - **14,** 1-1,2-1,3-1,4-1,5-1,6-1,7-1,8-1,9-1,10-1,11-1,12-1,13-1,14-1
HCSB - **14,** 1-1,2-1,3-1,4-1,5-1,6-1,7-1,8-1,9-1,10-1,11-1,12-1,13-1,14-1
NASV - **14,** 1-1,2-1,3-1,4-1,5-1,6-1,7-1,8-1,9-1,10-1,11-1,12-1,13-1,14-1
NCV - **14,** 1-1,2-1,3-1,4-1,5-1,6-1,7-1,8-1,9-1,10-1,11-1,12-1,13-1,14-1
NIV - **14,** 1-1,2-1,3-1,4-1,5-1,6-1,7-1,8-1,9-1,10-1,11-1,12-1,13-1,14-1
NKJV - **16,** 1-1,2-1,3-1,4-1,5-1,6-1,7-1,8-1,9-1,10-1,11-1,12-1,13-1,14-1,15-1,16-1
NLT - **16,** 1-1,2-1,3-1,4-1,5-1,6-**2**1,7-1,8-1,9-1,10-1,11-1,12-1,13-1,14-1,15-1,16-1
NRSV - **15,** 1-1,2-1,3-1,4-1,5-1,6-1,7-1,8-1,9-1,10-1,11-1,12-1,13-1,14-1,15-1
Conclusion: Only the NLT made the verse more complex.

813. Luke 9:15 And they did so, and made them all sit down.
AV - **10,** 1-1,2-1,3-1,4-1,5-1,6-1,7-1,8-1,9-1,10-1
ESV - **10,** 1-1,2-1,3-1,4-1,5-1,6-1,7-1,8-1,9-1,10-1
HCSB - **9,** 1-1,2-1,3-1,4-1,5-1,6-1,7-1,8-1,9-1
NASV - **9,** 1-1,2-1,3-1,4-1,5-1,6-1,7-1,8-1,9-1
NCV - **11,** 1-1,2-1,3-**3**,4-1,5-1,6-1,7-1,8-1,9-**2**,10-1,11-1
NIV - **8,** 1-1,2-**3**,3-1,4-1,5-1,6-**4**,7-1,8-1
NKJV - **10,** 1-1,2-1,3-1,4-1,5-1,6-1,7-1,8-1,9-1,10-1
NLT - **6,** 1-1,2-1,3-**2**,4-1,5-1,6-1
NRSV - **9,** 1-1,2-1,3-1,4-1,5-1,6-1,7-1,8-1,9-1
Conclusion: Only three modern versions are more complex than the King James Bible.

814. Luke 12:12* For the **Holy** Ghost shall teach you in the same hour what ye ought to say.
AV - **16,** 1-1,2-1,3-1,4-1,5-1,6-1,7-1,8-1,9-1,10-1,11-1,12-1,13-1,14-1,15-1,16-1
ESV - **16,** 1-1,2-1,3-1,4-1,5-1,6-1,7-1,8-1,9-1,10-**2**,11-1,12-1,13-1,14-1,15-1,16-1
HCSB - **15,** 1-1,2-1,3-1,4-1,5-1,6-1,7-1,8-1,9-1,10-**2**,11-1,12-1,13-1,14-1,15-1
NASV - **16,** 1-1,2-1,3-1,4-1,5-1,6-1,7-1,8-1,9-1,10-**2**,11-1,12-1,13-1,14-1,15-1,16-1
NCV - **13,** 1-1,2-1,3-1,4-1,5-1,6-1,7-1,8-1,9-1,10-1,11-1,12-1,13-1
NIV - **14,** 1-1,2-1,3-1,4-1,5-1,6-1,7-1,8-1,9-1,10-1,11-1,12-1,13-1,14-1
NKJV - **16,** 1-1,2-1,3-1,4-1,5-1,6-1,7-1,8-1,9-1,10-**2**,11-1,12-1,13-1,14-1,15-1,16-1
NLT - **15,** 1-1,2-1,3-1,4-1,5-1,6-1,7-1,8-1,9-1,10-1,11-1,12-1,13-1,14-1,15-1
NRSV - **16,** 1-1,2-1,3-1,4-1,5-1,6-1,7-1,8-1,9-1,10-**2**,11-1,12-1,13-1,14-1,15-1,16-1
Conclusion: Five modern versions are more complex than the King James Bible.

815. Luke 14:4 And they held their peace. And he took him, and healed him, and let him go;
AV - **16,** 1-1,2-1,3-1,4-1,5-1,6-1,7-1,8-1,9-1,10-1,11-1,12-1,13-1,14-1,15-1,16-1
ESV - **15,** 1-1,2-1,3-**2**,4-**2**,5-1,6-1,7-1,8-1,9-1,10-1,11-1,12-1,13-1,14-1,15-**2**
HCSB - **14,** 1-1,2-1,3-1,4-**2**,5-1,6-1,7-1,8-1,9-1,10-1,11-1,12-1,13-1,14-**2**
NASV - **17,** 1-1,2-1,3-1,4-**2**,5-1,6-1,7-1,8-1,9-1,10-1,11-1,12-1,13-1,14-1,15-1,16-1,17-**2**
NCV - **18,** 1-1,2-1,3-1,4-1,5-**2**,6-1,7-**2**,8-1,9-1,10-1,11-1,12-1,13-1,14-1,15-1,16-1,17-1,18-**2**
NIV - **17,** 1-1,2-1,3-**2**,4-**2**,5-1,6-**2**,7-1,8-1,9-1,10-1,11-1,12-1,13-1,14-1,15-1,16-1,17-**2**
NKJV - **15,** 1-1,2-1,3-1,4-**2**,5-1,6-1,7-1,8-1,9-1,10-1,11-1,12-1,13-1,14-1,15-1
NLT - **17,** 1-1,2-1,3-**2**,4-1,5-**2**,6-1,7-1,8-1,9-1,10-1,11-1,12-1,13-1,14-1,15-1,16-1,17-**2**
NRSV - **15,** 1-1,2-1,3-1,4-**2**,5-1,6-1,7-1,8-1,9-1,10-1,11-1,12-1,13-1,14-1,15-**2**

Conclusion: All eight modern versions are more complex than the King James Bible.

816. Luke 18:21 And he said, All these have I kept from my youth up.
AV - **12,** 1-1,2-1,3-1,4-1,5-1,6-1,7-1,8-1,9-1,10-1,11-1,12-1
ESV - **11,** 1-1,2-1,3-1,4-1,5-1,6-1,7-1,8-1,9-1,10-1,11-1
HCSB - **10,** 1-1,2-1,3-1,4-1,5-1,6-1,7-1,8-1,9-1,10-1
NASV - **12,** 1-1,2-1,3-1,4-1,5-1,6-1,7-1,8-1,9-1,10-1,11-1,12-1
NCV - **15,** 1-1,2-1,3-**2,**4-1,5-1,6-1,7-**2,**8-1,9-1,10-**2,**11-1,12-1,13-1,14-1,15-1
NIV - **12,** 1-1,2-1,3-1,4-1,5-1,6-1,7-1,8-1,9-1,10-1,11-1,12-1
NKJV - **12,** 1-1,2-1,3-1,4-1,5-1,6-1,7-1,8-1,9-1,10-1,11-1,12-1
NLT - **12,** 1-1,2-1,3-**2,**4-1,5-**2,**6-1,7-1,8-**3,**9-1,10-1,11-1,12-1
NRSV - **10,** 1-1,2-**2,**3-1,4-1,5-1,6-1,7-1,8-1,9-1,10-1
Conclusion: Only three modern versions are more complex than the King James Bible.

817. Luke 18:26 And they that heard it said, Who then can be saved?
AV - **10,** 1-1,2-1,3-1,4-1,5-1,6-1,7-1,8-1,9-1,10-1
ESV - **10,** 1-1,2-1,3-1,4-1,5-1,6-1,7-1,8-1,9-1,10-1
HCSB - **10,** 1-1,2-1,3-1,4-1,5-1,6-1,7-1,8-1,9-1,10-1
NASV - **10,** 1-1,2-1,3-1,4-1,5-1,6-1,7-1,8-1,9-1,10-1
NCV - **12,** 1-1,2-1,3-**2,**4-1,5-1,6-1,7-1,8-1,9-1,10-1,11-1,12-1
NIV - **10,** 1-1,2-1,3-1,4-1,5-1,6-1,7-1,8-1,9-1,10-1
NKJV - **11,** 1-1,2-1,3-1,4-1,5-1,6-1,7-1,8-1,9-1,10-1,11-1
NLT - **13,** 1-1,2-1,3-1,4-1,5-1,6-1,7-1,8-1,9-1,10-1,11-1,12-1,13-1
NRSV - **10,** 1-1,2-1,3-1,4-1,5-1,6-1,7-1,8-1,9-1,10-1
Conclusion: Only the NCV made the verse more complex.

818. Luke 19:10 For the Son of man is come to seek and to save that which was lost.
AV - **16,** 1-1,2-1,3-1,4-1,5-1,6-1,7-1,8-1,9-1,10-1,11-1,12-1,13-1,14-1,15-1,16-1
ESV - **13,** 1-1,2-1,3-1,4-1,5-1,6-1,7-1,8-1,9-1,10-1,11-1,12-1,13-1
HCSB - **14,** 1-1,2-1,3-1,4-1,5-1,6-1,7-1,8-1,9-1,10-1,11-1,12-1,13-1,14-1
NASV - **16,** 1-1,2-1,3-1,4-1,5-1,6-1,7-1,8-1,9-1,10-1,11-1,12-1,13-1,14-1,15-1,16-1
NCV - **12,** 1-1,2-1,3-1,4-1,5-1,6-1,7-1,8-1,9-**2,**10-1,11-1,12-1
NIV - **15,** 1-1,2-1,3-1,4-1,5-1,6-1,7-1,8-1,9-1,10-1,11-1,12-1,13-1,14-1,15-1
NKJV - **16,** 1-1,2-1,3-1,4-1,5-1,6-1,7-1,8-1,9-1,10-1,11-1,12-1,13-1,14-1,15-1,16-1
NLT - **14,** 1-1,2-1,3-1,4-1,5-1,6-1,7-1,8-1,9-1,10-1,11-1,12-1,13-1,14-1
NRSV - **14,** 1-1,2-1,3-1,4-1,5-1,6-1,7-1,8-1,9-1,10-1,11-1,12-1,13-1,14-1
Conclusion: Only the NCV made the verse more complex.

819. Luke 19:34 And they said, The Lord hath need of him.
AV - **8,** 1-1,2-1,3-1,4-1,5-1,6-1,7-1,8-1
ESV - **8,** 1-1,2-1,3-1,4-1,5-1,6-1,7-1,8-1
HCSB - **6,** 1-1,2-1,3-1,4-1,5-1,6-1
NASV - **8,** 1-1,2-1,3-1,4-1,5-1,6-1,7-1,8-1
NCV - **7,** 1-1,2-**3,**3-**2,**4-1,5-**2,**6-1,7-1

NIV - **6,** 1-1,2-**2,**3-1,4-1,5-1,6-1
NKJV - **9,** 1-1,2-1,3-1,4-1,5-1,6-1,7-1,8-1,9-1
NLT - **9,** 1-1,2-1,3-**3,**4-**2,**5-**2,**6-1,7-1,8-1,9-1
NRSV - **6,** 1-1,2-1,3-1,4-1,5-1,6-1
Conclusion: Only three modern versions are more complex than the King James Bible. The NCV and NLT did a good job of making this simple statement complex.

820. Luke 19:36 And as he went, they spread their clothes in the way.
AV - **11,** 1-1,2-1,3-1,4-1,5-1,6-1,7-1,8-1,9-1,10-1,11-1
ESV - 12, 1-1,2-1,3-1,4-1,5-**2,**6-1,7-1,8-1,9-1,10-1,11-1,12-1
HCSB - 13, 1-1,2-1,3-1,4-**2,**5-**2,**6-1,7-1,8-**2,**9-1,10-1,11-1,12-1,13-1
NASV - 12, 1-1,2-1,3-1,4-**2,**5-1,6-1,7-**2,**8-1,9-1,10-1,11-1,12-1
NCV - 14, 1-1,2-1,3-1,4-1,5-1,6-**2,**7-1,8-1,9-1,10-1,11-1,12-1,13-**2,**14-1
NIV - 11, 1-1,2-1,3-1,4-**2,**5-**2,**6-1,7-1,8-1,9-1,10-1,11-1
NKJV - 11, 1-1,2-1,3-1,4-1,5-**2,**6-1,7-1,8-1,9-1,10-1,11-1
NLT - 16, 1-1,2-1,3-1,4-**2,**5-1,6-1,7-1,8-1,9-1,10-**2,**11-1,12-1,13-1,14-**2,**15-1,16-1
NRSV - 12, 1-1,2-1,3-1,4-**2,**5-**2,**6-1,7-**2,**8-1,9-1,10-1,11-1,12-1
Conclusion: All eight modern versions are more complex than the King James Bible. The NCV inserted the names "Jesus" and "Jerusalem" but this was not counted against it since these names would be accepted as proper names under other circumstances.

821. Luke 21:35 For as a snare shall it come on all them that dwell on the face of the whole earth.
AV - **19,** 1-1,2-1,3-1,4-1,5-1,6-1,7-1,8-1,9-1,10-1,11-1,12-1,13-1,14-1,15-1,16-1,17-1,18-1,19-1
ESV - 15, 1-1,2-1,3-1,4-1,5-**2,**6-1,7-1,8-1,9-1,10-1,11-1,12-1,13-1,14-1,15-1
HCSB - **18,** 1-1,2-1,3-1,4-1,5-1,6-1,7-1,8-1,9-1,10-1,11-1,12-1,13-1,14-1,15-1,16-1,17-1,18-1
NASV - 16, 1-1,2-1,3-1,4-1,5-**2,**6-1,7-1,8-1,9-1,10-1,11-1,12-1,13-1,14-1,15-1,16-1
NCV - 8, 1-1,2-1,3-1,4-1,5-1,6-**2,**7-1,8-1
NIV - 16, 1-1,2-1,3-1,4-1,5-**2,**6-1,7-1,8-1,9-1,10-1,11-1,12-1,13-1,14-1,15-1,16-1
NKJV - **19,** 1-1,2-1,3-1,4-1,5-1,6-1,7-1,8-1,9-1,10-1,11-1,12-1,13-1,14-1,15-1,16-1,17-1,18-1,19-1
NLT - 14, 1-1,2-1,3-1,4-1,5-1,6-1,7-1,8-1,9-**2,**10-**4,**11-**2,**12-1,13-1,14-1
NRSV - 18, 1-1,2-1,3-1,4-1,5-1,6-1,7-1,8-**2,**9-1,10-1,11-1,12-1,13-1,14-1,15-1,16-1,17-1,18-1
Conclusion: Six modern versions are more complex than the King James Bible. In a strange twist, the HCSB, NLT and NRSV begin the verse with the last three words of a sentence. They all read; "like a trap. For..."

822. Luke 22:63* And the men that held **Jesus** mocked him, and smote him.
AV - **11,** 1-1,2-1,3-1,4-1,5-1,6-1,7-1,8-1,9-1,10-1,11-1
ESV - 16, 1-1,2-1,3-1,4-1,5-1,6-**2,**7-1,8-1,9-**3,**10-1,11-**2,**12-1,13-1,14-1,15-1,16-1
HCSB - 10, 1-1,2-1,3-1,4-**2,**5-1,6-**2,**7-**2,**8-1,9-**2,**10-1
NASV - 15, 1-1,2-1,3-1,4-1,5-1,6-**2,**7-1,8-1,9-**3,**10-1,11-**2,**12-1,13-1,14-**2,**15-1
NCV - 14, 1-1,2-1,3-1,4-1,5-**2,**6-1,7-**2,**8-**2,**9-1,10-1,11-1,12-1,13-**2,**14-1
NIV - 11, 1-1,2-1,3-1,4-1,5-**2,**6-1,7-**2,**8-**2,**9-1,10-**2,**11-1
NKJV - 11, 1-1,2-1,3-1,4-1,5-1,6-1,7-1,8-1,9-1,10-1,11-1
NLT - 11, 1-1,2-1,3-1,4-1,5-1,6-1,7-**2,**8-**2,**9-1,10-**2,**11-1

NRSV - 14, 1-1,2-1,3-1,4-1,5-1,6-**2**,7-1,8-**2**,9-1,10-1,11-1,12-1,13-1,14-1
Conclusion: Seven modern versions are more complex than the King James Bible.

823. Luke 23:31 For if they do these things in a green tree, what shall be done in the dry?
AV - 17, 1-1,2-1,3-1,4-1,5-1,6-1,7-1,8-1,9-1,10-1,11-1,12-1,13-1,14-1,15-1,16-1,17-1
ESV - 18, 1-1,2-1,3-1,4-1,5-1,6-1,7-1,8-1,9-1,10-1,11-1,12-1,13-1,14-**2**,15-1,16-1,17-1,18-1
HCSB - 18, 1-1,2-1,3-1,4-1,5-1,6-1,7-1,8-1,9-1,10-1,11-1,12-1,13-1,14-**2**,15-1,16-1,17-1,18-1
NASV - 18, 1-1,2-1,3-1,4-1,5-1,6-1,7-1,8-1,9-1,10-1,11-1,12-1,13-1,14-**2**,15-1,16-1,17-1,18-1
NCV - 17, 1-1,2-1,3-1,4-1,5-1,6-1,7-1,8-1,9-1,10-1,11-1,12-1,13-**2**,14-1,15-1,16-1,17-1
NIV - 18, 1-1,2-1,3-1,4-1,5-1,6-1,7-1,8-1,9-1,10-1,11-1,12-1,13-1,14-**2**,15-1,16-1,17-1,18-1
NKJV - 17, 1-1,2-1,3-1,4-1,5-1,6-1,7-1,8-1,9-1,10-1,11-1,12-1,13-1,14-1,15-1,16-1,17-1
NLT - 18, 1-1,2-1,3-1,4-1,5-1,6-1,7-1,8-1,9-1,10-1,11-1,12-1,13-1,14-**2**,15-1,16-1,17-1,18-1
NRSV - 17, 1-1,2-1,3-1,4-1,5-1,6-1,7-1,8-1,9-1,10-1,11-1,12-1,13-**2**,14-1,15-1,16-1,17-1
Conclusion: All eight modern versions are more complex than the King James Bible. All the versions with eighteen words read identical; also, the NCV and NRSV read identical.

824. Luke 24:30 And it came to pass, as he sat at meat with them, he took bread, and blessed it, and brake, and gave to them.
AV - 24, 1-1,2-1,3-1,4-1,5-1,6-1,7-1,8-1,9-1,10-1,11-1,12-1,13-1,14-1,15-1,16-1,17-1,18-1,19-1,20-1,21-1,22-1,23-1,24-1
ESV - 21, 1-1,2-1,3-1,4-1,5-**2**,6-1,7-1,8-1,9-1,10-1,11-1,12-1,13-1,14-1,15-1,16-1,17-1,18-1,19-1,20-1,21-1
HCSB - 24, 1-1,2-1,3-1,4-1,5-**2**,6-1,7-1,8-**2**,9-1,10-1,11-1,12-1,13-1,14-1,15-1,16-1,17-1,18-1,19-1,20-1,21-1,22-1,23-1,24-1
NASV - 25, 1-1,2-1,3-1,4-**2**,5-1,6-1,7-**2**,8-1,9-1,10-1,11-1,12-1,13-1,14-1,15-1,16-1,17-1,18-**2**,19-1,20-1,21-**2**,22-**2**,23-1,24-1,25-1
NCV - 21, 1-1,2-1,3-1,4-1,5-1,6-**2**,7-1,8-1,9-1,10-1,11-1,12-1,13-1,14-1,15-**3**,16-1,17-1,18-1,19-1,20-1,21-1
NIV - 22, 1-1,2-1,3-1,4-1,5-1,6-**2**,7-1,8-1,9-1,10-1,11-1,12-1,13-1,14-1,15-1,16-1,17-**2**,18-1,19-1,20-1,21-1,22-1
NKJV - 26, 1-1,2-1,3-1,4-1,5-1,6-1,7-1,8-1,9-1,10-1,11-**2**,12-1,13-1,14-1,15-1,16-1,17-1,18-1,19-1,20-1,21-1,22-1,23-1,24-1,25-1,26-1
NLT - 22, 1-1,2-1,3-1,4-1,5-1,6-1,7-1,8-1,9-1,10-1,11-1,12-1,13-1,14-1,15-1,16-1,17-1,18-1,19-1,20-1,21-1,22-1
NRSV - 20, 1-1,2-1,3-1,4-1,5-1,6-**2**,7-1,8-1,9-1,10-1,11-1,12-1,13-1,14-1,15-1,16-1,17-1,18-1,19-1,20-1
Conclusion: Seven modern versions are more complex than the King James Bible. Amazing only the NLT did not make the verse more complex. The NASV is the most difficult to read.

825. John 1:4 In him was life; and the life was the light of men.
AV - 12, 1-1,2-1,3-1,4-1,5-1,6-1,7-1,8-1,9-1,10-1,11-1,12-1
ESV - 12, 1-1,2-1,3-1,4-1,5-1,6-1,7-1,8-1,9-1,10-1,11-1,12-1
HCSB - 12, 1-1,2-1,3-1,4-1,5-1,6-1,7-1,8-1,9-1,10-1,11-1,12-1
NASV - 12, 1-1,2-1,3-1,4-1,5-1,6-1,7-1,8-1,9-1,10-1,11-1,12-1

NCV - 14, 1-1,2-1,3-1,4-1,5-1,6-1,7-1,8-1,9-1,10-1,11-1,12-1,13-1,14-**2**
NIV - **12,** 1-1,2-1,3-1,4-1,5-1,6-1,7-1,8-1,9-1,10-1,11-1,12-1
NKJV - **12,** 1-1,2-1,3-1,4-1,5-1,6-1,7-1,8-1,9-1,10-1,11-1,12-1
NLT - 16, 1-1,2-1,3-1,4-1,5-1,6-**4**,7-1,8-1,9-**3**,10-1,11-1,12-1,13-1,14-1,15-1,16-**4**
NRSV - 13, 1-1,2-1,3-1,4-1,5-1,6-1,7-1,8-1,9-1,10-1,11-1,12-1,13-**2**
Conclusion: Only three modern versions are more complex than the King James Bible. The NLT is the most difficult to read.

826. John 1:6 There was a man sent from God, whose name was John.
AV - **11,** 1-1,2-1,3-1,4-1,5-1,6-1,7-1,8-1,9-1,10-1,11-1
ESV - **11,** 1-1,2-1,3-1,4-1,5-1,6-1,7-1,8-1,9-1,10-1,11-1
HCSB - **11,** 1-1,2-1,3-1,4-1,5-1,6-1,7-1,8-1,9-1,10-1,11-1
NASV - **11,** 1-1,2-1,3-1,4-1,5-1,6-1,7-1,8-1,9-1,10-1,11-1
NCV - **11,** 1-1,2-1,3-1,4-1,5-1,6-1,7-1,8-1,9-1,10-1,11-1
NIV - **13,** 1-1,2-1,3-1,4-1,5-1,6-1,7-1,8-1,9-1,10-1,11-1,12-1,13-1
NKJV - **11,** 1-1,2-1,3-1,4-1,5-1,6-1,7-1,8-1,9-1,10-1,11-1
NLT - **7,** 1-1,2-1,3-1,4-1,5-1,6-1,7-1
NRSV - **11,** 1-1,2-1,3-1,4-1,5-1,6-1,7-1,8-1,9-1,10-1,11-1
Conclusion: All versions read the same.

827. John 1:10 He was in the world, and the world was made by him, and the world knew him not.
AV - **18,** 1-1,2-1,3-1,4-1,5-1,6-1,7-1,8-1,9-1,10-1,11-1,12-1,13-1,14-1,15-1,16-1,17-1,18-1
ESV - **19,** 1-1,2-1,3-1,4-1,5-1,6-1,7-1,8-1,9-1,10-1,11-1,12-1,13-1,14-1,15-1,16-1,17-1,18-1,19-1
HCSB - 19, 1-1,2-1,3-1,4-1,5-1,6-1,7-1,8-1,9-1,10-**3**,11-1,12-1,13-1,14-1,15-1,16-1,17-1,18-**3**,19-1
NASV - **19,** 1-1,2-1,3-1,4-1,5-1,6-1,7-1,8-1,9-1,10-1,11-1,12-1,13-1,14-1,15-1,16-1,17-1,18-1,19-1
NCV - **20,** 1-1,2-1,3-1,4-1,5-1,6-1,7-1,8-1,9-1,10-1,11-1,12-1,13-1,14-1,15-1,16-1,17-1,18-1,19-1,20-1
NIV - 19, 1-1,2-1,3-1,4-1,5-1,6-1,7-1,8-1,9-1,10-1,11-1,12-1,13-1,14-1,15-1,16-1,17-1,18-**3**,19-1
NKJV - **19,** 1-1,2-1,3-1,4-1,5-1,6-1,7-1,8-1,9-1,10-1,11-1,12-1,13-1,14-1,15-1,16-1,17-1,18-1,19-1
NLT - 14, 1-1,2-1,3-**2**,4-1,5-**2**,6-1,7-1,8-**3**,9-1,10-1,11-1,12-**2**,13-**3**,14-1
NRSV - 20, 1-1,2-1,3-1,4-1,5-1,6-1,7-1,8-1,9-1,10-**2**,11-**2**,12-1,13-1,14-1,15-1,16-1,17-1,18-1,19-1,20-1
Conclusion: Four modern versions are more complex than the King James Bible. Through heroic efforts, the NLT again managed to be the most difficult to read.

828. John 1:13 Which were born, not of blood, nor of the will of the flesh, nor of the will of man, but of God.
AV - **22,** 1-1,2-1,3-1,4-1,5-1,6-1,7-1,8-1,9-1,10-1,11-1,12-1,13-1,14-1,15-1,16-1,17-1,18-1,19-1,20-1,21-1,22-1
ESV - **22,** 1-1,2-1,3-1,4-1,5-1,6-1,7-1,8-1,9-1,10-1,11-1,12-1,13-1,14-1,15-1,16-1,17-1,18-1,19-1,20-1,21-1,22-1
HCSB - **22,** 1-1,2-1,3-1,4-1,5-1,6-1,7-1,8-1,9-1,10-1,11-1,12-1,13-1,14-1,15-1,16-1,17-1,18-1,19-1,20-1,21-1,22-1

NASV - **22,** 1-1,2-1,3-1,4-1,5-1,6-1,7-1,8-1,9-1,10-1,11-1,12-1,13-1,14-1,15-1,16-1,17-1,18-1,19-1,20-1,21-1,22-1

NCV - **22,** 1-1,2-1,3-1,4-**2,**5-1,6-**2,**7-1,8-**2,**9-**2,**10-1,11-1,12-**2,**13-**2,**14-**2,**15-1,16-**2,**17-**2,**18-1,19-1,20-1,21-1,22-1

NIV - **18,** 1-**2,**2-1,3-1,4-1,5-**3,**6-**2,**7-1,8-1,9-**2,**10-**3,**11-1,12-1,13-**2,**14-1,15-1,16-1,17-1,18-1

NKJV - **22,** 1-1,2-1,3-1,4-1,5-1,6-1,7-1,8-1,9-1,10-1,11-1,12-1,13-1,14-1,15-1,16-1,17-1,18-1,19-1,20-1,21-1,22-1

NLT - **21,** 1-1,2-1,3-**2,**4-1,5-1,6-1,7-**3,**8-1,9-**3,**10-1,11-**2,**12-**2,**13-1,14-1,15-1,16-1,17-1,18-1,19-1,20-1,21-1

NRSV - **22,** 1-1,2-1,3-1,4-1,5-1,6-1,7-1,8-1,9-1,10-1,11-1,12-1,13-1,14-1,15-1,16-1,17-1,18-1,19-1,20-1,21-1,22-1

Conclusion: Only three modern versions are more complex than the King James Bible. The NCV, NIV and NLT ran a stiff competition, but the NLT worked hard to become the most difficult to read.

829. John 1:24* And they which were sent were of the **Pharisees**.
AV - **9,** 1-1,2-1,3-1,4-1,5-1,6-1,7-1,8-1,9-1
ESV - **8,** 1-1,2-1,3-1,4-1,5-1,6-1,7-1,8-1
HCSB - **8,** 1-1,2-1,3-1,4-1,5-1,6-1,7-1,8-1
NASV - **8,** 1-1,2-1,3-1,4-1,5-1,6-1,7-1,8-1
NCV - **8,** 1-1,2-1,3-1,4-1,5-1,6-1,7-1,8-1
NIV - **7,** 1-1,2-1,3-1,4-1,5-1,6-1,7-1
NKJV - **9,** 1-1,2-1,3-1,4-1,5-1,6-1,7-1,8-1,9-1
NLT - **7,** 1-1,2-1,3-1,4-1,5-1,6-1,7-1
NRSV - **8,** 1-1,2-1,3-1,4-1,5-1,6-1,7-1,8-1
Conclusion: All versions read the same.

830. John 3:6* That which is born of the flesh is flesh; and that which is born of the **Spirit** is **spirit**.
AV - **19,** 1-1,2-1,3-1,4-1,5-1,6-1,7-1,8-1,9-1,10-1,11-1,12-1,13-1,14-1,15-1,16-1,17-1,18-1,19-1
ESV - **19,** 1-1,2-1,3-1,4-1,5-1,6-1,7-1,8-1,9-1,10-1,11-1,12-1,13-1,14-1,15-1,16-1,17-1,18-1,19-1
HCSB - 17, 1-**3,**2-1,3-1,4-1,5-1,6-1,7-1,8-1,9-1,10-**3,**11-1,12-1,13-1,14-1,15-1,16-1,17-1
NASV - **19,** 1-1,2-1,3-1,4-1,5-1,6-1,7-1,8-1,9-1,10-1,11-1,12-1,13-1,14-1,15-1,16-1,17-1,18-1,19-1
NCV - 13, 1-**2,**2-1,3-1,4-1,5-**2,**6-**2,**7-1,8-**3,**9-1,10-1,11-1,12-1,13-1
NIV - **12,** 1-1,2-1,3-1,4-1,5-1,6-1,7-1,8-1,9-1,10-1,11-1,12-1
NKJV - **19,** 1-1,2-1,3-1,4-1,5-1,6-1,7-1,8-1,9-1,10-1,11-1,12-1,13-1,14-1,15-1,16-1,17-1,18-1,19-1
NLT - 15, 1-**2,**2-1,3-**3,**4-**2,**5-**2,**6-1,7-1,8-1,9-1,10-1,11-1,12-1,13-1,14-**3,**15-1
NRSV - **17,** 1-1,2-1,3-1,4-1,5-1,6-1,7-1,8-1,9-1,10-1,11-1,12-1,13-1,14-1,15-1,16-1,17-1
Conclusion: Only three modern versions are more complex than the King James Bible. The NCV and the NLT are tied for being the most difficult to read.

831. John 4:4* And he must needs go through **Samaria**.
AV - **7,** 1-1,2-1,3-1,4-1,5-1,6-1,7-1
ESV - **7,** 1-1,2-1,3-1,4-1,5-1,6-1,7-1
HCSB - 6, 1-1,2-1,3-1,4-**2,**5-1,6-1
NASV - **7,** 1-1,2-1,3-1,4-1,5-1,6-1,7-1

NCV - 13, 1-1,2-1,3-1,4-1,5-1,6-1,7-1,8-1,9-1,10-1,11-**2**,12-1,13-1
NIV - **7,** 1-1,2-1,3-1,4-1,5-1,6-1,7-1
NKJV - 7, 1-1,2-1,3-**2**,4-1,5-1,6-1,7-1
NLT - **9,** 1-1,2-1,3-1,4-1,5-1,6-1,7-1,8-1,9-1
NRSV - 7, 1-1,2-1,3-1,4-1,5-1,6-1,7-1
Conclusion: Only three modern versions are more complex than the King James Bible.

832. John 5:40 And ye will not come to me, that ye might have life.
AV -**12,** 1-1,2-1,3-1,4-1,5-1,6-1,7-1,8-1,9-1,10-1,11-1,12-1
ESV - 12, 1-1,2-1,3-**2**,4-1,5-1,6-1,7-1,8-1,9-1,10-1,11-1,12-1
HCSB - 14, 1-1,2-1,3-1,4-1,5-**2**,6-1,7-1,8-1,9-1,10-1,11-1,12-1,13-1,14-1
NASV - 14, 1-1,2-1,3-1,4-**3**,5-1,6-1,7-1,8-1,9-1,10-1,11-1,12-1,13-1,14-1
NCV - 11, 1-1,2-1,3-**2**,4-1,5-1,6-1,7-1,8-1,9-1,10-1,11-1
NIV - 10, 1-1,2-1,3-**2**,4-1,5-1,6-1,7-1,8-1,9-1,10-1
NKJV - 13, 1-1,2-1,3-1,4-**2**,5-1,6-1,7-1,8-1,9-1,10-1,11-1,12-1,13-1
NLT - 11, 1-1,2-1,3-**2**,4-1,5-1,6-1,7-1,8-1,9-**2**,10-1,11-1
NRSV - 10, 1-1,2-1,3-**2**,4-1,5-1,6-1,7-1,8-1,9-1,10-1
Conclusion: All eight modern versions are more complex than the King James Bible.

833. John 5:42 But I know you, that ye have not the love of God in you.
AV - **14,** 1-1,2-1,3-1,4-1,5-1,6-1,7-1,8-1,9-1,10-1,11-1,12-1,13-1,14-1
ESV - 14, 1-1,2-1,3-1,4-1,5-1,6-1,7-1,8-1,9-1,10-1,11-1,12-1,13-**2**,14-1
HCSB - 13, 1-1,2-1,3-1,4-1,5-1,6-1,7-1,8-1,9-1,10-1,11-1,12-**2**,13-1
NASV - 15, 1-1,2-1,3-1,4-1,5-1,6-1,7-1,8-1,9-1,10-1,11-1,12-1,13-1,14-1,15-**2**
NCV - **14,** 1-1,2-1,3-1,4-1,5-1,6-1,7-1,8-1,9-1,10-1,11-1,12-1,13-1,14-1
NIV - **18,** 1-1,2-1,3-1,4-1,5-1,6-1,7-1,8-1,9-1,10-1,11-1,12-1,13-1,14-1,15-1,16-1,17-1,18-1
NKJV - **15,** 1-1,2-1,3-1,4-1,5-1,6-1,7-1,8-1,9-1,10-1,11-1,12-1,13-1,14-1,15-1
NLT - 10, 1-**2**,2-1,3-1,4-1,5-1,6-1,7-1,8-1,9-**2**,10-1
NRSV - **14,** 1-1,2-1,3-1,4-1,5-1,6-1,7-1,8-1,9-1,10-1,11-1,12-1,13-1,14-1
Conclusion: Four modern versions are more complex than the King James Bible.

834. John 6:48 I am that bread of life.
AV - **6,** 1-1,2-1,3-1,4-1,5-1,6-1
ESV - **6,** 1-1,2-1,3-1,4-1,5-1,6-1
HCSB - **6,** 1-1,2-1,3-1,4-1,5-1,6-1
NASV - **6,** 1-1,2-1,3-1,4-1,5-1,6-1
NCV - **7,** 1-1,2-1,3-1,4-1,5-1,6-1,7-1
NIV - **6,** 1-1,2-1,3-1,4-1,5-1,6-1
NKJV - **6,** 1-1,2-1,3-1,4-1,5-1,6-1
NLT - **7,** 1-1,2-1,3-1,4-1,5-1,6-1,7-1
NRSV - **6,** 1-1,2-1,3-1,4-1,5-1,6-1
Conclusion: All versions read the same.

835. John 7:11 Then the Jews sought him at the feast, and said, Where is he?
AV - **13,** 1-1,2-1,3-1,4-1,5-1,6-1,7-1,8-1,9-1,10-1,11-1,12-1,13-1
ESV - **14,** 1-1,2-1,3-1,4-**2,**5-1,6-1,7-1,8-1,9-1,10-1,11-**2,**12-1,13-1,14-1
HCSB - **14,** 1-1,2-1,3-1,4-**2,**5-1,6-1,7-1,8-1,9-**3,**10-1,11-**2,**12-1,13-1,14-1
NASV - **15,** 1-1,2-1,3-1,4-1,5-**2,**6-1,7-1,8-1,9-1,10-1,11-1,12-**2,**13-1,14-1,15-1
NCV - **15,** 1-1,2-1,3-1,4-1,5-**2,**6-1,7-**2,**8-1,9-1,10-1,11-**2,**12-1,13-1,14-1,15-1
NIV - **16,** 1-1,2-1,3-1,4-1,5-1,6-1,7-1,8-**2,**9-1,10-1,11-1,12-**2,**13-1,14-1,15-1,16-1
NKJV - **13,** 1-1,2-1,3-1,4-1,5-1,6-1,7-1,8-1,9-1,10-1,11-1,12-1,13-1
NLT - **18,** 1-1,2-**2,**3-**2,**4-1,5-1,6-1,7-1,8-1,9-1,10-**3,**11-1,12-1,13-**2,**14-1,15-**3,**16-1,17-1,18-1
NRSV - **13,** 1-1,2-1,3-**2,**4-1,5-1,6-1,7-1,8-**3,**9-1,10-**2,**11-1,12-1,13-1
Conclusion: Seven modern versions are more complex than the King James Bible. The NLT is the most difficult to read.

836. John 7:29 But I know him: for I am from him, and he hath sent me.
AV - **14,** 1-1,2-1,3-1,4-1,5-1,6-1,7-1,8-1,9-1,10-1,11-1,12-1,13-1,14-1
ESV - **12,** 1-1,2-1,3-1,4-1,5-1,6-1,7-1,8-1,9-1,10-1,11-1,12-1
HCSB - **12,** 1-1,2-1,3-1,4-**2,**5-1,6-1,7-1,8-1,9-1,10-1,11-1,12-1
NASV - **12,** 1-1,2-1,3-1,4-**2,**5-1,6-1,7-1,8-1,9-1,10-1,11-1,12-1
NCV - **13,** 1-1,2-1,3-1,4-1,5-**2,**6-1,7-1,8-1,9-1,10-1,11-1,12-1,13-1
NIV - **12,** 1-1,2-1,3-1,4-**2,**5-1,6-1,7-1,8-1,9-1,10-1,11-1,12-1
NKJV - **12,** 1-1,2-1,3-1,4-1,5-1,6-1,7-1,8-1,9-1,10-1,11-1,12-1
NLT - **15,** 1-1,2-1,3-1,4-1,5-**2,**6-1,7-1,8-1,9-1,10-1,11-1,12-1,13-1,14-1,15-1
NRSV - **12,** 1-1,2-1,3-1,4-**2,**5-1,6-1,7-1,8-1,9-1,10-1,11-1,12-1
Conclusion: Six modern versions are more complex than the King James Bible.

837. John 8:32 And ye shall know the truth, and the truth shall make you free.
AV - **13,** 1-1,2-1,3-1,4-1,5-1,6-1,7-1,8-1,9-1,10-1,11-1,12-1,13-1
ESV - **13,** 1-1,2-1,3-1,4-1,5-1,6-1,7-1,8-1,9-1,10-1,11-1,12-1,13-1
HCSB - **12,** 1-1,2-1,3-1,4-1,5-1,6-1,7-1,8-1,9-1,10-1,11-1,12-1
NASV - **13,** 1-1,2-1,3-1,4-1,5-1,6-1,7-1,8-1,9-1,10-1,11-1,12-1,13-1
NCV - **13,** 1-1,2-1,3-1,4-1,5-1,6-1,7-1,8-1,9-1,10-1,11-1,12-1,13-1
NIV - **13,** 1-1,2-1,3-1,4-1,5-1,6-1,7-1,8-1,9-1,10-1,11-1,12-1,13-1
NKJV - **13,** 1-1,2-1,3-1,4-1,5-1,6-1,7-1,8-1,9-1,10-1,11-1,12-1,13-1
NLT - **13,** 1-1,2-1,3-1,4-1,5-1,6-1,7-1,8-1,9-1,10-1,11-1,12-1,13-1
NRSV - **13,** 1-1,2-1,3-1,4-1,5-1,6-1,7-1,8-1,9-1,10-1,11-1,12-1,13-1
Conclusion: All versions read the same.

838. John 8:38* I speak that which I have seen with my **Father**: and ye do that which ye have seen with your **father**.
AV - **21,** 1-1,2-1,3-1,4-1,5-1,6-1,7-1,8-1,9-1,10-1,11-1,12-1,13-1,14-1,15-1,16-1,17-1,18-1,19-1,20-1,21-1
ESV - **20,** 1-1,2-1,3-1,4-1,5-1,6-1,7-1,8-1,9-1,10-1,11-1,12-1,13-1,14-1,15-1,16-1,17-1,18-1,19-1,20-1

HCSB - **23,** 1-1,2-1,3-1,4-1,5-1,6-1,7-1,8-1,9-**2,**10-1,11-1,12-1,13-1,14-**2,**15-1,16-1,17-1,18-1,19-1,20-1,21-1,22-1,23-1

NASV - **23,** 1-1,2-1,3-1,4-1,5-1,6-1,7-1,8-1,9-1,10-1,11-1,12-**2,**13-1,14-**2,**15-1,16-1,17-1,18-1,19-1,20-1,21-1,22-1,23-1

NCV - **19,** 1-1,2-1,3-**2,**4-1,5-1,6-1,7-1,8-1,9-1,10-1,11-1,12-1,13-1,14-1,15-1,16-1,17-1,18-1,19-1

NIV - **22,** 1-1,2-1,3-**2,**4-1,5-1,6-1,7-1,8-1,9-1,10-1,11-1,12-**2,**13-1,14-1,15-1,16-1,17-1,18-1,19-1,20-1,21-1,22-1

NKJV - **19,** 1-1,2-1,3-1,4-1,5-1,6-1,7-1,8-1,9-1,10-1,11-1,12-1,13-1,14-1,15-1,16-1,17-1,18-1,19-1

NLT - **22,** 1-1,2-1,3-**2,**4-1,5-1,6-1,7-1,8-1,9-1,10-1,11-1,12-1,13-1,14-1,15-1,16-1,17-**3,**18-1,19-**2,**20-1,21-1,22-1

NRSV - **23,** 1-1,2-**2,**3-1,4-1,5-1,6-1,7-1,8-1,9-1,10-**2,**11-1,12-1,13-1,14-1,15-1,16-1,17-1,18-1,19-1,20-1,21-1,22-1,23-1

Conclusion: Six modern versions are more complex than the King James Bible.

839. John 8:40* But now ye seek to kill me, a man that hath told you the truth, which I have heard of God: this did not **Abraham**.

AV - **25,** 1-1,2-1,3-1,4-1,5-1,6-1,7-1,8-1,9-1,10-1,11-1,12-1,13-1,14-1,15-1,16-1,17-1,18-1,19-1,20-1,21-1,22-1,23-1,24-1,25-1

ESV - **26,** 1-1,2-1,3-1,4-1,5-1,6-1,7-1,8-1,9-1,10-1,11-1,12-1,13-1,14-1,15-1,16-1,17-1,18-1,19-1,20-1,21-1,22-1,23-1,24-1,25-1,26-1

HCSB - **26,** 1-1,2-1,3-1,4-1,5-**2,**6-1,7-1,8-1,9-1,10-1,11-1,12-1,13-1,14-1,15-1,16-1,17-1,18-1,19-1,20-1,21-1,22-1,23-1,24-1,25-1,26-1

NASV - **28,** 1-1,2-1,3-1,4-1,5-1,6-1,7-**2,**8-1,9-1,10-1,11-1,12-1,13-1,14-1,15-1,16-1,17-1,18-1,19-1,20-1,21-1,22-1,23-1,24-1,25-1,26-1,27-1,28-1

NCV - **27,** 1-1,2-1,3-1,4-1,5-1,6-1,7-1,8-1,9-1,10-1,11-1,12-1,13-1,14-1,15-1,16-1,17-1,18-1,19-**2,**20-1,21-1,22-1,23-1,24-1,25-**2,**26-1,27-1

NIV - **28,** 1-1,2-1,3-1,4-1,5-1,6-**3,**7-1,8-1,9-1,10-1,11-1,12-1,13-1,14-1,15-1,16-1,17-1,18-1,19-1,20-1,21-1,22-1,23-1,24-1,25-1,26-1,27-1,28-1

NKJV - **25,** 1-1,2-1,3-1,4-1,5-1,6-1,7-1,8-1,9-1,10-1,11-1,12-1,13-1,14-1,15-1,16-1,17-1,18-1,19-1,20-1,21-1,22-1,23-1,24-1,25-1

NLT - **24,** 1-**2,**2-1,3-1,4-**2,**5-1,6-1,7-1,8-**2,**9-1,10-1,11-1,12-1,13-1,14-1,15-1,16-1,17-1,18-1,19-1,20-**2,**21-1,22-1,23-1,24-1

NRSV - **27,** 1-1,2-1,3-1,4-1,5-**2,**6-1,7-1,8-1,9-1,10-1,11-1,12-1,13-1,14-1,15-1,16-1,17-1,18-1,19-1,20-1,21-1,22-1,23-1,24-1,25-1,26-1,27-1

Conclusion: Six modern versions are more complex than the King James Bible. The NLT is the most difficult to read.

840. John 9:1* And as **Jesus** passed by, he saw a man which was blind from his birth.

AV - **15,** 1-1,2-1,3-1,4-1,5-1,6-1,7-1,8-1,9-1,10-1,11-1,12-1,13-1,14-1,15-1

ESV - **11,** 1-1,2-1,3-1,4-1,5-1,6-1,7-1,8-1,9-1,10-1,11-1

HCSB - **12,** 1-1,2-1,3-1,4-**2,**5-1,6-1,7-1,8-1,9-1,10-1,11-1,12-1

NASV - **11,** 1-1,2-1,3-1,4-1,5-1,6-1,7-1,8-1,9-1,10-1,11-1

NCV - **14,** 1-1,2-1,3-1,4-**2,**5-**2,**6-1,7-1,8-1,9-1,10-1,11-1,12-1,13-1,14-1

NIV - **11,** 1-1,2-1,3-1,4-**2,**5-1,6-1,7-1,8-1,9-1,10-1,11-1

NKJV - **14,** 1-1,2-1,3-1,4-1,5-1,6-1,7-1,8-1,9-1,10-1,11-1,12-1,13-1,14-1
NLT - 15, 1-1,2-1,3-1,4-**2**,5-**2**,6-1,7-1,8-1,9-1,10-1,11-1,12-1,13-1,14-1,15-1
NRSV - 11, 1-1,2-1,3-1,4-**2**,5-1,6-1,7-1,8-1,9-1,10-1,11-1
Conclusion: Five modern versions are more complex than the King James Bible.

841. John 9:5 As long as I am in the world, I am the light of the world.
AV - **15,** 1-1,2-1,3-1,4-1,5-1,6-1,7-1,8-1,9-1,10-1,11-1,12-1,13-1,14-1,15-1
ESV - **15,** 1-1,2-1,3-1,4-1,5-1,6-1,7-1,8-1,9-1,10-1,11-1,12-1,13-1,14-1,15-1
HCSB - **15,** 1-1,2-1,3-1,4-1,5-1,6-1,7-1,8-1,9-1,10-1,11-1,12-1,13-1,14-1,15-1
NASV - **13,** 1-1,2-1,3-1,4-1,5-1,6-1,7-1,8-1,9-1,10-1,11-1,12-1,13-1
NCV - **13,** 1-1,2-1,3-1,4-1,5-1,6-1,7-1,8-1,9-1,10-1,11-1,12-1,13-1
NIV - **13,** 1-1,2-1,3-1,4-1,5-1,6-1,7-1,8-1,9-1,10-1,11-1,12-1,13-1
NKJV - **15,** 1-1,2-1,3-1,4-1,5-1,6-1,7-1,8-1,9-1,10-1,11-1,12-1,13-1,14-1,15-1
NLT - **15,** 1-1,2-1,3-1,4-1,5-1,6-1,7-1,8-1,9-1,10-1,11-1,12-1,13-1,14-1,15-1
NRSV - **15,** 1-1,2-1,3-1,4-1,5-1,6-1,7-1,8-1,9-1,10-1,11-1,12-1,13-1,14-1,15-1
Conclusion: All versions read the same.

842. John 10:30* I and my **Father** are one.
AV - **6,** 1-1,2-1,3-1,4-1,5-1,6-1
ESV - **6,** 1-1,2-1,3-1,4-1,5-1,6-1
HCSB - **6,** 1-1,2-1,3-1,4-1,5-1,6-1
NASV - **6,** 1-1,2-1,3-1,4-1,5-1,6-1
NCV - **6,** 1-1,2-1,3-1,4-1,5-1,6-1
NIV - **6,** 1-1,2-1,3-1,4-1,5-1,6-1
NKJV - **6,** 1-1,2-1,3-1,4-1,5-1,6-1
NLT - **6,** 1-1,2-1,3-1,4-1,5-1,6-1
NRSV - **6,** 1-1,2-1,3-1,4-1,5-1,6-1
Conclusion: While it would seem that all versions read the same, there is a seemingly minor difference that makes a major change. All modern versions, except the NKJV, remove the personal pronoun "my" from the text and say only, "the" Father, thus excluding the relationship between God the Father and God the Son. The NKJV reads "My."

843. John 11:35* **Jesus** wept.
AV - **2,** 1-1,2-1
ESV - **2,** 1-1,2-1
HCSB - **2,** 1-1,2-1
NASV - **2,** 1-1,2-1
NCV - **2,** 1-1,2-1
NIV - **2,** 1-1,2-1
NKJV - **2,** 1-1,2-1
NLT - **3,** 1-1,2-1,3-1
NRSV - 4, 1-1,2-**2**,3-1,4-1
Conclusion: Only the NRSV managed to make the verse more complex.

844. John 11:46* But some of them went their ways to the **Pharisees**, and told them what things **Jesus** had done.
AV - **18,** 1-1,2-1,3-1,4-1,5-1,6-1,7-1,8-1,9-1,10-1,11-1,12-1,13-1,14-1,15-1,16-1,17-1,18-1
ESV - **15,** 1-1,2-1,3-1,4-1,5-1,6-1,7-1,8-1,9-1,10-1,11-1,12-1,13-1,14-1,15-1
HCSB - **15,** 1-1,2-1,3-1,4-1,5-1,6-1,7-1,8-1,9-1,10-1,11-1,12-1,13-1,14-1,15-1
NASV - **17,** 1-1,2-1,3-1,4-1,5-1,6-1,7-1,8-1,9-1,10-1,11-1,12-1,13-1,14-1,15-1,16-1,17-1
NCV - **15,** 1-1,2-1,3-1,4-1,5-1,6-1,7-1,8-1,9-1,10-1,11-1,12-1,13-1,14-1,15-1
NIV - **15,** 1-1,2-1,3-1,4-1,5-1,6-1,7-1,8-1,9-1,10-1,11-1,12-1,13-1,14-1,15-1
NKJV - 16, 1-1,2-1,3-1,4-1,5-1,6-**2,**7-1,8-1,9-1,10-1,11-1,12-1,13-1,14-1,15-1,16-1
NLT - **13,** 1-1,2-1,3-1,4-1,5-1,6-1,7-1,8-1,9-1,10-1,11-1,12-1,13-1
NRSV - **15,** 1-1,2-1,3-1,4-1,5-1,6-1,7-1,8-1,9-1,10-1,11-1,12-1,13-1,14-1,15-1
Conclusion: Amazingly, this is one of the rare occasions when the NKJV is the only modern version to make the verse more complex.

845. John 12:43 For they loved the praise of men more than the praise of God.
AV - **13,** 1-1,2-1,3-1,4-1,5-1,6-1,7-1,8-1,9-1,10-1,11-1,12-1,13-1
ESV - 17, 1-1,2-1,3-1,4-1,5-**2,**6-1,7-1,8-1,9-1,10-1,11-1,12-1,13-**2,**14-1,15-1,16-1,17-1
HCSB - **11,** 1-1,2-1,3-1,4-1,5-1,6-1,7-1,8-1,9-1,10-1,11-1
NASV - 13, 1-1,2-1,3-1,4-1,5-**3,**6-1,7-1,8-**2,**9-1,10-1,11-**3,**12-1,13-1
NCV - 10, 1-1,2-1,3-1,4-1,5-**2,**6-1,7-1,8-1,9-1,10-1
NIV - **11,** 1-1,2-1,3-1,4-1,5-1,6-1,7-1,8-1,9-1,10-1,11-1
NKJV - **13,** 1-1,2-1,3-1,4-1,5-1,6-1,7-1,8-1,9-1,10-1,11-1,12-1,13-1
NLT - 11, 1-1,2-1,3-1,4-**2,**5-1,6-1,7-1,8-1,9-1,10-1,11-1
NRSV - 13, 1-1,2-1,3-1,4-**2,**5-**2,**6-1,7-1,8-1,9-**2,**10-1,11-1,12-1,13-1
Conclusion: Five modern versions are more complex than the King James Bible.

846. John 13:13* Ye call me **Master** and Lord: and ye say well; for so I am.
AV - **14,** 1-1,2-1,3-1,4-1,5-1,6-1,7-1,8-1,9-1,10-1,11-1,12-1,13-1,14-1
ESV - **14,** 1-1,2-1,3-1,4-1,5-1,6-1,7-1,8-1,9-1,10-1,11-1,12-1,13-1,14-1
HCSB - **13,** 1-1,2-1,3-1,4-1,5-1,6-1,7-1,8-1,9-1,10-1,11-1,12-1,13-1
NASV - **14,** 1-1,2-1,3-1,4-1,5-1,6-1,7-1,8-1,9-1,10-1,11-1,12-1,13-1,14-1
NCV - 16, 1-1,2-1,3-1,4-1,5-1,6-1,7-1,8-1,9-1,10-1,11-**2,**12-1,13-1,14-1,15-1,16-1
NIV - 15, 1-1,2-1,3-1,4-1,5-1,6-1,7-1,8-**2,**9-1,10-1,11-1,12-1,13-1,14-1,15-1
NKJV - **14,** 1-1,2-1,3-1,4-1,5-1,6-1,7-1,8-1,9-1,10-1,11-1,12-1,13-1,14-1
NLT - 15, 1-1,2-1,3-1,4-1,5-1,6-1,7-1,8-1,9-1,10-1,11-**2,**12-1,13-1,14-1,15-1
NRSV - **16,** 1-1,2-1,3-1,4-1,5-1,6-1,7-1,8-1,9-1,10-1,11-1,12-1,13-1,14-1,15-1,16-1
Conclusion: While only three modern versions are more complex than the King James Bible, all modern versions replaced "Master" with "Teacher."

847. John 14:20* At that day ye shall know that I am in my **Father**, and ye in me, and I in you.
AV - **20,** 1-1,2-1,3-1,4-1,5-1,6-1,7-1,8-1,9-1,10-1,11-1,12-1,13-1,14-1,15-1,16-1,17-1,18-1,19-1,20-1
ESV - **20,** 1-1,2-1,3-1,4-1,5-1,6-1,7-1,8-1,9-1,10-1,11-1,12-1,13-1,14-1,15-1,16-1,17-1,18-1,19-1,20-1

HCSB - **21,** 1-1,2-1,3-1,4-1,5-1,6-1,7-1,8-1,9-1,10-1,11-1,12-1,13-1,14-1,15-1,16-1,17-1,18-1,19-1,20-1,21-1

NASV - **20,** 1-1,2-1,3-1,4-1,5-1,6-1,7-1,8-1,9-1,10-1,11-1,12-1,13-1,14-1,15-1,16-1,17-1,18-1,19-1,20-1

NCV - **23,** 1-1,2-1,3-1,4-1,5-1,6-1,7-1,8-1,9-1,10-1,11-1,12-1,13-1,14-1,15-1,16-1,17-1,18-1,19-1,20-1,21-1,22-1,23-1

NIV - 22, 1-1,2-1,3-1,4-1,5-1,6-**3**,7-1,8-1,9-1,10-1,11-1,12-1,13-1,14-1,15-1,16-1,17-1,18-1,19-1,20-1,21-1,22-1

NKJV - **20,** 1-1,2-1,3-1,4-1,5-1,6-1,7-1,8-1,9-1,10-1,11-1,12-1,13-1,14-1,15-1,16-1,17-1,18-1,19-1,20-1

NLT - 26, 1-1,2-1,3-1,4-1,5-1,6-1,7-**2**,8-1,9-1,10-1,11-1,12-1,13-1,14-1,15-1,16-1,17-1,18-1,19-1,20-1,21-1,22-1,23-1,24-1,25-1,26-1

NRSV - **20,** 1-1,2-1,3-1,4-1,5-1,6-1,7-1,8-1,9-1,10-1,11-1,12-1,13-1,14-1,15-1,16-1,17-1,18-1,19-1,20-1

Conclusion: Only the NIV and NLT made the verse more complex.

848. John 19:3 And said, Hail, King of the Jews! and they smote him with their hands.

AV - **14,** 1-1,2-1,3-1,4-1,5-1,6-1,7-1,8-1,9-1,10-1,11-1,12-1,13-1,14-1

ESV - 17, 1-1,2-1,3-1,4-1,5-1,6-**2**,7-1,8-1,9-1,10-1,11-1,12-1,13-1,14-1,15-1,16-1,17-1

HCSB - 19, 1-1,2-1,3-**4**,4-1,5-1,6-1,7-1,8-1,9-1,10-1,11-1,12-1,13-1,14-1,15-1,16-1,17-**2**,18-1,19-1

NASV - 23, 1-1,2-1,3-**2**,4-1,5-1,6-1,7-1,8-1,9-1,10-1,11-1,12-1,13-1,14-1,15-1,16-1,17-1,18-1,19-1,20-1,21-1,22-1,23-1

NCV - 20, 1-1,2-1,3-1,4-1,5-1,6-**2**,7-1,8-1,9-1,10-1,11-1,12-1,13-1,14-1,15-1,16-1,17-1,18-1,19-1,20-1

NIV - 21, 1-1,2-1,3-1,4-1,5-1,6-**2**,7-1,8-**2**,9-**2**,10-1,11-1,12-1,13-1,14-1,15-1,16-1,17-1,18-1,19-1,20-1,21-1

NKJV - **15,** 1-1,2-1,3-1,4-1,5-1,6-1,7-1,8-1,9-1,10-1,11-1,12-1,13-1,14-1,15-1

NLT - 14, 1-1,2-1,3-1,4-1,5-1,6-1,7-1,8-1,9-1,10-1,11-1,12-**2**,13-1,14-1

NRSV - 18, 1-1,2-1,3-**2**,4-1,5-1,6-1,7-**2**,8-1,9-1,10-1,11-1,12-1,13-1,14-**2**,15-1,16-1,17-1,18-1

Conclusion: Seven modern versions are more complex than the King James Bible.

849. John 19:21* Then said the chief priests of the Jews to **Pilate**, Write not, The King of the Jews; but that he said, I am King of the Jews.

AV - **27,** 1-1,2-1,3-1,4-1,5-1,6-1,7-1,8-1,9-1,10-1,11-1,12-1,13-1,14-1,15-1,16-1,17-1,18-1,19-1,20-1,21-1,22-1,23-1,24-1,25-1,26-1,27-1

ESV - 29, 1-1,2-1,3-1,4-1,5-1,6-1,7-1,8-1,9-1,10-1,11-1,12-1,13-1,14-1,15-1,16-1,17-1,18-1,19-1,20-**2**,21-1,22-1,23-1,24-1,25-1,26-1,27-1,28-1,29-1

HCSB - **28,** 1-1,2-1,3-1,4-1,5-1,6-1,7-1,8-1,9-1,10-1,11-1,12-1,13-1,14-1,15-1,16-1,17-1,18-1,19-1,20-1,21-1,22-1,23-1,24-1,25-1,26-1,27-1,28-1

NASV - 29, 1-1,2-1,3-1,4-1,5-1,6-1,7-1,8-1,9-**2**,10-1,11-1,12-1,13-1,14-1,15-1,16-1,17-1,18-1,19-1,20-1,21-1,22-1,23-1,24-1,25-1,26-1,27-1,28-1,29-1

NCV - 25, 1-1,2-**2**,3-1,4-1,5-1,6-1,7-1,8-1,9-1,10-1,11-1,12-1,13-1,14-1,15-1,16-1,17-1,18-1,19-1,20-1,21-1,22-1,23-1,24-1,25-1

NIV - **28,** 1-1,2-1,3-1,4-1,5-1,6-1,7-**3,**8-1,9-1,10-1,11-1,12-1,13-1,14-1,15-1,16-1,17-1,18-1,19-1,20-1,21-1,22-1,23-1,24-1,25-1,26-1,27-1,28-1

NKJV, **28,** 1-**2,**2-1,3-1,4-1,5-1,6-1,7-1,8-1,9-1,10-1,11-1,12-1,13-1,14-1,15-1,16-1,17-1,18-1,19-1,20-1,21-1,22-1,23-1,24-1,25-1,26-1,27-1,28-1

NLT - **26,** 1-1,2-1,3-**2,**4-1,5-**3,**6-1,7-1,8-1,9-1,10-1,11-1,12-1,13-1,14-1,15-1,16-1,17-1,18-1,19-1,20-1,21-1,22-1,23-1,24-1,25-1,26-1

NRSV - **28,** 1-1,2-1,3-1,4-1,5-1,6-1,7-1,8-1,9-1,10-1,11-1,12-1,13-1,14-1,15-1,16-1,17-1,18-1,19-1,20-1,21-1,22-1,23-1,24-1,25-1,26-1,27-1,28-1

Conclusion: Six modern versions are more complex than the King James Bible.

850. John 20:24* But **Thomas**, one of the twelve, called **Didymus**, was not with them when **Jesus** came.

AV - **15,** 1-1,2-1,3-1,4-1,5-1,6-1,7-1,8-1,9-1,10-1,11-1,12-1,13-1,14-1,15-1

ESV - **16,** 1-1,2-1,3-1,4-1,5-1,6-1,7-1,8-1,9-1,10-1,11-1,12-1,13-1,14-1,15-1,16-1

HCSB - **15,** 1-1,2-1,3-1,4-1,5-1,6-1,7-1,8-1,9-1,10-1,11-1,12-1,13-1,14-1,15-1

NASV - **15,** 1-1,2-1,3-1,4-1,5-1,6-1,7-1,8-1,9-1,10-1,11-1,12-1,13-1,14-1,15-1

NCV - **16,** 1-1,2-1,3-1,4-1,5-1,6-1,7-1,8-1,9-1,10-1,11-1,12-1,13-1,14-1,15-1,16-1

NIV - **16,** 1-1,2-1,3-1,4-1,5-1,6-1,7-1,8-1,9-1,10-1,11-1,12-1,13-**3,**14-1,15-1,16-1

NKJV - **16,** 1-1,2-1,3-1,4-1,5-1,6-1,7-1,8-1,9-1,10-1,11-1,12-1,13-1,14-1,15-1,16-1

NLT - **17,** 1-1,2-1,3-1,4-1,5-**3,**6-1,7-**2,**8-1,9-1,10-1,11-1,12-1,13-1,14-**2,**15-1,16-1,17-1

NRSV - **18,** 1-1,2-1,3-1,4-1,5-1,6-1,7-1,8-1,9-1,10-1,11-1,12-1,13-1,14-1,15-1,16-1,17-1,18-1

Conclusion: Only the NIV and the NLT made the verse more complex.

851. Acts 5:3* But **Peter** said, **Ananias**, why hath **Satan** filled thine heart to lie to the **Holy** Ghost, and to keep back part of the price of the land?

AV - **27,** 1-1,2-1,3-1,4-1,5-1,6-1,7-1,8-1,9-1,10-1,11-1,12-1,13-1,14-1,15-1,16-1,17-1,18-1,19-1,20-1,21-1,22-1,23-1,24-1,25-1,26-1,27-1

ESV - **29,** 1-1,2-1,3-1,4-1,5-1,6-1,7-1,8-1,9-1,10-1,11-1,12-1,13-1,14-1,15-1,16-1,17-1,18-1,19-1,20-1,21-1,22-**2,**23-1,24-1,25-1,26-**2,**27-1,28-1,29-1

HCSB - **26,** 1-1,2-1,3-1,4-1,5-1,6-1,7-1,8-1,9-1,10-1,11-1,12-1,13-1,14-1,15-1,16-1,17-1,18-1,19-1,20-1,21-1,22-1,23-**2,**24-1,25-1,26-1

NASV - **27,** 1-1,2-1,3-1,4-1,5-1,6-1,7-1,8-1,9-1,10-1,11-1,12-1,13-1,14-1,15-1,16-1,17-1,18-1,19-1,20-1,21-1,22-1,23-1,24-1,25-1,26-1,27-1

NCV - **31,** 1-1,2-1,3-1,4-1,5-1,6-1,7-1,8-1,9-1,10-1,11-1,12-1,13-1,14-1,15-1,16-1,17-1,18-1,19-1,20-1,21-1,22-**2,**23-1,24-1,25-1,26-**2,**27-1,28-**2,**29-1,30-1,31-1

NIV - **36,** 1-1,2-1,3-1,4-1,5-1,6-1,7-1,8-1,9-1,10-1,11-1,12-1,13-1,14-1,15-1,16-1,17-1,18-1,19-1,20-1,21-1,22-1,23-1,24-1,25-1,26-1,27-**2,**28-1,29-1,30-1,31-**2,**32-1,33-**2,**34-1,35-1,36-1

NKJV - **28,** 1-1,2-1,3-1,4-1,5-1,6-1,7-1,8-1,9-1,10-1,11-1,12-1,13-1,14-1,15-1,16-1,17-1,18-1,19-1,20-1,21-1,22-1,23-1,24-1,25-1,26-1,27-1,28-1

NLT - **27,** 1-1,2-1,3-1,4-1,5-1,6-1,7-1,8-1,9-1,10-1,11-1,12-1,13-1,14-1,15-1,16-1,17-1,18-1,19-1,20-1,21-1,22-1,23-1,24-1,25-**2,**26-1,27-**2**

NRSV - **26,** 1-1,2-1,3-1,4-1,5-1,6-1,7-1,8-1,9-1,10-1,11-1,12-1,13-1,14-1,15-1,16-1,17-1,18-1,19-1,20-1,21-1,22-1,23-**2,**24-1,25-1,26-1

Conclusion: Six modern versions are more complex than the King James Bible.

852. Acts 7:1 Then said the high priest, Are these things so?
AV - **9,** 1-1,2-1,3-1,4-1,5-1,6-1,7-1,8-1,9-1
ESV - **9,** 1-1,2-1,3-1,4-1,5-1,6-1,7-1,8-1,9-1
HCSB - **7,** 1-1,2-1,3-1,4-1,5-1,6-1,7-1
NASV - **8,** 1-1,2-1,3-1,4-1,5-1,6-1,7-1,8-1
NCV - **10,** 1-1,2-1,3-1,4-1,5-1,6-1,7-1,8-1,9-1,10-1
NIV - **10,** 1-1,2-1,3-1,4-1,5-1,6-1,7-1,8-1,9-**2,**10-1
NKJV - **9,** 1-1,2-1,3-1,4-1,5-1,6-1,7-1,8-1,9-1
NLT - **10,** 1-1,2-1,3-1,4-1,5-1,6-1,7-1,8-1,9-**4,**10-1
NRSV - **10,** 1-1,2-1,3-1,4-1,5-1,6-1,7-1,8-1,9-1,10-1
Conclusion: Only th NIV and NLT made the verse more complex.

853. Acts 7:47* But **Solomon** built him an house.
AV - **6,** 1-1,2-1,3-1,4-1,5-1,6-1
ESV - **10,** 1-1,2-1,3-1,4-1,5-1,6-1,7-1,8-1,9-1,10-1
HCSB - **9,** 1-1,2-1,3-1,4-1,5-1,6-1,7-1,8-1,9-1
NASV - **10,** 1-1,2-1,3-1,4-1,5-1,6-1,7-1,8-1,9-1,10-1
NCV - **9,** 1-1,2-1,3-1,4-1,5-1,6-1,7-1,8-1,9-1
NIV - **10,** 1-1,2-1,3-1,4-1,5-1,6-1,7-1,8-1,9-1,10-1
NKJV - **6,** 1-1,2-1,3-1,4-1,5-1,6-1
NLT - **8,** 1-1,2-1,3-1,4-1,5-1,6-**4,**7-1,8-1
NRSV - **10,** 1-1,2-1,3-1,4-1,5-1,6-1,7-1,8-1,9-1,10-1
Conclusion: Only the NLT made the verse more complex.

854. Acts 7:50 Hath not my hand made all these things?
AV - **8,** 1-1,2-1,3-1,4-1,5-1,6-1,7-1,8-1
ESV - **8,** 1-1,2-1,3-1,4-1,5-1,6-1,7-1,8-1
HCSB - **8,** 1-1,2-1,3-1,4-1,5-1,6-1,7-1,8-1
NASV - **10,** 1-1,2-1,3-1,4-1,5-1,6-1,7-1,8-1,9-1,10-1
NCV - **7,** 1-**3,**2-1,3-1,4-1,5-1,6-1,7-1
NIV - **8,** 1-1,2-1,3-1,4-1,5-1,6-1,7-1,8-1
NKJV - **8,** 1-1,2-1,3-1,4-1,5-1,6-1,7-1,8-1
NLT - **8,** 1-1,2-1,3-1,4-1,5-1,6-**2,**7-1,8-1
NRSV - **8,** 1-1,2-1,3-1,4-1,5-1,6-1,7-1,8-1
Conclusion: Only the NCV and the NLT made the verse more complex.

855. Acts 7:54 When they heard these things, they were cut to the heart, and they gnashed on him with their teeth.
AV - **19,** 1-1,2-1,3-1,4-1,5-1,6-1,7-1,8-1,9-1,10-1,11-1,12-1,13-1,14-1,15-1,16-1,17-1,18-1,19-1
ESV - **16,** 1-1,2-1,3-1,4-1,5-1,6-1,7-1,8-1,9-**2,**10-1,11-1,12-1,13-1,14-1,15-1,16-1
HCSB - **17,** 1-1,2-1,3-1,4-1,5-1,6-1,7-1,8-**2,**9-1,10-1,11-1,12-1,13-1,14-1,15-1,16-1,17-1
NASV - **19,** 1-1,2-1,3-1,4-1,5-1,6-1,7-1,8-1,9-1,10-1,11-1,12-1,13-1,14-**2,**15-**2,**16-1,17-1,18-1,19-1
NCV - **19,** 1-1,2-1,3-**2,**4-1,5-1,6-1,7-**2,**8-**3,**9-1,10-1,11-1,12-1,13-1,14-1,15-**2,**16-1,17-1,18-1,19-1
NIV - **13,** 1-1,2-1,3-1,4-1,5-1,6-1,7-**3,**8-1,9-1,10-1,11-1,12-1,13-1

NKJV - **19,** 1-1,2-1,3-1,4-1,5-1,6-1,7-1,8-1,9-1,10-1,11-1,12-1,13-1,14-1,15-1,16-1,17-1,18-1,19-1
NLT - 17, 1-1,2-1,3-**2,**4-1,5-**5,**6-1,7-1,8-**4,**9-1,10-1,11-1,12-1,13-1,14-1,15-1,16-1,17-1
NRSV - 14, 1-1,2-1,3-1,4-1,5-1,6-1,7-**2,**8-**2,**9-1,10-1,11-1,12-1,13-1,14-1
Conclusion: Seven modern versions are more complex than the King James Bible.

856. Acts 9:35* And all that dwelt at **Lydda** and **Saron** saw him, and turned to the Lord.
AV - **15,** 1-1,2-1,3-1,4-1,5-1,6-1,7-1,8-1,9-1,10-1,11-1,12-1,13-1,14-1,15-1
ESV - 16, 1-1,2-1,3-1,4-**3,**5-1,6-1,7-1,8-1,9-1,10-1,11-1,12-1,13-1,14-1,15-1,16-1
HCSB - **15,** 1-1,2-1,3-1,4-1,5-1,6-1,7-1,8-1,9-1,10-1,11-1,12-1,13-1,14-1,15-1
NASV - **16,** 1-1,2-1,3-1,4-1,5-1,6-1,7-1,8-1,9-1,10-1,11-1,12-1,13-1,14-1,15-1,16-1
NCV - 19, 1-1,2-1,3-**2,**4-**2,**5-1,6-1,7-1,8-1,9-1,10-1,11-1,12-1,13-1,14-1,15-1,16-1,17-1,18-1,19-1
NIV - **15,** 1-1,2-1,3-1,4-1,5-1,6-1,7-1,8-1,9-1,10-1,11-1,12-1,13-1,14-1,15-1
NKJV - **15,** 1-1,2-1,3-1,4-1,5-1,6-1,7-1,8-1,9-1,10-1,11-1,12-1,13-1,14-1,15-1
NLT - 18, 1-1,2-1,3-1,4-**4,**5-1,6-1,7-1,8-1,9-1,10-1,11-**2,**12-**2,**13-1,14-1,15-1,16-1,17-1,18-1
NRSV - 15, 1-1,2-1,3-1,4-**3,**5-1,6-1,7-1,8-1,9-1,10-1,11-1,12-1,13-1,14-1,15-1
Conclusion: Four modern versions are more complex than the King James Bible. The NLT is the most difficult to read.

857. Acts 10:13* And there came a voice to him, Rise, **Peter**; kill, and eat.
AV - **12,** 1-1,2-1,3-1,4-1,5-1,6-1,7-1,8-1,9-1,10-1,11-1,12-1
ESV - **12,** 1-1,2-1,3-1,4-1,5-1,6-1,7-1,8-1,9-1,10-1,11-1,12-1
HCSB - **12,** 1-1,2-1,3-1,4-1,5-1,6-1,7-1,8-1,9-1,10-1,11-1,12-1
NASV - **11,** 1-1,2-1,3-1,4-1,5-1,6-1,7-1,8-1,9-1,10-1,11-1
NCV - **12,** 1-1,2-1,3-1,4-1,5-1,6-1,7-1,8-1,9-1,10-1,11-1,12-1
NIV - **11,** 1-1,2-1,3-1,4-1,5-1,6-1,7-1,8-1,9-1,10-1,11-1
NKJV - **11,** 1-1,2-1,3-1,4-1,5-1,6-1,7-1,8-1,9-1,10-1,11-1
NLT - **13,** 1-1,2-1,3-1,4-1,5-1,6-1,7-1,8-1,9-1,10-1,11-1,12-1,13-1
NRSV - 12, 1-1,2-1,3-1,4-1,5-1,6-**2,**7-1,8-1,9-1,10-1,11-1,12-1
Conclusion: Only the NRSV made the verse more complex.

858. Acts 13:30 But God raised him from the dead:
AV - **7,** 1-1,2-1,3-1,4-1,5-1,6-1,7-1
ESV - **7,** 1-1,2-1,3-1,4-1,5-1,6-1,7-1
HCSB - **7,** 1-1,2-1,3-1,4-1,5-1,6-1,7-1
NASV - **7,** 1-1,2-1,3-1,4-1,5-1,6-1,7-1
NCV - **8,** 1-1,2-1,3-1,4-1,5-1,6-1,7-1,8-1
NIV - **7,** 1-1,2-1,3-1,4-1,5-1,6-1,7-1
NKJV - **7,** 1-1,2-1,3-1,4-1,5-1,6-1,7-1
NLT - **7,** 1-1,2-1,3-1,4-1,5-1,6-1,7-1
NRSV - **7,** 1-1,2-1,3-1,4-1,5-1,6-1,7-1
Conclusion: All versions read the same.

859. Acts 16:30 And brought them out, and said, Sirs, what must I do to be saved?
AV - **14,** 1-1,2-1,3-1,4-1,5-1,6-1,7-1,8-1,9-1,10-1,11-1,12-1,13-1,14-1

ESV - **15,** 1-1,2-1,3-1,4-1,5-1,6-1,7-1,8-1,9-1,10-1,11-1,12-1,13-1,14-1,15-1
HCSB - **15,** 1-1,2-1,3-**3,**4-1,5-1,6-1,7-1,8-1,9-1,10-1,11-1,12-1,13-1,14-1,15-1
NASV - **16,** 1-1,2-**2,**3-1,4-1,5-1,6-1,7-1,8-1,9-1,10-1,11-1,12-1,13-1,14-1,15-1,16-1
NCV - **14,** 1-1,2-1,3-1,4-**2,**5-1,6-1,7-1,8-1,9-1,10-1,11-1,12-1,13-1,14-1
NIV - **15,** 1-1,2-1,3-1,4-1,5-1,6-1,7-1,8-1,9-1,10-1,11-1,12-1,13-1,14-1,15-1
NKJV - **15,** 1-1,2-1,3-1,4-1,5-1,6-1,7-1,8-1,9-1,10-1,11-1,12-1,13-1,14-1,15-1
NLT - **15,** 1-1,2-1,3-1,4-1,5-1,6-1,7-1,8-1,9-1,10-1,11-1,12-1,13-1,14-1,15-1
NRSV - **15,** 1-1,2-1,3-1,4-1,5-**2,**6-1,7-1,8-1,9-1,10-1,11-1,12-1,13-1,14-1,15-1
Conclusion: Four modern versions are more complex than the King James Bible.

860. Acts 20:14* And when he met with us at **Assos**, we took him in, and came to **Mitylene**.
AV - **16,** 1-1,2-1,3-1,4-1,5-1,6-1,7-1,8-1,9-1,10-1,11-1,12-1,13-1,14-1,15-1,16-1
ESV - **16,** 1-1,2-1,3-1,4-1,5-1,6-1,7-1,8-1,9-1,10-1,11-1,12-1,13-1,14-1,15-1,16-1
HCSB - **15,** 1-1,2-1,3-1,4-1,5-1,6-1,7-1,8-1,9-1,10-1,11-1,12-1,13-1,14-1,15-1
NASV - **16,** 1-1,2-1,3-1,4-1,5-1,6-1,7-1,8-1,9-1,10-1,11-1,12-1,13-1,14-1,15-1,16-1
NCV - **13,** 1-1,2-1,3-1,4-1,5-1,6-1,7-1,8-1,9-**2,**10-1,11-1,12-1,13-1
NIV - **15,** 1-1,2-1,3-1,4-1,5-1,6-1,7-1,8-1,9-1,10-**2,**11-1,12-1,13-1,14-1,15-1
NKJV - **16,** 1-1,2-1,3-1,4-1,5-1,6-1,7-1,8-1,9-1,10-1,11-1,12-1,13-1,14-1,15-1,16-1
NLT - **10,** 1-1,2-1,3-1,4-1,5-1,6-1,7-1,8-**3,**9-1,10-1
NRSV - **15,** 1-1,2-1,3-1,4-1,5-1,6-1,7-1,8-1,9-1,10-1,11-1,12-1,13-1,14-1,15-1
Conclusion: Only three modern versions are more complex than the King James Bible.

861. Acts 20:37* And they all wept sore, and fell on Paul's neck, and kissed him,
AV - **13,** 1-1,2-1,3-1,4-1,5-1,6-1,7-1,8-1,9-1,10-1,11-1,12-1,13-1
ESV - **16,** 1-1,2-1,3-1,4-1,5-**2,**6-1,7-1,8-1,9-1,10-1,11-1,12-**2,**13-1,14-1,15-1,16-1
HCSB - **15,** 1-1,2-1,3-1,4-1,5-1,6-1,7-**2,**8-1,9-**3,**10-1,11-**3,**12-1,13-1,14-1,15-1
NASV - **13,** 1-1,2-1,3-**2,**4-1,5-1,6-**2,**7-1,8-**2,**9-1,10-1,11-**4,**12-1,13-1
NCV - **31,** 1-1,2-1,3-1,4-1,5-**2,**6-1,7-1,8-1,9-1,10-1,11-**2,**12-1,13-1,14-**2,**15-1,16-1,17-1,18-1,19-**2,**20-1,21-1,22-1,23-1,24-1,25-1,26-1,27-1,28-1,29-1,30-1,31-1
NIV - **10,** 1-1,2-1,3-1,4-1,5-1,6-**2,**7-1,8-1,9-1,10-1
NKJV - **13,** 1-1,2-1,3-1,4-1,5-**2,**6-1,7-1,8-1,9-1,10-1,11-1,12-1,13-1
NLT - **10,** 1-1,2-1,3-1,4-1,5-1,6-**2,**7-1,8-1,9-1,10-1
NRSV - **13,** 1-1,2-1,3-1,4-**2,**5-**2,**6-1,7-1,8-1,9-**2,**10-1,11-1,12-1,13-1
Conclusion: All eight modern versions are more complex than the King James Bible. The translators of the NCV went to great lengths to complicate this simple verse beyond all reason.

862. Acts 27:37# And we were in all in the ship two **hundred threescore** and **sixteen** souls.
AV - **14,** 1-1,2-1,3-1,4-1,5-1,6-1,7-1,8-1,9-1,10-1,11-1,12-1,13-1,14-1
ESV - **9,** 1-1,2-1,3-1,4-1,5-1,6-**2,**7-1,8-1,9-1
HCSB - **10,** 1-1,2-1,3-1,4-1,5-1,6-1,7-1,8-1,9-1,10-1
NASV - **13,** 1-1,2-1,3-1,4-1,5-1,6-1,7-1,8-1,9-1,10-1,11-1,12-1,13-**2**
NCV - **10,** 1-1,2-1,3-1,4-1,5-1,6-1,7-**2,**8-1,9-1,10-1
NIV - **8,** 1-**4,**2-1,3-1,4-1,5-1,6-1,7-1,8-1
NKJV - **14,** 1-1,2-1,3-1,4-1,5-1,6-1,7-1,8-1,9-1,10-1,11-**2,**12-1,13-1,14-1

NLT - **8,** 1-1,2-1,3-1,4-1,5-1,6-1,7-1,8-1
NRSV - 12, 1-1,2-1,3-1,4-1,5-1,6-1,7-1,8-1,9-**2,**10-1,11-1,12-1
Conclusion: Six modern versions are more complex than the King James Bible. This is one of those rare times when the NLT is more conservative than most other modern versions.

863. Romans 3:15 Their feet are swift to shed blood:
AV - **7,** 1-1,2-1,3-1,4-1,5-1,6-1,7-1
ESV - **7,** 1-1,2-1,3-1,4-1,5-1,6-1,7-1
HCSB - **7,** 1-1,2-1,3-1,4-1,5-1,6-1,7-1
NASV - **7,** 1-1,2-1,3-1,4-1,5-1,6-1,7-1
NCV - 7, 1-1,2-1,3-**2,**4-**2,**5-1,6-1,7-**2**
NIV - **7,** 1-1,2-1,3-1,4-1,5-1,6-1,7-1
NKJV - **7,** 1-1,2-1,3-1,4-1,5-1,6-1,7-1
NLT - 5, 1-1,2-1,3-1,4-**2,**5-**2**
NRSV - **7,** 1-1,2-1,3-1,4-1,5-1,6-1,7-1
Conclusion: In their consistent complexity, only the NCV and NLT found a way to complicate this simple verse.

864. Romans 3:17 And the way of peace have they not known:
AV - **9,** 1-1,2-1,3-1,4-1,5-1,6-1,7-1,8-1,9-1
ESV - **9,** 1-1,2-1,3-1,4-1,5-1,6-1,7-1,8-1,9-1
HCSB - **9,** 1-1,2-1,3-1,4-1,5-1,6-1,7-1,8-1,9-1
NASV - **9,** 1-1,2-1,3-1,4-1,5-1,6-1,7-1,8-1,9-1
NCV - **8,** 1-1,2-1,3-1,4-1,5-1,6-1,7-1,8-1
NIV - **9,** 1-1,2-1,3-1,4-1,5-1,6-1,7-1,8-1,9-1
NKJV - **9,** 1-1,2-1,3-1,4-1,5-1,6-1,7-1,8-1,9-1
NLT - **7,** 1-1,2-1,3-1,4-1,5-1,6-1,7-1
NRSV - **9,** 1-1,2-1,3-1,4-1,5-1,6-1,7-1,8-1,9-1
Conclusion: All versions read the same.

865. Romans 6:7 For he that is dead is freed from sin.
AV - **9,** 1-1,2-1,3-1,4-1,5-1,6-1,7-1,8-1,9-1
ESV - **11,** 1-1,2-1,3-1,4-1,5-1,6-1,7-1,8-1,9-1,10-1,11-1
HCSB - 11, 1-1,2-1,3-**2,**4-1,5-1,6-1,7-1,8-1,9-1,10-1,11-1
NASV - **9,** 1-1,2-1,3-1,4-1,5-1,6-1,7-1,8-1,9-1
NCV - 10, 1-**3,**2-1,3-1,4-1,5-1,6-1,7-1,8-1,9-1,10-**2**
NIV - 10, 1-**2,**2-**3,**3-1,4-1,5-1,6-1,7-1,8-1,9-1,10-1
NKJV - **10,** 1-1,2-1,3-1,4-1,5-1,6-1,7-1,8-1,9-1,10-1
NLT - 15, 1-1,2-1,3-1,4-1,5-1,6-1,7-1,8-1,9-1,10-1,11-1,12-1,13-**2,**14-1,15-1
NRSV - 8, 1-1,2-**2,**3-1,4-1,5-1,6-1,7-1,8-1
Conclusion: Five modern versions are more complex than the King James Bible.

866. Romans 8:2* For the law of the **Spirit** of life in Christ **Jesus** hath made me free from the law of sin and death.

AV - **22,** 1-1,2-1,3-1,4-1,5-1,6-1,7-1,8-1,9-1,10-1,11-1,12-1,13-1,14-1,15-1,16-1,17-1,18-1,19-1,20-1,21-1,22-1

ESV - **22,** 1-1,2-1,3-1,4-1,5-1,6-1,7-1,8-1,9-1,10-1,11-1,12-1,13-1,14-1,15-1,16-1,17-1,18-1,19-1,20-1,21-1,22-1

HCSB - **21,** 1-**2**,2-1,3-1,4-1,5-1,6-1,7-1,8-1,9-1,10-1,11-1,12-1,13-1,14-1,15-1,16-1,17-1,18-1,19-1,20-1,21-1

NASV - **23,** 1-1,2-1,3-1,4-1,5-1,6-1,7-1,8-1,9-1,10-1,11-1,12-1,13-1,14-1,15-1,16-1,17-1,18-1,19-1,20-1,21-1,22-1,23-1

NCV - **22,** 1-1,2-1,3-1,4-1,5-1,6-1,7-1,8-1,9-1,10-1,11-1,12-1,13-1,14-1,15-1,16-1,17-1,18-1,19-1,20-1,21-1,22-1

NIV - **21,** 1-**2**,2-1,3-1,4-1,5-1,6-1,7-1,8-1,9-1,10-1,11-1,12-1,13-1,14-1,15-1,16-1,17-1,18-1,19-1,20-1,21-1

NKJV - **22,** 1-1,2-1,3-1,4-1,5-1,6-1,7-1,8-1,9-1,10-1,11-1,12-1,13-1,14-1,15-1,16-1,17-1,18-1,19-1,20-1,21-1,22-1

NLT - **25,** 1-1,2-**2**,3-1,4-**2**,5-1,6-1,7-1,8-**2**,9-1,10-1,11-1,12-**2**,13-1,14-1,15-1,16-1,17-1,18-1,19-**2**,20-1,21-1,22-1,23-1,24-1,25-1

NRSV - **23,** 1-1,2-1,3-1,4-1,5-1,6-1,7-1,8-1,9-1,10-1,11-1,12-1,13-1,14-1,15-1,16-1,17-1,18-1,19-1,20-1,21-1,22-1,23-1

Conclusion: Only three modern versions are more complex than the King James Bible. The NLT is the most difficult to read.

867. Romans 15:33* Now the God of peace be with you all. **Amen.**

AV - **10,** 1-1,2-1,3-1,4-1,5-1,6-1,7-1,8-1,9-1,10-1

ESV - **10,** 1-1,2-1,3-1,4-1,5-1,6-1,7-1,8-1,9-1,10-1

HCSB - **9,** 1-1,2-1,3-1,4-1,5-1,6-1,7-1,8-1,9-1

NASV - **10,** 1-1,2-1,3-1,4-1,5-1,6-1,7-1,8-1,9-1,10-1

NCV - **10,** 1-1,2-1,3-1,4-1,5-1,6-1,7-1,8-1,9-1,10-1

NIV - **9,** 1-1,2-1,3-1,4-1,5-1,6-1,7-1,8-1,9-1

NKJV - **10,** 1-1,2-1,3-1,4-1,5-1,6-1,7-1,8-1,9-1,10-1

NLT - **14,** 1-1,2-1,3-1,4-1,5-1,6-1,7-1,8-1,9-1,10-1,11-1,12-1,13-1,14-1

NRSV - **10,** 1-1,2-1,3-1,4-1,5-1,6-1,7-1,8-1,9-1,10-1

Conclusion: All versions read the same.

868. Romans 16:24* The grace of our Lord **Jesus** Christ be with you all. **Amen.**

AV - **12,** 1-1,2-1,3-1,4-1,5-1,6-1,7-1,8-1,9-1,10-1,11-1,12-1

ESV - The verse is omitted from this version.

HCSB - **[11,** 1-1,2-1,3-1,4-1,5-1,6-1,7-1,8-1,9-1,10-1,11-1**]**

NASV - **[12,** 1-1,2-1,3-1,4-1,5-1,6-1,7-1,8-1,9-1,10-1,11-1,12-1**]**

NCV - **[13,** 1-1,2-1,3-1,4-1,5-1,6-1,7-1,8-1,9-1,10-1,11-1,12-1,13-1**]**

NIV - The verse is omitted from this version.

NKJV - **12,** 1-1,2-1,3-1,4-1,5-1,6-1,7-1,8-1,9-1,10-1,11-1,12-1

NLT - The verse is omitted from this version.

NRSV - The verse is omitted from this version.

Conclusion: Four modern versions omit the verse while three place it in brackets. Only the NKJV reads as the King James Bible

869. 1 Corinthians 3:23 And ye are Christ's; and Christ is God's.
AV - **8,** 1-1,2-1,3-1,4-1,5-1,6-1,7-1,8-1
ESV - **8,** 1-1,2-1,3-1,4-1,5-1,6-1,7-1,8-1
HCSB - 9, 1-1,2-1,3-**2**,4-1,5-1,6-1,7-1,8-1,9-1
NASV - 10, 1-1,2-1,3-**2**,4-1,5-1,6-1,7-1,8-**2**,9-1,10-1
NCV - 10, 1-1,2-1,3-**2**,4-1,5-1,6-1,7-1,8-**2**,9-1,10-1
NIV - **10,** 1-1,2-1,3-1,4-1,5-1,6-1,7-1,8-1,9-1,10-1
NKJV - **8,** 1-1,2-1,3-1,4-1,5-1,6-1,7-1,8-1
NLT - 10, 1-1,2-1,3-**2**,4-1,5-1,6-1,7-1,8-**2**,9-1,10-1
NRSV - 10, 1-1,2-1,3-**2**,4-1,5-1,6-1,7-1,8-**2**,9-1,10-1
Conclusion: Five modern versions are more complex than the King James Bible.

870. 1 Corinthians 4:18 Now some are puffed up, as though I would not come to you.
AV - **13,** 1-1,2-1,3-1,4-1,5-1,6-1,7-1,8-1,9-1,10-1,11-1,12-1,13-1
ESV - 11, 1-1,2-1,3-**3**,4-1,5-1,6-1,7-1,8-1,9-**2**,10-1,11-1
HCSB - 14, 1-1,2-1,3-1,4-**3**,5-1,6-1,7-1,8-1,9-1,10-1,11-1,12-**2**,13-1,14-1
NASV - 13, 1-1,2-1,3-1,4-**2**,5-**3**,6-1,7-1,8-1,9-1,10-1,11-**2**,12-1,13-1
NCV - 15, 1-1,2-1,3-1,4-**2**,5-1,6-**2**,7-1,8-1,9-1,10-1,11-1,12-1,13-1,14-1,15-1
NIV - 14, 1-1,2-1,3-1,4-1,5-**2**,6-**3**,7-1,8-1,9-1,10-1,11-1,12-**2**,13-1,14-1
NKJV - 13, 1-1,2-1,3-1,4-1,5-1,6-1,7-1,8-1,9-1,10-1,11-**2**,12-1,13-1
NLT - 13, 1-1,2-1,3-1,4-1,5-**2**,6-**3**,7-**2**,8-1,9-1,10-1,11-**2**,12-1,13-**2**
NRSV -15, 1-1,2-1,3-1,4-1,5-**2**,6-1,7-1,8-1,9-1,10-**2**,11-1,12-1,13-1,14-**2**,15-**3**
Conclusion: All eight modern versions are more complex than the King James Bible. The NLT is the most difficult to read.

871. 1 Corinthians 10:15 I speak as to wise men; judge ye what I say.
AV - **11,** 1-1,2-1,3-1,4-1,5-1,6-1,7-1,8-1,9-1,10-1,11-1
ESV - 12, 1-1,2-1,3-1,4-1,5-**3**,6-**2**,7-1,8-1,9-**2**,10-1,11-1,12-1
HCSB - 13, 1-1,2-1,3-**2**,4-1,5-1,6-1,7-**2**,8-1,9-1,10-**2**,11-1,12-1,13-1
NASV - **11,** 1-1,2-1,3-1,4-1,5-1,6-1,7-1,8-1,9-1,10-1,11-1
NCV - 15, 1-1,2-1,3-**2**,4-1,5-1,6-1,7-1,8-**4**,9-**2**,10-1,11-1,12-**2**,13-1,14-1,15-1
NIV - 11, 1-1,2-1,3-1,4-**3**,5-**2**,6-1,7-1,8-**2**,9-1,10-1,11-1
NKJV - 12, 1-1,2-1,3-1,4-1,5-1,6-1,7-1,8-1,9-**2**,10-1,11-1,12-1
NLT - 14, 1-1,2-1,3-**4**,4-**2**,5-**2**,6-1,7-**2**,8-1,9-1,10-1,11-1,12-**2**,13-1,14-1
NRSV - 12, 1-1,2-1,3-1,4-1,5-**3**,6-**2**,7-1,8-1,9-**2**,10-1,11-1,12-1
Conclusion: Seven modern versions are more complex than the King James Bible. Strangely, only the NASV did not make the verse more complex. Usually, it's the NKJV.

872. 1 Corinthians 14:18 I thank my God, I speak with tongues more than ye all:
AV - **12,** 1-1,2-1,3-1,4-1,5-1,6-1,7-1,8-1,9-1,10-1,11-1,12-1

ESV - **13,** 1-1,2-1,3-1,4-1,5-1,6-1,7-1,8-1,9-1,10-1,11-1,12-1,13-1
HCSB - 14, 1-1,2-1,3-1,4-1,5-1,6-1,7-1,8-**2,**9-**3,**10-1,11-1,12-1,13-1,14-1
NASV - **11,** 1-1,2-1,3-1,4-1,5-1,6-1,7-1,8-1,9-1,10-1,11-1
NCV - 16, 1-1,2-1,3-1,4-1,5-1,6-1,7-1,8-**3,**9-1,10-1,11-**3,**12-1,13-1,14-1,15-1,16-1
NIV - **13,** 1-1,2-1,3-1,4-1,5-1,6-1,7-1,8-1,9-1,10-1,11-1,12-1,13-1
NKJV - 12, 1-1,2-1,3-1,4-1,5-1,6-1,7-1,8-1,9-1,10-1,11-1,12-1
NLT - 13, 1-1,2-1,3-1,4-1,5-1,6-1,7-1,8-1,9-1,10-1,11-**2,**12-1,13-1
NRSV - **13,** 1-1,2-1,3-1,4-1,5-1,6-1,7-1,8-1,9-1,10-1,11-1,12-1,13-1
Conclusion: Only three modern versions made the verse more complex.

873. 1 Corinthians 15:5*And that he was seen of **Cephas**, then of the twelve:
AV - **11,** 1-1,2-1,3-1,4-1,5-1,6-1,7-1,8-1,9-1,10-1,11-1
ESV - 10, 1-1,2-1,3-1,4-**2,**5-1,6-1,7-1,8-1,9-1,10-1
HCSB - 10, 1-1,2-1,3-1,4-**2,**5-1,6-1,7-1,8-1,9-1,10-1
NASV - 10, 1-1,2-1,3-1,4-**2,**5-1,6-1,7-1,8-1,9-1,10-1
NCV - 13, 1-1,2-1,3-1,4-1,5-1,6-1,7-1,8-1,9-1,10-1,11-1,12-1,13-**3**
NIV - 11, 1-1,2-1,3-1,4-**2,**5-1,6-1,7-1,8-1,9-1,10-1,11-1
NKJV - **11,** 1-1,2-1,3-1,4-1,5-1,6-1,7-1,8-1,9-1,10-1,11-1
NLT - 10, 1-1,2-1,3-1,4-1,5-1,6-1,7-1,8-1,9-1,10-1
NRSV - 10, 1-1,2-1,3-1,4-**2,**5-1,6-1,7-1,8-1,9-1,10-1
Conclusion: Six modern versions are more complex than the King James Bible.

874. 1 Corinthians 15:16 For if the dead rise not, then is not Christ raised:
AV - **11,** 1-1,2-1,3-1,4-1,5-1,6-1,7-1,8-1,9-1,10-1,11-1
ESV - 13, 1-1,2-1,3-1,4-1,5-1,6-1,7-1,8-1,9-1,10-1,11-1,12-1,13-**2**
HCSB - **12,** 1-1,2-1,3-1,4-1,5-1,6-1,7-1,8-1,9-1,10-1,11-1,12-1
NASV - 13, 1-1,2-1,3-1,4-1,5-1,6-1,7-1,8-1,9-1,10-1,11-1,12-1,13-**2**
NCV - 12, 1-1,2-1,3-1,4-1,5-1,6-1,7-1,8-1,9-1,10-1,11-1,12-**2**
NIV - 14, 1-1,2-1,3-1,4-1,5-1,6-1,7-1,8-1,9-1,10-1,11-1,12-1,13-1,14-**2**
NKJV - 12, 1-1,2-1,3-1,4-1,5-1,6-1,7-1,8-1,9-1,10-1,11-1,12-**2**
NLT - 15, 1-1,2-1,3-1,4-1,5-1,6-**4,**7-1,8-1,9-1,10-1,11-1,12-1,13-1,14-1,15-1
NRSV - **13,** 1-1,2-1,3-1,4-1,5-1,6-1,7-1,8-1,9-1,10-1,11-1,12-1,13-1
Conclusion: Six modern versions are more complex than the King James Bible.

875. 1 Corinthians 15:17 And if Christ be not raised, your faith is vain; ye are yet in your sins.
AV - **16,** 1-1,2-1,3-1,4-1,5-1,6-1,7-1,8-1,9-1,10-1,11-1,12-1,13-1,14-1,15-1,16-1
ESV - 18, 1-1,2-1,3-1,4-1,5-1,6-1,7-1,8-1,9-1,10-1,11-**2,**12-1,13-1,14-1,15-1,16-1,17-1,18-1
HCSB - 17, 1-1,2-1,3-1,4-1,5-1,6-1,7-1,8-1,9-1,10-1,11-**2,**12-1,13-1,14-1,15-1,16-1,17-1
NASV - 17, 1-1,2-1,3-1,4-1,5-1,6-1,7-1,8-1,9-1,10-1,11-**2,**12-1,13-1,14-1,15-1,16-1,17-1
NCV - 21, 1-1,2-1,3-1,4-1,5-1,6-1,7-1,8-1,9-1,10-1,11-1,12-**2,**13-1,14-1,15-1,16-1,17-1,18-**2,**19-1,20-1,21-1
NIV - 17, 1-1,2-1,3-1,4-1,5-1,6-1,7-1,8-1,9-1,10-1,11-**2,**12-1,13-1,14-1,15-1,16-1,17-1
NKJV - 16, 1-1,2-1,3-1,4-1,5-1,6-1,7-1,8-1,9-1,10-**2,**11-1,12-1,13-1,14-1,15-1,16-1

NLT - 20, 1-1,2-1,3-1,4-1,5-1,6-1,7-1,8-1,9-1,10-1,11-1,12-**2**,13-1,14-1,15-1,16-1,17-**2**,18-1,19-1,20-1
NRSV - 17, 1-1,2-1,3-1,4-1,5-1,6-1,7-1,8-1,9-1,10-**2**,11-1,12-1,13-1,14-1,15-1,16-1,17-1
Conclusion: All eight modern versions are more complex than the King James Bible.

876. 1 Corinthians 15:56 The sting of death is sin; and the strength of sin is the law.
AV - 14, 1-1,2-1,3-1,4-1,5-1,6-1,7-1,8-1,9-1,10-1,11-1,12-1,13-1,14-1
ESV - 14, 1-1,2-1,3-1,4-1,5-1,6-1,7-1,8-1,9-**2**,10-1,11-1,12-1,13-1,14-1
HCSB - 15, 1-1,2-1,3-1,4-1,5-1,6-1,7-1,8-1,9-1,10-**2**,11-1,12-1,13-1,14-1,15-1
NASV - 14, 1-1,2-1,3-1,4-1,5-1,6-1,7-1,8-1,9-**2**,10-1,11-1,12-1,13-1,14-1
NCV - 14, 1-1,2-**2**,3-1,4-1,5-1,6-1,7-1,8-1,9-**2**,10-1,11-1,12-1,13-1,14-1
NIV - 14, 1-1,2-1,3-1,4-1,5-1,6-1,7-1,8-1,9-**2**,10-1,11-1,12-1,13-1,14-1
NKJV - **14,** 1-1,2-1,3-1,4-1,5-1,6-1,7-1,8-1,9-1,10-1,11-1,12-1,13-1,14-1
NLT - 16, 1-1,2-1,3-1,4-1,5-1,6-1,7-**2**,8-1,9-1,10-1,11-1,12-1,13-1,14-1,15-1,16-**2**
NRSV - 14, 1-1,2-1,3-1,4-1,5-1,6-1,7-1,8-1,9-**2**,10-1,11-1,12-1,13-1,14-1
Conclusion: Seven modern versions are more complex than the King James Bible.

877. 1 Corinthians 16:13 Watch ye, stand fast in the faith, quit you like men, be strong.
AV - 13, 1-1,2-1,3-1,4-1,5-1,6-1,7-1,8-1,9-1,10-1,11-1,12-1,13-1
ESV - 12, 1-1,2-**2**,3-1,4-1,5-1,6-1,7-1,8-1,9-1,10-1,11-1,12-1
HCSB - 11, 1-1,2-**2**,3-1,4-1,5-1,6-1,7-1,8-1,9-1,10-1,11-1
NASV - 14, 1-1,2-1,3-1,4-**2**,5-1,6-1,7-1,8-1,9-1,10-1,11-1,12-1,13-1,14-1
NCV - 12, 1-1,2-**2**,3-**3**,4-1,5-1,6-1,7-1,8-1,9-**2**,10-1,11-1,12-1
NIV - 15, 1-1,2-1,3-1,4-1,5-1,6-1,7-1,8-1,9-1,10-1,11-1,12-1,13-**2**,14-1,15-1
NKJV - **10,** 1-1,2-1,3-1,4-1,5-1,6-1,7-1,8-1,9-1,10-1
NLT - 12, 1-1,2-1,3-1,4-1,5-1,6-1,7-1,8-1,9-1,10-**3**,11-1,12-1
NRSV - 11, 1-1,2-**2**,3-1,4-1,5-1,6-1,7-1,8-1,9-**3**,10-1,11-1
Conclusion: Seven modern versions are more complex than the King James Bible.

878. 1 Corinthians 16:23* The grace of our Lord **Jesus** Christ be with you.
AV - **10,** 1-1,2-1,3-1,4-1,5-1,6-1,7-1,8-1,9-1,10-1
ESV - **9,** 1-1,2-1,3-1,4-1,5-1,6-1,7-1,8-1,9-1
HCSB - **9,** 1-1,2-1,3-1,4-1,5-1,6-1,7-1,8-1,9-1
NASV - **9,** 1-1,2-1,3-1,4-1,5-1,6-1,7-1,8-1,9-1
NCV - **9,** 1-1,2-1,3-1,4-1,5-1,6-1,7-1,8-1,9-1
NIV - **9,** 1-1,2-1,3-1,4-1,5-1,6-1,7-1,8-1,9-1
NKJV - **10,** 1-1,2-1,3-1,4-1,5-1,6-1,7-1,8-1,9-1,10-1
NLT - **10,** 1-1,2-1,3-1,4-1,5-1,6-1,7-1,8-1,9-1,10-1
NRSV - **9,** 1-1,2-1,3-1,4-1,5-1,6-1,7-1,8-1,9-1
Conclusion: All eight versions structure the verse with words of single syllables, but every modern version, with the exception of the NKJV deletes the word "Christ."

879. 1 Corinthians 16:24* My love be with you all in Christ **Jesus. Amen.**
AV - **10,** 1-1,2-1,3-1,4-1,5-1,6-1,7-1,8-1,9-1,10-1

ESV - **10,** 1-1,2-1,3-1,4-1,5-1,6-1,7-1,8-1,9-1,10-1
HCSB - **10,** 1-1,2-1,3-1,4-1,5-1,6-1,7-1,8-1,9-1,10-1
NASV - **10,** 1-1,2-1,3-1,4-1,5-1,6-1,7-1,8-1,9-1,10-1
NCV - **10,** 1-1,2-1,3-1,4-1,5-1,6-1,7-1,8-1,9-1,10-1
NIV - **10,** 1-1,2-1,3-1,4-1,5-1,6-1,7-1,8-1,9-1,10-1
NKJV - **10,** 1-1,2-1,3-1,4-1,5-1,6-1,7-1,8-1,9-1,10-1
NLT - **9 ,** 1-1,2-1,3-1,4-1,5-1,6-1,7-1,8-1,9-1
NRSV - **10,** 1-1,2-1,3-1,4-1,5-1,6-1,7-1,8-1,9-1,10-1
Conclusion: All versions read the same.

880. 2 Corinthians 1:2* Grace be to you and peace from God our **Father**, and from the Lord **Jesus** Christ.
AV - **16,** 1-1,2-1,3-1,4-1,5-1,6-1,7-1,8-1,9-1,10-1,11-1,12-1,13-1,14-1,15-1,16-1
ESV - **14,** 1-1,2-1,3-1,4-1,5-1,6-1,7-1,8-1,9-1,10-1,11-1,12-1,13-1,14-1
HCSB - **14,** 1-1,2-1,3-1,4-1,5-1,6-1,7-1,8-1,9-1,10-1,11-1,12-1,13-1,14-1
NASV - **14,** 1-1,2-1,3-1,4-1,5-1,6-1,7-1,8-1,9-1,10-1,11-1,12-1,13-1,14-1
NCV - **14,** 1-1,2-1,3-1,4-1,5-1,6-1,7-1,8-1,9-1,10-1,11-1,12-1,13-1,14-1
NIV - **14,** 1-1,2-1,3-1,4-1,5-1,6-1,7-1,8-1,9-1,10-1,11-1,12-1,13-1,14-1
NKJV - **14,** 1-1,2-1,3-1,4-1,5-1,6-1,7-1,8-1,9-1,10-1,11-1,12-1,13-1,14-1
NLT - **14,** 1-1,2-1,3-1,4-1,5-1,6-1,7-1,8-1,9-1,10-1,11-1,12-1,13-1,14-1
NRSV - **14,** 1-1,2-1,3-1,4-1,5-1,6-1,7-1,8-1,9-1,10-1,11-1,12-1,13-1,14-1
Conclusion: All versions read the same.

881. 2 Corinthians 3:4 And such trust have we through Christ to God-ward:
AV - **10,** 1-1,2-1,3-1,4-1,5-1,6-1,7-1,8-1,9-1,10-1
ESV - 11, 1-1,2-1,3-1,4-**3,**5-1,6-1,7-1,8-1,9-1,10-1,11-1
HCSB - 10, 1-1,2-1,3-1,4-1,5-1,6-**3,**7-1,8-1,9-1,10-1
NASV - 8, 1-1,2-**3,**3-1,4-1,5-1,6-1,7-1,8-1
NCV - 12, 1-1,2-1,3-1,4-1,5-**2,**6-1,7-1,8-1,9-1,10-**2,**11-**2,**12-1
NIV - 10, 1-1,2-**3,**3-1,4-1,5-1,6-1,7-1,8-1,9-1,10-1
NKJV - **9,** 1-1,2-1,3-1,4-1,5-1,6-1,7-1,8-1,9-1
NLT - 15, 1-1,2-1,3-**3,**4-1,5-1,6-1,7-**2,**8-1,9-1,10-1,11-1,12-1,13-1,14-1,15-1
NRSV - 11, 1-1,2-1,3-1,4-**3,**5-1,6-1,7-1,8-1,9-1,10-1,11-1
Conclusion: Seven modern versions are more complex than the King James Bible.

882. 2 Corinthians 5:7 (For we walk by faith, not by sight:)
AV - **8,** 1-1,2-1,3-1,4-1,5-1,6-1,7-1,8-1
ESV - **8,** 1-1,2-1,3-1,4-1,5-1,6-1,7-1,8-1
HCSB - **8,** 1-1,2-1,3-1,4-1,5-1,6-1,7-1,8-1
NASV - **8,** 1-1,2-1,3-1,4-1,5-1,6-1,7-1,8-1
NCV - 12, 1-1,2-1,3-1,4-1,5-1,6-**2,**7-1,8-1,9-1,10-1,11-1,12-1
NIV - **7,** 1-1,2-1,3-1,4-1,5-1,6-1,7-1
NKJV - **8,** 1-1,2-1,3-1,4-1,5-1,6-1,7-1,8-1
NLT - 9, 1-1,2-1,3-1,4-1,5-**3,**6-1,7-1,8-1,9-**2**

NRSV - **8,** 1-1,2-1,3-1,4-1,5-1,6-1,7-1,8-1

Conclusion: Only the NCV and the NLT managed to make this simple statement more complex. I don't think I'd want the translators of either of these two modern versions to write an instruction manual for anything.

883. 2 Corinthians 11:22* Are they **Hebrews**? so am I. Are they **Israelites**? so am I. Are they the seed of **Abraham**? so am I.

AV - **21,** 1-1,2-1,3-1,4-1,5-1,6-1,7-1,8-1,9-1,10-1,11-1,12-1,13-1,14-1,15-1,16-1,17-1,18-1,19-1,20-1,21-1

ESV - **19,** 1-1,2-1,3-1,4-1,5-1,6-1,7-1,8-1,9-1,10-1,11-1,12-1,13-1,14-**2,**15-1,16-1,17-1,18-1,19-1

HCSB - **21,** 1-1,2-1,3-1,4-1,5-1,6-1,7-1,8-1,9-1,10-1,11-1,12-1,13-1,14-1,15-1,16-1,17-1,18-1,19-1,20-1,21-1

NASV - **20,** 1-1,2-1,3-1,4-1,5-1,6-1,7-1,8-1,9-1,10-1,11-1,12-1,13-1,14-1,15-**3,**16-1,17-1,18-1,19-1,20-1

NCV, 20, 1-1,2-1,3-1,4-1,5-1,6-1,7-1,8-1,9-1,10-1,11-1,12-1,13-1,14-1,15-1,16-1,17-**3,**18-1,19-1,20-1

NIV - **19,** 1-1,2-1,3-1,4-1,5-1,6-1,7-1,8-1,9-1,10-1,11-1,12-1,13-1,14-1,15-1,16-**3,**17-1,18-1,19-1

NKJV - **21,** 1-1,2-1,3-1,4-1,5-1,6-1,7-1,8-1,9-1,10-1,11-1,12-1,13-1,14-1,15-1,16-1,17-1,18-1,19-1,20-1,21-1

NLT - **20,** 1-1,2-1,3-1,4-1,5-1,6-1,7-1,8-1,9-1,10-1,11-1,12-1,13-1,14-1,15-**3,**16-1,17-1,18-1,19-1,20-1

NRSV - **20,** 1-1,2-1,3-1,4-1,5-1,6-1,7-1,8-1,9-1,10-1,11-1,12-1,13-1,14-1,15-**3,**16-1,17-1,18-1,19-1,20-1

Conclusion: Six modern versions are more complex than the King James Bible.

884. Galatians 1:3* Grace be to you and peace from God the **Father**, and from our Lord **Jesus** Christ,

AV - **16,** 1-1,2-1,3-1,4-1,5-1,6-1,7-1,8-1,9-1,10-1,11-1,12-1,13-1,14-1,15-1,16-1

ESV - **14,** 1-1,2-1,3-1,4-1,5-1,6-1,7-1,8-1,9-1,10-1,11-1,12-1,13-1,14-1

HCSB - **14,** 1-1,2-1,3-1,4-1,5-1,6-1,7-1,8-1,9-1,10-1,11-1,12-1,13-1,14-1

NASV - **14,** 1-1,2-1,3-1,4-1,5-1,6-1,7-1,8-1,9-1,10-1,11-1,12-1,13-1,14-1

NCV - **14,** 1-1,2-1,3-1,4-1,5-1,6-1,7-1,8-1,9-1,10-1,11-1,12-1,13-1,14-1

NIV - **14,** 1-1,2-1,3-1,4-1,5-1,6-1,7-1,8-1,9-1,10-1,11-1,12-1,13-1,14-1

NKJV - **14,** 1-1,2-1,3-1,4-1,5-1,6-1,7-1,8-1,9-1,10-1,11-1,12-1,13-1,14-1

NLT - **14,** 1-1,2-1,3-1,4-1,5-1,6-1,7-1,8-1,9-1,10-1,11-1,12-1,13-1,14-1

NRSV - **14,** 1-1,2-1,3-1,4-1,5-1,6-1,7-1,8-1,9-1,10-1,11-1,12-1,13-1,14-1

Conclusion: All versions read the same.

885. Ephesians 1:2* Grace be to you, and peace, from God our **Father**, and from the Lord **Jesus** Christ.

AV - **16,** 1-1,2-1,3-1,4-1,5-1,6-1,7-1,8-1,9-1,10-1,11-1,12-1,13-1,14-1,15-1,16-1

ESV - **14,** 1-1,2-1,3-1,4-1,5-1,6-1,7-1,8-1,9-1,10-1,11-1,12-1,13-1,14-1

HCSB - **14,** 1-1,2-1,3-1,4-1,5-1,6-1,7-1,8-1,9-1,10-1,11-1,12-1,13-1,14-1

NASV - **14,** 1-1,2-1,3-1,4-1,5-1,6-1,7-1,8-1,9-1,10-1,11-1,12-1,13-1,14-1

NCV - **14,** 1-1,2-1,3-1,4-1,5-1,6-1,7-1,8-1,9-1,10-1,11-1,12-1,13-1,14-1
NIV - **14,** 1-1,2-1,3-1,4-1,5-1,6-1,7-1,8-1,9-1,10-1,11-1,12-1,13-1,14-1
NKJV - **14,** 1-1,2-1,3-1,4-1,5-1,6-1,7-1,8-1,9-1,10-1,11-1,12-1,13-1,14-1
NLT - **14,** 1-1,2-1,3-1,4-1,5-1,6-1,7-1,8-1,9-1,10-1,11-1,12-1,13-1,14-1
NRSV - **14,** 1-1,2-1,3-1,4-1,5-1,6-1,7-1,8-1,9-1,10-1,11-1,12-1,13-1,14-1
Conclusion: All versions read the same.

886. Ephesians 4:20 But ye have not so learned Christ;
AV - **7,** 1-1,2-1,3-1,4-1,5-1,6-1,7-1
ESV - **9,** 1-1,2-1,3-1,4-1,5-1,6-1,7-1,8-1,9-1
HCSB - **10,** 1-1,2-1,3-1,4-1,5-1,6-1,7-1,8-**2**,9-1,10-1
NASV - **9,** 1-1,2-1,3-1,4-1,5-1,6-1,7-1,8-1,9-1
NCV - **10,** 1-1,2-1,3-1,4-1,5-1,6-1,7-1,8-1,9-1,10-1
NIV - **10,** 1-1,2-**3**,3-1,4-1,5-1,6-1,7-1,8-1,9-1,10-1
NKJV - **7,** 1-1,2-1,3-1,4-1,5-1,6-1,7-1
NLT - **8,** 1-1,2-1,3-**2**,4-1,5-1,6-1,7-**2**,8-1
NRSV - **8,** 1-1,2-1,3-1,4-1,5-1,6-1,7-1,8-1
Conclusion: Only three modern versions are more complex than the King James Bible.

887. Ephesians 4:21* If so be that ye have heard him, and have been taught by him, as the truth is in **Jesus**:
AV - **20,** 1-1,2-1,3-1,4-1,5-1,6-1,7-1,8-1,9-1,10-1,11-1,12-1,13-1,14-1,15-1,16-1,17-1,18-1,19-1,20-1
ESV - **19,** 1-1,2-**3**,3-1,4-1,5-1,6-1,7-**2**,8-1,9-1,10-1,11-1,12-1,13-1,14-1,15-1,16-1,17-1,18-1,19-1
HCSB - **15,** 1-**3**,2-1,3-1,4-1,5-1,6-1,7-1,8-1,9-1,10-**2**,11-1,12-1,13-1,14-1,15-1
NASV - **18,** 1-1,2-**2**,3-1,4-1,5-1,6-1,7-1,8-1,9-1,10-1,11-1,12-1,13-1,14-1,15-1,16-1,17-1,18-1
NCV - **22,** 1-**3**,2-1,3-1,4-1,5-1,6-1,7-1,8-1,9-1,10-**2**,11-1,12-1,13-1,14-1,15-1,16-1,17-1,18-1,19-1,20-1,21-1,22-1
NIV - **19,** 1-**2**,2-1,3-1,4-1,5-1,6-1,7-1,8-1,9-1,10-1,11-1,12-**3**,13-1,14-1,15-1,16-1,17-1,18-1,19-1
NKJV - **18,** 1-1,2-**2**,3-1,4-1,5-1,6-1,7-1,8-1,9-1,10-1,11-1,12-1,13-1,14-1,15-1,16-1,17-1,18-1
NLT - **15,** 1-1,2-1,3-1,4-1,5-**2**,6-1,7-1,8-1,9-1,10-1,11-1,12-1,13-1,14-1,15-1
NRSV - **17,** 1-1,2-**2**,3-1,4-1,5-1,6-**2**,7-1,8-1,9-1,10-1,11-1,12-1,13-1,14-1,15-1,16-1,17-1
Conclusion: All eight modern versions are more complex than the King James Bible. Once again the NKJV mirrors the NASV.

888. Philippians 1:21 For to me to live is Christ, and to die is gain.
AV - **12,** 1-1,2-1,3-1,4-1,5-1,6-1,7-1,8-1,9-1,10-1,11-1,12-1
ESV - **12,** 1-1,2-1,3-1,4-1,5-1,6-1,7-1,8-1,9-1,10-1,11-1,12-1
HCSB - **9,** 1-1,2-1,3-**2**,4-1,5-1,6-1,7-**2**,8-1,9-1
NASV - **12,** 1-1,2-1,3-1,4-1,5-1,6-1,7-1,8-1,9-1,10-1,11-1,12-1
NCV - **17,** 1-1,2-1,3-1,4-**2**,5-**3**,6-1,7-**2**,8-**2**,9-1,10-1,11-1,12-**2**,13-1,14-1,15-**2**,16-1,17-1
NIV - **12,** 1-1,2-1,3-1,4-1,5-1,6-1,7-1,8-1,9-1,10-1,11-1,12-1
NKJV - **12,** 1-1,2-1,3-1,4-1,5-1,6-1,7-1,8-1,9-1,10-1,11-1,12-1
NLT - **13,** 1-1,2-1,3-1,4-**2**,5-1,6-**2**,7-1,8-1,9-1,10-**2**,11-1,12-**2**,13-**2**

NRSV - 10, 1-1,2-1,3-1,4-**2**,5-1,6-1,7-1,8-**2**,9-1,10-1

Conclusion: While only four modern versions are more complex than the King James Bible, the NCV and NLT are again masterpieces of complexity.

889. Philippians 2:21* For all seek their own, not the things which are **Jesus** Christ's.

AV - **12,** 1-1,2-1,3-1,4-1,5-1,6-1,7-1,8-1,9-1,10-1,11-1,12-1

ESV - 11, 1-1,2-1,3-1,4-1,5-1,6-**3**,7-1,8-1,9-1,10-1,11-1

HCSB - 10, 1-1,2-1,3-1,4-1,5-**3**,6-1,7-1,8-1,9-1,10-1

NASV - 13, 1-1,2-1,3-1,4-1,5-1,6-1,7-1,8-**3**,9-1,10-1,11-1,12-1,13-1

NCV - 16, 1-**2**,2-**2**,3-1,4-**4**,5-**2**,6-1,7-1,8-1,9-1,10-1,11-1,12-1,13-1,14-1,15-1,16-1

NIV - 13, 1-1,2-**4**,3-1,4-1,5-1,6-1,7-1,8-**3**,9-1,10-1,11-1,12-1,13-1

NKJV - **13,** 1-1,2-1,3-1,4-1,5-1,6-1,7-1,8-1,9-1,10-1,11-1,12-1,13-1

NLT - **15,** 1-1,2-1,3-**2**,4-1,5-**2**,6-1,7-**2**,8-1,9-1,10-1,11-1,12-**2**,13-1,14-1,15-1

NRSV - 12, 1-1,2-1,3-1,4-1,5-1,6-1,7-**2**,8-1,9-1,10-1,11-1,12-1

Conclusion: Seven modern versions are more complex than the King James Bible. It is a shame and a sham to call either the NCV or the NLT "easier to read."

890. Philippians 4:23* The grace of our Lord **Jesus** Christ be with you all. **Amen.**

AV - **12,** 1-1,2-1,3-1,4-1,5-1,6-1,7-1,8-1,9-1,10-1,11-1,12-1

ESV - **11,** 1-1,2-1,3-1,4-1,5-1,6-1,7-1,8-1,9-1,10-1,11-1

HCSB - **11,** 1-1,2-1,3-1,4-1,5-1,6-1,7-1,8-1,9-1,10-1,11-1

NASV - **11,** 1-1,2-1,3-1,4-1,5-1,6-1,7-1,8-1,9-1,10-1,11-1

NCV - **11,** 1-1,2-1,3-1,4-1,5-1,6-1,7-1,8-1,9-1,10-1,11-1

NIV - **12,** 1-1,2-1,3-1,4-1,5-1,6-1,7-1,8-1,9-1,10-1,11-1,12-1

NKJV - **12,** 1-1,2-1,3-1,4-1,5-1,6-1,7-1,8-1,9-1,10-1,11-1,12-1

NLT - **12,** 1-1,2-1,3-1,4-1,5-1,6-1,7-1,8-1,9-1,10-1,11-1,12-1

NRSV - **11,** 1-1,2-1,3-1,4-1,5-1,6-1,7-1,8-1,9-1,10-1,11-1

Conclusion: All versions read the same.

891. Colossians 1:4* Since we heard of your faith in Christ **Jesus**, and of the love which ye have to all the saints,

AV - **20,** 1-1,2-1,3-1,4-1,5-1,6-1,7-1,8-1,9-1,10-1,11-1,12-1,13-1,14-1,15-1,16-1,17-1,18-1,19-1,20-1

ESV - **20,** 1-1,2-1,3-1,4-1,5-1,6-1,7-1,8-1,9-1,10-1,11-1,12-1,13-1,14-1,15-1,16-1,17-1,18-1,19-1,20-1

HCSB - **20,** 1-1,2-1,3-1,4-1,5-1,6-1,7-1,8-1,9-1,10-1,11-1,12-1,13-1,14-1,15-1,16-1,17-1,18-1,19-1,20-1

NASV - **19,** 1-1,2-1,3-1,4-1,5-1,6-1,7-1,8-1,9-1,10-1,11-1,12-1,13-1,14-1,15-1,16-1,17-1,18-1,19-1

NCV - 22, 1-**2**,2-1,3-1,4-1,5-**2**,6-1,7-1,8-1,9-1,10-1,11-1,12-1,13-1,14-1,15-1,16-1,17-1,18-1,19-1,20-1,21-1,22-**2**

NIV - **20,** 1-**2**,2-1,3-1,4-1,5-1,6-1,7-1,8-1,9-1,10-1,11-1,12-1,13-1,14-1,15-1,16-1,17-1,18-1,19-1,20-1

NKJV - **17,** 1-1,2-1,3-1,4-1,5-1,6-1,7-1,8-1,9-1,10-1,11-1,12-1,13-1,14-1,15-1,16-1,17-1

NLT - 18, 1-1,2-1,3-1,4-1,5-1,6-1,7-1,8-1,9-1,10-1,11-1,12-1,13-1,14-1,15-1,16-1,17-1,18-**2**

NRSV - 21, 1-**2**,2-1,3-1,4-1,5-1,6-1,7-1,8-1,9-1,10-1,11-1,12-1,13-1,14-1,15-1,16-1,17-1,18-1,19-1,20-1,21-1

Conclusion: Four modern versions are more complex than the King James Bible. The NCV is the most difficult to read.

892. Colossians 3:3 For ye are dead, and your life is hid with Christ in God.
AV - **13,** 1-1,2-1,3-1,4-1,5-1,6-1,7-1,8-1,9-1,10-1,11-1,12-1,13-1
ESV - 13, 1-1,2-1,3-1,4-1,5-1,6-1,7-1,8-1,9-**2**,10-1,11-1,12-1,13-1
HCSB - 14, 1-1,2-1,3-1,4-1,5-1,6-1,7-1,8-1,9-**2**,10-1,11-1,12-1,13-1,14-1
NASV - 13, 1-1,2-1,3-1,4-1,5-1,6-1,7-1,8-1,9-**2**,10-1,11-1,12-1,13-1
NCV - 16, 1-1,2-1,3-**2**,4-1,5-1,6-1,7-1,8-1,9-1,10-1,11-1,12-1,13-1,14-1,15-1,16-1
NIV - 13, 1-1,2-1,3-1,4-1,5-1,6-1,7-1,8-1,9-**2**,10-1,11-1,12-1,13-1
NKJV - 12, 1-1,2-1,3-1,4-1,5-1,6-1,7-1,8-**2**,9-1,10-1,11-1,12-1
NLT - 16, 1-1,2-1,3-1,4-1,5-1,6-1,7-1,8-1,9-1,10-1,11-1,12-**2**,13-1,14-1,15-1,16-1
NRSV - 13, 1-1,2-1,3-1,4-1,5-1,6-1,7-1,8-1,9-**2**,10-1,11-1,12-1,13-1
Conclusion: All eight modern versions are more complex than the King James Bible.

893. 1 Thessalonians 3:8 For now we live, if ye stand fast in the Lord.
AV - **11,** 1-1,2-1,3-1,4-1,5-1,6-1,7-1,8-1,9-1,10-1,11-1
ESV - 12, 1-1,2-1,3-1,4-1,5-1,6-1,7-1,8-**2**,9-1,10-1,11-1,12-1
HCSB - **11,** 1-1,2-1,3-1,4-1,5-1,6-1,7-1,8-1,9-1,10-1,11-1
NASV - 12, 1-1,2-1,3-1,4-**2**,5-1,6-1,7-1,8-1,9-1,10-1,11-1,12-1
NCV - 12, 1-1,2-1,3-1,4-**2**,5-1,6-1,7-1,8-1,9-1,10-1,11-1,12-1
NIV - 13, 1-1,2-1,3-1,4-**2**,5-1,6-1,7-1,8-1,9-**2**,10-1,11-1,12-1,13-1
NKJV - **11,** 1-1,2-1,3-1,4-1,5-1,6-1,7-1,8-1,9-1,10-1,11-1
NLT - 15, 1-1,2-1,3-1,4-1,5-1,6-1,7-1,8-1,9-1,10-1,11-**2**,12-1,13-1,14-1,15-1
NRSV - 13, 1-1,2-1,3-1,4-1,5-1,6-1,7-**3**,8-1,9-1,10-1,11-1,12-1,13-1
Conclusion: Six modern versions are more complex than the King James Bible.

894. 1 Thessalonians 5:19* Quench not the **Spirit**.
AV - **4,** 1-1,2-1,3-1,4-1
ESV - **5,** 1-1,2-1,3-1,4-1,5-1
HCSB - 4, 1-1,2-**2**,3-1,4-1
NASV - **5,** 1-1,2-1,3-1,4-1,5-1
NCV - **10,** 1-1,2-1,3-1,4-1,5-1,6-1,7-1,8-1,9-1,10-1
NIV - **7,** 1-1,2-1,3-1,4-1,5-1,6-1,7-1
NKJV - **5,** 1-1,2-1,3-1,4-1,5-1
NLT - 6, 1-1,2-1,3-**2**,4-1,5-1,6-1
NRSV - **5,** 1-1,2-1,3-1,4-1,5-1
Conclusion: Only the HCSB and NLT made the verse more complex. You can be sure the translators of the NCV worked hard to squeeze this simple four word statement down to a mere ten words.

895. 1 Thessalonians 5:21 Prove all things; hold fast that which is good.
AV - **9,** 1-1,2-1,3-1,4-1,5-1,6-1,7-1,8-1,9-1
ESV - 8, 1-1,2-1,3-**4**,1,4-1,5-1,6-1,7-1,8-1
HCSB - **10,** 1-1,2-1,3-1,4-1,5-1,6-1,7-1,8-1,9-1,10-1
NASV - 11, 1-1,2-**3**,3-**4**,4-1,5-**3**,6-1,7-1,8-1,9-1,10-1,11-1
NCV - 7, 1-1,2-1,3-**4**,4-1,5-1,6-1,7-1
NIV - 7, 1-1,2-**4**,3-1,4-1,5-1,6-1,7-1
NKJV - **8,** 1-1,2-1,3-1,4-1,5-1,6-1,7-1,8-1
NLT - 12, 1-1,2-1,3-**4**,4-1,5-1,6-1,7-1,8-1,9-1,10-1,11-1,12-1
NRSV - 9, 1-1,2-1,3-**4**,1,4-1,5-1,6-1,7-1,8-1,9-1
Conclusion: Six modern versions are more complex than the King James Bible. The NCV is the most difficult to read.

896. 1 Thessalonians 5:28* The grace of our Lord **Jesus** Christ be with you. **Amen.**
AV - **11,** 1-1,2-1,3-1,4-1,5-1,6-1,7-1,8-1,9-1,10-1,11-1
ESV - **10,** 1-1,2-1,3-1,4-1,5-1,6-1,7-1,8-1,9-1,10-1
HCSB - **11,** 1-1,2-1,3-1,4-1,5-1,6-1,7-1,8-1,9-1,10-1,11-1
NASV - **10,** 1-1,2-1,3-1,4-1,5-1,6-1,7-1,8-1,9-1,10-1
NCV - **10,** 1-1,2-1,3-1,4-1,5-1,6-1,7-1,8-1,9-1,10-1
NIV - **10,** 1-1,2-1,3-1,4-1,5-1,6-1,7-1,8-1,9-1,10-1
NKJV - **11,** 1-1,2-1,3-1,4-1,5-1,6-1,7-1,8-1,9-1,10-1,11-1
NLT - **11,** 1-1,2-1,3-1,4-1,5-1,6-1,7-1,8-1,9-1,10-1,11-1
NRSV - **10,** 1-1,2-1,3-1,4-1,5-1,6-1,7-1,8-1,9-1,10-1
Conclusion: All versions read the same.

897. 2 Thessalonians 3:18* The grace of our Lord **Jesus** Christ be with you all. **Amen.**
AV - **12,** 1-1,2-1,3-1,4-1,5-1,6-1,7-1,8-1,9-1,10-1,11-1,12-1
ESV - **11,** 1-1,2-1,3-1,4-1,5-1,6-1,7-1,8-1,9-1,10-1,11-1
HCSB - **12,** 1-1,2-1,3-1,4-1,5-1,6-1,7-1,8-1,9-1,10-1,11-1,12-1
NASV - **11,** 1-1,2-1,3-1,4-1,5-1,6-1,7-1,8-1,9-1,10-1,11-1
NCV - **11,** 1-1,2-1,3-1,4-1,5-1,6-1,7-1,8-1,9-1,10-1,11-1
NIV - **11,** 1-1,2-1,3-1,4-1,5-1,6-1,7-1,8-1,9-1,10-1,11-1
NKJV - **12,** 1-1,2-1,3-1,4-1,5-1,6-1,7-1,8-1,9-1,10-1,11-1,12-1
NLT - **12,** 1-1,2-1,3-1,4-1,5-1,6-1,7-1,8-1,9-1,10-1,11-1,12-1
NRSV - **12,** 1-1,2-1,3-1,4-1,5-1,6-1,7-1,8-1,9-1,10-1,11-1,12-1
Conclusion: All versions read the same.

898. 1 Timothy 2:13* For **Adam** was first formed, then Eve.
AV - **7,** 1-1,2-1,3-1,4-1,5-1,6-1,7-1
ESV - **7,** 1-1,2-1,3-1,4-1,5-1,6-1,7-1
HCSB - 7, 1-1,2-1,3-1,4-**3**,5-1,6-1,7-1
NASV - 11, 1-1,2-1,3-1,4-1,5-1,6-1,7-1,8-**3**,9-1,10-1,11-1
NCV - 8, 1-**2**,2-1,3-1,4-1,5-1,6-1,7-1,8-1
NIV - **7,** 1-1,2-1,3-1,4-1,5-1,6-1,7-1

NKJV - **7,** 1-1,2-1,3-1,4-1,5-1,6-1,7-1
NLT - 11, 1-1,2-1,3-1,4-1,5-1,6-1,7-**3**,8-1,9-1,10-1
NRSV - **7,** 1-1,2-1,3-1,4-1,5-1,6-1,7-1
Conclusion: Four modern versions are more complex than the King James Bible.

899. 1 Timothy 3:5 (For if a man know not how to rule his own house, how shall he take care of the church of God?)
AV - **22,** 1-1,2-1,3-1,4-1,5-1,6-1,7-1,8-1,9-1,10-1,11-1,12-1,13-1,14-1,15-1,16-1,17-1,18-1,19-1,20-1,21-1,22-1
ESV - 19, 1-1,2-1,3-**2**,4-1,5-1,6-1,7-1,8-1,9-**2**,10-1,11-1,12-**2**,13-1,14-1,15-1,16-1,17-1,18-1,19-1
HCSB - 20, 1-1,2-**3**,3-1,4-1,5-1,6-1,7-1,8-1,9-**2**,10-1,11-1,12-**2**,13-1,14-1,15-1,16-1,17-1,18-1,19-1,20-1
NASV - 23, 1-1,2-1,3-1,4-1,5-1,6-1,7-1,8-1,9-1,10-**2**,11-1,12-1,13-**2**,14-1,15-1,16-1,17-1,18-1,19-1,20-1,21-1,22-1,23-1
NCV - 19, 1-1,2-**2**,3-1,4-1,5-1,6-1,7-1,8-1,9-1,10-**3**,11-1,12-1,13-1,14-**2**,15-1,16-1,17-1,18-1,19-1
NIV - 20, 1-1,2-**2**,3-1,4-1,5-1,6-1,7-1,8-**2**,9-1,10-1,11-1,12-1,13-**3**,14-1,15-1,16-1,17-1,18-1,19-1,20-1
NKJV - 23, 1-1,2-1,3-1,4-1,5-1,6-1,7-1,8-1,9-1,10-1,11-1,12-1,13-1,14-1,15-1,16-1,17-1,18-1,19-1,20-1,21-1,22-1,23-1
NLT - 17, 1-1,2-1,3-1,4-1,5-**2**,6-**2**,7-1,8-1,9-**2**,10-1,11-1,12-1,13-1,14-1,15-1,16-1,17-1
NRSV - 20, 1-1,2-1,3-**2**,4-1,5-1,6-1,7-1,8-1,9-**2**,10-1,11-1,12-**2**,13-1,14-1,15-1,16-1,17-1,18-1,19-1,20-1
Conclusion: All eight modern versions are more complex than the King James Bible.

900. 2 Timothy 1:13* Hold fast the form of sound words, which thou hast heard of me, in faith and love which is in Christ **Jesus**.
AV - **22,** 1-1,2-1,3-1,4-1,5-1,6-1,7-1,8-1,9-1,10-1,11-1,12-1,13-1,14-1,15-1,16-1,17-1,18-1,19-1,20-1,21-1,22-1
ESV - 23, 1-**2**,2-1,3-**2**,4-1,5-1,6-1,7-1,8-1,9-1,10-1,11-1,12-1,13-1,14-1,15-1,16-1,17-1,18-1,19-1,20-1,21-1,22-1,23-1
HCSB - 24, 1-1,2-1,3-1,4-1,5-**2**,6-1,7-1,8-**2**,9-1,10-1,11-1,12-1,13-1,14-1,15-1,16-1,17-1,18-1,19-1,20-1,21-1,22-1,23-1,24-1
NASV - 22, 1-**2**,2-1,3-**2**,4-1,5-1,6-1,7-1,8-1,9-1,10-1,11-1,12-1,13-1,14-1,15-1,16-1,17-1,18-1,19-1,20-1,21-1,22-1
NCV - 20, 1-**2**,2-1,3-**2**,4-1,5-**2**,6-**2**,7-1,8-1,9-1,10-1,11-1,12-1,13-1,14-1,15-1,16-1,17-1,18-1,19-1,20-1
NIV - 19, 1-1,2-1,3-1,4-1,5-1,6-1,7-1,8-1,9-**2**,10-1,11-1,12-**2**,13-1,14-1,15-1,16-1,17-1,18-1,19-1
NKJV - 22, 1-1,2-1,3-1,4-**2**,5-1,6-1,7-1,8-1,9-1,10-1,11-1,12-1,13-1,14-1,15-1,16-1,17-1,18-1,19-1,20-1,21-1,22-1
NLT - 26, 1-1,2-1,3-1,4-1,5-**2**,6-1,7-**2**,8-**2**,9-1,10-1,11-1,12-1,13-1,14-**2**,15-1,16-1,17-1,18-1,19-1,20-1,21-1,22-1,23-1,24-1,25-1,26-1
NRSV - 23, 1-1,2-1,3-1,4-**2**,5-1,6-1,7-**2**,8-1,9-1,10-1,11-1,12-1,13-1,14-1,15-1,16-1,17-1,18-1,19-1,20-1,21-1,22-1,23-1
Conclusion: All eight modern versions are more complex than the King James Bible.

901. 2 Timothy 4:12* And **Tychicus** have I sent to **Ephesus**.
AV - **7,** 1-1,2-1,3-1,4-1,5-1,6-1,7-1
ESV - **6,** 1-1,2-1,3-1,4-1,5-1,6-1
HCSB - **6,** 1-1,2-1,3-1,4-1,5-1,6-1
NASV - **7,** 1-1,2-1,3-1,4-1,5-1,6-1,7-1
NCV - **5,** 1-1,2-1,3-1,4-1,5-1
NIV - **5,** 1-1,2-1,3-1,4-1,5-1
NKJV - **7,** 1-1,2-1,3-1,4-1,5-1,6-1,7-1
NLT - **5,** 1-1,2-1,3-1,4-1,5-1
NRSV - **6,** 1-1,2-1,3-1,4-1,5-1,6-1
Conclusion: All versions read the same.

902. Philemon 1:3* Grace to you, and peace, from God our **Father** and the Lord **Jesus** Christ.
AV - **14,** 1-1,2-1,3-1,4-1,5-1,6-1,7-1,8-1,9-1,10-1,11-1,12-1,13-1,14-1
ESV - **14,** 1-1,2-1,3-1,4-1,5-1,6-1,7-1,8-1,9-1,10-1,11-1,12-1,13-1,14-1
HCSB - **14,** 1-1,2-1,3-1,4-1,5-1,6-1,7-1,8-1,9-1,10-1,11-1,12-1,13-1,14-1
NASV - **14,** 1-1,2-1,3-1,4-1,5-1,6-1,7-1,8-1,9-1,10-1,11-1,12-1,13-1,14-1
NCV - **14,** 1-1,2-1,3-1,4-1,5-1,6-1,7-1,8-1,9-1,10-1,11-1,12-1,13-1,14-1
NIV - **14,** 1-1,2-1,3-1,4-1,5-1,6-1,7-1,8-1,9-1,10-1,11-1,12-1,13-1,14-1
NKJV - **14,** 1-1,2-1,3-1,4-1,5-1,6-1,7-1,8-1,9-1,10-1,11-1,12-1,13-1,14-1
NLT - **14,** 1-1,2-1,3-1,4-1,5-1,6-1,7-1,8-1,9-1,10-1,11-1,12-1,13-1,14-1
NRSV - **14,** 1-1,2-1,3-1,4-1,5-1,6-1,7-1,8-1,9-1,10-1,11-1,12-1,13-1,14-1
Conclusion: All versions read the same.

903. Hebrews 7:10* For he was yet in the loins of his **father**, when **Melchisedec** met him.
AV - **14,** 1-1,2-1,3-1,4-1,5-1,6-1,7-1,8-1,9-1,10-1,11-1,12-1,13-1,14-1
ESV - 14, 1-1,2-1,3-1,4-1,5-1,6-1,7-1,8-1,9-1,10-**3**,11-1,12-1,13-1,14-1
HCSB - 11, 1-1,2-1,3-1,4-1,5-**2**,6-1,7-**3**,8-1,9-1,10-1,11-1
NASV - **14,** 1-1,2-1,3-1,4-1,5-1,6-1,7-1,8-1,9-1,10-1,11-1,12-1,13-1,14-1
NCV - 18, 1-1,2-1,3-1,4-1,5-1,6-1,7-1,8-1,9-1,10-1,11-**2**,12-1,13-1,14-**3**,15-1,16-1,17-1,18-1
NIV - 14, 1-**2**,2-1,3-1,4-1,5-1,6-1,7-1,8-1,9-1,10-1,11-**2**,12-1,13-1,14-**3**
NKJV - **14,** 1-1,2-1,3-1,4-1,5-1,6-1,7-1,8-1,9-1,10-1,11-1,12-1,13-1,14-1
NLT - 22, 1-1,2-**2**,3-1,4-**2**,5-1,6-1,7-1,8-1,9-1,10-1,11-1,12-1,13-1,14-1,15-1,16-**2**,17-1,18-1,19-**3**,20-1,21-1,22-1
NRSV - 14, 1-1,2-1,3-1,4-1,5-1,6-1,7-1,8-1,9-1,10-**3**,11-1,12-1,13-1,14-1
Conclusion: Six modern versions are more complex than the King James Bible.

904. Hebrews 11:18* Of whom it was said, That in **Isaac** shall thy seed be called:
AV - **13,** 1-1,2-1,3-1,4-1,5-1,6-1,7-1,8-1,9-1,10-1,11-1,12-1,13-1
ESV - 12, 1-1,2-1,3-1,4-1,5-1,6-1,7-1,8-1,9-1,10-**2**,11-1,12-1
HCSB - 13, 1-**2**,2-1,3-1,4-1,5-1,6-1,7-1,8-1,9-1,10-1,11-1,12-1,13-1
NASV - 15, 1-1,2-1,3-1,4-1,5-1,6-1,7-1,8-1,9-1,10-1,11-1,12-**3**,13-1,14-1,15-1
NCV - 12, 1-1,2-1,3-1,4-1,5-**3**,6-1,7-**2**,8-1,9-1,10-1,11-1,12-1

NIV - 17, 1-**2**,2-1,3-1,4-1,5-1,6-1,7-1,8-1,9-1,10-1,11-1,12-1,13-1,14-**2**,15-1,16-1,17-**2**
NKJV - **12,** 1-1,2-1,3-1,4-1,5-1,6-1,7-1,8-1,9-1,10-1,11-1,12-1
NLT - 17, 1-**2**,2-1,3-1,4-1,5-1,6-1,7-1,8-1,9-1,10-1,11-1,12-1,13-1,14-**2**,15-1,16-1,17-**2**
NRSV - 17, 1-1,2-1,3-1,4-1,5-1,6-1,7-1,8-1,9-1,10-1,11-1,12-**3**,13-1,14-1,15-1,16-1,17-1
Conclusion: Seven modern versions are more complex than the King James Bible. Only the NIV and the NRSV made the verse more complex. The fact that verse structure for both of these versions is identical makes it look as though the translators of the NLT simply copied the NIV.

905. Hebrews 13:25* Grace be with you all. **Amen**.
AV - **6,** 1-1,2-1,3-1,4-1,5-1,6-1
ESV - **6,** 1-1,2-1,3-1,4-1,5-1,6-1
HCSB - **6,** 1-1,2-1,3-1,4-1,5-1,6-1
NASV - **5,** 1-1,2-1,3-1,4-1,5-1
NCV - **5,** 1-1,2-1,3-1,4-1,5-1
NIV - **5,** 1-1,2-1,3-1,4-1,5-1
NKJV - **6,** 1-1,2-1,3-1,4-1,5-1,6-1
NLT - **7,** 1-1,2-1,3-1,4-1,5-1,6-1,7-1
NRSV - **6,** 1-1,2-1,3-1,4-1,5-1,6-1
Conclusion: All versions read the same.

906. James 4:15 For that ye ought to say, If the Lord will, we shall live, and do this, or that.
AV - **18,** 1-1,2-1,3-1,4-1,5-1,6-1,7-1,8-1,9-1,10-1,11-1,12-1,13-1,14-1,15-1,16-1,17-1,18-1
ESV - 17, 1-**2**,2-1,3-1,4-1,5-1,6-1,7-1,8-1,9-1,10-1,11-1,12-1,13-1,14-1,15-1,16-1,17-1
HCSB - 16, 1-**2**,2-1,3-1,4-1,5-1,6-1,7-1,8-1,9-1,10-1,11-1,12-1,13-1,14-1,15-1,16-1
NASV - 18, 1-**2**,2-1,3-1,4-1,5-1,6-1,7-1,8-1,9-1,10-1,11-1,12-1,13-1,14-**2**,15-1,16-1,17-1,18-1
NCV - **16,** 1-1,2-1,3-1,4-1,5-1,6-1,7-1,8-1,9-1,10-1,11-1,12-1,13-1,14-1,15-1,16-1
NIV - 19, 1-**2**,2-1,3-1,4-1,5-1,6-1,7-1,8-1,9-1,10-1,11-1,12-1,13-1,14-1,15-1,16-1,17-1,18-1,19-1
NKJV - 17, 1-**2**,2-1,3-1,4-1,5-1,6-1,7-1,8-1,9-1,10-1,11-1,12-1,13-1,14-1,15-1,16-1,17-1
NLT - **20,** 1-1,2-1,3-1,4-1,5-1,6-1,7-1,8-1,9-1,10-1,11-1,12-1,13-1,14-1,15-1,16-1,17-1,18-1,19-1,20-1
NRSV - 17, 1-**2**,2-1,3-1,4-1,5-1,6-1,7-1,8-1,9-**2**,10-1,11-1,12-1,13-1,14-1,15-1,16-1,17-1
Conclusion: Six modern versions are more complex than the King James Bible. In the strangest of turns, it is only the NCV and NLT that do not alter the syllable count!

907. 1 John 2:16* For all that is in the world, the lust of the flesh, and the lust of the eyes, and the pride of life, is not of the **Father**, but is of the world.
AV - **33,** 1-1,2-1,3-1,4-1,5-1,6-1,7-1,8-1,9-1,10-1,11-1,12-1,13-1,14-1,15-1,16-1,17-1,18-1,19-1,20-1,21-1,22-1,23-1,24-1,25-1,26-1,27-1,28-1,29-1,30-1,31-1,32-1,33-1
ESV - 32, 1-1,2-1,3-1,4-1,5-1,6-1,7-1,8-1,9-**2**,10-1,11-1,12-1,13-1,14-1,15-**2**,16-1,17-1,18-1,19-1,20-1,21-1,22-**3**,23-1,24-1,25-1,26-1,27-1,28-1,29-1,30-1,31-1,32-1
HCSB - 26, 1-1,2-1,3-1,4-1,5-1,6-1,7-1,8-1,9-1,10-1,11-1,12-1,13-1,14-1,15-1,16-**2**,17-1,18-1,19-1,20-1,21-1,22-1,23-1,24-1,25-1,26-1
NASV - 34, 1-1,2-1,3-1,4-1,5-1,6-1,7-1,8-1,9-1,10-1,11-1,12-1,13-1,14-1,15-1,16-1,17-1,18-1,19-1,20-1,21-**2**,22-1,23-1,24-1,25-1,26-1,27-1,28-1,29-1,30-1,31-1,32-1,33-1,34-1

NCV - 42, 1-1,2-1,3-1,4-1,5-1,6-1,7-1,8-**2**,9-1,10-1,11-1,12-**2**,13-1,14-**2**,15-1,16-**2**,17-1,18-1,19-1,20-1,21-**2**,22-1,23-1,24-1,25-1,26-1,27-1,28-1,29-1,30-1,31-1,32-1,33-1,34-1,35-1,36-1,37-1,38-1,39-1,40-1,41-1,42-1

NIV - 33, 1-1,2-**4**,3-1,4-1,5-1,6-1,7-**2**,8-1,9-**2**,10-1,11-1,12-1,13-1,14-1,15-1,16-1,17-1,18-**2**,19-1,20-1,21-1,22-1,23-1,24-1,25-1,26-1,27-1,28-1,29-1,30-1,31-1,32-1,33-1

NKJV - **32,** 1-1,2-1,3-1,4-1,5-1,6-1,7-1,8-1,9-1,10-1,11-1,12-1,13-1,14-1,15-1,16-1,17-1,18-1,19-1,20-1,21-1,22-1,23-1,24-1,25-1,26-1,27-1,28-1,29-1,30-1,31-1,32-1

NLT - 34, 1-1,2-1,3-1,4-**2**,5-**2**,6-1,7-**2**,8-1,9-**3**,10-**2**,11-1,12-**2**,13-1,14-**4**,15-1,16-1,17-1,18-1,19-1,20-1,21-**3**,22-1,23-**3**,24-1,25-1,26-1,27-1,28-1,29-1,30-1,31-1,32-1,33-1,34-1

NRSV - 30, 1-1,2-1,3-1,4-1,5-1,6-1,7-1,8-1,9-**2**,10-1,11-1,12-1,13-1,14-1,15-1,16-1,17-1,18-1,19-1,20-1,21-1,22-1,23-1,24-1,25-1,26-1,27-1,28-1,29-1,30-1

Conclusion: Seven modern versions are more complex than the King James Bible. At 42 words the NCV was the longest rendering, but the NLT managed to be the most complex in only 34 words.

908. 1 John 5:12 He that hath the Son hath life; and he that hath not the Son of God hath not life.
AV - **19,** 1-1,2-1,3-1,4-1,5-1,6-1,7-1,8-1,9-1,10-1,11-1,12-1,13-1,14-1,15-1,16-1,17-1,18-1,19-1

ESV - 18, 1-**2**,2-1,3-1,4-1,5-1,6-1,7-**2**,8-1,9-1,10-1,11-1,12-1,13-1,14-1,15-1,16-1,17-1,18-1

HCSB - 24, 1-1,2-**2**,3-1,4-1,5-1,6-1,7-1,8-1,9-1,10-1,11-**2**,12-1,13-1,14-1,15-1,16-1,17-1,18-1,19-1,20-1,21-1,22-1,23-1,24-1

NASV - **22,** 1-1,2-1,3-1,4-1,5-1,6-1,7-1,8-1,9-1,10-1,11-1,12-1,13-1,14-1,15-1,16-1,17-1,18-1,19-1,20-1,21-1,22-1

NCV - 19, 1-**2**,2-1,3-1,4-1,5-1,6-1,7-1,8-**2**,9-1,10-1,11-1,12-1,13-1,14-1,15-1,16-1,17-1,18-1,19-1

NIV - **20,** 1-1,2-1,3-1,4-1,5-1,6-1,7-1,8-1,9-1,10-1,11-1,12-1,13-1,14-1,15-1,16-1,17-1,18-1,19-1,20-1

NKJV - **20,** 1-1,2-1,3-1,4-1,5-1,6-1,7-1,8-1,9-1,10-1,11-1,12-1,13-1,14-1,15-1,16-1,17-1,18-1,19-1,20-1

NLT - 16, 1-**2**,2-1,3-1,4-1,5-1,6-1,7-**2**,8-1,9-1,10-1,11-1,12-1,13-1,14-1,15-1,16-1

NRSV - 18, 1-**2**,2-1,3-1,4-1,5-1,6-1,7-**2**,8-1,9-1,10-1,11-1,12-1,13-1,14-1,15-1,16-1,17-1,18-1

Conclusion: Five modern versions are more complex than the King James Bible.

909. Revelation 1:14 His head and his hairs were white like wool, as white as snow; and his eyes were as a flame of fire;
AV - **22,** 1-1,2-1,3-1,4-1,5-1,6-1,7-1,8-1,9-1,10-1,11-1,12-1,13-1,14-1,15-1,16-1,17-1,18-1,19-1,20-1,21-1,22-1

ESV - **21,** 1-1,2-1,3-1,4-1,5-1,6-1,7-1,8-1,9-1,10-1,11-1,12-1,13-1,14-1,15-1,16-1,17-1,18-1,19-1,20-1,21-1

HCSB - 17, 1-1,2-1,3-1,4-1,5-1,6-1,7-1,8-1,9-1,10-1,11-1,12-1,13-1,14-1,15-1,16-**2**,17-1

NASV - **21,** 1-1,2-1,3-1,4-1,5-1,6-1,7-1,8-1,9-1,10-1,11-1,12-1,13-1,14-1,15-1,16-1,17-1,18-1,19-1,20-1,21-1

NCV - **20,** 1-1,2-1,3-1,4-1,5-1,6-1,7-1,8-1,9-1,10-1,11-1,12-1,13-1,14-1,15-1,16-1,17-1,18-1,19-1,20-1

NIV - 19, 1-1,2-1,3-1,4-1,5-1,6-1,7-1,8-1,9-1,10-1,11-1,12-1,13-1,14-1,15-1,16-1,17-1,18-**2**,19-1

NKJV - **20,** 1-1,2-1,3-1,4-1,5-1,6-1,7-1,8-1,9-1,10-1,11-1,12-1,13-1,14-1,15-1,16-1,17-1,18-1,19-1,20-1

NLT - **21,** 1-1,2-1,3-1,4-1,5-1,6-1,7-1,8-1,9-1,10-1,11-1,12-1,13-1,14-1,15-1,16-1,17-1,18-1,19-
1,20-1,21-1

NRSV - **21,** 1-1,2-1,3-1,4-1,5-1,6-1,7-1,8-1,9-1,10-1,11-1,12-1,13-1,14-1,15-1,16-1,17-1,18-1,19-
1,20-1,21-1

Conclusion: Only the HCSB and the NIV made the verse more complex.

910. Revelation 7:5*# Of the tribe of **Juda** were sealed twelve **thousand**. Of the tribe of **Reuben**
were sealed twelve **thousand**. Of the tribe of Gad were sealed twelve **thousand**.

AV - **27,** 1-1,2-1,3-1,4-1,5-1,6-1,7-1,8-1,9-1,10-1,11-1,12-1,13-1,14-1,15-1,16-1,17-1,18-1,19-1,20-
1,21-1,22-1,23-1,24-1,25-1,26-1,27-1

ESV - **20,** 1-1,2-1,3-1,4-1,5-1,6-1,7-1,8-1,9-1,10-1,11-1,12-1,13-1,14-1,15-1,16-1,17-1,18-1,19-
1,20-1

HCSB - **19,** 1-1,2-1,3-1,4-1,5-1,6-1,7-1,8-1,9-1,10-1,11-1,12-1,13-1,14-1,15-1,16-1,17-1,18-1,19-1

NASV - **23,** 1-1,2-1,3-1,4-1,5-1,6-1,7-1,8-1,9-1,10-1,11-1,12-1,13-1,14-1,15-1,16-1,17-1,18-1,19-
1,20-1,21··1,22-1,23-1

NCV - **26,** 1-1,2-1,3-1,4-1,5-1,6-1,7-1,8-1,9-1,10-1,11-1,12-1,13-1,14-1,15-1,16-1,17-1,18-1,19-
1,20-1,21-1,22-1,23-1,24-1,25-1,26-1

NIV - **20,** 1-1,2-1,3-1,4-1,5-1,6-1,7-1,8-1,9-1,10-1,11-1,12-1,13-1,14-1,15-1,16-1,17-1,18-1,19-1,20-
1

NKJV - **27,** 1-1,2-1,3-1,4-1,5-1,6-1,7-1,8-1,9-1,10-1,11-1,12-1,13-1,14-1,15-1,16-1,17-1,18-1,19-
1,20-1,21-1,22-1,23-1,24-1,25-1,26-1,27-1

NLT - **10,** 1-1,2-1,3-1,4-1,5-1,6-1,7-1,8-1,9-1,10-1

NRSV - **22,** 1-1,2-1,3-1,4-1,5-1,6-1,7-1,8-1,9-1,10-1,11-1,12-1,13-1,14-1,15-1,16-1,17-1,18-1,19-
1,20-1,21-1,22-1

Conclusion: All versions read the same.

911. Revelation 7:6*# Of the tribe of **Aser** were sealed twelve **thousand**. Of the tribe of **Nepthalim**
were sealed twelve **thousand**. Of the tribe of **Manasses** were sealed twelve **thousand**.

AV - **27,** 1-1,2-1,3-1,4-1,5-1,6-1,7-1,8-1,9-1,10-1,11-1,12-1,13-1,14-1,15-1,16-1,17-1,18-1,19-1,20-
1,21-1,22-1,23-1,24-1,25-1,26-1,27-1

ESV - **18,** 1-1,2-1,3-1,4-1,5-1,6-1,7-1,8-1,9-1,10-1,11-1,12-1,13-1,14-1,15-1,16-1,17-1,18-1

HCSB - **18,** 1-1,2-1,3-1,4-1,5-1,6-1,7-1,8-1,9-1,10-1,11-1,12-1,13-1,14-1,15-1,16-1,17-1,18-1

NASV - **21,** 1-1,2-1,3-1,4-1,5-1,6-1,7-1,8-1,9-1,10-1,11-1,12-1,13-1,14-1,15-1,16-1,17-1,18-1,19-
1,20-1,21-1

NCV - **21,** 1-1,2-1,3-1,4-1,5-1,6-1,7-1,8-1,9-1,10-1,11-1,12-1,13-1,14-1,15-1,16-1,17-1,18-1,19-
1,20-1,21-1

NIV - **18,** 1-1,2-1,3-1,4-1,5-1,6-1,7-1,8-1,9-1,10-1,11-1,12-1,13-1,14-1,15-1,16-1,17-1,18-1

NKJV - **27,** 1-1,2-1,3-1,4-1,5-1,6-1,7-1,8-1,9-1,10-1,11-1,12-1,13-1,14-1,15-1,16-1,17-1,18-1,19-
1,20-1,21-1,22-1,23-1,24-1,25-1,26-1,27-1

NLT - **10,** 1-1,2-1,3-1,4-1,5-1,6-1,7-1,8-1,9-1,10-1

NRSV - **21,** 1-1,2-1,3-1,4-1,5-1,6-1,7-1,8-1,9-1,10-1,11-1,12-1,13-1,14-1,15-1,16-1,17-1,18-1,19-
1,20-1,21-1

Conclusion: All versions read the same.

912. Revelation 7:7*# Of the tribe of **Simeon** were sealed twelve **thousand**. Of the tribe of **Levi** were sealed twelve **thousand**. Of the tribe of **Issachar** were sealed twelve **thousand**.

AV - **27,** 1-1,2-1,3-1,4-1,5-1,6-1,7-1,8-1,9-1,10-1,11-1,12-1,13-1,14-1,15-1,16-1,17-1,18-1,19-1,20-1,21-1,22-1,23-1,24-1,25-1,26-1,27-1

ESV - **18,** 1-1,2-1,3-1,4-1,5-1,6-1,7-1,8-1,9-1,10-1,11-1,12-1,13-1,14-1,15-1,16-1,17-1,18-1

HCSB - **18,** 1-1,2-1,3-1,4-1,5-1,6-1,7-1,8-1,9-1,10-1,11-1,12-1,13-1,14-1,15-1,16-1,17-1,18-1

NASV - **21,** 1-1,2-1,3-1,4-1,5-1,6-1,7-1,8-1,9-1,10-1,11-1,12-1,13-1,14-1,15-1,16-1,17-1,18-1,19-1,20-1,21-1

NCV - **21,** 1-1,2-1,3-1,4-1,5-1,6-1,7-1,8-1,9-1,10-1,11-1,12-1,13-1,14-1,15-1,16-1,17-1,18-1,19-1,20-1,21-1

NIV - **18,** 1-1,2-1,3-1,4-1,5-1,6-1,7-1,8-1,9-1,10-1,11-1,12-1,13-1,14-1,15-1,16-1,17-1,18-1

NKJV - **27,** 1-1,2-1,3-1,4-1,5-1,6-1,7-1,8-1,9-1,10-1,11-1,12-1,13-1,14-1,15-1,16-1,17-1,18-1,19-1,20-1,21-1,22-1,23-1,24-1,25-1,26-1,27-1

NLT - **10,** 1-1,2-1,3-1,4-1,5-1,6-1,7-1,8-1,9-1,10-1

NRSV - **21,** 1-1,2-1,3-1,4-1,5-1,6-1,7-1,8-1,9-1,10-1,11-1,12-1,13-1,14-1,15-1,16-1,17-1,18-1,19-1,20-1,21-1

Conclusion: All versions read the same.

913. Revelation 7:8*# Of the tribe of **Zabulon** were sealed twelve **thousand**. Of the tribe of **Joseph** were sealed twelve **thousand**. Of the tribe of **Benjamin** were sealed twelve **thousand**.

AV - **27,** 1-1,2-1,3-1,4-1,5-1,6-1,7-1,8-1,9-1,10-1,11-1,12-1,13-1,14-1,15-1,16-1,17-1,18-1,19-1,20-1,21-1,22-1,23-1,24-1,25-1,26-1,27-1

ESV - **20,** 1-1,2-1,3-1,4-1,5-1,6-1,7-1,8-1,9-1,10-1,11-1,12-1,13-1,14-1,15-1,16-1,17-1,18-1,19-1,20-1

HCSB - **19,** 1-1,2-1,3-1,4-1,5-1,6-1,7-1,8-1,9-1,10-1,11-1,12-1,13-1,14-1,15-1,16-1,17-1,18-1,19-1

NASV - **23,** 1-1,2-1,3-1,4-1,5-1,6-1,7-1,8-1,9-1,10-1,11-1,12-1,13-1,14-1,15-1,16-1,17-1,18-1,19-1,20-1,21-1,22-1,23-1

NCV - **27,** 1-1,2-1,3-1,4-1,5-1,6-1,7-1,8-1,9-1,10-1,11-1,12-1,13-1,14-1,15-1,16-1,17-1,18-1,19-1,20-1,21-1,22-1,23-1,24-1,25-1,26-1,27-1

NIV - **18,** 1-1,2-1,3-1,4-1,5-1,6-1,7-1,8-1,9-1,10-1,11-1,12-1,13-1,14-1,15-1,16-1,17-1,18-1

NKJV - **27,** 1-1,2-1,3-1,4-1,5-1,6-1,7-1,8-1,9-1,10-1,11-1,12-1,13-1,14-1,15-1,16-1,17-1,18-1,19-1,20-1,21-1,22-1,23-1,24-1,25-1,26-1,27-1

NLT - **10,** 1-1,2-1,3-1,4-1,5-1,6-1,7-1,8-1,9-1,10-1

NRSV - **22,** 1-1,2-1,3-1,4-1,5-1,6-1,7-1,8-1,9-1,10-1,11-1,12-1,13-1,14-1,15-1,16-1,17-1,18-1,19-1,20-1,21-1,22-1

Conclusion: All versions read the same.

914. Revelation 21:13 On the east three gates; on the north three gates; on the south three gates; and on the west three gates.

AV - **21,** 1-1,2-1,3-1,4-1,5-1,6-1,7-1,8-1,9-1,10-1,11-1,12-1,13-1,14-1,15-1,16-1,17-1,18-1,19-1,20-1,21-1

ESV - **21,** 1-1,2-1,3-1,4-1,5-1,6-1,7-1,8-1,9-1,10-1,11-1,12-1,13-1,14-1,15-1,16-1,17-1,18-1,19-1,20-1,21-1

HCSB - **23,** 1-1,2-1,3-1,4-1,5-1,6-1,7-1,8-1,9-1,10-1,11-1,12-1,13-1,14-1,15-1,16-1,17-1,18-1,19-1,20-1,21-1,22-1,23-1

NASV - **25,** 1-1,2-1,3-1,4-1,5-1,6-1,7-1,8-1,9-1,10-1,11-1,12-1,13-1,14-1,15-1,16-1,17-1,18-1,19-1,20-1,21-1,22-1,23-1,24-1,25-1

NCV - **20,** 1-1,2-1,3-1,4-1,5-1,6-1,7-1,8-1,9-1,10-1,11-1,12-1,13-1,14-1,15-1,16-1,17-1,18-1,19-1,20-1

NIV - **20,** 1-1,2-1,3-1,4-1,5-1,6-1,7-1,8-1,9-1,10-1,11-1,12-1,13-1,14-1,15-1,16-1,17-1,18-1,19-1,20-1

NKJV - **21,** 1-1,2-1,3-1,4-1,5-1,6-1,7-1,8-1,9-1,10-1,11-1,12-1,13-1,14-1,15-1,16-1,17-1,18-1,19-1,20-1,21-1

NLT - **12,** 1-1,2-1,3-1,4-1,5-1,6-1,7-1,8-1,9-1,10-1,11-1,12-1

NRSV - **21,** 1-1,2-1,3-1,4-1,5-1,6-1,7-1,8-1,9-1,10-1,11-1,12-1,13-1,14-1,15-1,16-1,17-1,18-1,19-1,20-1,21-1

Conclusion: All versions read the same.

915. Revelation 21:25 And the gates of it shall not be shut at all by day: for there shall be no night there.

AV - **19,** 1-1,2-1,3-1,4-1,5-1,6-1,7-1,8-1,9-1,10-1,11-1,12-1,13-1,14-1,15-1,16-1,17-1,18-1,19-1

ESV - **16,** 1-1,2-1,3-1,4-1,5-1,6-1,7-1,8-1,9-1,10-1,11-1,12-1,13-1,14-1,15-1,16-1

HCSB - 14, 1-1,2-1,3-1,4-1,5-1,6-**2**,7-1,8-**2**,9-1,10-1,11-**2**,12-1,13-1,14-1

NASV - 16, 1-1,2-1,3-**2**,4-1,5-1,6-1,7-1,8-1,9-1,10-1,11-1,12-1,13-1,14-**2**,15-1,16-1

NCV - 16, 1-1,2-**2**,3-1,4-1,5-**2**,6-1,7-1,8-1,9-**2**,10-1,11-**2**,12-1,13-1,14-1,15-1,16-1

NIV - 16, 1-1,2-1,3-1,4-1,5-1,6-1,7-**2**,8-1,9-1,10-1,11-1,12-1,13-1,14-1,15-1,16-1

NKJV - **16,** 1-1,2-1,3-1,4-1,5-1,6-1,7-1,8-1,9-1,10-1,11-1,12-1,13-1,14-1,15-1,16-1

NLT - 17, 1-1,2-1,3-1,4-**2**,5-1,6-1,7-1,8-1,9-1,10-1,11-1,12-**2**,13-1,14-1,15-1,16-1,17-1

NRSV - 15, 1-1,2-1,3-1,4-**2**,5-1,6-1,7-1,8-1,9-1,10-1,11-1,12-1,13-1,14-1,15-1

Conclusion: Six modern versions are more complex than the King James Bible. The HCSB and NCV are the most difficult to read.

916. Revelation 22:21* The grace of our Lord **Jesus** Christ be with you all. **Amen**.

AV - **12,** 1-1,2-1,3-1,4-1,5-1,6-1,7-1,8-1,9-1,10-1,11-1,12-1

ESV - **10,** 1-1,2-1,3-1,4-1,5-1,6-1,7-1,8-1,9-1,10-1

HCSB - **12,** 1-1,2-1,3-1,4-1,5-1,6-1,7-1,8-1,9-1,10-1,11-1,12-1

NASV - **10,** 1-1,2-1,3-1,4-1,5-1,6-1,7-1,8-1,9-1,10-1

NCV - **10,** 1-1,2-1,3-1,4-1,5-1,6-1,7-1,8-1,9-1,10-1

NIV - 11, 1-1,2-1,3-1,4-1,5-1,6-1,7-1,8-1,9-1,10-**2**,11-1

NKJV - **12,** 1-1,2-1,3-1,4-1,5-1,6-1,7-1,8-1,9-1,10-1,11-1,12-1

NLT - 12, 1-1,2-1,3-1,4-1,5-1,6-1,7-1,8-1,9-1,10-1,11-**2**,12-**2**

NRSV - **12,** 1-1,2-1,3-1,4-1,5-1,6-1,7-1,8-1,9-1,10-1,11-1,12-1

Conclusion: Only the NIV and the NLT made the verse more complex.

Part 3

Conclusions

And God said, Let there be light: and there was light.
Genesis 1:3

Conclusions

Any honest person reading this study has to see that, in spite of claims to the contrary, modern versions are more complex than the King James Bible. I am sure that some insincere anti-King James types will feel it necessary to somehow disparage this study because they tremble at the concept of a perfect Bible, even while paying it lip service. Facts trump both opinion and prejudice. Therefore the hollow cries of those who place no value on truth are overruled by the roar of facts.

The eight modern translations all complicated the humble, unassuming language of our King James Bible in varying degrees. Here are the figures from the least to the greatest:

New King James Version ....inserted multi-syllable words 126 times.
English Standard Version ....inserted multi-syllable words 189 times.
New American Standard Version ....inserted multi-syllable words 218 times.
New Revised Standard Version ....inserted multi-syllable words 277 times.
Holman Christian Study Bible ....inserted multi-syllable words 306 times.
New International Version ....inserted multi-syllable words 327 times.
New Century Version ....inserted multi-syllable words 423 times.
New Living Translation ....inserted multi-syllable words 482 times.

Following are the percentage of times these modern versions complicated the simple truth of Scripture from the least to the greatest:

New King James Version ....complicated Scripture 14% of the time.
English Standard Version ....complicated Scripture 21% of the time.
New American Standard Version ....complicated Scripture 24% of the time.
New Revised Standard Version ....complicated Scripture 30% of the time.
Holman Christian Study Bible ....complicated Scripture 33% of the time.
New International Version ....complicated Scripture 36% of the time.
New Century Version ....complicated Scripture 46% of the time.
New Living Translation ....complicated Scripture 53% of the time.

The statistics given above are undeniable testimony that there is no truth to the charge "the King James Bible is too hard to read" nor to the statement that modern versions are easier to read. How can they be easier to read if they complicate Scripture?

As would be expected, the New King James Version wandered the least from perfection but it still managed to complicate the simple delivery of the King James Bible 126 times. The proponents of the NKJV may somehow attempt to interpret this number as virtuous. Look at it this way, every time one of these versions inserted complexity into a reading they were a thief who was "stealing simplicity" from the reader. Thus, although the New King James Version stole simplicity from the reader "only" 126 times, it is still a **thief**. You don't thank a thief who steals $126 from you for **not** stealing $482. A thief is a thief and a corrupted version is a corrupted version.

I think it ironic that of the modern version which you would expect to be the easiest to read, the New Living Translation was, in fact, the most complex, complicating simplicity 482 times. Doesn't it stun you that anyone could claim the Authorized Version is too hard to read and should be replaced with the likes of the masterfully complex New Living Translation?

So whether you prefer the mildly complex New King James Version or the one of the "complexity heavyweights" like the New Century Version or the New Living Translation, you still end up with a version that is inferior to the simplicity of the King James Bible.

Unfortunately, most of the false charges brought against the King James Bible are just that, prejudicial charges leveled not from sincerity but from an ulterior desire to replace the excellency found in God's Authorized Version with **anything** else. That's why the **legitimate** problems inherent with modern versions that this study documents will be ignored by the insincere critics of the King James Bible. In other words, they will bemoan the King James Bible as not being worthy of usage because it is "too hard to read," yet **when the facts** reveal that the King James is easy to read and it is the modern translations that are "too hard to read", they will suddenly fall mute or say it doesn't matter. Why? Because critics **really don't care** how difficult or simple **any** version is to read. They only care about destroying the high regard Christians have for the King James Bible, a regard that has survived for centuries. Therefore, they make up phoney arguments in an effort to supplant the King James Bible with **any** other version. But as this study has proven, **any other version** is harder to read than the King James Bible. Therefore, if you are either reading or using for study **any** modern version, you are using a translation that is both harder to read and inferior to the King James Bible.

What will you do with this information?

Part 4

Miscellaneous Information

But your eyes have seen all the great acts of the LORD which he did.
Deuteronomy 11:7

Immutable Words

Here are the verses which have words that I call "immutable." This refers to words which are multi-syllable but **not** the choice of the translators. I have included them in the master list in the study but listed them below in case a reader would like to identify them and delete them from their own personal count. Their master list number is included.

154. Numbers 31:22* Only the gold, and the **silver**, the brass, the iron, the tin, and the lead,
AV - **15,** 1-1,2-1,3-1,4-1,5-1,6-1,7-1,8-1,9-1,10-1,11-1,12-1,13-1,14-1,15-1
ESV - 14, 1-2,2-1,3-1,4-1,5-1,6-1,7-1,8-1,9-1,10-1,11-1,12-1,13-1,14-1
HCSB - 9, 1-2,2-1,3-1,4-1,5-1,6-1,7-1,8-1,9-1
NASV - 15, 1-2,2-1,3-1,4-1,5-1,6-1,7-1,8-1,9-1,10-1,11-1,12-1,13-1,14-1,15-1
NCV - 9, 1-1,2-**2**,3-1,4-1,5-1,6-1,7-1,8-1,9-1
NIV - **6,** 1-1,2-1,3-1,4-1,5-1,6-1
NKJV - 14, 1-2,2-1,3-1,4-1,5-1,6-1,7-1,8-1,9-1,10-1,11-1,12-1,13-1,14-1
NLT - **10,** 1-**3**,2-1,3-1,4-1,5-1,6-1,7-1,8-1,9-1,10-1
NRSV - **7,** 1-1,2-1,3-1,4-1,5-1,6-1,7-1
Conclusion: Six modern versions are more complex than the King James Bible.

756. Daniel 5:4* They drank wine, and praised the gods of gold, and of **silver**, of brass, of iron, of wood, and of stone.
AV - **21,** 1-1,2-1,3-1,4-1,5-1,6-1,7-1,8-1,9-1,10-1,11-1,12-1,13-1,14-1,15-1,16-1,17-1,18-1,19-1,20-1,21-1
ESV - **16,** 1-1,2-1,3-1,4-1,5-1,6-1,7-1,8-1,9-1,10-1,11-1,12-1,13-1,14-1,15-1,16-1
HCSB - **18,** 1-1,2-1,3-1,4-1,5-1,6-1,7-1,8-1,9-1,10-1,11-1,12-1,13-1,14-1,15-1,16-1,17-1,18-1
NASV - **18,** 1-1,2-1,3-1,4-1,5-1,6-1,7-1,8-1,9-1,10-1,11-1,12-1,13-1,14-1,15-1,16-1,17-1,18-1
NCV - 19, 1-1,2-1,3-1,4-**2**,5-1,6-1,7-1,8-1,9-1,10-1,11-1,12-1,13-1,14-1,15-1,16-1,17-1,18-1,19-1
NIV - **19,** 1-1,2-1,3-1,4-1,5-1,6-1,7-1,8-1,9-1,10-1,11-1,12-1,13-1,14-1,15-1,16-1,17-1,18-1,19-1
NKJV - **17,** 1-1,2-1,3-1,4-1,5-1,6-1,7-1,8-1,9-1,10-1,11-1,12-1,13-1,14-1,15-1,16-1,17-1
NLT - 18, 1-1,2-1,3-1,4-1,5-1,6-1,7-1,8-1,9-**2**,10-1,11-1,12-1,13-1,14-1,15-1,16-1,17-1,18-1
NRSV - **17,** 1-1,2-1,3-1,4-1,5-1,6-1,7-1,8-1,9-1,10-1,11-1,12-1,13-1,14-1,15-1,16-1,17-1
Conclusion: Only the NCV and the NLT made the verse more complex.

765. Haggai 2:8* The **silver** is mine, and the gold is mine, saith the LORD of hosts.
AV - **14,** 1-1,2-1,3-1,4-1,5-1,6-1,7-1,8-1,9-1,10-1,11-1,12-1,13-1,14-1
ESV - 14, 1-1,2-1,3-1,4-1,5-1,6-1,7-1,8-1,9-1,10-**2**,11-1,12-1,13-1,14-1
HCSB - 14, 1-1,2-1,3-1,4-1,5-**2**,6-1,7-1,8-1,9-**4**,10-1,11-1,12-1,13-1,14-1
NASV - 14, 1-1,2-1,3-1,4-1,5-1,6-1,7-1,8-1,9-1,10-**2**,11-1,12-1,13-1,14-1
NCV - **14,** 1-1,2-1,3-1,4-1,5-1,6-1,7-1,8-1,9-1,10-1,11-1,12-1,13-1,14-1
NIV - 13, 1-1,2-1,3-1,4-1,5-**2**,6-1,7-1,8-1,9-**4**,10-1,11-1,12-1,13-1
NKJV - **14,** 1-1,2-1,3-1,4-1,5-1,6-1,7-1,8-1,9-1,10-1,11-1,12-1,13-1,14-1
NLT - **15,** 1-1,2-1,3-1,4-1,5-1,6-1,7-1,8-1,9-1,10-1,11-1,12-1,13-1,14-1,15-1
NRSV - **14,** 1-1,2-1,3-1,4-1,5-1,6-1,7-1,8-1,9-1,10-1,11-1,12-1,13-1,14-1
Conclusion: Four modern versions are more complex than the King James Bible. Rather than "Lord of Hosts" the NCV says "Lord All-Powerful" the NIV says, "Lord Almighty" and the NLT says "Lord of Heaven's Armies" none of these were held against these modern versions.

790. Mark 15:25* And it was the third hour, and they **crucified** him.
AV - **10,** 1-1,2-1,3-1,4-1,5-1,6-1,7-1,8-1,9-1,10-1
ESV - **10,** 1-1,2-1,3-1,4-1,5-1,6-1,7-1,8-1,9-1,10-1
HCSB - 11, 1-1,2-1,3-1,4-1,5-1,6-1,7-**2**,8-1,9-1,10-1,11-1
NASV - **9,** 1-1,2-1,3-1,4-1,5-1,6-1,7-1,8-1,9-1
NCV - 11, 1-1,2-1,3-1,4-**2**,5-1,6-1,7-**2**,8-1,9-1,10-1,11-1
NIV - **9,** 1-1,2-1,3-1,4-1,5-1,6-1,7-1,8-1,9-1
NKJV - **10,** 1-1,2-1,3-1,4-1,5-1,6-1,7-1,8-1,9-1,10-1
NLT - 11, 1-1,2-1,3-1,4-**2**,5-1,6-1,7-**2**,8-1,9-1,10-1,11-1
NRSV - 11, 1-1,2-1,3-1,4-**2**,5-1,6-1,7-**2**,8-1,9-1,10-1,11-1
Conclusion: Four modern versions are more complex than the King James Bible.

791. Mark 15:27* And with him they **crucify** two thieves; the one on his right hand, and the other on his left.
AV - **19,** 1-1,2-1,3-1,4-1,5-1,6-1,7-1,8-1,9-1,10-1,11-1,12-1,13-1,14-1,15-1,16-1,17-1,18-1,19-1
ESV - 16, 1-1,2-1,3-1,4-1,5-1,6-1,7-**2**,8-1,9-1,10-1,11-1,12-1,13-1,14-1,15-1,16-1
HCSB - 15, 1-1,2-1,3-1,4-**3**,5-1,6-1,7-1,8-1,9-1,10-1,11-1,12-1,13-1,14-1,15-1
NASV - 15, 1-1,2-1,3-1,4-**2**,5-1,6-1,7-1,8-1,9-1,10-1,11-1,12-1,13-1,14-1,15-1
NCV - 19, 1-1,2-**2**,3-1,4-1,5-**2**,6-1,7-**2**,8-**2**,9-1,10-1,11-1,12-1,13-1,14-1,15-1,16-**2**,17-1,18-1,19-1
NIV - 15, 1-1,2-1,3-1,4-**2**,5-1,6-1,7-1,8-1,9-1,10-1,11-1,12-1,13-1,14-1,15-1
NKJV - 17, 1-1,2-1,3-1,4-**2**,5-1,6-1,7-**2**,8-1,9-1,10-1,11-1,12-1,13-1,14-**2**,15-1,16-1,17-1
NLT - 15, 1-1,2-**6**,3-1,4-1,5-1,6-1,7-1,8-1,9-1,10-1,11-1,12-1,13-1,14-1,15-1
NRSV - 16, 1-1,2-1,3-1,4-1,5-1,6-1,7-**2**,8-1,9-1,10-1,11-1,12-1,13-1,14-1,15-1,16-1
Conclusion: While all eight modern versions are more complex than the King James Bible this is one of those rare occasions when the NKJV was more complex than ever other modern version except the NCV, which made the verse the most complex.

Honorable Mention Verses

Genesis 28:10* And **Jacob** went out from **Beersheba**, and went toward **Haran**.
AV - **10,** 1-1,2-1,3-1,4-1,5-1,6-1,7-1,8-1,9-1,10-1
ESV - **7,** 1-1,2-1,3-1,4-1,5-1,6-1,7-1
HCSB - **7,** 1-1,2-1,3-1,4-1,5-1,6-1,7-1
NASV - 9, 1-1,2-1,3-**3**,4-1,5-1,6-1,7-1,8-1,9-1
NCV - **8,** 1-1,2-1,3-1,4-1,5-1,6-1,7-1,8-1
NIV - **8,** 1-1,2-1,3-1,4-1,5-1,6-1,7-1,8-1
NKJV - **10,** 1-1,2-1,3-1,4-1,5-1,6-1,7-1,8-1,9-1,10-1
NLT - 8, 1-**2**,2-1,3-1,4-1,5-1,6-**2**,7-1,8-1
NRSV - **7,** 1-1,2-1,3-1,4-1,5-1,6-1,7-1
Conclusion: Only the NASV and NLT are more complex than the King James Bible. The NLT is the most difficult to read.

Genesis 32:1* And **Jacob** went on his way, and the **angels** of God met him.
AV - **13,** 1-1,2-1,3-1,4-1,5-1,6-1,7-1,8-1,9-1,10-1,11-1,12-1,13-1
ESV - **12,** 1-1,2-1,3-1,4-1,5-1,6-1,7-1,8-1,9-1,10-1,11-1,12-1
HCSB - **10,** 1-1,2-1,3-1,4-1,5-1,6-1,7-1,8-1,9-1,10-1
NASV - **13,** 1-1,2-1,3-1,4-1,5-1,6-1,7-1,8-1,9-1,10-1,11-1,12-1,13-1
NCV - 12, 1-1,2-1,3-**2**,4-1,5-1,6-1,7-1,8-1,9-1,10-1,11-1,12-1
NIV - 13, 1-1,2-**2**,3-1,4-1,5-1,6-1,7-1,8-1,9-1,10-1,11-1,12-1,13-1
NKJV - **13,** 1-1,2-1,3-1,4-1,5-1,6-1,7-1,8-1,9-1,10-1,11-1,12-1,13-1
NLT - 14, 1-1,2-1,3-**2**,4-1,5-1,6-1,7-**2**,8-1,9-1,10-1,11-1,12-1,13-1,14-1
NRSV - **12,** 1-1,2-1,3-1,4-1,5-1,6-1,7-1,8-1,9-1,10-1,11-1,12-1
Conclusion: Only three modern versions are more complex than the King James Bible.

Genesis 49:9* **Judah** is a **lion's** whelp: from the prey, my son, thou art gone up: he stooped down, he couched as a **lion**, and as an old **lion**; who shall rouse him up?
AV - **32,** 1-1,2-1,3-1,4-1,5-1,6-1,7-1,8-1,9-1,10-1,11-1,12-1,13-1,14-1,15-1,16-1,17-1,18-1,19-1,20-1,21-1,22-1,23-1,24-1,25-1,26-1,27-1,28-1,29-1,30-1,31-1,32-1
ESV - 30, 1-1,2-1,3-1,4-1,5-1,6-1,7-1,8-1,9-1,10-1,11-1,12-1,13-1,14-1,15-1,16-1,17-1,18-1,19-1,20-1,21-1,22-1,23-1,24-1,25-1,26-**2**,27-1,28-1,29-1,30-1
HCSB - 29, 1-1,2-1,3-1,4-1,5-1,6-1,7-1,8-1,9-**2**,10-1,11-1,12-1,13-1,14-1,15-1,16-1,17-1,18-1,19-1,20-1,21-1,22-1,23-1,24-**2**,25-1,26-1,27-1,28-1,29-1
NASV - **31,** 1-1,2-1,3-1,4-1,5-1,6-1,7-1,8-1,9-1,10-1,11-1,12-1,13-1,14-1,15-1,16-1,17-1,18-1,19-1,20-1,21-1,22-1,23-1,24-1,25-1,26-1,27-1,28-1,29-1,30-1,31-1
NCV - 33, 1-1,2-1,3-1,4-1,5-1,6-1,7-1,8-1,9-**2**,10-1,11-**2**,12-1,13-1,14-1,15-1,16-1,17-1,18-1,19-1,20-1,21-1,22-1,23-1,24-1,25-1,26-1,27-1,28-1,29-1,30-**2**,31-1,32-1,33-1
NIV - 30, 1-1,2-1,3-1,4-1,5-1,6-1,7-1,8-1,9-**2**,10-1,11-1,12-1,13-1,14-1,15-1,16-1,17-1,18-1,19-1,20-1,21-1,22-1,23-1,24-1,25-**2**,26-1,27-1,28-1,29-1,30-1
NKJV - **31,** 1-1,2-1,3-1,4-1,5-1,6-1,7-1,8-1,9-1,10-1,11-1,12-1,13-1,14-1,15-1,16-1,17-1,18-1,19-1,20-1,21-1,22-1,23-1,24-1,25-1,26-1,27-1,28-1,29-1,30-1,31-1
NLT - 29, 1-1,2-1,3-1,4-1,5-1,6-1,7-1,8-1,9-1,10-**2**,11-**2**,12-1,13-1,14-1,15-1,16-1,17-1,18-1,19-1,20-1,21-1,22-1,23-1,24-**2**,25-1,26-1,27-1,28-1,29-1

Samuel C. Gipp Ph.D.

NRSV - 31, 1-1,2-1,3-1,4-1,5-1,6-1,7-1,8-1,9-1,10-1,11-1,12-1,13-1,14-1,15-1,16-1,17-1,18-1,19-1,20-1,21-1,22-1,23-1,24-1,25-1,26-**2**,27-1,28-1,29-1,30-1,31-1
Conclusion: Six modern versions are more complex than the King James Bible.

Leviticus 21:22* He shall eat the bread of his God, both of the most **holy**, and of the **holy**.
AV - **17,** 1-1,2-1,3-1,4-1,5-1,6-1,7-1,8-1,9-1,10-1,11-1,12-1,13-1,14-1,15-1,16-1,17-1
ESV - **18,** 1-1,2-1,3-1,4-1,5-1,6-1,7-1,8-1,9-1,10-1,11-1,12-1,13-1,14-1,15-1,16-1,17-1,18-1
HCSB - 20, 1-1,2-1,3-1,4-1,5-1,6-1,7-1,8-1,9-1,10-1,11-1,12-**4**,13-1,14-1,15-1,16-1,17-1,18-1,19-1,20-1
NASV - **17,** 1-1,2-1,3-1,4-1,5-1,6-1,7-1,8-1,9-1,10-1,11-1,12-1,13-1,14-1,15-1,16-1,17-1
NCV - 12, 1-1,2-1,3-1,4-1,5-1,6-1,7-1,8-1,9-**2**,10-1,11-1,12-1
NIV - **16,** 1-1,2-1,3-1,4-1,5-1,6-1,7-1,8-1,9-1,10-1,11-1,12-1,13-1,14-1,15-1,16-1
NKJV - **15,** 1-1,2-1,3-1,4-1,5-1,6-1,7-1,8-1,9-1,10-1,11-1,12-1,13-1,14-1,15-1
NLT - 19, 1-**3**,2-1,3-1,4-1,5-1,6-1,7-1,8-**2**,9-1,10-1,11-**3**,12-1,13-1,14-**3**,15-1,16-1,17-1,18-1,19-**3**
NRSV - **18,** 1-1,2-1,3-1,4-1,5-1,6-1,7-1,8-1,9-1,10-1,11-1,12-1,13-1,14-1,15-1,16-1,17-1,18-1
Conclusion: While only three modern versions are more complex than the King James Bible, the NLT did its usual masterful job of complicating the most simple of statements.

Numbers 19:5* And one shall burn the **heifer** in his sight; her skin, and her flesh, and her blood, with her dung, shall he burn:
AV - **23,** 1-1,2-1,3-1,4-1,5-1,6-1,7-1,8-1,9-1,10-1,11-1,12-1,13-1,14-1,15-1,16-1,17-1,18-1,19-1,20-1,21-1,22-1,23-1
ESV - **22,** 1-1,2-1,3-1,4-1,5-1,6-1,7-1,8-1,9-1,10-1,11-1,12-1,13-1,14-1,15-1,16-1,17-1,18-1,19-1,20-1,21-1,22-1
HCSB - 21, 1-1,2-1,3-1,4-1,5-1,6-1,7-1,8-1,9-1,10-1,11-1,12-1,13-1,14-1,15-1,16-1,17-1,18-**2**,19-1,20-1,21-1
NASV - 23, 1-1,2-1,3-1,4-1,5-1,6-1,7-1,8-1,9-1,10-1,11-1,12-1,13-1,14-1,15-1,16-1,17-1,18-1,19-1,20-**2**,21-1,22-1,23-1
NCV - 22, 1-1,2-1,3-1,4-1,5-1,6-1,7-1,8-1,9-**2**,10-1,11-1,12-1,13-1,14-1,15-1,16-1,17-1,18-**3**,19-1,20-1,21-1,22-1
NIV - 15, 1-1,2-1,3-**2**,4-1,5-1,6-1,7-1,8-1,9-1,10-1,11-1,12-1,13-1,14-1,15-**2**
NKJV - 21, 1-1,2-1,3-1,4-1,5-1,6-1,7-1,8-1,9-1,10-1,11-1,12-1,13-1,14-1,15-1,16-1,17-1,18-**2**,19-1,20-1,21-1
NLT - 14, 1-1,2-1,3-**2**,4-1,5-1,6-1,7-1,8-1,9-1,10-1,11-1,12-1,13-1,14-1
NRSV - **22,** 1-1,2-1,3-1,4-1,5-1,6-1,7-1,8-1,9-1,10-1,11-1,12-1,13-1,14-1,15-1,16-1,17-1,18-1,19-1,20-1,21-1,22-1
Conclusion: Six modern versions are more complex than the King James Bible.

Numbers 26:46* And the name of the **daughter** of **Asher** was **Sarah**.
AV - **10,** 1-1,2-1,3-1,4-1,5-1,6-1,7-1,8-1,9-1,10-1
ESV - **10,** 1-1,2-1,3-1,4-1,5-1,6-1,7-1,8-1,9-1,10-1
HCSB - **8,** 1-1,2-1,3-1,4-1,5-1,6-1,7-1,8-1
NASV - **9,** 1-1,2-1,3-1,4-1,5-1,6-1,7-1,8-1,9-1
NCV - 7, 1-1,2-**2**,3-1,4-1,5-1,6-1,7-1
NIV - **6,** 1-1,2-1,3-1,4-1,5-1,6-1
NKJV - **10,** 1-1,2-1,3-1,4-1,5-1,6-1,7-1,8-1,9-1,10-1
NLT - 7, 1-1,2-**2**,3-1,4-1,5-1,6-1,7-1
NRSV - **10,** 1-1,2-1,3-1,4-1,5-1,6-1,7-1,8-1,9-1,10-1
Conclusion: Only the NCV and the NLT found a way to make the verse more complex.

Deuteronomy 14:12* But these are they of which ye shall not eat: the **eagle**, and the **ossifrage**, and the **ospray**,
AV - **18,** 1-1,2-1,3-1,4-1,5-1,6-1,7-1,8-1,9-1,10-1,11-1,12-1,13-1,14-1,15-1,16-1,17-1,18-1
ESV - **18,** 1-1,2-1,3-1,4-1,5-1,6-1,7-1,8-1,9-1,10-1,11-1,12-1,13-1,14-1,15-1,16-1,17-1,18-1
HCSB - **17,** 1-1,2-1,3-1,4-1,5-1,6-1,7-1,8-1,9-1,10-1,11-1,12-1,13-1,14-1,15-1,16-1,17-1
NASV - **18,** 1-1,2-1,3-1,4-1,5-1,6-1,7-1,8-1,9-1,10-1,11-1,12-1,13-1,14-1,15-1,16-1,17-1,18-1
NCV - **10,** 1-1,2-1,3-1,4-1,5-1,6-1,7-1,8-1,9-1,10-1
NIV - **13,** 1-1,2-1,3-1,4-1,5-1,6-1,7-1,8-1,9-1,10-1,11-1,12-1,13-1
NKJV - **12,** 1-1,2-1,3-1,4-1,5-1,6-1,7-1,8-1,9-1,10-1,11-1,12-1
NLT - **17,** 1-1,2-1,3-1,4-1,5-1,6-1,7-1,8-1,9-1,10-1,11-1,12-1,13-1,14-1,15-1,16-1,17-1
NRSV - **16,** 1-1,2-1,3-1,4-1,5-1,6-1,7-1,8-1,9-1,10-1,11-1,12-1,13-1,14-1,15-1,16-1
Conclusion: All versions read the same.

Deuteronomy 32:1* Give ear, O ye **heavens**, and I will speak; and hear, O earth, the words of my mouth.
AV - **18,** 1-1,2-1,3-1,4-1,5-1,6-1,7-1,8-1,9-1,10-1,11-1,12-1,13-1,14-1,15-1,16-1,17-1,18-1
ESV - **18,** 1-1,2-1,3-1,4-1,5-1,6-1,7-1,8-1,9-1,10-1,11-1,12-1,13-1,14-1,15-1,16-1,17-1,18-1
HCSB - 15, 1-1,2-**3,**3-1,4-1,5-1,6-1,7-1,8-**2,**9-1,10-1,11-1,12-1,13-1,14-1,15-1
NASV - **18,** 1-1,2-1,3-1,4-1,5-1,6-1,7-1,8-1,9-1,10-1,11-1,12-1,13-1,14-1,15-1,16-1,17-1,18-1
NCV - 12, 1-1,2-1,3-1,4-1,5-1,6-1,7-**2,**8-1,9-1,10-1,11-1,12-1
NIV - 15, 1-**2,**2-1,3-1,4-1,5-1,6-1,7-1,8-1,9-1,10-1,11-1,12-1,13-1,14-1,15-1
NKJV - **17,** 1-1,2-1,3-1,4-1,5-1,6-1,7-1,8-1,9-1,10-1,11-1,12-1,13-1,14-1,15-1,16-1,17-1
NLT - 15, 1-**2,**2-1,3-1,4-1,5-1,6-1,7-1,8-1,9-1,10-1,11-1,12-1,13-1,14-1,15-1
NRSV - **17,** 1-1,2-1,3-1,4-1,5-1,6-1,7-1,8-1,9-1,10-1,11-1,12-1,13-1,14-1,15-1,16-1,17-1
Conclusion: Four modern versions are more complex than the King James Bible.

Deuteronomy 33:22* And of Dan he said, Dan is a **lion's** whelp: he shall leap from **Bashan**.
AV - **15,** 1-1,2-1,3-1,4-1,5-1,6-1,7-1,8-1,9-1,10-1,11-1,12-1,13-1,14-1,15-1
ESV - **14,** 1-1,2-1,3-1,4-1,5-1,6-1,7-1,8-1,9-1,10-1,11-1,12-1,13-1,14-1
HCSB - 13, 1-1,2-1,3-**2,**4-1,5-1,6-1,7-1,8-1,9-1,10-**2,**11-1,12-1,13-1
NASV - **14,** 1-1,2-1,3-1,4-1,5-1,6-1,7-1,8-1,9-1,10-1,11-1,12-1,13-1,14-1
NCV - 19, 1-1,2-1,3-1,4-**2,**5-1,6-**2,**7-1,8-1,9-1,10-1,11-1,12-1,13-1,14-1,15-1,16-1,17-1,18-1,19-1
NIV - 13, 1-**2,**2-1,3-1,4-1,5-1,6-1,7-1,8-1,9-1,10-**2,**11-1,12-1,13-1
NKJV - **15,** 1-1,2-1,3-1,4-1,5-1,6-1,7-1,8-1,9-1,10-1,11-1,12-1,13-1,14-1,15-1
NLT - 17, 1-1,2-1,3-1,4-**2,**5-1,6-1,7-1,8-1,9-1,10-1,11-1,12-1,13-1,14-**2,**15-1,16-1,17-1
NRSV - **15,** 1-1,2-1,3-1,4-1,5-1,6-1,7-1,8-1,9-1,10-1,11-1,12-1,13-1,14-1,15-1
Conclusion: Four modern versions are more complex than the King James Bible.

1 Samuel 23:6* And it came to pass, when **Abiathar** the son of **Ahimelech** fled to **David** to **Keilah**, that he came down with an **ephod** in his hand.
AV - **26,** 1-1,2-1,3-1,4-1,5-1,6-1,7-1,8-1,9-1,10-1,11-1,12-1,13-1,14-1,15-1,16-1,17-1,18-1,19-1,20-1,21-1,22-1,23-1,24-1,25-1,26-1
ESV - **22,** 1-1,2-1,3-1,4-1,5-1,6-1,7-1,8-1,9-1,10-1,11-1,12-1,13-1,14-1,15-1,16-1,17-1,18-1,19-1,20-1,21-1,22-1
HCSB - **16,** 1-1,2-1,3-1,4-1,5-1,6-1,7-1,8-1,9-1,10-1,11-1,12-1,13-1,14-1,15-1,16-1
NASV - 25, 1-1,2-1,3-1,4-**2,**5-1,6-1,7-1,8-1,9-1,10-1,11-1,12-1,13-1,14-1,15-1,16-1,17-1,18-1,19-1,20-1,21-1,22-1,23-1,24-1,25-1
NCV - **19,** 1-1,2-1,3-1,4-1,5-1,6-1,7-1,8-1,9-1,10-1,11-1,12-1,13-1,14-1,15-1,16-1,17-1,18-1,19-1
NIV - **19,** 1-1,2-1,3-1,4-1,5-1,6-1,7-1,8-1,9-1,10-1,11-1,12-1,13-1,14-1,15-1,16-1,17-1,18-1,19-1

NKJV - 24, 1-1,2-1,3-**2**,4-1,5-1,6-1,7-1,8-1,9-1,10-1,11-1,12-1,13-1,14-1,15-1,16-1,17-1,18-1,19-1,20-1,21-1,22-1,23-1,24-1
NLT - **17,** 1-1,2-1,3-1,4-1,5-1,6-1,7-1,8-1,9-1,10-1,11-1,12-1,13-1,14-1,15-1,16-1,17-1
NRSV - **19,** 1-1,2-1,3-1,4-1,5-1,6-1,7-1,8-1,9-1,10-1,11-1,12-1,13-1,14-1,15-1,16-1,17-1,18-1,19-1
Conclusion: Only the NASV and the NKJV made the verse more complex.

1 Kings 15:11* And **Asa** did that which was right in the eyes of the LORD, as did **David** his **father**.
AV - **18,** 1-1,2-1,3-1,4-1,5-1,6-1,7-1,8-1,9-1,10-1,11-1,12-1,13-1,14-1,15-1,16-1,17-1,18-1
ESV - **18,** 1-1,2-1,3-1,4-1,5-1,6-1,7-1,8-1,9-1,10-1,11-1,12-1,13-1,14-1,15-1,16-1,17-1,18-1
HCSB - **15,** 1-1,2-1,3-1,4-1,5-1,6-1,7-1,8-1,9-1,10-1,11-1,12-1,13-1,14-1,15-1
NASV - **15,** 1-1,2-1,3-1,4-1,5-1,6-1,7-1,8-1,9-1,10-1,11-1,12-1,13-1,14-1,15-1
NCV - **14,** 1-1,2-1,3-1,4-1,5-1,6-1,7-1,8-1,9-1,10-1,11-1,12-1,13-1,14-1
NIV - **17,** 1-1,2-1,3-1,4-1,5-1,6-1,7-1,8-1,9-1,10-1,11-1,12-1,13-1,14-1,15-1,16-1,17-1
NKJV - **16,** 1-1,2-1,3-1,4-1,5-1,6-1,7-1,8-1,9-1,10-1,11-1,12-1,13-1,14-1,15-1,16-1
NLT - **16,** 1-1,2-1,3-1,4-1,5-1,6-1,7-1,8-1,9-1,10-1,11-1,12-1,13-1,14-1,15-1,16-1
NRSV - **17,** 1-1,2-1,3-1,4-1,5-1,6-1,7-1,8-1,9-1,10-1,11-1,12-1,13-1,14-1,15-1,16-1,17-1
Conclusion: Both the HCSB and NCV changed "father" to "ancestor" but since the two syllable word, "father" was accepted in the other versions checked "ancestor" was not counted against these two.

1 Kings 22:40* So **Ahab** slept with his **fathers**; and **Ahaziah** his son reigned in his stead.
AV - **14,** 1-1,2-1,3-1,4-1,5-1,6-1,7-1,8-1,9-1,10-1,11-1,12-1,13-1,14-1
ESV - **14,** 1-1,2-1,3-1,4-1,5-1,6-1,7-1,8-1,9-1,10-1,11-1,12-1,13-1,14-1
HCSB - 14, 1-1,2-**2**,3-1,4-1,5-1,6-1,7-1,8-1,9-1,10-**2**,11-1,12-1,13-1,14-1
NASV - 15, 1-1,2-1,3-1,4-1,5-1,6-1,7-1,8-1,9-1,10-1,11-**2**,12-1,13-1,14-1,15-1
NCV - 12, 1-1,2-1,3-1,4-1,5-1,6-1,7-1,8-**2**,9-1,10-1,11-1,12-1
NIV - 13, 1-1,2-**2**,3-1,4-1,5-1,6-1,7-1,8-1,9-1,10-**3**,11-1,12-1,13-1
NKJV - 14, 1-1,2-1,3-**2**,4-1,5-1,6-1,7-1,8-1,9-1,10-1,11-1,12-1,13-1,14-1
NLT - 11, 1-1,2-1,3-1,4-1,5-1,6-1,7-1,8-**2**,9-1,10-1,11-1
NRSV - 12, 1-1,2-1,3-1,4-1,5-1,6-1,7-1,8-1,9-1,10-1,11-**3**,12-1
Conclusion: Seven modern versions are more complex than the King James Bible. The NRSV changed "father" to "ancestor" but since the two syllable word, "father" was accepted in the other versions checked "ancestor" was not counted against it.

2 Kings 15:22* And **Menahem** slept with his **fathers**; and **Pekahiah** his son reigned in his stead.
AV - **14,** 1-1,2-1,3-1,4-1,5-1,6-1,7-1,8-1,9-1,10-1,11-1,12-1,13-1,14-1
ESV - **14,** 1-1,2-1,3-1,4-1,5-1,6-1,7-1,8-1,9-1,10-1,11-1,12-1,13-1,14-1
HCSB - 14, 1-1,2-**2**,3-1,4-1,5-1,6-1,7-1,8-1,9-1,10-**2**,11-1,12-1,13-1,14-1
NASV - 15, 1-1,2-1,3-1,4-1,5-1,6-1,7-1,8-1,9-1,10-1,11-**2**,12-1,13-1,14-1,15-1
NCV - 12, 1-1,2-1,3-1,4-1,5-1,6-1,7-1,8-**2**,9-1,10-1,11-1,12-1
NIV - 13, 1-1,2-**2**,3-1,4-1,5-1,6-1,7-1,8-1,9-1,10-**3**,11-1,12-1,13-1
NKJV - 14, 1-1,2-1,3-**2**,4-1,5-1,6-1,7-1,8-1,9-1,10-1,11-1,12-1,13-1,14-1
NLT - 10, 1-1,2-1,3-1,4-1,5-1,6-1,7-**2**,8-1,9-1,10-1
NRSV - 11, 1-1,2-1,3-1,4-1,5-1,6-1,7-1,8-1,9-1,10-**3**,11-1
Conclusion: Seven modern versions are more complex than the King James Bible. The NRSV changed "fathers" to "ancestors" but since the two syllable word, "fathers" was accepted in other cases "ancestors" was not counted against it.

2 Kings 20:21* And **Hezekiah** slept with his **fathers**: and **Manasseh** his son reigned in his stead.
AV - **14,** 1-1,2-1,3-1,4-1,5-1,6-1,7-1,8-1,9-1,10-1,11-1,12-1,13-1,14-1
ESV - **14,** 1-1,2-1,3-1,4-1,5-1,6-1,7-1,8-1,9-1,10-1,11-1,12-1,13-1,14-1
HCSB - 14, 1-1,2-**2**,3-1,4-1,5-1,6-1,7-1,8-1,9-1,10-**2**,11-1,12-1,13-1,14-1
NASV - 15, 1-1,2-1,3-1,4-1,5-1,6-1,7-1,8-1,9-1,10-1,11-**2**,12-1,13-1,14-1,15-1
NCV - 12, 1-1,2-1,3-1,4-1,5-1,6-1,7-1,8-**2**,9-1,10-1,11-1,12-1
NIV - 13, 1-1,2-**2**,3-1,4-1,5-1,6-1,7-1,8-1,9-1,10-**3**,11-1,12-1,13-1
NKJV - 14, 1-1,2-1,3-**2**,4-1,5-1,6-1,7-1,8-1,9-1,10-1,11-1,12-1,13-1,14-1
NLT - 10, 1-1,2-1,3-1,4-1,5-1,6-1,7-**2**,8-1,9-1,10-1
NRSV - 11, 1-1,2-1,3-1,4-1,5-1,6-1,7-1,8-1,9-1,10-**3**,11-1
Conclusion: This verse is the mirror image of 2 Kings 15:22; seven modern versions are more complex than the King James Bible. The NRSV changed "fathers" to "ancestors" but since the two syllable word, "fathers" was accepted in other cases "ancestors" was not counted against it.

1 Chronicles 2:17* And **Abigail** bare **Amasa**: and the **father** of **Amasa** was **Jether** the **Ishmeelite**.
AV - **13,** 1-1,2-1,3-1,4-1,5-1,6-1,7-1,8-1,9-1,10-1,11-1,12-1,13-1
ESV - **12,** 1-1,2-1,3-1,4-1,5-1,6-1,7-1,8-1,9-1,10-1,11-1,12-1
HCSB - **11,** 1-1,2-1,3-1,4-1,5-1,6-1,7-1,8-1,9-1,10-1,11-1
NASV - **12,** 1-1,2-1,3-1,4-1,5-1,6-1,7-1,8-1,9-1,10-1,11-1,12-1
NCV - **13,** 1-1,2-1,3-1,4-1,5-1,6-1,7-1,8-1,9-1,10-1,11-1,12-1,13-1
NIV - **12,** 1-1,2-1,3-1,4-1,5-1,6-1,7-1,8-1,9-1,10-1,11-1,12-1
NKJV - **12,** 1-1,2-1,3-1,4-1,5-1,6-1,7-1,8-1,9-1,10-1,11-1,12-1
NLT - 15, 1-1,2-**2**,3-1,4-1,5-1,6-1,7-1,8-1,9-1,10-1,11-1,12-1,13-1,14-1,15-1
NRSV - **12,** 1-1,2-1,3-1,4-1,5-1,6-1,7-1,8-1,9-1,10-1,11-1,12-1
Conclusion: Only the NLT made the verse more complex. The HCSB, NCV and NIV added the word "mother" in describing Abigail. Since "father" was not counted aginst any version neither was "mother."

1 Chronicles 2:45* And the son of **Shammai** was **Maon**: and **Maon** was the **father** of **Bethzur**.
AV - **14,** 1-1,2-1,3-1,4-1,5-1,6-1,7-1,8-1,9-1,10-1,11-1,12-1,13-1,14-1
ESV - **9,** 1-1,2-1,3-1,4-1,5-1,6-1,7-1,8-1,9-1
HCSB - **8,** 1-1,2-1,3-1,4-1,5-1,6-1,7-1,8-1
NASV - **13,** 1-1,2-1,3-1,4-1,5-1,6-1,7-1,8-1,9-1,10-1,11-1,12-1,13-1
NCV - **14,** 1-1,2-1,3-1,4-1,5-1,6-1,7-1,8-1,9-1,10-1,11-1,12-1,13-1,14-1
NIV - **14,** 1-1,2-1,3-1,4-1,5-1,6-1,7-1,8-1,9-1,10-1,11-1,12-1,13-1,14-1
NKJV - **15,** 1-1,2-1,3-1,4-1,5-1,6-1,7-1,8-1,9-1,10-1,11-1,12-1,13-1,14-1,15-1
NLT - **12,** 1-1,2-1,3-1,4-1,5-1,6-1,7-1,8-1,9-1,10-1,11-1,12-1
NRSV - **12,** 1-1,2-1,3-1,4-1,5-1,6-1,7-1,8-1,9-1,10-1,11-1,12-1
Conclusion: All versions read the same.

1 Chronicles 2:51* **Salma** the **father** of **Bethlehem**, **Hareph** the **father** of **Bethgader**.
AV - **10,** 1-1,2-1,3-1,4-1,5-1,6-1,7-1,8-1,9-1,10-1
ESV - **11,** 1-1,2-1,3-1,4-1,5-1,6-1,7-1,8-1,9-1,10-1,11-1
HCSB - **7,** 1-1,2-1,3-1,4-1,5-1,6-1,7-1
NASV - **11,** 1-1,2-1,3-1,4-1,5-1,6-1,7-1,8-1,9-1,10-1,11-1
NCV - **14,** 1-1,2-1,3-1,4-1,5-1,6-1,7-1,8-1,9-1,10-1,11-1,12-1,13-1,14-1
NIV - **12,** 1-1,2-1,3-1,4-1,5-1,6-1,7-1,8-1,9-1,10-1,11-1,12-1
NKJV - **12,** 1-1,2-1,3-1,4-1,5-1,6-1,7-1,8-1,9-1,10-1,11-1,12-1
NLT - **11,** 1-1,2-1,3-1,4-1,5-1,6-1,7-1,8-1,9-1,10-1,11-1

NRSV - **9,** 1-1,2-1,3-1,4-1,5-1,6-1,7-1,8-1,9-1
Conclusion: All versions read the same.

1 Chronicles 2:52* And **Shobal** the **father** of **Kirjathjearim** had sons; **Haroeh**, and half of the **Manahethites**.
AV - **14,** 1-1,2-1,3-1,4-1,5-1,6-1,7-1,8-1,9-1,10-1,11-1,12-1,13-1,14-1
ESV - 13, 1-1,2-1,3-1,4-1,5-1,6-1,7-**2**,8-1,9-1,10-1,11-1,12-1,13-1
HCSB - 15, 1-1,2-1,3-1,4-**3**,5-1,6-1,7-1,8-1,9-1,10-1,11-1,12-1,13-1,14-1,15-1
NASV - **12,** 1-1,2-1,3-1,4-1,5-1,6-1,7-1,8-1,9-1,10-1,11-1,12-1
NCV - **14,** 1-1,2-1,3-1,4-1,5-1,6-1,7-1,8-1,9-**3**,10-1,11-1,12-1,13-1,14-1
NIV - 14, 1-1,2-**3**,3-1,4-1,5-1,6-1,7-1,8-1,9-1,10-1,11-1,12-1,13-1,14-1
NKJV - 17, 1-1,2-1,3-1,4-1,5-1,6-1,7-1,8-1,9-**3**,10-1,11-1,12-1,13-1,14-1,15-**3**,16-1,17-1
NLT - 13, 1-1,2-**3**,3-1,4-1,5-1,6-1,7-1,8-1,9-1,10-1,11-1,12-1,13-1
NRSV - 12, 1-1,2-1,3-1,4-1,5-1,6-**2**,7-1,8-1,9-1,10-1,11-1,12-1
Conclusion: Seven modern versions are more complex than the King James Bible. Remarkably, the NKJV made the verse more complex.

1 Chronicles 5:15* **Ahi** the son of **Abdiel**, the son of **Guni**, chief of the house of their **fathers**.
AV - **16,** 1-1,2-1,3-1,4-1,5-1,6-1,7-1,8-1,9-1,10-1,11-1,12-1,13-1,14-1,15-1,16-1
ESV - 14, 1-1,2-1,3-1,4-1,5-1,6-1,7-1,8-1,9-1,10-1,11-1,12-1,13-1,14-**2**
HCSB - 13, 1-1,2-1,3-1,4-1,5-1,6-1,7-1,8-1,9-1,10-1,11-1,12-1,13-**2**
NASV - 15, 1-1,2-1,3-1,4-1,5-1,6-1,7-1,8-1,9-1,10-1,11-1,12-1,13-1,14-1,15-**2**
NCV - 16, 1-1,2-1,3-1,4-1,5-1,6-1,7-1,8-1,9-1,10-1,11-1,12-1,13-**2**,14-1,15-1,16-1
NIV - **13,** 1-1,2-1,3-1,4-1,5-1,6-1,7-1,8-1,9-1,10-1,11-1,12-1,13-1
NKJV - **15,** 1-1,2-1,3-1,4-1,5-1,6-1,7-1,8-1,9-1,10-1,11-1,12-1,13-1,14-1,15-1
NLT - 13, 1-1,2-1,3-1,4-1,5-1,6-1,7-1,8-1,9-1,10-**2**,11-1,12-1,13-1
NRSV - 12, 1-1,2-1,3-1,4-1,5-1,6-1,7-1,8-1,9-1,10-1,11-1,12-1
Conclusion: Five modern versions are more complex than the King James Bible.

2 Chronicles 5:4* And all the **elders** of **Israel** came; and the **Levites** took up the ark.
AV - **14,** 1-1,2-1,3-1,4-1,5-1,6-1,7-1,8-1,9-1,10-1,11-1,12-1,13-1,14-1
ESV - **14,** 1-1,2-1,3-1,4-1,5-1,6-1,7-1,8-1,9-1,10-1,11-1,12-1,13-1,14-1
HCSB - **13,** 1-1,2-1,3-1,4-1,5-1,6-1,7-1,8-1,9-1,10-1,11-1,12-1,13-1
NASV - **14,** 1-1,2-1,3-1,4-1,5-1,6-1,7-1,8-1,9-1,10-1,11-1,12-1,13-1,14-1
NCV - 13, 1-1,2-1,3-1,4-1,5-1,6-1,7-**2**,8-1,9-1,10-**2**,11-1,12-1,13-1
NIV - 14, 1-1,2-1,3-1,4-1,5-1,6-1,7-1,8-**2**,9-1,10-1,11-1,12-1,13-1,14-1
NKJV - **14,** 1-1,2-1,3-1,4-1,5-1,6-1,7-1,8-1,9-1,10-1,11-1,12-1,13-1,14-1
NLT - 13, 1-1,2-1,3-1,4-1,5-1,6-1,7-**2**,8-1,9-1,10-1,11-1,12-1,13-1
NRSV - 13, 1-1,2-1,3-1,4-1,5-1,6-1,7-1,8-1,9-1,10-1,11-**2**,12-1,13-1
Conclusion: Four modern versions are more complex than the King James Bible.

2 Chronicles 6:7* Now it was in the heart of **David** my **father** to build an house for the name of the LORD God of **Israel**.
AV - **23,** 1-1,2-1,3-1,4-1,5-1,6-1,7-1,8-1,9-1,10-1,11-1,12-1,13-1,14-1,15-1,16-1,17-1,18-1,19-1,20-1,21-1,22-1,23-1
ESV - **24,** 1-1,2-1,3-1,4-1,5-1,6-1,7-1,8-1,9-1,10-1,11-1,12-1,13-1,14-1,15-1,16-1,17-1,18-1,19-1,20-1,21-1,22-1,23-1,24-1

HCSB - 23, 1-1,2-1,3-1,4-1,5-1,6-1,7-1,8-1,9-1,10-1,11-1,12-1,13-1,14-**2**,15-1,16-1,17-1,18-1,19-1,20-1,21-1,22-1,23-1

NASV - 24, 1-1,2-1,3-1,4-1,5-1,6-1,7-1,8-1,9-1,10-1,11-1,12-1,13-1,14-1,15-1,16-1,17-1,18-1,19-1,20-1,21-1,22-1,23-1,24-1

NCV - 15, 1-1,2-1,3-1,4-**2**,5-1,6-1,7-1,8-**2**,9-1,10-1,11-1,12-1,13-1,14-1,15-1

NIV - 22, 1-1,2-1,3-1,4-1,5-1,6-1,7-1,8-1,9-1,10-1,11-1,12-**2**,13-1,14-1,15-1,16-1,17-1,18-1,19-1,20-1,21-1,22-1

NKJV - 23, 1-1,2-1,3-1,4-1,5-1,6-1,7-1,8-1,9-1,10-1,11-1,12-1,13-1,14-**2**,15-1,16-1,17-1,18-1,19-1,20-1,21-1,22-1,23-1

NLT - 22, 1-1,2-1,3-1,4-1,5-1,6-1,7-**2**,8-1,9-1,10-1,11-**2**,12-1,13-**2**,14-1,15-1,16-1,17-1,18-1,19-1,20-1,21-1,22-1

NRSV - 21, 1-1,2-1,3-1,4-1,5-1,6-1,7-1,8-1,9-1,10-1,11-1,12-1,13-1,14-1,15-1,16-1,17-1,18-1,19-1,20-1,21-1

Conclusion: Five modern versions are more complex than the King James Bible. Each of these five replaced "house" with "temple." While this multi-syllable word would be accepted under other conditions it was not here. That is because the discussion between God, David and Nathan the Prophet concerned building a "house" for the Lord, which ultimately led to the Temple. The NLT adds the name "Solomon" to the verse but this wasn't counted against it.

Job 15:18* Which wise men have told from their **fathers**, and have not hid it:
AV - 13, 1-1,2-1,3-1,4-1,5-1,6-1,7-1,8-1,9-1,10-1,11-1,12-1,13-1
ESV - 11, 1-1,2-1,3-1,4-1,5-1,6-**2**,7-**2**,8-1,9-1,10-1,11-1
HCSB - 13, 1-1,2-1,3-**2**,4-1,5-1,6-1,7-1,8-1,9-1,10-**2**,11-1,12-1,13-1
NASV - 12, 1-1,2-1,3-1,4-1,5-1,6-1,7-1,8-1,9-**2**,10-1,11-1,12-1
NCV - 16, 1-1,2-1,3-1,4-1,5-1,6-1,7-1,8-1,9-1,10-1,11-1,12-1,13-1,14-1,15-**2**,16-**2**
NIV - 11, 1-1,2-1,3-1,4-1,5-**2**,6-**2**,7-**2**,8-**2**,9-1,10-1,11-1
NKJV - 12, 1-1,2-1,3-1,4-1,5-1,6-1,7-**2**,8-**3**,9-**2**,10-1,11-1,12-1
NLT - 19, 1-1,2-1,3-1,4-**2**,5-1,6-1,7-**2**,8-1,9-1,10-1,11-1,12-1,13-1,14-1,15-1,16-1,17-1,18-1,19-1
NRSV - 10, 1-1,2-1,3-1,4-1,5-1,6-1,7-1,8-1,9-1,10-**2**

Conclusion: All eight modern versions are more complex than the King James Bible. This is one of the rare times when the NKJV was among the most complex, barely being edged out by the NIV as the most complex. The HCSB, NCV and NRSV replaced "fathers" with "ancestors" but, although this word is in and of itself more complex than "fathers," it was not counted them.

Job 28:6* The stones of it are the place of **sapphires**: and it hath dust of gold.
AV - 15, 1-1,2-1,3-1,4-1,5-1,6-1,7-1,8-1,9-1,10-1,11-1,12-1,13-1,14-1,15-1
ESV - 13, 1-1,2-1,3-1,4-1,5-1,6-1,7-1,8-1,9-1,10-1,11-1,12-1,13-1
HCSB - 11, 1-1,2-1,3-1,4-1,5-1,6-1,7-1,8-**3**,9-1,10-1,11-1
NASV - 12, 1-1,2-1,3-1,4-1,5-1,6-1,7-1,8-1,9-1,10-1,11-**2**,12-1
NCV - 12, 1-1,2-1,3-1,4-1,5-1,6-1,7-1,8-1,9-1,10-**2**,11-1,12-1
NIV - 12, 1-1,2-1,3-1,4-1,5-1,6-1,7-1,8-1,9-**2**,10-**2**,11-1,12-1
NKJV - 12, 1-1,2-1,3-1,4-1,5-1,6-1,7-1,8-1,9-1,10-**2**,11-1,12-1
NLT - 12, 1-1,2-1,3-1,4-**2**,5-1,6-1,7-1,8-1,9-1,10-1,11-**2**,12-1
NRSV - 12, 1-1,2-1,3-1,4-1,5-1,6-1,7-1,8-1,9-1,10-1,11-**2**,12-1

Conclusion: Seven modern versions are more complex than the King James Bible. Seven out of the eight used the word "sapphires" as did the Authorized Version. The NLT replaced "sapphires" with "precious lapis lazuli." None of these three words were counted against it although most people know what a "sapphire" is but might be a bit perplexed by the term "lapis lazuli."

Job 28:6* The stones of it are the place of **sapphires**: and it hath dust of gold.
AV - **15,** 1-1,2-1,3-1,4-1,5-1,6-1,7-1,8-1,9-1,10-1,11-1,12-1,13-1,14-1,15-1
ESV - **13,** 1-1,2-1,3-1,4-1,5-1,6-1,7-1,8-1,9-1,10-1,11-1,12-1,13-1
HCSB - 11, 1-1,2-1,3-1,4-1,5-1,6-1,7-1,8-**3**,9-1,10-1,11-1
NASV - 12, 1-1,2-1,3-1,4-1,5-1,6-1,7-1,8-1,9-1,10-1,11-**2**,12-1
NCV - 12, 1-1,2-1,3-1,4-1,5-1,6-1,7-1,8-1,9-1,10-**2**,11-1,12-1
NIV - 12, 1-1,2-1,3-1,4-1,5-1,6-1,7-1,8-1,9-**2**,10-**2**,11-1,12-1
NKJV - 12, 1-1,2-1,3-1,4-1,5-1,6-1,7-1,8-1,9-1,10-**2**,11-1,12-1
NLT - 12, 1-1,2-1,3-1,4-**2**,5-**3**,6-1,7-1,8-1,9-1,10-1,11-**2**,12-1
NRSV - 12, 1-1,2-1,3-1,4-1,5-1,6-1,7-1,8-1,9-1,10-1,11-**2**,12-1
Conclusion: Seven modern versions are more complex than the King James Bible. In an effort to be easier to read (right!) the NLT is the only modern version that altered the word "sapphires" which it replaced with "lapis lazuli" The NLT is the most difficult to read.

Psalm 58:6 Break their teeth, O God, in their mouth: break out the great teeth of the young **lions**, O LORD.
AV - **19,** 1-1,2-1,3-1,4-1,5-1,6-1,7-1,8-1,9-1,10-1,11-1,12-1,13-1,14-1,15-1,16-1,17-1,18-1,19-1
ESV - **18,** 1-1,2-1,3-1,4-1,5-1,6-1,7-1,8-1,9-1,10-1,11-1,12-1,13-1,14-1,15-1,16-1,17-1,18-1
HCSB - **15,** 1-1,2-1,3-1,4-1,5-1,6-1,7-1,8-1,9-1,10-1,11-1,12-1,13-1,14-1,15-1
NASV - 18, 1-1,2-1,3-**2**,4-1,5-1,6-1,7-1,8-1,9-1,10-1,11-1,12-1,13-1,14-1,15-1,16-1,17-1,18-1
NCV - **15,** 1-1,2-1,3-1,4-1,5-1,6-1,7-1,8-1,9-1,10-1,11-1,12-1,13-1,14-1,15-1
NIV - **17,** 1-1,2-1,3-1,4-1,5-1,6-1,7-1,8-1,9-1,10-1,11-1,12-1,13-1,14-1,15-1,16-1,17-1
NKJV - **18,** 1-1,2-1,3-1,4-1,5-1,6-1,7-1,8-1,9-1,10-1,11-1,12-1,13-1,14-1,15-1,16-1,17-1,18-1
NLT - **14,** 1-1,2-1,3-1,4-1,5-1,6-1,7-1,8-1,9-1,10-1,11-1,12-1,13-1,14-1
NRSV - **18,** 1-1,2-1,3-1,4-1,5-1,6-1,7-1,8-1,9-1,10-1,11-1,12-1,13-1,14-1,15-1,16-1,17-1,18-1
Conclusion: Only the NASV made the verse more complex.

Psalm 124:8* Our help is in the name of the LORD, who made **heaven** and earth.
AV - **14,** 1-1,2-1,3-1,4-1,5-1,6-1,7-1,8-1,9-1,10-1,11-1,12-1,13-1,14-1
ESV - **14,** 1-1,2-1,3-1,4-1,5-1,6-1,7-1,8-1,9-1,10-1,11-1,12-1,13-1,14-1
HCSB - 15, 1-1,2-1,3-1,4-1,5-1,6-1,7-1,8-1,9-1,10-1,11-**2**,12-1,13-1,14-1,15-1
NASV - **14,** 1-1,2-1,3-1,4-1,5-1,6-1,7-1,8-1,9-1,10-1,11-1,12-1,13-1,14-1
NCV - **11,** 1-1,2-1,3-1,4-1,5-1,6-1,7-1,8-1,9-1,10-1,11-1
NIV - 15, 1-1,2-1,3-1,4-1,5-1,6-1,7-1,8-1,9-1,10-1,11-**2**,12-1,13-1,14-1,15-1
NKJV - **14,** 1-1,2-1,3-1,4-1,5-1,6-1,7-1,8-1,9-1,10-1,11-1,12-1,13-1,14-1
NLT - **11,** 1-1,2-1,3-1,4-1,5-1,6-1,7-1,8-1,9-1,10-1,11-1
NRSV - **14,** 1-1,2-1,3-1,4-1,5-1,6-1,7-1,8-1,9-1,10-1,11-1,12-1,13-1,14-1
Conclusion: Only the HCSB and the NIV made the verse more complex.

Psalm 134:3 The LORD that made **heaven** and earth bless thee out of **Zion**.
AV - **12,** 1-1,2-1,3-1,4-1,5-1,6-1,7-1,8-1,9-1,10-1,11-1,12-1
ESV - **13,** 1-1,2-1,3-1,4-1,5-1,6-1,7-1,8-1,9-1,10-1,11-1,12-1,13-1
HCSB - 12, 1-1,2-1,3-1,4-**2**,5-1,6-1,7-1,8-1,9-1,10-1,11-1,12-1
NASV - **13,** 1-1,2-1,3-1,4-1,5-1,6-1,7-1,8-1,9-1,10-1,11-1,12-1,13-1
NCV - **14,** 1-1,2-1,3-1,4-1,5-1,6-1,7-1,8-1,9-1,10-1,11-1,12-1,13-1,14-1
NIV - 13, 1-1,2-1,3-1,4-1,5-**2**,6-1,7-1,8-1,9-1,10-1,11-1,12-1,13-1
NKJV - **11,** 1-1,2-1,3-1,4-1,5-1,6-1,7-1,8-1,9-1,10-1,11-1
NLT - 12, 1-1,2-1,3-1,4-1,5-1,6-1,7-1,8-1,9-1,10-1,11-1,12-**4**
NRSV - 12, 1-1,2-1,3-1,4-**2**,5-1,6-1,7-1,8-1,9-1,10-1,11-1,12-1

Conclusion: Four modern versions are more complex than the King James Bible. The NLT replaced "Zion" with "Jerusalem." Since the literal translation should have been "Zion" this was counted against this version.

Psalm 148:1* Praise ye the LORD. Praise ye the LORD from the **heavens**: praise him in the heights.
AV - **16,** 1-1,2-1,3-1,4-1,5-1,6-1,7-1,8-1,9-1,10-1,11-1,12-1,13-1,14-1,15-1,16-1
ESV - **14,** 1-1,2-1,3-1,4-1,5-1,6-1,7-1,8-1,9-1,10-1,11-1,12-1,13-1,14-1
HCSB - 12, 1-**4**,2-1,3-1,4-1,5-1,6-1,7-1,8-1,9-1,10-1,11-1,12-1
NASV - **14,** 1-1,2-1,3-1,4-1,5-1,6-1,7-1,8-1,9-1,10-1,11-1,12-1,13-1,14-1
NCV - 15, 1-1,2-1,3-1,4-1,5-1,6-1,7-1,8-1,9-1,10-1,11-1,12-1,13-**2**,14-1,15-1
NIV - 15, 1-1,2-1,3-1,4-1,5-1,6-1,7-1,8-1,9-1,10-1,11-1,12-1,13-1,14-1,15-**2**
NKJV - **14,** 1-1,2-1,3-1,4-1,5-1,6-1,7-1,8-1,9-1,10-1,11-1,12-1,13-1,14-1
NLT - **14,** 1-1,2-1,3-1,4-1,5-1,6-1,7-1,8-1,9-1,10-1,11-1,12-1,13-1,14-1
NRSV - **14,** 1-1,2-1,3-1,4-1,5-1,6-1,7-1,8-1,9-1,10-1,11-1,12-1,13-1,14-1
Conclusion: Only three modern versions are more complex than the King James Bible.

Psalm 148:2* Praise ye him, all his **angels**: praise ye him, all his hosts.
AV - **12,** 1-1,2-1,3-1,4-1,5-1,6-1,7-1,8-1,9-1,10-1,11-1,12-1
ESV - **10,** 1-1,2-1,3-1,4-1,5-1,6-1,7-1,8-1,9-1,10-1
HCSB - **10,** 1-1,2-1,3-1,4-1,5-1,6-1,7-1,8-1,9-1,10-1
NASV - **10,** 1-1,2-1,3-1,4-1,5-1,6-1,7-1,8-1,9-1,10-1
NCV - **12,** 1-1,2-1,3-1,4-1,5-1,6-1,7-1,8-1,9-1,10-2,11-1,12-2
NIV - 11, 1-1,2-1,3-1,4-1,5-1,6-1,7-1,8-1,9-1,10-**3**,11-1
NKJV - **10,** 1-1,2-1,3-1,4-1,5-1,6-1,7-1,8-1,9-1,10-1
NLT - **12,** 1-1,2-1,3-1,4-1,5-1,6-1,7-1,8-1,9-1,10-2,11-1,12-2
NRSV - **10,** 1-1,2-1,3-1,4-1,5-1,6-1,7-1,8-1,9-1,10-1
Conclusion: Only the NIV made the verse more complex. The NCV and the NLT replaced "all his hosts" with "armies of heaven" while the NIV says "heavenly host" which was held against it.

Isaiah 43:15* I am the LORD, your **Holy** One, the **creator** of **Israel**, your King.
AV - **13,** 1-1,2-1,3-1,4-1,5-1,6-1,7-1,8-1,9-1,10-1,11-1,12-1,13-1
ESV - **13,** 1-1,2-1,3-1,4-1,5-1,6-1,7-1,8-1,9-1,10-1,11-1,12-1,13-1
HCSB - **13,** 1-1,2-1,3-1,4-1,5-1,6-1,7-1,8-1,9-1,10-1,11-1,12-1,13-1
NASV - **13,** 1-1,2-1,3-1,4-1,5-1,6-1,7-1,8-1,9-1,10-1,11-1,12-1,13-1
NCV - **13,** 1-1,2-1,3-1,4-1,5-1,6-1,7-1,8-1,9-1,10-1,11-1,12-1,13-1
NIV - **11,** 1-1,2-1,3-1,4-1,5-1,6-1,7-1,8-1,9-1,10-1,11-1
NKJV - **13,** 1-1,2-1,3-1,4-1,5-1,6-1,7-1,8-1,9-1,10-1,11-1,12-1,13-1
NLT - **11,** 1-1,2-1,3-1,4-1,5-1,6-1,7-1,8-1,9-1,10-1,11-1
NRSV - **13,** 1-1,2-1,3-1,4-1,5-1,6-1,7-1,8-1,9-1,10-1,11-1,12-1,13-1
Conclusion: All versions read the same.

Hosea 2:21* And it shall come to pass in that day, I will hear, saith the LORD, I will hear the **heavens**, and they shall hear the earth;
AV - **26,** 1-1,2-1,3-1,4-1,5-1,6-1,7-1,8-1,9-1,10-1,11-1,12-1,13-1,14-1,15-1,16-1,17-1,18-1,19-1,20-1,21-1,22-1,23-1,24-1,25-1,26-1
ESV - 21, 1-1,2-1,3-1,4-1,5-1,6-1,7-**2**,8-**2**,9-1,10-1,11-1,12-1,13-**2**,14-1,15-1,16-1,17-1,18-1,19-**2**,20-1,21-1
HCSB - 22, 1-1,2-1,3-1,4-1,5-1,6-**2**,7-1,8-1,9-**4**,10-1,11-1,12-**2**,13-1,14-1,15-1,16-1,17-1,18-1,19-**2**,20-1,21-1,22-1

NASV - **27,** 1-1,2-1,3-1,4-**2**,5-1,6-1,7-1,8-1,9-1,10-1,11-**2**,12-**2**,13-1,14-1,15-1,16-1,17-**2**,18-1,19-1,20-1,21-1,22-1,23-1,24-**2**,25-1,26-1,27-1

NCV - **25,** 1-1,2-1,3-1,4-1,5-1,6-1,7-1,8-1,9-1,10-1,11-1,12-1,13-1,14-1,15-1,16-1,17-1,18-1,19-1,20-1,21-1,22-1,23-1,24-1,25-1

NIV - **22,** 1-1,2-1,3-1,4-1,5-1,6-**2**,7-**2**,8-1,9-1,10-1,11-1,12-**2**,13-1,14-1,15-1,16-1,17-1,18-1,19-1,20-**2**,21-1,22-1

NKJV - **26,** 1-1,2-1,3-1,4-1,5-1,6-1,7-1,8-1,9-1,10-1,11-1,12-**2**,13-1,14-1,15-1,16-1,17-1,18-**2**,19-1,20-1,21-1,22-1,23-1,24-**2**,25-1,26-1

NLT - **28,** 1-1,2-1,3-1,4-1,5-1,6-**2**,7-1,8-1,9-1,10-1,11-1,12-**2**,13-1,14-1,15-1,16-1,17-1,18-1,19-1,20-1,21-1,22-1,23-1,24-**2**,25-1,26-1,27-1,28-1

NRSV - **20,** 1-1,2-1,3-1,4-1,5-1,6-**2**,7-1,8-1,9-1,10-1,11-1,12-**2**,13-1,14-1,15-1,16-1,17-1,18-**2**,19-1,20-1

Conclusion: Seven modern versions are more complex than the King James Bible. This is one of those extremely rare cases where the NCV is the **only** modern version that does not complicate the verse.

Matthew 14:1* At that time **Herod** the **tetrarch** heard of the fame of **Jesus,**
AV - **12,** 1-1,2-1,3-1,4-1,5-1,6-1,7-1,8-1,9-1,10-1,11-1,12-1
ESV - **12,** 1-1,2-1,3-1,4-1,5-1,6-1,7-1,8-1,9-1,10-1,11-1,12-1
HCSB - 11, 1-1,2-1,3-1,4-1,5-1,6-1,7-1,8-1,9-**2**,10-**2**,11-1
NASV - 11, 1-1,2-1,3-1,4-1,5-1,6-1,7-1,8-1,9-1,10-**2**,11-1
NCV - 13, 1-1,2-1,3-1,4-1,5-1,6-**2**,7-1,8-1,9-1,10-1,11-**2**,12-**2**,13-1
NIV - 11, 1-1,2-1,3-1,4-1,5-1,6-1,7-1,8-1,9-**2**,10-**2**,11-1
NKJV - 11, 1-1,2-1,3-1,4-1,5-1,6-1,7-1,8-1,9-**2**,10-**2**,11-1
NLT - 10, 1-1,2-1,3-1,4-1,5-**2**,6-1,7-1,8-1,9-**2**,10-1
NRSV - 10, 1-1,2-1,3-1,4-1,5-1,6-**2**,7-1,8-**2**,9-**2**,10-1

Conclusion: Seven modern versions are more complex than the King James Bible. Both the NCV and the NLT added the word "Gallilee while the NLT also included the name "Antipas." Neither of these were counted against them.

Matthew 26:6* Now when **Jesus** was in **Bethany**, in the house of **Simon** the **leper,**
AV - **13,** 1-1,2-1,3-1,4-1,5-1,6-1,7-1,8-1,9-1,10-1,11-1,12-1,13-1
ESV - **13,** 1-1,2-1,3-1,4-1,5-1,6-1,7-1,8-1,9-1,10-1,11-1,12-1,13-1
HCSB - 18, 1-1,2-1,3-1,4-1,5-1,6-1,7-1,8-1,9-1,10-1,11-1,12-1,13-1,14-1,15-1,16-**3**,17-1,18-1
NASV - **13,** 1-1,2-1,3-1,4-1,5-1,6-1,7-1,8-1,9-1,10-1,11-1,12-1,13-1
NCV - **14,** 1-1,2-1,3-1,4-1,5-1,6-1,7-1,8-1,9-1,10-1,11-1,12-1,13-1,14-1
NIV - **16,** 1-1,2-1,3-1,4-1,5-1,6-1,7-1,8-1,9-1,10-1,11-1,12-1,13-1,14-1,15-1,16-1
NKJV - 13, 1-1,2-1,3-1,4-1,5-1,6-1,7-1,8-1,9-1,10-1,11-1,12-1,13-1
NLT - 17, 1-**2**,2-1,3-1,4-1,5-1,6-1,7-1,8-1,9-1,10-1,11-1,12-1,13-1,14-1,15-**4**,16-1,17-1
NRSV - **13,** 1-1,2-1,3-1,4-1,5-1,6-1,7-1,8-1,9-1,10-1,11-1,12-1,13-1

Conclusion: Only the HCSB and the NLT made the verse more complex. Both the HCSB and the NCV replaced "the leper" with "skin disease" and this was not counted against them. The HCSB added the "serious" with no Greek authority and this was counted against it. The NLT said of Simon, "a man who had previously had leprosy." There is no Greek authority for this addition.

Mark 10:7* For this cause shall a man leave his **father** and **mother**, and cleave to his wife;
AV - **16,** 1-1,2-1,3-1,4-1,5-1,6-1,7-1,8-1,9-1,10-1,11-1,12-1,13-1,14-1,15-1,16-1
ESV - 15, 1-**2**,2-1,3-1,4-1,5-1,6-1,7-1,8-1,9-1,10-1,11-1,12-1,13-1,14-1,15-1
HCSB - 17, 1-1,2-1,3-**2**,4-1,5-1,6-1,7-1,8-1,9-1,10-1,11-1,12-1,13-1,14-1,15-1,16-1,17-1
NASV - 11, 1-1,2-1,3-**2**,4-1,5-1,6-1,7-1,8-1,9-1,10-1,11-1

NCV - 15, 1-1,2-1,3-1,4-1,5-1,6-1,7-1,8-1,9-1,10-1,11-1,12-**3**,13-1,14-1,15-1
NIV - 17, 1-1,2-1,3-**2**,4-1,5-1,6-1,7-1,8-1,9-1,10-1,11-1,12-1,13-1,14-**3**,15-1,16-1,17-1
NKJV - 17, 1-1,2-1,3-**2**,4-1,5-1,6-1,7-1,8-1,9-1,10-1,11-1,12-1,13-1,14-1,15-1,16-1,17-1
NLT - 16, 1-1,2-**2**,3-1,4-1,5-1,6-1,7-1,8-1,9-1,10-1,11-1,12-1,13-1,14-1,15-1,16-1
NRSV - 17, 1-1,2-1,3-**2**,4-1,5-1,6-1,7-1,8-1,9-1,10-1,11-1,12-1,13-1,14-1,15-1,16-1,17-1
Conclusion: All eight modern versions are more complex than the King James Bible. Not one of the modern versions believes a man should "cleave" to his wife. Six of them say either "be joined to" or "be united with" which is obviously weaker than "cleave. The ESV does say "hold fast to" which is a little better, and much better than the NASV which deletes the phrase all together.

Luke 1:73* The oath which he sware to our **father Abraham,**
AV - **9,** 1-1,2-1,3-1,4-1,5-1,6-1,7-1,8-1,9-1
ESV - **12,** 1-1,2-1,3-1,4-1,5-1,6-1,7-1,8-1,9-1,10-1,11-1,12-1
HCSB - 15, 1-1,2-1,3-1,4-1,5-1,6-1,7-1,8-1,9-1,10-1,11-1,12-**2**,13-1,14-1,15-**3**
NASV - **9,** 1-1,2-1,3-1,4-1,5-1,6-1,7-1,8-1,9-1
NCV - 5, 1-1,2-**2**,3-1,4-1,5-1
NIV - **8,** 1-1,2-1,3-1,4-1,5-1,6-1,7-1,8-1
NKJV - 9, 1-1,2-1,3-1,4-1,5-1,6-1,7-1,8-1,9-1
NLT - 11, 1-1,2-**3**,3-1,4-1,5-1,6-1,7-1,8-1,9-1,10-1,11-1
NRSV - **12,** 1-1,2-1,3-1,4-1,5-1,6-1,7-1,8-1,9-1,10-1,11-1,12-1
Conclusion: Only three modern versions are more complex than the King James Bible.

Luke 4:28* And all they in the **synagogue,** when they heard these things, were filled with wrath,
AV - **15,** 1-1,2-1,3-1,4-1,5-1,6-1,7-1,8-1,9-1,10-1,11-1,12-1,13-1,14-1,15-1
ESV - **13,** 1-1,2-1,3-1,4-1,5-1,6-1,7-1,8-1,9-1,10-1,11-1,12-1,13-1
HCSB - 10, 1-1,2-1,3-1,4-1,5-**3**,6-1,7-1,8-1,9-1,10-**2**
NASV - 16, 1-1,2-1,3-1,4-**2**,5-1,6-1,7-1,8-1,9-1,10-1,11-1,12-1,13-1,14-1,15-1,16-1
NCV - 14, 1-1,2-1,3-1,4-**2**,5-1,6-1,7-1,8-1,9-1,10-1,11-1,12-**2**,13-**2**,14-1
NIV - 12, 1-1,2-1,3-**2**,4-1,5-1,6-1,7-1,8-**3**,9-1,10-1,11-1,12-1
NKJV - **15,** 1-1,2-1,3-1,4-1,5-1,6-1,7-1,8-1,9-1,10-1,11-1,12-1,13-1,14-1,15-1
NLT - 11, 1-1,2-1,3-1,4-1,5-1,6-**2**,7-1,8-1,9-1,10-1,11-**3**
NRSV - **12,** 1-1,2-1,3-1,4-1,5-1,6-1,7-1,8-1,9-1,10-1,11-1,12-1
Conclusion: Five modern versions are more complex than the King James Bible.

Luke 4:44 And he preached in the **synagogues** of **Galilee.**
AV - **8,** 1-1,2-1,3-1,4-1,5-1,6-1,7-1,8-1
ESV - 9, 1-1,2-1,3-1,4-**2**,5-1,6-1,7-1,8-1,9-1
HCSB - 9, 1-1,2-1,3-1,4-**2**,5-1,6-1,7-1,8-1,9-1
NASV - 10, 1-1,2-1,3-1,4-1,5-**2**,6-1,7-1,8-1,9-1,10-1
NCV - 10, 1-1,2-1,3-1,4-1,5-**2**,6-1,7-1,8-1,9-1,10-1
NIV - 10, 1-1,2-1,3-1,4-1,5-**2**,6-1,7-1,8-1,9-1,10-1
NKJV - 9, 1-1,2-1,3-1,4-**2**,5-1,6-1,7-1,8-1,9-1
NLT - 11, 1-1,2-1,3-**3**,4-1,5-**2**,6-**2**,7-**2**,8-1,9-1,10-**2**,11-1
NRSV - 11, 1-1,2-1,3-**3**,4-**3**,5-1,6-**2**,7-1,8-1,9-1,10-1,11-1
Conclusion: While all eight modern versions are more complex than the King James Bible and the NRSV was more complicated than six of the modern versions it was the NLT that showed it stuff and rendered the most complex version. The ESV, NASV, NCV, NIV, NLT and the NRSV all replaced "Galilee" with "Judea."

Luke 7:18* And the **disciples** of John shewed him of all these things.
AV - **11,** 1-1,2-1,3-1,4-1,5-1,6-1,7-1,8-1,9-1,10-1,11-1
ESV - 12, 1-1,2-1,3-1,4-1,5-**3**,6-1,7-1,8-1,9-1,10-1,11-1,12-1
HCSB - 16, 1-1,2-1,3-1,4-1,5-1,6-**2**,7-1,8-1,9-1,10-1,11-1,12-**2**,13-1,14-1,15-1,16-1
NASV - 11, 1-1,2-1,3-1,4-1,5-**3**,6-1,7-1,8-**2**,9-1,10-1,11-1
NCV - 15, 1-1,2-1,3-1,4-1,5-**2**,6-1,7-1,8-1,9-1,10-1,11-1,12-1,13-1,14-1,15-1
NIV - 12, 1-1,2-1,3-1,4-1,5-**2**,6-1,7-1,8-1,9-**2**,10-1,11-1,12-1
NKJV - 12, 1-1,2-1,3-1,4-1,5-1,6-**3**,7-1,8-1,9-**3**,10-1,11-1,12-1
NLT - 21, 1-1,2-1,3-1,4-1,5-1,6-1,7-1,8-1,9-**2**,10-**4**,11-1,12-1,13-**2**,14-1,15-1,16-1,17-1,18-1,19-1,20-1,21-1
NRSV - 17, 1-1,2-1,3-1,4-1,5-**3**,6-1,7-1,8-1,9-1,10-1,11-1,12-1,13-**2**,14-1,15-1,16-1,17-1
Conclusion: All eight modern versions are more complex than the King James Bible. The HCSB, NLT and the NRSV all had the word "disciples" in the verse twice. This was not counted against them. The NCV is the only translation that didn't say "disciples" but instead "followers", which was in the verse twice. This was not counted against it. The NLT is the most difficult to read.

Luke 22:1* Now the feast of **unleavened** bread drew nigh, which is called the **Passover**.
AV - **13,** 1-1,2-1,3-1,4-1,5-1,6-1,7-1,8-1,9-1,10-1,11-1,12-1,13-1
ESV - **13,** 1-1,2-1,3-1,4-1,5-1,6-1,7-1,8-1,9-1,10-1,11-1,12-1,13-1
HCSB - 12, 1-1,2-1,3-1,4-1,5-1,6-1,7-1,8-1,9-1,10-1,11-**2**,12-1
NASV - 13, 1-1,2-1,3-1,4-1,5-1,6-1,7-1,8-1,9-1,10-1,11-1,12-1,13-**3**
NCV - 14, 1-1,2-1,3-**2**,4-1,5-1,6-1,7-1,8-1,9-1,10-1,11-1,12-1,13-1,14-1
NIV - 11, 1-1,2-1,3-1,4-1,5-1,6-1,7-1,8-1,9-1,10-1,11-**3**
NKJV - **12,** 1-1,2-1,3-1,4-1,5-1,6-1,7-1,8-1,9-1,10-1,11-1,12-1
NLT - 12, 1-1,2-**3**,3-1,4-1,5-1,6-1,7-1,8-**2**,9-1,10-1,11-1,12-**3**
NRSV - 13, 1-1,2-1,3-**3**,4-1,5-1,6-1,7-1,8-1,9-1,10-1,11-1,12-1,13-1
Conclusion: Six modern versions are more complex than the King James Bible.

John 2:13* And the Jews' **passover** was at hand, and **Jesus** went up to **Jerusalem**,
AV - **13,** 1-1,2-1,3-1,4-1,5-1,6-1,7-1,8-1,9-1,10-1,11-1,12-1,13-1
ESV - **14,** 1-1,2-1,3-1,4-1,5-1,6-1,7-1,8-1,9-1,10-1,11-1,12-1,13-1,14-1
HCSB - **11,** 1-1,2-1,3-1,4-1,5-1,6-1,7-1,8-1,9-1,10-1,11-1
NASV - **13,** 1-1,2-1,3-1,4-1,5-1,6-1,7-1,8-1,9-1,10-1,11-1,12-1,13-1
NCV - 14, 1-1,2-1,3-1,4-**2**,5-1,6-1,7-1,8-**2**,9-1,10-1,11-1,12-1,13-1,14-1
NIV - 14, 1-1,2-1,3-1,4-**2**,5-1,6-1,7-1,8-**2**,9-1,10-1,11-1,12-1,13-1,14-1
NKJV - **15,** 1-1,2-1,3-1,4-1,5-1,6-1,7-1,8-1,9-1,10-1,11-1,12-1,13-1,14-1,15-1
NLT - 14, 1-1,2-1,3-**2**,4-1,5-1,6-1,7-**2**,8-1,9-**4**,10-1,11-1,12-1,13-1,14-1
NRSV - **13,** 1-1,2-1,3-1,4-1,5-1,6-1,7-1,8-1,9-1,10-1,11-1,12-1,13-1
Conclusion: Only three modern versions are more complex than the King James Bible. The NLT is the most difficult to read.

John 10:14* I am the good **shepherd**, and know my sheep, and am known of mine.
AV - **14,** 1-1,2-1,3-1,4-1,5-1,6-1,7-1,8-1,9-1,10-1,11-1,12-1,13-1,14-1
ESV - **14,** 1-1,2-1,3-1,4-1,5-1,6-1,7-1,8-1,9-1,10-1,11-1,12-1,13-1,14-1
HCSB - **14,** 1-1,2-1,3-1,4-1,5-1,6-1,7-1,8-1,9-1,10-1,11-1,12-1,13-1,14-1
NASV - **15,** 1-1,2-1,3-1,4-1,5-1,6-1,7-1,8-1,9-1,10-1,11-1,12-1,13-1,14-1,15-1
NCV - **14,** 1-1,2-1,3-1,4-1,5-1,6-1,7-1,8-1,9-1,10-1,11-1,12-1,13-1,14-1
NIV - **14,** 1-1,2-1,3-1,4-1,5-1,6-1,7-1,8-1,9-1,10-1,11-1,12-1,13-1,14-1

NKJV - **16,** 1-1,2-1,3-1,4-1,5-1,6-1,7-1,8-1,9-1,10-1,11-1,12-1,13-1,14-1,15-1,16-1
NLT - **14,** 1-1,2-1,3-1,4-1,5-1,6-1,7-1,8-1,9-1,10-1,11-1,12-1,13-1,14-1
NRSV - **14,** 1-1,2-1,3-1,4-1,5-1,6-1,7-1,8-1,9-1,10-1,11-1,12-1,13-1,14-1
Conclusion: All versions read the same.

John 10:23* And **Jesus** walked in the **temple** in **Solomon's** porch.
AV - **9,** 1-1,2-1,3-1,4-1,5-1,6-1,7-1,8-1,9-1
ESV - 12, 1-1,2-1,3-1,4-**2**,5-1,6-1,7-1,8-1,9-1,10-**3**,11-1,12-1
HCSB - 10, 1-1,2-1,3-**2**,4-1,5-1,6-1,7-**2**,8-1,9-1,10-**3**
NASV - 15, 1-1,2-1,3-**2**,4-1,5-1,6-1,7-**2**,8-1,9-1,10-1,11-1,12-1,13-**3**,14-1,15-1
NCV - 10, 1-1,2-1,3-1,4-**2**,5-1,6-1,7-1,8-1,9-1,10-1
NIV - 11, 1-1,2-1,3-1,4-1,5-1,6-1,7-**3**,8-**2**,9-1,10-1,11-**3**
NKJV - **9,** 1-1,2-1,3-1,4-1,5-1,6-1,7-1,8-1,9-1
NLT - 13, 1-1,2-1,3-1,4-1,5-1,6-**2**,7-1,8-1,9-**2**,10-1,11-1,12-1,13-**3**
NRSV - 12, 1-1,2-1,3-1,4-**2**,5-1,6-1,7-1,8-1,9-1,10-**3**,11-1,12-1
Conclusion: Seven modern versions are more complex than the King James Bible.

John 11:5* Now **Jesus** loved **Martha**, and her **sister**, and **Lazarus**.
AV - **9,** 1-1,2-1,3-1,4-1,5-1,6-1,7-1,8-1,9-1
ESV - **9,** 1-1,2-1,3-1,4-1,5-1,6-1,7-1,8-1,9-1
HCSB - **7,** 1-1,2-1,3-1,4-1,5-1,6-1,7-1
NASV - **9,** 1-1,2-1,3-1,4-1,5-1,6-1,7-1,8-1,9-1
NCV - **8,** 1-1,2-1,3-1,4-1,5-1,6-1,7-1,8-1
NIV - **8,** 1-1,2-1,3-1,4-1,5-1,6-1,7-1,8-1
NKJV - **9,** 1-1,2-1,3-1,4-1,5-1,6-1,7-1,8-1,9-1
NLT - 8, 1-1,2-**2**,3-1,4-1,5-1,6-1,7-1,8-1
NRSV - 10, 1-**4**,2-1,3-1,4-1,5-1,6-1,7-1,8-1,9-1,10-1
Conclusion: Only the NLT and the NRSV found a way to make this simple verse more complex.

John 11:12* Then said his **disciples**, Lord, if he sleep, he shall do well.
AV - **12,** 1-1,2-1,3-1,4-1,5-1,6-1,7-1,8-1,9-1,10-1,11-1,12-1
ESV - 15, 1-1,2-1,3-1,4-1,5-1,6-1,7-1,8-1,9-1,10-1,11-**2**,12-**2**,13-1,14-1,15-**3**
HCSB - 16, 1-1,2-1,3-1,4-1,5-1,6-1,7-1,8-1,9-1,10-1,11-**2**,12-2,13-1,14-1,15-1,16-1
NASV - 15, 1-1,2-1,3-1,4-1,5-1,6-1,7-1,8-1,9-1,10-1,11-**2**,12-**2**,13-1,14-1,15-**3**
NCV - 15, 1-1,2-1,3-1,4-1,5-1,6-1,7-1,8-1,9-**2**,10-**2**,11-1,12-1,13-1,14-1,15-1
NIV - 11, 1-1,2-1,3-**2**,4-1,5-1,6-1,7-1,8-1,9-1,10-1,11-**2**
NKJV - **12,** 1-1,2-1,3-1,4-1,5-1,6-1,7-1,8-1,9-1,10-1,11-1,12-1
NLT - 13, 1-1,2-1,3-1,4-1,5-1,6-1,7-1,8-**2**,9-1,10-1,11-1,12-1,13-**2**
NRSV - 16, 1-1,2-1,3-1,4-1,5-1,6-1,7-1,8-1,9-1,10-**2**,11-**2**,12-1,13-1,14-1,15-1,16-1
Conclusion: Seven modern versions are more complex than the King James Bible. The NCV replaced "disciples" with "followers" but this was not held against it.

2 Corinthians 1:18 But as God is true, our word **toward** you was not yea and nay.
AV - **14,** 1-1,2-1,3-1,4-1,5-1,6-1,7-1,8-1,9-1,10-1,11-1,12-1,13-1,14-1
ESV - 16, 1-1,2-**2**,3-1,4-1,5-1,6-**2**,7-1,8-1,9-1,10-1,11-1,12-1,13-1,14-1,15-1,16-1
HCSB - 13, 1-1,2-1,3-1,4-**2**,5-1,6-**2**,7-1,8-1,9-1,10-1,11-1,12-1,13-1
NASV - 14, 1-1,2-1,3-1,4-1,5-**2**,6-1,7-1,8-1,9-1,10-1,11-1,12-1,13-1,14-1
NCV - 20, 1-1,2-1,3-1,4-1,5-**2**,6-1,7-1,8-1,9-**2**,10-1,11-1,12-1,13-1,14-1,15-1,16-**2**,17-1,18-1,19-1,20-1

NIV - 16, 1-1,2-1,3-**2**,4-1,5-1,6-1,7-**2**,8-1,9-**2**,10-1,11-1,12-1,13-1,14-1,15-1,16-1
NKJV - 14, 1-1,2-1,3-1,4-1,5-**2**,6-1,7-1,8-1,9-1,10-1,11-1,12-1,13-1,14-1
NLT - 17, 1-1,2-**2**,3-1,4-1,5-1,6-**2**,7-1,8-1,9-1,10-1,11-1,12-1,13-**2**,14-**2**,15-1,16-1,17-1
NRSV - 16, 1-1,2-**2**,3-1,4-1,5-1,6-**2**,7-1,8-1,9-1,10-1,11-1,12-1,13-1,14-1,15-1,16-1
Conclusion: All eight modern versions are more complex than the King James Bible.

1 John 1:10 If we say that we have not sinned, we make him a **liar**, and his word is not in us.
AV - **20,** 1-1,2-1,3-1,4-1,5-1,6-1,7-1,8-1,9-1,10-1,11-1,12-1,13-1,14-1,15-1,16-1,17-1,18-1,19-1,20-1
ESV - **19,** 1-1,2-1,3-1,4-1,5-1,6-1,7-1,8-1,9-1,10-1,11-1,12-1,13-1,14-1,15-1,16-1,17-1,18-1,19-1
HCSB - **19,** 1-1,2-1,3-1,4-1,5-1,6-1,7-1,8-1,9-1,10-1,11-1,12-1,13-1,14-1,15-1,16-1,17-1,18-1,19-1
NASV - **20,** 1-1,2-1,3-1,4-1,5-1,6-1,7-1,8-1,9-1,10-1,11-1,12-1,13-1,14-1,15-1,16-1,17-1,18-1,19-1,20-1
NCV - 19, 1-1,2-1,3-1,4-1,5-1,6-1,7-1,8-1,9-1,10-1,11-1,12-1,13-1,14-1,15-1,16-1,17-**2**,18-1,19-**2**
NIV - **24,** 1-1,2-1,3-1,4-1,5-1,6-1,7-1,8-1,9-1,10-1,11-1,12-1,13-1,14-1,15-1,16-1,17-1,18-1,19-1,20-1,21-1,22-1,23-1,24-1
NKJV - **20,** 1-1,2-1,3-1,4-1,5-1,6-1,7-1,8-1,9-1,10-1,11-1,12-1,13-1,14-1,15-1,16-1,17-1,18-1,19-1,20-1
NLT - 24, 1-1,2-1,3-1,4-1,5-1,6-1,7-1,8-1,9-1,10-**2**,11-1,12-1,13-1,14-1,15-**2**,16-1,17-1,18-1,19-1,20-1,21-1,22-1,23-1,24-1
NRSV - **20,** 1-1,2-1,3-1,4-1,5-1,6-1,7-1,8-1,9-1,10-1,11-1,12-1,13-1,14-1,15-1,16-1,17-1,18-1,19-1,20-1
Conclusion: Only the NCV and the NLT made the verse more complex.

Single Syllable Word Verses with No Names or Numbers

1. Genesis 1:3 And God said, Let there be light: and there was light.
11 words

2. Genesis 8:16 Go forth of the ark, thou, and thy wife, and thy sons, and thy sons' wives with thee.
18 words

3. Genesis 26:30 And he made them a feast, and they did eat and drink.
12 words

4. Genesis 35:13 And God went up from him in the place where he talked with him.
14 words

5. Genesis 38:17 And he said, I will send thee a kid from the flock. And she said, Wilt thou give me a pledge, till thou send it?
25 words

6. Genesis 49:12 His eyes shall be red with wine, and his teeth white with milk.
13 words

7. Exodus 4:13 And he said, O my Lord, send, I pray thee, by the hand of him whom thou wilt send.
19 words

8. Exodus 4:24 And it came to pass by the way in the inn, that the LORD met him, and sought to kill him.
21 words

9. Exodus 14:14 The LORD shall fight for you, and ye shall hold your peace.
12 words

10. Exodus 15:3 The LORD is a man of war: the LORD is his name.
12 words

11. Exodus 20:13 Thou shalt not kill.
4 words

12. Exodus 20:15 Thou shalt not steal.
4 words

13. Exodus 21:24 Eye for eye, tooth for tooth, hand for hand, foot for foot,
12 words

14. Exodus 33:20 And he said, Thou canst not see my face: for there shall no man see me, and live.
18 words

15. Exodus 40:14 And thou shalt bring his sons, and clothe them with coats:
11 words

16. Leviticus 24:12 And they put him in ward, that the mind of the LORD might be showed them.
16 words

17. Numbers 6:24 The LORD bless thee, and keep thee:
7 words

18. Numbers 31:11 And they took all the spoil, and all the prey, both of men and of beasts.
16 words

19. Deuteronomy 3:22 Ye shall not fear them: for the LORD your God he shall fight for you.
15 words

20. Deuteronomy 4:29 But if from thence thou shalt seek the LORD thy God, thou shalt find him, if thou seek him with all thy heart and with all thy soul.
28 words

21. Deuteronomy 5:4 The LORD talked with you face to face in the mount out of the midst of the fire,
18 words

22. Deuteronomy 5:17 Thou shalt not kill.
4 words

23. Deuteronomy 6:5 And thou shalt love the LORD thy God with all thine heart, and with all thy soul, and with all thy might.
22 words

24. Deuteronomy 6:13 Thou shalt fear the LORD thy God, and serve him, and shalt swear by his name.
16 words

25. Deuteronomy 10:20 Thou shalt fear the LORD thy God; him shalt thou serve, and to him shalt thou cleave, and swear by his name.
22 words

26. Deuteronomy 11:7 But your eyes have seen all the great acts of the LORD which he did.
15 words

27. Deuteronomy 14:4 These are the beasts which ye shall eat: the ox, the sheep, and the goat,
15 words

28. Deuteronomy 14:11 Of all clean birds ye shall eat.
7 words

29. Deuteronomy 14:20 But of all clean fowls ye may eat.
8 words

30. Deuteronomy 21:12 Then thou shalt bring her home to thine house; and she shall shave her head, and pare her nails;
19 words

A Study of Verses Composed of Single Syllable Words

31. Deuteronomy 24:12 And if the man be poor, thou shalt not sleep with his pledge:
13 words

32. Deuteronomy 28:34 So that thou shalt be mad for the sight of thine eyes which thou shalt see.
16 words

33. Deuteronomy 28:44 He shall lend to thee, and thou shalt not lend to him: he shall be the head, and thou shalt be the tail.
23 words

34. Deuteronomy 33:25 Thy shoes shall be iron and brass; and as thy days, so shall thy strength be.
16 words

35. Judges 5:27 At her feet he bowed, he fell, he lay down: at her feet he bowed, he fell: where he bowed, there he fell down dead.
25 words

36. 1 Samuel 6:10 And the men did so; and took two milch kine, and tied them to the cart, and shut up their calves at home:
23 words

37. 2 Samuel 22:32 For who is God, save the LORD? and who is a rock, save our God?
15 words

38. 2 Kings 4:15 And he said, Call her. And when he had called her, she stood in the door.
16 words

39. 2 Kings 22:11 And it came to pass, when the king had heard the words of the book of the law, that he rent his clothes.
23 words

40. 2 Chronicles 34:19 And it came to pass, when the king had heard the words of the law, that he rent his clothes.
20 words

41. Job 1:11 But put forth thine hand now, and touch all that he hath, and he will curse thee to thy face.
20 words

42. Job 2:5 But put forth thine hand now, and touch his bone and his flesh, and he will curse thee to thy face.
21 words

43. Job 3:2 And Job spake, and said.
5 words

44. Job 5:27 Lo this, we have searched it, so it is; hear it, and know thou it for thy good.
18 words

45. Job 6:12 Is my strength the strength of stones? or is my flesh of brass?
13 words

46. Job 8:2 How long wilt thou speak these things? and how long shall the words of thy mouth be like a strong wind?
21 words

47. Job 9:2 I know it is so of a truth: but how should man be just with God?
16 words

48. Job 9:35 Then would I speak, and not fear him; but it is not so with me.
15 words

49. Job 10:5 Are thy days as the days of man? are thy years as man's days,
14 words

50. Job 10:13 And these things hast thou hid in thine heart: I know that this is with thee.
16 words

51. Job 12:7 But ask now the beasts, and they shall teach thee; and the fowls of the air, and they shall tell thee:
21 words

52. Job 12:11 Doth not the ear try words? and the mouth taste his meat?
12 words

53. Job 13:19 Who is he that will plead with me? for now, if I hold my tongue, I shall give up the ghost.
21 words

54. Job 17:15 And where is now my hope? as for my hope, who shall see it?
14 words

55. Job 18:10 The snare is laid for him in the ground, and a trap for him in the way.
17 words

56. Job 20:11 His bones are full of the sin of his youth, which shall lie down with him in the dust.
19 words

57. Job 25:6 How much less man, that is a worm? and the son of man, which is a worm?
17 words

58. Job 27:23 Men shall clap their hands at him, and shall hiss him out of his place.
15 words

59. Job 28:14 The depth saith, It is not in me: and the sea saith, It is not with me.
17 words

60. Job 29:15 I was eyes to the blind, and feet was I to the lame.
13 words

61. Job 31:4 Doth not he see my ways, and count all my steps?
11 words

62. Job 31:20 If his loins have not blessed me, and if he were not warmed with the fleece of my sheep;
19 words

63. Job 39:5 Who hath sent out the wild ass free? or who hath loosed the bands of the wild ass?
18 words

64. Job 41:7 Canst thou fill his skin with barbed irons? or his head with fish spears?
14 words

65. Psalms 18:1 I will love thee, O LORD, my strength.
8 words

66. Psalms 18:31 For who is God save the LORD? or who is a rock save our God?
15 words

67. Psalms 20:9 Save, LORD: let the king hear us when we call.
10 words

68. Psalms 22:19 But be not thou far from me, O LORD: O my strength, haste thee to help me.
17 words

69. Psalms 25:4 Show me thy ways, O LORD; teach me thy paths.
10 words

70. Psalms 33:4 For the word of the LORD is right; and all his works are done in truth.
16 words

71. Psalms 34:9 O fear the LORD, ye his saints: for there is no want to them that fear him.
17 words

72. Psalm 37:31 The law of his God is in his heart; none of his steps shall slide.
15 words

73. Psalms 38:15 For in thee, O LORD, do I hope: thou wilt hear, O Lord my God.
15 words

74. Psalms 39:7 And now, Lord, what wait I for? my hope is in thee.
12 words

75. Psalms 50:13 Will I eat the flesh of bulls, or drink the blood of goats?
13 words

76. Psalms 54:1 Save me, O God, by thy name, and judge me by thy strength.
13 words

77. Psalms 54:2 Hear my prayer, O God; give ear to the words of my mouth.
13 words

78. Psalm 56:10 In God will I praise his word: in the LORD will I praise his word.
15 words

79. Psalm 57:7 My heart is fixed, O God, my heart is fixed: I will sing and give praise.
16 words

80. Psalms 63:4 Thus will I bless thee while I live: I will lift up my hands in thy name.
17 words

81. Psalms 67:7 God shall bless us; and all the ends of the earth shall fear him.
14 words

82. Psalms 71:5 For thou art my hope, O Lord GOD: thou art my trust from my youth.
15 words

83. Psalms 71:12 O God, be not far from me: O my God, make haste for my help.
15 words

84. Psalms 73:4 For there are no bands in their death: but their strength is firm.
13 words

85. Psalms 73:21 Thus my heart was grieved, and I was pricked in my reins.
12 words

86. Psalms 75:5 Lift not up your horn on high: speak not with a stiff neck.
13 words

87. Psalms 84:5 Blessed is the man whose strength is in thee; in whose heart are the ways of them.
17 words

88. Psalms 95:5 The sea is his, and he made it: and his hands formed the dry land.
15 words

89. Psalms 102:27 But thou art the same, and thy years shall have no end.
12 words

90. Psalms 104:17 Where the birds make their nests: as for the stork, the fir trees are her house.
16 words

91. Psalms 108:11 Wilt not thou, O God, who hast cast us off? and wilt not thou, O God, go forth with our hosts?
21 words

92. Psalms 109:1 Hold not thy peace, O God of my praise;
9 words

93. Psalms 109:27 That they may know that this is thy hand; that thou, LORD, hast done it.
15 words

94. Psalms 110:5 The Lord at thy right hand shall strike through kings in the day of his wrath.
16 words

95. Psalms 115:5 They have mouths, but they speak not: eyes have they, but they see not:
14 words

96. Psalms 115:11 Ye that fear the LORD, trust in the LORD: he is their help and their shield.
16 words

97. Psalms 115:13 He will bless them that fear the LORD, both small and great.
12 words

98. Psalms 118:13 Thou hast thrust sore at me that I might fall: but the LORD helped me.
15 words

99. Psalms 119:113 I hate vain thoughts: but thy law do I love.
10 words

100. Psalms 119:126 It is time for thee, LORD, to work: for they have made void thy law.
15 words

101. Psalms 120:7 I am for peace: but when I speak, they are for war.
12 words

102. Psalm 121:6 The sun shall not smite thee by day, nor the moon by night.
13 words

103. Psalms 126:5 They that sow in tears shall reap in joy.
9 words

104. Psalms 130:5 I wait for the LORD, my soul doth wait, and in his word do I hope.
16 words

105. Psalms 135:2 Ye that stand in the house of the LORD, in the courts of the house of our God,
18 words

106. Psalms 135:16 They have mouths, but they speak not; eyes have they, but they see not;
14 words

107. Psalms 137:4 How shall we sing the Lord's song in a strange land?
11 words

108. Psalms 138:4 All the kings of the earth shall praise thee, O LORD, when they hear the words of thy mouth.
19 words

109. Psalms 139:1 O LORD, thou hast searched me, and known me.
9 words

110. Psalms 139:23 Search me, O God, and know my heart: try me, and know my thoughts:
14 words

111. Psalms 145:10 All thy works shall praise thee, O LORD; and thy saints shall bless thee.
14 words

112. Psalm 146:1 Praise ye the LORD. Praise the LORD, O my soul.
10 words

113. Psalm 148:3 Praise ye him, sun and moon: praise him, all ye stars of light.
13 words

114. Proverbs 3:2 For length of days, and long life, and peace, shall they add to thee.
14 words

115. Proverbs 5:5 Her feet go down to death; her steps take hold on hell.
12 words

116. Proverbs 20:9 Who can say, I have made my heart clean, I am pure from my sin?
15 words

117. Proverbs 22:23 For the LORD will plead their cause, and spoil the soul of those that spoiled them.
16 words

118. Proverbs 22:25 Lest thou learn his ways, and get a snare to thy soul.
12 words

119. Proverbs 23:19 Hear thou, my son, and be wise, and guide thine heart in the way.
14 words

120. Proverbs 31:2 What, my son? and what, the son of my womb? and what, the son of my vows?
17 words

121. Proverbs 31:31 Give her of the fruit of her hands; and let her own works praise her in the gates.
18 words

122. Ecclesiastes 3:3 A time to kill, and a time to heal; a time to break down, and a time to build up;
20 words

123. Ecclesiastes 3:4 A time to weep, and a time to laugh; a time to mourn, and a time to dance;
18 words

124. Ecclesiastes 3:8 A time to love, and a time to hate; a time of war, and a time of peace.
18 words

125. Ecclesiastes 10:2 A wise man's heart is at his right hand; but a fool's heart at his left.
16 words

126. Song of Solomon 4:7 Thou art all fair, my love; there is no spot in thee.
12 words

127. Song of Solomon 7:3 Thy two breasts are like two young roes that are twins.
11 words

128. Isaiah 3:21 The rings, and nose jewels,
5 words

129. Isaiah 6:4 And the posts of the door moved at the voice of him that cried, and the house was filled with smoke.
21 words

130. Isaiah 14:15 Yet thou shalt be brought down to hell, to the sides of the pit.
14 words

131. Isaiah 27:5 Or let him take hold of my strength, that he may make peace with me; and he shall make peace with me.
22 words

132. Isaiah 42:2 He shall not cry, nor lift up, nor cause his voice to be heard in the street.
17 words

133. Isaiah 42:18 Hear, ye deaf; and look, ye blind, that ye may see.
11 words

134. Isaiah 66:9 Shall I bring to the birth, and not cause to bring forth? saith the LORD: shall I cause to bring forth, and shut the womb? saith thy God.
28 words

135. Jeremiah 17:14 Heal me, O LORD, and I shall be healed; save me, and I shall be saved: for thou art my praise.
21 words

136. Jeremiah 22:29 O earth, earth, earth, hear the word of the LORD.
10 words

137. Jeremiah 29:13 And ye shall seek me, and find me, when ye shall search for me with all your heart.
18 words

138. Lamentations 3:27 It is good for a man that he bear the yoke in his youth.
14 words

139. Lamentations 3:59 O LORD, thou hast seen my wrong: judge thou my cause.
11 words

140. Lamentations 5:17 For this our heart is faint; for these things our eyes are dim.
13 words

141. Ezekiel 6:7 And the slain shall fall in the midst of you, and ye shall know that I am the LORD.
19 words

142. Ezekiel 26:13 And I will cause the noise of thy songs to cease; and the sound of thy harps shall be no more heard.
22 words

143. Ezekiel 28:8 They shall bring thee down to the pit, and thou shalt die the deaths of them that are slain in the midst of the seas.
25 words

144. Ezekiel 34:3 Ye eat the fat, and ye clothe you with the wool, ye kill them that are fed: but ye feed not the flock.
23 words

145. Ezekiel 34:15 I will feed my flock, and I will cause them to lie down, saith the Lord GOD.
17 words

146. Daniel 2:33: His legs of iron, his feet part of iron and part of clay.
13 words

147. Daniel 12:13 But go thou thy way till the end be: for thou shalt rest, and stand in thy lot at the end of the days.
24 words

148. Zechariah 14:6 And it shall come to pass in that day, that the light shall not be clear, nor dark:
18 words

149. Matthew 5:8 Blessed are the pure in heart: for they shall see God.
11 words

150. Matthew 5:38 Ye have heard that it hath been said, An eye for an eye, and a tooth for a tooth:
19 words

151. Matthew 7:1 Judge not, that ye be not judged.
7 words

152. Matthew 7:9 Or what man is there of you, whom if his son ask bread, will he give him a stone?
19 words

153. Matthew 10:34 Think not that I am come to send peace on earth: I came not to send peace, but a sword.
20 words

154. Matthew 11:15 He that hath ears to hear, let him hear.
9 words

155. Matthew 12:16 And charged them that they should not make him known:
10 words

156. Matthew 13:9 Who hath ears to hear, let him hear.
8 words

157. Matthew 13:16 But blessed are your eyes, for they see: and your ears, for they hear.
14 words

158. Matthew 13:46 Who, when he had found one pearl of great price, went and sold all that he had, and bought it.
20 words

159. Matthew 18:11 For the Son of man is come to save that which was lost.
13 words

160. Matthew 25:33 And he shall set the sheep on his right hand, but the goats on the left
16 words

161. Mark 6:42 And they did all eat, and were filled.
8 words

162. Mark 8:30 And he charged them that they should tell no man of him.
12 words

163. Mark 10:8 And they twain shall be one flesh: so then they are no more twain, but one flesh.
17 words

164. Mark 13:17 But woe to them that are with child, and to them that give suck in those days!
17 words

165. Mark 13:33 Take ye heed, watch and pray: for ye know not when the time is.
14 words

166. Mark 14:46 And they laid their hands on him, and took him.
10 words

167. Mark 16:10 And she went and told them that had been with him, as they mourned and wept.
16 words

168. Luke 2:28 Then took he him up in his arms, and blessed God, and said,
13 words

169. Luke 6:46 And why call ye me, Lord, Lord, and do not the things which I say?
15 words

170. Luke 9:15 And they did so, and made them all sit down.
10 words

171. Luke 14:4 And they held their peace. And he took him, and healed him, and let him go;
16 words

172. Luke 18:21 And he said, All these have I kept from my youth up.
12 words

173. Luke 18:26 And they that heard it said, Who then can be saved?
10 words

174. Luke 19:10 For the Son of man is come to seek and to save that which was lost.
16 words

175. Luke 19:34 And they said, The Lord hath need of him.
8 words

176. Luke 19:36 And as he went, they spread their clothes in the way.
11 words

177. Luke 21:35 For as a snare shall it come on all them that dwell on the face of the whole earth.
19 words

178. Luke 23:31 For if they do these things in a green tree, what shall be done in the dry?
17 words

179. Luke 24:30 And it came to pass, as he sat at meat with them, he took bread, and blessed it, and brake, and gave to them.
24 words

180. John 1:4 In him was life; and the life was the light of men.
12 words

181. John 1:6 There was a man sent from God, whose name was John.
11 words

182. John 1:10 He was in the world, and the world was made by him, and the world knew him not.
18 words

183. John 1:13 Which were born, not of blood, nor of the will of the flesh, nor of the will of man, but of God.
22 words

184. John 5:40 And ye will not come to me, that ye might have life.
12 words

185. John 5:42 But I know you, that ye have not the love of God in you.
14 words

186. John 6:48 I am that bread of life.
6 words

187. John 7:11 Then the Jews sought him at the feast, and said, Where is he?
13 words

188. John 7:29 But I know him: for I am from him, and he hath sent me.
14 words

189. John 8:32 And ye shall know the truth, and the truth shall make you free.
13 words

190. John 9:5 As long as I am in the world, I am the light of the world.
15 words

191. John 12:43 For they loved the praise of men more than the praise of God.
13 words

192. John 19:3 And said, Hail, King of the Jews! and they smote him with their hands.
14 words

193. Acts 7:1 Then said the high priest, Are these things so?
9 words

194. Acts 7:50 Hath not my hand made all these things?
8 words

195. Acts 7:54 When they heard these things, they were cut to the heart, and they gnashed on him with their teeth.
19 words

196. Acts 13:30 But God raised him from the dead:
7 words

197. Acts 16:30 And brought them out, and said, Sirs, what must I do to be saved?
14 words

198. Romans 3:15 Their feet are swift to shed blood:
7 words

199. Romans 3:17 And the way of peace have they not known:
9 words

200. Romans 6:7 For he that is dead is freed from sin.
9 words

201. 1 Corinthians 3:23 And ye are Christ's; and Christ is God's.
8 words

202. 1 Corinthians 4:18 Now some are puffed up, as though I would not come to you.
13 words

203. 1 Corinthians 10:15 I speak as to wise men; judge ye what I say.
11 words

204. 1 Corinthians 14:18 I thank my God, I speak with tongues more than ye all:
12 words

205. 1 Corinthians 15:16 For if the dead rise not, then is not Christ raised:
11 words

206. 1 Corinthians 15:17 And if Christ be not raised, your faith is vain; ye are yet in your sins.
16 words

207. 1 Corinthians 15:56 The sting of death is sin; and the strength of sin is the law.
14 words

208. 1 Corinthians 16:13 Watch ye, stand fast in the faith, quit you like men, be strong.
13 words

209. 2 Corinthians 3:4 And such trust have we through Christ to God-ward:
10 words

210. 2 Corinthians 5:7 (For we walk by faith, not by sight:)
8 words

211. Ephesians 4:20 But ye have not so learned Christ;
7 words

212. Philippians 1:21 For to me to live is Christ, and to die is gain.
12 words

213. Colossians 3:3 For ye are dead, and your life is hid with Christ in God.
13 words

214. 1 Thessalonians 3:8 For now we live, if ye stand fast in the Lord.
11 words

215. 1 Thessalonians 5:21 Prove all things; hold fast that which is good.
9 words

216. 1 Timothy 3:5 (For if a man know not how to rule his own house, how shall he take care of the church of God?)
22 words

217. James 4:15 For that ye ought to say, If the Lord will, we shall live, and do this, or that.
18 words

218. 1 John 5:12 He that hath the Son hath life; and he that hath not the Son of God hath not life.
19 words

219. Revelation 1:14 His head and his hairs were white like wool, as white as snow; and his eyes were as a flame of fire;
22 words

220. Revelation 21:13 On the east three gates; on the north three gates; on the south three gates; and on the west three gates.
21 words

221. Revelation 21:25 And the gates of it shall not be shut at all by day: for there shall be no night there.
19 words

(You preachers can put these together for a sermon however you wish.)

Single Syllable Word Verses with No Names or Numbers Plus Data

1. Genesis 1:3 And God said, Let there be light: and there was light.
AV - **11,** 1-1,2-1,3-1,4-1,5-1,6-1,7-1,8-1,9-1,10-1,11-1
ESV - **11,** 1-1,2-1,3-1,4-1,5-1,6-1,7-1,8-1,9-1,10-1,11-1
HCSB - **11,** 1-1,2-1,3-1,4-1,5-1,6-1,7-1,8-1,9-1,10-1,11-1
NASV - **11,** 1-1,2-1,3-1,4-1,5-1,6-1,7-1,8-1,9-1,10-1,11-1
NCV - **11,** 1-1,2-1,3-1,4-1,5-1,6-1,7-1,8-1,9-1,10-1,11-1
NIV - **11,** 1-1,2-1,3-1,4-1,5-1,6-1,7-1,8-1,9-1,10-1,11-1
NKJV - **11,** 1-1,2-1,3-1,4-1,5-1,6-1,7-1,8-1,9-1,10-1,11-1
NLT - **11,** 1-1,2-1,3-1,4-1,5-1,6-1,7-1,8-1,9-1,10-1,11-1
NRSV - **11,** 1-1,2-1,3-1,4-1,5-1,6-1,7-1,8-1,9-1,10-1,11-1
Conclusion: All versions read the same.

2. Genesis 8:16 Go forth of the ark, thou, and thy wife, and thy sons, and thy sons' wives with thee.
AV - **18,** 1-1,2-1,3-1,4-1,5-1,6-1,7-1,8-1,9-1,10-1,11-1,12-1,13-1,14-1,15-1,16-1,17-1,18-1
ESV - **18,** 1-1,2-1,3-1,4-1,5-1,6-1,7-1,8-1,9-1,10-1,11-1,12-1,13-1,14-1,15-1,16-1,17-1,18-1
HCSB - **16,** 1-1,2-1,3-1,4-1,5-1,6-1,7-1,8-1,9-1,10-1,11-1,12-1,13-1,14-1,15-1,16-1
NASV - **18,** 1-1,2-1,3-1,4-1,5-1,6-1,7-1,8-1,9-1,10-1,11-1,12-1,13-1,14-1,15-1,16-1,17-1,18-1
NCV - **15,** 1-1,2-1,3-1,4-1,5-1,6-1,7-1,8-1,9-1,10-1,11-1,12-1,13-1,14-1,15-1
NIV - **15,** 1-1,2-1,3-1,4-1,5-1,6-1,7-1,8-1,9-1,10-1,11-1,12-1,13-1,14-1,15-1
NKJV - **18,** 1-1,2-1,3-1,4-1,5-1,6-1,7-1,8-1,9-1,10-1,11-1,12-1,13-1,14-1,15-1,16-1,17-1,18-1
NLT - **16,** 1-1,2-1,3-1,4-1,5-1,6-1,7-1,8-1,9-1,10-1,11-1,12-1,13-1,14-1,15-1,16-1
NRSV - **18,** 1-1,2-1,3-1,4-1,5-1,6-1,7-1,8-1,9-1,10-1,11-1,12-1,13-1,14-1,15-1,16-1,17-1,18-1
Conclusion: All versions read the same.

3. Genesis 26:30 And he made them a feast, and they did eat and drink.
AV - **12,** 1-1,2-1,3-1,4-1,5-1,6-1,7-1,8-1,9-1,10-1,11-1,12-1
ESV - **11,** 1-1,2-1,3-1,4-1,5-1,6-1,7-1,8-1,9-1,10-1,11-1
HCSB - 12, 1-1,2-1,3-**2,**4-1,5-**2,**6-1,7-1,8-1,9-1,10-1,11-1,12-1
NASV - **11,** 1-1,2-1,3-1,4-1,5-1,6-1,7-1,8-1,9-1,10-1,11-1
NCV - 12, 1-1,2-1,3-**2,**4-1,5-1,6-1,7-1,8-1,9-1,10-1,11-1,12-1
NIV - **12,** 1-1,2-1,3-1,4-1,5-1,6-1,7-1,8-1,9-1,10-1,11-1,12-1
NKJV - **11,** 1-1,2-1,3-1,4-1,5-1,6-1,7-1,8-1,9-1,10-1,11-1
NLT - 16, 1-1,2-1,3-**2,**4-1,5-**3,**6-1,7-1,8-**3,**9-1,10-**2,**11-1,12-1,13-1,14-1,15-1,16-**3**
NRSV - **11,** 1-1,2-1,3-1,4-1,5-1,6-1,7-1,8-1,9-1,10-1,11-1
Conclusion: Three modern versions are more complex than the King James Bible. The NLT is the most difficult to read.

4. Genesis 35:13 And God went up from him in the place where he talked with him.
AV - **14,** 1-1,2-1,3-1,4-1,5-1,6-1,7-1,8-1,9-1,10-1,11-1,12-1,13-1,14-1
ESV - 15, 1-1,2-1,3-1,4-1,5-1,6-1,7-1,8-1,9-1,10-1,11-1,12-1,13-**2,**14-1,15-1
HCSB - 14, 1-1,2-1,3-**2,**4-1,5-1,6-1,7-1,8-1,9-1,10-1,11-1,12-**2,**13-1,14-1

NASV - 15, 1-1,2-1,3-1,4-1,5-1,6-1,7-1,8-1,9-1,10-1,11-1,12-1,13-**2**,14-1,15-1
NCV - **4,** 1-1,2-1,3-1,4-1
NIV - **15,** 1-1,2-1,3-1,4-1,5-1,6-1,7-1,8-1,9-1,10-1,11-1,12-1,13-1,14-1,15-1
NKJV - **14,** 1-1,2-1,3-1,4-1,5-1,6-1,7-1,8-1,9-1,10-1,11-1,12-1,13-1,14-1
NLT - 13, 1-1,2-1,3-1,4-1,5-1,6-1,7-1,8-1,9-1,10-1,11-**2**,12-1,13-1
NRSV - 15, 1-1,2-1,3-1,4-1,5-1,6-1,7-1,8-1,9-1,10-1,11-1,12-1,13-**2**,14-1,15-1
Conclusion: Five modern versions are more complex than the King James Bible. The verse is brief in the NCV because this version cuts the verse short and adds the latter portion to verse fourteen.

5. Genesis 38:17 And he said, I will send thee a kid from the flock. And she said, Wilt thou give me a pledge, till thou send it?
AV -   **25,** 1-1,2-1,3-1,4-1,5-1,6-1,7-1,8-1,9-1,10-1,11-1,12-1,13-1,14-1,15-1,16-1,17-1,18-1,19-1,20-1,21-1,22-1,23-1,24-1,25-1
ESV - 25, 1-1,2-**2**,3-1,4-1,5-1,6-1,7-1,8-1,9-1,10-1,11-1,12-1,13-1,14-1,15-1,16-1,17-1,18-1,19-1,20-1,21-1,22-**2**,23-1,24-1,25-1
HCSB - 26, 1-1,2-1,3-1,4-1,5-1,6-1,7-1,8-1,9-1,10-1,11-1,12-**2**,13-1,14-1,15-1,16-**2**,17-1,18-1,19-1,20-1,21-1,22-1,23-1,24-1,25-1,26-1
NASV - 25, 1-1,2-1,3-**2**,4-1,5-1,6-1,7-1,8-1,9-1,10-1,11-1,12-1,13-1,14-1,15-1,16-**2**,17-1,18-1,19-1,20-1,21-1,22-**2**,23-1,24-1,25-1
NCV - 28, 1-1,2-**2**,3-1,4-1,5-1,6-1,7-1,8-1,9-1,10-1,11-1,12-1,13-1,14-**2**,15-1,16-1,17-1,18-**2**,19-1,20-1,21-1,22-1,23-**3**,24-**2**,25-1,26-1,27-1,28-1
NIV - 24, 1-1,2-1,3-1,4-1,5-1,6-1,7-1,8-1,9-1,10-1,11-1,12-1,13-1,14-1,15-**2**,16-1,17-1,18-1,19-**2**,20-1,21-1,22-1,23-1,24-1
NKJV - 25, 1-1,2-1,3-1,4-1,5-1,6-1,7-1,8-1,9-1,10-1,11-1,12-1,13-1,14-1,15-1,16-1,17-1,18-1,19-1,20-1,21-1,22-1,23-1,24-1,25-1
NLT - 27, 1-1,2-1,3-1,4-1,5-1,6-1,7-1,8-1,9-1,10-1,11-**2**,12-1,13-1,14-1,15-1,16-1,17-1,18-1,19-**3**,20-1,21-1,22-1,23-1,24-1,25-1,26-1,27-1
NRSV - 25, 1-1,2-**2**,3-1,4-1,5-1,6-1,7-1,8-1,9-1,10-1,11-1,12-1,13-1,14-1,15-**2**,16-1,17-1,18-1,19-1,20-1,21-1,22-**2**,23-1,24-1,25-1
Conclusion: Seven modern versions are more complex than the King James Bible. The NCV and the NLT are the most difficult to read.

6. Genesis 49:12 His eyes shall be red with wine, and his teeth white with milk.
AV - **13,** 1-1,2-1,3-1,4-1,5-1,6-1,7-1,8-1,9-1,10-1,11-1,12-1,13-1
ESV - 12, 1-1,2-1,3-1,4-**2**,5-1,6-1,7-1,8-1,9-1,10-**2**,11-1,12-1
HCSB - 13, 1-1,2-1,3-1,4-**2**,5-1,6-1,7-1,8-1,9-1,10-1,11-**2**,12-1,13-1
NASV - **12,** 1-1,2-1,3-1,4-1,5-1,6-1,7-1,8-1,9-1,10-1,11-1,12-1
NCV - **20,** 1-1,2-1,3-1,4-1,5-1,6-1,7-**2**,8-1,9-1,10-1,11-1,12-1,13-1,14-1,15-1,16-1,17-1,18-**2**,19-1,20-1
NIV - **12,** 1-1,2-1,3-1,4-1,5-**2**,6-1,7-1,8-1,9-1,10-**2**,11-1,12-1
NKJV - 12, 1-1,2-1,3-1,4-**2**,5-1,6-1,7-1,8-1,9-1,10-**2**,11-1,12-1
NLT - **13,** 1-1,2-1,3-1,4-**2**,5-1,6-1,7-1,8-1,9-1,10-1,11-**2**,12-1,13-1
NRSV - 12, 1-1,2-1,3-1,4-**2**,5-1,6-1,7-1,8-1,9-1,10-**2**,11-1,12-1
Conclusion: Seven modern versions are more complex than the King James Bible.

7. Exodus 4:13 And he said, O my Lord, send, I pray thee, by the hand of him whom thou wilt send.
AV - **19,** 1-1,2-1,3-1,4-1,5-1,6-1,7-1,8-1,9-1,10-1,11-1,12-1,13-1,14-1,15-1,16-1,17-1,18-1,19-1
ESV - 10, 1-1,2-1,3-1,4-1,5-1,6-1,7-1,8-1,9-**2**,10-1
HCSB - 7, 1-1,2-1,3-1,4-1,5-1,6-**2**,7-1
NASV - 13, 1-1,2-1,3-1,4-1,5-1,6-1,7-1,8-1,9-**2**,10-1,11-**2**,12-1,13-1
NCV - 8, 1-1,2-1,3-1,4-1,5-1,6-1,7-**2**,8-1
NIV - 12, 1-1,2-1,3-1,4-1,5-1,6-1,7-1,8-**2**,9-1,10-1,11-1,12-1
NKJV - 17, 1-1,2-1,3-1,4-1,5-1,6-1,7-1,8-1,9-1,10-1,11-1,12-1,13-**2**,14-1,15-1,16-1,17-1
NLT - 9, 1-1,2-1,3-**2**,4-**2**,5-1,6-1,7-1,8-**2**,9-1
NRSV - 10, 1-1,2-1,3-1,4-1,5-1,6-1,7-1,8-1,9-**2**,10-1
Conclusion: All eight modern versions are more complex than the King James Bible. The NLT is the most difficult to read.

8. Exodus 4:24 And it came to pass by the way in the inn, that the LORD met him, and sought to kill him.
AV - **21,** 1-1,2-1,3-1,4-1,5-1,6-1,7-1,8-1,9-1,10-1,11-1,12-1,13-1,14-1,15-1,16-1,17-1,18-1,19-1,20-1,21-1
ESV - 18, 1-1,2-1,3-**2**,4-1,5-1,6-1,7-1,8-1,9-1,10-1,11-1,12-1,13-1,14-1,15-1,16-1,17-1,18-1
HCSB - 21, 1-1,2-1,3-1,4-1,5-1,6-**3**,7-**2**,8-1,9-**2**,10-1,11-1,12-1,13-**3**,14-1,15-1,16-1,17-1,18-1,19-1,20-1,21-1
NASV - 23, 1-1,2-1,3-1,4-1,5-1,6-1,7-**2**,8-1,9-1,10-1,11-1,12-1,13-1,14-1,15-1,16-1,17-1,18-1,19-1,20-1,21-1,22-1,23-1
NCV - 27, 1-1,2-1,3-1,4-1,5-1,6-1,7-1,8-1,9-1,10-1,11-1,12-1,13-**2**,14-1,15-1,16-1,17-1,18-1,19-1,20-1,21-1,22-1,23-1,24-1,25-1,26-1,27-1
NIV - 17, 1-1,2-1,3-**2**,4-1,5-1,6-1,7-1,8-1,9-1,10-1,11-1,12-1,13-1,14-1,15-1,16-1,17-1
NKJV - 21, 1-1,2-1,3-1,4-1,5-1,6-1,7-1,8-1,9-1,10-1,11-**3**,12-1,13-1,14-1,15-1,16-1,17-1,18-1,19-1,20-1,21-1
NLT - 28, 1-1,2-1,3-1,4-1,5-1,6-1,7-1,8-1,9-1,10-1,11-1,12-1,13-1,14-1,15-1,16-1,17-1,18-1,19-1,20-1,21-**3**,22-1,23-1,24-1,25-1,26-1,27-1,28-1
NRSV - **20,** 1-1,2-1,3-1,4-1,5-1,6-1,7-1,8-1,9-1,10-1,11-1,12-1,13-1,14-1,15-1,16-1,17-1,18-1,19-1,20-1
Conclusion: Seven modern versions are more complex than the King James Bible. The HCSB is the most difficult to read.

9. Exodus 14:14 The LORD shall fight for you, and ye shall hold your peace.
AV - **12,** 1-1,2-1,3-1,4-1,5-1,6-1,7-1,8-1,9-1,10-1,11-1,12-1
ESV - 13, 1-1,2-1,3-1,4-1,5-1,6-1,7-1,8-1,9-1,10-1,11-1,12-1,13-**2**
HCSB - 10, 1-1,2-1,3-1,4-1,5-1,6-1,7-1,8-1,9-1,10-**2**
NASV - 10, 1-1,2-1,3-1,4-1,5-1,6-1,7-1,8-1,9-1,10-**2**
NCV - 12, 1-1,2-**2**,3-1,4-1,5-**2**,6-1,7-1,8-1,9-1,10-1,11-1,12-1
NIV - 12, 1-1,2-1,3-1,4-1,5-1,6-1,7-1,8-1,9-**2**,10-1,11-1,12-1
NKJV - **12,** 1-1,2-1,3-1,4-1,5-1,6-1,7-1,8-1,9-1,10-1,11-1,12-1
NLT - 10, 1-1,2-1,3-**2**,4-1,5-1,6-1,7-1,8-1,9-1,10-1
NRSV - 13, 1-1,2-1,3-1,4-1,5-1,6-1,7-1,8-1,9-1,10-**2**,11-1,12-1,13-1
Conclusion: Seven modern versions are more complex than the King James Bible.

10. Exodus 15:3 The LORD is a man of war: the LORD is his name.
AV - **12,** 1-1,2-1,3-1,4-1,5-1,6-1,7-1,8-1,9-1,10-1,11-1,12-1
ESV - **12,** 1-1,2-1,3-1,4-1,5-1,6-1,7-1,8-1,9-1,10-1,11-1,12-1
HCSB - 9, 1-1,2-1,3-1,4-1,5-**2**,6-1,7-1,8-1,9-1

NASV - **10,** 1-1,2-1,3-1,4-1,5-**2,**6-1,7-1,8-1,9-1,10-1
NCV - **10,** 1-1,2-1,3-1,4-1,5-**2,**6-1,7-1,8-1,9-1,10-1
NIV - **10,** 1-1,2-1,3-1,4-1,5-**2,**6-1,7-1,8-1,9-1,10-1
NKJV - **12,** 1-1,2-1,3-1,4-1,5-1,6-1,7-1,8-1,9-1,10-1,11-1,12-1
NLT - **9,** 1-1,2-1,3-1,4-1,5-**2,**6-1,7-1,8-1,9-1
NRSV - **10,** 1-1,2-1,3-1,4-1,5-**2,**6-1,7-1,8-1,9-1,10-1

Conclusion: Six modern versions are more complex than the King James Bible. In the HCSB and the NLT the sixth word in the verse is transliterated, "Yahweh" but it was counted as one syllable because it is a name.

11. Exodus 20:13 Thou shalt not kill.
AV - **4,** 1-1,2-1,3-1,4-1
ESV - **4,** 1-1,2-1,3-1,4-**2**
HCSB - **3,** 1-1,2-1,3-**2**
NASV - **4,** 1-1,2-1,3-1,4-**2**
NCV - **5,** 1-1,2-1,3-1,4-**2,**5-**2**
NIV - **4,** 1-1,2-1,3-1,4-**2**
NKJV - **4,** 1-1,2-1,3-1,4-**2**
NLT - **4,** 1-1,2-1,3-1,4-**2**
NRSV - **4,** 1-1,2-1,3-1,4-**2**

Conclusion: All eight modern versions are more complex than the King James Bible. The NCV is the most difficult to read.

12. Exodus 20:15 Thou shalt not steal.
AV - **4,** 1-1,2-1,3-1,4-1
ESV - **4,** 1-1,2-1,3-1,4-1
HCSB - **3,** 1-1,2-1,3-1
NASV - **4,** 1-1,2-1,3-1,4-1
NCV - **4,** 1-1,2-1,3-1,4-1
NIV - **4,** 1-1,2-1,3-1,4-1
NKJV - **4,** 1-1,2-1,3-1,4-1
NLT - **4,** 1-1,2-1,3-1,4-1
NRSV - **4,** 1-1,2-1,3-1,4-1

Conclusion: All versions read the same.

13. Exodus 21:24 Eye for eye, tooth for tooth, hand for hand, foot for foot,
AV - **12,** 1-1,2-1,3-1,4-1,5-1,6-1,7-1,8-1,9-1,10-1,11-1,12-1
ESV - **12,** 1-1,2-1,3-1,4-1,5-1,6-1,7-1,8-1,9-1,10-1,11-1,12-1
HCSB -**12,** 1-1,2-1,3-1,4-1,5-1,6-1,7-1,8-1,9-1,10-1,11-1,12-1
NASV - **12,** 1-1,2-1,3-1,4-1,5-1,6-1,7-1,8-1,9-1,10-1,11-1,12-1
NCV - **12,** 1-1,2-1,3-1,4-1,5-1,6-1,7-1,8-1,9-1,10-1,11-1,12-1
NIV - **12,** 1-1,2-1,3-1,4-1,5-1,6-1,7-1,8-1,9-1,10-1,11-1,12-1
NKJV - **12,** 1-1,2-1,3-1,4-1,5-1,6-1,7-1,8-1,9-1,10-1,11-1,12-1
NLT - **20,** 1-1,2-1,3-1,4-1,5-1,6-1,7-1,8-1,9-1,10-1,11-1,12-1,13-1,14-1,15-1,16-1,17-1,18-1,19-1,20-1
NRSV - **12,** 1-1,2-1,3-1,4-1,5-1,6-1,7-1,8-1,9-1,10-1,11-1,12-1

Conclusion: All versions read the same. The NLT found a longer way to say the same thing.

Samuel C. Gipp Ph.D.

14. Exodus 33:20 And he said, Thou canst not see my face: for there shall no man see me, and live.
AV - **18,** 1-1,2-1,3-1,4-1,5-1,6-1,7-1,8-1,9-1,10-1,11-1,12-1,13-1,14-1,15-1,16-1,17-1,18-1
ESV - 16, 1-1,2-1,3-1,4-1,5-**2**,6-1,7-1,8-1,9-1,10-1,11-1,12-1,13-1,14-1,15-1,16-1
HCSB - 16, 1-1,2-1,3-**2**,4-1,5-**2**,6-1,7-1,8-1,9-1,10-1,11-1,12-1,13-1,14-1,15-1,16-1
NASV - 16, 1-1,2-1,3-1,4-1,5-**2**,6-1,7-1,8-1,9-1,10-1,11-1,12-1,13-1,14-1,15-1,16-1
NCV - 14, 1-1,2-1,3-**2**,4-1,5-1,6-1,7-**2**,8-1,9-1,10-1,11-1,12-1,13-1,14-1
NIV - 16, 1-1,2-1,3-1,4-1,5-**2**,6-1,7-1,8-1,9-1,10-1,11-1,12-1,13-1,14-1,15-1,16-1
NKJV - 16, 1-1,2-1,3-1,4-1,5-**2**,6-1,7-1,8-1,9-1,10-1,11-1,12-1,13-1,14-1,15-1,16-1
NLT - 17, 1-1,2-1,3-1,4-1,5-1,6-**3**,7-1,8-1,9-1,10-1,11-1,12-1,13-1,14-1,15-1,16-1,17-1
NRSV - 16, 1-1,2-1,3-1,4-1,5-**2**,6-1,7-1,8-1,9-1,10-1,11-1,12-1,13-1,14-1,15-1,16-1
Conclusion: All eight modern versions are more complex than the King James Bible.

15. Exodus 40:14 And thou shalt bring his sons, and clothe them with coats:
AV - **11,** 1-1,2-1,3-1,4-1,5-1,6-1,7-1,8-1,9-1,10-1,11-1
ESV - 11, 1-1,2-1,3-1,4-1,5-1,6-**2**,7-1,8-1,9-1,10-1,11-1
HCSB - 10, 1-1,2-1,3-1,4-1,5-**2**,6-1,7-1,8-1,9-1,10-**2**
NASV - 10, 1-1,2-1,3-1,4-1,5-1,6-1,7-1,8-**2**,9-1,10-1
NCV - 10, 1-1,2-1,3-1,4-1,5-1,6-1,7-**2**,8-1,9-1,10-1
NIV - 8, 1-1,2-1,3-1,4-1,5-1,6-1,7-1,8-**2**
NKJV - 11, 1-1,2-1,3-1,4-1,5-1,6-1,7-1,8-1,9-1,10-1,11-**2**
NLT - 10, 1-1,2-**2**,3-1,4-1,5-1,6-1,7-1,8-1,9-1,10-**2**
NRSV - 11, 1-1,2-1,3-1,4-1,5-1,6-1,7-1,8-1,9-**2**,10-1,11-1
Conclusion: All eight modern versions are more complex than the King James Bible. The NCT says "Aaron's" where most say "his" but this was not counted as multi-syllable.

16. Leviticus 24:12 And they put him in ward, that the mind of the LORD might be showed them.
AV - **16,** 1-1,2-1,3-1,4-1,5-1,6-1,7-1,8-1,9-1,10-1,11-1,12-1,13-1,14-1,15-1,16-1
ESV - 17, 1-1,2-1,3-1,4-1,5-1,6-**3**,7-1,8-1,9-1,10-1,11-1,12-1,13-1,14-1,15-1,16-1,17-1
HCSB - 15, 1-1,2-1,3-1,4-1,5-**3**,6-**2**,7-1,8-1,9-**3**,10-1,11-1,12-1,13-1,14-1,15-1
NASV - 18, 1-1,2-1,3-1,4-1,5-**3**,6-1,7-1,8-1,9-**2**,10-1,11-1,12-1,13-1,14-1,15-1,16-1,17-1,18-1
NCV - 20, 1-1,2-**2**,3-1,4-1,5-1,6-1,7-**3**,8-1,9-1,10-**2**,11-1,12-1,13-1,14-**2**,15-1,16-1,17-1,18-1,19-1,20-1
NIV - 17, 1-1,2-1,3-1,4-1,5-**3**,6-**2**,7-1,8-1,9-1,10-1,11-1,12-1,13-1,14-1,15-1,16-1,17-1
NKJV - 17, 1-1,2-1,3-1,4-1,5-1,6-**3**,7-1,8-1,9-1,10-1,11-1,12-1,13-1,14-1,15-1,16-1,17-1
NLT - 18, 1-1,2-1,3-1,4-1,5-1,6-**3**,7-**2**,8-1,9-1,10-1,11-1,12-1,13-**2**,14-1,15-**2**,16-1,17-1,18-1
NRSV - 18, 1-1,2-1,3-1,4-1,5-1,6-**3**,7-**2**,8-1,9-**3**,10-1,11-1,12-1,13-1,14-1,15-1,16-1,17-1,18-1
Conclusion: All eight modern versions are more complex than the King James Bible.

17. Numbers 6:24 The LORD bless thee, and keep thee:
AV - **7,** 1-1,2-1,3-1,4-1,5-1,6-1,7-1
ESV - **7,** 1-1,2-1,3-1,4-1,5-1,6-1,7-1
HCSB - 7, 1-1,2-1,3-1,4-1,5-1,6-**2**,7-1
NASV - **7,** 1-1,2-1,3-1,4-1,5-1,6-1,7-1
NCV - **8,** 1-1,2-1,3-1,4-1,5-1,6-1,7-1,8-1
NIV - **7,** 1-1,2-1,3-1,4-1,5-1,6-1,7-1
NKJV - **7,** 1-1,2-1,3-1,4-1,5-1,6-1,7-1

NLT - 8, 1-1,2-1,3-1,4-1,5-1,6-1,7-**2**,8-1
NRSV - 7, 1-1,2-1,3-1,4-1,5-1,6-1,7-1
Conclusion: Only the HCSB and the NLT made the verse more complex.

18. Numbers 31:11 And they took all the spoil, and all the prey, both of men and of beasts.
AV - 16, 1-1,2-1,3-1,4-1,5-1,6-1,7-1,8-1,9-1,10-1,11-1,12-1,13-1,14-1,15-1,16-1
ESV - 15, 1-1,2-1,3-1,4-1,5-1,6-1,7-1,8-1,9-**2**,10-1,11-1,12-1,13-1,14-1,15-1
HCSB - 15, 1-1,2-1,3-**2**,4-1,5-1,6-1,7-1,8-1,9-1,10-1,11-**2**,12-1,13-**2**,14-1,15-**3**
NASV - 15, 1-1,2-1,3-1,4-1,5-1,6-1,7-1,8-1,9-1,10-1,11-1,12-1,13-1,14-1,15-1
NCV - 10, 1-1,2-1,3-1,4-1,5-1,6-**2**,7-1,8-**3**,9-1,10-1
NIV - 12, 1-1,2-1,3-1,4-1,5-**2**,6-1,7-1,8-**3**,9-1,10-**2**,11-1,12-**3**
NKJV - 14, 1-1,2-1,3-1,4-1,5-1,6-1,7-1,8-1,9-1,10-**2**,11-1,12-1,13-1,14-1
NLT - 12, 1-**2**,2-1,3-1,4-**2**,5-1,6-**2**,7-1,8-**2**,9-1,10-1,11-**2**,12-**3**
NRSV - 14, 1-1,2-1,3-1,4-1,5-1,6-1,7-1,8-1,9-1,10-**2**,11-1,12-**2**,13-1,14-**3**
Conclusion: Seven modern versions are more complex than the King James Bible. The NLT is the most difficult to read.

19. Deuteronomy 3:22 Ye shall not fear them: for the LORD your God he shall fight for you.
AV - 15, 1-1,2-1,3-1,4-1,5-1,6-1,7-1,8-1,9-1,10-1,11-1,12-1,13-1,14-1,15-1
ESV - 16, 1-1,2-1,3-1,4-1,5-1,6-1,7-1,8-1,9-1,10-1,11-1,12-1,13-1,14-1,15-1,16-1
HCSB - 13, 1-1,2-1,3-**2**,4-1,5-1,6-1,7-1,8-1,9-1,10-1,11-1,12-1,13-1
NASV - 15, 1-1,2-1,3-1,4-1,5-1,6-1,7-1,8-1,9-1,10-1,11-1,12-1,13-**2**,14-1,15-1
NCV - 14, 1-1,2-1,3-**2**,4-1,5-1,6-**2**,7-1,8-1,9-1,10-1,11-1,12-1,13-1,14-1
NIV - 15, 1-1,2-1,3-1,4-**2**,5-1,6-1,7-1,8-1,9-1,10-1,11-**2**,12-1,13-1,14-1,15-1
NKJV - 14, 1-1,2-1,3-1,4-1,5-1,6-1,7-1,8-1,9-1,10-1,11-**2**,12-1,13-1,14-1
NLT - 17, 1-1,2-1,3-1,4-**2**,5-1,6-1,7-**2**,8-1,9-1,10-1,11-1,12-1,13-1,14-1,15-1,16-1,17-1
NRSV - 15, 1-1,2-1,3-1,4-1,5-1,6-1,7-1,8-1,9-1,10-1,11-1,12-1,13-1,14-1,15-1
Conclusion: Six modern versions are more complex than the King James Bible.

20. Deuteronomy 4:29 But if from thence thou shalt seek the LORD thy God, thou shalt find him, if thou seek him with all thy heart and with all thy soul.
AV - 28, 1-1,2-1,3-1,4-1,5-1,6-1,7-1,8-1,9-1,10-1,11-1,12-1,13-1,14-1,15-1,16-1,17-1,18-1,19-1,20-1,21-1,22-1,23-1,24-1,25-1,26-1,27-1,28-1
ESV - 29, 1-1,2-1,3-1,4-1,5-1,6-1,7-1,8-1,9-1,10-1,11-1,12-1,13-1,14-1,15-1,16-1,17-1,18-1,19-**2**,20-1,21-1,22-1,23-1,24-1,25-1,26-1,27-1,28-1,29-1
HCSB - **28,** 1-1,2-1,3-1,4-1,5-1,6-1,7-1,8-1,9-1,10-1,11-1,12-1,13-1,14-1,15-1,16-1,17-1,18-1,19-1,20-1,21-1,22-1,23-1,24-1,25-1,26-1,27-1,28-1
NASV - **28,** 1-1,2-1,3-1,4-1,5-1,6-1,7-1,8-1,9-1,10-1,11-1,12-1,13-1,14-1,15-1,16-1,17-1,18-1,19-1,20-1,21-1,22-1,23-1,24-1,25-1,26-1,27-1,28-1
NCV - 25, 1-1,2-**2**,3-1,4-1,5-1,6-1,7-1,8-1,9-1,10-1,11-1,12-1,13-1,14-1,15-1,16-1,17-1,18-1,19-1,20-1,21-1,22-1,23-1,24-1,25-**2**
NIV - 28, 1-1,2-1,3-1,4-1,5-1,6-1,7-1,8-1,9-1,10-1,11-1,12-1,13-1,14-1,15-1,16-1,17-1,18-1,19-1,20-1,21-1,22-1,23-1,24-1,25-1,26-1,27-1,28-1
NKJV - **28,** 1-1,2-1,3-1,4-1,5-1,6-1,7-1,8-1,9-1,10-1,11-1,12-1,13-1,14-1,15-1,16-1,17-1,18-1,19-1,20-1,21-1,22-1,23-1,24-1,25-1,26-1,27-1,28-1

NLT - **28,** 1-1,2-1,3-1,4-1,5-1,6-1,7-**2**,8-1,9-1,10-1,11-1,12-1,13-1,14-1,15-1,16-1,17-1,18-1,19-1,20-1,21-1,22-1,23-1,24-1,25-1,26-1,27-1,28-1

NRSV - **25,** 1-1,2-1,3-1,4-1,5-1,6-1,7-1,8-1,9-1,10-1,11-1,12-1,13-1,14-1,15-1,16-1,17-1,18-**2**,19-1,20-1,21-1,22-1,23-1,24-1,25-1

Conclusion: Four modern versions are more complex than the King James Bible.

21. Deuteronomy 5:4 The LORD talked with you face to face in the mount out of the midst of the fire,

AV - **18,** 1-1,2-1,3-1,4-1,5-1,6-1,7-1,8-1,9-1,10-1,11-1,12-1,13-1,14-1,15-1,16-1,17-1,18-1

ESV - **18,** 1-1,2-1,3-1,4-1,5-1,6-1,7-1,8-1,9-1,10-1,11-**2**,12-1,13-1,14-1,15-1,16-1,17-1,18-1

HCSB - **14,** 1-1,2-1,3-1,4-1,5-1,6-1,7-1,8-1,9-1,10-1,11-1,12-1,13-1,14-**2**

NASV - **17,** 1-1,2-1,3-1,4-1,5-1,6-1,7-1,8-1,9-1,10-1,11-**2**,12-1,13-1,14-1,15-1,16-1,17-1

NCV - **14,** 1-1,2-1,3-1,4-1,5-1,6-1,7-1,8-1,9-1,10-1,11-1,12-1,13-1,14-**2**

NIV - **15,** 1-1,2-1,3-1,4-1,5-1,6-1,7-1,8-1,9-1,10-1,11-1,12-1,13-1,14-1,15-**2**

NKJV - **17,** 1-1,2-1,3-1,4-1,5-1,6-1,7-1,8-1,9-1,10-1,11-**2**,12-1,13-1,14-1,15-1,16-1,17-1

NLT - **17,** 1-1,2-1,3-1,4-1,5-1,6-1,7-1,8-1,9-1,10-1,11-1,12-1,13-1,14-1,15-1,16-1,17-1

NRSV - **15,** 1-1,2-1,3-1,4-1,5-1,6-1,7-1,8-1,9-1,10-1,11-**2**,12-1,13-1,14-1,15-1

Conclusion: Seven modern versions are more complex than the King James Bible.

22. Deuteronomy 5:17 Thou shalt not kill.

AV - **4,** 1-1,2-1,3-1,4-1

ESV - **4,** 1-1,2-1,3-1,4-**2**

HCSB - **3,** 1-1,2-1,3-**2**

NASV - **4,** 1-1,2-1,3-1,4-**2**

NCV - **5,** 1-1,2-1,3-1,4-**2**,5-**2**

NIV - **4,** 1-1,2-1,3-1,4-**2**

NKJV - **4,** 1-1,2-1,3-1,4-**2**

NLT - **4,** 1-1,2-1,3-1,4-**2**

NRSV - **4,** 1-1,2-1,3-1,4-**2**

Conclusion: All eight modern versions are more complex than the King James Bible. The NCV is the most difficult to read.

23. Deuteronomy 6:5 And thou shalt love the LORD thy God with all thine heart, and with all thy soul, and with all thy might.

AV - **22,** 1-1,2-1,3-1,4-1,5-1,6-1,7-1,8-1,9-1,10-1,11-1,12-1,13-1,14-1,15-1,16-1,17-1,18-1,19-1,20-1,21-1,22-1

ESV - **21,** 1-1,2-1,3-1,4-1,5-1,6-1,7-1,8-1,9-1,10-1,11-1,12-1,13-1,14-1,15-1,16-1,17-1,18-1,19-1,20-1,21-1

HCSB - **18,** 1-1,2-1,3-1,4-1,5-1,6-1,7-1,8-1,9-1,10-1,11-1,12-1,13-1,14-1,15-1,16-1,17-1,18-1

NASV - **21,** 1-1,2-1,3-1,4-1,5-1,6-1,7-1,8-1,9-1,10-1,11-1,12-1,13-1,14-1,15-1,16-1,17-1,18-1,19-1,20-1,21-1

NCV - **16,** 1-1,2-1,3-1,4-1,5-1,6-1,7-1,8-1,9-1,10-1,11-1,12-1,13-1,14-1,15-1,16-1

NIV - **19,** 1-1,2-1,3-1,4-1,5-1,6-1,7-1,8-1,9-1,10-1,11-1,12-1,13-1,14-1,15-1,16-1,17-1,18-1,19-1

NKJV - **20,** 1-1,2-1,3-1,4-1,5-1,6-1,7-1,8-1,9-1,10-1,11-1,12-1,13-1,14-1,15-1,16-1,17-1,18-1,19-1,20-1

NLT - **19,** 1-1,2-1,3-1,4-1,5-1,6-1,7-1,8-1,9-1,10-1,11-1,12-1,13-1,14-1,15-1,16-1,17-1,18-1,19-1

NRSV - **21,** 1-1,2-1,3-1,4-1,5-1,6-1,7-1,8-1,9-1,10-1,11-1,12-1,13-1,14-1,15-1,16-1,17-1,18-1,19-1,20-1,21-1

Conclusion: All versions read the same.

24. Deuteronomy 6:13 Thou shalt fear the LORD thy God, and serve him, and shalt swear by his name.
AV - **16,** 1-1,2-1,3-1,4-1,5-1,6-1,7-1,8-1,9-1,10-1,11-1,12-1,13-1,14-1,15-1,16-1
ESV - **20,** 1-1,2-1,3-1,4-1,5-1,6-1,7-1,8-1,9-1,10-1,11-1,12-1,13-1,14-1,15-1,16-1,17-1,18-1,19-1,20-1
HCSB - 14, 1-1,2-1,3-1,4-1,5-1,6-**2**,7-1,8-1,9-1,10-1,11-1,12-1,13-1,14-1
NASV - 18, 1-1,2-1,3-1,4-**2**,5-1,6-1,7-1,8-1,9-1,10-1,11-1,12-**2**,13-1,14-1,15-1,16-1,17-1,18-1
NCV - 17, 1-**2**,2-1,3-1,4-1,5-1,6-1,7-1,8-**2**,9-1,10-1,11-1,12-1,13-**3**,14-1,15-1,16-1,17-1
NIV - 15, 1-1,2-1,3-1,4-1,5-1,6-1,7-1,8-**2**,9-1,10-1,11-1,12-1,13-1,14-1,15-1
NKJV - **17,** 1-1,2-1,3-1,4-1,5-1,6-1,7-1,8-1,9-1,10-1,11-1,12-1,13-1,14-1,15-1,16-1,17-1
NLT - 21, 1-1,2-1,3-1,4-1,5-1,6-1,7-1,8-1,9-1,10-1,11-1,12-1,13-1,14-1,15-1,16-1,17-1,18-1,19-**2**,20-1,21-1
NRSV - 19, 1-1,2-1,3-1,4-1,5-1,6-1,7-1,8-1,9-1,10-1,11-1,12-1,13-1,14-1,15-1,16-**2**,17-1,18-1,19-1
Conclusion: Six modern versions are more complex than the King James Bible. The NCV is the most difficult to read.

25. Deuteronomy 10:20 Thou shalt fear the LORD thy God; him shalt thou serve, and to him shalt thou cleave, and swear by his name.
AV - **22,** 1-1,2-1,3-1,4-1,5-1,6-1,7-1,8-1,9-1,10-1,11-1,12-1,13-1,14-1,15-1,16-1,17-1,18-1,19-1,20-1,21-1,22-1
ESV - **23,** 1-1,2-1,3-1,4-1,5-1,6-1,7-1,8-1,9-1,10-1,11-1,12-1,13-1,14-1,15-1,16-1,17-1,18-1,19-1,20-1,21-1,22-1,23-1
HCSB - 21, 1-1,2-1,3-1,4-1,5-1,6-1,7-1,8-1,9-1,10-**2**,11-1,12-**2**,13-**2**,14-1,15-1,16-1,17-1,18-1,19-1,20-1,21-1
NASV - **22,** 1-1,2-1,3-1,4-1,5-1,6-1,7-1,8-1,9-1,10-1,11-1,12-1,13-1,14-1,15-1,16-1,17-1,18-1,19-1,20-1,21-1,22-1
NCV - 19, 1-**2**,2-1,3-1,4-1,5-1,6-1,7-1,8-1,9-1,10-**2**,11-1,12-1,13-1,14-1,15-1,16-**3**,17-1,18-1,19-1
NIV - **19,** 1-1,2-1,3-1,4-1,5-1,6-1,7-1,8-1,9-1,10-1,11-1,12-1,13-1,14-1,15-1,16-1,17-1,18-1,19-1
NKJV - **24,** 1-1,2-1,3-1,4-1,5-1,6-1,7-1,8-1,9-1,10-1,11-1,12-1,13-1,14-1,15-1,16-1,17-1,18-1,19-1,20-1,21-1,22-1,23-1,24-1
NLT - 22, 1-1,2-1,3-1,4-1,5-1,6-1,7-1,8-1,9-**2**,10-1,11-1,12-1,13-1,14-1,15-1,16-1,17-1,18-1,19-1,20-1,21-1,22-**2**
NRSV - 25, 1-1,2-1,3-1,4-1,5-1,6-1,7-1,8-1,9-**2**,10-1,11-1,12-**2**,13-1,14-1,15-1,16-1,17-1,18-1,19-1,20-1,21-1,22-1,23-1,24-1,25-1
Conclusion: Four modern versions are more complex than the King James Bible.

26. Deuteronomy 11:7 But your eyes have seen all the great acts of the LORD which he did.
AV - **15,** 1-1,2-1,3-1,4-1,5-1,6-1,7-1,8-1,9-1,10-1,11-1,12-1,13-1,14-1,15-1
ESV - **16,** 1-1,2-1,3-1,4-1,5-1,6-1,7-1,8-1,9-1,10-1,11-1,12-1,13-1,14-1,15-1,16-1
HCSB - 12, 1-1,2-1,3-1,4-1,5-1,6-**2**,7-1,8-1,9-1,10-1,11-1,12-1
NASV - **16,** 1-1,2-1,3-1,4-1,5-1,6-1,7-1,8-1,9-1,10-1,11-1,12-1,13-1,14-1,15-1,16-1
NCV - **13,** 1-1,2-1,3-1,4-1,5-1,6-1,7-1,8-1,9-1,10-1,11-1,12-1,13-1
NIV - **16,** 1-1,2-1,3-1,4-1,5-1,6-1,7-1,8-1,9-1,10-1,11-1,12-1,13-1,14-1,15-1,16-1
NKJV - 14, 1-1,2-1,3-1,4-1,5-1,6-**2**,7-1,8-1,9-1,10-1,11-1,12-1,13-1,14-1
NLT - 15, 1-1,2-1,3-1,4-1,5-1,6-1,7-**2**,8-1,9-1,10-**2**,11-1,12-1,13-1,14-1,15-1
NRSV - **16,** 1-1,2-1,3-1,4-1,5-1,6-1,7-1,8-1,9-1,10-**2**,11-1,12-1,13-1,14-1,15-1,16-1
Conclusion: Four modern versions are more complex than the King James Bible.

27. Deuteronomy 14:4 These are the beasts which ye shall eat: the ox, the sheep, and the goat,
AV - **15,** 1-1,2-1,3-1,4-1,5-1,6-1,7-1,8-1,9-1,10-1,11-1,12-1,13-1,14-1,15-1
ESV - 13, 1-1,2-1,3-1,4-**3,**5-1,6-1,7-1,8-1,9-1,10-1,11-1,12-1,13-1
HCSB - 13, 1-1,2-1,3-1,4-**3,**5-1,6-1,7-1,8-1,9-1,10-1,11-1,12-1,13-1
NASV - 14, 1-1,2-1,3-1,4-**3,**5-1,6-1,7-1,8-1,9-1,10-1,11-1,12-1,13-1,14-1
NCV - 10, 1-1,2-1,3-1,4-**3,**5-1,6-1,7-1,8-**2,**9-1,10-1
NIV - 13, 1-1,2-1,3-1,4-1,**3,**5-1,6-1,7-1,8-1,9-1,10-1,11-1,12-1,13-1
NKJV - 14, 1-1,2-1,3-1,4-**3,**5-1,6-1,7-1,8-1,9-1,10-1,11-1,12-1,13-1,14-1
NLT - 13, 1-1,2-1,3-1,4-**3,**5-1,6-1,7-1,8-1,9-1,10-1,11-1,12-1,13-1
NRSV - 13, 1-1,2-1,3-1,4-**3,**5-1,6-1,7-1,8-1,9-1,10-1,11-1,12-1,13-1
Conclusion: All eight modern versions are more complex than the King James Bible. Ironically the NCV has the smallest word count but the highest syllable count.

28. Deuteronomy 14:11 Of all clean birds ye shall eat.
AV - **7,** 1-1,2-1,3-1,4-1,5-1,6-1,7-1
ESV - **6,** 1-1,2-1,3-1,4-1,5-1,6-1
HCSB - **6,** 1-1,2-1,3-1,4-1,5-1,6-1
NASV - **6,** 1-1,2-1,3-1,4-1,5-1,6-1
NCV - **6,** 1-1,2-1,3-1,4-1,5-1,6-1
NIV - **6,** 1-1,2-1,3-1,4-1,5-1,6-1
NKJV - **6,** 1-1,2-1,3-1,4-1,5-1,6-1
NLT - 9, 1-1,2-1,3-1,4-1,5-1,6-1,7-1,8-**6,**9-1
NRSV - **6,** 1-1,2-1,3-1,4-1,5-1,6-1
Conclusion: It is remarkable that, when all other modern versions kept such a short verse to single syllable words the one that would be expected to be the simplest, the NLT, is once again the most difficult to read.

29. Deuteronomy 14:20 But of all clean fowls ye may eat.
AV - **8,** 1-1,2-1,3-1,4-1,5-1,6-1,7-1,8-1
ESV - **7,** 1-1,2-1,3-1,4-1,5-1,6-1,7-1
HCSB - 9, 1-1,2-1,3-1,4-1,5-**3,**6-1,7-1,8-**2,**9-**2**
NASV - 6, 1-1,2-1,3-1,4-**2,**5-1,6-1
NCV - 11, 1-**2,**2-1,3-1,4-1,5-1,6-1,7-1,8-1,9-1,10-1,11-1
NIV - 10, 1-1,2-**2,**3-1,4-**2,**5-1,6-1,7-1,8-1,9-1,10-1
NKJV - **6,** 1-1,2-1,3-1,4-1,5-1,6-1
NLT - 13, 1-1,2-1,3-1,4-1,5-**2,**6-1,7-1,8-1,9-**2,**10-1,11-1,12-**6,**13-1
NRSV - 7, 1-1,2-1,3-1,4-**2,**5-1,6-1,7-**2**
Conclusion: Six modern versions are more complex than the King James Bible. Once again the NLT is the most difficult to read.

30. Deuteronomy 21:12 Then thou shalt bring her home to thine house; and she shall shave her head, and pare her nails;
AV - **19,** 1-1,2-1,3-1,4-1,5-1,6-1,7-1,8-1,9-1,10-1,11-1,12-1,13-1,14-1,15-1,16-1,17-1,18-1,19-1
ESV - **17,** 1-1,2-1,3-1,4-1,5-1,6-1,7-1,8-1,9-1,10-1,11-1,12-1,13-1,14-1,15-1,16-1,17-1
HCSB - 16, 1-1,2-1,3-1,4-1,5-1,6-**2,**7-1,8-1,9-1,10-1,11-1,12-1,13-1,14-1,15-1,16-1
NASV - **19,** 1-1,2-1,3-1,4-1,5-1,6-1,7-1,8-1,9-1,10-1,11-1,12-1,13-1,14-1,15-1,16-1,17-1,18-1,19-1

NCV - **15,** 1-1,2-1,3-**2,**4-1,5-1,6-1,7-1,8-1,9-1,10-1,11-1,12-1,13-1,14-1,15-1
NIV - **14,** 1-1,2-1,3-**2,**4-1,5-1,6-1,7-1,8-1,9-1,10-1,11-1,12-1,13-1,14-1
NKJV - **19,** 1-1,2-1,3-1,4-1,5-1,6-1,7-1,8-1,9-1,10-1,11-1,12-1,13-1,14-1,15-1,16-1,17-1,18-1,19-1
NLT - **19,** 1-1,2-1,3-**2,**4-1,5-1,6-1,7-1,8-1,9-1,10-1,11-1,12-1,13-1,14-1,15-1,16-1,17-1,18-1,19-1
NRSV - **17,** 1-1,2-1,3-1,4-1,5-1,6-1,7-1,8-1,9-1,10-1,11-1,12-1,13-1,14-1,15-1,16-1,17-1
Conclusion: Four modern versions are more complex than the King James Bible.

31. Deuteronomy 24:12 And if the man be poor, thou shalt not sleep with his pledge:
AV - **13,** 1-1,2-1,3-1,4-1,5-1,6-1,7-1,8-1,9-1,10-1,11-1,12-1,13-1
ESV - **14,** 1-1,2-1,3-1,4-1,5-1,6-1,7-1,8-1,9-1,10-1,11-1,12-1,13-1,14-1
HCSB - 18, 1-1,2-1,3-1,4-1,5-1,6-1,7-1,8-1,9-1,10-1,11-1,12-1,13-**2,**14-1,15-1,16-**2,**17-1,18-**4**
NASV - **13,** 1-1,2-1,3-1,4-1,5-1,6-1,7-1,8-1,9-1,10-1,11-1,12-1,13-1
NCV - 18, 1-1,2-1,3-1,4-**2,**5-1,6-1,7-1,8-1,9-1,10-1,11-1,12-1,13-1,14-1,15-1,16-1,17-1,18-**2**
NIV - 16, 1-1,2-1,3-1,4-1,5-1,6-1,7-1,8-1,9-1,10-1,11-1,12-1,13-1,14-1,15-1,16-**3**
NKJV - 13, 1-1,2-1,3-1,4-1,5-1,6-1,7-1,8-1,9-1,10-1,11-1,12-1,13-**3**
NLT - **21,**1-1,2-1,3-**2,**4-1,5-1,6-1,7-1,8-1,9-1,10-1,11-1,12-**4,**13-1,14-1,15-1,16-1,17-1,18-1,19-1,20-1,21-**3**
NRSV - 17, 1-1,2-1,3-**2,**4-1,5-1,6-1,7-1,8-1,9-1,10-1,11-1,12-**2,**13-**2,**14-1,15-1,16-1,17-1
Conclusion: Six modern versions are more complex than the King James Bible. Once again the NLT is the most difficult to read.

32. Deuteronomy 28:34 So that thou shalt be mad for the sight of thine eyes which thou shalt see.
AV - **16,** 1-1,2-1,3-1,4-1,5-1,6-1,7-1,8-1,9-1,10-1,11-1,12-1,13-1,14-1,15-1,16-1
ESV - 13, 1-1,2-1,3-1,4-1,5-**2,**6-1,7-1,8-1,9-1,10-1,11-1,12-1,13-1
HCSB - 9, 1-1,2-1,3-1,4-**2,**5-1,6-1,7-1,8-1,9-1
NASV - 12, 1-1,2-1,3-1,4-**2,**5-1,6-1,7-1,8-1,9-1,10-1,11-1,12-1
NCV - **10,** 1-1,2-1,3-1,4-1,5-1,6-1,7-1,8-1,9-1,10-1
NIV - **8,** 1-1,2-1,3-1,4-1,5-1,6-1,7-1,8-1
NKJV - 14, 1-1,2-1,3-1,4-1,5-**2,**6-1,7-**2,**8-1,9-1,10-1,11-1,12-1,13-1,14-1
NLT - 13, 1-1,2-1,3-1,4-1,5-**2,**6-1,7-1,8-1,9-**3,**10-1,11-1,12-**2,**13-1
NRSV - 11, 1-1,2-**2,**3-1,4-1,5-1,6-1,7-1,8-1,9-1,10-1,11-1
Conclusion: Six modern versions are more complex than the King James Bible. It is surprising to see the NKJV, which usually tends to be more conservative, be one of the most complex. But, never fear, the NLT is the most difficult to read.

33. Deuteronomy 28:44 He shall lend to thee, and thou shalt not lend to him: he shall be the head, and thou shalt be the tail.
AV - **23,** 1-1,2-1,3-1,4-1,5-1,6-1,7-1,8-1,9-1,10-1,11-1,12-1,13-1,14-1,15-1,16-1,17-1,18-1,19-1,20-1,21-1,22-1,23-1
ESV - **23,** 1-1,2-1,3-1,4-1,5-1,6-1,7-1,8-1,9-1,10-1,11-1,12-1,13-1,14-1,15-1,16-1,17-1,18-1,19-1,20-1,21-1,22-1,23-1
HCSB - **22,** 1-1,2-1,3-1,4-1,5-1,6-1,7-1,8-1,9-1,10-1,11-1,12-1,13-1,14-1,15-1,16-1,17-1,18-1,19-1,20-1,21-1,22-1
NASV - **23,** 1-1,2-1,3-1,4-1,5-1,6-1,7-1,8-1,9-1,10-1,11-1,12-1,13-1,14-1,15-1,16-1,17-1,18-1,19-1,20-1,21-1,22-1,23-1

NCV - **29,** 1-**3**,2-1,3-1,4-**2**,5-1,6-1,7-1,8-1,9-1,10-1,11-1,12-**2**,13-1,14-1,15-1,16-1,17-1,18-1,19-1,20-1,21-1,22-1,23-1,24-1,25-1,26-1,27-1,28-1,29-1

NIV - **23,** 1-1,2-1,3-1,4-1,5-1,6-1,7-1,8-1,9-1,10-1,11-1,12-1,13-1,14-1,15-1,16-1,17-1,18-1,19-1,20-1,21-1,22-1,23-1

NKJV - **23,** 1-1,2-1,3-1,4-1,5-1,6-1,7-1,8-1,9-1,10-1,11-1,12-1,13-1,14-1,15-1,16-1,17-1,18-1,19-1,20-1,21-1,22-1,23-1

NLT - **24,** 1-1,2-1,3-1,4-**2**,5-1,6-1,7-1,8-1,9-1,10-1,11-1,12-1,13-1,14-1,15-1,16-1,17-1,18-1,19-1,20-1,21-1,22-1,23-1,24-1

NRSV - **23,** 1-1,2-1,3-1,4-1,5-1,6-1,7-1,8-1,9-1,10-1,11-1,12-1,13-1,14-1,15-1,16-1,17-1,18-1,19-1,20-1,21-1,22-1,23-1

Conclusion: Only the NCV and the NLT made the verse more complex. The NCV is the most difficult to read.

34. Deuteronomy 33:25 Thy shoes shall be iron and brass; and as thy days, so shall thy strength be.

AV - **16,** 1-1,2-1,3-1,4-1,5-1,6-1,7-1,8-1,9-1,10-1,11-1,12-1,13-1,14-1,15-1,16-1

ESV - **16,** 1-1,2-1,3-1,4-1,5-1,6-1,7-1,8-1,9-1,10-1,11-1,12-1,13-1,14-1,15-1,16-1

HCSB - **19,** 1-1,2-1,3-1,4-1,5-1,6-1,7-1,8-1,9-1,10-1,11-1,12-1,13-1,14-1,15-1,16-1,17-1,18-1,19-1

NASV - **18,** 1-1,2-1,3-1,4-1,5-1,6-1,7-1,8-1,9-**3**,10-1,11-1,12-1,13-1,14-1,15-1,16-**3**,17-1,18-1

NCV - **19,** 1-1,2-1,3-1,4-1,5-1,6-1,7-1,8-1,9-1,10-1,11-1,12-1,13-1,14-1,15-1,16-1,17-1,18-1,19-1

NIV - **17,** 1-1,2-1,3-1,4-1,5-1,6-1,7-1,8-1,9-1,10-1,11-1,12-1,13-1,14-1,15-**2**,16-1,17-1

NKJV - **15,** 1-1,2-**2**,3-1,4-1,5-1,6-1,7-1,8-1,9-1,10-1,11-1,12-1,13-1,14-1,15-1

NLT - **18,** 1-1,2-1,3-1,4-1,5-1,6-1,7-1,8-1,9-1,10-1,11-1,12-1,13-1,14-1,15-**3**,16-1,17-1,18-1

NRSV - **14,** 1-1,2-1,3-1,4-1,5-1,6-1,7-1,8-1,9-1,10-1,11-1,12-1,13-1,14-1

Conclusion: Four modern versions are more complex than the King James Bible.

35. Judges 5:27 At her feet he bowed, he fell, he lay down: at her feet he bowed, he fell: where he bowed, there he fell down dead.

AV - **25,** 1-1,2-1,3-1,4-1,5-1,6-1,7-1,8-1,9-1,10-1,11-1,12-1,13-1,14-1,15-1,16-1,17-1,18-1,19-1,20-1,21-1,22-1,23-1,24-1,25-1

ESV - **24,** 1-**2**,2-1,3-1,4-1,5-1,6-1,7-1,8-1,9-1,10-1,11-**2**,12-1,13-1,14-1,15-1,16-1,17-1,18-1,19-1,20-1,21-1,22-1,23-1,24-1

HCSB - **24,** 1-1,2-**2**,3-1,4-1,5-1,6-1,7-1,8-1,9-1,10-1,11-1,12-**2**,13-1,14-1,15-1,16-1,17-1,18-1,19-1,20-**2**,21-1,22-1,23-1,24-1

NASV - **23,** 1-**2**,2-1,3-1,4-1,5-1,6-1,7-1,8-1,9-1,10-**2**,11-1,12-1,13-1,14-1,15-1,16-1,17-1,18-1,19-1,20-1,21-1,22-1,23-1

NCV - **25,** 1-1,2-1,3-1,4-1,5-1,6-1,7-1,8-1,9-1,10-1,11-1,12-1,13-1,14-1,15-1,16-1,17-1,18-1,19-1,20-1,21-1,22-1,23-1,24-1,25-1

NIV - **24,** 1-1,2-1,3-1,4-1,5-1,6-1,7-1,8-1,9-1,10-1,11-1,12-1,13-1,14-1,15-1,16-1,17-1,18-1,19-1,20-1,21-1,22-1,23-1,24-1

NKJV - **24,** 1-1,2-1,3-1,4-1,5-1,6-1,7-1,8-1,9-1,10-1,11-1,12-1,13-1,14-1,15-1,16-1,17-1,18-1,19-1,20-1,21-1,22-1,23-1,24-1

NLT - **17,** 1-1,2-1,3-1,4-1,5-1,6-1,7-1,8-1,9-1,10-1,11-1,12-1,13-1,14-1,15-1,16-1,17-1

NRSV - **24,** 1-1,2-1,3-1,4-1,5-1,6-1,7-1,8-1,9-1,10-1,11-1,12-1,13-1,14-1,15-1,16-1,17-1,18-1,19-1,20-1,21-1,22-1,23-1,24-1

Conclusion: Only three modern versions are more complex than the King James Bible.

36. 1 Samuel 6:10 And the men did so; and took two milch kine, and tied them to the cart, and shut up their calves at home:

AV - **23,** 1-1,2-1,3-1,4-1,5-1,6-1,7-1,8-1,9-1,10-1,11-1,12-1,13-1,14-1,15-1,16-1,17-1,18-1,19-1,20-1,21-1,22-1,23-1

ESV - **22,** 1-1,2-1,3-1,4-1,5-1,6-1,7-1,8-1,9-1,10-1,11-1,12-1,13-1,14-1,15-1,16-1,17-1,18-1,19-1,20-1,21-1,22-1

HCSB - **21,** 1-1,2-1,3-1,4-1,5-1,6-1,7-1,8-1,9-1,10-1,11-1,12-1,13-1,14-1,15-1,16-**2**,17-1,18-1,19-1,20-1,21-1

NASV - **23,** 1-1,2-1,3-1,4-1,5-1,6-1,7-1,8-1,9-1,10-1,11-1,12-1,13-1,14-1,15-1,16-1,17-1,18-1,19-1,20-1,21-1,22-1,23-1

NCV - **31,** 1-1,2-**2**,3-1,4-1,5-1,6-1,7-1,8-**3**,9-1,10-1,11-1,12-1,13-1,14-1,15-1,16-1,17-1,18-1,19-1,20-1,21-1,22-1,23-1,24-1,25-1,26-1,27-1,28-1,29-1,30-1,31-1

NIV - **20,** 1-1,2-1,3-1,4-1,5-1,6-1,7-1,8-1,9-1,10-1,11-1,12-1,13-1,14-1,15-1,16-1,17-1,18-1,19-1,20-1

NKJV - **22,** 1-1,2-1,3-1,4-1,5-1,6-1,7-1,8-1,9-1,10-1,11-1,12-1,13-1,14-1,15-1,16-1,17-1,18-1,19-1,20-1,21-1,22-1

NLT - **23,** 1-1,2-1,3-**3**,4-1,5-**2**,6-1,7-1,8-1,9-1,10-1,11-1,12-1,13-1,14-1,15-1,16-**2**,17-1,18-1,19-1,20-1,21-1,22-1,23-1

NRSV - **22,** 1-1,2-1,3-1,4-1,5-1,6-1,7-1,8-1,9-1,10-1,11-1,12-1,13-1,14-1,15-1,16-1,17-1,18-1,19-1,20-1,21-1,22-1

Conclusion: Only three modern versions are more complex than the King James Bible.

37. 2 Samuel 22:32 For who is God, save the LORD? and who is a rock, save our God?

AV - **15,** 1-1,2-1,3-1,4-1,5-1,6-1,7-1,8-1,9-1,10-1,11-1,12-1,13-1,14-1,15-1

ESV - **15,** 1-1,2-1,3-1,4-1,5-1,6-1,7-1,8-1,9-1,10-1,11-1,12-1,13-**2**,14-1,15-1

HCSB - **15,** 1-1,2-1,3-1,4-1,5-**2**,6-1,7-1,8-1,9-1,10-1,11-1,12-1,13-**2**,14-1,15-1

NASV - **15,** 1-1,2-1,3-1,4-1,5-**2**,6-1,7-1,8-1,9-1,10-1,11-1,12-1,13-**2**,14-1,15-1

NCV - **13,** 1-1,2-1,3-1,4-**2**,5-1,6-1,7-1,8-1,9-1,10-1,11-**2**,12-1,13-1

NIV - **15,** 1-1,2-1,3-1,4-1,5-**2**,6-1,7-1,8-1,9-1,10-1,11-1,12-1,13-**2**,14-1,15-1

NKJV - **15,** 1-1,2-1,3-1,4-1,5-**2**,6-1,7-1,8-1,9-1,10-1,11-1,12-1,13-**2**,14-1,15-1

NLT - **15,** 1-1,2-1,3-1,4-1,5-**2**,6-1,7-1,8-1,9-1,10-1,11-1,12-1,13-1,14-**2**,15-1

NRSV - **15,** 1-1,2-1,3-1,4-1,5-1,6-1,7-1,8-1,9-1,10-1,11-1,12-1,13-**2**,14-1,15-1

Conclusion: All eight modern versions are more complex than the King James Bible.

38. 2 Kings 4:15 And he said, Call her. And when he had called her, she stood in the door.

AV - **16,** 1-1,2-1,3-1,4-1,5-1,6-1,7-1,8-1,9-1,10-1,11-1,12-1,13-1,14-1,15-1,16-1

ESV - **15,** 1-1,2-1,3-1,4-1,5-1,6-1,7-1,8-1,9-1,10-1,11-1,12-1,13-1,14-1,15-**2**

HCSB - **14,** 1-1,2-1,3-1,4-1,5-1,6-1,7-1,8-1,9-1,10-1,11-1,12-1,13-1,14-**2**

NASV - **14,** 1-1,2-1,3-1,4-1,5-1,6-1,7-1,8-1,9-1,10-1,11-1,12-1,13-1,14-**2**

NCV - **21,** 1-1,2-1,3-1,4-**2**,5-1,6-1,7-1,8-1,9-1,10-**2**,11-**2**,12-1,13-1,14-1,15-1,16-1,17-1,18-1,19-1,20-1,21-**2**

NIV - **15,** 1-1,2-1,3-1,4-1,5-1,6-1,7-1,8-1,9-1,10-1,11-1,12-1,13-1,14-1,15-**2**

NKJV - **15,** 1-1,2-1,3-1,4-1,5-1,6-1,7-1,8-1,9-1,10-1,11-1,12-1,13-1,14-1,15-**2**

NLT - **16,** 1-1,2-1,3-1,4-1,5-1,6-1,7-1,8-1,9-1,10-1,11-1,12-1,13-1,14-1,15-1,16-**2**

NRSV - **14,** 1-1,2-1,3-1,4-1,5-1,6-1,7-1,8-1,9-1,10-1,11-1,12-1,13-1,14-1

Conclusion: Seven modern versions are more complex than the King James Bible. The NCV seemed to go out of its way to make this verse difficult to read.

Samuel C. Gipp Ph.D.

39. 2 Kings 22:11 And it came to pass, when the king had heard the words of the book of the law, that he rent his clothes.

AV - **23,** 1-1,2-1,3-1,4-1,5-1,6-1,7-1,8-1,9-1,10-1,11-1,12-1,13-1,14-1,15-1,16-1,17-1,18-1,19-1,20-1,21-1,22-1,23-1

ESV - **16,** 1-1,2-1,3-1,4-1,5-1,6-1,7-1,8-1,9-1,10-1,11-1,12-1,13-1,14-1,15-1,16-1

HCSB - **16,** 1-1,2-1,3-1,4-1,5-1,6-1,7-1,8-1,9-1,10-1,11-1,12-1,13-1,14-1,15-1,16-1

NASV - **16,** 1-1,2-1,3-1,4-1,5-1,6-1,7-1,8-1,9-1,10-1,11-1,12-1,13-1,14-1,15-1,16-1

NCV - **22,** 1-1,2-1,3-1,4-1,5-1,6-1,7-1,8-1,9-1,10-1,11-1,12-**2,**13-1,14-1,15-1,16-1,17-1,18-1,19-1,20-**2,**21-1,22-1

NIV - **16,** 1-1,2-1,3-1,4-1,5-1,6-1,7-1,8-1,9-1,10-1,11-1,12-1,13-1,14-1,15-1,16-1

NKJV - **20,** 1-1,2-1,3-**2,**4-1,5-1,6-1,7-1,8-1,9-1,10-1,11-1,12-1,13-1,14-1,15-1,16-1,17-1,18-1,19-1,20-1

NLT - **19,** 1-1,2-1,3-1,4-1,5-1,6-1,7-**2,**8-1,9-1,10-1,11-1,12-1,13-1,14-1,15-1,16-1,17-1,18-1,19-**2**

NRSV - **16,** 1-1,2-1,3-1,4-1,5-1,6-1,7-1,8-1,9-1,10-1,11-1,12-1,13-1,14-1,15-1,16-1

Conclusion: Only three modern versions are more complex than the King James Bible. This is one of the rare times that the NKJV was more complex than either the NCV, HCSB, NASV, NIV or NRSV.

40. 2 Chronicles 34:19 And it came to pass, when the king had heard the words of the law, that he rent his clothes.

AV - **20,** 1-1,2-1,3-1,4-1,5-1,6-1,7-1,8-1,9-1,10-1,11-1,12-1,13-1,14-1,15-1,16-1,17-1,18-1,19-1,20-1

ESV - **14,** 1-1,2-1,3-1,4-1,5-1,6-1,7-1,8-1,9-1,10-1,11-1,12-1,13-1,14-1

HCSB - **13,** 1-1,2-1,3-1,4-1,5-1,6-1,7-1,8-1,9-1,10-1,11-1,12-1,13-1

NASV - **13,** 1-1,2-1,3-1,4-1,5-1,6-1,7-1,8-1,9-1,10-1,11-1,12-1,13-1

NCV - **19,** 1-1,2-1,3-1,4-1,5-1,6-1,7-1,8-1,9-**2,**10-1,11-1,12-1,13-1,14-1,15-1,16-1,17-**2,**18-1,19-1

NIV - **13,** 1-1,2-1,3-1,4-1,5-1,6-1,7-1,8-1,9-1,10-1,11-1,12-1,13-1

NKJV - **17,** 1-1,2-1,3-**2,**4-1,5-1,6-1,7-1,8-1,9-1,10-1,11-1,12-1,13-1,14-1,15-1,16-1,17-1

NLT - **16,** 1-1,2-1,3-1,4-1,5-1,6-1,7-**2,**8-1,9-1,10-1,11-1,12-1,13-1,14-1,15-1,16-**2**

NRSV - **13,** 1-1,2-1,3-1,4-1,5-1,6-1,7-1,8-1,9-1,10-1,11-1,12-1,13-1

Conclusion: Only three modern versions are more complex than the King James Bible.

41. Job 1:11 But put forth thine hand now, and touch all that he hath, and he will curse thee to thy face.

AV - **20,** 1-1,2-1,3-1,4-1,5-1,6-1,7-1,8-1,9-1,10-1,11-1,12-1,13-1,14-1,15-1,16-1,17-1,18-1,19-1,20-1

ESV - **19,** 1-1,2-1,3-1,4-1,5-1,6-1,7-1,8-1,9-1,10-1,11-1,12-1,13-1,14-1,15-1,16-1,17-1,18-1,19-1

HCSB - **19,** 1-1,2-1,3-1,4-1,5-1,6-1,7-1,8-**4,**9-1,10-1,11-1,12-1,13-1,14-**2,**15-1,16-1,17-1,18-1,19-1

NASV - **20,** 1-1,2-1,3-1,4-1,5-1,6-1,7-1,8-1,9-1,10-1,11-1,12-1,13-1,14-1,15-**2,**16-1,17-1,18-1,19-1,20-1

NCV - **18,** 1-1,2-1,3-1,4-1,5-1,6-1,7-**2,**8-**4,**9-1,10-1,11-1,12-1,13-1,14-1,15-1,16-1,17-1,18-1

NIV - **19,** 1-1,2-1,3-1,4-1,5-1,6-1,7-1,8-**4,**9-1,10-1,11-1,12-1,13-1,14-**2,**15-1,16-1,17-1,18-1,19-1

NKJV - **21,** 1-1,2-1,3-1,4-1,5-1,6-1,7-1,8-1,9-1,10-1,11-1,12-1,13-1,14-1,15-1,16-**2,**17-1,18-1,19-1,20-1,21-1

NLT - **18,** 1-1,2-1,3-1,4-1,5-1,6-**2,**7-**4,**8-1,9-1,10-1,11-1,12-1,13-**2,**14-1,15-1,16-1,17-1,18-1

NRSV - **20,** 1-1,2-1,3-1,4-1,5-1,6-1,7-1,8-1,9-1,10-1,11-1,12-1,13-1,14-1,15-1,16-1,17-1,18-1,19-1,20-1

Conclusion: Six modern versions are more complex than the King James Bible.

42. Job 2:5 But put forth thine hand now, and touch his bone and his flesh, and he will curse thee to thy face.

AV - **20,** 1-1,2-1,3-1,4-1,5-1,6-1,7-1,8-1,9-1,10-1,11-1,12-1,13-1,14-1,15-1,16-1,17-1,18-1,19-1,20-1

ESV - **20,** 1-1,2-1,3-1,4-1,5-1,6-1,7-1,8-1,9-1,10-1,11-1,12-1,13-1,14-1,15-1,16-1,17-1,18-1,19-1,20-1

HCSB - 20, 1-1,2-1,3-1,4-1,5-1,6-1,7-1,8-1,9-1,10-1,11-1,12-1,13-1,14-1,15-**2**,16-1,17-1,18-1,19-1,20-1
NASV - 20, 1-**3**,2-1,3-1,4-1,5-1,6-1,7-1,8-1,9-1,10-1,11-1,12-1,13-1,14-1,15-1,16-1,17-1,18-1,19-1,20-1
NCV - 19, 1-1,2-1,3-1,4-1,5-1,6-1,7-**2**,8-1,9-1,10-1,11-1,12-1,13-1,14-1,15-1,16-1,17-1,18-1,19-1
NIV - 20, 1-1,2-1,3-1,4-1,5-1,6-1,7-1,8-1,9-1,10-1,11-1,12-1,13-1,14-1,15-**2**,16-1,17-1,18-1,19-1,20-1
NKJV - 22, 1-1,2-1,3-1,4-1,5-1,6-1,7-1,8-1,9-1,10-1,11-1,12-1,13-1,14-1,15-1,16-1,17-**2**,18-1,19-1,20-1,21-1,22-1
NLT - 17, 1-1,2-1,3-1,4-1,5-1,6-**2**,7-1,8-1,9-1,10-1,11-1,12-**2**,13-1,14-1,15-1,16-1,17-1
NRSV - 21, 1-1,2-1,3-1,4-1,5-1,6-1,7-1,8-1,9-1,10-1,11-1,12-1,13-1,14-1,15-1,16-1,17-1,18-1,19-1,20-1,21-1
Conclusion: Six modern versions are more complex than the King James Bible.

43. Job 3:2 And Job spake, and said.
AV - **5,** 1-1,2-1,3-1,4-1,5-1
ESV - **3,** 1-1,2-1,3-1
HCSB - **2,** 1-1,2-1
NASV - **3,** 1-1,2-1,3-1
NCV - **1,** 1-1
NIV - **2,** 1-1,2-1
NKJV - **5,** 1-1,2-1,3-1,4-1,5-1
NLT - **2,** 1-1,2-1
NRSV - **2,** 1-1,2-1
Conclusion: All versions read the same. For this verse the NCV simply has the lone word, "saying:" with no capital letter or any other word. I imagine this qualifies this verse as "the shortest verse in the bible" concerning the NCV.

44. Job 5:27 Lo this, we have searched it, so it is; hear it, and know thou it for thy good.
AV - **18,** 1-1,2-1,3-1,4-1,5-1,6-1,7-1,8-1,9-1,10-1,11-1,12-1,13-1,14-1,15-1,16-1,17-1,18-1
ESV - **16,** 1-**2**,2-1,3-1,4-1,5-1,6-1,7-1,8-1,9-1,10-1,11-1,12-1,13-1,14-1,15-1,16-1
HCSB - **15,** 1-1,2-1,3-**5**,4-1,5-1,6-1,7-1,8-1,9-1,10-1,11-1,12-**3**,13-1,14-1,15-**2**
NASV - **16,** 1-**2**,2-1,3-1,4-1,5-**5**,6-1,7-1,8-1,9-1,10-1,11-1,12-1,13-1,14-1,15-1,16-**2**
NCV - **18,** 1-1,2-1,3-1,4-1,5-1,6-1,7-1,8-1,9-1,10-1,11-1,12-1,13-**2**,14-1,15-1,16-1,17-1,18-1
NIV - **16,** 1-1,2-1,3-**3**,4-1,5-1,6-1,7-1,8-1,9-1,10-1,11-1,12-1,13-**2**,14-1,15-1,16-**2**
NKJV - **15,** 1-**2**,2-1,3-1,4-1,5-1,6-1,7-1,8-1,9-1,10-1,11-1,12-1,13-1,14-1,15-**2**
NLT - **20,** 1-1,2-1,3-**2**,4-1,5-1,6-1,7-1,8-1,9-1,10-1,11-1,12-**2**,13-1,14-1,15-**2**,16-1,17-**2**,18-1,19-1,20-**2**
NRSV - **15,** 1-1,2-1,3-1,4-1,5-1,6-1,7-1,8-1,9-1,10-1,11-1,12-1,13-1,14-1,15-**2**
Conclusion: All eight modern versions are more complex than the King James Bible. The NLT is the most difficult to read.

45. Job 6:12 Is my strength the strength of stones? or is my flesh of brass?
AV - **13,** 1-1,2-1,3-1,4-1,5-1,6-1,7-1,8-1,9-1,10-1,11-1,12-1,13-1
ESV - **12,** 1-1,2-1,3-1,4-1,5-1,6-1,7-1,8-1,9-1,10-1,11-1,12-1
HCSB - **12,** 1-1,2-1,3-1,4-1,5-1,6-1,7-1,8-1,9-1,10-1,11-1,12-1
NASV - **12,** 1-1,2-1,3-1,4-1,5-1,6-1,7-1,8-1,9-1,10-1,11-1,12-1
NCV - **13,** 1-1,2-1,3-1,4-1,5-1,6-1,7-1,8-1,9-1,10-1,11-1,12-1,13-1
NIV - **11,** 1-1,2-1,3-1,4-1,5-1,6-1,7-1,8-1,9-1,10-1,11-1
NKJV - **12,** 1-1,2-1,3-1,4-1,5-1,6-1,7-1,8-1,9-1,10-1,11-1,12-1

NLT - **12,** 1-1,2-1,3-1,4-1,5-1,6-1,7-1,8-1,9-1,10-1,11-1,12-1
NRSV - **12,** 1-1,2-1,3-1,4-1,5-1,6-1,7-1,8-1,9-1,10-1,11-1,12-1
Conclusion: All versions read the same.

46. Job 8:2 How long wilt thou speak these things? and how long shall the words of thy mouth be like a strong wind?
AV - **21,** 1-1,2-1,3-1,4-1,5-1,6-1,7-1,8-1,9-1,10-1,11-1,12-1,13-1,14-1,15-1,16-1,17-1,18-1,19-1,20-1,21-1
ESV - **17,** 1-1,2-1,3-1,4-1,5-1,6-1,7-1,8-1,9-1,10-1,11-1,12-1,13-1,14-1,15-1,16-1,17-1
HCSB - **16,** 1-1,2-1,3-1,4-1,5-1,6-1,7-**2,**8-1,9-1,10-1,11-1,12-1,13-1,14-1,15-1,16-1
NASV - **17,** 1-1,2-1,3-1,4-1,5-1,6-1,7-1,8-1,9-1,10-1,11-1,12-1,13-1,14-1,15-1,16-**2,**17-1
NCV - **14,** 1-1,2-1,3-1,4-1,5-1,6-1,7-1,8-1,9-1,10-1,11-1,12-1,13-1,14-1
NIV - **13,** 1-1,2-1,3-1,4-1,5-1,6-1,7-1,8-1,9-1,10-1,11-1,12-**3,**13-1
NKJV - **18,** 1-1,2-1,3-1,4-1,5-1,6-1,7-1,8-1,9-1,10-1,11-1,12-1,13-1,14-1,15-1,16-1,17-1,18-1
NLT - **14,** 1-1,2-1,3-1,4-1,5-1,6-1,7-1,8-1,9-1,10-1,11-1,12-1,13-**3,**14-1
NRSV - **17,** 1-1,2-1,3-1,4-1,5-1,6-1,7-1,8-1,9-1,10-1,11-1,12-1,13-1,14-1,15-1,16-1,17-1
Conclusion: Four modern versions are more complex than the King James Bible.

47. Job 9:2 I know it is so of a truth: but how should man be just with God?
AV - **16,** 1-1,2-1,3-1,4-1,5-1,6-1,7-1,8-1,9-1,10-1,11-1,12-1,13-1,14-1,15-1,16-1
ESV - **18,** 1-**2,**2-1,3-1,4-1,5-1,6-1,7-1,8-1,9-1,10-1,11-1,12-1,13-1,14-1,15-1,16-1,17-**2,**18-1
HCSB - **17,** 1-1,2-1,3-1,4-1,5-1,6-1,7-1,8-1,9-1,10-1,11-1,12-1,13-**2,**14-1,15-**3,**16-**2,**17-1
NASV - **19,** 1-1,2-1,3-1,4-1,5-1,6-1,7-1,8-1,9-1,10-1,11-1,12-1,13-1,14-1,15-1,16-1,17-1,18-**2,**19-1
NCV - **18,** 1-1,2-1,3-1,4-1,5-1,6-1,7-1,8-1,9-1,10-1,11-**3,**12-1,13-1,14-1,15-1,16-**2,**17-1,18-1
NIV - **16,** 1-**2,**2-1,3-1,4-1,5-1,6-1,7-1,8-1,9-1,10-1,11-1,12-**2,**13-1,14-**3,**15-**2,**16-1
NKJV - **15,** 1-**2,**2-1,3-1,4-1,5-1,6-1,7-1,8-1,9-1,10-1,11-1,12-1,13-**3,**14-**2,**15-1
NLT - **20,** 1-1,2-1,3-1,4-1,5-1,6-1,7-1,8-1,9-**3,**10-1,11-1,12-1,13-1,14-**2,**15-1,16-**2,**17-**3,**18-1,19-1,20-1
NRSV - **16,** 1-**2,**2-1,3-1,4-1,5-1,6-1,7-1,8-1,9-1,10-1,11-1,12-**2,**13-1,14-1,15-**2,**16-1
Conclusion: All eight modern versions are more complex than the King James Bible. The New Living Translation is the most difficult to read.

48. Job 9:35 Then would I speak, and not fear him; but it is not so with me.
AV - **15,** 1-1,2-1,3-1,4-1,5-1,6-1,7-1,8-1,9-1,10-1,11-1,12-1,13-1,14-1,15-1
ESV - **15,** 1-1,2-1,3-1,4-1,5-**2,**6-1,7-1,8-1,9-1,10-1,11-1,12-1,13-1,14-1,15-**2**
HCSB - **19,** 1-1,2-1,3-1,4-1,5-1,6-1,7-1,8-1,9-1,10-1,11-1,12-1,13-1,14-1,15-1,16-1,17-1,18-1,19-1
NASV - **16,** 1-1,2-1,3-1,4-1,5-1,6-1,7-1,8-1,9-1,10-1,11-1,12-1,13-1,14-1,15-1,16-**2**
NCV - **15,** 1-1,2-1,3-1,4-1,5-**2,**6-**2,**7-**2,**8-1,9-1,10-1,11-1,12-**2,**13-1,14-1,15-1
NIV - **18,** 1-1,2-1,3-1,4-1,5-1,6-**2,**7-1,8-1,9-1,10-1,11-1,12-1,13-1,14-1,15-1,16-1,17-1,18-**2**
NKJV - **15,** 1-1,2-1,3-1,4-1,5-1,6-1,7-1,8-1,9-1,10-1,11-1,12-1,13-1,14-1,15-1
NLT - **17,** 1-1,2-1,3-1,4-1,5-1,6-1,7-**2,**8-1,9-1,10-1,11-**2,**12-1,13-1,14-1,15-1,16-1,17-1
NRSV - **20,** 1-1,2-1,3-1,4-1,5-**2,**6-1,7-1,8-1,9-1,10-1,11-1,12-1,13-1,14-1,15-1,16-1,17-i,18-1,19-1,20-1
Conclusion: Six modern versions are more complex than the King James Bible. The NCV is the most difficult to read.

49. Job 10:5 Are thy days as the days of man? are thy years as man's days,
AV - **14,** 1-1,2-1,3-1,4-1,5-1,6-1,7-1,8-1,9-1,10-1,11-1,12-1,13-1,14-1

ESV - **15,** 1-1,2-1,3-1,4-1,5-1,6-1,7-1,8-1,9-1,10-1,11-1,12-1,13-1,14-1,15-1
HCSB - 16, 1-1,2-1,3-1,4-1,5-1,6-1,7-1,8-**2**,9-1,10-1,11-1,12-1,13-1,14-1,15-1,16-1
NASV - 15, 1-1,2-1,3-1,4-1,5-1,6-1,7-1,8-1,9-**2**,10-1,11-1,12-1,13-1,14-1,15-1
NCV - 14, 1-1,2-1,3-1,4-1,5-1,6-1,7-1,8-**2**,9-1,10-1,11-1,12-1,13-1,14-1
NIV - 16, 1-1,2-1,3-1,4-1,5-1,6-1,7-1,8-**2**,9-1,10-1,11-1,12-1,13-1,14-1,15-1,16-1
NKJV - 20, 1-1,2-1,3-1,4-1,5-1,6-1,7-1,8-1,9-**2**,10-1,11-1,12-1,13-1,14-1,15-1,16-1,17-1,18-1,19-**2**,20-1
NLT - 13, 1-1,2-1,3-**2**,4-1,5-1,6-1,7-1,8-1,9-1,10-1,11-1,12-1,13-1
NRSV - 14, 1-1,2-1,3-1,4-1,5-1,6-1,7-1,8-**2**,9-1,10-1,11-1,12-1,13-**2**,14-1
Conclusion: Seven modern versions are more complex than the King James Bible.

50. Job 10:13 And these things hast thou hid in thine heart: I know that this is with thee.
AV - **16,** 1-1,2-1,3-1,4-1,5-1,6-1,7-1,8-1,9-1,10-1,11-1,12-1,13-1,14-1,15-1,16-1
ESV - 15, 1-1,2-1,3-1,4-1,5-1,6-1,7-1,8-1,9-1,10-1,11-1,12-1,13-1,14-1,15-**2**
HCSB - 16, 1-1,2-1,3-**2**,4-1,5-1,6-1,7-1,8-1,9-1,10-1,11-1,12-1,13-1,14-1,15-**2**,16-1
NASV - 16, 1-1,2-1,3-1,4-1,5-1,6-**2**,7-1,8-1,9-1,10-1,11-1,12-1,13-1,14-1,15-**2**,16-1
NCV - 15, 1-1,2-1,3-1,4-1,5-1,6-1,7-**2**,8-1,9-1,10-1,11-1,12-1,13-1,14-1,15-1
NIV - 7, 1-1,2-1,3-1,4-**2**,5-1,6-1,7-**2**
NKJV - 16, 1-1,2-1,3-1,4-1,5-1,6-**2**,7-1,8-1,9-1,10-1,11-1,12-1,13-1,14-1,15-1,16-1
NLT - 18, 1-1,2-1,3-1,4-1,5-1,6-**2**,7-1,8-1,9-1,10-1,11-1,12-1,13-1,14-1,15-1,16-1,17-1,18-1
NRSV - 15, 1-1,2-1,3-1,4-1,5-1,6-1,7-1,8-1,9-1,10-1,11-1,12-1,13-1,14-1,15-**2**
Conclusion: All eight modern versions are more complex than the King James Bible.

51. Job 12:7 But ask now the beasts, and they shall teach thee; and the fowls of the air, and they shall tell thee:
AV - **21,** 1-1,2-1,3-1,4-1,5-1,6-1,7-1,8-1,9-1,10-1,11-1,12-1,13-1,14-1,15-1,16-1,17-1,18-1,19-1,20-1,21-1
ESV - 19, 1-1,2-1,3-1,4-1,5-1,6-1,7-1,8-1,9-1,10-1,11-1,12-1,13-1,14-**2**,15-1,16-1,17-1,18-1,19-1
HCSB - 20, 1-1,2-1,3-1,4-**3**,5-1,6-1,7-1,8-**2**,9-1,10-1,11-1,12-1,13-1,14-1,15-1,16-1,17-1,18-1,19-1,20-1
NASV - 21, 1-1,2-1,3-1,4-1,5-1,6-1,7-1,8-1,9-1,10-1,11-1,12-1,13-1,14-1,15-1,16-**2**,17-1,18-1,19-1,20-1,21-1
NCV - 21, 1-1,2-1,3-1,4-**3**,5-1,6-1,7-1,8-1,9-1,10-1,11-1,12-1,13-1,14-1,15-1,16-1,17-1,18-1,19-1,20-1,21-1
NIV - 20, 1-1,2-1,3-1,4-**3**,5-1,6-1,7-1,8-1,9-1,10-1,11-1,12-1,13-1,14-1,15-1,16-1,17-1,18-1,19-1,20-1
NKJV - 21, 1-1,2-1,3-1,4-1,5-1,6-1,7-1,8-1,9-1,10-1,11-1,12-1,13-1,14-1,15-1,16-1,17-1,18-1,19-1,20-1,21-1
NLT - 20, 1-1,2-1,3-1,4-**3**,5-1,6-1,7-1,8-1,9-1,10-1,11-1,12-1,13-1,14-1,15-1,16-1,17-1,18-1,19-1,20-1
NRSV - 19, 1-1,2-1,3-1,4-**3**,5-1,6-1,7-1,8-1,9-1,10-1,11-1,12-1,13-1,14-1,15-1,16-1,17-1,18-1,19-1
Conclusion: Seven modern versions are more complex than the King James Bible. The HCSB is the most difficult to read.

52. Job 12:11 Doth not the ear try words? and the mouth taste his meat?
AV - **12,** 1-1,2-1,3-1,4-1,5-1,6-1,7-1,8-1,9-1,10-1,11-1,12-1
ESV - 11, 1-1,2-1,3-1,4-1,5-1,6-1,7-1,8-1,9-**2**,10-1,11-1
HCSB - 10, 1-**2**,2-1,3-1,4-1,5-1,6-1,7-1,8-**2**,9-1,10-1
NASV - 12, 1-1,2-1,3-1,4-1,5-1,6-1,7-1,8-1,9-**2**,10-1,11-1,12-1
NCV - **9,** 1-1,2-1,3-1,4-1,5-1,6-1,7-1,8-1,9-1
NIV - **11,** 1-1,2-1,3-1,4-1,5-1,6-1,7-1,8-1,9-1,10-1,11-1
NKJV - **12,** 1-1,2-1,3-1,4-1,5-1,6-1,7-1,8-1,9-1,10-1,11-1,12-1
NLT - 14, 1-1,2-1,3-1,4-1,5-1,6-1,7-1,8-1,9-1,10-1,11-1,12-**4**,13-**2**,14-1

NRSV - 11, 1-1,2-1,3-1,4-1,5-1,6-1,7-1,8-1,9-**2**,10-1,11-1
Conclusion: Five modern versions are more complex than the King James Bible. The NLT is the most difficult to read.

53. Job 13:19 Who is he that will plead with me? for now, if I hold my tongue, I shall give up the ghost.
AV - **21,** 1-1,2-1,3-1,4-1,5-1,6-1,7-1,8-1,9-1,10-1,11-1,12-1,13-1,14-1,15-1,16-1,17-1,18-1,19-1,20-1,21-1
ESV - 16, 1-1,2-1,3-1,4-1,5-1,6-**2**,7-1,8-1,9-1,10-1,11-1,12-1,13-1,14-**2**,15-1,16-1
HCSB - 12, 1-1,2-**2**,3-**2**,4-1,5-1,6-1,7-1,8-1,9-1,10-**2**,11-1,12-1
NASV - 13, 1-1,2-1,3-**2**,4-1,5-1,6-1,7-1,8-1,9-1,10-1,11-**2**,12-1,13-1
NCV - 17, 1-1,2-1,3-1,4-**2**,5-1,6-1,7-**2**,8-1,9-1,10-**2**,11-1,12-1,13-1,14-1,15-1,16-1,17-1
NIV - 14, 1-1,2-**2**,3-1,4-**2**,5-**2**,6-1,7-1,8-1,9-1,10-1,11-1,12-**2**,13-1,14-1
NKJV - 16, 1-1,2-1,3-1,4-1,5-1,6-**2**,7-1,8-1,9-1,10-1,11-1,12-1,13-1,14-1,15-1,16-**2**
NLT - 20, 1-1,2-1,3-**2**,4-1,5-1,6-**2**,7-1,8-1,9-1,10-1,11-1,12-1,13-1,14-1,15-1,16-**2**,17-**2**,18-1,19-1,20-1
NRSV - 16, 1-1,2-1,3-1,4-1,5-1,6-**2**,7-1,8-1,9-1,10-1,11-1,12-1,13-1,14-**2**,15-1,16-1
Conclusion: All eight modern versions are more complex than the King James Bible.

54. Job 17:15 And where is now my hope? as for my hope, who shall see it?
AV - **14,** 1-1,2-1,3-1,4-1,5-1,6-1,7-1,8-1,9-1,10-1,11-1,12-1,13-1,14-1
ESV - **10,** 1-1,2-1,3-1,4-1,5-1,6-1,7-1,8-1,9-1,10-1
HCSB - 12, 1-1,2-1,3-1,4-1,5-1,6-1,7-1,8-1,9-**2**,10-1,11-1,12-1
NASV - 10, 1-1,2-1,3-1,4-1,5-1,6-1,7-1,8-**2**,9-1,10-1
NCV - 12, 1-1,2-1,3-1,4-1,5-1,6-1,7-1,8-1,9-**2**,10-1,11-1,12-1
NIV - 12, 1-1,2-1,3-1,4-1,5-1,6-1,7-1,8-1,9-**2**,10-1,11-1,12-1
NKJV - 13, 1-1,2-1,3-1,4-1,5-1,6-1,7-1,8-1,9-**2**,10-1,11-1,12-1,13-1
NLT - **9,** 1-1,2-1,3-1,4-1,5-1,6-1,7-**3**,8-1,9-1
NRSV - **10,** 1-1,2-1,3-1,4-1,5-1,6-1,7-1,8-1,9-1,10-1
Conclusion: Six modern versions are more complex than the King James Bible.

55. **Job 18:10** The snare is laid for him in the ground, and a trap for him in the way.
AV - **17,** 1-1,2-1,3-1,4-1,5-1,6-1,7-1,8-1,9-1,10-1,11-1,12-1,13-1,14-1,15-1,16-1,17-1
ESV - 16, 1-1,2-1,3-1,4-**2**,5-1,6-1,7-1,8-1,9-1,10-1,11-1,12-1,13-1,14-1,15-1,16-1
HCSB - 18, 1-1,2-1,3-1,4-**2**,5-1,6-1,7-1,8-1,9-1,10-1,11-1,12-1,13-1,14-1,15-1,16-**2**,17-1,18-1
NASV - 17, 1-1,2-1,3-1,4-1,5-1,6-**2**,7-1,8-1,9-1,10-1,11-1,12-1,13-1,14-1,15-1,16-1,17-1
NCV - 13, 1-1,2-1,3-1,4-1,5-1,6-**2**,7-1,8-1,9-1,10-1,11-1,12-1,13-1
NIV - 15, 1-1,2-1,3-1,4-**2**,5-1,6-1,7-1,8-1,9-1,10-1,11-1,12-1,13-1,14-1,15-1
NKJV - 17, 1-1,2-1,3-1,4-**2**,5-1,6-1,7-1,8-1,9-1,10-1,11-1,12-1,13-1,14-1,15-1,16-1,17-1
NLT - 14, 1-1,2-1,3-1,4-**2**,5-1,6-1,7-1,8-1,9-1,10-1,11-1,12-**2**,13-1,14-1
NRSV - **16,** 1-1,2-1,3-1,4-1,5-1,6-1,7-1,8-1,9-1,10-1,11-1,12-1,13-1,14-1,15-1,16-1
Conclusion: Seven modern versions are more complex than the King James Bible.

56. Job 20:11 His bones are full of the sin of his youth, which shall lie down with him in the dust.
AV - **19,** 1-1,2-1,3-1,4-1,5-1,6-1,7-1,8-1,9-1,10-1,11-1,12-1,13-1,14-1,15-1,16-1,17-1,18-1,19-1
ESV - 18, 1-1,2-1,3-1,4-1,5-1,6-1,7-**2**,8-**2**,9-1,10-1,11-1,12-1,13-1,14-1,15-1,16-1,17-1,18-1
HCSB - 18, 1-1,2-1,3-1,4-1,5-1,6-1,7-**2**,8-**2**,9-1,10-1,11-1,12-1,13-1,14-1,15-1,16-1,17-1,18-1
NASV - 17, 1-1,2-1,3-1,4-1,5-1,6-1,7-**2**,8-**2**,9-1,10-1,11-1,12-1,13-1,14-1,15-1,16-1,17-1

NCV - **21,** 1-1,2-1,3-1,4-1,5-1,6-1,7-1,8-1,9-1,10-1,11-1,12-1,13-1,14-1,15-1,16-1,17-1,18-1,19-1,20-1,21-1
NIV - **14,** 1-1,2-**2,**3-**2,**4-1,5-1,6-1,7-1,8-1,9-1,10-1,11-1,12-1,13-1,14-1
NKJV - **18,** 1-1,2-1,3-1,4-1,5-1,6-1,7-**2,**8-**2,**9-1,10-1,11-1,12-1,13-1,14-1,15-1,16-1,17-1,18-1
NLT - **11,** 1-1,2-1,3-1,4-1,5-1,6-1,7-1,8-1,9-1,10-1,11-1
NRSV - **14,** 1-1,2-**2,**3-1,4-1,5-1,6-1,7-1,8-1,9-1,10-1,11-1,12-1,13-1,14-1
Conclusion: Six modern versions are more complex than the King James Bible. In an extremely rare turnabout the NCV and NLT are the only modern version that **do not** make the verse more complex.

57. Job 25:6 How much less man, that is a worm? and the son of man, which is a worm?
AV - **17,** 1-1,2-1,3-1,4-1,5-1,6-1,7-1,8-1,9-1,10-1,11-1,12-1,13-1,14-1,15-1,16-1,17-1
ESV - **17,** 1-1,2-1,3-1,4-1,5-1,6-1,7-1,8-**2,**9-1,10-1,11-1,12-1,13-1,14-1,15-1,16-1,17-1
HCSB - **17,** 1-1,2-1,3-1,4-1,5-1,6-1,7-1,8-**2,**9-1,10-1,11-1,12-1,13-1,14-1,15-1,16-1,17-1
NASV - **13,** 1-1,2-1,3-1,4-1,5-1,6-**2,**7-1,8-1,9-1,10-1,11-1,12-1,13-1
NCV - **12,** 1-**2,**2-1,3-1,4-1,5-1,6-1,7-1,8-**2,**9-1,10-1,11-**2,**12-1
NIV - **18,** 1-1,2-1,3-1,4-1,5-1,6-1,7-1,8-1,9-**2,**10-1,11-1,12-1,13-1,14-1,15-1,16-**2,**17-1,18-1
NKJV - **17,** 1-1,2-1,3-1,4-1,5-1,6-1,7-1,8-**2,**9-1,10-1,11-1,12-1,13-1,14-1,15-1,16-1,17-1
NLT - **10,** 1-1,2-**4,**3-**2,**4-1,5-**2,**6-1,7-**2,**8-1,9-1,10-1
NRSV - **17,** 1-1,2-1,3-1,4-1,5-**2,**6-1,7-1,8-1,9-**2,**10-1,11-1,12-**2,**13-**2,**14-1,15-1,16-1,17-1
Conclusion: All eight modern versions are more complex than the King James Bible. Both the NLT and the NRSV have four words that are multi-syllable, but the NLT manages to achieve that with only ten words, and one of those even has four syllables.

58. Job 27:23 Men shall clap their hands at him, and shall hiss him out of his place.
AV - **15,** 1-1,2-1,3-1,4-1,5-1,6-1,7-1,8-1,9-1,10-1,11-1,12-1,13-1,14-1,15-1
ESV - **13,** 1-1,2-1,3-1,4-1,5-1,6-1,7-1,8-**2,**9-1,10-1,11-1,12-1,13-1
HCSB - **12,** 1-1,2-1,3-1,4-1,5-1,6-1,7-1,8-1,9-1,10-1,11-1,12-1
NASV - **14,** 1-1,2-1,3-1,4-1,5-1,6-1,7-1,8-1,9-1,10-1,11-1,12-1,13-1,14-1
NCV - **22,** 1-1,2-1,3-1,4-1,5-1,6-1,7-1,8-1,9-**2,**10-1,11-1,12-1,13-1,14-**2,**15-1,16-1,17-1,18-1,19-1,20-1,21-1,22-1
NIV - **13,** 1-1,2-1,3-1,4-1,5-1,6-**3,**7-1,8-**2,**9-1,10-1,11-1,12-1,13-1
NKJV - **15,** 1-1,2-1,3-1,4-1,5-1,6-1,7-1,8-1,9-1,10-1,11-1,12-1,13-1,14-1,15-1
NLT - **8,** 1-1,2-**3,**3-1,4-1,5-1,6-1,7-1,8-1
NRSV - **13,** 1-1,2-1,3-1,4-1,5-1,6-1,7-1,8-**2,**9-1,10-1,11-1,12-1,13-1
Conclusion: Five modern versions are more complex than the King James Bible.

59. Job 28:14 The depth saith, It is not in me: and the sea saith, It is not with me.
AV - **17,** 1-1,2-1,3-1,4-1,5-1,6-1,7-1,8-1,9-1,10-1,11-1,12-1,13-1,14-1,15-1,16-1,17-1
ESV - **17,** 1-1,2-1,3-1,4-1,5-1,6-1,7-1,8-1,9-1,10-1,11-1,12-1,13-1,14-1,15-1,16-1,17-1
HCSB - **16,** 1-1,2-**2,**3-1,4-1,5-1,6-1,7-1,8-1,9-1,10-1,11-1,12-**2,**13-1,14-1,15-1,16-1
NASV - **17,** 1-1,2-1,3-1,4-1,5-1,6-1,7-1,8-1,9-1,10-1,11-1,12-1,13-1,14-1,15-1,16-1,17-1
NCV - **15,** 1-1,2-1,3-**2,**4-1,5-1,6-1,7-1,8-1,9-1,10-1,11-1,12-1,13-1,14-1,15-1
NIV - **16,** 1-1,2-1,3-1,4-1,5-1,6-1,7-1,8-1,9-1,10-1,11-1,12-1,13-1,14-1,15-1,16-1
NKJV - **17,** 1-1,2-1,3-1,4-1,5-1,6-1,7-1,8-1,9-1,10-1,11-1,12-1,13-1,14-1,15-1,16-1,17-1
NLT - **14,** 1-1,2-1,3-1,4-1,5-1,6-1,7-**2,**8-1,9-1,10-1,11-1,12-1,13-1,14-1
NRSV - **17,** 1-1,2-1,3-1,4-1,5-1,6-1,7-1,8-1,9-1,10-1,11-1,12-1,13-1,14-1,15-1,16-1,17-1

Conclusion: Only three modern versions are more complex than the King James Bible.

60. Job 29:15 I was eyes to the blind, and feet was I to the lame.
AV - **13,** 1-1,2-1,3-1,4-1,5-1,6-1,7-1,8-1,9-1,10-1,11-1,12-1,13-1
ESV - **11,** 1-1,2-1,3-1,4-1,5-1,6-1,7-1,8-1,9-1,10-1,11-1
HCSB - **11,** 1-1,2-1,3-1,4-1,5-1,6-1,7-1,8-1,9-1,10-1,11-1
NASV - **11,** 1-1,2-1,3-1,4-1,5-1,6-1,7-1,8-1,9-1,10-1,11-1
NCV - **11,** 1-1,2-1,3-1,4-1,5-1,6-1,7-1,8-1,9-1,10-1,11-1
NIV - **11,** 1-1,2-1,3-1,4-1,5-1,6-1,7-1,8-1,9-1,10-1,11-1
NKJV - **13,** 1-1,2-1,3-1,4-1,5-1,6-1,7-1,8-1,9-1,10-1,11-1,12-1,13-1
NLT - **12,** 1-1,2-1,3-1,4-1,5-1,6-1,7-1,8-1,9-1,10-1,11-1,12-1
NRSV - **11,** 1-1,2-1,3-1,4-1,5-1,6-1,7-1,8-1,9-1,10-1,11-1
Conclusion: All versions read the same.

61. Job 31:4 Doth not he see my ways, and count all my steps?
AV - **11,** 1-1,2-1,3-1,4-1,5-1,6-1,7-1,8-1,9-1,10-1,11-1
ESV - 11, 1-1,2-1,3-1,4-1,5-1,6-1,7-1,8-**2**,9-1,10-1,11-1
HCSB - 11, 1-1,2-1,3-1,4-1,5-1,6-1,7-1,8-**2**,9-1,10-1,11-1
NASV - 11, 1-1,2-1,3-1,4-1,5-1,6-1,7-1,8-**2**,9-1,10-1,11-1
NCV - 10, 1-1,2-1,3-1,4-1,5-1,6-1,7-**2**,8-1,9-1,10-1
NIV - **11,** 1-1,2-1,3-1,4-1,5-1,6-1,7-1,8-1,9-1,10-1,11-1
NKJV - **11,** 1-1,2-1,3-1,4-1,5-1,6-1,7-1,8-1,9-1,10-1,11-1
NLT - 11, 1-**2**,2-1,3-1,4-**3**,5-1,6-1,7-1,8-**2**,9-1,10-1,11-1
NRSV - 11, 1-1,2-1,3-1,4-1,5-1,6-1,7-1,8-**2**,9-1,10-1,11-1
Conclusion: Six modern versions are more complex than the King James Bible. Once again, the NLT is the most difficult to read.

62. Job 31:20 If his loins have not blessed me, and if he were not warmed with the fleece of my
 sheep;
AV - **19,** 1-1,2-1,3-1,4-1,5-1,6-1,7-1,8-1,9-1,10-1,11-1,12-1,13-1,14-1,15-1,16-1,17-1,18-1,19-1
ESV - 19, 1-1,2-1,3-**2**,4-1,5-1,6-1,7-1,8-1,9-1,10-1,11-1,12-1,13-1,14-1,15-1,16-1,17-1,18-1,19-1
HCSB - 15, 1-1,2-1,3-1,4-1,5-1,6-1,7-1,8-**2**,9-**2**,10-1,11-1,12-1,13-1,14-1,15-1
NASV - **20,** 1-1,2-1,3-1,4-1,5-1,6-1,7-1,8-1,9-1,10-1,11-1,12-1,13-1,14-1,15-1,16-1,17-1,18-1,19-1,20-1
NCV - 15, 1-1,2-**2**,3-1,4-1,5-1,6-**2**,7-1,8-1,9-1,10-1,11-1,12-1,13-1,14-1,15-1
NIV - 16, 1-1,2-1,3-1,4-1,5-1,6-1,7-1,8-1,9-**2**,10-1,11-1,12-1,13-1,14-1,15-1,16-1
NKJV - **19,** 1-1,2-1,3-1,4-1,5-1,6-1,7-1,8-1,9-1,10-1,11-1,12-1,13-1,14-1,15-1,16-1,17-1,18-1,19-1
NLT - 13, 1-1,2-1,3-1,4-1,5-1,6-1,7-**3**,8-1,9-**2**,10-1,11-1,12-1,13-1
NRSV - **17,** 1-1,2-1,3-1,4-1,5-1,6-1,7-1,8-1,9-1,10-1,11-1,12-1,13-1,14-1,15-1,16-1,17-1
Conclusion: Five modern versions are more complex than the King James Bible.

63. Job 39:5 Who hath sent out the wild ass free? or who hath loosed the bands of the wild ass?
AV - **18,** 1-1,2-1,3-1,4-1,5-1,6-1,7-1,8-1,9-1,10-1,11-1,12-1,13-1,14-1,15-1,16-1,17-1,18-1
ESV - 17, 1-1,2-1,3-1,4-1,5-1,6-**2**,7-1,8-1,9-1,10-1,11-1,12-1,13-1,14-1,15-1,16-1,17-**2**
HCSB - 14, 1-1,2-1,3-1,4-1,5-**2**,6-1,7-1,8-**2**,9-1,10-1,11-**2**,12-1,13-1,14-**2**
NASV - 16, 1-1,2-1,3-1,4-1,5-1,6-**2**,7-1,8-1,9-1,10-1,11-1,12-1,13-1,14-1,15-1,16-**2**

NCV - **11,** 1-1,2-1,3-1,4-1,5-**2**,6-1,7-1,8-1,9-**2**,10-1,11-1
NIV - **11,** 1-1,2-1,3-1,4-1,5-**2**,6-1,7-1,8-1,9-**2**,10-1,11-1
NKJV - **13,** 1-1,2-1,3-1,4-1,5-**2**,6-1,7-1,8-1,9-1,10-1,11-1,12-1,13-**3**
NLT - **11,** 1-1,2-1,3-1,4-1,5-**2**,6-1,7-**2**,8-1,9-**2**,10-1,11-1
NRSV - **17,** 1-1,2-1,3-1,4-1,5-1,6-1,7-1,8-1,9-1,10-1,11-1,12-1,13-1,14-1,15-1,16-1,17-1

Conclusion: Seven modern versions are more complex than the King James Bible. Only the NRSV retained the Authorized Version's "ass" where six of the remaining seven changed it to "donkey" both times. But, for some reason the NKJV used "donkey" for the first reference and "onager" in the second. The HCSB is the most difficult to read.

64. Job 41:7 Canst thou fill his skin with barbed irons? or his head with fish spears?
AV - **14,** 1-1,2-1,3-1,4-1,5-1,6-1,7-1,8-1,9-1,10-1,11-1,12-1,13-1,14-1
ESV - **13,** 1-1,2-1,3-1,4-1,5-1,6-1,7-**2**,8-1,9-1,10-1,11-1,12-**2**,13-1
HCSB - **13,** 1-1,2-1,3-1,4-1,5-1,6-1,7-**2**,8-1,9-1,10-1,11-1,12-**2**,13-1
NASV - **13,** 1-1,2-1,3-1,4-1,5-1,6-1,7-**2**,8-1,9-1,10-1,11-1,12-**2**,13-1
NCV - **15,** 1-1,2-1,3-1,4-1,5-1,6-**2**,7-1,8-1,9-1,10-1,11-1,12-1,13-1,14-**2**,15-1
NIV - **13,** 1-1,2-1,3-1,4-1,5-1,6-1,7-**2**,8-1,9-1,10-1,11-1,12-**2**,13-1
NKJV - **13,** 1-1,2-1,3-1,4-1,5-1,6-1,7-**2**,8-1,9-1,10-1,11-1,12-**2**,13-1
NLT - **13,** 1-1,2-1,3-1,4-1,5-1,6-1,7-1,8-1,9-1,10-1,11-1,12-1,13-**2**
NRSV - **13,** 1-1,2-1,3-1,4-1,5-1,6-1,7-**2**,8-1,9-1,10-1,11-1,12-**2**,13-1

Conclusion: All eight modern versions are more complex than the King James Bible.

65. Psalms 18:1 I will love thee, O LORD, my strength.
AV - **8,** 1-1,2-1,3-1,4-1,5-1,6-1,7-1,8-1
ESV - **7,** 1-1,2-1,3-1,4-1,5-1,6-1,7-1
HCSB - **6,** 1-1,2-1,3-1,4-1,5-1,6-1
NASV - **7,** 1-1,2-1,3-1,4-1,5-1,6-1,7-1
NCV - **8,** 1-1,2-1,3-1,4-1,5-1,6-1,7-1,8-1
NIV - **7,** 1-1,2-1,3-1,4-1,5-1,6-1,7-1
NKJV - **8,** 1-1,2-1,3-1,4-1,5-1,6-1,7-1,8-1
NLT - **8,** 1-1,2-1,3-1,4-1,5-1,6-1,7-1,8-1
NRSV - **7,** 1-1,2-1,3-1,4-1,5-1,6-1,7-1

Conclusion: All versions read the same.

66. Psalms 18:31 For who is God save the LORD? or who is a rock save our God?
AV - **15,** 1-1,2-1,3-1,4-1,5-1,6-1,7-1,8-1,9-1,10-1,11-1,12-1,13-1,14-1,15-1
ESV - **15,** 1-1,2-1,3-1,4-1,5-1,6-1,7-1,8-1,9-1,10-1,11-1,12-1,13-**2**,14-1,15-1
HCSB - **15,** 1-1,2-1,3-1,4-1,5-**2**,6-1,7-1,8-1,9-1,10-1,11-1,12-1,13-**2**,14-1,15-1
NASV - **15,** 1-1,2-1,3-1,4-1,5-**2**,6-1,7-1,8-1,9-1,10-1,11-1,12-1,13-**2**,14-1,15-1
NCV - **13,** 1-1,2-1,3-1,4-**2**,5-1,6-1,7-1,8-1,9-1,10-1,11-**2**,12-1,13-1
NIV - **15,** 1-1,2-1,3-1,4-1,5-**2**,6-1,7-1,8-1,9-1,10-1,11-1,12-1,13-**2**,14-1,15-1
NKJV - **15,** 1-1,2-1,3-1,4-1,5-**2**,6-1,7-1,8-1,9-1,10-1,11-1,12-1,13-**2**,14-1,15-1
NLT - **15,** 1-1,2-1,3-1,4-1,5-**2**,6-1,7-1,8-1,9-1,10-1,11-1,12-1,13-1,14-**2**,15-1
NRSV - **15,** 1-1,2-1,3-1,4-1,5-**2**,6-1,7-1,8-1,9-1,10-1,11-1,12-1,13-**2**,14-1,15-1

Conclusion: All eight modern versions are more complex than the King James Bible. With the exception of the NRSV these results mirror those of 2 Samuel 22:32. In 2 Samuel 22:32 the NRSV uses a one syllable word for its fifth word in the verse. In Psalm 18:1 it uses a two syllable word as its fifth word.

67. Psalms 20:9 Save, LORD: let the king hear us when we call.
AV - **10,** 1-1,2-1,3-1,4-1,5-1,6-1,7-1,8-1,9-1,10-1
ESV - 12, 1-1,2-1,3-1,4-1,5-1,6-1,7-1,8-**2**,9-1,10-1,11-1,12-1
HCSB - 16, 1-1,2-1,3-**3**,4-1,5-1,6-1,7-1,8-1,9-**2**,10-1,11-1,12-1,13-1,14-1,15-1,16-1
NASV - 13, 1-1,2-1,3-1,4-1,5-1,6-1,7-**2**,8-1,9-1,10-1,11-1,12-1,13-1
NCV - 11, 1-1,2-1,3-1,4-1,5-**2**,6-1,7-1,8-1,9-1,10-1,11-1
NIV - 10, 1-1,2-1,3-1,4-1,5-1,6-**2**,7-1,8-1,9-1,10-1
NKJV - 10, 1-1,2-1,3-1,4-1,5-1,6-**2**,7-1,8-1,9-1,10-1
NLT - 12, 1-1,2-**3**,3-1,4-1,5-1,6-1,7-1,8-**2**,9-1,10-1,11-1,12-1
NRSV - 12, 1-1,2-**3**,3-1,4-1,5-1,6-1,7-1,8-**2**,9-1,10-1,11-1,12-1
Conclusion: All eight modern versions are more complex than the King James Bible.

68. Psalms 22:19 But be not thou far from me, O LORD: O my strength, haste thee to help me.
AV - **17,** 1-1,2-1,3-1,4-1,5-1,6-1,7-1,8-1,9-1,10-1,11-1,12-1,13-1,14-1,15-1,16-1,17-1
ESV - 18, 1-1,2-1,3-1,4-1,5-1,6-1,7-1,8-1,9-1,10-1,11-1,12-1,13-1,14-1,15-**2**,16-1,17-1,18-1
HCSB - 14, 1-1,2-1,3-1,4-1,5-1,6-1,7-**2**,8-1,9-1,10-1,11-**2**,12-1,13-1,14-1
NASV - 16, 1-1,2-1,3-1,4-1,5-1,6-1,7-1,8-1,9-1,10-1,11-1,12-1,13-**2**,14-1,15-1,16-**2**
NCV - 14, 1-1,2-1,3-1,4-1,5-1,6-**2**,7-1,8-1,9-1,10-1,11-**2**,12-1,13-1,14-1
NIV - 16, 1-1,2-1,3-1,4-1,5-1,6-1,7-1,8-1,9-1,10-1,11-1,12-1,13-**2**,14-1,15-1,16-1
NKJV - 17, 1-1,2-1,3-1,4-1,5-1,6-1,7-1,8-1,9-1,10-1,11-1,12-1,13-1,14-**2**,15-1,16-1,17-1
NLT - 16, 1-1,2-1,3-1,4-1,5-1,6-1,7-**2**,8-1,9-1,10-1,11-1,12-1,13-**2**,14-1,15-1,16-1
NRSV - 17, 1-1,2-1,3-1,4-1,5-1,6-1,7-1,8-1,9-**2**,10-1,11-1,12-1,13-1,14-**2**,15-1,16-1,17-1
Conclusion: All eight modern versions are more complex than the King James Bible.

69. Psalms 25:4 Show me thy ways, O LORD; teach me thy paths.
AV - **10,** 1-1,2-1,3-1,4-1,5-1,6-1,7-1,8-1,9-1,10-1
ESV - **12,** 1-1,2-1,3-1,4-1,5-1,6-1,7-1,8-1,9-1,10-1,11-1,12-1
HCSB - **11,** 1-1,2-1,3-1,4-1,5-1,6-1,7-1,8-1,9-1,10-1,11-1
NASV - **11,** 1-1,2-1,3-1,4-1,5-1,6-1,7-1,8-1,9-1,10-1,11-1
NCV - **10,** 1-1,2-1,3-1,4-1,5-1,6-1,7-1,8-1,9-1,10-1
NIV - **10,** 1-1,2-1,3-1,4-1,5-1,6-1,7-1,8-1,9-1,10-1
NKJV - **10,** 1-1,2-1,3-1,4-1,5-1,6-1,7-1,8-1,9-1,10-1
NLT - 15, 1-1,2-**2**,3-1,4-1,5-1,6-1,7-1,8-1,9-1,10-1,11-1,12-1,13-1,14-1,15-1
NRSV - **12,** 1-1,2-1,3-1,4-1,5-1,6-1,7-1,8-1,9-1,10-1,11-1,12-1
Conclusion: Only the NLT made the verse more complex.

70. Psalms 33:4 For the word of the LORD is right; and all his works are done in truth.
　AV - **16,** 1-1,2-1,3-1,4-1,5-1,6-1,7-1,8-1,9-1,10-1,11-1,12-1,13-1,14-1,15-1,16-1
ESV - 16, 1-1,2-1,3-1,4-1,5-1,6-1,7-1,8-**2**,9-1,10-1,11-1,12-1,13-1,14-1,15-1,16-**3**
HCSB - 14, 1-1,2-1,3-1,4-1,5-1,6-1,7-1,8-1,9-1,10-1,11-1,12-1,13-1,14-**3**
NASV - 16, 1-1,2-1,3-1,4-1,5-1,6-1,7-1,8-**2**,9-1,10-1,11-1,12-1,13-1,14-1,15-1,16-**3**

NCV - **10,** 1-1,2-1,3-1,4-1,5-1,6-**4**,7-1,8-1,9-1,10-1
NIV - 17, 1-1,2-1,3-1,4-1,5-1,6-1,7-1,8-1,9-1,10-1,11-1,12-1,13-**2**,14-1,15-1,16-1,17-1
NKJV - **16,** 1-1,2-1,3-1,4-1,5-1,6-1,7-1,8-1,9-1,10-1,11-1,12-1,13-1,14-1,15-1,16-1
NLT - 15, 1-1,2-1,3-1,4-1,5-1,6-1,7-1,8-1,9-1,10-1,11-1,12-1,13-**4**,14-1,15-1
NRSV - 16, 1-1,2-1,3-1,4-1,5-1,6-1,7-1,8-**2**,9-1,10-1,11-1,12-1,13-1,14-1,15-1,16-**3**
Conclusion: Seven modern versions are more complex than the King James Bible.

71. Psalms 34:9 O fear the LORD, ye his saints: for there is no want to them that fear him.
AV - **17,** 1-1,2-1,3-1,4-1,5-1,6-1,7-1,8-1,9-1,10-1,11-1,12-1,13-1,14-1,15-1,16-1,17-1
ESV - **15,** 1-1,2-1,3-1,4-1,5-1,6-1,7-1,8-1,9-1,10-1,11-1,12-1,13-1,14-1,15-1
HCSB - 13, 1-1,2-1,3-1,4-1,5-1,6-1,7-1,8-1,9-1,10-1,11-1,12-1,13-**2**
NASV - **17,** 1-1,2-1,3-1,4-1,5-1,6-1,7-1,8-1,9-1,10-1,11-1,12-1,13-1,14-1,15-1,16-1,17-1
NCV - 17, 1-1,2-1,3-**2**,4-1,5-1,6-1,7-1,8-1,9-1,10-1,11-1,12-1,13-1,14-1,15-**4**,16-1,17-1
NIV - 13, 1-1,2-1,3-1,4-1,5-1,6-1,7-1,8-1,9-1,10-1,11-1,12-1,13-**2**
NKJV - **16,** 1-1,2-1,3-1,4-1,5-1,6-1,7-1,8-1,9-1,10-1,11-1,12-1,13-1,14-1,15-1,16-1
NLT - 17, 1-1,2-1,3-1,4-1,5-1,6-**2**,7-**2**,8-1,9-1,10-1,11-1,12-1,13-1,14-1,15-1,16-1,17-1
NRSV - 16, 1-1,2-1,3-1,4-1,5-1,6-1,7-**2**,8-1,9-1,10-1,11-1,12-1,13-1,14-1,15-1,16-1
Conclusion: Five modern versions are more complex than the King James Bible.

72. Psalm 37:31 The law of his God is in his heart; none of his steps shall slide.
AV - **15,** 1-1,2-1,3-1,4-1,5-1,6-1,7-1,8-1,9-1,10-1,11-1,12-1,13-1,14-1,15-1
ESV - **14,** 1-1,2-1,3-1,4-1,5-1,6-1,7-1,8-1,9-1,10-1,11-1,12-1,13-1,14-1
HCSB - 15, 1-1,2-**3**,3-1,4-1,5-1,6-1,7-1,8-1,9-1,10-1,11-1,12-1,13-1,14-1,15-**2**
NASV - **14,** 1-1,2-1,3-1,4-1,5-1,6-1,7-1,8-1,9-1,10-1,11-1,12-1,13-1,14-1
NCV - 17, 1-1,2-**2**,3-1,4-1,5-1,6-1,7-1,8-1,9-1,10-1,11-1,12-1,13-1,14-1,15-1,16-1,17-1
NIV - **14,** 1-1,2-1,3-1,4-1,5-1,6-1,7-1,8-1,9-1,10-1,11-1,12-1,13-1,14-1
NKJV - **15,** 1-1,2-1,3-1,4-1,5-1,6-1,7-1,8-1,9-1,10-1,11-1,12-1,13-1,14-1,15-1
NLT - 15, 1-1,2-1,3-1,4-1,5-1,6-1,7-1,8-1,9-1,10-1,11-**2**,12-1,13-1,14-1,15-1
NRSV - **14,** 1-1,2-1,3-1,4-1,5-1,6-1,7-1,8-1,9-1,10-1,11-1,12-1,13-1,14-1
Conclusion: Only three modern versions are more complex than the King James Bible.

73. Psalms 38:15 For in thee, O LORD, do I hope: thou wilt hear, O Lord my God.
AV - **15,** 1-1,2-1,3-1,4-1,5-1,6-1,7-1,8-1,9-1,10-1,11-1,12-1,13-1,14-1,15-1
ESV - 18, 1-1,2-1,3-1,4-1,5-1,6-1,7-1,8-1,9-1,10-1,11-1,12-1,13-1,14-1,15-1,16-1,17-1,18-**2**
HCSB - 13, 1-1,2-1,3-1,4-1,5-1,6-1,7-1,8-1,9-1,10-**2**,11-1,12-1,13-1
NASV - 14, 1-1,2-1,3-1,4-1,5-1,6-1,7-1,8-1,9-1,10-**2**,11-1,12-1,13-1,14-1
NCV - 11, 1-1,2-1,3-1,4-1,5-1,6-1,7-**2**,8-1,9-1,10-1,11-1
NIV - 13, 1-1,2-1,3-1,4-1,5-1,6-1,7-1,8-1,9-**2**,10-1,11-1,12-1,13-1
NKJV - **14,** 1-1,2-1,3-1,4-1,5-1,6-1,7-1,8-1,9-1,10-1,11-1,12-1,13-1,14-1
NLT - 17, 1-1,2-1,3-1,4-**2**,5-1,6-1,7-1,8-1,9-1,10-1,11-**2**,12-1,13-1,14-1,15-1,16-1,17-1
NRSV - 20, 1-1,2-1,3-1,4-1,5-1,6-1,7-1,8-1,9-1,10-1,11-1,12-1,13-1,14-1,15-1,16-1,17-1,18-1,19-1,20-**2**
Conclusion: Seven modern versions are more complex than the King James Bible.

74. Psalms 39:7 And now, Lord, what wait I for? my hope is in thee.
AV - **12,** 1-1,2-1,3-1,4-1,5-1,6-1,7-1,8-1,9-1,10-1,11-1,12-1

ESV - **14,** 1-1,2-1,3-1,4-1,5-1,6-1,7-1,8-1,9-1,10-1,11-1,12-1,13-1,14-1
HCSB - **12,** 1-1,2-1,3-1,4-1,5-1,6-1,7-1,8-1,9-1,10-1,11-1,12-1
NASV - **13,** 1-1,2-1,3-1,4-1,5-1,6-1,7-1,8-1,9-1,10-1,11-1,12-1,13-1
NCV - **11,** 1-1,2-1,3-1,4-1,5-1,6-1,7-1,8-1,9-1,10-1,11-1
NIV - **13,** 1-1,2-1,3-1,4-1,5-1,6-1,7-1,8-1,9-1,10-1,11-1,12-1,13-1
NKJV - **13,** 1-1,2-1,3-1,4-1,5-1,6-1,7-1,8-1,9-1,10-1,11-1,12-1,13-1
NLT - **15,** 1-1,2-1,3-1,4-1,5-1,6-1,7-1,8-1,9-1,10-1,11-1,12-1,13-1,14-1,15-1
NRSV - **14,** 1-1,2-1,3-1,4-1,5-1,6-1,7-1,8-1,9-1,10-1,11-1,12-1,13-1,14-1
Conclusion: All versions read the same.

75. Psalms 50:13 Will I eat the flesh of bulls, or drink the blood of goats?
AV - **13,** 1-1,2-1,3-1,4-1,5-1,6-1,7-1,8-1,9-1,10-1,11-1,12-1,13-1
ESV - **13,** 1-1,2-1,3-1,4-1,5-1,6-1,7-1,8-1,9-1,10-1,11-1,12-1,13-1
HCSB - **13,** 1-1,2-1,3-1,4-1,5-1,6-1,7-1,8-1,9-1,10-1,11-1,12-1,13-1
NASV - **14,** 1-1,2-1,3-1,4-1,5-1,6-1,7-1,8-1,9-1,10-1,11-1,12-1,13-1,14-1
NCV - **13,** 1-1,2-1,3-1,4-1,5-1,6-1,7-1,8-1,9-1,10-1,11-1,12-1,13-1
NIV - **13,** 1-1,2-1,3-1,4-1,5-1,6-1,7-1,8-1,9-1,10-1,11-1,12-1,13-1
NKJV - **13,** 1-1,2-1,3-1,4-1,5-1,6-1,7-1,8-1,9-1,10-1,11-1,12-1,13-1
NLT - **14,** 1-1,2-1,3-1,4-1,5-1,6-1,7-1,8-1,9-1,10-1,11-1,12-1,13-1,14-1
NRSV - **13,** 1-1,2-1,3-1,4-1,5-1,6-1,7-1,8-1,9-1,10-1,11-1,12-1,13-1
Conclusion: All versions read the same.

76. Psalms 54:1 Save me, O God, by thy name, and judge me by thy strength.
AV - **13,** 1-1,2-1,3-1,4-1,5-1,6-1,7-1,8-1,9-1,10-1,11-1,12-1,13-1
ESV - **13,** 1-1,2-1,3-1,4-1,5-1,6-1,7-1,8-1,9-**3**,10-1,11-1,12-1,13-1
HCSB - **12,** 1-1,2-1,3-1,4-1,5-1,6-1,7-1,8-**3**,9-1,10-1,11-1,12-1
NASV - **13,** 1-1,2-1,3-1,4-1,5-1,6-1,7-1,8-1,9-**3**,10-1,11-1,12-1,13-1
NCV - **16,** 1-1,2-1,3-1,4-**2**,5-1,6-1,7-1,8-1,9-1,10-1,11-1,12-1,13-1,14-1,15-1,16-**3**
NIV - **12,** 1-1,2-1,3-1,4-1,5-1,6-1,7-1,8-**3**,9-1,10-1,11-1,12-1
NKJV - **13,** 1-1,2-1,3-1,4-1,5-1,6-1,7-1,8-1,9-**3**,10-1,11-1,12-1,13-1
NLT - **14,** 1-1,2-1,3-1,4-**2**,5-1,6-1,7-1,8-**2**,9-1,10-**2**,11-1,12-1,13-1,14-1
NRSV - **13,** 1-1,2-1,3-1,4-1,5-1,6-1,7-1,8-1,9-**3**,10-1,11-1,12-1,13-1
Conclusion: All eight modern versions are more complex than the King James Bible.

77. Psalms 54:2 Hear my prayer, O God; give ear to the words of my mouth.
AV - **13,** 1-1,2-1,3-1,4-1,5-1,6-1,7-1,8-1,9-1,10-1,11-1,12-1,13-1
ESV - **13,** 1-1,2-1,3-1,4-1,5-1,6-1,7-1,8-1,9-1,10-1,11-1,12-1,13-1
HCSB - **11,** 1-1,2-1,3-1,4-1,5-**2**,6-1,7-1,8-1,9-1,10-1,11-1
NASV - **13,** 1-1,2-1,3-1,4-1,5-1,6-1,7-1,8-1,9-1,10-1,11-1,12-1,13-1
NCV - **9,** 1-1,2-1,3-1,4-1,5-**2**,6-1,7-1,8-1,9-1
NIV - **12,** 1-1,2-1,3-1,4-1,5-1,6-**2**,7-1,8-1,9-1,10-1,11-1,12-1
NKJV - **13,** 1-1,2-1,3-1,4-1,5-1,6-1,7-1,8-1,9-1,10-1,11-1,12-1,13-1
NLT - **11,** 1-**2**,2-1,3-1,4-1,5-1,6-1,7-1,8-**3**,9-1,10-1,11-1
NRSV - **13,** 1-1,2-1,3-1,4-1,5-1,6-1,7-1,8-1,9-1,10-1,11-1,12-1,13-1
Conclusion: Four modern versions are more complex than the King James Bible.

78. Psalm 56:10 In God will I praise his word: in the LORD will I praise his word.
AV - **15,** 1-1,2-1,3-1,4-1,5-1,6-1,7-1,8-1,9-1,10-1,11-1,12-1,13-1,14-1,15-1
ESV - **13,** 1-1,2-1,3-1,4-1,5-1,6-1,7-1,8-1,9-1,10-1,11-1,12-1,13-1
HCSB - **13,** 1-1,2-1,3-1,4-1,5-1,6-1,7-1,8-1,9-1,10-1,11-1,12-1,13-1
NASV - **13,** 1-1,2-1,3-1,4-1,5-1,6-1,7-1,8-1,9-1,10-1,11-1,12-1,13-1
NCV - **15,** 1-1,2-1,3-1,4-1,5-1,6-1,7-1,8-1,9-1,10-1,11-1,12-1,13-1,14-1,15-1
NIV - **13,** 1-1,2-1,3-1,4-1,5-1,6-1,7-1,8-1,9-1,10-1,11-1,12-1,13-1
NKJV - **15,** 1-1,2-1,3-1,4-1,5-1,6-1,7-1,8-1,9-1,10-1,11-1,12-1,13-1,14-1,15-1
NLT - **18,** 1-1,2-1,3-1,4-1,5-1,6-1,7-1,8-**2**,9-1,10-1,11-1,12-1,13-1,14-1,15-1,16-1,17-1,18-**2**
NRSV - **13,** 1-1,2-1,3-1,4-1,5-1,6-1,7-1,8-1,9-1,10-1,11-1,12-1,13-1
Conclusion: Only the NLT made the verse more complex.

79. Psalm 57:7 My heart is fixed, O God, my heart is fixed: I will sing and give praise.
AV - **16,** 1-1,2-1,3-1,4-1,5-1,6-1,7-1,8-1,9-1,10-1,11-1,12-1,13-1,14-1,15-1,16-1
ESV - **16,** 1-1,2-1,3-1,4-**2**,5-1,6-1,7-1,8-1,9-1,10-**2**,11-1,12-1,13-1,14-1,15-1,16-**3**
HCSB - **16,** 1-1,2-1,3-1,4-**2**,5-1,6-1,7-1,8-1,9-1,10-**2**,11-1,12-1,13-1,14-1,15-1,16-**2**
NASV - **18,** 1-1,2-1,3-1,4-**2**,5-1,6-1,7-1,8-1,9-1,10-**2**,11-1,12-1,13-1,14-1,15-1,16-1,17-1,18-**2**
NCV - **15,** 1-1,2-1,3-1,4-**2**,5-1,6-1,7-1,8-1,9-**2**,10-1,11-1,12-1,13-1,14-1,15-1
NIV - **16,** 1-1,2-1,3-1,4-**2**,5-1,6-1,7-1,8-1,9-1,10-**2**,11-1,12-1,13-1,14-1,15-1,16-**2**
NKJV - **16,** 1-1,2-1,3-1,4-**2**,5-1,6-1,7-1,8-1,9-1,10-**2**,11-1,12-1,13-1,14-1,15-1,16-1
NLT - **19,** 1-1,2-1,3-1,4-**3**,5-1,6-1,7-1,8-1,9-1,10-1,11-1,12-**3**,13-1,14-**2**,15-1,16-1,17-1,18-1,19-**2**
NRSV - **16,** 1-1,2-1,3-1,4-**2**,5-1,6-1,7-1,8-1,9-1,10-**2**,11-1,12-1,13-1,14-1,15-1,16-**3**
Conclusion: All eight modern versions are more complex than the King James Bible. The NLT is the most difficult to read.

80. Psalms 63:4 Thus will I bless thee while I live: I will lift up my hands in thy name.
AV - **17,** 1-1,2-1,3-1,4-1,5-1,6-1,7-1,8-1,9-1,10-1,11-1,12-1,13-1,14-1,15-1,16-1,17-1
ESV - **19,** 1-1,2-1,3-1,4-1,5-1,6-1,7-1,8-1,9-1,10-1,11-1,12-1,13-1,14-1,15-1,16-1,17-1,18-1,19-1
HCSB - **19,** 1-1,2-1,3-1,4-1,5-1,6-1,7-1,8-1,9-1,10-1,11-1,12-1,13-1,14-1,15-1,16-1,17-1,18-1,19-1
NASV - **19,** 1-1,2-1,3-1,4-1,5-1,6-1,7-1,8-1,9-1,10-1,11-1,12-1,13-1,14-1,15-1,16-1,17-1,18-1,19-1
NCV - **20,** 1-1,2-1,3-1,4-1,5-1,6-1,7-1,8-1,9-1,10-1,11-1,12-1,13-1,14-1,15-1,16-1,17-1,18-1,19-1,20-1
NIV - **19,** 1-1,2-1,3-1,4-1,5-1,6-1,7-1,8-1,9-1,10-1,11-1,12-1,13-1,14-1,15-1,16-1,17-1,18-1,19-1
NKJV - **17,** 1-1,2-1,3-1,4-1,5-1,6-1,7-1,8-1,9-1,10-1,11-1,12-1,13-1,14-1,15-1,16-1,17-1
NLT - **17,** 1-1,2-1,3-1,4-1,5-1,6-1,7-1,8-1,9-1,10-**2**,11-1,12-1,13-1,14-1,15-1,16-1,17-1
NRSV -**21,** 1-1,2-1,3-1,4-1,5-1,6-1,7-1,8-1,9-1,10-1,11-1,12-1,13-1,14-1,15-1,16-1,17-1,18-1,19-1,20-1,21-1
Conclusion: Only the NLT made the verse more complex.

81. Psalms 67:7 God shall bless us; and all the ends of the earth shall fear him.
AV - **14,** 1-1,2-1,3-1,4-1,5-1,6-1,7-1,8-1,9-1,10-1,11-1,12-1,13-1,14-1
ESV - **13,** 1-1,2-1,3-1,4-1,5-1,6-1,7-1,8-1,9-1,10-1,11-1,12-1,13-1
HCSB - **14,** 1-1,2-1,3-1,4-1,5-1,6-1,7-1,8-1,9-1,10-1,11-1,12-1,13-1,14-1
NASV - **13,** 1-1,2-1,3-1,4-1,5-1,6-1,7-1,8-1,9-1,10-1,11-1,12-1,13-1
NCV - **12,** 1-1,2-**2**,3-1,4-1,5-**2**,6-1,7-**2**,8-1,9-1,10-1,11-1,12-1
NIV - **14,** 1-1,2-1,3-1,4-1,5-1,6-1,7-1,8-1,9-1,10-1,11-1,12-1,13-1,14-1
NKJV - **14,** 1-1,2-1,3-1,4-1,5-1,6-1,7-1,8-1,9-1,10-1,11-1,12-1,13-1,14-1

NLT - **14,** 1-1,2-1,3-1,4-1,5-1,6-1,7-**2**,8-1,9-**2**,10-1,11-**2**,12-1,13-1,14-1
NRSV - **15,** 1-1,2-1,3-**3**,4-1,5-1,6-1,7-1,8-1,9-1,10-1,11-1,12-1,13-1,14-**2**,15-1
Conclusion: Only three modern versions are more complex than the King James Bible.

82. Psalms 71:5 For thou art my hope, O Lord GOD: thou art my trust from my youth.
AV - **15,** 1-1,2-1,3-1,4-1,5-1,6-1,7-1,8-1,9-1,10-1,11-1,12-1,13-1,14-1,15-1
ESV - **14,** 1-1,2-1,3-1,4-1,5-1,6-1,7-1,8-1,9-1,10-1,11-1,12-1,13-1,14-1
HCSB - 12, 1-1,2-1,3-1,4-1,5-1,6-1,7-1,8-1,9-**3**,10-1,11-1,12-1
NASV - 15, 1-1,2-1,3-1,4-1,5-1,6-1,7-1,8-1,9-1,10-1,11-1,12-**3**,13-1,14-1,15-1
NCV - 13, 1-1,2-1,3-1,4-1,5-1,6-1,7-1,8-**2**,9-1,10-1,11-1,12-1,13-1
NIV - 14, 1-1,2-1,3-1,4-1,5-1,6-1,7-1,8-**3**,9-1,10-1,11-**3**,12-1,13-1,14-1
NKJV - **15,** 1-1,2-1,3-1,4-1,5-1,6-1,7-1,8-1,9-1,10-1,11-1,12-1,13-1,14-1,15-1
NLT - 14, 1-1,2-1,3-1,4-**2**,5-1,6-1,7-1,8-1,9-**2**,10-1,11-1,12-1,13-1,14-**2**
NRSV - **14,** 1-1,2-1,3-1,4-1,5-1,6-1,7-1,8-1,9-1,10-1,11-1,12-1,13-1,14-1
Conclusion: Five modern versions made the verse more complex. As Psalm 68:15 illustrated how the NKJV often slavishly follows the NASV this verse indicates its other favorite version to duplicate, the King James Bible.

83. Psalms 71:12 O God, be not far from me: O my God, make haste for my help.
AV - **15,** 1-1,2-1,3-1,4-1,5-1,6-1,7-1,8-1,9-1,10-1,11-1,12-1,13-1,14-1,15-1
ESV - **15,** 1-1,2-1,3-1,4-1,5-1,6-1,7-1,8-1,9-1,10-1,11-1,12-1,13-1,14-1,15-1
HCSB - 13, 1-1,2-1,3-1,4-1,5-1,6-1,7-1,8-1,9-1,10-**2**,11-1,12-1,13-1
NASV - 15, 1-1,2-1,3-1,4-1,5-1,6-1,7-1,8-1,9-1,10-1,11-1,12-**2**,13-1,14-1,15-1
NCV - 11, 1-1,2-1,3-1,4-1,5-1,6-1,7-1,8-**2**,9-1,10-1,11-1
NIV - 15, 1-1,2-1,3-1,4-1,5-1,6-1,7-1,8-1,9-**2**,10-1,11-1,12-1,13-1,14-1,15-1
NKJV - **16,** 1-1,2-1,3-1,4-1,5-1,6-1,7-1,8-1,9-1,10-1,11-1,12-1,13-1,14-1,15-1,16-1
NLT - 12, 1-1,2-1,3-1,4-1,5-**2**,6-1,7-1,8-1,9-**2**,10-1,11-1,12-1
NRSV - **16,** 1-1,2-1,3-1,4-1,5-1,6-1,7-1,8-1,9-1,10-1,11-1,12-1,13-1,14-1,15-1,16-1
Conclusion: Five modern versions are more complex than the King James Bible. The NLT is the most difficult to read.

84. Psalms 73:4 For there are no bands in their death: but their strength is firm.
AV - **13,** 1-1,2-1,3-1,4-1,5-1,6-1,7-1,8-1,9-1,10-1,11-1,12-1,13-1
ESV - 13, 1-1,2-1,3-1,4-1,5-1,6-**2**,7-1,8-1,9-**2**,10-1,11-1,12-1,13-1
HCSB - 14, 1-1,2-1,3-1,4-**2**,5-1,6-**2**,7-1,8-1,9-1,10-1,11-**2**,12-1,13-1,14-1
NASV - 13, 1-1,2-1,3-1,4-1,5-1,6-1,7-1,8-1,9-1,10-1,11-**2**,12-1,13-1
NCV - 9 , 1-1,2-1,3-1,4-**3**,5-1,6-1,7-**2**,8-1,9-1
NIV - 10, 1-1,2-1,3-1,4-**2**,5-1,6-**2**,7-1,8-**2**,9-1,10-1
NKJV - **13,** 1-1,2-1,3-1,4-1,5-1,6-1,7-1,8-1,9-1,10-1,11-1,12-1,13-1
NLT - 14, 1-1,2-1,3-1,4-1,5-1,6-**2**,7-1,8-1,9-**2**,10-1,11-1,12-**2**,13-1,14-1
NRSV - 11, 1-1,2-1,3-1,4-1,5-1,6-1,7-**2**,8-1,9-1,10-1,11-1
Conclusion: Seven modern versions are more complex than the King James Bible.

86. Psalms 73:21 Thus my heart was grieved, and I was pricked in my reins.
AV - **12,** 1-1,2-1,3-1,4-1,5-1,6-1,7-1,8-1,9-1,10-1,11-1,12-1

ESV - 11, 1-1,2-1,3-1,4-1,5-**3**,6-1,7-1,8-1,9-1,10-1,11-1
HCSB - 10, 1-1,2-1,3-**2**,4-**3**,5-1,6-1,7-**3**,8-**2**,9-1,10-**2**
NASV - 10, 1-1,2-1,3-1,4-1,5-**3**,6-1,7-1,8-1,9-1,10-**2**
NCV - 9, 1-1,2-1,3-1,4-1,5-1,6-1,7-1,8-1,9-**2**
NIV - 9, 1-1,2-1,3-1,4-1,5-1,6-1,7-1,8-**2**,9-**3**
NKJV - **12,** 1-1,2-1,3-1,4-1,5-1,6-1,7-1,8-1,9-1,10-1,11-1,12-1
NLT - 15, 1-1,2-1,3-**3**,4-1,5-1,6-1,7-1,8-**2**,9-1,10-1,11-1,12-1,13-1,14-1,15-**2**
NRSV - 11, 1-1,2-1,3-1,4-1,5-**3**,6-1,7-1,8-1,9-1,10-1,11-1
Conclusion: Seven modern versions are more complex than the King James Bible. The HCSB is the most difficult to read.

87. Psalms 75:5 Lift not up your horn on high: speak not with a stiff neck.
AV - **13,** 1-1,2-1,3-1,4-1,5-1,6-1,7-1,8-1,9-1,10-1,11-1,12-1,13-1
ESV - 13, 1-1,2-1,3-1,4-1,5-1,6-1,7-1,8-1,9-1,10-1,11-1,12-**2**,13-1
HCSB - 11, 1-1,2-1,3-1,4-1,5-1,6-1,7-**2**,8-**2**,9-1,10-1,11-**4**
NASV - 14, 1-1,2-1,3-1,4-1,5-1,6-1,7-1,8-1,9-1,10-1,11-1,12-1,13-**4**,14-1
NCV - 11, 1-1,2-1,3-1,4-1,5-1,6-**2**,7-**2**,8-**2**,9-1,10-1,11-**2**
NIV - 13, 1-1,2-1,3-1,4-1,5-1,6-**2**,7-**2**,8-1,9-1,10-1,11-1,12-**2**,13-1
NKJV - **15,** 1-1,2-1,3-1,4-1,5-1,6-1,7-1,8-1,9-1,10-1,11-1,12-1,13-1,14-1,15-1
NLT - 14, 1-1,2-1,3-1,4-1,5-1,6-**3**,7-1,8-1,9-**2**,10-1,11-1,12-1,13-1,14-**3**
NRSV - 13, 1-1,2-1,3-1,4-1,5-1,6-1,7-1,8-1,9-1,10-1,11-1,12-**3**,13-1
Conclusion: Seven modern versions are more complex than the King James Bible.

87. Psalms 84:5 Blessed is the man whose strength is in thee; in whose heart are the ways of them.
AV - **17,** 1-1,2-1,3-1,4-1,5-1,6-1,7-1,8-1,9-1,10-1,11-1,12-1,13-1,14-1,15-1,16-1,17-1
ESV - 16, 1-1,2-1,3-1,4-1,5-1,6-1,7-1,8-1,9-1,10-1,11-1,12-1,13-1,14-**2**,15-1,16-**2**
HCSB - 15, 1-**2**,2-1,3-1,4-**2**,5-1,6-1,7-1,8-1,9-1,10-1,11-1,12-1,13-1,14-1,15-**3**
NASV - 18, 1-1,2-1,3-1,4-1,5-1,6-1,7-1,8-1,9-1,10-1,11-1,12-1,13-1,14-1,15-1,16-**2**,17-1,18-**2**
NCV - 14, 1-**2**,2-1,3-1,4-1,5-1,6-1,7-1,8-1,9-1,10-1,11-1,12-**2**,13-1,14-**4**
NIV - 15, 1-1,2-1,3-1,4-1,5-1,6-1,7-1,8-1,9-1,10-1,11-1,12-1,13-1,14-1,15-**3**
NKJV - 15, 1-1,2-1,3-1,4-1,5-1,6-1,7-1,8-1,9-1,10-1,11-1,12-1,13-1,14-1,15-**3**
NLT - 20, 1-1,2-1,3-1,4-1,5-1,6-1,7-1,8-1,9-1,10-1,11-1,12-1,13-1,14-1,15-1,16-1,17-1,18-**3**,19-1,20-**4**
NRSV - 16, 1-**2**,2-1,3-1,4-1,5-1,6-1,7-1,8-1,9-1,10-1,11-1,12-1,13-1,14-**2**,15-1,16-**2**
Conclusion: All eight modern versions are more complex than the King James Bible.

88. Psalms 95:5 The sea is his, and he made it: and his hands formed the dry land.
AV - **15,** 1-1,2-1,3-1,4-1,5-1,6-1,7-1,8-1,9-1,10-1,11-1,12-1,13-1,14-1,15-1
ESV - **15,** 1-1,2-1,3-1,4-1,5-1,6-1,7-1,8-1,9-1,10-1,11-1,12-1,13-1,14-1,15-1
HCSB - **13,** 1-1,2-1,3-1,4-1,5-1,6-1,7-1,8-1,9-1,10-1,11-1,12-1,13-1
NASV - **18,** 1-1,2-1,3-1,4-1,5-1,6-1,7-1,8-1,9-1,10-1,11-1,12-1,13-1,14-1,15-1,16-1,17-1,18-1
NCV - 16, 1-1,2-1,3-1,4-**2**,5-1,6-1,7-1,8-1,9-1,10-**3**,11-1,12-1,13-1,14-1,15-1,16-1
NIV - **15,** 1-1,2-1,3-1,4-1,5-1,6-1,7-1,8-1,9-1,10-1,11-1,12-1,13-1,14-1,15-1
NKJV - **15,** 1-1,2-1,3-1,4-1,5-1,6-1,7-1,8-1,9-1,10-1,11-1,12-1,13-1,14-1,15-1
NLT - 16, 1-1,2-1,3-**2**,4-1,5-1,6-1,7-1,8-1,9-1,10-1,11-1,12-1,13-1,14-1,15-1,16-1
NRSV - **17,** 1-1,2-1,3-1,4-1,5-1,6-1,7-1,8-1,9-1,10-1,11-1,12-1,13-1,14-1,15-1,16-1,17-1

Conclusion: Only the NCV and the NLT made the verse more complex.

89. Psalms 102:27 But thou art the same, and thy years shall have no end.
AV - **12,** 1-1,2-1,3-1,4-1,5-1,6-1,7-1,8-1,9-1,10-1,11-1,12-1
ESV - **11,** 1-1,2-1,3-1,4-1,5-1,6-1,7-1,8-1,9-1,10-1,11-1
HCSB - **11,** 1-1,2-1,3-1,4-1,5-1,6-1,7-1,8-1,9-1,10-**2**,11-1
NASV - **14,** 1-1,2-1,3-1,4-1,5-1,6-1,7-1,8-1,9-1,10-1,11-1,12-1,13-1,14-1
NCV - **10,** 1-1,2-1,3-**2**,4-1,5-1,6-1,7-1,8-1,9-**2**,10-1
NIV - **11,** 1-1,2-1,3-**2**,4-1,5-1,6-1,7-1,8-1,9-1,10-**2**,11-1
NKJV - **12,** 1-1,2-1,3-1,4-1,5-1,6-1,7-1,8-1,9-1,10-1,11-1,12-1
NLT - **9,** 1-1,2-1,3-1,4-**2**,5-1,6-1,7-1,8-1,9-**3**
NRSV - **11,** 1-1,2-1,3-1,4-1,5-1,6-1,7-1,8-1,9-1,10-1,11-1
Conclusion: Four modern versions are more complex than the King James Bible.

90. Psalms 104:17 Where the birds make their nests: as for the stork, the fir trees are her house.
AV - **16,** 1-1,2-1,3-1,4-1,5-1,6-1,7-1,8-1,9-1,10-1,11-1,12-1,13-1,14-1,15-1,16-1
ESV - **16,** 1-1,2-1,3-1,4-1,5-1,6-1,7-1,8-1,9-1,10-1,11-1,12-1,13-1,14-1,15-1,16-1
HCSB - **15,** 1-1,2-1,3-1,4-1,5-1,6-1,7-1,8-1,9-1,10-1,11-1,12-1,13-1,14-1,15-1
NASV - **15,** 1-1,2-1,3-1,4-1,5-1,6-1,7-1,8-1,9-1,10-1,11-1,12-1,13-1,14-1,15-1
NCV - **14,** 1-1,2-1,3-1,4-1,5-1,6-1,7-1,8-1,9-1,10-1,11-1,12-1,13-1,14-1
NIV - **15,** 1-1,2-1,3-1,4-1,5-1,6-1,7-1,8-1,9-1,10-1,11-1,12-1,13-1,14-1,15-1
NKJV - **15,** 1-1,2-1,3-1,4-1,5-1,6-1,7-1,8-1,9-1,10-1,11-1,12-1,13-1,14-1,15-1
NLT - **15,** 1-1,2-1,3-1,4-1,5-1,6-1,7-1,8-1,9-1,10-1,11-1,12-1,13-1,14-1,15-**3**
NRSV - **16,** 1-1,2-1,3-1,4-1,5-1,6-1,7-1,8-1,9-1,10-1,11-1,12-1,13-1,14-1,15-1,16-1
Conclusion: Only the NLT made the verse more complex.

91. Psalms 108:11 Wilt not thou, O God, who hast cast us off? and wilt not thou, O God, go forth with our hosts?
AV - **21,** 1-1,2-1,3-1,4-1,5-1,6-1,7-1,8-1,9-1,10-1,11-1,12-1,13-1,14-1,15-1,16-1,17-1,18-1,19-1,20-1,21-1
ESV - **17,** 1-1,2-1,3-1,4-**3**,5-1,6-1,7-1,8-1,9-1,10-1,11-1,12-1,13-1,14-1,15-1,16-1,17-**2**
HCSB - **15,** 1-1,2-1,3-1,4-**3**,5-1,6-1,7-1,8-1,9-1,10-1,11-1,12-1,13-1,14-1,15-**2**
NASV - **19,** 1-1,2-1,3-1,4-**2**,5-1,6-1,7-**3**,8-1,9-1,10-1,11-1,12-1,13-1,14-1,15-1,16-1,17-**2**,18-1,19-1
NCV - **14,** 1-1,2-**2**,3-1,4-1,5-**3**,6-1,7-1,8-1,9-1,10-1,11-1,12-1,13-1,14-**2**
NIV - **19,** 1-1,2-1,3-1,4-1,5-1,6-1,7-1,8-1,9-1,10-**3**,11-1,12-1,13-1,14-**2**,15-1,16-1,17-1,18-1,19-**2**
NKJV - **22,** 1-1,2-1,3-1,4-1,5-1,6-1,7-1,8-1,9-1,10-1,11-1,12-1,13-1,14-1,15-1,16-1,17-1,18-1,19-1,20-1,21-1,22-**2**
NLT - **14,** 1-1,2-1,3-**3**,4-1,5-1,6-1,7-1,8-1,9-1,10-**2**,11-1,12-1,13-1,14-**2**
NRSV - **17,** 1-1,2-1,3-1,4-**3**,5-1,6-1,7-1,8-1,9-1,10-1,11-1,12-1,13-1,14-1,15-1,16-1,17-**2**
Conclusion: All eight modern versions are more complex than the King James Bible.

92. Psalms 109:1 Hold not thy peace, O God of my praise;
AV - **9,** 1-1,2-1,3-1,4-1,5-1,6-1,7-1,8-1,9-1
ESV - **8,** 1-1,2-1,3-**2**,4-1,5-1,6-1,7-1,8-1
HCSB - **8,** 1-1,2-1,3-1,4-1,5-1,6-1,7-1,8-**2**
NASV - **9,** 1-1,2-1,3-1,4-1,5-1,6-1,7-1,8-1,9-**2**

NCV - **8,** 1-1,2-1,3-1,4-1,5-1,6-1,7-1,8-**2**
NIV - **9,** 1-1,2-1,3-1,4-1,5-1,6-1,7-1,8-**2**,9-**2**
NKJV - **9,** 1-1,2-1,3-1,4-**2**,5-1,6-1,7-1,8-1,9-1
NLT - **10,** 1-1,2-1,3-1,4-1,5-1,6-1,7-1,8-**2**,9-1,10-**2**
NRSV - **9,** 1-1,2-1,3-1,4-**2**,5-1,6-1,7-1,8-1,9-1
Conclusion: All eight modern versions are more complex than the King James Bible.

93. Psalms 109:27 That they may know that this is thy hand; that thou, LORD, hast done it.
AV - **15,** 1-1,2-1,3-1,4-1,5-1,6-1,7-1,8-1,9-1,10-1,11-1,12-1,13-1,14-1,15-1
ESV - **14,** 1-1,2-1,3-1,4-1,5-1,6-1,7-1,8-1,9-1,10-1,11-1,12-1,13-1,14-1
HCSB - **16,** 1-1,2-1,3-1,4-1,5-1,6-1,7-1,8-1,9-1,10-1,11-1,12-1,13-1,14-1,15-1,16-1
NASV - **14,** 1-1,2-1,3-1,4-1,5-1,6-1,7-1,8-1,9-1,10-1,11-1,12-1,13-1,14-1
NCV - **19,** 1-1,2-1,3-1,4-1,5-1,6-1,7-**2**,8-1,9-1,10-1,11-1,12-1,13-1,14-1,15-1,16-1,17-1,18-1,19-1
NIV - **15,** 1-1,2-1,3-1,4-1,5-1,6-1,7-1,8-1,9-1,10-1,11-1,12-1,13-1,14-1,15-1
NKJV - **15,** 1-1,2-1,3-1,4-1,5-1,6-1,7-1,8-1,9-1,10-1,11-1,12-1,13-1,14-1,15-1
NLT - **15,** 1-1,2-1,3-1,4-1,5-1,6-1,7-1,8-**2**,9-1,10-1,11-1,12-1,13-1,14-1,15-**2**
NRSV - **14,** 1-1,2-1,3-1,4-1,5-1,6-1,7-1,8-1,9-1,10-1,11-1,12-1,13-1,14-1
Conclusion: Only the NCV and the NLT made the verse more complex.

94. Psalms 110:5 The Lord at thy right hand shall strike through kings in the day of his wrath.
AV - **16,** 1-1,2-1,3-1,4-1,5-1,6-1,7-1,8-1,9-1,10-1,11-1,12-1,13-1,14-1,15-1,16-1
ESV - **17,** 1-1,2-1,3-1,4-1,5-1,6-1,7-1,8-1,9-1,10-**2**,11-1,12-1,13-1,14-1,15-1,16-1,17-1
HCSB - **16,** 1-1,2-1,3-1,4-1,5-1,6-1,7-1,8-1,9-1,10-1,11-1,12-1,13-1,14-1,15-1,16-**2**
NASV - **17,** 1-1,2-1,3-1,4-1,5-1,6-1,7-1,8-1,9-1,10-**2**,11-1,12-1,13-1,14-1,15-1,16-1,17-1
NCV - **16,** 1-1,2-1,3-1,4-**2**,5-1,6-1,7-1,8-1,9-1,10-1,11-**2**,12-**2**,13-1,14-1,15-1,16-1
NIV - **17,** 1-1,2-1,3-1,4-1,5-1,6-1,7-1,8-1,9-1,10-1,11-1,12-1,13-1,14-1,15-1,16-1,17-1
NKJV - **17,** 1-1,2-1,3-1,4-1,5-1,6-1,7-1,8-1,9-1,10-**3**,11-1,12-1,13-1,14-1,15-1,16-1,17-1
NLT - **20,** 1-1,2-1,3-1,4-1,5-1,6-1,7-1,8-1,9-**2**,10-1,11-1,12-1,13-1,14-1,15-**2**,16-1,17-1,18-1,19-**2**,20-**2**
NRSV - **17,** 1-1,2-1,3-1,4-1,5-1,6-1,7-1,8-1,9-1,10-**2**,11-1,12-1,13-1,14-1,15-1,16-1,17-1
Conclusion: Seven modern versions are more complex than the King James Bible. The NLT is the most difficult to read.

95. Psalms 115:5 They have mouths, but they speak not: eyes have they, but they see not:
AV - **14,** 1-1,2-1,3-1,4-1,5-1,6-1,7-1,8-1,9-1,10-1,11-1,12-1,13-1,14-1
ESV - **12,** 1-1,2-1,3-1,4-1,5-1,6-1,7-1,8-1,9-1,10-1,11-1,12-1
HCSB - **10,** 1-1,2-1,3-1,4-1,5-**2**,6-1,7-1,8-1,9-**2**,10-1
NASV - **14,** 1-1,2-1,3-1,4-1,5-1,6-**2**,7-1,8-1,9-1,10-1,11-1,12-1,13-**2**,14-1
NCV - **14,** 1-1,2-1,3-1,4-1,5-1,6-**2**,7-1,8-1,9-1,10-1,11-1,12-1,13-**2**,14-1
NIV - **10,** 1-1,2-1,3-1,4-1,5-**2**,6-1,7-1,8-1,9-**2**,10-1
NKJV - **16,** 1-1,2-1,3-1,4-1,5-1,6-1,7-1,8-1,9-1,10-1,11-1,12-1,13-1,14-1,15-1,16-1
NLT - **11,** 1-1,2-1,3-1,4-1,5-**2**,6-1,7-1,8-1,9-1,10-**2**,11-1
NRSV - **12,** 1-1,2-1,3-1,4-1,5-1,6-1,7-1,8-1,9-1,10-1,11-1,12-1
Conclusion: Five modern versions are more complex than the King James Bible.

96. Psalms 115:11 Ye that fear the LORD, trust in the LORD: he is their help and their shield.
AV - **16,** 1-1,2-1,3-1,4-1,5-1,6-1,7-1,8-1,9-1,10-1,11-1,12-1,13-1,14-1,15-1,16-1
ESV - **16,** 1-1,2-1,3-1,4-1,5-1,6-1,7-1,8-1,9-1,10-1,11-1,12-1,13-1,14-1,15-1,16-1
HCSB - **15,** 1-1,2-1,3-1,4-1,5-1,6-1,7-1,8-1,9-1,10-1,11-1,12-1,13-1,14-1,15-1
NASV - **16,** 1-1,2-1,3-1,4-1,5-1,6-1,7-1,8-1,9-1,10-1,11-1,12-1,13-1,14-1,15-1,16-1
NCV - 15, 1-1,2-1,3-**2**,4-1,5-1,6-1,7-1,8-1,9-1,10-1,11-1,12-**2**,13-1,14-1,15-**3**
NIV - **14,** 1-1,2-1,3-1,4-1,5-1,6-1,7-1,8-1,9-1,10-1,11-1,12-1,13-1,14-1
NKJV - **16,** 1-1,2-1,3-1,4-1,5-1,6-1,7-1,8-1,9-1,10-1,11-1,12-1,13-1,14-1,15-1,16-1
NLT - 16, 1-1,2-1,3-1,4-1,5-1,6-1,7-1,8-1,9-1,10-1,11-1,12-1,13-**2**,14-1,15-1,16-1
NRSV - **16,** 1-1,2-1,3-1,4-1,5-1,6-1,7-1,8-1,9-1,10-1,11-1,12-1,13-1,14-1,15-1,16-1
Conclusion: Only two modern versions are more complex than the King James Bible. The NCV is the most difficult to read.

97. Psalms 115:13 He will bless them that fear the LORD, both small and great.
AV - **12,** 1-1,2-1,3-1,4-1,5-1,6-1,7-1,8-1,9-1,10-1,11-1,12-1
ESV - **14,** 1-1,2-1,3-1,4-1,5-1,6-1,7-1,8-1,9-1,10-1,11-1,12-1,13-1,14-1
HCSB - **12,** 1-1,2-1,3-1,4-1,5-1,6-1,7-1,8-1,9-1,10-1,11-1,12-1
NASV - 14, 1-1,2-1,3-1,4-1,5-1,6-1,7-1,8-1,9-1,10-1,11-**3**,12-1,13-1,14-1
NCV - 14, 1-1,2-1,3-1,4-1,5-1,6-1,7-**2**,8-1,9-1,10-1,11-**2**,12-1,13-1,14-**2**
NIV - 12, 1-1,2-1,3-1,4-1,5-1,6-1,7-1,8-1,9-1,10-1,11-1,12-**2**
NKJV - **12,** 1-1,2-1,3-1,4-1,5-1,6-1,7-1,8-1,9-1,10-1,11-1,12-1
NLT - 12, 1-1,2-1,3-1,4-1,5-1,6-1,7-1,8-1,9-1,10-1,11-1,12-**2**
NRSV - **12,** 1-1,2-1,3-1,4-1,5-1,6-1,7-1,8-1,9-1,10-1,11-1,12-1
Conclusion: Four modern versions are more complex than the King James Bible. The NCV is the most difficult to read.

98. Psalms 118:13 Thou hast thrust sore at me that I might fall: but the LORD helped me.
AV - **15,** 1-1,2-1,3-1,4-1,5-1,6-1,7-1,8-1,9-1,10-1,11-1,12-1,13-1,14-1,15-1
ESV - 14, 1-1,2-1,3-1,4-1,5-1,6-1,7-1,8-1,9-**2**,10-1,11-1,12-1,13-1,14-1
HCSB - **13,** 1-1,2-1,3-1,4-1,5-1,6-1,7-1,8-1,9-1,10-1,11-1,12-1,13-1
NASV - 14, 1-1,2-1,3-1,4-**4**,5-1,6-1,7-1,8-1,9-**2**,10-1,11-1,12-1,13-1,14-1
NCV - 13, 1-1,2-1,3-1,4-**2**,5-1,6-1,7-**2**,8-**3**,9-1,10-1,11-1,12-1,13-1
NIV - **13,** 1-1,2-1,3-1,4-1,5-1,6-1,7-1,8-1,9-1,10-1,11-1,12-1,13-1
NKJV - 13, 1-1,2-1,3-1,4-**4**,5-1,6-1,7-1,8-1,9-1,10-1,11-1,12-1,13-1
NLT - 13, 1-1,2-**3**,3-1,4-1,5-1,6-1,7-1,8-1,9-1,10-1,11-1,12-**2**,13-1
NRSV - 14, 1-1,2-1,3-1,4-1,5-1,6-1,7-1,8-1,9-**2**,10-1,11-1,12-1,13-1,14-1
Conclusion: Six modern versions are more complex than the King James Bible. The NCV is the most difficult to read.

99. Psalms 119:113 I hate vain thoughts: but thy law do I love.
AV - **10,** 1-1,2-1,3-1,4-1,5-1,6-1,7-1,8-1,9-1,10-1
ESV - 10, 1-1,2-1,3-1,4-**2**,5-**2**,6-1,7-1,8-1,9-1,10-1
HCSB - 10, 1-1,2-1,3-1,4-**2**,5-**2**,6-1,7-1,8-1,9-1,10-**3**
NASV - 12, 1-1,2-1,3-1,4-1,5-1,6-**2**,7-**2**,8-1,9-1,10-1,11-1,12-1
NCV - 9, 1-1,2-1,3-**2**,4-**2**,5-1,6-1,7-1,8-1,9-**2**

NIV - 10, 1-1,2-1,3-**2,**4-**2,**5-1,6-1,7-1,8-1,9-1,10-1
NKJV - 10, 1-1,2-1,3-1,4-**2,**5-**2,**6-1,7-1,8-1,9-1,10-1
NLT - 11, 1-1,2-1,3-1,4-1,5-**3,**6-**3,**7-1,8-1,9-1,10-1,11-**3**
NRSV - 10, 1-1,2-1,3-1,4-**2,**5-**2,**6-1,7-1,8-1,9-1,10-1
Conclusion: All eight modern versions are more complex than the King James Bible. Just as the NKJV often mimics the NASV it appears the ESV often does the same thing using the NRSV as its template.

100. Psalms 119:126 It is time for thee, LORD, to work: for they have made void thy law.
AV - 15, 1-1,2-1,3-1,4-1,5-1,6-1,7-1,8-1,9-1,10-1,11-1,12-1,13-1,14-1,15-1
ESV - 14, 1-1,2-1,3-1,4-1,5-1,6-1,7-1,8-1,9-1,10-1,11-1,12-1,13-1,14-**2**
HCSB - 14, 1-1,2-1,3-1,4-1,5-1,6-1,7-1,8-1,9-1,10-1,11-1,12-**2,**13-1,14-1
NASV - 14, 1-1,2-1,3-1,4-1,5-1,6-1,7-1,8-1,9-1,10-1,11-1,12-**2,**13-1,14-1
NCV - 15, 1-1,2-1,3-1,4-1,5-1,6-1,7-1,8-1,9-**2,**10-**2,**11-**2,**12-1,13-**3,**14-1,15-**2**
NIV - 14, 1-1,2-1,3-1,4-1,5-1,6-1,7-1,8-1,9-1,10-1,11-1,12-1,13-**2,**14-**2**
NKJV - 17, 1-1,2-1,3-**3,**4-1,5-1,6-1,7-1,8-1,9-1,10-1,11-1,12-1,13-1,14-1,15-1,16-1,17-1
NLT - 16, 1-1,2-1,3-1,4-1,5-1,6-1,7-1,8-1,9-1,10-1,11-**2,**12-**2,**13-1,14-**4,**15-1,16-**3**
NRSV - 14, 1-1,2-1,3-1,4-1,5-1,6-1,7-1,8-1,9-1,10-1,11-1,12-1,13-1,14-**2**
Conclusion: All eight modern versions are more complex than the King James Bible. The translators of the NCV and NLT should be credited for their fertile imaginations in managing to make such a simple verse so overwhelmingly complicated.

101. Psalms 120:7 I am for peace: but when I speak, they are for war.
AV - 12, 1-1,2-1,3-1,4-1,5-1,6-1,7-1,8-1,9-1,10-1,11-1,12-1
ESV - 12, 1-1,2-1,3-1,4-1,5-1,6-1,7-1,8-1,9-1,10-1,11-1,12-1
HCSB - 12, 1-1,2-1,3-1,4-1,5-1,6-1,7-1,8-1,9-1,10-1,11-1,12-1
NASV - 12, 1-1,2-1,3-1,4-1,5-1,6-1,7-1,8-1,9-1,10-1,11-1,12-1
NCV - 7, 1-1,2-1,3-1,4-1,5-1,6-1,7-1
NIV - 14, 1-1,2-1,3-1,4-1,5-1,6-1,7-1,8-1,9-1,10-1,11-1,12-1,13-1,14-1
NKJV - 12, 1-1,2-1,3-1,4-1,5-1,6-1,7-1,8-1,9-1,10-1,11-1,12-1
NLT - 13, 1-1,2-1,3-1,4-1,5-1,6-1,7-1,8-1,9-1,10-1,11-1,12-1,13-1
NRSV - 12, 1-1,2-1,3-1,4-1,5-1,6-1,7-1,8-1,9-1,10-1,11-1,12-1
Conclusion: All versions read the same.

102. Psalm 121:6 The sun shall not smite thee by day, nor the moon by night.
AV - 13, 1-1,2-1,3-1,4-1,5-1,6-1,7-1,8-1,9-1,10-1,11-1,12-1,13-1
ESV - 13, 1-1,2-1,3-1,4-1,5-1,6-1,7-1,8-1,9-1,10-1,11-1,12-1,13-1
HCSB - 13, 1-1,2-1,3-1,4-1,5-1,6-1,7-1,8-1,9-1,10-1,11-1,12-1,13-1
NASV - 13, 1-1,2-1,3-1,4-1,5-1,6-1,7-1,8-1,9-1,10-1,11-1,12-1,13-1
NCV - 16, 1-1,2-1,3-**2,**4-1,5-1,6-**2,**7-1,8-1,9-1,10-1,11-1,12-**2,**13-1,14-1,15-1,16-1
NIV - 13, 1-1,2-1,3-1,4-1,5-1,6-1,7-1,8-1,9-1,10-1,11-1,12-1,13-1
NKJV - 13, 1-1,2-1,3-1,4-1,5-1,6-1,7-1,8-1,9-1,10-1,11-1,12-1,13-1
NLT - 13, 1-1,2-1,3-1,4-1,5-1,6-1,7-1,8-1,9-1,10-1,11-1,12-1,13-1
NRSV - 13, 1-1,2-1,3-1,4-1,5-1,6-1,7-1,8-1,9-1,10-1,11-1,12-1,13-1
Conclusion: Only the NCV made the verse more complex, and that royally.

103. Psalms 126:5 They that sow in tears shall reap in joy.
AV - **9,** 1-1,2-1,3-1,4-1,5-1,6-1,7-1,8-1,9-1
ESV - **11,** 1-1,2-1,3-1,4-1,5-1,6-1,7-1,8-1,9-1,10-1,11-1
HCSB - **11,** 1-1,2-1,3-1,4-1,5-1,6-1,7-1,8-1,9-1,10-1,11-1
NASV - 10, 1-1,2-1,3-1,4-1,5-1,6-1,7-1,8-1,9-**2,**10-**2**
NCV - 12, 1-1,2-1,3-1,4-1,5-1,6-1,7-1,8-1,9-1,10-1,11-**2,**12-1
NIV - **11,** 1-1,2-1,3-1,4-1,5-1,6-1,7-1,8-1,9-1,10-1,11-1
NKJV - **9,** 1-1,2-1,3-1,4-1,5-1,6-1,7-1,8-1,9-1
NLT - 11, 1-1,2-1,3-1,4-1,5-1,6-1,7-**2,**8-1,9-1,10-1,11-1
NRSV - **11,** 1-1,2-1,3-1,4-1,5-1,6-1,7-1,8-1,9-1,10-1,11-1
Conclusion: Only three modern versions are more complex than the King James Bible. The NASV is the most difficult to read.

104. Psalms 130:5 I wait for the LORD, my soul doth wait, and in his word do I hope.
AV - **16,** 1-1,2-1,3-1,4-1,5-1,6-1,7-1,8-1,9-1,10-1,11-1,12-1,13-1,14-1,15-1,16-1
ESV - **14,** 1-1,2-1,3-1,4-1,5-1,6-1,7-1,8-1,9-1,10-1,11-1,12-1,13-1,14-1
HCSB - **14,** 1-1,2-1,3-1,4-1,5-1,6-1,7-1,8-1,9-1,10-1,11-1,12-1,13-1,14-1
NASV - **16,** 1-1,2-1,3-1,4-1,5-1,6-1,7-1,8-1,9-1,10-1,11-1,12-1,13-1,14-1,15-1,16-1
NCV - **13,** 1-1,2-1,3-1,4-1,5-1,6-1,7-1,8-1,9-1,10-1,11-1,12-1,13-1
NIV - **16,** 1-1,2-1,3-1,4-1,5-1,6-1,7-1,8-1,9-1,10-1,11-1,12-1,13-1,14-1,15-1,16-1
NKJV - **15,** 1-1,2-1,3-1,4-1,5-1,6-1,7-1,8-1,9-1,10-1,11-1,12-1,13-1,14-1,15-1
NLT - 20, 1-1,2-1,3-**2,**4-1,5-1,6-1,7-1,8-1,9-1,10-**2,**11-1,12-1,13-1,14-1,15-1,16-1,17-1,18-1,19-1,20-1
NRSV - **14,** 1-1,2-1,3-1,4-1,5-1,6-1,7-1,8-1,9-1,10-1,11-1,12-1,13-1,14-1
Conclusion: Only the NLT made the verse more complex.

105. Psalms 135:2 Ye that stand in the house of the LORD, in the courts of the house of our God,
AV - **18,** 1-1,2-1,3-1,4-1,5-1,6-1,7-1,8-1,9-1,10-1,11-1,12-1,13-1,14-1,15-1,16-1,17-1,18-1
ESV - **17,** 1-1,2-1,3-1,4-1,5-1,6-1,7-1,8-1,9-1,10-1,11-1,12-1,13-1,14-1,15-1,16-1,17-1
HCSB - **17,** 1-1,2-1,3-1,4-1,5-1,6-1,7-1,8-1,9-1,10-1,11-1,12-1,13-1,14-1,15-1,16-1,17-1
NASV - **18,** 1-1,2-1,3-1,4-1,5-1,6-1,7-1,8-1,9-1,10-1,11-1,12-1,13-1,14-1,15-1,16-1,17-1,18-1
NCV - 13, 1-1,2-1,3-1,4-1,5-1,6-1,7-**2,**8-1,9-1,10-1,11-**2,**12-1,13-**2**
NIV - 18, 1-1,2-1,3-**3,**4-1,5-1,6-1,7-1,8-1,9-1,10-1,11-1,12-1,13-1,14-1,15-1,16-1,17-1,18-1
NKJV - **18,** 1-1,2-1,3-1,4-1,5-1,6-1,7-1,8-1,9-1,10-1,11-1,12-1,13-1,14-1,15-1,16-1,17-1,18-1
NLT - **18,** 1-1,2-1,3-1,4-1,5-1,6-1,7-1,8-1,9-1,10-1,11-1,12-1,13-1,14-1,15-1,16-1,17-1,18-1
NRSV - **18,** 1-1,2-1,3-1,4-1,5-1,6-1,7-1,8-1,9-1,10-1,11-1,12-1,13-1,14-1,15-1,16-1,17-1,18-1
Conclusion: Only the NCV and the NIV made the verse more complex. The NCV is the most difficult to read.

106. Psalms 135:16 They have mouths, but they speak not; eyes have they, but they see not;
AV - **14,** 1-1,2-1,3-1,4-1,5-1,6-1,7-1,8-1,9-1,10-1,11-1,12-1,13-1,14-1
ESV - **14,** 1-1,2-1,3-1,4-1,5-1,6-1,7-1,8-1,9-1,10-1,11-1,12-1,13-1,14-1
HCSB - 10, 1-1,2-1,3-1,4-1,5-**2,**6-1,7-1,8-1,9-**2,**10-1
NASV - **16,** 1-1,2-1,3-1,4-1,5-1,6-1,7-1,8-1,9-1,10-1,11-1,12-1,13-1,14-1,15-1,16-1
NCV - 14, 1-1,2-1,3-1,4-1,5-1,6-**2,**7-1,8-1,9-1,10-1,11-1,12-1,13-**2,**14-1
NIV - 11, 1-1,2-1,3-1,4-1,5-**2,**6-1,7-1,8-1,9-1,10-**2,**11-1

NKJV - **16,** 1-1,2-1,3-1,4-1,5-1,6-1,7-1,8-1,9-1,10-1,11-1,12-1,13-1,14-1,15-1,16-1
NLT - **11,** 1-1,2-1,3-1,4-1,5-**2**,6-1,7-1,8-1,9-1,10-**2**,11-1
NRSV - **16,** 1-1,2-1,3-1,4-1,5-1,6-1,7-1,8-1,9-1,10-1,11-1,12-1,13-1,14-1,15-1,16-1
Conclusion: Four modern versions are more complex than the King James Bible.

107. Psalms 137:4 How shall we sing the Lord's song in a strange land?
AV - **11,** 1-1,2-1,3-1,4-1,5-1,6-1,7-1,8-1,9-1,10-1,11-1
ESV - **11,** 1-1,2-1,3-1,4-1,5-1,6-1,7-1,8-1,9-1,10-**2**,11-1
HCSB - **10,** 1-1,2-1,3-1,4-1,5-1,6-1,7-1,8-1,9-**2**,10-1
NASV - **11,** 1-1,2-1,3-1,4-1,5-1,6-1,7-1,8-1,9-1,10-**2**,11-1
NCV - **15,** 1-1,2-1,3-**2**,4-1,5-1,6-**2**,7-1,8-1,9-1,10-1,11-1,12-1,13-1,14-**2**,15-**2**
NIV - **14,** 1-1,2-1,3-1,4-1,5-1,6-1,7-1,8-1,9-1,10-1,11-1,12-1,13-**2**,14-1
NKJV - **11,** 1-1,2-1,3-1,4-1,5-1,6-1,7-1,8-1,9-1,10-**2**,11-1
NLT - **15,** 1-1,2-1,3-1,4-1,5-1,6-1,7-1,8-1,9-1,10-1,11-1,12-1,13-1,14-**2**,15-1
NRSV - **11,** 1-1,2-1,3-1,4-1,5-1,6-1,7-1,8-1,9-1,10-**2**,11-1
Conclusion: All eight modern versions are more complex than the King James Bible. Once again, the NCV is the most difficult to read.

108. Psalms 138:4 All the kings of the earth shall praise thee, O LORD, when they hear the words of thy mouth.
AV - **19,** 1-1,2-1,3-1,4-1,5-1,6-1,7-1,8-1,9-1,10-1,11-1,12-1,13-1,14-1,15-1,16-1,17-1,18-1,19-1
ESV - **21,** 1-1,2-1,3-1,4-1,5-1,6-1,7-1,8-1,9-1,10-1,11-1,12-1,13-1,14-1,15-1,16-1,17-1,18-1,19-1,20-1,21-1
HCSB - **17,** 1-1,2-1,3-1,4-1,5-1,6-1,7-1,8-1,9-1,10-1,11-1,12-1,13-1,14-1,15-1,16-1,17-**2**
NASV - **22,** 1-1,2-1,3-1,4-1,5-1,6-1,7-1,8-1,9-1,10-1,11-1,12-1,13-1,14-1,15-1,16-1,17-1,18-1,19-1,20-1,21-1,22-1
NCV - **17,** 1-1,2-1,3-1,4-1,5-1,6-1,7-1,8-1,9-1,10-1,11-1,12-1,13-1,14-1,15-1,16-1,17-1
NIV - **19,** 1-1,2-1,3-1,4-1,5-1,6-1,7-1,8-1,9-1,10-1,11-1,12-1,13-1,14-1,15-1,16-1,17-1,18-1,19-1
NKJV - **19,** 1-1,2-1,3-1,4-1,5-1,6-1,7-1,8-1,9-1,10-1,11-1,12-1,13-1,14-1,15-1,16-1,17-1,18-1,19-1
NLT - **18,** 1-**3**,2-1,3-1,4-1,5-1,6-1,7-1,8-1,9-1,10-1,11-1,12-1,13-1,14-1,15-1,16-1,17-1,18-1
NRSV - **20,** 1-1,2-1,3-1,4-1,5-1,6-1,7-1,8-1,9-1,10-1,11-1,12-1,13-1,14-1,15-1,16-1,17-1,18-1,19-1,20-1
Conclusion: Only the HCSB and the NLT made the verse more complex.

109. Psalms 139:1 O LORD, thou hast searched me, and known me.
AV - **9,** 1-1,2-1,3-1,4-1,5-1,6-1,7-1,8-1,9-1
ESV - **9,** 1-1,2-1,3-1,4-1,5-1,6-1,7-1,8-1,9-1
HCSB - **8,** 1-1,2-1,3-1,4-1,5-1,6-1,7-1,8-1
NASV - **9,** 1-1,2-1,3-1,4-1,5-1,6-1,7-1,8-1,9-1
NCV - **10,** 1-1,2-1,3-1,4-**3**,5-1,6-1,7-1,8-1,9-**2**,10-1
NIV - **10,** 1-1,2-1,3-1,4-1,5-1,6-1,7-1,8-1,9-1,10-1
NKJV - **9,** 1-1,2-1,3-1,4-1,5-1,6-1,7-1,8-1,9-1
NLT - **12,** 1-1,2-1,3-1,4-1,5-**3**,6-1,7-1,8-1,9-1,10-**4**,11-1,12-1
NRSV - **9,** 1-1,2-1,3-1,4-1,5-1,6-1,7-1,8-1,9-1
Conclusion: Once again the NCV and the NLT are the most difficult to read.

110. Psalms 139:23 Search me, O God, and know my heart: try me, and know my thoughts:
AV - **14,** 1-1,2-1,3-1,4-1,5-1,6-1,7-1,8-1,9-1,10-1,11-1,12-1,13-1,14-1
ESV - **14,** 1-1,2-1,3-1,4-1,5-1,6-1,7-1,8-1,9-1,10-1,11-1,12-1,13-1,14-1
HCSB - **13,** 1-1,2-1,3-1,4-1,5-1,6-1,7-1,8-1,9-1,10-1,11-1,12-1,13-**2**
NASV - **15,** 1-1,2-1,3-1,4-1,5-1,6-1,7-1,8-1,9-1,10-1,11-1,12-1,13-1,14-**2**,15-1
NCV - **14,** 1-1,2-**3**,3-1,4-1,5-1,6-1,7-1,8-1,9-1,10-1,11-1,12-1,13-**2**,14-1
NIV - **15,** 1-1,2-1,3-1,4-1,5-1,6-1,7-1,8-1,9-1,10-1,11-1,12-1,13-1,14-**2**,15-1
NKJV - **14,** 1-1,2-1,3-1,4-1,5-1,6-1,7-1,8-1,9-1,10-1,11-1,12-1,13-1,14-**4**
NLT - **15,** 1-1,2-1,3-1,4-1,5-1,6-1,7-1,8-1,9-1,10-1,11-1,12-1,13-1,14-**2**,15-1
NRSV - **14,** 1-1,2-1,3-1,4-1,5-1,6-1,7-1,8-1,9-1,10-1,11-1,12-1,13-1,14-1
Conclusion: Six modern versions are more complex than the King James Bible. The NCV is the most difficult to read.

111. Psalms 145:10 All thy works shall praise thee, O LORD; and thy saints shall bless thee.
AV - **14,** 1-1,2-1,3-1,4-1,5-1,6-1,7-1,8-1,9-1,10-1,11-1,12-1,13-1,14-1
ESV - **17,** 1-1,2-1,3-1,4-1,5-1,6-1,7-1,8-1,9-1,10-1,11-1,12-1,13-1,14-1,15-1,16-1,17-1
HCSB - **13,** 1-1,2-1,3-1,4-1,5-1,6-1,7-1,8-1,9-1,10-**2**,11-1,12-1,13-1
NASV - **17,** 1-1,2-1,3-1,4-1,5-1,6-1,7-1,8-1,9-1,10-1,11-1,12-1,13-**2**,14-1,15-1,16-1,17-1
NCV - **16,** 1-1,2-**4**,3-1,4-1,5-1,6-1,7-1,8-1,9-1,10-1,11-**2**,12-1,13-1,14-1,15-1,16-1
NIV - **14,** 1-1,2-1,3-1,4-1,5-1,6-1,7-1,8-1,9-1,10-1,11-1,12-1,13-**2**,14-1
NKJV - **14,** 1-1,2-1,3-1,4-1,5-1,6-1,7-1,8-1,9-1,10-1,11-1,12-1,13-1,14-1
NLT - **15,** 1-1,2-1,3-1,4-1,5-1,6-1,7-1,8-1,9-1,10-1,11-**2**,12-**3**,13-1,14-1,15-1
NRSV - **17,** 1-1,2-1,3-1,4-1,5-1,6-1,7-1,8-1,9-1,10-1,11-1,12-1,13-1,14-**2**,15-1,16-1,17-1
Conclusion: Six modern versions are more complex than the King James Bible.

112. Psalm 146:1 Praise ye the LORD. Praise the LORD, O my soul.
AV - **10,** 1-1,2-1,3-1,4-1,5-1,6-1,7-1,8-1,9-1,10-1
ESV - **9,** 1-1,2-1,3-1,4-1,5-1,6-1,7-1,8-1,9-1
HCSB - **6,** 1-1,2-1,3-1,4-1,5-1,6-1
NASV - **9,** 1-1,2-1,3-1,4-1,5-1,6-1,7-1,8-1,9-1
NCV - **9,** 1-1,2-1,3-1,4-1,5-1,6-**2**,7-1,8-1,9-1
NIV - **9,** 1-1,2-1,3-1,4-1,5-1,6-1,7-1,8-1,9-1
NKJV - **9,** 1-1,2-1,3-1,4-1,5-1,6-1,7-1,8-1,9-1
NLT - **11,** 1-1,2-1,3-1,4-1,5-1,6-1,7-1,8-1,9-1,10-1,11-1
NRSV - **9,** 1-1,2-1,3-1,4-1,5-1,6-1,7-1,8-1,9-1
Conclusion: Only the NCV made the verse more complex. The HCSB inserted "Hallelujah" for "Praise the LORD" but this was not counted against it.

113. Psalm 148:3 Praise ye him, sun and moon: praise him, all ye stars of light.
AV - **13,** 1-1,2-1,3-1,4-1,5-1,6-1,7-1,8-1,9-1,10-1,11-1,12-1,13-1
ESV - **11,** 1-1,2-1,3-1,4-1,5-1,6-1,7-1,8-1,9-1,10-**2**,11-1
HCSB - **11,** 1-1,2-1,3-1,4-1,5-1,6-1,7-1,8-1,9-1,10-**2**,11-1
NASV - **11,** 1-1,2-1,3-1,4-1,5-1,6-1,7-1,8-1,9-1,10-1,11-1
NCV - **11,** 1-1,2-1,3-1,4-1,5-1,6-1,7-1,8-1,9-1,10-**2**,11-1
NIV - **11,** 1-1,2-1,3-1,4-1,5-1,6-1,7-1,8-1,9-1,10-**2**,11-1

NKJV - **12,** 1-1,2-1,3-1,4-1,5-1,6-1,7-1,8-1,9-1,10-1,11-1,12-1
NLT - 11, 1-1,2-1,3-1,4-1,5-1,6-1,7-1,8-1,9-1,10-**2**,11-1
NRSV - 11, 1-1,2-1,3-1,4-1,5-1,6-1,7-1,8-1,9-1,10-**2**,11-1
Conclusion: Six modern versions are more complex than the King James Bible.

114. Proverbs 3:2 For length of days, and long life, and peace, shall they add to thee.
AV - **14,** 1-1,2-1,3-1,4-1,5-1,6-1,7-1,8-1,9-1,10-1,11-1,12-1,13-1,14-1
ESV - **15,** 1-1,2-1,3-1,4-1,5-1,6-1,7-1,8-1,9-1,10-1,11-1,12-1,13-1,14-1,15-1
HCSB - 13, 1-1,2-1,3-1,4-1,5-1,6-**2**,7-1,8-1,9-1,10-1,11-1,12-1,13-**2**
NASV - **15,** 1-1,2-1,3-1,4-1,5-1,6-1,7-1,8-1,9-1,10-1,11-1,12-1,13-1,14-1,15-1
NCV - 13, 1-1,2-1,3-1,4-1,5-1,6-1,7-1,8-1,9-1,10-1,11-1,12-1,13-**3**
NIV - 13, 1-1,2-1,3-1,4-**2**,5-1,6-1,7-**2**,8-1,9-1,10-1,11-1,12-**4**
NKJV - **14,** 1-1,2-1,3-1,4-1,5-1,6-1,7-1,8-1,9-1,10-1,11-1,12-1,13-1,14-1
NLT - 15, 1-1,2-1,3-1,4-1,5-1,6-1,7-1,8-**2**,9-1,10-1,11-1,12-1,13-1,14-1,15-**4**
NRSV - 15, 1-1,2-1,3-1,4-1,5-1,6-1,7-1,8-1,9-1,10-**3**,11-**2**,12-1,13-1,14-1,15-1
Conclusion: Five modern versions are more complex than the King James Bible.

115. Proverbs 5:5 Her feet go down to death; her steps take hold on hell.
AV - **12,** 1-1,2-1,3-1,4-1,5-1,6-1,7-1,8-1,9-1,10-1,11-1,12-1
ESV - 13, 1-1,2-1,3-1,4-1,5-1,6-1,7-1,8-1,9-**2**,10-1,11-1,12-1,13-1
HCSB - **12,** 1-1,2-1,3-1,4-1,5-1,6-1,7-1,8-1,9-1,10-1,11-1,12-1
NASV - **12,** 1-1,2-1,3-1,4-1,5-1,6-1,7-1,8-1,9-1,10-1,11-1,12-1
NCV - 15, 1-1,2-1,3-1,4-1,5-1,6-1,7-1,8-1,9-1,10-1,11-**2**,12-1,13-1,14-1,15-1
NIV - **13,** 1-1,2-1,3-1,4-1,5-1,6-1,7-1,8-1,9-1,10-1,11-1,12-1,13-1
NKJV - **12,** 1-1,2-1,3-1,4-1,5-1,6-1,7-1,8-1,9-1,10-1,11-1,12-1
NLT - **13,** 1-1,2-1,3-1,4-1,5-1,6-1,7-1,8-1,9-1,10-1,11-1,12-1,13-1
NRSV - 13, 1-1,2-1,3-1,4-1,5-1,6-1,7-1,8-1,9-**2**,10-1,11-1,12-1,13-1
Conclusion: Only three modern versions, the ESV, NCV and the NRSV, made the verse more complex.
The NCV, NIV and NLT say "grave" in place of "hell." The ESV, HCSB, NASV and NRSV say "Sheol" which was counted as one syllable. Only the NKJV says "hell" like the Authorized Version.

116. Proverbs 20:9 Who can say, I have made my heart clean, I am pure from my sin?
AV - **15,** 1-1,2-1,3-1,4-1,5-1,6-1,7-1,8-1,9-1,10-1,11-1,12-1,13-1,14-1,15-1
ESV - **15,** 1-1,2-1,3-1,4-1,5-1,6-1,7-1,8-1,9-1,10-1,11-1,12-1,13-1,14-1,15-1
HCSB - **15,** 1-1,2-1,3-1,4-1,5-1,6-1,7-1,8-1,9-1,10-1,11-1,12-1,13-1,14-1,15-1
NASV - **14,** 1-1,2-1,3-1,4-1,5-1,6-1,7-1,8-1,9-1,10-1,11-1,12-1,13-1,14-1
NCV - 13, 1-1,2-1,3-1,4-1,5-1,6-1,7-**3**,8-1,9-1,10-**2**,11-1,12-**3**,13-1
NIV - 15, 1-1,2-1,3-1,4-1,5-1,6-1,7-1,8-1,9-1,10-1,11-1,12-1,13-1,14-**2**,15-1
NKJV - **15,** 1-1,2-1,3-1,4-1,5-1,6-1,7-1,8-1,9-1,10-1,11-1,12-1,13-1,14-1,15-1
NLT - **15,** 1-1,2-1,3-1,4-1,5-1,6-1,7-1,8-1,9-1,10-1,11-1,12-1,13-1,14-1,15-1
NRSV - **15,** 1-1,2-1,3-1,4-1,5-1,6-1,7-1,8-1,9-1,10-1,11-1,12-1,13-1,14-1,15-1
Conclusion: Only the NCV and the NIV made the verse more complex. The NCV is the most difficult to read.

117. Proverbs 22:23 For the LORD will plead their cause, and spoil the soul of those that spoiled them.
AV - **16,** 1-1,2-1,3-1,4-1,5-1,6-1,7-1,8-1,9-1,10-1,11-1,12-1,13-1,14-1,15-1,16-1
ESV - **15,** 1-1,2-1,3-1,4-1,5-1,6-1,7-1,8-1,9-1,10-1,11-1,12-1,13-1,14-1,15-1
HCSB - 15, 1-1,2-1,3-1,4-1,5-1,6-1,7-1,8-1,9-1,10-1,11-**2**,12-1,13-1,14-**2**,15-1
NASV - 16, 1-1,2-1,3-1,4-1,5-1,6-1,7-1,8-1,9-1,10-1,11-1,12-1,13-1,14-1,15-1,16-1
NCV - 19, 1-1,2-1,3-1,4-**2**,5-1,6-1,7-1,8-1,9-1,10-1,11-1,12-1,13-1,14-1,15-1,16-1,17-**2**,18-1,19-1
NIV - 15, 1-1,2-1,3-1,4-1,5-1,6-1,7-1,8-1,9-1,10-1,11-**2**,12-1,13-1,14-**2**,15-1
NKJV - 16, 1-1,2-1,3-1,4-1,5-1,6-1,7-1,8-1,9-**2**,10-1,11-1,12-1,13-1,14-1,15-**2**,16-1
NLT - 13, 1-1,2-1,3-1,4-1,5-1,6-**3**,7-1,8-1,9-**2**,10-**3**,11-1,12-**2**,13-1
NRSV - 14, 1-1,2-1,3-1,4-1,5-1,6-1,7-1,8-**2**,9-1,10-1,11-1,12-1,13-**2**,14-1
Conclusion: Six modern versions are more complex than the King James Bible. The NLT did its usual masterful job of complicating the simple.

118. Proverbs 22:25 Lest thou learn his ways, and get a snare to thy soul.
AV - **12,** 1-1,2-1,3-1,4-1,5-1,6-1,7-1,8-1,9-1,10-1,11-1,12-1
ESV - 11, 1-1,2-1,3-1,4-1,5-1,6-1,7-**3**,8-**2**,9-1,10-1,11-1
HCSB - 12, 1-1,2-1,3-1,4-1,5-1,6-1,7-1,8-**3**,9-**2**,10-1,11-1,12-1
NASV - 12, 1-1,2-1,3-1,4-1,5-1,6-1,7-1,8-1,9-1,10-1,11-1,12-**2**
NCV - 15, 1-1,2-1,3-1,4-1,5-1,6-1,7-1,8-1,9-1,10-1,11-1,12-1,13-1,14-1,15-**2**
NIV - 10, 1-1,2-1,3-1,4-1,5-1,6-1,7-1,8-1,9-**2**,10-**2**
NKJV - 12, 1-1,2-1,3-1,4-1,5-1,6-1,7-1,8-1,9-1,10-1,11-1,12-1
NLT - 12, 1-1,2-1,3-1,4-1,5-1,6-1,7-1,8-1,9-1,10-**3**,11-1,12-1
NRSV - 12, 1-1,2-1,3-1,4-1,5-1,6-1,7-1,8-**3**,9-**2**,10-1,11-1,12-1
Conclusion: Seven modern versions are more complex than the King James Bible.

119. Proverbs 23:19 Hear thou, my son, and be wise, and guide thine heart in the way.
AV - **14,** 1-1,2-1,3-1,4-1,5-1,6-1,7-1,8-1,9-1,10-1,11-1,12-1,13-1,14-1
ESV - 13, 1-1,2-1,3-1,4-1,5-1,6-1,7-1,8-**2**,9-1,10-1,11-1,12-1,13-1
HCSB - 13, 1-**2**,2-1,3-1,4-1,5-1,6-1,7-1,8-1,9-1,10-1,11-1,12-1,13-1
NASV - 13, 1-**2**,2-1,3-1,4-1,5-1,6-1,7-1,8-**2**,9-1,10-1,11-1,12-1,13-1
NCV - 13, 1-**2**,2-1,3-1,4-1,5-1,6-1,7-1,8-1,9-1,10-1,11-1,12-1,13-1
NIV - 14, 1-**2**,2-1,3-1,4-1,5-1,6-1,7-1,8-1,9-1,10-1,11-1,12-1,13-1,14-1
NKJV - **13,** 1-1,2-1,3-1,4-1,5-1,6-1,7-1,8-1,9-1,10-1,11-1,12-1,13-1
NLT - 13, 1-1,2-1,3-**2**,4-1,5-1,6-1,7-1,8-1,9-1,10-1,11-1,12-1,13-1
NRSV - 13, 1-1,2-1,3-1,4-1,5-1,6-1,7-1,8-**2**,9-1,10-1,11-1,12-1,13-1
Conclusion: Seven modern versions are more complex than the King James Bible.

120. Proverbs 31:2 What, my son? and what, the son of my womb? and what, the son of my vows?
AV - **17,** 1-1,2-1,3-1,4-1,5-1,6-1,7-1,8-1,9-1,10-1,11-1,12-1,13-1,14-1,15-1,16-1,17-1
ESV - 22, 1-1,2-1,3-1,4-**2**,5-1,6-1,7-1,8-1,9-1,10-**2**,11-1,12-1,13-1,14-1,15-1,16-1,17-1,18-**2**,19-1,20-1,21-1,22-1
HCSB - **16,** 1-1,2-1,3-1,4-1,5-1,6-1,7-1,8-1,9-1,10-1,11-1,12-1,13-1,14-1,15-1,16-1
NASV - **18,** 1-1,2-1,3-1,4-1,5-1,6-1,7-1,8-1,9-1,10-1,11-1,12-1,13-1,14-1,15-1,16-1,17-1,18-1
NCV - **14,** 1-1,2-1,3-1,4-1,5-1,6-1,7-1,8-1,9-1,10-1,11-1,12-1,13-1,14-1
NIV - **13,** 1-1,2-1,3-1,4-1,5-1,6-1,7-1,8-1,9-1,10-1,11-1,12-1,13-1

NKJV - **15,** 1-1,2-1,3-1,4-1,5-1,6-1,7-1,8-1,9-1,10-1,11-1,12-1,13-1,14-1,15-1

NLT - **13,** 1-1,2-1,3-1,4-1,5-1,6-1,7-1,8-1,9-1,10-1,11-1,12-1,13-1

NRSV - **13,** 1-1,2-1,3-1,4-1,5-1,6-1,7-1,8-1,9-1,10-1,11-1,12-1,13-1

Conclusion: Only the ESV made the verse more complex. The NCV renders the verse in all single syllable words as do the remaining modern versions, but where the other versions all share the same basic format, the rendering of the NCV is both stunning and humorous. It merits reproduction here. Where it came from one can only guess.

      Pro. 31:2 (NCV) "My son, I gave birth to you. You are the son I prayed for."

121. Proverbs 31:31 Give her of the fruit of her hands; and let her own works praise her in the gates.

AV - **18,** 1-1,2-1,3-1,4-1,5-1,6-1,7-1,8-1,9-1,10-1,11-1,12-1,13-1,14-1,15-1,16-1,17-1,18-1

ESV - **17,** 1-1,2-1,3-1,4-1,5-1,6-1,7-1,8-1,9-1,10-1,11-1,12-1,13-1,14-1,15-1,16-1,17-1

HCSB - 17, 1-1,2-1,3-1,4-**2,**5-1,6-1,7-**2,**8-1,9-1,10-1,11-1,12-1,13-1,14-1,15-1,16-**2,**17-1

NASV - 16, 1-1,2-1,3-1,4-**2,**5-1,6-1,7-1,8-1,9-1,10-1,11-1,12-1,13-1,14-1,15-1,16-1

NCV - 18, 1-1,2-1,3-1,4-**2,**5-1,6-1,7-1,8-1,9-1,10-1,11-1,12-1,13-**2,**14-1,15-1,16-1,17-1,18-1

NIV - 18, 1-1,2-1,3-1,4-**2,**5-1,6-1,7-1,8-1,9-1,10-1,11-1,12-1,13-1,14-1,15-1,16-1,17-1,18-1

NKJV - **18,** 1-1,2-1,3-1,4-1,5-1,6-1,7-1,8-1,9-1,10-1,11-1,12-1,13-1,14-1,15-1,16-1,17-1,18-1

NLT - 14, 1-**2,**2-1,3-1,4-1,5-1,6-1,7-1,8-1,9-1,10-1,11-**3,**12-**2,**13-1,14-1

NRSV - 20, 1-1,2-1,3-1,4-1,5-1,6-1,7-1,8-1,9-1,10-1,11-1,12-1,13-1,14-1,15-1,16-1,17-1,18-1,19-**2,**20-1

Conclusion: Six modern versions are more complex than the King James Bible. The HCSB and the NLT made the verse more complex.

122. Ecclesiastes 3:3 A time to kill, and a time to heal; a time to break down, and a time to build up;

AV - **20,** 1-1,2-1,3-1,4-1,5-1,6-1,7-1,8-1,9-1,10-1,11-1,12-1,13-1,14-1,15-1,16-1,17-1,18-1,19-1,20-1

ESV - **20,** 1-1,2-1,3-1,4-1,5-1,6-1,7-1,8-1,9-1,10-1,11-1,12-1,13-1,14-1,15-1,16-1,17-1,18-1,19-1,20-1

HCSB - **19,** 1-1,2-1,3-1,4-1,5-1,6-1,7-1,8-1,9-1,10-1,11-1,12-1,13-1,14-1,15-1,16-1,17-1,18-1,19-1

NASV - **20,** 1-1,2-1,3-1,4-1,5-1,6-1,7-1,8-1,9-1,10-1,11-1,12-1,13-1,14-1,15-1,16-1,17-1,18-1,19-1,20-1

NCV - 22, 1-1,2-1,3-1,4-1,5-1,6-1,7-1,8-1,9-1,10-1,11-1,12-1,13-1,14-1,15-1,16-1,17-**2,**18-1,19-1,20-1,21-1,22-1

NIV - **19,** 1-1,2-1,3-1,4-1,5-1,6-1,7-1,8-1,9-1,10-1,11-1,12-1,13-1,14-1,15-1,16-1,17-1,18-1,19-1

NKJV - **20,** 1-1,2-1,3-1,4-1,5-1,6-1,7-1,8-1,9-1,10-1,11-1,12-1,13-1,14-1,15-1,16-1,17-1,18-1,19-1,20-1

NLT - **20,** 1-1,2-1,3-1,4-1,5-1,6-1,7-1,8-1,9-1,10-1,11-1,12-1,13-1,14-1,15-1,16-1,17-1,18-1,19-1,20-1

NRSV - **20,** 1-1,2-1,3-1,4-1,5-1,6-1,7-1,8-1,9-1,10-1,11-1,12-1,13-1,14-1,15-1,16-1,17-1,18-1,19-1,20-1

Conclusion: Only the NCV made the verse more complex.

123. Ecclesiastes 3:4 A time to weep, and a time to laugh; a time to mourn, and a time to dance;

AV - **18,** 1-1,2-1,3-1,4-1,5-1,6-1,7-1,8-1,9-1,10-1,11-1,12-1,13-1,14-1,15-1,16-1,17-1,18-1

ESV - **18,** 1-1,2-1,3-1,4-1,5-1,6-1,7-1,8-1,9-1,10-1,11-1,12-1,13-1,14-1,15-1,16-1,17-1,18-1

HCSB - **18,** 1-1,2-1,3-1,4-1,5-1,6-1,7-1,8-1,9-1,10-1,11-1,12-1,13-1,14-1,15-1,16-1,17-1,18-1

NASV - **18,** 1-1,2-1,3-1,4-1,5-1,6-1,7-1,8-1,9-1,10-1,11-1,12-1,13-1,14-1,15-1,16-1,17-1,18-1

NCV - **23,** 1-1,2-1,3-1,4-1,5-1,6-1,7-1,8-1,9-1,10-1,11-1,12-1,13-1,14-1,15-1,16-1,17-1,18-1,19-1,20-1,21-1,22-1,23-1

NIV - **18,** 1-1,2-1,3-1,4-1,5-1,6-1,7-1,8-1,9-1,10-1,11-1,12-1,13-1,14-1,15-1,16-1,17-1,18-1

NKJV - **18,** 1-1,2-1,3-1,4-1,5-1,6-1,7-1,8-1,9-1,10-1,11-1,12-1,13-1,14-1,15-1,16-1,17-1,18-1

NLT - **18,** 1-1,2-1,3-1,4-1,5-1,6-1,7-1,8-1,9-1,10-1,11-1,12-1,13-1,14-1,15-1,16-1,17-1,18-1

NRSV - **18,** 1-1,2-1,3-1,4-1,5-1,6-1,7-1,8-1,9-1,10-1,11-1,12-1,13-1,14-1,15-1,16-1,17-1,18-1
Conclusion: All versions read the same.

124. Ecclesiastes 3:8 A time to love, and a time to hate; a time of war, and a time of peace.
AV - **18,** 1-1,2-1,3-1,4-1,5-1,6-1,7-1,8-1,9-1,10-1,11-1,12-1,13-1,14-1,15-1,16-1,17-1,18-1
ESV - **18,** 1-1,2-1,3-1,4-1,5-1,6-1,7-1,8-1,9-1,10-1,11-1,12-1,13-1,14-1,15-1,16-1,17-1,18-1
HCSB - **18,** 1-1,2-1,3-1,4-1,5-1,6-1,7-1,8-1,9-1,10-1,11-1,12-1,13-1,14-1,15-1,16-1,17-1,18-1
NASV - **18,** 1-1,2-1,3-1,4-1,5-1,6-1,7-1,8-1,9-1,10-1,11-1,12-1,13-1,14-1,15-1,16-1,17-1,18-1
NCV - **22,** 1-1,2-1,3-1,4-1,5-1,6-1,7-1,8-1,9-1,10-1,11-1,12-1,13-1,14-1,15-1,16-1,17-1,18-1,19-1,20-1,21-1,22-1
NIV - **18,** 1-1,2-1,3-1,4-1,5-1,6-1,7-1,8-1,9-1,10-1,11-1,12-1,13-1,14-1,15-1,16-1,17-1,18-1
NKJV - **18,** 1-1,2-1,3-1,4-1,5-1,6-1,7-1,8-1,9-1,10-1,11-1,12-1,13-1,14-1,15-1,16-1,17-1,18-1
NLT - **18,** 1-1,2-1,3-1,4-1,5-1,6-1,7-1,8-1,9-1,10-1,11-1,12-1,13-1,14-1,15-1,16-1,17-1,18-1
NRSV - **18,** 1-1,2-1,3-1,4-1,5-1,6-1,7-1,8-1,9-1,10-1,11-1,12-1,13-1,14-1,15-1,16-1,17-1,18-1
Conclusion: All versions read the same.

125. Ecclesiastes 10:2 A wise man's heart is at his right hand; but a fool's heart at his left.
AV - **16,** 1-1,2-1,3-1,4-1,5-1,6-1,7-1,8-1,9-1,10-1,11-1,12-1,13-1,14-1,15-1,16-1
ESV - **16,** 1-1,2-1,3-1,4-1,5-**2,**6-1,7-1,8-1,9-1,10-1,11-1,12-1,13-1,14-1,15-1,16-1
HCSB - **15,** 1-1,2-1,3-1,4-1,5-1,6-1,7-1,8-1,9-1,10-1,11-1,12-1,13-1,14-1,15-1
NASV - **19,** 1-1,2-1,3-1,4-1,5-**2,**6-1,7-1,8-1,9-1,10-1,11-1,12-1,13-1,14-1,15-**2,**16-1,17-1,18-1,19-1
NCV - **17,** 1-1,2-1,3-1,4-1,5-1,6-1,7-1,8-1,9-1,10-1,11-1,12-1,13-1,14-1,15-1,16-1,17-1
NIV - **18,** 1-1,2-1,3-1,4-1,5-1,6-**2,**7-1,8-1,9-1,10-1,11-1,12-1,13-1,14-1,15-1,16-1,17-1,18-1
NKJV - **16,** 1-1,2-1,3-1,4-1,5-1,6-1,7-1,8-1,9-1,10-1,11-1,12-1,13-1,14-1,15-1,16-1
NLT - **13,** 1-1,2-1,3-**2,**4-**2,**5-1,6-1,7-1,8-1,9-1,10-1,11-1,12-1,13-1
NRSV - **18,** 1-1,2-1,3-1,4-1,5-1,6-**2,**7-1,8-1,9-1,10-1,11-1,12-1,13-1,14-1,15-1,16-1,17-1,18-1
Conclusion: Five modern versions are more complex than the King James Bible.

126. Song of Solomon 4:7 Thou art all fair, my love; there is no spot in thee.
AV - **12,** 1-1,2-1,3-1,4-1,5-1,6-1,7-1,8-1,9-1,10-1,11-1,12-1
ESV - **12,** 1-1,2-1,3-**4,**4-**3,**5-1,6-1,7-1,8-1,9-1,10-1,11-1,12-1
HCSB - **11,** 1-1,2-1,3-**4,**4-**3,**5-1,6-**2,**7-1,8-1,9-**4,**10-1,11-1
NASV - **13,** 1-1,2-1,3-1,4-**3,**5-**4,**6-**2,**7-1,8-1,9-1,10-1,11-**2,**12-1,13-1
NCV - **16,** 1-1,2-**2,**3-**4,**4-**2,**5-1,6-1,7-**3,**8-1,9-1,10-1,11-**2,**12-1,13-1,14-1,15-1,16-1
NIV - **12,** 1-1,2-**3,**3-1,4-1,5-1,6-**2,**7-1,8-1,9-1,10-1,11-1,12-1
NKJV - **13,** 1-1,2-1,3-1,4-1,5-1,6-1,7-1,8-1,9-1,10-1,11-1,12-1,13-1
NLT - **10,** 1-1,2-1,3-**4,**4-**3,**5-1,6-**2,**7-**3,**8-1,9-**3,**10-1
NRSV - **12,** 1-1,2-1,3-**4,**4-**3,**5-1,6-1,7-1,8-1,9-1,10-1,11-1,12-1
Conclusion: Seven modern versions are more complex than the King James Bible. The modern versions produce an amazing array of complexity.

127. Song of Solomon 7:3 Thy two breasts are like two young roes that are twins.
AV - **11,** 1-1,2-1,3-1,4-1,5-1,6-1,7-1,8-1,9-1,10-1,11-1
ESV - **11,** 1-1,2-1,3-1,4-1,5-1,6-1,7-1,8-1,9-1,10-1,11-**2**
HCSB - **10,** 1-1,2-1,3-1,4-1,5-1,6-1,7-1,8-1,9-1,10-**2**

NASV - 11, 1-1,2-1,3-1,4-1,5-1,6-1,7-1,8-1,9-1,10-1,11-**2**
NCV - 11, 1-1,2-1,3-1,4-1,5-1,6-1,7-1,8-1,9-1,10-1,11-**2**
NIV - 10, 1-1,2-1,3-1,4-1,5-1,6-1,7-1,8-1,9-1,10-**2**
NKJV - 11, 1-1,2-1,3-1,4-1,5-1,6-1,7-1,8-1,9-1,10-1,11-**2**
NLT - 11, 1-1,2-1,3-1,4-1,5-1,6-1,7-1,8-1,9-1,10-1,11-**2**
NRSV - 11, 1-1,2-1,3-1,4-1,5-1,6-1,7-1,8-1,9-1,10-1,11-**2**
Conclusion: All eight modern versions are more complex than the King James Bible. In case you are wondering, the two syllable word added to every modern version is "gazelle" and in all eight it appears at the end of the verse.

128. Isaiah 3:21 The rings, and nose jewels,
AV - **5,** 1-1,2-1,3-1,4-1,5-1
ESV - 6, 1-1,2-**2**,3-1,4-1,5-1,6-1
HCSB - 4, 1-**2**,2-1,3-1,4-1
NASV - 4, 1-**2**,2-1,3-1,4-1
NCV - 5, 1-1,2-**2**,3-1,4-1,5-1
NIV - 6, 1-1,2-**2**,3-1,4-1,5-1,6-1
NKJV - **6,** 1-1,2-1,3-1,4-1,5-1,6-1
NLT - **2,** 1-1,2-1
NRSV - 6, 1-1,2-**2**,3-1,4-1,5-1,6-1
Conclusion: Six modern versions are more complex than the King James Bible.

129. Isaiah 6:4 And the posts of the door moved at the voice of him that cried, and the house was filled with smoke.
AV - **21,** 1-1,2-1,3-1,4-1,5-1,6-1,7-1,8-1,9-1,10-1,11-1,12-1,13-1,14-1,15-1,16-1,17-1,18-1,19-1,20-1,21-1
ESV - 21, 1-1,2-1,3-**3**,4-1,5-1,6-**2**,7-1,8-1,9-1,10-1,11-1,12-1,13-1,14-1,15-1,16-1,17-1,18-1,19-1,20-1,21-1
HCSB - 19, 1-1,2-**3**,3-1,4-1,5-**2**,6-1,7-1,8-1,9-1,10-1,11-1,12-1,13-1,14-1,15-**2**,16-1,17-1,18-1,19-1
NASV - 22, 1-1,2-1,3-**3**,4-1,5-1,6-**2**,7-**2**,8-1,9-1,10-1,11-1,12-1,13-1,14-1,15-1,16-1,17-1,18-**2**,19-1,20-**2**,21-1,22-1
NCV - 16, 1-1,2-**2**,3-1,4-1,5-1,6-**2**,7-1,8-1,9-1,10-1,11-1,12-1,13-**2**,14-1,15-1,16-1
NIV - 18, 1-1,2-1,3-1,4-1,5-1,6-1,7-1,8-**2**,9-1,10-**2**,11-1,12-1,13-1,14-**2**,15-1,16-1,17-1,18-1
NKJV - 23, 1-1,2-1,3-1,4-1,5-1,6-1,7-1,8-**2**,9-1,10-1,11-1,12-1,13-1,14-1,15-1,16-1,17-1,18-1,19-1,20-1,21-1,22-1,23-1
NLT - 16, 1-1,2-**2**,3-1,4-1,5-**2**,6-1,7-1,8-**3**,9-1,10-1,11-**2**,12-**2**,13-1,14-1,15-1,16-1
NRSV - 19, 1-1,2-**2**,3-1,4-1,5-**2**,6-1,7-1,8-1,9-**2**,10-1,11-1,12-1,13-1,14-1,15-1,16-1,17-1,18-1,19-1
Conclusion: All eight modern versions are more complex than the King James Bible.

130. Isaiah 14:15 Yet thou shalt be brought down to hell, to the sides of the pit.
AV - **14,** 1-1,2-1,3-1,4-1,5-1,6-1,7-1,8-1,9-1,10-1,11-1,12-1,13-1,14-1
ESV - 14, 1-1,2-1,3-1,4-1,5-1,6-1,7-1,8-1,9-1,10-1,11-**2**,12-1,13-1,14-1
HCSB - 15, 1-1,2-1,3-1,4-1,5-1,6-1,7-1,8-1,9-**2**,10-1,11-**2**,12-**2**,13-1,14-1,15-1
NASV - 14, 1-**4**,2-1,3-1,4-1,5-1,6-1,7-1,8-1,9-1,10-1,11-**3**,12-1,13-1,14-1
NCV - 16, 1-1,2-1,3-1,4-1,5-1,6-1,7-1,8-1,9-1,10-1,11-1,12-**2**,13-1,14-1,15-1,16-1
NIV - **14,** 1-1,2-1,3-1,4-1,5-1,6-1,7-1,8-1,9-1,10-1,11-1,12-1,13-1,14-1
NKJV - 15, 1-1,2-1,3-1,4-1,5-1,6-1,7-1,8-1,9-1,10-1,11-**2**,12-1,13-1,14-1,15-1

NLT - **17,** 1-**2**,2-1,3-1,4-1,5-1,6-1,7-1,8-1,9-1,10-1,11-1,12-1,13-1,14-1,15-1,16-**2**,17-1
NRSV - **13,** 1-1,2-1,3-1,4-1,5-1,6-1,7-1,8-1,9-1,10-1,11-1,12-1,13-1
Conclusion: Six modern versions are more complex than the King James Bible. The ESV, HCSB, NASV and NRSV all replace "hell" with "Sheol" but it was not counted as a multi-syllable word. None of the eight versions examined contain the word "hell."

131. Isaiah 27:5 Or let him take hold of my strength, that he may make peace with me; and he shall make peace with me.
AV - **22,** 1-1,2-1,3-1,4-1,5-1,6-1,7-1,8-1,9-1,10-1,11-1,12-1,13-1,14-1,15-1,16-1,17-1,18-1,19-1,20-1,21-1,22-1
ESV - 20, 1-1,2-1,3-1,4-1,5-1,6-1,7-1,8-**3**,9-1,10-1,11-1,12-1,13-1,14-1,15-1,16-1,17-1,18-1,19-1,20-1
HCSB - **18,** 1-1,2-1,3-1,4-1,5-1,6-1,7-1,8-1,9-1,10-1,11-1,12-1,13-1,14-1,15-1,16-1,17-1,18-1
NASV - 19, 1-1,2-1,3-1,4-**2**,5-1,6-1,7-**3**,8-1,9-1,10-1,11-1,12-1,13-1,14-1,15-1,16-1,17-1,18-1,19-1
NCV - 23, 1-1,2-1,3-**3**,4-1,5-1,6-1,7-1,8-**2**,9-1,10-1,11-1,12-1,13-1,14-1,15-1,16-1,17-1,18-1,19-1,20-1,21-1,22-1,23-1
NIV - 22, 1-1,2-1,3-1,4-1,5-1,6-1,7-1,8-1,9-**2**,10-1,11-1,12-1,13-1,14-1,15-1,16-1,17-1,18-1,19-1,20-1,21-1,22-1
NKJV - **22,** 1-1,2-1,3-1,4-1,5-1,6-1,7-1,8-1,9-1,10-1,11-1,12-1,13-1,14-1,15-1,16-1,17-1,18-1,19-1,20-1,21-1,22-1
NLT - 20, 1-**2**,2-1,3-1,4-1,5-1,6-1,7-1,8-1,9-1,10-1,11-1,12-1,13-1,14-1,15-1,16-1,17-1,18-1,19-1,20-1
NRSV - 21, 1-1,2-1,3-1,4-1,5-1,6-1,7-1,8-1,9-**3**,10-1,11-1,12-1,13-1,14-1,15-1,16-1,17-1,18-1,19-1,20-1,21-1
Conclusion: Six modern versions are more complex than the King James Bible.

132. Isaiah 42:2 He shall not cry, nor lift up, nor cause his voice to be heard in the street.
AV - **17,** 1-1,2-1,3-1,4-1,5-1,6-1,7-1,8-1,9-1,10-1,11-1,12-1,13-1,14-1,15-1,16-1,17-1
ESV - 17, 1-1,2-1,3-1,4-1,5-**2**,6-1,7-1,8-1,9-1,10-1,11-1,12-1,13-1,14-1,15-1,16-1,17-1
HCSB - **15,** 1-1,2-1,3-1,4-1,5-1,6-1,7-1,8-1,9-1,10-1,11-1,12-1,13-1,14-1,15-1
NASV - **17,** 1-1,2-1,3-1,4-1,5-1,6-1,7-1,8-1,9-1,10-1,11-1,12-1,13-1,14-1,15-1,16-1,17-1
NCV - 13, 1-1,2-1,3-1,4-1,5-1,6-1,7-1,8-1,9-1,10-**2**,11-1,12-1,13-1
NIV - **14,** 1-1,2-1,3-1,4-1,5-1,6-1,7-1,8-1,9-1,10-1,11-1,12-1,13-1,14-1
NKJV - **19,** 1-1,2-1,3-1,4-1,5-1,6-1,7-1,8-1,9-1,10-1,11-1,12-1,13-1,14-1,15-1,16-1,17-1,18-1,19-1
NLT - 10, 1-1,2-1,3-1,4-1,5-1,6-1,7-1,8-1,9-1,10-**2**
NRSV - **16,** 1-1,2-1,3-1,4-1,5-1,6-1,7-1,8-1,9-1,10-1,11-1,12-1,13-1,14-1,15-1,16-1
Conclusion: Only three modern versions are more complex than the King James Bible.

133. Isaiah 42:18 Hear, ye deaf; and look, ye blind, that ye may see.
AV - **11,** 1-1,2-1,3-1,4-1,5-1,6-1,7-1,8-1,9-1,10-1,11-1
ESV - **11,** 1-1,2-1,3-1,4-1,5-1,6-1,7-1,8-1,9-1,10-1,11-1
HCSB - 11, 1-**2**,2-1,3-1,4-1,5-1,6-1,7-1,8-1,9-1,10-1,11-1
NASV - **11,** 1-1,2-1,3-1,4-1,5-1,6-1,7-1,8-1,9-1,10-1,11-1
NCV - **13,** 1-1,2-1,3-1,4-1,5-1,6-1,7-1,8-1,9-1,10-1,11-1,12-1,13-1
NIV - **8,** 1-1,2-1,3-1,4-1,5-1,6-1,7-1,8-1
NKJV - **11,** 1-1,2-1,3-1,4-1,5-1,6-1,7-1,8-1,9-1,10-1,11-1
NLT - 10, 1-**2**,2-1,3-1,4-1,5-1,6-1,7-1,8-1,9-1,10-1
NRSV - 14, 1-**2**,2-1,3-1,4-1,5-1,6-1,7-1,8-1,9-1,10-1,11-1,12-1,13-1,14-1

Conclusion: Only three modern versions are more complex than the King James Bible.

134. Isaiah 66:9 Shall I bring to the birth, and not cause to bring forth? saith the LORD: shall I cause to bring forth, and shut the womb? saith thy God.
AV - **28,** 1-1,2-1,3-1,4-1,5-1,6-1,7-1,8-1,9-1,10-1,11-1,12-1,13-1,14-1,15-1,16-1,17-1,18-1,19-1,20-1,21-1,22-1,23-1,24-1,25-1,26-1,27-1,28-1
ESV - **30,** 1-1,2-1,3-1,4-1,5-1,6-1,7-1,8-1,9-1,10-1,11-1,12-1,13-1,14-1,15-1,16-1,17-1,18-1,19-1,20-1,21-1,22-1,23-1,24-1,25-1,26-1,27-1,28-1,29-1,30-1
HCSB - **27,** 1-1,2-1,3-1,4-**2,**5-1,6-1,7-1,8-1,9-1,10-1,11-1,12-**3,**13-1,14-1,15-1,16-1,17-1,18-1,19-1,20-1,21-**3,**22-1,23-1,24-1,25-1,26-1,27-1
NASV - **27,** 1-1,2-1,3-1,4-1,5-1,6-1,7-1,8-1,9-1,10-1,11-1,12-**4,**13-1,14-1,15-1,16-1,17-1,18-1,19-1,20-1,21-**4,**22-1,23-1,24-1,25-1,26-1,27-1
NCV - **40,** 1-1,2-1,3-1,4-1,5-1,6-1,7-1,8-1,9-1,10-**2,**11-**3,**12-**2,**13-1,14-1,15-1,16-1,17-1,18-1,19-1,20-1,21-1,22-1,23-1,24-1,25-1,26-1,27-1,28-1,29-1,30-1,31-1,32-**2,**33-1,34-1,35-1,36-1,37-1,38-1,39-1,40-1
NIV - **29,** 1-1,2-1,3-1,4-1,5-1,6-**2,**7-1,8-1,9-1,10-1,11-1,12-**4,**13-1,14-1,15-1,16-1,17-1,18-1,19-1,20-1,21-1,22-1,23-1,24-1,25-1,26-**4,**27-1,28-1,29-1
NKJV - **27,** 1-1,2-1,3-1,4-1,5-1,6-1,7-1,8-1,9-1,10-1,11-1,12-**4,**13-1,14-1,15-1,16-1,17-1,18-1,19-1,20-**4,**21-1,22-1,23-1,24-1,25-1,26-1,27-1
NLT - **32,** 1-1,2-1,3-**2,**4-1,5-1,6-**2,**7-1,8-1,9-1,10-1,11-1,12-1,13-1,14-1,15-**3,**16-1,17-1,18-1,19-1,20-1,21-1,22-1,23-**2,**24-1,25-1,26-**2,**27-1,28-**2,**29-1,30-1,31-1,32-1
NRSV - **23,** 1-1,2-1,3-**2,**4-1,5-1,6-1,7-1,8-**3,**9-1,10-1,11-1,12-1,13-1,14-1,15-1,16-1,17-**3,**18-1,19-1,20-1,21-1,22-1,23-1
Conclusion: Seven modern versions are more complex than the King James Bible. In a strange twist, the ESV has 30 words in the verse and they are all single syllable.

135. Jeremiah 17:14 Heal me, O LORD, and I shall be healed; save me, and I shall be saved: for thou art my praise.
AV - **21,** 1-1,2-1,3-1,4-1,5-1,6-1,7-1,8-1,9-1,10-1,11-1,12-1,13-1,14-1,15-1,16-1,17-1,18-1,19-1,20-1,21-1
ESV - **21,** 1-1,2-1,3-1,4-1,5-1,6-1,7-1,8-1,9-1,10-1,11-1,12-1,13-1,14-1,15-1,16-1,17-1,18-1,19-1,20-1,21-1
HCSB - **20,** 1-1,2-1,3-1,4-1,5-1,6-1,7-1,8-1,9-1,10-1,11-1,12-1,13-1,14-1,15-1,16-1,17-1,18-1,19-1,20-1
NASV - **21,** 1-1,2-1,3-1,4-1,5-1,6-1,7-1,8-1,9-1,10-1,11-1,12-1,13-1,14-1,15-1,16-1,17-1,18-1,19-1,20-1,21-1
NCV - **23,** 1-1,2-1,3-1,4-1,5-1,6-1,7-**2,**8-1,9-1,10-1,11-1,12-1,13-1,14-1,15-**2,**16-1,17-1,18-1,19-1,20-1,21-1,22-1,23-1
NIV - **23,** 1-1,2-1,3-1,4-1,5-1,6-1,7-1,8-1,9-1,10-1,11-1,12-1,13-1,14-1,15-1,16-1,17-1,18-1,19-1,20-1,21-1,22-1,23-1
NKJV - **21,** 1-1,2-1,3-1,4-1,5-1,6-1,7-1,8-1,9-1,10-1,11-1,12-1,13-1,14-1,15-1,16-1,17-1,18-1,19-1,20-1,21-1
NLT - **26,** 1-1,2-1,3-1,4-1,5-1,6-1,7-1,8-1,9-1,10-**2,**11-1,12-1,13-1,14-1,15-1,16-1,17-1,18-1,19-**2,**20-1,21-1,22-1,23-1,24-1,25-1,26-**2**
NRSV - **21,** 1-1,2-1,3-1,4-1,5-1,6-1,7-1,8-1,9-1,10-1,11-1,12-1,13-1,14-1,15-1,16-1,17-1,18-1,19-1,20-1,21-1
Conclusion: Only the NCV and the NLT made the verse more complex.

136. Jeremiah 22:29 O earth, earth, earth, hear the word of the LORD.
AV - **10,** 1-1,2-1,3-1,4-1,5-1,6-1,7-1,8-1,9-1,10-1
ESV - **10,** 1-1,2-1,3-1,4-1,5-1,6-1,7-1,8-1,9-1,10-1
HCSB - **9,** 1-1,2-1,3-1,4-1,5-1,6-1,7-1,8-1,9-1

NASV - **10,** 1-1,2-1,3-1,4-1,5-1,6-1,7-1,8-1,9-1,10-1
NCV - 11, 1-1,2-1,3-1,4-1,5-**2,**6-1,7-1,8-1,9-1,10-1,11-1
NIV - **10,** 1-1,2-1,3-1,4-1,5-1,6-1,7-1,8-1,9-1,10-1
NKJV - **10,** 1-1,2-1,3-1,4-1,5-1,6-1,7-1,8-1,9-1,10-1
NLT - 11, 1-1,2-1,3-1,4-1,5-**2,**6-1,7-1,8-**2,**9-1,10-1,11-1
NRSV - **10,** 1-1,2-1,3-1,4-1,5-1,6-1,7-1,8-1,9-1,10-1
Conclusion: Only the NCV and the NLT made the verse more complex. The ESV, NASV, NCV, NIV and the NRSV replaced "earth" with "land" which greatly curtails the scope of the prophecy. The NCV rendered "earth" as, "land of Judah." This was counted against it because, although "Judah" would be accepted as a proper name elsewhere, there is no authority for the insertion in this case. The NLT is the most difficult to read.

137. Jeremiah 29:13 And ye shall seek me, and find me, when ye shall search for me with all your heart.
AV - **18,** 1-1,2-1,3-1,4-1,5-1,6-1,7-1,8-1,9-1,10-1,11-1,12-1,13-1,14-1,15-1,16-1,17-1,18-1
ESV - **15,** 1-1,2-1,3-1,4-1,5-1,6-1,7-1,8-1,9-1,10-1,11-1,12-1,13-1,14-1,15-1
HCSB - **16,** 1-1,2-1,3-1,4-1,5-1,6-1,7-1,8-1,9-1,10-1,11-1,12-1,13-1,14-1,15-1,16-1
NASV - **16,** 1-1,2-1,3-1,4-1,5-1,6-1,7-1,8-1,9-1,10-1,11-1,12-1,13-1,14-1,15-1,16-1
NCV - **19,** 1-1,2-1,3-1,4-1,5-1,6-1,7-1,8-1,9-1,10-1,11-1,12-1,13-1,14-1,15-1,16-1,17-1,18-1,19-1
NIV - **15,** 1-1,2-1,3-1,4-1,5-1,6-1,7-1,8-1,9-1,10-1,11-1,12-1,13-1,14-1,15-1
NKJV - **17,** 1-1,2-1,3-1,4-1,5-1,6-1,7-1,8-1,9-1,10-1,11-1,12-1,13-1,14-1,15-1,16-1,17-1
NLT - 10, 1-1,2-1,3-1,4-1,5-1,6-**4,**7-1,8-1,9-1,10-1
NRSV - **17,** 1-1,2-1,3-1,4-1,5-1,6-1,7-1,8-1,9-1,10-1,11-1,12-1,13-1,14-1,15-1,16-1,17-1
Conclusion: Only the NLT made the verse more complex, which although it had the smallest word count inserted a four syllable word.

138. Lamentations 3:27 It is good for a man that he bear the yoke in his youth.
AV - **14,** 1-1,2-1,3-1,4-1,5-1,6-1,7-1,8-1,9-1,10-1,11-1,12-1,13-1,14-1
ESV - **14,** 1-1,2-1,3-1,4-1,5-1,6-1,7-1,8-1,9-1,10-1,11-1,12-1,13-1,14-1
HCSB - **15,** 1-1,2-1,3-1,4-1,5-1,6-1,7-1,8-1,9-1,10-1,11-1,12-1,13-1,14-1,15-1
NASV - **15,** 1-1,2-1,3-1,4-1,5-1,6-1,7-1,8-1,9-1,10-1,11-1,12-1,13-1,14-1,15-1
NCV - 12, 1-1,2-1,3-1,4-1,5-**2,**6-1,7-1,8-1,9-1,10-1,11-1,12-1
NIV - **14,** 1-1,2-1,3-1,4-1,5-1,6-1,7-1,8-1,9-1,10-1,11-1,12-1,13-1,14-1
NKJV - **13,** 1-1,2-1,3-1,4-1,5-1,6-1,7-1,8-1,9-1,10-1,11-1,12-1,13-1
NLT - 18, 1-1,2-1,3-1,4-1,5-1,6-**2,**7-1,8-**2,**9-1,10-1,11-**2,**12-1,13-1,14-1,15-1,16-1,17-1,18-**3**
NRSV - **11,** 1-1,2-1,3-1,4-1,5-1,6-1,7-1,8-1,9-1,10-1,11-1
Conclusion: Only the NCV and the NLT made the verse more complex. The NLT mustered an olympic effort to complicate the simple.

139. Lamentations 3:59 O LORD, thou hast seen my wrong: judge thou my cause.
AV - **11,** 1-1,2-1,3-1,4-1,5-1,6-1,7-1,8-1,9-1,10-1,11-1
ESV - **13,** 1-1,2-1,3-1,4-1,5-1,6-1,7-1,8-1,9-1,10-1,11-1,12-1,13-1
HCSB - **11,** 1-1,2-1,3-1,4-1,5-1,6-1,7-1,8-1,9-1,10-1,11-1
NASV - 10, 1-1,2-1,3-1,4-1,5-1,6-1,7-**3,**8-1,9-1,10-1
NCV - **15,** 1-1,2-1,3-1,4-1,5-1,6-1,7-1,8-1,9-1,10-1,11-1,12-1,13-1,14-1,15-1
NIV - 13, 1-1,2-1,3-1,4-1,5-1,6-1,7-1,8-1,9-1,10-1,11-**2,**12-1,13-1

NKJV - **12,** 1-1,2-1,3-1,4-1,5-1,6-1,7-1,8-1,9-1,10-1,11-1,12-1
NLT - **18,** 1-1,2-1,3-1,4-1,5-1,6-1,7-1,8-1,9-1,10-1,11-1,12-1,13-1,14-1,15-1,16-1,17-1,18-1
NRSV - **13,** 1-1,2-1,3-1,4-1,5-1,6-1,7-1,8-1,9-1,10-1,11-1,12-1,13-1
Conclusion: Only the NASV and the NIV made the verse more complex.

140. Lamentations 5:17 For this our heart is faint; for these things our eyes are dim.
AV - **13,** 1-1,2-1,3-1,4-1,5-1,6-1,7-1,8-1,9-1,10-1,11-1,12-1,13-1
ESV - **15,** 1-1,2-1,3-1,4-1,5-1,6-**2**,7-1,8-1,9-1,10-1,11-1,12-1,13-1,14-1,15-1
HCSB - **14,** 1-**2**,2-1,3-1,4-1,5-1,6-1,7-1,8-**2**,9-1,10-1,11-1,12-1,13-1,14-1
NASV - **15,** 1-**2**,2-1,3-1,4-1,5-1,6-1,7-1,8-**2**,9-1,10-1,11-1,12-1,13-1,14-1,15-1
NCV - **12,** 1-**2**,2-1,3-1,4-1,5-1,6-1,7-1,8-1,9-1,10-1,11-1,12-1
NIV - **15,** 1-**2**,2-1,3-1,4-1,5-1,6-1,7-1,8-**2**,9-1,10-1,11-1,12-1,13-1,14-1,15-1
NKJV - **15,** 1-**2**,2-1,3-1,4-1,5-1,6-1,7-1,8-**2**,9-1,10-1,11-1,12-1,13-1,14-1,15-1
NLT - **13,** 1-1,2-1,3-1,4-1,5-1,6-**2**,7-1,8-1,9-1,10-1,11-1,12-1,13-1
NRSV - **16,** 1-**2**,2-1,3-1,4-1,5-1,6-1,7-1,8-**2**,9-1,10-1,11-1,12-1,13-1,14-1,15-1,16-1
Conclusion: All eight modern versions are more complex than the King James Bible.

141. Ezekiel 6:7 And the slain shall fall in the midst of you, and ye shall know that I am the LORD.
AV - **19,** 1-1,2-1,3-1,4-1,5-1,6-1,7-1,8-1,9-1,10-1,11-1,12-1,13-1,14-1,15-1,16-1,17-1,18-1,19-1
ESV - **17,** 1-1,2-1,3-1,4-1,5-1,6-1,7-1,8-1,9-1,10-1,11-1,12-1,13-1,14-1,15-1,16-1,17-1
HCSB - **15,** 1-1,2-1,3-1,4-1,5-**2**,6-1,7-1,8-1,9-1,10-1,11-1,12-1,13-1,14-1,15-1
NASV - **15,** 1-1,2-1,3-1,4-1,5-**2**,6-1,7-1,8-1,9-1,10-1,11-1,12-1,13-1,14-1,15-1
NCV - **18,** 1-1,2-**2**,3-1,4-1,5-1,6-1,7-1,8-**2**,9-1,10-1,11-1,12-1,13-1,14-1,15-1,16-1,17-1,18-1
NIV - **16,** 1-1,2-**2**,3-1,4-1,5-1,6-**2**,7-1,8-1,9-1,10-1,11-1,12-1,13-1,14-1,15-1,16-1
NKJV - **16,** 1-1,2-1,3-1,4-1,5-1,6-1,7-1,8-1,9-1,10-1,11-1,12-1,13-1,14-1,15-1,16-1
NLT - **17,** 1-1,2-1,3-1,4-1,5-**2**,6-1,7-**2**,8-1,9-1,10-1,11-1,12-1,13-1,14-**2**,15-1,16-1,17-1
NRSV - **16,** 1-1,2-1,3-1,4-1,5-1,6-1,7-1,8-1,9-1,10-1,11-1,12-1,13-1,14-1,15-1,16-1
Conclusion: Five modern versions are more complex than the King James Bible. Again, the NLT won the prize for complexity.

142. Ezekiel 26:13 And I will cause the noise of thy songs to cease; and the sound of thy harps shall be no more heard.
AV - **22,** 1-1,2-1,3-1,4-1,5-1,6-1,7-1,8-1,9-1,10-1,11-1,12-1,13-1,14-1,15-1,16-1,17-1,18-1,19-1,20-1,21-1,22-1
ESV - **20,** 1-1,2-1,3-1,4-1,5-1,6-**2**,7-1,8-1,9-1,10-1,11-1,12-1,13-1,14-1,15-1,16-1,17-1,18-1,19-1,20-1
HCSB - **22,** 1-1,2-1,3-1,4-1,5-1,6-1,7-1,8-1,9-1,10-1,11-1,12-1,13-1,14-1,15-1,16-1,17-1,18-1,19-1,20-**2**,21-1,22-1
NASV - **20,** 1-1,2-1,3-1,4-**2**,5-1,6-1,7-1,8-1,9-1,10-1,11-1,12-1,13-1,14-1,15-1,16-1,17-1,18-1,19-1,20-1
NCV - **16,** 1-1,2-1,3-1,4-1,5-1,6-1,7-1,8-**2**,9-1,10-1,11-1,12-1,13-1,14-1,15-1,16-**3**
NIV - **20,** 1-1,2-1,3-1,4-1,5-1,6-1,7-1,8-**2**,9-1,10-1,11-1,12-**2**,13-1,14-1,15-1,16-1,17-1,18-1,19-1,20-1
NKJV - **22,** 1-1,2-1,3-1,4-1,5-1,6-1,7-1,8-1,9-1,10-1,11-1,12-1,13-1,14-1,15-1,16-1,17-1,18-1,19-1,20-1,21-1,22-1
NLT - **20,** 1-1,2-1,3-1,4-1,5-**2**,6-1,7-1,8-1,9-1,10-1,11-1,12-1,13-1,14-1,15-1,16-1,17-1,18-**2**,19-1,20-**2**
NRSV - **18,** 1-1,2-1,3-**2**,4-1,5-**2**,6-1,7-1,8-1,9-1,10-1,11-1,12-1,13-1,14-1,15-1,16-1,17-1,18-1

Conclusion: Seven modern versions are more complex than the King James Bible. The NLT is the most difficult to read.

143. Ezekiel 28:8 They shall bring thee down to the pit, and thou shalt die the deaths of them that are slain in the midst of the seas.
AV - **25,** 1-1,2-1,3-1,4-1,5-1,6-1,7-1,8-1,9-1,10-1,11-1,12-1,13-1,14-1,15-1,16-1,17-1,18-1,19-1,20-1,21-1,22-1,23-1,24-1,25-1
ESV - **23,** 1-1,2-1,3-1,4-1,5-1,6-**2**,7-1,8-1,9-1,10-1,11-1,12-1,13-1,14-1,15-1,16-1,17-1,18-1,19-1,20-1,21-1,22-1,23-1
HCSB - **21,** 1-1,2-1,3-1,4-1,5-1,6-1,7-1,8-1,9-1,10-1,11-1,12-1,13-1,14-**3**,15-1,16-1,17-1,18-1,19-1,20-1,21-1
NASV - **25,** 1-1,2-1,3-1,4-1,5-1,6-1,7-1,8-1,9-1,10-1,11-1,12-1,13-1,14-1,15-1,16-1,17-1,18-1,19-1,20-1,21-1,22-1,23-1,24-1,25-1
NCV - **17,** 1-1,2-1,3-1,4-1,5-1,6-1,7-1,8-1,9-**3**,10-1,11-1,12-1,13-1,14-1,15-1,16-1,17-1
NIV - **21,** 1-1,2-1,3-1,4-1,5-1,6-1,7-1,8-1,9-1,10-1,11-1,12-1,13-1,14-**3**,15-1,16-1,17-1,18-1,19-1,20-1,21-1
NKJV - **23,** 1-1,2-1,3-1,4-1,5-1,6-**2**,7-1,8-1,9-1,10-1,11-1,12-1,13-1,14-1,15-1,16-1,17-1,18-1,19-1,20-1,21-1,22-1,23-1
NLT - **22,** 1-1,2-1,3-1,4-1,5-1,6-1,7-1,8-1,9-1,10-1,11-1,12-1,13-1,14-1,15-1,16-1,17-1,18-1,19-1,20-1,21-**2**,22-1
NRSV - **21,** 1-1,2-1,3-1,4-1,5-1,6-1,7-1,8-1,9-1,10-1,11-1,12-1,13-1,14-**3**,15-1,16-1,17-1,18-1,19-1,20-1,21-1
Conclusion: Seven modern versions are more complex than the King James Bible.

144. Ezekiel 34:3 Ye eat the fat, and ye clothe you with the wool, ye kill them that are fed: but ye feed not the flock.
AV - **23,** 1-1,2-1,3-1,4-1,5-1,6-1,7-1,8-1,9-1,10-1,11-1,12-1,13-1,14-1,15-1,16-1,17-1,18-1,19-1,20-1,21-1,22-1,23-1
ESV - **22,** 1-1,2-1,3-1,4-1,5-1,6-1,7-**2**,8-1,9-1,10-1,11-1,12-**2**,13-1,14-1,15-1,16-1,17-1,18-1,19-1,20-1,21-1,22-1
HCSB - **18,** 1-1,2-1,3-1,4-1,5-1,6-1,7-1,8-1,9-**2**,10-1,11-**2**,12-1,13-1,14-1,15-1,16-1,17-1,18-1
NASV - **19,** 1-1,2-1,3-1,4-1,5-1,6-1,7-**2**,8-1,9-1,10-1,11-1,12-**2**,13-1,14-1,15-1,16-**2**,17-**2**,18-1,19-1
NCV - **24,** 1-1,2-1,3-1,4-1,5-1,6-1,7-1,8-1,9-**2**,10-1,11-1,12-1,13-1,14-1,15-1,16-1,17-1,18-1,19-1,20-1,21-1,22-1,23-1,24-1
NIV - **23,** 1-1,2-1,3-1,4-1,5-1,6-**2**,7-1,8-1,9-1,10-1,11-**2**,12-1,13-1,14-**3**,15-1,16-1,17-1,18-1,19-1,20-1,21-1,22-1,23-1
NKJV - **21,** 1-1,2-1,3-1,4-1,5-1,6-1,7-**2**,8-1,9-1,10-1,11-1,12-**2**,13-1,14-**2**,15-1,16-1,17-1,18-1,19-1,20-1,21-1
NLT - **18,** 1-1,2-1,3-1,4-1,5-1,6-1,7-1,8-1,9-**2**,10-1,11-1,12-**3**,13-1,14-1,15-1,16-1,17-1,18-1
NRSV - **21,** 1-1,2-1,3-1,4-1,5-1,6-1,7-**2**,8-1,9-1,10-1,11-1,12-**2**,13-1,14-**2**,15-1,16-1,17-1,18-1,19-1,20-1,21-1
Conclusion: All eight modern versions are more complex than the King James Bible.

145. Ezekiel 34:15 I will feed my flock, and I will cause them to lie down, saith the Lord GOD.
AV - **17,** 1-1,2-1,3-1,4-1,5-1,6-1,7-1,8-1,9-1,10-1,11-1,12-1,13-1,14-1,15-1,16-1,17-1
ESV - **21,** 1-1,2-**2**,3-1,4-1,5-1,6-**2**,7-1,8-1,9-1,10-1,11-1,12-**2**,13-1,14-1,15-1,16-1,17-1,18-**2**,19-1,20-1,21-1
HCSB - **18,** 1-1,2-1,3-1,4-1,5-1,6-1,7-1,8-1,9-1,10-1,11-1,12-1,13-1,14-**4**,15-1,16-1,17-1,18-1
NASV - **16,** 1-1,2-1,3-1,4-1,5-1,6-1,7-1,8-1,9-1,10-1,11-1,12-1,13-**2**,14-1,15-1,16-1
NCV - **14,** 1-1,2-1,3-1,4-1,5-1,6-1,7-1,8-1,9-1,10-1,11-1,12-1,13-1,14-1
NIV - **15,** 1-1,2-**2**,3-1,4-1,5-1,6-1,7-1,8-1,9-1,10-1,11-1,12-**2**,13-1,14-**3**,15-1

NKJV - **16,** 1-1,2-1,3-1,4-1,5-1,6-1,7-1,8-1,9-1,10-1,11-1,12-1,13-1,14-1,15-1,16-1
NLT - **20,** 1-1,2-**2**,3-1,4-1,5-1,6-1,7-1,8-1,9-1,10-1,11-1,12-1,13-1,14-1,15-1,16-1,17-1,18-1,19-**3**,20-1
NRSV - **20,** 1-1,2-**2**,3-1,4-1,5-1,6-**2**,7-1,8-1,9-1,10-1,11-1,12-1,13-1,14-1,15-1,16-1,17-1,18-1,19-1,20-1
Conclusion: Six modern versions are more complex than the King James Bible.

146. Daniel 2:33: His legs of iron, his feet part of iron and part of clay.
AV - **13,** 1-1,2-1,3-1,4-1,5-1,6-1,7-1,8-1,9-1,10-1,11-1,12-1,13-1
ESV - **13,** 1-1,2-1,3-1,4-1,5-1,6-1,7-**2**,8-1,9-1,10-1,11-**2**,12-1,13-1
HCSB - **14,** 1-1,2-1,3-1,4-1,5-1,6-1,7-1,8-1,9-**2**,10-1,11-1,12-**2**,13-1,14-1
NASV - **13,** 1-1,2-1,3-1,4-1,5-1,6-1,7-**2**,8-1,9-1,10-1,11-**2**,12-1,13-1
NCV - **23,** 1-1,2-**2**,3-1,4-1,5-1,6-1,7-1,8-1,9-1,10-1,11-1,12-1,13-1,14-1,15-1,16-**2**,17-1,18-1,19-1,20-**2**,21-1,22-1,23-1
NIV - **14,** 1-1,2-1,3-1,4-1,5-1,6-1,7-**2**,8-1,9-1,10-1,11-**2**,12-1,13-1,14-1
NKJV - **13,** 1-1,2-1,3-1,4-1,5-1,6-1,7-**2**,8-1,9-1,10-1,11-**2**,12-1,13-1
NLT - **15,** 1-1,2-1,3-1,4-1,5-1,6-1,7-1,8-1,9-1,10-**4**,11-1,12-1,13-1,14-1,15-1
NRSV - **13,** 1-1,2-1,3-1,4-1,5-1,6-1,7-**2**,8-1,9-1,10-1,11-**2**,12-1,13-1
Conclusion: All eight modern versions are more complex than the King James Bible. The NCV made the verse more complex.

147. Daniel 12:13 But go thou thy way till the end be: for thou shalt rest, and stand in thy lot at the end of the days.
AV - **24,** 1-1,2-1,3-1,4-1,5-1,6-1,7-1,8-1,9-1,10-1,11-1,12-1,13-1,14-1,15-1,16-1,17-1,18-1,19-1,20-1,21-1,22-1,23-1,24-1
ESV - **24,** 1-1,2-1,3-1,4-1,5-1,6-1,7-1,8-1,9-1,10-1,11-1,12-1,13-1,14-1,15-1,16-1,17-**3**,18-1,19-1,20-1,21-1,22-1,23-1,24-1
HCSB - **25,** 1-1,2-1,3-1,4-1,5-1,6-1,7-1,8-1,9-1,10-1,11-1,12-1,13-1,14-1,15-1,16-1,17-1,18-1,19-**3**,20-1,21-1,22-1,23-1,24-1,25-1
NASV - **29,** 1-1,2-1,3-1,4-1,5-1,6-1,7-1,8-1,9-1,10-1,11-1,12-1,13-1,14-**2**,15-**2**,16-1,17-1,18-1,19-**2**,20-1,21-1,22-**3**,23-**2**,24-1,25-1,26-1,27-1,28-1,29-1
NCV - **26,** 1-1,2-1,3-1,4-1,5-1,6-1,7-1,8-**2**,9-1,10-1,11-1,12-1,13-1,14-1,15-1,16-1,17-1,18-1,19-1,20-1,21-1,22-1,23-1,24-**2**,25-1,26-**2**
NIV - **28,** 1-1,2-1,3-1,4-1,5-1,6-1,7-1,8-1,9-1,10-1,11-1,12-1,13-1,14-1,15-1,16-1,17-1,18-1,19-1,20-1,21-1,22-1,23-1,24-1,25-**2**,26-1,27-**3**,28-**4**
NKJV - **24,** 1-1,2-1,3-1,4-1,5-1,6-1,7-1,8-1,9-1,10-1,11-1,12-1,13-1,14-1,15-**2**,16-1,17-1,18-**4**,19-1,20-1,21-1,22-1,23-1,24-1
NLT - **32,** 1-1,2-1,3-1,4-1,5-1,6-1,7-**2**,8-1,9-1,10-1,11-1,12-1,13-1,14-1,15-1,16-1,17-1,18-1,19-1,20-1,21-1,22-1,23-1,24-**2**,25-1,26-**2**,27-1,28-**4**,29-1,30-**2**,31-1,32-1
NRSV - **19,** 1-1,2-1,3-1,4-1,5-1,6-1,7-1,8-1,9-1,10-1,11-1,12-1,13-**2**,14-1,15-1,16-1,17-1,18-1,19-1
Conclusion: All eight modern versions are more complex than the King James Bible.

148. Zechariah 14:6 And it shall come to pass in that day, that the light shall not be clear, nor dark:
AV - **18,** 1-1,2-1,3-1,4-1,5-1,6-1,7-1,8-1,9-1,10-1,11-1,12-1,13-1,14-1,15-1,16-1,17-1,18-1
ESV - **11,** 1-1,2-1,3-1,4-1,5-1,6-1,7-1,8-1,9-1,10-1,11-1
HCSB - **14,** 1-1,2-1,3-1,4-1,5-1,6-1,7-1,8-1,9-1,10-**2**,11-1,12-**2**,13-1,14-**3**
NASV - **12,** 1-1,2-1,3-1,4-1,5-1,6-1,7-1,8-1,9-1,10-**4**,11-1,12-**2**

NCV - **11,** 1-1,2-1,3-1,4-1,5-1,6-1,7-1,8-1,9-1,10-1,11-1
NIV - **12,** 1-1,2-1,3-1,4-1,5-1,6-1,7-1,8-1,9-1,10-1,11-1,12-1
NKJV - 18, 1-1,2-1,3-1,4-1,5-1,6-1,7-1,8-1,9-1,10-1,11-1,12-1,13-1,14-1,15-1,16-1,17-1,18-**3**
NLT - 11, 1-1,2-1,3-1,4-1,5-**2**,6-1,7-1,8-1,9-1,10-**2**,11-1
NRSV - 11, 1-1,2-1,3-1,4-1,5-1,6-1,7-1,8-**2**,9-1,10-1,11-1
Conclusion: Five modern versions are more complex than the King James Bible. The HCSB made the verse more complex.

149. Matthew 5:8 Blessed are the pure in heart: for they shall see God.
AV - **11,** 1-1,2-1,3-1,4-1,5-1,6-1,7-1,8-1,9-1,10-1,11-1
ESV - **11,** 1-1,2-1,3-1,4-1,5-1,6-1,7-1,8-1,9-1,10-1,11-1
HCSB - 11, 1-1,2-1,3-1,4-1,5-1,6-1,7-**2**,8-1,9-1,10-1,11-1
NASV - **11,** 1-1,2-1,3-1,4-1,5-1,6-1,7-1,8-1,9-1,10-1,11-1
NCV - **12,** 1-1,2-1,3-1,4-1,5-1,6-1,7-1,8-1,9-1,10-1,11-1,12-1
NIV - **11,** 1-1,2-1,3-1,4-1,5-1,6-1,7-1,8-1,9-1,10-1,11-1
NKJV - **11,** 1-1,2-1,3-1,4-1,5-1,6-1,7-1,8-1,9-1,10-1,11-1
NLT - 12, 1-1,2-**2**,3-1,4-1,5-1,6-1,7-1,8-1,9-1,10-1,11-1,12-1
NRSV - **11,** 1-1,2-1,3-1,4-1,5-1,6-1,7-1,8-1,9-1,10-1,11-1
Conclusion: Only the HCSB and the NLT made the verse more complex.

150. Matthew 5:38 Ye have heard that it hath been said, An eye for an eye, and a tooth for a tooth:
AV - **19,** 1-1,2-1,3-1,4-1,5-1,6-1,7-1,8-1,9-1,10-1,11-1,12-1,13-1,14-1,15-1,16-1,17-1,18-1,19-1
ESV - **18,** 1-1,2-1,3-1,4-1,5-1,6-1,7-1,8-1,9-1,10-1,11-1,12-1,13-1,14-1,15-1,16-1,17-1,18-1
HCSB - **18,** 1-1,2-1,3-1,4-1,5-1,6-1,7-1,8-1,9-1,10-1,11-1,12-1,13-1,14-1,15-1,16-1,17-1,18-1
NASV - **18,** 1-1,2-1,3-1,4-1,5-1,6-1,7-1,8-1,9-1,10-1,11-1,12-1,13-1,14-1,15-1,16-1,17-1,18-1
NCV - **18,** 1-1,2-1,3-1,4-1,5-1,6-1,7-1,8-1,9-1,10-1,11-1,12-1,13-1,14-1,15-1,16-1,17-1,18-1
NIV - **14,** 1-1,2-1,3-1,4-1,5-1,6-1,7-1,8-1,9-1,10-1,11-1,12-1,13-1,14-1
NKJV - **18,** 1-1,2-1,3-1,4-1,5-1,6-1,7-1,8-1,9-1,10-1,11-1,12-1,13-1,14-1,15-1,16-1,17-1,18-1
NLT - 24, 1-1,2-1,3-1,4-1,5-1,6-1,7-1,8-1,9-**3**,10-1,11-1,12-1,13-**3**,14-1,15-1,16-1,17-1,18-1,19-1,20-1,21-1,22-1,23-1,24-1
NRSV - **18,** 1-1,2-1,3-1,4-1,5-1,6-1,7-1,8-1,9-1,10-1,11-1,12-1,13-1,14-1,15-1,16-1,17-1,18-1
Conclusion: Only the NLT made the verse more complex.

151. Matthew 7:1 Judge not, that ye be not judged.
AV - **7,** 1-1,2-1,3-1,4-1,5-1,6-1,7-1
ESV - **7,** 1-1,2-1,3-1,4-1,5-1,6-1,7-1
HCSB - **9,** 1-1,2-1,3-1,4-1,5-1,6-1,7-1,8-1,9-1
NASV - **10,** 1-1,2-1,3-1,4-1,5-1,6-1,7-1,8-1,9-1,10-1
NCV - **8,** 1-1,2-1,3-1,4-1,5-1,6-1,7-1,8-1
NIV - **9,** 1-1,2-1,3-1,4-1,5-1,6-1,7-1,8-1,9-1
NKJV - **7,** 1-1,2-1,3-1,4-1,5-1,6-1,7-1
NLT - 10, 1-1,2-1,3-1,4-**2**,5-1,6-1,7-1,8-1,9-1,10-1
NRSV - **10,** 1-1,2-1,3-1,4-1,5-1,6-1,7-1,8-1,9-1,10-1
Conclusion: Only the NLT found a way to make such a simple statement complex.

152. Matthew 7:9 Or what man is there of you, whom if his son ask bread, will he give him a stone?
AV - **19,** 1-1,2-1,3-1,4-1,5-1,6-1,7-1,8-1,9-1,10-1,11-1,12-1,13-1,14-1,15-1,16-1,17-1,18-1,19-1
ESV - **17,** 1-1,2-1,3-1,4-1,5-1,6-1,7-1,8-1,9-1,10-1,11-1,12-1,13-1,14-1,15-1,16-1,17-1
HCSB - 16, 1-1,2-1,3-**2**,4-1,5-1,6-1,7-1,8-1,9-1,10-1,11-1,12-1,13-1,14-1,15-1,16-1
NASV - 20, 1-1,2-1,3-1,4-1,5-1,6-**2**,7-1,8-1,9-1,10-1,11-1,12-1,13-1,14-1,15-1,16-1,17-1,18-1,19-1,20-1
NCV - 14, 1-1,2-1,3-**2**,4-1,5-1,6-1,7-1,8-1,9-1,10-1,11-1,12-1,13-1,14-1
NIV - **14,** 1-1,2-1,3-1,4-1,5-1,6-1,7-1,8-1,9-1,10-1,11-1,12-1,13-1,14-1
NKJV - 19, 1-1,2-1,3-1,4-1,5-1,6-**2**,7-1,8-1,9-1,10-1,11-1,12-1,13-1,14-1,15-1,16-1,17-1,18-1,19-1
NLT - 18, 1-1,2-**2**,3-1,4-1,5-**2**,6-1,7-1,8-1,9-1,10-1,11-1,12-1,13-1,14-1,15-1,16-1,17-1,18-**2**
NRSV - 16, 1-1,2-1,3-**3**,4-**2**,5-1,6-1,7-1,8-1,9-1,10-1,11-1,12-1,13-1,14-1,15-1,16-1
Conclusion: Six modern versions are more complex than the King James Bible. The NLT is the most difficult to read.

153. Matthew 10:34 Think not that I am come to send peace on earth: I came not to send peace, but a sword.
AV - **20,** 1-1,2-1,3-1,4-1,5-1,6-1,7-1,8-1,9-1,10-1,11-1,12-1,13-1,14-1,15-1,16-1,17-1,18-1,19-1,20-1
ESV - **23,** 1-1,2-1,3-1,4-1,5-1,6-1,7-1,8-1,9-1,10-1,11-1,12-1,13-1,14-1,15-1,16-1,17-1,18-1,19-1,20-1,21-1,22-1,23-1
HCSB - 21, 1-1,2-**2**,3-1,4-1,5-1,6-1,7-1,8-1,9-1,10-1,11-1,12-1,13-1,14-1,15-1,16-1,17-1,18-1,19-1,20-1,21-1
NASV - 22, 1-1,2-1,3-1,4-1,5-1,6-1,7-1,8-1,9-1,10-1,11-1,12-1,13-1,14-1,15-1,16-1,17-1,18-1,19-1,20-1,21-1,22-1
NCV - **21,** 1-1,2-1,3-1,4-1,5-1,6-1,7-1,8-1,9-1,10-1,11-1,12-1,13-1,14-1,15-1,16-1,17-1,18-1,19-1,20-1,21-1
NIV - 23, 1-1,2-1,3-**2**,4-1,5-1,6-1,7-1,8-1,9-1,10-1,11-1,12-1,13-1,14-1,15-1,16-1,17-1,18-1,19-1,20-1,21-1,22-1,23-1
NKJV - **21,** 1-1,2-1,3-1,4-1,5-1,6-1,7-1,8-1,9-1,10-1,11-1,12-1,13-1,14-1,15-1,16-1,17-1,18-1,19-1,20-1,21-1
NLT - 21, 1-1,2-**3**,3-1,4-1,5-1,6-1,7-1,8-1,9-1,10-1,11-1,12-1,13-1,14-1,15-1,16-1,17-1,18-1,19-1,20-1,21-1
NRSV - **23,** 1-1,2-1,3-1,4-1,5-1,6-1,7-1,8-1,9-1,10-1,11-1,12-1,13-1,14-1,15-1,16-1,17-1,18-1,19-1,20-1,21-1,22-1,23-1
Conclusion: Only the HCSB, the NIV and the NLT made the verse more complex.

154. Matthew 11:15 He that hath ears to hear, let him hear.
AV - **9,** 1-1,2-1,3-1,4-1,5-1,6-1,7-1,8-1,9-1
ESV - **9,** 1-1,2-1,3-1,4-1,5-1,6-1,7-1,8-1,9-1
HCSB - 6, 1-**3**,2-1,3-1,4-1,5-1,6-**2**
NASV - **9,** 1-1,2-1,3-1,4-1,5-1,6-1,7-1,8-1,9-1
NCV - **7,** 1-1,2-1,3-1,4-1,5-1,6-1,7-1
NIV - **9,** 1-1,2-1,3-1,4-1,5-1,6-1,7-1,8-1,9-1
NKJV - **9,** 1-1,2-1,3-1,4-1,5-1,6-1,7-1,8-1,9-1
NLT - 9, 1-**3**,2-1,3-1,4-1,5-1,6-1,7-**2**,8-1,9-**3**
NRSV - 5, 1-1,2-**3**,3-1,4-1,5-**2**
Conclusion: Only three modern versions are more complex than the King James Bible. The NLT is the most difficult to read.

155. Matthew 12:16 And charged them that they should not make him known:
AV - **10,** 1-1,2-1,3-1,4-1,5-1,6-1,7-1,8-1,9-1,10-1
ESV - 8, 1-1,2-**2**,3-1,4-1,5-1,6-1,7-1,8-1

HCSB - **8,** 1-1,2-1,3-1,4-1,5-1,6-1,7-1,8-1
NASV - **9,** 1-1,2-1,3-1,4-1,5-1,6-1,7-1,8-1,9-1
NCV - 11, 1-1,2-1,3-1,4-1,5-**2,**6-1,7-1,8-1,9-1,10-1,11-1
NIV - 8, 1-**2,**2-1,3-1,4-1,5-1,6-1,7-1,8-1
NKJV - **9,** 1-1,2-1,3-1,4-1,5-1,6-1,7-1,8-1,9-1
NLT - 10, 1-1,2-1,3-1,4-1,5-1,6-1,7-**2,**8-1,9-1,10-1
NRSV - 9, 1-1,2-1,3-**2,**4-1,5-1,6-1,7-1,8-1,9-1
Conclusion: Five modern versions are more complex than the King James Bible. The NCV inserted "Jesus" for "him" but it was not counted as a multi-syllable word.

156. Matthew 13:9 Who hath ears to hear, let him hear.
AV - **8,** 1-1,2-1,3-1,4-1,5-1,6-1,7-1,8-1
ESV - **7,** 1-1,2-1,3-1,4-1,5-1,6-1,7-1
HCSB - 6, 1-**3,**2-1,3-1,4-1,5-1,6-**2**
NASV - **7,** 1-1,2-1,3-1,4-1,5-1,6-1,7-1
NCV - 8, 1-1,2-1,3-1,4-1,5-1,6-1,7-1,8-**2**
NIV - **7,** 1-1,2-1,3-1,4-1,5-1,6-1,7-1
NKJV - **9,** 1-1,2-1,3-1,4-1,5-1,6-1,7-1,8-1,9-1
NLT - 9, 1-**3,**2-1,3-1,4-1,5-1,6-1,7-**2,**8-1,9-**3**
NRSV - 5, 1-1,2-**3,**3-1,4-1,5-**2**
Conclusion: Four modern versions are more complex than the King James Bible. The NLT is the most difficult to read.

157. Matthew 13:16 But blessed are your eyes, for they see: and your ears, for they hear.
AV - **14,** 1-1,2-1,3-1,4-1,5-1,6-1,7-1,8-1,9-1,10-1,11-1,12-1,13-1,14-1
ESV - **14,** 1-1,2-1,3-1,4-1,5-1,6-1,7-1,8-1,9-1,10-1,11-1,12-1,13-1,14-1
HCSB - 16, 1-1,2-1,3-1,4-1,5-1,6-**2,**7-1,8-1,9-1,10-1,11-1,12-1,13-**2,**14-1,15-1,16-1
NASV - 14, 1-1,2-1,3-1,4-1,5-1,6-**2,**7-1,8-1,9-1,10-1,11-1,12-**2,**13-1,14-1
NCV - 15, 1-1,2-1,3-1,4-1,5-**2,**6-1,7-1,8-1,9-1,10-1,11-1,12-1,13-1,14-1,15-1
NIV - 14, 1-1,2-1,3-1,4-1,5-1,6-**2,**7-1,8-1,9-1,10-1,11-1,12-**2,**13-1,14-1
NKJV - **14,** 1-1,2-1,3-1,4-1,5-1,6-1,7-1,8-1,9-1,10-1,11-1,12-1,13-1,14-1
NLT - **14,** 1-1,2-1,3-1,4-1,5-1,6-**2,**7-1,8-1,9-1,10-1,11-1,12-**2,**13-1,14-1
NRSV - **14,** 1-1,2-1,3-1,4-1,5-1,6-1,7-1,8-1,9-1,10-1,11-1,12-1,13-1,14-1
Conclusion: Five modern versions are more complex than the King James Bible.

158. Matthew 13:46 Who, when he had found one pearl of great price, went and sold all that he had, and bought it.
AV - **20,** 1-1,2-1,3-1,4-1,5-1,6-1,7-1,8-1,9-1,10-1,11-1,12-1,13-1,14-1,15-1,16-1,17-1,18-1,19-1,20-1
ESV - 18, 1-1,2-1,3-**2,**4-1,5-1,6-1,7-1,8-**2,**9-1,10-1,11-1,12-1,13-1,14-1,15-1,16-1,17-1,18-1
HCSB - 16, 1-1,2-1,3-1,4-1,5-**2,**6-1,7-1,8-1,9-1,10-1,11-**4,**12-1,13-1,14-1,15-1,16-1
NASV - 19, 1-1,2-**2,**3-**2,**4-1,5-1,6-1,7-1,8-**2,**9-1,10-1,11-1,12-1,13-1,14-1,15-1,16-1,17-1,18-1,19-1
NCV - 17, 1-1,2-1,3-1,4-1,5-**2,**6-**4,**7-1,8-1,9-1,10-1,11-1,12-**4,**13-1,14-1,15-1,16-1,17-1
NIV - 18, 1-1,2-1,3-1,4-1,5-1,6-1,7-**2,**8-1,9-1,10-**2,**11-1,12-1,13-**4,**14-1,15-1,16-1,17-1,18-1
NKJV - **20,** 1-1,2-1,3-1,4-1,5-1,6-1,7-1,8-1,9-1,10-1,11-1,12-1,13-1,14-1,15-1,16-1,17-1,18-1,19-1,20-1
NLT - 16, 1-1,2-1,3-**3,**4-1,5-1,6-1,7-1,8-**2,**9-1,10-1,11-**4,**12-1,13-1,14-1,15-1,16-1

NRSV - **18,** 1-1,2-**2,**3-1,4-1,5-1,6-1,7-1,8-1,9-1,10-1,11-1,12-1,13-1,14-1,15-1,16-1,17-1,18-1
Conclusion: Seven modern versions are more complex than the King James Bible.

159. Matthew 18:11 For the Son of man is come to save that which was lost.
AV - **13,** 1-1,2-1,3-1,4-1,5-1,6-1,7-1,8-1,9-1,10-1,11-1,12-1,13-1
ESV - The verse is omitted.
HCSB - **[11,** 1-1,2-1,3-1,4-1,5-1,6-1,7-1,8-1,9-1,10-1,11-1]
NASV - **[13,** 1-1,2-1,3-1,4-1,5-1,6-1,7-1,8-1,9-1,10-1,11-1,12-1,13-1]
NCV - **[9,** 1-1,2-1,3-1,4-1,5-1,6-1,7-1,8-1,9-**2]**
NIV - The verse is omitted.
NKJV - **13,** 1-1,2-1,3-1,4-1,5-1,6-1,7-1,8-1,9-1,10-1,11-1,12-1,13-1
NLT - The verse is omitted.
NRSV - The verse is omitted.
Conclusion: Four modern versions omit the verse entirely. The HCSB, the NASV and the NCV have the verse in brackets. Only the NKJV does not put the verse in brackets.

160. Matthew 25:33 And he shall set the sheep on his right hand, but the goats on the left
AV - **16,** 1-1,2-1,3-1,4-1,5-1,6-1,7-1,8-1,9-1,10-1,11-1,12-1,13-1,14-1,15-1,16-1
ESV - **15,** 1-1,2-1,3-1,4-1,5-1,6-1,7-1,8-1,9-1,10-1,11-1,12-1,13-1,14-1,15-1
HCSB - **14,** 1-1,2-1,3-1,4-1,5-1,6-1,7-1,8-1,9-1,10-1,11-1,12-1,13-1,14-1
NASV - **15,** 1-1,2-1,3-1,4-1,5-1,6-1,7-1,8-1,9-1,10-1,11-1,12-1,13-1,14-1,15-1
NCV - **17,** 1-1,2-1,3-1,4-1,5-1,6-1,7-1,8-1,9-1,10-1,11-1,12-1,13-1,14-1,15-1,16-1,17-1
NIV - **14,** 1-1,2-1,3-1,4-1,5-1,6-1,7-1,8-1,9-1,10-1,11-1,12-1,13-1,14-1
NKJV - **16,** 1-1,2-1,3-1,4-1,5-1,6-1,7-1,8-1,9-1,10-1,11-1,12-1,13-1,14-1,15-1,16-1
NLT - **15,** 1-1,2-1,3-1,4-1,5-1,6-1,7-1,8-1,9-1,10-1,11-1,12-1,13-1,14-1,15-1
NRSV - **16,** 1-1,2-1,3-1,4-1,5-1,6-1,7-1,8-1,9-1,10-1,11-1,12-1,13-1,14-1,15-1,16-1
Conclusion: All versions read the same.

161. Mark 6:42 And they did all eat, and were filled.
AV - **8,** 1-1,2-1,3-1,4-1,5-1,6-1,7-1,8-1
ESV - **7,** 1-1,2-1,3-1,4-1,5-1,6-1,7-**3**
HCSB - **5,** 1-**4,**2-1,3-1,4-1,5-1
NASV - **6,** 1-1,2-1,3-1,4-1,5-1,6-**3**
NCV - **7,** 1-1,2-1,3-**2,**4-1,5-1,6-1,7-**3**
NIV - **6,** 1-1,2-1,3-1,4-1,5-1,6-**3**
NKJV - **7,** 1-1,2-1,3-1,4-1,5-1,6-1,7-1
NLT - **8,** 1-1,2-1,3-1,4-1,5-1,6-1,7-1,8-**2**
NRSV - **6,** 1-1,2-1,3-1,4-1,5-1,6-1
Conclusion: Six modern versions are more complex than the King James Bible. The NCV is the most difficult to read.

162. Mark 8:30 And he charged them that they should tell no man of him.
AV - **12,** 1-1,2-1,3-1,4-1,5-1,6-1,7-1,8-1,9-1,10-1,11-1,12-1
ESV - **11,** 1-1,2-1,3-**2,**4-1,5-1,6-1,7-1,8-1,9-1,10-**2,**11-1
HCSB - **11,** 1-1,2-1,3-**2,**4-1,5-1,6-1,7-1,8-1,9-1,10-**2,**11-1

NASV - 10, 1-1,2-1,3-1,4-1,5-1,6-1,7-1,8-1,9-**2**,10-1
NCV - 11, 1-1,2-1,3-1,4-**3**,5-1,6-1,7-1,8-**3**,9-1,10-1,11-1
NIV - 9, 1-1,2-1,3-1,4-1,5-1,6-1,7-**3**,8-**2**,9-1
NKJV - 13, 1-1,2-1,3-**2**,4-1,5-1,6-1,7-1,8-1,9-1,10-1,11-1,12-**2**,13-1
NLT - 10, 1-1,2-1,3-1,4-1,5-1,6-1,7-1,8-**3**,9-**2**,10-1
NRSV - 11, 1-1,2-1,3-**2**,4-**2**,5-1,6-1,7-1,8-1,9-**3**,10-**2**,11-1
Conclusion: All eight modern versions are more complex than the King James Bible. The NRSV is the most difficult to read.

163. Mark 10:8 And they twain shall be one flesh: so then they are no more twain, but one flesh.
AV - 17, 1-1,2-1,3-1,4-1,5-1,6-1,7-1,8-1,9-1,10-1,11-1,12-1,13-1,14-1,15-1,16-1,17-1
ESV - 15, 1-1,2-1,3-1,4-**2**,5-1,6-1,7-1,8-1,9-1,10-1,11-**2**,12-1,13-1,14-1,15-1
HCSB - 16, 1-1,2-1,3-1,4-1,5-**2**,6-1,7-1,8-1,9-1,10-1,11-1,12-**2**,13-1,14-1,15-1,16-1
NASV - 16, 1-1,2-1,3-1,4-1,5-**2**,6-1,7-1,8-1,9-1,10-1,11-1,12-**2**,13-1,14-1,15-1,16-1
NCV - 14, 1-1,2-1,3-1,4-1,5-**2**,6-1,7-1,8-1,9-1,10-1,11-1,12-1,13-1,14-1
NIV - 15, 1-1,2-1,3-1,4-1,5-**2**,6-1,7-1,8-1,9-1,10-1,11-1,12-**2**,13-1,14-1,15-1
NKJV - 16, 1-1,2-1,3-1,4-1,5-**2**,6-1,7-1,8-1,9-1,10-1,11-1,12-**2**,13-1,14-1,15-1,16-1
NLT - 15, 1-1,2-1,3-1,4-1,5-**3**,6-**2**,7-1,8-1,9-1,10-1,11-1,12-**2**,13-1,14-1,15-1
NRSV - 16, 1-1,2-1,3-1,4-1,5-**2**,6-1,7-1,8-1,9-1,10-1,11-1,12-**2**,13-1,14-1,15-1,16-1
Conclusion: All eight modern versions are more complex than the King James Bible. The NLT is the most difficult to read.

164. Mark 13:17 But woe to them that are with child, and to them that give suck in those days!
AV - 17, 1-1,2-1,3-1,4-1,5-1,6-1,7-1,8-1,9-1,10-1,11-1,12-1,13-1,14-1,15-1,16-1,17-1
ESV - 17, 1-1,2-**2**,3-1,4-**2**,5-1,6-1,7-**2**,8-1,9-1,10-1,11-1,12-1,13-**2**,14-**2**,15-1,16-1,17-1
HCSB - 10, 1-1,2-1,3-**2**,4-**2**,5-1,6-**2**,7-**2**,8-1,9-1,10-1
NASV - 17, 1-1,2-1,3-1,4-1,5-1,6-1,7-**2**,8-1,9-1,10-1,11-1,12-1,13-**2**,14-**2**,15-1,16-1,17-1
NCV - 17, 1-1,2-1,3-1,4-1,5-**3**,6-1,7-1,8-1,9-1,10-**2**,11-1,12-1,13-**2**,14-1,15-1,16-**2**,17-**2**
NIV - 14, 1-1,2-**2**,3-1,4-1,5-1,6-1,7-1,8-1,9-1,10-**2**,11-**2**,12-1,13-**2**,14-**2**
NKJV - 17, 1-1,2-1,3-1,4-1,5-1,6-1,7-**2**,8-1,9-1,10-1,11-1,12-1,13-**2**,14-**2**,15-1,16-1,17-1
NLT - 15, 1-1,2-**3**,3-1,4-1,5-1,6-1,7-**2**,8-**2**,9-1,10-1,11-**2**,12-**2**,13-1,14-1,15-1
NRSV - 16, 1-1,2-1,3-1,4-1,5-1,6-**2**,7-1,8-1,9-1,10-1,11-1,12-**2**,13-**2**,14-1,15-1,16-1
Conclusion: All eight modern versions are more complex than the King James Bible.

165. Mark 13:33 Take ye heed, watch and pray: for ye know not when the time is.
AV - 14, 1-1,2-1,3-1,4-1,5-1,6-1,7-1,8-1,9-1,10-1,11-1,12-1,13-1,14-1
ESV - 15, 1-1,2-1,3-1,4-1,5-**2**,6-1,7-1,8-1,9-1,10-1,11-1,12-1,13-1,14-1,15-1
HCSB - 12, 1-1,2-1,3-**2**,4-1,5-1,6-1,7-1,8-1,9-1,10-1,11-1,12-**2**
NASV - 17, 1-1,2-1,3-1,4-1,5-1,6-**2**,7-1,8-1,9-1,10-1,11-1,12-1,13-1,14-**3**,15-1,16-1,17-1
NCV - 14, 1-1,2-**2**,3-**2**,4-1,5-**2**,6-**2**,7-1,8-1,9-1,10-1,11-1,12-1,13-1,14-1
NIV - 14, 1-1,2-1,3-1,4-1,5-**2**,6-1,7-1,8-1,9-1,10-1,11-1,12-1,13-1,14-1
NKJV - 14, 1-1,2-1,3-1,4-1,5-1,6-1,7-1,8-1,9-1,10-1,11-1,12-1,13-1,14-1
NLT - 15, 1-1,2-1,3-1,4-1,5-1,6-1,7-1,8-1,9-1,10-1,11-1,12-1,13-1,14-1,15-**2**
NRSV - 13, 1-**2**,2-1,3-**2**,4-1,5-1,6-1,7-1,8-1,9-1,10-1,11-1,12-1,13-1
Conclusion: Seven modern versions are more complex than the King James Bible.

A Study of Verses Composed of Single Syllable Words

166. Mark 14:46 And they laid their hands on him, and took him.
AV - **10,** 1-1,2-1,3-1,4-1,5-1,6-1,7-1,8-1,9-1,10-1
ESV - **9,** 1-1,2-1,3-1,4-1,5-1,6-1,7-1,8-1,9-1
HCSB - 9, 1-1,2-1,3-1,4-1,5-1,6-1,7-1,8-**3**,9-1
NASV - **8,** 1-1,2-1,3-1,4-1,5-1,6-1,7-1,8-1
NCV - 8, 1-1,2-1,3-**2**,4-1,5-1,6-1,7-**3**,8-1
NIV - 7, 1-1,2-1,3-1,4-1,5-1,6-**3**,7-1
NKJV - **10,** 1-1,2-1,3-1,4-1,5-1,6-1,7-1,8-1,9-1,10-1
NLT - 8, 1-1,2-1,3-**2**,4-1,5-1,6-1,7-**3**,8-1
NRSV - 9, 1-1,2-1,3-1,4-1,5-1,6-1,7-1,8-**3**,9-1
Conclusion: Five modern versions are more complex than the King James Bible. Both the NCV and the NIV inserted the name "Jesus" but this was not counted against them since "Jesus" would be accepted as a proper name under other circumstances.

167. Mark 16:10 And she went and told them that had been with him, as they mourned and wept.
AV - **16,** 1-1,2-1,3-1,4-1,5-1,6-1,7-1,8-1,9-1,10-1,11-1,12-1,13-1,14-1,15-1,16-1
ESV - **15,** 1-1,2-1,3-1,4-1,5-1,6-1,7-1,8-1,9-1,10-1,11-1,12-1,13-1,14-1,15-1
HCSB - 17, 1-1,2-1,3-1,4-**3**,5-1,6-1,7-1,8-1,9-1,10-1,11-1,12-1,13-1,14-1,15-**2**,16-1,17-**2**
NASV - 17, 1-1,2-1,3-1,4-**3**,5-1,6-1,7-1,8-1,9-1,10-1,11-1,12-1,13-1,14-1,15-**2**,16-1,17-**2**
NCV - 17, 1-**2**,2-1,3-1,4-1,5-1,6-1,7-1,8-1,9-1,10-**3**,11-1,12-1,13-1,14-1,15-1,16-1,17-**2**
NIV - 16, 1-1,2-1,3-1,4-1,5-1,6-1,7-1,8-1,9-1,10-1,11-1,12-1,13-1,14-**2**,15-1,16-**2**
NKJV - **15,** 1-1,2-1,3-1,4-1,5-1,6-1,7-1,8-1,9-1,10-1,11-1,12-1,13-1,14-1,15-1
NLT - 16, 1-1,2-1,3-1,4-1,5-**3**,6-1,7-1,8-**2**,9-1,10-**2**,11-1,12-1,13-1,14-1,15-1,16-**2**
NRSV - 17, 1-1,2-1,3-1,4-1,5-1,6-1,7-1,8-1,9-1,10-1,11-1,12-1,13-1,14-1,15-**2**,16-1,17-**2**
Conclusion: Six modern versions are more complex than the King James Bible. The NCV inserts the names "Mary" and "Jesus" but this was not counted against it since these names would be accepted as a proper names under other circumstances.

168. Luke 2:28 Then took he him up in his arms, and blessed God, and said,
AV - **13,** 1-1,2-1,3-1,4-1,5-1,6-1,7-1,8-1,9-1,10-1,11-1,12-1,13-1
ESV - **12,** 1-1,2-1,3-1,4-1,5-1,6-1,7-1,8-1,9-1,10-1,11-1,12-1
HCSB - **11,** 1-1,2-1,3-1,4-1,5-1,6-1,7-1,8-1,9-1,10-1,11-1
NASV - 12, 1-1,2-1,3-1,4-1,5-**2**,6-1,7-1,8-1,9-1,10-1,11-1,12-1
NCV - 10, 1-1,2-1,3-1,4-**2**,5-1,6-1,7-1,8-1,9-1,10-1
NIV - 14, 1-1,2-1,3-1,4-1,5-1,6-1,7-1,8-1,9-1,10-1,11-1,12-1,13-1,14-**2**
NKJV - **12,** 1-1,2-1,3-1,4-1,5-1,6-1,7-1,8-1,9-1,10-1,11-1,12-1
NLT - 10, 1-1,2-1,3-1,4-1,5-1,6-1,7-1,8-1,9-1,10-**2**
NRSV - 10, 1-1,2-1,3-1,4-1,5-1,6-1,7-1,8-1,9-1,10-**2**
Conclusion: Five modern versions are more complex than the King James Bible. The HCSB, NCV, NIV, NLT and the NRSV insert the name "Simeon" but this was not counted against them since "Simeon" would be accepted as a proper name under other circumstances.

169. Luke 6:46 And why call ye me, Lord, Lord, and do not the things which I say?
AV - **15,** 1-1,2-1,3-1,4-1,5-1,6-1,7-1,8-1,9-1,10-1,11-1,12-1,13-1,14-1,15-1
ESV - **14,** 1-1,2-1,3-1,4-1,5-1,6-1,7-1,8-1,9-1,10-1,11-1,12-1,13-1,14-1

HCSB - **14,** 1-1,2-1,3-1,4-1,5-1,6-1,7-1,8-1,9-1,10-1,11-1,12-1,13-1,14-1
NASV - **14,** 1-1,2-1,3-1,4-1,5-1,6-1,7-1,8-1,9-1,10-1,11-1,12-1,13-1,14-1
NCV - **14,** 1-1,2-1,3-1,4-1,5-1,6-1,7-1,8-1,9-1,10-1,11-1,12-1,13-1,14-1
NIV - **14,** 1-1,2-1,3-1,4-1,5-1,6-1,7-1,8-1,9-1,10-1,11-1,12-1,13-1,14-1
NKJV - **16,** 1-1,2-1,3-1,4-1,5-1,6-1,7-1,8-1,9-1,10-1,11-1,12-1,13-1,14-1,15-1,16-1
NLT - **16,** 1-1,2-1,3-1,4-1,5-1,6-**2**1,7-1,8-1,9-1,10-1,11-1,12-1,13-1,14-1,15-1,16-1
NRSV - **15,** 1-1,2-1,3-1,4-1,5-1,6-1,7-1,8-1,9-1,10-1,11-1,12-1,13-1,14-1,15-1
Conclusion: Only the NLT made the verse more complex.

170. Luke 9:15 And they did so, and made them all sit down.
AV - **10,** 1-1,2-1,3-1,4-1,5-1,6-1,7-1,8-1,9-1,10-1
ESV - **10,** 1-1,2-1,3-1,4-1,5-1,6-1,7-1,8-1,9-1,10-1
HCSB - **9,** 1-1,2-1,3-1,4-1,5-1,6-1,7-1,8-1,9-1
NASV - **9,** 1-1,2-1,3-1,4-1,5-1,6-1,7-1,8-1,9-1
NCV - **11,** 1-1,2-1,3-**3**,4-1,5-1,6-1,7-1,8-1,9-**2**,10-1,11-1
NIV - **8,** 1-1,2-**3**,3-1,4-1,5-1,6-**4**,7-1,8-1
NKJV - **10,** 1-1,2-1,3-1,4-1,5-1,6-1,7-1,8-1,9-1,10-1
NLT - **6,** 1-1,2-1,3-**2**,4-1,5-1,6-1
NRSV - **9,** 1-1,2-1,3-1,4-1,5-1,6-1,7-1,8-1,9-1
Conclusion: Only three modern versions are more complex than the King James Bible.

171. Luke 14:4 And they held their peace. And he took him, and healed him, and let him go;
AV - **16,** 1-1,2-1,3-1,4-1,5-1,6-1,7-1,8-1,9-1,10-1,11-1,12-1,13-1,14-1,15-1,16-1
ESV - **15,** 1-1,2-1,3-**2**,4-**2**,5-1,6-1,7-1,8-1,9-1,10-1,11-1,12-1,13-1,14-1,15-**2**
HCSB - **14,** 1-1,2-1,3-1,4-**2**,5-1,6-1,7-1,8-1,9-1,10-1,11-1,12-1,13-1,14-**2**
NASV - **17,** 1-1,2-1,3-1,4-**2**,5-1,6-1,7-1,8-1,9-1,10-1,11-1,12-1,13-1,14-1,15-1,16-1,17-**2**
NCV - **18,** 1-1,2-1,3-1,4-1,5-**2**,6-1,7-**2**,8-1,9-1,10-1,11-1,12-1,13-1,14-1,15-1,16-1,17-1,18-**2**
NIV - **17,** 1-1,2-1,3-**2**,4-**2**,5-1,6-**2**,7-1,8-1,9-1,10-1,11-1,12-1,13-1,14-1,15-1,16-1,17-**2**
NKJV - **15,** 1-1,2-1,3-1,4-**2**,5-1,6-1,7-1,8-1,9-1,10-1,11-1,12-1,13-1,14-1,15-1
NLT - **17,** 1-1,2-1,3-**2**,4-1,5-**2**,6-1,7-1,8-1,9-1,10-1,11-1,12-1,13-1,14-1,15-1,16-1,17-**2**
NRSV - **15,** 1-1,2-1,3-1,4-**2**,5-1,6-1,7-1,8-1,9-1,10-1,11-1,12-1,13-1,14-1,15-**2**
Conclusion: All eight modern versions are more complex than the King James Bible.

172. Luke 18:21 And he said, All these have I kept from my youth up.
AV - **12,** 1-1,2-1,3-1,4-1,5-1,6-1,7-1,8-1,9-1,10-1,11-1,12-1
ESV - **11,** 1-1,2-1,3-1,4-1,5-1,6-1,7-1,8-1,9-1,10-1,11-1
HCSB - **10,** 1-1,2-1,3-1,4-1,5-1,6-1,7-1,8-1,9-1,10-1
NASV - **12,** 1-1,2-1,3-1,4-1,5-1,6-1,7-1,8-1,9-1,10-1,11-1,12-1
NCV - **15,** 1-1,2-1,3-**2**,4-1,5-1,6-1,7-**2**,8-1,9-1,10-**2**,11-1,12-1,13-1,14-1,15-1
NIV - **12,** 1-1,2-1,3-1,4-1,5-1,6-1,7-1,8-1,9-1,10-1,11-1,12-1
NKJV - **12,** 1-1,2-1,3-1,4-1,5-1,6-1,7-1,8-1,9-1,10-1,11-1,12-1
NLT - **12,** 1-1,2-1,3-**2**,4-1,5-**2**,6-1,7-1,8-**3**,9-1,10-1,11-1,12-1
NRSV - **10,** 1-1,2-**2**,3-1,4-1,5-1,6-1,7-1,8-1,9-1,10-1
Conclusion: Only three modern versions are more complex than the King James Bible.

173. Luke 18:26 And they that heard it said, Who then can be saved?
AV - **10,** 1-1,2-1,3-1,4-1,5-1,6-1,7-1,8-1,9-1,10-1
ESV - **10,** 1-1,2-1,3-1,4-1,5-1,6-1,7-1,8-1,9-1,10-1
HCSB - **10,** 1-1,2-1,3-1,4-1,5-1,6-1,7-1,8-1,9-1,10-1
NASV - **10,** 1-1,2-1,3-1,4-1,5-1,6-1,7-1,8-1,9-1,10-1
NCV - 12, 1-1,2-1,3-**2**,4-1,5-1,6-1,7-1,8-1,9-1,10-1,11-1,12-1
NIV - **10,** 1-1,2-1,3-1,4-1,5-1,6-1,7-1,8-1,9-1,10-1
NKJV - **11,** 1-1,2-1,3-1,4-1,5-1,6-1,7-1,8-1,9-1,10-1,11-1
NLT - **13,** 1-1,2-1,3-1,4-1,5-1,6-1,7-1,8-1,9-1,10-1,11-1,12-1,13-1
NRSV - **10,** 1-1,2-1,3-1,4-1,5-1,6-1,7-1,8-1,9-1,10-1
Conclusion: Only the NCV made the verse more complex.

174. Luke 19:10 For the Son of man is come to seek and to save that which was lost.
AV - **16,** 1-1,2-1,3-1,4-1,5-1,6-1,7-1,8-1,9-1,10-1,11-1,12-1,13-1,14-1,15-1,16-1
ESV - **13,** 1-1,2-1,3-1,4-1,5-1,6-1,7-1,8-1,9-1,10-1,11-1,12-1,13-1
HCSB - **14,** 1-1,2-1,3-1,4-1,5-1,6-1,7-1,8-1,9-1,10-1,11-1,12-1,13-1,14-1
NASV - **16,** 1-1,2-1,3-1,4-1,5-1,6-1,7-1,8-1,9-1,10-1,11-1,12-1,13-1,14-1,15-1,16-1
NCV - 12, 1-1,2-1,3-1,4-1,5-1,6-1,7-1,8-1,9-**2**,10-1,11-1,12-1
NIV - **15,** 1-1,2-1,3-1,4-1,5-1,6-1,7-1,8-1,9-1,10-1,11-1,12-1,13-1,14-1,15-1
NKJV - **16,** 1-1,2-1,3-1,4-1,5-1,6-1,7-1,8-1,9-1,10-1,11-1,12-1,13-1,14-1,15-1,16-1
NLT - **14,** 1-1,2-1,3-1,4-1,5-1,6-1,7-1,8-1,9-1,10-1,11-1,12-1,13-1,14-1
NRSV - **14,** 1-1,2-1,3-1,4-1,5-1,6-1,7-1,8-1,9-1,10-1,11-1,12-1,13-1,14-1
Conclusion: Only the NCV made the verse more complex.

175. Luke 19:34 And they said, The Lord hath need of him.
AV - **8,** 1-1,2-1,3-1,4-1,5-1,6-1,7-1,8-1
ESV - **8,** 1-1,2-1,3-1,4-1,5-1,6-1,7-1,8-1
HCSB - **6,** 1-1,2-1,3-1,4-1,5-1,6-1
NASV - **8,** 1-1,2-1,3-1,4-1,5-1,6-1,7-1,8-1
NCV - 7, 1-1,2-**3**,3-**2**,4-1,5-**2**,6-1,7-1
NIV - 6, 1-1,2-**2**,3-1,4-1,5-1,6-1
NKJV - **9,** 1-1,2-1,3-1,4-1,5-1,6-1,7-1,8-1,9-1
NLT - 9, 1-1,2-1,3-**3**,4-**2**,5-**2**,6-1,7-1,8-1,9-1
NRSV - **6,** 1-1,2-1,3-1,4-1,5-1,6-1
Conclusion: Only three modern versions are more complex than the King James Bible. The NCV and NLT did a good job of making this simple statement complex.

176. Luke 19:36 And as he went, they spread their clothes in the way.
AV - **11,** 1-1,2-1,3-1,4-1,5-1,6-1,7-1,8-1,9-1,10-1,11-1
ESV - 12, 1-1,2-1,3-1,4-1,5-**2**,6-1,7-1,8-1,9-1,10-1,11-1,12-1
HCSB - 13, 1-1,2-1,3-1,4-**2**,5-**2**,6-1,7-1,8-**2**,9-1,10-1,11-1,12-1,13-1
NASV - 12, 1-1,2-1,3-1,4-**2**,5-1,6-1,7-**2**,8-1,9-1,10-1,11-1,12-1
NCV - 14, 1-1,2-1,3-1,4-1,5-1,6-**2**,7-1,8-1,9-1,10-1,11-1,12-1,13-**2**,14-1
NIV - 11, 1-1,2-1,3-1,4-**2**,5-**2**,6-1,7-1,8-1,9-1,10-1,11-1
NKJV - 11, 1-1,2-1,3-1,4-1,5-**2**,6-1,7-1,8-1,9-1,10-1,11-1

NLT - **16,** 1-1,2-1,3-1,4-**2,**5-1,6-1,7-1,8-1,9-1,10-**2,**11-1,12-1,13-1,14-**2,**15-1,16-1
NRSV - **12,** 1-1,2-1,3-1,4-**2,**5-**2,**6-1,7-**2,**8-1,9-1,10-1,11-1,12-1
Conclusion: All eight modern versions are more complex than the King James Bible. The NCV inserted the names "Jesus" and "Jerusalem" but this was not counted against it since these names would be accepted as proper names under other circumstances.

177. Luke 21:35 For as a snare shall it come on all them that dwell on the face of the whole earth.
AV - **19,** 1-1,2-1,3-1,4-1,5-1,6-1,7-1,8-1,9-1,10-1,11-1,12-1,13-1,14-1,15-1,16-1,17-1,18-1,19-1
ESV - **15,** 1-1,2-1,3-1,4-1,5-**2,**6-1,7-1,8-1,9-1,10-1,11-1,12-1,13-1,14-1,15-1
HCSB - **18,** 1-1,2-1,3-1,4-1,5-1,6-1,7-1,8-1,9-1,10-1,11-1,12-1,13-1,14-1,15-1,16-1,17-1,18-1
NASV - **16,** 1-1,2-1,3-1,4-1,5-**2,**6-1,7-1,8-1,9-1,10-1,11-1,12-1,13-1,14-1,15-1,16-1
NCV - **8,** 1-1,2-1,3-1,4-1,5-1,6-**2,**7-1,8-1
NIV - **16,** 1-1,2-1,3-1,4-1,5-**2,**6-1,7-1,8-1,9-1,10-1,11-1,12-1,13-1,14-1,15-1,16-1
NKJV - **19,** 1-1,2-1,3-1,4-1,5-1,6-1,7-1,8-1,9-1,10-1,11-1,12-1,13-1,14-1,15-1,16-1,17-1,18-1,19-1
NLT - **14,** 1-1,2-1,3-1,4-1,5-1,6-1,7-1,8-1,9-**2,**10-**4,**11-**2,**12-1,13-1,14-1
NRSV - **18,** 1-1,2-1,3-1,4-1,5-1,6-1,7-1,8-**2,**9-1,10-1,11-1,12-1,13-1,14-1,15-1,16-1,17-1,18-1
Conclusion: Six modern versions are more complex than the King James Bible. In a strange twist, the HCSB, NLT and NRSV begin the verse with the last three words of a sentence. They all read; "like a trap. For..."

178. Luke 23:31 For if they do these things in a green tree, what shall be done in the dry?
AV - **17,** 1-1,2-1,3-1,4-1,5-1,6-1,7-1,8-1,9-1,10-1,11-1,12-1,13-1,14-1,15-1,16-1,17-1
ESV - **18,** 1-1,2-1,3-1,4-1,5-1,6-1,7-1,8-1,9-1,10-1,11-1,12-1,13-1,14-**2,**15-1,16-1,17-1,18-1
HCSB - **18,** 1-1,2-1,3-1,4-1,5-1,6-1,7-1,8-1,9-1,10-1,11-1,12-1,13-1,14-**2,**15-1,16-1,17-1,18-1
NASV - **18,** 1-1,2-1,3-1,4-1,5-1,6-1,7-1,8-1,9-1,10-1,11-1,12-1,13-1,14-**2,**15-1,16-1,17-1,18-1
NCV - **17,** 1-1,2-1,3-1,4-1,5-1,6-1,7-1,8-1,9-1,10-1,11-1,12-1,13-**2,**14-1,15-1,16-1,17-1
NIV - **18,** 1-1,2-1,3-1,4-1,5-1,6-1,7-1,8-1,9-1,10-1,11-1,12-1,13-1,14-**2,**15-1,16-1,17-1,18-1
NKJV - **17,** 1-1,2-1,3-1,4-1,5-1,6-1,7-1,8-1,9-1,10-1,11-1,12-1,13-1,14-1,15-1,16-1,17-1
NLT - **18,** 1-1,2-1,3-1,4-1,5-1,6-1,7-1,8-1,9-1,10-1,11-1,12-1,13-1,14-**2,**15-1,16-1,17-1,18-1
NRSV - **17,** 1-1,2-1,3-1,4-1,5-1,6-1,7-1,8-1,9-1,10-1,11-1,12-1,13-**2,**14-1,15-1,16-1,17-1
Conclusion: All eight modern versions are more complex than the King James Bible. All the versions with eighteen words read identical; also, the NCV and NRSV read identical.

179. Luke 24:30 And it came to pass, as he sat at meat with them, he took bread, and blessed it, and brake, and gave to them.
AV - **24,** 1-1,2-1,3-1,4-1,5-1,6-1,7-1,8-1,9-1,10-1,11-1,12-1,13-1,14-1,15-1,16-1,17-1,18-1,19-1,20-1,21-1,22-1,23-1,24-1
ESV - **21,** 1-1,2-1,3-1,4-1,5-**2,**6-1,7-1,8-1,9-1,10-1,11-1,12-1,13-1,14-1,15-1,16-1,17-1,18-1,19-1,20-1,21-1
HCSB - **24,** 1-1,2-1,3-1,4-1,5-**2,**6-1,7-1,8-**2,**9-1,10-1,11-1,12-1,13-1,14-1,15-1,16-1,17-1,18-1,19-1,20-1,21-1,22-1,23-1,24-1
NASV - **25,** 1-1,2-1,3-1,4-**2,**5-1,6-1,7-**2,**8-1,9-1,10-1,11-1,12-1,13-1,14-1,15-1,16-1,17-1,18-**2,**19-1,20-1,21-**2,**22-**2,**23-1,24-1,25-1
NCV - **21,** 1-1,2-1,3-1,4-1,5-1,6-**2,**7-1,8-1,9-1,10-1,11-1,12-1,13-1,14-1,15-**3,**16-1,17-1,18-1,19-1,20-1,21-1
NIV - **22,** 1-1,2-1,3-1,4-1,5-1,6-**2,**7-1,8-1,9-1,10-1,11-1,12-1,13-1,14-1,15-1,16-1,17-**2,**18-1,19-1,20-1,21-1,22-1

NKJV - 26, 1-1,2-1,3-1,4-1,5-1,6-1,7-1,8-1,9-1,10-1,11-**2**,12-1,13-1,14-1,15-1,16-1,17-1,18-1,19-1,20-1,21-1,22-1,23-1,24-1,25-1,26-1

NLT - **22,** 1-1,2-1,3-1,4-1,5-1,6-1,7-1,8-1,9-1,10-1,11-1,12-1,13-1,14-1,15-1,16-1,17-1,18-1,19-1,20-1,21-1,22-1

NRSV - 20, 1-1,2-1,3-1,4-1,5-1,6-**2**,7-1,8-1,9-1,10-1,11-1,12-1,13-1,14-1,15-1,16-1,17-1,18-1,19-1,20-1

Conclusion: Seven modern versions are more complex than the King James Bible. Amazing only the NLT did not make the verse more complex. The NASV is the most difficult to read.

180. John 1:4 In him was life; and the life was the light of men.
AV - **12,** 1-1,2-1,3-1,4-1,5-1,6-1,7-1,8-1,9-1,10-1,11-1,12-1
ESV - **12,** 1-1,2-1,3-1,4-1,5-1,6-1,7-1,8-1,9-1,10-1,11-1,12-1
HCSB - **12,** 1-1,2-1,3-1,4-1,5-1,6-1,7-1,8-1,9-1,10-1,11-1,12-1
NASV - **12,** 1-1,2-1,3-1,4-1,5-1,6-1,7-1,8-1,9-1,10-1,11-1,12-1
NCV - 14, 1-1,2-1,3-1,4-1,5-1,6-1,7-1,8-1,9-1,10-1,11-1,12-1,13-1,14-**2**
NIV - **12,** 1-1,2-1,3-1,4-1,5-1,6-1,7-1,8-1,9-1,10-1,11-1,12-1
NKJV - **12,** 1-1,2-1,3-1,4-1,5-1,6-1,7-1,8-1,9-1,10-1,11-1,12-1
NLT - 16, 1-1,2-1,3-1,4-1,5-1,6-**4**,7-1,8-1,9-**3**,10-1,11-1,12-1,13-1,14-1,15-1,16-**4**
NRSV - 13, 1-1,2-1,3-1,4-1,5-1,6-1,7-1,8-1,9-1,10-1,11-1,12-1,13-**2**

Conclusion: Only three modern versions are more complex than the King James Bible. The NLT is the most difficult to read.

181. John 1:6 There was a man sent from God, whose name was John.
AV - **11,** 1-1,2-1,3-1,4-1,5-1,6-1,7-1,8-1,9-1,10-1,11-1
ESV - **11,** 1-1,2-1,3-1,4-1,5-1,6-1,7-1,8-1,9-1,10-1,11-1
HCSB - **11,** 1-1,2-1,3-1,4-1,5-1,6-1,7-1,8-1,9-1,10-1,11-1
NASV - **11,** 1-1,2-1,3-1,4-1,5-1,6-1,7-1,8-1,9-1,10-1,11-1
NCV - **11,** 1-1,2-1,3-1,4-1,5-1,6-1,7-1,8-1,9-1,10-1,11-1
NIV - **13,** 1-1,2-1,3-1,4-1,5-1,6-1,7-1,8-1,9-1,10-1,11-1,12-1,13-1
NKJV - **11,** 1-1,2-1,3-1,4-1,5-1,6-1,7-1,8-1,9-1,10-1,11-1
NLT - **7,** 1-1,2-1,3-1,4-1,5-1,6-1,7-1
NRSV - **11,** 1-1,2-1,3-1,4-1,5-1,6-1,7-1,8-1,9-1,10-1,11-1

Conclusion: All versions read the same.

182. John 1:10 He was in the world, and the world was made by him, and the world knew him not.
AV - **18,** 1-1,2-1,3-1,4-1,5-1,6-1,7-1,8-1,9-1,10-1,11-1,12-1,13-1,14-1,15-1,16-1,17-1,18-1
ESV - **19,** 1-1,2-1,3-1,4-1,5-1,6-1,7-1,8-1,9-1,10-1,11-1,12-1,13-1,14-1,15-1,16-1,17-1,18-1,19-1
HCSB - 19, 1-1,2-1,3-1,4-1,5-1,6-1,7-1,8-1,9-1,10-**3**,11-1,12-1,13-1,14-1,15-1,16-1,17-1,18-**3**,19-1
NASV - **19,** 1-1,2-1,3-1,4-1,5-1,6-1,7-1,8-1,9-1,10-1,11-1,12-1,13-1,14-1,15-1,16-1,17-1,18-1,19-1
NCV - **20,** 1-1,2-1,3-1,4-1,5-1,6-1,7-1,8-1,9-1,10-1,11-1,12-1,13-1,14-1,15-1,16-1,17-1,18-1,19-1,20-1
NIV - 19, 1-1,2-1,3-1,4-1,5-1,6-1,7-1,8-1,9-1,10-1,11-1,12-1,13-1,14-1,15-1,16-1,17-1,18-**3**,19-1
NKJV - **19,** 1-1,2-1,3-1,4-1,5-1,6-1,7-1,8-1,9-1,10-1,11-1,12-1,13-1,14-1,15-1,16-1,17-1,18-1,19-1
NLT - 14, 1-1,2-1,3-**2**,4-1,5-**2**,6-1,7-1,8-**3**,9-1,10-1,11-1,12-**2**,13-**3**,14-1
NRSV - 20, 1-1,2-1,3-1,4-1,5-1,6-1,7-1,8-1,9-1,10-**2**,11-**2**,12-1,13-1,14-1,15-1,16-1,17-1,18-1,19-1,20-1

Conclusion: Four modern versions are more complex than the King James Bible. Through heroic efforts, the NLT again managed to be the most difficult to read.

Samuel C. Gipp Ph.D.

183. John 1:13 Which were born, not of blood, nor of the will of the flesh, nor of the will of man, but of God.

AV - **22,** 1-1,2-1,3-1,4-1,5-1,6-1,7-1,8-1,9-1,10-1,11-1,12-1,13-1,14-1,15-1,16-1,17-1,18-1,19-1,20-1,21-1,22-1

ESV - **22,** 1-1,2-1,3-1,4-1,5-1,6-1,7-1,8-1,9-1,10-1,11-1,12-1,13-1,14-1,15-1,16-1,17-1,18-1,19-1,20-1,21-1,22-1

HCSB - **22,** 1-1,2-1,3-1,4-1,5-1,6-1,7-1,8-1,9-1,10-1,11-1,12-1,13-1,14-1,15-1,16-1,17-1,18-1,19-1,20-1,21-1,22-1

NASV - **22,** 1-1,2-1,3-1,4-1,5-1,6-1,7-1,8-1,9-1,10-1,11-1,12-1,13-1,14-1,15-1,16-1,17-1,18-1,19-1,20-1,21-1,22-1

NCV - **22,** 1-1,2-1,3-1,4-**2,**5-1,6-**2,**7-1,8-**2,**9-**2,**10-1,11-1,12-**2,**13-**2,**14-**2,**15-1,16-**2,**17-**2,**18-1,19-1,20-1,21-1,22-1

NIV - **18,** 1-**2,**2-1,3-1,4-1,5-**3,**6-**2,**7-1,8-1,9-**2,**10-**3,**11-1,12-1,13-**2,**14-1,15-1,16-1,17-1,18-1

NKJV - **22,** 1-1,2-1,3-1,4-1,5-1,6-1,7-1,8-1,9-1,10-1,11-1,12-1,13-1,14-1,15-1,16-1,17-1,18-1,19-1,20-1,21-1,22-1

NLT - **21,** 1-1,2-1,3-**2,**4-1,5-1,6-1,7-**3,**8-1,9-**3,**10-1,11-**2,**12-**2,**13-1,14-1,15-1,16-1,17-1,18-1,19-1,20-1,21-1

NRSV - **22,** 1-1,2-1,3-1,4-1,5-1,6-1,7-1,8-1,9-1,10-1,11-1,12-1,13-1,14-1,15-1,16-1,17-1,18-1,19-1,20-1,21-1,22-1

Conclusion: Only three modern versions are more complex than the King James Bible. The NCV, NIV and NLT ran a stiff competition, but the NLT worked hard to become the most difficult to read.

184. John 5:40 And ye will not come to me, that ye might have life.

AV - **12,** 1-1,2-1,3-1,4-1,5-1,6-1,7-1,8-1,9-1,10-1,11-1,12-1

ESV - **12,** 1-1,2-1,3-**2,**4-1,5-1,6-1,7-1,8-1,9-1,10-1,11-1,12-1

HCSB - **14,** 1-1,2-1,3-1,4-1,5-**2,**6-1,7-1,8-1,9-1,10-1,11-1,12-1,13-1,14-1

NASV - **14,** 1-1,2-1,3-1,4-**3,**5-1,6-1,7-1,8-1,9-1,10-1,11-1,12-1,13-1,14-1

NCV - **11,** 1-1,2-1,3-**2,**4-1,5-1,6-1,7-1,8-1,9-1,10-1,11-1

NIV - **10,** 1-1,2-1,3-**2,**4-1,5-1,6-1,7-1,8-1,9-1,10-1

NKJV - **13,** 1-1,2-1,3-1,4-**2,**5-1,6-1,7-1,8-1,9-1,10-1,11-1,12-1,13-1

NLT - **11,** 1-1,2-1,3-**2,**4-1,5-1,6-1,7-1,8-1,9-**2,**10-1,11-1

NRSV - **10,** 1-1,2-1,3-**2,**4-1,5-1,6-1,7-1,8-1,9-1,10-1

Conclusion: All eight modern versions are more complex than the King James Bible.

185. John 5:42 But I know you, that ye have not the love of God in you.

AV - **14,** 1-1,2-1,3-1,4-1,5-1,6-1,7-1,8-1,9-1,10-1,11-1,12-1,13-1,14-1

ESV - **14,** 1-1,2-1,3-1,4-1,5-1,6-1,7-1,8-1,9-1,10-1,11-1,12-1,13-**2,**14-1

HCSB - **13,** 1-1,2-1,3-1,4-1,5-1,6-1,7-1,8-1,9-1,10-1,11-1,12-**2,**13-1

NASV - **15,** 1-1,2-1,3-1,4-1,5-1,6-1,7-1,8-1,9-1,10-1,11-1,12-1,13-1,14-1,15-**2**

NCV - **14,** 1-1,2-1,3-1,4-1,5-1,6-1,7-1,8-1,9-1,10-1,11-1,12-1,13-1,14-1

NIV - **18,** 1-1,2-1,3-1,4-1,5-1,6-1,7-1,8-1,9-1,10-1,11-1,12-1,13-1,14-1,15-1,16-1,17-1,18-1

NKJV - **15,** 1-1,2-1,3-1,4-1,5-1,6-1,7-1,8-1,9-1,10-1,11-1,12-1,13-1,14-1,15-1

NLT - **10,** 1-**2,**2-1,3-1,4-1,5-1,6-1,7-1,8-1,9-**2,**10-1

NRSV - **14,** 1-1,2-1,3-1,4-1,5-1,6-1,7-1,8-1,9-1,10-1,11-1,12-1,13-1,14-1

Conclusion: Four modern versions are more complex than the King James Bible.

186. John 6:48 I am that bread of life.
AV - **6,** 1-1,2-1,3-1,4-1,5-1,6-1
ESV - **6,** 1-1,2-1,3-1,4-1,5-1,6-1
HCSB - **6,** 1-1,2-1,3-1,4-1,5-1,6-1
NASV - **6,** 1-1,2-1,3-1,4-1,5-1,6-1
NCV - **7,** 1-1,2-1,3-1,4-1,5-1,6-1,7-1
NIV - **6,** 1-1,2-1,3-1,4-1,5-1,6-1
NKJV - **6,** 1-1,2-1,3-1,4-1,5-1,6-1
NLT - **7,** 1-1,2-1,3-1,4-1,5-1,6-1,7-1
NRSV - **6,** 1-1,2-1,3-1,4-1,5-1,6-1
Conclusion: All versions read the same.

187. John 7:11 Then the Jews sought him at the feast, and said, Where is he?
AV - **13,** 1-1,2-1,3-1,4-1,5-1,6-1,7-1,8-1,9-1,10-1,11-1,12-1,13-1
ESV - **14,** 1-1,2-1,3-1,4-**2**,5-1,6-1,7-1,8-1,9-1,10-1,11-**2**,12-1,13-1,14-1
HCSB - **14,** 1-1,2-1,3-1,4-**2**,5-1,6-1,7-1,8-1,9-**3**,10-1,11-**2**,12-1,13-1,14-1
NASV - **15,** 1-1,2-1,3-1,4-1,5-**2**,6-1,7-1,8-1,9-1,10-1,11-1,12-**2**,13-1,14-1,15-1
NCV - **15,** 1-1,2-1,3-1,4-1,5-**2**,6-1,7-**2**,8-1,9-1,10-1,11-**2**,12-1,13-1,14-1,15-1
NIV - **16,** 1-1,2-1,3-1,4-1,5-1,6-1,7-1,8-**2**,9-1,10-1,11-1,12-**2**,13-1,14-1,15-1,16-1
NKJV - **13,** 1-1,2-1,3-1,4-1,5-1,6-1,7-1,8-1,9-1,10-1,11-1,12-1,13-1
NLT - **18,** 1-1,2-**2**,3-**2**,4-1,5-1,6-1,7-1,8-1,9-1,10-**3**,11-1,12-1,13-**2**,14-1,15-**3**,16-1,17-1,18-1
NRSV - **13,** 1-1,2-1,3-**2**,4-1,5-1,6-1,7-1,8-**3**,9-1,10-**2**,11-1,12-1,13-1
Conclusion: Seven modern versions are more complex than the King James Bible. The NLT is the most difficult to read.

188. John 7:29 But I know him: for I am from him, and he hath sent me.
AV - **14,** 1-1,2-1,3-1,4-1,5-1,6-1,7-1,8-1,9-1,10-1,11-1,12-1,13-1,14-1
ESV - **12,** 1-1,2-1,3-1,4-1,5-1,6-1,7-1,8-1,9-1,10-1,11-1,12-1
HCSB - **12,** 1-1,2-1,3-1,4-**2**,5-1,6-1,7-1,8-1,9-1,10-1,11-1,12-1
NASV - **12,** 1-1,2-1,3-1,4-**2**,5-1,6-1,7-1,8-1,9-1,10-1,11-1,12-1
NCV - **13,** 1-1,2-1,3-1,4-1,5-**2**,6-1,7-1,8-1,9-1,10-1,11-1,12-1,13-1
NIV - **12,** 1-1,2-1,3-1,4-**2**,5-1,6-1,7-1,8-1,9-1,10-1,11-1,12-1
NKJV - **12,** 1-1,2-1,3-1,4-1,5-1,6-1,7-1,8-1,9-1,10-1,11-1,12-1
NLT - **15,** 1-1,2-1,3-1,4-1,5-**2**,6-1,7-1,8-1,9-1,10-1,11-1,12-1,13-1,14-1,15-1
NRSV - **12,** 1-1,2-1,3-1,4-**2**,5-1,6-1,7-1,8-1,9-1,10-1,11-1,12-1
Conclusion: Six modern versions are more complex than the King James Bible.

189. John 8:32 And ye shall know the truth, and the truth shall make you free.
AV - **13,** 1-1,2-1,3-1,4-1,5-1,6-1,7-1,8-1,9-1,10-1,11-1,12-1,13-1
ESV - **13,** 1-1,2-1,3-1,4-1,5-1,6-1,7-1,8-1,9-1,10-1,11-1,12-1,13-1
HCSB - **12,** 1-1,2-1,3-1,4-1,5-1,6-1,7-1,8-1,9-1,10-1,11-1,12-1
NASV - **13,** 1-1,2-1,3-1,4-1,5-1,6-1,7-1,8-1,9-1,10-1,11-1,12-1,13-1
NCV - **13,** 1-1,2-1,3-1,4-1,5-1,6-1,7-1,8-1,9-1,10-1,11-1,12-1,13-1
NIV - **13,** 1-1,2-1,3-1,4-1,5-1,6-1,7-1,8-1,9-1,10-1,11-1,12-1,13-1
NKJV - **13,** 1-1,2-1,3-1,4-1,5-1,6-1,7-1,8-1,9-1,10-1,11-1,12-1,13-1

NLT - **13,** 1-1,2-1,3-1,4-1,5-1,6-1,7-1,8-1,9-1,10-1,11-1,12-1,13-1
NRSV - **13,** 1-1,2-1,3-1,4-1,5-1,6-1,7-1,8-1,9-1,10-1,11-1,12-1,13-1
Conclusion: All versions read the same.

190. John 9:5 As long as I am in the world, I am the light of the world.
AV - **15,** 1-1,2-1,3-1,4-1,5-1,6-1,7-1,8-1,9-1,10-1,11-1,12-1,13-1,14-1,15-1
ESV - **15,** 1-1,2-1,3-1,4-1,5-1,6-1,7-1,8-1,9-1,10-1,11-1,12-1,13-1,14-1,15-1
HCSB - **15,** 1-1,2-1,3-1,4-1,5-1,6-1,7-1,8-1,9-1,10-1,11-1,12-1,13-1,14-1,15-1
NASV - **13,** 1-1,2-1,3-1,4-1,5-1,6-1,7-1,8-1,9-1,10-1,11-1,12-1,13-1
NCV - **13,** 1-1,2-1,3-1,4-1,5-1,6-1,7-1,8-1,9-1,10-1,11-1,12-1,13-1
NIV - **13,** 1-1,2-1,3-1,4-1,5-1,6-1,7-1,8-1,9-1,10-1,11-1,12-1,13-1
NKJV - **15,** 1-1,2-1,3-1,4-1,5-1,6-1,7-1,8-1,9-1,10-1,11-1,12-1,13-1,14-1,15-1
NLT - **15,** 1-1,2-1,3-1,4-1,5-1,6-1,7-1,8-1,9-1,10-1,11-1,12-1,13-1,14-1,15-1
NRSV - **15,** 1-1,2-1,3-1,4-1,5-1,6-1,7-1,8-1,9-1,10-1,11-1,12-1,13-1,14-1,15-1
Conclusion: All versions read the same.

191. John 12:43 For they loved the praise of men more than the praise of God.
AV - **13,** 1-1,2-1,3-1,4-1,5-1,6-1,7-1,8-1,9-1,10-1,11-1,12-1,13-1
ESV - 17, 1-1,2-1,3-1,4-1,5-**2**,6-1,7-1,8-1,9-1,10-1,11-1,12-1,13-**2**,14-1,15-1,16-1,17-1
HCSB - **11,** 1-1,2-1,3-1,4-1,5-1,6-1,7-1,8-1,9-1,10-1,11-1
NASV - 13, 1-1,2-1,3-1,4-1,5-**3**,6-1,7-1,8-**2**,9-1,10-1,11-**3**,12-1,13-1
NCV - 10, 1-1,2-1,3-1,4-1,5-**2**,6-1,7-1,8-1,9-1,10-1
NIV - **11,** 1-1,2-1,3-1,4-1,5-1,6-1,7-1,8-1,9-1,10-1,11-1
NKJV - **13,** 1-1,2-1,3-1,4-1,5-1,6-1,7-1,8-1,9-1,10-1,11-1,12-1,13-1
NLT - 11, 1-1,2-1,3-1,4-**2**,5-1,6-1,7-1,8-1,9-1,10-1,11-1
NRSV - 13, 1-1,2-1,3-1,4-**2**,5-**2**,6-1,7-1,8-1,9-**2**,10-1,11-1,12-1,13-1
Conclusion: Five modern versions are more complex than the King James Bible.

192. John 19:3 And said, Hail, King of the Jews! and they smote him with their hands.
AV - **14,** 1-1,2-1,3-1,4-1,5-1,6-1,7-1,8-1,9-1,10-1,11-1,12-1,13-1,14-1
ESV - 17, 1-1,2-1,3-1,4-1,5-1,6-**2**,7-1,8-1,9-1,10-1,11-1,12-1,13-1,14-1,15-1,16-1,17-1
HCSB - 19, 1-1,2-1,3-**4**,4-1,5-1,6-1,7-1,8-1,9-1,10-1,11-1,12-1,13-1,14-1,15-1,16-1,17-**2**,18-1,19-1
NASV - 23, 1-1,2-1,3-**2**,4-1,5-1,6-1,7-1,8-1,9-1,10-1,11-1,12-1,13-1,14-1,15-1,16-1,17-1,18-1,19-1,20-1,21-1,22-1,23-1
NCV - 20, 1-1,2-1,3-1,4-1,5-1,6-**2**,7-1,8-1,9-1,10-1,11-1,12-1,13-1,14-1,15-1,16-1,17-1,18-1,19-1,20-1
NIV - 21, 1-1,2-1,3-1,4-1,5-1,6-**2**,7-1,8-**2**,9-**2**,10-1,11-1,12-1,13-1,14-1,15-1,16-1,17-1,18-1,19-1,20-1,21-1
NKJV - **15,** 1-1,2-1,3-1,4-1,5-1,6-1,7-1,8-1,9-1,10-1,11-1,12-1,13-1,14-1,15-1
NLT - 14, 1-1,2-1,3-1,4-1,5-1,6-1,7-1,8-1,9-1,10-1,11-1,12-**2**,13-1,14-1
NRSV - 18, 1-1,2-1,3-**2**,4-1,5-1,6-1,7-**2**,8-1,9-1,10-1,11-1,12-1,13-1,14-**2**,15-1,16-1,17-1,18-1
Conclusion: Seven modern versions are more complex than the King James Bible.

193. Acts 7:1 Then said the high priest, Are these things so?
AV - **9,** 1-1,2-1,3-1,4-1,5-1,6-1,7-1,8-1,9-1
ESV - **9,** 1-1,2-1,3-1,4-1,5-1,6-1,7-1,8-1,9-1
HCSB - **7,** 1-1,2-1,3-1,4-1,5-1,6-1,7-1

NASV - **8,** 1-1,2-1,3-1,4-1,5-1,6-1,7-1,8-1
NCV - **10,** 1-1,2-1,3-1,4-1,5-1,6-1,7-1,8-1,9-1,10-1
NIV - **10,** 1-1,2-1,3-1,4-1,5-1,6-1,7-1,8-1,9-**2**,10-1
NKJV - **9,** 1-1,2-1,3-1,4-1,5-1,6-1,7-1,8-1,9-1
NLT - **10,** 1-1,2-1,3-1,4-1,5-1,6-1,7-1,8-1,9-**4**,10-1
NRSV - **10,** 1-1,2-1,3-1,4-1,5-1,6-1,7-1,8-1,9-1,10-1
Conclusion: Only th NIV and NLT made the verse more complex.

194. Acts 7:50 Hath not my hand made all these things?
AV - **8,** 1-1,2-1,3-1,4-1,5-1,6-1,7-1,8-1
ESV - **8,** 1-1,2-1,3-1,4-1,5-1,6-1,7-1,8-1
HCSB - **8,** 1-1,2-1,3-1,4-1,5-1,6-1,7-1,8-1
NASV - **10,** 1-1,2-1,3-1,4-1,5-1,6-1,7-1,8-1,9-1,10-1
NCV - **7,** 1-**3**,2-1,3-1,4-1,5-1,6-1,7-1
NIV - **8,** 1-1,2-1,3-1,4-1,5-1,6-1,7-1,8-1
NKJV - **8,** 1-1,2-1,3-1,4-1,5-1,6-1,7-1,8-1
NLT - **8,** 1-1,2-1,3-1,4-1,5-1,6-**2**,7-1,8-1
NRSV - **8,** 1-1,2-1,3-1,4-1,5-1,6-1,7-1,8-1
Conclusion: Only the NCV and the NLT made the verse more complex.

195. Acts 7:54 When they heard these things, they were cut to the heart, and they gnashed on him with their teeth.
AV - **19,** 1-1,2-1,3-1,4-1,5-1,6-1,7-1,8-1,9-1,10-1,11-1,12-1,13-1,14-1,15-1,16-1,17-1,18-1,19-1
ESV - **16,** 1-1,2-1,3-1,4-1,5-1,6-1,7-1,8-1,9-**2**,10-1,11-1,12-1,13-1,14-1,15-1,16-1
HCSB - **17,** 1-1,2-1,3-1,4-1,5-1,6-1,7-1,8-**2**,9-1,10-1,11-1,12-1,13-1,14-1,15-1,16-1,17-1
NASV - **19,** 1-1,2-1,3-1,4-1,5-1,6-1,7-1,8-1,9-1,10-1,11-1,12-1,13-1,14-**2**,15-**2**,16-1,17-1,18-1,19-1
NCV - **19,** 1-1,2-1,3-**2**,4-1,5-1,6-1,7-**2**,8-**3**,9-1,10-1,11-1,12-1,13-1,14-1,15-**2**,16-1,17-1,18-1,19-1
NIV - **13,** 1-1,2-1,3-1,4-1,5-1,6-1,7-**3**,8-1,9-1,10-1,11-1,12-1,13-1
NKJV - **19,** 1-1,2-1,3-1,4-1,5-1,6-1,7-1,8-1,9-1,10-1,11-1,12-1,13-1,14-1,15-1,16-1,17-1,18-1,19-1
NLT - **17,** 1-1,2-1,3-**2**,4-1,5-**5**,6-1,7-1,8-**4**,9-1,10-1,11-1,12-1,13-1,14-1,15-1,16-1,17-1
NRSV - **14,** 1-1,2-1,3-1,4-1,5-1,6-1,7-**2**,8-**2**,9-1,10-1,11-1,12-1,13-1,14-1
Conclusion: Seven modern versions are more complex than the King James Bible.

196. Acts 13:30 But God raised him from the dead:
AV - **7,** 1-1,2-1,3-1,4-1,5-1,6-1,7-1
ESV - **7,** 1-1,2-1,3-1,4-1,5-1,6-1,7-1
HCSB - **7,** 1-1,2-1,3-1,4-1,5-1,6-1,7-1
NASV - **7,** 1-1,2-1,3-1,4-1,5-1,6-1,7-1
NCV - **8,** 1-1,2-1,3-1,4-1,5-1,6-1,7-1,8-1
NIV - **7,** 1-1,2-1,3-1,4-1,5-1,6-1,7-1
NKJV - **7,** 1-1,2-1,3-1,4-1,5-1,6-1,7-1
NLT - **7,** 1-1,2-1,3-1,4-1,5-1,6-1,7-1
NRSV - **7,** 1-1,2-1,3-1,4-1,5-1,6-1,7-1
Conclusion: All versions read the same.

197. Acts 16:30 And brought them out, and said, Sirs, what must I do to be saved?
AV - **14,** 1-1,2-1,3-1,4-1,5-1,6-1,7-1,8-1,9-1,10-1,11-1,12-1,13-1,14-1
ESV - **15,** 1-1,2-1,3-1,4-1,5-1,6-1,7-1,8-1,9-1,10-1,11-1,12-1,13-1,14-1,15-1
HCSB - 15, 1-1,2-1,3-**3**,4-1,5-1,6-1,7-1,8-1,9-1,10-1,11-1,12-1,13-1,14-1,15-1
NASV - 16, 1-1,2-**2**,3-1,4-1,5-1,6-1,7-1,8-1,9-1,10-1,11-1,12-1,13-1,14-1,15-1,16-1
NCV - 14, 1-1,2-1,3-1,4-**2**,5-1,6-1,7-1,8-1,9-1,10-1,11-1,12-1,13-1,14-1
NIV - **15,** 1-1,2-1,3-1,4-1,5-1,6-1,7-1,8-1,9-1,10-1,11-1,12-1,13-1,14-1,15-1
NKJV - **15,** 1-1,2-1,3-1,4-1,5-1,6-1,7-1,8-1,9-1,10-1,11-1,12-1,13-1,14-1,15-1
NLT - **15,** 1-1,2-1,3-1,4-1,5-1,6-1,7-1,8-1,9-1,10-1,11-1,12-1,13-1,14-1,15-1
NRSV - 15, 1-1,2-1,3-1,4-1,5-**2**,6-1,7-1,8-1,9-1,10-1,11-1,12-1,13-1,14-1,15-1
Conclusion: Four modern versions are more complex than the King James Bible.

198. Romans 3:15 Their feet are swift to shed blood:
AV - **7,** 1-1,2-1,3-1,4-1,5-1,6-1,7-1
ESV - **7,** 1-1,2-1,3-1,4-1,5-1,6-1,7-1
HCSB - **7,** 1-1,2-1,3-1,4-1,5-1,6-1,7-1
NASV - **7,** 1-1,2-1,3-1,4-1,5-1,6-1,7-1
NCV - 7, 1-1,2-1,3-**2**,4-**2**,5-1,6-1,7-**2**
NIV - **7,** 1-1,2-1,3-1,4-1,5-1,6-1,7-1
NKJV - **7,** 1-1,2-1,3-1,4-1,5-1,6-1,7-1
NLT - 5, 1-1,2-1,3-1,4-**2**,5-**2**
NRSV - **7,** 1-1,2-1,3-1,4-1,5-1,6-1,7-1
Conclusion: In their consistent complexity, only the NCV and NLT found a way to complicate this simple verse.

199. Romans 3:17 And the way of peace have they not known:
AV - **9,** 1-1,2-1,3-1,4-1,5-1,6-1,7-1,8-1,9-1
ESV - **9,** 1-1,2-1,3-1,4-1,5-1,6-1,7-1,8-1,9-1
HCSB - **9,** 1-1,2-1,3-1,4-1,5-1,6-1,7-1,8-1,9-1
NASV - **9,** 1-1,2-1,3-1,4-1,5-1,6-1,7-1,8-1,9-1
NCV - **8,** 1-1,2-1,3-1,4-1,5-1,6-1,7-1,8-1
NIV - **9,** 1-1,2-1,3-1,4-1,5-1,6-1,7-1,8-1,9-1
NKJV - **9,** 1-1,2-1,3-1,4-1,5-1,6-1,7-1,8-1,9-1
NLT - **7,** 1-1,2-1,3-1,4-1,5-1,6-1,7-1
NRSV - **9,** 1-1,2-1,3-1,4-1,5-1,6-1,7-1,8-1,9-1
Conclusion: All versions read the same.

200. Romans 6:7 For he that is dead is freed from sin.
AV - **9,** 1-1,2-1,3-1,4-1,5-1,6-1,7-1,8-1,9-1
ESV - **11,** 1-1,2-1,3-1,4-1,5-1,6-1,7-1,8-1,9-1,10-1,11-1
HCSB - 11, 1-1,2-1,3-**2**,4-1,5-1,6-1,7-1,8-1,9-1,10-1,11-1
NASV - **9,** 1-1,2-1,3-1,4-1,5-1,6-1,7-1,8-1,9-1
NCV - 10, 1-**3**,2-1,3-1,4-1,5-1,6-1,7-1,8-1,9-1,10-**2**
NIV - 10, 1-**2**,2-**3**,3-1,4-1,5-1,6-1,7-1,8-1,9-1,10-1
NKJV - **10,** 1-1,2-1,3-1,4-1,5-1,6-1,7-1,8-1,9-1,10-1

NLT - **15,** 1-1,2-1,3-1,4-1,5-1,6-1,7-1,8-1,9-1,10-1,11-1,12-1,13-**2**,14-1,15-1
NRSV - **8,** 1-1,2-**2**,3-1,4-1,5-1,6-1,7-1,8-1
Conclusion: Five modern versions are more complex than the King James Bible.

201. 1 Corinthians 3:23 And ye are Christ's; and Christ is God's.
AV - **8,** 1-1,2-1,3-1,4-1,5-1,6-1,7-1,8-1
ESV - **8,** 1-1,2-1,3-1,4-1,5-1,6-1,7-1,8-1
HCSB - 9, 1-1,2-1,3-**2**,4-1,5-1,6-1,7-1,8-1,9-1
NASV - 10, 1-1,2-1,3-**2**,4-1,5-1,6-1,7-1,8-**2**,9-1,10-1
NCV - 10, 1-1,2-1,3-**2**,4-1,5-1,6-1,7-1,8-**2**,9-1,10-1
NIV - **10,** 1-1,2-1,3-1,4-1,5-1,6-1,7-1,8-1,9-1,10-1
NKJV - **8,** 1-1,2-1,3-1,4-1,5-1,6-1,7-1,8-1
NLT - 10, 1-1,2-1,3-**2**,4-1,5-1,6-1,7-1,8-**2**,9-1,10-1
NRSV - 10, 1-1,2-1,3-**2**,4-1,5-1,6-1,7-1,8-**2**,9-1,10-1
Conclusion: Five modern versions are more complex than the King James Bible.

202. 1 Corinthians 4:18 Now some are puffed up, as though I would not come to you.
AV - **13,** 1-1,2-1,3-1,4-1,5-1,6-1,7-1,8-1,9-1,10-1,11-1,12-1,13-1
ESV - 11, 1-1,2-1,3-**3**,4-1,5-1,6-1,7-1,8-1,9-**2**,10-1,11-1
HCSB - 14, 1-1,2-1,3-1,4-**3**,5-1,6-1,7-1,8-1,9-1,10-1,11-1,12-**2**,13-1,14-1
NASV - 13, 1-1,2-1,3-1,4-**2**,5-**3**,6-1,7-1,8-1,9-1,10-1,11-**2**,12-1,13-1
NCV - 15, 1-1,2-1,3-1,4-**2**,5-1,6-**2**,7-1,8-1,9-1,10-1,11-1,12-1,13-1,14-1,15-1
NIV - 14, 1-1,2-1,3-1,4-1,5-**2**,6-**3**,7-1,8-1,9-1,10-1,11-1,12-**2**,13-1,14-1
NKJV - 13, 1-1,2-1,3-1,4-1,5-1,6-1,7-1,8-1,9-1,10-1,11-**2**,12-1,13-1
NLT - 13, 1-1,2-1,3-1,4-1,5-**2**,6-**3**,7-**2**,8-1,9-1,10-1,11-**2**,12-1,13-**2**
NRSV -**15,** 1-1,2-1,3-1,4-1,5-**2**,6-1,7-1,8-1,9-1,10-**2**,11-1,12-1,13-1,14-**2**,15-**3**
Conclusion: All eight modern versions are more complex than the King James Bible. The NLT is the most difficult to read.

203. 1 Corinthians 10:15 I speak as to wise men; judge ye what I say.
AV - **11,** 1-1,2-1,3-1,4-1,5-1,6-1,7-1,8-1,9-1,10-1,11-1
ESV - 12, 1-1,2-1,3-1,4-1,5-**3**,6-**2**,7-1,8-1,9-**2**,10-1,11-1,12-1
HCSB - 13, 1-1,2-1,3-**2**,4-1,5-1,6-1,7-**2**,8-1,9-1,10-**2**,11-1,12-1,13-1
NASV - **11,** 1-1,2-1,3-1,4-1,5-1,6-1,7-1,8-1,9-1,10-1,11-1
NCV - 15, 1-1,2-1,3-**2**,4-1,5-1,6-1,7-1,8-**4**,9-**2**,10-1,11-1,12-**2**,13-1,14-1,15-1
NIV - 11, 1-1,2-1,3-1,4-**3**,5-**2**,6-1,7-1,8-**2**,9-1,10-1,11-1
NKJV - 12, 1-1,2-1,3-1,4-1,5-1,6-1,7-1,8-1,9-**2**,10-1,11-1,12-1
NLT - 14, 1-1,2-1,3-**4**,4-**2**,5-**2**,6-1,7-**2**,8-1,9-1,10-1,11-1,12-**2**,13-1,14-1
NRSV - 12, 1-1,2-1,3-1,4-1,5-**3**,6-**2**,7-1,8-1,9-**2**,10-1,11-1,12-1
Conclusion: Seven modern versions are more complex than the King James Bible. Strangely, only the NASV did not make the verse more complex. Usually, it's the NKJV.

204. 1 Corinthians 14:18 I thank my God, I speak with tongues more than ye all:
AV - **12,** 1-1,2-1,3-1,4-1,5-1,6-1,7-1,8-1,9-1,10-1,11-1,12-1
ESV - **13,** 1-1,2-1,3-1,4-1,5-1,6-1,7-1,8-1,9-1,10-1,11-1,12-1,13-1

HCSB - 14, 1-1,2-1,3-1,4-1,5-1,6-1,7-1,8-**2**,9-**3**,10-1,11-1,12-1,13-1,14-1
NASV - 11, 1-1,2-1,3-1,4-1,5-1,6-1,7-1,8-1,9-1,10-1,11-1
NCV - 16, 1-1,2-1,3-1,4-1,5-1,6-1,7-1,8-**3**,9-1,10-1,11-**3**,12-1,13-1,14-1,15-1,16-1
NIV - **13,** 1-1,2-1,3-1,4-1,5-1,6-1,7-1,8-1,9-1,10-1,11-1,12-1,13-1
NKJV - 12, 1-1,2-1,3-1,4-1,5-1,6-1,7-1,8-1,9-1,10-1,11-1,12-1
NLT - 13, 1-1,2-1,3-1,4-1,5-1,6-1,7-1,8-1,9-1,10-1,11-**2**,12-1,13-1
NRSV - 13, 1-1,2-1,3-1,4-1,5-1,6-1,7-1,8-1,9-1,10-1,11-1,12-1,13-1
Conclusion: Only three modern versions made the verse more complex.

205. 1 Corinthians 15:16 For if the dead rise not, then is not Christ raised:
AV - **11,** 1-1,2-1,3-1,4-1,5-1,6-1,7-1,8-1,9-1,10-1,11-1
ESV - 13, 1-1,2-1,3-1,4-1,5-1,6-1,7-1,8-1,9-1,10-1,11-1,12-1,13-**2**
HCSB - **12,** 1-1,2-1,3-1,4-1,5-1,6-1,7-1,8-1,9-1,10-1,11-1,12-1
NASV - 13, 1-1,2-1,3-1,4-1,5-1,6-1,7-1,8-1,9-1,10-1,11-1,12-1,13-**2**
NCV - 12, 1-1,2-1,3-1,4-1,5-1,6-1,7-1,8-1,9-1,10-1,11-1,12-**2**
NIV - 14, 1-1,2-1,3-1,4-1,5-1,6-1,7-1,8-1,9-1,10-1,11-1,12-1,13-1,14-**2**
NKJV - 12, 1-1,2-1,3-1,4-1,5-1,6-1,7-1,8-1,9-1,10-1,11-1,12-**2**
NLT - 15, 1-1,2-1,3-1,4-1,5-1,6-**4**,7-1,8-1,9-1,10-1,11-1,12-1,13-1,14-1,15-1
NRSV - **13,** 1-1,2-1,3-1,4-1,5-1,6-1,7-1,8-1,9-1,10-1,11-1,12-1,13-1
Conclusion: Six modern versions are more complex than the King James Bible.

206. 1 Corinthians 15:17 And if Christ be not raised, your faith is vain; ye are yet in your sins.
AV - **16,** 1-1,2-1,3-1,4-1,5-1,6-1,7-1,8-1,9-1,10-1,11-1,12-1,13-1,14-1,15-1,16-1
ESV - 18, 1-1,2-1,3-1,4-1,5-1,6-1,7-1,8-1,9-1,10-1,11-**2**,12-1,13-1,14-1,15-1,16-1,17-1,18-1
HCSB - 17, 1-1,2-1,3-1,4-1,5-1,6-1,7-1,8-1,9-1,10-1,11-**2**,12-1,13-1,14-1,15-1,16-1,17-1
NASV - 17, 1-1,2-1,3-1,4-1,5-1,6-1,7-1,8-1,9-1,10-1,11-**2**,12-1,13-1,14-1,15-1,16-1,17-1
NCV - **21,** 1-1,2-1,3-1,4-1,5-1,6-1,7-1,8-1,9-1,10-1,11-1,12-**2**,13-1,14-1,15-1,16-1,17-1,18-**2**,19-1,20-1,21-1
NIV - 17, 1-1,2-1,3-1,4-1,5-1,6-1,7-1,8-1,9-1,10-1,11-**2**,12-1,13-1,14-1,15-1,16-1,17-1
NKJV - 16, 1-1,2-1,3-1,4-1,5-1,6-1,7-1,8-1,9-1,10-**2**,11-1,12-1,13-1,14-1,15-1,16-1
NLT - 20, 1-1,2-1,3-1,4-1,5-1,6-1,7-1,8-1,9-1,10-1,11-1,12-**2**,13-1,14-1,15-1,16-1,17-**2**,18-1,19-1,20-1
NRSV - 17, 1-1,2-1,3-1,4-1,5-1,6-1,7-1,8-1,9-1,10-**2**,11-1,12-1,13-1,14-1,15-1,16-1,17-1
Conclusion: All eight modern versions are more complex than the King James Bible.

207. 1 Corinthians 15:56 The sting of death is sin; and the strength of sin is the law.
AV - **14,** 1-1,2-1,3-1,4-1,5-1,6-1,7-1,8-1,9-1,10-1,11-1,12-1,13-1,14-1
ESV - 14, 1-1,2-1,3-1,4-1,5-1,6-1,7-1,8-1,9-**2**,10-1,11-1,12-1,13-1,14-1
HCSB - 15, 1-1,2-1,3-1,4-1,5-1,6-1,7-1,8-1,9-1,10-**2**,11-1,12-1,13-1,14-1,15-1
NASV - 14, 1-1,2-1,3-1,4-1,5-1,6-1,7-1,8-1,9-**2**,10-1,11-1,12-1,13-1,14-1
NCV - 14, 1-1,2-**2**,3-1,4-1,5-1,6-1,7-1,8-1,9-**2**,10-1,11-1,12-1,13-1,14-1
NIV - 14, 1-1,2-1,3-1,4-1,5-1,6-1,7-1,8-1,9-**2**,10-1,11-1,12-1,13-1,14-1
NKJV - **14,** 1-1,2-1,3-1,4-1,5-1,6-1,7-1,8-1,9-1,10-1,11-1,12-1,13-1,14-1
NLT - 16, 1-1,2-1,3-1,4-1,5-1,6-1,7-**2**,8-1,9-1,10-1,11-1,12-1,13-1,14-1,15-1,16-**2**
NRSV - 14, 1-1,2-1,3-1,4-1,5-1,6-1,7-1,8-1,9-**2**,10-1,11-1,12-1,13-1,14-1
Conclusion: Seven modern versions are more complex than the King James Bible.

394

208. 1 Corinthians 16:13 Watch ye, stand fast in the faith, quit you like men, be strong.
AV - **13,** 1-1,2-1,3-1,4-1,5-1,6-1,7-1,8-1,9-1,10-1,11-1,12-1,13-1
ESV - 12, 1-1,2-**2**,3-1,4-1,5-1,6-1,7-1,8-1,9-1,10-1,11-1,12-1
HCSB - 11, 1-1,2-**2**,3-1,4-1,5-1,6-1,7-1,8-1,9-1,10-1,11-1
NASV - 14, 1-1,2-1,3-1,4-**2**,5-1,6-1,7-1,8-1,9-1,10-1,11-1,12-1,13-1,14-1
NCV - 12, 1-1,2-**2**,3-**3**,4-1,5-1,6-1,7-1,8-1,9-**2**,10-1,11-1,12-1
NIV - 15, 1-1,2-1,3-1,4-1,5-1,6-1,7-1,8-1,9-1,10-1,11-1,12-1,13-**2**,14-1,15-1
NKJV - 10, 1-1,2-1,3-1,4-1,5-1,6-1,7-1,8-1,9-1,10-1
NLT - 12, 1-1,2-1,3-1,4-1,5-1,6-1,7-1,8-1,9-1,10-**3**,11-1,12-1
NRSV - 11, 1-1,2-**2**,3-1,4-1,5-1,6-1,7-1,8-1,9-**3**,10-1,11-1
Conclusion: Seven modern versions are more complex than the King James Bible.

209. 2 Corinthians 3:4 And such trust have we through Christ to God-ward:
AV - **10,** 1-1,2-1,3-1,4-1,5-1,6-1,7-1,8-1,9-1,10-1
ESV - 11, 1-1,2-1,3-1,4-**3**,5-1,6-1,7-1,8-1,9-1,10-1,11-1
HCSB - 10, 1-1,2-1,3-1,4-1,5-1,6-**3**,7-1,8-1,9-1,10-1
NASV - 8, 1-1,2-**3**,3-1,4-1,5-1,6-1,7-1,8-1
NCV - 12, 1-1,2-1,3-1,4-1,5-**2**,6-1,7-1,8-1,9-1,10-**2**,11-**2**,12-1
NIV - 10, 1-1,2-**3**,3-1,4-1,5-1,6-1,7-1,8-1,9-1,10-1
NKJV - 9, 1-1,2-1,3-1,4-1,5-1,6-1,7-1,8-1,9-1
NLT - 15, 1-1,2-1,3-**3**,4-1,5-1,6-1,7-**2**,8-1,9-1,10-1,11-1,12-1,13-1,14-1,15-1
NRSV - 11, 1-1,2-1,3-1,4-**3**,5-1,6-1,7-1,8-1,9-1,10-1,11-1
Conclusion: Seven modern versions are more complex than the King James Bible.

210. 2 Corinthians 5:7 (For we walk by faith, not by sight:)
AV - **8,** 1-1,2-1,3-1,4-1,5-1,6-1,7-1,8-1
ESV - **8,** 1-1,2-1,3-1,4-1,5-1,6-1,7-1,8-1
HCSB - **8,** 1-1,2-1,3-1,4-1,5-1,6-1,7-1,8-1
NASV - **8,** 1-1,2-1,3-1,4-1,5-1,6-1,7-1,8-1
NCV - 12, 1-1,2-1,3-1,4-1,5-1,6-**2**,7-1,8-1,9-1,10-1,11-1,12-1
NIV - **7,** 1-1,2-1,3-1,4-1,5-1,6-1,7-1
NKJV - **8,** 1-1,2-1,3-1,4-1,5-1,6-1,7-1,8-1
NLT - 9, 1-1,2-1,3-1,4-1,5-**3**,6-1,7-1,8-1,9-**2**
NRSV - **8,** 1-1,2-1,3-1,4-1,5-1,6-1,7-1,8-1
Conclusion: Only the NCV and the NLT managed to make this simple statement more complex. I don't think I'd want the translators of either of these two modern versions to write an instruction manual for anything.

211. Ephesians 4:20 But ye have not so learned Christ;
AV - **7,** 1-1,2-1,3-1,4-1,5-1,6-1,7-1
ESV - **9,** 1-1,2-1,3-1,4-1,5-1,6-1,7-1,8-1,9-1
HCSB - 10, 1-1,2-1,3-1,4-1,5-1,6-1,7-1,8-**2**,9-1,10-1
NASV - 9, 1-1,2-1,3-1,4-1,5-1,6-1,7-1,8-1,9-1
NCV - 10, 1-1,2-1,3-1,4-1,5-1,6-1,7-1,8-1,9-1,10-1
NIV - 10, 1-1,2-**3**,3-1,4-1,5-1,6-1,7-1,8-1,9-1,10-1
NKJV - 7, 1-1,2-1,3-1,4-1,5-1,6-1,7-1

Samuel C. Gipp Ph.D.

NLT - 8, 1-1,2-1,3-**2**,4-1,5-1,6-1,7-**2**,8-1
NRSV - **8,** 1-1,2-1,3-1,4-1,5-1,6-1,7-1,8-1
Conclusion: Only three modern versions are more complex than the King James Bible.

212. Philippians 1:21 For to me to live is Christ, and to die is gain.
AV - **12,** 1-1,2-1,3-1,4-1,5-1,6-1,7-1,8-1,9-1,10-1,11-1,12-1
ESV - **12,** 1-1,2-1,3-1,4-1,5-1,6-1,7-1,8-1,9-1,10-1,11-1,12-1
HCSB - 9, 1-1,2-1,3-**2**,4-1,5-1,6-1,7-**2**,8-1,9-1
NASV - **12,** 1-1,2-1,3-1,4-1,5-1,6-1,7-1,8-1,9-1,10-1,11-1,12-1
NCV - 17, 1-1,2-1,3-1,4-**2**,5-**3**,6-1,7-**2**,8-**2**,9-1,10-1,11-1,12-**2**,13-1,14-1,15-**2**,16-1,17-1
NIV - **12,** 1-1,2-1,3-1,4-1,5-1,6-1,7-1,8-1,9-1,10-1,11-1,12-1
NKJV - **12,** 1-1,2-1,3-1,4-1,5-1,6-1,7-1,8-1,9-1,10-1,11-1,12-1
NLT - 13, 1-1,2-1,3-1,4-**2**,5-1,6-**2**,7-1,8-1,9-1,10-**2**,11-1,12-**2**,13-**2**
NRSV - 10, 1-1,2-1,3-1,4-**2**,5-1,6-1,7-1,8-**2**,9-1,10-1
Conclusion: While only four modern versions are more complex than the King James Bible, the NCV and NLT are again masterpieces of complexity.

213. Colossians 3:3 For ye are dead, and your life is hid with Christ in God.
AV - **13,** 1-1,2-1,3-1,4-1,5-1,6-1,7-1,8-1,9-1,10-1,11-1,12-1,13-1
ESV - 13, 1-1,2-1,3-1,4-1,5-1,6-1,7-1,8-1,9-**2**,10-1,11-1,12-1,13-1
HCSB - 14, 1-1,2-1,3-1,4-1,5-1,6-1,7-1,8-1,9-**2**,10-1,11-1,12-1,13-1,14-1
NASV - 13, 1-1,2-1,3-1,4-1,5-1,6-1,7-1,8-1,9-**2**,10-1,11-1,12-1,13-1
NCV - 16, 1-1,2-1,3-**2**,4-1,5-1,6-1,7-1,8-1,9-1,10-1,11-1,12-1,13-1,14-1,15-1,16-1
NIV - 13, 1-1,2-1,3-1,4-1,5-1,6-1,7-1,8-1,9-**2**,10-1,11-1,12-1,13-1
NKJV - 12, 1-1,2-1,3-1,4-1,5-1,6-1,7-1,8-**2**,9-1,10-1,11-1,12-1
NLT - 16, 1-1,2-1,3-1,4-1,5-1,6-1,7-1,8-1,9-1,10-1,11-1,12-**2**,13-1,14-1,15-1,16-1
NRSV - 13, 1-1,2-1,3-1,4-1,5-1,6-1,7-1,8-1,9-**2**,10-1,11-1,12-1,13-1
Conclusion: All eight modern versions are more complex than the King James Bible.

214. 1 Thessalonians 3:8 For now we live, if ye stand fast in the Lord.
AV - **11,** 1-1,2-1,3-1,4-1,5-1,6-1,7-1,8-1,9-1,10-1,11-1
ESV - 12, 1-1,2-1,3-1,4-1,5-1,6-1,7-1,8-**2**,9-1,10-1,11-1,12-1
HCSB - **11,** 1-1,2-1,3-1,4-1,5-1,6-1,7-1,8-1,9-1,10-1,11-1
NASV - 12, 1-1,2-1,3-1,4-**2**,5-1,6-1,7-1,8-1,9-1,10-1,11-1,12-1
NCV - 12, 1-1,2-1,3-1,4-**2**,5-1,6-1,7-1,8-1,9-1,10-1,11-1,12-1
NIV - 13, 1-1,2-1,3-1,4-**2**,5-1,6-1,7-1,8-1,9-**2**,10-1,11-1,12-1,13-1
NKJV - **11,** 1-1,2-1,3-1,4-1,5-1,6-1,7-1,8-1,9-1,10-1,11-1
NLT - 15, 1-1,2-1,3-1,4-1,5-1,6-1,7-1,8-1,9-1,10-1,11-**2**,12-1,13-1,14-1,15-1
NRSV - 13, 1-1,2-1,3-1,4-1,5-1,6-1,7-**3**,8-1,9-1,10-1,11-1,12-1,13-1
Conclusion: Six modern versions are more complex than the King James Bible.

215. 1 Thessalonians 5:21 Prove all things; hold fast that which is good.
AV - **9,** 1-1,2-1,3-1,4-1,5-1,6-1,7-1,8-1,9-1
ESV - 8, 1-1,2-1,3-**4**,1,4-1,5-1,6-1,7-1,8-1
HCSB - **10,** 1-1,2-1,3-1,4-1,5-1,6-1,7-1,8-1,9-1,10-1

NASV - 11, 1-1,2-**3**,3-**4**,4-1,5-**3**,6-1,7-1,8-1,9-1,10-1,11-1
NCV - 7, 1-1,2-1,3-**4**,4-1,5-1,6-1,7-1
NIV - 7, 1-1,2-**4**,3-1,4-1,5-1,6-1,7-1
NKJV - 8, 1-1,2-1,3-1,4-1,5-1,6-1,7-1,8-1
NLT - 12, 1-1,2-1,3-**4**,4-1,5-1,6-1,7-1,8-1,9-1,10-1,11-1,12-1
NRSV - 9, 1-1,2-1,3-**4**,1,4-1,5-1,6-1,7-1,8-1,9-1

Conclusion: Six modern versions are more complex than the King James Bible. The NCV is the most difficult to read.

216. 1 Timothy 3:5 (For if a man know not how to rule his own house, how shall he take care of the church of God?)
AV - 22, 1-1,2-1,3-1,4-1,5-1,6-1,7-1,8-1,9-1,10-1,11-1,12-1,13-1,14-1,15-1,16-1,17-1,18-1,19-1,20-1,21-1,22-1
ESV - 19, 1-1,2-1,3-**2**,4-1,5-1,6-1,7-1,8-1,9-**2**,10-1,11-1,12-**2**,13-1,14-1,15-1,16-1,17-1,18-1,19-1
HCSB - 20, 1-1,2-**3**,3-1,4-1,5-1,6-1,7-1,8-1,9-**2**,10-1,11-1,12-**2**,13-1,14-1,15-1,16-1,17-1,18-1,19-1,20-1
NASV - 23, 1-1,2-1,3-1,4-1,5-1,6-1,7-1,8-1,9-1,10-**2**,11-1,12-1,13-**2**,14-1,15-1,16-1,17-1,18-1,19-1,20-1,21-1,22-1,23-1
NCV - 19, 1-1,2-**2**,3-1,4-1,5-1,6-1,7-1,8-1,9-1,10-**3**,11-1,12-1,13-1,14-**2**,15-1,16-1,17-1,18-1,19-1
NIV - 20, 1-1,2-**2**,3-1,4-1,5-1,6-1,7-1,8-**2**,9-1,10-1,11-1,12-1,13-**3**,14-1,15-1,16-1,17-1,18-1,19-1,20-1
NKJV - 23, 1-1,2-1,3-1,4-1,5-1,6-1,7-1,8-1,9-1,10-1,11-1,12-1,13-1,14-1,15-1,16-1,17-1,18-1,19-1,20-1,21-1,22-1,23-1
NLT - 17, 1-1,2-1,3-1,4-1,5-**2**,6-**2**,7-1,8-1,9-**2**,10-1,11-1,12-1,13-1,14-1,15-1,16-1,17-1
NRSV - 20, 1-1,2-1,3-**2**,4-1,5-1,6-1,7-1,8-1,9-**2**,10-1,11-1,12-**2**,13-1,14-1,15-1,16-1,17-1,18-1,19-1,20-1

Conclusion: All eight modern versions are more complex than the King James Bible.

217. James 4:15 For that ye ought to say, If the Lord will, we shall live, and do this, or that.
AV - 18, 1-1,2-1,3-1,4-1,5-1,6-1,7-1,8-1,9-1,10-1,11-1,12-1,13-1,14-1,15-1,16-1,17-1,18-1
ESV - 17, 1-**2**,2-1,3-1,4-1,5-1,6-1,7-1,8-1,9-1,10-1,11-1,12-1,13-1,14-1,15-1,16-1,17-1
HCSB - 16, 1-**2**,2-1,3-1,4-1,5-1,6-1,7-1,8-1,9-1,10-1,11-1,12-1,13-1,14-1,15-1,16-1
NASV - 18, 1-**2**,2-1,3-1,4-1,5-1,6-1,7-1,8-1,9-1,10-1,11-1,12-1,13-1,14-**2**,15-1,16-1,17-1,18-1
NCV - 16, 1-1,2-1,3-1,4-1,5-1,6-1,7-1,8-1,9-1,10-1,11-1,12-1,13-1,14-1,15-1,16-1
NIV - 19, 1-**2**,2-1,3-1,4-1,5-1,6-1,7-1,8-1,9-1,10-1,11-1,12-1,13-1,14-1,15-1,16-1,17-1,18-1,19-1
NKJV - 17, 1-**2**,2-1,3-1,4-1,5-1,6-1,7-1,8-1,9-1,10-1,11-1,12-1,13-1,14-1,15-1,16-1,17-1
NLT - 20, 1-1,2-1,3-1,4-1,5-1,6-1,7-1,8-1,9-1,10-1,11-1,12-1,13-1,14-1,15-1,16-1,17-1,18-1,19-1,20-1
NRSV - 17, 1-**2**,2-1,3-1,4-1,5-1,6-1,7-1,8-1,9-**2**,10-1,11-1,12-1,13-1,14-1,15-1,16-1,17-1

Conclusion: Six modern versions are more complex than the King James Bible. In the strangest of turns, it is only the NCV and NLT that do not alter the syllable count!

218. 1 John 5:12 He that hath the Son hath life; and he that hath not the Son of God hath not life.
AV - 19, 1-1,2-1,3-1,4-1,5-1,6-1,7-1,8-1,9-1,10-1,11-1,12-1,13-1,14-1,15-1,16-1,17-1,18-1,19-1
ESV - 18, 1-**2**,2-1,3-1,4-1,5-1,6-1,7-**2**,8-1,9-1,10-1,11-1,12-1,13-1,14-1,15-1,16-1,17-1,18-1
HCSB - 24, 1-1,2-**2**,3-1,4-1,5-1,6-1,7-1,8-1,9-1,10-1,11-**2**,12-1,13-1,14-1,15-1,16-1,17-1,18-1,19-1,20-1,21-1,22-1,23-1,24-1
NASV - 22, 1-1,2-1,3-1,4-1,5-1,6-1,7-1,8-1,9-1,10-1,11-1,12-1,13-1,14-1,15-1,16-1,17-1,18-1,19-1,20-1,21-1,22-1

NCV - **19,** 1-**2**,2-1,3-1,4-1,5-1,6-1,7-1,8-**2**,9-1,10-1,11-1,12-1,13-1,14-1,15-1,16-1,17-1,18-1,19-1
NIV - **20,** 1-1,2-1,3-1,4-1,5-1,6-1,7-1,8-1,9-1,10-1,11-1,12-1,13-1,14-1,15-1,16-1,17-1,18-1,19-1,20-1
NKJV - **20,** 1-1,2-1,3-1,4-1,5-1,6-1,7-1,8-1,9-1,10-1,11-1,12-1,13-1,14-1,15-1,16-1,17-1,18-1,19-1,20-1
NLT - 16, 1-**2**,2-1,3-1,4-1,5-1,6-1,7-**2**,8-1,9-1,10-1,11-1,12-1,13-1,14-1,15-1,16-1
NRSV - 18, 1-**2**,2-1,3-1,4-1,5-1,6-1,7-**2**,8-1,9-1,10-1,11-1,12-1,13-1,14-1,15-1,16-1,17-1,18-1
Conclusion: Five modern versions are more complex than the King James Bible.

219. Revelation 1:14 His head and his hairs were white like wool, as white as snow; and his eyes were as a flame of fire;
AV - **22,** 1-1,2-1,3-1,4-1,5-1,6-1,7-1,8-1,9-1,10-1,11-1,12-1,13-1,14-1,15-1,16-1,17-1,18-1,19-1,20-1,21-1,22-1
ESV - **21,** 1-1,2-1,3-1,4-1,5-1,6-1,7-1,8-1,9-1,10-1,11-1,12-1,13-1,14-1,15-1,16-1,17-1,18-1,19-1,20-1,21-1
HCSB - 17, 1-1,2-1,3-1,4-1,5-1,6-1,7-1,8-1,9-1,10-1,11-1,12-1,13-1,14-1,15-1,16-**2**,17-1
NASV - **21,** 1-1,2-1,3-1,4-1,5-1,6-1,7-1,8-1,9-1,10-1,11-1,12-1,13-1,14-1,15-1,16-1,17-1,18-1,19-1,20-1,21-1
NCV - **20,** 1-1,2-1,3-1,4-1,5-1,6-1,7-1,8-1,9-1,10-1,11-1,12-1,13-1,14-1,15-1,16-1,17-1,18-1,19-1,20-1
NIV - 19, 1-1,2-1,3-1,4-1,5-1,6-1,7-1,8-1,9-1,10-1,11-1,12-1,13-1,14-1,15-1,16-1,17-1,18-**2**,19-1
NKJV - **20,** 1-1,2-1,3-1,4-1,5-1,6-1,7-1,8-1,9-1,10-1,11-1,12-1,13-1,14-1,15-1,16-1,17-1,18-1,19-1,20-1
NLT - **21,** 1-1,2-1,3-1,4-1,5-1,6-1,7-1,8-1,9-1,10-1,11-1,12-1,13-1,14-1,15-1,16-1,17-1,18-1,19-1,20-1,21-1
NRSV - **21,** 1-1,2-1,3-1,4-1,5-1,6-1,7-1,8-1,9-1,10-1,11-1,12-1,13-1,14-1,15-1,16-1,17-1,18-1,19-1,20-1,21-1
Conclusion: Only the HCSB and the NIV made the verse more complex.

220. Revelation 21:13 On the east three gates; on the north three gates; on the south three gates; and on the west three gates.
AV - **21,** 1-1,2-1,3-1,4-1,5-1,6-1,7-1,8-1,9-1,10-1,11-1,12-1,13-1,14-1,15-1,16-1,17-1,18-1,19-1,20-1,21-1
ESV - **21,** 1-1,2-1,3-1,4-1,5-1,6-1,7-1,8-1,9-1,10-1,11-1,12-1,13-1,14-1,15-1,16-1,17-1,18-1,19-1,20-1,21-1
HCSB - **23,** 1-1,2-1,3-1,4-1,5-1,6-1,7-1,8-1,9-1,10-1,11-1,12-1,13-1,14-1,15-1,16-1,17-1,18-1,19-1,20-1,21-1,22-1,23-1
NASV - **25,** 1-1,2-1,3-1,4-1,5-1,6-1,7-1,8-1,9-1,10-1,11-1,12-1,13-1,14-1,15-1,16-1,17-1,18-1,19-1,20-1,21-1,22-1,23-1,24-1,25-1
NCV - **20,** 1-1,2-1,3-1,4-1,5-1,6-1,7-1,8-1,9-1,10-1,11-1,12-1,13-1,14-1,15-1,16-1,17-1,18-1,19-1,20-1
NIV - **20,** 1-1,2-1,3-1,4-1,5-1,6-1,7-1,8-1,9-1,10-1,11-1,12-1,13-1,14-1,15-1,16-1,17-1,18-1,19-1,20-1
NKJV - **21,** 1-1,2-1,3-1,4-1,5-1,6-1,7-1,8-1,9-1,10-1,11-1,12-1,13-1,14-1,15-1,16-1,17-1,18-1,19-1,20-1,21-1
NLT - **12,** 1-1,2-1,3-1,4-1,5-1,6-1,7-1,8-1,9-1,10-1,11-1,12-1
NRSV - **21,** 1-1,2-1,3-1,4-1,5-1,6-1,7-1,8-1,9-1,10-1,11-1,12-1,13-1,14-1,15-1,16-1,17-1,18-1,19-1,20-1,21-1
Conclusion: All versions read the same.

221. Revelation 21:25 And the gates of it shall not be shut at all by day: for there shall be no night there.
AV - **19,** 1-1,2-1,3-1,4-1,5-1,6-1,7-1,8-1,9-1,10-1,11-1,12-1,13-1,14-1,15-1,16-1,17-1,18-1,19-1
ESV - **16,** 1-1,2-1,3-1,4-1,5-1,6-1,7-1,8-1,9-1,10-1,11-1,12-1,13-1,14-1,15-1,16-1
HCSB - 14, 1-1,2-1,3-1,4-1,5-1,6-**2**,7-1,8-**2**,9-1,10-1,11-**2**,12-1,13-1,14-1
NASV - 16, 1-1,2-1,3-**2**,4-1,5-1,6-1,7-1,8-1,9-1,10-1,11-1,12-1,13-1,14-**2**,15-1,16-1
NCV - 16, 1-1,2-**2**,3-1,4-1,5-**2**,6-1,7-1,8-1,9-**2**,10-1,11-**2**,12-1,13-1,14-1,15-1,16-1
NIV - 16, 1-1,2-1,3-1,4-1,5-1,6-1,7-**2**,8-1,9-1,10-1,11-1,12-1,13-1,14-1,15-1,16-1
NKJV - **16,** 1-1,2-1,3-1,4-1,5-1,6-1,7-1,8-1,9-1,10-1,11-1,12-1,13-1,14-1,15-1,16-1
NLT - 17, 1-1,2-1,3-1,4-**2**,5-1,6-1,7-1,8-1,9-1,10-1,11-1,12-**2**,13-1,14-1,15-1,16-1,17-1

NRSV - 15, 1-1,2-1,3-1,4-**2**,5-1,6-1,7-1,8-1,9-1,10-1,11-1,12-1,13-1,14-1,15-1

Conclusion: Six modern versions are more complex than the King James Bible. The HCSB and NCV are the most difficult to read.

Miscellaneous Facts

The Authorized Version

1. The longest verse made up of single syllable words in the Old Testament, including names, has 38 words in it.

     1. Genesis 36:17 And these are the sons of Reuel Esau's son; duke Nahath, duke Zerah, duke Shammah, duke Mizzah: these are the dukes that came of Reuel in the land of Edom; these are the sons of Bashemath Esau's wife.   **38 words**

2. There are eight verses that qualify for the shortest verses made up of single syllable words in the Old Testament, including names, they all have 4 words in them.

     1. Exodus 1:3 Issachar, Zebulun, and Benjamin,   **4 words**

     2. Joshua 15:58 Halhul, Bethzur, and Gedor,   **4 words**

     3. Ezra 10:32 Benjamin, Malluch, and Shemariah.   **4 words**

     4. Ezra 10:37 Mattaniah, Mattenai, and Jaasau,   **4 words**

     5. Ezra 10:41 Azareel, and Shelemiah, Shemariah,   **4 words**

     6. Ezra 10:42 Shallum, Amariah, and Joseph.   **4 words**

     7. Nehemiah 10:26 And Ahijah, Hanan, Anan,   **4 words**

     8. Nehemiah 12:6 Shemaiah, and Joiarib, Jedaiah,   **4 words**

3. The longest verse made up of single syllable words in the New Testament, including names, has 33 words in it.

     1. 1 John 2:16 For all that is in the world, the lust of the flesh, and the lust of the eyes, and the pride of life, is not of the **Father**, but is of the world.   **33 words**

4. The shortest verse made up of single syllable words in the New Testament, including names, has 2 words in it.

     1. John 11:35 Jesus wept.   **2 words**

5. There are two verses that qualify as the longest verses made up of single syllable words in the Old Testament. Excluding names or numbers, they both have 28 words in them.

     1. Deuteronomy 4:29 But if from thence thou shalt seek the LORD thy God, thou shalt find him, if thou seek him with all thy heart and with all thy soul. **28 words**

     2. Isaiah 66:9 Shall I bring to the birth, and not cause to bring forth? saith the LORD: shall I cause to bring forth, and shut the womb? saith thy God.   **28 words**

6. There are three verses that qualify for the shortest verses made up of single syllable words in the Old Testament. Excluding names or numbers, they both have 4 words in them.

     1. Exodus 20:13 Thou shalt not kill.   **4 words**

     2. Exodus 20:15 Thou shalt not steal.   **4 words**

A Study of Verses Composed of Single Syllable Words

3. Deuteronomy 5:17 Thou shalt not kill.   **4 words**

7. The longest verse made up of single syllable words in the New Testament, excluding names or numbers, has 24 words in it.

    1. Luke 24:30 And it came to pass, as he sat at meat with them, he took bread, and blessed it, and brake, and gave to them.   **24 words**

8. The shortest verse made up of single syllable words in the New Testament, excluding names or numbers, has 6 words in it.

    1. John 6:48 I am that bread of life.   **6 words**

Modern Versions

1. The longest verse in a modern version, the New Century Version, has 79 words in it.

The New Century Version combined 1 Chronicles 4:34-38 to produce a massive, seventy-nine word verse which reads:

    1 Chronicles 4:34-38 The men in this list were leaders of their family groups: Meshobab, Jamlech, Joshah son of Amaziah, Joel, Jehu son of Joshibiah (Joshibiah was the son of Seraiah, who was the son of Asiel), Elioenai, Jaakobah, Jeshohaiah, Asaiah, Adiel, Jesimiel, Benaiah, and Ziza. (Ziza was the son of Shiphi, who was the son of Allon. Allon was the son of Jedaiah, who was the son of Shimri. And Shimri was the son of Shemaiah.) These families grew very large. **79 words**

2. The longest non-combined verse in a modern version, the New Century Version, has 48 words in it.

    1. Numbers 16:1 Korah, Dathan, Abiram, and On turned against Moses. (Korah was the son of Izhar, the son of Kohath, the son of Levi; Dathan and Abiram were brothers, the sons of Eliab; and On was the son of Peleth; Dathan, Abiram, and On were from the tribe of Reuben.) - **48 words**

3. Verses with 40 or more words in Modern Versions
Old Testament

        1. NLT, **Genesis 36:17***   40 words
        2. NCV, **1 Chronicles 9:12***   40 words
        3. NCV, **Isaiah 66:9**   40 words
        4. NCV, **1 Chronicles 12:3***   42 words
        5. NCV, **Numbers 16:1***   48 words
New Testament
        6. NCV, **1 John 2:16***   42 words

Except for one reference from the New Living Translation, the New Century Version has an obvious corner on the market on wordy verses. In fact, it also has the shortest verse.

4. Shortest verse in a modern version, the New Century Version.

    1. Job 3:2 saying: **1 word**

Samuel C. Gipp Ph.D.

5. The only verse where the New King James Version is the only modern version that has a multi-syllable word.

John 11:46* But some of them went their ways to the **Pharisees**, and told them what things **Jesus** had done.

AV - **18,** 1-1,2-1,3-1,4-1,5-1,6-1,7-1,8-1,9-1,10-1,11-1,12-1,13-1,14-1,15-1,16-1,17-1,18-1

ESV - **15,** 1-1,2-1,3-1,4-1,5-1,6-1,7-1,8-1,9-1,10-1,11-1,12-1,13-1,14-1,15-1

HCSB - **15,** 1-1,2-1,3-1,4-1,5-1,6-1,7-1,8-1,9-1,10-1,11-1,12-1,13-1,14-1,15-1

NASV - **17,** 1-1,2-1,3-1,4-1,5-1,6-1,7-1,8-1,9-1,10-1,11-1,12-1,13-1,14-1,15-1,16-1,17-1

NCV - **15,** 1-1,2-1,3-1,4-1,5-1,6-1,7-1,8-1,9-1,10-1,11-1,12-1,13-1,14-1,15-1

NIV - **15,** 1-1,2-1,3-1,4-1,5-1,6-1,7-1,8-1,9-1,10-1,11-1,12-1,13-1,14-1,15-1

NKJV - **16,** 1-1,2-1,3-1,4-1,5-1,6-**2**,7-1,8-1,9-1,10-1,11-1,12-1,13-1,14-1,15-1,16-1

NLT - **13,** 1-1,2-1,3-1,4-1,5-1,6-1,7-1,8-1,9-1,10-1,11-1,12-1,13-1

NRSV - **15,** 1-1,2-1,3-1,4-1,5-1,6-1,7-1,8-1,9-1,10-1,11-1,12-1,13-1,14-1,15-1

6. The longest verse made up of single syllable words in a Modern Version, excluding names or numbers, has 30 words in it.

Isaiah 66:9 Shall I bring to the birth, and not cause to bring forth? saith the LORD: shall I cause to bring forth, and shut the womb? saith thy God.

AV - **28,** 1-1,2-1,3-1,4-1,5-1,6-1,7-1,8-1,9-1,10-1,11-1,12-1,13-1,14-1,15-1,16-1,17-1,18-1,19-1,20-1,21-1,22-1,23-1,24-1,25-1,26-1,27-1,28-1

ESV - **30,** 1-1,2-1,3-1,4-1,5-1,6-1,7-1,8-1,9-1,10-1,11-1,12-1,13-1,14-1,15-1,16-1,17-1,18-1,19-1,20-1,21-1,22-1,23-1,24-1,25-1,26-1,27-1,28-1,29-1,30-1

HCSB - **27,** 1-1,2-1,3-1,4-**2**,5-1,6-1,7-1,8-1,9-1,10-1,11-1,12-**3**,13-1,14-1,15-1,16-1,17-1,18-1,19-1,20-1,21-**3**,22-1,23-1,24-1,25-1,26-1,27-1

NASV - **27,** 1-1,2-1,3-1,4-1,5-1,6-1,7-1,8-1,9-1,10-1,11-1,12-**4**,13-1,14-1,15-1,16-1,17-1,18-1,19-1,20-1,21-**4**,22-1,23-1,24-1,25-1,26-1,27-1

NCV - **40,** 1-1,2-1,3-1,4-1,5-1,6-1,7-1,8-1,9-1,10-**2**,11-**3**,12-**2**,13-1,14-1,15-1,16-1,17-1,18-1,19-1,20-1,21-1,22-1,23-1,24-1,25-1,26-1,27-1,28-1,29-1,30-1,31-1,32-**2**,33-1,34-1,35-1,36-1,37-1,38-1,39-1,40-1

NIV - **29,** 1-1,2-1,3-1,4-1,5-1,6-**2**,7-1,8-1,9-1,10-1,11-1,12-**4**,13-1,14-1,15-1,16-1,17-1,18-1,19-1,20-1,21-1,22-1,23-1,24-1,25-1,26-**4**,27-1,28-1,29-1

NKJV - **27,** 1-1,2-1,3-1,4-1,5-1,6-1,7-1,8-1,9-1,10-1,11-1,12-**4**,13-1,14-1,15-1,16-1,17-1,18-1,19-1,20-**4**,21-1,22-1,23-1,24-1,25-1,26-1,27-1

NLT - **32,** 1-1,2-1,3-**2**,4-1,5-1,6-**2**,7-1,8-1,9-1,10-1,11-1,12-1,13-1,14-1,15-**3**,16-1,17-1,18-1,19-1,20-1,21-1,22-1,23-**2**,24-1,25-1,26-**2**,27-1,28-**2**,29-1,30-1,31-1,32-1

NRSV - **23,** 1-1,2-1,3-**2**,4-1,5-1,6-1,7-1,8-**3**,9-1,10-1,11-1,12-1,13-1,14-1,15-1,16-1,17-**3**,18-1,19-1,20-1,21-1,22-1,23-1

In a strange twist, the English Standard Version has 30 words in the verse and they are all single syllable.

Other Materials

Other Helpful books from:
DayStar Publishing

* A Charted History of the Bible*

By James Kahler. The first book every Christian should have to help them understand how we got our Bible. Easy to read charts with brief, but informative synopsis on important events in the history of the Bible. $5.95

* Gipp's Understandable History of the Bible *

By Samuel C. Gipp. A thorough study of the history of the Bible with information on King James, the translators, where Bible manuscripts came from, the Greek witnesses and numerous comparisons of various modern versions. $24.95

* Bread of Life *

By Ted Warmack. A wonderfully complete general study of the Bible covering numerous subjects of interest to Christians, both old and new. Workbook sized and easy to read. $17.95

* The Bible Believer's Guide to Dispensationalism *

By David E. Walker. For the student who wants to better understand how to "rightly divide" the Word of truth. $21.95

* Biblical Youth Work *

By Jim Krohn. One of the leading youth men in the country shows how you can have a successful youth work without compromising or dropping your standards. $12.95

* Living With Pain *

By Samuel C. Gipp. Millions live in constant pain everyday. Dr. Gipp, who has suffered a broken neck has lived with daily pain for over three decades. In this book he helps those who are hurting to deal with their pain. $3.95

* Life's Great Moments *

By Jim White. We've all heard of "Murphy's Law." Jim White says, "Murphy was an optimist!" Read about the most amazing and hilarious happenings in this man's life. $8.95

*For His Pleasure *

By Samuel C. Gipp. Ever wonder why God put you on earth? Ever wonder what your purpose for existing is? This book will help you know what you should be doing every single day of your life. A must read for all Christians. $9.95

* Corruptions in the New King James Bible *

By Jack Munday. Many Christians are fooled into thinking the NKJV is a King James Bible without the "thee's" and "thou's." Jack Munday exposes the drastic changes found in the New King James Version. $7.95

*Basic Bible Doctrines *

By David E. Walker. Two individual volumes explain what happened to the new Christian when they were saved and to start them in the right direction in their Bible. $7.95 ea.

* Old Paths Preaching Methods *

By James A. Lince. Before he went home to be with the Lord, Bro. Lince recorded and published this work which has been a real help to both preachers and Christians. $13.95

* The Answer Book *

By Samuel C. Gipp. This book has become a classic. It answers over 60 charges brought against the King James Bible. In publication for almost two decades, it is still in great demand. Nothing in this book has been refuted. $6.95

* In Spirit and in Truth *

By Jeff Williams. This book explains the errors of the Charismatic Movement. In a workbook format with answers to be filled in, this book deals with tongues, healing, signs & wonders and other errors of this movement. $14.95

* Fight On! *

By Samuel C. Gipp. Short, one-page, stories which will encourage the reader to "Fight On!" as others have before them. $24.95

* More Fight On! Stories*

By Samuel C. Gipp. A second volume of the popular **Fight On!** series. Three hundred more pages of short stories which will encourage the reader to keep going through tough times. $24.95

* The Geneva Bible, the Trojan Horse *

By Samuel C. Gipp. The Geneva Bible, a predecessor of the King James, was a good translation, but it wasn't perfect. Today, in an attempt the pry the King James Bible out of Christians and get them to use anything else, an edition called the "1599" is being promoted as superior to the King James Bible. Find out why it isn't. $5.95

* Rightly Dividing God's Word *

By Victor Shingler. Another look at how to correctly interpret Scripture. $8.95

* The Song of Solomon *

By Jeff Williams. The only commentary on this great book written by a real Bible believer. $19.95

* Who Is The god Beside Jehovah? *

By Jack Munday. Christians are shown what is incorrect about the Jehovah's Witness cult. Jack Munday does his usual thorough investigation of their errant teachings. $9.95

* Is Our English Bible Inspired? *

By Samuel C. Gipp. This book is a "one night read" that defends our Bible and explains the importance of preservation in the transmission of Scripture across the centuries. It also defines the difference between a "King James Man" and a "Textus Receptus Man." $4.95

** Valiant for the Truth **

A two-year course suitable for Christian schools, home schoolers, Bible institutes, Youth Groups or individuals who simply want to be able to answer those who relentlessly attack the authority of their Bible. Produced in two series', 11 and 12, each series contains twelve lessons that simplify the most difficult answers to questions about the authority of the King James Bible. $59.95 per series

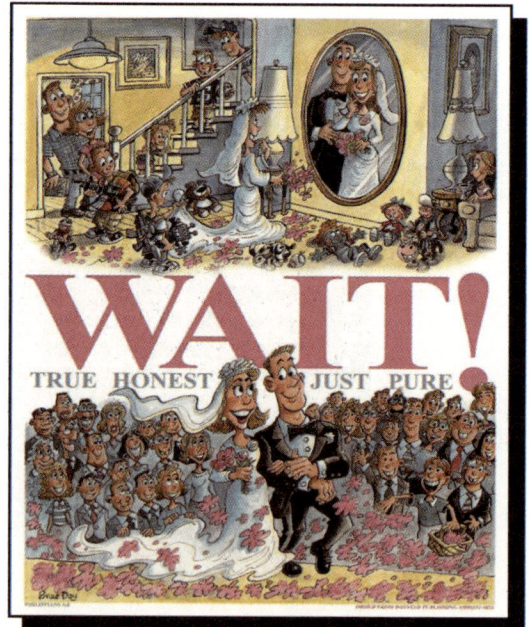

DayStar Publishing also has
sermons and lessons on CD and DVD,
hard-hitting bumper sticker,
as well as over a dozen posters for teens,
youth ministries or just for fun!

Check out DayStarPublishing.com or call 1-800-311-1823

Notes